Ireland under the Normans
1169–1333

Goddard Henry Orpen

with an introduction by Seán Duffy

FOUR COURTS PRESS

This book was typeset
in 10.5 on 12.5 Ehrhardt for
FOUR COURTS PRESS LTD
7 Malpas Street, Dublin 8, Ireland
www.fourcourtspress.ie
and in North America
FOUR COURTS PRESS
c/o IPG, 814 N. Franklin Street, Chicago, IL 60610.

ISBN 978-1-84682-818-8

PRINTING HISTORY
First published by the Clarendon Press, Oxford: volumes 1–2 (1169–1216) in 1911 and volumes 3–4 (1216–1333) in 1920; reprinted lithographically by Oxford University Press, 1968. The text was re-set for the Four Courts Press edition, hardback, 2005; paperback, 2019.

Printed in England
by TJ International, Padstow, Cornwall.

IRELAND UNDER THE NORMANS, 1169–1333

CONTENTS

MAPS & CHARTS

PUBLISHER'S NOTE

Sometime around 1999, we considered re-issuing Orpen's *Ireland under the Normans* (originally published by the Clarendon Press) as had been suggested to us by many academics and by Pádraic Ó Táilliúr and Joe Collins. The work was still in copyright; we eventually ran to earth a grandson of Orpen living in Wexford, but the matter of copyright management was never clarified. Now that the work is out of copyright, we are issuing this new, re-set edition in one volume.

We rejected the idea of meddling with Orpen's text by copy-editing it – not least the footnotes, which are quite casual in style.

Some of the contents have been re-arranged for this edition: for example, the notes on chief governors (now largely supplanted by the list in *NHI*, ix) have all been placed at the start of the book, as has the foreword to volumes 3 and 4; maps are retained – but not as fold-outs; and the original two indexes have been integrated.

With regard to the footnotes: in the first edition they start on each page at number one. For this edition we have renumbered the notes consecutively for each chapter. We have also incorporated into the text or footnotes (as may be) a cross-reference – ('[see *Add.*]') – drawing the reader's attention to the 'Addenda et Corrigenda to volumes I and II' that appeared in the fourth volume of the OUP edition, pp 307ff and which appear here at pp 589ff.

Readers of the book (and consultors of the index) will note that the original volume number is given in left-hand page running heads, and the page numbers of the original text appear as shoulder notes (the original shoulder notes have not been reproduced). This evidence of the original pagination is essential for using the index, but it also has the advantage that this edition can be used by readers who wish to follow up references to the first edition of the work.

We would like to thank Dr Seán Duffy and the editor of *Irish Historical Studies*, for permission to use, as an introduction to this volume, Dr Duffy's 'revisit to Orpen' published in *IHS* in 2000.

INTRODUCTION TO THIS EDITION*

Seán Duffy

Almost a century after the publication, in 1911, of the first two volumes of his magnum opus (the third and fourth appeared together in 1920), Goddard Henry Orpen's *Ireland under the Normans* remains controversial. The way to test this is not to read the polite comments of this generation of his successors but to go to a university library, take all four volumes off the shelf, and expose one's eyes to the palimpsest of student marginalia added down through the decades. Pencilled emotions ranging from anger and outrage to ridicule and blasphemy litter the pages and tarnish the author's memory, every bit as much the reprint (dating, interestingly, from 1968) as the original edition.

When the first two volumes, covering the period 1169–1216, were published they were warmly greeted in certain quarters, British journals in particular carrying laudatory reviews. But in nationalist Ireland grave offence was taken not simply at some of the author's apparently callous and hurtful statements but at his basic thesis, a thesis which Orpen set out clearly in the preface to his first volume:

> In the course of my study of the twelfth and thirteenth centuries (which has been spread over many years) ... I have been led to regard the domination of the English Crown and of its ministers in Ireland, during the thirteenth century, and indeed up to the invasion of Edward Bruce in 1315, as having been much more complete than has been generally recognized, and to think that due credit has not been given to the new rulers for creating the comparative peace and order and the manifest progress and prosperity that Ireland enjoyed, during that period, wherever their rule was effective ...
>
> ... it is, I think, manifest that the most prominent effect of the Anglo-Norman occupation was not, as has been represented, an increase of turmoil, but rather the introduction over large parts of Ireland of a measure of peace and prosperity quite unknown before.[1]

One can well imagine that to Irish nationalist readers, in the heady atmosphere surrounding the publication by Asquith, in April 1912, of the third home rule bill, Orpen's

*This introduction (pp xi–xxiii) was first published as an independent essay in 'Historical revisit: Goddard Henry Orpen, *Ireland under the Normans, 1169–1333* (1911-20)' in *Irish Historical Studies*, xxxii, no. 126 (November 2000), pp 246–59, and is reproduced by the kind permission of the editor. The biographical details of the original edition of Orpen are: *Ireland under the Normans, 1169–1333*. By Goddard Henry Orpen. 4 vols (vols i and ii, 1911; vols iii and iv, 1920). 1 Orpen, *Ireland under the Normans*, i, pp 7–8, 10–11.

allusions to the order, peace, progress, and prosperity that flowed from the English connexion seemed designed to undermine the case for Irish self-rule. The union debate was certainly a subtext in Orpen's work. He used, for instance, the marriage of Strongbow and Aoife as a metaphor for the union of England and Ireland. Describing it as 'a sign which all might read that the invaders had come to stay', he notes how some contemporaries may have failed to realize this, and concludes: 'But there was something else which the Irish at any rate did not foresee, but which we, looking back over the centuries, can see clearly enough. The union of Strongbow and Eva was the symbol of that union between the two islands which, for better or worse, has lasted ever since.'[2]

If Orpen here appears agnostic as to the benefits of English intevention, he reveals his true conviction in commenting on the early death of Strongbow (again with more than a hint that the latter euphemistically represents England itself) that it 'was a real misfortune, not just for the Anglo-Norman colony, but for Ireland. If Ireland was to benefit by Norman rule and Norman organization, and by the higher civilization and greater industrial energy of the new colonists, there was needed a man whom the other colonists would recognize as being, by birth, antecedents, and abilities, their natural superior.'[3] Ireland needed to be conquered, Orpen believed, because its people 'were still in a lower plane of civilization than had been reached elswehere', and conquest, which was in fact 'rendered inevitable by the previous anarchy', was 'effected primarily by superior weapons and better discipline in the field', while 'the position won was maintained and peace secured by that instinct for organized rule which is the mark of progressive races all the world over'.[4]

Orpen saw in the marriage of Strongbow and Aoife 'the first clash of English feudalism with Celtic tribalism the first clash of those discordant ideas which were to lead to so much hardship and misunderstanding in the future between the two races'.[5] This is a point of view which it is perfectly reasonable to hold but what angered those of Orpen's critics who saw themselves on the 'Celtic' rather than the Norman side of the equation was an apparent gratuitous descent into insult in describing some of the basic differences between them. On the Norman capture of Waterford, for instance, Orpen remarked that here 'we see the difference between the Celt and the Norman. The Celt would have plundered and burnt the town and then left it. The Norman plunders, no doubt, but puts a garrison in to hold the place, and, if necessary, fortifies it.'[6] Condescension outdid insult when Orpen, in a passage worthy of the pen of Sir John Davies, James I's attorney-general for Ireland, castigated the Normans for not showing 'a wiser statesmanship' by recognizing that the Irish 'were not to be emended by the use of hard names and exaggerated language, but by patient teaching, wholesome example, and the gradual introduction and enforcement of better laws'.[7]

Foremost amongst Orpen's critics was Eoin MacNeill, not remembered today primarily for the gifted historian he was and for his remarkable expertise in the sources for the history of early medieval Ireland (the chair of which he had held in University College, Dublin since 1909), but rather as a public and political figure of some stature.[8]

2 Ibid., pp 201–2. 3 Ibid., p. 358. 4 Ibid., p. 309; ii, p. 324. 5 Ibid., i, p. 200. 6 Ibid., p. 197. 7 Ibid., p. 309. 8 See F.X. Martin and F.J. Byrne (eds), *The scholar revolutionary: Eoin MacNeill, 1867–1945, and*

MacNeill had published a restrained and dignified review of Orpen's first two volumes in the *Journal of the Royal Society of Antiquaries of Ireland* immediately upon their appearance in 1911.[9] Perhaps moderation was called for in the journal of a society in which Orpen had published many ground-breaking contributions over the years and of which he would later be president. However, in 1917, following his release from the life imprisonment to which he had been sentenced in the aftermath of the Easter rising, MacNeill delivered a series of public lectures on medieval Ireland which were published in 1919 as *Phases of Irish history*, in which he bitterly assaulted Orpen's work.

One of his bugbears was Orpen's persistent use of the terms 'tribe' and 'tribal' to describe Irish dynasties and inter-dynastic conflicts, and as an explanation for one of the weaknesses as he saw it in the Irish body politic. For instance, while Orpen did not condone the unlicensed Anglo-Norman expansion from Leinster into Munster in 1174, he did note: 'Human nature being what it is, however, such encroachments are the inevitable result when a strong conquering and as yet united race gets a foothold among a weak ill-knit congeries of tribes'.[10] MacNeill's response to this was to state in his public lecture on 'Medieval Irish institutions' (Chapter X in *Phases of Irish history*), that

> Ireland in the twelfth century, says Mr Orpen, was still in the tribal state. This is written to justify the Norman invasion. The Normans were not in the tribal state.[11]

MacNeill explained that he himself avoided the use of this term because 'others have used it with the deliberate intent to create the impression that the structure of society in Ireland down to the twelfth century, and in parts of Ireland down to the seventeenth century, finds its modern parallel among the Australian or Central African aborigines'.[12]

He believed that Orpen was under the misapprehension that (to use the sample he cites) everybody who lived in, to use the examples he cites, the territory of Diarmait Mac Murchada bore that surname, or that everybody in Clandeboye was an O'Neill, and went on to cite what he calls 'clans' of Norman origin in Ireland and declared that Orpen must accept them as, by extension, 'tribal': 'Every one of these great families was precisely as much and as little a tribe as any Irish tribe that Mr Orpen has in contemplation; as much and as little a tribe as the Plantagenets or the Bourbons or the Hapsburgs or the Hohenzollerns.'[13] It was an unfair reproach since at no point in all of Orpen's four volumes had he ever shown signs of such ignorance of the structures of medieval Irish society – the contrary, in fact – and one cannot help but feel that part of the impulse behind MacNeill's angry response was simple annoyance at the pejorative way in which Orpen seemed to employ his 'tribal' terminology.

Rather than poking fun at Orpen before a receptive public audience MacNeill would have been better employed exploring more fully the implications of Orpen's line of argument: that if twelfth-century Ireland was simply an 'ill-knit congeries of tribes', it

the making of the new Ireland (Shannon, 1973). 9 *R.S.A.I. Jn.*, xli (1911), pp 277–82. 10 Orpen, *Ireland under the Normans*, i, p. 330. 11 Eoin Mac Neill, *Phases of Irish history* (Dublin, 1919), p. 292. 12 Ibid., p. 290. 13 Ibid., pp 293–4.

was not a country, it was not a 'small nation' whose sovereignty could be infringed or right to self-determination denied (to use the sort of parlance current at the very moment of MacNeill's assault). Orpen was quite clear where he stood on this matter. In volume two, when absolving Ruaidrí Ó Conchobair, the high-king, of any blame for not putting up a more effective resistence to the invaders, he states:

> It was the clan-system and the weakness and irresolution inherent in it, rather than lack of courage and determination in any individual, that rendered continuous and united opposition to the foreigners impossible. There was no national sense of country   only a 'tribal patriotism' and consequent anarchy.[14]

This is a statement with which one could certainly choose to disagree, and which Eoin MacNeill more so than any of his peers was perfectly positioned to contest, citing solid evidence. Instead, he chose the easy option of playing to the gallery in a public lecture on 'Ireland's golden age' (later, Chapter VIII of *Phases of Irish history*) and, without naming the target of his attack, launched into a most cruel and personalized tirade:

> When I see the eulogist of Anglo-Norman feudalism in Ireland sitting in judgement upon the political institutions of a people which he has never studied and does not at all understand, I call to mind the estimate formed by 'the ancient philosophers of Ireland' about Victorius of Aquitaine   that he was deserving of compassion rather than of ridicule.[15]

Yet ridicule is what he proceeded to feed to his willing listeners, just as in the foreword to the published version he could enunciate the noble principle that 'Neither apathy nor antipathy can ever bring out the truth of history', and then proceed to commit to print some of the most bilious antipathy to flow from the pen of an Irish historian of the twentieth century in reference to one of his peers. He said of Orpen's approach to writing about the medieval Irish that 'every item [was] culled out that might suggest comparison with the head-hunters of New Guinea and the Hottentot', a grossly unfair caricature of Orpen's not inconsiderable efforts to try to understand pre-Norman Irish society and of his purpose in writing. Employing a statement from Bede with which his audience was presumably familiar, and which no doubt produced raucous laughter, he declared that 'we can still use the scrapings of our Irish vellum as a cure for the foreign snake-bite', the clear implication of which was that Goddard Orpen, Dublin born and bred, was a foreigner in his own land.[16]

MacNeill then alluded to the use by Orpen (still unnamed) of phrases like 'the tribal state' of medieval Ireland and implied that the latter had called the Irish 'a barbarous people', when in fact what Orpen had written, in a passage heavily critical of certain aspects of Norman rule, was that 'it is plain that the Normans regarded the Irish as an uncooth and barbarous people and the fit spoil of their conquerors'.[17]

14 Orpen, *Ireland under the Normans*, ii, p. 182. 15 MacNeill, *Phases*, p. 240. 16 Ibid. 17 Orpen, *Ireland under the Normans*, ii, p. 335.

MacNeill next asked his audience how it was that in the midst of this barbarism there had existed 'schools everywhere, not schools but universities books everywhere, "the countless multitude of the books of Éire"'. He then launched headlong into an anti-intellectual rant on the the source-materials for the history of Anglo-Norman Ireland, comparing the literature and achievements of Ireland's golden age with

> the pomp and circumstance of Feudalism, with its archiepiscopal viceroys, its incastellations and its subinfeudations, its charters and its statutes, its registers and its inquisitions, but during four centuries not one school of note, not even one, and one abortive university, no literature except the melancholy records of anti-national statecraft, and whatever learning there was for the most part suborned to the purposes of a dominating officialdom, just as in our own day we have seen the highest achievements of science and invention suborned to the service of the war departments.[18]

This was not the stuff of a history lecture, rather a political rally, and one, at that, likely to incite to hatred. But, then, MacNeill was not now wearing the mortarboard of a university professor (though the chair which he had forfeited in 1916 had been restored to him two years later)[19] but was speaking and writing as a politician, elected in 1918 as MP for Derry City and the National University of Ireland, and by the following year Minister for Finance in the First Dáil.

It is most unfortunate that a scholar of Eoin MacNeill's integrity and stature should have let his emotions enter the historical debate in this way, as it left no room for a just assessment of the very real achievement of Orpen's first two volumes, and gave licence to scholars of lesser standing to join the pack when the other two volumes, covering the period 1216–1333, appeared in 1920. Obviously stung by some of the more robust criticism that had greeted the first half of his project, Orpen concluded the foreward to the latter half with the following heart-felt statement:

> In the immediate future Ireland is likely to focus upon herself a large share of political attention, and many ill-founded assertions regarding her past history as well as her present condition will doubtless continue to be made by politicians of all parties. It might indeed be thought that what happened upwards of seven centuries ago can have no practical bearing on our present-day problems. Nevertheless the appeal to history will inevitably be made...it has been my aim to examine the Anglo-Norman period from a mediaeval standpoint, and not to allow any modern political nostrum to colour the presentation of the picture drawn. All those who are sincerely desirous of understanding the Irish problem with the single-minded object of arriving at the best solution for all concerned, should therefore welcome an endeavour to set forth the facts of that occupation with as much exactness of statement and indifferency of judgement as is humanly possible.[20]

This was not to be.

18 MacNeill, *Phases*, p. 240. **19** Martin and Byrne (eds), *The scholar revolutionary*, pp 387–90. **20** Orpen,

To pick but one example, within months the Irish Jesuit journal *Studies* carried a lengthy review of the latter two volumes by Fr John McErlean, a member of the order and an ecclesiastical historian and Gaelic scholar of some merit.[21] The review appeared in September 1921 and it was perhaps inevitable that it would be coloured by circumstance, though the level of personalized vitriol which had earlier marked MacNeill's assault and now reappeared was unworthy of its author. As a cleric, the brunt of Fr McErlean's criticism was reserved for Orpen's treatment of the church in Anglo-Norman Ireland and, in perhaps his most uncharitable outburst, stated that Orpen judged 'the progress of the church from a thoroughly unchristian standpoint' or, again, that he was unable 'to view the Christian religion from the Christian standpoint'. This specific sectarian tone is matched by sweeping insult:

> ... neither Mr Orpen's ability nor his admiration for the invaders has succeeded in imparting a living human interest to what is little else than a dreary catalogue of murder and fraud, spoliation and chicane, disguised in the legal phraseology of a semi-civilised feudalism. The general dullness might have been to a great extent dispelled, had the author taken a wider view of his subject, or had his sympathies lain with those who kept up during that whole period a long and desperate struggle to maintain or regain their independence against successive hordes of invaders. There alone could he have found those high and noble motives to which the human heart will always respond despite the lapse of time. But viewed from the author's standpoint, the material could hardly be anything but dull and deadening.[22]

It is difficult to believe that the work thus described is the same about which Edmund Curtis, then Erasmus Smith's professor of modern history at the University of Dublin (Trinity College), could write, at precisely that same point:

> Dr Orpen maintains to the full in these two volumes that careful scholarship which, when its first two volumes appeared, at once placed him in the foremost ranks of real Irish historians a band, unfortunately, not too numerous. He shows again here his determination to get to the root of things, to take nothing for granted, and to verify his statements to the utmost available degree. His work on chronology, pedigree, and baronial tenure is impeccable, and constantly he revises our views and adds to our knowledge of this period ... Dr Orpen is a true pioneer in a field which, before him, was almost untouched, and every student of mediaeval Irish history will find his work absolutely indispensable.[23]

Of course, Orpen was a Trinity graduate (in classics) of many years' standing, a foundation scholar of the college, and was in fact awarded a doctorate in letters *honoris causa* by the university in June 1921 in recognition of his contribution to the study of

Ireland under the Normans, iii, p. 9. *R.S.A.I. Jn.*, li (1921), pp 81–2. **21** *Studies*, x (1921), 471–6. **22** Ibid., p. 472. **23** *R.S.A.I.Jn.*, li (1921), pp 81–2.

medieval Ireland. Curtis may well have played a part in securing this for him, and it might be argued that some such connexion accounts for his generous assessment of *Ireland under the Normans*.

But it is far more likely that Curtis was simply being fair-minded. He was, after all, a man who shared with Eoin MacNeill a similar vision of medieval Ireland,[24] so much so that when Brendan Bradshaw made his famous plea for a return to the pre-revisionist tradition of Irish historical scholarship he cited as his ideal 'the vision of its great luminaries Eoin MacNeill and Edmund Curtis'.[25] When, in 1923, Curtis published his own *History of medieval Ireland from 1110 to 1513* his very opening words made reference to Orpen and his work as 'an invaluable guide for part of my period, and it is a pleasure to acknowledge my great indebtedness to him'. Curtis may even have produced his own monograph to act a single-volume complement to Orpen since he openly declares the main difference between the two (apart from the chronological scope) to be the fact that *Ireland under the Normans* is 'professedly devoted to the history of the Norman colonists, whereas I have devoted more attention to the native side'.[26] It seems, therefore, that where others saw only the faults in Orpen's work, Edmund Curtis recognized the depth of the achievement encapsulated in *Ireland under the Normans*, and the folly of condemning to oblivion the work's many positive attributes, solely on the ground of antipathy towards its author's (very commonly-held) prejudices.

And prejudices, not objections on the grounds of historical accuracy, are at the core of the reaction to Orpen. Orpen's four volumes are cluttered with the prejudices of his class and age, as F.J. Byrne put it, his 'touching faith in the cultural superiority of the Anglo-Normans as a race, his Victorian belief in the civilizing destiny of England, and his very English [*sic*] trust in the trappings of law and order as essential prerequisites of civilization'.[27] It is this that angered MacNeill and others, rather than factual error. Professor Byrne, a successor to MacNeill's chair, has recognized what the latter understandably, perhaps, in the midst of a war of independence could not, that Orpen 'did his best to paint as accurate a picture as he knew how of Gaelic Ireland and its institutions', and that 'Orpen's view of pre-Norman Irish society, if partial in more senses than one, contains much truth'.[28] He is, in fact, a very astute observer of the conditions of life and the body politic in pre-Norman Ireland. He is all too aware, for instance, that 'theoretically there was a regular chain of subordination from the tiller of the ground through his immediate lord leading up, link by link, to the *ard-rí* or chief king of Ireland', and that, as more recent Irish historians have pointed out, 'in theory the organization bore a certain superficial resemblance to the feudal system'; the problem was, as Orpen saw it – and it is a view well supported by the evidence, no matter how vehemently MacNeill may argue to the contrary – that this theory was not matched by practice, and that 'the provincial king seldom acknowledged the superi-

24 See James Lydon, 'Historical revisit: Edmund Curtis, *A history of medieval Ireland* (1923, 1938)', *I.H.S.*, xxxi, no. 124 (Nov. 1999), pp 535–48. 25 Brendan Bradshaw, 'Nationalism and historical scholarship in modern Ireland' in *I.H.S.*, xxvi, no. 104 (Nov. 1989), p. 350. 26 Edmund Curtis, *A history of medieval Ireland from 1110 to 1513* (Dublin, 1923), Foreword. 27 F.J. Byrne, 'MacNeill the historian', in Martin and Byrne (eds), *The scholar revolutionary*, p. 25. 28 Ibid., p. 27.

ority of any other unless under compulsion and then, as a rule, only as long as the compulsion lasted'.[29]

If MacNeill objected to Orpen's (never more than implicit) comparison of the inhabitants of medieval Ireland with aboriginal tribal communities in other continents, it was out of concern that the Irish might still be considered 'uncivilized', whereas it is in fact a perfectly legitimate exercise to look to Africa and elsewhere for parallels with early Irish society: Kenneth Nicholls, for example, opened his pioneering *Gaelic and gaelicised Ireland in the middle ages* with a comparison between medieval Ireland and Abyssinia.[30] MacNeill's objection to the term 'tribal' had the same basis, although, as Byrne points out, 'the modern student would concur in the designation of Irish law as fundamentally tribal', the only qualification being that no ethnic or linguistic distinction existed between 'tribes', rather a remarkable uniformity in customs and institutions.

It was the redoubtable Professor Binchy of the Dublin Institute for Advanced Studies (spiritual successor to MacNeill as the leading authority on early Irish law) who, a half-century ago, put his finger on the essence of the dispute between Orpen and MacNeill. In an essay on 'Secular institutions' in early medieval Ireland, he noted on the subject of law and order that some believe that these cannot exist in the absence of formal structures for their enforcement, and added:

> Well, this was the conclusion reached by a fair-minded, scholarly (though I think subconsciously prejudiced) historian, the late Goddard Henry Orpen, who held that prior to the coming of the Normans anarchy reigned in Ireland. This view was hotly contested by MacNeill, as those of you who have read his great work 'Phases of Irish History' will remember. It has always seemed to me that these two eminent scholars, despite their violent collision, started out from precisely the same suppressed premise: that law and order were impossible in any society where the State had not substantially the same functions as in the late Victorian era in which they both grew up! Orpen's study of the Irish evidence convinced him that the Irish kings had nothing like these functions; hence, he concluded, Gaelic Ireland was anarchical. MacNeill, tacitly admitting the same suppressed premise, sought to disprove Orpen's facts and to show that in each *túath* law was promulgated, applied and enforced by the king's authority. I disagree completely with MacNeill in this, but I dissent just as emphatically from Orpen's conclusion. If comparative legal history teaches us anything, it is that legal order has in fact obtained among communities where, as in ancient Ireland, the State exists only in embryo.[31]

29 Orpen, *Normans*, i, pp 20–1. 30 Kenneth Nicholls, *Gaelic and gaelicised Ireland in the middle ages* (Dublin, 1972), p. 3. 31 D.A. Binchy, 'Secular institutions', in Myles Dillon (ed.), *Early Irish society* (Dublin, 1954), p. 62. On this matter, see Donnchadh Ó Corráin, 'Nationality and kingship in pre-Norman Ireland', in T.W. Moody (ed.), *Nationality and the pursuit of national independence*, Historical Studies XI (Belfast, 1978), pp 1–35.

If Orpen and MacNeill shared something of the same starting-point in terms of the value-system they inherited, they also had other things in common, and it is a great pity that political circumstances and perhaps differing allegiances prevented the latter and others from recognizing this. For instance, it was evidently part of MacNeill's purpose in publishing *Phases of Irish history* to instill in his readers a pride in Ireland's past, a sense of self-belief and self-worth, and to contribute his own particular talents to the urgent and proper task, as he would have seen it, of casting off the legacy of colonialism. The book is infused with a love of Ireland and with a pride in the past achievements of the country and its people. How unfortunate that he could not recognize in his nemesis, Goddard Orpen, 'the eulogist of Anglo-Norman feudalism in Ireland', a similar love for the land of his birth.

Orpen was fifteen years MacNeill's senior, born into a legal family in Dublin in 1852, and was educated in Tipperary and at Trinity College, but then left Ireland to practise at the English bar. However, it was in England that he began in earnest his studies into medieval Irish history, and while resident there he published, at the age of forty, his first major work, an edition of the contemporary Norman-French poem on the English invasion of Ireland, to which he himself gave the title that has clung to it ever since, *The song of Dermot and the earl*.[32] Eight years later he returned to Ireland when his wife inherited Monksgrange, in the Blackstairs mountains on the borders of Wexford and Carlow, and there he lived for the rest of his life until his death, just short of his eightieth birthday in May 1932. *Ireland under the Normans* is Orpen's single greatest accomplishment but the entire corpus of his published writings on medieval Ireland is doubly impressive, and has stood the test of time possibly even more successfully than the former.

Because we now take it for granted, it is difficult to believe that it was Goddard Orpen, for instance, who, in a series of ground-breaking articles and in the teeth of much resistance and not a little resentment, first conclusively proved that the many hundreds of 'motes' which dot the Irish countryside are not 'Danish' mounds or prehistoric sepulchres but motte-and-bailey castles erected by the Anglo-Normans (albeit sometimes on the site of earlier monuments). He established this by sheer graft and by the type and degree of fieldwork which very few professionally-trained archaeologists half his years and in this age of mechanized travel could rival. He has visited the sites about which he writes, whether they be in the furthest reaches of Ireland or for that matter, in South Wales. With an extraordinary eye for topographical detail, he seems to know and to love every nook and cranny about which he writes, and particularly in the case of castles and defensive structures, describes them with the skill and assurance denied all but the most gifted of archaeologists and architectural historians: this is all the more important in view of the extent to which so many of the sites he surveys have since become degraded or been destroyed.

Orpen's pride in Ireland and in things Irish is not something confined to the Anglo-Norman contribution. In *Ireland under the Normans* he is, for instance, scathing in his

32 *The song of Dermot and the earl*, ed. and trans. G.H. Orpen (Oxford, 1892). Recently a new edition of the Song has been published: Evelyn Mullally, *The deeds of the Normans in Ireland* (Dublin, 2002).

criticism of Ruaidrí O Conchobair's father, Tairdelbach, high-king of Ireland, *c.*1120–56, repeatedly labelling him as an unscrupulous and violent ruler (a description, it must be said, from which it is hard to dissent). Yet, when writing of the high-king's death, Orpen declares that 'After the lapse of seven and a half centuries we too may forgive Turlough much, and remember him as the young King of Erin for whom 'the cross of Cong' – one of the noblest surviving examples of native Irish craft – was made in the year 1123', adding in a footnote, 'Let us try too to remember the name – Maelisa son of Bratan O'Echan – of the wonderful craftsman who made the shrine'.[33] These are the words of a man who rejoices, equally with Eoin MacNeill, in the artistic achievements of ancient Ireland, but who, as an Irishman, feels entitled, in lauding the patrons of such creations, to bemoan their more destructive actions. And it is entirely incorrect to state that Orpen lacks sympathy or empathy for the Irish. In describing the divisive aftermath of Brian Bóruma's death at the battle of Clontarf, he remarks: 'Few pages of Irish history are more bitter reading for an Irishman than those which tell of the subsequent fortunes of the shattered battalion of the Dalcassians, the brave remnants of Brian's own tribe.'[34] He can spare a thought for what might have been: 'Had Ireland been allowed to go her own way unheeded by Europe, she might in time, and after much suffering, have evolved a better ordered system with some hope of progress in it, and the world might have seen a Celtic civilization, where Celtic imagination and Celtic genius, free and unfettered, would assuredly have contributed something towards the solution of human problems, which, as it is, mankind has missed for ever. But it was not to be.'[35]

And it was not to be because of the Anglo-Norman invasion, for which Orpen is assumed to be an unequivocal apologist, though his view on the latter is by no means as straightforward. As an apologist, Orpen might, for example, have taken refuge behind the frequently-repeated nonsense that the English under Henry II had little interest in Ireland and only reluctantly became involved in its affairs when Diarmait Mac Murchada's overtures to the Normans of South Wales made royal intervention unavoidable. Instead, he argues convincingly that Henry had lusted after involvement in Ireland almost from the moment he ascended the throne, and that Mac Murchada's request for aid was music to Henry's ears: 'No doubt', he comments candidly, 'pretexts for war, when required, are in general easily manufactured, but here was an admirable one offered by Dermot, ready made to Henry's hand.' As to the actions of men who sought foreign aid for their own advancement, like Mac Murchada – who aught to be the hero of a Norman apologist – Orpen declares that 'if such princes were wiser and more patriotic than their fellows, they might have learnt and observed the great historic lesson that such a course was a likely way to enslave both themselves and their country'.[36]

Orpen was of the view that the Anglo-Norman invasion of Ireland was a mixed blessing. For all his much-vaunted 'Pax Normannica', he was aware that the alleged turmoil of pre-Norman Ireland (for which MacNeill so vehemently castigated him) was not ended by the invasion; rather it continued, but it was, in his own words, 'turmoil

33 Orpen, *Ireland under the Normans*, i, pp 60–1; cf. pp 46, 51. 34 Ibid., p. 32. 35 Ibid., p. 27. 36 Ibid., p. 82.

now caused partly, but not exclusively, by the efforts of the newcomers to extend their domination'.[37] Of Henry II's actions in 1172 in establishing Strongbow as lord of Leinster and granting the kingdom of Meath to Hugh de Lacy, he confesses that the king had thereby 'rendered inevitable a conflict between English and Irish aims and interests'.[38] When, in 1177, the kingdoms of Cork (Mac Carthaig's Desmond) and Limerick (Ó Briain's Thomond) were similarly granted away to Anglo-Norman feudatories, he admits that it is 'impossible to reconcile these sweeping grants with our ideas of equitable dealing'.[39] And he shows the extent to which he appreciated the motivations of the Irish in making war on the colonists, saying that they 'had always the feeling rankling in their minds that the invaders had robbed them of the best lands, and they remained always ready, when opportunity should occur, to raid and plunder as of old, and if possible recover the land they had lost'.[40]

Orpen does not regard it as part of the role of the historian to mete out blame, but his story does have its villains. However, just as these are not the Anglo-Norman settlers in Ireland whom he admires for what he sees as their courage and adventuresome spirit on this new frontier, neither are his villains, as some suppose, the native Irish. In fact, Orpen vents most of his spleen on the policies of Ireland's lord, the king of England. He has little good to say of Henry II, of whose policy in South Wales and Ireland in 1171 he states: 'it was Henry's cue thoughout this expedition to appear as the friend of the natives, Welsh and Irish, and the stern oppressor of the Anglo-Norman marcher-lords, his real object being to secure the control of the Crown over both'.[41] Of the 1185 expedition to Ireland by Henry's son John, and the Irish response it evoked, he has very bitter words: 'A proud and sensitive people never willingly submits to the rule of a master, however mighty, who despises them.' Here we see something of Goddard Orpen's respect for the Irish, not the contempt his detractors allege. He proceeds to describe the incident recorded by Giraldus Cambrensis when John and his youthful entourage pulled the beards of the Irish lords who had greeted them on their arrival, and adds that 'this rude plucking of the beards was only a symbol of that want of consideration for the native Irish which exhibited itself in more harmful ways'.[42]

Some more recent historians have attempted to rehabilitate King John, the late W.L. Warren making the colourful if somewhat meaningless statement that he was 'the most successful high-king Ireland had ever seen',[43] while the late F.X. Martin went one step further with the even more improbable suggestion that 'John, so often described as the worst of the kings of England, was, paradoxically, the best for Ireland'.[44] Oddly enough, this latter point had specifically been addressed by Orpen over sixty years earlier, who could remark of his day that it 'has been the fashion, especially with writers who have seldom a good word for English policy in Ireland, to bestow a considerable measure of

37 Ibid., ii, p. 328. 38 Ibid., i, p. 284. 39 Ibid., ii, p. 33. 40 Ibid., p. 328. 41 Ibid., i, pp 253–4. 42 Ibid., ii, p. 97. 43 W.L. Warren, 'King John and Ireland', in J.F. Lydon (ed.), *England and Ireland in the later middle ages: essays in honour of Jocelyn Otway-Ruthven* (Dublin, 1981), pp 26–42, at p. 39. 44 F.X. Martin, 'John and Ireland, 1185–1216' in A. Cosgrove (ed.), *NHI*, ii (Oxford, 1987, p. 132). I have attempted a reassessment in 'John and Ireland: the origins of England's Irish problem', in Stephen Church (ed.), *King John: new interpretations* (Woodbridge, 1999), pp 221-45.

praise upon the action of King John in that country'. He concluded, however, that 'if we have correctly read the record of his rule, this praise is wholly undeserved ... For the native Irish themselves, in common with too many of his contemporaries, he had no sort of regard', and was 'always ready to grant away their territories (for a consideration) to his favourites'.[45]

John's successors, in Orpen's eyes, were little better. In discussing the change in English government policy under John's son, Henry III, which involved authorizing the confiscation of Connacht from its king, Áed son of Cathal Crobderg Ó Conchobair, and the grant by royal charter of most of the province to Richard de Burgh, Orpen states that 'when all is said that can fairly be said in favour of the new policy, the fact remains that it involved harsh treatment of King Cathal's son, and was not unnaturally regarded by him and his followers as an act of treachery and deception'.[46] Henry's son Edward I is sometimes regarded as the greatest of England's medieval kings, but Orpen is again severe in his criticism of the lack of attention he displayed towards his lordship of Ireland. He states that had Edward devoted his whole attention 'even for a short period' to the business of governing the country, 'he could not have failed to perceive that there were several parts of Ireland which required "pacification" to enable an orderly government to be carried on there'. In a passage not far removed from MacNeill's caustic summary of English governmental procedure quoted above, Orpen notes that peace 'was not to be produced by the magic of mandates from Gascony or even from Westminster, or to be enforced by the entry of fines on the pipe roll'. Instead, he states, it required the highest efforts of statesmanship, and adequate military power, 'guided by principles of justice and fair dealing'.[47]

This statement captures some of the recurrent themes of *Ireland under the Normans*. To take the latter point first, one of the reasons, as Orpen sees it, that the Normans failed to conquer Ireland was because of the sense of injustice their actions produced among the Irish, specifically arising from their denial of access to legal remedy. In commenting on some of the failures of the first fifty years of Norman rule, he (a lawyer, of course) remarks on how the western world had learnt from experience that 'to make a united and contented nation, equal rights before the law must be secured to all'; unfortunately, 'such a conception was, however, entirely beyond the ken of the statesmen of the twelfth and thirteenth centuries'. By denying the native population access to the law, 'those who guided the destinies of the colony were not', he argues, 'far-seeing enough to perceive the ultimate effect of a half-conquest carried out in such a spirit'.[48]

This lack of statesmanship, he believed, came from the top, and here we see in Goddard Orpen the authentic voice of the Anglo-Irishman through the ages. He criticizes Henry III and his English officials, not the Anglo-Irishmen who governed in Henry's name. The reason?

> They [the Anglo-Irish] were men who spent most if not all of their lives in Ireland, who held lands there, and had the interests of the colony at heart, and

45 Orpen, *Ireland under the Normans*, ii, pp 319–20. 46 Ibid., iii, pp 163–4. 47 Ibid., p. 271. 48 Ibid., ii, p. 334.

> who, if they took little thought of the interests of the native Irish population, at least understood them and their ways as no official fresh from England could do.[49]

Resentment at the intrusion of English-born officials was almost as old as the Anglo-Irish colony itself, and here, in 1920, Goddard Orpen articulates it with the same conviction that his forebears had for centuries past. Nine years earlier, in volume one, he had been, if anything, more forthright. Ostensibly discussing the efforts to which Henry II went in 1170 to choke off the supply of men and provisions to the insubordinate Strongbow and his men in Ireland, Orpen launches into an attack on English policy worthy of a Swift or a Grattan:

> Henry's embargo, then, must rather be regarded as the first example of that perversity which in after years too often characterized England's policy towards Ireland, *and from which, perhaps, it is not yet wholly free*, a perversity which manifests itself in first encouraging the formation of an English colony in Ireland for the greater glory and security of the English Crown, and then, not from any regard to the native Irish, but from motives of suspicion and jealousy, thwarting the efforts of that colony whenever it seemed likely to be successful and prosperous.[50]

This statement brings us as close as we are likely to get to the perspective of Goddard Henry Orpen on the period of Irish history about which he wrote with such fervour and such skill. He wrote from the standpoint of an Anglo-Irishman, confident in the belief that generations of people of his background had striven to give of their best to Ireland and that, on balance, in spite of the divisions to which their presence gave rise and their many mistakes and injustices – which he is ready to acknowledge – theirs was a positive contribution. If blame is to be meted out – and he does not believe it to be part of the function of the historian either to praise or blame[51] – it does not belong with those who made Ireland their home for better or worse, but with an English government which cared neither for native nor newcomer, but sought merely to exploit both for its own ends.

Goddard Henry Orpen's four-volume *Ireland under the Normans* offers so many insights into the *Weltanschauung* of its author and his class that it is rewarding of study for this purpose alone. But it would be a dreadful shame if sight was lost of the fact that his is a work of quite the most stupendous scholarship. Every monograph which has since appeared on this era of Irish history has simply paraphrased him, tweaked some of the minutiae of his account, added some details where a new source has been unearthed, or sought to tell the same story in a different tone. His work has not been surpassed and it cannot be superseded because it is the *fons et origo* of the professional historiography of Anglo-Norman Ireland.

49 Ibid., iii, p. 296. 50 Ibid., i, p. 219 (my italics). 51 Ibid., p. 143.

I refer the reader to the Publisher's Note, which explains Four Courts Press policy as regards the preparation of this edition; it is a policy that seems sensible to me.

The publishers, I note, have reproduced Orpen's footnotes. Because these do not agree with modern practice, bibliographical references for the main sources quoted by Orpen are given below:

Ancient Laws of Ireland	*Ancient laws and institutes of Ireland*, 6 vols (Dublin, 1865–1901).
Anglo-Norman church	*See* Stokes, *Anglo-Norman church.*
Ann. Boyle	A.M. Freeman, 'The annals in Cotton MS Titus A XXV' in *Rev. Celt.*, 41 (1924), pp 301–30, 42 (1925), pp 283–305, 43 (1926), pp 358–84, 44 (1927), pp 226–61.
Ann. Camb.	*Annales Cambriae*, ed. J. Williams, Rolls Series (London, 1860).
Ann. Clonmacnois	*Annals of Clonmacnoise*, ed. Denis Murphy (Dublin: Royal Society of Antiquaries of Ireland, 1896).
Ann. Loch Cé	*Annals of Loch Cé*, ed. W.M. Hennessy, 2 vols, Rolls Series (London, 1871, reflex facsimile, Irish Manuscripts Commission, Dublin, 1939).
Ann. Mon. Paris, Chron. Mai	*Annales Monastici*, ed. H.R. Luard, 4 vols (London, 1864). Matthew Paris, *Chronica Majora*, ed. H.R. Luard, Rolls Series 57, 7 vols (London, 1872–84).
Ann. Tigernach	'The annals of Tigernach', ed. Whitley Stokes in Rev. Celt., 16 (1895), pp 374–419, 17 (1896), pp 6–3 3, 119–263, 337–420; 18 (1897), pp 9–59, 150–97, 367–303.
Ann. Ulster	*Annála Uladh: Annals of Ulster*, ed. W.M. Hennessy and B. MacCarthy, 4 vols (Dublin, 1887–1901).
Annals of Inisfallen Dublin MS	Unpublished MS in TCD library.
d-Arbois de Jubainville, Lit. Celtique/Cours de Litt.	H. d'Arbois de Jubainville, *Introduction a l'étude de la littéra ture celtique*, Cours de littérature celtique, i (Paris, 1883).
Berry, Early statutes	*Statutes and ordinances, and acts of the parliament of Ireland, King John to Henry V*, ed. H.F. Berry (Dublin, 1907)
Black Book of Limerick	J. MacCaffrey, *The black book of Limerick* (Dublin, 1906).
Bodleian Annals of Inisfallen	MS Rawl. since published by S. Mac Airt, *Annals of Inisfallen.*
Book of Howth	Carew calendar.
Book of Leinster (Facsimile)	*The Book of Leinster, sometime called the Book of Glendalough* ..., ed. R. Atkinson (facsimile, Royal Irish Academy, 1880).
Books of Rights	*Leabhar na g-Ceart or the Book of Rights*, ed. J. O'Donovan (Dublin: Celtic Society, 1847).
Bray's Conquest of Ireland	in Cal. Carew Manuscripts, vol. 6.
Br(ehon) Laws	*See* Anc. Laws of Ireland
Brut y Tywys	*Brut y Tywysogion* or the *Chronicle of the princes*, ed. J. Williams ap Ithel, Rolls Series (London, 1860).
Bugge, The place of Dublin	A. Bugge, *Contributions to the history of the Norsemen in Ireland*, 3 vols (Christiania, 1900).
Cal.	*See* Cal. Docs Ireland.
Cal. Anc. Records of Dublin	*Calendar of ancient records of Dublin in the possession of the municipal corporation*, ed. J.T. Gilbert, 19 vols (Dublin, 1889–1944).

Cal. Christ Church Deeds	'Calendar of Christ Church deeds' in *Reports of the Deputy Keeper of the Public Records in Ireland*, 20th (1888), appendix vii), 23rd (1891), appendix iii; 24th (1892), appendix, viii, 27th (1896), appendix; reprinted in one vol., ed. M.J. McEnery and R. Refausse (2000).
Cal. Charter Rolls	*Calendar of the charter rolls*, 1226–1516 (London, 1903–27).
Cal. Docs. France (Round)	J.H. Round, *Calendar of documents preserved in France* (London: Public Record Office, 1899).
Cal. Docs. Ireland	*Calendar of documents relating to Ireland preserved in her Majesty's Public Record Office*, London, ed. H.S. Sweetman and G.F. Handcock, 5 vols (London: Public Record Office, 1875–86).
Cal. Liber Albus Ch.Ch.	H.J. Lawlor, 'A calendar of the Liber Niger and Liber Albus of Christ Church, Dublin' in *Proceedings of the Royal Irish Academy*, xxvii, C (1908), pp. 1–93.
Cal. Lib. Niger	H.J. Lawlor, 'A calendar of the Liber Niger and Liber Albus of Christ Church, Dublin' in *Proceedings of the Royal Irish Academy*, xxvii, C (1908), pp. 1–93.
Cal. Justiciary Rolls	*Calendar of the justiciary rolls*, ed. J. Mills et al., 3 vols (Dublin, 1905) 1956
Cal. of Oengus	*Félire Oengusso*; ed. W. Stokes, *Henry Bradshaw Society*, 2nd edn (London, 1905).
Cal. Pat. Rolls	*Calendar of the patent rolls* (London, 1891–)
Calendar	*See* Cal. Docs Ireland
Camb. Eversus	John Lynch (Gratianus Lucius), *Cambrensus eversus, seu potius historica fides in rebus Hibernicis Giraldo Cambrensi abrogata ... 1662*, ed. Matthew Kelly, 3 vols (Dublin: Celtic Society, 1848–52).
Camden, Britannia (1695)	William Camden, *Camden's Britannia newly translated into English* (London, 1695)
Campion, (reprint 1809)	Ware, James, *Ancient Irish histories: the works of Spencer, Campion, Hanmer and Marlebury* (Dublin, 1809)
Car. Cal	See Cal. Misc.
Carew, Cal. Misc.	*Calendar of the Carew manuscripts preserved in the archiepiscopal library at Lambeth*, 1515–74 ..., 6 vols (London, 1867–73).
Cathréim *Thoirdhealbhaigh*	Standish Hayes O'Grady, ed., *Caithréim Thoirdhealbhaigh, The Triumphs of Turlough* (Dublin, 1929)
C.D.I.	*See* Cal. Docs. Ireland
Carte's *Life of Ormond* (ed. 1851)	T. Carte, *History of the life of James, the first duke of Ormond* (6 vols, London, 1851)
Chartae &/Chartae Priv. et Immun.	*Chartae, privilegia et immunitates ... 1171–1395* (printed for the Irish Record Commission, 1829–30, published Dublin, 1889).
Chart. John	See Rot. chart.
Chart. St. Mary's Dub.	*Chartularies of St Mary's Abbey, Dublin, 1162–1370*, ed. J.T. Gilbert, 2 vols, Rolls Series (London, 1884–6).
Chron. Manniae	*Chronica regum Manniae et Insumarum*, ed. P.A. Munch, 2 vols, Manx Society [Publications], xxii–xxiii (1874).

Close Roll	*Calendar of the close rolls* (London, 1892–); *Close Rolls of the reign of Henry III*, 14 vols (London, 1902–38).
Clyn's Annals	John Clyn, *Annals of Ireland*; ed. R. Butler (Irish Archaeological Society, 1849).
Coleman, *Ancient dominican foundations in Ireland*	Ambrose Coleman, *The Irish Dominicans of the seventeenth century by Father John O'Heyne first published in Louvain in 1706 reprinted with a translation and historical sketches of all the ancient Dominican foundations in Ireland* (Dundalk, 1902).
Colt Hoare, Sir Richard	*See* Hoare, Richard Colt.
Coote's Survey of Queen's Co.	C. Coote, *General view of the agriculture and manusfactures of the Queen's county with observations on the means of their improvement drawn up in the year 1801 for the consideration and under the direction of the Dublin Society* (Dublin, 1801).
Council book of Cork (Caulfield)	R. Caulfield, *The council book of the corporation of the city of Cork* (Guildford, Surrey, 1876).
Cox	R. Cox, *Hibernia Anglicana* (London, 1689).
Crede mihi	*Crede mihi*, ed. J.T. Gilbert (Dublin, 1897).
D'Alton, *History of Ireland*	D'Alton, Edward Alfred. *History of Ireland, from the earliest times to the present day* (London, 1910).
Davies, Discovery &	Sir John Davies, *A discovery of the true causes which Ireland was never entirely subdued ... until ... his majesty's happy reign* (1787 edn).
Davies, *Report of cases* (ed. 1762)	J. Davies, *A report of cases and matters in law resolved and adjudged in the king's courts in Ireland* (Dublin, 1762).
Dict. Nat. Biog.	*Dictionary of national biography*, ed. L. Stephen and S. Lee, 66 vols (London, 1885–1901; reprinted with corrections 22 vols, London 1908–9).
Diceto, R. de	*Radulphi de Diceto opera historica*, ed. W. Stubbs, 2 vols, Rolls Series (London, 1876).
Dublin Annals of Inisfallen	*See* Annals of Inisfallen, Dublin manuscript.
Dugdale, Monasticon/Dugdale, Mon. Angl.	Dugdale, William, *Monasticon Anglicanum*, new edn, ed. John Caley, Henry Ellis and Bulkeley Bandinel, 6 vols in 8, (London, 1817–30, 1846 reprint).
Dymmok, Tracts I. A.S./ Dymmok's 'Treatice of Ireland'	John Dymmok, 'A treatice of Ireland', ed. R. Butler in *Tracts relating to Ireland*, ii (Irish Archaeological Society, 1843), pp 1–90.
Eng. Hist. Review	*English Historical Review* (London, 1886–).
Excerpta Fine Rolls (Roberts)	C. Roberts (ed.), *Excerpta e Rotulis Finium in Turri Londinensi asservatis, Henry III, 1216-72* (London, 1835–6)
Eyton, Itin.	R.W. Eyton, *Court, household and itinerary of King Henry II* (London, 1878).
Eyton, Shropshire	R.W. Eyton, 12 vols, *Antiquities of Shropshire* (London, 1854–60).
Fac(similes) Nat. MSS. (of)	*Facsimilies of the national manuscripts of Ireland*, ed. J.T. Gilbert, 4 vols (Dublin, 1874–84).
Fantosme	*Chronicles, Stephen, Henry II and Richard I*; ed. R. Howlett, iii (Rolls Series, London, 1890).
Feudal England	*See* Round's *Feudal England*.

H. Litton Falkiner	C.L. Falkiner in *Proceedings of the Royal Irish Academy*, xxvi (1906–7), pp 275 ff.
Fiants Eliz.	'Calendar to fiants of the reign of Henry VIII ... [etc.] in *Reports of the Deputy Keeper of the Public records in Ireland*, 7–22 (Dublin, 1875–90); reprinted as *The Irish fiants of the Tudor soverigns*, 4 vols (London, 1994).
Florence of Worcester	*Florentii Wigorniensis monachi chronicon ex chronicis* (English Historical Society, 1848).
F(our) M(asters)	*Annála rioghachta Éireann: Annals of the kingdom of Ireland by the Four Masters from the earliest period to the year 1616*, ed. and trans. John O'Donovan, 7 vols (Dublin 1845–51; reprint New York, 1966).
Fraser, J.G., *Psyche's Task*	J.G. Fraser, *Psyche's task: a discourse concerning the influence of superstition on the growth of institutions* (London, 1909).
Freeman, *Norman Conquest*	E.A. Freeman, *The history of the Norman conquest of England*, 6 vols (Oxford, 1867–9).
Gerv[ase]. Cant.	Gervase of Canterbury, *Historical works*, ed. William Stubbs, 2 vols, Rolls Series (London, 1879–80).
Gesta Hen.	*Gesta Henrici secundi Benedicti abbatis*, ed. W. Stubbs, 2 vols, Rolls Series (London, 1867).
Gesta Ricardi	*Chronicles, Stephen, Henry II and Richard I*, ed. R. Howlett, iii (Rolls Series, London, 1886).
Gilbert, History of Dublin	J.T. Gilbert, *History of the city of Dublin*, 3 vols (Dublin, 1845–9).
Gilbert, Viceroys of Ireland	J.T. Gilbert, *History of the viceroys of Ireland* (Dublin, 1865).
Gir. Camb.	*Giraldi Cambrensis opera*, ed. J.S. Brewer, J.F. Dimock and G.F. Warner, 8 vols, Rolls Series (London, 1861–91).
Gir. Camb Itin. Camb.	in *Giraldi Cambrensis opera*, vi, ed. J.F. Dimock, Rolls Series (London, 1868).
Gormanston Reg(ister)	Manuscript destroyed in the Public Record Office of Ireland in 1922, now extant only in *Calendar of the Gormanston Register*, ed. J. Mill and M.J. McEnery (Dublin, 1916).
Grace's annals	Jacobus Grace, *Annales Hiberniae*, ed. R. Butler (I.A.S., Dublin, 1842).
Green, *Short history* (illus. edn 1893)	J.R. Green, *A short history of the English people*, illustrated edition, 4 vols (London, 1892–4).
Hal(l)iday, *Scandinavian (kingdom of) Dublin*	C. Haliday, *The Scandinavian kingdom of Dublin*, 2nd edn (Dublin, 1884).
Hanmer, Chronicle	'Doctor Hanmer's Chronicle of Ireland' in James Ware, *Ancient Irish histories*, ii (Dublin, 1633).
Harris's Ware, Antiq. (ed. 1764)	J. Ware, *The history and antiquities of Ireland*, ed. Walter Harris (Dublin, 1764).
Hearne, Liber Niger Scaccarii	Thomas Hearne, *Liber Niger scaccarii* (London, 1774).
Hist(oirc) and Mun. Docs. of Ireland	*Historic and municipal documents of Ireland, 1172–1320*, ed. J.T. Gilbert (London, 1970).
H(ist). M(SS) C(om). 9th Rep. part I	*Historical Manuscripts Commission, report* (London, 1874–)
History of St. Canice (Graves and Prim)	J. Graves and J.G.A. Prim, *The history, architecture and antiquities of the cathedral church of St Canice, Kilkenny* (Dublin, 1857).

History and Antiquities of the Cathedral of St. Canice (Graves and Prim)	J. Graves, and J.G.A. Prim (eds), *The history, architecture and antiquities of the Cathedral Church of St Canice, Kilkenny* (Dublin, 1857).
Hoare, Richard Colt	*Journal of a tour of Ireland, A.D. 1806* (London, 1807).
Hogan's Ireland in 1598	*The description of Ireland and the state thereof as it is at this present anno in 1598*, ed. E. Hogan (Dublin, 1878).
Hogan's Onomasticon	E. Hogan, *Onomasticon Goedelicum* (Dublin, 1910).
Hore, History of Wexford	P.H. Hore, *History of the town and county of Wexford*, 6 vols (London, 1900–11).
Hoveden/Hoveden, Roger	*See* Roger of Howden
Hy Fiachrach	J. O'Donovan ed., *The genealogies* [..] of *Hy Fiachrach, commonly called O'Dowd's country* (Irish Archaeological Society, Dublin, 1844).
Inquis. Lageniae	*Inquisitionum in officio rotulorum cancellaria Hiberniae asservatarum repertorium*, 2 vols (Dublin, 1826–9).
Inquis. P.M.	*Calendar of inquisitions post mortem* (London, 1904–).
Irish abridgement of the Expugnatio in *EHR*	Whitley Stokes, 'The Irish abridgement of the *Expugnatio Hibernia*' in *English Historical Review*, 20 (1905), pp. 77–115.
Irish Arc. Soc. Misc.	*Miscellany of the Irish Archaeological Society* (Dublin, 1846).
Irish close rolls	*See* Rot. Canc. Cal. (Dublin, 1828).
Irish pipe roll 45 Hen. III	*Fac. Nat. MSS. Ireland*, ii, no. 7.
John Lackland	K. Norgate, *John Lackland* (London, 1902).
John of Salisbury, Metalogicus	*Metalogicon*, ed. C.C.J. Webb (Oxford, 1909).
Johannis Sarisb. Opera ed. Giles	John of Salisbury, *Opera omnia*, ed. J.A. Giles, 5 vols (London, 1848).
Journ. Brit. Arch. Assoc.	Journal of the British Archaeological Society.
Journ. R.S.A.I.	Journal of the Royal Society of Antiquaries of Ireland.
Joyce, *Short History of Ireland*	P.W. Joyce, *A short history of Ireland from the earliest times to 1608* (London & New York, 1893).
Joyce, Social Hist.	P.W. Joyce, *A social history of ancient Ireland*, 2 vols, (Dublin, 1903).
Just. Rolls	*See* Cal. Justiciary Rolls
Keating's History (I.T.S.)	Keating, Geoffrey, *Foras feasa ar Éirinn: the history of Ireland*, ed. David Comyn and P.S. Dineen, 4 vols, Ir. Texts Soc., iv, viii, ix, xv (1901–14).
Kilk. Arch. Soc.	*Transactions of the Kilkenny Achaeological Society*, 2 vols (Dublin, 1850–54); continued as *Proceedings and Transactions of the Kilkenny and South east of Ireland Archaeological Society*, 1 vol. (1854–5); *Journal of the Kilkenny and South East of Ireland Archaeological Society*, 6 vols (1856–67); continued as *Journal of the Royal Society of Antiquaries of Ireland* with consecutive enumeration dating back to 1850 and the title applied retrospectively.
King, *Church history of Ireland*	Robert King, *Church history of Ireland* (1851).
Knox, *History of Mayo*	H.T. Knox, *The history of Mayo to the close of the 16th century*, (Dublin, 1908).
Letter to the earl of Salisbury (ed. 1787)	Sir John Davies, *Historical tracts*, i (London, 1786).
Laud MS. Annals	Printed in *Chartul. St. Mary's Dublin*, ii, pp 303–98.

Liber Niger of Ch(rist) Ch(urch) (Cal.)	See Cal. Liber Niger.
Liber Primus Kilkenniensis	MS in custody of Kilkenny Corporation, ed. Charles McNeill (Dublin, 1931).
Liberate 5 John	*Rotuli de liberate et de misis et praestitis, regnante Johanne* (London, 1844).
Lanigan	J. Lanigan, *An ecclesiastical history of Ireland* (Dublin, 1822).
Leland's *History of Ireland*	T. Leland, *History of Ireland from the invasion of Henry II* (London, 1773).
Liber Albus Ossoriensis	H.F. Berry, 'Ancient charters in the Liber Albus Ossoriensis' in *Proceedings of the Royal Irish Academy,* xvii, C (1908), pp 115–25.
Liber Niger Alani	MS in custody of Representative Church Body Library, Dublin, ed. Charles McNeill (Dublin, 1850).
Liber Niger Scaccarii	*Liber Niger Scaccarii*; ed. Thomas Hearne (1728).
Lingard	J. Lingard, *The history of England from the first invasion by the Romans* 6th edn, 10 vols (London, 1854–5).
Lodge	John Lodge, *Peerage of Ireland* (Dublin, 1754).
Lodge, Westmeath	John Lodge, *Peerage of Ireland*, s.vi., 'Westmeath'.
Lynch's *Legal institutions*	William Lynch, *A view of the legal institutions, honorary hereditary offices, and feudal baronies established in Ireland during the reign of Henry II* (London, 1830).
MacGeogeghan, Abbé	J. MacGeogeghan, *The history of Ireland ancient and modern* (Paris, 1758; English edn Dublin 1844).
Maine, Early institutions	H.S. Maine, *Lectures on the early history of institutions* (London, 1875).
Marlebrugh's Chronicle	TCD MS E. 30
Mason's History of St Patrick's	W.M. Mason, *History and antiquities of the collegiate church of St Patrick near Dublin, from its foundation in 1190 to the year 1819* (Dublin, 1820).
Metalogicus	*See* John of Salisbury
Migne	Migne, *Patrologia Latina*
Miss Norgate, *Minority of Hen. III*	Kate Norgate, *The minority of Henry III* (1912).
Monasticon Diocesis Oxoniensis; ed. George Oliver	George Oliver, *Monasticon diocesis Exoniensis* (Exeter, 1846).
Moran, Dr	P.F. Moran, *Occasional papers* (Dublin, 1890).
Norgate's Angevin kings	K. Norgate, *England under the Angevin kings*, 2 vols (London, 1887).
Norman Conquest	*See* Freeman, *Norman Conquest.*
O'Curry, Manners and customs	E. O'Curry, *On the manners and customs of the ancient Irish* (London, 1873).
O'Donovan, *Celtic Miscellany*	John O'Donovan (ed.), *Miscellany of the Celtic Society* (Dublin, 1849)
O'Flaherty, *West Connacht*	Roderick O'Flaherty, *A chorographical description of West or h-Iar Connaught,* ed. J. Hardiman (Dublin, 1846).
O'Donovan's supplement to O'Reilly's Dictionary	Edward O'Reilly, *An Irish-English dictionary,* new edn with supplement by John O'Donovan (Dublin, 1864).
Ord. Survey Letters Q.C.	Manuscripts in the Library of the Royal Irish Academy cf. Orpen's edition of the *Song*, p. 254.

Ord. Vit. (Duchesne)	Orderic Vitalis, 'Historia ecclesiastica', in André Duchesne, *Flistoriae Normannorum scriptores* (Paris, 1619).
Owen, *Old Pembroke families*	Henry Owen, *Old Pembroke families in the ancient county palatine of Pembroke* (London, 1902).
Owen's Pembrokeshire	*Description of Pembrokeshire*, ed. H. Owen, 3 vols, Cymmrodorion Society (London, 1892–1906).
Papal letters (Bliss)	*Calendar of entries in the papal registers relating to Great Britain and Ireland: papal letters, 1198–1304* [*etc.*], ed. W.H. Bliss [and others], (London, 1893–).
Pipe Roll	*The great rolls of the pipe of the reign of Henry the second, 5th to 34th years*, 30 vols., Pipe Roll Society (London, 1884–1925).
Pipe Roll 12 and 13 John	National Archives Dublin, ed. O. Davies and D.B. Quinn, in *WJA*, 3rd ser, vi, supplement (1941).
Pollock and Maitland, Hist. of Eng. Law	Pollock and Maitland (eds), *History of English law before the time of Edward I* (Cambridge, 1895).
Proceedings, R.I.A.	Proceedings of the Royal Irish Academy
Professor G.T. Stokes, *Ireland and the Celtic Church*	Dr G.T. Stokes, *Ireland and the Celtic Church* (London, 1886).
R. de Diceto	*See* Diceto, R. de.
R. de Hovedon	*See* Howden, Roger of.
Ralph (de) Diceto	*See* Diceto, R. de.
Ramsay Angevin empire	J.H. Ramsay, *The Angevin empire, or the three reigns of Henry II, Richard I and John* (*A.D. 1154–1216*) (London, 1903).
Reeves, Eccl. Ant.	W. Reeves, *Ecclesiastical antiquities of Down, Connor and Dromore* (Dublin, 1847).
Reg. All Hallows	*Registrum prioratus omnium sanctorum*, ed. Richard Butler (Dublin: Irish Archaeological Society, 1845).
Reg. St Thomas/ Reg. St Thomas's, Dublin	*Register of the Abbey of St Thomas the Martyr,* Dublin, ed. J.T. Gilbert, Rolls Series (London, 1889).
Rep. D.K.	*Reports of the Deputy Keeper of the Public Records in Ireland.*
Rev. Thomas Olden, *Church of Ireland*	Thomas Olden, *The national churches: the Church of Ireland* (London, 1892).
Robert of Torigny	*Chronicles, Stephen, Henry II and Richard I*, ed. R. Howlett, iv (Rolls Series, London, 1890).
Rog. Hoveden/Rog. Howden	Roger of Howden, *Chronica Rogeri de Houedone*, ed. W. Stubbs, 4 vols, Rolls Series (London, 1868–71).
Rog(er) (de, of) Wend(over)	*Chronica Rogeri de Wendover*, ed. H.G. Howlett, 3 vols, Rolls Series (London, 1886–89).
Rot. Canc(ellaire) Cal (Tresham)	*Rotul patentium et clausorum cancellariae Hiberniae calendarum*, ed. E. Tresham, 2 vols (Dublin, 1828).
Rot. chart.	*Rotuli chartarum in Turri Londiniensi asservati, 1199–1216* (London, 1837)
Rot. claus.	*Rotuli literrarum clausarum in Turri Londiniensi asservati* (London, 1835).
Rot. de Finibus	*Rotuli de Oblatis et Finibus* (London, 1835)
Rot. de Prest(ito) 12 John	*Rotuli de libertate et de misis et praestitis regnante Johanne* (London, 1844).
Rogers, *Six Centuries of Work and Wages*	James E. Thorol Rogers, *Six centuries of work and wages: the history of English labour* (London, 1884).

Rot. Misae	*Rotuli de libertate et de misis et praestitis regnante Johanne* (London, 1844).
Rot. Pat	*Rotuli litterarum patentium in Turri Londineniensi asservati* (London, 1835).
Round, *Commune of London*	J.H. Round, *Commune of London* (London, 1899).
Round, *Feudal England*	J.H. Round, *Feudal England* (London, 1909).
Royal (&c.) letters (ed. Shirley)	W.W. Shirley, *Royal and other historical letters illustrative of the reign of Henry III*, 2 vols (London, 1862).
Rymer, *Foedera*	Thomas Rymer, *Foedera, conventiones, litterae* ... 4 vols (London, 1816; 69).
Silva Gadelica	S. Hayes O'Grady, *Silva Gadelica: a collection of tales in Irish*, 2 vols (London, 1892).
Skene, *Celtic Scotland*	W.F. Skene, *Celtic Scotland* (Edinburgh, 1880).
Song/Song of Dermot	*The Song of Dermot and the earl*; ed. G.H. Orpen (Oxford, 1892).
Smith's *Waterford* (1746)	C. Smith, *The ancient and present state of the county and city of Waterford* (Dublin, 1746).
Spencer, *View of the state of Ireland*	Edmund Spenser, *A view of the state of Ireland* (1810 edn)
Stokes Anglo-Norman Church	G.T. Stokes, *Ireland and the Anglo-Norman church* (London, 1889).
Stokes, Margaret	*Early Christian architecture in Ireland* (London, 1878).
Story of Perugia (Medieval towns)	M. Symonds and L. Duff Gordon, *Story of Perugia*, Medieval towns series (London, various editions).
Stubbs, *Select Charters*	Stubbs, W. (ed.), *Select charters and other illustrations of English constitutional history*, 9th edn., by H.W.C. Davis (Oxford, 1913).
Theiner, *Vet. Mon.*	A. Theiner, *Vetera monumenta Hibernium et Scotorum* (Rome, 1864).
Topog(r). poems	*The topographical poems of John O'Dubhagain and Giolla na naomh O'Huidhrin*, ed. John O'Donovan (Irish Archaeological Society, 1862).
Tout, *The political history of England*	T.F. Tout, *The history of England from the accession of Henry III to the death of Edward III (1216-1377)* (London etc., 1905).
Tracts I.A.S.	*Tracts relating to Ireland*, 2 vols (Irish Archaeological Society, 1841–4).
Tribes of Hy Many (ed. O'Donovan)	J. O'Donovan, *The tribes and customs of Hy Many* (Irish Archaeological Society, 1843).
Ussher's Sylloge	Ussher, James, *Sylloge veterum epistolarum Hibernicarum* (Dublin, 1632) reprinted in Ussher, James, *The whole works of the most reverend James Ussher*, ed. C.R. Elrington, 17 vols (Dublin, 1847–64).
Vallencey Collectanea de Rebus Hib.	C. Vallencey, *Collectanea de rebus Hibernicis*, 6 vols (Dublin, 1770–1804).
Vickers, *England in the later Middle Ages*	K.H. Vickers, *England in the later Middle Ages* (London, 1914).

Walsingham, *Historia Anglicana*	Thomas Walsingham, *Thomae Walsingham, quondam monachi S. Albani, Historia Anglicana*, ed. H.T. Riley, Rolls Series 28., 2 vols. (London, 1863–4).
Walter of Coventry	*Memoriale fratris Walteri de Coventria*, ed. W. Stubbs, 2 vols, Rolls Series (London, 1872–3).
Ware	James Ware, *Ancient Irish histories* (Dublin, 1809).
Ware-Harris, *Writers of Ireland*	Ware-Harris, *Writers of Ireland* (Dublin, 1764).
Ware's Annals	In *Chart. St Marys, Dublin*, ii.
Wars of the Gaedhil with the Gaill	*War of the Gaedhil with the Gaill, or the invasions of Ireland by the Danes and other Norsemen*, ed. J.H. Todd, Rolls Series (London, 1867).
White, Stephen	*Apologia pro Hibernia adversus Cambri calumnias*, ed. Matthew Kelly (1849).
Wilkins' Concilia	D. Wilkins, *Concilia magna Britanniae et Hiberniae*, 4 vols (London, 1737).
William of Malmesbury, Gesta Reg.	*Willelmi Malmesbiriensis de gestis regum*, ed. W. Stubbs, 2 vols, Rolls Series (London, 1887–89).
William of Newburgh	*Chronicles, Stephen, Henry II and Richard I*, ed. R. Howlett, i–ii, Rolls Series (London, 1885).
T. Wright, (Louthiana)	T. Wright, *Louthiana or an introduction to the antiquities of Ireland* (London, 1748).

PREFACE

(to the first edition of volumes 1 and 2)

Much of the story of Ireland has never been adequately told. Her early traditions, indeed, regarded by the annalists and by Geoffrey Keating and others as sober history, have in recent times been more scientifically treated from varying points of view, as legend with a dim substratum of fact, as mythology with a still dimmer basis, as folklore growing out of deep-rooted primitive custom. The footprints of St. Patrick and of the early saints have been followed over the length and breadth of the island. The traces of her missionaries have been sought for and found throughout western Europe. Her wonderful handiwork, executed under the patronage of her Church, on vellum, in metal, on stone, has been praised with justifiable pride, and has taken its place – no mean one – in the history of the evolution of art. Her primitive literature is gradually being given to the world by competent scholars. But when we come to the more fully attested history of later times, the raids of the Wikings in the ninth and tenth centuries have indeed been described and duly deplored, but only scant recognition has been
[i, 6] accorded to the contribution made by the Northmen to peaceful progress in the formation of seaport towns and the furthering of foreign trade. Throughout the whole historic period down to the coming of the Normans, the turmoil of inter-tribal conflicts has been the despair of writers who seek to tell a connected story, and in general they have passed it over rapidly, though perhaps not rapidly enough for their readers. The Norman invasion, the most far-reaching event that occurred in Ireland since the introduction of Christianity, has of course been repeatedly handled, but the importance of the invasion, and the interest that attaches to it and to the settlement of the new-comers that followed it, seem to demand for the period a much fuller study than any hitherto attempted. Then for the next three centuries, with the exception of some few unconnected episodes, the history of Ireland has been left in great obscurity, until in the sixteenth century she once more emerges into the light, and it is seen that English domination has sunk to its lowest ebb – that, though there are still two peoples in the island, over large parts of it descendants of English settlers have adopted Irish customs and have become as lawless and almost as rude as the Irish themselves, while in purely Irish districts little real advance from the position in the twelfth century has been effected. From this time forward Irish history has been treated more adequately, though not always with the freedom from passion becoming to historical
[i, 7] writers.

The object I had in view in the preparation of this work was, primarily, to give a more adequate as well as a more accurate account of the Anglo-Norman invasion of

Ireland, and of the settlement consequent thereon, than had hitherto been published; while it was my expectation that a closer study of the period would enable a more just estimate to be formed of the influence for good or for evil of the domination of the new people. A beginning would thus have been made towards filling up the gap in Irish history to which allusion has been made. In the course of my study of the twelfth and thirteenth centuries (which has been spread over many years) I have not only had occasion to correct many mis-statements of fact which have passed current, unquestioned, from writer to writer, but I have been led to regard the domination of the English Crown and of its ministers in Ireland, during the thirteenth century, and indeed up to the invasion of Edward Bruce in the year 1315, as having been much more complete than has been generally recognized, and to think that due credit has not been given to the new rulers for creating the comparative peace and order and the manifest progress and prosperity that Ireland enjoyed, during that period, wherever [i, 8]
their rule was effective.

With a view to ascertaining the main facts which led up to the invasion, I have commenced the present work with a survey, mainly derived from the Irish annals, of the immediately preceding period. This is followed by a brief study, based chiefly on the Brehon Law Tracts, of some of those customs and institutions which were at the time peculiar to Ireland and which subsequently affected the relation between the two races. For the period of the actual invasion we are fortunate in having two independent and virtually contemporary accounts. One of these, that of Gerald de Barry, has indeed long been known and utilized, but owing to his connexion with the invaders and to his inevitable want of sympathy with the Irish, it has been the fashion to discredit his statements and to represent his judgement as hopelessly warped. His observations on the social state of the country have been regarded as calumnies inspired by malevolence, the miraculous stories he tells have been held up as proofs of abnormal credulity, while he has even been charged with the deliberate forgery of important historical documents. That his sympathies were with the invaders, and in particular with those of his relatives who took a leading part in the invasion, should of course always be carefully borne in mind, but a study of his writings has led me to regard him not only [i, 9]
as an extraordinarily acute observer, and one who for his time was not peculiarly credulous, but also as a writer who (allowance being made for certain obvious prepossessions) faithfully recorded what he saw and heard. Following good classical authority, and from artistic motives, he has put speeches more or less imaginary into the mouths of his protagonists, and even ascribed to them written messages which perhaps are not verbally authentic; but the charge of deliberate forgery I reject as not merely non-proven, but in the highest degree improbable.

The other authority which I think we may regard as virtually contemporary is the Old French poem which some years ago I edited under the title of 'The Song of Dermot and the Earl.' This has come to be recognized as a primary authority for the period of the invasion, but the information to be obtained from it, corroborating, supplementing, and sometimes correcting the account in the 'Expugnatio', has never been fully incorporated in regular Irish histories; and in particular the evidence it affords as

to the distribution of fiefs among the early settlers, their manorial centres, and the type of castle usually erected by them, has never been fully co-ordinated with evidence to
[i, 10] be obtained from charters and other sources, and from especially recent topographical research. These omissions I have endeavoured to supply.

But the fragmentary 'Song' breaks off before the death of Strongbow in 1176, and Gerald de Barry gives us only a few disjointed facts after the death of Hugh de Lacy, a decade later. Then there is a brief period of considerable obscurity until, with the accession of King John, the series of English records begins to cast a more certain light. From this time forward patient research in many quarters, coupled with the exercise of a sound judgement and other qualities essential to the historian, should result in the production of a trustworthy and fairly full history of Ireland for the next three centuries. The present modest contribution towards fulfiling this great task proceeds no further than the close of the reign of King John. I offer it with a full consciousness of its many defects – some of them due to the need of having first to establish the facts – but whatever its value, it is at least the result of an independent study of the primary sources. Even in this short period – less than half a century from the time when the first invader set foot in Ireland – it is, I think, manifest that the most prominent effect of the Anglo-Norman occupation was not, as has been represented,
[i, 11] an increase in turmoil, but rather the introduction over large parts of Ireland of a measure of peace and prosperity quite unknown before.

I have not thought it part of my duty to pass moral judgements on anybody. Such judgements, even if unwarped by prepossessions, usually ignore historical perspective and take little account of the moral standards of the period, and are therefore not only unfair but uninstructive. The most important function of an historian, after he has carefully ascertained the facts of a case, is to understand them in their relation to other facts, and to give an intelligible account of the whole. To understand an action he must regard it from the point of view of the actor and with reference to the circumstances in which the actor stood. When he has really done this he will seldom care to pass severe moral judgements. More often he will find that 'tout comprendre est tout pardonner'.

Goddard H. Orpen

To Mr. Mills and Mr. McEnery, of the Public Record Office, Dublin, I owe thanks for their courtesy and assistance, and in particular for letting me use not only the original Gormanston Register, but also some proof sheets of the forthcoming Calendar to the Register which is being prepared in the Office. To the National Library of Ireland I am much indebted for the ease of of my researches among its well-arranged shelves.

FOREWORD

(to volumes 3 and 4)

Encouraged by the reception given to the first two volumes of this work, I lost no time before commencing to fulfil the promise held out at the close of Volume II, and endeavouring to complete my study of what may be regarded as the Anglo-Norman period of Irish history. Some explanation then seems to be required to account for the lapse of time before my self-imposed task was done.

In the first place, these new volumes are to an increasing extent pioneer work. Most of the ground now covered has never been properly surveyed before. It was necessary to examine more systematically many fields of inquiry which had been at best hastily run over, and to explore for the first time others which had been entirely ignored or left unnoticed. The recent publication of various calendars of public records has rendered available many authentic sources of our history which were practically beyond the reach of previous writers. These had to be examined and compared with the bald and isolated entries in Irish and Anglo-Norman annals. In result, the records and annalistic entries were often found to explain each other and bring both into relation with preceding and subsequent facts. There were still, however, many documents and some
[iii, 6] collections of documents which had to be examined in the original. Among the most important of these collections were the 'Red Book of the Earl of Kildare', which, by the courtesy of Lord Frederick Fitz Gerald, I was enabled to study at leisure, and the 'Gormanston Register', then lying in manuscript in the Public Record Office at Dublin, but since (in 1916) calendared. These collections not only add to our knowledge of the history and possessions of some great Irish families, but incidentally help to determine the extent and progress from time to time of Anglo-Norman domination. For the episode of the Normans in Thomond it was essential to consult the *Caithréim Toirdelbaig*, a fourteenth-century tract recounting from an Irish point of view the wars of Thomond in the times of Thomas de Clare and his son Richard (1275–1318). To the kindness of Dr., now Sir Norman, Moore, I was indebted for the loan of the scholarly rendering (still unpublished) of this MS. by the late Standish Hayes O'Grady. For the important period of the invasion of Edward Bruce, which proved to be the turning-point of Anglo-Norman influence, the entries in the Annals of Loch Cé and in some Anglo-Norman annals are unusually full. These last-mentioned annals are now known as Additional MS. 4792 in the British Museum and Laud MS. 526 in the Bodleian Library, and they have been published by J.T. Gilbert in his Chartularies of St. Mary's Abbey, Dublin. The accuracy of the dates supplied
[iii, 7] by these annals, as shown, whenever they can be verified, points to a contemporary

source. The Scottish tradition as preserved by Archdeacon Barbour, and the Irish account in the late tract entitled Cath Fochairte Brighite, were also consulted, and though these were found to be often inaccurate and unhistorical, they supply some details which may be regarded as authentic. The above sources taken in connexion with the public records of the time have enabled me to give a much fuller and more coherent account of this fateful period than any that has hitherto appeared. To Mr. H.T. Knox I owe the gift of careful transcripts of the lengthy inquisitions concerning the lands of the Earl of Ulster, who was murdered in 1333. Abstracts of the inquisitions relating to Connaught had already been made and annotated by Mr. Knox, while those relating to Ulster were similarly handled by me in a series of papers contributed to the Royal Society of Antiquaries of Ireland. These inquisitions throw much fresh light on the dominant position of the Norman barons in these two provinces in former years, as well as on the extent to which that position was lost owing to the disturbances following on the murder of the earl. It is unnecessary to specify here other sources of Irish history for the period covered, as I have thought it right to give throughout the work precise references to the principal authorities on which I rely; but as further accounting for the delay in publication I may add that when these and other
preliminary studies were completed, and the results from all sources compared and [iii, 8]
welded, as far as might be, into a coherent whole, the outbreak of the World-War diverted and absorbed all energy and attention, and the final revision and publication of the work was necessarily postponed to happier times.

Of the defects of these volumes no one can be more conscious than myself. One obvious imperfection is perhaps inherent in the subject. Writers of history have always had to compromise between observing the strict chronological order of the events within their purview and following out the course of particular movements to their ultimate issues, or at least to some convenient stage, but they are generally enabled to find a sort of epic unity in the influence on events of successive kings or their chief ministers. The history of mediaeval Ireland, however, presents the difficulty in an aggravated form. Not only was the influence of the English kings and their justiciars in Ireland, though far from negligible, often entirely overshadowed by that of the local magnates, whether Anglo-Norman or Irish, but the course of events in one province or sometimes even in smaller districts was in general unaffected by what happened in others. I have therefore frequently found it advisable to treat such districts separately; though such treatment has inevitably involved serious anticipations of the general chronological arrangement, as well as occasional repetition due to the need of recalling to mind relevant facts more conveniently mentioned in detail elsewhere.

Another difficulty presented by Irish as contrasted with English history in the thir- [iii, 9]
teenth century is that there were no contemporary historians in Ireland, such for example as those connected with the school of St. Albans in England, who aimed at supplying a connected narrative of events, exhibiting them in the relation of cause of effect, and explaining their significance. It was impossible, therefore, without an undue exercise of the imagination to unfold in any detail a continuous drama of Irish history. The story has to be laboriously pieced together from isolated annalistic entries, from

various public records and other documents, and from scattered indications of facts gleaned from many quarters, far and wide – and there were intervals of time between the acts of our drama without any obliging chorus or messenger to tell us what has happened in the interludes. As some compensation the writer is exempt from the risk of accepting too readily what may be only a distorted view of facts as seen by a prejudiced contemporary, or one designedly coloured with a view to influence opinion. While if due care be taken and a ripe judgement exercised, the narrative pieced together as above indicated, however imperfect, is at least so far as it goes based for the most part on the best and most easily-tested evidence, that is to say, on documents not designed to influence posterity, but intended for immediate use in the ordinary course of administration or business.

In the immediate future Ireland is likely to focus upon herself a large share of political attention, [iii, 10] and many ill-founded assertions regarding her past history as well as her present condition will doubtless continue to be made by politicians of all parties. It might indeed be thought that what happened upwards of seven centuries ago can have no practical bearing on our present-day problems. Nevertheless the appeal to history will inevitably be made, and as a matter of fact the Anglo-Norman occupation of Ireland is by many regarded as the 'fons et origo mali'. It certainly had far-reaching effects. Now it has been my aim to examine the Anglo-Norman period from a mediaeval standpoint, and not to allow any modern political nostrum to colour the presentation of the picture drawn. All those who are sincerely desirous of understanding the Irish problem with the single-minded object of arriving at the best solution for all concerned, should therefore welcome an endeavour to set forth the facts of that occupation with as much exactness of statement and indifferency of judgement as is humanly possible.

CHIEF GOVERNORS OF IRELAND

IN THE REIGNS OF HENRY II, RICHARD I, AND JOHN

HUGH DE LACY: appointed *custos* of Dublin (Gesta Hen. i. 30, Gir. Camb. v. 286) and *justiciarius Hiberniae* (Rog. Hoveden, ii. 34) in April 1172; summoned to Normandy, *c.* April (?) 1173.

WILLIAM FITZ AUDELIN: sent to transact the king's business, *Regis loco et vice*, *c.* April 1173 (see chap. ix, note A). He held office probably for about five months.

RICHARD DE CLARE, EARL OF STRIGUIL: appointed *custos regni*, *c.* August 1173 (Gir. Camb. v. 298, ' Song,' 2904–5); died *c.* June 1, 1176 (Gir. Camb. v. 332).

RAYMOND FITZ WILLIAM: appointed procurator provisionally by the king's commissioners on the death of Richard de Clare (Gir. Camb. v. 334).

WILLIAM FITZAUDELIN: appointed procurator by Henry, *c.* June 1176 (Gir. Camb. v. 334, Gesta Hen. i. 195).

HUGH DE LACY: appointed procurator general, *c.* May 1177 (Gir. Camb. v. 347), or *custos* of Dublin (Gesta Hen. i. 164). At the same time Henry created his son John *Rex Hiberniae*, but it is probable that he did not interfere before 1185.

JOHN DE LACY, constable of Chester and RICHARD DE PEC jointly appointed *ad curam regiminis*, *c.* May 1, 1181 (Gir. Camb. v. 355), or as *custodes* of Dublin (Gesta Hen. i. 270).

HUGH DE LACY: re-appointed in the winter of 1181–2 (Gir. Camb. v. 356).

[16] PHILIP OF WORCESTER: appointed procurator, *c.* Sept. 1, 1184 (Gir. Camb. v. 359).

JOHN FILIUS REGIS: in Ireland as *dominus* from April 25, 1185 (Gir. Camb. v. 380) to December 17, 1185 (R. de Diceto, ii. 39).

JOHN DE COURCY: appointed by Henry, *c.* December 1185 (Gir. Camb. v. 392). He was still justiciar when John was Earl of Mortain (Reg. St. Thomas, p. 383).

? WILLIAM LE PETIT: stated by Harris to have been Chief Governor in 1191.

? PETER PIPARD: *justiciarius* in 1194 (Marlburgh's Chronicle, Trin. Coll. Dub. MS. E. 3. 20, p. 135).

HAMO DE VALOGNES: *justiciarius*, 1196 (Annals of Inisfallen) to *c.* 1198 (Papal Letters (Bliss), vol. i, p. 3).

? PETER PIPARD and WILLIAM LE PETIT: joint justiciars, *c.* 1198–9 (Chart. St. Mary's, vol. i, p. 144; vol. ii, p. 28). [See *Add.*]

MEILER FITZ HENRY: his appointment as *capitalis justiciarius* is entered on Rot. Chart. 2 John, but writs are addressed to him as justiciar from *c.* July 1199. He remained justiciar until the autumn of 1208, when he appears to have been superseded by Hugh de Lacy.

HUGH DE LACY: EARL OF ULSTER: probably Chief Governor for a few months from the autumn of 1208 (Annals of Inisfallen, and Harris).

JOHN DE GRAY, BISHOP OF NORWICH: justiciar probably from the winter of 1208–9, when William de Braose seems to have fled to Ireland (Hist. Guillaume le Maréchal, Rot. Misae, pp. 144, 149).

KING JOHN: in Ireland June 20, 1210, to August 25, 1210 (Rot. de Prestito).

JOHN DE GRAY: remained as justiciar until superseded by Archbishop Henri de Londres, but he appears to have been summoned to attend the king on the Welsh campaign of 1211 (Four Masters, *sub anno* 1210, and cf. Roger of Wendover, vol. ii, p. 60), when Richard de Tuit was [17]
left as deputy in his stead; and again in April 1213, when he attended the muster at Barham Down with 500 knights (Roger of Wendover, vol. ii, p. 67), and when probably Geoffrey de Marisco was his deputy.

HENRI DE LONDRES, ARCHBISHOP OF DUBLIN: appointed justiciar on July 23, 1213 (Rot. Pat., 15 John, p. 102).

GEOFFREY DE MARISCO: appointed justiciar on July 6, 1215 (Rot. Pat., 17 John, p. 148).

The above list differs in several particulars from that compiled by Walter Harris in his edition of Ware's Antiquities (1764), p. 102. Harris's list, though generally followed by later writers, can be shown to be incorrect in many particulars (see *c.*xvii, § 1). The principal authorities for the above list are in each case given. The only really obscure period is from the termination of John de Courcy's term of office to the appointment of Meiler Fitz Henry.

IN THE REIGN OF HENRY III [iii, 13]

GEOFFREY DE MARISCO, who had been appointed justiciar by King John on July 6, 1215, was retained in that office under the Regency up to July 1221: Rot. Claus., 5 Hen. III, p. 476 b.

HENRY DE LONDRES, ARCHBISHOP OF DUBLIN, appointed July 3, 1221: Pat. Roll, 5 Hen. III, m. 3.

WILLIAM MARSHAL THE YOUNGER, EARL OF PEMBROKE, appointed May 2, 1224: Pat. Roll, 8 Hen. III, m. 8. During William's absence in England in the winter of 1224–5 Geoffrey de Marisco was his deputy: Rot. Claus, 9 Hen. III, vol. ii, p. 69 b.

GEOFFREY DE MARISCO, reappointed June 25, 1226: Pat. Roll, 10 Hen. III, m. 4.

RICHARD DE BURGH, appointed February 13, 1228: Pat. Roll, 12 Hen. III, m. 6.

HUBERT DE BURGH, Earl of Kent and justiciar of England, on June 16, 1232, was granted the office of justiciar of Ireland for life with power to appoint a deputy, and Richard de Burgh, as Hubert's deputy, was ordered to be intentive to Hubert: Pat. Roll, 16 Hen. III, m. 4. Hubert, however, was dismissed in disgrace on July 29, 1232, and there is no evidence that he ever acted as justiciar of Ireland.

MAURICE FITZ GERALD, second baron of Offaly, appointed September 2, 1232: Close Roll, 16 Hen. III, m. 4.

JOHN FITZ GEOFFREY, appointed November 4, 1245: Cal. Pat. Rolls, 30 Hen. III, p. 465. He had previously acted during the absence of Maurice Fitz Gerald on the king's expedition to Wales

from September 1245: Close Roll, 29 Hen. III, m. 2. On Februrary 14, 1254, the king made a grant of Ireland to his eldest son Prince Edward: Charter Roll, 37 & 38 Hen. III, Cal. Docs.
[iii, 14] Ireland, vol. ii, nos. 326, 371. John Fitz Geoffrey, though absent with the king in Bordeaux and afterwards with the prince, was seemingly continued as justiciar, with Richard de la Rochelle, seneschal of Prince Edward, as his lieutenant, until the appointment as justiciar of Alan de la Zuche. From 1254 to 1276 the appointments of justiciars do not appear on the rolls, and the precise dates cannot be fixed.

ALAN DE LA ZUCHE, justiciar from shortly before June 27, 1256: Cal. Docs. Ireland, vol. ii, no. 506.

STEPHEN LONGESPEE, justiciar from before October 21, 1258: Ibid., no. 600.

WILLIAM DE DENE, justiciar by October 2, 1260: Ibid., no. 683.

RICHARD DE LA ROCHELLE, justiciar by October 28, 1261: Ibid., no. 715. He was imprisoned by the Geraldines on December 6, 1264. In consequence of the caption of the justiciar, and during the confusion caused by the Barons' War in England, the king, ostensibly on behalf of his son, committed the custody of Ireland to several persons in succession, namely on February 26, 1265, to Fulk de Saunford, Archbishop of Dublin: Ibid., nos. 758, 766; on or before May 6, 1265, to Roger Waspail: Ibid., no. 771; and on June 10, 1265, to Hugh de Taghmun, Bishop of Meath. On April 28, 1266, however, the king again addressed a writ to Richard de la Rochelle as justiciar or his deputy.

DAVID DE BARRY, justiciar from Michaelmas 1266: Pipe Roll (Ireland), 51 Hen. III, 35 Rep. D.K., p. 48; and Laud MS. Annals, Chart. St. Mary's, vol. ii, p. 316.

ROBERT D'UFFORD, justiciar from *c.* Michaelmas 1268; Laud MS. as above, and cf. Cal. Docs. Ireland, vol. ii, nos. 849, 970. On his returning to England in March 1270 Richard of Exeter performed the functions of justiciar: Annales de Monte Fernandi, and cf. 36 Rep. D.K., p. 54.

JAMES D'AUDLEY, justiciar from Michaelmas 1270 to June 23, 1272, when he broke his neck in Thomond: Cal. Docs. Ireland, vol. ii, nos. 889–90; Annales de Monte Fernandi, 1272.

[iv, 5] IN THE PERIOD 1272–1332

MAURICE FITZ MAURICE, younger son (eldest surviving) of Maurice Fitz Gerald II, deputed by the lieutenants of Prince Edward as justiciar from *c.* August 1272: Cal. Pat. Rolls, 56 Hen. III, p. 674.

MAURICE FITZ MAURICE, confirmed in the office of justiciar by the king on December 7, 1272: Cal. Fine Rolls, 1 Ed. I, p. 1.

GEOFFREY DE GEYNVILLE, justiciar from August 1273 to the summer of 1276: see his accounts, Pipe Roll (Ireland), 7 Ed. I, 36th Rep. D.K., pp. 40, 41.

ROBERT D'UFFORD, appointed justiciar June 17, 1276: Cal. Pat. Roll, 4 Ed. I, p. 149. When absent in England during parts of 1279 and 1280, his *locum tenens* was Stephen de Fulburne, bishop of Waterford: Cal., nos. 1596, 1646; Laud MS. Annals in Chart. St. Mary's, vol. ii, p. 318.

STEPHEN DE FULBURNE, Bishop of Waterford, and treasurer of Ireland, appointed justiciar November 21, 1281: Cal. Pat. Roll, 10 Ed. I, p. 1. William Fitz Roger, prior of Kilmainham, was his deputy in 1283 (36th Rep. D.K., p. 70); and again in July 1285: Cal., vol. iii, no. 814. Stephen de Fulburne was translated to the see of Tuam on July 11, 1286, and died July 3, 1288: 37th Rep. D.K., p. 34.

JOHN DE SAUNFORD, Archbishop of Dublin, on July 7, 1288, was appointed by the King's Council 'Keeper of Ireland until the king should otherwise decide': Cal., vol. iii, no. 559. William d'Oddingeseles and Walter l'Enfant were his deputies in 1290 in some operations against O'Melaghlin of Meath: ibid., p. 270.

WILLIAM DE VESCY, appointed justiciar September 12, 1290: Cal. Pat. Roll, 18 Ed. I, p. 387. On his going to England early in 1294 in connexion with his dispute with John Fitz Thomas, Walter de la Haye, escheator of Ireland, was his *locum tenens*: Cal., vol. iv, no. 147; Laud MS. Annals, Chart. St. Mary's, vol. ii, p. 328.

WILLIAM FITZ ROGER, Prior of Kilmainham, assigned by the King's Council as Keeper after the [iv, 6] removal of William de Vescy, from June 4, 1294, to October 19 in the same year: Cal., vol. iv, pp. 120–1.

WILLIAM D'ODDINGESELES, appointed justiciar October 18, 1294: Cal. Pat. Roll, 22 Ed. I, p. 99. He died in office in April 1295: Cal., vol. iv, p. 121; Laud MS. Annals, Chart St. Mary's, vol. ii, p. 324.

THOMAS FITZ MAURICE (of Desmond), assigned by the King's Council as Keeper of Ireland, April 19, 1295: Cal., vol. iv, p. 121.

JOHN WOGAN, lord of Picton Castle in Pembrokeshire, appointed justiciar October 18, 1295: Cal. Pat. Roll, 23 Ed. I, p. 155. Among his *locum tenentes* were for some months from October 1299, Richard de Burgh, Earl of Ulster (Justiciary Roll, vol. i); from August 1301 to March 1302, William de Ros, Prior of Kilmainham (Cal., vol. iv, no. 801); Maurice de Rochefort, from June 30 to September 29, 1302 (Cal., vol. v, no. 71); Edmund le Botiller, from October 1304 to May 1305 (Justiciary Roll, vol. ii, where he is called *custos*). On June 16, 1208, Piers Gaveston, Earl of Cornwall, came to Ireland with viceregal powers, but in the autumn, when John Wogan crossed to England, he left William de Burgh as *custos* during his absence: Laud MS. Annals, Chart. St. Mary's, vol. ii, p. 337. Gaveston returned to England on June 23, 1309, and John Wogan remained in office. In 1312 Edmund le Botiller was once more his *locum tenens*: ibid., p. 341.

THEOBALD DE VERDUN, appointed justiciar April 30, 1313 (Cal. Pat. Rolls, 6 Ed. II, p. 568), came to Ireland as justiciar on December 31, 1314: Laud MS., as above, p. 343; but was soon summoned to Newcastle against the Scots.

EDMUND LE BOTILLER, appointed justiciar on January 4, 1315; Cal. Pat. Rolls, 8 Ed. II, p. 207.

ROGER DE MORTIMER, of Wigmore (afterwards Earl of March), who had been appointed keeper of Ireland November 23, 1316 (Cal. Pat. Rolls, 10 Ed. II, p. 563), landed at Youghal April 7, 1317: Laud MS., as above, p. 301. He returned to England about May 1318, leaving William FitzJohn, Archbishop of Cashel, as *custos*: ibid., p. 358.

ALEXANDER DE BYKENORE, Archbishop of Dublin, appointed justiciar August 11, 1318 (Cal. [iv, 6] Pat. Rolls, 12 Ed. II, p. 196), entered Dublin as justiciar October 9, 1318: Laud MS., p. 359.

ROGER DE MORTIMER, again justiciar on March 16, 1319 (Cal. Pat. Rolls, 12 Ed. II, p. 317), returned to England in 1320, leaving Thomas Fitz John, Earl of Kildare, as deputy: ibid., p. 361.

RALPH DE GORGES, appointed justiciar February 1, 1321 (Cal. Pat. Rolls, 14 Ed. II, p. 558); but he seems not to have come to Ireland.

JOHN DE BERMINGHAM, Earl of Louth, appointed justiciar May 21, 1321: Cal. Pat. Rolls, 14 Ed. II, p. 588.

JOHN DARCY (LE NEVEU), justiciar November 18, 1323 (Cal. Pat. Rolls, 17 Ed. II, p. 348); he was 'going to Ireland' on August 18, 1324.

THOMAS FITZ JOHN, Earl of Kildare, appointed justiciar March 12, 1327: Cal. Pat. Rolls, 1 Ed. III, p. 29. He died April 1328.

BROTHER ROGER OUTLAW, Prior of Kilmainham and chancellor, seems to have been justiciar April 1328.

JOHN DARCY (LE NEVEU), appointed justiciar August 21, 1328: Cal. Pat. Rolls, 2 Ed. III, p. 316.

JOHN DARCY (LE COSYN), appointed justiciar February 19, 1329: Cal. Pat. Rolls, 3 Ed. III, p. 373.

ANTHONY DE LUCY, appointed justiciar February 27, 1331: Cal. Pat. Rolls, 5 Ed. III, p. 83. Four days later William de Burgh, Earl of Ulster, was appointed king's deputy in Ireland, to take with the advice of the justiciar and council all measures necessary for the preservation of peace there: Foedera, vol. ii, p. 811.

JOHN DARCY (LE COSYN), appointed justiciar September 30, 1332: Cal. Pat. Rolls, 6 Ed. III, p. 340.

NOTE:—In the above list of Chief Governors their various deputies or *locum tenentes* are not all mentioned.

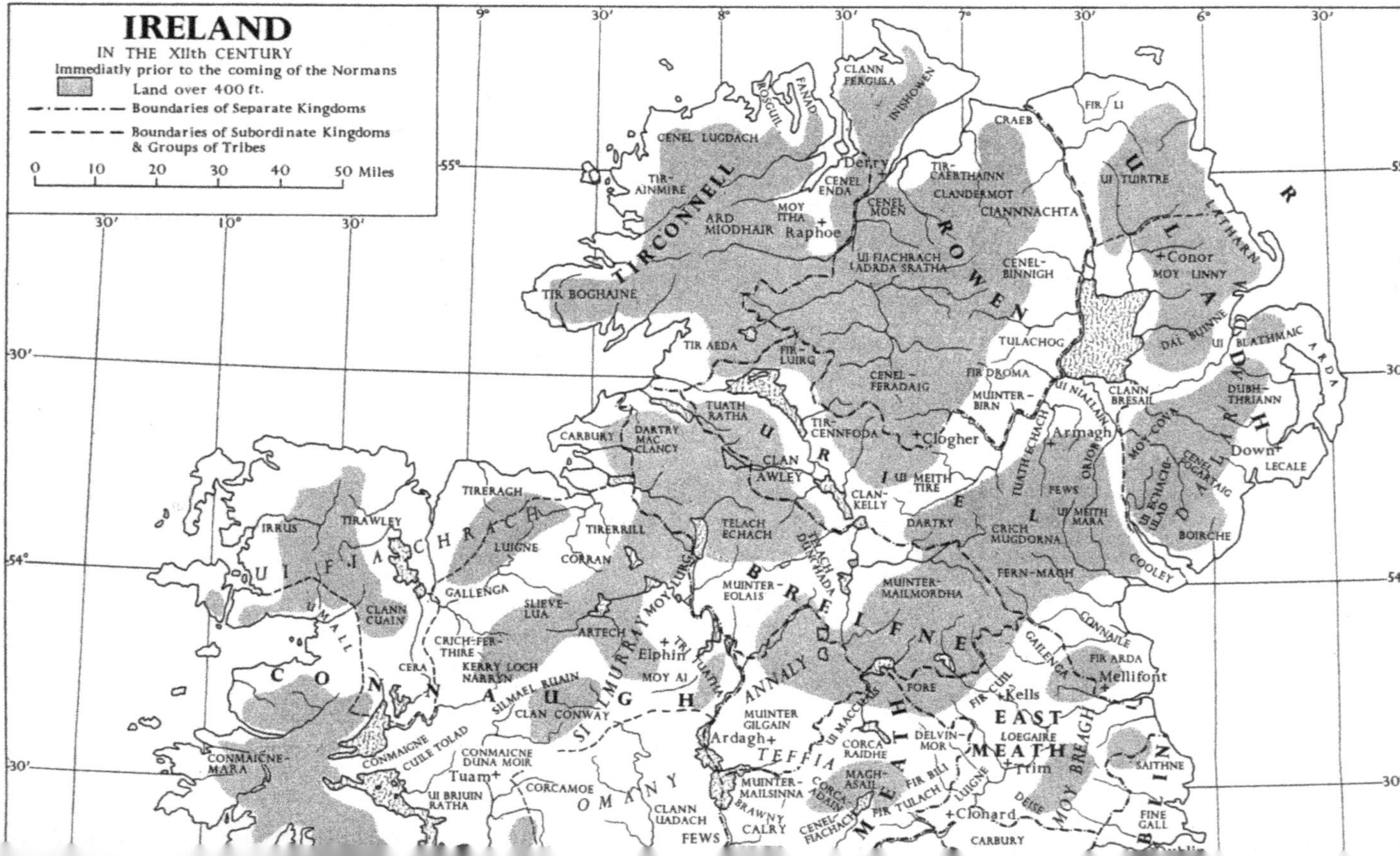
IRELAND
IN THE XIIth CENTURY
Immediatly prior to the coming of the Normans
Land over 400 ft.
Boundaries of Separate Kingdoms
Boundaries of Subordinate Kingdoms & Groups of Tribes
0 10 20 30 40 50 Miles
TIRCONNELL
CENEL LUGDACH
TIR-AINMIRE
TIR BOGHAINE
ARD MIODHAIR
MOY ITHA
Raphoe
FANAD
ROSGUIL
CLANN FERGUSA
INISHOWEN
Derry
CENEL ENDA
CENEL MOEN
TIR-CAERTHAINN
CLANDERMOT
CIANNNACHTA
CRAEB
ROWEN
UI FIACHRACH ARDA SRATHA
CENEL-BINNIGH
TULACHOG
FIR DROMA
MUINTER-BIRN
CENEL-FERADAIG
TIR-CENNFODA
Clogher
UI MEITH TIRE
CLAN-KELLY
TIR AEDA
FIR-LUIRG
TUATH RATHA
CLAN AWLEY
DARTRY MAC CLANCY
CARBURY
TELACH ECHACH
TELACH DUNCHADA
FIR LI
UI TUIRTRE
LATHARN
Conor
MOY LINNY
DAL BUINNE
UI BLATHMAIC
ARDA
ULAIDH
DUBH-THRIANN
Down
LECALE
CLANN BRESAIL
UI NIALLAIN
Armagh
TUATH ECHACH
ORIOR
FEWS
UI MEITH MARA
MOY COVA
CENEL FOGARTAIG
UI ECHACH ULAD
BOIRCHE
COOLEY
DARTRY
CRICH MUGDORNA
FERN-MAGH
MUINTER-MAILMORDHA
BREFNE
MUINTER-EOLAIS
ANNALY
CONNAILE
FIR ARDA
Mellifont
GAILENGA
FIR CUIL
Kells
EAST MEATH
LOEGAIRE
Trim
MOY BREAGH
SAITHNE
FINE GALL
DEISE
Clonard
CARBURY
LUIGNE
FIR TULACH
FIR BILI
DELVIN-MOR
CORCA RAIDHE
MAGH-ASAIL
CORCA ADAIN
CENEL FIACHACH
FORE
UI MACCUAIS
MUINTER GILGAIN
Ardagh
TEFFIA
MUINTER-MAILSINNA
BRAWNY
CALRY
FEWS
CLANN UADACH
OMANY
TIRERAGH
LUIGNE
GALLENGA
TIRERRILL
CORRAN
SLIEVE-LUA
ARTECH
MOY LURG
Elphin
TRI TUATHA
MOY AI
SIL MURRAY
CONNAUGH
CLAN CONWAY
SILMAEL RUAIN
KERRY LOCH NARRYN
CRICH-FER-THIRE
CERA
IRRUS
TIRAWLEY
UI FIACHRACH
CLANN CUAIN
UMALL
CONMAICNE-MARA
CONMAIGNE CUILE TOLAD
CONMAICNE DUNA MOIR
Tuam
UI BRIUIN RATHA
CORCAMOE

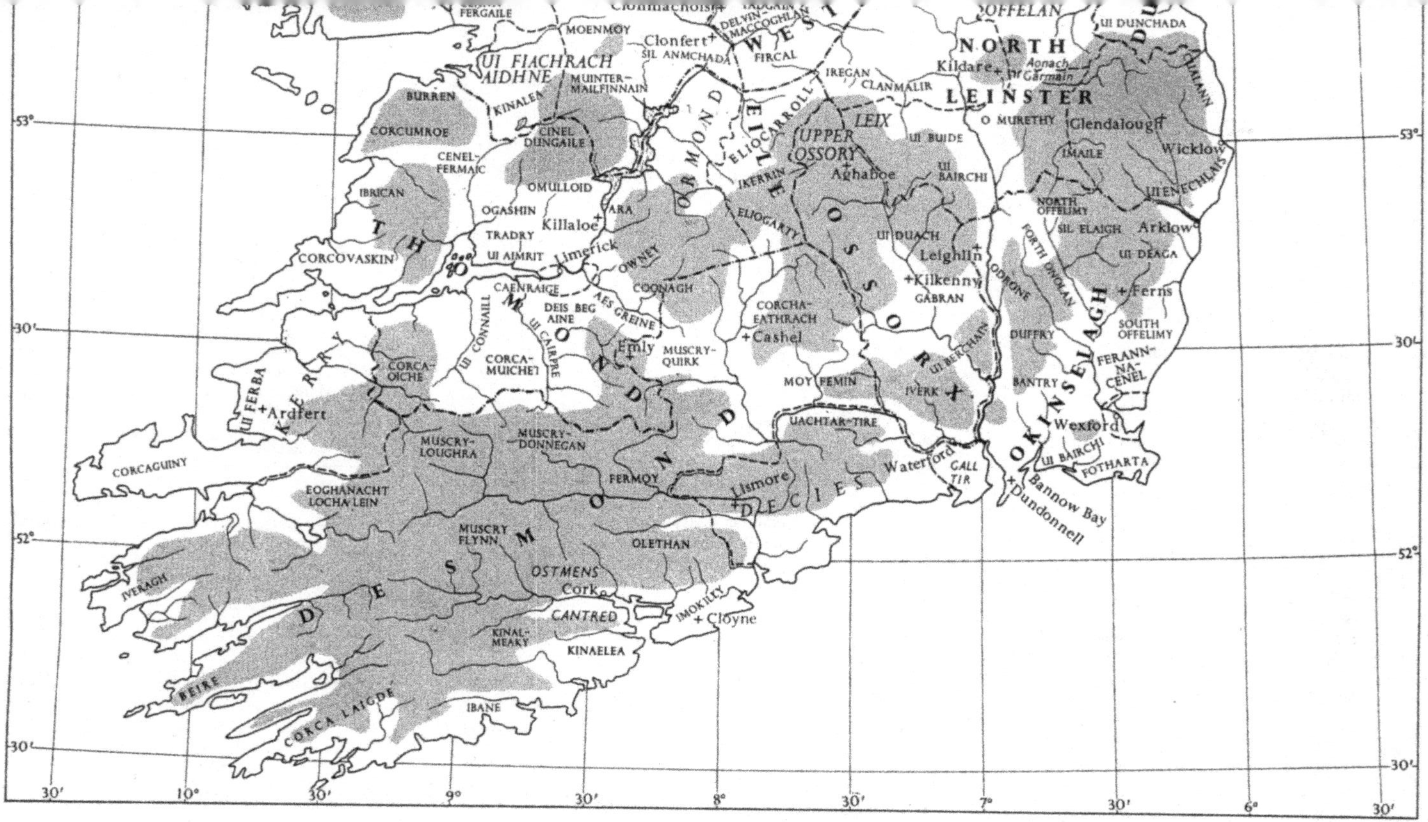
FERGAILE
Clonmacnoise
MOENMOY
Clonfert
SIL ANMCHADA
DELVIN-MACCOGHLAN
WEST
FIRCAL
OFFELAN
NORTH
LEINSTER
UI DUNCHADA
Kildare
Aonach Carmain
UI FIACHRACH AIDHNE
MUINTER-MAILFINNAIN
KINALEA
IREGAN
CLANMALIR
BURREN
CORCUMROE
CINEL DUNGAILE
ORMOND
ELIOCARROLL
UPPER OSSORY
LEIX
UI BUIDE
O MURETHY
Glendalough
CUALANN
IMAILE
Wicklow
CENEL-FERMAIC
IBRICAN
OMULLOID
IKERRIN
Aghaboe
UI BAIRCHI
UI ENECHLAIS
OGASHIN
Killaloe
ARA
ELIOGARTY
NORTH OFFELIMY
SIL ELAIGH
Arklow
TRADRY
UI DUACH
UI DEAGA
THOMOND
CORCOVASKIN
UI AIMRIT
Limerick
OWNEY
Leighlin
FORTH ONOLAN
CAENRAIGE
COONAGH
Kilkenny
ODRONE
Ferns
DEIS BEG AINE
AES GREINE
GABRAN
OSSORY
UI CONNAILL
CORCHA-EATHRACH
SOUTH OFFELIMY
UI CAIRPRE
Cashel
DUFFRY
KERRY
UI FERBA
Emly
MUSCRY-QUIRK
UI BERCHAIN
FERANN-NA-CENEL
CORCA-OICHE
CORCA-MUICHET
MOY FEMIN
IVERK
BANTRY
Ardfert
UACHTAR-TIRE
Wexford
MUSCRY-LOUGHRA
MUSCRY-DONNEGAN
UI BAIRCHI
FOTHARTA
CORCAGUINY
FERMOY
Waterford
GALL TIR
Lismore
Bannow Bay
Dundonnell
EOGHANACHT LOCHA LEIN
DECIES
MUSCRY FLYNN
OLETHAN
DESMOND
OSTMENS
Cork
IVERAGH
CANTRED
IMOKILLY
Cloyne
KINAL-MEAKY
KINAELEA
BEIRE
CORCA LAIGDE
IBANE
53°
30′
52°
10°
9°
8°
7°
6°

DESCENDANTS OF NEST, DAUGHTER OF RHYS AF TEWDWR

by

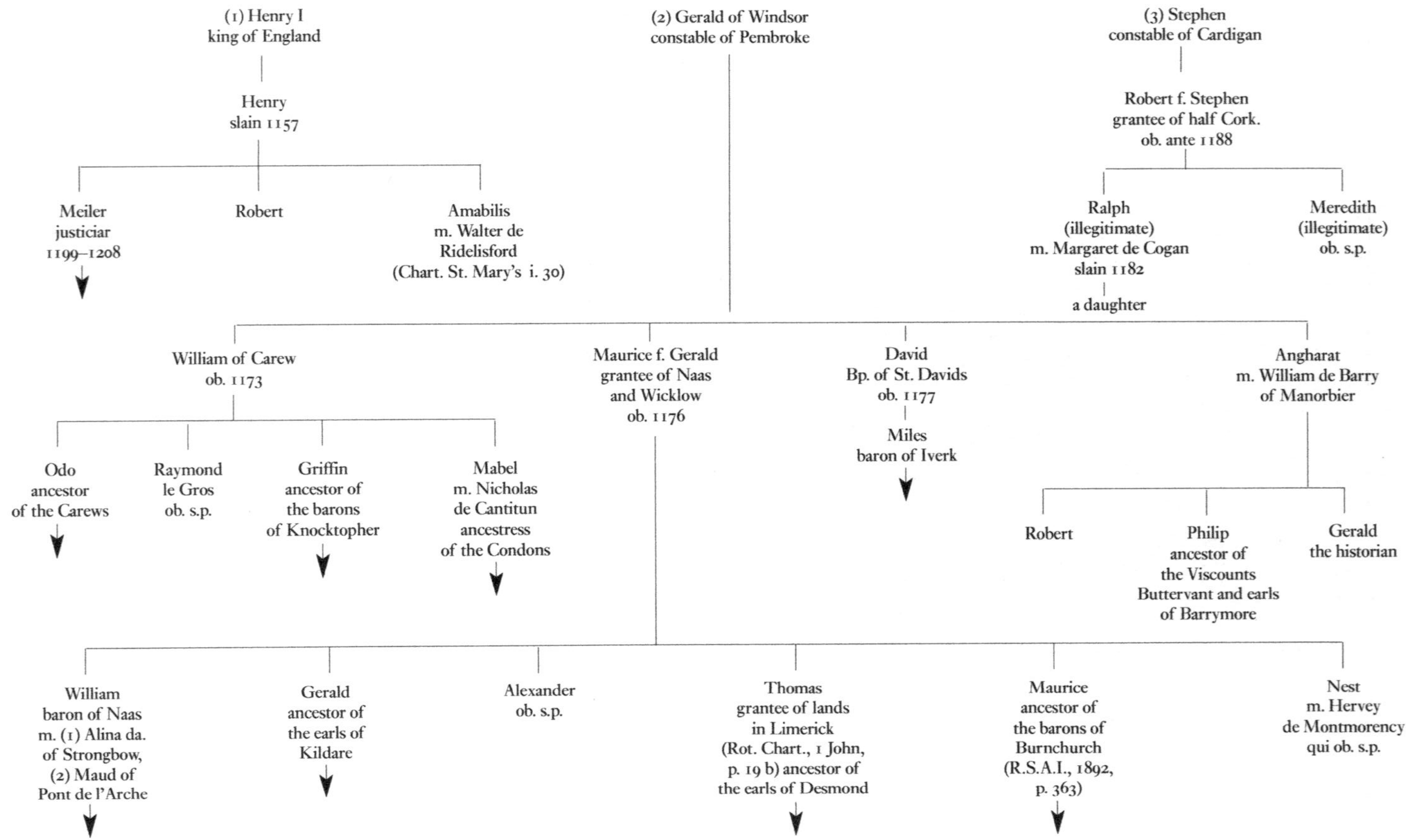

[19]

CHAPTER I

ANARCHIC IRELAND
NINTH TO ELEVENTH CENTURIES

'O Mary! It is a great deed that has been done in Erin on this day, the Kalends of August: Diarmaid Mac Donnchada Mic Murchada, King of Leinster and of the Foreigners, to have been banished by the men of Erin over the sea eastwards! Uch, uch, O Lord! what shall I do?'[1]

These words, written in Irish on the margin of a page in the Book of Leinster, express the feelings of some devoted adherent of Dermot Mac Murrough upon the occasion of Dermot's expulsion from Ireland in the year 1166. Verily it was a great deed that was done in Erin on that day; greater even than this poor follower of the fallen king, unless endowed with prophetic insight, could have foreseen; a deed big with the destinies of Erin for many a long century to come.

But although the expulsion of Dermot, by supplying a pretext for interference, led directly to the Anglo-Norman invasion and to the ultimate subjection of Ireland to the
[20] English Crown, great national movements are never really due to mere personal action or individual volition. Had Dermot never been expelled, or had he never invoked Norman aid, we may rest assured that the ultimate result would not have been very different. In the state of Ireland, viewed relatively to that of England in the twelfth century, we must seek for the more deep-seated conditions which invited the invasion and rendered the ultimate subjection inevitable.

Ireland was still in the tribal state. The allegiance of the free-born Irishman was given in the first place to the head of his family, kindred, or sept (*fine*), and through the family head (*cenn fine*) to the chief of the tribe of which his family formed an element, related by real or supposed remoter kinship and connected by common ownership of land. The Irishman's country was the *tuath* or territory belonging to his tribe. There was often a tangible bond of union between his particular tribe and certain neighbouring ones, connected perhaps by traditional kinship or actual conquest, linked together under a sub-king, and forming a *mór-tuath*. A still weaker bond bound this *mór-tuath* with its sub-king to the provincial king, while the provincial king seldom acknowledged the superiority of any other unless under compulsion, and then,
[21] as a rule, only so long as the compulsion lasted. In theory indeed this was not so. Theoretically there was a regular chain of subordination from the tiller of the ground through his immediate lord, leading up, link by link, to the *ard-rí* or chief king of Ireland. In theory the organization bore a certain superficial resemblance to the feudal system, but it was based in its lower stages on loans of cattle and food rents, and in the

1 Book of Leinster, f. 200 a.

higher ranks on more or less arbitrary tributes, and not in any case on gifts of lands, and there was no adequate legal machinery for enforcing the observance of rights and the performance of duties.

It is usual to speak of the five provinces of Ireland, the names of which, though not the exact boundaries, are still represented by Ulster, Munster, Leinster, Connaught, and Meath, as if they were definite units each under one king. This was perhaps the theory, and, when there was a strong king in any particular province, may have been the fact in that province, during the period of his strength; but it was seldom, if ever, literally true of them all. Had it been so, it would not have been necessary for the provincial kings to be again and again exacting hostages from their supposed subordinates. This is the principal criterion of kingship laid down in the Brehon Law Tracts: 'He is not a king who has not hostages in fetters, to whom the rent of a king is not given, to whom the fines of law are not paid.'[2] The principal groups of tribes in Ulster [22]
(the modern province) were the Cinel Owen (seated in Tyrone and Londonderry), the Cinel Connell (in Donegal), the Ulidians (in Down and Antrim), and the Oirghialla (or people of Uriel, i.e. Louth, Armagh, and Monaghan). There was really no recognized king of this province,[3] though in general the king of the Cinel Owen, whose traditional seat was the fort of Ailech near Derry, was the most powerful; but more often than not the kings of the other groups appear to have been quite independent of him, and whenever he claimed supremacy it was necessary to reduce them to subjection. Breffny, a district comprising the modern counties of Leitrim and Cavan, with which at times parts of Longford were held, though nominally classed with Connaught, was often independent and even opposed to that province. The kingdom of Ossory, corresponding to the modern diocese of that name, and including besides Kilkenny the three western baronies of Queen's County, was sometimes claimed as subordinate to Munster and sometimes as subject to Leinster, and yet was really more often independent of both. From the dawn of history for a period of six centuries (i.e. from the [23]
middle of the fifth to the middle of the eleventh century) the so-called kings of Leinster were almost without exception chosen from the groups of tribes that clustered round the Curragh of Kildare, and they seldom had any effective authority in Southern Leinster. When the tribe of Okinselagh, seated in the diocese of Ferns, gave kings to Leinster, the tribes of Leix, Offaly, Offelan, and Omurethy (i.e. Northern Leinster), as well as Ossory, were often opposed to them. Munster in later times was generally divided into Thomond or North Munster and Desmond or South Munster, and these districts were constantly at war with each other. Meath, the traditional seat of the *ard-rí*, was more homogeneous, but its boundaries, though generally coinciding with the modern diocese, varied at different times. Dublin and the adjoining district were generally held independently under the Danish kings, while, on the other hand, Offaly and Offelan sometimes gave hostages to the King of Meath. In the twelfth century Meath was again and again partitioned in the most arbitrary manner, and was more than once subjected to 'foreign kings'.

2 Ancient Laws of Ireland, vol. iv, p. 51. 3 In the Book of Rights the kings of Ailech, of Oirghialla, and of Uladh are treated as co-ordinate and quite independent of each other.

But if the authority of the provincial kings was frequently defied, that of the *ard-*
[24] *rí* or supreme King of Ireland, if acknowledged at all, was little more than nominal. The Book of Rights contains an elaborate account of the tributes stated to be due from the provincial kings (of which as many as twelve are enumerated) to the *ard-rí*, and from the sub-kings to the provincial kings, as well as of the 'stipends' to be paid by the latter in each case to the former, but this elaborate account must be regarded as a claim put forward by a king of Munster who aspired to the head kingship of Ireland, rather than as a system ever regularly carried out. Certainly the supreme king could not count upon military assistance from the provincial kings even to resist an invasion of Ireland. Thus when Brian, always acknowledged to be the most powerful monarch Ireland ever had, summoned his great army to crush the Danes of Dublin and to repel the fresh Scandinavian hordes invited to the conquest of Ireland by Sitric, the northern province universally held aloof; so did the King of Connaught with the major part of the province; while Leinster actually fought on the enemy's side.[4] To the same weakness, as we shall find, must largely be ascribed the inability of Rory O'Conor to cope with the handful of Norman knights who fought under Strongbow.

The theoretical organization, then, of Ireland, consisting of five provinces ruled by
[25] five kings in subordination to a supreme king, did not in historic times square with the facts. If we wish to get a truer idea of political forces in Ireland, at any rate after the period of the Norse invasions, we must regard the country as split up into about 185 tribes, of which some were grouped together in comparative permanence, and some were generally subordinate to the principal groups. But we must be prepared to find these tribes and groups of tribes ever and again forming new combinations of a more or less temporary nature, either by way of alliance or of conquest, and exercising an independent judgement as to joining or holding aloof from any particular general hosting. In fact the question of peace or war in any particular instance seems to have been decided independently by each petty group of clansmen, and in their decision they appear to have been more often actuated by their own immediate interests, or even by their petty jealousies, than by any large survey of the good of the whole. If now we go a step further back and seek the cause of this—how it was that Ireland, even in the latter half of the twelfth century, remained in the tribal state, with one tribe or shifting combination of tribes incessantly at war with other tribes and combinations, while Europe generally was settling down into strong centralized monarchies—
[26] we shall find that it was because Ireland lay outside the march of events in Europe. Her Celtic immigrants had brought with them from the common Aryan home a body of primitive custom, which had remained almost unchanged and had never been quickened in its development by contact with more advanced systems. She had never felt the shock of the Roman legions. Her institutions had never been pressed into a new mould by Roman law and government. She had never known the Pax Romana. She had, however, been happily exempt from the rush of barbarians which followed the downfall of the power of Rome in other lands, and to this is probably due much of

4 Ann. Loch Cé, vol. i, p. 7.

her early civilization and comparative advance in the seventh and eighth centuries, when her missionary monks helped to preserve some of the learning of the past and to hand on the torch of a higher faith to succeeding generations. Christianity too had come to her gradually and peaceably, and had not been imposed by the sword of a conquering race from without, as was the case with the continental Saxons. It left her tribal system untouched, or rather the Church took the mould of the tribe, and the 'family of the saint' was organized and held property somewhat on the analogy of that of the secular chieftain. Hence some of those ecclesiastical peculiarities which afterwards attracted so much attention. Had Ireland been allowed to go her way unheeded [27]
by Europe, she might in time, and after much suffering, have evolved a better ordered system with some hope of progress in it, and the world might have seen a Celtic civilization where Celtic imagination and Celtic genius, free and unfettered, would assuredly have contributed something towards the solution of human problems, which, as it is, mankind has missed for ever. But it was not to be. In the ninth and tenth centuries the 'Land Leapers' from the North, 'merciless soure and hardie,' swept across the land, pillaging, burning, and destroying. The Irish, with their loose tribal organization, were incapable of offering an effective resistance. The same cause, by a curious compensation, saved them from final defeat and subjugation. There was no national army which, once destroyed, would leave the country open to the invader. There was no capital city, the taking of which would mark the downfall of the national government. There was little to plunder except in the ecclesiastical centres. So the Northmen never subjugated Ireland, nor made it a Scandinavian kingdom. They finally settled down in the walled towns they had built on the sea-coast, and from Pagans and pirates became Christians and traders. But the evil they had done lived after them. Their example in plundering churches and monasteries, to which art, [28]
learning, and culture were largely confined, was only too aptly followed by the Irish themselves. The march of Irish civilization was arrested, nay, put back. The primitive literature of Ireland, which seems to have survived her Christianization, and even to have been preserved in the vernacular by Christian writers, was to a large extent lost. The authority of the *ard-rí*, never very great, was diminished, and was only co-extensive with his might. The power of the subordinate chiefs was increased, the influence of the Church, which even at home had never advanced beyond the missionary stage, was on the wane, and the turmoil and anarchy were greater than ever.

But, it may be said, the Scandinavian invasions came to an end. The power of the Northmen was finally crushed at Clontarf, and there remained a century and a half before Ireland was again interfered with by any extern power. Why did she not evolve into something great in this time? Why did she not at least consolidate herself into one nation?

The battle of Clontarf marks an important epoch in Irish history, but not exactly in the way in which it is popularly remembered. It certainly did not rid Ireland of 'the foreigners'. The Norsemen remained as before in possession of the walled city of Dublin and of the sea-board towns which they had created on the east and south coasts, whence [29]
they dominated the adjoining districts, and occasionally joined in the internal contests

of the Irish themselves. It is true that the defeat put an end to the last great attempt of the Scandinavian race to gain the upper hand in Ireland. Just at the moment when the Danes in England were succeeding in uniting all elements under one powerful monarchy, and making her for the first time in history one nation, all chance (if chance there were) of a like result in Ireland was at an end. But, indeed, the wise government of Swegen and Cnut succeeded in winning the allegiance of the various kingdoms of England because they were akin to the English. They brought no novel institutions with them, above all no novel system of land tenure, and even their language was closely allied to English. Their kinsfolk would have had an incomparably more difficult task in Celtic Ireland, and they could hardly have succeeded where the Normans ultimately failed. At any rate, for good or for evil, the possibility of a Scandinavian domination of Ireland was at an end. Yet it may be questioned whether the result of the battle was not in other respects more disastrous to the conquerors than to the conquered. The battle of Clontarf marks the downfall of the hopes of Brian to establish a strong monarchy in
[30] Ireland, and the failure of the most promising attempt ever made to make Celtic Ireland a nation. Whatever Brian's motive may have been, whether purely patriotic or largely personal, he went nearer to effecting this great object than any Irishman before or since.

When no more than a sort of outlaw with a handful of followers in the wilds of Thomond, Brian is said to have spurred on his brother Mahon to declare undying war to the foreigners, and to have aided him to win back his province of Thomond from their clutches. On succeeding in 976 to his brother's throne, he amply avenged his brother's treacherous murder and forced all Munster to acknowledge him as king. In 999 he defeated the men of Leinster and their allies the Norsemen of Dublin at Glenmama.[5] Then, not hesitating in pursuit of his great object to ally himself with the foreigners, he entered Meath and forced the *ard-rí* Malachy to yield to him the crown of Ireland (A.D. 1002). Finally, still accompanied by the Norsemen, he marched tri-
[31] umphantly through the north of Ireland[6] and obtained successively the hostages of the Ulidians, the Cinel Owen, and the Cinel Connell. Having thus by the right of the sword made himself master of Ireland, he used his power well. A glowing picture of Brian's rule is given us in what may be regarded as a 'Brian Saga':[7]

> He proclaimed peace throughout Erin. He hanged and killed and destroyed the robbers and thieves and plunderers of Erin. He extirpated, banished, and ruined the foreigners in every district. He killed their kings and their chieftains, their men of renown and valour. He enslaved their stewards and their mercenaries, their comely, large, cleanly youths, and their smooth, youthful maidens. So that after the banishment of the foreigners the poet sang:
>
> From Tory island to pleasant Cleena,
> While carrying with her a ring of gold,

5 As to the site of this battle see Journ. R.S.A.I., vol. xxxvi (1906), p. 78. 6 There is an interesting proof of Brian's visit to Armagh on one of these expeditions (Four Masters, 1004) in the shape of an entry in the Book of Armagh made *in conspectu Briani imperatoris Scotorum*, recognizing the supremacy of the see of Armagh: Facsimiles Nat. MSS. Irel., vol. i, pl. xxv. 7 Wars of the Gaedhil with the Gaill, R.S., pp 136–40.

In the days of Brian, the brilliant, the fearless,
A woman might wander alone through Erin.

He rebuilt churches and sanctuaries, destroyed by the Norsemen. He purchased books beyond the sea to supply the place of those that had been burned and 'drowned' by the plunderers. By him were erected the church of Killaloe,[8] and the church of Inish Caltra, and the bell-tower of Tomgraney, and many other works. By him were made [32] bridges and causeways and high roads. He strengthened the duns and fastnesses and islands (crannogs) and royal forts of Munster; and continued in this way, peaceful and prosperous, for twelve years[9] in the chief sovereignty of Erin.

Making large allowances for the poetry and partisanship of the passage condensed above, there seems no reason to doubt that Brian laid the foundations of a real monarchy in Ireland. But Brian fell at Clontarf, and the edifice he had commenced fell with him. He left no successor strong enough to maintain the position he had won for himself with the sword. Nay, the very success of his career made it much more difficult for even any of the legitimate line of titular monarchs to make his rule a reality. Few pages of Irish history are more bitter reading for an Irishman than those which tell of the subsequent fortunes of the shattered battalion of the Dalcassians, the brave remnants of Brian's own tribe. No sooner had they buried their dead on the field of battle than dissensions, we are told,[10] broke out among the leaders of Brian's army. Cian, son of Molloy, and Donnell, son of Duvdavorenn, leaders of the men of Desmond, [33] took counsel together against the Dal Cais; and the men of Desmond, noting how few of the Dal Cais had survived and how many of them were wounded, said one to the other— 'The attention of Brian's son will be on you to seek for lordship and power such as his father had, and should he reach his home it will be more difficult to meet him than now.' Accordingly they demanded hostages of Donough, son of Brian, and insisted on the observance of the rule according to which the sovereignty of Munster should belong alternately to the Eoghanachts and Dal Cais, tribes which drew their descent respectively from Eoghan Mor and Cormac Cas, sons of Oilioll Olum, King of Munster in the third century—a rule which had already been ignored when Brian succeeded his brother Mahon. But Donough replied that it was not voluntarily they had been subject to his father nor to his father's brother; for the whole of Munster had been wrested by Brian from the foreigners, when the men of Desmond were unable to contest it with them, and he refused to give them hostages. Thereupon the men of Desmond arose and took their arms to give battle to the Dal Cais, and badly would the latter have fared, brave as they were—their very wounded, we are told, stuffed their wounds with moss [see *Add.*] and insisted on standing by their comrades—only that [34] their treacherous foes fell out amongst themselves over the division of the expected

8 Not, of course, any part of the existing cathedral, but perhaps the stone-roofed church of St. Flannan with its early Romanesque doorway, which still stands close by. 9 The writer says 'for fifteen years'. But Brian cannot be said to have been King of Ireland until after the deposition of Malachy in 1002. 10 Wars of the Gaedhil with the Gaill, pp 212–17.

spoils. 'Wilt thou give me an equal division of half Munster, as much of it as we may both conquer?' said Donnell, son of Duvdavorenn. 'That will I not give, indeed,' said the son of Molloy. 'If thou give it not, then,' said Donnell, 'on my word I shall not go with thee against the Dal Cais, because I am not better pleased to be under thee than under the son of Brian Borumha, unless for the profit of land and territory for myself.' Thus the conspiracy fell through, and before the year was out a battle was fought between the conspirators, and Cian, son of Molloy, and two of his brothers were slain, and 'a prodigious slaughter' was made around them.[11] In the following year Donnell, son of Duvdavorenn, led an army to Limerick to challenge the Crown of Munster, but he was defeated and slain by the sons of Brian.[12] Thus ended this conspiracy, but it was not the only piece of treachery that the heroes of Dal Cais had to meet on their return from Clontarf. They had reached the ford across the Barrow at Athy, and had refreshed themselves with the waters, and had cleansed their wounds, when they found Donough, son of Gillapatrick, King of Ossory, with the men of Leix, lying in
[35] wait for them in battle array on the further side, 'for they were natural enemies to each other.' The men of Ossory straightway demanded hostages, which Donough O'Brien indignantly refused. When the wounded men heard of this demand, 'their strength and their fury grew so that every man of them was able for battle,' and they bade their comrades drive stakes into the ground 'to which they could put their backs standing during the battle'. The men of Ossory, however, intimidated by this wonderful courage in the Dal Cais, both whole and wounded, declined the battle.

This whole story, embellished as it doubtless is to heighten the glory of the Dal Cais, shows clearly the evil results to the country at large of the clan system. The chieftain, if he did not fight merely for his own hand, had no higher conception of duty than to increase the power of his clan; with this object in view, he was stayed by no scruples. The clansman, while ready to lay down his life for his chief, felt no enthusiasm for a national cause. The sentiment for 'country', in any sense more extended than that of his own tribal territory, was alike to him and to his chief unknown.

Just as Brian had disturbed the old rule of alternate succession in Munster between
[36] the descendants of Cormac Cas and those of Eoghan Mor, so, but with still more fatal effect, he had put an end to the custom, acquiesced in for upwards of five centuries, according to which the *ard-rí* of Ireland was chosen alternately from the two great houses of the Hy Neill race, or descendants of Niall of the Nine Hostages, King of Ireland at the close of the fourth century. Henceforth the prize of the sovereignty of Ireland was open to all comers. What Brian had won by the sword an O'Brien, or an O'Conor, or a Mac Murrough, might win by the same means. For the moment the deposed King Malachy was allowed to resume the crown which he had been forced to yield to Brian. There is evidence indeed that the succeeding generation regarded Brian as a mere usurper. For just as English jurists speak of the year of the Restoration as the twelfth year of Charles II, ignoring the intervening rule of Cromwell, or as French Royalists regard the period 1793–1814 as part of the reign of Louis XVIII, so the annalist Tigernach, who died in 1088, takes no account of Brian's reign, but states that

11 Ann. Ulster, 1014. 12 Ibid. 1015

Malachy reigned for forty-three years, just as if there had been no interruption, and in this reckoning he is followed by the annalists generally.[13] From the death of Malachy (1022), however, up to the year of Dermot's expulsion (1166), there never was a uni- [37]
versally acknowledged king of Ireland. In the phrase of the annalists, there were only kings *co fressabbra*, 'with opposition.'

At first perhaps Donough, Brian's son, who High had foully got rid of his elder brother Teig, was the chief aspirant to the throne, but he never obtained the submission of either Ulster or Connaught, and his nephew Turlough O'Brien, aided by his foster-father Dermot Mac Maelnamo, waged constant war with him, until at length, in 1064, Turlough wrested the crown of Munster from his uncle's grasp. Even before this Dermot Mac Maelnamo, King of Leinster and Dublin, was the most powerful of the provincial kings, and by some is reckoned King of Ireland,[14] but in 1072 he was defeated and slain by Conor O'Melaghlin, King of Meath, son of Malachy. Turlough O'Brien was now styled King of Ireland 'with opposition'. He, too, failed to exact [38]
hostages from Ulster. He died in 1086. His son, Murtough O'Brien, was opposed by Donnell O'Loughlin, King of Ailech or Ulster, who now revived the almost lapsed claims of the royal line of Niall Mor. They fought almost incessantly for a quarter of a century without decisive result. Both are claimed by their respective partisans as kings of Ireland. A new claimant now appeared in the person of Turlough O'Conor, King of Connaught, in whose time we first hear of Dermot MacMurrough.

13 Ann. Tigernach, 1022. So Ann. Clonmacnois, Ann. Ulster, Ann. Loch Cé. 14 See Ann. Clonmacnois, 1041, where the criterion of an *ard-rí co fressabbra* is given. The name Maelnamo (pronounced with a short penultimate), in Irish *Máel na mbó*, probably means 'chief of the kine'. Cf. Mael-duin, 'chief of the fortress', *Máel doborchon*, *Máel mílchon*, 'chief of the otters' and 'greyhounds' respectively. *Máel* properly means 'bald'. When used with a saint's name, as in *Máelpatric*, it means the tonsured one (i.e. servant) of the saint. Like the Welsh *moel* it is often applied to a bare hill or mountain-top. The transition from the head or top of a man or mountain to 'head' in the sense of 'chief' is easily paralleled.

[39] CHAPTER II

DERMOT, KING OF LEINSTER, 1126–66

To follow the fortunes of Dermot Mc Murrough prior to his expulsion in 1166 will lead us into a tortuous maze of inter-provincial and inter-tribal fighting, but if we wish to understand the causes which led to his expulsion and—what is more important—gain even a glimpse of the anarchy that revelled throughout Ireland up to the coming of the Normans, we cannot entirely pass over this page of history, amply evidenced as it is by unimpeachable Irish authorities. We shall, however, omit to notice all fighting except what had a direct bearing on Dermot's position and fortunes, and merely endeavour to piece together what remains into an intelligible narrative.

Dermot was son of Donough Mc Murrough, King of Southern Leinster, and was born in 1110.[1] His father was one of a long line of kings of Okinselagh, who in recent
[40] times had won recognition as Kings of Leinster and of Dublin, and who once at any rate, in the person of Dermot, son of Maelnamo, had even aspired to the overlordship of Ireland. This Donough Mc Murrough, Dermot's father, was slain in 1115 in the battle of Dublin by Donnell, son of Murtough O'Brien, and the Foreigners of Dublin.[2] Giraldus says that the citizens of Dublin murdered Dermot's father while sitting in the hall of one of his chief men which he used for his court of justice, and that, adding insult to injury, the citizens buried him along with a dog. There is no authority in the annals for these particulars, which are, however, repeated by Keating, and were probably current in Leinster as part of the story in Giraldus's time. Donough Mc Murrough was succeeded by another member of the family, and then by his son Enna, both of whom are styled kings of Leinster. Enna died in 1126, and was immediately succeeded as lord of Okinselagh by Dermot, then in his seventeenth year.[3]

[40] The youthful King of Okinselagh had, however, a long struggle before he was the acknowledged King of Leinster. For the past decade Turlough O'Conor, King of Connaught, had been striving to reduce the provinces of the south of Ireland, with a view to gaining for himself the practically vacant throne of Ireland. His general method was to harry each province in turn, force it into submission, and then divide

1 This date follows from the statement in the Book of Leinster (f. 20) that Dermot died in the sixty-first year of his age. See Song of Dermot, note l. 1729. 2 Ann. Tigernach [under this head I refer to the continuation of Tigernach's annals, 1088–1178, one of the most valuable native authorities for this period, edited by W. Stokes in Revue Celtique, vol. xviii], Ann. Ulster, &c. Donough Mc Murrough was two years in joint kingship with Conor O'Conor, King of Offaly, when they were both slain: Book of Leinster (Facsimile, p. 39 d). 3 According to the Book of Leinster, Dermot reigned forty-six years. His reign must therefore have been reckoned from the year 1126.

it between two or more kings. But the process had to be repeated in each case more than once. In 1115 he divided Meath between two of the O'Melaghlins, one of whom immediately killed the other.[4] In 1118 he divided Munster, which had been united since the time of Brian Borumha, between an O'Brien and a Mc Carthy, and hurled the royal palace of Kincora, 'both stone and wood,' into the Shannon.[5] In 1120 he expelled Murrough O'Melaghlin, the surviving King of Meath, and when the so-called *ard-rí*, Donnell O'Loughlin, came to his assistance, Turlough made a 'false peace' with them.[6] Five years later he again expelled Murrough O'Melaghlin and placed three kings over Meath, one of whom was immediately killed.[7] Again and again Turlough constructed a wicker bridge across the Shannon at Athlone and defended it [42]
with a fortress, in order that, as one annalist puts it, 'he might at his pleasure have access to take the spoils of West Meath,'[8] but each time, at the first opportunity, the king of the country thus threatened destroyed both bridge and fortress. In 1121 he laid waste Desmond 'from Magh Feimhin to Tralee, both lands and churches, namely, seventy churches or a little more', until, in the simple but expressive words of another annalist, 'he caused the people of Munster to cry aloud.'[9] In the same year he made another plundering excursion as far as Lismore and 'obtained cattle-spoils innumerable'. On his next expedition in 1123 to Desmond he was bought off with hostages, including the king's son, but before another year was out he had the usual ground—a general rising against him—for putting the hostages to death.[10]

Upon the death of Enna Mc Murrough, King of Leinster, in 1126, Turlough made a hosting into Leinster and exacted hostages. In the course of the same year he [43]
deposed 'the son of Mac Murrough', presumably Dermot, and set up his own son Conor as King of Leinster and Dublin, to which position, of course, he had no sort of hereditary or elective claim. This is only one out of many examples of the forcible breaking up of the old rules whereby the provincial kings were chosen from certain ruling families of the leading tribes of the province. If the plan had succeeded it might have formed part of the meritorious policy of consolidating Ireland under one king, but it was premature and utterly failed. In the same year Turlough formed a great encampment in Ormond from August 1 to February 1, a veritable pirates' nest, from which he sent out plundering parties to Connello (co. Limerick), Glanmire (co. Cork), and to the south of Ossory, 'and carried off many kine and a great number of captives'. This was the signal for 'a great storm of war throughout Ireland in general', not to be allayed by Cellach, the co-arb of St. Patrick, though he was for a year and a month endeavouring to pacify the country.[11] The men of Munster and of Leinster once more revolted against Turlough, and their hostages were again forfeited. The Leinstermen deposed the king that had been forced upon them, but in 1127 they had to accept [44]

4 Ann. Tigernach, Four Masters. 5 Ann. Tigernach. 6 Ann. Ulster, Ann. Loch Cé, Ann. Tigernach, 1120. 7 Ann. Ulster, 1125. The continuator of Tigernach says that Turlough divided Meath into four parts and gave one part to Tiernan O'Rourke, who now 'submitted to him and made an alliance with him as to doing his will'. 8 Ann. Clonmacnois, 1132. Turlough made at least four other bridges for plundering purposes at Athlone (Four Masters, 1120, 1129, 1140, 1155), and each time the bridge was destroyed within a few years. 9 Ann. Ulster, Ann. Tigernach (continuation). 10 The fullest account is given by the continuator of Tigernach. 11 Ann. Tigernach, Ann. Loch Cé, Ann. Ulster, Four Masters, 1126.

another nominee of Turlough, namely Donnell son of Mac Faelain.[12] He came of a family from which several kings of Leinster had been chosen in the centuries which preceded the rise to power of Okinselagh, and he might have been ultimately accepted by the North Leinster clans; but the young prince of Okinselagh, in whose family the sovereignty of Leinster had been for three quarters of a century, was not prepared to waive his claims. Accordingly, in 1128 Turlough made a foray-hosting into Okinselagh, to Wexford, and thence round Leinster to Dublin, and wrought great destruction of cattle on the route; 'but the ill-fame of that hosting,' we are told, 'rested on Tiernan O'Rourke.'[13] Thus early do we find the King of Connaught and Tiernan O'Rourke in hostile relations with Dermot. It does not appear whether Dermot formally submitted to Turlough at this time. Probably he did or was ignored, as we do not hear of his taking any steps to assert his claims for some years. He was probably biding his time until he should be strong enough to assert his rights.

One ugly deed, which may have had a political motive, is ascribed to him, or at least
[45] to his tribe. When Donnell son of MacFaelain was set up as king by Turlough O'Conor, fighting took place between the tribes of Offaly and Offelan as to which of the two tribes should have the appointment of the new abbess of Kildare, and Carroll, the new king's brother, was slain.[14] Three years later Dermot appears to have settled the question in a peculiarly revolting fashion. The house of the abbess was captured and burned by the men of Okinselagh and many were slain 'and the nun herself was carried off a prisoner and put into a man's bed.'[15] The motive was evidently similar to that which induced so many in high position to blind their rivals when they got them into their power—namely, while keeping clear of actual murder, to incapacitate the victim from holding office. Probably the appointment of the successor of St. Bridget was regarded as a prerogative of the King of Leinster.

Meanwhile Turlough O'Conor continued his merciless raids on Munster by land and sea. In 1127 he drove Cormac McCarthy into the monastery at Lismore, and
[46] divided Munster into two (or three) parts[16] and carried off thirty hostages. He had a fleet of 190 vessels on Lough Derg, and from this base devastated the adjoining cantreds of Munster. This fleet was an important element in his destructive strength, and it was not only on the Shannon that he had ships. His sea-fleet plundered as far as Tory Island and Tirconnell in the north and Valentia and Cork in the south.[17] But we need not follow Turlough in his raids any further. During a long reign of fifty years he was perhaps the most turbulent of his contemporaries, but it must not be supposed that much better conditions prevailed under rulers elsewhere. In the north the Cinel Owen were repeatedly fighting with the men of Uladh and with the Cinel Connell, and the subordinate clans were frequently at war with each other. Meath was almost incessantly fighting with Connaught, and Tiernan O'Rourke was always joining in, first on one side and then on the other, according as he saw some momentary advan-

12 Ann. Ulster, 1127, where see editor's note. 13 Ann. Ulster, Ann. Loch Cé, 1128. 14 Ann. Ulster, 1127. 15 Ann. Loch Cé, 1132; cf. Ann. Clonmacnois, 1135. Neither the Four Masters nor the continuator of Tigernach have this entry. That in the Annals of Ulster is defective. 16 Ann. Tigernach. The Four Masters say that Turlough divided Munster into three parts. 17 Four Masters, 1130.

tage to be gained by himself. Meath was itself split into opposing factions, and Munster was only once able to combine to resist Turlough's oppression.

To return to Dermot Mc Murrough. In 1134 he suffered a defeat at the hands of the men of Ossory, but later in the same year, aided by the Ostmen of Dublin, he avenged himself by inflicting a slaughter on Conor O'Brien, the men of Ossory, and [47]
the Ostmen of Waterford.[18]

Dermot was now a prince whose alliance was worth seeking. In 1137, accompanied by his late opponent Conor O'Brien, and aided by the Ostmen of Dublin and Wexford with a fleet of two hundred ships, he laid siege to Waterford, and obtained the hostages, not only of that town, but of Donough Mc Carthy (perhaps one of the kings [48]
set up by Turlough O'Conor in 1127) and of the neighbouring district of the Decies. But more than this. According to the Four Masters, Conor O'Brien gave hostages to Dermot and submitted to him as king in consideration of Dermot's securing to him the obedience of the Mc Carthys of Desmond.[19]

About the same time Dermot made a treaty alliance with Murrough O'Melaghlin, King of Meath, whereby Dermot, quite after the manner of modern principalities and powers, undertook to come to Murrough's assistance with his forces and at his own charges 'against any one with as great an army', provided that Murrough would be pleased to suffer him to enjoy without disturbance the territories of Offelan and Offaly. These territories in the north of Leinster had recently been burnt and spoiled by the men of East Meath.[20] In 1138, in pursuance of this treaty, Dermot came to the assistance of the King of Meath against the formidable combination of Turlough O'Conor, Tiernan O'Rourke, and Donough O'Carroll of Uriel, who once more 'mustered their forces to contest unjustly his own lands with O'Melaghlin'. The two armies were encamped for a week in close proximity, but eventually separated without a bat- [49]
tle and without one giving hostages to the other.[21]

Dermot, though now a power to be reckoned with in the south of Ireland, had enemies within his own borders. Among these were Donnell MacFaelain, Murtough Mac

18 1 Ann. Loch Cé, 1134. In the Annals of Tigernach this war is ascribed to the maledictions of the clerics of Ireland and Connaught, uttered apparently at the time of the consecration of Cormac's chapel at Cashel, which took place earlier in the year. The entries are misplaced and probably incomplete, but a careful reading will, I think, show that the facts as originally recorded must have been as follows:— At the time of the consecration a peace was arranged between Connaught and Leth Mogha (or Southern Ireland) by the Archbishop of Connaught and the co-arb of St. Jarlaith of Tuam. The Dalcassians, however, could not resist the temptation to destroy or otherwise desecrate the cathach of St. Jarlaith. ['The cathach' was a reliquary brought into battle to ensure victory, and the Dalcassians no doubt attributed their numerous defeats to the virtue of this reliquary.] Thereupon the archbishop and the co-arb of St. Jarlaith (who had brought the cathach with him) pronounced a malediction on the Dalcassians, which was fulfilled within the year by Conor O'Brien's defeat and by a slaughter of the Dalcassians inflicted by the men of Desmond; cf. Chronicon Scotorum, 1130, where, however, the editor misunderstands the word *cathach*. The O'Donnells also had a cathach (Ann. Ulster, 1497), which contained a coyy of the Psalter believed to have been written by St. Columba. It is now in the Library of the R.I.A. The Cinel Owen probably had another: Ann. Ulster, 1182. **19** Four Master, 1137. It does not appear that Dermot did anything further to carry out this agreement. Next year Cormac McCarthy was treacherously killed by Turlough O'Brien, Conor's brother, and in 1139 the Clann Carthy were expelled from Munster by the race of Brian. **20** Ann. Clonmacnois, 1136. **21** Four Masters, 1138.

Gillamocholmog, and Murrough O'Toole, all lords of North Leinster tribes. They belonged to families which from the seventh to the middle of the eleventh centuries had habitually supplied kings of Leinster, and they no doubt resented Dermot's claim to be their overlord. Donnell MacFaelain is styled by the Four Masters *righdhamhna* of Leinster.[22] This term, usually anglicized Roydamna, has been translated 'royal heir 'and even 'crown prince', but these are most misleading renderings. The word means literally 'the makings of a king', and a roydamna might more properly be regarded as a fully qualified candidate for the succession to the throne if a vacancy should occur. How exactly he was marked out from the rest of the *rigraid* or kingfolk is obscure. He was certainly not regularly elected by the tribes concerned, as the 'tanist', an officer of a later period, was. There might be more than one roydamna at the same time. Indeed,
[50] at the period of which we speak at any rate, it would seem that the provincial kings themselves were seldom formally elected. They appear usually to have had to fight their way to the throne, battle-axe in hand. The roydamnas, as may well be imagined, were often objects of jealousy and suspicion to the monarch even after he was seated on his throne. So now Dermot got rid of his possible rivals in the ruthless way not unusual among the provincial kings, namely by either killing or blinding them. In the year 1141 seventeen of the kingfolk of Leinster, including those above mentioned, were 'removed' for him in this way by his brother Murrough,[23] an act which in the words of one chronicler 'brought all Leinster far under hand'. Thus did Dermot, like many of his compeers, secure his throne with the corpses and pierced eye-balls of his rivals. One horror, however, often added in the case of other kings, was wanting in his case. The slaughtered and mutilated victims were not of his own household.

Dermot's alliance with Conor O'Brien did not last long. In 1141 Conor forced the
[51] Ostmen of Dublin to submit to him, and in the same year a great army led by the O'Briens raided first Connaught and then Okinselagh as far as Wexford.[24] Next year Conor O'Brien died, and the sovereignty of all Munster was assumed by his brother Turlough. He proceeded to carry on incessant war with Connaught. Dermot now was either forced or found it prudent to give hostages to Turlough O'Conor and join him in a fruitless march into Munster, with the result that his territory was immediately raided by Turlough O'Brien.[25]

Murrough O'Melaghlin, King of Meath, no longer supported by Dermot, was now treacherously taken prisoner by Turlough O'Conor 'while he was under the protection of the relics and guarantees of Ireland'. A long list of these relics and guarantees is given by the Four Masters;[26] but no oaths, however sacred, bound Turlough O'Conor, who in an unscrupulous age seems to have been pre-eminent in unscrupulousness. He gave the kingdom of Meath, 'from the Shannon to the sea,' to his own son Conor, who, however, was killed next year by one of his new subjects, 'for he con-

22 He was presumably the Donnell son of Mac Faelain set up as King of Leinster by Turlough O'Conor in 1127. 23 Ann. Tigernach, 1141. This, our best authority, ascribes the act to Murchad son of Murchad, but on the *cui bono* principle we cannot acquit Dermot (to whom the Four Masters and the Annals of Clonmacnois ascribe it) of responsibility for the crime. 24 Four Masters, 1141. 25 Ibid. 1142. 26 Ibid.

sidered him a stranger in sovereignty over the men of Meath.'[27] The kingdom of Meath was now once more the subject of forced partitions and reparations. After delivering a battle 'like the Day of Judgement' on the unfortunate Meathmen, [52]
Turlough divided East Meath between Tiernan O'Rourke and Dermot Mc Murrough, while both remained under his protection.[28] We can imagine what the result of this arrangement might have been had it lasted for any time. But it was set aside within the year. The clergy, headed by the honoured name of Gilla Mac Liag or Gelasius, Co-arb of St. Patrick, or, as we should say, Archbishop of Armagh, now intervened. The Church had been directly outraged by Turlough's action towards his son Rory, the future *ard-rí*, whom he had imprisoned in 1143 in violation of its protection, as well as by his action towards Murrough O'Melaghlin, and no doubt the clergy sincerely desired to stay the incessant wars which were reducing Ireland to sheer anarchy. A great hosting and convention of the clergy was now held, and Rory, at their intercession, was set free. This was followed by a great assembly of the men of Ireland convened by the two Turloughs at Terryglas in Ormond, where, in accordance with the wishes of the clerics and laymen, 'they made the perfect peace of Ireland so long as they should be alive'. One immediate consequence was that Murrough O'Melaghlin was restored. He had, however, to share his kingdom with his son Murtough, and Meath had to pay an eric of 400 cows for the killing of Turlough's [53]
son. Leinster would seem not to have been included in the peace, as it was raided in the same year by Turlough O'Brien. Indeed the 'perfect peace' did not last a twelvemonth. In the very next year (1145) there was great war, 'so that Ireland was a trembling sod' convulsed by the movements of the Kings of Connaught and Munster and Meath and Breffny.[29] As Dermot was not concerned, beyond having his territory again raided by Turlough O'Brien, we, happily, may pass over these convulsions.

A new power soon appeared on the scene. Since the days of Donnell O'Loughlin, the northern province, though its various tribe-groups fought frequently amongst themselves, had seldom interfered in the disputes of the rest of Ireland. But now Murtough son of Niall O'Loughlin, King of the Cinel Owen and representative of the claims of the northern Ui Neill to the crown of Ireland, comes prominently into notice. After a succession of campaigns, 1147–9, he subdued the Ulidians and obtained their hostages, and the Oirghialla (or men of Uriel) and the Cinel Connell submitted to him. Next Tiernan O'Rourke and Dermot Mac Murrough 'came into his house', the usual expression for submission. In 1150, when he is styled by the Four Masters King of Ireland, he made a royal journey into Meath, where the hostages of [54]
Connaught were brought to him without a hosting—a significant proof of his power. He divided Meath between O'Conor, O'Rourke, and O'Carroll; and 'through the curse of the co-arb of Patrick and the clergy', Murrough O'Melaghlin was once more banished. But Turlough O'Conor never really submitted to him while life lasted, nor did Turlough's great enemy and namesake, Turlough O'Brien. The end of the latter's power, however, was at hand. In 1151 Turlough O'Conor led an army into Munster and, joined by Dermot Mac Murrough and others, met the army of Turlough

1143. 27 Ibid. 1144. 28 Ann. Tigernach, Four Masters, 1144. 29 Ibid. 1145.

O'Brien at Moinmor, and cut them to pieces. 'Until sand of sea and stars of heaven are numbered,' says one annalist, 'no one will reckon all the sons of kings and chiefs and great lords of the men of Munster that were killed there, so that of the three battalions of Munster that had come thither none escaped save only one shattered battalion.'[30]

We have now reached the year 1152, when the rape of Dervorgil took place. In this year the two most powerful chieftains in Ireland, Murtough O'Loughlin and Turlough O'Conor, met and 'made friendship under the Staff of Jesus and under the relics of Columkille'. Afterwards, in company with Dermot Mac Murrough, they made a new
[55] division of Meath, restoring Murrough O'Melaghlin to the western half, and putting his son Melaghlin over the eastern half. Tiernan O'Rourke, who had claims upon Meath under former partitions, did not accept this new arrangement. He was defeated by the new alliance, and even his territory of Clonmaicne (the present county of Longford and the southern half of Leitrim) was taken from him and given to a more amenable member of the family, and a stronghold of his, Daingean Bona Cuilinn,[31] near the Shannon, was burned. It was on this occasion that Dermot carried off Dervorgil, his old enemy's wife, with her cattle and furniture, the lady consenting to the abduction, and her own brother Melaghlin, the new king of East Meath, instigating Dermot to the act 'for some abuses of her husband, Tiernan, done to her before'.[32] Violent and bad a man as Dermot undoubtedly was, he was not worse or more violent than Tiernan O'Rourke. We first hear of the latter in the year 1124, when he had a son old enough to be killed, apparently in battle, and from that time to the day of his death there is hardly a year in which a predatory excursion or some killing or fighting by him is not recorded. Though he married the daughter of Murrough O'Melaghlin, King of
[56] Meath, he was always fighting against the O'Melaghlins, raiding their territory, and aiding in and profiting by the numerous partitions to which that unhappy kingdom was subjected. No wonder the O'Melaghlins distrusted and hated him. In 1140 his own subjects expelled him, but he recovered his chieftainship again. In 1152 he must have been at least sixty years of age, while his rival Dermot was forty-two, and Dervorgil herself had attained the ripe age of forty-four.[33] It is impossible that in an age of lawless violence, treachery, and loose sexual relations,[34] this elopement or abduction of a faithless wife could have been regarded as a very serious moral offence. To O'Rourke, however, it was a grievous personal insult, and one which he seems never to have forgotten or forgiven. That it was the sole cause of Dermot's expulsion fourteen years afterwards, as stated both by Giraldus and by the writer of the Song of Dermot, and affirmed by by some of the Irish annals,[35] is, considering the lapse of time, too much to assert; but by making a mortal enemy of Tiernan O'Rourke, who, as we shall see, was the actual agent of Dermot's expulsion, it directly contributed to

30 Ann. Tigernach, 1151. 31 Now Dangan, in the parish of Kilmore, county of Roscommon (O'Donovan). 32 Four Masters, Ann. Tigernach, Ann. Clonmacnois, 1152. 33 She died in 1193 at the monastery of Mellifont, in the eighty-fifth year of her age. 34 In this very year the great synod of Kells, under Cardinal Papiron, found it necessary to pass enactments against concubinage and irregular unions. Four Masters, 1152. 35 Ann. Clonmacnois, 1164; Ann. Tigernach, 1166.

that result, and we cannot wonder that the popular imagination should have exaggerated the personal element in the cause, and that a later age should have seen a dramatic fitness in the consequence. [57]

Next year Tiernan O'Rourke submitted to Turlough O'Conor and left him hostages, and O'Conor marched against Dermot and took away Dervorgil and her cattle from him, 'so that she was in the power of the men of Meath.'[36] According to a subsequent entry in the Four Masters she returned to her lawful husband.[37] There seems no reason to doubt that she continued to live with him. We next hear of her in the year 1157 as a benefactress of the newly consecrated church of the Cistercian Abbey at Mellifont, near Drogheda. To it she gave 'three score ounces of gold, and a chalice of gold on the altar of Mary (to whom these churches were usually dedicated), and a cloth for each of the nine other altars that were in that church'. Her husband, Tiernan O'Rourke, was present among other kings and seventeen bishops, together with the legate and the Archbishop of Armagh, on the consecration day when these munifi- [58] cent gifts were made.[38] Recent excavations on this site disclose the base of a magnificent cruciform[39] building of the transition period, which must, however, represent a later construction. Ten years afterwards, Dervorgil completed the church of the Nuns at Clonmacnois,[40] the remains of which to this day afford a beautiful example of the Hiberno-Romanesque style. In 1186 she retired from the world to the monastery she had endowed at Mellifont,[41] and here, in the eighty-fifth year of her age, in the year 1193, she died.[42]

To return to Dermot. In 1153 we find him releasing from fetters O'More, the lord of Leix, one of his nominally subordinate chieftains, after he had been blinded against the guarantee of laity and clergy.[43] To blind a chieftain was to render him incapable of ruling, and this particularly odious method, as it seems to us, of incapacitating rivals and opponents was only too common in this age. In this very year, for instance, Melaghlin, son of Murrough O'Melaghlin, who now upon his father's death claimed to be sole king of Meath, blinded his nephew, son of his elder brother, to put an end to rival claims, and Teig O'Brien, who had been set up as king of half Munster by [59] Turlough O'Conor, was blinded by his brother to incapacitate him from reigning. In 1136 Turlough O'Conor blinded his own son Hugh, no doubt because he was considered dangerous. And when his son Rory, or Roderic (as he is usually called), the last king of Ireland, succeeded him, his first act was to imprison three of his brothers and to blind the eldest. This revolting practice was not peculiar to Ireland. The Welsh chronicles at this period[44] 'contain numerous entries of the same barbarity, to which was sometimes added a further mutilation to make sure that the blind victim, already incapacitated from ruling, should leave no children after him to avenge his wrongs. We find even Henry II adopting the custom of the country and, in his rage at his want of

36 O'Conor marched to a place called Doire-an-ghabhlain, 'the oak wood of the Fork,' which O'Donovan failed to identify. Perhaps it is the place now called Old Gowlin, on the western side of the Blackstairs. 37 Cf. Ann. Tigernach, 1153: 'The daughter of Murrough O'Melaghlin came again to O'Rourke by flight from Leinster.' 38 Four Masters, Ann. Tigernach, 1157. 39 Fifty-fifth Report, Commissioners of Public Works in Ireland, 1887. 40 Four Masters, 1167. 41 Ann. Loch Cé, Ann. Ulster, 1186. 42 Ibid. 1193. 43 Four Masters. 44 Brut y Tywys. for the years 1110, 1124–8, 1151.

success against the Welsh, blinding his hostages, sons of the Welsh chieftains.[45] As regards the blinding of hostages, however, it must be borne in mind that this punishment was, perhaps not unnaturally, regarded as more merciful than putting them to death, and the system of taking hostages for good behaviour would have been unmeaning if, on breach of the conditions, punishment in some form had not followed. The
[60] blinding of rivals was a consequence of the custom by which the chief was chosen from the recognized ruling family or families. All who were eligible were naturally suspicious of each other.

For the next three years Dermot's power, at no time very great, seems to have been on the wane. In 1154 he was defeated by the men of Ossory, and his territory of Omurethy was plundered by Tiernan O'Rourke. In 1156, however, Turlough O'Conor died, and there was a re-arrangement of parties. In spite of his almost incessant plundering (to no good purpose) of four-fifths of Ireland, and in spite of his cruelty, treachery, and general unscrupulousness, Turlough O'Conor is magniloquently described as 'the Augustus of the west of Europe, flood of glory and princeliness and veneration for churches and clerics, head of the prosperity and wealth of the world, one who so long as he was alive never lost a battle or a hard conflict, the one man coming from the blood of Adam's children whose mercy and bounty, charity and generosity, were best.'[46] This extraordinary obituary notice is followed by a recital of Turlough's dying munificence to the Church, which may account for the extravagance of the monkish eulogy. After the lapse of seven and a half centuries we too may forgive Turlough much, and remember him as the young King of Erin for whom 'the
[61] cross of Cong' —one of the noblest surviving examples of native Irish craft—was made in the year 1123.[47]

Just before Turlough O'Conor's death, Tulough O'Brien was forced to give him hostages for half Munster, and on Rory O'Conor's accession to the throne of Connaught Turlough submitted to him. Tiernan O'Rourke, too, had made a temporary peace with Turlough O'Conor.[48] Dermot, on the other hand, soon afterwards gave hostages to Murtough O'Loughlin, now unquestionably the most powerful king in Ireland, and Murtough in return secured to Dermot his whole province of Leinster.[49] A dispute was going on as to the kingship of Meath between Dermot O'Melaghlin and his brother Donough. The latter had been appointed king by Murtough O'Loughlin in the previous year, but had been deposed by the Meathmen. He was now assisted by Dermot Mc Murrough and the Ostmen of Dublin to defeat Tiernan O'Rourke and regain his kingdom. Then followed a struggle for power between Rory and Murtough, which we need not follow in detail. They did not at first meet in battle, but each king in turn made a foray-hosting to support his own nomi-
[62] nees in Meath and Munster and depose the nominees of his rival, with consequent turmoil, fighting, and plundering among all concerned. In 1159 Tiernan O'Rourke definitively cast in his lot with Rory O'Conor and turned against Murtough

45 Ibid. 1164 (*recte* 1165). 46 Ann. Tigernach, 1156. The Four Masters repeat most of this eulogy. 47 Ann. Tigernach, 1123. Let us try too to remember the name—Maelisa, son of Bratan O'Echan—of the wonderful craftsman who made the shrine. 48 Four Masters, 1156. 49 Ann. Ulster, 1156.

O'Loughlin, but the latter for the time crushed the combination at the bloody battle of Ardee, and asserted his supremacy over nearly all Ireland.[50] This victory was followed up by hostings into Connaught and Meath, and finally, in 1161, Rory gave hostages to Murtough.[51]

Dermot was now secure in his kingdom of Leinster, and high in favour with the northern powers, both lay and clerical. The latter indeed, under Gilla MacLiag or Gelasius, Archbishop of Armagh, come very much into evidence about this time. In 1157 the clergy, assembled to consecrate the church of the Cistercian monastery at Mellifont, excommunicated Donough O'Maghlin, King of Meath, for a recent offence to the Church, and he was banished for a time. In 1158 Gelasius held a synod in Meath, when Flaherty O'Brollaghan, Abbot of Derry, was given a bishop's chair with jurisdiction over all the Columban communities throughout Ireland.[52] And now, in 1162, a synod of the clergy of Ireland was held at Clane, on the Liffey, in the presence and under the protection of Dermot Mc Murrough. It was presided over by [63] Gelasius, and attended by twenty-six bishops. The synod formally abolished the 'scandalous custom', which had been vehemently denounced by St. Bernard, whereby the co-arbship of St. Patrick at Armagh passed by hereditary succession for fifteen generations, and in eight cases had been filled by married laymen. They also endeavoured to secure uniformity of doctrine and the supremacy of Armagh by providing that no one should be a lector (*fer léginn*) in any church in Ireland except an alumnus of Armagh.[53] In this year Dermot obtained great sway over the Ostmen of Dublin, 'such as was not obtained before for a long time.' Upon the death of Grene (or Gregory), the Bishop of Dublin and Archbishop of Leinster, who, like his predecessors, had been consecrated by the Archbishop of Canterbury, Lorcan O'Toole, son of the King of Omurethy and Abbot of Glendalough, was consecrated Archbishop of Leinster by Gelasius. Lorcan was Dermot's brother-in-law, and may have owed his elevation to Dermot's influence both with the Ostmen and with Gelasius and the *ard-rí*. To this period must be ascribed Dermot's grant of Balidubgaill (Baldoyle) to the Priory of All Hallows, close to Dublin.[54]

For a few years there was no change in the political situation. O'Loughlin contin- [64]
ued to hold the commanding position and to support Dermot in the possession of Leinster, but there was no real settlement or lasting peace. Rory O'Conor and Tiernan O'Rourke were merely biding their time and watching for an opportunity to crush their foes. The opportunity came in the fateful year 1166.

O'Loughlin had more than once had occasion to assert by the strong hand his supremacy over the kingdom of Uladh or Ulidia, a district represented by the modern counties of Down and Antrim. In 1165 the people of this region turned against O'Loughlin, who accordingly entered their territory with a large army, harried the land, killed a countless number of the inhabitants, and expelled the king, Eochy Mac Dunlevy. Later on in the same year, at the intercession of Donough O'Carroll, Prince

50 Ann. Ulster, Ann. Tigernach, Four Masters, 1159. 51 Ibid. 1161. 52 Ann. Ulster, 1158; cf. ibid. 1161. 53 Ann. Ulster, 1162. 54 Reg. All Hallows (Irish Arch. Soc.), p. 50. L[aurentius], Archbishop of Dublin, is the first witness.

of Uriel, Mac Dunlevy was restored to his kingdom, on giving as pledges a son of every chieftain in Ulidia and his own daughter to O'Loughlin.[55] The very next year, however, Eochy Mac Dunlevy was blinded by O'Loughlin, and some of the principal men of Ulidia were put to death 'in despite of the protection of the successor of Patrick and of the Staff of Jesus and of Donough O'Carroll, King of Uriel'.[56]

[65] This base act of treachery and violation of oaths and guarantees was immediately followed by the defection of Ulidia and Uriel from O'Loughlin, and led to his defeat and death soon afterwards. It was also the signal for Rory O'Conor to assert his supremacy, and for Tiernan O'Rourke to avenge himself upon his enemy, Dermot Mac Murrough, now deprived of O'Loughlin's powerful protection.[57] O'Conor, accompanied by O'Rourke, marched through Meath, where he received hostages from Dermot O'Melaghlin, to Dublin. The Ostmen of Dublin submitted to him, and he was there inaugurated king 'as honourably as any king of the Gael was ever inaugurated'.[58] From thence, accompanied by the Ostmen, he went to the monastery of Mellifont, near Drogheda, and received hostages from Donough O'Carroll, King of Uriel. It was the turn of Leinster next, and Dermot, unsupported by his great ally, and
[66] not able to count on the fidelity of the Leinster tribes, could only stand at bay in his hereditary principality of Okinselagh. The Song of Dermot tells how one after the other of Dermot's *urrighs* or subkings deserted him, and of his futile efforts to retain their allegiance. Rory marched through Leinster, where the petty Kings of Offelan and Offaly, always jealous of Okinselagh, at once submitted to him and received their stipends as his *urrighs*. Dermot endeavoured to stay his progress at a wood called Fid Dorcha, 'the dark wood,' which appears to have been the gate of Okinselagh in the north,[59] but O'Conor forced the pass. Dermot, in desperation, and that there might be the less for his enemies to plunder, burned the royal city of Ferns, and gave four hostages to O'Conor, and 'got no glory save the corpses of the men of Okinselagh'.[60] With this submission O'Conor appears to have been satisfied. He did not recognize Dermot as King of Leinster, from which position he had been *de facto* deposed, but he left him in possession of his hereditary principality of Okinselagh, and, taking hostages from Ossory on the way, returned home to Connaught. He remained, how-
[67] ever, only four nights in his house, when he fared forth on a hosting to Assaroe, where the Cinel Connell submitted to him. During his absence there, Donough O'Carroll and Tiernan O'Rourke, at the instigation of the Cinel Owen themselves, who had abandoned their lord, marched with their forces into Tirowen to take vengeance on O'Loughlin. O'Loughlin, now under the ban of the Church, and more completely

55 Ann. Ulster, 1165. 56 Ann. Ulster, 1166. 57 I follow the order of events as given by the continuator of Tigernach (1166), where they form a consecutive narrative. With this the Annals of Ulster agree in the main, but the Four Masters give the entries as to the killing of O'Loughlin and O'Conor's incursion into Tirconnel before his march on Meath, Dublin, Uriel and Leinster. 58 Four Masters. The continuator of Tigernach says that the Foreigners gave the kingship to Rory, and he gave 4,000 cows to the Foreigners. This enormous 'stipend' shows the political importance of Dublin at this time. 59 This 'dark wood' was probably the woody fastness afterwards known as 'the Leverocke', co. Carlow: Dymmok, Tracts I.A.S., vol. ii, p. 26; Car. MSS., No. 635. Inquis. Lageniae, Carlow, 6 Car. I), and it was necessary to traverse it to get to Ferns from the north. 60 Ann. Tigernach, 1166.

deserted by his own men than even Dermot, was slain at a place called by the Four Masters Leiter Luin, somewhere in the Fews of Armagh. 'A great marvel and wonderful deed was then done: to wit, the King of Ireland to fall without battle, without contest, after his dishonouring the successor of Patrick, and the Staff of Jesus, and the successor of Colum-cille, and the Gospel of Martin, and many clergy besides.'[61]

It is a common form with the annalists to attribute to a miracle or to the supernatural agency of the offended saints the deaths of persons who had outraged the Church, whether by plundering church property or by killing those under its special protection. In the case of Murtough O'Loughlin, however, there are substantial grounds for attributing the sudden and complete collapse of his hitherto irresistible power to the action of the clergy of the north of Ireland, and especially to that of Flaherty O'Brollaghan, the co-arb of Columkille. The entry in the Annals of Ulster [68]
continues as follows:—'Howbeit his body was carried to Armagh and buried there, in spite of the co-arb of Columkille with his community; and Columkille himself [i.e. the co-arb ?] and the head of the students of Derry fasted[62] regarding it, i.e. regarding his being carried to [Christian] burial.' There are many indications that about this period the Church in Ireland was endeavouring by every means in its power to bring about a higher standard of fair dealing between man and man, and to enforce a more rigorous fidelity to the plighted word.

Dermot, weakened and humiliated by the defection of the Ostmen, the north Leinster tribes, and Ossory, and by the loss of his great protector in the north, was not long allowed to remain in possession even of the territory of his own group of tribes. Tiernan O'Rourke, fresh from his victory over O'Loughlin and confident in the support of O'Conor, was not the man to let slip the opportunity of paying off an old score. Accordingly he made an alliance with Dermot O'Melaghlin, whose territory in Meath he had frequently harried and claimed as his own, and towards whose house, in spite of his marriage alliance, he had been a lifelong foe, and their united forces, [69]
accompanied by the Ostmen of Dublin and the revolted Leinstermen, made a hosting against Dermot Mc Murrough, 'in order to take vengeance upon him for O'Rourke's wife.' This is the motive expressly assigned for the hosting by our best authority, and we may well believe that it was the one which mainly actuated Tiernan O'Rourke; but other motives probably influenced his allies. Dermot O'Melaghlin, for instance, had an old score of his own to wipe out, for Mc Murrough had more than once supported the rival claims of his brother, Donough O'Melaghlin, to the throne of Meath. Besides, Dermot O'Melaghlin had just taken hostages from Offaly and Offelan, and probably aimed at securing for himself a large slice of Dermot's lost kingdom. The Ostmen and the North Leinster tribes always chafed under the yoke of Okinselagh, and had many deeds of violence to avenge. In the face of this combination Dermot, deserted even by some of his immediate neighbours, and feeling that resistance was useless, fled over sea, hunted out of Ireland by his relentless foe. The victorious army proceeded to demolish Dermot's stone house (*tech cloiche*) at Ferns, and to burn the

61 Ann. Ulster, 1166. 62 This is a late example of the custom of fasting to compel the granting of a request, as to which see *infra*, p. 106 [p. 36].

wooden defences of his entrenchment (*longport*). The leaders then divided Okinselagh between Donough Mac Gillapatrick, King of Ossory, and Murrough Mc Murrough, [70] Dermot's brother, and sent their hostages to Rory O'Conor.[63] Enna Mc Murrough, Dermot's son and roydamna of Leinster, did not escape, but was captured by the King of Ossory, and in 1168, after Dermot's return, was blinded by his captor.

Rory O'Conor had now no rival to the throne of Ireland, and he soon afterwards made a 'great army-circuit', and obtained hostages from all the principal tribe-groups of Ireland except the Cinel Owen, and even from these he exacted hostages in the next year.

Such is the brief outline of Dermot's political life and surroundings up to the time of his banishment. It is usual to describe him as a particularly turbulent, cruel, and unscrupulous Irish king. But this description is certainly not borne out by the Irish annals. In turbulence, in the matter of plundering expeditions into the territories of others, in cruelty to kith and kin, in falseness to the sworn word, his record is far surpassed by those of at least half a dozen of his compeers. This was probably not due to any leanings towards moderation and virtue—when he had Normans to back him he was ready [71] to use his power without scruple—but simply to weakness. Except in 1137, when he acted with Conor O'Brien and besieged Waterford, and again in 1151–2, when he gave hostages to Turlough O'Conor, then regarded as *ard-rí*, and acted with him against his own bitter foes, Turlough O'Brien and Tiernan O'Rourke, and perhaps once or twice when he defended Meath against O'Rourke's aggression, he does not seem to have joined in any of the incessant fighting that went on outside his kingdom during the forty years of his rule. His own family and tribe were always loyal to him, and this can hardly be said of any other Irish king. A study of the annals shows that in Dermot's time, and indeed generally throughout history, Leinster was the weakest of the provinces. The tribes of North Leinster, of Ossory, and of Okinselagh, never willingly submitted to the same ruler. The Ostmen were in general practically independent, and Dermot, like most of his predecessors, had no really loyal followers outside his own tribe-group. He appears to have been frequently engaged in endeavouring to keep in subjection the various members of his kingdom and in repelling attacks from without, and had it not been for the powerful aid of Murtough O'Loughlin, who may be regarded as the legitimate [72] *ard-rí*, he could not have held out as long as he did. After all is said that can be fairly said, Dermot's great crime, for which his name has since been held in detestation, was bringing the foreigners into Ireland, the foreigners who came to stay and ultimately to rule. From this act he came to be known distinctively as *Diarmat na nGall*, or Dermot of the Foreigners, while his brother, who was set up as King of Okinselagh in his room, was called *Murchadh na nGaedhal*, or Murrough of the Irish.

However bad a man Dermot may have been, he was a munificent patron of the Church and was always befriended by his own clergy. About the middle of the century

63 Ann. Tigernach, 1166. The Four Masters speak of Murrough alone as being set up as king. Probably the district to the west of the mountains in the modern county of Carlow was annexed to Ossory. In 1169 St. Mullins appears to have been under domination of the King of Ossory (Song of Dermot, p. 85) and in 1170 O'Ryan of Odrone fought with Ossory against Raymond at Baginbun.

he founded the Cistercian abbey de Valle Salutis at Baltinglass, and the nunnery of St. Mary de Hogges, close to Dublin.[64] To this nunnery he subordinated the cells of Kilclehin (Kilculliheen, just opposite Waterford) and Athady (Aghade, co. Carlow). Where Trinity College, Dublin, now stands he founded, shortly before his expulsion, the priory of All Hallows, and endowed it with the land of Baldoyle together with its men (serfs).[65] About the same time he confirmed a gift of lands by Dermot O'Ryan, chief of Idrone, for the construction of a Benedictine monastery at Killenny ('Old Abbey,' now Barrow Mount, co. Kilkenny) by a charter which is still extant.[66] Finally, [73]
about the year 1161, he founded and endowed an Augustinian monastery at Ferns, near his own royal seat.[67] The ruins existing on the site include an interesting example of the transition from the old Celtic round tower to the later square tower or belfry, viz. a tower square below and round above. At this abbey Dermot took refuge in the year 1166, after burning his house as already mentioned. The Song of Dermot supplies a graphic picture of the deserted king going about disguised as a monk and endeavouring vainly to rally his disaffected sub-kings around him.

Dermot married Mor, only daughter of Murtough O'Toole, King of Omurethy (or Southern Kildare), and sister of the famous Laurence O'Toole, Abbot of Glendalough, and afterwards (1162) Archbishop of Dublin. Six children of Dermot are mentioned. Three sons, namely, Donnell Kavanagh, an illegitimate son of whom we shall hear more, eponymous ancestor of the clan Kavanagh; Enna, reputed ancestor of the Kinselaghs, taken prisoner in 1166 and blinded in 1168 by Donnell Mac Gillapatrick of Ossory; and Conor, put to death as a hostage by Rory O'Conor in 1170. And three [74]
daughters, namely, Aife (Eva) afterwards married to Strongbow, Urlacam married to Donnell O'Brien, King of Thomond, and (probably) Dervorgil,[68] married to Donnell Mac Gillamocholmog, a sub-king whose territory lay to the south-west of Dublin. These marriage connexions may have had something to do with the friendly relations which generally subsisted among Dermot's sons-in-law.

Like other provincial kings, Dermot, when in power, no doubt had his court officials and household officers, but we know little about them. One of the witnesses to his Ferns charter is described as his chancellor. Maurice Regan, to whom we are principally indebted for the materials woven into the Song of Dermot, was his *latimer*, or Latin-writer, and appears as his confidential agent and messenger. In his All Hallows' charter Dermot speaks of Edan, or Aedh O'Kaelly (*O'Caellaighe*), Bishop of Louth or Clogher, as his spiritual father and confessor, and his foster-brother was an O'Caellaighe, probably of the same family.[69] Aedh Mac Criffan, who is believed to have [75]

64 Ware. 65 Reg. All Hallows, Dub. (Ir. Arch. Soc.), p. 50. 66 Facsimiles Nat. MSS. Irel., pt. 2, p. lxii. Both this and the last mentioned charter are witnessed by Dermot's brother-in-law, Archbishop Laurence, i.e. in or after 1162. 67 See Dugdale, Mon. Angl., vol. vi, p. 1141, for this charter. It is witnessed by six bishops and by Laurence O'Toole while Abbot of Glendalough, i.e. before 1162. 68 She is called Dervorgil filia or inien (*inghen*) Mac Murchada in Chart. St. Mary's, Dub., vol. i, Nos. 4, 5, 6. 69 The son of Dermot's foster-brother O'Caellaighe was one of the hostages killed in 1170 (Four Masters). The family was probably that of O'Caellaighe, kings of Upper Ossory in the twelfth century, the last of whom was slain in 1172 (Ann. Tigernach). This fosterage relationship probably explains the connexion of Dermot with the Bishop of Louth which puzzled the editor of the Register of All Hallows (see note, p. 125).

superintended the compilation of the famous Book of Leinster, under Dermot's patronage, was his *fer léginn* or lector. This book, perhaps the chief treasure of Dermot's library, contains one of the most valuable collections of Celtic lore which have survived to us. In it Aedh is addressed by Finn Mac Gorman, Bishop of Kildare (who appears to have been the actual compiler of part of the book), as 'the chief historian of Leinster in wisdom, and knowledge, and the cultivation of books, and science, and learning'.[70]

We may here add the personal description of Dermot supplied by Gerald de Barry, who was intimate with those who had known him in the closing years of his life. 'Dermot was tall of stature and of stout build. A man of warlike spirit and a brave one in his nation, with a voice hoarse from frequent shouting in the din of battle. One who preferred to be feared rather than to be loved, who put down the nobles and exalted the lowly, who was obnoxious to his own people and an object of hatred to strangers. His hand was against every man, and every man's hand against his.'

70 See marginal note, Book of Leinster (facsimile), p. 288.

DERMOT SEEKS FOREIGN AID, 1166–7

From a place called Corcoran[1] on the coast of Imokilly, a little south of Youghal, Dermot, the once powerful King of Leinster, on the first day of August 1166, with some few followers, stole away, a fugitive from his native land. After a fair passage he landed at Bristol, even then an important port and commercial centre, and one well known to the Norse merchants of Dublin, Wexford, and Waterford. He and all his company were entertained by Robert Fitz Harding at his house near the monastery of St. Augustine, just outside Bristol. This fact, which we know from the Song of Dermot, is peculiarly interesting, for Robert Fitz Harding is a name well known in the annals of Bristol. He was an old man in 1166, having been born in 1085. He was reeve [78]
of Bristol and had purchased land in the immediate neighbourhood of the town, viz. the manor of Bedminster, including the vill of Redcliff on the other side of the river, and the vill of Billeswick to the south west, where he had founded an abbey for Augustinian canons. He had supported Earl Robert of Gloucester and Matilda in the struggle with Stephen, and had won the favour of Matilda's son, who rewarded him with the fief of Berkeley. It was probably through the trading relations that had subsisted for some time between the Ostmen of Dublin and the merchants of Bristol that Dermot had become acquainted with the reeve of the latter town, and was able to count on his hospitality and friendship. These trading relations afterwards supplied a motive for Henry's effort to colonize the depleted city of Dublin with his men of Bristol, and in this connexion it is worth noting that among the earliest citizens of the Anglo-Norman town was 'John son of Jordan son of Harding',[2] possibly a nephew of Dermot's host.

After staying a while in Bristol Dermot summoned his followers and told them that he had resolved to go to Normandy to hold parley with King Henry. Accordingly he journeyed to Normandy and set out to seek the king. But the King of England was [79]
sometimes as hard to find in those days as a criminal in hiding is to-day. Where exactly Dermot came up with him is not clear, but it was somewhere in the more distant parts of Aquitaine.[3] Henry, we know, was always on the move. His dominions extended from

1 Song of Dermot, l. 221. See this place identified, Journ. R.S.A.I. 1903, p. 418 and 1904, pp. 191-2. The chronicle says that Dermot brought with him 'Awelaf Okinad e plus de seisante treis'. This last number seems to have been used at the time for any small figure, just as 60,000 seems to have been used for any large figure; cf. Fantosme, 1. 161, *meins de seisante mil e plus de seisante treis*, and see Round, Feudal England, p. 291. 2 Hist. and Mun. Docs. of Ireland (Gilbert), p. 40. 3 Giraldus (v. 227) says vaguely that Henry was 'in remotis et trasmarinis Aquitannicae Galliae partibus'. The Song of Dermot (ll. 258-9) seems to mention the place of meeting, but it is not easy to identify it. 'A une cité l'ad

the Tweed to the Pyrenees, and throughout this vast region his busy mind and active body knew no rest. He spent the Christmas of 1166 at Poitiers and then went south into Guienne and Gascony. 'The Song' indicates that Dermot had no small difficulty in finding him. He went 'up and down, forwards and back, he sent messages and made inquiries', until at last he came up with him and gained audience.

Now what induced Dermot to take this long and troublesome journey? He would never have undertaken it unless he had good reason for believing that his suit would be successful. But what grounds had he for believing this? Had he gone for assistance in the first instance, as he did afterwards, to South Wales, we could have easily under-
[80] stood his action. Again and again Norse and Irish of the east coast had assisted the Welsh, both against the Normans and in their own intestine feuds, and Dermot might well expect to receive from the Welsh payment in kind. Indeed we find a tolerably close connexion between Leinster and Wales reaching back to the dawn of history. But there was no such obligation on a Norman king[4]—rather the reverse—and no precedent for seeking aid in that quarter. It certainly looks as if Dermot knew of Henry's meditated expedition into Ireland, and had perhaps even heard of Adrian's Bull. At any rate, it is very probable that Fitz Harding knew all about Henry's designs. He was his intimate and trusted friend. When Henry was nine years old, Geoffrey of Anjou had sent him to Bristol to his uncle, Earl Robert of Gloucester, and he lived in Bristol Castle for four years. Then was formed his friendship with Robert Fitz Harding, which remained unbroken for life. When Henry came to England again in 1152 he was assisted by Fitz Harding, who was rewarded, as we have seen, with the fief of Berkeley, and no doubt every time Henry went into Wales he saw Fitz Harding on the way. Fitz
[81] Harding, Henry's trusted and favoured vassal, must have known of Henry's ambitious views with regard to Ireland, and it was probably on Fitz Harding's advice that Dermot took the unprecedented course of appealing to the Angevin king.

The Song of Dermot gives us an account of Dermot's interview with Henry. It tells us how Dermot 'very courteously saluted him' and then puts the following speech into Dermot's mouth:

> May God who dwells on high
> Ward and save you, King Henry,
> And likewise give you
> Heart and courage and inclination
> To avenge my shame and my misfortune
> That my own people have brought upon me!
> Hear, noble King Henry,
> Whence I was born, of what country.
> Of Ireland I was born a lord,
> In Ireland acknowledged king;

trové,/Que seigñ esteit clamé.' 4 Some 'ships from Dublin and other cities in Ireland' had indeed come to assist Henry in his Welsh expedition of 1165, but these were fitted out by the Ostmen and not by Dermot. Brut y Tywys. 1164 (*recte* 1165).

But wrongfully my own people
Have cast me out of my kingdom.
To you I come to make plaint, good sire,
In the presence of the barons of your empire.
Your liegeman I shall become
Henceforth all the days of my life.
On condition that you be my helper,
So that I lose not everything,
You I shall acknowledge as sire and lord,
In the presence of your barons and earls.

However he phrased it, Dermot's story fell upon willing ears. Henry had long cast hungry eyes towards Ireland. In the struggle with the Welsh which had now been [82] going on for three-fourths of a century, had not the Irish always harboured Welsh fugitives? Nay, had they not frequently given active assistance to Welsh insurgents, and, worse still, supported rebellious Norman vassals? Shortly after coming to the throne Henry had meditated an expedition into Ireland, and had obtained the famous Bull 'Laudabiliter' sanctioning the invasion; but the scheme, which was laid before a council at Winchester about Michaelmas 1158, did not commend itself to the Empress Matilda, and the expedition was postponed.[5] No doubt pretexts for war, when required, are in general easily manufactured, but here was an admirable one offered by Dermot, ready made to Henry's hand. For an exiled prince to seek restitution by aid of a foreign force was no unusual proceeding, nor one repugnant to the average morality of the time. True, if such princes were wiser and more patriotic than their fellows, they might have learnt and observed the great historic lesson that such a course was a likely way to enslave both themselves and their country. The story of Vortigern and Hengist, whether true or false, was at any rate believed. A similar story was told of the [83] introduction of the Romans under Claudius into Britain. The Normans appear to have got their first foothold in South Wales on the invitation of a disaffected native chieftain, and Henry's expedition to Gwynedd or North Wales in 1157 was ostensibly undertaken to reinstate a dispossessed prince. But exceptional patriotism and exceptional wisdom are not to be looked for in banished princes. Even Harold, son of Godwin, did not hesitate in the year 1050 to seek Irish aid to restore him to the position from which he had been expelled. Instances of Irish tribes using the assistance of the Ostmen of Dublin and Waterford, or even invoking the aid of the northmen of the Isles,[6] to get the upper hand over their fellow countrymen, are not rare, and at the great battle of Clontarf Irishmen fought on the side of Brodir and of Sitric. But if there was nothing peculiarly disgraceful to Dermot, according to the ideas of the time, in his application, there was certainly nothing to bring discredit on Henry in his lis-

5 Robert of Torigny, p. 186, says that the project was not approved by the Empress Matilda, Henry's mother, and was postponed. The evidence as to Laudabiliter will be considered later on. 6 In 1154 Murtough O'Loughlin hired the fleets of Aran, Cantire, Man, and the Scottish coast, to fight the fleet of Turlough O'Conor: Four Masters, 1154.

tening to it and expecting to gain advantage to himself by acceding to it. *Do ut des* is an old maxim in international politics. Dermot's offer suited Henry's ambitious pro-
[84] jects much too well to be ignored, but at the moment Henry was unable to take full advantage of it. His contest with Becket, now in full swing, had stirred up many enemies against him, and his whole attention was devoted to counteracting their machinations.

Accordingly, as Henry was just then unable to organize an expedition into Ireland on Dermot's behalf, he did what he could in the circumstances to secure Dermot's allegiance and keep the opportunity open for carrying out his own designs later on. He accepted Dermot's proffered homage and oath of fealty, promised to help him as soon as he could, loaded him with presents,[7] and gave him Letters Patent[8] to the following effect:—

'Henry, King of England, Duke of Normandy and Aquitaine, and Count of Anjou, to all his liegemen, English, Normans, Welsh, and Scots, and to all nations subject to his sway, greeting. Whensoever these letters shall come unto you know that we have received Dermot, Prince of Leinster, into our grace and favour; wherefore whosoever within the bounds of our territories shall be willing to give him aid, as our vassal and
[85] liegeman, in recovering his dominion, let him be assured of our favour and licence in that behalf.'

Dermot then returned to Bristol, where he was again entertained by Robert Fitz Harding, this time by Henry's express command. Here Dermot stayed for some weeks, and, having Henry's purse to draw upon, lived in good style.[9] From the ships trading with Ireland he was able to get news of what was going on in his own country and among his own people; but though he caused Henry's Letters to be read in public, and made liberal promises of land and pay to all and sundry who might help him, he failed in this quarter to obtain the aid he sought. Bristol at this time was a thriving and growing commercial town, and was hardly the place to yield adventurers of the type required by Dermot. At length, however, there came to him the man he wanted in the person of Richard Fitz Gilbert, called by his contemporaries Earl of Striguil and known to all time as 'Strongbow', whose fortress of Striguil stood on the cliff overhanging the Wye, where the stately ruins of the castle of Chepstow now stand.

Richard Fitz Gilbert came of the great family of Clare, so called from one of the many fiefs in Suffolk which had been given by William the Conqueror to Richard's
[86] great-grandfather, who was known in Normandy as Richard de Bienfaite. We first read of the de Clares in Wales in the reign of Henry I. About the year 1109, in consequence of the burnings and plunderings of Owain ab Cadwgan (of whom as the ravisher of Nest we shall hear again), Henry confiscated Cadwgan's territory in Ceredigion (Cardigan), and gave the lands to Gilbert, son of Richard de Bienfaite, known as Gilbert of Tonbridge, if he could win it.[10] This practice of issuing 'territorial letters of marque 'was only too common with the Norman and Angevin kings,

7 The Pipe Roll of the 12th Hen. II records gifts to certain Irishmen. This perhaps refers to Dermot, who, according to Giraldus (p. 228), was 'regiae munificentiae donariis honoratus plurimum et oneratus.' 8 Gir. Camb. v. 227. 9 Song of Dermot, ll. 300-5. 10 Brut y Tywys. 1107, Ann. Camb. 1111.

and we shall meet with parallels hereafter. Gilbert appears to have accomplished his purpose with some success, and to have built castles at the mouths of the rivers Ystwith and Teivi. He was succeeded by his eldest son, Richard Fitz Gilbert, afterwards created Earl of Hertford, who appears to have carried on the work of colonization and peaceful rule so successfully that this part of Wales was 'like a second England'.[11] The accession of Stephen to the throne, however, threw all England into commotion, and gave the signal in Wales for many attempts to throw off the yoke of the foreigner. The year 1136 opened with a successful outbreak [12] against the Norman and Flemish settlements in Gower, and soon afterwards Richard Fitz Gilbert was way- [87]
laid and killed, and the Welsh overran and ravaged all his lands in Ceredigion. In October in the same year, Stephen, Constable of Aberteivi (father of Robert Fitz Stephen, of whom we shall hear much), and the sons of Gerald the Steward (ancestor of the Geraldines of Ireland) met with a bloody defeat. The bridge over the Teivi was broken down, and 'it was a wretched spectacle,' says one chronicler, 'to see crowds passing to and fro across a bridge formed by the horrible mass of human corpses and horses drowned in the river.' Stephen, after some unavailing efforts to recover the position, thought it prudent or necessary to leave the Welsh to themselves.

Strongbow's father was Gilbert Fitz Gilbert, younger brother of Richard, Earl of Hertford. He appears as owner of Striguil from perhaps as early as 1138, when he seems to have succeeded his uncle, Walter de Clare, the founder of Tintern. About the same time he was made Earl of Pembroke by Stephen.[13] In 1144 he subdued Dyved (Pembrokeshire) and erected the castle of Caermarthen.[14] In 1147 he broke with [88]
Stephen, who refused to give him the forfeited de Clare castles in England,[15] and shortly afterwards he died.

The sobriquet Strongbow appears to have been given in Wales to Gilbert Fitz Gilbert,[16] but it has clung to his better known son, Richard Fitz Gilbert de Clare, whose fortunes we shall have to trace. His mother was Elizabeth, daughter of Robert de Beaumont, Earl of Leicester. He succeeded his father as Earl of Pembroke, and with this title we find him as one of the witnesses to Stephen's proclamation of the Treaty of Wallingford, by which Henry was recognized as successor to the throne (1153).[17] We know little or nothing of him during the years that elapsed from the death of his father to his interview with Dermot Mac Murrough.[16] It is probable that his earldom of Pembroke, like others of Stephen's creation, was forfeited on Henry's [89]
accession, as he is always styled Earl of Striguil by contemporary writers. Gerald, in a series of punning antitheses which cannot be fully reproduced, describes him as 'a man whose past was brighter than his prospects, whose blood was better than his

11 Gesta Stephani, p. 12. 12 The authorities for this outbreak are Cont. Florence of Worchester, 1136-7; Gesta Stephani, pp. 11-14; Brut y Tywys. 1135; Ann. Camb. 1136. 13 Ord. Vit. (Duchesne), p. 917. The statement that he held the office of Marshal has been shown to be founded on an error; Round, Commune of London, p. 302. 14 Brut y Tywys. 1144. Ann. Camb. 1145. 15 Gesta Stephani, pp. 127-9. 16 Ann. Camb. 1149, where he is described as 'Gilbertus comes qui Strongboga dictus est'. His son Richard is not called Strongbow by any contemporary authority. The earliest mention of the name appears to be in a Tintern Abbey Charter (May 22, 1223), the correct text of which was given for the first time by Mr. Round, Commune of London, p. 309.

brains, and whose claims of succession were larger than his lands in possession'. As a past supporter of Stephen he was out of favour with the king, and from a variety of causes he had lost the lands in Dyved and Ceredigion and about Caermarthen, which had been won by his grandfather and held at times by his uncle and by his father. It appears that about the year 1158 Henry had re-granted the lands of Ceredigion to one Roger de Clare, who was probably second son of Richard of Tonbridge, and cousin of Strongbow. This may have been one of Strongbow's grievances against Henry, as he no doubt considered that he had an hereditary claim to these lands. Rhys ap Gruffudd, Prince of South Wales, however, not satisfied with the territories assigned to him by Henry, had again and again overrun Ceredigion and burned the Norman castles there and in Dyved, failing only at Caermarthen itself. Indeed, owing to his patriotic energy the power of the Normans and of their Flemish dependants throughout South Wales had been much curtailed.

[90] In 1165,[19] in conjunction with the princes of Gwynedd and Powys, Rhys dared to withstand Henry in person, and the latter, after beating in vain against the rocks of Berwyn, had been obliged to retire without effecting anything. In the autumn of the same year the Lord Rhys took the castles of Aberteivi and Cilgerran and threw Robert Fitz Stephen, constable of the latter, into prison, and in the following year he successfully resisted the efforts of the Normans to recover the ground they had lost. Thus even if Strongbow in 1166 had not, strictly speaking, forfeited his claim to the lands in Ceredigion and Dyved, it seems pretty clear that he could have enjoyed no effective possession of them. He appears, in fact, when Dermot net him to have been a man who, having been brought up to greatness, had fallen upon evil days, and who therefore was all the more ready to endeavour to repair his fortunes by a bold adventure in another country.[18] As Lord Marcher of Striguil, however, he was still a power in the land; and as a de Clare he had a name to conjure with. We may be quite sure, too, that in the incessant border warfare of South Wales he had gained an experience in fighting against large bodies of light-armed, swift-footed, impetuous foes, in a difficult
[91] country, which was afterwards invaluable to him under not dissimilar circumstances in Ireland.

After a lengthy conference Dermot came to agreement with Strongbow. The earl was to collect a force and to come to Ireland in the ensuing spring to aid Dermot in recovering his throne, and in return Dermot was to give his eldest daughter Eva (Aoife) to the earl to wife and the succession of the kingdom after his death. Whatever might be said for the legality of this arrangement had Dermot been dealing with a Norman seignory, it was of course inoperative under Irish law, whereby the provincial kings were, in theory at any rate, selected by the tribesmen from one or more ruling families. Still, as the position of a new chief depended in the last resort on his power to compel recognition and the delivery of hostages, which were often not yielded until after a fierce contest, Strongbow may possibly have expected that the force of his arms, after winning the throne for Dermot, might be able to hold it for himself. But it is very

17 Rymer, Foedera, vol. i, p. 18. 18 We find Richard Fitz Gilbert and Roger, Earl of Clare, witnesses to a royal charter 'apud Dover in transitu Regis' in January, 1156: Eyton's Itin, p. 16.

improbable that he looked forward to occupying the precise position of a Celtic king. He expected rather to fill in Ireland a position similar to that which his father and grandfather before him had filled in Wales, and he only valued Dermot's undertaking in so far as it was likely to help him to win for himself that position. He was, in fact, [92]
about to extend to Ireland a method of acquisition which had already been successfully adopted in Wales. What title had he or any Norman in Wales but the title of the sword, backed by the licence of a king ill recognized in Wales? True, Norman and Angevin kings had more than once led armies into Wales, and had recently wrested from the native princes an unwilling homage and oath of fealty, but the royal armies had followed, and not preceded, the granting of the original licence and the victory of the private sword, and in the case of Ireland the royal armies would no doubt follow in the same way. Even the proposed native marriage had its successful precedent. It was in all probability largely owing to the marriage of Gerald of Windsor with the daughter of the King of South Wales that Gerald and the sons of Gerald had been able to hold their own in Dyved,[21] whence other adventurers, unconnected with the native princes, had been again and again expelled. There was only one point in which the parallel was perhaps incomplete. Strongbow's grandfather, Gilbert de Clare of [93]
Tonbridge, had received a personal licence from his sovereign, Henry I, before he made sword-land for himself in Ceredigion, and so no doubt had most of the other adventurers in Wales. But the licence which Dermot had obtained from Henry II was in general terms and addressed to all and sundry. It would be safer, therefore, to get special leave from the king before embarking on this new adventure; otherwise the earl might forfeit the lands he already possessed, as well as those to which he had hereditary claims, without being allowed to retain those which he might acquire in Ireland. This thought seems to have made him hesitate and delay[22] for two years to fulfil his part of the bargain with Dermot.

Meanwhile Dermot had to content himself with the conditional undertaking from Strongbow, and, despairing of obtaining further assistance in the neighbourhood of Bristol, he set out along the coast route through South Wales to St. Davids. Dermot probably took this journey, not, as Gerald suggests, for the pleasure of inhaling the scent of his beloved country, or of feasting his eyes with the sight of his native land [94]
(though the distance is such that it is difficult, even on the clearest day, to distinguish between mountains and clouds), but with the much more practical expectation of securing further aid either from the Welsh themselves or from the Norman adventurers still holding their own in those parts. Indeed it is possible that Strongbow himself may have directed him to this district, with which, as having been included in his lost lordship, he must have been familiar. Certain it is that the men whose services Dermot

19 Brut y Tywys. 1164. Ann. Camb. 1166. **20** Wm. of Newburgh, vol. i, p. 167. **21** So Bernard of Newmarch, who won for himself the territory of Brecknock, married a native wife, Nest, granddaughter of Gruffudd ap Llywelyn: Gir. Camb. vi. 28. Similarly William Martin, grandson of Martin of Tours strengthened his position in Kemes by his marriage with Angharad, daughter of Rhys ap Gruffudd: Owen's Pembrokeshire, Preface, vii, and p. 39. **22** The Earl of Striguil is stated to have formed one of the escort of the Princess Matilda on her leaving England, probably late in September 1167, for her marriage with Henry, Duke of Saxony: R. de Diceto, vol. i, p. 330.

was now to secure, and who afterwards took so prominent a part in the invasion of Ireland, belonged to a family which had been long connected in feudal relation with the de Clares, though their kinsman, Gerald de Barry, takes no notice of the connexion. This remarkable family, though thorough Normans in character and training, were linked together by common descent from a Welsh princess, Nest, daughter of Rhys ap Tewdwr, the last independent king of South Wales, and grandfather of Rhys ap Gruffudd, who at this time, in the estimation of the Welsh, was the lawful prince.

In an age and country of loose morals, this lady was perhaps conspicuous for her laxity. At one time she had a royal lover in the person of Henry I, by whom she had a
[95] son named Henry, who was slain in Anglesea in 1157.[23] He left two sons, Meyler and Robert, both of whom settled in Ireland, the former figuring conspicuously among her early invaders and rulers. Early in the twelfth century, Gerald, younger son of Walter Fitz Other, castellan of Windsor, married Nest. We first hear of this remarkable man in Wales in the year 1097, when he was castellan of Pembroke under Arnulf de Montgomery.[24] This castle was originally but a slender fortress surrounded by an earthen vallum and a palisade, as indeed we may be pretty sure were nearly all the first castles built by the Normans in Wales; but its splendid position on a rock, washed on three sides by a pill or arm of the sea, rendered it strong enough to withstand more than one siege.[25] Gerald's grandson, the historian Gerald de Barry, tells us that Gerald married Nest in order to make himself and his dependants more secure. There can indeed be little doubt that Gerald's union with a Welsh princess was of material aid to
[96] him and his sons in holding their own among the warlike clans of South Wales. About the year 1108 [26] Nest was carried off from her husband by Owain ap Cadwgan from the new castle which Gerald had just built at a spot called Kenarth, or Kengarth Bychan.[27] The Chronicle of the Princes gives a graphic account of the rape, and we are left to suspect that in her case, as in that of Dervorgil, *rapta nimirum fuit quia rapi voluit*. 'They took Nest with her two sons and a daughter, and also another son that he (Gerald) had by a concubine.' Who this last son was is not clear, but William, the eldest son of Gerald, is afterwards in the same chronicle called 'the Bastard'. Gerald de Barry, however, calls him the eldest son by Nest, and gives no hint of his illegitimacy. The other children may have been Maurice, ancestor of the earls of Leinster and of Desmond, David, afterwards Bishop of St. Davids, and Angharat, afterwards wife of William de Barry and mother of Gerald the historian. At least, these are all of Nest's children believed to have been children of Gerald. These children, shortly after
[97] Owain carried them off, were restored to their father at the intercession of Nest, who, we are told, said to Owain, 'If thou wilt have me faithful to thee and remain with thee,

23 Brut y Tywys. 1156; Ann. Camb. 1156; Gir. Camb. vi. 130. 24 Brut y Tywys. 1095. Gir. Camb. vi. 89. In 1102, at the time of his rebellion against Henry I, Arnulf sent Gerald to Ireland to ask for the daughter of Murtough O'Brien, King of Ireland, in marriage and for military assistance, both of which he obtained. Brut y Tywys. 1100. 25 Brut y Tywys. 1092, 1094; Gir. Camb. vi. 90. 26 Brut y Tywys. 1106; Ann. Camb. 1110. 27 Cenn-garth would mean an eminence which is enclosed or fortified, or has an enclosure or fortification upon it. Rhys, Arch. Camb., 1895, p. 23. From one of the later MSS. of the Brut this appears to have been regarded as referring to a rebuilding of Pembroke Castle itself. But this is doubtful, and some think the site intended was that of Carew Castle.

send my children to their father.' Whether she remained with Owain, who afterwards became a sort of outlaw and was finally killed by Gerald, or whether she returned to her husband, we are not told, but her 'faith unfaithful' did not 'keep her falsely true', for, in addition to three other sons and a daughter of doubtful paternity,[28] she had a son by yet another husband or lover (it is uncertain which), namely Stephen, the Constable of Aberteivi, now known as Cardigan. This son was Robert Fitz Stephen, of whom also we shall hear much. He outlived his half-brothers, and may have been their junior.

When Dermot was journeying through Wales, Robert Fitz Stephen was a prisoner of Rhys ap Gruffudd.[29] Rhys, as we have seen, was very much dissatisfied with the districts assigned to him by Henry in 1157, and had on more than one occasion opposed the king and ravaged the lands occupied by the Normans, especially Ceredigion. In the year 1165, in one of these efforts to recover his hereditary dominions, he took the castle of Cilgerran on the Teivi, a little above Cardigan, and imprisoned his cousin, Robert Fitz Stephen, its castellan. Gerald de Barry tells us that Rhys had just released [98]
Robert Fitz Stephen after three years' imprisonment, on condition that he would join him against Henry, a condition which Fitz Stephen was reluctant to perform. Now, however, at the intercession of David FitzGerald, Bishop of St. Davids, and of his brother Maurice, Rhys, at Dermot's request, consented to a new disposition of his prisoner. It was accordingly arranged that Robert Fitz Stephen and Maurice Fitz Gerald should cross over to Ireland in the ensuing spring to aid Dermot in recovering his territories, Dermot on his part promising to grant to them the town of Wexford with two adjoining cantreds in fee. This was obviously an arrangement to suit all parties. Rhys, who no doubt sympathized with Dermot, but was quite unable to spare any native troops, would get rid of a number of foreigners from his territories; Fitz Stephen was to get his liberty without onerous conditions; and both he and Maurice would have a better prospect of winning sword-land for themselves in Ireland than they had at that moment in Wales, where Rhys was carrying all before him, and was no longer leaving even his aunt's descendants unassailed. Dermot, on his side, was obtaining valuable aid at the cost of a town which did not belong to him, but was held adversely by the Norsemen, and of the adjoining districts, which, as lying between the [99]
two Norse towns of Wexford and Waterford, were probably at no time very remunerative to him.

This arrangement having been made, Dermot proceeded on his journey to Ty Dewi, or St. Davids, the extreme western point of Wales, where he was only the distance of one day's sail from his hereditary kingdom. Here he was probably entertained by David Fitz Gerald, the bishop of the place, who, we are told, sympathized warmly with the unfortunate exile. The rule of celibacy among the clergy was not strictly observed in Celtic districts at that time, and the bishop had a son named Milo or Miles, who afterwards fought valiantly for Dermot, received from Strongbow a large grant of lands in Southern Ossory, and was the ancestor of the Geraldine barons of Iverk.

28 Their names were William Hay, Hoel, Walter; and Gledewis: Gir. Camb., De rebus, vol. i, p. 59. **29** Gir. Camb. v. 229; Song of Dermot, ll. 374–99.

The bishop's palace, the splendid ruins of which remain at St. Davids, was not then in existence, nor was the present beautiful cathedral. No doubt they were represented by more modest structures. The little river Alun still babbles by the cathedral close, but the famous slab that bridged it, the Lechlawar, has not only ceased to speak, but has ceased in any recognizable shape to exist. A few carved and inscribed tombstones have alone survived the wreck of centuries. Gerald's description of the surroundings
[100] is, however, still applicable. 'Menevia,' as he calls St. Davids, 'is situated in a most remote corner of land upon the Irish Ocean, with soil stony and barren, neither clothed with woods, diversified by rivers, nor adorned by meadows, ever exposed to the winds and tempests,' though happily no longer 'subject to the hostile attacks of the Flemings on one side and of the Welsh on the other'.[30] The coast is rocky, but indented with numerous little bays and natural havens. From one of these Dermot embarked early in August 1167, and landing, perhaps at Glascarrig, on the coast of Wexford, made his way straight to Ferns. Why he did not wait to return in company with his promised auxiliaries is not clear. His bold resolve can hardly have been due merely to impatience at the sufferings of his continued exile, as stated by Gerald. It is more probable that it was owing to the receipt of intelligence of a movement in his favour among his own tribesmen. Certainly we hear of no opposition from his brother, Murrough 'of the Irish', who had been set up as king in his room, nor from the men of Okinselagh.

30 Gir. Camb. vi. 102.

CHAPTER IV [101]

SOCIAL AND PHYSICAL ASPECTS OF IRELAND

Before resuming our narrative it will be useful to consider some aspects of the social state of Ireland in the period immediately prior to the coming of the Normans, and to glance at its physical aspect.

In its physical features Ireland in the twelfth century was in some respects very different from the Ireland of to-day. It was more watery and much more woody. Even now, in the western and northern regions, the island abounds in great shallow lakes. A line drawn from Dundalk to Kenmare will leave nearly all these lakes on its north-western side. But there is reason to believe that in the twelfth century and earlier the water levels were everywhere higher than they are to-day, and that much of the lowlands, even south-east of the above line, was marshy and dotted with small lakes which have since been drained away. As an example we may mention the place called Lagore (*Loch Gabhar*), near Ratoath in East Meath. In 934 'the island' (i.e. the crannog or fortified island) here was destroyed by Olaf, grandson of Ivar.[1] The site is well [102]
known, but the lake has been drained away, and now there remains a small low-lying plain with a low mound in the middle. The place has yielded vast quantities of bones and many weapons and other articles.[2]

Probably the climate was more humid than it is at present, but indeed the description of it given by Gerald de Barry applies to most districts to-day. He lays much stress on the rains and general moisture, which in spite of a fertile soil prevented the due ripening of the corn. 'What the Spring germinates and brings forth, and the Summer nourishes and advances, can with difficulty,' he says, 'be garnered in Autumn owing to the excessive rain.'[3] No Irish farmer will discredit the statement; he will only wonder how without time-saving machinery crops could have been garnered at all.

Ireland was also much more woody than at any subsequent time. Indeed the woods appear to have covered the greater part of the island known to Gerald. 'There are,' he says, 'in places beautiful champaign lands, but in comparison with the forest regions they are of small extent.'[4] Even at the close of the sixteenth century there were several [103]
woody fastnesses in each of the four provinces, of which but slight, if any, remains are to be seen to-day.[5] Through these woods tracks were cut in places, and from time to time cleared, and when we read of a fight in a 'pass' it is often a pass through the woods that is intended.

1 Ann. Ulster, 934. In 851 the islands in the east of Bregha (East Meath) are mentioned. 2 Proceedings R.I.A. (1840), vol. i, p. 420. 3 Gir. Camb. v 27. 4 Ibid., p. 26. 5 See the list in Dymmok's 'Treatice of Ireland' (159).

Communication was difficult, especially between the provinces. There were, of course, roads of some sort in all inhabited places, besides a few main roads [6] (though no such roads as the Romans left behind them in England), but there were few permanent bridges over the larger rivers.

When we turn from the land to the people, and try to form an accurate picture of their political organization, their social customs, and their manner of living generally in the period immediately preceding the Norman invasion, we are confronted with a mass of scattered material embodied in Irish literary remains of various dates and
[104] degrees of credibility. To collect, sift, and present in synthetic form the facts to be deduced from these Irish sources, so as to give as complete and as authentic a picture as possible, is fortunately beyond the scope of this work.[7] We shall here attempt to explain briefly those customs and institutions only which principally distinguished the native Irish from the Norman invaders, and which must be borne in mind if we would rightly understand the subsequent history of the two peoples. The most authentic information as to these customs and institutions is to be gathered from the Brehon Law Tracts,[8] and accordingly to these we shall first direct our attention.

There was no regular machinery in Ireland for the enactment of laws or for the judicial enforcement of customs normally observed. The so-called Brehon Law was really a body of customs which had no known commencement, but which had been observed more or less faithfully from time immemorial. These customs, speaking generally, were not peculiar to Ireland. Probably the nucleus from which they grew was at one time the common heritage of the whole Aryan family of races [see *Add.*]. But in
[105] Ireland customary law had been developed from within, and was almost entirely uninfluenced by contact with other peoples. Until the coming of the Normans—and then only partially—Ireland never felt the direct influence of a race more advanced than herself. She never experienced the stern discipline of Roman domination, nor acquired from the law-givers of modern Europe a conception of the essential condition of a progressive society, the formation of a strong state able to make and, above all, enforce the laws. Some modification in her ancient customs no doubt took place owing to the influence of Christian missionaries, but the great change they effected mainly concerned religious beliefs and observances, and left political, legal, and social institutions almost untouched. That an attempt was made by the early Christian Church to introduce the death-penalty for murder instead of pecuniary compensation may be reasonably inferred from the case of the murder of Odhran, St. Patrick's charioteer, as traditionally reported in the introduction to the Senchus Mor, the oldest of the Brehon Law Tracts. But the attempt failed, and indeed the history of Ireland many centuries later has shown that nothing short of an entirely new judicial system, backed

6 See Joyce, Social Hist., vol. ii, p. 303. When Giraldus (v. 26) says of Ireland, amongst other characteristics, that it was 'terra deserta, invia, sed aquosa' (modelling his language on Psalm lxii. 3) he does not mean, as has been supposed, that it was all 'trackless' any more than that it was all 'desert 'or all 'marshy'. He was no doubt referring to the vast regions of bog, forest, and mountain-land only. 7 This is to be the less regretted as a praiseworthy, though somewhat uncritical, attempt 'at opening up the entire field' has been recently made by Dr. P. W. Joyce in his Social History of Ancient Ireland (1903). 8 Ancient Laws of Ireland. Five volumes have been published and a useful Glossary.

by a powerful executive, could effect this reform. Accordingly the body of primitive customs which the Gaels brought with them to Ireland was slowly developed and expanded from within, first by the Druids, and then by their christianized successors, [106] the brehons.

The brehons were a class, tending to become hereditary, of persons who alone possessed an intimate knowledge of these immemorial customs, and who for a fee offered themselves as skilled arbitrators to decide disputes in accordance therewith. No adequate machinery, however, existed either for compelling the submission of a dispute to the arbitration of a brehon or for enforcing obedience to the award when given. Much of the Senchus Mor is taken up with the law of Distress as a method of inducing the defendant, or party distrained, to consent to arbitration. In the case of persons of distinction it was necessary for the plaintiff to begin by fasting (*troscad*) on his debtor's doorstep until he received a pledge of submission to law.[9] This curious custom has been shown to have existed until recently among the Hindoos, by whom it was called 'sitting dharna'.[10] Its attested existence at the two extremities of the Aryan world affords an interesting indication of a common origin. But it may be asked, What if the defendant forcibly resisted the distrain or let his creditor starve? It is not enough [107] to reply that in that case he would render himself liable to increased penalties. How were these to be enforced? The Druid, who like the Brahmin was priest as well as judge, could threaten immediate supernatural terrors, which in most cases would be effective, but the christianized brehon could rely on this aid only in a secondary degree. The ultimate sanction of his award was, after all, only public opinion. Contumacy might be followed by social ostracism.[11] This absence of an effective sanction was the greatest defect in the whole system.

Most of the Brehon Law Tracts consist of an ancient text, to which have been subsequently added glosses, or explanations of words and phrases, and more lengthened commentaries. The tracts do not form a code of laws, or even a systematic digest. In all probability they were the work of the brehons, and were used as textbooks in their law schools. Only in a long course of time did they assume their present shape. Some [108] of the tracts have the appearance of a law professor's notebook, into which headings only of presumably well-known rules, or even mere titles of departments of law, were copied as texts for exegetical dissertation. In utilizing these tracts as evidence of customs existing in the twelfth century, we are met at the outset by the difficulty of dating works of such gradual growth. The text of the Senchus Mor, the most important and probably the oldest of these tracts, has been variously assigned by competent

9 Brehon Laws, vol. i, p. 112, l. 15. There are many allusions in the religious legends and romantic tales of Ireland to 'fasting' to obtain an advantage over an opponent, or to compel the granting of a request. See Joyce, Social Hist., vol. i, pp. 207. An example from the Annals as late as the year 1166 was referred to *supra*, p. 68 [p. 20]. 10 See Maine, Early Institutions, pp. 297–301. 11 So with the continental Gauls: —'Si qui aut privatus aut populus eorum (Druidum) decreto non stetit, sacrificiis interdicunt. Haec poena apud eos est gravissima. Quibus ita est interdictum, hi numero impiorum ac sceleratorum habentur, his omnes decedunt, aditum sermonemque defugiunt, ne quid ex contagione incommodi accipiant, neque his petentibus ius redditur neque honos ullus communicatur': Caesar, Bell. Gall. vi. 13. It was the primitive 'boycott'.

scholars to about the year 800, or to about two centuries later.[12] This at first sight leaves [109] a wide margin of possible error as to the date of the original text, but, as suggested in the note, the two opinions are not irreconcilable, and in any case there can be no doubt that the glosses and commentaries extend to a much later period. While some of the customs embodied in these tracts can be traced back to a period even long anterior to the eighth century, it is improbable that elaborate dissertations on obsolete customs would be copied into textbooks in the fourteenth century, and purely antiquarian matter can in general be distinguished. Moreover, seeing that the picture of society presented by the Brehon tracts can be shown by other testimony to be in many important respects essentially true of purely Irish districts up to the close of the sixteenth century, and in view of the undoubted almost stationary nature of Irish society, we cannot be far wrong in assuming that at least those customs which are elaborated in the comsmentaries were in full force in the twelfth century and even somewhat later.

Owing to the confused and often contradictory statements in the tracts, and especially in the commentaries, and to the obscurity surrounding the technical terms employed, it is almost impossible to gain a clear and consistent view of these customs. Different modern writers have drawn very different conclusions from them, and I can [110] only give the brief results of my own independent study of the published tracts and of other sources, without being at all confident that they are in all respects correct.[13]

First as regards the customary methods of holding land. According to the theory of Celtic law the land belonged to the tribe that occupied it. At the stage reached in the twelfth century the land of Ireland appears to have been divided into about 185 cantreds (*tricha céd* or *tuatha*),[14] and these may be regarded as so many distinct tribal [111] territories. Some of this land, however, from an early date appears to have been held by certain families in severalty. Thus a certain portion was assigned as mensal land to

12 M. D'Arbois de Jubainville fixes on the former date: Lit. Celtique, vol. vii, pp. 332–46. The oldest MSS. into which the Senchus Mor has been copied date from the fourteenth century, and some of the glosses and commentaries may be no earlier, but the text is cited in the Lebor na h. Uidre and Liber Hymnorum, MSS. dating from c. 1100. Both the introduction and the glossed text of the Senchus Mor are cited in Cormac's Glossary, and this work is believed to have been written by Cormac Mac Cuilennain (ob. 907). The Senchus Mor mentions no law-book, nor does the word *lebor* occur in the text. It, however, speaks of the *recht litre*, meaning the Canon Law, probably the collection of c. 700. These and other indications point, in M. D'Arbois' opinion, to c. 800 as the date of the text. Dr. Whitley Stokes, from a consideration of the verbal forms, believed that the Senchus Mor was compiled in, or perhaps slightly before, the eleventh century. The two opinions may be reconciled if we suppose the verbal forms to have been modernized in a recension of about the later date. 13 Of previous writers I have found M. D'Arbois de Jubainville (Études sur le Droit Celtique) the most illuminating, and, in a less degree, Sir Henry Maine (Early History of Institutions). Dr. Atkinson's Glossary is useful for checking the published translations. It leaves, however, many of the most difficult points undecided, and has not escaped the severe criticism of Dr. Stokes. 14 Keating, Hist. of Ireland (Ir. Texts Soc.), vol. i, p. 128. Each cantred contained 30 ballybetaghs, and each ballybetagh 12 *seisreachs* or ploughlands. Giraldus (vol. v, p. 145) gives 176 cantreds, each cantred containing 100 vills. The term *tricha céd* means 'thirty hundreds', and if we suppose each ballybetagh to be estimated to contain 100 homesteads, and each vill 30 homesteads, we can reconcile the two methods of subdivision. A ploughland contained 120 Irish acres, each of which, Keating says, was equivalent to 2 or 3 English acres. Taking the Irish acre as equivalent to 2½ English acres, the 66,600 ploughlands of Ireland would amount in round numbers to 20,000,000 statute acres, which is almost exactly the area of Ireland. Dividing this by 185, we get 108,000 acres as the average area of a tuath or cantred.

the chief for the time being of the tribe. Other portions were acquired by professional men, or rather families, as, for instance, brehons, physicians, chroniclers, &c., as emoluments of their profession.[15] Besides these, it appears that in course of time chiefs of septs and other wealthy and powerful individuals managed to acquire lands which were not subject to partition like ordinary tribe-land, but were occupied by the family under their head, and descended in the family as lands of inheritance according to certain rules based on the four-fold family organization.[16] Notwithstanding these exceptional cases, and, apart from church land and monastic land, the greater part of the [112] land appears to have been regarded as belonging to the tribe. Much of this would be waste land of the tribe and commons on which the tribesmen could pasture their cattle, while the rest, mostly arable and meadow land, was divided from time to time among the free tribesmen. In the twelfth century there was probably land and to spare for all, but land without cattle to stock and work it was of no value, and accordingly a man was poor or wealthy, not primarily according to the amount of land he held, but in proportion to the head of cattle he possessed.

Cattle, then, formed the principal wealth of the community, as indeed of all primitive communities, and the ordinary tribesman obtained the requisite number of cattle from his own chief or from some other wealthy noble. A considerable section of the Senchus Mor deals with the relationship thus constituted between the chief or nobles and individual tribesmen.[17] The editor speaks of this section as the 'Law of Tenures', and renders the two contracts mentioned as '*saer*-stock and *daer*-stock tenure', and translates the words *ceile* and *ceilsine* as 'tenant 'and 'tenancy'. But this rendering is [113] misleading, as suggesting that the relationship was one of landlord and tenant, and that the laws concern the tenure of land. Had this been so in the twelfth century the conflict between Celtic and Norman or English ideas would have been much less acute than it actually was. Of course a tribesman might hire land which belonged to his chief in severalty, but his share in the tribe-land was his of ancient right, and was in no way due to his chief. No translation is entirely free from objection, but it would be less misleading to speak of the correlation as that of 'lord' or 'chief' and 'vassal', as not necessarily connoting the tenure of land. A contract for the letting of cattle is known as *cheptel* in French law, but there seems to be no simple equivalent in modern English law. With this explanation we may call the contract a cattle-bailment, and for convenience speak of the parties to it as bailor and bailee, but as the contract (if such it

15 Br. Laws, vol. iii, p. 50, l. 2. 16 Ibid., p. 48, l. 15. The four-fold family organization is known as the Gelfine system, the principal rules concerning which will be found in Br. Laws, vol. iii, pp. 334, vol. iv, pp. 38–42 and 282, &c. Exactly how this joint-family was organized is too obscure to be discussed here. It must suffice to say that it consisted, when complete, of seventeen related males, distributed into four divisions of four men each, with a fifth man, who seems to have been the chief, in the Gelfine division. These four classes succeeded to the acquired property, and were liable for the crimes of the members according to certain rules. Moreover, for some purposes they seem to have represented the entire sept or kindred. When the number seventeen was complete, and a duly qualified member was born into the Gelfine division, the eldest of those most distantly related to the chief seems to have gone out of the family. The chief appears to have been selected from a restricted number of qualified persons by a rule similar to that of Tanistry, by which the tribal chief was selected. 17 Br Laws. vol. ii, pp. 194–340.

should be called) undoubtedly created, or rather regulated, a quasi-feudal relation, we shall in general regard it as a contract of vassalage and call the parties thereto king or chief and vassal.

Two kinds of cattle-bailment are described, one called free (*saerrath*) and the other base or servile (*daerrath*).

[114] In the free contract the bailee, in return for a certain number of cattle, had to render the value of one-third in food-rents, or rents in kind, every year to the bailor,[18] who would in general be either the tribal king or the chief of the bailee's sept. This amounted to interest at 331 per cent. If nothing was paid for three years, compound interest became due,[19] and the amount was liable to be penally increased if the bailee made default.[20] Besides this, the bailee or vassal was bound to assist the chief in erecting his *dún*, or in reaping his harvest, or by joining in his hostings. Homage, too, had to be paid. It consisted in standing up (*ureirghe*) before the sitting lord.[21] The contract lasted normally for seven years, and then apparently the original loan had to be restored.[22] A man was obliged to accept cattle on these terms from his own king, and probably from the chief of his sept, but from no one else.[23] If he entered into the contract with others he could terminate it at any time on restoring the stock.[24] If the chief, on the other hand, recalled his stock, the bailee could elect to become a base vassal, and
[115] then the chief would be obliged to give the additional stock required by that contract or forfeit the stock already given.[25]

Regarded as a business contract, this arrangement is so oppressive as to be in fact economically impossible. The arrangement, or rather custom, should, I think, be regarded as resulting essentially from status and not from contract. The king or chief had the right of being maintained by his principal vassals, and he gave them a certain amount of cattle, not as a mere business transaction—not as the capital out of which alone the vassals might be expected to make the food-rents due—but primarily as a mark of their subjection and as a measure of their obligations. The free vassal, if not wealthy enough to support his obligations, could only escape from them by surrendering some of his liberties and accepting the position of a base vassal.

The relationship between the tribal king and his free vassals seems analogous to that between the provincial king and the tribal kings. The Book of Rights enumerates the stipends (*tuarastla*) given by the provincial kings to their subordinate kings, and the tributes and refections (*císa*, *biathaidh*) paid by the subordinate kings to the provin-
[116] cial kings. In each case the stipend is very much less than the tribute, and there is no doubt that the acceptance of a stipend was a mark of submission.[26]

18 Br. Laws, vol. ii, p. 194, ll. 15–16. **19** Ibid., p. 196; l. 7, and 198, l. 20 et seq. **20** Ibid., p.198, l. 9; 194, ll. 6–9, and 219, l. 15 and comm., where a defaulting bailee of three cows is shown to owe no less than forty-two cows at the end of the seven years! **21** Ibid., p. 194, ll. 9–14. 5 **22** Ibid., p. 204, ll. 5–11. **23** Ibid., p. 208, ll. 1–10; p. 210, ll. 4–8. **24** Ibid., p 206, l. 6. **25** Br. Laws, vol. ii, p. 212, ll. 1–18. **26** So when Malachi II 'went into Brian's house', i.e. submitted to him, Brian gave him twelve score steeds, 'and there was not one of the twelve score men who accompanied Malachy who would deign to carry a led horse with him,' so reluctant were they to admit vassalage to Brian. To get out of the difficulty Malachy made a present of the horses to Brian's son: Wars of the Gaedhil with the Gaill, p. 132. Compare the story of Gormlaith and the tunic which Brian had given to the King of Leinster as a mark of vassalage: ibid., p. 143.

In the contract of base vassalage a certain number of cattle were delivered to the vassal proportional to the food-rents to be paid and the services to be performed by him (*tuircreic*), and in addition a further number of cattle equivalent in value to the honour-price of the vassal (*seoit turcluide*).[27] This addition was in effect a purchase of the honour-price of the vassal, who thus underwent a diminution of status. It was in fact this parting with his honour-price that constituted the base or servile element in his relation to his lord, for the food-rents to which the base vassal became liable were very much lighter than those of the free vassal,[28] while the services to be performed were of a similar character.[29] If the base vassal were injured or killed, his chief, and not [117]
himself or his family, became entitled to the amount recoverable as honour-price.[30] His oath, too, was valueless, and, unlike the free vassal, he could not give evidence against his chief.[31] Elaborate rules were devised by the brehons to prevent the capricious termination of the contract on either side. When entering into the contract the base vassal had to give notice of its terms to his tribe, who might refuse to sanction an excessive delivery of stock, as in the event of the vassal absconding the tribe became liable, and the land or part of it might become forfeited to the chief.[32] This was probably one of the ways in which the nobles became entitled to land in severalty.

By means of these food-rents, or rents in kind, the chiefs, both of the tribe and of the septs or families into which the tribe was divided, were supplied and maintained with their suites, and it was their custom to obtain what was due, or part of it, on visitation to the houses of the vassals, both free and base—a custom which seems to indicate less disparity in the manner of living of the various classes than might otherwise be supposed. It is probable that in course of time this custom came to be regarded as [118]
the right of the chieftain quite independently of the delivery of cattle on which it was originally based, and to be looked upon as a rent due for the land held by the tribesmen as tenants. It and analogous customs, or abuses of customs, known by various names, such as cuddy, coshery, bonnaght, coigny and livery, &c—whether as practised by Irish chiefs or imitated and perhaps further abused by Anglo-Irish lords—though more than once forbidden by statute, lived on in Munster and in Irish districts to Elizabethan times, and were denounced by Sir John Davies as evil customs which made the lords absolute tyrants, the land waste, and the tenants very slaves and villeins.[33]

Even up to the beginning of the seventeenth century by far the greater part of the land in the Irish districts continued to be divisible from time to time among the tribesmen, and the parts that were not so divisible appear to have been held by joint families rather than by individuals—at least the succession of owners was regulated by what Davies calls the law of Tanistry. In his official capacity Davies investigated the state of Mac Mahon's, Maguire's, and O'Reilly's countries, or Monaghan, Fermanagh, and [119]

27 Br. Laws, vol. ii, p. 222, l. 9, and p. 226, l. 13. **28** Ibid., pp. 254–60. **29** Namely erecting the *dún* and harvest work, ibid., p. 256, l. 9; also joining in the chief's hostings, ibid., vol. iii, p. 494. **30** Br. Laws, vol. iii, p. 334, ll. 12–15. **31** Ibid., vol. ii, p. 344, l. 14. **32** Ibid., vol. ii, p. 222, l. 16; pp. 228, 230, 258, l. 10. **33** A Discovery, &c. (ed. 1787), pp. 131, 134. As to these exactions and others, see Harris's Ware, Antiq. (ed. 1764), p.74.

Cavan respectively. He gives the fullest details as to Fermanagh. There were here fifty-one and a half ballybetaghs divisible among the tribesmen by the custom of gavelkind and chargeable to Maguire with about 240 beeves annually. Of lands not so chargeable there were (1) the church lands, which were considerable and found in every barony, but of which the extent is not given; (2) the mensal lands of Maguire, amounting to four ballybetaghs, the occupiers of which paid food-rents, (3) lands given to certain septs, such as Chroniclers, Rhymers, and Galloglasses, amounting to two ballybetaghs; and (4) there was 'a chief of every sept who had certain services, duties, and demesnes that ever passed to the tanist of that sept and never were subject to division'.[34] This chief was the 'canfiny or caput cognationis' mentioned in the 'Resolution of the judges touching gavelkind in 1606,[35] and we can hardly doubt that he represented the Gelfine chief of the Brehon Law Tracts.[36]

[120] The distinction drawn in modern law between crimes, or offences regarded as affecting the State, and torts, or private wrongs, was unknown to the Celtic world. All offences were regarded as affecting individuals alone. The great object of the Brehon Law was to induce those who were wronged to forgo the right of private vengeance, and to submit their claims to the arbitrament of the brehons. This aim, when effected, was no small victory over violence, but humanity had elsewhere already found that sterner methods are required than those adopted by the brehons. When the submission to law was made, the work of the brehons mainly resolved itself into estimating the damages or penalties to be paid by the wrongdoer in the particular circumstances of the case. This is most strikingly shown in the law of murder. There was no public prosecution. If the family of the victim consented to forgo their right of vengeance the brehon assessed the composition to be paid, and determined, according to certain rules, the persons by whom and the persons to whom the payments were to be made.

The composition for murder (*eric*) consisted of (1) 'body-fine '(*coirp-dire*), apparently fixed for all free men at seven cumals[37] or twenty-one cows; (2) 'honour-price'
[121] (*enech-lann* or *log enech*, literally 'face-price'), varying, with the dignity of the victim, from one cumal for a bo-aire or cow-chief, the highest of the non-noble classes, to twenty-eight cumals for the chief king.[38]

The right of private vengeance was at one time not only freely admitted, but in the case of the family of the murdered man was recognized as a sacred duty. This was, of course, not peculiar to Ireland, nor to Celtic peoples. Probably all the branches of the Aryan family of races [see *Add.*] passed through this stage, as also some non-Aryans—

34 Letter to the Earl of Salisbury (ed. 1787), pp. 2438. 35 See the Irish Custom of Gavelkind, Davies, Report of Cases (ed. 1762), p. 134; and compare the Case of Tanistry, ibid., p. 78. 36 'Canfiny' represents the Irish *ceann-fine*, head of the line, sept, or family, of the same lineage or surname. For his qualifications see Br. Laws, vol. ii, p. 278, 11. 19–25. In this section I think the word *fine* in general refers to the 'sept' or 'family', and not to the 'tribe'. 37 Br. Laws. vol. iii, p. 350, l. 4. A *cumal* meant originally a 'bondmaid', but was used as a measure of value, equivalent (generally) to three cows. 38 Br. Laws, vol. ii, p. 226, l. 13, and p. 224, ll. 8 and 9. A different scale is given in the *Crith gabhlach*, ibid., vol. iv, and yet another in the *Uraicecht Bece* or Small Primer, vol. v. The principal passages in the Brehon Law Tracts concerning the composition for murder are, vol. iii, pp. 68, 98 (where 'malice aforethought' is a faulty translation, as the commentary shows), and 536, vol. iv, pp. 240–61.

for example, the Hebrews. But agreeably to the habit of non-interference by the ruling powers with the mutual relations of families, and the absence of any executive machinery, the right of private vengeance continued to be exercised in Ireland to a late period, and influenced to the last the rules of Brehon Law for the composition of homicide. This is shown by the curious distinction made between 'necessary' and 'unnecessary' homicide. Necessary, or (to use a term which better expresses the idea) 'obligatory' homicide was when the killing was motived by vengeance for the previous [122]
killing of a near relative of the avenger. It was classed with cases of accidental homicide, probably as involving no moral obliquity. Unnecessary or non-obligatory homicide was where the killing was intentional, but the motive was not what was regarded as legitimate vengeance but something else, such as private gain.[39] In all these cases, at the time the commentaries were written, a composition might be arranged, but a significant distinction was made as to the persons on whom the liability fell. In the case of obligatory homicide (to which must be added 'the four "obligatory" woundings which defile not the purity of the hand)[40] this liability did not fall exclusively on the actual slayer, but was shared in certain proportions by those who were entitled to the honour-price of the victim for whose death vengeance had been taken—that is to say, by those on whom the duty of vengeance fell.[41] In the case of unnecessary or non- [123]
obligatory crimes the liability fell primarily on the criminal and on his movable property, and the family might either deliver up the criminal and keep his land or give the land for his crime.[42] This, indeed, affords a further distinction, for in cases of obligatory crimes the family had no such choice. The old rule in this case was 'a man is better than land',[43] and this evidently meant that it was better to sacrifice his land than to give up the righteous avenger.

The above appear to be the general principles which regulated the composition in cases of homicide. To pursue the matter further would lead us into a maze of doubtful detail. It is important, however, to note that in most cases of homicide motived by vengeance for a previous homicide, the debts incurred in consequence of the two homicides would cancel each other, or if the honour-piece of the victims were not equal, the difference alone would require adjustment.

This 'compounding of felony' was one of the principal features in the Brehon Law which caused it to be condemned by English Acts of Parliament as no law, but a bad custom,[44] and which led Edmund Spenser to describe it as a wild law by which many [124]
murders among the Irish were smothered up. Spenser also notices that the brehons for the most part adjudge a better share of the eric to the head of the sept than to the parties grieved.[45] This would occur in many cases, as, for instance, if it were for the killing of a base vassal who had parted with his honour-price to the chief, or a *fuidhir*, a

39 Br. Laws, vol. iii, p. 68, ll. 12–14, and vol. iv, p. 248, l. 25. For the translation of *indethbire torba*, see D'Arbois de Jubainville, Cours de Litt., vol. vii, p. 182, and Atkinson's Glossary, s.v. *dethbire*. These scholars take the words differently, but agree as to the fundamental meaning of the distinction. 40 Br. Laws, vol. iv, p. 252, l. 17 et seq., and p. 244, l. 20 et seq., where *cenmota* = besides, not except. 41 In addition to the above passages, see vol. iv, p. 254, ll. 12–14. 42 Br. Laws, vol. iv, p. 246, ll. 23–9. 43 Ibid., p. 246, l. 15. 44 Early Statutes (Berry), pp. 389, 436. 45 View of the State of Ireland (1810), p. 7.

numerous class of bondmen whose erics went to their lord.[46] The brehon's fee was ordinarily one-twelfth of the fine, but if he levied the fine in circumstances of difficulty he might take as much as two-thirds.[47]

The position of women in Ireland presented some peculiarities. The Irish maiden was in her father's power until marriage, and he was expected to pay for her fosterage and to wed her to a man of equal family.[48] The contract of marriage was accompanied by a nuptial gift (*coibche*) from the husband, equivalent to half the honour-price of the bride's father,[49] and this was paid, not to the wife, but to her father, or if the marriage took place after the death of her father half of it was paid to the chief of the sept.[50]
[125] The wife on her side brought a contribution (*tinól*) of cattle or goods, part of which passed to the husband and part was regarded as her separate property.[51] Neither as daughter nor as wife had she any share in the tribe-land,[52] but during her first marriage her position was one of considerable independence and dignity. A broad distinction must, however, be made between the first or chief wife (*cétmuintir*) and subsequent wives taken on repudiation of the first wife, as well as various temporary
[126] or irregular partners or concubines who were not regarded as lawful wives, but whose rights, though far inferior to that of the *cétmuintir*, were carefully regulated by law, and whose offspring seem to have been under no disability.[53] If the wife's property was equal to that of her husband, and if their marriage state was equally free and lawful, the wife was called 'a wife of equal rank', and no contract, unless for the common benefit of the couple, was binding without the consent of both.[54] Husband and wife could separate at any time by mutual consent, when a fair division of the property and its increase should be made. For this division elaborate rules are given.[55] Seven grounds are enumerated entitling the woman to separate from her husband.[56] Some of these are not recognized in modern law, as where the husband circulates a false story about his wife or a satire until she is laughed at. The wife of equal rank, we may assume, would generally be a *cétmuintir*, but a *cétmuintir*, even without property and though she had no children, held an equally high position in the eye of the law.

On the other hand, even a first wife, though she had faithfully performed her
[127] duties, was liable to be displaced by the husband introducing into the house a new

46 Br. Laws, vol. v, p. 512, l. 7. 47 Ibid., vol. iii, p. 316, l. 26 and commentary. 48 Ibid.,vol. ii, p. 346, l. 6. 49 Ibid., vol. v, p. 288, l. 18. 50 Ibid.,vol. iii, p. 314, l. 5; vol. iv, p. 62, l. 9. 51 Br. Laws, vol. ii, p. 346, l. 9, and compare p. 378, l. 29, with p. 386, l. 3. *Tinól* means the 'act of collecting', and it was probably subscribed by the bride's father and friends. A similar custom survived in Westmeath up to the close of tho seventeenth century; see Piers' Description of Westmeath in Collectanea de Rebus Hib. (Vallancy), vol. i, p. 122. 52 In the ancient leading case of Ciannacht. overruling two previous unjust (blotch-producing) decisions of Sencha (iv, pp. 9–17), and in the case of Seither (ibid., pp. 17–19), the successful plaintiffs appear to have been daughters of the Picts of Uladh who had intermarried with the Feini in the south, and who claimed lands in their native country, where matriarchal rules of descent still survived. So far as these interesting cases were tentatively used in much later times as precedents, they seem to have been applied only to land which had come to be regarded as heritable, or at least as separated for the time being from ordinary partible tribe-land (vol. iv, pp. 39–47); such as lands belonging to the gelfine when the male succession failed (p. 40, l. 19, and p. 42, l. 18), and *orba cruibh no sliasta* ('hand and thigh land') of the mother, and unoccupied land (p. 44, l. 14). 53 As to the various species of concubines, see vol. ii, p. 396, l. 27, to p. 404, l. 13, and Glossary, s.v. *Dormaine*. 54 Br. Laws, vol. ii, p. 356, l. 29. She was be *cuitchernsa*. apparently *co-tigernasa*, 'of equal lordship': see Glossary. 55 Vol. ii, pp. 363–77. 56 Vol. v, p. 292, heptad 52.

wife[57] to whom he had given a nuptial present (*coibche*). This *coibche* would then be forfeited to the first wife, and honour-price would have to be paid to her by the new wife and by the husband, and the marriage would be dissolved—unless indeed the first wife remained with her husband, when a new *coibche* would be due to her.[58] Indeed, the Brehon Law Tracts alone make it quite plain that repudiations by the husband were frequent, and temporary unions very common, and that both were fully recognized by the law.[59] In all cases the contract was sealed, as it were, by the *coibche* or nuptial gift from the man, but provision was made in the law to regulate the payment of no fewer than twenty-one of these nuptial gifts in respect of the same woman on successive marriages. A continually decreasing portion of each gift went to the wife's father, if alive, or one-half of the father's share to the chief of the sept if the father [128]
were no longer living.[60] It is said in the Senchus Mor that Beltene (May Day) was usually the time of making these separations,[61] and this is enough to suggest a connexion with the traditions as to annual marriages taking place at the great aonachs or fairs held on Beltene, Lugnasad, and Samain, or May 1, August 1, and November 1 respectively. The tradition of these marriages and separations was particularly vivid at Teltown in County Meath, where the ancient fair of Tailtiu was held on the Lugnasad.[62] A 'Teltown marriage' is an expression used for an irregular union. In Cormac's Glossary [129]
it is said that a hillock at the fair of Tailtiu was called *tulach na coibche*, and this use of the technical law-term makes the identity of the custom as revealed in the Law Tracts with that preserved on the spot by tradition quite certain.

The laxity of Irish marriage customs was repeatedly noticed by foreign ecclesiastics in the eleventh and twelfth centuries. Thus Lanfranc, Archbishop of Canterbury, writing in 1074 to Gothric, King of Dublin, says: 'It is reported that in your kingdom men take wives of their own family (*parentela*) or of that of their deceased wives, and that others at their own caprice and will leave their lawfully wedded wives, and that

57 This new wife is frequently called an *adaltrach* or adulteress. We cannot call her a concubine, for her subsequent legal position, if she had sons, appears to have been equivalent to that of the *cétmuintir* (vol. ii, p. 378, l. 16; pp. 384, l. 17), and she was one of the four lawful wives (vol. v, p. 286, ll. 18–20). 58 Vol. ii, p. 382, l. 15 et seq., and vol. v, p. 72, l. 17. 59 As an example taken.from the highest ranks: Gormfhlaith, sister of Maelmordha; King of Leinster, was married to, and repudiated by, Amlaf, King of Dublin, Malachy II, of Ireland, and Brian Borumha, successively. 60 Br. Laws, vol. ii, p. 346, ll. 9–13; vol. iii, p. 314, l. 15; vol. iv, p. 62, l. 9 et seq. The passage cited from vol. iv seems to explain the supposed contradiction noticed in the note to vol. iii, p. 314, and to render superfluous the explanation offered in the Glossary s.v. *coibche*. The chief had no share, at least in the first three nuptial gifts, if the father was alive; after that he perhaps had a share, whether the father was alive or not, as in the discreditable case mentioned by way of analogy. The passage in vol. iii, p. 316, ll. 14–16, must mean that the shares of father or chief vest absolutely only if the wife is justified in separating. If she was not justified the whole *coibche* had to be repaid to the husband: ibid. ll. 17–20, and vol. iv, p. 64, ll. 6–9. 61 Vol. ii, p. 390, ll. 18–21. The husband had to give a sack of provisions to the wife (under notice to quit) every month up to the end of the year, i.e. to the next May Day, when the formal separation took place. (Hence the phrase, 'to give the sack' ?) Separations also took place at the other quarters of the year: ibid., p. 370, ll. 24–7. 62 See Book of Rights, p. 243, note h. The custom died hard. Campion, writing in 1571, says: 'Yea even at this day, where the cleargie is fainte, they (the Irish) can be content to marrie for a yeare and a day of probation, and at the yeares end to return her home uppon any light quarrels, if the gentlewomans friendes bee weake and unable to avenge the injury '(Reprint, 1809, p. 23).

some give their own wives to others and by an infamous exchange receive the wives of others in return.'[63] At the same time and in the same strain he wrote to Turlough O'Brien, King of Ireland.[64] At the beginning of the twelfth century Anselm, writing to Murtough O'Brien, King of Ireland, says: 'We hear that marriages in your kingdom
[130] are dissolved without any cause and wives exchanged, and that blood relations under colour of marriage or otherwise do not fear to unite openly and without blame, contrary to canonical prohibition.'[65] The language of St. Bernard, referring to the year 1124 and to the north of Ireland, though more vague in its charges, is still more bitter.[66] We are thus prepared for the language attributed to Popes Adrian IV and Alexander III in the third quarter of the twelfth century. Making due allowance for ecclesiastical counsels of perfection in these matters, it must be admitted that there was much in Irish marriage customs which must have appeared, even to average foreign lay opinion, as reprehensible.[67]

It was the custom of the chiefs and nobles of the Irish to send their children, especially their sons, to be fostered in some other family away from home. A section of the
[131] Senchus Mor is devoted to the rules as to fosterage, the fees to be paid according to the rank of the father, the duties of the foster-parent, his liability for the crimes of his foster-son, and so on. All writers speak of the warm friendship that always existed between the foster-son and his foster-father and foster-brothers, and Giraldus contrasts it with the enmity that often arose between natural brothers and blood relations.[68] Of the latter the Annals supply numerous examples. The root cause of this enmity probably explains the origin of fosterage. The sons of a chief, perhaps by different wives, were all equally eligible for the chieftainship. Hence mutual jealousies and enmities, and hence probably the necessity of having the sons reared in different families and away from home.

This was one of the Irish customs adopted in after years by some of the border Anglo-Irish lords, with the natural result that the children in many cases grew up Irish in speech, in manners, in habits of thought, and in sympathies. It was not only to prevent them from 'degendring from their auncient dignities', but also because the ties created by fosterage led to 'espials and forewarnings' which impeded the action of the government, that attempts were made to prohibit the English from fostering, as well
[132] as from intermarrying, with the Irish, and that the practice was reprobated by Edmund Spenser and Sir John Davies.[69]

The Brehon Law Tracts contain a mine of information as to the customs of the Irish and the real facts of their social state, but, owing to a variety of uncertainties, it is a mine difficult to work, and at times so obscure that we cannot be certain of having

63 Ussher's Sylloge, ep. 26. 64 Ibid., ep. 27. 65 Ussher's Sylloge, ep. 35. In epistle 37, apparently to the same king, Anselm says: 'Dicitur enim quod viri ita libere uxores suas uxoribus aliorum commutant, sicut quilibet equum equo, aut quamlibet aliam rem re alia ab illo commutat; aut pro libitu et sine ratione relinquunt.' 66 De vita S. Malachiae, Migne, vol. clxxxii, col. 1034, 67 Marriage by *coibche* was, I think, what is referred to by the Stat. of Kilkenny, § 2, which prohibits *alliance par . . . concubinaunce ou de caif* [*e*]. Early Statutes, p. 432, and cf. Hardiman's edition, Tracts I.A.S., vol. ii, p. 8. *Caife* might very fairly represent the sound of *coibche*. 68 v. 167. 69 31 Ed. III, § 8. Early Statutes, p. 412; also Stat. of Kilkenny, ibid., p. 432; Spenser, View of the State of Ireland (Reprint), pp. 110–12; Davies, Discovery (1787), p. 135.

extracted the genuine ore of fact. We cannot pursue the search in this quarter any further. When we turn to the pages of Gerald de Barry we are confronted with no uncertainties of language or of dates, but though our author was a man of remarkable observation and acuteness he had little opportunity of observing more than the surface of Irish life and manners, and, bearing in mind his relationship with the invaders, we must make allowance for that want of sympathy which those whose heart is engaged in any militant cause inevitably display towards their opponents. As to the facts of the invasion, with which we shall have to deal in detail hereafter, he must have learnt them almost entirely from the invaders, and principally from his uncle Robert Fitz Stephen and his cousin Raymond le Gros. As to his description of Ireland and [133]
the Irish, so far as he did not draw his account from personal observation, he must have derived it largely from the Irish themselves—probably from the clergy, with whom alone he could readily converse. Living in a credulous age, he was not a peculiarly credulous man, and most of his stories of a miraculous nature can be shown to have been believed in by the Irish themselves. Like Herodotus, he may have been occasionally gulled or misled by his informants; but, again like Herodotus, he seems to have faithfully recorded what he heard. At any rate, these stories which have cast an undeserved discredit on his work are, except to the folklorist, of no importance. For the rest, there is no reason to think that he has anywhere wilfully perverted the truth as he saw it.

The following is a summary of his most pertinent observations:[70]

Irish children, he says, are not scientifically treated, as is usual elsewhere, but are left almost entirely to Nature, who, however, manages to rear them up to full strength with tall, handsome figures, regular features, and fresh complexions. But though richly endowed by Nature, the barbarous fashion of their beards and clothes and their ignorance mark their uncivilized state. They are slightly clad in woollen clothing, mostly [134]
black,[71] the colour of their sheep, and arranged in barbarous fashion. They wear close-fitting hoods, made of patchwork, extending over the shoulders and down to the elbows, and under this a *phalanga* instead of a mantle (*pallium*). They also wear woollen trews, or hose and breeches in one, usually dyed some colour.[72] For riding they use neither saddle nor riding-boots nor spurs, but urge on their horses with a crooked stick.[73] Reins serve as bit and bridle. In war they wear no defensive armour. They use a short spear, a pair of javelins, and a large battle-axe, well wrought and tempered, which they borrowed from the Ostmen. This they wield with one hand with such force that neither conical helmet nor coat of mail can protect the person. Hand-stones (*lapides pugillares*),[74] when other weapons fail, they hurl more dexterously than any [135]
other nation, so as to inflict great loss on the enemy.

70 v. 150 et seq. 71 'Black, yellowish, grey, and drab clothes for the sons of the Feini grades': Br. Laws, vol. ii, p. 148, l. 3. 72 The Irish *falaing*, or cloak reaching down below the knees, and the trews, are well illustrated in a thirteenth century copy of the Topographia Hibernica: MS. Roy 13, B. viii, Brit. Mus. See reproductions, Green's Short History (illustrated ed., 1893), pp. 901, 903; and the close fitting hood, *cochull*, in MS. Harl. 1319, reproduced ibid., opp. p. 904. 73 The crooked stick (*echflesc, each-lasc*=horse-rod) probably had a goad at its curved end. See Joyce, Social Hist., vol. ii, p. 417. 74 *Lapides pugillares* looks like a translation of the *lia láimbe láich*, or 'champion's hand-stone', frequently mentioned in the ancient tales

The Irish, he says, are a rude people, living on animal produce and little advanced from the pastoral stage. While shunning the labour of agriculture, they are not attracted by the refinements, and dislike the restraints, of town-life, and cannot shake off the bucolic ways to which they have hitherto been accustomed. They use most of their land as rough pasture, little is cultivated and still less sown,[75] and this though much of the land is naturally fertile. There are few fruit-bearing trees, foreign sorts not having been planted. Chestnut, beech, maple (*aralus* ?), and box-trees are not indigenous, but yew-trees are more plentiful than elsewhere, and were often planted in ancient cemeteries. The forests abound in fir-trees![76] Metallic veins are not turned to account, and gold, which is much in request, is imported by merchants.[77] They do not
[136] profitably employ their time in making linen or woollen cloth, or any other sort of merchandise, nor in any kind of mechanical art.[78] Sunk in sloth, they think the height of luxury is to have no work to do, and what they most dearly prize is the enjoyment of liberty.

Gerald praises highly the musical attainments of the Irish. 'In this art,' he says, 'they far surpass any people I have met.' They use and delight in two instruments alone: the cithara (or harp, Ir. *crott*) and the tympanum (Ir. *timpan*).[79]

In another place he speaks with enthusiastic appreciation of the illuminations in a book of the Gospels which he saw at Kildare. His fine description of it would apply to
[137] the well-known Book of Kells. 'However often and however closely I scrutinize it,' he concludes, 'I am always astounded afresh, and always find more and more to admire in it.'[80]

In speaking of the illicit marriages of the Irish, Gerald uses the intemperate language habitual with ecclesiastics.[81] He stigmatizes the Irish as treacherous and keeping faith with no man. Then he gives us some interesting details as to their usages in making a solemn covenant of friendship. First they enter into an alliance of gossipred,[82] then they go in procession thrice round a church; afterwards they enter the

(O'Curry, Manners and Customs, vol. i, p. 263 et seq.; Joyce, Social Hist., vol. i, p. 100). It seems to have been artificially prepared and kept ready for use in the hollow of the shield. **75** Yet the Irish cultivated wheat, oats, barley, and rye, also flax and *glaisin* (some blue dye-plant: woad ?). **76** Compare the list of trees in Br. Laws, vol. iv, pp. 147–8, with which the above account, as far as it goes, agrees. It is curious to note the absence of beech. Was there a prehistoric plague of the *cryptococcus fagi*? **77** See Joyce, Social Hist., vol. i, p. 554. Surface-washing for gold was probably practised by the Irish, and they may have attempted mining; but there are several allusions to the importation of torques and gold ore in Irish literature, and probably some Irish gold was obtained by plunder or commerce from Britain and Gaul. **78** This passage cannot mean that the Irish were ignorant of these arts, nor can it mean that they never practised them, but that the people as a whole preferred idleness to industry. Gerald has already indicated that they made their woollen clothing from their own sheep, and, as a matter of fact, spinning and weaving were done by the women from very early times: Joyce, Social Hist., c. xxvi. Irish goldsmith work has never been surpassed, and the Irish were proficient in several arts. **79** The *timpan* was not a drum, but an instrument like a psaltery, with brass strings, and played with a plectrum. It is probably that represented in the illustrated MS. of the Topographia, and reproduced in Green's Short History (illustrated ed., 1893), p. 899. **80** v. 123–4. **81** 'Nondum matrimonia contrahunt; non incestus vitant; . . . fratres, pluribus per Hiberniam locis, fratrum defunetorum usores non dico ducunt, sed traducunt,' &c.: v. 164. **82** 'Primo compaternitatis foedera jungunt.' *Alliance par compaternitee* between English and Irish was made felony by the Stat. of Kilkenny (1366). It is usually translated 'gossipred', but it was not confined to the relation constituted at baptism.

church and before the altar, in the presence of the relics of the saints, with many solemn oaths, and after the celebration of the mass and the prayers of the priests, they form what purports to be an indissoluble alliance. Finally, for the better confirmation of friendship, and as it were for the perfecting of the business, each drinks the other's blood voluntarily shed for the purpose.[83] This last ceremony, Gerald observes, was [138]
derived from the rites of their pagan ancestors, who used to confirm their treaties with blood. The statement that the blood covenant was used by the Irish has been hotly denied by Irish writers,[84] but not only are there references to it in early Irish literature,[85] but according to the Annals it was practised in Thomond nearly a century after Gerald wrote.[86]

Gerald praises the clergy highly for their piety and exemplary continence. The principal defect he finds in them arises, he thinks, from their monastic training. They make good monks, but indifferent pastors. They were too fond of leading a contemplative life within the precincts of their churches, while neglecting the duty of preaching to the people and correcting their faults.

There is only one other passage in the writings of Giraldus that need be referred to here. It is important as showing conclusively—what in any case we should be led to [139]
infer—that at the time of the Norman invasion the Irish, broadly speaking, used no castles. It also seems to prove, if I understand it rightly, that the dry-stone cahers and strong earthen ringforts, many of which still remain in Ireland, were at that time unused. After stating that Turgesius the Norwegian had subdued the whole island [early in the ninth century] and encastled it (*incastellavit*) in suitable places, he proceeds: 'Hence among these remains and vestiges of the past you will find here up to this day both many great entrenchments, very deep, and circular, and often three-fold, and also walled castles still entire, but vacant and deserted. For the Irish pay no regard to castles, but use the woods as their strongholds and the marshes as their entrenchments.'[87]

This last sentence is clear enough, and agrees with all we know. In the whole history of the Norman invasion there is no allusion to the siege or taking of an Irish fortress. The walled towns of the Northmen alone offered resistance. We may disre- [140]
gard Gerald's theory that the entrenchments and walled castles of which he speaks were all erected by the Norwegians. The latter must refer to the dry-stone cahers now to be seen principally in the western parts of Ireland, but also in other parts, as, for instance, the great stone fort of Aileach or Greenan Ely near Derry, which was for ages the seat of the northern kings, but which was destroyed by Murtough O'Brien in 1101

83 v. 167. 84 e. g. Keating, Hist., vol. i, p. 19. 85 Silva Gadelica (Ir. text), p. 376, and cf. Joyce, Social Hist., vol. ii, p. 510. 86 Ann. Ulster, vol. ii, p. 356, and editor's note, Ann. Loch Cé, 1277. Thomas de Clare treacherously killed Brian Roe O'Brien 'after they had poured their blood into the same vessel, and after they had formed gossipred, and after they had exchanged mutual vows by the relics, bells, and croziers of Munster'. Clearly the whole ceremony as described by Giraldus. 87 Gir. Camb. v. 182. I have endeavoured to translate the passage quite literally. The original is as follows: 'Unde et fossata infinita, alta nimis, rotunda quoque, et pleraque triplicia; castella etiam murata, et adhuc integra, vacua tamen et deserta, ex reliquiis illis et antiquitatis vestigiis hic usque in hodiernum multa reperies. Hibernicus enim populus castella non curat. Silvis namque pro castris, paludibus utitur pro fossatis.'

and apparently never afterwards occupied.[88] The great circular and often three-fold entrenchments can, I think, only be the stronger examples of ring-forts which we generally call duns or raths, such as those at Tara, Emain Macha, Rathcroghan, and Dun Aillinn, seats of the principal kings which were all deserted long before Gerald wrote.[89]

88 Ann. Ulster and Four Masters, 1101. There is also in Leinster a well-preserved, though but little known, dry-stone caher, called Rathgall, three miles due east of Tullow. It is comparable in size to the largest of those in the west. I mention it in particular because it is very probable that Gerald's observant eye saw it, and that he had it in his mind when he wrote the passage quoted. It is only four miles from Raymond le Gros's mote-castle near Tullow, and Gerald can hardly have failed to visit his favourite cousin there. [See *Add.*] 89 See the Prologue to the Cal. of Oengus, 165, 177, 189, 193. This work is now ascribed by Dr. W. Stokes to about the year 800 (edition, Henry Bradshaw Society, 1905).

CHAPTER V [141]

THE FIRST CONQUERORS, 1167–9

It was in August 1167 that Dermot returned to Ireland from his exile. Though he did not wait for Strongbow or Fitz Stephen, he did not come quite alone. He was accompanied by a knight of Pembrokeshire named Richard Fitz Godebert (who appears to have been a Fleming from Roch Castle, near Haverford), and a small body of troops.[1] Dermot at once recovered his hereditary kingdom of Okinselagh, apparently without opposition, but he was not allowed to remain long unmolested. His return was the signal for Rory O'Conor and Dermot's mortal enemy, Tiernan O'Rourke, with Dermot O'Melaghlin and the Ostmen of Dublin, to take the field against him. This was, in fact, the same combination that had dethroned him early in 1166, and they marched to the same dark wood, Fid-dorcha,[2] where they had previously defeated him. Dermot, [142] who must have seen that a contest was hopeless, treated for peace. A week was spent in negotiations, but before they were concluded a party of nobles stole out from O'Conor's camp to seek a combat, and six of them were killed in a conflict with Dermot's horsemen. A general engagement followed, Dermot was put to flight 'with his Saxons', and ten-score heads of Leinstermen and the heads of two of the foreign knights were collected by the victors.[3]

Notwithstanding their victory, O'Conor and O'Rourke, instead of once more expelling Dermot, came to terms with him. The *ard-rí* accepted hostages from Dermot and left him in possession of ten cantreds of his tribe-lands, probably about the whole of the present county of Wexford, while O'Rourke accepted 100 ounces of gold as his *lóg-enech*, or honour-piece, for the wrong done him by Dermot in carrying off his wife. Those who think that the rape of Dervorgil had nothing to do with Dermot's expulsion, inasmuch as it happened fourteen years before that event, must have overlooked this payment to the injured husband, a payment which was exactly in accordance with [143] Brehon Law, and which shows beyond question that the original cause of the feud between Tiernan and Dermot had by no means been forgotten.

The *ard-rí* has been severely blamed by modern writers for not crushing Dermot utterly when he was in his power. I do not know that it is the duty of an historian to mete out either praise or blame. His first duty with regard to human actions, after hav-

1 Song of Dermot, ll. 404–19. He was probably son of Godebert Flandrensis of Ros. See *infra*, p. 392 [p. 148]. 2 Ann. Tigernach. According to the Four Masters, Rory marched to Cill Osnadh, now Kellistown, co. Carlow. This would be exactly in the direction of the fastness of 'the Leverocke' (*leamhrach*, elm-wood?), which we have already shown to be probably the Fid-dorcha: *supra*, p. 66 [p. 19]. 3 The Four Masters, state that 'the son of the King of Britain (Rhys?), who was the battle-prop of the island of Britain', was among the slain. But for this no early authority is known.

ing carefully ascertained them and faithfully recorded them, is to understand them. In this case it is not difficult to understand Rory's action. Had he foreseen that Dermot would bring in more foreigners, who would oust many an Irish chieftain from his territory, he would, without doubt, have remorselessly exterminated him and his. But it is, perhaps happily, not given to man to see far into the future, and Rory, having obtained Dermot's submission, having seen that due reparation according to law was given to O'Rourke, may well have thought that Dermot had received a sufficient lesson, and that justice was amply vindicated. Dermot, it must be recollected, was no longer the powerful king of a province, but the petty chieftain of a *mór-túath*, or approximately the modern county of Wexford. One possible check on Dermot's power
[144] Rory seems to have omitted. Had he set up a strong king of Leinster in Dermot's room and over Dermot, he would have erected a power whose interest it would have been to watch Dermot's movements with argus eyes, and control them with an iron hand. Perhaps inevitable tribe-jealousies prevented this, but in any case it had long been the policy of those who sought to obtain the over-lordship of Ireland, in order to augment their own power, to subdivide rather than to consolidate the provincial kingdoms. Murrough Mac Murrough appears never to have been recognized as king of North Leinster nor of Ossory. Both he and, afterwards, his son Murtough were at most only kings of South Leinster.

During the ensuing year 1168 it would seem that Dermot made no overt attempt to break his engagement with the *ard-rí*, or to reassert his claims to the throne of Leinster. The remnant of Richard Fitz Godebert's little band would have brought back news of their want of success and of Dermot's submission, and we cannot wonder if Strongbow and Fitz Stephen hesitated to carry out their engagements at the time stipulated. Dermot, however, had no intention of relinquishing his purpose, and was merely biding his time for a favourable opportunity of throwing off the mask of submission.

It was probably in the winter of 1168–9 that Dermot sent his trusty 'latimer',
[145] Maurice Regan, to Wales, as Regan himself, through the pen of the Norman rhymer, informs us,[4] to remind Fitz Stephen and Fitz Gerald of their promises, and to whip up further recruits:

> Whoever shall wish for land or pence,
> Horses, trappings, or chargers,
> Gold or silver, I shall give them
> A very ample pay.
> Whoever may wish for soil or sod,
> Richly shall I enfeoff them.

Urged on by some such message, Robert The Fitz Stephen now bestirred himself and got together a force of thirty knights—'milites,' Gerald calls them[5]—of his own kinsmen and retainers, and sixty other horsemen clad in coats of mail (*loricati*), as well as about three hundred archers on foot, the flower of the south of Wales. Having

4 Song of Dermot, ll. 420–38.

embarked his men in three ships, he landed at Bannow Bay on the south coast of Wexford about May 1, 1169. Such was the small beginning of a movement of peoples destined in a brief period to have big results for Ireland. Among his principal followers were his nephews Meiler FitzHenry and Miles, son of the Bishop of St. Davids, whom we have already mentioned, and Robert de Barry, elder brother of the historian. With the expedition, which was evidently dispatched with Strongbow's knowledge and [146]
approval, was sent Hervey de Montmorency, Strongbow's paternal uncle, to investigate the position of affairs on the spot and report to Strongbow.

Gerald de Barry, who misses no opportunity of placing Hervey's character and actions in an unfavourable light, describes him here as a man of fallen fortunes, without military equipment or pecuniary resources, who came over as a spy on behalf of his nephew rather than as a soldier. At a later period he gives the following sketch of his personal appearance and moral character: 'Hervey was a tall, handsome man, with prominent grey eyes, pleasing presence, comely countenance, and polished address ... But in proportion as Nature had endowed his outward appearance with many graces, so she had deformed the inner man with the stains of many vices. From youth upwards he had abandoned himself to all kinds of venery. . . He was a malicious, double-faced informer, a cunning, smooth-tongued rogue, and his honeyed words were fraught with venom. Shallow and shifty, he was constant only in inconstancy'[6]—with more to the same effect. Hervey, it is evident, was not a Geraldine; nay, more—as a military commander he was the principal rival of Raymond, the pattern and paragon of Geraldine [147]
perfection. How Hervey was Strongbow's uncle, as stated by Gerald, was long unknown, but it has recently been shown[7] that Adeliz de Clermont, Strongbow's paternal grandmother, married a de Montmorency as her second husband, and bore to him Hervey, who accordingly was half-brother to Strongbow's father.

Gerald, indeed, gives us personal descriptions of all the protagonists in the drama of the conquest, and making due allowance for his bias in favour of his relatives, and for his evident prejudice in the cases of Strongbow and Hervey, we can form from his descriptions some idea of their appearances and main characteristics. He says of his uncle, Robert Fitz Stephen, that he was a burly, healthy-looking man, somewhat above middle height, and with a comely countenance. A good liver, open-handed, generous, and jovial, but too much given to wine and women. A man of singular courage and energy, but, like a second Marius, the sport of fickle Fortune, now and again prosperous, but more often weighed down by adversity. He describes his cousin, Meiler Fitz Henry, as a swarthy man with stern black eyes and piercing look. Below the middle [148]
height, but very strong for his size. His chest was broad, his waist narrow, his limbs bony and sinewy. A courageous and eager soldier, who shrank from no enterprise, whether to be undertaken alone or in company with others. The first to plunge into battle and the last to leave the field, he knew no alternative but death or victory.

5 The *milites* were not necessarily dubbed knights, but were fully equipped men-at-arms, such as tenants *in capite* and were bound by the conditions of their tenure to furnish to the Crown. 6 Gir. Camb. v. 327. 7 By Mr. Round, Feudal England, p. 519. The impossibility of the previously received pedigree, and the error on which it was founded, had already been indicated in a note to the Song, p. 266. 8 Even the 'to-

This little band of warriors was joined next day by Maurice de Prendergast, who came from the district of Rhos in Pembrokeshire, where the name Prendergast survives as that of a suburb of Haverford. In all probability he was one of the principal Flemish settlers there. He brought with him ten men-at-arms and a considerable body of archers in two ships. These men, who remained apart under Maurice's command, and, as we shall see, mostly followed his fortunes, were also probably Flemings by descent. Probably, too, Fitz Stephen brought with him some of the Flemings who had fought by his side in Wales. The Four Masters, indeed, speak of the whole band as 'the fleet of the Flemings'. The leaders, however, other than Maurice de Prendergast, were Normans, though they had the blood of Welsh princes in their veins. Fitz Stephen's archers were selected from 'the youth of Wales', but though the names of many of the early settlers in Ireland can be traced to South Wales, and especially to Pembrokeshire,
[149] there is not much positive evidence that many men of pure Welsh descent settled at this time in Ireland. The names are, for the most part, apparently Norman or English, with only an occasional Welsh name, but with, in Wexford especially, a fair sprinkling of what seem to be Flemish names. Names, however, are not always conclusive of origin.[8] Surnames taken from placenames in South Wales may not all have belonged to Normans. Thus the descendants of Godebert the Fleming took the name of de la Roche from the rock-castle near Haverford.

This little army of invaders, probably not exceeding 600 men in all, landed on what was then an island in Bannow Bay, on the southern coast of the present County Wexford. As the walled towns of Waterford and Wexford were held by Norsemen independently of Dermot, they could not land in either of the harbours connected with those towns, and if the map of Wexford be studied, or, better still, if the coast-line itself be examined, it will be found difficult to discover a more favourable landing-place
[150] for vessels of light draught.[9] They drew up their ships on the sandy beach, and sent messengers at once to Dermot to apprise him of their arrival, and he immediately sent forward his illegitimate son, Donnell Kavanagh, to welcome them. The island of Bannow is now joined to the mainland on the eastern side by a narrow neck of sand washed up by the sea. At one time there was evidently a channel here. The island, however, is low and unprotected by cliffs, so that it was not a strong place or one that could well be held in the face of a hostile country. Fortunately, however, for the invaders, the adjoining country was not hostile. The people of the district, Gerald tells us, had formerly deserted Dermot in his misfortune, but now that his luck had turned they flocked together to support him.[10] In any case, Dermot lost no time in joining them with 500 men, and on the following day the combined troops marched to attack the Scandinavian stronghold of Wexford, distant about sixteen English miles.

name' le Waleis (afterwards Walsh) does not necessarily imply pure Welsh blood. Raymond le Gros had a nephew David *agnomine Walensis non cognomine, natione Kambrensis non cognatione*: Gir. Camb. v. 321. 9 The bay no longer affords good anchorage even for shallow vessels. It is nearly drained at low water, and there is a dangerous bar. But that this was not always so is indicated by the once prosperous towns of Bannow and Clonmines situated on its shores. See paper by the Rev. James Graves, Kilk. Arch. Soc., 1850, p. 187. 10 The chieftains of the adjoining districts, the modern baronies of Forth and Bargy, were

Wexford, known to the Irish as Loch Garman, owed its importance and probably its origin to the Ostmen, as they were called, whether Danes or Norwegians, and had been [151] held by them for about three hundred years. It was a walled town, and though the Irish had several times inflicted an overthrow on the foreigners of Loch Garman, they were quite incapable of taking the town by storm. The extensive harbour, almost enclosed by Rosslare Point and the Raven, afforded ample shelter for the Danish vessels, which carried on a trade with South Wales and Bristol only inferior to that of Dublin and Waterford. As long as the sea communication remained open the town could not be reduced by siege, even supposing the Irish were capable of conducting lengthy siege operations. Dermot, however, claimed to be overlord of the 'Foreigners of Wexford', and in 1161 Donnell Kavanagh gained a victory over them. Whatever the result of this may have been, the Ostmen, we may be sure, were among the first to throw off their allegiance when Dermot was in difficulties. Apart, however, from any claim of right by Dermot, Fitz Stephen, as a prudent general, could not leave so important a post in hostile hands in his rear. Accordingly Wexford was the first objective of the invaders. What sort of stronghold it was we have scanty means of judging. Like Dublin and Waterford, it was a walled town running down to the water's edge. These walls included towers or turrets (*propugnacula*) at intervals, and were defended on the outside by a ditch, beyond [152] which there was rising ground. So much we can glean from Gerald's narrative. Probably the later walls, which still exist in places and can be traced all round on the land side, follow in part the lines of the old walls, though embracing a larger area towards the north. We do not hear of any castle or citadel in the town.

When the townsmen heard of Dermot's approach they boldly sallied forth to the number of two thousand, confident in the issue of a battle with their old foe; but they soon perceived that it was a new sort of enemy they had to deal with. Instead of a horde of naked Irish kerns armed with pikes and darts, with perhaps a body of galloglasses, as they were afterwards termed, wielding in one hand the broad battleaxe borrowed from the Danes themselves, they saw before them an orderly body of men drawn up in even ranks, armed with the bow which carried death at a distance, and flanked on either side by a squadron of horsemen, with long lances, glittering kite-shaped shields, and helmets and coats of mail.[11] The Ostmen of Wexford were no doubt not wholly unused to armour. Their compatriots at Clontarf, a century and a half before, are said to have been encased in mail, but in the interval they had given up their old piratical life, and had [153] become Christians and traders. They had certainly now no such armour as they saw on the Norman chivalry before them, nor were they archers or horsemen. Accordingly, in these changed circumstances, they changed their tactics, and after firing the suburbs, so as to deprive the enemy of shelter, they retired within the ramparts.

Fitz Stephen at once made his preparations for the attack. On the rising ground behind the town he placed his archers so as to command the turrets on the walls.[12]

O'Lorcain and O'Duibhginn: Topog. Poems, p. 93, note (468, 470). Both of them are mentioned in the Song as being at a later period on Strongbow's side: ll. 3214, 3217. 11 The accounts of the battle of Clontarf all mention the *lúrech* (= *lorica*) on the Danes, but it was probably of leather reinforced with metal rings and studs. 12 The existing walls run some way up the hill behind the town, but the ground still

Under the shelter of their arrows, the men in mail proceeded to fill up in places the ditch which surrounded the walls on the outside.[13] Over the places thus levelled a rush was made to scale the walls with ladders or some extemporized substitute. The townsmen, however, stood to the defence, and, hurling great beams and stones from the battlements on the heads of the assailants, for the time repulsed the assault. According to the Song, eighteen of the English were killed, while the townsfolk lost but three.
[154] Gerald mentions that his elder brother, Robert de Barry, as he led the escalade, was struck on the helmet by a stone, and, falling headlong to the bottom of the ditch, was with difficulty rescued by his comrades. Withdrawing then from the walls, the assailants rushed to the neighbouring strand and set fire to all the ships they could lay their hands on. One band of youths boarded a merchant vessel from England, laden with corn and wine, when the sailors cut the hawser, and the vessel, driven by the west wind, stood out towards the sea, so that the boarding-party were barely able to escape by taking again to their boats and rowing to land. Night closed in without the invaders obtaining any real advantage.

Next morning, after mass was solemnized in full parade, Fitz Stephen proceeded to renew the attack, but this time with more circumspection than before. Despairing of taking the walls by a mere rush, he was preparing to adopt some of the devices of that military science for which the Normans were famous, when the besieged, abandoning all hope of defending their town, sent envoys to treat for peace. Mainly by the mediation of two bishops, terms were arranged. The townsmen submitted to Dermot, and gave him four hostages for their future fidelity. No violence was done, but the town was
[155] henceforth held by the victors. Pleased with his first success, and by way of encouraging his allies, Dermot is said to have at once redeemed his promise to Fitz Stephen, and assigned to him and his half-brother, Maurice Fitz Gerald (who had not yet arrived) the town of Wexford with all its dependent territory. To Hervey de Montmorency he gave two cantreds adjoining the sea between Wexford and Waterford.[14] This latter gift would seem to indicate that Hervey, perhaps as representing Strongbow, was a much more important personage in Dermot's eyes than one would gather from the pages of Gerald. These lands, which probably included the present baronies of Bargy and Shelburne, were afterwards re-granted or confirmed to Hervey by Strongbow.[15]

After the taking of Wexford, Dermot brought his allies with him to Ferns, where they stayed for three weeks to heal their wounded and to refresh themselves. Then
[156] Dermot proposed an expedition against the King of Ossory,[16] to which his allies, ready

rises beyond them. 13 'Virius armatis fossata replentibus': Gir. Camb. v. 232. This phrase has, I think, been mistranslated 'lining the ditches with those of his troops who wore armour' (Giles). 'The men in mail lined the ditches' (Barnard). For the operation as above rendered cf. Caesar, De Bello Gallico, vii. 82. 14 Gir. Camb. v. 233. According to the Song of Dermot, the delivery of Wexford to Fitz Stephen, and the grant of the adjoining land at Carrick to Maurice Fitz Gerald, took place at a later period, after the earlier raids and just before Raymond's landing; and this appears more probable: ll. 1392–9. Henry afterwards took Wexford into his own hands, but ultimately gave it to Strongbow (Song of Dermot, 1. 2902), so that it merged in the lordship of Leinster. 15 Song of Dermot, ll. 3070–1, and see note. 16 The principal authority for this Ossorian expedition is Song of Dermot, ll. 520–823. Giraldus, v. 233–6, includes both

for any fighting, agreed. The kingdom, as it was usually called, of Ossory corresponded to the present diocese of that name, and included, besides the entire county of Kilkenny, three baronies in the western part of Queen's County [Leix]. It thus extended from the Slieve Bloom mountains to the meeting of the three rivers near Waterford, and was separated from Okinselagh by the lower reaches of the river Barrow. This large district was sometimes reckoned as part of Munster and sometimes as part of Leinster, but was perhaps more often practically independent of both. Dermot, however, claimed its submission. In 1152 Ossory may have furnished him with troops in the fateful expedition against Tiernan O'Rourke,[17] but subsequently he met with more than one reverse at its hands, and it was no doubt due to the defection of Ossory along with that of other subordinate chieftainries that Dermot was unable to make any stand against his enemies in 1160. In that year, as we have seen, the King of Ossory had shared in the partition of Dermot's principality of Okinselagh, and had taken prisoner Dermot's son, Enna, who had probably been left behind as Dermot's representative. In 1168 Donough Mac Gillapatrick had deliberately blinded Enna, styled by the annal- [157]
ists 'rigdamna of Leinster', to dispose of his claims. Dermot had therefore special grounds for his animosity against the King of Ossory, who, however, at this time appears to have been Donnell, son of Donough Mac Gillapatrick.[18]

After the success at Wexford, many of the men of Leinster returned to their allegiance, and Dermot's troops were reinforced partly by them and partly by a body of the Ostmen of Wexford, until he had 3,000 fighting men under his command. It is probable that the army entered Ossory by the well-known route called the *Bealach Gabhráin*, or Pass of Gowran, and that it was somewhere along this route that Donnell Mac Gillapatrick attempted to stop him. It is quite certain that large districts in Leinster and in other parts of Ireland were at this time, and for centuries afterwards, covered with natural forests quite impassable for cavalry, or indeed, with safety, for any [158]
troops. Through these forests narrow tracks were cut to the open places or plains where the cattle fed, and such agriculture as was in vogue was carried on. The upper slopes of the hills were also generally bare, and thither the cattle used to be driven in summer to feed. When we read of a 'pass' it is often one of these tracks through the forests that is meant, and not a defile between mountains. It was in some such forest-track that Mac Gillapatrick of Ossory now endeavoured to arrest Dermot's predatory expedition. He defended it in the usual way, but with more than the usual care and completeness. He caused a barricade to be made consisting of a triple fosse and vallum, and on the top of each vallum he erected a sort of stockade of intertwined branches (*haie*). Behind this barricade he sat down with five thousand men awaiting the enemy. Here the battle lasted from morning until eventide, until at last the English, though with consider-

this expedition, and one to be presently described, under the same heading, *de expugnatione Ossiriae*; cf. Ann. Tigernach, 1169. 17 Song of Dermot, l. 75. 18 Gerald calls him Duvenaldus, which represents Domhnall (Donnell), not Donnchadh (Donough), while in the Song of Dermot he is called Macdonchid (variously spelled), i.e. Mac Donnchadha, or son of Donnough; cf. note, 1. 560. Perhaps this Donough died in the winter of 1169, and was succeeded in half Ossory by his son Donnell. The Ossorian succession at this period is, however, rather obscure; partly because there were three contemporaneous kings in Ossory, and two of them were of the family of Mac Gillapatrick and were each named Donnell.

able loss, forced their way through. They now advanced into the plain and laid waste the country, collecting what spoil they could. They did not penetrate very far, however, but took a northerly direction, and then endeavoured to return to their own country, apparently by the shorter but more difficult route through the *fásach* or wilderness of
[159] the Dinin and across the Slievemargy hills to the valley of the Barrow. On this march they very nearly met with a disaster. Mac Gillapatrick had rallied his men, and was hanging about the rear of the retreating army as it was about to enter a pass where Dermot had on three occasions met with a defeat. The Irish troops, who were under the command of Donnell Kavanagh, fearing lest they should be defeated for the fourth time, fled in a panic through the woods, leaving only forty-three men with their commander. The little body of Normans were now in a tight place, as their horse could not operate amid the woods and swamps of the pass. Accordingly Maurice de Prendergast, who was in command, urged his men forward as rapidly as possible, so as to gain the hard open country on the upper slopes of the hills, where the cavalry could act. At the same time he set a little ambuscade of fifty archers in a thicket at the side of the pass to take the enemy in the rear. Meanwhile the men of Ossory, to the number of two thousand, were impetuously pursuing the retreating invaders until the hard open ground was reached, when the latter turned, and, charging their pursuers, speared them with their long lances and scattered them in utter rout. Dermot's men, who had fled to the woods earlier in the day, now returned and joined in the *mêlée*, cutting off with their broad axes the heads of those who were thrown to the ground by the charge of the
[160] horse. Thus what seemed at first like the flight of the invaders was turned into the defeat of the pursuers, and to Dermot as he rested by the Barrow were brought some two hundred of the heads of his enemies. Here Gerald gives us a horrible picture of the savagery of the times, or at least of the brutality of Dermot. 'To see to whom the heads belonged he turned them over one by one; then thrice did he clap his hands and leap for joy, and, giving thanks to the Most High, burst into exultant song. Aye, and even the head of one whom he hated above the rest, he took up by the ears and hair, and in a most blood thirsty and brutal manner tore away with his teeth the lips and nose.'[19]

[161] Overruling the bolder proposal made by Fitz Stephen, that they should remain where they were for the night and on the morrow continue the contest with the King

19 This action of Dermot may perhaps indicate the late survival in Ireland of a once widespread superstition noticed by Dr. J.G. Fraser (Psyche's Task, pp. 56–8), viz. that one way of allaying the avenging ghost of a murdered man was to taste the blood of the slain, and so, by making him part of oneself, and establishing in the strictest sense a blood-covenant with him, one could convert him from an enemy into an ally. He refers *inter alia* to a 'still widespread opinion in Calabria that if a murderer is to escape he must suck his victim's blood from the reeking blade of the dagger with which he did the deed'. An historic example from Italy, which at any rate offers analogies to Dermot's action, occurred at the massacre of the Baglioni in Perugia in 1500, when 'one of the noble murderers tore from a great wound in his (the victim's) side the still quivering heart, into which he drove his teeth with savage fury'. (See the contemporary chronicle of Matarazzo, quoted in The Story of Perugia, Mediaeval Town Series, p. 65.) The fear of the avenging spirit was not confined to the case of murder, but was felt even when the victim was slain in battle, as in Dermot's case. Probably the common custom of decapitating the slain arose from a similar belief. For the usage of the blood-covenant in Ireland at this time and even later, see Giraldus, v. 167, Ann. Ulster, 1275, and editor's note, vol. ii, p. 356, and *supra*, p. 137 [pp. 47–8].

of Ossory, Dermot marched his men along by the Barrow to Old Leighlin, situated on a hill two miles west of the river, where they spent the night. and where the leaders were possibly entertained in the monastery of St. Laserian. Next day they returned to Ferns for another brief period of rest.

Such was the dread inspired by Dermot's auxiliaries, the fame of whose exploits now began to be noised abroad, that many disaffected tribes of Leinster returned to their allegiance; but there were important chieftains in North Leinster, always jealous of Okinselagh, who still held out. Among these was Faelan Mac Fhaelain or Mackelan (as the name was anglicized), lord of Offelan, the tribal territory of the O'Byrnes, who at this time occupied the north-eastern part of the present County Kildare, including Naas. Mackelan came of a family which, in centuries gone by, had given more than one king to Leinster, and a member of this family had, as we have seen, been set up as king [162]
by Turlough O'Conor in 1127, and had eventually been slain by Dermot. Naturally, the present chief bore Dermot no goodwill, and had been one of the first to turn against him. So now Dermot, with the aid of his Norman allies, drove him out of Offelan, raided his territory, and carried off a great spoil.[20] The next to suffer was O'Toole, the chieftain of Omurethy, a district comprising the southern half of the present County Kildare. This chieftain was brother of Lorcan or Laurence O'Toole, Archbishop of Dublin, and brother-in-law of Dermot himself; but family ties are seldom allowed to stand in the way of the ambition of monarchs, and Dermot proceeded to spoil the district of Glendalough,[21] which must even thus early have been subject to O'Toole.

The Irish, though brave and inured to fighting, could not stand against the far-reaching arrows, the long lances, and the military skill of the Normans. Many of them, however, preferred to see their homesteads burned, their lands laid waste, and their cattle spoiled, rather than give in their submission to Dermot. The King of Ossory, for example, still held out, and a fresh expedition[22] was accordingly organized into his territory on a larger scale than before. Donnell Kavanagh had now five thousand men [163]
under his command, and then there was the contingent of Ostmen from Wexford, who, we are told, hated Dermot and fought under compulsion, and were consequently viewed with suspicion, besides the foreign contingent, with whom Dermot himself always marched, perhaps for greater safety. From the indications given in the Song of Dermot, we can gather the route they took with some particularity. They marched into the district of the Fotharta Fea, now known as the barony of Forth, in County Carlow, having, no doubt, passed the mountains by the cutting through which the Slaney flows, and they encamped for the night by the river Burren,[23] some of them occupying an old disused fort,[24] in which circumstance we may perhaps discover the cause of the curious event that followed. Our two Norman authorities tell how the camp was aroused in the night by a phantom army and put to panic flight. 'Suddenly,' says Gerald, 'as it were countless thousands of warriors burst in upon them on all sides, seeming to over-

20 Song of Dermot, ll. 846–75. 21 Ibid., ll. 884–917, and notes. 22 Ibid., ll. 920–1055. 23 *Sur l'ewe de Macburtin* (Song of Dermot, ll. 957–68) where Macburtin probably represents Mag Boirenn, or the plain of the Burren. 24 Probably '*le langport*' (Ir. *longphort* = encampment or fort) of the Song of Dermot, l. 1000, is the *castellarium quoddam antiquum* of Gerald.

[164] whelm everything in their furious charge, while the rattling of their armour, the mighty crash of their battle-axes, and their fearful shouts filled the air.' The Normans thought that they were being treacherously attacked by the men of Wexford, who in their turn thought that they were being entrapped by Dermot, while in reality no one was hurt except those who were in the confusion knocked on the head by their panic-stricken comrades. Knowing the belief that Irish peasants in the more backward parts have to this day in fairy hosts, and how they associate them and their hostings with the old forts or raths that dot the land, we may shrewdly suspect that some of Dermot's followers, imbued with the same superstitious beliefs, saw the fairy hosts issue from the old rath in which the army slept, and that from them the panic spread to the rest of the troops.

Next morning they pursued their march, and advanced into Ossory until they came to 'a river of great vehemence', presumably the Nore, where they encamped for the night. Mac Gillapatrick did not dispute with them the passage of the Nore, but fortified the pass of Achadh-ur against them. Achadh-ur was the ancient name of the little town now called Freshford, on the river Nuenna, about three miles above its junction with the Nore. It was a place of some importance, as is testified by the beau-
[165] tiful romanesque doorway of the church—a doorway which was probably erected early in the century of which we write. As one approaches this town from the side of Kilkenny and the Nore, the hills to the south come close to the road, and leave a comparatively narrow passage between them and the Nuenna. This spot may have been that chosen by Mac Gillapatrick to meet the invader. He trenched the pass in the usual manner, with a hedge of stakes and intertwined branches on the top of his earthen rampart. This post he bravely held against the attack of the Wexford men, but he could not withstand the terrible shafts that sped from the Norman bows, nor the onset of the mail-clad spearmen. He preferred flight, however, to submission, and was vainly pursued by Dermot to the borders of his country. Then Dermot returned to Ferns with a great spoil.

And now occurred the first division in the ranks of the invaders.[25] For some reason, at which we can only vaguely guess, Maurice de Prendergast and about two hundred men, perhaps in the main the Flemings he had brought with him, wished to return to Wales. The character of this man as it appears in the Song is that of a chivalrous warrior who would keep his word even with an enemy, and he may have been disgusted
[166] with Dermot's brutality. Gerald, however, after telling of his arrival in Ireland, never mentions his name, but when Rory's great hosting into Okinselagh (to be mentioned immediately) was threatened he says that many of Dermot's friends deserted him, some even going openly over to the enemy,[26] and it may well be that this was the occasion of Prendergast's defection. Perhaps on seeing the opposition that had arisen against them throughout the greater part of Ireland, Prendergast and his men may have despaired of ultimate success and may have resolved to return to Wales. In any case, he parted in bad terms with Dermot, and drawing off two hundred of his men—

25 Song of Dermot, ll. 1056–1151, **26** v. 237.

about one-third of the foreign contingent—set out for Wexford. Dermot at once sent a message to the ship-captains of Wexford charging them to give no assistance to Prendergast, but to obstruct his design in every way they could. Prendergast, baulked in this way, immediately sent word to Donnell Mac Gillapatrick, Dermot's great enemy, to offer him his services. That chieftain gladly accepted the offer, assured him of safe-conduct, and promised him ample reward. Accordingly Prendergast, turning aside from Wexford, took the road to St. Mullins, on the Barrow, in the present county of Carlow. This did not suit Dermot at all, and his son Donnell Kavanagh, with five hundred men, endeavoured to bar his way. A battle was fought, evidently in the pass of [167] Pollmounty, a narrow defile between the hills on the direct route to St. Mullins, and Prendergast forced his way through. St. Mullins was an ancient ecclesiastical centre, and the remains of a round tower, a carved cross, and numerous churches may still be seen there. Here after three days, Donnell, King of Ossory, arrived with a company of troops, and on the altar and shrine of St. Moling took oath never to betray Maurice de Prendergast or his men. The King of Ossory was now able to take the offensive against Dermot, and with the aid of Maurice, who in consequence of his new service received the name of 'Maurice of Ossory', harried Dermot's territory. Dermot, it will be noted, was not the only Irish king who was ready to employ foreigners to fight his battles for him.

It was probably about this time that Rory O'Conor, attended by Tiernan O'Rourke, Dermot O'Conor O'Melaghlin, and the Ostmen of Dublin (again the same combination as before), led a hosting into Okinselagh. According to the Four Masters, this vast array 'deemed the Flemings', as the followers of Fitz Stephen are called, 'not worth notice'—so incorrectly did they calculate the forces of the future. O'Conor simply exacted Dermot's son as a hostage and retired.[27] A different complexion is given to the [168] hosting by Gerald de Barry, who also supplies some new details.[28] According to him, the *ard-rí*, alarmed at Dermot's successes and apprehensive of evil from the introduction of foreigners, came with his vast host to crush Dermot and exterminate the foreigners while they were as yet few in numbers. Dermot at this crisis found himself deserted by his fairweather friends, some of whom secretly disappeared while others openly joined the foe.

Among the latter, as we have seen, must probably be included Maurice de Prendergast and his Flemings. Thus in his hour of need Dermot found himself with very few firm supporters, besides Fitz Stephen and his men. He therefore retired with those who remained faithful to him 'to a place not far from Ferns which, surrounded as it was by dense woods, steep mountains, and watery marshes, formed a natural fastness very difficult of access'. From this description we can locate the site of Dermot's retreat with much confidence somewhere near Mount Leinster to the west of Ferns, in the district still known as the Duffry. This district, situated in the parish of Templeshanbo, remained for centuries one of the most inaccessible fastnesses of Leinster. As [169] its name, the *Dubh-tir*, 'black or dark country,' indicates, it was covered with dark

27 Four Masters, Ann. Tigernach, 1169. 28 Gir. Camb. v. 236–44. The Song of Dermot does not mention this hosting.

woods. It is bounded on the west and north by the steep sides of Mount Leinster and its adjacent spurs (the *praerupti montes* of Gerald), it is coursed by numerous mountain streams, while in the lowlands to the east the remains of bogs and marshes may still be discerned. Here they felled trees and plashed the woods in the method well known to the Irish; they broke up the surface of the level ground with deep pits and trenches, leaving only narrow and tortuous entrances and exits, through which they could easily pass, but in which the enemy would be hopelessly entangled. Having thus strengthened a naturally strong position, they awaited with great resolution the advance of the army of Ireland.

Rory, on his arrival, at first sent to Fitz Stephen messengers, who endeavoured by the proffer and promise of valuable gifts, and by every argument, to persuade him to return in peace and amity to his own country. Failing with him, the messengers then urged Dermot to unite with the men of Ireland in exterminating the foreigners, promising in that event the peaceable restoration of all Leinster to Dermot, together with the firm friendship of the *ard-rí*. But Dermot, to his credit be it said, would not
[170] agree to this treachery. It would seem there was nothing for it but to fight, and Gerald puts long speeches into the mouths of O'Conor, Dermot, and Fitz Stephen, all, as it were, animating their respective followers for the approaching battle. But we may pass over these speeches, all the more as there was no fighting. Perhaps on learning how few the foreigners were, Rory may have thought their presence a matter of no importance, as seems to be the statement of the Irish annals; perhaps he may have shrunk from attacking them in their present strong position, as Gerald says. Indeed, the two motives are not absolutely inconsistent with each other, and may have been actuated partly by the one and partly by the other. In either case we may accept the statement of Gerald that through intervention of good men (meaning thereby clergy, who seem always to have supported Dermot) and by the grace of Heaven, peace at length established upon the following conditions: that Leinster should be left to Dermot, who should acknowledge Rory as *ard-rí* and yield him due submission. To secure this compact Dermot handed over his son Conor as a hostage to Rory, who on his part promised that if Dermot fulfilled his engagements he would give his daughter in marriage to Dermot's
[171] son. Besides these conditions, which were publicly proclaimed and confirmed by the oaths of the parties, it was secretly agreed between Dermot and Rory that Dermot should bring no more foreigners into Ireland, and moreover that he should send back those whom he had brought as soon as he had reduced Leinster to submission.

Such is Gerald's account of the matter, but without questioning that it correctly represents the view taken by his friends[29] and states truly the conditions of peace, we may doubt if it gives a correct impression of the main object of Rory's expedition. Since his inauguration as King of Ireland in 1166, Rory had been very active in making hostings throughout the various divisions of his kingdom, obtaining hostages from the subordinate kings, dividing their territories, settling disputes, and generally making his power felt. A brief account of these proceedings, derived mainly from the Four

29 Gerald must have derived his account of the military events of this year mainly from his uncle, Robert Fitz Stephen.

Masters, will show what Rory's general policy was, and will serve to put in truer perspective his Leinster expedition.

In 1167 Rory followed up his hostings of the previous year by leading an expedition into Tirowen, where Murtough O'Loughlin, his former rival, had recently been slain. Here he divided the territory between Niall O'Loughlin and Aedh O'Neill, and [172] exacted hostages from each. Then on the return of Dermot Mc Murrough, as we have seen, he exacted hostages from him for Okinselagh, and obtained a large money compensation for the affront done to Tiernan O'Rourke. In Munster, Murtough O'Brien, who had expelled his father Turlough in 1165, and had apparently been recognized in 1166 by Rory O'Conor, whose half-brother he was, as King of Thomond, was killed in 1168 by Conor O'Brien—the representative of an elder branch. Conor was himself, with his conspirators, immediately afterwards killed, and Donnell O'Brien, of whom we shall hear much, a brother of Murtough, then assumed the kingdom of Munster. Rory O'Conor, however, led an army into Munster, divided the kingdom between Dermot Mac Carthy and Donnell O'Brien, obtained hostages from the former, and levied an eric of 720 cows on Desmond for the killing of Murtough O'Brien. In Meath in the same year, the king, Dermot O'Melaghlin, in revenge of his father, killed the lord of Delvin, who was under the protection of Connaught, and Rory at the head of an army exacted an eric of 800 cows. Dermot O'Melaghlin was deposed by the people of East Meath in revenge for the payment of the aforesaid cows. He recovered his position by fighting, and joined in the hosting into Okinselagh in 1169. But later in the [173] same year[30] he was slain by his nephew, Donnell of Bregia. Thereupon Rory again interfered, expelled Donnell of Bregia, and divided Meath between himself and Tiernan O'Rourke.

Thus in Ulster, Munster, and Meath, the activity of the *ard-rí* was directed to secure the submission of the provincial kings by the exaction of hostages, and to weaken their power by dividing their territories. Much might be said for this policy had it been effective, but these enforced divisions only resulted in chronic fighting among the dissatisfied chieftains. We now come to Rory's expedition into Leinster, which seems to have taken place late in 1169. His object, primarily at least, was not to get rid of the handful of foreigners, in his eyes almost a negligible quantity, still less was it to expel Dermot, but to obtain his submission, exact more important hostages, and regularize his position in Leinster. These objects he for the moment obtained, and the settlement was for the moment as effective or ineffective[31] as the settlement of the other portions of Ireland.

With the return of Rory's army the first great danger that threatened the invaders [174] passed away, and the first opportunity that Ireland had of ridding herself of the foreigner was lost. Soon afterwards Dermot heard to his great joy of the arrival of two ships at Wexford bearing Maurice Fitz Gerald, Fitz Stephen's half-brother, accompa-

30 The entries in Four Masters, 1169, are, as often, out of chronological order. Dermot O'Melaghlin's death is recorded prior to his joining in the hosting. 31 In 1169 Conor O'Loughlin assumed the kingship of the Cinel Owen. In 1170 Donnell O'Brien was at war with O'Conor, and Donnell of Bregia was back again in Meath, turned against O'Conor and O'Rourke, and submitted to Dermot: Four Masters.

nied by ten knights, thirty mounted retainers, and about one hundred archers on foot.[32] This reinforcement went far to fill the gap caused by the defection of Maurice de Prendergast and his men. Maurice Fitz Gerald at this time must have been upwards of sixty years of age. He is described by his nephew Gerald de Barry as an upright and discreet man, remarkable for his good faith and energy, modest as a maiden, true to his word, and famed for his courage. He was the common ancestor of the two great houses of the Geraldines, that of Leinster and that of Desmond, both of which houses played so important a part in the subsequent history of Ireland.

We must now return to 'Maurice of Ossory' and tell how he fared under his new master.[33] The territory adjoining Ossory on the north was Leix (included in Mary's reign in Queen's County), of which the O'Mores were the ruling family. It was no part
[175] of Ossory, but was properly subject to the King of Leinster. With the aid of Prendergast the King of Ossory made a successful raid into the territory of Leix, and eventually O'More promised to submit to Mac Gillapatrick and give hostages on a fixed day three or four days ahead. A truce for that period was accordingly granted. Meantime O'More besought Dermot, as King of Leinster, to come to his aid, and he with Fitz Stephen and Fitz Gerald came promptly into Leix. When Prendergast was informed of this, and knew that he would have to fight, not against an Irish host, but against a superior number of his own late comrades, he recommended a retreat. This was successfully carried out, though the retreating army was pursued by Dermot to the borders of Ossory. Dermot then returned to Ferns, taking care, however, to bring with him hostages from O'More of Leix. The men of Ossory now began to grumble at having to give pay to English soldiers who no longer brought them victory, and some even proposed to massacre them and divide their goods. The king, however, would not agree to this treachery, but with regret gave leave to Prendergast to return to his own country, and probably informed him of the meditated plot. The foreigners were now at Kilkenny, making preparations for their immediate return, when they heard that the
[176] men of Ossory had plashed the passes through which they had to go and had laid an ambuscade for them with two thousand well-armed men. The king, who was no doubt innocent of this treachery, or at any rate helpless to prevent it, was at Fertagh, a place about fifteen miles away. Prendergast accordingly required all his address and craft to get himself out of the tight place in which he found himself. He sent word to Mac Gillapatrick that he was willing to serve him for another period, and took care that the news should be spread through the country. Those in ambush then returned to their homes, whereupon Prendergast and his men secretly took horse and rapidly escaped to Waterford, whence they sailed for Wales.

Early in the next year (1170), Dermot, emboldened by the accession to his forces of Fitz Gerald and his men, determined to march on Dublin and attempt to obtain the submission of the Ostmen of that city. We have already mentioned that Dermot Mac Maelnamo, great-grandfather of Dermot Mac Murrough, had been recognized as King of Dublin, and that Donough MacMurrough, Dermot's father, had been slain

32 Gir. Camb. v. 244; Song, ll. 1157–75. 33 Song. ll. 1176–1391.

by the foreigners of Dublin and, according to the current story, buried ignominiously with a dog. In 1162 Dermot himself appears to have been recognized as overlord of Dublin. He had, therefore, claims on Dublin as well as a blood-feud with its inhabi- [177]
tants. While, then, Fitz Stephen was left behind, fortifying a rock known as the Carrick,[34] on the right bank of the Slaney a couple of miles above Wexford, Fitz Gerald, accompanied by Dermot, took the command of the army and marched to the Dyflinarskirri or Scandinavian district in the immediate neighbourhood of Dublin. No attempt was made to take the city, but the adjoining regions were soon laid waste by plunder, fire, and sword, and at length the citizens, who seem to have shrunk from meeting the Normans in the open, sued for peace and gave security for their future fidelity and due submission.[35]

It was probably soon after this that Donnell O'Brien, king of half Munster, turned against the *ard-rí* and forfeited his hostages.[36] As we have seen, Rory had divided Munster between him and Dermot Mac Carthy in 1168. Next year Donnell treacherously blinded his brother, Brian of Slieve Bloom, who had assumed the principality of Ormond, near that mountain, in 1168. This may have been done merely to get rid of a rival to his throne, but evidently Donnell was not satisfied with the division of his [178]
patrimony made by the *ard-rí*. He had pretension to be king of all Munster, as his father Turlough had been before him, and he resented the interference of Rory O'Conor and withdrew his allegiance. Donnell was son-in-law to Dermot Mac Murrough, and he now sought and readily obtained the assistance of some of his father-in-law's foreign allies in his struggle with the *ard-rí* Robert Fitz Stephen, with a band of men including Meiler Fitz Henry and Robert de Barry, marched across Ireland to Limerick to aid in repelling the advance of the *ard-rí*. O'Conor brought a huge fleet, probably down the Shannon, and ravaged Munster therefrom, while his men of Connaught advanced into Thomond and Ormond, and the plank bridge of Killaloe was burned. We have no particulars of the part played by the Normans in this expedition, and are merely told that Rory, after getting the worst of several conflicts, was obliged to retire.[37] Next year the *ard-rí* continued the contest and forced fresh hostages from Donnell. The temporary assistance of the foreigners was of little avail to Donnell, but the foreigners themselves had learned the way to Limerick, and had learned, moreover, that they could go with a small expeditionary force across Ireland and return in safety.

34 Song of Dermot, l. 1397, note, where the true site of this stronghold is shown. 35 Gir. Camb. v. 245. Ann. Tigernach, 1170: 'Mac Murchada received the Kingship of the Foreigners of Leinster.' 36 Four Masters, Ann. Tigernach, 1170. 37 Gir. Camb. v. 245

[179] CHAPTER VI

THE COMING OF STRONGBOW, 1170

Dermot had now, at the close of the year 1169, by the aid of his Norman auxiliaries, made himself master, in a sense, of all Leinster, including Ossory, from Dublin to Wexford. That is to say, he had overrun the various tribal territories included in Leinster, with the exception perhaps of Offaly, as to which nothing is said, and had presumably obtained submission and exacted hostages from their chiefs. The recognition was, no doubt, in many cases forced, but he was nevertheless once more the recognized King of Leinster, able to make his power felt exactly in the same way as other provincial kings, when their authority was disputed, were able to make their power felt. He had, moreover, an ally, if not a subordinate, in his son-in-law, Donnell O'Brien, King of Thomond, who had recently, with the aid of Fitz Stephen, successfully withstood the *ard-rí*. The time had now come when, if he was to carry out the secret clause
[180] in his treaty with the *ard-rí*, he should send his foreign mercenaries home, but so far was he from fulfilling that engagement that he now, we are told, looked beyond the confines of Leinster, and hoped with the aid of his Norman troops to subdue the King of Connaught and win for himself the high-kingship of Ireland. He disclosed his design in confidence to Fitz Stephen and Fitz Gerald, who replied that it might easily be accomplished if he could obtain further troops from England. He then urged them to invite over their kindred and countrymen in greater numbers to Ireland, and he is even said to have made to each of them the same offer that he had made to Strongbow, namely, his daughter's hand and the succession of the kingdom, if they would carry out the execution of his project. But as they both happened to be lawfully wedded, they were unable to avail themselves of this offer, and finally Dermot resolved to write to Richard Fitz Gilbert, Earl of Striguil, to remind him of his promise and urge its prompt fulfilment. Strongbow was told, in language, we may be sure, much less flowery than that which Gerald reports to us, that all Leinster had now been subdued, and that if he would come with a strong force it would be easy to conquer the rest of Ireland.[1]

While Strongbow had now, in consequence of Fitz Stephen's success, more
[180] inducement than ever to risk his life and fortunes in the Irish adventure, he had, in Dermot's new proposal, fresh ground for hesitation. Henry's general licence was, as we have seen, a licence to aid Dermot in the recovery of his dominion in Leinster, but Dermot's new proposal was to conquer all Ireland. In these circumstances Strongbow thought it prudent to seek Henry's express sanction to the enterprise, and having

1 Gir. Camb. v. 246.

obtained an interview with the king he besought him either to restore to him the lands which belonged to him by hereditary right or to grant him leave to accept Dermot's offer and seek his fortune in Ireland.[2] Henry appears to have avoided committing himself to a positive answer; but Strongbow, laying hold of some words of his, spoken, according to Gerald, more in jest than in earnest, which he interpreted as favourable to the project, set about making his preparations. When winter was past, about the first of May, he sent on before him into Ireland Raymond, a young man of his household, with ten knights and seventy archers.[3]

Raymond was a son of William Fitz Gerald, and therefore nephew to both Robert Fitz Stephen and Maurice Fitz Gerald, and the fact that he was a member of Strongbow's household, and sent forward at the head of his little force by Strongbow, [182]
is a further indication that the earlier expedition of the Geraldines was undertaken in concert with Strongbow, and not altogether independently of him. One of the knights sent by Strongbow with Raymond was Walter Bluet.[4] Raglan Castle, in Monmouthshire, is said to have been granted to him in consideration of soldiers, money, and arms furnished to Strongbow for his expedition to Ireland.[5]

Gerald de Barry gives a description[6] of his cousin Raymond, which, though probably more applicable to a somewhat later period of his life, may be substantially reproduced here. He was of little more than average height, but very stout (hence he was often called Raymond le Gros). He had rather curly yellow hair, large round grey eyes, a somewhat prominent nose, and a high-coloured, jovial, pleasant countenance; and although undoubtedly corpulent, he made up for the heaviness of his body by his light-heartedness and high spirits. He was a man of simple habits, not luxurious in either food or dress, patient and hardy, and equally inured to heat and cold. He was [183]
careful of his men, and would spend nights in going the rounds of his sentinels and challenging them to keep them on the alert. It was owing to his vigilance that the men in his command had the good fortune of rarely, if ever, being overwhelmed in rash undertakings or being caught by surprise. In short, he was a kind and prudent man, a skilful and daring soldier, and a consummate general.

Raymond, we are told, landed at a certain sea-cliff called Dundonnell 'about four[teen] miles from Waterford on the southern coast of Wexford', where he threw up a somewhat slight fortification made of earth and boughs of trees.[7] The name Dundonnell, pointing to an ancient Celtic or, possibly, Scandinavian fort, is now forgotten, and the place is called Baginbun. Common fame derives this strange name from the two greatest ships in which the Englishmen there arrived. It used sometimes to be written 'Bagg and Bunn', and *la Bague* and *la Bonne* are not improbable names

2 Ibid., p. 247. So Gervase of Canterbury (vol. i, p. 234) says of Earl Richard, *licentiam abeundi petiit et obtinuit.* 3 Ibid. p. 248. 4 Song of Dermot, l. 1497. Walter Bluet witnessed several charters granted by Strongbow to St. Mary's Abbeys at Dublin and Dunbrody. 5 Journ. Brit. Arch. Assoc., vol. x, p. 319. 6 Gir. Camb. v. 323. 7 The authorities for Raymond's landing-place and the subsequent battle are Gir. Camb. v. 248–53, and the Song of Dermot, ll. 1400–99. Gerald calls the place *Dundunnolf* and the Song *Dordonuil*, &c. The Irish Abridgement of the Expugnatio gives the true form *Dun Domhnaill* (*anglice* Dundonnell). For its identification with Baginbun see my papers in the Journ. R.S.A.I. 1898, pp. 155–60, and 1904, pp. 354–7, and compare Mr. Westropp's description, ibid. 1906, p. 257.

[184] of Norman ships. Tradition has linked the spot with the landing of Fitz Stephen, and the earthworks there with the name of Strongbow, and has retained the memory of a fateful battle fought in the neighbourhood; but from contemporary evidence we know that neither Strongbow nor Fitz Stephen landed here, and there is no reason to suppose that either of them entrenched himself or fought a battle in this district. But the position of the headland, and the character of the great earthwork there, point clearly to Raymond's landing-place and fortification as indicated in the authorities, and the fateful battle may well have been the fight to be presently described.

Baginbun is a rocky headland rising abruptly from the sea on the south coast of County Wexford, between Bannow Bay and the Hook. A minor point of the headland jutting out towards the east is cut off by some ancient earthworks, after the manner of a 'cliff-castle'. This probably represents the early Scandinavian or Celtic *dún*. The whole headland, embracing about thirty acres, is also marked off from the mainland by a huge trench, 700 feet long and 40 feet wide, with inner and outer earthen ramparts, and this entrenchment was in all probability the work of Raymond le Gros.

[185] At this fortress, then, Raymond was joined by Hervey de Montmorency with three knights, and (we must suppose) a small troop of men. We hear nothing of Robert Fitz Stephen and the Geraldines, who may have been absent in Thomond assisting Donnell O'Brien, Dermot's son-in-law, in his revolt against the *ard-rí*. Dermot himself, weakened by the defection of Maurice de Prendergast, and perhaps by the absence of Robert Fitz Stephen, did not stir. It was probably thought wiser to make no move until Strongbow came. Meanwhile Raymond and his little band, probably not much more than a hundred all told, were in great danger of being overwhelmed, and they had ample need of strong entrenchments and stout hearts. Accordingly Raymond collected cattle, drove them within his lines, and awaited the event. This followed speedily in the shape of a determined attack by the Ostmen of Waterford.

The men of Waterford may well have thought that the time had come for them to strike the first blow. With the warning they had received in the fall of Wexford in the previous year, they may well have foreseen that their town would be attacked next. It would be better to extirpate this little band of foreigners entrenched so near the mouth of their fiord before they were reinforced by further troops. They had heard of the exploits of Fitz Stephen, and they knew what masters of the art of war were these
[186] Norman kinsmen of theirs, with whom, however, they had lost all sense of kinship. Therefore they did not despise Raymond's little force, though it numbered hardly a hundred men. They took counsel with their neighbours, with whom they seem to have been on good terms, and organized a force some three thousand strong. O'Phelan, Prince of the Decies, a large district adjoining their territory on the west, assisted them, and a contingent came from Ossory, across the river, and even from O'Ryan, chieftain of Odrone, in the modern county of Carlow.[8] They crossed the river Suir, and having formed into three bands marched towards Raymond's camp. The two

8 In the partition of Dermot's territory made in 1166 Odrone had probably been annexed to Ossory: *supra*, p. 70 [p. 21].

accounts of the ensuing battle which have come down to us, though not exactly inconsistent with each other, differ somewhat in details. Reconciling them as well as we can, we infer that Raymond determined to sally forth and meet his opponents in the open. Whatever his motive may have been, this movement seems to have been a mistake, and nearly led to a disaster. His little band could not resist so great a multitude, but turned and fled back to their camp. So closely were they pursued that some of the enemy got inside the entrenchments before the barricades could be closed. Then Raymond, see- [187]
ing the jeopardy that he and his men were in, faced the foe, and cut down with his sword the first of his pursuers who crossed the threshold. It was probably at this moment that a curious incident, preserved by the old French chronicle, occurred. Raymond, as we have seen, had collected a number of cattle within his lines at Baginbun, and these, either taking fright at the turmoil, or, as would seem more probable, being designedly driven forth, rushed wildly through the entrance of the fort and met the impetuous onset of the attacking party. 'This was the first company/That sallied from the fort, I trow,' says the Norman Rhymer, with a touch of humour. The maddened cattle disconcerted and put into confusion the ranks of the Irish, and then Raymond, who had meanwhile rallied his men, raised his battle-cry of St. David and, throwing himself upon the disordered crowd, turned what seemed very nearly a crushing defeat into a complete victory. Upwards of 500 are said to have been killed, and numbers were thrown from the cliffs into the sea. In the quaint words of an early translator of the Expugnatio, 'Here the pride of Waterford fell; here al his myght went to noght. Her-of come [to] the Englysshe hope and comfort; and to the Iresshe dred and wanhope; for it was neuer there-to-for I-herd, that of so fewe men so grett a slaght [188]
was done.'

The glory of victory was quickly tarnished by a deed of unusual severity. The English had taken seventy of the principal townsmen of Waterford prisoners, and the question arose what was to be done with them. Raymond and Hervey, as we are told by Raymond's cousin, took opposite sides on this question. Raymond pleaded on behalf of mercy to those who were no longer resisting but were vanquished, and urged that they should be held to ransom. Hervey argued that mercy was out of place while the people generally were unsubdued, that they had come to conquer and not to spare, that the prisoners were more numerous than the guards, and were an ever-present danger in their midst in the event of a further attack. In the end the sterner counsels prevailed, and the wretched captives had their limbs broken and were cast headlong from the cliffs into the sea.

Notwithstanding the completeness of this victory Raymond remained very quietly at Baginbun for some three months,[9] waiting for Strongbow's arrival before attempting anything further. Meanwhile the earl was completing his preparations and was [189]
marching along the coast-route of South Wales to St. Davids, gathering fresh recruits as he went. This was part of the route so graphically described for us in Gerald's Itinerary through Wales. Starting from his castle of Striguil on the cliff overhanging

9 It is possible that the date (about the calends of May) given by Gerald for Raymond's arrival is too early. The Song of Dermot says that Strongbow arrived very soon after the battle: *bien tost apres*, l. 1501.

the Wye; he would march through Netherwent, famous for its archers, many of whom, no doubt, he brought with him, to the ancient Roman town of Caerleon, the city of the legions, and so to Newport and 'the noble fortress on the Taff' (Cardiff), first perhaps a mere 'mote-castle' erected within the Roman *castrum* by Robert Fitz Hamon, the conqueror of Morganwg, but rebuilt magnificently by Robert, Earl of Gloucester, son of Henry I. Next he would advance through Morganwg to Neath and the Flemish settlements at Gower, where such names as Scurlege Castle and Horton remind us of the Scurlocks and Hores, early settlers in Wexford. Then he would reach Caermarthen, where his father, Gilbert Fitz Gilbert, had built the castle, and thence to Haverford, and perhaps St. Davids, to the famous shrine.[10] At Haverford he appears to have persuaded Maurice de Prendergast, who, as we have seen, had returned to his home in the neighbourhood, to try his fortunes in Ireland once more. Indeed, it is
[190] probable that many of Strongbow's followers came from the cantrefs about Haverford and Pembroke, inasmuch as the names of many of those who are believed to have accompanied him, as well as of those who are known to have been among the first settlers in Ireland, can with great probability be traced to these regions.

We may here quote Gerald's description of the earl. In reading it we must bear in mind that Strongbow did not belong to the noble progeny of the Castellan of Pembroke. He did not belong even to one of the allied families connected by a common descent from Nesta. True, his fortunes were to a large extent linked with those of the great Geraldine clan. He had fought by their side against the common enemy in South Wales, and now he had come to their assistance in Ireland, and had ranged himself with them against the natives, whether Norse or Celtic, and later on he enfeoffed them with rich lands. He is not, therefore, to be classed with William Fitz Audelin and other late-comers, who were jealous of the Geraldines and craftily deprived them of the best fruits of their valour, leaving to them the remote and barren marches next the enemy, while themselves keeping the rich and safe lands beside the coast. Nevertheless we can detect a jealousy of Strongbow in the mind of our historian, a jealousy which
[191] shows itself in an endeavour to belittle his powers and his performances, a jealousy which was probably but the reflection of a feeling amongst the Geraldines that Strongbow had come over after they had shown the way and borne the brunt of the danger, and by his greater name and greater success had overshadowed their more sterling qualities and had secured the greater reward.

This is the manner of man he was according to Gerald de Barry: 'A man with reddish hair, freckled skin, grey eyes, feminine features, thin voice, and short neck. For the rest, he was tall in stature, open-handed, and kindly in disposition. What he could not accomplish by force he would effect by gentle speech. As a private individual he was more disposed to be led than to lead. In time of peace he had more the air of an ordinary soldier than of a commander, but in war he was a commander rather than a fighter. He was daring enough in carrying out the plans of his subordinates, but of his own initiative he would never take the offensive or stake everything on personal val-

10 This is stated in the Irish Abridgement of the Expugnatio, § 19. See English Historical Review, 1905.

our. In actual battle his standard was ever a sure rallying-point for his men. In defeat, as in victory, he was calm and unmoved, neither driven to despair by adversity nor unduly elated by prosperity.' [11]

Making allowance for the evident bias of this picture, we think we can gather from [192] it, and still more certainly from what we know of Strongbow's doings, that he was really a man of higher stamp than any of the descendants of Nesta. He was not so reckless a fighter as Meiler Fitz Henry, nor so bold a general in the field as Raymond le Gros, but he had military and, above all, statesmanlike qualities denied to them, which fitted him for the work of subduing Ireland and subjecting her people to Norman rule. Perhaps the difference was partly racial, for he had no Welsh blood in his veins. He would gain his end by the sword if necessary, but if possible by the gentler arts of persuasion and compromise. Much as we may admire the courage which the first conquerors showed in facing fearful odds, and wonder at the success of their expeditions, they had really effected little towards gaining a permanent foothold in Ireland or in pacifying, as distinguished from plundering, Leinster, and at the time of Strongbow's arrival their prospects were far from assured. In the six remaining years of Strongbow's life the Anglo-Norman settlement in Leinster became an accomplished fact, and the whole face of the province was changed.

At the last moment, when his preparations were complete and Strongbow was ready to embark, messengers came from the king forbidding the expedition;[12] but it [193] was too late to draw back, and Strongbow sailed from Milford Haven with a force consisting of 200 knights and about 1,000 other troops, probably lancers and archers.[13] He landed near Waterford, probably where King Henry landed in the following year, at Crook, or more precisely at the landing-place now called Passage, a little below the confluence of the three rivers, the exact date being the eve of St. Bartholomew, August 23, 1170. Next day Raymond joined him with forty knights, including perhaps some of the earlier comers, and on the morning of the 25th the united forces advanced to the assault of Waterford.

Waterford was at this time a walled town. The ancient walls have been traced, and it appears that they formed a small triangle, containing about fifteen statute acres, with the base along the right bank of the river.[14] Reginald's Tower, believed to be the *turris Raghnaldi* mentioned by Gerald, still exists, and marks the eastern limit of this base. [194] Other towers marking the other two angles have disappeared. The ancient Irish name for the harbour or estuary was Loch Dá Caech (i.e. the lough or estuary of the two blind ones), but it was afterwards generally called Port Láirge, probably from Laraic, a Scandinavian chieftain.[15] The Northmen, however, called it Vedrafiordr, meaning 'weather-haven', and this is the name now represented by Waterford. The 'foreigners of Port Láirge' are first mentioned towards the close of the ninth century.[16] Reinforcements throng in early in the next century and 'place a stronghold (*longport*)

11 Geraldine Gir. Camb. v 272. 12 Wm. of Newburgh, vol. i, p. 168. 13 Giraldus, p. 254. The Song, l. 1503, says *Bien quinz cent od sei mena*. The entries in the Irish annals are meagre and confused. That in the Annals of Tigernach (followed by the Four Masters) lumps together the arrivals of Robert Fitz Stephen and Richard Fitz Gilbert and the captures of Wexford and Waterford. 14 Smith's Waterford (1746), p. 169. Cf. Cal. Docs. Irel., vol. i, no. 763. 15 Four Masters, 951, note. 16 Ibid., 888.

there'.[17] Among them is Raghnall, grandson of Ivar, one of the clan that founded dynasties in Dublin and Limerick as well as in Waterford. With him comes Earl Ottir the Black, 'and the whole of Munster,' in the exuberant language of the Irish shanachy,[18] 'became filled with immense floods, and countless sea-vomitings of ships and boats and fleets, so that there was not a harbour nor a landing port nor a *dún* nor a fortress nor a fastness in all Munster without fleets of Danes and pirates.' In the course of the tenth century the Northmen settled down into a more peaceful life as
[195] traders in their seaport towns—occasionally, no doubt, fighting and raiding, but less frequently than the Irish themselves raided and fought. They became Christians too, of a sort, and those of Waterford, following the example of their kinsmen in Dublin, applied in 1096 to Anselm, Archbishop of Canterbury, to ordain one Malchus, a monk of Winchester, as their bishop.[19] By this time the town had become of considerable size and importance. Its inhabitants held the country near Waterford, and the name of the barony of Gaultier, 'the land of the foreigners,' marks their occupation. It is even possible that the round stone forts at the promontory of Hook and at Dunmore date from the Norse period, and are to be ranked with Reginald's Tower as among the few relics of Scandinavian masonry which have survived to our times.[20]

[196] As in the case of their kin at Wexford, the Ostmen of Waterford[21] were able for a time to repulse their assailants from the walls. Twice they had beaten them off, when Raymond, who is stated by his kinsman to have been in command, perceived a little house jutting out from the wall and supported by a post on the outside. He at once summoned the whole force to the assault at this spot, and sent some mail-clad men to hew down the post. When this was done the house fell, dragging a considerable portion of the wall with its ruins and laying open a practicable breach. Rushing over the debris and through this breach, the assailants stormed the town, butchered the citizens in crowds, and gained a bloody victory. In Raghnall's or Reginald's tower, which is mentioned by name, two Norse leaders, named Sitric, were taken and put to the sword. A third leader, named Raghnall, and Melaghlin O'Phelan, Prince of the Decies, taken in the same place, were spared at the intervention of Dermot, who with Fitz Stephen and Maurice Fitz Gerald arrived shortly afterwards.

[197] Thus fell Waterford, a city which the Irish seem never to have taken, not at least since the days of Dermot's great-grandfather, Diarmaid Mac Maelnamo, and certainly

17 Ibid., 910, 912, 915; Ann. Ulster, 913, 914. **18** Wars of the Gaedhil with the Gaill, p. 41. **19** Ussher's Sylloge, epist. 34, ed. Elrington, vol. iv, p. 518; Eadmer's Hist. R. S., pp. 76-7. **20** The Hook Tower has, however, been virtually rebuilt to form a lighthouse, and Reginald's Tower appears to have been restored and perhaps remodelled by the Normans. The masonry of the upper part is very similar to that of the Norman addition to the town walls, and is of quite a different character from the lower part. The town walls were extended by the Normans in the early part of the thirteenth century so as to include a larger area to the south and west, and the existing remains of walls and mural towers probably date from about that time. Those at the eastern side appear to follow the lines of the Scandinavian walls. Grants of customs to enable the citizens to enclose the town were repeatedly made by Henry III (Cal. Docs. Ireland, vol. i, nos. 1163, 2133, 2613). **21** The authorities for the capture of Waterford are Giraldus, vol. v, p. 254-5; Song of Dermot, ll. 1499-1539 The Annals of Tigernach (followed and corrected by the Four Masters) states that Mac Gillamuire, the officer of the fort at Waterford, was taken prisoner, but it appears that this was Raghnall's patronymic. See note to Song, l. 1506.

never to have garrisoned and held. Dermot himself, indeed, as we have mentioned, aided by Conor O'Brien and the Danish fleets of Dublin and Wexford, had besieged it in 1137 and exacted hostages, but it does not appear that the city was taken or plundered. Now Strongbow placed a garrison in the city, locating the guards, as we may suppose, in the Danish towers. Herein we see the difference between the Celt and the Norman. The Celt would have plundered and burnt the town and then left it. The Norman plunders, no doubt, but puts a garrison in to hold the place, and, if necessary, fortifies it.

Strongbow had now given earnest, as it were, that he would fulfil his engagement with Dermot, and Dermot now showed himself ready to fulfil his part of the bargain. This was promptly done, and Dermot's daughter, Aoife or Eva, was given in marriage to the earl, and the treaty, according to which Strongbow was to succeed Dermot as King of Leinster, was confirmed, so far at least as such a treaty could be confirmed without the free sanction of the tribes concerned.

A famous fresco preserved in the precincts of the House of Commons has for its subject the marriage of Strongbow and Eva. The knight and his lady stand in the open [198]
battlefield, amid flaming houses and with the bodies of the dead and dying strewn around. Far be it from me to question the prescriptive right of the painter to treat his subject in an imaginative way, and to introduce any setting that serves to help out his thought; but in view of the statements of recent historians it is almost necessary to remark that Maclise's picture is not a contemporary record, and cannot be used, as the Bayeux Tapestry has been used, to fill up the gaps of contemporary writers. There is no other authority for this scene, which on the face of it is utterly improbable. In all probability the marriage ceremony took place in the Christ Church of the Holy Trinity at Waterford[22] some days after the taking of the town. It is true that Gerald, in a heavily loaded Latin sentence (of which he was probably proud), lumps together a great number of events: he says in a breath, as it were, that the two Sitrics were taken in Reginald's tower and put to the sword; that Reginald and Melaghlin O'Phelan were taken in the same place, but that their lives were spared at the intercession of Dermot, who had just then arrived with Maurice and Fitz Stephen; that a garrison was placed in the city; that Dermot's daughter Eva was there married to the earl, her father giv- [199]
ing her away and confirming the treaty; and that the united army marched towards Dublin. It is obvious that all these events did not take place on the same day. Dermot could hardly have received notice of Strongbow's arrival in time to enable him to summon his men and reach Waterford in the middle of the assault, which according to Giraldus took place on the day next but one to Strongbow's arrival. But we are not dependent on inferences for the conclusion that some days elapsed between the taking of the town and the marriage of Strongbow and Eva. According to the express statement of the Song of Dermot, which indeed is not inconsistent with that of Giraldus, it was after the earl had taken Waterford that he sent messengers to Dermot to acquaint him with this fact and to invite the king to join him with his English troops,

22 The crypt of this church seems to have been a replica of that at Christ Church, Dublin (Journ. R.S.A.I. 1894, p. 73); but probably both were Norman.

and it was in joyful response to this message that Dermot came with the English barons and his daughter, and fulfilled, as far as in him lay, his part of the bargain.[23]

But, indeed, the marriage of Eva and Strongbow stands in need of none of these lurid accompaniments to heighten its dramatic effect. No marriage like it had ever
[200] taken place in Ireland before. Irish ladies of the highest rank had indeed wedded with Norman knights. Murtough O'Brien, King of Munster and (with opposition) of Ireland, had, for instance, given his daughter in marriage to Arnulf de Montgomery, the first founder of Pembroke Castle. But these ladies had gone to live on their lords' lands and had followed their lords' fortunes, while Eva was to endow her lord with a broad fifth of Ireland. It is true that according to Celtic law it was not in her power, nor in Dermot's power, to do this. In theory and in normal practice the successor to the chieftainship was chosen from some ruling family by the subject tribes, but it must be remembered that it was no uncommon occurrence for different members of the privileged family or families to fight for the succession, and even for a ruler to be imposed from without in opposition to the local choice. The succession was, however, never regarded as simply hereditary, nor in recent times, at any rate, was it ever held or handed on by a woman. This marriage then, with its professed object, was something entirely new in Ireland. It marks the first clash of English feudalism with Celtic tribalism—the first clash of those discordant ideas which were to lead to so much hardship and misunderstanding in the future between the two races. It is not, indeed,
[201] to be supposed that Strongbow was so ignorant of Celtic customs as to imagine that he was getting by this marriage a clear and indisputable title to the kingship of Leinster. He must have been familiar with the tribal customs of Wales, which, though breaking down, were not very dissimilar to those of Ireland. In all probability, as already remarked, he did not look forward to the position of a tribal chief at all, but rather to that of a feudal lord over a vast fief which he knew he must sooner or later hold of the Crown. Dermot, indeed, who was utterly unscrupulous in the furtherance of his ambition and revenge, may have intended to force a tanist upon his subjects, or at least to appear to Strongbow to be doing so; but Strongbow himself probably regarded the marriage as merely strengthening a position which he knew full well must be won and held by the sword; just as Gerald of Windsor and Bernard of Newmarch had strengthened the positions they had won in Wales by their marriage alliances with the families of the legitimate princes. But this marriage was more than the mark of clashing ideas: it was a sign which all might read that the invaders had come to stay. They were not mere marauders who ravage and plunder and run off with the spoil. They were not mere mercenaries who when they had won Dermot's battles for him would return with their pay whence they came. They had come to stay
[202] and to rule. Thus much those who were clear-visioned amongst the spectators of this wedding may have foreseen. But there was something else which the Irish at any rate did not foresee, but which we, looking back across the centuries, can see clearly enough. This union of Strongbow and Eva was the symbol of that union between the two islands which, for better or worse, has lasted ever since.

23 Song of Dermot, ll. 1516–39.

A council of war was now held at which Strongbow, Dermot, Raymond, Maurice de Prendergast, Meiler Fitz Henry, and other leaders were present, and it was determined that the next move should be on Dublin. This, we may be sure, was a project which commended itself to Dermot. He had, as we have seen, an old claim on the allegiance of Dublin and a blood-feud with its inhabitants. But apart from personal motives, there were excellent strategic reasons pointing in the same direction. Wexford and Waterford had fallen, but the greatest of the Norse strongholds remained intact. The Ostmen of Dublin had, indeed, nominally submitted to Dermot in the early part of the year, but something more than nominal submission was now required. It was obvious that if Dermot was to hold Leinster securely it was desirable to take and hold Dublin. Moreover, Dermot, as we have seen, did not now limit his ambition to Leinster. With the aid of his foreign troops he hoped to take vengeance on his old [203]
enemy Tiernan O'Rourke and on Rory O'Conor himself. He had not forgotten or forgiven those who had expelled him from his kingdom of Leinster. He had even ultimate aims on the high-kingship of Ireland. In these wider aims, we may be quite certain, his English allies, with a view to their own succession, actively encouraged him. From their point of view it was absolutely essential to gain possession of Dublin. Once inside its walls they would know how to hold it, and they would have a new base, accessible by sea, in the middle of the east coast from which to extend their operations. Dublin, though held by foreigners and not the seat of the King of Ireland, nor the mother city of the Irish Church, was undoubtedly the chief town, and was rapidly coming to be regarded, in a less technical sense, as the metropolis of Ireland. In order to understand its position better, it will be well here to glance briefly at its past history.

Dublin had been for upwards of three centuries in Scandinavian hands.[24] It owed
its origin and importance as a town and seaport to them. The name, *Dubh-linn*, means [204]
the 'black pool', and was in early times applied by the Irish to the mouth of the Liffey, and not to a town at all. It seems to have been the North men who first applied the name, under the form Dyflin, to the town. The Irish always called the town *Baile atha cliath*, meaning 'the town of the ford (or crossing) of hurdles', a name which apparently owed its origin to a bridge of hurdles by which the ancient road *slighe Cualann* from Tara crossed the Liffey above the 'black pool', until it was superseded by the bridge of the Ostmen.

As we have seen, the battle of Clontarf, though it permanently weakened the Northmen and put an end to all possibility of uniting Ireland under a Scandinavian dynasty, did not seriously affect the position they had gained in Ireland. They retained their hold of Dublin, Wexford, Waterford, Cork, and Limerick, until the coming of their remote kinsfolk the Normans. They joined occasionally in the tribal warfare of the Irish, but they devoted themselves more and more to trade and peaceful arts. Their

24 The foreigners of Dublin are generally called by modern writers Danes, but Dr. Alexander Bugge has shown that the dynasty was probably Norwegian throughout: The Royal Race of Dublin (1900). Giraldus, too, speaks not only of the earlier invasion under Turgesius (Thorgils) as Norwegian, but says that the later comers under Amlaf Sitric and Ivar came from Norway and the northern isles. They were called in his time Ostmanni: Gir. Camb. v. 182-7.

trade with Bristol was not confined to a traffic in slaves, and the town of Chester appears to have had definite trading rights with Dublin in the time of Henry I.[25] They
[205] were Christians of a sort even before the battle of Clontarf, but they now more fully adopted the cross of Christ as their symbol of victory instead of the discredited Raven banner. Dunan or Donatus was the first Ostman Bishop of Dublin (circa 1038), and in his time the Cathedral of the Holy Trinity, commonly called Christ Church, is said to have been founded.[26]

It is not known by whom Dunan was consecrated, but after his death, in 1074, the clergy and laity of Dublin chose a priest named Patrick and sent him to Lanfranc, Archbishop of Canterbury, to be consecrated.[27] This ceremony Lanfranc performed at St. Paul's Cathedral after receiving Patrick's profession of canonical obedience, and copies of Lanfranc's letters sent by the hand of the newly consecrated bishop to 'Gothric glorious King of Ireland' and to 'Terdelvac magnificent King of Ireland' have been preserved.[28] This Gothric was in all probability the Godfrey, son of Amlaf, son of Raghnall, King of Ath Cliath, whose death is recorded in the next year.[29]
[206] Terdelvac was of course Turlough O'Brien, King of Munster, who, since the death of Dermot Mac Maelnamo, was the most powerful chieftain in the south of Ireland, and had probably been acknowledged by the citizens of Dublin as their overlord. Following the example of Bishop Patrick, the three succeeding bishops of Dublin were all consecrated in England, and promised obedience to the See of Canterbury, while they maintained an attitude of independence, if not of antagonism, towards the See of Armagh and the Celtic Church.[30]

In 1028 Sitric Silkbeard went on a pilgrimage to Rome, but his family seem to have maintained their position in Dublin up to the year 1052. In that year Dermot, son of Maelnamo, King of Leinster, then the most prominent king in Ireland, plundered Fine Gall, drove out Echmarcach, and assumed the kingship of the foreigners.[31] Dermot was slain in 1072, and thenceforward the Northmen, though generally ruled by their own countrymen, were often obliged to give hostages to the more prominent Irish kings. Indeed, during the century and a half of anarchy, of which we have already
[207] given a slight sketch, it seems to have been more and more recognized that any chieftain who had pretensions to the crown of Ireland should first of all obtain the adhesion of the foreigners of Ath-cliath. We have seen that Malachi II, Brian Borumha, and Dermot Mac Maelnamo all entered Dublin and took hostages, and in each case their claims to the chief power may be said to date from the submission of Dublin. Next Turlough O'Brien secured the adhesion of Dublin before making his first (unsuccessful) attempt to obtain hostages from the northern chieftains,[32] and again in 1080 it was at Dublin that he received the submission of Meath and of the clergy of

25 See Round's Feudal England, p. 465, where a writ from Henry II (c. 1175-6) is cited, directing that the burgesses of Chester might buy and sell in Dublin, and have the same rights, liberties, and free customs which they used to have in the time of Henry I. **26** Liber Niger of Christ Church. **27** Ussher's Works (Elrington's ed.), vol. iv, p. 488. It appears from this letter that even at this time the Norsemen expressly termed Dublin *Hiberniae insulae metropolis.* **28** Ibid., pp. 490, 492. **29** Ann. Ulster, 1075. **30** See their professions of canonical obedience, Ussher's Sylloge, p. 120, also Epistle no. 40; and cf. Ware's Bishops. **31** Ann. Tigernach, Four Masters, 1152; Ann. Ulster, vol. i, p. 591, note. **32** Four Masters, 1075.

the north.[33] Murtough, his son, the year after his accession to the throne of Munster, defeated the Leinstermen at Rath Edair (Howth), and apparently secured the allegiance of Dublin.[34] In 1118 Turlough O'Conor, now preparing to contest the throne, marched on Dublin and exacted hostages.[35] In 1154 Murtough O'Loughlin, Turlough's most formidable foe and successor, obtained the submission of the Ostmen of Dublin, and gave them 1,200 cows as their wages or stipend to secure their fealty and future services in war.[36] Finally, on O'Loughlin's death in 1166, Rory O'Conor [208]
marched on Dublin, took hostages, and was there inaugurated as *ard-rí*, and he levied a tax of 4,000 cows upon the men of Ireland for the stipend of the foreigners.[37] These facts go to show the increasing political importance of Dublin. Though inhabited and directly ruled by foreigners, and not the seat of the *ard-rí*, it had gradually come to be regarded as in some sort the capital of Ireland.

At the time of which we treat, Haskulf, son of Raghnall, son of Thorkil, was King of Dublin.[38] He had thrown off his allegiance to Dermot, and had, as we have seen, submitted to Rory O'Conor, and along with O'Rourke had been one of the principal instruments of Dermot's expulsion. On hearing of Dermot's impending expedition against Dublin, Haskulf sent to his overlord for assistance, and Rory promptly came [209]
to his aid, accompanied by O'Rourke, O'Melaghlin, and O'Carroll, with the forces of Breffny, Meath, and Uriel. The regular route from Wexford to Dublin followed up the course of the Slaney to the west of the Wicklow Mountains, and approached Dublin by way of Naas and Clondalkin. A possible alternative at this side was the defile of Glen Saggart. There was also a less frequented coast route through the Windgate near Bray, and a route through Enniskerry and the Scalp, both narrow defiles. Rory, expecting Dermot by some one of these routes, lay at Clondalkin, five miles south-west of Dublin, with his main army, and sent out troops to plash and beset the passes through the woods and hold the narrow defiles against Dermot's advance. Informed of this by his scouts, when already some way on his march, Dermot avoided the traps laid for him, and leading his army across the mountain ridge to Glendalough reached Dublin by a mountain track[39] perhaps approximately that now followed by the military road from Sally Gap by Glencree and Killakee to the woods of Rathfarnham—thus turning the Irish position.

We may be quite sure that Strongbow came to the walls of Dublin intending to take possession of the town by assault if necessary, and having taken it, to put a garrison into [210]
it and hold it against all comers. The Irish custom of taking hostages for good behav-

33 Ann. Tigernach, Four Masters, 1080. 34 Ibid. 1087. 35 Ann. Ulster, Ann. Loch Cé, Four Masters, 1118. 36 Four Masters, 1154. Four years previously, on the occasion of an advance by Murtough O'Loughlin, 'the Foreigners made a year's peace between the North and the South of Ireland,' indicating that they held the balance between the contending sides. 37 Ann. Tigernach, Four Masters, 1166. The enormous number of cows constituting its 'stipend' indicates the pre-eminence of Dublin. On the same occasion the stipends to Uriel, Offaly, Offelan, and Ossory were only 240 cows apiece. This acceptance of cows from the overlord was the regular symbol of subjection to him. 38 He is called Asgall son of Raghnall son of Turcall by the Four Masters, 1170. Gerald calls him Hasculphus, and in the Song he is named Hesculf or Esculf Macturkil or Mactorkil. Raghnall son of Turcall, King of the Foreigners of Dublin, was slain in 1146, and Brodar son of Turcall, King of Dublin, in 1160: Ann. Tigernach. 39 *Per devexa montium de Glindelachan latera*: Gir. Camb. v. 256; cf. Song of Dermot, ll. 1570–1623.

iour was a poor substitute for placing a garrison in a secure fortress, when that was practicable. The townsfolk, with the example of Waterford before their eyes, endeavoured at once to make terms with Dermot. Perhaps they had lost some of their dash and daring, now that they had become Christians, and no longer believed that the Valkyries, Odin's corse-choosers, were waiting on the battlefield to bring all who fell bravely fighting to Odin's hall. At any rate, they sent envoys to Dermot headed by their archbishop Lorcan or Laurence O'Toole, who was Dermot's brother-in-law. It was due in particular to his mediation that negotiations for peace were entered on. Maurice Regan, Dermot's trusty servant and secretary, to whom we owe so much of our information, was dispatched to the town with Dermot's terms, which were that the citizens should return to their allegiance and should surrender to him thirty hostages for their good behaviour. The position of a hostage at this time was far from enviable. Even if well treated by his jailor, his eyes or his life were always liable to be forfeited upon breach of the conditions which
[211] those who had surrendered him had undertaken to observe. This forfeiture was constantly exacted by the highest and best in the land, and indeed had it been otherwise the system of hostages would have been unmeaning and useless. We can then well believe the statement that a difficulty arose when it came to the selecting of the hostages. None but the more influential citizens would of course be accepted, and these were the very ones who could best resist the imposition of the hated office. The negotiations were therefore protracted, and apparently extended over three days.

Meanwhile two young leaders, Miles de Cogan and Raymond le Gros, who were posted near the city, becoming impatient at the delay, rushed suddenly with their following at the walls and gained access to the town. The Ostmen were evidently taken unawares, for they seem to have made no stand against the storming party. Many of them were killed, but the greater number, led by Haskulf, succeeded in escaping with their more valuable effects to their boats and galleys, which were moored in the river ready for this contingency, and sailed off to their kinsfolk in the Hebrides and Man. This exploit, in which we may suspect a treacherous breach of truce, was performed without the order or the knowledge of either Dermot or Strongbow, who were
[212] encamped somewhat further from the city. Thus Dublin fell on the day of St. Matthew the Apostle, September 21, 1170.

But what was the Irish army under the *ard-rí* doing all this time? It is clear that they departed without fighting, but why? To this question our Norman authorities do not give any complete answer. From the Song, indeed, we should infer that when Rory saw himself out-manoeuvred by Dermot's march across the mountains, he simply retired and disbanded his army. The Irish Annals,[40] however, throw a somewhat different light on the action of the *ard-rí*. Rory had summoned his army to defend the Ostmen of Dublin, who had recently submitted to him, against the threatened attack of Dermot

40 Four Masters, Ann. Tigernach, Ann. Ulster, 1170. The Four Masters give the clearest account, and probably preserve the meaning of the original entry. The passage in the Annals of Tigernach which states that 'the Foreigners assented to the burning of the town, since they perceived that to be with Mac Murchada was to revolt against the King of Ireland', is unintelligible as it stands. Probably we should read *Gaedhil* for *Gaill*, i.e. 'the Irish' for 'the Foreigners'.

and the English, and he remained on the 'Green of Ath-Cliath' (near Kilmainham) ready to fight in their defence. But instead of showing fight against Dermot, the men of Dublin prepared to submit to him, and with this view had entered independently into negotiations with him. Rory regarded this impending submission as a repudiation of their allegiance to him. After three days, while the negotiations were still going on, [213]
a thunderstorm broke over the town, and the lightning set it on fire. This 'act of God' was regarded as showing the displeasure of Heaven against the Ostmen for having 'deserted from the Connaughtmen and the people of North Ireland in general'. Accordingly O'Conor left the traitors to their fate and returned with his whole army. The subsequent surprise and sacking of the town was looked upon as a 'miracle', or just judgement, on the Ostmen 'for having violated their word to the men of Ireland'. Such is the view the annalists seek to convey, and we may accept it as helping to explain Rory's inaction; but we may suspect that, had not the Irish, unsupported by the Ostmen, felt themselves unable to cope with the Norman force in the open ground in the neighbourhood of Dublin, they would not have departed without forcing a battle.

The Northmen had been driven out of Dublin before, but never by any one who knew how to hold a town, and they had always succeeded in regaining their position. But now the town was occupied by one who was a master in the military art, and we may be quite sure that its fortifications were made stronger than ever. Dermot had amply avenged himself on the citizens of Dublin, but he still burned for vengeance on [214]
Tiernan O'Rourke[41] and the men of Meath and Breffny who had been the immediate agents of his expulsion. Accordingly an army was led by Dermot and his knights into East Meath, and they plundered Clonard and burned Kells and many another place in the valleys of the Boyne and Blackwater celebrated from of old for some religious house. Then they invaded O'Rourke's proper territory as far as Slieve Gory, a hilly district in the barony of Clankee, in the county of Cavan, and carried off many prisoners and cows to their camp. Donnell of Bregia, the reinstating of whom may have formed a pretext for this incursion, and the men of East Meath, now turned against O'Rourke and O'Conor and gave hostages to Dermot. The next step was for Tiernan O'Rourke to put to death the hostages of East Meath which he held, and for O'Conor to put to death the hostages which Dermot had given him for Leinster. These latter were Dermot's own son, Conor, his grandson, son of Donnell Kavanagh, and the son of his [215]
foster-brother O'Caellaighe. They were put to death at the instigation of O'Rourke, 'for O'Rourke had pledged his conscience that Rory should not be King of Ireland unless they were put to death.'[42] Gerald, indeed, purports to give us the correspondence that passed between Rory and Dermot on the subject, and Rory's letter is so exactly in keep-

41 Tiernan O'Rourke was, as we have seen, hereditary chieftain of Breffny, a district embracing the modern counties of Cavan and Leitrim. He is called by Gerald *Rex Medensium*, and the expression at this time was not incorrect. For in the previous year Dermot O'Melaghlin, the hereditary King of Meath, had been murdered by his nephew Donnell O'Melaghlin, known as Donnell of Bregia, and O'Conor had in consequence expelled Donnell and divided Meath into two parts, keeping the western part to himself and giving East Meath to his staunch ally Tiernan. At this time, then, Tiernan's territory extended right across Ireland from the mouth of the Erne to the mouth of the Boyne. 42 Ann. Tigernach, Ann. Ulster, Four Masters, 1170; Gir. Camb. v. 257.

ing with the facts that we may take it as in substance correct. 'Contrary to the terms of our treaty,' he writes, 'you have invited a host of foreigners into this island. So long, however, as you confined your operations within your ancient kingdom of Leinster, we bore it patiently; but now, inasmuch as, unmindful of your oath and reckless of the fate of your hostage, you have passed the limits assigned and insolently crossed even your hereditary boundaries, for the future you must either restrain the irruptions of your foreign troops or I shall certainly send to you the decapitated head of your son.' To this warning Dermot arrogantly replied that he would not desist from his enterprise until he had subdued Connaught, which belonged to him by ancestral right,[43] and won for
[216] himself the monarchy of Ireland. We cannot wonder that Rory kept his word.

In the face of this new and extended invasion of the foreigners, while the *ard-rí* felt called upon to do no more than wreak his vengeance on Dermot's hostages, an assembly of clergy convened at Armagh came to the inept conclusion that it was a just judgement for the sins of the people in carrying on a slave trade with England, and they accordingly decreed that throughout the island all English slaves should be set free.[44] In times past Bristol had been the great centre of this trade with the Ostmen, but through the exertions of Wulfstan, Bishop of Worcester, the iniquitous traffic had been abandoned.[45] Possibly during the anarchy of Stephen's reign it had to some extent revived.

A few other items may be gleaned from the Irish Annals. It appears that the people of Uriel, as well as those of Meath, gave hostages to Dermot[46] and assisted him against O'Rourke.[47] The latter made reprisals upon his enemies and harried again the north-
[217] ern part of Meath and Fingall, but the serious fighting for the year was over. Dermot retired to his former seat at Ferns, never to leave it again, and Strongbow, on October 1, leaving Dublin under the care of Miles de Cogan, set out for Waterford 'with an ample suite'. According to the Four Masters, the garrison left here had met with a reverse at the hands of Dermot Macarthy and the men of Desmond, and it may be that Strongbow thought it necessary to strengthen it. He had, however, a greater difficulty to contend with. The King of England had become alarmed at the news of Strongbow's successes, magnified perhaps by report. It would never do to allow anything like an independent kingdom to be erected in Ireland. It was difficult enough to keep in hand the lords who had carved out for themselves lordships in Wales, among whom were these very de Clares and Fitz Geralds. It might become impossible to control them in the sea-divided Ireland. Besides, he had designs on that country of his own, when he could find time and opportunity to prosecute them. Accordingly he issued an edict placing the Irish ports under a sort of paper blockade, and ordering all his subjects there to return before the following Easter on pain of forfeiting their lands and being banished from the kingdom for ever.

This move of Henry's put Strongbow into great straits, for not only could he no
[218] longer obtain reinforcements[48] or supplies from Wales, but he was in danger of losing

43 By this expression Dermot probably alluded to his descent from Dermot Mac Maelnamo, who by some was reckoned King of Ireland. The remark is significant as bearing out what has already been stated, that since the usurpation of Brian Borumha any chieftain might aspire to the crown of Ireland. 44 Gir. Camb. v. 258. 45 William of Malmesbury. 46 Ann. Tigernach. 47 Four Masters. 48 That some individu-

his followers, who, to avoid outlawry, would have to obey the royal edict. Accordingly, after consulting his friends, he dispatched Raymond to the king, then in Aquitaine, with the following letter: 'It was with your licence, my lord, if I remember rightly, that I crossed over to Ireland to aid your liege man Dermot in recovering his territories. Wherefore whatever lands I have had the good fortune to acquire here either from his patrimony or from that of any one else, inasmuch as I owe them all to your gracious favour, I shall hold them at your will and disposal.' [49]

The terms of this letter, and the undertaking contained in it, sufficiently indicate what Strongbow understood to be the motive of Henry's action. It was not any regard for the rights of the Irish; it was simply the apprehension of trouble and risk to the English crown if a strong, independent kingdom were established in Ireland. If there had really been any danger of Strongbow's setting up an independent kingdom there, Henry's determination thus early to counteract such a project would have been amply [219]
justified. The whole subsequent history of the relation between England and the quasi-independent kingdom of Scotland shows what troubles and perils such a relationship necessarily involves. But there was certainly no immediate prospect of Strongbow's succeeding in any such enterprise, even if, as is unlikely, he ever entertained the idea. Henry's embargo, then, must rather be regarded as the first example of that perversity which in after years too often characterized England's policy towards Ireland, and from which, perhaps, it is not yet wholly free, a perversity which manifests itself in first encouraging the formation of an English colony in Ireland for the greater glory and security of the English Crown, and then, not from any regard to the native Irish, but from motives of suspicion and jealousy, thwarting the efforts of that colony whenever it seemed likely to be successful and prosperous.

als nevertheless came to Ireland from England at this time 'against the king's command', and were fined for so doing appears from the Pipe Roll, Henry II, pp. 29, 92. 49 Gir. Camb. v 259.

CHAPTER VII

[221]

STRONGBOW AS DERMOT'S SUCCESSOR, 1171

Dermot MacMurrough did not live long to enjoy his recovered kingdom. In the spring of 1171 he died, and was buried at Ferns.[1] The Irish annalists, in recording the event, show their bitter feeling by alleging that he died an evil death—'without unction, without the Body of Christ, without penance, without a will'—and ascribing it to the miracle of the saints whose churches he had destroyed. A more friendly hand, however, has made the following entry in the Book of Leinster:' 'Diarmait son of Dunchadh son of Murchadh [reigned] forty six [years]. And he was King of all South Erin and also of Meath. He died at Ferna after the victory of unction and penance in the sixty-first year of his age.'[2] There seems no reason why we should not accept the dates indicated by this entry, which comes at the end of a long list of the Kings of Leinster. It would refer the commencement of his reign to the year 1126 (if we count
[222] inclusively), and that was the year of the death of the preceding king, Enna Mac Murrough. He is described by Giraldus as *plenus dierum* at his death, but sixty-one was old for an Irish warrior king, and as he headed his army on arduous expeditions to the last, he must have retained much of his vigour.[3]

Dermot's death was the signal for the revolt of the Irish of Leinster against Earl Richard. It is plain that the tribes were not ready without a struggle to accept the arrangement, entirely unknown to Irish legal custom, by which the crown of Leinster
[223] was to pass, on Dermot's death, to his foreign son-in-law. Only three Irishmen of any note are said to have remained faithful to Strongbow. These were Donnell Kavanagh, his brother-in-law, who had hitherto accompanied him in his victories; O'Reilly of Tirbriuin or Breffny, whose family had a long-standing blood-feud with the O'Rourkes of the same district, and this O'Reilly had probably been expelled from his country by Tiernan O'Rourke; and Aulaff O'Garvy, a petty chieftain of the district

1 Gir. Camb. v. 263; Song of Dermot, ll. 1728–31. 2 Book of Leinster (Facsimile), p. 39 (d). 3 O'Donovan states that Dermot was in his sixty-second year at the time of the rape of Dervorgil (1152): notes to Four Masters, vol. ii, pp. 4 and 96. From this it would follow that he was in his eighty-first year at his death in 1171. But O'Donovan's statement seems to result from a miscalculation founded on an unsupported statement of Dr. O'Conor that Dermot was expelled in his seventieth year (1166): see note to Song of Dermot, l. 1729. The Book of Leinster contains the only early data on the subject, and its statements are consistent with Dermot's pedigree and the succession of kings. His father, Dunchad Mac Murchada, was killed at Dublin in 1115 (Ann. Ulster, Ann. Tigernach, Ann. Loch Cé), when Dermot, *ex hypothesi*, was only five years old. The next king, Diarmait Mac Enna, died in 1117. He was succeeded by Enna Mac Dunchada Maic Murchada (presumably an elder brother of Dermot), who died in 1126 (ibid.), from which date Dermot's reign is reckoned. He would then have been in his seventeenth year. As we have seen, however, some years elapsed before he gained real power.

about Rathvilly, co. Carlow.[4] The Leinster tribes were incited to revolt by Murtough MacMurrough, son of Dermot's brother, Murrough 'of the Irish,' who had been set up as King of Okinselagh on Dermot's banishment. But the combination against Strongbow was not confined to Leinster. The *ard-rí* O'Conor lent a willing ear to the request for assistance, and summoned 'the Irish of all Ireland' to accompany him to the siege of Dublin.[5] Lorcan, or Laurence O'Toole, the Archbishop of Dublin, according to a report mentioned by Gerald, is said to have been especially zealous in [224] beating up allies, not hesitating to call in foreigners to expel foreigners. In conjunction with Rory O'Conor, he sent letters to Gottred, King of Man, and the wikings of the western isles, urging them to blockade the city by sea. Some of these chieftains, induced by promise of reward, and also thinking that their own independence would be imperilled by the success of the English adventurers, straightway sailed to the mouth of the Liffey with a fleet of thirty ships, thus effectually cutting off Dublin from any supplies which, in spite of Henry's embargo, might come by sea. Meanwhile, the vast host assembled by O'Conor invested the city on every side. Castleknock, about four miles to the west of the city, was the head-quarters of the *ard-rí*, while still nearer, on the other side of the river, Donnell O'Brien, who had recently submitted to O'Conor, was at Kilmainham. On the north, at Clontarf, lay MacDunlevy, King of Ulidia, or Eastern Ulster, while Murtough MacMurrough blocked the southern coast road at Dalkey.

For nearly two months the investment lasted, and provisions began to fail. No attempt seems to have been made to take the town by assault, or even to commence siege operations. The walls and ditches had probably been strengthened by the Normans during the winter, and, at any rate, the Irish were quite unversed in the art [225] of conducting a regular siege. They probably did not advance within bowshot of the walls, but seem to have been satisfied with a somewhat loose investment. There were some skirmishes between the opposing parties for the space of a fortnight, and a party of horsemen, we are told,[6] was sent by O'Conor to cut down the corn of the Saxons, from which we may perhaps infer that the month of August had been reached. Still, the inactivity of this huge investing army[7] is hard to explain, unless, as seems proba- [226]

4 Song of Dermot, ll. 1734–41; cf. ll. 1788 and 1909. 5 The authorities for O'Conor's siege are the Song of Dermot, ll. 1746 to 1966; Gir. Camb. v. 265–70; Ann. Tigernach, 1171. The two last place Haskulf's expedition before O'Conor's hosting, but for the reasons given *infra*, pp. 245–6 [p. 90], I am inclined to think that the Song of Dermot preserves the true sequence. The Four Masters follow the Annals of Tigernach, and the siege is not mentioned in the Annals of Ulster nor in those of Loch Ce. 6 Ann. Tigernach, 1171, followed with slight variations by the Four Masters. 7 Giraldus says ' cum infinita totius fere Hiberniae multitudine ' (p. 265), and speaks of O'Conor's division as alone comprising 30,000 men (p. 268). Such large numerical calculations may be disregarded, but it was little exaggeration to say that all Ireland sent contingents to this siege. From Giraldus (p. 269) we learn that besides those mentioned above the following chieftains were also present:— In the southern army *Machelanus*, i.e. Faelan Mac Failain (Mackelan), King of Offelan; *Machtalewi*, a Leinster chieftain of uncertain locality (see Song of Dermot, note, p. 318); *Gillemeholmoch*, i.e. Domhnall Mac Gillamocholmog, King of Ui Donchadha; and *Otuethelis*, i.e. Ua Tuathail (O'Toole), King of Ui Muireadhaigh. In the northern army *Ororicius Medensis*, i.e. Tighearnan Ua Ruairc (O'Rourke), King of Breifne, with claims over Meath; *Ocaruelus Urielensis*, i.e. Murchadh Ua Cearbhaill, King of Oirghialla (Murrough O'Carrol, King of Uriel); *Machsachelinus*, i.e. (probably) Domhnall Breagach

ble, they were waiting for the expected arrival of Haskulf, son of Thorkil, the exiled lord of Dublin, before undertaking the assault of the town.

Unable to obtain supplies by either land or sea, the earl found his stock of provisions nearly exhausted, when a new cause of anxiety arose. Donnell Kavanagh with a few followers managed to slip into the beleaguered city with the intelligence that Robert Fitz Stephen was besieged in his castle of Carrick, and that if not relieved within three days it would be all over with him.[8] Thereupon Strongbow summoned his principal followers to a council of war. The Song of Dermot gives us the names of several. They include some with whom we are already familiar and others of whom we shall hear again: Robert de Quency, Walter de Ridelisford, Maurice de Prendergast, Miles de Cogan, Meiler Fitz Henry, Miles, son of David Fitz gerald, the bishop,
[227] Richard de Marreis, and Walter Bluet. To these we must add from Giraldus, Raymond le Gros and Maurice Fitz Gerald.[9] When the barons were assembled in council the earl laid before them the desperate state of affairs, and proposed to make terms with O'Conor, to offer 'to become his man and hold Leinster of him'. This proposal was adopted, and the Archbishop Laurence O'Toole,[10] accompanied by Maurice de Prendergast, was sent to the King of Connaught with the message. Rory O'Conor, however, confident in his strength, would have none of these terms. He was willing indeed to leave to Strongbow the cities the Norsemen had hitherto held, Dublin, Waterford, and Wexford, but not another rood of ground in all Ireland would he give them, and, he added, that if the earl did not accept this offer he would assault the city on the morrow.

[228] On hearing this reply the bold course was adopted to sally forth and attack the camp of the King of Connaught. It might seem a forlorn hope, but it was better than to be starved to death cooped up within the walls of the town, and there was Fitz Stephen's peril to be remembered. Gerald de Barry here puts into the mouth of his uncle a speech which, though it probably represents correctly enough the motives and feelings of the besieged garrison, need not here be given at length. One bitter sentence, however, is so remarkable at this early date, and has been so applicable to the English

Ua Maelseachlainn (O'Melaghlin), King of Meath; and *Ocadesi*, i.e. Ua Cathasaigh (O'Casey), lord of Saithne. Tirowen, Tirconnell, Desmond, and Ossory seem to be the only important districts not represented. The Song of Dermot, l. 1753, says *seisant*[*e*] *mil*[*e*] *erent armez*, but as already mentioned (*supra*, p. 77 [p. 24]), this phrase merely means 'a very large number'. 8 This is the statement as given by Giraldus, p. 266. According to the Song of Dermot (ll. 1790), Donnell Kavanagh told the earl of Fitz Stephen's actual capture and imprisonment. This may be correct; in which case Strongbow's subsequent march towards Wexford was undertaken in the hope of forcing his captors 'to liberate the imprisoned Robert' (l. 2023). 9 Gir. Camb., vol. v, p. 266, where Raymond is said to have just returned from court, i.e. from his mission to Henry II. Two of the sons of Maurice Fitz Gerald, Gerald and Alexander, were also in Dublin (Gir. Camb., p. 268). His wife and younger children appear to have been left under the care of Fitz Stephen (ibid., p. 266). After l. 1802, in the transcript of the Song of Dermot, one or more lines are missing, and *Morice le fiz Gerout* and *le gros Reymun* may have been mentioned here. 10 The presence of Laurence O'Toole in the beleaguered city, and his undertaking this mission of peace, discredit his alleged zeal in organizing the hosting against the Normans. After all, Giraldus merely mentions this antagonistic zeal as a report (*ut ferebatur*), and we may venture to disbelieve it. The archbishop is not mentioned in the Irish verisons.

colony almost at any time in the centuries that have since elapsed, that I cannot forbear quoting it: 'What are we waiting for?' he exclaims, 'Are we looking for help from our own people? Nay, such is our position, that to the Irish we are Englishmen, and to the English, Irishmen.'[11]

Accordingly, three companies of about 200 men each, under the command of Miles de Cogan, Raymond le Gros, and Earl Richard respectively, prepared for an immediate sortie.[12] Each company consisted of about 30 or 40 knights on horseback, 60 bow- [229] men, and 100 foot-soldiers In addition there were a few Irishmen under Donnell Kavanagh, and some of the citizens of Dublin. A sufficient guard had, of course, to be left in the town. Crossing the Liffey, perhaps by the wicker bridge erected by the Norsemen, Miles, who led the little band, set out rapidly towards Finglas. This is still the name of a little village about three miles nearly north of Dublin. It is the site of an ancient abbey ascribed to St. Cainnech. Here they turned to attack Rory's camp at Castleknock, about three miles to the south-west. The object of the tour seems to have been to surprise the camp and take it in the flank. At any rate, the huge disorderly force was quite unprepared for an attack, and was soon put to utter rout. The king himself is said to have been bathing, we may suppose in the Liffey hard by, and to have barely escaped.[13] The pursuit lasted till evening, when the victors returned to the city, [230] laden with victuals and spoils. It was an astounding victory. Rory's army is said to have numbered 30,000 men, and they were utterly discomfited by a tiny band of a few hundreds. Allowing for gross exaggeration in the former figure, the result shows what superior arms and discipline can do. The effect was immediate and far-reaching. The remaining armies to the north and south of Dublin at once dispersed in terror, and Rory O'Conor never made another attempt to oust the foreigners from Dublin.

Having thus effectually raised the siege, Earl Richard delivered Dublin to the custody of Miles de Cogan, and straightway set out for the relief of Fitz Stephen. He took the upper road to the west of the Wicklow Mountains, through the present counties of Kildare and Carlow.

The present county of Wexford is girt round by natural obstacles, formidable to a twelfth-century invader. Washed on the south and east by the sea, it was protected on the north by a difficult hill and forest region, while on the west it is cut off by a high mountain range and a deep river. As we have seen, when O'Conor came to attack Dermot Mac Murrough in 1166 and again in 1167, he forced the pass through 'the Dark Wood' on the north leading from the Fotharta, now the barony of Forth, County [231]

11 'Ea jam lege tenemur, ut sicut Hibernicis Angli sic et Anglis Hibernici simus,' Gir. Camb., p. 267; cf. Camb. Eversus, vol. iii, p. 167. The allusion, no doubt, was to Henry's embargo, and perhaps to the unfavourable report brought back by Raymond. 12 The two accounts of this sortie agree substantially even in many details, but it is characteristic of Gerald that he speaks of Raymond as being in the foremost company and the first to make the attack, while the Song clearly shows that Miles de Cogan was in the van and in command of the whole force. 13 'Rotherico vero, qui tunc forte in balneis sedebat, vix elapso,' Gir. Camb., p. 269. The Song, ll. 1949–50, says, ' A hundred and more were slain while bathing where they were beset.' The Annals of Tigernach, however, state that O'Conor had 'marched to meet the Leinstermen (what Leinstermen (?) and the cavalry of Breffny and Uriel went to cut down the Englishmen's corn', when 'the Earl and Miles de Cogan entered the camp of Leth Cuinn and killed a multitude of their rabble, and carried off their provisions, their armour, and their sumpter-horses'.

Carlow. From this southwards to the Barrow there are only two narrow gates through the range of mountains. One, the Pass of Pollmounty, at the south end of the range, where a little stream makes its way to join the Barrow. Here it was that Donnell Kavanagh endeavoured to arrest the desertion of Maurice de Prendergast in 1169. The other, Scollagh Gap, a high defile leading from Odrone (now the barony of Idrone) between Mount Leinster and Blackstairs into Okinselagh. This last appears to have been the entrance towards which Strongbow was marching, and here, in the 'Pass of Odrone', as it is called by Giraldus, he was opposed by O'Ryan, chieftain of the district, who had formed a barricade of fallen trees across the narrow route.[14] A
[232] sharp engagement followed, in which O'Ryan was killed by an arrow shot by a monk named Nichol, and Meiler Fitz Henry was stunned by the blow of a stone. These incidents, trivial as they are, help us to understand the extraordinary success of the invaders against almost any odds. The Irish had no weapon of greater precision or more deadly effect than a stone[15] with which to reply to an arrow dealing death from afar. When their leader fell, the Irish dispersed, and the earl and his men got safely through the defile and descended towards Wexford to succour Fitz Stephen.[16]

We must now turn for a moment to Fitz Stephen, to see how he had fared while these events were in progress. At the time of the rising he was in Wexford. He sent a small force, about thirty-six of his men, to aid Earl Richard in Dublin, but he soon found himself obliged to abandon Wexford and shut himself up in his newly constructed 'castle' at Carrick on Slaney.[17] We can identify this spot with confidence, and
[233] from the site and the contemporary descriptions we can form an idea of this, the first Norman castle erected in Ireland. It was situated on high ground on the right or south bank of the Slaney, just before the river widens into a shallow estuary. On the side next the river the rock descends precipitously, but on the land side there is a gradual ascent. A level space on the top—shaped approximately like a gibbous moon, with dimensions of about 130 x 90 feet—is now cut off by a high earthen vallum and wide fosse. Fitz Stephen's fortress is described by Giraldus as 'an ill fortified camp, weakly enclosed with a wooden palisade and a rampart of earth.'[18] It probably, therefore, did not con-

14 This identification, though new, is, I think, tolerably certain. Gerald tells us (p. 270) that the earl marched from Dublin towards Wexford *superiore per Odronam via,* and that the army of the Leinstermen met him in *passu Odronae, quanquam in sui natura arcto nimis et invio, concidibus tamen plurimum arte munto*, and that after the fight the earl *ad campana indemnis evasit* (p. 272), and he speaks of the force as descending to the territory of Wexford. (p. 273). This all points to Scollagh Gap as the scene of the fight. In fact, even at the present day, it is the only route between the barony of Idrone and the County Wexford. There are indeed no trees in the actual defile, but on the approach to it from the west there is a natural wood, called Coonogue wood, which very probably in the twelfth century closed the entrance. The Song (l. 2018) says the wood was afterwards called 'the Earl's pass', but this name has been forgotten. 15 Gerald notices the dexterity of the Irish at hurling by hand *lapides pugillares*; see *supra*, chap. iv, p. 134 [p. 46]. 16 The authorities for the fight in the Pass of Odrone are the Song, ll. 1967–2020; Gir. Camb. v. 270–2. 17 The authorities for the siege of Carrick are Giraldus, pp. 270–3, and Song of Dermot, ll. 1768–97. 18 'Municipium immunitissimum virgis tenuiter et cespite clausum,' Gir. Camb., p. 266. He also mentions its *fossata* (p. 270). For proofs of this identification, a description and plan of the site, and its subsequent history, see a contribution by the present writer to Hore's Hist. of Wexford, pp. 22–34. The site is now marked by a Crimean monument resembling (from a distance) an ancient Insh Round Tower.

tain a mote or mound of earth within. It was rather a kind of 'promontory castle', strong by nature along one curved side and strengthened by art on the other. Within this enclosure a wooden tower (*bretesche* or *turris lignea*) was probably erected. From it a small body of resolute archers could keep a large force of unarmoured men for some time at bay.

For some days indeed Fitz Stephen, with only five men-at-arms and a few archers, successfully resisted every attack; but at length the assailants succeeded in obtaining his [234] surrender by the weapons of deceit and perjury. The Bishops of Wexford and Kildare, and other persons in religious garb, says Giraldus, came up to the entrenchments, and all most solemnly took their oaths on holy relics that Dublin had fallen, that the earl, Fitz Gerald, Raymond, and all the English had been slain, and that the hosts of Connaught and Leinster were marching on Wexford. They further protested that they were acting in Fitz Stephen's interest, in order that they might send him and his men safe to Wales before the arrival of his enemies. Giving credence to these asseverations, Fitz Stephen surrendered, whereupon his treacherous assailants killed some of his men, ill-treated the rest with wounds and blows, and flung the survivors into prison.

News of this disaster met the earl when descending into the territory about Wexford. He also learnt that the inhabitants had burned the town and had put their prisoners on the island of Beg-erin.[19] They further threatened that if he should dare to come near them they would send him the severed heads of his friends. Checkmated [235] here, the earl in much bitterness of spirit turned to Waterford, where the garrison had held its own.

Strongbow now set about securing his position as Dermot's successor in Leinster. This he aimed at accomplishing rather by diplomacy, backed where needful by a show of strength, than by actual fighting. First of all, he organized an expedition against Donnell Mac Gillapatrick, King of Ossory. Ossory was by far the most important of the sub-kingdoms nominally subject to the King of Leinster. Indeed, more often than not it was practically independent, and in recent times its king had been frequently at war with King Dermot. Since the coming of the Normans more than one hazardous expedition had been made into Ossory without any permanent result. Obviously Strongbow needed all available strength to overawe its king. Accordingly he invited Donnell O'Brien, King of Thomond, to join the expedition. This prince, having married a daughter of Dermot Mac Murrough, was connected with the earl; but he is found at one time fighting on his side, and at another time against him, in a somewhat bewildering fashion.[20] Fitz Stephen had assisted him in driving Rory O'Conor out of [236] Thomond in 1170, but in 1171 O'Brien had to give hostages to the *ard-rí*, and we find

19 Begerin or Begery is, or rather was, a small island in Wexford harbour associated with St. Ibhar. It is now joined to the mainland by reclamation. It contains the ruins of a small church and some ancient cross-inscribed stones. 20 Donnell O'Brien seems to have supported Strongbow's claim to succeed Dermot MacMurrough in Leinster, but to have resisted him—at this period at least—when he sought to extend his conquests beyond the limits of that kingdom. Perhaps he was for accepting the offer Strongbow made when besieged in Dublin, and separated from the *ard-rí* on that account. This supposition would help to explain the dispersal of Rory's host and O'Brien's present alliance with Strongbow.

him accompanying the *ard-rí* in the great hosting against the earl in Dublin. Now he came with about 2,000 men to aid Strongbow against the King of Ossory. They met at Odoth (Ir. *ui Duach*), a district roughly corresponding to the barony of Fassadinin, in the County Kilkenny. Here the King of Ossory came to a parley with them under the safe-conduct of his former friend, Maurice de Prendergast. O'Brien's counsel was to seize the King of Ossory as a traitor, and the barons seemed willing to agree; when Maurice de Prendergast intervened, upbraided the barons with being false to their oaths, and 'swore by his sword' that he would kill the first man that laid his hand on the king. Then, Strongbow delivered up Mac Gillapatrick to Maurice de Prendergast, and Maurice brought him back in safety to his woody fastness, slaying on the way some of O'Brien's men who were pillaging the land. This story, which redounds to the credit of Maurice de Prendergast, is told with considerable detail in the Song of
[237] Dermot.[21] It ends with an interesting legal incident. The barons accused Maurice of having rescued a traitor, whereupon—

> 'Maurice folded his glove and gave it to his lord as a pledge that he would redress in his court whatever transgression he had committed. And the renowned English vassals went sufficient security for him.'

The expedition then broke up. O'Brien went back to Limerick, and the earl to Ferns. Here, at the seat of the old royal power, Strongbow was more successful in establishing himself as Dermot's successor. With the aid of Donnell Kavanagh, he captured a neighbouring petty chieftain who had deserted and repudiated Dermot in 1166, and now refused allegiance to Strongbow. He seems to have been Murrough O'Brain of the Duffry,[22] a woody district lying between Enniscorthy and the mountains to the west. He and his son were beheaded and their bodies thrown to dogs. On
[238] the other hand, a much more important personage, Murtough MacMurrough, son of Dermot's brother, Murrough 'of the Irish', came to terms with the earl. He, like his father before him, was acknowledged as King of Okinselagh by those tribesmen of the territory who had fallen away from Dermot, and those who after Dermot's death had refused to acknowledge Strongbow. The earl is now said to have 'granted to him the kingdom of Okinselagh', and at the same time to have 'bailled the pleas of Leinster to Donnell Kavanagh'.[23] By these expressions I think we must understand that Strongbow at this time granted a large portion of the district of Okinselagh to Murtough, perhaps to be held as a sort of fief under him on quasi-feudal terms, and that Donnell Kavanagh was appointed as an Irish seneschal with jurisdiction over pleas between Irishmen in Leinster. Even if no formal charter or grant was executed, some such

21 ll. 2035–154. Probably, as we shall see, Donnell Mac Gillapatrick was left in possession of a large part of Central Ossory. We shall find him later on assisting the English. 22 Song of Dermot, ll. 2161–80; cf. ll. 141 and 3215 and notes. The name was not, however, anglicized O'Brien, but O'Brin and (later) O'Breen. O'Dubhagain places the Siol Brain in the Duffry (Topog. Poems, p. 91), and probably the very individuals, 'Murchad Uabrain' and 'Dalbach' his son, are among the witnesses to a charter of Dermot Mac Murrough: Fac. Nat. MSS. Ireland, pt. 2, pl. lxiii. 23 Song of Dermot, ll. 2181–8.

arrangement seems to have been made. For though a very full list is afterwards given of the fiefs created by Strongbow in Leinster, it will be observed that a large portion of what was then known as the kingdom of Okinselagh was not distributed among his Norman and Welsh followers, and that this portion, though afterwards perhaps somewhat encroached upon, remained for centuries distinctively Irish, and was not planted with colonists in the same way as the parts granted to his followers were. Moreover, a [239]
few years later we are expressly told that Murtough Mac Murrough and Donnell Kavanagh, as well as most of the other Leinster chieftains, were on Strongbow's side, and had given him hostages for their fidelity. Murtough Mac Murrough is styled lord of Okinselagh in the entry in the Irish Annals recording his death, which occurred in 1193, and Donnell Kavanagh was killed by two Irishmen in 1175. There is nothing to show that they were not faithful to the English to the last.[24]

It was probably after Strongbow had left Dublin upon the dispersal of Rory O'Conor's army, and before the arrival of Henry II in Ireland (October 18), that Dublin was the object of two separate attacks.[25] The first was headed by Tiernan O'Rourke, and consisted of the men of Breffny and Uriel, and the second was an attempt to regain the town by Haskulf Mac Thorkil, the former Norse governor. The glory of successfully resisting both these attempts belonged primarily to Miles de [240]
Cogan, to whom Earl Richard had entrusted the custody of the city when he, with most of the leading Normans, departed. The attack by O'Rourke's army was met by de Cogan outside the walls 'on the green of Ath-cliath', when a number of chiefs were killed, including O'Rourke's son, royal heir (*rigdamna*) of Breffny.[26] Haskulf's attempt to recover his patrimony, which perhaps preceded this last, was a much more formidable affair, and is told in great detail and with evident local knowledge in the Song of Dermot.[27] Haskulf had collected a large fleet of sea-rovers from Norway and 'the islands' (Orkneys and Hebrides, and the Isle of Man), and he had the assistance of a noted berserker, John 'the Wode', or the Mad, said to be nephew of the King of Norway.[28] It is probable that Haskulf's expedition was originally planned to synchronize with O'Conor's hosting, but, happily perhaps for the Norman invaders, he came [241]
too late. 'At the Steine' they landed and encamped, preparatory to attacking the city. The Steine was the name of an open piece of land to the east of the city, extending southwards from the Liffey. It was so called from a Menhir or Standing Stone, probably erected by the Northmen in days gone by at their landing-place. On part of this

24 When, about a century later, in the accounts of the minister of Roger Bigod, Earl of Norfolk, we get a detailed picture of Anglo-Norman organization in this district, we find that fees were paid to the chief of the Mc Murroughs and to his brother, and that robes (the earl's livery) were given to them as to other officers of the earl. They were evidently left in possession of considerable tracts of land in North Wexford and Southern Carlow, and lived on good terms with the earl. 25 For the time when the Norse attack took place see note at the close of this chapter. 26 Ann. Tigernach, Ann. Ulster, 1171, where the editor has wrongly punctuated the passage, the date '16th of the Kalends of November' obviously referring to Henry's arrival. Giraldus dates this attack *circa Kalendas Septembris* (p. 274). It is not mentioned in the Song. 27 Song of Dermot, ll. 2255–492. Cf. Gir. Camb. v. 263–5; Ann. Tigernach, Ann. Ulster, 1171. 28 Song of Dermot, ll. 2264–8; John (the Mad) from the islands of Orc, Ann. Ulster, 1171; 'duce Johanne agnomine the Wode, quod Latine sonat Insano vel Vehementi,' Gir. Camb., p. 264.

piece of land, where Trinity College now stands, stood the priory of All Hallows, founded by Dermot MacMurrough. Miles de Cogan now made preparations to resist the attack. First we are told of an amusing parley between him and Donnell Mac Gillamocholmog. The latter was petty king of a district close to Dublin on the south, and knew well what he had to expect if he opposed unsuccessfully Haskulf's return. He had, indeed, joined Rory O'Conor's abortive hosting against the Normans in Dublin a little earlier in the summer, but on the dispersal of the Irish forces he had made peace with Miles and had given him hostages. Probably Miles was not very confident of his fidelity, and preferred not to have him within the walls. Accordingly he said to him: 'I will return you your hostages on these conditions, that you stand aside and watch the coming battle, aiding neither us nor them, but if with God's help we discomfit these men, then that you and your force aid us to overthrow them; while if
[242] we be recreant, that you aid them with all your might in cutting us to pieces and destroying us.' This advice suited Gillamocholmog exactly, so he placed himself with his men outside the city, on the summit of the 'hogges' or Howe overlooking the Steine. This was an artificial mound, the existence of which on Hoggen Green, a little to the south of the entrance to Trinity College, up to the year 1685 is well attested.[29]

John the Wode advanced with his men in well-ordered ranks towards the city. It was a very different army from Rory's undisciplined, ill-armed host. They were 'born warriors, in Danish fashion completely clad in iron; some in long coats of mail, others with iron plates cunningly fastened to their tunics, and all bearing round shields painted red and rimmed with iron. Men with iron hearts as well as iron arms'.[30] We do not read that they had bows, but they carried formidable battleaxes. To meet such men Miles and his little garrison had need of all their courage and resource.

The attack was delivered against the eastern gate of the city, called Saint Mary's Gate. Its site is well known. The church of St. Mary del Dam stood outside the walls close to it—so-called from a mill-dam on a little stream, the Poddle, now built over.
[243] The gate was afterwards known as Damas Gate, and the street leading up to it Damas Street, now refined in pronunciation into Dame Street. It was the direct route from the Steine. While the Norsemen were advancing towards the eastern gate, Miles de Cogan secretly dispatched his brother Richard with a small force of thirty horsemen out of a gate on the opposite side of the town, directing him to make a detour and fall upon the camp of the enemy in the rear. At the same time he manned the battlemented wall with archers and men with darts to resist the attack. While the assault was going on, Richard de Cogan fell upon the camp unexpectedly, and John the Wode, hearing the noise and the shouting in his rear, turned back to succour his men. Then Miles made a sortie with 300 men, and took the enemy in the rear as they were engaged with his brother Richard. In vain did John the Wode perform prodigies of valour, lopping off with one blow of his mighty battleaxe the armoured leg of a horseman, and killing nine or ten of the English. Taken in front and rear at the same time, the Norsemen fled for their ships. Now was the time for Gillamocholmog to join in on

29 See the Scandinavian Kingdom of Dublin, by C. Halliday, pp. 162–6. **30** Gir. Camb., vol. v, p. 264.

the winning side. 'Up now, brave sirs!' he shouted to his men, 'Let us aid the rightful English! Up now quickly. To good Richard and Miles we shall bring aid!' And thereupon the Irish, with javelins and darts, rushed upon the flying foe. Many were killed on the field, and many were drowned while endeavouring to reach their ships. John the [244] Wode was slain, and Haskulf was taken prisoner. The latter, it is said, might have ransomed his life, had it not been for his reckless outburst before Miles in the justice-hall to which he had been brought. 'We came this time,' he cried, 'a small band, but it is only the beginning. If I live, we shall soon return in much greater numbers.' This audacious speech cost him his head.

NOTE TO CHAPTER VII, pp. 82 and 88 [223 and 239] [245]

The time of the Norse attack on Dublin

With regard to the time at which the Norse attack took place, the authorities conflict. Giraldus places it 'about Pentecost' (May 16), before Rory's siege (p. 263 [97]), while the Song (l. 2256) says it occurred while Strongbow 'was with his lord', i.e. about the middle of September. For reasons partly given in the notes to the Song, I incline to think the sequence there observed was the true one. The narrative in the Song for the period from Dermot's death to the landing of Henry is more continuous and much fuller in its details than that of Giraldus. It reads like the story of an eyewitness throughout, and wherever it can be tested it appears to be accurate. It follows Strongbow's movements, and accounts for both his absence and that of Fitz Stephen from Dublin at the time of the Norse attack. Also the sequence there given harmonizes with the changed attitude of Gillamocholmog on the two occasions. Moreover, where actual documents dated at the time are not available, a date fixed approximately by reference to another event is more likely to be correct than a precise date given by such a writer as Giraldus (with whom chronology was a weak point) many years after the event. Furthermore, the order preserved in the Song seems to explain the long inactivity of Rory O'Conor and his allies before Dublin. They must have been waiting for something before attempting a serious assault, and [246] this 'something' may well have been the arrival of Haskulf. It would be strange if, when seeking for assistance from Godred, King of Man, and the wikings of the islands, they had omitted to communicate with Haskulf, the dispossessed lord of Dublin, to whose aid they had come in the preceding autumn. But Haskulf may well have been late, and the intended combination upset by Strongbow's brilliant sortie. Thus the order of events as given in the Song seems to explain much that is hard to account for if we suppose that order reversed. On the other hand, it must be noted that in the Annals of Tigernach, followed by the Four Masters, the entry as to Haskulf's attack precedes that as to Rory's siege, but these entries are quite independent of each other, and entries in the annals do not always follow the chronological order. Thus, for example, in 1169, the Four Masters record the death of Dermot O'Melaghlin, King of Meath, and afterwards mention him as accompanying O'Conor hosting into Okinselagh.

[247] CHAPTER VIII

HENRY II IN IRELAND, 1171–2

Before the summer of 1171 was ended Strongbow was master of the three principal seaport towns of Ireland, namely, Dublin, Waterford, and Wexford, and partly by arms and partly by diplomacy had done much to strengthen his position as Dermot's successor in Leinster. He had successfully repelled all outside attempts, whether Norse or Irish, to oust him from his position, and by the power and prestige of his arms, aided by the wisdom of his policy, he had won the acquiescence of the principal tribes of Leinster to his rule. He knew well, however, that there was another and a more formidable power with which he must reckon before he could hope to secure to himself the fruits of his conquest. It was in defiance of Henry's express orders that he had set sail a year previously from Milford Haven, and his lands at home had in consequence been taken from him by the king. He had been sorely hampered in his operations by
[248] Henry's embargo, which had effectually prevented him from getting adequate supplies and reinforcements in the spring of the year. He had then sent Raymond on a fruitless embassy to endeavour to gain the King's favour to his expedition, and on Raymond's return with dispiriting news, just before the great attempt to overwhelm the invaders in Dublin, he had dispatched his uncle, Hervey de Montmorency, on a second embassy with the same object. Hervey appears to have found Henry at Argentan, in the act of holding a council of his barons with reference to his proposed expedition to Ireland. This was in the month of July. Hervey offered on the part of the earl to surrender to the king the cities of Dublin and Waterford, and the other strongholds which the earl held in right of his wife, and the king, we are told, promised on his doing so to restore to the earl his lands in England (Wales) and Normandy, to leave him in possession of the rest of what he had acquired by his marriage, and to appoint him constable or seneschal of Ireland.[1] We may, however, doubt if the terms of the arrangement were quite so definitely fixed at this time. For when Hervey returned to Ireland, early in September, he came with the news that the king was on his way to Ireland with a large army, and, whatever the nature of his report may have been, he
[249] strongly urged the earl to cross the channel and meet the king. Accordingly the earl at once set sail, and found the king either at Newnham in Gloucestershire, where he had already mustered a considerable army,[2] or at Pembroke.

1 Robert of Torigny, p. 252, where, however, the names of the ambassadors are not mentioned. 2 Gir. Camb., vol. v, p. 273. According to the Song (l. 2230) the earl found Henry at Pembroke, and this may be right. According to the Brut, Henry entered Wales soon after September 8, and reached Pembroke on the 21st, where, or at St. Davids, he stayed until October 16, when he sailed for Ireland: cf. Eyton's Itin. The

The time was indeed in many respects opportune for Henry to make his long meditated expedition to Ireland. If he were to claim the benefit of Strongbow's conquests, to make Strongbow's proffered submission to him a reality, and to take advantage of the opening thus afforded to obtain the submission of the still independent Irish kings, now was the time for him to act. Moreover, an expedition to Ireland at this moment would gain him a respite from the meeting with the cardinal legates who had been dispatched by the Pope to deal with Henry's supposed complicity in the murder of Becket. Time would dull the edge of the horror which all Christendom felt on hearing of the archbishop's tragic end, and Henry, as the acknowledged lord of Ireland, would be in a bet- [250]
ter position to make terms with the Pope. True, he could not at this moment enter Ireland masquerading as a sort of crusader, and, with the blessing of the present occupant of the Holy See, professing to reform the moral iniquities of that country. But he might do something there to bring about a closer conformity with the Church of Rome, and the papal blessing and sanction would be sure to follow. Accordingly, in July he held a council of the barons at Argentan, and obtained their approval of his Irish expedition.[3] Early in August he landed at Portsmouth, having left orders with the bailiffs of the ports on both sides of the channel to prevent any papal envoys from following him.[4] Then he made preparations for the assembling of a fleet of the chivalry of England somewhere near the Welsh border, probably at Newnham in Gloucestershire, where, according to Gerald de Barry, Strongbow is said to have met him.

According to Gerald, too, it was only after much altercation, and by the address of Hervey, that the royal ire was appeased: the earl undertaking to surrender to the king Dublin and the neighbouring cantreds, the other maritime towns, and all castles, and to renew the oath of fealty for the rest of his conquests. These terms do not appear to [251]
differ essentially from those offered on the earl's behalf at the council of Argentan. They included, however, the surrender not only of the towns of Dublin, Waterford, and Wexford, but also of the lands now comprised in the county of Dublin and the littoral as far south as Arklow. So far as appears, there were no stonebuilt castles to surrender, except perhaps a Norse stronghold at Wicklow.[5] By these terms, as one writer notices,[6] Strongbow was indeed giving up the more valuable portions of his conquest; but he was left in possession of an extensive fief, now to be held of the king; while if Henry was to exercise any control over the adventurers, and to extend his domination, as he hoped, over the unconquered parts of Ireland, it was absolutely essential for him to hold the seaport towns in his own hands. This important question having been thus satisfactorily settled, Henry pursued the coast road which led through South Wales [252]
towards St. Davids.

later date for the meeting would seem to suit Strongbow's movements as recorded in the Song best. On the other hand, Gerald is precise in his mention of the place, which, at any rate, was probably the muster-ground of the feudal host. 3 Robert of Torigny, 1171. 4 Gesta Hen., vol. i, p. 24. 5 'The Castellum Wikingelonense is spoken of as already in existence in the summer of 1173, when it, together with the town of Wexford, was granted by Henry to Earl Richard: Gir. Camb., vol. v, p. 298. It was perhaps a Scandinavian stronghold occupying the site of the Black Castle at Wicklow. on a rocky point jutting out into the sea immediately south of the harbour. See Eng. Hist. Rev. 1907, p. 250. The castle, however, is not mentioned in Strongbow's grant of Wicklow to Maurice Fitz Gerald: Gormanston Register, f. 190. 6 William of Newburgh, vol. i, p. 168.

Six years had elapsed since Henry's last expedition into Wales, when he was beaten back from the rocks of Berwyn by the ceaseless rain, and Rhys, the Prince of South Wales, was now much perturbed at his approach. Probably he had been summoned to the muster-ground at Newnham; at any rate he hastened to meet Henry, whose goodwill he was anxious to secure.[7] Ireland, however, was now Henry's objective, and he had no intention of frittering away his strength in Wales. Moreover, it was important for him to secure the peaceful passage of his army along the route to Pembroke, and Rhys was easily able to purchase his goodwill by a promise of 300 horses and 4,000 cows, and an undertaking to give him hostages for good behaviour. Ultimately, indeed, Henry took only 36 horses, saying that 'it was not for want of them they were accepted, but to express his thanks to Rhys', and he gave him time as to the delivery of hostages and the rest of the promised tribute. Rhys had indeed reason to view with satisfaction Henry's expedition. He had found that the previous Irish expeditions had
[253] relieved him of the presence of several of his most dangerous rivals and of their supporters, thus enabling him to consolidate his power. He had just built 'a castle of stone and mortar' at Aberteivi (Cardigan), to replace the Norman structure which he had demolished when he captured its constable, Robert Fitz Stephen, as already mentioned. He also held Cilgerran Castle, perched on a rock hard by. And now Henry, so far from making him restore these places to the de Clares, regularized his position by giving him, according to the Welsh Chronicle, the whole district of Ceredigion, now Cardiganshire, the vale of the Towy, and other debatable lands.[8] While showing this favour to the native prince, Henry, with real or assumed anger, threatened the Norman barons of South Wales for having given Earl Richard a passage through to Ireland, but, except that he put royal garrisons into their castles, nothing came of his threats.[9] As we shall see, it was Henry's cue throughout this expedition to appear as the friend of the natives, Welsh and Irish, and the stern represser of the Anglo-Norman march-
[254] lords; his real object being to secure the control of the Crown over both.

Henry reached Pembroke about September 21. After a few days he went on the usual pilgrimage to St. Davids, and made an offering at the shrine. Here, attended by Earl Richard and some others, he was informally entertained on Michaelmas Day by the bishop, David Fitz Gerald. Shortly after dinner he mounted horse and returned to Pembroke in heavy rain.[10] The distance from St. Davids to Pembroke is sixteen miles over a very hilly country. We cannot wonder that Henry's suite found his extraordinary activity irksome at times.[11]

Henry was detained at Pembroke for seventeen days longer by unfavourable winds. While he was there a deputation came from the men of Wexford to announce to him

7 According to the Brut y Tywys., p. 21l, Henry, giving out that he would go and subdue Ireland, 'convoked to him all the princes of England and Wales.' Accordingly Rhys went to meet him about September 8. 8 Brut y Tywys. 1171, where a detailed account is given of Henry's movements in Wales and of his interviews with Rhys. 9 Gir. Camb., vol. v, p. 274. The account here given of Henry's anger towards the *proceres* of South Wales seems to confirm the statement of William of Newburgh that Henry had expressly forbidden Strongbow's expedition. 10 Brut y Tywys., p. 215. To avoid an excess of expense to the bishop, Henry declined a formal banquet, and the company, we are told, 'dined standing.' 11 For the view taken by Henry's clerks of his restless activity see Norgate's Angevin Kings, vol. i, p. 411.

that they had captured 'his felon', Robert Fitz Stephen, who had often, they said, waged war against him in Wales and in England, and had lately come to Ireland to destroy their country. They had put him in prison, and would give him up to the king to deal with according to his pleasure. Evidently they were anxious to curry favour with the powerful king now approaching their shores. Henry assured them of his [255] favour, provided they surrendered their prisoner to him to deal with. His anger against Fitz Stephen was assumed, we are told, to ensure the prisoner's safe delivery into his hands,[12] but Henry was also anxious to impress the Irish with the idea that he was coming as their friend and protector.

On October 16, all being ready and the wind at last favourable, the king embarked 'at the Cross' below Pembroke,[13] and landed next day at Crook, near Waterford, the exact landing-place being probably the ferry-point now called Passage, about a mile [256] from the old church of Crook,[14] and five miles from Waterford. His army consisted of five hundred knights and their esquires, and a large body of archers, about 4,000 in all.[15] A fleet of 400 ships was required to transport the men with their horses, arms, and provisions.[16] Among the knights who accompanied Henry were William Fitz Audelin, the king's dapifer, Humphrey de Bohun, his constable, Hugh de Lacy, Robert Fitz Bernard, sheriff of Devon, and Bertram de Verdun.[17]

Henry's army seems to have consisted almost entirely of English tenants in [257] chivalry. Many of the tenants in chief, however, sent money instead of men for the Irish expedition, and there are many entries in the Pipe Rolls concerning the scutage, at the rate of £1 per knight's fee, of those who neither went to Ireland nor sent men or money there.[18] The Pipe Rolls show further how this army was supplied during the

12 Song of Dermot, ll. 2497–578. Perhaps this was the embassy alluded to by Gervase of Canterbury (vol. i, p. 235). He says that the Irish sent ambassadors to Henry in 1171, to ask him to take over the lordship of the country and relieve them from the aggression of Earl Richard: 'ut in Hiberniam veniret, eisque contra importunitatem Ricardi comitis succurreret, sibique dominium Hiberniae assumeret.' The deputation of the *traiterez duzze de Weyseford* seems to have been distinct from the embassy composed of Murtough Mac Murrough and the burgesses of Wexford, mentioned in the account of the Sheriff of Winevhester: Pipe Roll, 19 Hen. II (1172–3). They appear to have gone as far as Winchester, where they were entertained at the king's expense, and presented with six robes, costing the considerable sum of £10 14*s*. 11*d*. 13 Song of Dermot, l. 2590: *a la Croiz en mer entra*. This appears to have been the usual place of embarkation. John, too, in 1210, embarked *apud Crucem super mare, subtus Penbroc*: Rot. de Prest., 12 John, pp. 177, 246. The place is probably now occupied by Pembroke Dock on Milford Haven. It is not mentioned in other accounts of Henry's embarkation, and is thus an indication of the independence and accuracy of the Song. 14 Gesta Hen., vol. i, p. 25; Rog. Howden, vol. ii, p. 29: *apud Oroch*. This is the Irish *Cruach*, now represented by Crook, a parish which adjoins the landing-place at Passage. 15 Giraldus says 'cum militibus quasi quingentis, arcariis (*v.l.* satellitibus equestribus) quoque et sagittariis multis.' The Song says *quatre cent chevalers*, and gives the total, *quatre mil Engleis*. 16 Gesta Hen., vol. i, p. 25; Rog. Howden, vol. ii. 17 This list is given in the Song of Dermot, ll. 2601–10. According to the Gesta Hen. and Rog. Howden (*ut supra*), William Fitz Audelin and Robert Fitz Bernard had been sent to Ireland some time before and met Henry at Waterford. But we find both of these individuals witnessing a charter at Pembroke on October 7, 1171 (Round's Commune of London, p. 152), so that at most they can only have preceded the king by a few days. To the above list we may add from the witnesses to Henry's Dublin charter, William de Braose, Reginald de Curtenay, Hugh de Gunderville, Randulph de Glanville, Hugh de Cressy, and Reginald de Pavilly; and from Henry's charter to Hugh de Lacy, William de Albiny, William de Stoteville, Ralph de Verdun, William de Gerpunville (the king's falconer), and Robert de Ruilly. 18 In the Pipe Roll, 18 Hen.

six months of Henry's stay in Ireland. From almost all parts of England large quantities of wheat, oats, beans, cheeses, and hogs were forwarded, with canvas to cover the corn, and hand-mills to grind it. A moderate sum was spent on wine, part of which was bought in Waterford, and a few horses were sent, the feudal tenants of course supplying their own mounts. Engineering tools were also brought over in large quantities, viz. axes, spades, shovels, pickaxes, planks, nails, and a few *castella lignea* or ready-made wooden towers. For the king's own use the royal tent was conveyed to Ireland, also wearing apparel, skins, silks, cloths, 1,000 lb. of wax for his charters and other
[258] documents, and spices and electuaries for Joseph, his doctor. Most of these supplies were shipped from Bristol.

Though at the head of an imposing force, Henry did not come with the intention of forcibly imposing his rule over the Irish. The late period of the year would alone indicate that no extensive campaign was meditated. He came to regulate the conquests that had already been made by his subjects, to secure the supremacy of the Crown over them and their lands, and to receive the submission of as many of the remaining independent Irish princes as could be induced to come in.

On the day following his landing in Ireland, being St. Luke's Day, Henry entered Waterford, and there Strongbow formally surrendered the city to him and did homage for Leinster, which the king granted to him in fee.[19] The deed evidencing this grant is not forthcoming, but if we may judge from the copies of the grant of Meath to Hugh de Lacy, executed a few months later, it was made without any express reservations and was deemed at the time to confer cognizance of all pleas. In accordance with the terms arranged at Newnham, the lands granted did not include Dublin, nor the adjacent territory, nor the littoral as far south as Arklow, nor the town of Wexford. These
[259] lands, together with Waterford, were reserved by the king, and formed the original demesne of the Crown in Ireland. The rest of Leinster (excluding, of course, the 'kingdom of Meath'), probably defined 'as Dermot Mac Murrough held it', was to be held of the king and his heirs by the service of 100 knights. Henceforth Strongbow and his heirs were to hold the lordship of Leinster not on any fictitious Irish title, but as tenants-in-chief of the English Crown.

While Henry was staying at Waterford, the men of Wexford, in accordance with their undertaking, delivered up to him their prisoner, Robert Fitz Stephen. With an assumption of anger, designed to conciliate the Irish, and show that he meant to exercise his authority over the ' first conquerors', and hold them in check, Henry soundly upbraided Fitz Stephen for his unauthorized attack on Ireland, and caused him to be chained to another prisoner, and to be incarcerated in Reginald's Tower.[20]

And now, without delay, began the submission of the Irish kings. Dermot Mac Carthy, King of Desmond, came of his own accord to Henry at Waterford, took the oath of fealty, did homage, gave hostages, and agreed to pay tribute for his kingdom.[21]

II, mention is made of only 163 *coterelli* or mercenary troops in the king's service in Ireland, for whom garments were purchased. The word *coterelli* is rendered 'cottagers' by Sweetman, and this rendering led Professor G. T. Stokes to remark that Henry 'did not despise measures for the social and material improvement of the people'! 19 Song of Dermot, ll. 2613–22. 20 Gir. Camb., vol. v, p. 277. 21 Ibid. The

Henry then advanced to Lismore. His object was doubtless to have an interview [260] with Christian O'Conarchy, legate of the Pope, and at this time Bishop of Lismore. Christian had been a monk at the Cistercian monastery of Clairvaux, under St. Bernard, and in 1142 had been sent by him to Ireland as first abbot of Mellifont.[22] He had thus received a French training, and had been imbued from his youth with the reforming zeal of St. Bernard and St. Malachi. His position and training therefore marked him out as president of the council of clergy which shortly afterwards met at Cashel, and it was manifestly to arrange for this council that Henry made this detour into Munster. He was anxious to secure the support of the clergy to his action in Ireland, and by his efforts to improve their status and reform the Church he hoped to gain both their goodwill and that of Rome. He stayed for two days at Lismore, and, probably by arrangement with the bishop, selected a site for a castle there, but the [261] actual erection of it was postponed.[23] It was afterwards built by his son John in 1185 From Lismore Henry went on to Cashel, the seat of the Munster archbishopric, where in all probability he had an interview with Archbishop Donnell O'Huallaghan, respecting the proposed council, and arranged for its meeting at the archiepiscopal city. Soon afterwards, on November 6,[24] he sent Nicholas, his chaplain, and Ralph, Archdeacon of Llandaff, to summon the Irish bishops to the council.

On the morrow of Henry's arrival at Cashel, Donnell O'Brien, King of Thomond, came to meet him on the banks of the Suir, probably at the ford of Golden, and submitted to him in the same way as Dermot Mac Carthy had done. As part of the arrangement with these kings, Henry sent constables and officers of his own to Cork and Limerick, the chief towns of Desmond and Thomond respectively. Other princes of the south of Ireland followed suit, including Donnell MacGillapatrick of Ossory [262] and Melaghlin O'Phelan of the Decies.[25] Henry then returned to Waterford by the left bank of the Suir, passing Tibberaghny on the way, a place where his son erected another castle in 1185.[26]

Gesta Hen. and Roger of Howden speak of the Irish kings (except the King of Connaught) and of all the bishops and archbishops as submitting and swearing fealty to Henry while still at Waterford, but it is far more probable, as stated by Giraldus, that the kings severally submitted at different places on Henry's route, while most of the prelates can hardly have signified their submission before the meeting of the council of Cashel. In the Pipe Roll, 19 Hen. II, p. 51 (Winchester) is an entry of £6 for delivering the son of the King of Cork as a hostage, and also items for his corrody and that of Murchardus and the burgesses of Wexford. 22 Ware's Bishops. 23 Song of Dermot, 11. 2667–72. There is a typical mote and wedge-shaped bailey about a mile east of Lismore. It is probable that this was the site of John's *castellum*. See Eng. Hist. Review, 1907, p. 456. It is noteworthy that in going from Lismore to Cashel Henry may have crossed the Suir by the ford at Ardfinnan, and we are expressly told that he returned to Waterford by *Tibraccia* (Tibberaghny). It was at these three places, Lismore, Ardfinnan, and Tibberaghny, that John built castles in 1185. The sites had been probably selected by Henry. 24 This date is given in Gesta Hen., vol. i, p. 28. 25 In the above account of Henry's movements I have followed Giraldus (pp. 276–8). According to the Song of Dermot, which is here less circumstantial than usual, Henry went to Dublin from Waterford, and thence to Cashel and Lismore; then he marched about Leinster and returned to Dublin (ll. 2649–95). The Gesta Henrici and Roger of Howden do not expressly mention the visit to Lismore and Cashel, but speak of the preparations for the synod as taking place while Henry was at Waterford, and state that he arrived in Dublin at Martinmas (November 11). 26 The site of John's *Castrum apud Tibracciam* (Tibberaghny) is also marked by a mote: Eng. Hist. Review, 1907, p. 252.

On his return to Waterford, Henry released Robert Fitz Stephen, as his imprisonment had sufficiently served its purpose. At the same time, he deprived him of Wexford and the adjoining territory, which had been given to him by Dermot Mac Murrough, and so far as appears it was not until 1177 that Fitz Stephen was rewarded by a grant of lands in Ireland. The king evidently still viewed the first conquerors with suspicion. The Song of Dermot indeed does not mention Fitz Stephen's imprisonment by the king, but in a passage similar to that already referred to in the case of
[263] Maurice de Prendergast,[27] gives us an interesting glimpse of the legal procedure of the time. The lords of Wexford, it says, delivered up their prisoner to the king in the presence of his barons (i.e. in full court) and the king 'received the body', and in the presence of the men of Wexford formally accused him of the contempt he had committed (in invading Ireland without permission). Then Fitz Stephen 'folded his glove', and offered it to the king as a pledge that he would willingly give redress in the king's court according to the judgement of his peers, and thereupon his friends, French, Flemings, and Normans, went bail for him.[28]

Leaving Robert Fitz Bernard with a considerable garrison at Waterford, Henry, on
[264] November 1,[29] set out for Dublin by way of Ossory. Unfortunately, we have no details of his journey. He arrived at Dublin on the feast of St. Martin (November 11). Either on the way, or when at Dublin, Henry received the submission of all the principal Leinster chieftains. Among those specifically mentioned were Faelan Mac Faelain, King of Offelan or Northern Kildare; O'Toole, King of Omurethy or Southern Kildare; and Donnell Mac Gillamocholmog, whose territory lay in the vale of Dublin. Some of the northern chieftains also gave in their submission, such as Murrough O'Carroll, King of Uriel, and, most important of all, Dermot's old enemy, Tiernan O'Rourke, King of Breffny and part of O'Conor's Meath.[30] As to the attitude of Rory O'Conor, it is not at first sight easy to reconcile the authorities. According to Gerald de Barry, Rory came to the Shannon, probably at Athlone, to meet the king's messengers, Hugh de Lacy and William Fitz Audelin, and made his submission to them in the same way as Donnell O'Brien had done to Henry. According to other English authorities, Rory held aloof, claiming 'that the whole of Ireland was rightly his, and that all the other kings of the land ought to be placed under his authority'.[31] The older
[265] Irish annals, while stating that Henry received the pledges of Munster, Leinster, Breffny, Uriel, and Uladh or Eastern Ulster, say nothing about Connaught.[32] Probably

27 Supra, p. 237 [p. 87]. 28 Song of Dermot, ll. 2627–48 (where in l. 2646 we should probably restore *par l'esgart*, 'decision, judgement,' for *par la garde*). The procedure was that followed even a century later in Courts Baron, where the formula ran as follows: 'He shall wage his law with his folded glove (*de sun guant plyee*) and shall deliver it into the hand of the other, and then take his glove back and find pledge for his law' (Selden Soc. Publ., iv. 17, quoted in this connexion by Mr. Round, Commune of London, p. 153). The folded glove, according to Prof. Maitland, typified the chattel of value which in very old times was the *vadium*, *wed*, or gage constituting the contract, but was now supplanted by a contract with sureties, who had become the real security for the party's appearance in court. 29 Rog. Howden (vol. ii, p. 30) says that Henry stayed at Waterford for fifteen days, i.e. to November 1, but this must be taken to include his visit to Lismore and Cashel. 30 Gir. Camb., vol. v, p. 278. R. de Diceto, vol. i, p. 348, where O'Rourke is called monoculus'; cf. Ann. Tig. 1148. 31 Gervase Cant, vol. i, p. 235. Gesta Hen., vol. i, p. 26. 32 Ann. Ulster, Ann. Loch Cé, Ann. Tigernach, 1171. The Four Masters characteristically omit all mention of the

Rory, though anxious to obtain the king's peace, and willing to acknowledge Henry as overlord, was not satisfied to be placed on a par with the other kings who had recently submitted to him as *ard-rí*. He certainly did not do personal homage to Henry, or give him hostages, or 'come into his house', so that he cannot be said to have fully submitted to him in accordance either with English or with Irish procedure. And Henry took no steps to enforce his submission. To make a campaign against the *ard-rí* would not have suited the role which Henry desired to assume—the role of one whom the Irish had voluntarily accepted as their lord, who had come to protect them from the violence of the Anglo-Norman adventurers, to reform their Church, and bring order into their country. Besides, the wet season of the year and the difficult nature of the country would make such a campaign hazardous. At any rate, nothing was done to regulate Rory's position until four years later, when, by the Treaty of Windsor, as we shall see, a short-lived arrangement was made on the basis of Rory's overlordship of the other Irish kings outside the area of Anglo-Norman domination. [266]

Thus it appears that of all the principal tribe groups of Ireland the Cinel Owen and the Cinel Connell had alone shown no disposition to accept Henry as their overlord. Since the death of Murtough O'Loughlin, in 1166, no successor to his power had arisen in the north. According to the Four Masters, in 1167 Rory O'Conor, pursuing his usual policy, had divided Tirowen between Niall O'Loughlin and Aedh O'Neill,[33] but the division was not long observed. In 1169 Conor O'Loughlin, Murtough's son, assumed the kingship of the Cinel Owen, but was killed next year in the course of a blood-feud with a subordinate sept.[34] Niall O'Loughlin now assumed the kingship,[35] and appears to have been King of the Cinel Owen when Henry arrived in Ireland, but his authority was disputed by both the Ulidians and the Cinel Connell. In 1171 the Cinel Owen were fighting with the former, and in 1172 they were defeated by the latter, 'and great slaughter was put upon them.'[36] These northern tribes were too busy settling their own disputes to pay any attention to what was going on in the rest of Ireland, with which, indeed—except at intervals under Donnell and Murtough [267]
O'Loughlin—they had seldom concerned themselves since the days of Brian Borumha.

At Dublin Henry did not shut himself up in the fortress, as one in an enemy's country, but had a palace built for his use outside the walls, near the church of St. Andrew. It was a wonderful structure of wattle-work, erected at his request in the native style by the kings and great men who had submitted to him.[37] Evidently Henry was trying to please his new vassals by showing an appreciation of native craftsmanship, and living freely in their midst. Here he stayed, or here, at any rate, were his head-quarters, from the feast of St. Martin to the Purification (November 11 to February 2), and here, surrounded by his vassals, English and Irish, he kept Christmas with the usual festivities. Gerald expressly tells us that many Irish princes came to visit the king's court and marvelled at the splendid abundance of his table and the courtly [268]

submission of the Irish to Henry. 33 Four Masters, 1167. According to the Annals of Ulster only 'some of the Cinel Owen' submitted to Rory. 34 Ann. Ulster, Ann. Loch Cé, 1170. 35 Ann. Tigernach, 1170. He was slain in 1176. 36 Ann. Ulster, Ann. Loch Cé, 1171, 1172.

attention of his household, and learned to feast on cranes' flesh, a food they had hitherto viewed with abhorrence.

We have one authentic memorial of Henry's stay in Dublin, namely, the first Dublin charter, the original of which, executed in Dublin in the winter of 1171–2, is still preserved in the municipal archives. By this charter Henry granted to his men of Bristol (*Bristowa*) his city of Dublin (*Duvelina*), to be inhabited, together with all the liberties and free customs which they had at Bristol and throughout his entire land.[38] By a subsequent charter, executed probably in 1174 at St. Lo, in Normandy, Henry granted to 'his burgesses of Dublin' (i.e. whether men of Bristol or not) freedom from various tolls and duties throughout his lands. In 1185 John confirmed to his men of Bristol his father's grant, and in 1192 gave to the citizens of Dublin an extended charter similar to that granted by him to Bristol in 1188.[39] In the next century it became not uncommon for the great Anglo-Norman lords to grant ' the law of Bristol' [see
[269] *Add.*]. to the more promising vills that sprang up in their lands as the first step to an organized municipality. The little piece of parchment on which Henry's first charter to Dublin is written measures only 6½ x 5 inches, but it represents the source and origin of all municipal life in Ireland, and is surely a treasure which the municipality of Dublin may be proud to hold.

Henry, in fact, found Dublin largely depleted of inhabitants. There were indeed many survivors of the old Norse population, but the capital city of the new regime could not be entrusted to them, and accordingly they appear to have been settled on the north side of the river, in a suburb near St. Mary's Abbey, which came to be known as the *Villa Ostmannorum*, Ostmaneby, or (corruptly) Oxmantown.[40] It was clearly necessary to replenish the city, and Henry's selection of Bristol, the third city in England, as the source for the new colony, probably contributed to the commercial success of Anglo-Norman Dublin. The merchants of Bristol were no strangers to Dublin, and from no town in England could Dublin be so easily reached. Bristol had aided Henry's expedition, and it was from the port of Bristol that supplies were sent to his army.
[270] Whether any considerable number of Bristol men actually settled in Dublin at this time may, however, be first doubted. A roll of some 1,600 names of Dublin citizens, referred to about the close of the twelfth century, contains only fourteen names with the designation *de Bristollo* appended.[41] This in itself is not decisive, as many of the names have

37 'Ibi construi fecit juxta ecclesiam Sancti Andreae apostoli extra civitatem Duvelinae ad opus suum palatium regium, quod reges et ditiores terrae mirifice construxerunt ad opus ejus per praeceptum ipsius de virgis, ad morem patriae illius': Gesta Hen., vol. i, p. 28. 'Palatium regium miro artificio de virgis levigatis ad modum patriae illius constructum': Rog. Howden, vol. ii, p. 32. The old church of St. Andrew, as shown on Speed's map (1610), was just outside Damas Gate on the south side of Damas Street. 38 Reproduced in Facsimiles of Nat. MSS. of Ireland, and Cal. Anc. Records of Dublin (J. T. Gilbert), frontispiece. As late as the year 1887 this charter was produced as evidence in a court of law. 39 For all these charters and others see Hist. and Mun. Documents of Ireland (J. T. Gilbert). John's 1192 charter has also been preserved. 40 So in Waterford, Cork, and Limerick there was an Ostmen's quarter. 41 Hist. and Mun. Documents of Ireland, pp. 3–48. Many of the names are to be met with elsewhere. Thus I have noted (*inter alios*): Robert of Castle Cnoc (p. 20), Richard Gillemichel (p. 37), Elyas f. Norman (p. 39),William Blundel (p. 41), Walter de Stakepol (p. 44), in the Register of St. Thomas's Abbey, Dublin; William of Abbedestuna (= Abboteston) (p. 16), Norman Clater (p. 25), William Wiking (p. 44), Robert

no local designation appended, but only a patronymic, or frequently a 'to-name' taken from their trade (about 200) or from some other circumstance, and some of these may have belonged to Bristol. Besides, the list is defective at the commencement, and it is impossible to say how many membranes have been lost; but if the men of Bristol took advantage of Henry's charter in large numbers, it is at the commencement of the roll—for it appears to be chronologically arranged—that we should expect to find their names. However this may have been, the list seems to show that at the period it covers [271]
Dublin was inhabited by persons who came from many towns in England and Wales, and from a few towns in France and Scotland. Thus 37 are described as of Cardiff, 29 of Worcester, 28 of Gloucester, 27 of London, 14 of Bristol, 13 of Winchester and Bedford, 12 of Northampton, 11 of Exeter and Haverford, 10 of Hereford, 8 of Cardigan and Ludlow, 7 of Warwick, 6 of Lichfield, Chester, Striguil, Taunton, Bodmin, Coventry, and Oxford, and smaller numbers of many other towns.[42] About 14 others are described as Cornishmen, 11 as Flemings, about 6 as Francigenae, and only one as *Hiberniensis*. There is a slight sprinkling of Irish and of Scandinavian names in the list, and 56 are described as of various Anglo-Norman towns in Ireland.

It must not, however, be assumed that all these persons came directly to Dublin from the towns whose names they bore. Certainly Dublin citizens bore these and other local designations for many generations, and their progenitors may have been known [272]
by them in Bristol before migrating to Dublin. But making allowances for such cases, it seems pretty clear that the early citizens of Dublin drew their origin from very many towns besides Bristol. On the other hand, that the connexion with Bristol is not to be estimated by the fourteen names in this list is abundantly proved by the records of the thirteenth century, which show Bristol men holding property and rising to distinction in Dublin.[43] Indeed, Henry himself while in Dublin, perhaps before the date of his charter, made a special grant of a piece of land and houses outside the eastern gate of Dublin, between it and the bridge [over the Poddle] leading to St. Andrew's Church, to Aelelmus, brother of Hamund of Bristol,[44] or Adelelmus Dives, 'Aldelm the Rich,' [273]
as he is called in a later document.

the iremongere (= le Hyrnmangere) (p. 41), Alexander de Wavilla (p. 47), in the Chartulary of St. Mary's Abbey, Dublin; and Godfry de Wintone (p. 8), Rodbertus de Hichtrichburig (= Hehtredebiri) (p. 12), Johannes Hiberniensis (p. 13), Thomas de Blakemor (p. 23), and some going back to the time of Archbishop Laurence (1177), Robert de Deri (p. 16), Peter, brother of William (same page), in the Calendar of Christ Church Deeds; see nos. 468(f), 472, 476. 42 These included Leicester, Marlborough, Shrewsbury, York, Pembroke, St. Briavel, St. Austin's, Cirencester, Brecon, Southampton, Leominster, Lancaster, Furness, Dunstable, Caermarthen, Glasgow, Dumfries, Edinburgh, Carlisle, Stafford, Malmesbury, Monmouth, Wigmore, Swansea, Newport, Banbury, Reading, Cambridge (Grantebruche), Dorchester, Redcliff, Wells, Bath, Ripon, Tewkesbury, Lewes, Wallingford, and St. Albans; and in France, Toulouse, La Rochelle, Falaise, and Dinant. 43 The Chartulary of St. Mary's Abbey, Dublin, indicates that many Bristol men held property in Dublin. See, for instance, the grants from Roger Cordewaner (vol. i, pp. 214–16), who at one time was Mayor of Bristol (Reg. St. Thomas, p. 18), and William, his brother. Ralph of Bristol was Treasurer of St. Patrick's, Dublin, in 1219, and Bishop of Kildare in 1223–32. Geoffry of Bristol was Canon of St. Patrick's in 1223. William of Bristol was Mayor of Dublin 1287–8; Chartulary of St. Mary's, vol. i, p. 493. Robert of Bristol was Provost of Dublin in 1235; Cal. Christ Church Deeds, no. 48. 44 Chart. St. Mary's, Dublin, vol. i, p. 140, no. 118 (g). Adelelm, brother of Hamo, witnessed a Dublin deed circa 1190: Cal. Christ Church Deeds, no. 472; cf. 468a. His brother Roger

In the almost complete dearth of surviving records, Henry's charter of Dublin to the men of Bristol and his special grant to Aldelm the Rich stand almost alone as attested examples of Henry's dealings while in Ireland with the lands he had reserved to the Crown. We have, indeed, ample evidence that he confirmed to the priory of All Hallows, founded and endowed by Dermot Mac Murrough, the lands which it held before his coming to Ireland,[45] and he may have confirmed their lands to other reli-
[274] gious houses, as he certainly did somewhat later.[46] It appears also from a late enrolment[47] that in this year Henry granted the lands of Faithleg, near his landing-place at Crook in Waterford, to Ailward *juvenis*, as king's merchant, but we have no clear evidence of other grants out of the Crown lands at this time.

Some time in the winter of 1171–2 the council of clerics which Henry had summoned met at Cashel under the presidency of Christian O'Conarchy, Bishop of Lismore and Papal Legate. There were present Donatus, or Donnell O'Huallaghan,
[275] Archbishop of Cashel, Laurence, or Lorcan O'Toole, Archbishop of Dublin, and Catholicus, or Cadhla O'Duffy, Archbishop of Tuam, with the suffragans and co-bishops, together with abbots, archdeacons, priors, and deans, and many other dignitaries of the Irish Church. There were also present, commissioned by the king, Ralph, Abbot of Buildwas, Ralph, Archdeacon of Llandaff, Nicholas, the king's chaplain, and others.[48] Gelasius, or Gilla Mac Liag, the primate, on account of his great age, was not able to be present.[49] He was, however, entirely in favour of the new movement in the

also appears to have settled in Dublin: ibid., no. 468d; Chart. St. Mary's, vol. i, p. 173. This piece of land must have been quite close to, if it did not comprise, the site of the palace erected for Henry. Aldelm rented part of it to William Dubeldai (ibid., p. 10), who built on the Poddle (by licence from John in 1185: ibid., p. 223) a mill often mentioned in later documents. Elicia, daughter of Aldelm, and Scholastica, his grand-daughter, granted the plot and the rent of the mill to the monks of St. Mary's Abbey (ibid., pp. 325, 225), and the monks afterwards acquired the mill itself from members of the Dubeldai family (ibid., p. 222, and cf. p. 461). 45 Reg. All Hallows, Dublin, pp. 11–20. This charter was executed at Dublin and witnessed by Laurence, Archbishop of Dublin, Edan, Bishop of Louth, Richard, Earl of Striguil (R. Comite Destr[igoill), Hugh de Lacy, Ralph de Warner (probably Ralph de Warneville, Chancellor] (1173), afterwards (1180) Bishop of Lisieux), Robert Poer, and William his chancellor (?) [Who was this? Did William Fitz Audelin act as chancellor in Ireland ?] 46 It has indeed been contended that Henry, even
[221] before he came to Ireland, by a charter tested at Falaise confirmed their possessions to the monks of St. Mary's Abbey, Dublin, and by another charter confirmed Strongbow's grant of Kilmainham to the knights of St. John, but both contentions can be shown to be due to a somewhat similar misapprehension and to be very improbable; see *infra*, pp. 328 [p. 123], 365 [p. 137]. 47 Chief Rememb. Roll, Dublin, 38 Eliz. (cited Lynch's Legal Institutions, p. 107). Ailward juvenis was probably son of Ailward the chamberlain, at this time in the young king's suite. Close to Faithleg Church is a Norman mote, and in what was the attached bailey stand the ruins of a later stone castle which belonged to the Ailwards up to 1690. Henry's grant of Clontarf, Crook, &c., to the Templars may be confidently assigned to the time of his purgation, of which it was probably a condition. It is dated at Abryncae (Avranches), where Henry and all the chief witnesses can be shown to have probably been present on May 21, 1172, the day of the purgation. The witnesses include Rotrou, Archbishop of Rouen, Arnulf, Bishop of Lisieux, Henry, Bishop of Bayeux, and Richard, Archdeacon of Poitiers, besides Richard de Humez, Constable of Normandy, and other constant attendants of the king at this time. Cal. Docs. Ireland, vol. iii, p. 329. 48 Gir. Camb., vol. v, p. 281; cf. Gesta Hen., vol. i, p. 28; Rog. Howden, vol. ii, p. 31, where lists of the Irish bishops are given. Ralph Diceto and Rog. Wendover speak of Lismore as the place where the council met, probably confusing the see of the bishop-president with the place of assembly. The latter writer says that at the council 'the laws [*recte*, ecclesiastical regulations] of England' were gratefully received by all and confirmed by oath. 49

Church, and afterwards came to Dublin to signify his assent to all Henry's arrangements.[50] As a former pupil and friend of St. Malachi and his successor in the see of Armagh, he had devoted his efforts during a long episcopate towards securing the primacy of his see, and bringing about the conformity of the Irish Church with that of [276]
Western Christendom. Giraldus professes to give the Constitutions of Cashel in the very words in which they were promulgated. They were shortly to the following effect:

1. That the faithful shall desist from co-habitation with relations by blood or affinity, and shall contract and observe lawful marriages.

2. That children shall be catechized at the church doors, and shall be baptized in consecrated fonts within authorized churches.

3. That the faithful shall pay tithes of cattle, corn, and other produce to their parish church.

4. That church property shall be free from all secular imposts, and in particular that no petty kings nor lords nor magnates shall henceforth exact refection and lodging in church-lands, and that the detestable practice of exacting food four times a year from church-farms shall be abolished.

5. That in composition for homicide by laymen, clerics, though of kin to the perpetrators, shall pay no part of the fine [eric].

6. That the faithful taken with illness shall make their wills in the presence of their confessor and neighbours, reserving one-third of their movables for their funeral obsequies if they leave a legitimate wife and legitimate children, and one-half if they leave only a wife or legitimate children.

7. That to those who die after good confession due obsequies be paid with masses [277]
and vigils.

Finally, that all divine matters shall henceforth be conducted according to the observances of the Anglican Church.[51]

There is no reason to doubt that these constitutions, or canons, are correctly reported by Giraldus. They were directed to three objects: (1) to reform certain irregularities in the matters of baptism, marriage, and burial; (2) to give the clergy certain important privileges and immunities calculated to enrich them and secure their support to Henry's assumption of the overlordship of Ireland, (3) to bring about a closer conformity through the Anglican Church with Rome. All three objects were sure to find favour with the papal see.

It was probably at this synod that the Irish prelates swore fealty to Henry as their king and lord, and pledged themselves to conform in all things to the example of the English Church.[52] Each prelate too, we are told, gave him a letter with seal attached, [278]

Gelasius died on March 27, 1174, in the eighty-seventh year of his age and the thirty-seventh of his episcopacy: Ann. Ulster, 1174. **50** Gir. Camb., vol. v, p. 283, where he also mentions the interesting detail that Gelasius lived off the milk of one white cow which he brought with him wherever he went. **51** Gir. Camb., vol. v, p. 282. In Gesta Hen. and Rog. de Hoveden (as above) mention is made in general terms of the canons as to baptism, tithes, and marriages, the former adding statements as to the abuses in vogue, e.g. with regard to marriages: 'Plerique enim illorum [Hibernensium] quot volebant uxores habebant, et etiam cognatas suas germanas habere solebant sibi uxores.' **52** Gesta Hen., vol. i, p. 26; Roger Howden, vol. ii, p. 31; R. Diceto, vol. i, p. 351.

after the manner of a charter, confirming to him and his heirs the kingdom of Ireland.[53] These letters the king sent to Pope Alexander III to obtain the papal confirmation, which accordingly Henry obtained.

No mention is made at this time of 'the Bull Laudabiliter', which, as we have already stated, Henry had long ago obtained from Adrian IV, and we may conclude that no public use was made of it while Henry was in Ireland. It is, however, possible that it may have been privately communicated to the clergy, and this, if done, would further account for the readiness with which they accepted Henry as their overlord, and co-operated with his aims. However this may have been, Henry, as we shall see when we examine the evidence concerning the Bull,[54] had sound reasons for not making public use of the document before obtaining the sanction of the present occupant of the papal chair to his enterprise.

[279] About March 1 Henry reached Wexford. He was becoming very anxious to hear tidings of his dominions over sea, but owing to the stormy winter hardly a vessel crossed the channel, and no news was forthcoming. While here Henry attached to his household Raymond le Gros, Miles de Cogan, William Maskerel, and some others of the best men he could find in those parts, 'with a view,' says Gerald, 'to strengthen his own and weaken the earl's party.'[55] That he was still indeed apprehensive of the earl's power is plain from his creating a counterpoise to it in the person of Hugh de Lacy. While at Wexford he made a grant to Hugh of the land of Meath for the service of fifty knights, to hold as Murrough O'Melaghlin or any before or after him held it.[56] The ground or pretext for this grant was not exactly on all fours with the ground for granting Leinster to the earl. Dermot was the acknowledged King of Leinster, and Strongbow was regarded as in some sort his successor. Dermot is indeed described in
[280] the Book of Leinster as King of Leth Mogha (Southern Ireland) and Meath, but his claims to Meath were of quite recent date, and were not undisputed. The last undisputed King of Meath was Murrough O'Melaghlin, the father of Dervorgil, and he died in 1153. Since that time Meath had repeatedly been the subject of arbitrary partitions, though again and again an O'Melaghlin was proclaimed king. The latest of these partitions was in 1169, when Dermot O'Melaghlin was killed by Donnell of Bregia, his brother's son, and Rory O'Conor, in revenge for that deed, divided Meath into two parts, and gave the eastern half to Tiernan O'Rourke and kept the western half himself. After the taking of Dublin in 1170, Dermot Mac Murrough, as we have seen, led an army partly composed of his Norman allies through Meath and even into Breffny, and Donnell of Bregia and the people of East Meath turned against

53 'Et inde recepit ab unoquoque archiepiscopo et episcopo litteras suas in modum cartae extra sigillum pendentes, et confirmantes ei et haeredibus suum [?] regnum Hiberniae, et testimonium perhibentes ipsos eum et haeredes suos sibi in reges et dominos constituisse in perpetuum': Gesta Hen., vol. i, p. 26; cf. Roger Howden, vol. ii, p. 30. Both these writers, however, speak of the submission of the prelates as if it preceded the council of Cashel. We may doubt the accuracy of this description of the letters of the prelates. 54 See chap. ix. 55 Gir. Camb., vol. v, p. 284, 'ut et suum validiorem et comitis partem redderet exiliorem.' Miles de Cogan accompanied Henry when he left Ireland: Ann. Inisfallen, Dublin MS. 56 See note at end of this chapter. The Gesta Hen., vol. i, p. 30, and Roger Howden, vol. ii, p. 34, state that the service reserved in Henry's grant to Hugh de Lacy was 100 knights, but this appears to be a mistake.

O'Rourke and O'Conor, and gave hostages to Dermot. So at his death Dermot may have been regarded as overlord of Meath.

At last, after Mid-Lent, with a change of wind oversea to the east, news came both from England and Aquitaine. It was of so grave a nature that Henry had to give up whatever plans he had for further securing his foothold in Ireland, and prepare to [281]
return to face the storm that was gathering in both his English and his continental dominions. The cardinal legates commissioned by the Pope to inflict the extreme penalties of the Church on Henry's dominions, unless suitable reparation were made for Becket's murder, appear to have been in Normandy all the winter, and were now threatening an interdict unless the king forthwith came to meet them.

And 'as misfortunes never come singly', the king also learned that his son Henry, who had been crowned as a sort of subordinate colleague at Westminster in the preceding July [see *Add.*], was in a state of incipient rebellion with a discontented baronage at his back.

Accordingly Henry placed constables in charge of his seaport towns: at Dublin, Hugh de Lacy with a garrison of twenty knights, including Robert Fitz Stephen, Maurice Fitz Gerald, Meiler Fitz Henry, and Miles Fitz David; at Wexford, William Fitz Audelin, Philip de Hastings, and Philip de Braose, with thirty knights; and at Waterford, Robert Fitz Bernard, Humfrey de Bohun, and Hugh de Gundeville, with forty knights.[58] Hugh de Lacy, too, was appointed justiciar,[59] and this appointment, [282]
passing over the manifest claims of Richard of Striguil in favour of one who had taken no part in the conquest, is a further proof of Henry's jealousy of the earl, and of his desire to erect a counterpoise to his influence. Moreover, by giving the leading Geraldines posts in Dublin under Hugh de Lacy, taking Miles de Cogan[60] and, seemingly, Raymond le Gros away with him, and placing his own men in Wexford and Waterford, Henry seems to have aimed at further 'strengthening his own party and weakening that of Earl Richard'.

Having thus made his final arrangements, Henry set sail from Wexford at sunrise on Easter Monday, April 17, 1172, and after a prosperous voyage landed about noon at the port of St. Davids.[61] One month from that date he met the cardinal legates in Normandy.

Henry must have regarded his expedition to Ireland as an almost unqualified success. He regretted, indeed, having to leave before building castles in some strategic [283]
sites and completing the establishment of peace and order throughout the land.[62] But, so far as he had gone, almost everything had turned out exactly to his desire. He had

57 'Dolet quoque plurimum se regnum Hibernicum, quod aestate imminente tam incastellare quam firma stabilire pace statuerat, et in formam omnino redigere, tam intem pestive relicturum': Gir. Camb., p. 285. 58 Gir. Camb., p. 286; Song of Dermot, ll. 2709–24. In the Gesta Hen., vol. i, p. 30 and Roger Howden, vol. ii, p. 34, it is stated that the custody of both Waterford and Wexford was given to Robert Fitz Bemard, and that Henry ordered castles to be built in the three towns. This may be correct. At any rate, as we shall see, William Fitz Audelin did not long remain at Wexford. 59 Rog de Hoveden, vol. ii, p. 34. 60 The Song, l. 2759; Annals of Inisfallen; and cf. Gir. Camb., vol. v, p. 284. 61 His troops sailed the previous morning from Crook, near Waterford. The name of Henry's landing-place, which is left blank in the Gesta, is given in the Song as Portfinan. 62 Gir. Camb., vol. v, p. 285.

not unsheathed a sword, and yet he had received from the kings of three-fourths of Ireland an oath of fealty to him as overlord and a promise of tribute. Rory O'Conor indeed had submitted reluctantly (if at all) and subject to reservations, but his position could be arranged later on. The chieftains of the Cinel Owen and the Cinel Connell were alone in ignoring him, and this they had done, so far as appears, not in a spirit of defiance, but simply because they did not feel the pressure of his power, and did not concern themselves with what went on outside their borders. They, too, might be dealt with at another time. As to the clergy, he had entirely won them over to the support of the new regime, and by the measures adopted through them for the reform of abuses and the improvement of their status he had practically ensured the favour of Rome to his enterprise, and this would be useful to him in more ways than one. Above all—and this appears to have been his main object in coming to Ireland—by taking into his hand and garrisoning the seaport towns, he had effectually precluded Richard de Clare from founding an independent kingdom in Ireland.

[284] And yet appearances were deceptive. Henry was really far from having secured his own dominance over the kings who had so readily submitted to him, or an effective control over the lords to whom he had granted large fiefs. To the Irish kings their acknowledgement of Henry as overlord meant no more than the similar acknowledgement, which they had often given, and broken, to an *ard-rí*. Nay, as Henry would be far off across the seas, they probably expected it to mean a great deal less. And by granting on feudal conditions the greater part of Dermot's kingdom to Earl Richard, and, still more certainly, by similarly granting the entire kingdom of Meath to Hugh de Lacy, while conferring on these lords unlimited jurisdiction and complete control over their fiefs, Henry had rendered inevitable a conflict between English and Irish aims and interests.[63]

NOTE A

[285]

Grant of Meath to Hugh de Lacy

Transcribed from the Gormanston Register, f. 5.

Henricus Rex Anglie et dux Normannie et Acquitannie et comes Andegavie Archiepiscopis episcopis abbatibus comitibus baronibus justiciariis et omnibus ministris et fidelibus suis

63 It is worth noting that if we depended on the compilation of the Four Masters for our knowledge of Henry's expedition to Ireland all we should know is contained in the following entry at the end of the year 1171: 'The King of England, the second Henry, Duke of Normandy and Aquitaine, Earl of Andegavia, and lord of many other countries, came to Ireland this year. Two hundred and forty was the number of his ships, and he put in at Port-Lairge.' No notice is taken of the submission of the chieftains, though this is recorded in earlier annals. Such suppressions of unwelcome facts greatly impair the value of this compilation.

64 This list of witnesses, wanting in the Gormanston Register, is given by Mr. Round, Commune of London, p. 152, from MS. Hargrave 313, fol. 44 d (pencil). A similar list, with some differences of spelling, is given in the Liber Niger of Christ Church, f. 224 (Cal. no. 121). Radulfus de Aya was presumably the Radulphus de Haya who afterwards supported the young king in his rebellion: Gesta Hen., vol. i, p. 46.

Francis Anglis et Hiberniensibus totius terre sue salutem. Sciatis me dedisse et concessisse et presenti charta mea confirmasse Hugoni de Lacy pro servicio suo terram de Midia cum omnibus pertinenciis suis per seruicium quinquaginta militum sibi et heredibus suis Tenendam et habendam a me et ab heredibus meis sicuti Murcardus Ha Mulachlyn (*sic*) melius eam tenuit vel aliquis alius ante illum vel postea. Et de incremento illi dono omnia feoda que prebuit vel que prebebit circa Duueliniam dum Ballivus meus est ad faciendum mihi seruicium apud ciuitatem meam Duuelinie. Quare volo et firmiter precipio ut ipse Hugo et heredes sui post eum predictam terram habeant et teneant et omnes libertates et liberas consuetudines quas ibi habeo vel habere possum per prenominatum seruicium a me et ab heredibus meis bene et in pace libere et quiete et honorifice in bosco et plano in pratis et pascuis in aquis et molendinis in viuariis et stangnis in piscacionibus et venacionibus in viis et semitis et portubus maris et in omnibus aliis locis et aliis rebus ad eam pertinentibus cum omnibus libertatibus quas ibi habeo
vel illi dare possum et hac mea carta confirmaui. Testibus: Comite Ricardo filio Gilberti; [286]
Willelmo de Braosa; Willelmo de Albin[eio]; Reginaldo de Cortenay; Hugone de Gundevilla; Willelmo filio Aldelini dapifero; Hugone de Cresy; Willelmo de Stotevilla; Radulfo de Aya (*sic*); Reginaldo de Pavily; Radulfo de Verdun; Willelmo de Gerpunvilla; Roberto de Ruilli; Apud Wesefordam.

[287] # CHAPTER IX

'LAUDABILITER'

A heated controversy has raged at intervals during the last three hundred years over the document known as the 'Bull *Laudabiliter*', by which Pope Adrian IV has been supposed to have granted Ireland to Henry II.[1]

As long ago as 1615 it was denounced as a forgery by Stephen White [see *Add.*], an Irish Jesuit, of whom nothing else is known.[2] He was followed by John Lynch, a learned and estimable member of an old Anglo-Irish house, whose work, entitled Cambrensis Eversus, though showing a remarkable knowledge of Irish history and tradition, is, as regards its avowed object—to controvert Giraldus—in the main a
[288] pompous failure.[3] Three long chapters of this work, which was published in 1662, are devoted to a denunciation of the so-called Bulls of Adrian IV and Alexander III. This writer was followed by the Abbé Mac Geoghegan in his History of Ireland. Other writers, including such great Catholic historians as Dr. Lingard and Dr. Lanigan, have defended the authenticity of the 'Bull', and English writers generally have accepted it as genuine. In 1872, however, Dr. Moran, then Catholic Bishop of Ossory, re-examined the question and argued with great learning against the authenticity of the instrument, and he has since been followed by other distinguished Roman Catholic writers.

It would be out of place here to notice all the arguments which have been urged at various times against the authenticity of these documents. There is the less necessity to do so, as Miss Norgate, the historian of the Angevin kings, has recently reviewed the whole controversy with admirable temper and sound judgement, and, as regards the principal document, 'Laudabiliter,' has ably answered all serious objections that have been advanced to its authenticity.[4] As, however, great if undue importance has been attached to the question, I shall briefly tell the story of the Papal Sanctions as it may be gleaned from the contemporary authorities, adding only such comments as
[289] appear necessary to elucidate the same and to meet the main difficulties which have occurred to some minds.

On one important point, at any rate, I think I have something new to add. By assigning to its true date, about April 1173, Henry's Letter of Credence when sending William Fitz Audelin on a special mission of some sort to Ireland, I bring forward

1 Mr. Round points out that the so-called ' Bull' is only 'a letter commendatory': Commune of London, p. 172. Following Giraldus, we shall call it a 'privilege'. 2 Apologia pro Hibernia adversus Cambri calumnias, ed. Rev. Matthew Kelly, 1849. 3 Cambrensis Eversus, by 'Gratianus Lucius' (Dr. John Lynch), caps. 22–4, ed. Rev. Matthew Kelly, 1848–52. The editor answers effectively most of the author's arguments. 4 Eng Hist. Rev., vol. viii, pp 13–52.

some independent confirmation of Gerald's statement that Fitz Audelin was entrusted with the publication of the Papal Privilegia; and at the same time I prove that his mission, as already surmised by Mr. Round, took place about April 1173, and not, as has been generally assumed, in 1175, thus finally disposing of the argument against the truth of the story drawn from the supposed delay in publication.

It is true that the original documents are not now forthcoming, and that no copies of them are to be found in the Vatican archives, but then it appears that there are no documents relating to Ireland in the Roman archives earlier than the year 1215, and if all transcripts are to be rejected as such a good many pages from our most careful histories will have to be deleted. It appears to me that the account given by Gerald de Barry is throughout consistent with itself, is not disproved by any known facts, and is
confirmed on many substantial points by independent writers and authentic docu- [247]
ments; while to those best acquainted with the thought and policy of the time the disputed documents are in themselves in no way improbable. Better evidence than this we seldom obtain for any contemporary episode of the kind.

Nicholas Breakspear, Bishop of Albano, was elected Pope as Adrian IV about the same time as Henry II was crowned King of England. The king at once wrote to the Pope congratulating himself and his country on the elevation of an Englishman to the papal chair, and making suggestions to the Pope as to the work which lay before him.[5] In the same year, 1155—perhaps at the same time—he sent an embassy to the Pope, which included John of Salisbury, to whom was entrusted the commission to endeavour to obtain the papal sanction to Henry's meditated subjugation of Ireland to his rule. This sanction, John of Salisbury tells us, he obtained: 'At my prayer Adrian granted Ireland to the illustrious King of the English, Henry II, to be possessed as an inheritance, as his letter to this day testifies. For all islands by ancient right, by virtue
of the Donation of Constantine, the original donor of it, are said to belong to the [247]
Church of Rome. He also sent by me a golden ring adorned with an excellent emerald, by which investiture of the right to rule Ireland might be made; and this ring is still ordered to be kept in the State archives.'[6] This statement refers to the year 1155, and purports to have been written shortly after Adrian's death in 1159.

Now of John of Salisbury we know much. His character was one of transparent honesty. He was the devoted admirer of Thomas Becket, the trusted secretary and envoy of Archbishop Theobald, and the dearest friend of the English-born Pope.[7] No more suitable man for the delicate commission could have been selected. That he should have falsely concocted the above statement is unthinkable. Of course it has been asserted that the passage is a fraudulent interpolation, but this ready method of removing inconvenient evidence can only be admitted after stringent proof, which does not in this case appear to be forthcoming. Moreover, we have the statement of an entirely independent chronicler that at Michaelmas in this very year, 1155, Henry laid
before his barons at Winchester a scheme for conquering Ireland as a provision for his [247]

5 See Miss Norgate's Angevin Kings, vol. i, p. 497, note. The whole chapter gives an admirable account of the religious revival during 'the last years of Archbishop Theobald'. 6 Metalogicus, iv. 42. Johannis Sarisb. opera, ed. Giles, vol. v, p. 205. 7 Miss Norgate, Angevin Kings, vol. i, pp 480–91; Dict. Nat. Biog., vol. xxix, pp 439–41 (R.L. Poole).

brother William, but his mother, the Empress Matilda, dissuaded him from the project at the time.[8] Accordingly the project was laid aside until the events we have related forced Henry's hand. This independent evidence of Henry's intentions at the precise date can hardly have been taken into account by the supposed fabricator of the statement in the Metalogicus,with which it is incomplete harmony.

But it may be said, when Henry went to Ireland in 1171 why did he not make use of Adrian's Privilege if it existed? Then, if ever, was the time to publish it. A little consideration, however, will show that Henry could not have made any profitable public use of the document at that time. Adrian had died twelve years previously, and the existing Pope, Alexander III, was bitterly incensed at the moment against Henry on account of the conflict with Archbishop Thomas and the fearful tragedy in which that conflict had resulted. Until Henry had made his peace with Alexander it would have been perfectly futile to seek his confirmation of his predecessor's Privilege; while to have paraded the sanction of the deceased Pope at a moment when the existing Pope was threatening an interdict would have been to provoke a counterblast which would
[293] have far more than undone any possible advantage to be gained. This seems a simple and adequate explanation of the non-publication of 'Laudabiliter' at the time of Henry's expedition.

Henry took much more prudent steps to gain the approval of the present occupant of the papal chair. As we have seen, one of Henry's first acts in Ireland was to summon a synod of the clergy of Ireland to meet at Cashel. Gerald, who gives the fullest and clearest account of this synod, says that a public inquiry was made into the 'enormities and foul customs' (*enormitates*, *spurcitiae*) of the people of the land, which were carefully reduced to writing under the seal of the legate, Christian, Bishop of Lismore, who presided at the synod.[9] This synod seems to have taken place some time early in 1172. There were present at it on behalf of the king, Ralph, Abbot of Buildwas, Ralph, Archdeacon of Llandaff, Nicholas the chaplain, and others.[10] Referring to this synod, but without giving any precise date, Gerald afterwards[11] says that Henry, hav-
[294] ing sent an embassy to Rome[12] with the aforesaid letter concerning the 'foul customs' of the people, obtained from Alexander III, then Pope, a Privilege authorizing him both to rule the people of Ireland and, ill-instructed as they were in the rudiments of faith, to mould them by ecclesiastical rules and discipline into conformity with the usages of the Anglican Church. This Privilege, he continues, was sent to Ireland by the hands of Nicholas, Prior of Wallingford, and William Fitz Audelin,[13] and was forthwith publicly read with general approval before a synod of bishops convened at Waterford. Along with it was also read another Privilege, which the king had formerly obtained from Pope Adrian, Alexander's predecessor, through the agency of John of Salisbury, who had been sent to Rome to obtain it. By the hands of John, too, the same

8 Robert of Torigny (*anno* 1155), p. 86. 9 'Ubi, requisitis et auditis publice terrae illius et gentis tam enormitatibus quam spurcitiis, et in scriptum etiam sub sigillo legati Lismoriensis, qui ceteris ibidem dignitate tunc praeerat, ex industria redactis': Gir. Camb., p. 280. 10 Ibid., p. 281. 11 Ibid., p. 315. 12 This was probably soon after Henry's purgation before the legates at Avranches on May 21, 1172: see Norgate, Angevin Kings, vol. ii, p. 81. 13 Fitz Audelin, as we shall see, was probably sent on this mission in the spring of 1173: see Appendix to this chapter.

pope presented to the King of the English a golden ring in token of investiture, and this together with the Privilege, was forthwith deposited among the archives at Winchester.

Gerald then gives the contents of these two Privileges. That of Adrian may be closely rendered as follows: 'Adrian, bishop, servant of the servants of God, to our well-beloved son in Christ the illustrious King of the English greeting and apostolic benediction. Laudably and profitably doth your Majesty contemplate spreading the [295]
glory of your name on earth and laying up for yourself the reward of eternal happiness in heaven, in that, as becomes a catholic prince, you purpose to enlarge the boundaries of the Church, to proclaim the truths of the Christian religion to a rude and ignorant people, and to root out the growths of vice from the field of the Lord; and the better to accomplish this purpose you seek the counsel and goodwill of the apostolic see. In pursuing your object, the loftier your aim and the greater your discretion, the more prosperous, we are assured, with God's assistance, will be the progress you will make: for undertakings commenced in the zeal of faith and the love of religion are ever wont to attain to a good end and issue. Verily, as your Excellency doth acknowledge, there is no doubt that Ireland and all islands on which Christ the sun of righteousness has shone, and which have accepted the doctrines of the Christian faith, belong to the jurisdiction of the blessed Peter and the holy Roman Church; wherefore the more pleased are we to plant in them the seed of faith acceptable to God, inasmuch as our conscience warns us that in their case a stricter account will hereafter be required of us.

'Whereas then, well-beloved son in Christ, you have expressed to us your desire to enter the island of Ireland in order to subject its people to law and to root out from [296]
them the weeds of vice, and your willingness to pay an annual tribute to the blessed Peter of one penny from every house, and to maintain the rights of the churches of that land whole and inviolate: We therefore, meeting your pious and laudable desire with due favour and according a gracious assent to your petition, do hereby declare our will and pleasure that, with a view to enlarging the boundaries of the Church, restraining the downward course of vice, correcting evil customs, and planting virtue, and for the increase of the Christian religion, you shall enter that island and execute whatsoever may tend to the honour of God and the welfare of the land; and also that the people of that land shall receive you with honour and revere you as their lord: provided always that the rights of the churches remain whole and inviolate, and saving to the blessed Peter and the Holy Roman Church the annual tribute of one penny from every house. If then you should carry your project into effect, let it be your care to instruct that people in good ways of life, and so act, both in person and by agents whom you shall have found in faith, in word, and in deed fitted for the task, that the Church there may be adorned, that the Christian religion may take root and grow, and that all things appertaining to the honour of God and the salvation of souls may be so ordered that [297]
you may deserve at God's hands the fullness of an everlasting reward, and may obtain on earth a name renowned throughout the ages.'[14]

14 Adrian's Privilegium is also given by Rog. Wend., vol. i, p. 11. Ralph de Diceto, vol. i, p. 300. They

Alexander's Privilege, as given by Gerald, is little more than a brief confirmation of that of Adrian. It may be rendered as follows:

'Alexander, bishop, servant of the servants of God, to his well-beloved son in Christ the illustrious King of the English greeting and apostolic benediction. For as much as those concessions of our predecessors which are known to have been reasonably made deserve to be permanently confirmed, We, following in the footsteps of the venerable Pope Adrian, and paying heed to the satisfaction of your desire, ratify and confirm the concession of the said Pope made to you concerning the lordship of the kingdom of Ireland, saving to the blessed Peter and the Holy Roman Church in Ireland as in England the annual payment of one penny from every house, to the end that the foul customs (*spurcitiae*) of that country may be abolished, and the barbarous nation, reck-
[298] oned Christian in name,[15] may through your care assume the beauty of good morals, and that the church of those regions, hitherto disordered, may be set in order, and the people may henceforth through you attain the reality as well as the name of the Christian profession.'

It is not my purpose to discuss questions of textual criticism, but it is right to mention that an element of doubt is supposed to be thrown on the authenticity of Alexander's Privilege by the fact that in the manuscript of another of Gerald's works, De Principis Instructione, when introducing this Privilege, words are added meaning, 'as by some is asserted or pretended to have been obtained, or by others is denied to have ever been obtained.' These words, as the editor of the Expugnatio points out, have the appearance of a marginal note that has become incorporated with the text.[16] Possibly in consequence of the denial of authenticity so expressed, some of the later (fourteenth century) manuscripts of the Expugnatio omit all mention of Alexander's Privilege, and the omission is effected so clumsily that pure hash is made of the prefa-
[299] tory matter.[17] The editor is clearly right in saying that this bungling change could not possibly have been the work of Giraldus,[18] and it is not easy to see how the words throwing doubt on Alexander's Privilege could have been written by him either. It seems to me that these 'rectifications' of Gerald's original statement may be disregarded, and that the question of the authenticity of Alexander's Privilege must be determined on other grounds.

It will have been observed that Gerald's account of the original obtaining of Adrian's Privilege agrees closely with that given by John of Salisbury. The latter,

may have taken it from Giraldus, but their insertion of it at least shows that they did not consider it a forgery. Or are we to suppose that they were duped, or were in the conspiracy? It is also to be found in the Book of Leinster, Facsimile, p. 342. 15 This expression, *barbara natio quae Christiano censetur nomine,* recalls the language of St. Bernard respecting the inhabitants of St. Malachi's diocese, *Christiani nomine, re pagani*: Migne, vol. clxxxii, cap. viii, col. 1034. 16 Gir. Camb., vol. v, p. 318, note. 17 Ibid., pp 316, 313, notes. 18 Ibid., Preface, p. xliii. In the passage in the De Principis Instructione as edited by Mr. Brewer, Adrian, and not Alexander, appears as the pope from whom Henry obtained the *privilegia* after the council of Cashel; and Mr. Dimock, in the note to his remarks in the Preface to the Expugnatio (as above), supposes that Giraldus by this apparent slip may have himself given rise to the subsequent blundering rectification. But Mr. G. F. Warner, in the new edition of the De Principis Instructione (Gir. Camb., vol. viii, p. 195) shows that the slip was Mr. Brewer's, and not Giraldus's. The sole MS. reads *Alexandro tertio*, thus agreeing with the Expugnatio.

indeed, says that Adrian 'granted Ireland' to Henry 'to be possessed as an estate of inheritance', while the Privilege, as given by Gerald, contains no actual grant. We may, however, regard this expression of John of Salisbury as merely a loose and exaggerated way of describing the general effect of the Privilege. So the author of the Gesta [300] and Roger Hoveden still more emphatically say that Alexander 'by apostolic authority confirmed the kingdom to Henry and his heirs and appointed them kings of it for ever'.[19] This is certainly an incorrect description of any of the documents themselves, but it may perhaps be regarded as the view the court wished to be taken of those documents, and, curiously enough, it is the view which seems to have generally prevailed up to recent times. But though Adrian's Privilege contains no formal grant, temporal domination is implied throughout, and is indeed sanctioned and its acquisition encouraged when the Pope expresses his will and pleasure that the people of Ireland should receive Henry with honour and 'revere him as their lord' (*dominus*). This is the appropriate word to express territorial domination, and was in fact the title assumed by John in his charters and public documents. Adrian's Privilege is, in effect, a mere sanction on the part of the Pope to Henry's entering Ireland, if he should be minded to do so, with a view to effecting certain reforms there. Of course Henry could not do this without assuming the position of *dominus* of Ireland, and the Pope expressly recognizes this fact and uses his influence to prevail upon the Irish people to receive him as such.

The language employed in these Privileges, though indicating that in the opinion [301] of the Popes concerned there were many things in Ireland calling for reformation, deals only in generalities, and especially in the case of Adrian's Privilege does not go beyond what might be expected in a reforming Pope. Alexander, indeed, uses stronger language, and, as we may note, employs one of the very words (*spurcitae*) which Gerald uses in stating the subject of the inquiry which took place in connexion with the Council of Cashel.

But there are some other documents of really much greater significance as bearing on the action of the Pope after the date of Henry's expedition to Ireland. These are three letters of Alexander III, all dated Tusculum, the 20th of September, and almost certainly to be referred to the year 1172. One is addressed to Christian, Bishop of Lismore, legate of the apostolic see (who had presided at the Council of Cashel), the four Archbishops of Ireland (who are mentioned by name), and their suffragans. Another is addressed to Henry himself, and the third to the kings and princes of Ireland. These remarkable Letters were entered in the Black Book of the Exchequer of England,[20] and, though not mentioned by Gerald de Barry, they fully bear out his [302] account of the transactions between the prelates at the Council of Cashel and the Pope, and manifest the favour with which the Pope viewed Henry's recent action in Ireland. The following is the substance of these Letters, which are too long to quote in full:

19 Gesta Hen., vol. i, p. 28; Roger Hoveden, vol. i, p. 31. **20** These letters of Alexander are printed in the Liber Niger Scaccarii, ed. Tho. Hearne (1728), vol. i, pp 42–7; also in Rymer's Foedera, vol. i, pt. i, p. 45, and in Opp Alex. III, Migne, 200, col. 883–6.

In the first Alexander refers to the *vitiorum enormitates* made known to him by the letters of the prelates (*ex vestrarum serie literarum*) as well as by trustworthy statements of others, and rejoices that, as he learns from the prelates, those unlawful practices are, under Henry's influence, beginning to disappear [alluding probably to the decrees of the Council of Cashel]. He then commands the bishops to assist Henry in maintaining possession of the land and in extirpating those abominable practices (*ad extirpandam inde tantae abominationis spurcitiam*), and to visit with the censure of the Church any king, prince, or other person who should dare to contravene his oath of fealty to the said king (*juramenti debitum et fidelitatem praedicto Regi exhibitam*).

In the letter to Henry, after congratulating the king on his triumph, the Pope refers in similar strong language to the enormities and crimes (*enormitates et vicia*) of the
[303] Irish, specifically mentioning various unlawful sexual alliances, eating flesh in Lent, not paying tithes, and not showing due respect to churches and ecclesiastics. [Most of these subjects, it is to be noted, were dealt with by the Council of Cashel.] He gives as his authority for these charges the aforesaid letters of Christian, Bishop of Lismore, and the other Irish prelates, and the oral testimony of R[alph], Archdeacon of Llandaff, of whom he speaks highly. From this we may infer that Ralph, Archdeacon of Llandaff, who, as we have seen, was one of those present on the king's behalf at the Council of Cashel, was also one of the envoys sent on the embassy to Rome consequent on that council. He was just the person we might expect to be chosen for the purpose. Alexander then proceeds to express his thankfulness that Henry should have been inspired to undertake the subjugation of the Irish and to extirpate the abominable foulness (*abominationis spurcitiam*) alluded to, and he enjoins it upon him, 'for the remission of his sins,' to show still greater energy in the undertaking so laudably commenced. This expression seems to allude to Henry's sins against the Church, and could hardly have been written by anybody except the Pope himself. Finally, alluding, as Adrian had done, to the peculiar rights which the Church of Rome possessed over
[304] islands, Alexander urges Henry to preserve and extend in that land the rights of the blessed Peter. In the letter to the kings and princes, Alexander expresses his joy at learning that they had received Henry for their king and lord and had sworn fealty to him, commends them for having submitted of their own free will, and admonishes them to maintain their oath and fealty inviolate.

It will be observed that in these Letters Alexander repeatedly employs the strong words *enormitates* and *spurcitiae*, which Giraldus also employs when describing the subjects of the public inquiry instituted by the synod of Cashel, the results of which he tells us were written down under the seal of the legate and sent to Rome. Now this coincidence of language can seemingly be explained in only one of two ways: either Gerald and Alexander were both adopting, as they naturally would, the precise phrases used in the synodal inquiry, and embodied in the prelates' letter; or Gerald wrote the letters ascribed to Alexander. But seeing that Gerald makes no use or mention of Alexander's letters, this last supposition, on this ground alone, seems perfectly futile.

These letters, it will be seen, bear out the statement of Gerald de Barry even in details, and while the natural and, on the whole, well founded disbelief of Irishmen in

the justice of the sweeping and extravagant charges contained in the letters is quite [305]
intelligible and wholesome, it is hard to see why their authenticity should be called in question by any dispassionate historian. They have, indeed, been accepted as genuine by Roman Catholic writers and others who have laboured to prove that Adrian's Privilege was a forgery. Others again, with greater daring, but perhaps more consistently with their conclusions, have rejected all documents, from whatever source derived, implying a papal sanction to Henry's expedition, and have denied all statements concerning it to be found in the chronicles and writings of the time. This implies such a wholesale conspiracy of lying and forgery, and one that would have been so easily, and in many quarters so gladly, detected at the time, that it seems superfluous to deal seriously with it.

It may, however, be asked, Why did not Gerald transcribe these letters of Alexander, if they were in existence, seeing that they entirely support his account of the matter, instead of giving us only the Privileges of Adrian and Alexander? The simple answer seems to be that these latter were, as he says, published at Waterford, and were therefore available to him, while the three letters were very probably not available. There is no reason to suppose that either the prelates or the kings of Ireland
would publish the letters addressed to them, and Henry may well have thought that [306]
the simple confirmation of Adrian's Privilege was more to his purpose than the letter addressed to himself. It must be borne in mind that only recently and tentatively had Rome begun to exercise jurisdiction in Ireland, and there are signs that the clergy in many parts and the laity generally were not prepared to accept her decrees unreservedly. Henry was already assured of the support of the higher ranks of the clergy, but there were many in Ireland, both clerics and laymen, who would be certain to resent the intemperate denunciations contained in Alexander's letters to Henry and to the prelates, and their publication might be expected to do more harm than good to Henry's cause. Rome was going too fast and too far, and Henry may indeed have wished to be saved from his friends.

Only one other difficulty in accepting the contemporary accounts of this episode need here be noticed. Giraldus, it is said, states that the papal Privileges were for the first time published in Ireland by William Fitz Audelin at a synod in Waterford in 1175, or possibly at the earliest in 1174,[21] and it may be asked how we are to account for this delay in the production of such important documents. The answer is that
Giraldus gives no precise date, that the date usually accepted is only a hasty inference [307]
of the editor, and that Fitz Audelin's mission for the publication of the Privileges took place in 1173, probably in the month of April. As Alexander's letters, presumably sent at the same time, are dated September 20 (1172), there was no exceptional delay. Mr. Round, with his wholesome habit of investigating 'universally admitted facts', has already pointed out that the inference as to the date is a mistaken one, and has shown from the Pipe Roll that the mission probably took place between Michaelmas 1172 and Michaelmas 1173.[22] Following up this clue, I have, I think, identified the actual Letter of Credence given by Henry to William Fitz Audelin on this occasion, and have been

21 Gir. Camb. v. 315. 22 Commune of London, pp 182–4.

able to date it (approximately) April 1173. As the proof of this is rather tedious and technical, I have given it in a note appended to this chapter.

As we have seen, then, in none of the documents does the Pope purport to make a grant of the sovereignty of Ireland to Henry II. That sovereignty, or rather overlordship, so far as it existed, was won partly by the swords of the Norman adventurers, and was established more legally by the personal submission of the Irish kings and prelates.
[308] Adrian, for special reasons as to the welfare of the Church, warmly approved of Henry's meditated expedition; and Alexander, for similar reasons, still more warmly approved of the accomplished fact. The difference, however, between a formal grant of dominion and such a sanction from a mediaeval Pope is one that appeals to a lawyer rather than to a layman, and it is not surprising that in this case it has been habitually ignored.

It is probable that the authenticity of these documents would never have been contested were it not for the strong language employed in them characterizing the low state of morals and religion in Ireland. This strong language is to be found mainly in Alexander's letters (the evidence for which is entirely independent of Giraldus), and it may be largely discounted as being only the manner of ecclesiastical writing at the time. What the *enormitates vitiorum* and *spurcitiae* really were may be inferred with much confidence from the canons of the synod of Cashel, and are there seen to have been, with one exception, mostly matters of ritual, and above all the non-existence of the privileges elsewhere enjoyed by the Roman Church. The exception was the loose marriage customs that prevailed from of old among the lay-folk of Ireland. We have seen these customs condemned by foreign ecclesiastics such as Lanfranc, Anselm, and
[309] St. Bernard, and as late as 1152 by the synod over which Cardinal Papiro presided[23]—not to mention Giraldus and other contemporary writers. Our study of the marriage customs indicated in the Brehon Law Tracts[24] has rendered quite intelligible this persistent condemnation, and it is vain to assert that it was unfounded. A wider outlook than was possible at the time, however, would have shown that these customs were not a sign of degeneracy, but an indication that the people were still in a lower plane of civilization than had been reached elsewhere; and a wiser statesmanship would have known that they were not to be amended by the use of hard names and exaggerated language, but by patient teaching, wholesome example, and the gradual introduction and enforcement of better laws.

In short, from such study as I have been able to give to this episode, I cannot see any thing in these documents to warrant their being branded as forgeries. They hang well together, and fully bear out the account of the transaction given by Giraldus, and, considering the almost complete absence of records reaching back to this period, the main facts of his account are quite as fully substantiated by independent evidence as we have
[310] any grounds for expecting. The theory of wholesale forgery seems to me perfectly gratuitous and highly improbable. The Privileges, as we have them, were at any rate published to the world in the Expugnatio in 1188, and there is no sign that any voice was raised at Rome or elsewhere to denounce them.

23 Four Masters, 1152. The first canon was 'to put away concubines and lemans from men'—not from the clergy, as has been supposed. 24 *Supra*, pp 124–30 [pp. 43–5].

The importance of the papal action has, however, been exaggerated. Adrian's Privilege played no part—certainly no public part—in obtaining the submission of the princes and prelates of Ireland, and Alexander's action seems to have had no marked effect beyond probably confirming most of the clergy in their support of the new regime. Indeed, the action of the Popes may be regarded from another point of view as a grateful anticipation and recognition of the service Henry was proposing to do, or had done, to the Church of Rome in the way of extending her boundaries, supporting her jurisdiction, and bringing about a closer conformity to her usages, rather than as a means of conferring any very important benefit or assistance to Henry in Ireland. Moreover, Alexander's position must be borne in mind. There was a succession of anti-popes favoured by the emperor and other powers during his troubled pontificate, and Henry had been sorely tempted to throw his weight into the schismatic scale. To retain Henry's favour was vital to Alexander. Viewed as a matter of mundane policy, in securing Henry's support by sanctioning his action in Ireland, Alexander was get- [311]
ting more than he gave.

The Pope was not long in following up the opening thus made. In 1177, four years after March the publication of the papal Privileges at Waterford, Cardinal Vivian came to Ireland as legate of the Pope and summoned a synod of the bishops at Dublin. At this synod, according to Gerald, he made a public declaration of the right of the King of England to Ireland and of the confirmation of the Pope, and enjoined on clergy and people, under pain of anathema, not to presume to depart from their allegiance.[25] Here, fortunately, there is independent Irish evidence of the holding of this synod by Vivian, and an indication that its decrees were not relished by the Irish. The Four Masters, under 1177, record: 'Cardinal Vivianus arrived in Ireland: A synod of the clergy of Ireland, both bishops and abbots, about that cardinal in Dublin on the first Sunday in Lent, and they enacted many ordinances not now observed.'

NOTE A [312]

Date of the publication of the papal privileges

The date usually assigned by historians for the publication of 'Laudabiliter' is 1175, or perhaps 1174, but Mr. Round has pointed out (Commune of London, pp 181–4) that this date is not actually given by Giraldus, who alone mentions the publication, but is an inference drawn by Mr. Dimock from the supposed sequence of events indicated by Giraldus. But this sequence was misunderstood, and the precise inference unwarranted.

25 Gir. Camb. v. 345. The words *jus Anglorum regis in Hiberniam, et summi pontificis confirmationem, viva voce publice protestatur*, must refer to a proclamation by the papal emissary of the sanction of the existing Pope, Alexander III. When Vivian landed in England in July 1176 he was compelled to swear that he would do nothing against the king, before being allowed to proceed on his journey: Gesta Hen., vol. i, p. 118. His holding a council in Dublin is incidentally mentioned, ibid., p. 161.

In the first book of the Expugnatio, Giraldus carries the story, so far as Ireland is concerned, no further than the year 1172. He gives, however, some account of Henry's wars of 1173–4. In his preface to the second book he apologizes for no longer being able to detail the series of events fully, but says that he will jot down, *cursim et breviter*, the materials for history rather than attempt a regular historical narrative. The first four chapters of the second book then mention certain events in Ireland to be ascribed to the years 1173–4, and the fifth chapter, entitled *Privilegiorum impetratio*, opens as follows: 'Interea quanquam martiis plurimum intentus et detentus exercitiis, Anglorum rex, suae tamen inter agendum Hiberniae non immemor, cum
[313] praenotatis spurcitiarum literis in synodo Cassiliensi per industriam quaesitis directis ad curiam Romanam nunciis, ab Alexandro tertio tunc praesidente privilegium impetravit.' This Privilege, together with Adrian's Privilege, he then sent to Ireland by the hands of Nicholas, Prior of Wallingford, and William Fitz Audelin, who immediately summoned the Synod of Waterford and had them both publicly read. It is plain that the word *interea* may refer to any period of time between the date of the Council of Cashel (the winter 1171–2) and that of the last event mentioned in 1174. Moreover, Mr. Round quotes an entry on the Pipe Roll of 1173 which seems to show that William Fitz Audelin was actually sent to Ireland on a mission between Michaelmas 1172 and Michaelmas 1173, and so far to corroborate Gerald's statement. This entry is as follows: 'In Passagio Willelmi filii Aldelini et sociorum suorum et Hernesiorum suorum in Hyberniam xxvii sol. et vi den. per breve Ricardi de Luci' (p. 145). The Pipe Roll contains other writs by Richard de Luci, and, as pointed out in Eyton's Itinerary (p. 174), it is evident that in the spring and summer of 1173 he was acting as Viceroy in England.

But further, I venture to suggest that the Letter of Credence given at this time to William Fitz Audelin has been preserved and is well known, but has been wrongly referred to some other period. This document is given in Rymer's Foedera, i, p. 36, from Bibl. Cotton., Titus, B. XI, fol. 90, and referred to the year 1181, and is as follows:

> Henricus, Rex Angliae, dux Normanniae et Aquitaniae, et comes Andegaviae, archiepiscopis, episcopis, regibus, comitibus, baronibus, et omnibus fidelibus suis
> [314] Hiberniae, salutem. Sciatis me, Dei gratiâ, salvum esse et incolumem, et negotia mea benè et honorificè procedere; ego vero, quam cito potero, vacabo magnis negotiis meis Hiberniae.[26] Nunc autem ad vos mitto Willielmum filium Adelmi, dapiferum meum, cui commisi negotia mea tractanda et agenda mei loco et vice. Quare vobis mando et firmiter precipio, quod ei sicut michimet intendatis de agendis meis, et faciatis quicquid ipse vobis dixerit ex parte meâ; sicut amorem meum habere desideratis, et per fidem quam mihi debetis. Ego quoque ratum habebo et firmum quicquid ipse fecerit, tanquam egomet fecissem, et quicquid vos feceritis erga eum stabile habebo. Testibus,
>
> Galfrido archidiacono Cantuar'
> Ricardo archidiacono Pictaviens'
> Ricardo constabulario Apud Valunis.

Leland (History of Ireland, vol. i, p. 113) quotes this document, with the addition of *dominus Hiberniae* to Henry's titles, 'from an old parchment roll in possession of the Earl of Meath,' and supposes it to be the commission given to William Fitz Audelin when sent as procurator to Ireland in 1177. In this he is followed by Gilbert (Viceroys of Ireland, p. 41) and others. But this supposition is disproved by the fact that about May 1, 1173, the two archdeacon witnesses were elected Bishops of Winchester and Ely respectively, though they were not consecrated until the following year (Roger of Howden, vol. ii, pp 56, 69; Eyton's Itin., p. 175). Eyton places it about

26 Cf. the opening words of Giraldus quoted above, p. 312 [p. 116].

the end of July 1171, when Henry was leaving Normandy on his way to Ireland. But a little [315]
consideration might have shown that Henry could not have called himself *dominus Hiberniae* at that time, or (if this description be not part of the original document) could not have addressed his rescript to the archbishops, &c., and all his liege subjects (*omnibus fidelibus suis*) of Ireland, nor have enjoined them *per fidem quam mihi debetis* before he had obtained their oaths of fealty. The letter was certainly written after Henry had returned from Ireland, and probably after his reconciliation with the papacy and before the actual outbreak of hostilities with his sons. As far as Henry is concerned it might then be dated in October or November 1172, or in March or April 1173, when the king was in Normandy, but when we turn to the witnesses we find that the two archdeacons crossed from England to Normandy probably shortly before May 1173. The Pipe Roll (19 Hen. II, Southampton) has this entry: 'et in lib*er*ati*o*ne ix naviu*m* q*uae* debuer*un*t t*r*ansfretare c*um* Ric*ar*do de Luci et Ric*ardo* Pict*aviae* Archi*diacono* et Gaufri*do* Cant*uariensi* Archi*diacono* et aliis Baronib*us* p*re*cepto Reg*is* £13 15*s*. per breve Ricardi de Luci.' Pipe Roll Soc., vol. xix, p. 54, and see Eyton, Itin., p. 174, where the author takes the word *debuerunt* to mean no more than that Richard de Luci did not cross the sea. The two archdeacons, he says, would go to Normandy in prospect of their elections to bishoprics. The presence of Richard [de Humez], Constable [of Normandy], presents no difficulty. All this seems to fix March or April 1173 as the date of this rescript and of FitzAudelin's mission. We may add that as Hugh de Lacy was summoned about this time to the king's aid in Normandy, it would be
necessary to send some representative of the king to Ireland. Richard of Striguil was with the [316]
king in the beginning of August (Ralph de Diceto, vol. i, p. 375), and probably earlier, and was not entrusted with the custody of Ireland until the middle of that month at the earliest. See chapter x, pp 325–8 [pp. 122–3], *infra*, where another indication of the presence of William Fitz Audelin in Ireland at about this time is noted.

NOTE B [317]

Mr. Round's position

As I have more than once endorsed points made by Mr. Round in his contribution to the 'Laudabiliter' controversy, I should say that his conclusions are peculiar and differ widely from mine. He accepts Alexander's Black Book Letters as genuine, and as the real answer to Henry's embassy, but he thinks that Giraldus, instead of giving these, substituted 'a concocted confirmation of an equally concocted "Bull".'[27] He hardly attempts to explain why Giraldus should do this, but suggests that there was a conspiracy (which included among its active members not only Giraldus, but also the writer of the passage in the Metalogicus, the author of the Gesta Henrici, and Roger Hoveden, with Henry himself, presumably, in the background) to represent the Pope as actually granting or confirming the kingdom of Ireland to Henry and his heirs for ever (a representation not, I think, anywhere made by Giraldus), and that, as Alexander's real letters contained no such grant, Gerald substituted the document known as 'Laudabiliter' and its alleged confirmation, though, as Mr. Round emphatically asserts, 'Laudabiliter' contains no such grant either! A more futile forgery it would be hard to imagine. As to the method of the
forgery, Mr. Round thinks that Gerald employed largely the genuine letters of Alexander [318]
entered in the Liber Niger, and he maintains that 'Laudabiliter' does little more than para-

27 Commune of London, p. 194.

phrase and adapt the contents of Alexander's letter to Henry. I think Mr. Round greatly exaggerates the resemblance. But on the supposition that Gerald's statements are true, so far as there is a similarity between either the language or the sentiment of Alexander's letter and that of Adrian's Privilege, what can be more natural than that Alexander should to some extent echo the thought and even the phraseology of the document he was at the same time confirming? By way of proving that Gerald was capable of concocting the *privilegia*, Mr. Round adduces Dermot's letter to Strongbow, which certainly seems to contain much of Gerald's own fine writing. But surely the fact that Gerald, for literary effect, composed in his own words an epistle to represent Dermot's message, does not prove him—a mediaeval priest—morally capable of concocting, for political purposes, two great state documents, and of solemnly representing them as coming from the Papacy.

Having thus expressed the opinion that 'Laudabiliter' was a concoction, Mr. Round proceeds to show that this was not the view taken by the Papacy itself in after-times. He quotes a papal dispensation of 1290, which refers to Henry's invading Ireland 'at the wish of the papal see', and also a striking passage from the instructions of Innocent X to Rinuccini, which proves clearly that even in 1645 the Pope believed 'Laudabiliter' to be genuine. For Professor Thatcher's position as to 'Laudabiliter,' &c., see note at end of this volume [pp 151–2].

CHAPTER X [319]

STRONGBOW, LORD OF LEINSTER, 1172–6

After Henry's departure from Ireland, Earl Richard and Hugh de Lacy set about securing themselves in their possessions and making Henry's grants effective. They were not disturbed by any opposition from outside their lordships; the strong garrisons that Henry left in Dublin, Waterford, and Wexford were enough to secure them from attack.[1] The recent submissions of the chieftains of the south and east of Ireland effectually prevented any general combination against them, if such could in any circumstances have been organized, and the Cinel Owen and Cinel Connell, who alone had not submitted, were fighting bitterly amongst themselves.[2] Trouble, however, arose, as might have been foreseen, from some of the chieftains dispossessed by Henry's grants. Tiernan O'Rourke had indeed no hereditary rights in Meath, but, as we have seen, he had claims under the forcible partition of 1169. In 1170, however, the [320]
men of East Meath had turned against him, and had set up a native prince, who had given hostages to Dermot. Early in 1171 Tiernan made several raids into the district, drove off countless cattle, and—'war-dog,' as he is called by the annalist— burned the round tower of Tullyard 'with its fill of human beings'.[3] O'Rourke was one of those expressly named as having sworn fealty to Henry, but he had no idea of giving up his claims in East Meath to Henry's grantee, and there was an inevitable clash of interests between him and Hugh de Lacy. The latter advanced as far as Fore in West Meath[4] to take possession of his fief—a proceeding which Tiernan naturally resented. A meeting was arranged between the rival claimants at a place now known as the Hill of Ward, near Athboy,[5] with the result that O'Rourke was slain. There were charges of [321]
treachery on both sides, which it would be useless now to investigate. It appears, however, from the statements of the Irish annalists that O'Rourke had enemies in his own household: 'Tiernan O'Rourke, King of Breffny and Conmacne, a man of great power for a long time, was killed by the Saxons and by Donnell son of Annadh O'Rourke of his own clan along with them. He was beheaded also by them, and his head and body

1 'Interea sub regni custodibus tranquilla Hibernia pace respirante': Gir. Camb. v. 292. 2 Ann. Ulster, Four Masters, 1172. 3 Ann. Tigernach, Ann. Inisfallen, Four Masters, 1171, where see O'Donovan's note identifying the place. This is the last of several similar entries showing that these ecclesiastical towers were used, not only as belfries, but as keeps. See Table of 'References to Belfries' in the Irish Annals, compiled by Margaret Stokes, Early Christian Architecture in Ireland. 4 Ann. Tigernach, 1172. 5 The place is called Cnoc Tlachtgha in the Annals of Tigernach (followed by the Four Masters). This was one of the old centres of pre-Christian observances, and has been identified by O'Donovan with the Hill of Ward (perhaps an ignorant half-translation of *Cnoc an bháird*, 'the Bard's Hill'). Giraldus, who gives an elaborate defence of the occurrence, calls the place *Collis Ororicii*, evidently so named after the event.

were carried ignominiously to Dublin. The head was raised over the door of the fortress—a sore miserable sight for the Gael. The body was hung in another place with the feet upwards.'[6] In the same year this Donnell O'Rourke and the English made two incursions into Annaly, a district now included in the County Longford, killed its chief, Donnell O'Farrell, and carried off many cows and prisoners.[7] In the next year Donnell O'Rourke was slain by some of Tiernan's followers. One of his hands was
[322] struck off and sent to Rory O'Conor, 'who drove a nail through it on the top of the castle of Tuam' as a warning to traitors.[8]

As for the earl, before Henry's departure he went to Ferns, the old royal seat of Leinster, and there gave his daughter (by a former marriage, we must suppose) to Robert de Quency—probably a relative of Sayer de Quency, the future Earl of Winchester—appointed him Constable of Leinster, and gave him the Duffry in fee.[9] This was the district to the west of Ferns and Enniscorthy of which Murrough O'Brain, lately slain, had been chieftain. Afterwards the earl abode at Kildare. From this he made an incursion into Clanmalier,[10] a sub-district of Offaly, under the rule of O'Dempsy, a chieftain who refused to parley with the earl or give him hostages. When the earl was returning with his spoil to Kildare, his rearguard was attacked by O'Dempsy in a pass through the woods, and his constable, Robert de Quency, was killed.[11]

[323] Raymond le Gros now applied for the vacant constableship, and besought the earl to give him his sister Basilia in marriage. Strongbow refused, and Raymond, bitterly offended, returned to Wales, to his father's castle at Carew in Pembrokeshire.[12] Hervey de Montmorency, the earl's uncle, appears to have been appointed constable.

Hervey, as we have mentioned, had received a large grant from Dermot after the taking of Wexford, and this grant, comprising apparently the present baronies of Bargy and Shelburne in the south-west corner of the County Wexford, had been confirmed to him by Strongbow. It seems to have been in 1172 or, at latest, early in 1173, that Hervey gave a considerable portion of the latter barony to the monks of Buildwas in Shropshire, to found an abbey of the Cistercian Order. This date, somewhat earlier than that usually ascribed to Hervey's grant, seems to be fixed by Strongbow's con-
[324] firmation charter, among the witnesses to which was Robert de Quenci, who, as we

6 Ann. Ulster, 1172. 7 The Annals of Tigernach and those of Inisfallen (1172) specify the tribe-lands as Muintir Anghaille, Muintir Ghiollagain, and the town of Ardacha Eascoip Maoil (Ardagh), and state that Hugh de Lacy was the leader of the expeditions. Lands in these districts, which were included in the ancient kingdom of Meath, were afterwards granted by Hugh de Lacy to his followers. 8 Ann. Tigernach, 1173. 9 Song of Dermot, ll. 2741–50. 10 Clanmalier comprised the baronies of Portnahinch in Queen's County [Leix] and Upper Philipstown in King's County [Offaly]. See Book of Rights, pp 193, 216–17, and compare the map of Leis and Offalie reproduced in the Journ. R.S.A.I., 1862–3, p. 345. The O'Dempsys of Clanmalier were nominally subject to the O'Conors Faly. 11 Song of Dermot, ll. 2769–816. This affair is recorded in the Ann. Tigernach, 1172, as follows: 'An onfall by Cu Aifne, son of Aed Hua Conchobair Failge, on the earl's troops in Kildare, and some of the Foreigners and the Hui Failgi were killed there.' The Annals of Inisfallen, Dublin MS. (1172) has the following entry: 'Conaifne, son of Aedh O'Conor Failge, and O'Diomasa surprised the Earl of Striguil's forces at Kildare, where a few of the English were slain, among whom was Robert de Quincy, the earl's son-in-law.' The pass where the reverse occurred was probably a track through the woody fastness of Rosglas, near Monasterevan. 12 Song of Dermot, ll. 2827–60.

have seen, appears to have been slain before the earl was summoned to Normandy in 1173.[13]

The monastic buildings 'de Portu Sanctae Mariae de Dunbrothy', as the house was called, were not commenced until after the year 1182 [see *Add.*]. In this year the Abbot of Buildwas sent over a lay brother named Alan to inspect the site. Alan found the place a waste wilderness, and was obliged to use a hollow oak-tree as his lodging while the boundaries of the lands given were being marked out. On his certifying to the desolation of the site, the sterility of the land, and the fierceness of the barbarous people living in the neighbourhood, the Abbot of Buildwas made over all rights under Hervey's charter to St. Mary's Abbey, Dublin. The monks were soon busy in the [325] place,[14] erecting their buildings and converting the wilderness into a garden. They were granted protection by John in 1185.[15] Their privileges were confirmed and extended by William Marshal, Earl of Pembroke, and by subsequent lords of the soil, and for at least three centuries the Abbot of Dunbrody was a power in the land, and virtually supreme within his own borders. And now, at the confluence of the Suir and Barrow, the stately ruins of the abbey-church stand lonely amid the fields, to attest the former greatness of the house.

As we have seen, it was probably in March or April 1173 that Henry sent over to Ireland William Fitz Audelin on a special mission, with powers to act on the king's behalf, and about the same time both Hugh de Lacy and Richard Fitz Gilbert appear to have been summoned to Henry's aid in Normandy. The earl, we are told, came with a number of knights and was given the custody of the frontier fortress of Gisors.[16] Hugh de Lacy was entrusted with the defence of Verneuil, which was besieged by the [326] French king in July.[17] Early in August we find Strongbow in the force which Henry mustered for the relief of Verneuil.[18] 'By a double treachery', however, 'Louis, under cover of a truce, gained possession of the town, set it on fire, and retreated into his own domains before Henry could overtake him.'[19] We need not follow the fortunes of this war. Henry, we are told, was well pleased with the services of the earl, and gave him leave to return to Ireland. At last, indeed, Henry seems to have taken him into favour. He gave him the custody of the kingdom, sending with him Raymond (according to Gerald) as coadjutor. At the same time he granted to him Wexford, which

13 [See *Add.*] See these charters in the Chartulary of St. Mary's Abbey, vol. ii, pp 151–4. There is, however, a difficulty about their exact dates. Hervey's charter is witnessed by Felix [O'Dullany], Bishop of Ossory, but the obit of his predecessor, Donnell O'Fogarty, is given by the Four Masters in 1178, two years after Strongbow's death! Possibly *episcopo* is a transcriber's error for *abbate*, as Felix was called Abbot of Ossory, i.e. of Jerpoint, before he was translated to the see. Again, another witness is Domina Nesta, but from Giraldus (p. 314) we should certainly infer that Hervey's marriage with Nesta, daughter of Maurice Fitz Gerald, did not take place until 1174. Perhaps, however, this is another case in which we cannot take the order in which Giraldus mentions events as strictly chronological. Or it may be that a later copy of Hervey's charter was inserted in the Register. It is there said to have been executed in triplicate. 14 Chart. St. Mary's Abbey, Dublin, vol. i, pp 354–5. St. Mary's Abbey, Dublin, had already been subordinated to Ralph, Abbot of Buildwas, and his successors by Henry in 1175: ibid., p. 79. 15 Ibid., vol. ii, p. 167. 16 Song of Dermot, ll. 2886–7. The exact date is uncertain. Henry fortified and provisioned Gisors and other frontier fortresses in March: Gesta Hen., vol. i, p. 42. 17 Gesta Hen., vol. i, p. 49. 18 Ralph de Diceto, vol. i, p. 375, where Richard of Striguil is said to have lately come from Ireland. 19 Norgate's Angevin Kings, vol. ii, p. 147.

henceforth became merged in the lordship of Leinster, and the castle of Wicklow.[20] But a price had to be paid for this favour, and Henry, when sending back the earl to Ireland, summoned through him the garrisons he had left in the seaport towns, and
[327] apparently others as well, to aid him in his war with the revolted barons. Robert Fitz Stephen and Maurice de Prendergast are expressly mentioned, as well as Robert Fitz Bernard, who had been left in command of the garrison of Waterford.[21] Presumably William Fitz Audelin left at the same time. He cannot have been more than five months in Ireland as representative of the king, and, except his summoning the Synod of Waterford and publishing the papal Privileges, nothing is recorded of his brief governorship, which indeed has escaped the notice of historians. There is, however, one other clear indication of his presence as governor at this time. In pursuance of the king's precept he caused a legal inquisition to be made at Dublin as to the lands which had been properly given to the white monks of St. Mary's Abbey before his arrival in Ireland.[22] From the list of lands so found to belong to them it is clear that this inquisition must have been taken before, and with a view to, Henry's confirmatory grant of
[328] these precise lands to St. Mary's Abbey tested at Falaise,[23] and this grant should probably be referred to October 1174, when Henry and nearly all the witnesses can be shown to have been at Falaise, when the war was over.

Encouraged by the news of Henry's difficulties abroad and by the weakening of the garrisons in Ireland, the Irish chieftains who had so recently sworn fealty to Henry are said to have been in a state of rebellion against the king. The earl's own household
[329] troops, too, were discontented and threatening mutiny. There was soon no money wherewith to pay them, and under Hervey as constable there was no prospect of their being able to subsist by plunder. They therefore clamoured for Raymond to be appointed their commander, and threatened, if this were not done, to return to England or, worse, desert to the enemy. Accordingly, Raymond was appointed to the command

20 Song of Dermot, ll. 2894–905; Gir. Camb. v. 298. The Song says: 'Si li baillat la marine/Watreford e Dyveline.' These were the crown-lands. This appointment and grant took place at Rouen, where Henry was from August 10 to 21: Gesta Hen., vol. i, pp 56, 57. **21** Song of Dermot, ll. 2906–39; Giraldus *ut supra*. The Irish forces joined in the campaign against the Earl of Leicester and were present at the battle of Fornham, near St. Edmund's, October 1173. Then they are said to have been employed against William the Lion, King of Scotland, and after his capture in July 1174 to have passed over to Normandy to the king: Song, ll. 2946–85. Fantosme, l. 1057, expressly mentions Robert Fitz Bernard at Fornham. **22** Chart. St. Mary's Abbey, Dublin, vol. i, p. 138. **23** Ibid., p. 81. This confirmatory grant has been placed in July 1171: Dugdale, Monasticon, v. 363, ii; and Eyton, Itin., p. 158, who, however, says that 1175 is as likely as 1171. Gilbert (Preface, Chart. St. Mary's, vol. i, p. xviii) endeavours to support the earlier date by reference to some legal proceedings in 1282–3 (ibid., p. 297), in the course of which the abbot produced a charter from Henry II as evidence that the abbey had been founded and granted its liberty before liberties had been granted to the city of Dublin. But, as the same proceedings show, the comparison was with John's charter of 1192 or 1200 to the city. The persons to whom Henry's confirmatory charter is addressed: 'archiepiscopis, &c., et omnibus fidelibus suis Francis et Anglicis et Hyberniensibus,' sufficiently indicate that it could not have been granted before Henry's visit to Ireland. Besides, the places confirmed to St. Mary's include places granted by Strongbow (ibid., pp 78, 83), and Henry would never have confirmed a grant from Strongbow before receiving his submission. The Falaise charter must, however, have preceded the Feckenham charter (ibid., p. 79), which must be dated 1175, according to Mr. Round in July (Feudal England, p. 510), but according to Eyton's Itinerary, p. 196, in October.

of the troops. An incursion was immediately made into Offelan (a district in the north-east of the present County Kildare), which resulted in obtaining an immense booty and a fresh supply of horses and arms for the troops.[24] Offelan was in Leinster, and its chief was one of the foremost in opposing Dermot. As Dermot's successor, or rather, as grantee of Leinster, Strongbow would necessarily insist on submission here. Some other pretext must have been made for the next exploit. This was the plundering of Lismore, both the city and the adjoining territory. Lismore was in the territory of the Decies in Munster, and both Dermot Mac Carthy, King of Munster, and Melaghlin O'Phelan, King of the Decies, had submitted to Henry at Waterford, but only as subordinate kings submit to their overlord. This was the first instance in which [330]
the Normans advanced beyond the bounds of Leinster and Meath, and Giraldus himself disdains to excuse the earl for countenancing it.[25] Human nature being what it is, however, such encroachments are the inevitable result when a strong conquering and as yet united race gets a foothold among a weak, ill-knit congeries of tribes. If it was the first encroachment it was certainly not the last. Having collected their prey, the plunderers drove the cattle by the coast route to Waterford. The rest of their spoil they loaded in thirteen small vessels, some of which had come from Waterford, and others they had found in the port of Lismore itself. While they were waiting, apparently at Youghal haven, for a favourable breeze, a fleet of thirty-two ships from Cork, full of armed men under the command of Gilbert, son of Turgerius,[26] presumably an Ostman, attacked them. A naval combat ensued, one of the few recorded in Irish history. The Ostmen fought with stones (slings) and axes, the Normans, under Adam de Hereford, with bows and arbalests.[27] At length the men of Cork were defeated and the [331]
Ostman leader slain, and the victorious fleet, increased in number by the captured vessels, sailed in triumph to Waterford.[28] Raymond himself was not present at this fight, but, hearing of it, he immediately hastened to the district with a small band of troops, and meeting Dermot MacCarthy, who had come with an army to aid the men of Cork, he put him to flight at Lismore, and brought back 4,000 head of cattle to Waterford.

It was, perhaps, in consequence of this attack on Lismore that Donnell O'Brien, King of Thomond, and with pretensions to be King of Munster, now turned against Strongbow. As long as Strongbow confined his efforts to securing for himself Dermot's kingdom of Leinster, Donnell in general supported him, but in face of this attack on his neighbour, Dermot Mac Carthy, he may well have suspected Strongbow's ulterior aims, and thought that his own turn would come next. In any case, towards the close of

24 Gir. Camb. v. 308. Faelan Mac Faelain afterwards gave hostages to Strongbow: Song of Dermot, l. 3216. He lived to 1203, when he died in the monastery of Connell founded by Meiler Fitz Henry: Four Masters, 1203. 25 Gir. Camb. v. 382. 26 In the 'curia que fuit Gileberti filii Turgarii' was situated the church of St. Nicholas, Cork: Reg. St. Thomas's, Dublin, p. 209. 27 'Isti lapidibus et securibus acriter impetunt, illi vero tam sagittis, quam laminis ferreis quibus abundabant, promptissime resistunt.' *Laminae fereae* = quarrels. 28 Gir. Camb. v. 309. It is not quite clear in what *portus* the fight took place. In the Book of Howth and in Bray's Conquest of Ireland (Carew, Cal. Misc., pp 67, 291) Dungarvan is supplied as the scene of the battle. This is a good deal more than sixteen miles, the stated distance, from Cork. Youghal harbour, connected with Lismore by the navigable Blackwater, suits the distance better, and was probably regarded as the port of Lismore. The plundering of Lismore is mentioned in the Annals of Tigernach.

[332] 1173, in company with a battalion from the west of Connaught headed by Conor Maenmoy, son of Rory O'Conor, he led an expedition 'to attack the castle of Kilkenny and the foreigners who dwelt therein'. This is the first intimation we have that Strongbow had a castle in Kilkenny. Probably it was part of the agreement with Donnell Mac Gillapatrick that Strongbow should be allowed to erect and garrison a castle there. Like nearly all the early Anglo-Norman castles, it was probably a mote-castle, or an entrenched and stockaded mound of earth with a wooden tower on top. It was certainly not of any great strength, and at Donnell's approach the garrison evacuated it and retreated to Waterford. Donnell then destroyed the place and plundered the district round about. 'That reduction,' adds the annalist, 'was a grief to the Foreigners of Ireland.'[29]

Early in 1174 a new expedition was planned against Munster. The ever-victorious Raymond le Gros had returned to Wales in consequence of news he had received of the death of his father, William Fitz Gerald, and in his absence Hervey de Montmorency had once more been appointed constable. Hervey, we are told, now led
[333] the earl and his household troops to Cashel. The object probably was to make a reprisal for O'Brien's attack on Kilkenny. Hearing, however, that Rory O'Conor was coming to help the men of Munster, the earl sent to Dublin for reinforcements. A strong band, consisting of the Ostmen of Dublin, led by some of the garrison, immediately advanced to join the earl at Cashel. These reinforcements marched through Ossory to the neighbourhood of Thurles, where they encamped for the night. Next morning at dawn, Donnell O'Brien and Conor Maenmoy, Rory's son, who were fully informed by their scouts of these movements, surprised the Ostman force and after a sharp struggle utterly defeated them. Four hundred of the Ostmen (or, according to the older Irish annals, 700 foreigners) were slain, besides four Norman knights who led them. Outmanoeuvred and in great peril from the combination against him, the earl, when he heard of this misfortune, retreated in confusion to Waterford.[30]

[334] This was the first serious check the earl's arms had received, and though the victors returned home and did not follow up their success, the news of the mishap, we are told, was the signal for a rising of all Ireland against the English.[31] So far as appears, however, there was no rising in Leinster; but the Ostmen of Waterford and Wexford, no doubt on hearing of the calamity which had befallen their kinsfolk of Dublin,

29 Ann. Tigernach (continuation), Ann. Inisfallen (Dublin MS.), 1173. That there was a mote at Kilkenny Castle as late as 1307 appears from an extent of the lands of Joan, Countess of Gloucester and Hertford (35 Ed. I, no. 47, m. 34). 30 See the authorities collected in O'Donovan's note to Four Masters, 1174. There is, however, no such direct opposition between the brief entries in the older annals and the more detailed account given by Giraldus as O'Donovan intimates. In the Annals of Tigernach (followed with variations by the Four Masters) it seems indeed to be stated that the junction with the Dublin contingent had been effected before the battle. Even this is not quite certainly intended. But in any case the evidence of Gerald on such a point is preferable. His bias, moreover, would have been to exaggerate, not to minimize, the mishap, which occurred under Hervey's command, so as to give the greater glory to Raymond, who soon restored the position, and there are not wanting indications that he does exaggerate the evil plight of the earl. 31 Gerald's language (p. 311) is very emphatic and obviously exaggerated: 'casus istius occasione totus totius Hiberniae populus in Anglos unanimiter insurgunt.'

became disaffected, and this disaffection, in Waterford at any rate, 'where the earl was as one besieged,' was very serious, and afterwards broke out in open revolt. By the rising of all Ireland against the English we must understand the gathering of the clans of Ulster and Connaught, who were now being summoned by Rory for a hosting into Meath.

In these straits the earl sent a message to Raymond in Wales promising that he would give him his sister Basilia in marriage and the constableship of Leinster, as he had formerly asked, and urging him to come to his aid with strong force. Raymond, [335]
along with Meiler Fitz Henry and others of his kinsmen, immediately collected a force of thirty knights, 100 horse-soldiers, and 300 archers on foot, and conveyed them to Wexford in fifteen ships. They arrived just in time to quell a mutiny of the Ostmen here, and then set out to relieve Strongbow. It appears that the earl was at this time on an island in the Suir, near Waterford, now known as the Little Island, but then called Inis Teimle or Inis Doimhle, and that here Raymond came to meet him, and conducted him to Wexford.[32]

Raymond appears to have been unable to enter Waterford. The governor of the town, called Fretellus by Giraldus, endeavoured to follow the earl, but was slain with some of his companions by the Ostmen whom he had employed to convey him down the river in a boat. Having done this treacherous deed, the Ostmen returned to Waterford and excited a revolt, in which all the English who could be found in the [336]
open spaces and houses of the town were slaughtered, without regard to age or sex. The garrison in Reginald's Tower, however, succeeded in holding the town and quelling the mutiny. The Ostmen, except the leaders of the revolt, were pardoned, but were henceforth distrusted and reduced in status.[33]

The nuptials of Raymond and Basilia were now celebrated in Wexford, and on the following day Raymond set out, accompanied by his brother-in-law, to the relief of Hugh de Lacy's barons in Meath, whose territory at this moment was being raided by a huge army under Rory O'Conor.

The Irish annals do not mention this hosting of Rory O'Conor into Meath. Indeed, if we depended solely on Irish sources of information we should know very little about the doings of the Normans during the early years of the invasion, and especially during the three years that followed Henry's visit to Ireland. With the exception of the [337]
killing of O'Rourke and the battle of Thurles, they hardly mention anything bearing

32 Gir. Camb. v. 311–12. Song of Dermot, ll. 2994–3031, where the meeting-place of the earl and Raymond is called *iddle de Instepheni*. The Dublin copy of the Annals of Inisfallen state that the men of Waterford, on hearing of the defeat of Thurles, 'killed the two hundred who were guarding the town. Then the earl went on an island near the town and remained there a month, and then went back again to Dublin': Four Masters, 1174, note. According to the Song, Raymond landed with only 'three ships', another indication of probable exaggeration in Gerald's account. 33 This seems to be the meaning of Gerald's words: 'denuo proditores ad pacem cum deteriore tam opinione quam conditione sunt reversi' (p. 313). This reduction in status was perhaps the real historical foundation for the curious finding of the jury entered in the Plea Roll of the 4th Edward II (see Fac. Nat. MSS. of Ireland, vol. iii, Introd. vi, pl. vii, and App iii). At least the historical statement there made is not borne out by anything we know, and seems very improbable. It was probably in consequence of this revolt that the Ostmen were removed from Waterford and settled in the *villa Ostmannorum*.

on the fortunes of the invaders during these three years. From the Irish annals, however, we learn that Donnell Bregach O'Melaghlin, who in 1170 had turned against O'Conor and O'Rourke and given hostages to Dermot, and who had probably accepted the new régime, was killed in 1173 by his half-brother, Art O'Melaghlin, and that Art succeeded him in West Meath, while the kingdom of East Meath appears to have been assumed by Manus O'Melaghlin. Probably it was to assist these princes against the encroachments of the Normans, who were already beginning to build castles in Meath, that Rory now crossed the Shannon with a formidable army.

The Song of Dermot gives us several interesting particulars about this hosting.[34] In the first place, it shows that the hosting was on a very large scale, and consisted of contingents from all the principal tribes of Connaught and Ulster. It gives a list of the
[338] chieftains who joined in it, which must have been supplied by a contemporary Irish authority.[35] In the next place, we find there an authoritative contemporary description of the kind of castle erected by Hugh de Lacy at Trim, which, taken together with a similar description of the castle built by Richard le Fleming at Slane, has led to a fresh examination of the subject, and an entire revision of our ideas as to the type of the castles erected in Ireland by the first Anglo-Norman settlers.

We are told that Hugh de Lacy 'fortified a house at Trim, and threw a fosse around it, and then enclosed it with a herisson', or stockaded rampart.[36] He then placed a garrison in the house (*meysun*), appointed Hugh Tyrrell warden of the castle (*chastel*), and left for England. Rory O'Conor chose his time well for a last effort to oust the for-
[339] eigners from Meath. Hugh de Lacy was away with the king in Normandy,[37] Strongbow was only just emerging from his difficulties in Leinster, and the barons of Meath could expect no help from the depleted and disheartened garrison of Dublin.

On hearing of the gathering of the clans against him, Hugh Tyrrell sent a messenger in haste to seek succour from the earl, and the earl immediately assembled the host of Leinster and marched to Trim. But he arrived too late. The Irish were before him. Hugh Tyrrell, from lack of support, had evacuated the castle, and when the Irish came it was empty. Thereupon 'they threw down the mote and levelled it even with the ground, but first of all they put the house to flames'.[38] The Irish had departed before the earl arrived, and he found neither house nor cabin, big or little, to shelter him for the night in Trim. Straightway he mounted horse, pursued the retreating host, and came up with their rear. The Irish had no armour, and could not stand the charge of

34 ll. 3222–341. The account there given is not connected with the return and marriage of Raymond and his rescue of Strongbow—the sequence is interrupted by a long detailed account of the sub-infeudation of Leinster and Meath—but it evidently refers to the hosting mentioned by Giraldus, pp 311, 313. 35 Ibid., ll. 3238–9. The list includes, besides the Connaught princes, the kings of Meath, Breffny, Uriel, Uladh, the Cinel Owen, and the Cinel Connell—the whole of Leth Cuinn, in short. [*Corrigenda* in the notes to this passage: *Oharthire*, probably O'hEghra (O'Hara); *Poltilethban*, i.e. Poll tighe Liabhain, a place in O'Shaughnessy's country: Keating's Hist. (I.T.S.), vol. ii, p. 324. *Macgarragan*, Mac Carrghamhna, lord of Muintir Maoilsionna (in Westmeath): Topogr. Poems, p. 12.] 36 'A Trym ferma une meisun,/E fosse jeta envirun,/E pus l'enclost de hireson' (Song, ll. 3223–5). 37 Hugh de Lacy appears to have been with the king at Rouen about December 1174, and at Valognes in April 1175: Eyton's Itin., pp 187, 189. 38 'La mot[e] firent degeter,/Desque a la tere tut verser,/E la meysun tut premer/De fu ardant estenceler' (Song ii. 3300–3).

the Norman chivalry.[38a] But they scattered in every direction, and their pursuers only succeeded in cutting off a few. The earl then returned to Dublin, and Hugh Tyrrell [340] re-fortified his fortress (*forcelette*).

This castle, then, was not a strong structure of stone and mortar such as we are accustomed to associate with the term 'castle', but consisted simply of a wooden house or rather tower (*turris lignea* or *bretesche*) placed on the summit of an artificial mound or hillock of earth (mote, Latin *mota*), and surrounded at the base by a fosse and an earthen rampart bearing a stockade. Similarly at Slane, on the northern bank of the Boyne between Navan and Drogheda, where Hugh de Lacy gave twenty knights' fees to Richard le Fleming, the Song says that Richard 'raised a mote in order to harass his enemies'.[39] It then describes an attack by the Irish, the defence and ultimate destruction of the 'meyson', and the slaughter of its garrison. It is plain that this castle, like that at Trim, consisted of a wooden house or tower on a mote.

At Slane, on the top of the hill near the ancient monastery, the mote still exists. At Trim the re-erected mote was probably levelled when the great twenty-sided donjon and extensive courtyard, the ruins of which are among the finest in Ireland, were constructed. Motes, or fortified hillocks of earth wholly or partly artificial, are found in [341] considerable numbers in Ireland, but only in places to which the Normans are known to have penetrated at an early stage of the invasion. Indeed, nearly every undoubted example can be shown to be either at a known castle site, or actually connected with subsequent castle buildings, or, where no early castle is mentioned or can be detected, at what appears to have been the seat of an early Norman manor. They are usually from about twenty to forty feet in height, with very steep sides, and with a flat space on the summit from about thirty to a hundred feet across. At the base of the mote, and separated from it by its encircling ditch, is frequently found an enclosure (bawn, bailey, or courtyard), sometimes also artificially or naturally raised, and varying in shape and size and defences with the configuration of the ground or the needs of the builder. If not sufficiently protected by the natural or artificial steepness of the ground outside, this enclosure is usually guarded by an earthen rampart and outer ditch, the latter generally communicating with the ditch round the mote, and the whole fortress is sometimes surrounded by an additional outer rampart.

We have only to imagine one of the motes bearing on its flat summit a loop-holed and battlemented tower of wood, and girt round its upper edge by a stout palisade, and the earthen ramparts below similarly bearing wooden defences and enclosing the [342] buildings in the bailey, to obtain a picture of the type of castle first erected by the Normans in Ireland. But indeed the picture has been already drawn for us on the Bayeux Tapestry a century before the time of which we write, when castles of the same type were erected by the same race in somewhat conditions in England. The tower on high, the forerunner of the donjon keep, was connected with the bailey either by a light plank bridge of steps spanning the ditch at a steep incline, or by a stepped way borne by the inner rampart of the bailey, which in this case was carried across the ditch and up the slope of the mote.

38a [cavalry?]. 39 'Un[e] mot[e| fist cil jeter/Pur ses enemis grever' (Song, ll. 3178–9).

Partly by documentary evidence, but mainly by evidence of an archaeological nature, this type of castle has been shown to have been almost universally adopted by the first Norman invaders of Ireland. Except in the case of 'promontory fortresses', such as those already described at Baginbun and Carrick on Slaney, where a mote would not be required, and indeed would be difficult to erect, and in a few cases where an isolated rock formed a ready-made substitute, a mote, as above described, has been proved to exist, or to have formerly existed, at nearly every known early castle site.[40]

[343] Such a castle required little skilled labour, and only materials easy to obtain, but when completed it would afford a sure refuge in case of a sudden attack, and from the high-placed tower a handful of archers could keep an unarmoured host for some time at bay. The wooden materials, however, were liable to be burnt, if the attackers were numerous enough and sufficiently daring to get near. Hence we often read of the burning of these early castles, and as often of their rapid reconstruction. Gradually, and as opportunity occurred, the woodwork was in many cases replaced by stone towers and stone walls, but the original plan was in general substantially retained.

The passage summarized above from the Song of Dermot indicates further how it was that the Irish, in spite of their vast superiority in numbers, and even when united, could not hold their country against the invaders, and how it was that the invaders, on
[344] the other hand, failed to make their conquest complete. Without armour and with inferior weapons and discipline, the Irish, however numerous and however brave, could not face the death-dealing bolts of the crossbowmen or the charge of ironclad knights in the open field. They could only make a raid, burn, plunder, and retreat. The Normans, on the other hand, even if they overtook the retreating forces, could not adequately punish a foe that immediately dispersed among the woods and morasses.

Next year (1175) the Normans appear to have been active in Meath in making reprisals on the chieftains who took part in the hosting of the previous year. Thus we learn that they hanged Manus O'Melaghlin at Trim.[41] Probably he was tried and condemned as a traitor for the part he had played. They plundered Clonard and Durrow, and made raids into the territories of certain chieftains in West Meath who appear to have joined in Rory's hosting.[42] Indeed, the whole country from Athlone to Drogheda is said to have been laid waste by them.[43] Besides rebuilding the castles of Trim and
[345] Duleek, they erected castles at other places. From about this period we may date the complete occupation of East Meath and probably of part of West Meath as well.

40 The writer has examined this subject and adduced evidence to the above effect in the following papers: 'Mote and Bretesche Building in Ireland,' Eng. Hist. Rev., 1906, pp 417–44; 'Motes and Norman Castles in Ireland,' ibid. 1907, pp 228–54 and 440–67; 'Motes and Norman Castles in Ireland,' Journ. Roy. Soe. Antiquaries, Ireland, 1907, pp 123–52; 'Motes and Norman Castles in County Louth,' ibid. 1908, pp 241–69; 'Motes and Norman Castles in Ossory,' ibid. 1909, pp 313–42; also in monographs on the mote-castles of Foderedunolan, Athlone, Newcastle Mackynegan, Castlekevin, Killeedy, Shanid, Knockgraffon, Street, Ardowlan and Castlelost. And see Map, *infra*, vol. ii [pp 288–9]. 41 Ann. Tigernach, Four Masters, 1175. Art O'Melaghlin, on the other hand, appears to have been left in possession of West Meath or part of it. Three years later the Normans aided him in maintaining his position: ibid. 1178. 42 e.g. the Muintir Mail Sinna, whose chieftain, Mac Carrghamhna, is mentioned in the Song (l. 3255) under the form Macgarragan. 43 Ann. Tigernach, 1175.

Rory O'Conor did not make any effort this year to interrupt the re-settlement of Meath. As we shall see, he was now prepared to accept the domination of the foreigners both in Leinster and in Meath, and in the autumn was related to them by way of alliance and not of hostility.

About the 1st of October 1175 an expedition was organized by Raymond against Donnell O'Brien, King of Thomond. Strongbow must have desired to avenge the defeat at Thurles in the previous year, and may have authorized the expedition, but Raymond the constable was in sole command, and the earl himself appears to have been absent in England.[44] According to our best and most explicit Irish authority for the period, this seemingly rash expedition was undertaken 'at the invitation of Rory O'Conor, King of Ireland,' and Raymond was assisted by the Connaughtmen, who 'burnt the greater part of Thomond'.[45] This action of the *ard-rí* may at first sight seem [346]
improbable, but there is really no reason why we should doubt its occurrence. It was indeed in exact accordance with a provision in the Treaty of Windsor, just at this time being signed. We have, moreover, repeated examples of the kings of Connaught, of Thomond, and of Desmond, as well as those of subordinate districts, seeking aid from the Norman knights to subdue their enemies both within and without their borders. Rory's invitation, moreover, throws much light on the situation and explains much. It detracts somewhat from the hazardous nature of the expedition, and from Raymond's [347]
glory, and therefore perhaps was not mentioned by the writers on the Norman side. But it shows that Raymond had not to fear the combination which wrecked Hervey's attempt, and indeed, as the event proved, had only the Ostmen of Limerick to contend with. The preceding paragraph in the Annals of Tigernach states that Rory O'Conor made a hosting into Thomond, and banished Donnell O'Brien, and gave the kingdom to the son of Murrough O'Brien, his own mother's son.[46] The immediate occasion of this expulsion may have been the violent conduct of Donnell O'Brien, who earlier in the year had blinded Dermot, son of Teig O'Brien, and Mahon, son of Turlough

44 Giraldus, v. 321, gives the day of the month, and the Irish annals supply the year. If the date thus arrived at, October 1, 1175, be correct, it would seem that the earl was absent from Ireland, for Richard de Striguil was a witness to two of Henry's charters dated at Marlborough and Feckenham in this year, and the Marlborough charter, at any rate, seems to have been correctly placed in October 1175; Eyton's Itin., p. 196, but cf. Feudal England, p. 510. 45 Ann. Tigernach, 1175. The whole entry is thus rendered by Stokes: 'A hosting by Ruaidri Hua Conchobair into Thomond, and he banished Domnall Hua Briain into Ormond, and gave the kingship of Thomond to the son of Murchad Hua Briain to his own mother's son. At the invitation of the King of Ireland, Ruaidri Hua Conchobair, the Foreigners of Dublin and Waterford and Domnall Hua Gillapatraic, King of Ossory, came to Limerick, without being perceived by the Dal Cais, and plundered Limerick; and on this expedition the Connaughtmen burnt the greater part of Thomond.' The entry in the Four Masters, rendered in the same phraseology, would run as follows: 'A hosting by R. O'C. king of Ireland into Munster and he banished D. O'B. from Thomond, and on that expedition he greatly wasted the country.' It looks as if the Four Masters had adapted the commencement and the end of the entry in the earlier annals, while omitting all reference to the English; and yet, except as regards Rory's invitation, we have ample corroboration of the part omitted. 46 In Four Masters, 1168, it is stated that Murtough (then slain), son of Turlough O'Brien (ob. 1167), was son of Rory O'Conor's mother. This seems to indicate that at one time Turlough O'Brien had to wife the same lady as at some other time was wife of his great enemy, Turlough O'Conor (ob. 1156). The above Murrough must have been brother to Murtough. Rory O'Conor was imprisoned by his father as early as 1136 and again in 1143.

O'Brien, both of whom were descended from senior branches of the house. But this was by no means an unusual precaution to take, and, as Rory's own hands were not clean in this respect, it is perhaps more probable that his animosity was aroused by the killing of his kinsman, the son of Lethderg O'Conor, effected by O'Brien on the same
[348] day. At any rate, the hereditary feud between the O'Conors and the O'Briens was repeatedly breaking out, and contributed in no small degree to the ultimate loss of both kingdoms.

Raymond's expedition, then, was undertaken in favourable circumstances. His force consisted of 120 knights, 300 mounted archers, and 400 on foot. They assembled in Ossory, where O'Brien's old enemy, Donnell Mac Gillapatrick, undertook to guide them to Limerick. They reached the city in safety, but it 'was surrounded by a river, a wall, and a fosse, so that no man could pass over except by a treacherous ford'. As Gerald recounts the story, the honours of the day were all with his kinsfolk, but indeed he is substantially supported by the Song. First of all, David of Wales, a nephew of Raymond, without waiting for orders from his uncle, who was in the rear, rode his horse into the stream, and, crossing obliquely, was carried safely over. As, however, only one man followed him, the two proceeded to return, when his unfortunate follower was swept away by the impetuosity of the current. Next Meiler Fitz Henry outdid his kinsman's exploit by riding across and holding his ground on the other side in spite of enemies on the bank and missiles showered on him from the walls of the town. Attracted by the shouts, Raymond now came up, and, seeing Meiler's peril, animated
[349] his men to essay the ford. Then plunging into the stream he led tho whole force across without much loss, stormed the walls, and captured the town. 'It was a glorious victory,' and called forth a rhapsody from Gerald, but, like many another, it led to nothing. For the moment, however, all went well. Raymond provisioned and garrisoned the town, and having placed it in the custody of his cousin, Milo Fitz David, he returned with the rest of his force to Leinster.[47]

While Raymond was conducting this brilliant expedition to Limerick, Rory O'Conor was sending envoys to Henry to arrange a treaty of peace. These envoys were Catholicus, Archbishop of Tuam, Canthordis, Abbot of St. Brandon, and Master Laurence, described as chancellor of the King of Connaught. They found the king at Windsor, where, on the 6th of October 1175, in the presence of the council and of Laurence O'Toole, Archbishop of Dublin, the treaty was signed. By this treaty Henry 'granted to Rory, his liege man, King of Connaught, as long as he should faithfully serve him, that he should be king under him, prepared to do him service as his vassal; and that he should hold his land (of Connaught) well and peaceably, as he held it before his lord the King of England entered Ireland, rendering to him tribute'. As to
[350] the rest of the land and its inhabitants, Rory was to be overlord, and was to enforce the payment of tribute and due obedience to the English Crown, and for this purpose, if necessary, to call for the assistance of the king's constable and troops; and the annual tribute to be paid as well for Connaught as for the rest of the land was to be the tenth merchantable hide. The treaty was, however, subject to this proviso, that Rory was not

47 Gir. Camb. v. 320–3, 326; Song of Dermot, l. 3370 *ad finem*.

to interfere with the lands which the king retained in his dominion and in the dominion of his barons, namely Dublin, Meath, 'as fully as Murrough O'Melaghlin held it,' Wexford with the whole of Leinster, and Waterford with all the land between it and Dungarvan. The Irish who had fled were to return to the land of the king's barons in peace, and, at the will of their lords, either pay tribute or perform their accustomed services for their lands; and if any refused, Rory, at the requisition of their lords, was to compel them to return. And the King of Connaught was to take hostages from all who were committed to him, and to give hostages to the King of England.[48]

How little we can trust references in the Irish Annals to political dealings between [351]
England and Ireland may be exemplified by the only account of this treaty preserved by them. 'Cadla O'Duffy (Catholicus, Archbishop of Tuam) came out of England from the Son of the Empress, having with him the peace of Ireland and the kingship thereof, both Foreigner and Gael, to Rory O'Conor, and to every provincial king his province from the King of Ireland, and their tributes to Rory.' [49] Had the text of the treaty not been preserved, what should we make of this extraordinary account?

But this treaty was not workable. It was ostensibly based on the supposition that Rory O'Conor was a king in Ireland in the same sense that Henry was a king throughout his dominions across the water, able to rule and enforce obedience to his mandates. But we cannot imagine Rory O'Conor collecting tribute for the Saxon king from the chieftains of Ulster or from Donnell O'Brien, with whom he was at this moment at war, and restraining them from rebellion and disloyalty to the English Crown! Probably the endeavour to collect tribute for this purpose from his own subordinate chieftains in Connaught was the cause of his subsequent unpopularity.[50] As the next [352]
few years showed, Rory was not able to enforce obedience to himself even from his own sons.[51] If any attempt was to be made to enforce the terms of this treaty, assuredly the king's constable and the king's troops would have to be repeatedly requisitioned. Raymond, though a successful general, and the darling of his soldiers, had an enemy at home. Hervey de Montmorency, we are told, though he had recently allied himself with the Geraldines by marrying Nesta, daughter of Maurice Fitz Gerald, actuated by envy and malice, sent messengers to Henry, asserting that Raymond was designing to secure not only Limerick, but all Ireland, for himself and his friends.[52] It is probable that Henry did not approve of Raymond's aggressive methods, which were sure to

48 Gesta Hen., vol. i, p. 101–3; Rog. Howden, vol. i, pp 83, 84. It is probable that Strongbow had been summoned to the king with reference to this treaty. He was in the king's entourage at Marlborough, apparently in this month. See note, p. 345 [note 44, p. 130], *supra*. At this council Henry appointed Augustin, an Irishman, to the vacant see of Waterford, and sent him to Ireland with the archbishops of Dublin and Cashel to be consecrated: ibid. 49 Ann. Tigernach, 1175. This entry is repeated in the Dublin copy of the Annals of Inisfallen. The other annals, including the Four Masters, take no notice of the treaty whatsoever. 50 That he did collect some tribute from Connaught appears from the statement in the Annals of Loch Cé, 1186, that it was to Hugh de Lacy the tribute of Connaught was paid. 51 In 1177 Rory O'Conor's son, Murrough, brought Miles de Cogan and his knights to Roscommon 'to spoil Connaught through hatred of his father'. The Connaughtmen, however, laid waste the country before the invaders and eventually drove them out: Ann. Ulster. This rebellion was unsuccessful, and Murrough was blinded by his father. Ten years later, however, as we shall see, Conor Mainmoy, another son, succeeded in expelling his father and ruling in his stead. 52 Gir. Camb., p. 327.

[353] lead to disturbances. At any rate, early next year (1176) he sent four commissioners to recall Raymond, two of whom were to return with him, and the other two to stay in Ireland with the earl.[53]

Raymond was ready to obey the king's summons when intelligence came from the garrison he had left at Limerick that Donnell O'Brien with a large army was blockading the town, and that as their provisions were exhausted during the winter they were in need of immediate succour. The earl's troops refused to move without their favourite commander, so Raymond, with the approval of the king's commissioners, once more turned his standard towards Limerick. This time, in addition to his own band of 80 men-at-arms, 200 retainers, and 300 archers, he had with him some Irish contingents under Murtough Mac Murrough of Okinselagh and Donnell Mac Gillapatrick of Ossory, both of whom had definitively thrown in their lot with the invaders.[54] When on his way towards Cashel Raymond learnt that the men of Thomond had raised the siege of Limerick and had come to oppose him at 'the pass of Cashel'.

[354] The natural difficulties of this pass had been increased in the usual Celtic manner by felling trees, digging ditches, and running a strong barricade across it. Raymond divided his little band into three squadrons, and Donnell of Ossory, seeing how few they were, though well armed, warned them that unless they were victorious his Irish troops could not be trusted not to turn upon them. 'For we Irishmen,' he said, 'ever side with the winners, and fall upon those who flee.' Then Meiler, who led the first squadron, threw himself with his men like a mighty whirlwind into the pass, tore down the barricade, and clove a path with the sword through all who resisted him. This was on Easter Eve (April 3). On the following Tuesday the triumphant force entered Limerick.[55]

Raymond stayed at Limerick to repair the damage sustained during the siege, and shortly afterwards met Rory O'Conor and Donnell O'Brien in a parley, on the same day, but not in the same place. These two kings, it seems, were not yet at peace with one another. Rory had a fleet on Lough Derg, and at the close of the last year had laid Ormond waste and exacted hostages from the O'Briens of that district.[56] Now he came
[355] down Lough Derg in one of his ships, and anchored near the lower end of the lake. Donnell encamped not far off on the western side of the river, on the skirts of a wood. Raymond took up his position between the two, a little north of Killaloe. A long three-cornered parley followed, which resulted in both princes giving hostages and solemnly swearing to be faithful in future to the English king.[57] The Irish annals are silent about Raymond's intervention between the two kings, but they state that about this time Donnell made peace with Rory, and gave him hostages.[58] Raymond was, no doubt, acting under directions given him by Henry's commissioners, and he seems to have been actually carrying out the terms of the Treaty of Windsor, by which the

53 Gir. Camb., p. 328. Their names were Robert Poer, Osbert de Herlotera, William de Bendinges, and Adam de Gernemes (?) (perhaps 'Gernemue', Eyton's Itin.). 54 Donnell of Ossory and Donnell of Thomond were bitter foes. In the preceding year the son of the former was treacherously slain by the latter: Four Masters, 1175. 55 Gir. Camb. v. 329–30. Raymond approached Limerick via Cashel probably because he had joined Donnell Mac Gillapatrick somewhere in Ossory. 56 Ann. Tigernach, 1175. 57 Giraldus, p. 331. 58 Ann. Tigernach, 1176.

King of Connaught was to receive hostages from all who were committed to him, and himself to give hostages to the King of England.

When Raymond returned with his hostages to Limerick, he received envoys from Dermot Mac Carthy, King of Desmond, imploring aid, as a liege vassal of the King of England, against his eldest son, Cormac Liathanach, who had deprived him of his kingdom and thrown him into prison, and promising large gifts to Raymond as well as pay to his troops. Raymond accordingly led his victorious standards towards Cork, and by his aid Dermot Mac Carthy recovered his kingdom.[59] Thus were the forces of the [356]
crown from time to time requisitioned, but in this case not exactly as proposed by the Treaty of Windsor.

In the midst of these triumphs came the alarming news that Strongbow was dead. In conveying this intelligence to Raymond, great precautions were taken lest it should get abroad. The messenger, himself ignorant of its contents, bore a letter from Basilia containing this enigmatic sentence: 'The great jaw tooth which has troubled me so much has just dropped out. Wherefore, if thou hast any regard for me or even for thyself, delay not thy return.' This letter was privately read to Raymond by a clerk of his household, and Raymond, though he probably could not read, was shrewd enough to guess that the falling out of the tooth signified the death of the earl, who he knew was suffering from a serious illness. He had, in fact, died from blood-poisoning of the foot about the end of May,[60] but from fear of a rising among the Irish everything was done to conceal the fact until Raymond's return with his troops. In this emergency [357]
Raymond hastened back to Limerick, and took counsel with the most discreet of his household. It was agreed that in view of the earl's death, and Raymond's imminent departure for England, it would be necessary to give up for the present the attempt to hold a town so remote and so surrounded by enemies as Limerick, and withdraw the whole force to protect the coast-towns and the castles of Leinster. As a last resource, then, Raymond committed the custody of the town to Donnell O'Brien, as though to a baron of his lord the King of the English, and Donnell gave fresh hostages and took new oaths to preserve the town uninjured, to restore it at the king's command, and to keep the peace. Nevertheless, the garrison had hardly evacuated the place when Donnell broke down the bridge and fired the town.[61] Never again, if he could help it, would the old Danish walls afford protection to foreigners!

O'Brien may have been false to his repeated oaths of fealty, but he grimly held to this resolve, and, while he lived, never again did the English hold the city of Limerick. When Henry heard the whole story he is reported to have said, with insight at once generous and sound: 'Brilliant was the assault of Limerick, more brilliant still its relief, but only in its evacuation was there wisdom.'

When Raymond and his men reached Dublin, Richard of Striguil was buried in the [358]
church of the Holy Trinity, and Archbishop Laurence O'Toole performed the obsequies with due solemnity.

59 Giraldus, p. 331; cf. Ann. Tigernach, 1176 (followed by the Four Masters), where, however, Raymond is not mentioned. 60 Ralph de Diceto, vol. i, p. 407, says April 5; Giraldus (p. 332) says 'circa Kalendas Junii', and this is probably more correct. William Fitz Audelin was with the king up to the end of May: Eyton's Itin, pp 203–4. 61 Gir. Camb. v. 332–3.

As far as we can judge from the somewhat scanty indications which the facts as known to us afford, the untimely death of the Earl of Striguil was a real misfortune, not only for the Anglo-Norman colony, but for Ireland. If Ireland was to benefit by Norman rule and Norman organization, and by the higher civilization and greater industrial energy of the new colonists, there was needed a man whom the other colonists would recognize as being, by birth, antecedents, and abilities, their natural superior. It was not a soldier that was wanted, nor even a general capable of conducting extensive military operations, but a statesman actuated by the single purpose of making the Norman rule a success. Richard de Clare came of an illustrious house, had thrown in his lot with Ireland, had wedded an Irish wife, and his whole future depended on the success of his undertaking. It was not so with the court-official who followed him. Moreover, to judge by the earl's success in winning over most of the chieftains of Leinster to acquiesce in the Norman settlement, which he did (after showing his strength) more by persuasion and reasonable treatment than by the
[359] sword,[62] he was the man best fitted to carry on the work of pacification.

This, it is scarcely needful to say, was not the opinion of the native annalists. Their feeling towards Strongbow is plain from their ascribing his death to 'the miracles of Brigit and Columcille and the other saints whose churches he had destroyed.' But the native annalists not unnaturally fathered on Strongbow the evils which they deemed to have arisen from the English intervention in general. To him personally they do not ascribe any act of treachery or bad faith, or even of unusual severity, and with the exception of the revolt of the Ostmen of Waterford, Leinster, under his rule when viceroy and for many years afterwards, appears to have been quiet and prosperous.

The fine monument consisting of the recumbent effigy of a mail-clad knight still existing in the cathedral of the Holy Trinity (or, as it is commonly called, Christ Church), and known as Strongbow's Tomb, was not originally erected to Strongbow.
[360] An ancient inscription inserted in the wall of the south aisle records the fact that the original monument was broken by the fall of the roof and body of Christ Church in the year 1562, and though the inscription goes on to state that the monument was set up again in 1570 by Sir Henry Sidney, Lord Deputy of Ireland, there can be little doubt that the effigy of another knight was substituted for that of Strongbow. The existing effigy was never broken, and the arms exhibited on the shield are not those of the de Clares.[63] It appears that it was customary to provide in legal documents for the payment at Strongbow's tomb of moneys due, and therefore, lest debtors should go

62 Thus Murtough Mc Murrough and Donnell Kavanagh of Okinselagh, Donnell Mc Gillapatrick of Ossory, and Donnell Mc Gillamocholmog of the vale of Dublin, all seem to have had territory given to them and to have acquiesced in the Anglo-Norman settlement. See too the list of Leinster chieftains stated in the Song (ll. 3208–21) to have given hostages to Strongbow and to have been on his side. O'Toole is the only important king not mentioned. 63 This appears to have been first noticed by Sir Richard Colt Hoare in his Tour in Ireland 1806, p. 14, note, where he describes the arms on the monument as '*Argent, on a chief azure, three crosses crosslets fitchée of the field*', while the arms of the de Clares were *Gules, three chevronels or.* On the seal of Strongbow's grant of Aghaboe the knight bears a shield with a field *chevronée*, from which the three chevronels of de Clare are supposed by Boutell to have been derived.

free and the bonds of society be broken, it was necessary to provide for the continued existence of the tombstone.

Beside this tombstone is a smaller one, which as long ago as 1584 was described as the effigy of a youth cut in two and supporting his entrails with both his hands. About it a foolish legend is told that it represents Strongbow's son, who, it is said, was cut in two by his enraged father for showing cowardice in the face of the foe.[64] The story is [361]
purely apocryphal, and probably owes its origin to a misconception of the design of the monument. In the writer's opinion the figure is that of a kneeling lady holding up the folds of her robe with her two hands and wearing a wimple round her face. It should be placed upright, and probably formed part of the side of a sepulchral monument, whether Strongbow's or another's.

In a quite legitimate sense, however, we may regard Christ Church itself as a memorial of Strongbow. It is true that the fabric was probably not completed until half a century after his death, and that in the course of the long years that have rolled over its head it has suffered from many disastrous accidents and changes until in our own days it was completely restored on the original lines through the munificence of a Dublin citizen; yet there is reason to think that it was commenced under the auspices of Strongbow when viceroy in Dublin; and, even if this cannot be demonstrated, it was certainly among the first of the many splendid fanes which owed their origin to the energy, taste, and munificence of the Anglo-Norman colony of which Strongbow was the pioneer and chief.

The first foundation of a church dedicated to the Holy Trinity on the same site [362]
must indeed be ascribed to a much earlier time. It was certainly in existence when the Normans came, and had been richly endowed both by Irish kings of Leinster and by Scandinavian lords of Dublin.[65] A late, and in some respects clearly legendary, account of its origin is given in an entry in the Black Book of Christ Church.[66] The foundation is there ascribed to 'Sitruic, son of Ableb', meaning thereby Sitric, son of Olaf, who was lord of Dublin at the time of the battle of Clontarf. No part of this building, however, remains. Certain architectural features in the crypt, which runs under the whole building except the western bay of the nave, are pronounced by the competent authority of Mr. Street, the architect employed at the recent restoration, to be at the earliest of very late Romanesque character, or of about the end of the twelfth century; and though these features do not appear in the eastern part, Mr. Street considered that no [363]
long period elapsed between the commencement of the crypt and its completion. Whatever church existed on the site before the time of the English invasion was, he concludes, entirely removed in order to provide the necessary foundations for one on so large a scale. The choir and transepts were no doubt the first portions built above

64 By Richard Stanihurst, De rebus in Hibernia gestis (Antwerp, 1584), pp 171–3. 65 See the confirmation grant by Laurence, Archbishop of Dublin, c. 1178, Cal. Christ Church Deeds, No. 364 (a), and that by King John, Mar. 6, 1201, ibid., No. 364 (c), and Chart. Priv. et Immun., p. 12. From the latter we learn that gifts were made to the chureh by the following kings of Leinster: Donchad m. Domnail Remair, sl. 1089, F. M.; Enna Mac Donchada, ob. 1126, F. M.; and Diarmaid Mac Murchada, ob. 1171; as well as by Sitric son of Olaf and the sons of Thorkil. 66 Cal. Lib. Niger, Proc. R.I.A., xxvii (c), p. 69.

ground. The original choir was, however, replaced in the middle of the fourteenth century by a much longer structure. This was pulled down in 1871, and the present eastern termination built on what appears to have been the original lines. The form of the original choir was inferred from the plan of the crypt, which has a semicircular apse, round which the aisle is continued, and east of which are three small square-ended chapels, and with this the two western arches of the choir, which had not been disturbed, agreed. Now the entry in the Black Book before referred to (as calendared) goes on to state that Archbishop Laurence, Richard, Earl of Striguil, Robert Fitz Stephen, and Raymond le Gros, 'built the choir, with bells and two chapels, viz.
[364] of St. Edmund, king and martyr,[67] of St. Mary, called Alba, and St. Laud, and gave St. Michael's church for the Mensa.' Taking this tradition in connexion with the architectural evidence, it is probable that while Strongbow was viceroy a commencement was made to rebuild the old Norse cathedral. The choir, bell tower (blown down in 1316), and two eastern chapels were first erected, and of course the crypt underneath this portion of the church. The transepts which still remain belong to the transitional period, and were probably built very little later. Early in the next century the nave, which is Early English in style, was erected—all except the western bay, which appears to have been built, 'in order to lengthen and enlarge the church,' after the year 1234.[68] To restore the building as nearly as might be to its appearance at about this time was Mr. Street's professed aim, and, though he has not escaped criticism, the result is a small but beautiful structure with a continuity of existence from the days of
[365] Strongbow, and one of which all citizens of Dublin who care for historical associations may be justly proud.

Another foundation which may with even greater confidence be ascribed to Strongbow, though no remains of it exist to-day, is the Hospital of St. John of Jerusalem at Kilmainham, close to Dublin, on the west. Strongbow's charter is, unfortunately, not forthcoming, but the early title of the Knights Hospitallers here, commencing with Strongbow's grant of all the land of Kilmainham, was established in some legal proceedings between them and the mayor and citizens of Dublin in the year 1261.[69] The

67 This dedication was probably suggested by the great victory near St. Edmunds on October 17, 1174, to which the royal troops, including Robert Fitz Stephen and many of the barons of Ireland, marched 'praeferentes sibi vexillum Beati Eadmundi regis et martyris': Gesta Hen. i. 61, and cf. Song of Dermot, ll. 2946–79, and *ante*, p. 327, note 1 [p. 123, note 67]. This coincidence, which has hitherto escaped notice, seems to confirm the entry in the Black Book. Cf. note p. 366 [note 70, p. 138]. 68 Rot. Pat. 18 Hen. III, m. 4. This record gives us the date of the final completion of the nave. The choir and transepts must have been completed in the early years of the Anglo-Norman occupation, perhaps about 1178, the probable date of Archbishop Laurence's confirmatory grant. 69 Hist. and Mun. Docs. of Ireland (Gilbert), pp 495–9. Mr. C. Litton Falkiner, in a paper on the hospital (Proc. R.I.A., vol. xxvi (c), pp 275–317), has, however, fallen into error in supposing that in the proceedings of 1261 the jurors 'found that Strongbow's grant was made prior to Henry the Second's charter of 1172'. The charter to which they refer as subsequent to the grant to Kilmainham was one granted by Henry III ('dominus rex nunc'), that is to say, the Dublin charter of 1229 (Hist. and Mun. Docs. of Ireland, pp 89–90), confirming, *inter alia*, John's charter of 1200 (ibid., pp 57–60), which conferred the liberties relied on by the mayor. They also found that soon after Strongbow's grant Hugh Tyrel of Castleknock granted to the prior Kilmehauok (printed Kylmehanok), a place on the north side of the Liffey, opposite Kilmainham.

first prior of Kilmainham appears to have been Hugh de Clahull,[70] probably brother of Strongbow's marshal, John de Clahull, and the third prior from about the year 1200 was [366]
Maurice de Prendergast.[71] Though we cannot be quite sure, there seems to be no reason to doubt that he was the Maurice de Prendergast, one of the 'first conquerors', of whom we have already heard much. The priors of Kilmainham sat as spiritual peers in the Irish parliament, and played an important part for upwards of three centuries in the civil and military history of Ireland. The site of the hospital was strategically important as an outpost of Dublin on its most vulnerable side.

70 See list given by Mr. Falkiner, *ubi supra*, p. 316, and cf. Reg. St. Thomas's, pp 370–1, where he is also called Hugh of Kilmainan. 71 'St. Mary called Alba and St. Laud' (*supra*, p. 363 [p. 137]): The anomalous entry in the Liber Niger as calendared, apparently recording the erection of two chapels to three separate saints, and the obscurity of the above dedications, led me to suspect that the second chapel was really dedicated to St. Mary of Alba Landa or Ty Gwyn, a Cistercian monastery at Whitland in Pembrokeshire, with which the invaders from South Wales must have been very familiar. The Rev. Dr. Lawlor, editor of the Calendar, has now, at my request, kindly transcribed the whole entry (itself a transcript) for me. The critical passage runs thus: '... fecerunt chorum ecclesie metropolitane cum campanili et duabus capellis viz. Sc̃i Edmundi regis et martiris et [Sc̃e or Bt̃e] Marie que dicitur Alba et Sci Landi' (*sic*). The spelling of this last name, which is quite distinct and is so printed by Dugdale (vi. 1148), confirms the suspicion that some scribe, when copying an earlier record, made two saints out of Sce Marie de Alba Landa. If *de* in the supposed original entry were misread *dr* = *dicitur*, the other changes would be almost consequential.

[367] CHAPTER XI

THE SUB-INFEUDATION OF LEINSTER

Having now reached the death of the earl whose name is indissolubly linked with the conquest of Ireland, it will be useful to pause for a moment in our narrative and, so far as our limited vision permits, survey the nature and extent of the Anglo-Norman settlement in the country at this time. In spite of the occasional distant forays and expeditions we have noticed, this settlement, with the exception of the Scandinavian towns of Dublin and Waterford and certain neighbouring districts reserved to the crown, was entirely confined to the limits of the ancient kingdoms of Leinster and Meath, that is to say, to the two great lordships of Richard de Striguil and Hugh de Lacy respectively. Indeed, at the date of the earl's death considerable portions of the districts indicated had not yet been parcelled out among 'the barons'.

In the first place, then, certain lands were appropriated or retained by the Crown. These included Dublin and the greater part of the county of Dublin, and the whole
[368] littoral from Bray to Arklow. Also the town of Waterford and the adjoining district as far at least as Dungarvan. The district near Dublin had probably been dominated by the Norsemen of Dublin, and at any rate appears to have been excepted from Henry's grants to Richard de Striguil and Hugh de Lacy. Power was indeed given to Hugh de Lacy in his charter to deal with the lands about Dublin, but only while he was the king's bailiff, and only to enable him to perform the royal service at Dublin.[1] Some of these lands in the north of the county, which Hugh de Lacy had alienated contrary to the intention of this charter, were duly restored to their use as mensal lands of the viceroy by Philip of Worcester when he was sent to supersede Hugh as representative of the Crown in 1184.[2] South of the city the territory of an Irish tribe or group of tribes ruled over by Mac Gillamocholmog lay in the vale of Dublin, or the low land between the Liffey and the mountains, and this chieftain, who sided with the Normans, was confirmed as a feudal owner probably in such part of his territory as he
[369] held in severalty.[3] The lands of the see of Dublin were very extensive, and these were confirmed to Archbishop Laurence O'Toole. The principal archiepiscopal manors to the north of the river were Swords, Lusk, and Finglas, and to the south Clondalkin, Tallaght, Rathcoole, and Shankill.[4] The possessions of the see and abbacy of

1 'Et de incremento illi dono (i.e. the land of Meath) omnia feoda que prebuit vel que prebebit circa Duveliniam, dum Balivus meus est, ad faciendum mihi servitium apud civitatem meam Duvelinie.' 2 Gir. Camb. v. 359–60. 3 His seat at Liamain (corruptly 'Limerun', afterwards more correctly anglicized 'Leuan', and eventually Lyons), was at first confirmed to him and then resumed and added to the royal manor of Newcastle Lyons. C.D.I., vol. i, 569. His descendants retained a seat at Rathdown, co. Wicklow, for many generations. 4 Crede Mihi, no. i.

Glendalough were still more extensive, and seem to have included not only the mountainous districts of which Glendalough was the centre, but also much of the best lands on the skirts of the mountains.[5] Other lands, both north and south of the Liffey, belonged to Christ Church, Dublin,[6] and to the Cistercian Abbey of St. Mary.[7] Of the remaining lands the king from time to time granted portions to various tenants in chief. One of the most considerable of these grantees was Walter de Ridelisford, to whom Brien (Bray) and other lands were granted by Earl Richard as representative of the Crown.[8]

The land of Raheny, north of Dublin, was given by Strongbow to Vivien de [370] Cursun.[9] He also gave on behalf of the king, and with the assent of the citizens of Dublin, to Saveric Sellarius (Sadler) of Exeter a burgage 'in front of the monastery of St. Mary [del Dam] within the city, having a frontage in the road which is over against the gate of the castle'.[10] This document is of particular interest as showing that there was a castle of some sort—probably a mote castle—in Dublin at this time, and as indicating that its site is included in the present castle precincts. John, when Earl of Mortain, confirmed to Almaric de St. Laurent 'the land of Houede (Howth) as his father held the same',[11] and the lands of Howth have been held by the St. Lawrences as barons and earls of Howth up to our own day.

Finally, considerable portions were retained and formed into royal manors. Those in the vale of Dublin at the end of the century were Newcastle of Lyons, Saggart, Esker, and Crumlin.[12] On the littoral south of Bray the tribe land of ui Teigh (anglicized Othec or Othee), early in the next century at all events, was dominated by the [371] royal castle and manor of Newcastle Mc Kynegan.[13] Further south Wicklow Castle was for the time granted to Earl Richard,[14] and Arklow, a decade later, to Theobald Walter.[15]

The town of Waterford, as we have seen, was, from the time of Henry's visit to Ireland, retained in the king's hand, and in 1177 'the city with all the surrounding province' as far as Lismore, was given into the custody of Robert le Poer, the marshal.[16]

The principal, indeed the only connected, account of the sub-infeudation of the two great lordships of Leinster and Meath is contained in the Song of Dermot. We can, however, test its accuracy in many ways. In a few cases the original charters or trustworthy copies are forthcoming. In several cases we have transcripts of charters by

5 Ibid., nos. iii, xliv. The earliest confirmation of the lands of the abbacy was by Earl Richard as viceroy. It contains a long list of Irish names *sicut mihi in verbo veritatis Diarmicius rex testatus est*. 6 Calendar of Christ Church Deeds, nos. 1–6; 20th Rep., Deputy Keeper. 7 Chart. St. Mary's Abbey, Dublin, vol. i, pp. 78–83, 138. 8 Antiquissime litere patentes, no. 58. Perhaps 'Brien' stands for ui Briuin Cualann, which included Bray. 9 Chart. St. Mary's Abbey, Dublin, vol. i, p. 258. 10 Reg. St. Thomas's, p. 369. The site of St. Mary's Church was afterwards occupied by Cork House. 11 Rot. Canc. Cal. (Tresham), no. 16. 12 For the Norman settlement in this district see a careful paper by Mr. James Mills (now Deputy Keeper of the Records) in the Journal R.S.A.I. 1894, pp. 161–75. 13 See my paper on Novum Castrum McKynegan, Journ. R.S.A.I. 1908, p. 126. 14 Gir. Camb. v. 298. The earl granted it to Maurice Fitz Gerald: ibid., p. 314. 15 Arklow was probably given by John to Theobald Walter in 1185, or at any rate prior to 1189, when seisin of Leinster was given to William the Marshal; see Hist. Guill. le Maréchal, ll. 9609–16, and reference to the original charter in Carte's Life of Ormond, Introd., p. slvi. 16 Gesta Hen., vol. i, p. 161.

[372] the various feoffees dealing with portions of the lands stated to have been granted to them. Giraldus confirms the account in several particulars and mentions certain castles erected about five or six years afterwards on some of these manors; and still later records show us the original feoffees or their representatives in possession of lands in the districts indicated. The Irish annals, too, record the erection of certain castles and contain a few confirmatory entries, while recent archaeological research has disclosed the existence, or proofs of the former existence, of the earthworks of castles of the mote type at almost all the probable manorial centres. Thus the list of grants given in the Song is corroborated and supplemented in various ways, and has not been shown to be incorrect in any particular. With this list, then, as a basis, and supplementing it from all available sources, we can construct a rough survey of the primary distribution of the lands of Leinster and Meath as effected by Richard de Clare and Hugh de Lacy respectively. In this chapter we shall confine our view to the lordship of Leinster. Of course the effective occupation and exploitation of these lands took time, and to make the picture more complete and prove its general correctness we shall refer to some events which took place at a later period, but it will be our aim to deal with only those manors which originated with Earl Richard's grants.

[373] Unfortunately the Song, while recounting the earl's principal grants, does not state what places he retained as demesne lands and centres of his manors. We can only infer them from incidental allusions in the Song and elsewhere, and from the better-known organization of the lordship at a later time. We have, indeed, a complete list of the seignorial centres at the time of the partition of Leinster among Strongbow's granddaughters in 1247, but in several cases these are known to have originated in escheats or to have been of later formation. Others, however, appear to have been in existence at a very early period, and we shall mention such of these as may, in their origin, with probability be assigned to Strongbow's time.

WEXFORD was the principal town of the lordship from August 1173, when Henry, who had annexed it, restored it to the earl, and the mote there, with which the walls were connected, and on which a stone castle was afterwards built, was perhaps Strongbow's work.[17] This was, no doubt, the seat of his most important manor in South Leinster, and the adjoining districts, especially the barony of Forth, appear to have been very fully colonized from the first, and mainly by Flemings and others from
[374] South Wales. ROS (Old Ross), too, appears to have been the seat of a seignorial manor before the time of the elder Earl William Marshal, who established the port called, by way of distinction, *villa novi pontis* or *villa de Rosponte* and eventually New Ross, and the mote at Old Ross probably represents Strongbow's castle. It was surrounded by a forest delimited by Richard Marshal.[18] We hear of the earl dwelling with his household troops at KILDARE,[19] and this was probably his principal seat in North Leinster. The castle-site there is on a rock, but we do not hear of a castle at Kildare in Strongbow's time. The town of CARLOW was also probably the seat of a manor of Earl

17 Henry on leaving Ireland is said to have ordered a castle to be built at Wexford: Gesta Hen. i. 30. The mote may have been erected then. 18 Chart. St. Mary's, Dublin, ii. 154. 19 Song, ll. 2696, 2771, 2795.

Richard. He certainly does not appear to have parted with the place. A full charter was granted to the town by William Marshal (junior (?) circa 1225), from which it appears that the burgesses held under rents fixed before the close of the twelfth century.[20] It was a purely Anglo-Norman town, and must have grown up under the protection of [375]
an early castle. The existing castle ruins, though of later date, are well situated at the confluence of the Burren and the Barrow.

Probably, too, the rock fortress of DUNAMASE in Leix was retained by Strongbow. This no doubt was the site of the Celtic hill-fort called Dun Masg pillaged by the Northmen in 843.[21] The ruins of a late castle occupy the site, but in plan it is essentially of the mote and bailey type. The mote, however, was a natural rock precipitous on all sides but one, where there is a steep decline. The slope here was marked off by ditch and rampart into two, or perhaps three, baileys. The elder William Marshal claimed, and eventually succeeded in obtaining this castle from Meiler Fitz Henry,[22] and, as we shall see when we come to tell of the Earl Marshal's doings, it was probably on the ground that Dunamase was demesne land of Strongbow wrongfully retained by Meiler in collusion with King John. It was afterwards the principal seignorial stronghold in this division of Leinster.[23]

As we have seen, a mote-castle was erected at KILKENNY prior to 1173,when it [376]
was destroyed by Donnell O'Brien.[24] It was probably re-erected before the expedition to Limerick in 1175, but there is no clear indication of a developed manor here before the time of Earl William Marshal.

It seems probable, too, that the motes of ODAGH and CASTLECOMER, which appear as centres of already developed seignorial manors about the close of the twelfth century, should be attributed to Strongbow. The territory in which these motes are situated had been overrun by the invaders even in Dermot's lifetime, and it was at 'his court' at Odagh that Strongbow, in 1171, had the parley with Donnell Mac Gillapatrick, chief King of Ossory, from which, as already mentioned, the king was conducted in safety by Maurice de Prendergast.[25] Either then or later, King Donnell appears to have submitted to Strongbow, and we find him assisting the invaders in the two expeditions to Limerick (1175–6).[26] The mote at Kilkenny was probably erected with King Donnell's assent, and he is generally believed to have been left in possession of the greater part of the central plain of Kilkenny up to his death in 1185.[27] The castle of the Comar, or confluence (Castlecomer), was at any rate erected before the year [377]
1200, when it was burned by the O'Brennans.[28]

20 Chartae, &c., p. 37. This charter (absurdly ascribed to c. 1296) is almost identical *mutatis mutandis* with that granted by the elder William Marshal to Kilkenny prior to 1211; ibid., p. 33. From the names of the witnesses, however, I think it should be ascribed to William Marshal the younger; cf. the witnesses to his charter to Kilkenny (ibid., p. 34) and to his grant transcribed in the Register of St. Thomas's, p. 118. **21** Ann. Ulster, 843. **22** Histoire G. le Maréchal (Paul Meyer), ll. 14127–31; and cf. Rot. Pat. 17 John, pp. 153 b, 161 b, 180. **23** Cal. Docs. Ireland, vol. i, no. 2120. See too, Inquis. P. M., 11 Ed. I, on the lands of Roger le Mortimer: ibid., vol. ii, no. 2028. **24** *Supra*, p. 322 [p. 121], and see my paper on 'Motes and Norman Castles in Ossory', Journ. R.S.A.I. 1909. **25** *Supra*, p. 236 [p. 87]. **26** *Supra*, pp. 348, 353 [p. 131, p. 133]. **27** Between 1181 and 1185 King Donnell made a grant of Kilferagh, near Kilkenny, to John Cumin, Archbishop of Dublin: Crede Mihi, no. xxxii. **28** Liber Primus Kilkenniensis.

Thus it seems that not only the Norse town of Wexford, but also St. Brigit's Kildare, the confluence at Carlow, the rock fortress of Dunamase, and St. Cainnech's Kilkenny, afterwards the five *capita* of the quinquepartite lordship of Leinster, were all selected by Strongbow as among the principal centres of his vast fief, and it is not improbable that the motes of Old Ross, Castlecomer, and Odagh were also his works.

For Strongbow's principal grants we have clear and positive evidence. Taking first the modern county of Kildare, which seems to have been fully parcelled out among the earl's followers, we may describe it accurately enough for present purposes as being divided, at the time of the invasion, into three great tribal territories: Offelan in the north, Offaly (or rather part of that territory) in the middle, and Omurethy in the south. Giraldus speaks of three cantreds of Offelan, of which that farthest from Dublin was granted to Meiler Fitz Henry, the middle cantred to Maurice Fitz Gerald, and the cantred nearest to Dublin to the Hereford brothers.[29] The Song of Dermot and certain contemporary documents enable us to define these grants a little more closely.

[378] The earl's grants appear to have been as follows: CARBURY was granted to Meiler Fitz Henry.[30] This district is now represented by the barony of Carbury in County Kildare. It is the 'more remote cantred of Offelan' stated by Giraldus to have been given to Meiler as a 'marcher' or border baron.[31] Meiler granted four carucates of land at 'Karebri' to the abbey of Connell,[32] which he founded. The barony, together with all Meiler's lands in Leinster, afterwards escheated to the Marshals,[33] lords of Leinster, and still later, in the fourteenth century, Carbury was in the possession of the Bermingham family and became known as 'Bermingham's country'.[34] The late Tudor castle of Carbury was built immediately adjoining a mote, which occupies a striking position on the summit of a hill. In all probability this mote represents the first Norman castle.

[379] 'The cantred of OFFELAN nearest to Dublin' was given to Adam de Hereford,[35] and this large district was divided between him and his brothers John and Richard. Adam de Hereford has already been mentioned as commander in the naval encounter with the Ostmen of Cork in 1173. He retained in his own hands Saltus Salmonis (or Leixlip), from which the barony of Salt obtained its name, and also Cloncurry and Oughterard. To his brother John he gave Kill, Kildrought (Celbridge), Clonshanbo, and Mainham, including Rathcoffey; and to his brother Richard he gave Downings in the barony of Otymy, now Clane, and Richard's son Henry was afterwards lord of Otymy.[36]

The present castle at Leixlip is situated on a high promontory at the junction of the Rye and the Liffey. There are motes at Cloncurry, Castlewarden near Oughterard, Kill, Mainham, and Clane.

29 Gir. Camb. v. 314. 30 *Karebri donat al bon Meiler:* Song, l. 3084. 31 Gir. Camb., p. 314. The ui Cairbre were, however, a distinct race from the ui Faelain: Topog. Poems, p. 76. 32 C.D.I., vol. i, no. 273. This was in 1205. 33 The 'castle of Cabry' was to be delivered to Gilbert, Earl of Pembroke, in 1234: ibid., no. 2175. In 1249 the castle was assigned to Margaret, countess of Lincoln, widow of Walter, Earl Marshall: ibid. no. 2989. At the partition of Leinster 'Karberye' went with Kildare. 34 Ann. Clonmacnois, 1076 (translation by Connell Mageoghagan, 1627). Ann. Laud MS., Chart. St. Mary's, Dublin, vol. i, pp. 378, 396. 35 Gir. Camb., p. 314. The Song does not particularize: *Adam de Erford ensement/Donat riche feffement.* (ll. 3106–7.) 36 These particulars are given in the Register of St. Thomas's, Dublin, pp. 102–4; cf. the grants by the brothers Hereford, ibid., pp. 75–89, 142–4, &c.

The middle cantred of OFFELAN (which included Naas) and the cantred of WICKLOW were given to Maurice Fitz Gerald for the service of twelve knights.[37] In 1185 John, *dominus Hiberniae*, confirmed this grant as regards the cantred of Offelan [380] to William, son of Maurice FitzGerald, and his heirs (who were known as barons of Naas) to be held of the heirs of Earl Richard for the service of five knights.[38]

A few years later John confirmed to Gerald, son of Maurice Fitz Gerald, and ancestor of the barons of Offaly, earls of Kildare, and dukes of Leinster, the lands of Omolrov (?), Rathmore, Maynooth, Laraghbryan, Taghadoe, and Straffan, 'being the half-cantred which he held of the gift of William, son of Maurice, his brother.'[39] The other half-cantred remained with the barons of Naas. There is a high mote in the town of Naas with a terrace surrounding the mote about ten feet below the top. This terrace [381] is a feature not infrequently found. It probably carried a palisade for which afterwards, in some cases, a stone wall was substituted.

Offaly [or that part of Offaly lying] to the west of Offelan is said to have been granted to Robert de Bermingham.[40] This, taken literally, would include all that portion of King's County [Offaly], to the east of Tullamore; but only a small portion of this district was at first taken from the O'Conors Faly, and the original Bermingham fief appears to have been confined to Tethmoy, of which they were known as barons. This district was comprised in the baronies of Warrenstown and the northern part of Coolestown in King's County.[41]

Kildare and the adjacent territory [of Offaly] is said by Giraldus to have been given by the earl to Meiler FitzHenry, but afterwards, in 1181, to have been taken from him, and the province of Leix given him by way of exchange.[42] It is possible that such a [382] grant may have been made shortly before the earl's death, and that Meiler may have founded a claim thereon which was afterwards a cause of his conflict with William the Marshal; but there is good reason to think that during the earl's life Kildare was the principal manor of the lordship in North Leinster,[43] as it certainly was afterwards in the hands of the Marshals.[44]

An attempt was made by Meiler to gain a foothold in the territory of Leix thus given him in exchange. It was the tribe-land of the O'Mores, and from the greater por-

37 There is a transcript of this deed (in some respects obviously corrupt) in the Gormanston Register, f. 190, where the parcels are: ' Wykingl[o] et totam cantredam in quo Wykingl[o] sedet excepta villa Erkeks (?) et comoto illo in quo villa Erkek sedet ... cum his dedi etiam cantredam quem Makylan tenuit non propinquiorem Diuelin sed ab illo s[cilicet] propinquiorem (*sic*)'. Cf. Song, ll. 3086–95. Perhaps 'Erkek' = Arklow, written Herkelou, Gesta, i. 163. 38 Chartae Priv. et Immun., p. 5, where the parcels are: 'Unum canteredum terre quem Makelan tenuit non propinquiorem Duveline sed alium scilicet in quo villa de Nas sita est.' Wicklow had been resumed by the Crown: Gir. Camb. v 337. 39 Red Book of the Earl of Kildare. See transcript in Facsimiles National MSS. Ireland, vol. iii, pl. lx, and cf. Journ. R.S.A.I. 1879–82, p. 425. When I have no doubt, I give the modern forms of the names. There is also a mote at Rathmore, which seems to have been piled over a sepulchraı mound. 40 Song of Dermot, ll. 3104–5: *A Robert de Burmegam/Offali al west de Offelan*. 41 Tethmoy is one of the numerous anglicized forms (Toumuy, Totemoy, &c.) of the Irish *Tuath dá mhuighe*, i.e. the *tuath* or cantred of the two plains: Topog. Poems, p. 85, note 413. For the position of this district see the old map of Leis and Offalie, Journ R.S.A.I. 1862–3, p. 345. 42 Gir. Camb., p. 355. 43 The earl after his various expeditions generally returned to Kildare as his head-quarters and abode: Song of Dermot, ll. 2696, 2771, 2795. 44 C.D.I., vol. i, nos. 1872, 1950.

tion of it they were not dispossessed. A castle was built for Meiler in 1182 by Hugh de Lacy at TIMAHOE,[45] an ancient ecclesiastical centre, and half a mile west of the village is a mote, known as the Rath of Ballynaclogh, which probably represents Meiler's castle.[46] He also occupied and adapted the rock fortress of Dunamase, but eventually he gave this up to William the Marshal, and it became the principal manor of the
[383] Marshals in the district of Leix.[47] East of Dunamase and adjoining the Barrow lies the barony of REBAN. This was granted, probably by Earl Richard, to Robert de St. Michael.[48] The family of Michael supplied barons of Reban up to the time of Elizabeth.[49] Here may still be seen the remains of the original mote and bailey, close to the later stone castle. A district called 'LE NORRATH', a name now preserved in the barony of Narragh and Reban East, was granted to Eitz Robert Fitz Richard,[50] and a
[384] castle was built for him *apud Norrach* in 1182 by Hugh de Lacy.[51] In 1598 a Wesley (or Wellesley) was baronet of the Norragh.[52]

OBOY, a district lying between Timahoe and the Barrow in the barony of Ballyadams in Queen's County [Leix],[53] was granted to Robert de Bigarz, and here a castle was built for him in 1182 by Hugh de Lacy.[54] Its exact site is a matter of some uncertainty. The manor afterwards reverted to the Marshals, lords of Leinster.[55]

ARDRI was given to Thomas le Fleming.[56] Ardree is now the name of a small parish of 323 acres on the east side of the Barrow to the south of Athy. It was appar-
[385] ently here that a castle was built for Thomas Flandrensis by Hugh de Lacy in 1181;[57] but the farm with the old castle site was given along with the church of Ardree to the abbey of St. Thomas by Milo de Stanton early in the thirteenth century.[58] At this time

45 Gir. Camb., p. 356. 46 It has a raised circular bailey, the earthen walls of which are carried up the mound, as was frequently done in stone when a stone keep was built on a mote. Both mote and bailey are surrounded by a fosse and outer rampart. 47 Hist. Guil. le Maréchal, ll. 14128–9: *Son boen chastel otreia, / Donmas, al conte en heritage.* M. Meyer, by a blunder pardonable in a foreigner, places this castle in the County Clare (ibid., vol. iii, p. 195, note). 48 Robert de St. Michael witnessed Strongbow's grant of Aghaboe. He also witnessed a charter of his neighbour Robert Fitz Richard in the lifetime of Raymond le Gros: Chart. St. Mary's, Dublin, vol. i, p. 68. His son David de St. Michael married Margery, daughter of Thomas le Fleming, another neighbour, and granted the church of Reban to the abbey of St. Mary, *retenta in manu nostra capellaria Castelli nostri de Riban* (ibid., p. 115). This was, I think, before the close of the century. Margery was the widow of Robert de Bigarz, and after the death of David de St. Michael she married Roger Waspail (ibid., pp. 115, 116, and C.D.I., vol. i, no. 1392). She had by her second husband, David, a son, Richard de St. Michael, who fined for his father's land in 1215 (C.D.I., vol. i, no. 673), and confirmed his father's gift to the abbey of St. Mary: Chart. St. Mary's, Dublin, vol. i, p. 121. 49 Fiants, Eliz. (1582), no. 3882. 50 Song of Dermot, ll. 3122–5. 51 Gir. Camb., p. 356; cf. his grant, Reg. St. Thomas's, p. 228. 52 Hogan's Ireland in 1598, p. 47; Car. Cal. 1596, p. 191. 53 Oboy is an anglicized form of *ui Buidhe*. For the situation of this tribe see Book of Rights, p. 213, note. 54 Gir. Camb., p. 356, *apud Obowi*. Tullomoy in the barony preserves the name: *Tulach ua m-Buidhe*. There is a fine mote at Kilmorony in this barony on the Barrow, and as it is not far from Ardri and separated from it by the Barrow, it may be the site of Robert de Bigarz's castle. See quotation from Giraldus under Ardri, *infra*. 55 At the partition of Leinster 'Obboy' was assigned along with Dunamase to Roger de Mortimer, husband of Maude de Braose, who was daughter of Eva Mareschal: Chart. St. Mary's, Dublin, vol. ii, p. 403. 56 Song of Dermot, ll. 3112–13. 57 Gir. Camb. v. 356; 'Castellum Thomae Flandrensi non procul ab hoc [Obowi] in ulteriore videlicet Omurethi parte, Beruensis fluminis interlabentibus undis (erexit).' 58 Reg. St. Thomas's, Dublin, p. 162. For a description of this site see Eng. Hist. Review (1907), p. 249.

the manorial seat seems to have been at 'Mon' (i.e. Moone or Moone Abbey), afterwards a seignorial manor.

All the land between Oboy and Leighlin was granted by the earl to his marshal, John de Clahull.[59] This would cover the barony of SLIEVEMARGY in Queen's County. In 1181 a castle was built for John de Clahull above the Barrow, not far from Leighlin.[60] The site of this castle is probably marked by the mote of Killeshin. It is situated in a subdivision called Castlequarter, close to the old church of Killeshin. The [386] mote is twenty-five feet high, is surrounded by a square fosse, and contains traces of a rectangular building on the top. The tradition of an important Anglo-Norman town here, of which, except the mote and Celtic church, 'there is now [above ground] no trace,' has come down to our own times.[61]

Twenty knights' fees in Omurethi were granted to Walter de Ridelisford.[62] This was a large territory in the south of the County Kildare. A castle was erected for Walter de Ridelisford *apud Tristerdermoth* (Castledermot) in 1181.[63] In the early English versions of the Expugnatio, Kilcae or Kilca (i.e. Kilkea) is put instead of 'near Tristerdermoth' as the place where Walter de Ridelisford's castle was built.[64] Kilkea was undoubtedly a manor of his, and here, close to the old church and later castle, is a mote.

Passing now to the county of Carlow, the districts of FOTHERD (or Fotheret) and [387] ODRONE, together with GLASCARRIG on the east coast of Wexford near Cahore Point, were granted by Earl Richard to Raymond le Gros. Fotherd was given as a marriage portion with Basilia. The name is now preserved in the barony of Forth, but the ancient district granted to Raymond was more extensive, and included portions of the baronies of Rathvilly and Carlow as well.[65] A castle was built for Raymond at Fotheret Onolan in 1181, and this has been identified by means of contemporary charters with the mote of Castlemore near Tullow.[66] Raymond's manor of Odrone[67] was comprised in the barony of Idrone East. Raymond seems to have granted this land to his nephew, William de Carew, who had vills at Dunlech (Dunleckny) and also at Techmulin (St.

59 Song of Dermot, ll. 3100–3. That this was the situation of John de Clahull's lands appears also from a charter by which John Cumin, Archbishop of Dublin, *ad petitionem Johannis de Clahalla, domini fundi*, during a vacancy of the see of Leighlin, instituted Thurstin, a cleric, to the moiety of the churches of Sancti Congani de Clunussi (St. Comgan of Glen Uissen or Killeshin), Sancti Patricii de Slefta (Sletty), Sancti Congalli de Catherloc (Carlow), Sancte Brigide de Clodahc (Cloydagh, a parish in the north of Idrone West), and Sancti Ganulni de Clonena (Cloneen?): Crede Mihi, no. lv. This deed must be dated before the consecration of Herlewin, Bishop of Leighlin, c. 1201. 60 Gir. Camb., p. 355. John de Clahull, *marescallus*, witnessed Strongbow's grant to Savaric Saddler of Exeter: Reg. St. Thomas's, Dublin, p. 369. 61 Coote's Survey of Queen's Co., p. 194; Ord. Surv. Letters Q. C., vol. i, p. 105. 62 Song of Dermot, ll. 3096–9; Omurethi is the territory of *ui Muireadhaigh*, of which the O'Tooles were lords. 63 Gir. Camb., p. 355. As to the castle site see Eng. Hist. Review, 1907, p. 248. 64 The two earliest English versions have been published by the Early English Text Society (1896). Cf. Book of Howth Car. Cal., p. 98, and Bray's Conquest of Ireland, Ibid., p. 309. 65 Song of Dermot, ll. 3064–9. Fotherd, &c., represents the Irish Fotharta, of which there were several. This one was distinguished as Fotharta Fea or Fotharta Osnadhaigh. The ruling family was O'Nuallain (O'Nolan), hence the form in Giraldus and many Anglo-Norman charters. 66 Gir. Camb., p. 355. For the identification of Raymond's Castle with Castlemore Mote, see Journ R.S.A.I. 1906, pp. 368–82. 67 Odrone or Idrone represents the Irish *Ui Drona*, a tribal territory of which the O'Ryans were the ruling family.

Mullins).[68] There are motes in both places. Glascarrig he appears to have granted to
[388] one of his Cantitune nephews, and here, too, a little north of the slight ruins of the priory, close to the sea, may be seen the mote which probably represents the Norman fortress.

We have positive evidence of only two grants by Strongbow in Ossory, one at the north and the other at the south end of the ancient kingdom. In Upper Ossory the earl gave to Adam de Hereford 'half the vill of ACHEBO and the entire half of the cantred in which the vill is situated, as Dermot Ochelli (*O'Caelaidhe*) held the same in Ossory', to hold in fee by the service of five knights. The original deed with the seal appended has happily been preserved among the Ormond Muniments.[69]

The cathedral church of the diocese of Ossory was at this time at Aghaboe, and the remaining half of the vill and half-cantred were perhaps see-lands. Early in the thirteenth century the see-lands of Aghaboe were transferred by Hugh de Rous, the first Anglo-Norman bishop of Ossory, to William, Earl Marshal, 'in exchange for others in more convenient places'[70] — that is to say, nearer Kilkenny, the new episcopal seat, and at the time of the partition of Leinster

Aghaboe was a very rich seignorial manor and was assigned along with Dunamase
[389] to Eva de Braose. It was one of the last places retained by the English in Upper Ossory, but in 1346 Dermot Mac Gillapatrick, the one-eyed, burnt the vill of Aghaboe, including the church and shrine of St. Cainnech,[71] and three years later the castle was taken.[72] The castle site is marked by a square mote not far from the parish church, with foundations of a thick mortared wall round the top and traces of a wide fosse round the bottom.

In the southern portion of Ossory the earl gave the extensive tribe-land of Iverk (*Uibh Eirc*) to Miles, son of David, Bishop of St. Davids, and he became the first of the line of barons of Iverk.[73] Early in the thirteenth century his son David richly endowed the nunnery of Kilculliheen, close to Waterford on the Kilkenny side, and from his grant it appears that his chief manorial centres were 'the castle of Polsculi and the new castle of Clone'.[74] These places are now known as Portnascully, on a small tidal stream or 'pill' debouching into the Suir nearly mid-way between Carrick and
[390] Waterford, and Clone or Clonamery on the Nore below Inistioge. At Portnascully is a well-preserved and strongly fortified mote-and-bailey earthwork, and at Clone is an early stone castle or tower built on a mote. These earthworks probably date from the time of Miles Fitz David.

In the present county of Wexford it seems probable that the old royal seat at Ferns was left in the possession of Murtough Mc Murrough, who had, as we have seen,[75] come to terms with Strongbow. At any rate, a large district in the north of the county

68 Chart. St. Mary's, Dublin, vol. i, p. 112. 69 See transcript, Note A to this chapter. 70 For Earl William's Charter, see Liber Albus Ossoriensis, Proc R. I. A., vol xxvii (c), p 118. 71 Clyn's Annals, 1346. 72 See History of St. Canice (Graves and Prim), p. 19, note a. 73 Song, ll. 3108–11, and Journ. R.S.A.I. 1893, pp. 179–84. 74 Cal. Docs. Ireland, vol. i, no. 2485, from an *Inspeximus* dated June 10, 1240. This document shows that David's lands included the greater part of the present barony of Ida as well as that of Iverk. 75 *Supra*, p. 238 [p. 87–8].

as well as adjoining parts of the counties Wicklow and Carlow, appear not to have been granted by Strongbow to his followers.

The district of OFFELIMY by the sea, now represented by the barony of Ballaghkeen, was granted to Gilbert de Boreart (Boisrohard).[76] Before Henry II came to Ireland Strongbow had appointed this Gilbert custos of Waterford,[77] and he witnessed three of Strongbow's charters.[78] In the town-land of Ballymotymore in this barony there is a conspicuous mote.

The DUFFRY, a woody district to the west of the Slaney, extending from near Enniscorthy to the spurs of Mount Leinster, had been granted, as we have seen,[79] to [391]
Robert de Quency, the constable; but he was killed in 1172–3, leaving an infant or posthumous daughter, Maud, by his wife, who was a daughter of Strongbow. Maud de Quency was afterwards married to Philip, son of Maurice de Prendergast.[80] Philip succeeded in right of his wife to the Duffry, and was probably the builder of Enniscorthy Castle which is situated on a rock on the west side of the Slaney at the head of the tidal way. In 1227 he obtained from the Bishop of Ferns a surrender of that part of Enniscorthy which lies to the east of the river, about the ancient church of St. Senan. The town that grew up about the castle and the Anglo-Norman settlement in the neighbourhood should probably be ascribed to Philip de Prendergast and his son Gerald.[81]
'FERNEGENAL', a district corresponding with the barony of Shelmaliere East, was granted by the earl to Maurice de Prendergast for the service of ten knights, as an inducement to him to return to Ireland.[82] Afterwards Robert Fitz Godebert was enfeoffed of this district, or a large portion of its southern extremity, by Maurice. He was [392]
probably a brother of Richard FitzGodebert, the 'knight of Pembrokeshire' who accompanied Dermot on his return to Ireland in 1167, and son of Godebert, a Fleming of the hundred of Rhos (Rouse) near Haverford.[83] His sons took the name de la Roche from the castle there still known as Roch Castle. This descent of the Roches of Wexford, and presumably of the lords of Fermoy, appears from a charter to the monastery of St. Nicholas of Exeter, by which David, Henry, and Adam de Rupe granted the island of Begerin (in Wexford harbour) to the monastery *pro salute anime patris nostri Robert filii Godeberti.*[84] Early in the thirteenth century, Gerald de la Roche, son of David, divided the district between himself and his kinsman David Fitz Adam Sinad (Sinnott),[85] evidently also of Flemish descent, and hence the two portions became known as Roche's [393]
land and Sinnott's land.

76 Song, ll. 3114–17. In 1177 the land of Gilbert de Boisrohard was declared to be appurtenant to the service of Wexford. R. de Hoveden, ii. 134. 77 Song, ll. 2211–14. 78 Reg. St. Thomas's, p. 370; Chart. St. Mary's, vol. ii, p. 154; Gormanston Reg., f. 190. 79 *Supra*, p. 322 [p. 121]. 80 Song, ll. 2819–26 and 3040–57. 81 See Hore's Hist. of Co. Wexford, vol. vi. 82 Song of Dermot, ll. 3072–83. Fernegenal represents the Irish Fearann na gCenel: Topogr. Poems, p. 92 and note 471 [p. 50]. 83 *Supra*, p. 141. 84 Monasticon Diocesis Exoniensis, ed. George Oliver, Hist. of St. Nicholas, Exeter, *ex archivis civitatis Exoniae*, no. ix, p. 120. The charter is witnessed (*inter alios*) by Maurice de Prendergast, Philip Puher (Poer), Alexander de Brideshale, Robert and Henry de la Roche, Walter Hoel, and Roger Christopher, and must be dated before the close of the twelfth century, and probably about 1182. Adam, monk of St. Nicholas, *qui hanc elemosinam impetravit*, witnessed a charter by Miles de Cogan, Reg. St. Thomas's, p. 204; and charters by Margarite de Cogan, ibid., pp. 226, 227. 85 See deed quoted in the Annuary (1868–9) R.S.A.I., p. 52, note; and for further remarks concerning the Flemish element among the invaders, Note B at the end of this chapter.

'OBARTHY on the sea,' a name surviving in the barony of Bargy, was given or confirmed to Hervey de Montmorency.[86] His lands included also the present barony of Shelburne, where he founded and endowed the Abbey of Dunbrody, and where in 'the Island' (a portion of the parish of Kilmokea formerly surrounded by the Barrow) he probably had his *caput baroniae*.[87]

Thus it would appear that at the time of Earl Richard's death, while County Kildare and a large portion of County Carlow had been fully parcelled out into large fiefs, only the adjoining fringe of King's and Queen's County had been similarly dealt with. The settlement in Ossory had not proceeded very far, and in County Wexford the southern and eastern parts alone had been granted to the barons.

[394] NOTE A

*Strongbow's grant of Aghaboe**

Comes Ricardus filius Comitis Ricardi [*sic*] Gisleberti Amnibus Amicis suis et hominibus Francis Anglicis Walensibus hiberniensibus tam presentibus quam futuris Salutem. Sciatis me dedisse et concessisse Ade de hereford dimidiam uillam de achebo. et totum dimidium cantredum terre in quo uilla sedet cum totis pertinentibus suis. Sicut ochelli dermot scilicet illam melius tenuit in usseria per liberum seruicium quinque militum. Sibi et heredibus suis de me et heredibus meis libere et quiete et honorifice. In terra. In Aqua. In bosco. In plano. In Monasteriis. In Molendinis. In piscaturis. In stagnis. In viuariis. In foro. In domibus et castellis firmandis. In uiis. In semitis. et in omnibus libertatibus absque omnibus malis consuetudinibus tenendum et habendum in feodo et hereditate per liberum seruicium prenominatum. Scilicet. quinque militum. Quare uolo et firmiter precipio quatenus predictus Adam et heredes sui totum tenumentum suum de me et heredibus meis ita libere et quiete et honorifice teneant ut ille de hominibus meis qui melius et liberius tenumentum suum de me et heredibus meis tenuerit in hibernia. vel tenere debuerit. de tanto feodo. his testibus. Ramundo constabulario.

86 Song of Dermot, ll. 3070–1. Obarthi represents the Irish *Ui Bairrche.* 87 Hervey's fief must have reverted to the lord of Leinster. Much of it, however, had been alienated to the Church. What remained was afterwards known as the Barony of the Island, and along with the manor of Old Ross fell, at the partition, to the share of Matilda Mareschal, who married Hugh Bigod, Earl of Norfolk.

[395] * Transcribed from the photo-zincograph copy of the original: Nat. MSS of Ireland, vol. ii, pl. lxiii. The original charter and seal are thus described by the Rev. James Graves in the Journal of the Kilkenny Archaeological Society, vol. i, p. 502: 'The charter is written on a piece of thick vellum, measuring seven inches by six and a quarter, the hand is clear and bold, and the ink in good preservation; the seal appended to the document is about three inches in breadth and of rude workmanship. It bears on the obverse a mounted knight clad in a long surcoat, equipped with a heater-shaped shield, his head defended by a conical helmet furnished with a nasal, and bearing in his extended right hand a very broad sword, straight, and apparently two-edged. Of the inscription the word GILLEBERTI alone remains. The reverse is charged with the figure of a footman, wearing a surcoat reaching down half the leg; his body covered by a long shield, the right foot extended, and the spear brought down to the charge. A hood of mail and a flat skullcap with projecting rim protect the head; and the shield is charged with three chevronels, the well-known bearing of the de Clares.'

Griffino fratre suo. Roberto de sancto michaele. Ricardo de hereford. Johannes de hereford. [395]
hugone de gurnai. Waltero ridel [eford]. Johanne de clohalle. Rogero de Sanford. Willelmo Bret. Waltero filio pagani. Hugone de leia. hugone d luieuilla [*sic*].

NOTE B [395]

Flemish element among the settlers

The Flemish element among the early settlers impressed itself so strongly, especially in South Wexford, that a word or two on the subject will not be out of place. The district of Rhôs, near Haverford in Pembrokeshire, now the hundred of Roose, from which Maurice de Prendergast and his men seem to have come, was colonized by Flemings in the time of Henry I.[88]

It was afterwards, perhaps, further recruited by Henry II with some of Stephen's disbanded Flemish mercenaries. This Low Dutch settlement, which Freeman calls 'the last of a series of which the coming of Hengist was the first',[89] was very complete within its limits. The original Welsh inhabitants appear to have been driven out or exterminated, their language disappeared and was replaced by a dialect closely akin to the English of the day, and the local nomenclature was largely changed, so that the district came to be called ' Little England beyond Wales'.[90] Other Flemish settlements took place about the same time at Tenby and in the peninsula of Gower. A very similar phenomenon occurred in the baronies of Forth and Bargy in County Wexford. The original Irish inhabitants seem to have almost disappeared, and though the local [397]
nomenclature was only slightly changed, the people retained up to the eighteenth century peculiar customs and a peculiar Teutonic dialect which has been a standing puzzle to writers.[91] Their difference in personal appearance from the inhabitants of the Irish baronies in North Wexford has also been observed.[92] The explanation is not far to seek. These baronies were among the first to be occupied by the adventurers from South Wales, who were largely these very Flemings, and they brought over with them and retained their peculiar dialect, which developed somewhat on lines of its own, but never lost the characteristics which link it with Low Dutch dialects. The Four Masters were probably not far wrong in speaking of the forces which accompanied Fitz Stephen as the 'fleet of the Flemings'. Maurice de Prendergast, the Geraldines, and even Strongbow, probably brought many Flemings with them, and probably they were afterwards followed by their kinsfolk from the same quarter. George, in his Description of Pembrokeshire, notes that great numbers of the Irish went back to Pembroke about the time of Tyrone's rebellion, and adds 'as manye as come out of the countey of Weisford saye they understande noe Irishe, neyther doth anye well understande his Englishe'.[93]

But the Flemish element was not confined to South Wexford. Among the leading settlers else- [398]
where were some half-Normanized Flemings. The Roches followed their lords the Prendergasts to Cork. Mangunel, a Flemish name, was to be found in Cork.[94] A Fleming was baron of Slane, and a Fleming was given lands at Ardree, near Athy. Wilkin was a typical Flemish name, and we

88 William of Malmesbury, Gesta Reg., book v; Florence of Worcester; Brut y Tywys, 1105. 89 See Norman Conquest, vol. v, p. 209, and App. CC. 90 Camden's Britannia (1695), 631. 91 See Glossary of the Old Dialect of the English Colony in Forth and Bargy collected bv Jacob Poole and edited by William Barnes (1867), also 'An Account of the Barony of Forth,' written circa 1680, edited by Herbert Hore, Journ. R.S.A.I. 1862–3, pp 53–81. 92 See O'Donovan's note, Four Masters, 1169, p. 1172. 93 See Henry Owen's edition, Cymmrodorion Soc., 1892, p. 40. 94 Reg. St. Thomas's, p. 216. William Mangunel, a Fleming of Haverford, was expert in the art of divination with a ram's shoulder-blade: Gir. Camb. vi. 87. 95 Four Masters, 1200.

find a Wilkin of Castlewilkin, near Limerick.[95] Other undoubted examples might be added, and the fashion of adopting names in the Norman form, as in the case of the Roches, has probably obscured the Flemish origin of some families. When for convenience we speak of the invaders as Normans or Anglo-Normans, we must be understood to include these semi-Normanized Flemings, and also a sprinkling of Welshmen and Englishmen as well. Giraldus gives a good character to the Flemings of Wales: 'Gens fortis et robusta, gens lanificiis usitatissima, nunc ad aratrum nunc ad arma promtissima.'[96] These were qualities likely to be required in Ireland.

[399]

NOTE C

Professor Thatcher's position in relation to 'Laudabiliter' and the papal sanction of Henry's action in Ireland

When dealing with the subject of 'Laudabiliter' (vol. i, cap. ix) I considered it outside the scope of my purpose to discuss specifically the arguments of particular writers against the authenticity of the documents in question; but I was led to mention Mr Round's view, in a note, and perhaps it will be expected that I should notice the view taken still more recently by Professor Oliver J. Thatcher in his Studies concerning Adrian IV (Decennial Publications of the University of Chicago, 1st series, vol. iv, pp. 153–78).

Professor Thatcher, following in the main the late Professor Scheffer-Boichorst, accepts the passage in the Metalogicus (translated in part, *ante*, vol. i, pp. 290–1 [p. 108]) as the genuine statement of John of Salisbury, and also as a correct account of what actually occurred. He also accepts Alexander's three letters as genuine; but he regards 'Laudabiliter' as 'neither a genuine letter of Adrian IV, nor a forgery in the true sense of the word'. 'It was not', he says, 'written with the purpose of deceiving or of securing any material advantage.' He regards it as 'merely a Latin exercise of some twelfth-century student, who was practising himself in the art of letter-writing, and for this purpose chose to impersonate Adrian IV'. His position as regards the authenticity of the documents is similar to that of Mr Round, but he interprets the facts in an entirely different way. He holds, in short, that Adrian did actually make a feudal grant of Ireland to Henry and his heirs in the document, now lost, referred to by John of Salisbury, and did send a ring by which investiture might be made, but that no investiture was in fact made, the probable reason being that Henry did not wish to hold Ireland as a fief from the Papacy, but wanted to acquire it (with the papal sanction) as his own absolute dominion.

This view, representing the Pope as ready to make a grant of Ireland and Henry as refusing to accept the gift from the Pope's hands, is a curious inversion of the view usually taken by Irish writers. It is certainly one way—though not, I think the simplest—of accounting for the discrepancies between John of Salisbury's account and 'Laudabiliter'. But the question remains, why was 'Laudabiliter' inserted in the Expugnatio, and how was it that its spuriousness was not at once exposed?

This medieval student in letter-writing, it may be observed, cannot have been Giraldus. For
[400] when introducing Adrian's Privilege Giraldus refers to the agency of John of Salisbury in obtaining both it and the ring of investiture, mentioning the latter almost in John's own words, and Giraldus, even if we can suppose him capable of effectually disguising his own well-marked style, and—what is harder to believe—of daring to impersonate the Pope, would certainly have

96 vi. 83.

composed a document in closer conformity to John's account of it. Are we, then, to suppose that Giraldus inserted some student's exercise *by mistake* for the genuine article?

The principal argument adduced by Professor Thatcher against the authenticity of 'Laudabiliter'—apart from its discrepancy with John of Salisbury's account—is one that has been used before, viz. the close verbal similarity between some of the opening sentences and the commencement of another letter addressed by the same Pope to Louis VII. The similarity is indeed very close, but did the papal chancellery, even in the prefatory matter of its multitudinous correspondence, never repeat itself?

Of course, if 'Lauclabiliter' is to be regarded as a student's exercise Alexander's confirmation of it must be assigned to a similar lowly origin; but the only textual criticism offered is that, contrary to the rule of the papal chancellery, the words ' vos' and 'vester' are used in addressing Henry instead of 'tu' and 'tu us'. But surely this is a change which any courtier-scribe of the day, wishing to flatter the king with the greater dignity of the plural, would feel himself justified in making—more especially as it appears that Frederick I and Adrian IV had actually quarrelled about the usage.

We certainly cannot be confident that these documents are faithful and accurate transcripts of originals, such as we should expect a scholar to make to-day; but to regard 'Laudabiliter' as a mere student's exercise, which was solemnly inserted in the Expugnatio, for no apparent purpose, instead of the true version, and which has for centuries deceived not only the enemies of England but the Papacy itself, seems to me to be a very hazardous position to take up, and one which requires stronger evidence in its support than any that has as yet been produced. As, however; Professor Thatcher and (apparently) Mr Round both hold that Henry's expedition was in fact sanctioned by Pope Adrian as well as approved by Pope Alexander, the question of the precise form in which Adrian's sanction was given becomes on this view a matter of minor importance.

[5] CHAPTER XII

THE CONQUEST OF ULSTER, 1177–85

The untimely death of Richard of Stirguil was a heavy blow to the prospects of the Anglo-Norman colony, which, in Leinster at least, was beginning to settle down to peaceful progress and orderly rule. It left the king without a representative in Ireland, and the great fief of Leinster without a lord. The Countess Eva, daughter of King Dermot, had borne only one child to the earl, a daughter named Isabel, and she, an infant of not more than five years of age, was heiress to the earl's vast fief. The valuable feudal incidents of the wardship and marriage of this heiress now accrued to the king as *dominus*, and it was important for him at once to secure his rights. The commissioners sent to recall Raymond, seeing that it would be madness at this moment to execute their original commission, and that in the changed circumstances it was necessary to apply to the king for new instructions, left Raymond as procurator in Ireland,
[6] while they hastened to the king to acquaint him with the facts and learn his pleasure.[1]

Henry, however, had already conceived a distrust of Raymond, and indeed it is sufficiently obvious that Raymond was not fitted either to control the colony or to secure the interests of the Crown in Leinster. Accordingly Henry appointed his dapifer, William Fitz Audelin, whom he had previously on two occasions employed in Ireland, as procurator instead of Raymond, and sent him immediately to Ireland with orders to seize into the king's hand all the earl's castles (*munitiones*) in Leinster.[2]

Along with William Fitz Audelin came John de Courcy, Robert Fitz Stephen, and Miles de Cogan, each with ten men-at-arms. The two last, and probably all three, had fought for King Henry both in England and in France in his war with the barons, and might naturally expect their reward in Ireland now. John de Courcy may have accompanied Henry to Ireland in 1171, but this is the first time he came to stay in the country where he was soon to become famous. All three, according to Gerald de Barry,
[7] were joined in the commission with William Fitz Audelin. Of the latter Gerald gives a very unfavourable portrait: a courtly, luxurious man, smooth-spoken, but full of guile, a bully and a coward, greedy of gold, and a seeker after court favour.[3] Acting, as is hinted, and as was very probably the case, under instructions from Henry, he seems

1 Giraldus, v. 334. 2 Gesta Hen., vol. i, p. 125. The title 'procurator' is taken from Giraldus. 3 v. 337–8, with much more to the same effect. He has been strangely identified with William de Burgh, 'the conqueror of Connaught,' a man of a very different type. William Fitz Aldelin or Audelin, as the name should be written (not 'Aldelm'), was son of Aldelin de Aldefeld, and held a knight's fee in Yorkshire. His wife was Juliana, daughter of Robert Doisnell: see Round's Feudal England, p. 518, and the *cartae* of 1166 printed in Hearne's Liber Niger Scaccarii.

to have endeavoured to thwart in every way the bolder spirits of the conquest, and in particular the Geraldines. Maurice FitzGerald, the head of the clan, died about the 1st of September in this year. Strongbow had given to him Wicklow Castle, which had at first been reserved by Henry along with the maritime district south of Dublin, but was afterwards, as we have seen, granted to Strongbow. Now Fitz Audelin took the castle out of the hands of Maurice's sons, presumably to be held for the king during the minority of Strongbow's heir. Ferns was given to them by way of exchange, and they immediately set about building a castle there; but, according to Gerald, Walter 'Alemannus', or the German, a nephew of Fitz Audelin and Custos of Wexford (now [8]
also in the king's hand), bribed by Murtough Mc Murrough, Dermot's nephew, caused the castle to be destroyed.[4] Fitz Audelin is also said to have disappointed both Raymond and Fitz Stephen by refusing to give them any of the more secure lands near Dublin or Wexford, and leaving them only the more remote lands on the marches.

One adventurous spirit showed his discontent with Fitz Audelin's policy by organizing and carrying out a raid on his own account, which would seem to have been the act of a madman had it not been successful, and which resulted in subjecting a large portion of another province to English domination. This was John de Courcy, whose story is like a wild romance, and would hardly be believed were it not for many solid and enduring facts which testify to its essential truth.

Of his antecedents little is known. He came of a family seated at Stoke Courcy in Somersetshire and was related to William de Courcy (ob. 1176), dapifer of Henry II and at one time Seneschal of Normandy.[5] He probably accompanied Henry to Ireland, [9]
as the Song of Dermot expressly says that Henry, while in Ireland, granted to him 'Ulster, if he could conquer it'.[6] Niall O'Loughlin, King of the Cinel Owen, a group of tribes whose king, when strong enough, was recognized as high-king of the whole northern province, had alone among the principal kings of Ireland held entirely aloof from Henry during his visit, and Henry, who was himself unwilling to attempt a winter campaign in Ulster, may have half-jestingly granted a licence to John de Courcy to take the province if he could. As we have seen, the licence originally granted to Richard of Striguil a couple of years earlier is said to have been of a similar half-jesting nature.

John de Courcy is described as a tall fair man with big bones and muscular frame, of immense strength and remarkable daring. A born warrior, in action ever in the front, ever taking upon himself the brunt of the danger. So keen a fighter was he that [10]
even when in command he would forget the calmness that befits a general and become an impetuous soldier. In private life he was modest, sober-minded, and pious, and gave to God the glory of all his victories.[7]

4 Gir. Camb. v. 337. Wicklow Castle was afterwards restored to the Geraldines, and we find it belonging to the Baron of Naas in 1229: C.D.I., vol. i, no. 1757. It is probable that Ferns, the old royal seat of Leinster, was left at this time in the possession of Murtough Mc Murrough, who was friendly to the English, and had assisted Raymond at the relief of Limerick early in the year. 5 Along with his brother Jordan de Curci, John witnessed a grant by William de Curci, steward of the king, for the souls of his grandfather William de Curci and his father William, to the monks of St. Andrew of Stoke. Hist. MSS. Com., 9th Rep., Part 1, p. 353 b. 6 'A un Johan Uluestere, / Si a force la peust conquere, / De Curci out a nun Johan / Ki pus i suffri meint [a]han.' ll. 2733–6. 7 Gir. Camb. v. 344. John de Courcy was one of

Such a mettlesome warrior could not but grow restive under the timid and politic rule of Fitz Audelin. Accordingly, in spite of Fitz Audelin, he took the bit in his teeth. He gathered round him some of the garrison of Dublin who were discontented like himself, and with a little band of twenty-two men-at-arms and about three hundred others, supplemented perhaps by some of the Irish themselves,[8] boldly advanced into Ulster, where English arms had not yet attempted to penetrate. He marched rapidly through Meath and Uriel, and on the fourth day—about the 1st of February—he took by surprise the city of Down. This was an ancient ecclesiastical site associated with St. Patrick, and here the saint was believed to have been buried. It was also the chief seat of the kings of Uladh, or Ulidia, i.e. that part of the modern province of Ulster lying
[11] to the east of the Bann and the Newry river. The king, who was a member of the family called Mac Donlevy,[9] fled, but only to collect his host.

It happened that Cardinal Vivian was in the city of Down at this time on a mission from the Pope, and he endeavoured to make peace between de Courcy and the king, on the terms that the latter should pay tribute to the English and the former retire
[12] from the territory, but his good offices were fruitless.[10] In eight days Mac Donlevy returned with a huge army, said to number 10,000 men, to recapture the city. Meantime de Courcy had constructed a weak fort in a corner of the city,[11] but he preferred to meet the enemy in the open, on ground chosen by himself. Including his Irish auxiliaries he had perhaps 700 men.[12] A more than Homeric battle ensued, in which John de Courcy, his supposed brother-in-law Almaric de St. Lawrence, and Roger le Poer did wonders. We shall not attempt to describe the battle, for which indeed trustwor-
[13] thy details are wanting.[13] The Northerners fought with their usual courage, but in the

those with whom Gerald must have come into contact in 1185–6. **8** 'Associatis sibi Hyberniensibus illis qui parti eorum favebant': Gesta Hen., vol. i, p. 137. According to the Book of Howth (p. 81) John had 700 men at the battle of Down. **9** He is called 'Dunlevus' by Gerald, and the name appears as "Macdonleue' (representing Mac Duinnsleibhe) in the Song. The members of this family were always killing one another, and which of them was acknowledged king at this moment is hard to determine. See O'Donovan's notes to Four Masters, vol. iii, pp. 30 and 39, which however, do not seem to clear up the point. At any rate, Rory Mac Donlevy seems to have been in command both in 1177 (Ann. Inisfallen, Dublin MS.; Gesta Hen., vol. i, p. 137, where he is called Rodericus rex Ulvestere) and in 1178 (Ann. Inisfallen, Ann. Tigernach). For the ambiguity in the name *Uladh* or Ulster see O'Donovan's note to Four Masters, 1172, p. 7. In the twelfth century the name was (properly speaking) confined to the district represented by the modern counties of Down and Antrim. **10** Giraldus, v. 340. William of Newburgh, vol. i, p. 238, says that Vivian advised the Irish to fight for their country. According to the Gesta Henrici (vol. i, p. 137) Vivian met de Courcy's army while he was journeying along the coast on his way to Dublin. He may have returned to Down with it. He had come to Down from the Isle of Man, where 'Godredum regem legitime desponsari fecit cum uxore sua nomine Phingola (Finnghuala) filia Mac Loclen filii Murkartec regis Hyberniae, matre scilicet Olavi qui tunc trienniserat': Chron. Manniae, 1176. This is a late example of an Irish lady in high position entering into a marriage not recognized by the Church. Her grandfather was Murtough O'Loughlin, King of Ireland (with opposition), sl. 1166, and her father was, I suppose, Melaghlin O'Loughlin, who in this very year (1177) killed Aedh O'Neill, a former King of the Cinel Owen. **11** 'Exile municipium quod. in urbis angulo tenuiter erexerat': Gir. Camb. v. 340. **12** This is the number given in the Book of Howth. **13** Gir. Camb. v. 340–2. The fullest account, which reads like the tale of an Irish shanachy, is contained in the Book of Howth, pp. 81–4, in a passage not taken from Giraldus, but probably 'from a translation by Primate Dowdall made in 1551 out of a Latin book found with O'Neill in Armagh' (see the colophon, p. 117). This Latin book seems to have contained the *gestes* of

end were utterly defeated. The fight seems to have taken place in the low lands to the north of the city, which were intersected by the swamps of the river Quoile. Probably the narrow strips of firm land gave little advantage to numbers, and superior arms and discipline and, above all, the deadly arrows, turned the scale.

John de Courcy had now a breathing-space in which to fortify himself in his new possession. There can be little doubt that now was the time when the great mote, situated about a quarter of a mile to the north of the cathedral town, was erected, and that it was the *caislen* or *castrum* which he is said to have built at this time.[14] From this centre John de Courcy gradually extended his sway over Uladh, represented by by the counties of Down and Antrim, and over much of Uriel as well. But he was not always successful. Giraldus enumerates five battles, in three of which he was victorious and in the other two narrowly escaped with his life. He is, I think, substantially borne out [14]
by the Irish annals. The second battle was fought on the 24th of June, also at Down. It is described at some length in the Dublin copy of the Annals of Innisfallen. This time Rory Mac Donlevy, at the head of the Ulidians, was supported by Melaghlin O'Neill, lord of the Cinel Owen, and accompanied by the Archbishop of Armagh and others of the clergy, who bore numerous relics with them to secure the victory. The Cinel Owen and the Ulidians were defeated with the loss of 500 men. 'The Archbishop of Armagh, the Bishop of Down, and all the clergy were taken prisoners; and the English got possession of the croziers of St. Comgall and St. Dachiarog, the *Canoin Phatruic* [i.e. the Book of Armagh], besides a bell called *Ceolan an Tighearna*. They afterwards, however, set the bishops at liberty and restored the *Canoin Phatruic* and the bell, but they killed all the inferior clergy and kept the other noble relics,' which are stated to have remained in the hands of the English.[15] The third engagement was at Fir-Li, where De Courcy was raiding some cattle, when he was over- [15]
powered in a narrow pass and barely escaped with eleven of his knights to his *castrum* at Down. Fir-Li was a tribal district on the Bann in the north of Antrim, and this defeat at the hands of Cumee O'Flynn, lord of this district, is recorded in the Irish annals under the year 1178. The fourth battle was in Uriel, where de Courcy lost many of his men; and the fifth *apud pontem Ivori* (Newry) on is return from England, from which, however, he escaped to his own district victorious.[16]

John de Courcy. Mr. Brewer's account of the Book of Howth is very faulty; see Round, Commune of London, pp. 146–9. Roger de Hoveden (ii. 120) says: 'Johannes de Curci, amissa exercitus sui parte magna, victoria potitus est,' and adds that the bishop of Down was taken prisoner but was released at the entreaty of Cardinal Vivian. 14 This mote has in comparatively recent times been supposed to be Rath Celtair or the Fort of Celtar, a hero mentioned in early bardic story. But this has been disproved, and the real situation of Rath Celtair, which was known in John de Courcy's time, shown to have been on the hill where the cathedral now stands (see Eng. Hist. Review, 1907, p. 440, and the Journ. R.S.A.I. 1907, p. 137). In a map dated 1729 the mote is called 'English Mount'. 15 This passage from the Annals of Inisfallen is quoted in O'Donovan's note to Four Masters, vol. iii, p. 31. The older annals, in recording the names of the chieftains of the Cinel Owen who were killed, virtually corroborate this account. It is curious to note that the possession of the 'noble relics' seems to have been as much prized, presumably for battle-luck, by the victors as by the vanquished. 16 It is harder to identify these last two battles with the entries in the Annals, but the battle at Uriel is probably that mentioned in the Annals of Ulster in 1178, when John with his knights went pillaging from Dun (Downpatrick) to the Plain of Conaille (i.e. the low lands in Louth, a part

[16] A legend of the St. Lawrence family, as old as the Book of Howth,[17] locates pons Ivori at Howth, the ancient seat of the family, and here on the Ordnance Survey map may be seen the name 'Evora Bridge'. But the legend will not stand examination, and we may suspect that Evora Bridge owes its name to the legend, and lends it no support. The Irish name for Newry was *Iubhar cinn tragha*, 'yew-tree of the head of the strand.' By shortening it to Iubhar, prefixing the article (an), and adding a termination, the name Newry was evolved. Gerald's form represents the Irish sound without the article.

One would like to be able to trace more clearly the steps by which this remarkable man secured his position in Ulidia and dominated the whole country; but Giraldus, who alone throws any light on the subject, expressly tells us that he handles the mat-
[17] ter briefly and by way of episode, leaving to de Courcy's own writers to tell of his great exploits.[18] We may, however, indicate some of the conditions which probably aided him in accomplishing his purpose. In the first place, we have only to glance at the Irish annals for the period to see that the northern tribes, so far from being ready to combine steadily against the invaders, were incessantly fighting among themselves or with their neighbours in Connaught and in Ulidia. Thus the entries for the years 1177–80 are mainly concerned with the internal disputes of the subordinate tribes of Tir-owen. In 1181 we find the Cinel Connell inflicting a great defeat on Connaught, in which 'were killed sixteen sons of kings of Connaught and stark slaughter of Connaught besides'. Still more to the point, in the same year the Cinel Owen, under their king, Donnell O'Loughlin, 'gained a battle over the Ulidians and over Ui Tuirtri and over Fir-Li around Rory Mac Donlevy and Cumee O'Flynn,' who were hitherto John de
[18] Courcy's chief opponents; while again in the same year other tribes of the Cinel Owen 'took away many thousand of cows' from the same territories.[19] We may reasonably suspect that these chieftains, after this treatment by their neighbours, were ready to

of Uriel), and was attacked and defeated by Murrough O'Carroll, King of Uriel, and Mac Donlevy, King of Uladh, at Glenrigh (see, too, Four Masters and Ann. Inisfallen, MS. T.C.D.); and the fight at Newry may be that recorded in the Annals of Inisfallen (Dublin MS.) under the year 1180, where it is stated that John de Courcy plundered Machaire Conaille and Cuailgne and carried off 100 cows, but was pursued and overtaken by Murrough O'Carroll and others and defeated; and John de Courcy fled to Skreen Columbkille to the castle he had himself made there. This would be Castleskreen in Lecale, where the original mote may still be seen. O'Donovan, indeed, identifies the battle *apud pontem Ivori* with the first raid on Machaire Conaille and the defeat at Glenrigh, because Glenrigh was the old name for the vale of the Newry river. But this river was also the boundary of Uriel. Moreover, O'Donovan makes no attempt to identify the admitted defeat *apud Uriel*, or to trace in the pages of Giraldus the battle described in the Annals of Inisfallen, 1180. The equations suggested above seem substantially to reconcile the authorities. The last two battles, in fact, took place in very nearly the same place, but that *apud Uriel* was after a raid into Uriel and was admittedly a bad defeat, while that *apud pontem Ivori* might be characterized differently according to the sympathies of the writers. 17 Book of Howth (Car. Cal.), p. 90. The district about Howth and for a considerable distance to the north must have been subdued many years before this battle. 18 It is not improbable that Giraldus here actually alludes to some such work as was probably the original of those passages in the Book of Howth which tell of the *gestes* of John de Courcy, but in reading these stories as they have come down to us we note the entire absence of the acute observation, critical insight, and general moderation of statement for which Giraldus, by comparison with other writers of the time, is remarkable. 19 Ann. Ulster, Ann. Loch Cé, Four Masters.

invoke the assistance of de Courcy even at the price of submitting to his rule. Indeed the first entry in the next year (1182) goes far to prove the truth of this supposition. It tells of a new hosting of Donnell O'Loughlin to Dunbo in Dalriada[20] (a general name including the same districts in the north of Antrim), and of a battle there in which he was met and defeated by the Foreigners (i.e. John de Courcy's men). Furthermore, there is no record of any subsequent fighting between the Irish of Ulidia and John de Courcy, while on two occasions Rory Mac Donlevy was joined by the English on expeditions against Tir-owen and to Armagh. We may fairly conclude that there was no considerable displacement of the Irish population, but that after the first severe fighting the people settled down peaceably under their new rulers. Secondly, John de Courcy strengthened his position by marrying Affreca, daughter of Gottred, King of [19]
Man.[21] The Isle of Man was long connected with Ulidia, and the Northmen still lingered in some of the ports on the mainland. When in 1204 John de Courcy was driven out of Uladh, Reginald, King of Man, assisted him, because he was his brother-in-law.[22] He may have received assistance from the Manxmen before. At any rate, by his alliance with the King of Man, de Courcy did much to keep open communication by sea with England and with Dublin, and to secure his position generally.

Thirdly, he was a great builder of mote-castles,[23] and the motes dotted all over the counties of Down and Antrim indicate, more surely than any records which have survived, the precise centres of the manors created by him. Some few, indeed, we can positively connect with the castles mentioned in our scanty records, such as those at Downpatrick and Castleskreen (already mentioned), Mount Sandall near Coleraine, and one in Coleraine itself. Others can be shown with more or less probability to date from his time. Such are the so-called Crown Rath near Newry, the motes at Antrim, [20]
Donaghadee, Holywood, and Dromore, and the castle sites of Castlereagh, Clough, and others. The original castles at Carrickfergus, Carlingford, and Dundrum were on rock sites, and were probably built of stone from the first.

Fourthly, John de Courcy found a strong supporter in the Church, of which he was a munificent benefactor. He introduced Benedictine monks from the abbey of St. Werburgh in Chester into the priory of St. Patrick,[24] as he renamed the church of the Holy Trinity at Downpatrick. He confirmed the see of Down in its ancient possessions, and added largely thereto.[25] He also introduced Benedictine monks, from the

20 Dunbo is now the name of a townland and parish on the west side of the Bann, and according to O'Donovan Dalriada was bounded by that river. The point is immaterial for present purposes, as it is pretty plain that Donnell O'Loughlin was proceeding against Dalriada, and at one time, at any rate, the Fir-Li extended on both sides of the Bann. See Book of Rights, p. 123, note m. **21** According to the Annals of Inisfallen (MS. T.C.D.) this marriage took place in 1180. **22** Chron. Manniae (Manx Soc., vol. xxii), a. 1204, 1205. **23** 'Ultoniam undique locis idoneis incastellavit': Gir. Camb. v. 345. **24** Rot. Pat., 41 Ed. III, pt. 2, m. ii, an *inspeximus* of seven charters. The monks replaced the secular canons, but the church of Down was to be free from all subjection to the church of Chester. Malachi III, Bishop of Down, confirmed the grant, he remaining 'guardian and abbot of the black monks as in the church of Winchester or Coventry'. See Dugdale, Mon. Angl. (ed. 1830), vi, 1124. **25** John de Courcy's gifts to the see of Down were confirmed by Hugh de Lacy, Earl of Ulster, and are enumerated in an *inspeximus*, Rot. Pat., 16 Ed. III, pt. 2, m. 17. See Reeves, Eccl. Ant., p. 164.

priory at Stoke Courcy, into his new foundation, the priory of St. Andrew in the Ards,
[21] County Down.[26] He granted to the monks of St. Bega of Coupland, also Benedictines, the church of the island of Neddrum, now Mahee island, and two-thirds of the island itself, the remaining third being reserved to the see of Down.[27] He brought Cistericians from the abbey of Furness in Lancashire to Inishcourcy, now called Inch Abbey, near Downpatrick,[28] to atone, it is said, for having destroyed a Benedictine monastery in the neighbourhood; and he established Cruciferi or Crutched Friars in the priory of St. John the Baptist at Downpatrick.[29] He also endowed the house of St. Mary of Carrickfergus to the use of canons of the Premonstratensian order,[30] while
[22] his wife, Affreca, in 1193 founded the Cistercian monastery De Jugo Dei, the ruins of which are now known as the Grey Abbey, in Lower Ards.[31] He was also a benefactor of St. Thomas's Abbey[32] and of Christ Church, Dublin.[33]

Fifthly, and perhaps this was the real secret of his success, he was let alone. Until the period preceding his final expulsion in 1205 he was not interfered with either by king, justiciar, or brother baron. Though there is no evidence that he was ever created Earl of Ulster, he was *de facto* what the monk Jocelin called him, *Princeps Ulidiae*.[34] He practically exercised *jura regalia* even more completely than the great palatine lords of Leinster and Meath; he had a virtually unlimited jurisdiction, appointed his own feudal officers, created barons, and parcelled out the greater part of the territory among
[23] them. Unfortunately we have no authentic list of his barons,[35] and no account of his sub-infeudation, so that its extent is largely a matter of inference.

He had officers of his household just like any king or prince, and from his charters, several of which are known to us, we can tell some of their names. Thus it appears, from his charter granting jurisdiction to the Prior of Down, that Richard Fitz Robert was his seneschal, Roger de Courcy of Chester was his constable, and Adam his chamberlain.[36] Other witnesses to the same charater are William Savage, William Hach'

26 Dugdale, vi, 1123. This gift was confirmed by Pope Innocent III, Papal Letters, vol. i, p. 17. 27 Nine documents concerning Neddrum are summarized in Reeves, Eccl. Ant., pp 190–4, from a thirteenth-century roll, Cotton MSS., Brit. Mus. See also Dugdale, vi, 1127. Neddrum or Nendrum represents the Irish n-Oendruim, where there was formerly a Celtic monastery, the last abbot of which was 'burned in his own house': Four Masters, 974. The first abbot was Mochaoi (ob. 496, Four Masters), from whom the island was known as Inis Mochaoi or Mahee Island. John de Courcy's foundation is ascribed by Bishop Reeves to the year 1178. 28 Inishcourcy is a peninsula opposite to Downpatrick running into Strangford Lough. Its Irish name was Inis Cumhscraidh. The foundation of the abbey is ascribed to the year 1187: Ann. St. Mary's Abbey, Chart., vol. ii, p. 288. 29 Rot. Pat., 10 Ed. III, p. 2, m. 35, an *inspeximus* of six charters. 30 Royal Letters, no. 799; see Cal. Docs. Ireland, vol. i, no. 1227. 31 Chron. Manniae, 1204; Ann. Laud MS., Chart. St. Mary's, Dublin, vol. ii, p. 306. 32 Reg. St. Thomas's, Dublin, p. 221. 33 Christ Church Deeds, no. 10; cf. Liber Niger Ch. Ch., no. 9. This deed should be dated 1182–6. Amauri de Obda, one of the witnesses, is probably Almaric de St. Lawrence of Howth, brother-in-law to John de Courcy. 34 Dedication to his Life of St Patrick. 35 Sir John Davies in the Case of the County Palatine of Wexford mentions two of these barons, 'the baron Misset (a mistake for Bisset) and the baron Savage,' but there were many more. Thus King John addressed his mandate ordering the arrest of John de Courcy as follows: 'Rex omnibus Baronibus de Ultoniae,' &c.: Pat. Roll, 6 John. 36 See *inspeximus* of this charter in Dugdale from Pat. Roll, 41 Ed. III, p. 2, m. 11. These three officers witness other charters of John de Courcy. The other witnesses to this charter were William and Henry Copland, William de Curci, Philip de Hasting, Simon Passelew, Richard de Du[n]-donenald (i.e. Dundouenald or Dundonald, where there was an early

[Hacket], and William Saracen. In the list of hostages required from John de Courcy in 1204,[37] the sons of these six individuals are named with three others, and we may be pretty sure that the fathers were among John de Courcy's most trusted vassals.

castle now marked by a mote), and Reinard his brother, Walter de Loga[n]. Another charter (Reg. St. Thomas's, p. 222) was witnessed by Henry Purcell, constable, Roger Poer, marshal, and Adam, chamberlain. 37 Rot. Pat., 6 John, p. 55 b.

[25] CHAPTER XIII

THE OCCUPATION OF CORK, 1177–85

To return to the year 1177. After the battle of Down, Cardinal Vivian proceeded to Dublin, where he convened a synod of the bishops and abbots of Ireland. At this synod, according to Giraldus, he made a public declaration of the king's title to Ireland and of the papal confirmation thereof, and enjoined both clergy and laity, under pain of excommunication, to be true to their allegiance. Also, inasmuch as the Irish were accustomed to store their provisions in churches, he gave permission to the English troops, on any expedition, when they could not get food elsewhere, to take what they found in the churches on paying a just price.[1] This custom may seem at first sight
[26] curious and the licence given improbable; but there is independent evidence of the custom, and the statement throws light on the conduct of the Irish of Connaught in the face of an English expedition which took place soon afterwards in the same year, and which indeed seems to have been the immediate occasion for the licence. For this expedition we have the independent accounts of the Irish annals, which corroborate in a remarkable way the account of Giraldus. It appears that Murrough O'Conor, one of the sons of the King of Connaught, invited the English 'to destroy Connaught for evil towards his father'. What the exact pretext was we do not know. Possibly we have here only the first example of those jealousies and dissensions among the members of the O'Conor family which broke out again and again during the next century and gave the English full opportunity to interfere and dismember the province. But as not only Fitz Audelin, but also Cardinal Vivian, seem to have countenanced the expedition, we must suppose that some plausible case was made out for an interference in the affairs of Connaught, which certainly appears to have been a violation of the recent treaty between Henry and Rory.

With or without plausible grounds, however, Miles de Cogan, who was constable of the garrison of Dublin and custos of the city, with a band of 540 men crossed the
[27] Shannon and, guided by Murrough O'Conor, advanced as far as Roscommon and Tuam. The men of Connaught, not daring to oppose the invaders in the field, thwarted this expedition by the double-edged device of creating desolation before it throughout a large part of the province. They 'burned Tuam and the churches of the country besides, for evil towards the Foreigners'.[2] Giraldus explains this entry by his

1 Gir. Camb. v. 345. The Four Masters enigmatically state of this synod of the clergy that 'they enacted many ordinances not [now] observed'. When Vivian landed in England in July 1176 he was compelled to swear that he would do nothing against the king: Gesta Hen., vol. i, p. 118. The synod at Dublin is incidentally mentioned, ibid., p. 161. 2 Ann. Ulster, Ann. Loch Cé, 1177. The Annals of Tigernach and the

more ample statement. 'The Connaught men,' he says, 'with their own hands set fire to their towns and villages in every direction, and whatever provisions they could not conceal in underground chambers they burned together with the churches; and in order to bring scandal on our people and draw down upon their foes the vengeance of Heaven, they took down the crucifixes and images of the saints and strewed them on the plains before us.'[3] It seems, indeed, that it was the custom of the Irish, not only in [28]
Connaught but elsewhere, to store their corn in churches in the winter, and this custom enables us to understand how the burning of their own churches operated as 'evil to the Foreigners', and renders intelligible the statement of Giraldus as to the licence given by Cardinal Vivian. By these tactics the Connaught men, with whatever ultimate loss and hardship to themselves, gained their immediate object. The English took no prey and indeed barely escaped with their lives, and Murrough O'Conor was blinded by his father in revenge for the expedition.

Henry now recalled William Fitz Audelin, Miles de Cogan, and Robert Fitz Stephen. He may have been displeased at the Connaught expedition, but the grants which he soon afterwards made at the Council of Oxford show that his displeasure was not deep-seated. Fitz Audelin had been in office for only about ten months. At some time during this period, in the presence of Laurence the archbishop and Cardinal [29]
Vivian, he had founded, on the king's behalf, a church dedicated to St. Thomas the Martyr, just outside the western gate of Dublin, Thomas and endowed it with a carucate of land there.[4] This was the origin of the famous abbey of St. Thomas, which was served by Augustinian canons of the order of St. Victor, and soon became endowed by Anglo-Norman settlers from all parts of Ireland where they held lands.

The Register of Deeds of the abbey is one of our most important sources of information as to the extent and progress of the Anglo-Norman settlement up to near the close of the thirteenth-century. 'Its abbots were appointed subject to the approval of the king, they became members of his council in Ireland, peers of his parliament there, and administered justice in the court of the abbey.' The Liberty of Thomas-court survived the dissolution, and became the Liberty of the Brabazons, earls of Meath, and the last court-house building still exists to mark the spot where the famous abbey stood.[5]

Dublin Annals of Innisfallen give a detailed account of the places through which the English passed, and of how they escaped defeat at the Tochar mona Coinneadha (a causeway through a bog in the parish of Templetogher, County Galway) owing to the guidance of Murrough O'Conor. 3 Gir. Camb. v. 346. The statement that they burned all provisions 'quae hypogeis subterraneis abscondere non poterant', is interesting as apparently indicating that what antiquaries call 'rath-caves' or dry-stone chambers and passages to be found underneath many of the raths or ringforts of the country, were at this time in use. It has been absurdly taken to refer to crypts under the churches. Most of these churches were probably of wood, and at any rate contained no crypts. The practice of drawing down the wrath of Heaven on one's foes by strewing crucifixes, &c., on the ground was observed by the Anglo-Norman Archbishop Cumin in his quarrel with Hamo de Valognes, the justiciar, in 1197: Hoveden, iv, 29. 4 The charter is transcribed by Leland (vol. i, p. 127) from an ancient roll in the possession of the Earl of Meath. It is witnessed by the bishops of Meath, Kildare, and Waterford, and by some of the principal barons of Leinster, and some of the citizens of Dublin. It was confirmed by Henry, probably at the Council of Oxford in the same year. See too, Chartae Priv. et Immun., p. 2. 5 Journ. R.S.A.I. 1892, p. 41.

[30] One other 'remarkable deed' is ascribed to William Fitz Audelin at this time. He caused a most sacred relic, called the *Bachal Isa*, or 'Staff of Jesus', to be transferred from Armagh to Dublin.[6] The possessor of this staff at Armagh had been regarded as the true successor of Patrick, and it was probably brought to Dublin with the idea of assisting the cathedral church of that city in its claim to supremacy. It was used for centuries in Christ Church for the taking of solemn oaths, but was burned as an object of superstitious veneration at the Reformation.[7]

Hugh de Lacy was now appointed 'pro curator general' of Ireland in place of William Fitz Audelin. This new appointment appears to have been made at the Council of Oxford in May 1177,[8] when a number of appointments were made in the
[31] Irish establishment and some new and far-reaching grants were conferred. In the first place, Henry, with the authority of the Pope, constituted his son John, then a boy in the tenth year of his age, 'King of Ireland,' or perhaps we should say *Dominus* or Lord of Ireland,[9] that being the title which afterwards appears on John's writs. Moreover, the title *Dominus Hiberniae* appropriately expresses the feudal and territorial relation which it was desired to create, and accordingly Henry caused the new donees to whom grants were made at this council to do homage and take the oath of fealty to John as well as to himself for their lands. To these grants we must now turn.

First of all, he gave to Hugh de Lacy, by a new charter, the whole of Meath for the service, as is stated, of one hundred knights. This grant must have been confirmatory of the previous grant made at Wexford in 1172. The increased service—one hundred
[32] knights instead of fifty—may have been due to the fact that Hugh de Lacy was now appointed custos of the crown lands of Dublin and of the northern part of Leinster, now in the king's hand. In later times, however, we find that Meath owed only fifty services to the Crown[10] (or in money value £100), exactly as stated in the Song of Dermot with regard to the original grant, and as provided in King John's confirmatory grant to Walter de Lacy in 1208. In the next place, Henry granted to Robert Fitz Stephen and Miles de Cogan the kingdom of Cork from Cape St. Brendan (Brandon Head in Kerry) to the river (Blackwater) near Lismore, for the service of sixty knights. From this grant was excepted the city of Cork and the cantred of the Ostmen of the city, which the king retained in his own hands, giving the custody only to Fitz Stephen

6 Gir. Camb. v. 347 7 Four Masters, anno 1537, and O'Donovan's note, p. 1446. 8 In the Gesta Hen., vol. i, p. 161, it is said that Henry, apparently while still at Windsor, ordered Hugh, Earl of Chester, to go to Ireland to subdue it for Henry and his son John; but there is no indication anywhere that this Hugh ever went to Ireland, and the whole passage reads like a confused account of what was done at the Council of Oxford, which is told immediately afterwards in a fuller and more orderly fashion: ibid., pp. 162–5. The passage is omitted by Roger of Howden. 9 The distinction is an important one, but it is not, as is sometimes supposed, that the title of *Rex* is higher in degree than that of *Dominus*. The titles implied distinct relations and presupposed different ceremonies. The former title is national, the latter territorial. Strictly speaking, a person could not be *Rex* without having been elected and crowned, and could not be *Dominus* without having received homage and an oath of fealty from his vassal. Indeed from the feudal point of view it might be more important to be *Dominus* than *Rex* alone. Thus William the Marshal refused to fight for his king (John) against his lord (Philip Augustus): Hist. Guill. le Marechal, ll. 13060–256. 10 See the Irish Exchequer Memoranda of the reign of Edward I: Eng. Hist. Rev. 1903, vol. xviii, p. 505.

and de Cogan.[11] In the same way he granted the kingdom of Limerick (with the exception of the city and one cantred [of the Ostmen], which he retained in his own hands) to Herbert Fitz Herbert, William, brother of Earl Reginald of Cornwall, and Joel de la Pomerai, for the service of sixty knights. Later in the year, however, Henry [33]
granted the kingdom of Limerick to Philip de Braose, as the former grantees renounced the gift on the ground that the territory had not yet been won, and was not subject to the king.[12]

It is, of course, impossible to reconcile these sweeping grants with our ideas of equitable dealing; but it is the business of those who study historical actions to endeavour to understand the point of view of the actors, rather than to weigh their acts in modern scales of equity. It seems probable that Henry was by this time convinced that the Treaty of Windsor was utterly unworkable. It was based, as we have seen, on the hypothesis that Rory O'Conor was a real king, able to enforce his authority over all Ireland outside the portions which Henry retained in his direct dominion and in that of his barons. But events had shown that in this sense Rory was no king, at any rate outside his own province, and hardly within it. The conditions of the treaty could not possibly be enforced. Peace could not be maintained under it, and the aggressive spirit of the Norman barons was only too ready to take advantage of the inevitable dissensions that broke out among the Irish themselves. Henry may well have thought that [34]
the time had come to tear up this futile treaty and devise a new and more hopeful scheme of government. Besides, here was an opportunity to provide a lordship for his favourite son John. So John was made *Dominus Hiberniae*, and the policy was adopted of parcelling out his as yet unconquered territory among trusted vassals as rapidly and as completely as might be, leaving it to them to conquer, organize, and settle the lands thus granted to them. A commencement was made with the kingdoms of Cork and Limerick, or Desmond and Thomond, which had been torn by the recent struggle between the Kings of Connaught and Thomond, and by the intestine quarrel between the King of Desmond and his son.

It would have been more creditable, as well as probably more effective, if Henry had come himself with the armed forces of the Crown to impose his dominion over the length and breadth of Ireland, and to make a settlement which, while inflicting the minimum of hardship on Irish kinglets, might have introduced a better security for order and peaceful progress than any the Irish kinglets could offer. But Henry's energies, great as they were, were fully employed in other parts of his vast dominions, which extended from the North Sea to the Pyrenees. Ireland was only an inconsiderable fraction of these dominions, and accordingly Henry adopted there the less exact- [35]
ing method which had already been tried, with but partial success it is true, in Wales, of leaving the subjugation of the country in private hands. And this suggests a sounder ground for condemning the method—it was only partially successful in Ireland too.

11 This charter is printed in Littleton's Hen. II (App. III to vol. v) from Ware, and translated in Harris's Ware, Antiquities, p. 194. Among the witnesses connected with Ireland were Augustin, Bishop of Waterford, William Fitz Audelin, Hugh de Lacy, Maurice de Prendergast, Hervey de Montmorency, and Robert Fitz Stephen. 12 Gesta Hen., vol. i, p. 172; Roger Howden, vol. ii, pp. 133–6.

Henry next appointed custodians of the lands which were in his hand, including, of course, the great fief of Leinster, and named the places where the feudal services in respect of these lands should be paid or performed. He gave the custody of Wexford to William Fitz Audelin, his dapifer, that of Waterford to Robert le Poer, his marshal, and that of Dublin to Hugh de Lacy. Further, he defined the lands that were to be thenceforth appurtenant to each of these cities, and in doing so he seems to have had in view a further reduction of the late Earl Richard's fief.

Thus to the service of Wexford, at this time the *caput* of the lordship of Leinster, Henry appears to have assigned only the following lands: Arklow, the lands comprised in the present baronies which adjoin the eastern and southern coasts of the County Wexford, the baronies of Forth and Idrone in County Carlow, the southern part of the County Kildare, together with Leix, and the districts left to the O'Tooles in the inland
[36] parts of the County Wicklow.[13] These places were presumably intended to represent Strongbow's fief. To the service of Waterford Henry assigned not only all the land between the city and the Blackwater beyond Lismore,[14] but also the whole of Ossory, usually regarded as part of Leinster; while to the service of Dublin he assigned the lands of Offelan, Offaly, and Kildare, as well as Wicklow (i.e. the castle and lands held therewith) and Meath. It is possible that this distribution of services was intended only as a temporary arrangement, made for convenience, while the fief of Leinster was in the king's hand and Hugh de Lacy was custos of Dublin; but in view of the disputes and even warfare that afterwards occurred when William Marshal succeeded to the fief
[37] of Leinster, it seems probable that it was interpreted by John, if not intended by Henry, as defining the limits of that fief. It may be regarded as some confirmation of this view that Giraldus afterwards mentions with some bitterness that Kildare and the adjacent territory, which had been given by the earl to Meiler Fitz Henry, was taken away from him, and the rugged, woody, and hostile march lands of Leix given to him by way of exchange. Also, if Offelan, Offaly, and Kildare were at this time added to Meath, the increased service, that of one hundred knights instead of fifty required, according to the Gesta, by the new charter of Meath, would be intelligible.

The grantees of the kingdoms of Cork or Desmond, and Limerick or Thomond, set out in company in the month of November, each with a band of retainers, to take possession of their new fiefs. We can readily understand that this promised to be no easy matter. Rory O'Conor, indeed, was not likely to assert his overlordship or interfere in any way, but the provincial kings, Dermot McCarthy and Donnell O'Brien, might be expected to have a word to say. We might indeed have supposed that these princes would have united with all their forces against their common foe, but, so far

13 The scribe of the Gesta has blundered over some of the names, and the passage is corrupt in places, but, with the exception of the *tenementum Machtaloe* (as to the position of which I am uncertain), the districts above described are, I think, alone included. For *terra G. de Bisroharde* see Song of Dermot, ll. 3114–17 and note. Other less obvious equations are, Fernregwinal, the Fernegenal of the Song, l. 3074; Druua (read Druna): *ui Drona*, Idrone. Utmorthi is not a man's name in the genitive, but represents *ui Muireadhaigh*, usually anglicized Omurethy; and Leghlin: Leighlin was a separate tenement. 14 It will be remembered that by the Treaty of Windsor the western boundary of the royal demesne at Waterford was fixed so as to include Dungarvan only.

was this from being the case, that, according to an Irish authority, Murtough, son of Donnell O'Brien, actually assisted the foreigners against the King of Desmond, the hereditary foe of his house, and 'accompanied Fitz Stephen and de Cogan to Cork, [38] where they committed many depredations'.[15] This refers to the country about Cork, as there was already a Norman governor, Richard de Londres, in the city, who received them with honour. We are also told that 'the churches of the Plain of Munster were burnt by Donnell O'Brien' and the Norman leaders of the expedition.[16] Thus, as in so many other cases, it was by Irish aid that Dermot McCarthy and the lesser chieftains of Desmond were speedily overcome, and Fitz Stephen and de Cogan were enabled to win for themselves, not indeed the whole province at once, but seven of its cantreds near the city of Cork. These seven cantreds were then divided by lot between the grantees, the three eastern ones falling to Fitz Stephen, and the four western ones to de Cogan.[17]

Having thus arranged matters in Cork, the whole party of adventurers marched to Limerick to place Philip de Braose in possession of his fief. Donnell O'Brien was now no longer a welcome ally, but a formidable opponent, and 'for dread of the Dal Cais (Donnell's tribesmen),' we are told, the 'foreigners returned without obtaining their [39] desire'. When they reached the river in front of the town, they saw the desperate citizens (presumably Ostmen) once more setting fire to their buildings. Fitz Stephen and de Cogan were ready to attempt to cross the river and storm the town, or, if de Braose preferred, to construct a fortified camp for him on the opposite side of the river. But Philip, though personally brave, yielding to the pusillanimous advice of his friends, preferred to return safe home rather than to face the perils of fortune in so remote and so hostile a land.[18] Twenty-four years later Philip's grant was renewed to his unfortunate nephew, William de Braose,[19] and indeed before that time the city and much of the territory south of the Shannon was in the hands of the foreigners, but for the moment, at any rate, Limerick was left undisturbed.

The adventurers in Desmond for a time fared better. For the space of five years, we are told, they jointly governed the province in peace, restraining by their mild rule the impetuous spirits of the young men on both sides.[20] The families of the leaders [40] became united in marriage. Fitz Stephen, indeed, had no legitimate children, but he had two illegitimate sons with him. One of these, Meredith, died soon after the arrival in Cork, but the other, Ralph, was now married to Margarita, who seems to have been the only child and presumptive heiress of Miles de Cogan. Were it not for the illegitimacy of Ralph Fitz Stephen the two houses were likely to become one. Soon after the marriage was effected, however, this prosperous beginning was interrupted by a tragedy which nearly resulted in the destruction of the Anglo-Norman settlement in Desmond. Miles de Cogan, Ralph Fitz Stephen, and five other knights went in the

15 Ann. Inisfallen, Dublin MS., 1177. **16** Ibid., and Ann. Tigernach. The latter adds, 'and for dread of the Dal Cais they (the Foreigners) returned without (obtaining their) desire.' This seems to refer to the failure to get possession of Limerick. **17** Gir. Camb. v. 348. **18** Gir. Camb. v. 349. **19** Rot. Chart., 2 John, m. 15 (p. 84 b). **20** In the Register of St. Thomas's Abbey (pp. 201, 209, 211, 220) will be found several charters which show that Gregory, Bishop of Cork, and Reginald, Archdeacon (afterwards bishop), acted at this time with Miles de Cogan and Robert Fitz Stephen in endowing the new foundation of St. Thomas's, Dublin, with churches, lands, &c., in Cork and the neighbourhood.

direction of Lismore to meet the men of Waterford in a parley. While awaiting the advent of the latter they were treacherously attacked by Mac Tire, chieftain of
[41] Imokilly, and all slain.[21] This massacre led to a general rising of the Irish of Desmond against the English, and Robert Fitz Stephen was hemmed in by his enemies on all sides, in the town of Cork. Raymond le Gros, however, on hearing of his uncle's perilous condition, came to the rescue by sea from Waterford with a small band. With his usual success, he quickly dispersed the Irish and brought peace once more to the district. Richard de Cogan was now sent by the king to take the place of his brother Miles,[22] and in February 1183 Philip de Barry crossed over to Cork both to aid Fitz Stephen and to undertake the governance of Olethan, which had been granted to him by his uncle. Along with Philip came his brother Gerald, the historian, to whose observation and inquiries we owe much of our knowledge of recent and contemporary events.[23]

[42] We hear nothing more of Robert Fitz Stephen and little more of Raymond le Gros. Probably the former did not long survive the rising of 1182, though he was clearly alive when his nephew Gerald first came to Ireland in 1183.[24] When and how Raymond died is also quite uncertain. He was alive when John came to Ireland in 1185,[25] and must have been dead before the close of the century, when we find his widow Basilia married to Geoffrey Fitz Robert.[26] On the other hand, Raymond can hardly have died before 1189, as otherwise his death would surely be noticed in the Expugnatio, first published when Henry II was alive, and probably in that year.[27] Ware
[43] mentions a tradition that Raymond was buried at the abbey of Molana, situated on the Blackwater a little above Youghal, and this tradition may have been well founded, though both Raymond and his wife bequeathed their bodies to be buried in the abbey of St. Thomas, Dublin, of which they were munificent benefactors.[28] It is unfortunate

21 Gir. Camb. v. 350. The account in the Annals of Loch Cé states that besides Miles de Cogan and 'the two sons of Stephen' there were slain 'Mac Sleimne, Thomas Sugach ("the Merry"), Cenn Cuilenn ("Holly-head"), and Remunn.' Who were meant by these names is unknown. Remunn was certainly not Raymond le Gros (as stated in the Annals of Clonmacnois), nor Raymond Fitz Hugh (as supposed by the editors of the Annals of Loch Cé and of Ulster), for the latter witnessed a grant by Philip de Barry, which was also witnessed by Gerald the historian, and must be dated 1183: Reg. St. Thomas's, p. 205. Cenn Cuilinn cannot be a corruption of Reimundus Kantitunensis, as suggested by the editor of the Annals of Loch Cé, for, according to Gerald, he was slain in Ossory c. 1185: Gir. Camb. v. 386. **22** i.e. as bailiff of the king's demesnes in the city of Cork and its vicinity. **23** Gir. Camb., p. 351. 'Master Gerald the Archdeacon' [of Brecknock] was one of the witnesses to a grant made at this time by Philip de Barry of two carucates of land adjoining the bridge of Dungarvan [close to the town of Cork] and the site of a mill to the church of St. Thomas, Dublin: Reg. St. Thomas's, p. 205. **24** Gerald says that his brother, Philip de Barry, came at the end of February 1183 'ad avunculi subventionem', and describes himself as coming in the same ship and 'tam avunculum quam fratrem plurimum consilio juvans'. There is little doubt that it was from Fitz Stephen he derived most of the early story of the invasion. He does not expressly record his uncle's death, but the allusion to Raymond 'in hereditatem patruo succedens' (which appears in the early MSS.) implies it. **25** 'Reimundus filius Willelmi ' is one of the witnesses to John's confirmation charter to St. Mary's Abbey, tested at Dublin. See Chartulary, vol. i, pp. 85, 86. **26** Reg. St. Thomas's, Dublin, p. 112. Witnessed by John, Bishop of Leighlin, who was consecrated in 1198 (Papal Letters (Bliss), vol. i, p. 3) and died c.1201 (Ware). **27** For the date of the first edition of the Expugnatio, see Mr. Dimock's preface, pp. lvi–lviii. **28** Reg. St. Thomas's, pp. 113 (c. 1184), 111 (c. 1200).

that, owing to the imperfection of our records, the passing of Raymond, the most brilliant commander and the most picturesque figure in the army of the invaders, should be so obscure.

It is not possible to give a full account of the early sub-infeudation of the 'kingdom of Cork', or even to be sure how far it was carried out in the lifetime of the original grantees. In the case of FitzStephen, at any rate, it is pretty plain that, besides making large grants out of the three cantreds to the east of Cork originally, with the acquiescence of Dermot MacCarthy, allotted to him, he made what we may call 'speculative grants' of lands far removed from these cantreds. Thus by his charter to Philip de Barry he granted not only Olethan, but also two other cantreds, to be determined by lot.[29] What these two cantreds were ultimately decided to be, we know from John's confirmatory charter to William de Barry, Philip's son, made in 1207.[30] They were [44]
'Muscherie Dunegan' and 'Killede', of which the former is roughly represented by the barony of Orrery and Kilmore, County Cork, and the latter was comprised in the barony of Glenquin, County Limerick.[31] To Alexander, son of Maurice Fitz Gerald,[32] Fitz Stephen seems to have made a grant in Imokilly which was the origin of the Fitz [45]
Gerald property here. Other landholders in Fitz Stephen's time were, in Imokilly, Raymond Mangunel,[33] and Robert and Thomas des Auters or de Altaribus;[34] and in Fermoy, Alexander and Raymond Fitz Hugh.[35] Modern writers speak of Alexander Fitz Hugh as de Rupe or Roche, but in the charters he always appears as Alexander filius Hugonis, and Giraldus calls his brother Raymond 'Hugonides' and seems to include him in the noble band of his own kinsmen.

As to the four cantreds assigned to Miles de Cogan on the western side of Cork we have no direct information, but they perhaps included the barony of Muskerry and a broad strip along the coast between the harbours of Cork and Glandore. In 1207 King

29 'Olethan cum omnibus pertinentiis suis et duas alias cantredas in regno Corchaiae prout sorte obvenient ei pro servitio decem militum': Lodge, vol. i, Ware, p. 287, and Harris's Antiq., p. 195. 30 Chart., 9 John, m.5 (p.172), Cal. Docs. Irel., vol. i, no.340. 31 Muscherie Dunegan appears as the deanery of 'Muxydonnegan' or 'Muscridonegan' in the ecclesiastical taxations of 1302–6 (Cal. Docs. Irel., vol. v, pp. 277 and 314), and the parishes enumerated are comprised in the barony of Orrery and Kilmore with small adjacent parts of the baronies of Duhallow and Fermoy. The position of 'Killede' was long unknown, but that it is now represented by Killeedy in the barony of Glenquin, County Limerick, appears from an inquisition *post mortem* on the lands of John Fitz Thomas, 10 Ed. I, no. 21: 'Idem Johannes tenuit unum cantredum apud Kyllyde Hy Connil et castrum in eodem comitatu (Limerick) de Johanne de Barry pro duobus serviciis militum.' The ruins of a castle at Killeedy are situated on an artificial mound near a bend of a stream. The mound probably represents the original mote, and is an indication that the grant was utilized probably before the close of the twelfth century at latest. For the identification of Killeedy, co. Limerick, with the Killede of Philip's charter see the writer's paper, 'Notes on some Limerick Castles,' Journ. R.S.A.I., 1909, p. 30. 32 Alexander Fitz Maurice granted the church, &c., 'de villa mea que vocatur Killie' [Killeigh in Imokilly]. to the Abbey of St. Thomas, Reg. St. Thomas's, Dublin, p. 206. The lands probably passed to Alexander's brother, Gerald, who held the land of Oglassin in this district (Cal. Docs. Irel., vol. i, nos. 586, 598), and from him to his son Maurice, who may be regarded as the founder of Youghal. 33 Raymond Mangunel held Cahirultan, in the parish of Ballyoughtera, Imokilly; Reg. St. Thomas, Dublin, p. 216. 34 These brothers held Castlecor (Middleton) and Castlemartyr in Imokilly (ibid., p. 319); lands which afterwards were purchased by Richard de Carew (ibid., p. 200). 35 Alexander and Raymond Fitz Hugh held Kilcummer in Fermoy (ibid., p. 217), and the former afterwards founded the Priory de Ponte (Bridgetown); see the Charter in Dugdale, vi. 1146, and Cal. Charter Rolls, ii, p. 341.

John made large grants within these districts to Richard de Cogan, Philip de Prendergast, and Robert Fitz Martin, to hold of the king in fee. Also a grant to David
[46] de Rupe of the cantred of Rosselither (Rosscarbery).[36] These grants certainly seem to deal with Miles de Cogan's cantreds and to ignore the de Cogan seignory. Perhaps no effective settlement had been made in them during Miles's lifetime, but in any case arbitrary dealing of this sort with lands already granted was eminently characteristic of King John. Some grants by Miles de Cogan have been preserved in the Register of St. Thomas's, but with the exception of the grant of a knight's fee in Cridarim (*Crich Dairine*, i.e. Rosscarbery?) they were all made on behalf of the king and were concerned with houses and lands in or near the town of Cork, i.e. within the crown lands there. Among the witnesses to these charters were the following (who were also probably grantees of his lands): Richard and Geoffrey de Cogan, Richard de Pincheni, William de Bridesal, Roger de Chirchehille, Lucas de Londiniis, who married Leuki, daughter of Robert (p. 207), Roger of Oxford, and Richard Fitz Godebert, who may have been the knight of Pembrokeshire whom Dermot brought back with him in 1167, and whose sons probably took the name of de Rupe or Roche, as their cousins in the County Wexford did.

What became of the seignory of the lands included in the grant to Miles de Cogan
[47] and Robert Fitz Stephen has never been elucidated [see *Add.*]. It was indeed the subject of a claim made nearly four centuries later by Sir Peter Carew. However preposterous, after such a lapse of time, was Sir Peter's claim, it seems certain that throughout the greater part of the thirteenth century a Carew and a de Courcy shared in equal moieties the interests of the original grantees.[37]

Can we discover the heirs of the original grantees? We are expressly told that Raymond le Gros succeeded to the inheritance of his uncle, Robert Fitz Stephen, and obtained the custody of the town of Cork.[38] Raymond died childless, and his heir was
[48] probably his next brother, Odo de Carew. By what steps the seignory passed from Raymond's heir to the Robert de Carew who was tenant-in-chief in 1221 is obscure, but that it remained in the family for more than a century seems certain.[39] How the seignory was eventually lost to the Carews is perhaps clearer to us than to those who opposed Sir Peter Carew's claim in the latter part of the sixteenth century. An

36 Rot. Chart., 9 John, pp. 171–3, where 'Insovenach' is Inishannon, and its port is Kinsale Harbour. 37 Thus in the roll of services due to the king in the different counties of Ireland c. 1297–8 the total due from Cork is 61½ services. Of these 30 were due from Robert de Carew and the like number from Patrick Courcy, thus making up the original 60 services. The remaining services were due from Gerald de Prendergast: Irish Exchequer Memoranda transcribed Eng. Hist. Rev., vol. xviii (1903), p. 504; cf. Car. Cal. Misc., p. 232, and Cal. Docs. Irel. 1296, nos. 288, 473. A Patrick Courcy and Robert de Carew (predecessors of the above?) were among the magnates of Cork from as early as 1221: Cal. Docs. Irel., vol. i, nos. 1001, 2266. In the inquisition on the lands of Gerald de Prendergast in 1251 (Cal. Docs. Irel., vol. i, no. 3203) it was found that he held of the king *in capite* Bellonar and Dufglas (i. e. Beavor or Carrigaline and Douglas, south of the town of Cork) by the service of two knights. 38 Gir. Camb. v. 350. If, as is generally supposed, Robert Fitz Stephen was a bastard, Raymond's succession to his inheritance must have been due to a fresh grant. 39 From a confirmatory charter preserved in the Register of St. Thomas's, p. 200, it would seem probable that about 1224 Richard de Carew held the seignory of Fitz Stephen's moiety. Cf. for the date, charter, ibid., p. 213, and the confirmations by Marian O'Brien, Bishop of Cork, pp. 220–1.

attempted alienation without licence of the cantred of Fermoy by Maurice de Carew, then tenant-in-chief, was held in 1302 to work a forfeiture, as contrary to the newly enacted Statute of Quia Emptores, and David de Rupe (Roche), who held the cantred under Maurice de Carew, became tenant-in-chief.[40] Possibly at this time the *dominium* was more burdensome than it was worth. In the next generation Thomas de Carew, son of Maurice, released to David de Barry the manors of Olethan and Muscry-donegan, and consequently the latter, in the year 1336, became tenant-in-chief of the Crown.[41]

As to the moiety of Miles de Cogan, his heir was his daughter, Margarita de Cogan, [49]
the newly-made widow of Ralph Fitz Stephen.[42] She may possibly have had an only daughter and heiress, perhaps a posthumous child, by Ralph Fitz Stephen, but, as we have seen, her claims for the time appear to have been ignored. How the seignory passed to the de Courcys, as it seems to have done early in the thirteenth century, has not been precisely ascertained. Probably a de Courcy married a de Cogan heiress. Lodge, indeed, states that the Patrick de Courcy, who appears along with Robert de Carew as a magnate in Cork in 1221, married the daughter and heir of Miles de Cogan.[43] But for such a marriage there is no actual authority.[44]

40 See the Cal. Justiciary Rolls for 1302, pp. 383–5, where the proceedings are reported. This David de Rupe was son of Alexander, and grandson of David. 41 Irish Close Rolls, 32 Ed. III, no. 26. The father and grandfather of this David de Barry were both named David. 42 She was given by Robert Fitz Stephen, as her marriage portion with his son, one half of Inismor, ie. the Great Island in Cork Harbour, and she gave to St. Thomas's the church of Cloenmedli there, i. e. Clonmel in Great Island, not Clonmel Tipperary, as absurdly stated by the editor: Reg. St. Thomas's, Dublin, pp. 226–7. 43 Vol. vi, p 146. The treatment in Lodge, however, of the early pedigree of the barons of Kinsale does not inspire confidence.
44 It appears, however, from the Pipe Rolls, that in 1212 Thomas Bloet owed 500 marks 'for having all the [50]
land which belonged to Milo Cogan in Ireland with his niece (or granddaughter ?) in marriage': Cal. Docs. Irel., vol. i, nos. 422, 452. But this fine was still unpaid in 1227 (ibid., no. 1504), and in that year Kilmohanoc (now Kilmonoge) in Kinalea, which had formerly belonged to Miles de Cogan (Chart. St. Mary's, ii. 4), and appears to have been held by Thomas Bloet, was granted during pleasure to Richard de Cogan (Cal. Docs. Irel., i, nos. 1537, 1646), and was subsequently treated as an escheat: ibid., ii, nos. 262, 390. Meantime, in 1217, soon after the accession of Henry III, Margery Cogan (presumably the widow of Ralph Fitz Stephen) offered 100 marks 'to have the land of her inheritance in Desmond': Close Roll, 1 Hen. III, p. 297. This she seems to have obtained, and we find 'Margarita filia Milonis de Cogan' at about this date making a large grant in Rosselethry (Rosscarbery), and confirming her father's grant of Kilmohanoc to St. Mary's Abbey, Dublin; see Chartulary, vol. ii, p. 4. It looks as if the de Cogan seignory, over-ridden by John's grants of 1207, was, in part at least, restored to Margarita on the accession of Henry III. At this time she must have been at least fifty years of age; but she may have been long married to a de Courcy. It was customary for heiresses to retain their maiden names.

[51] CHAPTER XIV

HUGH DE LACY, LORD OF MEATH, 1172–86

While John de Courcy was carving out a lordship for himself in Ulster, and Robert Fitz Stephen and Miles de Cogan were endeavouring to establish themselves in Munster, Hugh de Lacy, the newly-appointed viceroy, was strengthening the position, both in Meath and in Leinster, by building castles and by the wisdom and moderation of his rule. This remarkable man, the fifth Baron Lacy by tenure, was descended from Walter, the first baron, who died in 1089. The family received their name from their original seat at Lassy in the Vire country in Normandy. The principal estates of the Lacy family lay on the borders of Wales at Ewias Lacy, Staunton Lacy, and Weobly. Ludlow Castle also belonged to them.[1] Hugh de Lacy is described by Giraldus[2] as a swarthy man with small black deep-set eyes, a flat nose, an ugly scar on his right cheek
[52] caused by a burn, a short neck, and a hairy, sinewy body. He was short and ill-made in person, but in character firm and resolute, and of French sobriety. He was very attentive to his private affairs, and in office a most vigilant public administrator. Although much experienced in military matters, he was not fortunate as a general. After his wife's death he fell into loose moral ways. He was very covetous, and immoderately ambitious of honour and renown.

Upon his first appointment, in April 1172, he did not remain many months in Ireland. He seems to have visited the country again in the early part of 1174, when he erected the mote-castle of Trim, but he left before its destruction by Rory O'Conor in that year. Thenceforward we can trace him in the entourage of the king up to the Council of Oxford in 1177, and he cannot have been long, if at all, in Ireland during these years.[3] He had, however, already made many grants of lands within his lordship.

[53] During his tenure of office we hear of little or no fighting either in Meath or in Leinster. An apparently unsuccessful attempt was made to gain a footing at Clonmacnois, where, however, the churches and bishop's houses were respected, and a battle was fought between Art O'Melaghlin and Melaghlin Beg, rival claimants to the kingship of Westmeath, in which the English joined on the side of the former.[4] Clearly

1 Dict. Nat. Biog. In 1165-6 Hugh de Lacy held 58¾ knights' fees and had nine tenants without knight service: Eyton, Shropshire, vol. v, p. 253. 2 v. 354. 3 Hugh de Lacy was at Canterbury on December 29, 1172: Gir. Camb. vii. 69. In 1173 he was at Alençon in April, defending Verneuil in July, and at Caen in December. He seems to have come to Ireland early in 1174: Song of Dermot, ll. 3222-31; but he was at Rouen in December. In 1175 he was at Valognes in April, at Northampton in August, and at Feckenham in October. In 1176 he was at Shrewsbury in January, and at Winchester in April; and in 1177 he was at Reading in April, and at Oxford in May: Eyton's Itin. 4 Ann. Tigernach, Four Masters, 1178. In the latter contest Murtough, son of the Sinnagh (i.e. O'Caharny surnamed the Fox), was slain. This is perhaps

Hugh de Lacy was no mere filibuster, though he was determined to hold with the strong hand and to rule the districts committed to his charge. With this object he erected many castles, of a type similar to the castles of Trim and Slane, both in Meath and in Leinster. He made it his first care, we are told, to invite back to peace the rural inhabitants who had been violently expelled from their territories—probably in the course of the reprisals which followed on Rory O'Conor's hosting of 1174—and to restore to them their farms and pasture lands. His next aim was to restrain the townsfolk and compel them to obey the laws and submit to governance. Thus he soon established peace in the land, and indeed, by his liberal treatment and affability, so gained [54]
the hearts of the Irish people—winning over even their chieftains to his side as to give rise to the suspicion that he meditated renouncing his allegiance and usurping the crown of Ireland for himself.[5]

That Henry was for some reason dissatisfied with Hugh de Lacy appears from the fact that in May 1181 he took from him the custody of Dublin and sent over in his place to that city John (de Lacy), Constable of Chester, and Richard de Pec, an itinerant justice. One reason given for this change is that Hugh had married, according to the custom of the country, the daughter of the King of Connaught without Henry's licence.[6] Henry was always suspicious of his Irish barons and jealously watchful lest they should get too powerful, and he may have thought that this alliance with Rory O'Conor's daughter, like Strongbow's marriage with Eva Mac Murrough, might lead to the acquisition of too great power. But that Hugh de Lacy had really any intention [55]
of 'usurping the crown of Ireland' is inconsistent with all we know of his character and actions.

Before departing, however, Hugh de Lacy advised with the new governors as to the erection of several castles in Leinster, which we have already mentioned when treating of the subinfeudation of that lordship. One other castle is expressly named as having been erected by him a little earlier. This was the *castrum Lechliniae* or castle of Leighlin, and from the description given it is very probable that its site is marked by an important mote, called Burgage or Ballyknockan mote, on the west bank of the Barrow, about half a mile below Leighlin bridge.[7] It appears that Henry had ordered that a fortress should be erected here, but Robert le Poer, the custos of Waterford, who, according to Gerald, was wanting in energy and valour and utterly unfit for border warfare, had failed to carry out the royal command.[8] A namesake now, but a very dif- [56]

noteworthy, as it was at the instigation of 'the Sinnagh' that Hugh de Lacy was murdered in 1186. 5 Gir. Camb. v. 353. William of Newburgh also says that Hugh de Lacy aspired to obtain the crown of Ireland for himself, vol. i, pp. 239–0. Early in 1179 some Irish men came to Windsor to complain of unjust treatment at the hands of Hugh de Lacy and William Fitz Audelin: Gesta Hen., vol. i, p. 221. 6 Gesta Hen., vol. i, p. 270. The marriage 'secundum morem patriae illius' was probably some sort of loose union repudiated by the Anglican Church, perhaps 'a Teltown marriage'. It took place in 1180: Ann. Inisfallen (MS. T.C.D.); cf. Gir. Camb.'s account of Hugh de Lacy's character. 7 Gir. Camb. v. 352: 'Super nobilem Beruae fluvium a latere Ossiriae trans Odronam in loco natura munito Lechliniae castrum erexit.' 8 'A quo Robertus Poer cui regio mandato injunctum id fuerat ante defecerat,' ibid. This sentence follows that last quoted, and has, I think, been misunderstood. According to the Annals of Inisfallen (Dublin copy), Robert Poer was killed in 1178 in an expedition against the O'Tooles of Hy Muireadhaigh (South Kildare). He was succeeded in Waterford by William Poer: Gir. Camb. v. 354. In the Pipe Roll, 25 Hen. II (1178–9),

ferent man, Roger le Poer, who had fought courageously under de Courcy at the battle of Down, was placed at the head of the garrison here, and gained great renown until he and many of his followers were cut off in Ossory about the year 1188. Of this mishap we have no details, but it is said to have led to a widespread conspiracy of the Irish against the English, and to the destruction of many castles.[9]

On November 14, 1180, Laurence O'Toole, the last Celtic archbishop of Dublin, died.[10] Since Henry's visit to Ireland, if not before, Laurence O'Toole, in common with the Irish clergy generally, seems to have loyally acquiesced in the new regime and cordially co-operated with the new rulers. Verifiable facts concerning him during this
[57] period are few. He was an assenting party at the Council of Cashel in 1172. He witnessed Strongbow's grant of the abbacy of Glendalough to 'Thomas his beloved cleric'. He saw the commencement of the building of the new and stately fane of the cathedral church of the Holy Trinity in Dublin. In it he buried Richard of Striguil, and to it, when Hugh de Lacy was constable, probably in 1178, he confirmed all its numerous possessions.[11] He was present at the Council at Windsor on the 6th of October 1175, and witnessed the treaty there made between Henry and Rory O'Conor.[12] In March 1179 he attended the general council of Lateran, when he was accompanied by Catholicus and five or six Irish bishops. On their way through England they obtained leave from Henry to go to Rome, on their solemnly swearing that they would seek
[58] nothing to the detriment of the king or his kingdom.[13] Giraldus states that Henry was afterwards displeased with Archbishop Laurence on the ground that he had obtained some privileges at the Lateran Council inconsistent with the royal dignity, and that consequently Henry detained the Archbishop both in England and in France, and that at length he died at Eu in Normandy.[14] The archbishop did indeed bring back two *privilegia* from Pope Alexander III: one confirming to him and his successors the rights and possessions (enumerated at length) of the see of Dublin, with metropolitan jurisdiction over the dioceses of Glendalough, Kildare, Ferns, Leighlin, and Ossory; the other making a like confirmation to Malchus, Bishop of Glendalough, and his successors, in each case threatening spiritual penalties on anybody interfering with those

p, 67, is the entry 'pro cc. summis frumenti missis Roberto Poherio in Hibernia xx. 1. per breve regis'. Corn was sent in the same year to Raymond Fitz William and to the officers of Hugh de Lacy. 9 Gir. Camb. v. 341, 354, 387. The date 1188 is from the Annals of Inisfallen, Dublin MS. 10 That this was the true date appears from a comparison of the statement in his Life, by Surius, as to the day of his death, Friday, November 14, with the year 1180 as given in the Irish annals, though his death is referred to early in 1181 in Gesta Hen., vol. i, p. 270. See Ussher's Sylloge, note to no. 48. Probably the date in the Gesta, *post Purificationem S. M.*, 1181, should really refer only to the seizure of the archbishopric into the king's hand, to which the account of the death of the archbishop is introductory. 11 Chartae Privil. et Immun., p. 2; Cal. Liber Albus, Ch. Ch., no. 42. This deed must be subsequent to 1173, when the predecessor of Eugenius, Bishop of Clonard, died (Ann. Ulster), and therefore subsequent to Hugh de Lacy's appointment as custos of Dublin in May 1177. It should probably be dated May 14, 1178, before the archbishop went to the Lateran Council. It shows that the churches of St. Michan, St. Michael, St. John the Evangelist, St, Bridget, and St. Paul, were all then in existence. Torquellus, the archdeacon, and some of the attesting presbyters have Scandinavian names. 12 Gesta Hen. i. 102; Hoveden, ii. 83. 13 Gesta Hen. i. 221. The prelates were assisted in the passage by the Crown: Pipe Roll, 25 Hen. II, and the sheriffs of London and Middlesex redeemed some pledges for Archbishop Laurence and for Brictius, Bishop of Limerick: ibid. To travel from Dublin to Rome in the twelfth century was an expensive matter. 14 Gir. Camb. v. 357.

possessions.[15] It is possible that Henry had already entertained the design of uniting the sees of Dublin and Glendalough, and in any case he may have resented this interference of the Pope. But the English Chroniclers, who had better means of knowing the facts, say nothing about Henry's displeasure. They state that the archbishop crossed the sea to the king in Normandy, bringing with him the son of Rory O'Conor [59]
as a hostage for the due performance of the treaty to pay tribute, and that, having obtained leave to return to his country, the archbishop got as far as Eu, where he was detained by illness and after a few days died.[16] It would seem, then, that the archbishop had returned to Ireland after attending the Lateran Council, and that it was on the occasion of a subsequent mission to Normandy[17] with the hostage of the King of Connaught that he died.

According to all testimony, Laurence O'Toole was a just and good man and had the best interest of his country at heart. Forty-six years after his death he was canonized as a saint. But, as has been well remarked, in those times of transition statesmen and not saints were needed,[18] and the next three archbishops belonged to the former category.

Henry at once sent over his officers to take possession of the temporalities of the see of Dublin. This was early in 1181, when the new custodians of Dublin were appointed.[19] In September Henry's nominee, John Cumin (or Comyn, as the name came to be written), a monk [see *Add.*] of the abbey of Evesham in Worcestershire, [60]
was elected by the bishops and clergy of England and some of the clergy of the metropolitan church of Dublin who had come to England for the purpose. He had at the time only deacon's orders, and was an ambassador, a iudge, an officer of the court, rather than a pastor.[20] On March 21, 1182, he was consecrated Archbishop of Dublin by Pope Lucius III at Velletri, and about the same time he obtained from the Pope a new privilege confirming to him and his successors the possessions, rights, and metropolitan jurisdiction of the see.[21] This document does not, like its predecessor, give a long list of Irish names denoting the churches, vills, and possessions of the see. In the phraseology of Norman law it mentions only the manor of Swords, the vill of Lusk, and the Great Vill (Finglas or Tallaght ?), and lumps the rest in general terms. It is [61]
noteworthy that it speaks of the see of Wexford, and not of Ferns, the old Celtic seat of the bishopric, and terms the see of Glendalough, *Insularum Episcopatus*. But historically its most important provision was that which forbade any archbishop or bishop from holding synods, hearing causes, or transacting any ecclesiastical business in the diocese without the assent of the Archbishop of Dublin—a provision which led to a lengthened dispute with the Primate of Armagh.

15 Crede Mihi, nos. i and iii. **16** Gesta Hen. i. 270; Hoveden, ii. 253. **17** Henry did not leave England for Normandy until April 1180: Eyton's Itin., p. 232. **18** Stokes, Anglo-Norman Church, p. 199. **19** Gest. Hen. i. 280. **20** In 1164 John Comyn or Cumin was ambassador at the court of the Emperor Frederic. In 1166–7 he was at Rome with reference to the dispute with Becket (by whom he was afterwards excommunicated), and again in December 1170, at the time of Becket's murder). In 1177 he was sent as ambassador to Spain. We find him repeatedly acting as a justice in eyre and amongst the king's entourage; see Eyton's Itin. of Hen. II. It is expressly stated in the Gesta Henrici (vol. i, p. 287) that John Cumin was honourably received by the Pope, and 'ab eodem factus est cardinalis, ut gratius imponeret ei summus Pontifex munus ordinationis et consecrationis'. So Giraldus was not alone, as Dimock thought, in calling Cumin a 'presbyter cardinalis': Gir. Camb., p. 358, n.

John Cumin's tenure of the see was remarkable for many changes in the direction of promoting its temporal power and welfare. He was instrumental in uniting with it the see of Glendalough, including ultimately the rich lands of the abbey, which were distinct from those of the bishopric. At the time of the synod of Kells (1152) Dublin seems to have been regarded as within the diocese of Glendalough, but there were two bishops in the diocese, the Celtic bishop of Glendalough and the bishop of the Ostmen of Dublin. At that synod, however, Cardinal Papiro, the papal legate, gave one of the four palls to Dublin, 'as being most fitted for a metropolitan city,' and probably as being already in connexion with Rome, and made a division of the diocese. Even at the coming of the Normans, however, all the endowments of the archiepiscopal see were
[62] in the near neighbourhood of Dublin. Glendalough was a purely Celtic monastery, in which the abbot was a more important personage than the bishop, though both bishopric and abbacy were extensively endowed. The absorption of the bishopric and rich abbatial possessions of Glendalough into the see of Dublin was an object early aimed at by the Anglo-Norman rulers, but it was not fully attained until after the death of William Piro, Bishop of Glendalough, in 1214.[22] Even before the union was completed, however, the archbishop became the largest landholder in the neighbourhood of Dublin, and, apart from his prerogatives as a prelate, exercised in his demesne lands all the rights and jurisdiction of a feudal baron.

Archbishop Cumin constituted the ancient parochial church of St. Patrick, which stood outside the walls of Dublin, a prebendal church, and in it created 'a college of clerics of approved life and learning, who should afford by their honest conversation an example of living for all, and by their learning an instruction to the illiterate'.[23] This collegiate church he endowed out of the possessions of the see, and assigned to it thir-
[63] teen churches, which became the original prebends of the new college.[24] He made no change with regard to the church of the Holy Trinity, which still remained the sole cathedral church with a prior and monastic chapter,[25] and it was not until the year 1219 that Cumin's successor, Archbishop Henry de Londres, by a new charter creating a dean and chapter, raised the collegiate church of St. Patrick to the rank of a cathedral. About the close of the twelfth century monastic chapters were out of favour with many English bishops, and there was a movement to substitute secular canons, over whom the bishops would have more control. Hence the raising of St. Patrick's to the rank of cathedral, and hence the anomaly of two cathedral churches in the same diocese. The co-existence of two cathedrals in Dublin, however, led, as might be expected, to disputes as to precedence, rights, and jurisdiction, which were not finally
[64] arranged until the year 1300.[26] Archbishop Cumin is said to have demolished the old

21 Crede Mihi, no. ii. 22 See Note appended to this chapter. 23 See the foundation charter in Mason's History of St. Patrick's, Appendix I. It must be dated in or prior to 1191, when it was confirmed by a Bull of Pope Celestine III: ibid., App. II. 24 The names of the original prebends are given in Celestine's Bull. They seem to have been, Swords, Clonmethan, Ireland's Eye (afterwards Howth), Finglas, Clondalkin, Imelach (Tavelach, Tallaght ?), Killesantan, Stahelach (Stahney, Taney ?), Donnachimelecha (now Burgage), Stagonil (included in Powerscourt), St. Nicholas of Dublin, Ballymore (Ballymore Eustace), Donaghmore (Yago). 25 Mason's Hist. of St. Patrick's, App. IV. 26 See the *Pacis compositio* in Mason's Hist. of St. Patrick's, App. VI.

parochial church of St. Patrick, and to have built for his new foundation a new edifice which was dedicated on St. Patrick's Day, 1191. The existing fabric, however, a fine example of Early English, belongs to a somewhat later date.[27] Like Christ Church, it has been recently restored and provided with suitable surroundings by the munificence of a family of which Dublin may well be proud. John Cumin is also believed to have built the palace of St. Sepulchre, close to his collegiate church, as an archiepiscopal residence. This became the seat of his adjoining manor or liberty, as it was called, of St. Sepulchre, wherein the archbishops of Dublin exercised jurisdiction up to recent times. The manor originally embraced the parishes of St. Kevin (now included in St. Peter's) and St. Nicholas Without.[28] The former residence of the archbishops was close to the church of the Holy Trinity,[29] but Cumin appears to have given this up
to the prior and canons for their offices.[30] In moving the archiepiscopal residence from [65]
beside the cathedral to the vicinity of his new collegiate church, Cumin was escaping from the jurisdiction of the civil and military authorities, with whom at one time he was in bitter conflict, and making his residence the *caput* of a liberty of his own.

Hugh de Lacy was not long under the cloud of the royal displeasure, and in the winter of 1181-2 he was again entrusted with the government of the country. This time a certain cleric, called Robert of Shrewsbury, was joined in commission with him as coadjutor and councillor, and a witness of his actions on the king's behalf. During the next three years he continued the work of castle-building, and we can trace the sites of his castles by the motes or mounds of earth that still remain at the places indicated in nearly every case. One of these was at Timahoe in Leix, marking an advance, which was perhaps not very permanent, in a hilly district in Queen's County [Leix]. The land here had lately been given to Meiler Fitz Henry as a recompense for some land which he claimed about Kildare, but it was yet to be conquered. At the same time
Hugh de Lacy gave his niece in marriage to Meiler,[31] but though some twenty four [66]
years later we hear of Meiler's son, it would seem that he was not the offspring of this marriage, as Giraldus, in the so-called preface to his second edition of the Expugnatio, written about the year 1210, expressly says that Meiler had no legitimate issue.[32] Other castles were built in the valley of the Barrow and in Hugh de Lacy's own lordship, especially in Westmeath, where the castles of Clonard, Killare,[33] Delvin, and others were now erected.

But in the summer of 1184 Henry's inveterate distrust of Hugh de Lacy, combined with his inordinate desire for the aggrandizement of the most worthless of his sons,

27 In 1225 protection was granted for four years for the preachers of the fabric of the church of St. Patrick, Dublin, going through Ireland to beg alms for that fabric: Rot. Pat., 9 Hen. III, Cal. no. 1241. This probably affords an indication of the date of the existing building. 28 For an account of the Manor of St. Sepulchre in the fourteenth century see papers by Mr. James Mills, Journ. R.S.A.I., 1889 and 1890. 29 Cal. Liber Niger, Ch. Ch., no. 140. 30 Cumin gave to the prior and canons 'aream curie sue ad officinas suas edificandas': Chartae, &c., p. 10. This probably included the old archiepiscopal residence. 31 Gir. Camb. v. 356. 32 Ibid. v. 409. The writer of the Histoire de Guillaume le Maréchal says of Meiler (l. 14134), *il n'aveit nut certein eir*, adding mistakenly, *Quer feme esposée n'out unques*. 33 The castle of Killare (*Cell-fair*) was erected in 1184: Ann. Ulster, Ann. Loch Cé. These annals also state that Art O'Melaghlin was killed treacherously by Dermot O'Brien at the instigation of the Foreigners, and that Melaghlin Beg took the kingship in his stead.

led to Hugh's final supersession and to a new scheme for the government of Ireland. To this scheme, and to John's visit to Ireland in 1185 as *Dominus Hiberniae*, we shall recur in chapter xvi.

Hugh de Lacy witnessed, as constable, John's Dublin Charter of 1185,[34] and was
[67] with John at Ardfinan,[35] but he was probably one of those who, we are told, disgusted with the insolence of the new-comers and the turn which affairs had taken, kept silent in the background and awaited the issue of events.[36] At any rate, after John's departure he was out of favour with the king. By one chronicler he is said to have disregarded the king's order to return,[37] given possibly in consequence of some report from John. Indeed, Irish annals, not, however, a good authority on such a point, state that John, on his return to England, complained that Hugh de Lacy had prevented the Irish kings from sending him either tribute or hostages. However this may have been, it is probable that he afforded the new government little or no assistance. In 1185, indeed, his lordship of Meath was invaded by the Cinel Owen under their chieftain, but they were repulsed by William le Petit, one of Hugh de Lacy's principal feudatories.[38] In July 1186, however, Hugh de Lacy's career was abruptly closed. He had built a castle within the precincts of an old Columban monastery at Durrow, near the borders of
[68] Westmeath (in the modern King's County) [Offaly], and, according to the oldest account, came out to look at it, when a youth with the curious name, Gilla gan-inathair[39] O'Meyey, suddenly cut off his head with one blow of a battle-axe which he had concealed about his person, and head and body both fell into the castle-ditch. The murderer then fled to his foster-father O'Caharny, called *an Sinnach* or 'the Fox', the chief of Teffia, at whose instigation the deed was done.[40]

When Henry heard the news that a certain Irishman had cut off Hugh de Lacy's head he is said to have rejoiced thereat,[41] for Hugh had in many ways displeased and disobeyed him. We have seen that Henry was angry with him for marrying Rory O'Conor's daughter, and was jealous of his great power and popularity. It was even rumoured that he aimed at making himself an independent king. He was, indeed, probably regarded by the Irish, unfamiliar with feudal relationships, as a king, and
[69] some of the Irish annals speak of him as such.[42] John and his followers may have given support to the rumour to hide their own utter discomfiture. But it is very unlikely that Hugh had any aspirations inconsistent with his loyalty to Henry or his position as a tenant of the Crown.

Hugh de Lacy was not a Geraldine. Nevertheless, of all the leaders portrayed in Gerald's pages, with the possible exception of Richard of Striguil, he appears to have

34 Hist. and Mun. Docs. of Ireland (Gilbert), p. 49. 35 Black Book of Limerick (Mac Caffrey), p. 103. 36 Gir. Camb. v. 391. 37 William of Newburgh, vol. i, p. 240. 38 Gir. Camb. v. 386. Melaghlin, son of Murtough O'Loughlin, was slain by the foreigners, probably in this raid: Ann. Ulster, 1185. 39 *Gilla gan-inathair*, 'the lad without bowels,' a sobriquet perhaps alluding to the extreme slimness which enabled him to outstrip his pursuers. 40 Ann. Loch Cé, 1186. 41 William of Newburgh, vol. i, p. 240. 42 Ann. Loch Cé, 1185: 'For it was Hugh de Lacy that was King of Erinn when the son of the King of the Saxons came.' And again, ibid. 1186, when recording his death, 'for he was King of Meath and Breffny and Uriel, and it was to him that the tribute of Connaught was paid.' The Four Masters in each case alter the expression, but probably on their own authority.

been the best equipped for the work of transformation taken in hand, and to have had just the qualities required at that moment for ruling Ireland and bringing peace and prosperity to the land. A strong, provident man, who took the necessary steps to make Norman rule effective, and gradually to supplant the antiquated clan system by an organization more fitted to preserve peace and promote progress; but one who at the same time did not despise the native Irish, but did his best to win their confidence and reconcile them to the new order of things. Like Strongbow, he had married an Irish wife and thrown in his fortunes with Ireland. He had made enemies, no doubt, among the chieftains whose power he had curtailed, but he was popular among the people, and his very popularity had aroused the suspicions of the English king. So far as we can see, the battle-axe of O'Meyey struck a bad blow for Ireland, and not only for the [70]
English colony, when it tumbled Hugh de Lacy's head into the castle-ditch at Durrow.

The subsequent history of Hugh de Lacy's remains is curious. In 1195 Matthew, Archbishop of Cashel and papal legate, and John Cumin, Archbishop of Dublin, removed the body of Hugh de Lacy from the Irish territory, probably at Durrow, where it had been buried, and solemnly interred it at the Cistercian monastery of Bective in Meath, but his head for some reason was either then or at some previous time deposited in the monastery of St. Thomas in Dublin.[43] A lengthened dispute arose between these two houses for the possession of the complete remains, which, after an appeal to the Pope, was finally settled in the year 1205 by a conclave of archbishops, bishops, abbots, priors, and other discreet and venerable persons, in favour of the canons of St. Thomas.[44] Hugh de Lacy, whatever his merits may have been, was not recognized as a saint, and it appears from further documents that the real dispute was not about his relics, but concerned certain lands which had been conferred along with his body upon the monastery of Bective.[45]

NOTE [71]

The gradual absorption of the see of Glendalough

The principal steps by which the bishopric and the abbatial lands of Glendalough were absorbed in the see of Dublin appear to have been as follows:

In 1185 John 'son of the king', when in Ireland, purported to effect the union of the sees *pro raritate populi et paupertate ecclesie Dublinensis*.[46] This grant clearly met with opposition and was inoperative. In 1192 John 'earl of Mortain and lord of Ireland', while confirming the abbacy of Glendalough and its lands to Abbot Thomas,[47] again granted the bishopric to the Archbishop of Dublin, 'so that, when the cathedral church should fall vacant the archbishop should take the bishopric into his hand until he should provide a pastor for it, and that the Bishop of Glen-

43 Grace's Annals, 1195; Annals, Laud MS., Chart. St. Mary's Abbey, Dublin, vol. ii, p. 307. 44 Reg. St. Thomas's, Dublin, p. 348. 45 Ibid., pp. 350, 352. The last document is wrongly dated 1240, or the bishop's name is wrongly given. Simon Rochford, Bishop of Meath, died in 1224. 46 Chartae Priv. et Immun., p. 4. Crede Midi, no. xxiv. 47 Chartae, &c., p. 6. Crede Mihi, no. xxxii.

dalough should be chaplain and vicar to the Archbishop of Dublin.'[48] John also gave to the archbishop (Cumin) and his successors the half-cantred of the abbey-lands of Glendalough which was next to the archbishop's castle of Ballymore (now Ballymore Eustace),[49] and the land [72] of Coillacht *in baroniam.*[50] Coillacht was a forest region which appears to have extended from the mountains about the upper basin of the river Doddagh to near Tallaght.[51] Later, in the reign of Richard I, John appears to have granted the whole abbacy of Glendalough to the archbishop, as a grant by him to this effect was confirmed by Matthew O'Heyney, Archbishop of Cashel and papal legate, who invoked 'the wrath of Almighty God and of the blessed apostles Peter and Paul if any one should presume to assail this confirmation'.[52] Nevertheless, Pope Innocent III in 1199, by a Bull, took the church of SS. Peter and Paul at Glendalough, with all the abbey-lands (enumerating them), under his protection, adding a similar comminatory clause.[53] Perhaps in consequence of the Pope's interference, King John in 1200 granted to Thomas, Abbot of Glendalough, for his life, forty carucates of the abbatial lands.[54] In 1213 John granted to Henry, Archbishop of Dublin, both the bishopric and the abbey of Glendalough, saving to Abbot Thomas during his life half a cantred to hold of the archbishop.[55] William Piro, the last recognized Bishop of Glendalough, died in 1214. Probably Abbot Thomas died about the same time. At any rate, in 1215, Innocent III, acting on the alleged intentions of Cardinal Papiro in 1152, that the two sees should be united on the death of the then Bishop of Glendalough, confirmed the transference of the bishopric of Glendalough to the Archbishop of Dublin.[56] The papal sanction to the absorption of Glendalough in the see of Dublin, which was confirmed in [73] 1216 by Honorius III,[57] appears to have been obtained through the personal exertions of Archbishop Henry, who went on an embassy from King John to Rome,[58] and who appears to have been armed by a testimonium from Felix O'Ruadhan, Archbishop of Tuam, and his suffragans, as to the intentions of Cardinal Papiro. This document, which reads like a piece of special pleading, ends with the following remarkable statement: 'The church in the mountains (i.e. the cathedral of Glendalough) was held in great reverence from the earliest times on account of St. Keywvyn, who lived as hermit there, but for nearly forty years it has become so deserted and desolate as to be used as a den for robbers, and more homicides are committed there than in any part of Ireland.'[59]

As part of the bargain with the Pope, a hospital for pilgrims to the shrine of St. James of Compostella, the patron saint of lepers, was founded by Archbishop Henry near the place of embarkation on the Stein at Dublin, and he endowed it partly out of the lands of the see of Glendalough.[60] The spot appears to be marked on Sir William Petty's map of the half-barony of Rathdown as 'Lowzy (i.e. Lazar) Hill'.[61] Thus ended the ancient Celtic bishopric of Glendalough, eaten up by its more stalwart Dano-Norman rival. When the power of the latter waxed faint in the fourteenth and fifteenth centuries there was, however, an unofficial revival of Irish bishops at Glendalough.

48 Chartae, &c., p. 6. Crede Mihi, no. xli. 49 Ibid., no. xxvi. 50 Ibid., no. xxvii. 51 Liber Niger Alani, p. 259. 52 Chartae, &c., p. 10. 53 Ibid., p. 11. 54 Rot. Chart., 2 John, p. 78 b. 55 Ibid., 15 John, p. 194 b. 56 Chartae, &c., p. 15. 57 Chartae, &c., p. 16. 58 Ibid., p. 18. 59 Cal. Christ Church Deeds, no. 20. 60 Chartae &c., as above, p. 18. 61 See Halliday's Scandinavian Dublin, map facing p. 151.

THE SUB-INFEUDATION OF MEATH

At the time of Hugh de Lacy's death, in 1186, the lordship of Meath 'from the Shannon to the sea was full of castles and of Foreigners'.[1] We can in general fix the sites of these castles by the motes which in nearly every case remain. There are upwards of sixty motes, big and little, within the lordship of Meath. They were not, however, all erected within Hugh de Lacy's lifetime, and we shall here notice only those which mark the centres of manors known to have been created by him. The principal castle and manor of the whole lordship was Trim, where, as already mentioned, the first mote-castle was destroyed in 1174. It was soon rebuilt, but the first regular stone castle—the keep of which is perhaps the massive twenty-sided structure still standing—appears not to have been erected until about 1220.[2]

Other seignorial castles in East Meath were: RATOATH, where Hugh de Lacy [76] appears to have retained a seignorial manor. He gave the tithes of Ratoath and Dunshaughlin, and a grange at the latter place, to the abbey of St. Thomas, Dublin, before 1183.[3] After the year 1196 Walter de Lacy gave the land of Ratoath to his brother Hugh,[4] who soon afterwards confirmed his father's grant of the church to the abbey of St. Thomas.[5] In the middle of the village of Ratoath is a very fine mote, which has not, I think, been described. It must suffice here to say that it is about fifty feet high and very steep, with a circular flat area on top of about twenty paces in diameter. At the base is a shield-shaped bailey, and both mote and bailey are surrounded with deep fosses and wide ramparts in a typical Norman manner. The whole is a magnificent specimen of a Norman earthwork, and there can be little doubt that it represents the elder Hugh de Lacy's castle.

CLONARD. The castle here was erected in 1182.[6] In 1200 'Clonard (i.e., probably, the new monastery) was burned by O'Keary to injure the English who were in it'.[7] [77] This was the site of the famous Celtic monastery of St. Finnian, which, however, appears not to have survived the repeated ravages of Norsemen and Irish. An Augustinian priory, dedicated to St. Peter, was founded here, probably by Hugh de Lacy. Even of this latter foundation nothing has been preserved except an octagonal Gothic

1 Ann. Loch Cé, 1186. Giraldus, speaking of the year 1181, says, 'Hactenus enim Media plurimum, Lagenia parum, fuerat incastellata': v. 355. 2 Ware's Annals, and compare *ante*, vol. i, pp. 338–42 [pp. 127–9]. 3 Reg. St. Thomas's, p. 280. Robert le Poer, who seems to have had the custody of Hugh de Lacy's lands after his death, confirmed this grant: ibid., p. 26. 4 Gormanston Register, f. 188 dors. The parcels include 'totam terram de Rathtowtht sicut melius et plenius eandem terram unquam tenui, et de incremento Treuthd' (Trevet Grange). 5 Reg. St. Thomas's, p. 8. 6 Gir. Camb. v. 356, where 'Clunaret' is the better reading; Ir. *Cluain-iráird.*

font, and the lofty mote of Hugh de Lacy's castle is the most conspicuous object in the deserted place. Clonard, in the twelfth century, and probably up to its burning in the year 1200, was the seat of a bishopric, afterwards removed to Trim. Eugene, the bishop from 1174 to 1194, appears to have acted from the first with the Anglo-Norman settlers in furthering the interests of the Church,[8] and in particular in endowing the abbey of St. Thomas, Dublin—to such an extent, indeed, as to impoverish the see of Meath and give rise to a dispute which was compromised in 1235.[9]

KELLS, the seat of a famous Columban monastery, marked still by its early stone-
[78] roofed church, its ecclesiastical round tower, and its beautiful crosses, was protected by Hugh de Lacy, and was probably the seat of a seignorial manor. 'A castle was in process of erection at Kells' as early as 1176, but in the same year, consequent on the destruction of the castle of Slane, it was razed and left desolate through fear of the Cinel Owen.[10] There is no further early mention of a castle at Kells. Hugh de Lacy granted to the canons of St. Mary at Kells a number of places with Irish names, presumably their former possessions,[11] and he is said to have re-edified the abbey. Walter de Lacy, in the reign of Richard I, granted a charter to the burgesses of Kells, conferring on them 'the law of Bristol' [see *Add.*].[12] Hugh de Lacy gave Emlagh, to the north-east of Kells, to Thomas de Craville,[13] but the barony of Kells does not appear to have been granted in one parcel, and we may perhaps conclude that the manor of Kells was retained in Hugh de Lacy's hands.

Similarly in the case of DULEEK. Hugh gave to Adam Dullard (whose brother was Pagan or Payn Dullard) certain lands which we may identify with Dollardstown
[79] and Painestown in this barony,[14] but there appears to have been no large grant made here. There was, however, a very early castle erected at Duleek. It was destroyed at the same time as Trim Castle, and afterwards restored.[15] At Duleek Hugh de Lacy founded a monastery for canons regular, and made it a cell of his favoured abbey at Llanthony. In the same barony at Colp, near the mouth of the Boyne, he also subjected another foundation to the same abbey. Duleek appears as an important manor of Theobald de Verdun,[16] who succeeded the de Lacys in a moiety of Meath, and it is probable that it was a seignorial manor throughout.

DROGHEDA [see *Add.*]. Though the castle here does not appear to be mentioned before 1203, when John gave 'to Nicholas de Verdun the custody of the [castle of the] bridge of Drogheda, as it was in the king's hand and as Nicholas's father [Bertram de Verdun] held it',[17] there can be little doubt that it was erected by Hugh de Lacy. The
[80] above entry shows that the castle was in existence about the time of Hugh de Lacy's

7 Four Masters, 1200. O'Keary (*Ua Ciardha)* was chieftain of Carbury (Cairbre), a district separated from Clonard by the river Boyne. 8 See, for instance, his precept enjoining the payment of tithes: Reg. St. Thomas's, Dublin, p. 259. 9 Ibid., pp. 246–52. 10 Ann. Ulster, 1176. 11 See this charter in Dugdale, Mon. Angl. vi. 1143. 12 Chartae Priv. et Immun., p. 10. Walter retained mills in Kells: Cal. Docs. Irel., vol. i, no. 1909. 13 Song, ll. 3166–73, and note. 14 Ibid., ll. 3164–5, and note. There is a terraced mote at Dollardstown. 'The land of Adam Dullart and Payn his brother' belonged to the Hospitallers before 1212: Papal Letters (Bliss), vol. i, p. 36. 15 Gir. Camb. v. 313. 16 In 1284 he was granted a yearly fair at his manor of Dyvelek; Cal. Docs. Irel., vol. ii, no. 2303. There was a mote at Duleek, but it has been nearly cleared away.

death, when Bertram de Verdun (who died on the crusade in 1192) was in Ireland. Besides, though the castle was retained as a royal castle when the other seignorial castles were restored to Walter de Lacy, compensation was paid to Walter and his successors, showing that it admittedly belonged originally to the de Lacys.[18]

The castle-site is marked by the 'Mill Mount', a formidable mote commanding the bridge across the Boyne, and connected with the later town walls on the Meath side. So important a site could hardly have been neglected by Hugh de Lacy.

In Westmeath Hugh de Lacy, in 1184, built a castle at KILLARE, within sight of the sacred hill of Usnech, near the spot where stood and still stands the 'stone of the divisions', the 'navel of Erin', where in prehistoric times the five provinces met.[19] This appears to have been at first the principal seat of the lordship in West Meath,[20] but in [81]
1187 the castle was destroyed and its garrison slain by the Irish.[21] The castle does not appear to have been rebuilt, but the mote remains to mark the site. Lough Sewdy, or BALLYMORE LOUGH SEWDY, as it came to be called,[22] was afterwards the principal seignorial manor in West Meath.

An early seignorial castle was erected at Fore (Ir. *Fabhar*, latinized *Favoria* and, by Giraldus, *Fovera*) in West Meath, where there was an ancient monastery founded by St. Fechin. The castle was one of those seized by King John in 1210 and restored to Walter de Lacy in 1215. It probably owed its origin to Hugh de Lacy, who was in occupation of the place *circa* 1180.[23] It appears to have been Hugh de Lacy, and not, [82]
as usually stated, his son Walter, who first gave to the monks of St. Taurin at Evreux the churches of Fore and the tithes, and St. Fechin's mill there, and the wood near the town for their habitation.[24] There is a mote at Fore.

Hugh de Lacy also retained in his own hand 'the lake and vill of Dissert (i.e. Lough Ennell, south of Mullingar, and Dysart on its western shore) and one knight's fee around the said vill'. The place was excepted from Hugh de Lacy's grant to William le Petit, to be presently mentioned. Malachi II, King of Ireland, lived at Dun na Sciath (a rath, still known by that name, or as 'Malachi's fort', on the border of the lake in the parish of Dysart), and died at Cro Inis,[25] a fortified island in the lake just opposite, and

17 Cal. Docs. Ireland, vol. i, no. 185. 18 For proof of this and a description of the site see my paper on 'Motes and Norman Castles in the County Louth', Journ. R.S.A.I. 1908, pp 246–50. 19 Gir. Camb. v. 356; Ann. Ulster, 1184, where the place is called Cill Fair; Four Masters, 1184 (Cill áir). Giraldus, speaking of the five sons of Dela, says: 'Et eam (Hiberniam) vacuam invenientes, in quinque portiones aequales inter se diviserunt; quarum capita in lapide quodam conveniunt apud Mediam juxta castrum de Kilair; qui lapis et umbelicus Hiberniae dicitur quasi in medio et meditullio terrae positus' (v. 144). 20 Hugh de Lacy's charter to William le Petit provides that the service due should be performed at Killare: 'inde servicium unius militis pro quibuslibet xxx carucatas [sic] terre predicte apud Killar faciendum'; see transcript, Song of Dermot, p. 310. 21 Four Masters, 1187. 22 It was restored to Walter de Lacy in 1215; C.D.I., no. 612, where it is corruptly printed Loxhundy. The Irish is *Loch Seimhdidhe*, of which Lough Sewdy is a phonetic rendering. The place long remained an important seat of the de Lacys, and a stone castle was built at Ballymore, of which some remains exist. A peninsula, called an island, in the lake seems to have been originally a fort of the O'Melaghlins. This was probably the site of Hugh de Lacy's castle. Abandoned for the stone castle of Ballymore, it was long afterwards, in 1641 and again in 1691, garrisoned and held as the strongest place in the neighbourhood. 23 Gir. Camb. v. 134, 354. 24 Cal. Docs. France (Round), vol. i, p. 105, where grants to St. Taurin from Walter de Lacy are also calendared. 25 Ann. Tigernach, Ann. Clonmacnois, 1022.

it is supposed that this was a seat of subsequent kings of Meath. There does not appear to have been a seignorial manor or early castle here, and it may be that Hugh de Lacy reserved it as a residence for the particular O'Melaghlin favoured at the time by him.

We now turn to Hugh de Lacy's principal feudatories. As in the case of the sub-infeudation of Leinster, our principal authority is the Song of Dermot. The Trouvère
[83] may have had a document[26] before him containing a list of Hugh's grants. Certainly most of his statements can be verified from other sources, and none of them has been shown to be inaccurate.

To Hugh Tyrel, who had been his custodian at Trim, Hugh de Lacy gave CASTLEKNOCK.[27] It would seem, however, that this grant was made by Hugh 'while he was the king's bailiff', and on behalf of the king. Certainly at a later time the three services due for Castleknock were paid to the Crown, and not to the lords of Meath.[28] The site of the castle, a little to the west of Phoenix Park, near Dublin, is well known. It is a fine example of a ditched and ramparted mote, with remains of a wall about seven feet thick enclosing an oval space on the top. On one end of this oval, on a secondary mound, there are remains of an octagonal tower. Hugh Tyrel and his successors were known as 'barons of Castleknock'. The castle was more than once ordered by John and Henry III to be prostrated as a danger to Dublin, but the owner, Richard Tyrel, appears to have avoided compliance with the order, and eventually, on
[84] giving his son as a hostage, was allowed to retain its custody.[29]

NAVAN and the land of ARDBRACCAN were granted to Jocelin de Nangle[30] or de Angulo, as the name appears in Latin documents (i.e. of Angle in Pembrokeshire). Jocelin is said to have founded St. Mary's Abbey at Navan in the twelfth century, and the town grew up under the Nangles. Four centuries later we find a Nangle baron of Navan.[31]

To Jocelin's son, Gilbert, Hugh de Lacy granted the barony of Morgallion.[32] His castle was at Nobber, a name which means 'the work' (Ir. *an obair*), and was perhaps what the Irish called the novel kind of castle, perched on an artificial hillock of earth, erected there. Gilbert de Nangle was outlawed in 1196, and the castle and lands reverted to Walter de Lacy, who granted them to his brother Hugh.[33]

Twenty knights' fees in the barony of Slane were granted to Richard le Fleming,
[85] who, as we have seen, erected the mote at Slane near the site of the ancient monastery.[34] In 1598 a Fleming was still Baron of Slane.[35]

26 In l. 3133 the writer expressly says *solum l'escrit*. **27** Song, ll. 3132–3. The Irish name for the place was simply *Cnucha*, and this name probably referred to the natural hill which rises a little to the east of the mote. **28** Irish Exchequer Memoranda, temp. Ed. I, Eng. Hist. Rev. 1903, p. 502. **29** Cal. Docs. Ireland, vol. i, nos. 515, 844, 1047, 1139. **30** Song, ll. 3144–7. There is a lofty mote at Navan formed out of a hillock of gravel, and a small one at Ardbraccan. **31** 'The Barnet of Navan, his name Nangle, his hous at the Navan,' Hogan's Ireland in 1598, p. 95; and indeed in 1636, Inquis. Lageniae, Meath, 23 Car. I. **32** Song, ll. 3142–3. There is a remarkable mote at Nobber. **33** Gormanston Register, f. 188 dors: 'totam terram de Mackergalinge . . . sicut eandem Gilbertus de Angulo . . . tenuit.' **34** Song, ll. 3174–201. For *Crandone* we should probably restore *Slan donat* (as suggested by Mr. Round, Commune of London, p. 142). **35** Hogan's Ireland in 1598.

Twenty knights' fees in the barony of Skreen were granted to Adam de Feipo, as well as the fee of one knight in the crown lands at Santry, near Dublin.[36] Hugh de Lacy built a castle for Adam de Feipo in Meath, presumably at Skreen,[37] where there is a mote in the grounds of the modern castle. A small town arose here. The Feipos were barons of Skreen up to the close of the fourteenth century, when an heiress carried the barony to the Marwards. The barony of Deece was granted to Hugh de Hose.[38] His castle at GALTRIM (where the mote remains) was one of those aban- [86] doned after the destruction of Slane Castle in 1176.[39] The Husseys, as the name came to be spelled, were still barons of Galtrim in 1598.[40] The barony of Lune was granted to William de Muset (Messet, Misset);[41] and a district in the barony of Lower Kells, including Emlagh, to Thomas de Cravile.[42]

In West Meath the barony of Magheradernon Wiiliam was granted to William le Petit.[43] His chief manor was at MULLINGAR, where the original mote and later stone castle of the Petits were finally removed in the last century to make way for a jail.[44] The barony was long known as 'Petit's Barony', and as late as 1596 was largely inhabited by Petits.[45] William le Petit was also given Rathkenny in Meath, and some [87] lands in the barony of Shrule, County Longford, and 'Chastelbrec', the position of which is uncertain.[46]

The barony of DELVIN was granted to Gilbert de Nungent (Nugent), 'which the O'Finelans held in the time of the Irish,' for the service of five knights.[47] Gilbert de Nugent is said to have married a sister of Hugh de Lacy, and Hugh built a castle for him,[48] the mote of which remains at Castletown Delvin, close to the later castle.[49]

36 Song, ll. 3156–7. For Santry, see Chart. St. Mary's, Dublin, ii. 95, and Exchequer Memoranda, Eng. Hist. Rev. 1903, p. 502. 37 Gir. Camb. v. 356. Adam speaks of the chapel of St. Nicholas ' que sita est in castello meo juxta Scrinium': Chart. St. Mary's, Dublin, ii. 21. 38 Song of Dermot, ll. 3162–3; Ware, quoting from Hugh de Lacy's charter or a transcript thereof, says that Hugh gave to Hose or Hussy 'all the land del Dies which Shaclin held'. This was clearly Mac Gilla Seachlainn, lord of Southern Breagh: Topogr. Poems, p. 12. The last chieftain of this name mentioned in the Four Masters was slain by Tighearnan O'Rourke in 1171. Cf. a charter from John de Hereford (to whom Hugh de Hose seems to have given lands in the barony): Reg. St. Thomas's, Dublin, p. 123. 39 Ann. Ulster, 1176. 40 Hogan's Ireland in 1598, p. 95: 'The barnet of Galtrim his name Hussy, his Hous Galtrim.' 41 Song of Dermot, l. 3159; cf. Harris's Ware, p. 193. The *caput baroniae* was probably Athboy. In 1213 Peter Messet, 'baro de Luyn juxta Trym,' died, and the inheritance passed to his three daughters, of whom the eldest married Lord de Vernaill, the second Talbot, the third Loundres: Annals Laud MS., Chart. St. Mary's, Dublin, vol. ii, p. 312. 42 Song of Dermot, ll. 316–73, where *Eymlath began* is Emlagh of St. Becan, and the other places mentioned are in the barony of Moygoish, co. Westmeath. 43 Song of Dermot, ll. 313–47. 44 Eng. Hist. Review, 1907, p. 237; and cf. Inquis. Lageniae, Westmeath, 6 Jac. I, where Thomas Pettit was found seised of the manor of Mullingar, including a watermill called 'the moate mylle' in the town. 45 Perambulation of the Pale, Car. Cal. 1596, p. 192. 46 In 1229 Nicholas le Petit was granted a market at 'his manor of Ratkenny', a fair at 'his manor of Dunboyny', and a free warren 'in the demesne of his manor of Admolinger': C.D.I., vol. i, no. 1673. Was Castlebrack a name give to William's castle at Dunboyne? 47 Song of Dermot, l. 3158. The charter is transcribed from Sir William Betham's Collections in Butler's Trim, p. 252, and is translated from an old copy in the Clarendon Collection in Lynch's Legal Institutions, p. 150. The original was seen by Ware. Cellach O'Findallan, Lord of Delbna Mor, is mentioned as assisting the foreigners of Dublin in killing Mulrony O'Keary, lord of Carbury. Ann. Tigernach, Four Masters, 1174. 48 Gir. Camb. v. 356; and Lodge, Westmeath. 49 The first stone castle at Delvin was probably built after 1220, when

[88] To Richard de Capella, *frater germanus* of Richard Gilbert de Nugent, lands were also given by Hugh de Lacy, but their position is not stated.[50] He succeeded to his brother as second baron of Delvin, and his daughter and heiress carried the barony to the Tuites for many generations.[51]

RATHWIRE (Ir. *Rath-Guaire*), in the barony of Farbill, was granted to Robert de Lacy, and Hugh is said to have built a castle for him there.[52] The mote remains with considerable foundations of a stone castle in the bailey.

KILBIXY, near Lough Iron, in the barony of Moygoish, was given to Geoffrey de Costentin, and a castle was erected here in 1192.[53] The mote remains, but nothing else, except the name 'Burgage lands', to testify to the ancient importance of the place.
[89] Near by, Geoffrey de Costentin founded a priory of canons regular at Tristernagh.[54]

The cantred of ARDNURCHER was given to Meiler Meiler Fitz Henry.[55] It is now a parish, more commonly known as 'Horseleap', in the barony of Moycashel. A castle was erected here in 1192.[56] Its site is well known. As in some other cases, the end of a natural ridge was selected, and this was cut off from the rest of the ridge by a double trench. An oblong mote with flat top, twenty-five by twelve paces, was formed. The summit is about thirty feet above the ditch at the upper side. There is a small raised bailey at one side, defended by a ditch. Two pieces of a massive wall seem to indicate where a bridge crossed this ditch to the bailey.

To Richard de Tuit was given 'a rich feoffment' including a district about GRA-
[90] NARD, in County Longford.[57] Here, in 1199, he erected a castle as a stronghold against O'Reilly in South Breifny. A high mote is to be seen here with traces of stone buildings on the top. Near Granard, in 1210, Richard de Tuit founded the Cistercian monastery of Larha, now Abbeylara, and in the same year his castle was visited by King John.

It would seem probable, then, that in Hugh de Lacy's lifetime little or no attempt was made to occupy the three western baronies of Westmeath, nor those parts of the ancient kingdom of Meath which are now included in King's County [Offaly] and Longford. Even those districts which were parcelled out among the barons were not

a year's service from the land of Meath was ordered to be given to Richard de Tuit 'to enable him to fortify (*firmare*) a castle in Delven': Cal. Docs. Ireland, vol. i, nos. 884, 970. This Richard de Tuit was, *jure uxoris*, third baron of Delvin. 50 Song of Dermot, ll. 3152–3. 51 Burke's Peerage, 'Marquis of Westmeath.' 52 Song of Dermot, ll. 3150–1 and note. Rathwire and Kilbixy were plundered and burned by Mageoghegan in 1450 (Four Masters). 53 Song of Dermot, ll. 315–45, where Kelberi and Ratheimarthi are corruptions for Kilbixi and Rathconarti, the latter being the ancient name of the barony now called Rathconrath. The castle is called *caislen Cille Bigsighe* (Ann. Loch Cé, 1192), i.e. the church of St. Bigseach. Walter de Lacy, in what was probably a confirmatory charter, granted to Geoffrey de Costentin 'five knights' fees in the theof of Kilbixi with a castle and fifteen knights' fees in the land of Conemake next adjoining to the said castle, beyond the water of Ethne (the river Inny) by the service of four knights': Harris's Ware, Antiq., p. 193. 54 The foundation charter is given in Dugdale's Mon. Angl. (1830),vol. vi, p. 1147. 55 Song of Dermot, ll. 3138–41. 56 *Caislen Atha an Urchair.* Ann. Loch Cé, 1192. The castle of Kilbixy, where the mote is also of an oblong shape, was erected in the same year. 57 Song of Dermot, ll. 3148–9. It is probable that Richard de Tuit was also given lands in a more settled district, perhaps at Tuitestown (5 miles to the north-west of Mullingar) and at Sonnagh (3 miles further), where we afterwards find Tuits. In several cases Hugh de Lacy gave lands on the marches of his lordship as well as lands nearer the centre to the same feoffee.

all occupied and turned to profit at once. Hugh de Lacy was himself building the castle of Durrow when he was murdered in 1186, and the border castles of Granard, Kilbixy, and Ardnurcher were not erected until the last decade in the century. Indeed, in several districts the Irish chieftains were never entirely dispossessed. The O'Melaghlins were styled kings of Meath for many generations, but they became confined to the barony of Clonlonan. The Mageoghegans in Moycashel, the O'Molloys in Fircall, the O'Caharneys in Kilcoursy, the MacCoghlans in Garrycastle, the O'Farrells in Annaly, and other ruling families, retained to the last their positions as chieftains of their respective tribes.

[91] CHAPTER XVI

JOHN DOMINUS HIBERNIAE, 1185

In 1184, while Hugh de Lacy was still justiciar, King Henry prepared to carry out a design which he had long meditated. At the Council of Oxford in 1177 he had, as we have seen, appointed his youngest son, John, 'Lord of Ireland,' and made the new grantees of lands there swear fealty and do homage to John as well as to himself. But John was too young to undertake the government, being then only in his tenth year. Now, in the summer of 1184, Henry sent John Cumin, the new archbishop, to Ireland to prepare for the coming of the prince. He also once more superseded Hugh de Lacy, and in September sent Philip of Worcester in his place with forty men-at-arms.[1] Philip
[92] is described as a sumptuous, open-handed man, and a brave soldier. We shall meet with a Philip of Worcester, presumably the same man, ten years later in Desmond. At this time not much is recorded of him. He revoked some grants of lands which had been improperly alienated by Hugh de Lacy in the north of the present county of Dublin, and restored the lands to their original purpose as mensal lands of the viceroy.[2] By his charter Hugh had power to grant fiefs in the neighbourhood of Dublin, but only while he was the king's bailiff, and to enable him to perform the king's service in Dublin. In March 1185 Philip of Worcester headed an expedition to Armagh, where he exacted a large tribute from the clergy. Hugh Tyrell, who accompanied him, carried off a large cauldron from the clergy, and brought it as far as the town of Louth. Here a fire broke out in the house in which he lodged, and the two horses which had drawn the boiler were burnt, and a great part of the town also. Frightened at this
[93] judgement, Hugh Tyrell restored the cauldron.[3] The stage in the evolution of morals when even men of light and leading did not scruple to pilfer a convent of monks was coincident with the stage in the evolution of reason when the same men were most subject to the influence of imaginary signs of divine wrath.

1 Gir. Camb. v. 359. Up to this moment Henry had vainly endeavoured to persuade his son Richard to give up Aquitaine to John: Gesta Hen. i. 311, 319. Gerald says, 'revocato Hugone de Laci,' but if Hugh went to the king he was back in Ireland next year, when he witnessed some of John's charters as constable. 2 'Terras quas Hugo de Laci alienaverat, terram videlicet Ocadhesi, et alias quam plures, ad regiam mensam cum omni solicitudine revocavit': Gir. Camb. v. 359–60. The 'terra Ocadhesi' (O'Casey) was equivalent to the barony of Balrothery West. Hugh seems to have granted all the ecclesiastical rights over this district to the Prior of Llanthony; see note by Bishop Reeves to Topogr. Poems, p. v, and Crede Mihi, lxiv. Cf. too, as to the tithes of Lusk in Balrothery East, Chart. St. Mary's, Dublin, i. 173. This deed was attested by 'Geroldus archidiaconus de Sancto David' and must be dated 1185–6. 3 Gir. Camb. v. 132, 360. The former passage indicates that a quarrel broke out within the year between Hugh de Lacy and Hugh Tyrell which caused great disturbance. The Annals of Ulster and Loch Cé, 1185, record that Philip of Worcester, accompanied by the Foreigners of Erin, remained at Armagh for six days in the middle of Lent. What-

On Mid-Lent Sunday, 1185, Henry at Windsor knighted his son John, and sent him to govern his lordship of Ireland.[4] He travelled by the coast-road of South Wales to Pembroke, where a numerous fleet had assembled in Milford Haven to transport him and his army. He was accompanied to this point by Ranulf de Glanville, Justiciar of England, who, in 1182, or perhaps a little earlier, had been appointed his tutor and guardian.[5] A favourable wind suddenly sprang up from the east, which might have been considered a good omen, but by taking advantage of it John had to omit the usual visit to the shrine of St. David—a sinister sign. He sailed on the evening of April 24, [94]
and arrived at noon next day in Waterford. He had with him about 300 knights and a large force of horse-soldiers and archers. Among those in the prince's ship was Gerald de Barry, the historian, who had been specially sent by the king to attend his son.[6] This was Gerald's second visit to the island, and, as before, he employed his time well in collecting materials for his Irish works. Among the officers of John's household who came with him to Ireland were Bertram de Verdun, his seneschal, William de Wendeval, his dapifer, and Alard Fitz William, his chamberlain. Others who witnessed his charters were Hugh de Lacy, constable, Philip of Worcester, Gilbert Pipard, and Theobald Walter. It is probable that the two last also came over with John.

Of the new-comers Theobald Walter, Philip of Worcester, Bertram de Verdun, and Gilbert (or perhaps his brother Roger) Pipard received from John about this time large grants of land, and became founders of great Anglo-Irish families. The most illustrious of these, and one conspicuous throughout the whole subsequent history of Ireland, was that of the Butlers, descended from Theobald Walter. He was son and eventual heir of Hervey Walter of Amounderness, in Lancashire. His elder brother, Hubert, afterwards Archbishop of Canterbury, was at this time one of the king's jus- [95]
tices. Ranulf de Glanville, Chief Justiciar of England, was his uncle by marriage, and the two brothers appear to have been reared in Ranulf's household, and to Ranulf's influence with John should probably be ascribed the favour shown to Theobald at this time.[7] In spite of statements to the contrary, it is probable that Theobald came to Ireland for the first time with John, and that it was John who gave him the office and emoluments of chief butler.

John's expedition to Ireland was a disastrous failure. So much is clear. Unfortunately, Gerald de Barry, who had such ample opportunities of knowing the facts, tells us little in detail concerning the expedition, though he indicates clearly enough in general terms the chief causes of its failure. At Waterford, immediately on John's arrival, [96]
the leading Irishmen of the neighbourhood, who had hitherto been loyal to the English and had lived peaceably, came to welcome the king's son as their lord and to give him the kiss of peace. But John's Norman retinue treated them with derision, some even rudely pulling their long beards in ridicule of the alien fashion. This irresponsible levity had its natural effect. The Irishmen, deeply incensed, betook themselves and their families to Donnell O'Brien, and disclosed to him and to Dermot Mc Carthy,

ever the object of the expedition, it does not appear to have been a regular raid. More probably it was an attempt to interfere in the election to the primacy, which took place in this year. 4 Gesta Hen. i. 336. 5 Ibid. i. 305. 6 Gir. Camb. v. 380–1.

and even to Rory O'Conor, the treatment they had received, adding that the king's son was a mere stripling surrounded and counselled by striplings like himself, and that from such a source there was no prospect for Irishmen of good government, or even of security. Influenced by these reports, these three chief kings of the south and west of Ireland, who, we are told, were prepared to wait upon John and offer him their submission as they had previously done to Henry, were induced to take a very different course. Laying aside for the moment their interminable quarrels, which had hitherto given opportunity to the advance of the foreigners, they formed a league together, and unanimously determined to defend with their lives their ancient liberties. This exam-
[97] ple was followed by the other native chieftains, who all held aloof from John and his giddy court.[8] 'We speak what we do know and testify what we have seen,' says Gerald solemnly, and we can believe him. A proud and sensitive people never willingly submits to the rule of a master, however mighty, who despises them.

But of course this rude plucking of the beards was only a symbol of that want of consideration for the native Irish which exhibited itself in more harmful ways. Continuing with the causes of the failure of the expedition, Gerald says: 'Contrary to our promises, we took away the deprived lands of our own Irishmen—those who from the first coming of Fitz Stephen and the earl had faithfully stood by us—and gave them to our newcomers. These Irishmen then went over to the enemy and became spies and guides for them instead of for us, having all the more power to injure us because of their former familiarity with our ways.'[9]

It is to be regretted that Gerald was not more explicit, but a careful consideration of John's acts in Ireland at this time, so far as they are known, tends to confirm and further elucidate this general statement. Almost the only military measure known to have been taken by John was the erection of castles at Tibberaghny, Ardfinan, and Lis-
[98] more.[10] Tibberaghny is on the borders of Ossory, north of the Suir and east of Carrick. Ardfinan and Lismore are near the frontiers of the territory known as the Decies. Motes remain at Tibberaghny and Lismore, probably indicating the exact positions of John's castles. Ardfinan was probably a 'promontory castle', situated on a precipitous rock, where the remains of a later, but still early, castle stand, commanding a ford over the Suir. The castles seem to have been erected with a view to holding the Decies, and as bases for an advance into parts of Munster not yet occupied. The Decies, though already regarded as crown lands—at least from the Blackwater beyond Lismore east-

7 That Hubert and probably Theobald were brought up by their aunt and Ranulf de Glanville appears from Hubert's charter to the Praemonstratensian House at West Dereham: Dugdale, Mon. Angl. vi, p. 899; and cf. Norgate's Angevin Kings, ii. 332, note. Theobald's relations are indicated in his foundation charter to the Cistercian house at Arklow (where he also held a fief from John, perhaps granted at this time): Dugdale, Mon. Angl. vi. 1128. His mother was Matilda de Valognes, and his second wife, mother of Theobald Walter II, was Matilda de Vavasor: Rot. Pat., 9 John, p. 74 b. By a former wife he had a daughter, Beatrice, who married (1) Thomas of Hereford and (2) Hugh Purcell, baron of Loughmoe; Reg. St. Thomas's, Dublin. Another daughter married Gerald de Prendergast: Inquis. P.M., 36 Hen. III. 8 Gir. Camb. v. 389. 9 Ibid., p. 390. 10 Ibid. v. 386. The erection of castles at Tipraid Fachtna and Ard Finain is mentioned in the Annals of Loch Cé, 1185. Ardfinan as well as Lismore was within the territory of the Deisi, which may be regarded as coterminous with the dioceses of Waterford and Lismore.

wards—had probably not yet been completely settled by the Normans. Melaghlin O'Faelain, the native prince, whose life had been spared at the taking of Waterford, was one of the first to submit to Henry on his arrival, and ever since he seems to have been true to his oath of fealty, and to have lived peaceably. It is probable that he was left undisturbed in part, at any rate, of his territory. But now it appears that he was one of those whom John's retinue treated disrespectfully, and who complained to Donnell [99]
O'Brien and the princes of Munster.[11] We may therefore infer that his territory was confiscated at this time, and that he was one of those to whom Gerald alludes when saying that John took away lands from faithful Irishmen and gave them to new-comers. This presumably was John's immediate answer to the disaffection which his inconsiderate conduct had provoked.

But further, it seems clear that, as a reply to the opposition shown by the princes of Munster, a reckless immature scheme was adopted for annexing the whole of the eastern part of Munster, where hitherto the native princes had been left undisturbed by the adventurers in Cork. From the Irish annals, as well as from the brief statements of Giraldus, we learn that out of his newly-erected castles John sent plundering parties into Munster. On two occasions, once in a neighbouring wood and once when taking a prey in the direction of Limerick, part of the garrison of Ardfinan was cut off by Donnell O'Brien, whose forces, however, suffered a defeat at Tibberaghny, in which two of the petty chieftains of Thomond fell.[12] Before the year was out Dermot [100]
McCarthy and several others were slain by the men of Cork and the followers of Theobald Walter on the occasion of a parley near Cork.[13]

It is clear, however, that no general league to take common action against the invaders can have been formed at this time between the Kings of Connaught and Munster, such as might perhaps be inferred from Gerald's language. The Irish annals state that in this year Rory O'Conor 'came from his pilgrimage', i.e. came out of the monastery of Cong, to which he had retired two years previously, when he left the reins of government in the hands of his son, Conor Maenmoy. Aided by Donnell O'Brien and the English of Cork, he destroyed the west of Connaught, both church and territory, in the endeavour to recover his kingdom from his son. A temporary [101]
peace was patched up between father and son, on the basis of a division of Connaught. This would of course involve the withdrawal of Donnell O'Brien from Connaught, and is probably the peace to which Gerald alludes. Later on in the year, however,

11 O'Faelain is expressly named in the Annals of Inisfallen (Dublin MS.). 12 Gir. Camb. v. 386; Ann. Loch Cé, Four Masters, 1185. Gerald mentions that an Irish noble named Oggravus was slain with many others at Tibberaghny. He was clearly Ruaidhri O'Gradha (O'Grady), who with Ruaidhri O'Conaing 'was slain by the Foreigners in the slaughter of Tipraid Fachtna': Ann. Loch Cé. These annals also state that 'the foster-brother of the son of the king of the Saxons' was slain in an engagement with Donnell O'Brien. Who was this foster-brother? In 1183 John was reared in Ranulf de Glanville's household, and Ranulf's sons would be John's foster-brothers. John's grant of Ormond was made to Ranulf de Glanville and Theobald Walter jointly. Ranulf, the justiciar, may have accepted this speculative grant for one of his sons and if we suppose that he sent this son to join Theobald in his venture, and that he was John's foster-brother slain by O'Brien, the hypothesis would seem to fulfil the conditions. 13 Gir. Camb. v. 386; Ann. Loch Cé, Four Masters, 1185.

Conor Maenmoy's son, Cathal Carrach, plundered and burned Killaloe in retaliation for the churches which the men of Munster had burned, and Thomond was pillaged by Conor Maenmoy at the head of some English mercenaries. These latter then came as far as Roscommon with Conor, 'who gave them 3,000 cows as wages.' Finally Conor Maenmoy assumed the entire kingship,[14] and next year expelled his father Rory. The league, then, must have consisted merely in a common resolve not to do homage or renew the oath of fealty to John. The peace, however, set free Donnell O'Brien, with
[102] whom Gerald's friends in Cork had probably been acting, and enabled him to concentrate the Irish forces of Munster against John's aggression.

But we have more certain evidence of John's intentions regarding Munster than is afforded by these encounters with Donnell O'Brien. John's grant to Theobald Walter of the large district afterwards known collectively as Ormond or East Munster, was tested at Waterford, and must be referred to this year. By it the borough of Killaloe and five and a half cantreds in 'the land of Limerick' were granted to Theobald and his uncle by marriage, Ranulf de Glanville, Chief Justiciar of England, for the service of twenty-two knights.[15] These cantreds appear to have been mentioned by name in the original deed, and the names are repeated in an agreement made between William de Braose and Theobald Walter in 1201 touching the lands of the latter, to which we shall have to recur.[16] They included the south-western extension of the present King's County [Offaly] and the whole of North Tipperary, with a portion of the County Limerick. At the time this was a speculative grant of lands not yet acquired, but before
[103] the close of the reign of Richard I, at any rate, Theobald seems to have been firmly seated in his new possessions.[17] It may be conjectured that a similar speculative grant in Southern Tipperary was made at this time to Philip of Worcester, and was the origin of the claims which, as we shall see, he made a few years later to lands in this district.[18]

Of John's personal movements in Ireland at this time little is known. A few points however, fixed by his charters, which indicate that he followed pretty closely his father's route. His grant to Theobald Walter was, as we have seen, tested at Waterford. At Lismore, where he built a castle, he granted a charter to the Cistercian monastery de Valle Salutis at Baltinglas, confirming to the monks the lands which they had of the

14 In the Annals of Loch Cé these entries are placed before, and in the Four Masters after, the entry as to John's visit to Ireland. Probably Rory agreed to the peace when Donnell O'Brien had to withdraw to meet the aggression of the garrisons of Ardfinan and Tibberaghny. Probably, too, the mercenaries, whom we hear of for the first time in Connaught, were deserters from John's army. In the Gesta Hen. (i. 339) it is said of John's army, 'Maxima pars equitum et peditum qui cum eo venerant ab eo recesserunt et ad Hibernenses contra eum pugnaturos perrexerunt.' 15 See Carte's Life of Ormond (ed. 1851), Introd., p. xlv. In Carte's time the original deed was at Kilkenny. Ranulf de Glanville, the justiciar, remained in that office up to 1189. He went on the crusade and died at the siege of Acre in 1190: Norgate, Angevin Kings, ii. 279. It is highly improbable that he ever came to Ireland. 16 Facsimiles Nat. MSS. of Ireland, vol. ii, no. lxvii. 17 Theobald's charter to the Cistercian monastery of Wodeny (Irish, *Uaithne*, variously anglicized Wetheny, Abbey Owney, Abington, &c.) was made in the reign of Richard I, circa 1197: Chartae, &c., p. 11, and cf. Carte's Life of Ormond, Introd., p. xlii. His principal seat seems to have been at Nenagh, near which he founded a priory of St. John Baptist circa 1200. 18 Philip of Worcester had a castle at the mote of Knockgraffon probably from 1192: Journ. R.S.A.I. xxxix (1909), p. 275.

gift of Dermot Mc Murrough before the coming to Ireland of Earl Richard.[19] At Ardfinan, where he built another castle, he made a grant of four ploughlands near Limerick to the cathedral church there.[20] Perhaps this was to ingratiate himself with the clergy there, in view of his hostilities with Donnell O'Brien. At Tibberaghny, where he also built a castle, he granted a charter of confirmation to the new Cistercian house founded by Hervey de Montmorency at Dunbrody, and gave it a letter of protection.[21] At Kildare he confirmed his father's charter granting Dublin to the men of Bristol.[22] Here he also confirmed William, son of Maurice Fitz Gerald, in his barony of Naas, and probably at the same time confirmed William's grant to his brother Gerald (ancestor of the earls of Leinster [see *Add.*]) of lands about Maynooth and Rathmore.[23] At Dublin, where he probably stayed most of his time, he granted to John Cumin, Archbishop of Dublin, and his successors the bishopric of Glendalough,[24] but this attempted union of the sees was for the time ineffectual. Also to the abbey of St. [105] Thomas a carucate of land at Wicklow.[25] Incidentally we learn that he made several grants of valuable plots of land and messuages outside the western gate of Dublin to members of his household and others.[26] Moreover, to this time should probably be referred the extensive Pipard and de Verdun grants in the present county of Louth. To these we shall recur in the next chapter.

[104]

John returned to England on December 17,[27] having been in Ireland for nearly eight months. In this brief period he had driven the Irish into open opposition, alienated the sympathy of the Anglo-Norman colony, dissipated the treasure entrusted to him, and frittered away his army to no purpose. He had shown no capacity either to govern with prudence or to fight with success. Gerald, whose words, from the point [106] of view of the invaders, are full of wisdom and good sense, explains in general terms, though clearly enough, the causes of John's failure to quell the storm which his contemptuous behaviour and reckless grants had stirred up.

The custody of the maritime towns and castles (i.e. principally, Dublin, Waterford, and Wexford, and perhaps Cork), with the adjacent lands and tributes, was given to men who, instead of using the revenue for the public good and the detriment of the enemy, squandered it in excessive eating and drinking. Then, though the country was not half subdued, both the civil and the military command was given into the hands

19 Cal. Pat. Rolls, anno 1337, p. 402. 20 Black Book of Limerick (Mac Caffrey, p. 103). The editor strangely fails to date this charter, which is the oldest in the book. 21 Chart. St. Mary's, Dublin, ii. 166, 168. 22 Hist. and Mun. Docs. Ireland (J.T. Gilbert), p. 49. 23 Chartae Priv. et Immun., p. 5. See too, Gormanston Register, f. 190 dors. One of the witnesses was Reimundus filius Willelmi. For John's grant to Gerald, son of Maurice Fitz Gerald, see Red Book of Kildare, H.M.C., 9th Rep., App., p. 265; and Facsimiles Nat. MSS. Ireland, vol. iii, pl. lx. 24 Chartae, &c., p. 4, and Crede Mihi, p. 5. 25 Ibid p. 5; cf. Reg. St. Thomas's, Dublin, p. 166. 26 The *porta occidentalis* itself was given by the citizens at John's request to Henry Mausanure, one of John's men: Hist. and Mun. Docs. (Gilbert), p. 56. To William de Wendewal, his dapifer, John gave a messuage between the church of St. Thomas and the curia of Bertram de Verdun, also very probably the gift of John at this time: Reg. St. Thomas's, Dublin, p. 417. To Philip of Worcester he gave land in front of the gate of the abbey of St. Thomas, ibid., p. 407. To Henry Tirel land near Kilmainham, ibid., pp. 383, 392. John had already provided for his chamberlain, Alard Fitz William, by a grant of lands near Waterford and 'entertainment' at various houses, 'by the service of six pair of lambskin gloves and one thabur': Lynch's Legal Institutions, p. 93. 27 Ralph de Diceto, ii. 39.

of carpet knights, who were more intent on spoiling good citizens than in attacking the foe—men who, reversing the politic maxim of the ancient Romans, oppressed those who had submitted while leaving the enemy unscathed. So that nothing was done, either by making incursions into the enemy's country, or by the erection of numerous castles[28] throughout the land, or by clearing the 'bad passes' through the woods, to bring about a more settled state of things. The bands of mercenaries were kept within the seaport towns, and, imitating their captains, gave themselves up to wine and
[107] women, so that the march lands were left undefended, and the intermediate villages and fortified posts were abandoned to the fire and sword of the enemy. Meanwhile the old soldiery, feeling themselves, in the growing insolence of the new-comers, despised and out of favour, kept quietly in the background, awaiting the issue of all this rioting and disorder. Thus the country went from bad to worse. Even in the towns, where alone there was the semblance of order, the veteran soldiers of the conquest, instead of being led against the enemy, were harassed with lawsuits. In this way the power of the colony was enfeebled, while the enemy became more daring in revolt; and thus were affairs mismanaged until the king recalled the new-comers as incompetent, not to say cowardly, and, turning once more to the men already experienced in the conquest of the island, entrusted John de Courcy with the administration of affairs.[29]

In all this Gerald evidently avoids laying the blame expressly on John. He had noth-
[108] ing good to say of him, so he says little or nothing. In the circumstances, we could hardly expect him to be more outspoken. Indeed, for a writer who was a courtier, and whose works were immediately published, we are astonished at his boldness in some passages, both here and elsewhere.

28 'Crebra castrorum constructione.' **29** Gir. Camb. v. 390–2. The account given in Gesta Hen. i. 339 is in the main consistent with Gerald's: 'Sed ipse Johannes parum ibi profecit, quia pro defectu indigenarum qui cum eo tenere debebant, et pro eo quod stipendia militibus et solidariis suis dare noluit, fere amisit totum exercitum suum in pluribus conflictibus quos sui fecerunt contra Hibernienses … Et sic praedictus Johannes, filius regis, ad opus suum omnia retinere cupiens, pro defectu auxilii terram Hiberniae relinquens, in Angliam rediit.'

CHAPTER XVII [109]

JOHN DE COURCY AND EASTERN IRELAND, 1186–1205

§1. The succession of chief governors

The period from the death of Hugh de Lacy to the beginning of John's reign is one of great obscurity in the history of the Anglo-Norman settlement in Ireland. Gerald de Barry, to whom we owe so much of our knowledge of the previous years, now fails us, and the great series of state papers and enrolments do not yet come to our help. Even the succession of justiciars is uncertain, for the list given by Walter Harris and followed by Gilbert and a host of writers is not correct. In tracing the progress of the English we must, to some extent, work backwards from their better ascertainable position at the commencement of the thirteenth century. For the stages of that progress we have some indications in the Irish annals, which record the erection of a few castles and mention certain English expeditions, but these annals are largely taken up
with the inter-tribal wars and plunderings.of the Irish themselves, which seldom had [110]
any permanent effect beyond weakening the Irish and giving the English opportunity to extend their influence. No useful purpose would be attained by mentioning these conflicts, except so far as they may help to explain English action, or had permanent results. A few charters which have been preserved throw a more certain light on some points, while recent archaeological research enables us to indicate with precision the principal manorial centres, and define more closely than has hitherto been done the area of Anglo Norman rule.

We shall first endeavour to ascertain who were the chief governors or justiciars of Ireland during this period.

On the failure of John's mission to Ireland in 1185, Henry, as we have seen, appointed John de Courcy as justiciar, and he remained in this capacity up to at least the beginning of the reign of Richard I.[1] Who succeeded him, and at what precise date, is uncertain. In the list of chief governors compiled by Walter Harris, and followed by Gilbert and other writers, 'Hugh de Lacy the younger, lord of Meath,'
appears as justiciar from 1189 to 1191. But Hugh de Lacy the younger was never lord [111]
of Meath, and it is very improbable that he was made justiciar at this time. His father, Hugh de Lacy, left at his death, by his first wife, Roheis de Monemue (Monmouth), two sons, viz. Walter, who afterwards succeeded to the lordship of Meath, and Hugh,

1 John de Courcy was justiciar after the time when John, the king's son, became Earl of Mortain; see Henry Tirel's charter, Reg. St. Thomas's, Dublin, p. 383, and Grant from Dublin Commonalty, Hist. and Mun. Docs. Ireland, p. 56.

who was created Earl of Ulster in 1205, and a daughter, Elayne, who married Richard de Beaufo.[2] Walter and Hugh were apparently minors at the time of their father's death, and Henry at once made arrangements for his son John to return to Ireland, and take the fief of Meath into his hand. John had got as far as Chester with this object, when Henry, on learning of the death of his son Geoffrey of Brittany, recalled
[112] him,[3] and sent Philip of Worcester to Ireland in John's place.[4] John's grant of Meath to Walter de Lacy was made in the reign of Richard I,[5] and it is probable that Walter did not get actual possession until 1194, when he did homage to Richard I for his lands, and when, we are told, he 'received the lordship of Meath and apprehended Peter Pipard, justiciar, with his comrades'.[6] If this be so, it is impossible to believe that Hugh de Lacy, Walter's younger brother, could have been justiciar in 1189–91. Moreover, the authority for this statement seems to be the Book of Howth, but the account there is quite untrustworthy, and actually confuses Hugh de Lacy the elder with his son of the same name.[7]

[113] The next justiciar, according to Harris, was William le Petit in 1191. This may be correct, but the authority is not forthcoming. He was a powerful baron in Meath, and, at any rate, appears as justiciar later. Then in the same year and up to 1194, when Peter Pipard is said to have been justiciar, Harris places William Marshal as governor. When we come to narrate the doings of this great man we shall see how extremely improbable it is that he was governor, or indeed in Ireland at all, at this time. In short, our scanty authorities only warrant us in stating that Peter Pipard was probably justiciar in 1194;[8] that Hamo de Valognes was justiciar from about 1196 to shortly before the

2 Dict. Nat. Biog. Richard de Bellofago was a witness to Hugh de Lacy's grant of Skreen to Adam de Feipo: Chart. St. Mary's, Dublin, vol. ii, p. 21. The family appear to have settled in Ireland. Almaric de Beaufo possessed the de Burgh castle of Esclone in County Limerick in 1215—C.D.I., vol. i, no. 585; and Isabella de Beaufo appears in 1245 as owner of the castle of Clonard in Meath: ibid., no. 2762. By his Irish wife, the daughter of Rory O'Conor, Hugh de Lacy had a son, William, who afterwards appears as a disturber of the peace and was ultimately killed by O'Reilly of Breifny in 1233 (Four Masters). Three brothers of William de Lacy, named Sir Henry Blund, Thomas Blund, and another, are mentioned, C.D.I., vol. i, no. 1203. Probably Hugh de Lacy's widow married a Blund. 3 Gesta Hen., vol. i, p. 350. Henry appears to have had a scheme at this time for crowning John king of Ireland,and had obtained from Pope Urban III his sanction and a crown of peacocks' feathers embroidered with gold (Rog. de Hoveden, vol. ii, pp. 306–7), but it came to nothing. 4 Chronicle of St. Werburg's Abbey, Chester, as quoted in Ware's Annals. 5 Gormanston Register, f. 5 dors. For Richard's confirmatory grant see ibid., f. 5. 6 Hist. Guill. le Marechal, ll. 10297–304, and Marlburgh's Chron. 1194: 'Walterus de Lacy recepit dominium de Media et Petrum Pipard justitiarium cum suis militibus deprehendit' (T.C.D. MS. E, 3, 20, p. 135). Was Peter Pipard intriguing with John against Walter de Lacy, just as Meiler Fitz Henry afterwards intrigued against William the Marshal? 7 Carew Calendar (Book of Howth), pp. 105–17. If the whole passage be read attentively it will be seen that the original compiler—adding, as he says, to the account of Giraldus some passages from an English translation made in 1551 by Primate Dowdall out of a Latin book found with O'Neill at Armagh—has attempted to weave into the narrative of Giraldus some traditional stories as to the death of Sir Almaric de St. Laurent, the taking of John de Courcy, and the subsequent career of the latter; but in doing so he has hopelessly confused the two Hughs. Probably he intended the elder Hugh throughout. The confusion becomes quite manifest when the murder of the elder Hugh at Durrow is spoken of as a just punishment for his malicious treatment of John de Courcy (pp. 116–17). 8 Marlburgh's Chron. (as above). The entry on the Coram Rege Roll relating to Peter Pipard's justiciarship (Cal. Docs. Irel., vol. i, no. 116) probably refers to 1198–9.

beginning of John's reign;[9] and that Peter Pipard and William le Petit were 'joint justiciars' for a short time in 1198–9,[10] until Meiler Fitz Henry was appointed by King John.[11] Meiler appears to have been justiciar continuously up to about the autumn of 1208, and Harris's list is again faulty in making Hugh de Lacy lord-deputy in 1203 to 1205.[12] There are many mandates to Meiler as justiciar during this period. Hugh de Lacy was, no doubt, carrying out the king's wishes (and his own) in chasing John de Courcy from Ulster, but this did not make him governor or displace Meiler. [114]

§2. *John de Courcy as justiciar and in Ulster*

Of John de Courcy's justiciarship we have few particulars. Giraldus tells us in general terms that under his vigorous rule the kingdom began to enjoy a more extended [115]
peace. The peace, however, was confined to the settled districts in the east of Ireland, as our author immediately goes on to say that de Courcy did not permit his troops to lie idle, but led them to the furthest parts of the land, to Cork and Connaught, and feared not to try the doubtful chances of war, which were sometimes in his favour and sometimes against him. This leads to the exclamation, 'Would that he had shown the prudence of a general as well as the bravery of a soldier!'[13]

The Irish annals say nothing about the expedition to Cork, which was presumably to aid the settlers there, but under the year 1188 give some details of the expedition to Connaught. This province was still torn by the conflict between Rory O'Conor and his son Conor Maenmoy. The peace patched up between them in 1185,[14] on the basis of a division of Connaught, did not last long. Before the year was out Conor Maenmoy 'assumed the sovereignty of Connaught', and next year he expelled his father.[15] The new king was hostile to the English, and in favour of taking active measures against them. In 1187 he made an attack on Meath, burned the newly erected mote-castle of Killare, and killed all the English who were in it.[16] It was probably to [116]
punish him for this outrage that John de Courcy, as justiciar, made an incursion into Connaught in the following year. He was accompanied by Conor O'Dermot, an illegitimate son of Rory O'Conor,[17] and we may perhaps infer that the pretext of the

9 Dublin Annals of Inisfallen, 1196. In the Charter Roll of the 1st John, Hamo de Valognes is repeatedly referred to as having been justiciar. He was apparently still justiciar in 1198: Papal Letters, vol. i, p. 3. 10 [See *Add.*] Chart. St. Mary's, Dublin, vol. i, p. 144; vol. ii, p. 28. This charter must be dated after Sept. 1198, when John, a Cistercian monk, was consecrated by the Pope Bishop of Leighlin: Papal Letters, vol. i, p. 3. Simon de Rocheford, another witness, is called 'elect of Meath'. He is usually stated to have succeeded Eugenius in 1194, but it is pretty clear that he was not consecrated Bishop of Meath until about 1198–9. 11 Rot. Chart., 2 John, p. 98 b. There are mandates to Meiler as justiciar before this date. The earliest is dated Sept. 4, 1199. Cal. Docs. Ireland, vol. i, no. 90. 12 Perhaps this second tenure of office was also suggested by the apocryphal story in the Book of Howth: Car. Cal., p. 111. 13 Gir Camb. v. 392. 14 *Supra*, p. 101 [pp. 190–1]. 15 Ann. Ulster, Ann. Loch Cé, 1186. 16 Four Masters, 1187. 17 This Conor, grandson of Dermot, seems to have been a son of Rory O'Conor. It was at his instigation that Conor Maenmoy was killed next year. He is then called in the Annals of Loch Cé (1189) 'own brother' of Conor Maenmoy; cf. Ann. Ulster, 1189. He may have been one of

incursion was the reinstatement of Rory O'Conor. The expedition was unsuccessful, however. Donnell O'Brien on this occasion came to the support of his former enemy, Conor Maenmoy, and the English, after fruitlessly burning some churches, endeavoured to return by way of Tirconnell. They got as far as Ballysadare, when, on learning that the Cinel Connell were assembled to oppose them, they once more turned through Connaught, and after suffering some loss in the Curlew Mountains they were forced to leave the country 'without a whit of triumph'.[18] Clearly John de Courcy was outgeneralled, and it is possible that he was soon afterwards superseded.

When John de Courcy surrendered his office of justiciar he no doubt retired to his
[117] lordship of Ulster, the southern part of which, at any rate, was already fully organized. As early as 1188 we read of the foreigners of the castle of Magh Cobha[19] making an incursion into Tirowen, and in 1189 Armagh was plundered; but no permanent settlement was made there, and the Newry river and Glenrigh may be regarded as the boundary of the lordship in this direction. Indeed, in many of the inland parts of the present counties of Down and Antrim the Irish tribes seem to have accepted the new order of things and to have been undisturbed.

For several years we hear little more of John de Courcy, and that 'little' has already been indicated in chapter xii. We may leave him building his castles, founding his religious establishments, and governing his lordship like an independent monarch, while
[118] we take a rapid survey of the other great feudal lordships and districts in the east of Ireland, and, so far as our scanty materials allow, note the progress made by the English colonists during the two decades that followed Hugh de Lacy's death. We shall then describe their expansion in Munster, and their dealings in Connaught during the same period.

§3. English Uriel

Between Ulster and Meath lay the Irish district of Oirghialla (anglicized Uriel), roughly equivalent at this time to the modern counties of Louth, Armagh, and Monaghan. The eastern portion of this district was overrun as early as 1176 by the English of Meath, and after 1177 by John de Courcy from Ulidia, but probably no organized settlement was made in it, except at Drogheda, and perhaps at Dundalk, until after John's visit to Ireland in 1185. At that time, or soon afterwards, John seems to have treated the modern county of Louth as already conquered, and to have granted two

Rory's numerous illegitimate progeny. He was killed in the same year by Cathal Carragh, son of Conor Maenmoy. 18 Ann. Ulster, Ann. Loch Cé, 1188. 19 Magh Cobha was the name of the plain extending from Dromore to Newry inhabited by the tribe of Ui Eathach Cobha, a name now preserved in the baronies of Iveagh. Perhaps the great mote at Dromore represents John de Courcy's castle. The castle of 'Maincove' is mentioned in the confirmation by Innocent III of John de Courcy's charter to St. Andrew de Stokes: Papal Letters, vol. i, p. 17. It was rebuilt in stone in 1252 (Ann. Ulster; C.D.I., vol. ii, no. 124), and demolished by Brian O'Neill in the following year: Ann. Ulster. It was restored c. 1260: Irish Pipe Roll, 45 Hen. III. See Facsimiles Nat. MSS. Ireland, pt. ii, pl. 73. The river Lagan, which flows by Dromore, was in Magh Cobha. See Hogan's Onomasticon.

large fiefs in it to two of his followers, while reserving a considerable slice for the Crown.[20] To Bertram de Verdun, his seneschal, he gave a district now represented by the barony of Dundalk, and perhaps the eastern half of the barony of Ferrard as well, [119]
and to Roger (or perhaps to Gilbert) Pipard he gave the barony of Ardee [see *Add.*]. Certainly this barony was afterwards held along with the parish of Donaghmoyne, in Farney, County Monaghan, by Roger, brother of Gilbert Pipard. The king retained the barony of Louth in his own hand, and portions of it were granted from time to time to smaller holders. The church-lands of Iniskeen, Dromiskin, Termonfeckin, Mellifont, and Monasterboice were, as usual, not interfered with. The abbey of Mellifont, founded by Donough O'Carroll in 1158, was now at the height of its fame, and here in 1189 died Donough's son, Murrough, the last king of undivided Uriel, and here in 1193 Dervorgil, the *teterrima causa belli*, ended her days at the age of eighty-five. Bertram de Verdun was made custodian of the Bridge of Drogheda. This expression would seem to include the castle of the bridge, often afterwards mentioned. This castle stood on the mote which still exists on the Meath side of the river. It was probably erected by Hugh de Lacy the elder to guard the bridge, and came into John's hand on Hugh's death. It was afterwards retained as a royal castle, and rent by way of compensation was paid to Walter de Lacy and his successors for more than a century. When the town was walled on the Meath side, the town walls were carried up the [120]
steep river bank to join the wall of the castle-bailey, and the mote and bailey then probably occupied the southern salient of the town walls.[21] At some subsequent time the wall on the eastern side was altered so as to include St. Mary's Church and a larger portion of the town. More recently the place was fitted up for barracks, but with all the changes of centuries the original mote and bailey plan has been in all essentials preserved up to the present day.

The *caput* of the de Verdun barony of Dundalk was at Castletown, about a mile to the west of the town, where an important mote marks the site of the first Norman castle. This mote has been supposed to be the *dún delga* of Cuchulainn, one of the principal figures in the Red Branch cycle of tales. It is possible that it occupies the site of an older Celtic fort, but as it stands it is essentially a Norman structure.[22] There was an ancient fishing-village at Dundalk before this, but 'the new vill' or 'Stradbally (street-town) of Dundalk' owed its origin to the Anglo-Norman settlers, and to the [121]
protection afforded by the castle-town. Bertram de Verdun remained in Ireland after John left at the close of 1185, when Gerald de Barry was his guest.[23]

The position of his house just outside the walls of Dublin, was long marked by the name 'Curia Bertrami'.[24] He is said to have founded the hospital of St. Leonard at Dundalk for Cruciferi, but how far he exploited his lands in Uriel is uncertain. He

20 References to the authorities for the statements in this section as to the Anglo-Norman settlement in Louth will be found in my paper on 'Motes and Norman Castles in Co. Louth', Journ. R.S.A.I. 1908, pp. 241–69. **21** This may be inferred from the murage grants, that of 1318 being 'in subsidium ville predicte claudende usque ad muros castri nostri ejusdem ville': Hist. and Mun. Docs. Ireland, p. 413. At the present day the remains of the town wall join the wall of the bailey on the west side. **22** See my paper, 'Motes and Norman Castles in Co. Louth' (as above), pp. 256–61. **23** Gir. Camb. i. 65.

accompanied Richard I on his crusade and died at Joppa in 1192. He was succeeded by his son Thomas, about whom little has hitherto been known. A remarkable document, however, preserved in the Gormanston Register, explains how Hugh de Lacy the younger obtained lands from Thomas de Verdun in the north of the present county of Louth, and throws light on the methods of expansion contemplated by the settlers. This document is, in the first place, an acknowledgement that Thomas de Verdun had given to Hugh de Lacy in frank marriage with Thomas's sister Leceline de Verdun the moiety of his land in Uriel, retaining, however, to himself and his heirs the castle of Dundalk and five knights' fees in its vicinity; and, in the second place, an agreement to divide equally between the parties whatever they may acquire in the
[122] 'land of war' in their respective parts of Uriel [see *Add.*].[25] Hence, probably, the division of the barony into Upper and Lower Dundalk.

Thomas de Verdun died in 1199, presumably without issue, and was succeeded by his brother Nicholas. The latter, in 1203, was given the custody of 'the bridge of Drogheda as his father held it',[26] and soon afterwards he obtained seisin of all his father's lands in Ireland.[27] He was the ancestor of a distinguished Anglo-Irish house, and his grandson, John de Verdun, by his marriage with Margaret de Lacy, one of the two granddaughters and co-heiresses of Walter de Lacy, became entitled to a moiety of the lordship of Meath.

The *caput* of Roger Pipard's barony was at Ardee, where a great mote known as
[123] 'Castle guard', though much mutilated, in all probability marks the spot.[28] Roger was brother of Gilbert Pipard, who accompanied Prince John to Ireland in 1185, and may have been the original grantee,[29] and of Peter Pipard, justiciar in 1194, and he was himself a trusted officer of King John. He founded the priory of St. John the Baptist at Ardee.[30] In 1193 he erected the castle of Donaghmoyne, where a strongly-defended mote, bearing the ruins of a later stone castle, still excites the wonder of the visitor by its size and strength.[31] Roger Pipard was a faithful servant of King John, and was made seneschal of Ulster and custodian of the castle of Rath (Dundrum), after the disseisin
[124] of Hugh de Lacy in 1210. For about a century he and his representatives were lords of Ardee. He died in 1225. His great-grandson, Ralph Pipard, in the beginning of the fourteenth century, surrendered all his Irish lands to Edward I. Among the feudatories of Roger Pipard were Ralph de Repenteni, lord of Drumcar and Killany, now parishes

24 See Gilbert's Hist. of Dublin, vol. i, p. 239. 25 Gormanston Register, f. 189 dors. This agreement must be dated between 1192 and 1199. The latter clause runs as follows: 'Et quicquid prefati Thomas et Hugo de Lacy poterint conquirere in terra gwerre in partibus suis terre de Ergallo totum inter se dimidiabunt sicut dimidiauerunt inter se terram pacis.' For the date of Thomas de Verdun's death I can only refer to Gilbert, Chart. St. Mary's, Dublin, vol. i, p. 66, note. [See *Add.*] 26 Liberate, 5 John, p. 59. 27 Rot. Claus., 7 John, m. 23 (p. 38). His principal manors were Dundalk and Clonmore; the latter was in the barony of Ferrard. One of his feudatories was Henry de Wotton, to whom he granted five knights' fees in the hilly district north of Dundalk: Chart. St. Mary's Abbey, Dublin, vol. i, p. 65. 28 This mote as figured in Louthiana (by T. Wright, 1748) shows the foundations of an octagonal keep surrounded by an octagonal parapet or wall on its summit. It was encircled by two ditches and ramparts, and had an earthen wall or approach crossing the ditches and running up the mote. 29 Gilbert Pipard accompanied Richard I on his crusade, and died at Brundusium: Gesta Ricardi, p. 150. 30 This foundation is placed by Ware in the year 1207.

at the east and west extremities of the barony; Ralph de Vernun, lord of 'Balisconan' (including Stabannon), whose daughter, Cecilia, married Geoffrey des Auters. Other tenants or sub-tenants were Hugh de Clinton (Clintonstown and Drumcashel in the parish of Stabannon), Geoffrey de Hadeshore, Peter de Maupas (Mapestown), and Robert Mor, all bearing names for many years distinguished in the County Louth.[32]

In John's barony of Louth the castle was already in existence in 1196, when it and the town were plundered and destroyed by Niall MacMahon and the Ulidians.[33] The castle was soon rebuilt, and in 1204 Meiler Fitz Henry, the justiciar, was ordered to take the city of Louth into the king's hand, and make what improvements he could in it.[34] The castle was probably situated on the mote which still exists near the glebe-house, and which appears to have been connected with the town trench. We read [125]
also of two subordinate manors in the neighbourhood, Castlefranc and Ays, the *capita* of which are now represented by the motes of Castlering and Mount Ash. In the eastern part of the barony of Louth the old Celtic monastery of Dromiskin had long ceased to exist, but the church-lands there were recognized as a manor belonging to the Archbishop of Armagh. Among the knights who followed John in 1210 to Carrickfergus were Robert de Mandeville and Ralph Gernon. To the former he seems to have granted the lands known from him as Mandevillestown[35] (now corruptly Mansfieldstown), and perhaps the latter was the first grantee of the manor of Killincoole, which, together with Gernonstown (now Castlebellingham), was held by a family of that name for centuries.[36] The first grantee of the manor of Darver is uncertain.[37]

§4. Meath [126]

Hugh de Lacy's murder in 1186 was probably an act of private revenge, and does not appear to have been followed by any general outbreak in Meath. His lands were taken into the king's hand, and it was probably not until 1194 that Hugh's son Walter got possession.[38] Walter continued his father's work of feudal organization, renewed the grant which had already been made of 'the law of Bristol' to the burgesses of Trim, and, perhaps for the first time, gave a similar charter to the burgesses of Kells.[39] To his brother, Hugh de Lacy, he gave the barony of Ratoath, and at the same time the confiscated lands of Gilbert de Nangle, in the barony of Morgallion.[40]

31 Ann. Loch Cé, 1193. In the year 1244 it was enclosed or fortified with stone, *do chumhdach do chlochaibh*: Ann. Ulster. The ruins at present existing may well date from this time. The earthworks consist of a lofty mote surrounded by a deep fosse and wide rampart. The westem end is further defended by a second fosse and rampart, and an excavated pond. At the eastern side is a lofty bailey, strongly fortified, and beyond this a second one at a lower level. 32 These and other names may be gleaned from among the benefactors of St. Mary's Abbey, Dublin. 33 Ann. Inisfallen, Dublin MS., 1196. 34 Rot. Pat., 5 John, p. 38; Rot. Claus., 6 John, p. 16 b. 35 See Close Roll, 13 Hen. III, m. 9; Calendar, vol, i, no. 1677, where 'Lune' stands for 'Luveth', and cf. nos. 1284 and 1681. 36 Richard, son and heir of William Gernon, was a tenant *in capite* of the Crown in 1229: Cal. Docs. Ireland, i, no. 1729, 38th Rep. D. K., p. 72. 37 Prior to 1286 the Manor of Derver was held by Richard of Exeter as tenant *in capite* of the Crown: Irish Pipe Roll, 16 Ed. I, 37th Rep. D. K., p. 35. A member of the family of Babe held it from the close of the fourteenth century to Stuart times. 38 *Supra*, p. 112 [p. 195]. 39 Chartae Priv. et Immun., p. 10.

The first Anglo-Norman Bishop of Meath was Simon de Rocheford (1198–1224). He founded an Augustinian priory at Newtown near Trim, the picturesque ruins of which still remain, and for about three centuries the chapel of the priory served as the cathedral church of the diocese. It was probably after the year 1200, when Clonard was
[127] burnt by the Irish, that the episcopal seat was moved here. Simon de Rocheford did much to consolidate and organize the diocese. In early times there were several bishops in Meath. As elsewhere, they were tribal rather than diocesan, but the rural deaneries of Meath may be taken as representing the ancient bishoprics. The policy of consolidation began with the Synod of Kells in 1152, but Simon de Rocheford carried it further by ordaining that 'in the churches of Trim, Kells, Slane, Skryne, and Dunshaughlin, which were at one time episcopal sees in Meath, but are now heads of rural deaneries, for the future archpresbyters be appointed'.[38]

During all this period we hear of no serious fighting with the native tribes. The whole of East Meath and much of West Meath had been parcelled out amongst Hugh de Lacy's barons, and the whole lordship was studded with mote-fortresses. The Irish inhabitants seem in general to have lived quite contentedly under their new lords. The late ruling family, the O'Melaghlins, still claimed to be kings of West Meath, but their power appears to have been gradually confined to the barony of Clonlonan. Almost the only recorded disturbance arose from outside. In 1187 Conor Maenmoy, who had
[128] expelled his father Rory from Connaught, made an unprovoked incursion into West Meath, and, assisted by Melaghlin Beg, burned and destroyed the castle of Killare and killed its garrison.[42] It is doubtful if it was ever rebuilt, but the position in the west of the lordship was strengthened by the erection of mote-castles at Rathconarty (now Rathconrath) in 1191, and at Ardnurcher and Kilbixy in 1192.[43] The two last were in lands granted to Meiler Fitz Henry and Geoffrey de Costentin respectively, and in process of time they were replaced by stone castles and small towns grew up under their protection. At Tristernagh, near Kilbixy, Geoffrey de Costentin, about the year 1200, founded a priory of canons regular.[44] In the same year Richard de Tuit erected a castle on a large mote at Granard in the present county of Longford, 'as a stronghold against O'Reilly of Breffny.'[45] This may be taken as the limit of the colony in this direction, though some other mote-fortresses were built in the south-eastern baronies
[129] of County Longford, then considered part of the ancient kingdom of Meath. A few years later Richard de Tuit founded the Cistercian abbey of Larha, near Granard. We do not know exactly when the mote at Athlone was erected to guard the important ford across the Shannon against the O'Conors, but it was probably before the year

40 Gormanston Register, f. 188 dors. *Supra*, pp. 76, 84 [pp. 180, 183]. John's confirmatory charter, as transcribed in the same Register, is dated December 4 a. r. 10 Richard I (1198), 'apud [In]sulam Andh[elys].' 41 Wilkins's Concilia, i, 547. 42 Four Masters, 1187. 43 Ann. Loch Cé, 1191, 1192. 44 Ware, quoting from the Register of Tristernagh. 45 Ann. Inisfallen (Dublin MS.), Ann. Loch Cé, 1199. The mote is about 40 feet high, and still retains traces of stone foundations round the top surface. There is a small bailey attached, and the whole is nearly surrounded by a mutilated earthen rampart. O'Donovan says that about fifty years before he wrote the arched vaults of a castle, built of cut stone and well cemented, were found within the mote: Four Masters, 1262, note o.

1199, when Cathal Crovderg burned the bawn of Athlone and carried off many cows from the foreigners.[46]

§5. *Dublin*

Dublin appears to have grown considerably, and to have become a flourishing commercial town during these twenty years. To this period must be referred the list of 1600 Dublin citizens, of which we have already given an analysis.[47] In the year 1192 John granted an extended charter to his citizens of Dublin—to those dwelling outside the walls as well as to those dwelling within.[48] The boundaries south of the Liffey extended from the river Dodder to Kilmainham, and on the north from Grangegorman to the river Tolka. The principal liberties granted by this charter were to the following effect: that citizens should not be obliged to plead beyond their walls except as regards external tenements, nor be liable to a general fine for murder; [130]
that they might clear themselves on any appeal by compurgation, instead of by wager of battle; that they should not be liable to forcible billeting; that (as before) they should be free from certain tolls throughout John's dominions; that they should not be amerced in fines except according to the law of their hundred-court; that the usages of the city should prevail as regards their lands, debts, and mortgages held or contracted therein; that no foreign merchant should buy corn, hides, or wool in the city except from a citizen, nor should open a wine-tavern except on board ship, nor sell cloth by retail in the city, nor tarry therein with his wares for more than forty days; that citizens, other than the principal debtor or sureties, should not be distrained anywhere for debts; that they might contract marriages for themselves, their sons, daughters, and widows, without licence of their lords, who should only have the custody during infancy of tenements of the lord's fee; that no assize of recognition should be held in the city; that the citizens should have all reasonable guilds as the burgesses of Bristol had; that the citizens, by common consent, might dispose freely of lands and messuages within the boundaries to be held in free burgage, and might freely build, subject to the rights of those to whom John had already given charters. This, the first extended charter granted in Ireland, was modelled on the charter given [131]
by John to Bristol in 1188, and was soon followed by others, similarly framed, and granted by the various feudal owners to the principal towns in their domains, as they grew to be of oonsequence.

As we have already noted, it was during this period that Archbishop Cumin converted the parochial church of St. Patrick de Insula into a collegiate church, and endowed it with thirteen prebends. Close by, at St. Sepulchre's, he appears to have had his principal residence. By moving outside the walls, however, he did not escape coming into conflict with Hamo de Valognes, who was justiciar in 1196–8. Hamo and his men are said to have done great injuries to the archbishop and the Church in

46 Ann. Loch Cé, 1199. 47 *Supra*, vol. i, pp. 270–1 [pp. 99–100]. 48 Hist. and Mun. Docs. Ireland, pp. 51–5.

1197. What these injuries were we are not told, but the archbishop took them so seriously that he excommunicated the offenders, and, pronouncing an interdict upon the archbishopric, went into exile. Like the men of Connaught in the face of Miles de Cogan's incursion in 1177, he 'ordered the crosses and images of the cathedral church to be laid on the ground and to be surrounded with thorns, that thus these malefactors might be smitten with fear and be checked in their intentions to rage against the property of the Church'. The carved Christ on the cross showed, it is
[132] said, miraculous signs of agony, but in vain. The archbishop appealed to King Richard and to Earl John, but without success.[49] In December 1204 the Pope threatened an interdict if John did not replace the archbishop in his favour.[50] Ultimately Hamo is said to have compensated the archbishop by a grant of 'twenty carucates of land in Ucunil'.[51] John Cumin had other quarrels about property with King John. Like Becket, when once made archbishop he was a great stickler for the rights of his see, which he left immensely richer than it was when he received it.

§6. The Crown lands and Leinster

In the crown lands of Dublin, Wicklow, and Waterford, as in the whole lordship of Leinster, we read of no fighting. As we saw when reviewing the sub-infeudation of Leinster, large tracts of country were left by Earl Richard in the hands of the Irish, either by arrangement with the native princes or because they were not thoroughly
[133] subdued. Thus in the northern part of the present county of Wexford and adjoining portions of the Counties Carlow and Wicklow, the tribes of Okinselagh seem to have been left by the earl under the rule of Murtough Mc Murrough. He lived on to 1193. We hear no more of the Mc Murroughs nor of any disturbance from them until the reign of Edward I. Indeed, even then the disturbance first arose from the O'Tooles and O'Byrnes. In Upper Ossory the Mac Gillapatricks still held sway; in parts of Leix the O'Mores, and in the western parts of Offaly the O'Conors and O'Dempsys held much of their own. The county of Kildare was, as we have seen, very fully parcelled out, and some of the tribes, such as the O'Tooles and O'Byrnes, retreated to the uplands of the County Wicklow, where they maintained their tribal organization and a lawless freedom, and were afterwards from time to time a source of danger and injury to the colony.

In 1189, after the accession of Richard I, Isabel de Clare, the heiress of Leinster and of many lands besides, was given in marriage to William Marshal, and soon afterwards he seems to have obtained seisin of his Irish lordship. With the possible exception of one or two brief visits, he did not come to Ireland until the close of the year

49 Roger de Hoveden (1197) iv. 29–30. 50 Cal. Papal Letters (Bliss) i. 18. 51 Crede Mihi, p. 66. This grant probably consisted of one knight's fee in Culballysiward (near Bruree in Upper Connello), together with a tenement in Bruree, given by Hamo, Lord of Iniskyfty, to the predecessor of John de Sanford, Archbishop of Dublin, as found by an inquisition of 1289 (quoted by Mr. Westropp, Journ. R.S.A.I. 1903, p. 29). Cf. Cal Liber Niger Alani, p. 771.

1206, and we shall reserve our account of him and his doings in Ireland to a subsequent chapter.

§7. *The downfall of John de Courcy* [134]

We must now return to John de Courcy, who after twenty years of prosperity in Ulster entered upon a stormy period which ended in his downfall. While the air in the north was still unruffled, however, acting apparently as an emissary of the government and accompanied by one of the de Lacys, probably his neighbour Hugh, he led an army in 1195 to Athlone, where he negotiated a peace with Cathal Crovderg O'Conor, King of Connaught, who had been making raids on the Anglo-Norman settlement in Munster. To this expedition we shall recur when we have described the events in Munster which led to it.

In 1197 Jordan de Courcy, John's brother, was slain by an Irishman of his household. This murder seems to mark a turning-point in John's career. Certainly after it he became more aggressive. He is said to have avenged his brother's death on certain petty kings, subjugating their territories and giving no small part of them to Duncan, son of Gilbert of Galloway, who had come to his aid.[52] This is the first we hear of a Scottish settlement in the neighbourhood of Coleraine, where large grants were afterwards made to Scots of Galloway by King John. Indeed, we need have no hesitation in connecting the erection in this year of the castle of Kilsantain or Kilsantail, identi- [135]
fied with the mote of Mount Sandel near Coleraine, and the devastation of the adjoining cantred of Keenaught in Tirowen,[53] with this expedition.

Since the year 1177 an intermittent struggle for the kingship of Tirowen appears to have been going on between the O'Loughlins and the O'Neills, the latter a name afterwards illustrious in the annals of Ireland, but now for the first time coming to the front. Between the years 1186 and 1201 no fewer than four kings of the Cinel Owen were killed and three deposed, while for several of these years Flaherty O'Muldory, King of Tirconnell, taking advantage of the weakness due to this intestine feud, had imposed his rule over Tirowen. In 1196 an O'Loughlin was killed by his own people, and it was apparently on behalf of another O'Loughlin that the first expedition from the castle of Kilsantail into Tirowen was made in 1197.[54] In that year Flaherty O'Muldory died, and for four years John de Courcy made repeated plundering expeditions, with varying success, to Derry and Inishowen, but no permanent settlement seems to have been effected.

In 1201 John de Courcy, in company with Hugh de Lacy, made an unsuccessful [136]
expedition into Connaught to assist Cathal Crovderg O'Conor, who had been expelled by his grand-nephew Cathal Carragh.[55] He seems, indeed, always to have welcomed the prospect of a fight and to have hearkened to the call of almost any dispossessed

52 Roger of Hoveden, iv. 25. 53 Ann. Ulster, Four Masters, 1197; Ann. Loch Cé, 1196. 54 Ann. Ulster, 1197; Ann. Loch Cé, 1196. John de Courcy's men 'were slaughtered to a large number around the son of Ardgal O'Loughlin'. 55 See below, p. 187 [p. 226].

chieftain, hoping no doubt to get profit to himself by the way. But in all his campaigning, which for the most part was unsuccessful, we seem to see the truth of Gerald de Barry's criticism that he was 'more of a soldier than of a general'. Within his lordship of Uladh, however, after the first few years of his occupation, we hear of no fighting. We may conclude that he dominated the whole country to the east of the Bann, Lough Neagh, and the Newry river,[56] and that the native tribes there acquiesced in his rule. To attain this result he must have been something of a statesman.

But the fall of this remarkable man was near at hand. He incurred the wrath of King John and succumbed to the treachery of his companions in arms, the de Lacys. John de Courcy's expeditions into Connaught will be better understood when the rela-
[137] tions of the rival claimants to the throne there with the English government and with William de Burgh have been examined. Here we may observe that these expeditions cannot have been the real cause of the king's ire against John de Courcy or of his ultimate ruin.[57] This supposition would not only seem to be excluded by the dates, but would fail to account for the royal favour bestowed on the de Lacys, one of whom at any rate shared in de Courcy's expedition. Some other cause of the royal ire must be sought. Probably de Courcy refused to do homage to John as king, and claimed to rule in Ulster independently.[58] Perhaps, too, there is truth in the tradition that he after-
[138] wards used very plain language with regard to John's treatment of Arthur of Brittany. Nothing would have been more likely to arouse John's vindictiveness. But, indeed, to judge by authenticated facts alone, John would appear to have behaved with unwonted forbearance, and the person whose conduct in the affair shows worst was not the king, but Hugh de Lacy, who was ready to do the bidding of the king, to his own advantage, but to the ruin of his former friend and companion in arms. The authenticated facts are as follows: On arriving in Meath after his forced retreat from Connaught in 1201, John de Courcy was treacherously arrested by the de Lacys, and would have been delivered up to the king, 'who had long wished to take him,' only that his release was obtained by his followers as the price of their ceasing to ravage the de Lacy's lands.[59] He returned to Uladh, and in July 1202 was offered a safe-conduct to and from the

56 The distribution of motes in Ulster, most of which were probably erected in John de Courcy's time, would alone indicate this. 57 In a mandate dated the 4th of September, 1199, the king bids Meiler Fitz Henry inquire whether Henry Tirel 'had sided with John de Courcy and W. de Lacy and aided them in destroying the king's land of Ireland': Cal. Docs. Ireland, vol. i, no. 90. This cannot refer to the Connaught expedition of 1201, and is unlikely to refer to that of 1195. It is more probable that it refers to John de Courcy's raids into Tirowen in 1198–9, though there is no mention in the annals of his being accompanied there by one of the de Lacys. According to the story of John de Courcy's treacherous arrest as told by Roger de Hoveden, Hugh de Lacy said he was John's liegeman. It is very probable that Hugh held lands of John in Ulster or perhaps in the north of the present County Louth. Perhaps the W. de Lacy of John's mandate was William de Lacy, son of the elder Hugh by the daughter of Rory O'Conor. 58 This is intimated in the Laud MS. Annals (Chart. St. Mary's, Dublin, ii. 309) and in the Book of Howth, p. 111. Roger de Hoveden (iv. 162), when giving, after the manner of chroniclers, a list of sovereigns synchronously reigning in the year 1201, winds up in a curious way with 'John de Courcy reigning in Ulster'. This has the air of being a court sarcasm current at the time. 59 Roger de Hoveden, iv. 176; Ann. Loch Cé, Ann. Inisfallen (Dublin), Ann. Ulster, 1201; cf. Ann. Clonmacnois, 1200, and Four Masters, 1199. The true date seems to be 1201.

king's court 'to treat of peace'.[60] This he must have ignored, for in 1203 Hugh de Lacy
followed him to Uladh, defeated him in a battle at Downpatrick, and banished him [139]
from his lordship.[61] In September a safe-conduct was issued to him to go to the king
and return 'if he does not make peace with us'.[62] Apparently he gave hostages at this
time and undertook to go to the king, but failed to perform his undertaking. On the
31st of August, 1204, the king ordered Meiler Fitz Henry and Walter de Lacy to
summon John de Courcy to come forthwith to the king's service, 'as he had sworn and
given hostages to do', and in default to confiscate his lands.[63] Probably the list of his
hostages entered on the Patent Roll for the 6th John are those referred to. The names
are those of his principal vassals or their sons.[64] At the same time the king ordered all [140]
the barons of Ulster, who had pledged their oaths and given hostages for John de
Courcy, to cause their lord to come to the king's service, and threatened in default to
betake himself to their hostages and their fiefs.[65] John de Courcy must have still proved
contumacious. A new expedition was made by Hugh de Lacy, apparently in Septem-
ber, a battle was fought, and John de Courcy was taken prisoner. He was, however,
permitted to go free, according to one account, 'on being crossed to go to Jerusalem'.
He appears, however, to have gone to Tirowen instead.[66] On the 21st of October a new
safe conduct was given to him to Mid-Lent,[67] and this was afterwards extended till
Easter, but there is nothing to show that he availed himself of it. The forfeiture was at
last deemed complete, and Hugh de Lacy got his reward. On the 29th of May, 1205,
the king granted to Hugh de Lacy all the land of Ulster, whereof the king belted him
earl, to hold of the king in fee as John de Courcy held it on the day when Hugh con-
quered and took him prisoner in the field, rendering the service of one knight for [141]
every cantred.[68] John de Courcy, however, made a further effort to recover his lordship.
He appealed to the Pope and obtained a worthless mandate addressed to the Arch-
bishop of Armagh, the Bishop of Down, and the Abbot of Ines, to order Hugh de
Lacy, if he had unjustly made war against John, to restore what he had taken.[69] He
obtained more tangible assistance from his brother-in-law Reginald, King of Man and

60 Rot. Pat., 4 John, m. 11 (p. 15 b). 61 Ann. Loch Cé, Ann. Clonmacnois, Four Masters, 1203, Ann. Ulster, 1204. 62 Rot. Pat., 5 John, m. 6 (p. 34 b). 63 Pat. Rot., 6 John, m. 9 (p. 45). 64 Pat. Roll., 6 John, m. 1 dors (p. 55 b). The names are Milo, son of John de Courcy juvenis; Robin, son of William Salvage; John de Courcy, son of Roger of Chester; Wilkin, son of Augustine de Ridal; Peter, son of William of Haket; Alexander, son of William Sarazein; John, son of Adam the chamberlain; John, son of Richard Fitz Robert. Of these names the following appear as witnesses to John de Courcy's charter granting full jurisdiction over their men and tenements to the prior and monks of the church of Down: William Savage, Roger of Chester, William Hacket, William Saracen, Adam the chamberlain, and Richard Fitz Robert: Pat. Roll, 42 Ed. III. Milo, son of John de Courcy, is supposed by Lodge to have been son of the conquerer of Ulster and ancestor of the Earls of Kildare. He may have been son of John, son of Roger of Chester. 65 Pat. Roll, 6 John, m. 9 (p. 45 b). 66 Ann. Loch Cé, 1204. In the Ann. Clonmacnois and Four Masters (1204) and Ann. Ulster (1205) it is stated that he sought protection in Tirowen—a further indication that there was a party which favoured him there. 67 Pat. Roll, 6 John, m. 7 (p. 47) and m. 4 (p. 50). 68 Rot. Chart., 7 John, p. 151; Pat. Rot., 6 John, p. 54. A little later (June 30) the king bade Meiler Fitz Henry place confidence in the representations of Hugh de Lacy, now sent by the king as a sort of coadjutor. The justiciar was not to wage war against the marchers except by advice of Walter and Hugh de Lacy and of the other subjects of the king whose fidelity and service are necessary to maintain war. 69 Papal Letters (Bliss), vol. i, Kal. Jul. 1205.

the Isles, and, having collected a large host and a fleet of one hundred ships, he landed at Strangford harbour and proceeded to lay siege to 'the castle of Rath'. This castle has been identified with the well-known castle of Dundrum,[70] the ruins of which include a fine circular donjon tower built on a platform of rock, and possibly dating from John de Courcy's time. It guards the only practicable approach by land into Lecale, and hence the importance of securing it at once. The castle, however, was apparently too strong to be taken by assault, and John commenced the tardier operations of a siege. The effort was of no avail. Walter de Lacy came with a large army and dispersed the invading force.[71] What happened to John de Courcy is obscure. He certainly never recovered his lordship. There are numerous legends, some of them of respectable antiquity,[72] but in the absence of confirmation we can place no reliance upon them. All we know for certain is that on the 14th of November, 1207, the king granted him
[143] licence to come to England and remain with his friends, adding that when it was the king's pleasure he should no longer remain the king would give him forty days' notice.[73] Probably John de Courcy accepted this permission and became reconciled with the king, as it seems that the king afterwards made use of his services. For, as we shall see, when King John came to Ireland in 1210, fulminating wrath and destruction on Hugh de Lacy and all his kith and kin, he seems to have brought John de Courcy with him, and to have employed him specially to bring into captivity some of the fugitives from Carrickfergus. And again at a later period, on the 20th of June, 1216, just at the moment when Louis of France, to whom London had opened its gates, was besieging Winchester, John issued a mandate to all his constables to aid John de Courcy and his followers in annoying the king's enemies and in securing any booty he might acquire from them.[74] This mandate can hardly refer to any one but the former lord of Ulster. There is some evidence that early in the reign of Henry III some of his
[144] English lands were restored to him;[75] but he must have died before the 22nd of September, 1219, when a mandate was issued to the justiciar of Ireland to cause Affreca, wife of the late John de Courcy, to have dower out of the tenements of her late husband.[76]

70 Journ. R.S.A.I. 1909, pp. 23–9. It may, however, be doubted whether the circular keep was introduced so early. 71 Chron. Manniae et Insularum, 1204 (Manx Society, vol. xxii). Reginald, King of Man, is here called John de Courey's son-in-law (*gener*). He was his brother-in-law. 72 The oldest form in which these stories have reached us is to be found in the Laud MS. Annals (printed Chart. St. Mary's Abbey, Dublin, vol. ii, pp. 308–10), a transcript dating from the fifteenth century. According to this it would appear that John de Courcy was captured by Hugh de Lacy in 1204 and thrown into prison. Afterwards King John sent for him to fight a duel as his champion against the champion of the King of France. The latter, however, hearing of de Courcy's prowess, declined the combat. The two kings, after witnessing a proof of de Courcy's extraordinary strength, rewarded him, and John gave him back his lordship of Ulster. Accordingly de Courcy made fifteen attempts to land in Ireland, but failed each time through contrary winds. He then, after staying a while with the monks of Chester, returned to France, where he died. 73 Rot. Pat., 9 John, p. 77. 74 Rot. Pat., 18 John, m. 7. 75 Rot. Claus., 2 Hen. III, m. 15 dors (p. 376), where his name occurs in a list apparently of those who had returned to their allegiance, and to whom seisin of their lands was to be given. See Mr. Round's article in the Dict. Nat. Biog., and cf. the curious certificate given by Hen. III in 1251, Cal. Docs. Ireland, vol. i, no. 3202. 76 Rot. Claus., 3 Hen. III, p. 401 b.

John de Courcy left no legitimate offspring,[77] and no records are forthcoming to connect him with the Patrick de Courcy who appears in 1221 as a tenant-in-chief in Cork,[78] and who may be regarded as a progenitor of the long line of barons of Kinsale. Some relationship between the two is very probable, though on this point history is mute. But history is not mute as to the effect of John de Courcy's rule in Uladh. From his time and to his orderly rule we may trace the early prosperity of Eastern Ulster;[79] and this prosperity, though in after ages nearly destroyed, was never wholly lost.

77 Gir. Camb. v 409 (written c.1210). 78 See *supra*, p. 49 [p. 170]. 79 Few monetary records survive; but in 1226, though following on a disturbed period, the sums received from the bailiwicks of Antrim, Carrickfergus, the Ards, Blathewic (Lr. Castlereagh), and Lecale, amounted to £936. Rot. Claus., 11 Hen. III, p. 205. Thirty-six years later the sum of £464 was received by the Crown from a few manors in the northern part of County Antrim: Facsimiles Nat. MSS. Irel., pt. ii, pl. 73.

[145] CHAPTER XVIII

THE OCCUPATION OF LIMERICK, 1192–1206

While throughout the eastern half of Ireland the inhabitants were everywhere settling down peaceably to the new order of things, a forward movement was made in Munster which led to some desultory fighting, and ultimately to a large expansion of the area of Anglo-Norman occupation. As we have seen, when John came to Ireland in 1185 his insolent conduct alienated the three great potentates of the west, Dermot Mc Carthy, Donnell O'Brien, and Rory O'Conor, and they abstained from doing him homage. At this time, it seems, he made what must be regarded as 'speculative grants' of large portions of the present County Tipperary to Theobald Walter, Philip of Worcester, and others. His newly erected castles at Ardfinan, Lismore, and Tibberaghny were used as bases for expeditions into Munster, which at first appear to have met with no success. In 1192, however, a new forward movement was made. The English advanced as far as
[146] Killaloe and a little beyond into Thomond, when they were checked by Donnell O'Brien. The expedition, however, resulted in the building of the two great mote fortresses of Kilfeacle and Knockgraffon.[1] The grassy fosse-encircled mounds remain with traces of later stone-castles on their summits or in their attached baileys, and from the size of the earthworks we can judge of their early importance. The mote of Kilfeacle lies close to the road between Tipperary and Cashel, near the ancient church- site, and the castle there was one of those restored to William de Burgh in 1203, and it became the *caput* of an important de Burgh manor.[2] We may perhaps infer that it was William de Burgh who erected it in 1192. This remarkable man, afterwards known to the Irish of Connaught as 'William the Conqueror', was brother to Hubert de Burgh, John's faithful minister,[3] and progenitor of the de Burghs or Burkes, earls of Ulster, and of the Burkes of Connaught and Munster. He has generally been represented by mod-
[147] ern writers as the same person as William Fitz Audelin, who first came to Ireland with Henry II, but for this identification there is no good authority and it must be rejected. He held two knights' fees about Ardoyne, near Tullow, from Theobald Walter,[4] and it is probable that he came to Ireland with John in 1185 and received a grant in Munster[5] about the same time as Theobald received his large grant there.

1 Four Masters, 1192; Ann. Inisfallen (Dublin MS.), 1192. According to the latter annals, in 1196 the castle of Kilfeacle was destroyed by Donnell mor na Curradh, son of Dermot Mc Carthy. But it must have been soon rebuilt again. 2 Liberate, 5 John, p. 67, and see the extent of the manors which belonged to Richard de Burgh in Munster at his death (1243): Inquis. P. M., 27 Hen. III, Cal. Docs. Ireland, vol. i, no. 2607; Cal. Inquis., vol. i, p. 6. 3 Hubert de Burgh, Earl of Kent, is called by Henry III uncle of Richard de Burgh, William's eldest son: Rot. Pat., 18 Hen. III, m. 3, Cal. Docs. Ireland, vol. i, no. 2217. 4 Reg. St. Thomas's, p. 104. This grant was before 1202, when it was ratified by Giovanni di Salerno, Cardinal Legate: ibid., p. 225. 5 Probably the

The mote of Knockgraffon lies not far from the Suir above Caher. It is similar in the arrangement of its defences to that at Kilfeacle, but is even a finer example. It bears traces of a stone building on its summit, and the remains of a stone castle in its bailey. Save for the neighbouring ruins of a church with some Early English features, it rises lonely from the swelling plain, conspicuous from afar, an imperishable memorial of the expedition of 1192. In 1202 it belonged to Philip of Worcester,[6] and perhaps it was for [148]
him it was erected.

Some arrangement seems to have been made with Donnell O'Brien, as in the next year (1193) he is said to have consented to the erection of the castle of Briginis in Thomond 'for the purpose of distressing Mac Carthy'.[7] The hereditary hatred of the Dalcassians for the Eoghanachts was stronger than any jealousy of the progress of the invader. Indeed, there are other grounds for thinking that friendly relations were formed with the house of O'Brien at this time. William de Burgh is stated by an early Irish genealogist to have married one of Donnell O'Brien's daughters,[8] and as Richard de Burgh, the eldest son of this union, appears to have come of age in 1214,[9] the marriage must have taken place in 1193 at latest. Like Hugh de Lacy in Meath and John de Courcy in Ulster, William de Burgh by this alliance undoubtedly strengthened his position in Munster.

Next year (1194) Donnell O'Brien died. He had been King of Thomond and the [149]
most powerful prince in Munster from the first coming of the Normans to Ireland. His marriage with a daughter of Dermot Mac Murrough, his hereditary feud with the house of O'Conor in Connaught and with the race of Eoghan in Munster, made him in general friendly to the invaders, except when they carried their aggression beyond Leinster and seemed to threaten Thomond. Then he more than once sternly and successfully repelled them. But towards the close of his career he seems to have entered into those closer relations with the English of Munster which formed a marked feature in the policy of his sons.

The succession to the throne of Thomond now becomes somewhat obscure, probably because no successor was universally recognized. We hear repeatedly of three sons of Donnell O'Brien, viz. Donough Cairbrech, Murtough Finn, and Conor Roe. One annalist tells us that Donough Cairbrech was made king by the English,[10] but it is probable that he was not accepted as such by the Irish of Thomond. The Four Masters state that Murtough O'Brien, son of the late king, 'assumed his father's place, using a phrase which implies that he was not formally chosen by the tribesmen. At any

grant by 'John son of the King of England and Duke (*dux* ?) of Ireland to William de Burgh of half a cantred at Tilra'ct in which is Kilsela to be holden by the service of two knights' (H.M.C., 3rd Rep., p. 231), means the half-cantred containing Kilsheelan, near Tibract, i.e. John's castle, now written Tibberaghny. Both Kilsheelan (written Kilsilan) and Tiperacht were de Burgh manors (Cal. Docs. Ireland, vol. i, no. 2607). The latter was granted to de Burgh in 1200; Rot. Chart., 2 John, p. 7 b. 6 Rot. Pat., 4 John, m. 10 (p. 16). For the mote of Knockgraffon see Journ. R.S.A.I. 1909, p. 275. 7 Ann. Inisfallen (Dublin MS.), 1193. 8 See the Tribes of Hy Many (ed. O'Donovan), p. 45, a tract from the Book of Leacan, a compilation (from earlier sources) of about the year 1418. 9 On the 11th July in this year John ordered seisin to be given to Richard de Burgh of his land in Ireland: Rot. Pat., 16 John, p. 118 b. 10 Ann. Inisfallen (Dublin MS), 1194.

[151]

TABLE OF OTHE DESCENDANTS OF BRIAN BORUMHA

- BRIAN BORUMHA, K.I., sl. at Clontarf 1014
  - Murrough sl. at Clontarf
    - Turlough, sl. at Clontarf
  - Teig sl. 1023 at the instigation of his brother Donough
    - TURLOUGH, K.I., ob. 1086
      - MURTOUGH MOR, K.I., ob. 1119
        - Donnell 'Short Hand' ob. 1135
          - Conor blinded 1158 by Turlough, K.M.
            - son blinded 1158 by Turlough, K.M.
              - Murtough blinded by foreigners or by Murtough Finn (Boyle) 1194
      - DERMOT, K.M., ob. 1118
        - CONOR 'of the Fortress', K.M. ob. 1142
          - Murtough sl. 1151
            - Conor sl. 1168 by Dermot Finn (F.M.)
            - Turlough (?)
              - Mahon blinded by Donnell Mor 1175 (Tig.)
        - TEIG, K.T. blinded by his brother Brian 1153 (Tig.)
          - Dermot blinded by Donnell Mor 1175 (Tig.)
        - TURLOUGH, K.M. ob. 1167
          - MURTOUGH, K.M. sl. by Conor grand-son of Conor 1168
            - Donough Murtough Finn 1194 sl. by (F.M.)
          - Brian 'of Slieve Bloom' blinded by Donnell Mor 1169 (F.M.)
            - Murtough took castles in Ely in 1208–12
          - Dermot Finn (?) blinded by Donnell Mor 1185 (A.L.C.)
          - DONNELL MOR, K.M. ob. 1194
            - Conor Roe sl. by Murtough Finn 1203
            - MURTOUGH FINN (K.T.) imprisoned by Donough Cairbrech 1208 ob. 1239
            - DONOUGH CAIRBRECH (K.T.) ob. 1242
  - DONOUGH, K.M. deposed 1064

rate, for some years we find the three brothers acting in harmony with each other and with the English, until in 1203 Conor Roe was slain by Murtough Finn.'[11] In 1208 [150] Murtough himself 'was taken prisoner by the English of Limerick in violation of the guarantee of three bishops and by order of his own brother Donough Cairbrech'.[12] In 1210, however, 'Mariadac', King of Limerick, is mentioned in an English Roll,[13] and this name represents Murtough. He died in 1239, but from about 1210 up to his death in 1242 Donough Cairbrech seems to have been king. There were other rivals to the throne, however, not sons of Donnell O'Brien, but with rights of seniority. Two of these were got out of the way at once by, or in the interests of, Murtough Finn. Donough, son of the late king's elder brother, was killed,[14] and Murtough, representative of the senior line traced from Murtough Mor, King of Munster, was blinded and otherwise incapacitated from ruling.[15] The following table will make the relationship clearer, and will serve to indicate the ruthless way in which the claims of seniority were from time to time met by the house of O'Brien.

Whoever is to be regarded as the titular king of Thomond at this time, the chief [152] power was soon to become centred in William de Burgh. It is pretty clear that William and his companions now, or very soon afterwards, made an alliance with his brothers-in-law, the sons of Donnell O'Brien. In all probability the foreigners were to be allowed to settle in Limerick and in the greater part of the kingdom south of the Shannon (mainly at the expense of the Eoghanachts), in return for their supporting the claims of Donnell O'Brien's sons to the kingship of Thomond, as against the representatives of elder branches of the house, and in return for protection against the interference of the O'Conors. That there was some such treaty or arrangement the events of the next few years seem to show.

At first sight these events as recorded in the Irish annals present a tangled skein, hard to unravel, and even after patient study we cannot be quite sure that we follow all the threads correctly. The bare fact of an incursion is mentioned without motive assigned, and sometimes the statement is so meagre that it is not easy to assign either cause or consequence. Two results are, however, plain enough from the clearer light of slightly subsequent English records: first, that before the close of the century the town of Limerick was finally occupied by the Anglo-Normans, and henceforth became an English [153] town; secondly, that the Anglo-Norman settlement and feudal organization soon extended over the greater part of the present counties of Limerick and Tipperary.

Interpreting the annalistic records as best we can in the light of established facts, the course of events seems to have been as follows:

The year after Donnell O'Brien's death 'Philip of Worcester came to Ireland to reinforce the English of Munster'.[16] Ten years previously he had been with John in

11 Ann. Loch Cé, 1203. 12 Four Masters, Ann. Clonmacnois, 1208. 13 Rot. de Prestito, 12 John, p. 196. 14 Four Masters, 1194. 15 Ann. Ulster, Ann. Loch Cé, Ann. Boyle, 1194. John O'Donoghue, in his Historical Memoirs of the O'Briens, makes Murtough Dall or 'the Blind' the immediate successor of Donnell Mor. There may be authority for this, but he seems to be mistaken in supposing him to be Donnell's son. 16 Ann. Inisfallen (Dublin MS.), 1195. Philip of Worcester is said to have founded the Benedictine Priory of Kilcumin (Kilcommon near Caher, co. Tipperary?), c. 1184 (Harris), but the dates is probably too early.

Ireland as justiciar, and he appears to have been again sent over to take the fief of Meath into the king's hand on Hugh de Lacy's death. The large grant which Philip had probably already received about Knockgraffon in Southern Tipperary supplied a personal motive for his interference, but we may be sure he did not come without John's assent and encouragement. William de Burgh was already in Munster, and the disputed succession to the throne of Thomond gave the adventurers an opportunity of making a bargain with the sons of Donnell O'Brien as the price of their support. The latter, at any rate, made no opposition to the renewed activity of the settlers in
[154] Munster, but the King of Connaught thought fit to interfere. 'Cathal Crovderg O'Conor and Mac Costello, with some of the English and Irish of Meath, marched into Munster until they reached Emly and Cashel, and they burned four large castles and some small ones.'[17] This raid, which appears to have been quite unprovoked, was primarily directed against William de Burgh, Philip of Worcester, and their companions, whose encroachment so near his southern border Cathal no doubt viewed with concern. But Cathal probably also meant to assert the ancient supremacy of Connaught over Munster. Very significant, too, is the part played by 'Mac Costello'. We have known him hitherto as Gilbert de Nangle, or de Angulo, to whom Hugh de Lacy had given the barony of Morgallion in Meath.[18] Gilbert, however, preferred the wild ways of the Irish to the more orderly life of a feudal baron. In 1193 we find him and his band of foreigners joining the Irish in plundering Inchcleraun, an island in Lough
[155] Ree,[19] and next year he led an expedition to Assaroe, on the border of Tirconnell, but 'without much profit'.[20] This was presumably on behalf of the King of Connaught. At any rate, in 1193 he took service under Cathal Crovderg in his raid against the Normans in Munster, and for this he and probably his brother Philip were outlawed and deprived of their lands in Meath. Gilbert seems to have remained permanently in Cathal's service, and was rewarded by a grant of the cantred of Maenmagh near Loughrea.[21] He is an early example of an hibernicized Norman (or perhaps Fleming), or at least of one who cast in his lot with the Irish.

While Cathal Crovderg was engaged in this raid there was also 'a hosting by John de Courcy and the son of Hugh de Lacy [probably the younger Hugh] to assume power', we are told, 'over the foreigners of Leinster and Munster.'[22] The motive assigned is ambiguous, but they were probably sent by the government to control the operations in Munster. They seem to have summoned Cathal to Athlone, whither he came with twelve hundred men, and the parley, we are simply told, resulted in his
[156] obtaining peace.[23] What the terms were we do not know, but he was probably recognized as King of Connaught on the promise of not interfering any more in Munster,

17 Four Masters, 1195; cf. Ann. Loch Cé, 1195, where Mac Costello is said to have been 'apprehended' [by John de Courcy], but the entry is incomplete. **18** *Supra*, p. 84 [p. 183]. He was called by the Irish Gillipert Mac Goisdealbh (son of Jocelin), a name which came to be written Mac Costello, and long afterwards the barony of Costello in Mayo took its name from the family. **19** Ann. Loch Cé, 1193. **20** Ann. Loch Cé, 1194. **21** In 1207 Gilbert was pardoned, and the cantred of Maenmagh, given to him by the king of Connaught, was confirmed to him: Rot. Claus., 8 John, p. 78 b. **22** Ann. Loch Cé, Ann. Ulster, Four Masters, 1195. **23** Ann. Loch Cé, 1195.

and of good behaviour generally. At any rate, he committed no further depredation on the English for the next four years.

At some time, however, during the reign of Richard I, John appears to have made a speculative grant of the whole or part of Connaught to William de Burgh,[24] who in his turn made a similar grant of ten cantreds in the north of Connaught to Hugh de Lacy.[25] This latter grant may have supplied the motive for Hugh de Lacy's hosting at this time, and the services of John de Courcy may have been similarly enlisted. To these grants we shall recur, but for the time, at any rate, they were inoperative, and were held in suspense by the peace of Athlone.

The city of Limerick, captured, relieved, and evacuated by Raymond le Gros twenty years previously, was now in Norman hands, and apparently with the consent of the O'Briens. Next year indeed we are told that Donnell, son of Dermot Mc [157]
Carthy, defeated the foreigners and afterwards expelled them from Limerick.[26] Whatever opposition there was came from the Eoghanachts. But the expulsion can only have been for the moment. Soon afterwards, probably in 1197, we find Hamo de Valognes, the justiciar, in Limerick, making grants of burgages in that town to the leaders of the forward movement, to whom he probably at the same time made the large grants of lands in the neighbouring districts which were confirmed by King John in 1199.[27] Indeed we know that John, before coming to the throne, and probably in 1197, granted to Hamo himself 'two cantreds in Hochenil (Ir. *Ui Conaill*) in the land of Limerick',[28] and about the same time he gave a charter to the city of Limerick conferring on the citizens all the liberties and free customs enjoyed by the citizens of
Dublin.[29] He also appears to have granted to Walter de Lacy a messuage in Limerick [158]
and three knights' fees in the cantred which he retained for his own use, i.e. that near Limerick.[30] How, or exactly when, the Normans obtained possession of the city of Limerick we are not told. We hear of neither siege nor capture, nor of warfare of any sort. Irish annalists are more ready to record and even magnify the defeats and disasters of the foreigners than to mention the stages of their advance. Thus they leave us here to infer that the Normans had got possession of Limerick from the statement that in 1196 Donnell Mc Carthy drove them out.

It must be borne in mind that Limerick, though in general politically subject to the King of Thomond, was still essentially an Ostman city. Its inhabitants in 1157, and again in 1171, are called Galls or Foreigners by the Four Masters; its first four bish-

24 John's grant to William de Burgh is referred to in his subsequent grant to Richard de Burgh (September 13, 1215) of 'all the land of Connaught which William, his father, held of the King': Rot. Chart., 17 John, p. 218 b. **25** Gormanston Register, f. 189. These cantreds were the Three Tuatha (Four Masters, 1189, note), Moylurg and Tirerrill as one cantred, Corran, Carbury-Drumcliff, Tireragh on the Moy, the two cantreds of Tirawley, Erris, Leyney, and Slieve-Lugha (South of Leyney). **26** Ann. Ulster, Four Masters, 1196; Ann. Loch Cé, 1195. It is probably to this temporary loss of Limerick that some fourteenth-century MSS. of the Expugnatio Hibernica refer: [urbs Limiricensis] 'longe post sub Hamone de Valoingnes justitiario fraudulenter destructa et per Meilerium recuperata': Rolls ed., p. 342. **27** King John's grants in 1199 refer to previous grants by Hamo of burgages in Limerick, and appear to be confirmatory. **28** See John's confirmatory grant, Rot. Chart., 1 John, p. 19. **29** Rot. Cancellarie Cal. (Tresham), p. 5, no. 13, and Chartae Priv. et Immun., p. 36. **30** Gormanston Register, f. 5 dors.

ops appear to have been of Scandinavian extraction; the surrounding district on both sides of the river was 'the cantred of the Ostmen'; the first provost of the city under its new charter was Syward, presumably an Ostman; and we shall find Ostmen jurors serving on the inquisition as to the lands of St. Mary's Church. It is probable that soon after the death of Donnell O'Brien the Ostmen of Limerick transferred their alle-
[159] giance to the Normans, to whom they were more akin, not only in race, but in habits and customs, than they were to the Irish. Probably, too, the sons of Donnell O'Brien, in return for Norman support, acquiesced in the Norman occupation of the town, as they appear to have subsequently acquiesced in the Norman occupation of the kingdom south of the Shannon. The immediate granting of a charter to Limerick similar to that given to Dublin in 1192 is a clear indication that Limerick was occupied by agreement and not by force, and at a later period, about 1210, we find forty carucates of land, part no doubt of 'the cantred of the Ostmen', secured to the citizens in burgage tenure.[31]

Indeed in the year 1197 the new settlers seem to have endeavoured to carry out their part of the bargain with the O'Briens. 'Donough Cairbrech brought the English into Thomond, where they slew Covey Macnamara, Conor O'Quin, and many others.'[32] Macnamara (Mac Conmara) was by hereditary right the chieftain to inaugurate the O'Brien, and O'Quin was a neighbouring chieftain. We cannot be far wrong in supposing that the object of this expedition was to force the tribes there to accept Donough Cairbrech as king and to inaugurate him in due form on the sacred mound
[160] of Magh Adhair. Whether the object was then effected or not, the grants of lands on both sides of the Shannon showered at this time on the leaders of the forward movement, and confirmed and perhaps added to by King John in 1199, were probably made with the consent of Donnell O'Brien's sons and at the cost of the Eoghanachts and other recalcitrant chieftains. That the hereditary enmity of the Dalcassians to the Eoghanachts had not at this time diminished in fervour we have clear evidence. In 1178 Donnell O'Brien had driven the greater part of the race of Eoghan out of his kingdom; and, in particular, the O'Coilens of Lower Connello and the O'Donovans of the valley of the Maigue were forced to fly southwards over Mangerton mountain.[33] Some of the Eoghanachts still remained or had returned, and in 1199 'the whole country along the Shannon was laid waste by a great war between English and Irish'.[34]

If we may trust a late Irish writer,[35] Coilen O'Coilein, chief of Ui Conaill Gabhra, was killed at this time by the seed of Maurice Fitz Gerald. In the ensuing year (1200)
[161] 'a great army was mustered by William de Burgo and all the English of Munster, joined by Murtough Finn, Conor Roe, and Donough Cairbrech, the three sons of Donnell Mor O'Brien, and they marched through Munster to Cork. They encamped for a week at Kinneigh, where Auliffe Mor O'Donovan and Mac Costello were slain. Then came Mahon O'Heynie, the Pope's Legate, and the bishops of Munster, and

31 Rot. Chart., 17 John, p. 211. 32 Annals of Inisfallen (Dublin MS.), 1197. 33 Annals of Inisfallen (Dublin MS.). See the passage quoted and commented on by O'Donovan, Four Masters, 1178, note *m*; and cf. the Bodleian Ann. Inisfallen, 1175, 1177. 34 Ibid., 1199. 35 Michael O'Clery (one of the 'Four Masters'), in his Book of Pedigrees; see Journ. R.S.A.I. 1879–82, p. 225.

made peace between the O'Briens [on the one side] and the Mac Carthys O'Donohoes and the rest of the Eugenians [on the other].'[36]

This helps us to understand how so much of the present county of Limerick was ready to receive new rulers. Lower Connello and the valley of the Maigue, territories of the O'Coilens and O'Donovans respectively, were among the first districts settled.

We have now reached the time when, with the beginning of John's reign, our regular records commence, in a stream thin at first, but gradually increasing in volume. Henceforth we are able to check, interpret, and supplement the Irish annals and English chronicles by a more authoritative source. In particular we are enabled to gain some idea of the extent of the new settlement of the Normans in the counties of Limerick and Tipperary about the year 1200, and to trace the beginnings of the more important manors there.

In September 1199, when Philip Augustus was commencing hostilities against John, [162]
the latter at Rouen and other places in Normandy made a number of grants of lands within the kingdom of Limerick on both sides of the Shannon. In most cases a grant of one or more burgages in the town of Limerick was also made, and these burgages are stated to have been already delivered to the grantees by Hamo de Valognes, when justiciar. We may infer that the grants themselves were really confirmatory of what had already been done in John's name by Hamo a year or two earlier. It is hard to identify some of the Irish place-names, disguised as they are by the strange spelling and positive blunders of scribes and transcribers. To attempt to do so in all cases would involve an unduly minute investigation, and we shall content ourselves with mentioning only such grants as seem to have been the origin of the more famous manors of later times.

To Hamo de Valognes himself John confirmed his grant of 'two cantreds in Hochenil in the land of Limerick', to hold by the service of ten knights.[37] The tribal territory designated appears to have included the whole western half of the present county, but Hamo's two cantreds were probably comprised in the present baronies of Upper and Lower Connello. A kite-shaped island in the river Deel, two miles from its [163]
source, was chosen by Hamo as the seat of his principal manor, and here in 1199 he built the castle of ASKEATON.[38] There is a rocky platform with precipitous sides in the middle of the island, and on this the ruined keep and inner ward of a later castle stand. This was no doubt the site of Hamo's castle. He was superseded as justiciar by Meiler Fitz Henry, but he got letters of protection and a special licence to colonize his lands.[39] In 1203, presumably after Hamo's death or forfeiture, John ordered the castle to be delivered to William de Burgh.[40] In 1207 Hamo's land and castles were restored to his son and heir Hamo, at the time a minor,[41] and in 1215 seisin was given to him.[42] All through the thirteenth century a Hamo de Valognes was tenant-in-chief in Lim-

36 Ann. Inisfallen (Dublin MS.), 1200. 37 Rot. Chart., 1 John, p. 19. 'Hochenil' represents the Irish *Ui Conaill* or Ui Conaill Gabhra: Topogr. Poems, p. 116. 38 Ann. Inisfallen (Dublin MS.), 1199. Askeaton represents the Irish *Eas Géibhtine*, 'the cataract of G.'—probably a man's name. In early records the castle is generally called Iniskefty (variously disguised), pointing, in an earlier stage of phonetic rendering, to *Inis Géibhtine.* 39 Rot. Chart., 2 John, p. 96 b. 40 Liberate, 5 John, p. 67. 41 Rot. Claus., 9 John, p. 96 b. At this time the custody was given to Hugh de Neville. 42 Rot. Pat., 17 John, p. 147.

[164] erick,[43] but about the middle of the next century the manor of Askeaton passed to the Earl of Desmond. The first Hamo appears to have granted the church of Askeaton (with others) to the abbey of Keynsham in Somerset,[44] and, as we have seen,[45] it was apparently with one knight's fee at Culballysiward and a tenement at Bruree, that he compensated Archbishop Cumin for the injuries he had done to him.

Three of the sons of Maurice Fitz Gerald shared in the exploitation of the land of Limerick, as they had, doubtless, shared in subduing such chieftains as resisted. Thomas, son of Maurice, now recognized as the progenitor of the House of Desmond, was probably granted at this time the lands which were afterwards known as the cantred of SHANID, and there can be little doubt that the castle-crowned mote of Shanid, long afterwards called 'Desmond's first and most ancient house', represents the seat of the manor created at this time.[46] His son John Fitz Thomas granted the church of 'Senode'
[165] (Shanid) to the church of St. Mary of Limerick,[47] and held the cantred called Shennede of the king in chief.[48] From him it descended to [see *Add.*] Thomas, son of Maurice (Fitz Gerald), the justiciar [see *Add.*], who died in 1298.[49] Probably about the same time the first-named Thomas's brother Gerald, who married the daughter of Hamo de Valognes [see *Add.*], and was ancestor of the earls of Kildare, obtained CROOM in the valley of the Maigue.[50] It was held by his successors until forfeited by Silken Thomas in the sixteenth century. These two castles supplied the war-cries of the two houses— 'Shanid aboo!' and 'Crom aboo!' —and each became the nucleus of several additional manors acquired from time to time. A third brother, William of Naas, was granted the castle of CARRICKITTLE in the parish of Kilteely, with five knights' fees near the castle.[51] Near the village of Kilteely there was a remarkable rock (now mostly quarried away) rising sheer out of the plain, on which the earl of Kildare
[166] built a castle in 1510. This was presumably the site of the twelfth-century castle.

William de Burgh had lands about Kilfeakle in the barony of Clanwilliam, County Tipperary. Here, as we have seen, a mote-castle was erected in 1192, and near at hand he founded the Augustinian priory of Athassel, about the year 1200.[52] Extensive ruins of this priory remain and attest its former magnificence. The main building has been assigned on architectural grounds to the middle of the thirteenth century.[53] The manor of Kilsheelan, too, on the Suir below Clonmel, where a mote marks the castle

43 In the time of Edward I, *Hamund de Valoniis* owed eight services to the Crown; Irish Exchequer Memoranda, Eng. Hist. Rev. 1903, p. 506. 44 Black Book of Limerick, no. lv (p. 47), to be read with no. xcv (p. 84). 45 *Supra*, p. 132, note [p. 203, note 51]. 46 In the Charter Roll, 1 John, p. 19 b, is a grant to Thomas son of Maurice of 'five knights' fees in the thwedum [Irish, *Tuath*] of Eleuri and cantred of Fontimel'. The position of this cantred is, however, doubtful. I have attempted to show that it may have included Shanid (Joum. R.S.A.I. 1909, pp. 34–9). In any case the manor of Shanid was held in chief by John FitzThomas, and the original grant probably dates from his father's time. 47 Black Book of Limerick (ed. Mac Caffrey), p. 114. 48 Cal. Inquis. P. M., Ed. I, vol. ii, p. 252. 49 Cal. Docs. Ireland, vol. iv, pp. 260, 340. 50 In 1215, when Gerald's son Maurice came of age, he obtained seisin of his father's lands and of the castle of Crumeth (Croom) of his inheritance: Rot. Pat., 17 John, p. 147. 51 Rot. Chart., 1 John, p. 196. David, third Baron of Naas, gave all his land of 'Karkytil' to his daughter Matilda in frank marriage with John Pincerna: Gormanston Register, f. 192 dors. 52 Ware. In 1206 King John confirmed the prior and canons in their possessions, without the demesne of William de Burgh, and granted them protection: Rot. Chart., 7 John, p.165. 53 See Paper by Dr. Cochrane, Journ. R.S.A.I. 1909, pp. 279–89.

site, probably belonged to William de Burgh from even an earlier period,[54] and both it
and Kilfeakle were important manors of his son Richard.[55] In 1199 John gave William
de Burgh ARDPATRICK with part of the cantred of Fontimel [*see Add.*].[56] This is sup-
posed to refer to the place now known as Knockpatrick, in the parish of Robertstown, [167]
north of Shanid. A castle is said to have been built at Ardpatrick in 1198,[57] but noth-
ing else is known to connect the de Burghs with the place. Perhaps it was forfeited by
William de Burgh along with other lands in 1203, and not restored.[58] In the year 1201
John is said to have given the tuath of CASTLECONAING (Castleconnell) to William
de Burgh, 'yet so that if he shall fortify the castle, and we shall desire to have it in our
own hands, we shall give him a reasonable exchange for it'.[59] The castle here was built
on an isolated flat-topped rock, close to the Shannon, above Limerick. The manor
belonged to William de Burgh's descendants for many centuries. At least one other
manor in the County Limerick belonged to William de Burgh. This was the manor of
ESCLON[60] (Ir. *Aes Cluana*), a district now comprised in the parish of Kilkeedy,[61] in the [168]
barony of Pubblebrian. The 'castle of Askelon' (under which more familiar title that
of Aes Cluana first appears) was 'restored' to Richard de Burgh in 1215,[62] and the
manor appears afterwards as belonging to him and his descendants, earls of Ulster. In
all probability the castle-site was that well known as Carrigogunnell (properly Carraig
Ui Coinnell, or the 'Rock of the O'Connells') though in the thirteenth century the cas-
tle is nearly always called, from the district or manor, the 'Castle of Esclon'.[63] The [169]
site—'a volcanic plateau of trap rock and ash falling in low cliffs at nearly every
point'— is marked out by nature as the castle-site of the district. Indeed, like that of
Castleconnell, it was probably occupied by a fortress in pre-Norman times. No part of
the existing building, however, is supposed to date from the thirteenth century.

54 The grant by 'John son of the King of England and Duke of Ireland to William de Burgh of half a cantred at Tilra'ct in which is Kilsela, to be holden by the service of two knights' (H.M.C. 3rd Rep., p. 231), probably refers to Kilsheelan. 55 Cal. Docs. Ireland, vol. i, nos. 2422, 2607. 56 Rot. Chart., 1 John, p. 19 b. 57 Ware's Annals, 1198. There is another Ardpatrick near Kilmallock. 58 Robert de Guher had a castle not far off from quite early in the thirteenth century. 59 Ware's Annals, and Ann. Inisfallen (Dublin MS.), 1201. It was probably the site of an Irish fortress. According to the Four Masters it was 'at their own house at *Caislén ui Conaing*' that Donnell O'Brien blinded two of his rivals to the throne, in 1175. 60 William de Burgh made a grant of some lands of his fee of Escluona to Donatus O'Brien, Bishop of Limerick, ob. 1207; Black Book of Limerick, p. 110. 61 'Ecclesia de Escluana alias Kylkyde cuius Rector est prior de Athissell': Taxation, 1418, Black Book of Limerick, p. 146. 62 Rot. Pat., 17 John, p. 147 b, where it appears as 'Askelon'. 63 Mr. Westropp, however, thinks that the two castles were distinct (see his Paper, showing great research, on Carrigogunnell Castle, Journ. R.S.A.I. 1907, pp 379–82); but his principal argument against their identity, viz. that 'Carrigogunnell was granted in 1209 (*sic*) to O'Brien, while Esclon was held by de Burgo', loses all force and indeed supports the opposite view, when we recollect that the manor of Esclon was in John's hand from 1206, when William de Burgh died (Rot. Pat., 7 John, p. 60 b), until 1213, when Richard, his son, came of age and obtained seisin of his father's lands (Rot. Pat., 16 John, p. 118 b). This very fact would enable John to deal with the castle and manor, and in the Annals of Inisfallen, the sole authority for the supposed inconsistent 'grant', it is merely stated that Donnough Cairbrech O'Brien at Waterford (i.e. in 1210) 'received a charter for Carrigogunnell and the lordship thereunto belonging, for which he was to pay a yearly rent of sixty marks' (see Four Masters, anno 1209, p. 163, note). John was quite capable of making a grant in fee of his minor's property, but after all it appears that he did nothing inconsistent with the minor's rights—at least, not by this charter.

Geoffrey de Marisco (or Mareis), who was Geoffrey nephew of Archbishop Cumin, and played an important, but not always creditable, part in the affairs of Ireland, had a manor at Anya (*Aine*, now KNOCKAINY), though it is not certain that he was the first grantee.[64] Near this, at Hospital, he founded a preceptory for knights of St. John before 1215.[65] In 1226 he was granted a fair at this manor, and also at Adare on the Maigue,[66] which may have belonged to him from the first. After his outlawry, [170] *c.*1236, both manors escheated to the Crown. Anya was for some time retained by the king, but Adare soon passed to the Fitz Geralds of Offaly.

Geoffrey Fitz Robert, baron of Kells in Ossory, appears to have been the first grantee of the manor of Grene or Esgrene[67] (*Aes Gréine*, now PALLAS GREEN). After his death it came into the king's hand, when it was let to the Bishop of Emly, who confirmed the gift of the church (evidently Geoffrey's gift) to the monastery of Kells.[68] In 1233 the manor was granted during pleasure to Maurice Fitz Gerald of Offaly.[69] About forty yards from the later castle-site at Pallas Green is a mote.

The castles erected by the lords of these manors were probably all of the keep and bailey plan. Like those found almost universally in the earlier settlements in the east of Ireland, the works at Shanid and Pallas Green, and perhaps at Adare, Aney, and other places, included a mote or artificial mound of earth as a substratum for the *turris* or keep. The castle-sites at Askeaton, Castleconnell, Esclon (Carrigogunnell), and [171] Carrickittle appear to have comprised an isolated rock forming a natural substitute for an artificial mound of earth. In these cases probably the tower and its defences were of stone from the first. In the occupation of the kingdom of Limerick south of the Shannon the settlers were assisted by the O'Briens, and seem to have met with comparatively slight opposition. Hence there was the less need of hastily throwing up earthworks. Rock-sites suitable to their purposes were often at hand, and being able now to obtain the skilled labour required and the necessary materials they could build more leisurely and more effectively in stone.

The property of the see of Limerick was respected, and in 1201 an inquisition was held by William de Burgh, who is described as 'Vicar of Munster', as to its lands. This inquisition was taken by the oaths of 36 jurors, composed of 12 Englishmen, 12 Ostmen, and 12 Irishmen (including Conor Roe O'Brien), and was certified by Meiler Fitz Henry, the justiciar.[70] At this time the bishop was Donough or Donatus O'Brien, presumably a member of the ruling family, who had been appointed about the time of the English occupation. John had already granted him protection, and the royal letter

64 Perhaps the grant of 'Katherain' with ten knights' fees to Geoffrey (Rot. Chart., 2 John, p. 80) refers to Aine, but the mandate (Cal. Docs. Ireland, vol. i, no. 529) that the men of Anya (i.e. the Hospitallers ?) were to hold their lands as in the time of William de Lacy seems to imply that the latter had been owner. 65 Ware's statement to the above effect is partly confirmed by the mandate in 1215 that 'the knights of the valley of Anya should have their liberty saving a moiety of their service to the king': Cal. Docs. Ireland, vol. i, no. 673; cf. nos. 675, 676. 66 Rot. Claus., 10 Hen III, p. 126. 67 Register of the Monastery of Kells. In the Charter Roll, 1 John, p. 28, is a grant to Geoffrey Fitz Robert of a fee of five knights at 'Radhoger' in the cantred of Huhene (Uaithne), which probably included Pallas Grean. 68 Rot. Claus., 18 John, p. 279; Register of Kells. 69 Cal. Docs. Ireland, vol. i, no. 2045. In 1234 Maurice was granted a fair at his manor of Gren: ibid., no. 2182. 70 Black Book of Limerick, nos. xxiii, xxiv.

speaks warmly of the bishop's devotion to John's interests.[71] About the same time the Cistercian abbey of Monasteranenagh was confirmed in the possession of a long list [172]
of lands about Lough Gur.[72]

Other grants were made by King John in September 1199, or soon afterwards—some of them dealing with lands to the north of the Shannon—but those mentioned above were historically the most important, and may suffice to show the system adopted in the feudalization of North Munster. The whole 'kingdom' was not conveyed in one vast fief to a single grantee to be sub-infeudated and organized by him, but the land was parcelled out by the king himself among a number of tenants-in chief, most of them holding five knights' fees or even smaller quantities, and rendering in knight-service one-third of that quota to the Crown.

In January 1201, however, John disturbed this arrangement, and with his usual capriciousness reverted to the former policy of making one supreme lord, by granting the honour of Limerick to William de Braose.[73] William was nephew of Philip de Braose, who had been granted the 'kingdom of Limerick' by King Henry in 1177, but, as we have seen, Philip had failed to prosecute his claims, and the grant had been treated as lapsed. William de Braose was a great landholder in Sussex and Devon, and
in the Breichiniog in Wales. He is represented by Giraldus as an excessively pious [173]
man, always prefacing his actions by saying, 'Let this be done in the name of the Lord,' paying his clerks extra for concluding his letters with the words 'by divine assistance', and never passing a church without saying a prayer.[74] Nevertheless, this piety did not restrain him from acts of the grossest cruelty and treachery, such as the massacre of the chieftains of Gwent at Abergavenny Castle in 1176.[75] William de Braose was connected with some of the magnates of England. Giles, one of his sons, was Bishop of Hereford. One of his daughters was married to Gruffudd ap Rhys, and another to Walter de Lacy. He had been a strong supporter of John's succession to the throne, and in the year 1200 John had granted him all the lands which he had acquired, or might in future acquire, from the king's enemies of Wales as an increase to his barony of Radnor.[76] Soon afterwards John thought further to reward him and benefit his own pocket by the sale to him of the honour of Limerick for 5,000 marks, to be paid at the rate of 500 marks a year. The honour was co-extensive with Henry's
grant to Philip de Braose, that is to say, it included the whole 'kingdom of Limerick', [174]
and was to be held by the service of sixty knights. There were some exceptions from the grant. The king retained in his demesne the city of Limerick, the gift of bishoprics and abbeys and all royalties, the cantred of the Ostmen, and the Holy Island. A special exception was made of the lands and tenements of William de Burgh, who was still in favour, and was to continue to hold of the king in chief.

This grant, as might have been anticipated, created a flutter among the settlers in North Munster. By it Theobald Walter and Philip of Worcester, who held vast districts in the County Tipperary, and the new grantees other than William de Burgh in

71 Ibid., no. xxxix, apparently before John's accession. 72 Rot. Chart., 2 John, p. 78. 73 Ibid., p. 84 b. 74 Gir. Camb.; Itin. Camb. 75 Brut y Tywys. 1175, p. 227. Giraldus minimizes the connexion of William de Braose with this affair. 76 Rot. Chart., 2 John, p. 66 b.

the County Limerick, were deprived of the privileged position of tenants-in-chief, and were reduced to the subordinate status of under-tenants owing fealty to William de Braose. Moreover, they would have to make terms with their new lord if they were to continue to hold their lands. Theobald Walter, indeed, procured a contemporaneous grant of his lands from William de Braose for the sum of 500 marks. By this grant, which is still extant, William granted to Theobald five and a half cantreds in Munster (being in fact the lands which Theobald had previously held under John's grant of 1185), to be held of William by the service of twenty-two knights.[77] Philip of Worcester, on the other hand, tried the arbitrament of the sword,[78] and 'a great war broke out'
[175] between him and William de Braose, and Magh Feimhin (a plain to the north of the Suir, including Knockgraffon) was wasted by them.[79] Even Meiler Fitz Henry, the justiciar, appears to have been reluctant to carry out the king's mandates touching the affair of William de Braose, until the king summoned him to come to him and put the government into commission consisting of Humphrey de Tickhill and Geoffrey de Costentin.[80] Then in August 1202, John sent a peremptory mandate to Philip of Worcester to deliver up to William de Braose all his lands and castles, including Knockgraffon, in the honour of Limerick.[81] Philip probably submitted, as we find him
[176] in 1207 and afterwards employed by John in confidential affairs of state,[82] and in 1215, after the outlawry of William de Braose, Philip was granted five cantreds in Southern Tipperary, including the castles of Knockgraffon, Kiltinan, and Ardmayle.[83]

With regard to the city of Limerick, John's policy was marked by even greater tergiversation. At first the custody was given to William de Burgh, but in the opening years of the thirteenth century, as we shall see in the next chapter, William de Burgh was actively engaged in the affairs of Connaught, and in 1203 came to loggerheads with Meiler, the justiciar, and fell under the suspicion of the king himself. Accordingly, on the 8th of July in this year, John gave the custody of Limerick to William de Braose at the yearly farm of 100 marks.[84] Disturbances, however, continued, and on the 2nd of November, 1204, John ordered Walter de Lacy, who acted as bailiff for his father-in-law, William de Braose, to deliver up the city to Meiler, as the king had been informed (probably by Meiler himself) that he could not maintain peace in his lands of Connaught and Cork, nor rule those lands unless he held in his hand the city of
[177] Limerick with the cantred[85] (of the Ostmen). It is not clear what action, if any, was immediately taken under this mandate. At any rate, on the 23rd of August, 1205, John once more gave the custody of Limerick to William de Braose.[86] At this moment the

77 Facsimiles Nat. MSS. Ireland, vol. ii, no. lxvii, and see supra, p. 102 [n. 191]. The parcels were as follows: the burgh of Kildelo (*Cill da lua*, Killaloe) with half the cantred called Truoheked Maleth (*Tricha ced o m-bloid*) in which the burgh is situated, and the entire cantred of Elykaruel (*Eile ui Cearbhaill*, the baronies of Clonlisk and Ballybrit, King's County), Elyhohogarthy (*Eile ui Fhogartaigh*, Eliogarty), Ewurmun (*Oir Mumhan*, Ormond), Areth and Wetheni (*Ara* and *Uaithne*, Ara and Owney, Tipperary), Owethenihokathelan (*Uaithne ui Cathalain*), and Owenihoiffernan (*Uaithne ui h-Ifearnain*)—these two last were districts in Owney beg, County Limerick: Topogr. Poems, p. 130. 78 Roger de Hoveden, iv. 153. 79 Ann. Inisfallen (Dublin MS.). 80 Rot. Pat., 3 John, p. 4. 81 Ibid., 4 John, p. 16 b. 82 Cal. Docs. Ireland, vol. i, nos. 377, 379, 385. 83 Rot. Pat., 17 John, p. 147 b. 84 Rot. Chart., 5 John, p. 107; cf. Ann. Loch Cé, 1203. 85 Rot. Pat., 6 John, p. 47. 86 Rot. Claus., 7 John, p. 47 b.

de Lacys were high in favour with the king, and Meiler was ordered to wage no war except by their advice.[87] It was probably in the winter of 1206–7 that Meiler, son of Meiler Fitz Henry, took Limerick by force.[88] Hence, it is said, great disturbances broke out between Meiler and the de Lacys in Meath. Before the 12th of February, 1207, William de Braose complained that Meiler and his son had seized his constablewick (Limerick), his knights, men, land, and chattels, although he had not been wanting in right; and John, with characteristic double-dealing, while ordering the knights, land, &c., to be restored, directed Meiler to retain the city of Limerick if it had been taken into the king's hand,[89] and on the 21st ordered that Meiler's son should not answer for [178]
the taking of Limerick except before the king.[90] It is easy to believe that William de Braose did not find his Irish lordship very profitable, but he was soon to lose it and everything else at the hands of his vindictive and ruthless master.

87 Ibid., p. 40. 88 Four Masters, 1205 (probably antedated by one year). Walter de Lacy appears to have been again bailiff for William de Braose in Limerick. See the king's letter to the barons of Meath, Feb. 21, 1207: Rot. Pat., 8 John, p. 69. Up to this date the barons had been quiet. 89 Rot. Claus., 8 John, p. 77 b. A month later the king seized Walter de Lacy's castle of Ludlow, and summoned him to stand to right in the king's court: Rot. Pat., 8 John, pp. 69 b, 70 b. 90 Rot. Pat., 8 John, p. 69. It is clear that these mandates refer to the forcible taking of Limerick by Meiler's son, wrongly placed by the Four Masters *sub anno* 1205. Miss Norgate has, I think, here missed the true sequence of events: John Lackland, pp. 144–5.

[179] CHAPTER XIX

WILLIAM DE BURGH IN CONNAUGHT, 1200–6

At the close of the twelfth century, when the settlers in the kingdom of Limerick were beginning to establish their manors, and to extend the feudal organization throughout the district, the aggressive action of Cathal Crovderg O'Conor and his conflict with his rival, Cathal Carragh, afforded at once a pretext and an occasion for the interference of the English in Connaught. Accordingly the affairs of that province now demand our attention.

Since 1177, when Murrough O'Conor brought Miles de Cogan into Connaught 'for evil towards his father',[1] no attempt against the king of that province seems to have been made by the English. In 1183 Rory O'Conor, we are told, 'went on his pilgrimage' to the monastery of Cong and left the sovereignty in the hands of his son, Conor Maenmoy.[2] Probably the ex-*ard-rí* was forced into this cloistral retirement by the more energetic spirit of his son. The latter was clearly not disposed to observe the restric-
[180] tions of the treaty of Windsor, and next year we find him in company with an O'Melaghlin invading Meath and destroying an unnamed castle.[3] In 1185 Rory 'came from his pilgrimage', but, like many another king, he found it easier to lay aside than to reassume the reins of authority. A general war broke out in Connaught among the 'roydamnas' or aspirants to the throne. These were Rory himself, Conor Maenmoy and Conor O'Dermot (sons of Rory), Cathal Carragh (son of Conor Maenmoy), and Cathal Crovderg, a younger brother of Rory. Rory obtained the assistance of Donnell O'Brien, and the English of Munster—assistance which took the form of burning and pillaging the churches of the west of Connaught. In spite of a patched-up peace, Cathal Carragh in retaliation burned and plundered Killaloe. Conor Maenmoy, who was aided by some English mercenaries, now once more assumed the kingship, and next year expelled his father from Connaught.[4] In 1187 Conor Maenmoy, anxious probably to secure his position by some exploit against the English, made an incursion
[181] into West Meath, and burned and demolished the castle of Killare.[5] It was in reply to this attack, and probably with the object of reinstating Rory O'Conor, that next year John de Courcy, the justiciar, and the English of Ireland, accompanied by two of Rory's sons, made the unsuccessful expedition already noticed into Connaught.[6] In 1189 Conor Maenmoy, who seems to have been a strong king, was murdered by his own people at the instigation of his brother, Conor O'Dermot.[7] The Sil Murray,

1 *Supra*, p. 26 [p. 161]. 2 Ann. Loch Cé, 1183. 3 Ann. Loch Cé, 1184—if indeed this entry be not anticipatory of the destruction of Killare in 1187 (Four Masters). 4 For these events see Ann. Ulster, Ann. Loch Cé, and Four Masters, 1185–6. 5 Four Masters, 1187. 6 *Supra*, p. 116 [pp 196–7]. 7 Ann. Loch

Rory's own tribe, now invited Rory to resume the kingship, but his own family would not support him. Cathal Crovderg must now be regarded as King of Connaught, though he was opposed by some influential tribesmen, and an attempt by the successor of Patrick (the Archbishop of Armagh) and others to reconcile him and Cathal Carragh proved unavailing.[8]

As for Rory O'Conor, we find him in 1191 going to Tirconnell, then to Tirowen, then to the English of Meath, and lastly to Munster, seeking in vain for assistance to recover his kingdom. Finally the Sil Murray gave him some lands in the south of the County Galway, and he died in 1198, in the monastery of Cong. Modern writers usually characterize him as a weak and irresolute prince, and regard it as the crowning [182]
misfortune of his country that he should have been *ard-rí* at the time of the English invasion. But the records in the Irish annals show that just before the coming of the English Rory O'Conor came more nearly to forcing his rule over the length and breadth of Ireland than any provincial king had succeeded in doing since the days of Brian. There is no reason to suppose that any one else would have fared better. It was the clan-system and the weakness and irresolution inherent in it, rather than lack of courage and determination in any individual, that rendered continuous and united opposition to the foreigners impossible. There was no national sense of country—only a 'tribal patriotism' and consequent anarchy.

From the above summary it appears that as early as 1185 there were some English in Connaught. They were mercenary troops employed by Conor Maenmoy in his struggle against his father, and probably consisted of a body of deserters in that year from John's army.[9] Then in 1193–5, as we have seen,[10] Gilbert de Nangle, with a band [183]
from Meath, took service under Cathal Crovderg and joined in Cathal's Munster raid of the latter year. For this Gilbert was outlawed, but he obtained the cantred of Maenmagh, a district about Loughrea, County Galway, from Cathal, and remained permanently in his service.

Cathal Crovderg's position as King of Connaught was probably recognized by the Peace of Athlone (1195), whatever the exact conditions of that peace may have been; and for the following four years he confined his military operations to his own province, where he was still opposed by influential chieftains. In 1199, however, he broke out again, burned the bawn of Athlone, killed many persons, and carried off many cows.[11] A mote-fortress appears to have been already erected here—perhaps under the conditions of the Peace of Athlone—to guard the ford (or wooden bridge) across the Shannon at this strategic point. The existing castle commands the gate of Connaught, and has had an eventful history, but in all the storm and stress through which it has passed it has embraced within its strong walls, up to the present battle-

Cé, 1189. Conor O'Dermot was killed in the same year as Cathal Carrach. 8 Four Masters, 1190. 9 *v. supra*, p. 101 [pp. 190–1]. Conor Maenmoy is described by the Four Masters (1189) as 'King of all Connaught both English and Irish', and after his death when the king of Tirconnell entered Connaught 'all the Conacians both English and Irish came to oppose him'. In the Gesta Hen. (i. 339) it is said of John's army, 'Maxima pars equitum et peditum qui cum eo venerant ab eo recesserunt, et ad Hibernenses contra eum pugnaturos perrexerunt.' 10 *v. supra*, p. 154 [p. 213]. 11 Ann. Loch Cé, 1199. The text has simply *bodhun Atha*, 'the bawn of the ford,' but as the editor says, *Ath-luain* (Athlone) is probably meant.

[184] ments on the river-side, a great mass of made earth, which, there is little doubt, represents a mote such as the Normans at this time usually raised for their fortresses.[12] Next year (1200) Cathal Crovderg, with Mc Costello in his company, followed up this exploit by a cattle-raid in West Meath.[13] These were unprovoked attacks. Now came the turning-point. He led a hosting against Cathal Carragh, with whom he had made peace in the previous year, and to whom he had assigned lands in the extreme south of the province. This is described by the annalist as 'a treacherous and malicious hosting, of which came the destruction of Connaught and his own destruction'.[14] It was indeed the occasion of renewed civil war in Connaught, with consequent ravaging and plundering of the province. The assistance of powerful Anglo-Norman lords was invoked by one side or the other. There was shifting of alliances, and a good deal of (at first sight) confused fighting. It resulted in the definite dependence of the kings of Connaught on the English Crown, and the gradual acquisition of lands or of claims to lands here and there in the province by William de Burgh and others, and ultimately,
[185] about a generation later, to the effective partition of the province and the virtual domination of William de Burgh's son. In order to see how the first stages of these important results were brought about it will be necessary to recount briefly the main facts of the conflict between the two Cathals, and, in particular, of the part played by the English therein, as they may be gleaned from the annals,[15] filling up gaps and testing the story, as far as may be, from the English records and other available sources.

Cathal Crovderg's attempt to entrap Cathal Carragh did not succeed, and a detachment sent to capture him was badly beaten. Cathal Carragh, however, knew that he could not stand up alone against the King of Connaught, so he invoked the assistance of William de Burgh, at this time governor of Limerick, and delivered to him his own
[186] son as a pledge for the pay of the foreigners. William de Burgh had a score to pay off against Cathal Crovderg for the Munster hosting of 1195, and perhaps for the burning of 'the bawn of Limerick and Castleconnell' early in 1200.[16] The King of Connaught had also forfeited the favour of the Crown by his attack on Athlone and raid into Meath. It is probable that William de Burgh thought the moment favourable to endeavour to make effective John's grant to him of Connaught, to which we have alluded. Accordingly he assembled a large force from Dublin and Leinster as well as from Limerick and Munster, and, accompanied by two of the sons of Donnell O'Brien and their Irish forces, came to the assistance of Cathal Carragh. Some of the

12 See my paper, 'Athlone Castle: Its Early History,' Journ. R.S.A.I. 1907, pp. 257–76. 13 Ann. Loch Cé, 1200. 14 Ibid. 15 The various annalists do not differ materially as to the chief events of these campaigns or as to their sequence, but vary as to the dates. The fullest and most coherent account, and apparently the true chronology, are given in the Annals of Loch Cé. Thus John de Courcy's intervention (and the death of Rory Mac Dunlevy) are fixed to the year 1201 by Roger de Hoveden. John, cardinal priest and papal legate, was in Ireland in August 1202 (Rot. Pat., 4 John, m. 10, Cal. no. 168). William de Burgh's turning against Cathal Crovderg seems to be fixed to the year 1203 by John's mandate of the 7th July of that year granting a safe-conduct to William (Rot. Pat., 5 John, p. 31 b), and by the grant of the custody of Limerick to William de Braose on the following day. 16 It is not quite certain that this took place before William's advance into Connaught. It is given as an isolated entry near the end of the entries for the year 1200 in the Annals of Loch Cé.

Connaught tribes at once gave hostages to Cathal Carragh, and Cathal Crovderg, unable to face the forces opposed to him, retreated to the north of Ireland to seek assistance there. Then the rest of Connaught was harried ruthlessly into submission, and Cathal Carragh assumed the nominal kingship.

Next year (1201) Cathal Crovderg made two attempts to recover his kingship. In the first he was accompanied by O'Neill, King of Tirowen, and O'Hegney, King of Fermanagh, but the combination failed through disunion in the camp. The northern [187]
chieftains, when they undertook the campaign, understood that there were no foreigners against them, and they refused to face William de Burgh. The consequence was they were cut off in detail. O'Hegney was slain, and O'Neill had to give hostages. In the second attempt Cathal Crovderg was assisted by John de Courcy and Hugh de Lacy. The latter, as we have seen, had received a speculative grant from William de Burgh of the northern third of Connaught,[17] but as he was ostensibly acting on behalf of Cathal Crovderg, whom William had just expelled from Connaught, he can hardly have been relying at this time on William's grant. It appears, in fact, that John, when Earl of Mortain [see *Add.*], had made a similarly speculative grant to Hugh de Lacy of six cantreds in the north of Connaught,[18] and it was probably in the hope of taking possession of these that Hugh made this second expedition in company with John de Courcy into Connaught. According to the Irish annals he marched through three of [188]
the cantreds granted to him by John, namely Corann, Moylurg, and Moy Ai. Then he went further south as far as Kilmacduagh in the attempt to recover the spoil which Cathal Carragh had driven off. The host, however, was caught in a pass through the woods, and defeated, and John de Courcy with difficulty led his army back by Tuam and Roscommon to Rinn-dúin, and so by boats across Lough Ree.[19]

And now a curious change of alliances took place, the cause of which is obscured by what seems to be a mutilation in the annals. Up to this point William de Burgh, and apparently the English government too, favoured Cathal Carragh; but now, at the moment when Cathal Crovderg had twice failed to recover his kingdom, the support of both William and the Crown was transferred to him. How is this change of policy to be explained? We are told that 'when the foreigners arrived in Meath (i.e. after the retreat across Lough Ree) they arrested Cathal Crovderg as a pledge for the payment of wages, and that he [Cathal] was taken to Dublin until he gave pledges for himself that he would obey the King of the Saxons'.[20] In all probability Cathal Crovderg at [189]

17 *Supra*; p. 156 [p. 214]. **18** See the cancelled charter of King John to Hugh de Lacy in 1204, confirming the grant of six cantreds in Connaught made by the king when Earl of Mortain: Rot. Chart., 6 John, p. 139 b. The cantreds were the Three Tuatha, Moylurg-Tirerrill, Moy Ai, Corran, Slieve Lugha, and Leyney, to be held of the king in fee by the service of twenty knights. It was not until about 1229 that Hugh de Lacy obtained an effective grant in Connaught, and then the grantor was William de Burgo's son Richard: Gormanston Register, f. 189. **19** Ann. Loch Cé, 1201. Rinn-dúin, 'the Point of the dun,' is a promontory jutting into Lough Ree. It was afterwards the site of an important castle, as to which see Journ. R.S.A.I. 1907, p. 274. **20** This is the translation of the passage as it originally stood in the Annals of Loch Cé, but the name Eoain (John) has been interlined, so as to make the passage mean that John de Courcy was taken to Dublin and gave the pledges. But it is probable that the statement as originally written was correct.

this time, in consideration of being recognized as King of Connaught by the English king, and being assisted to recover his throne, agreed to surrender some lands in Connaught to the Crown. We can even fix pretty confidently what these lands were. In November 1200 John had granted to Geoffrey de Costentin a cantred near Athlone afterwards known as the Fews of Athlone, and in April 1201 this grant was amplified by the addition of the adjoining cantred of Tirmany. Probably Cathal now agreed to the surrender of at least these cantreds. At any rate, it is certain that from this time forward Cathal Crovderg was supported by the Crown, even when William de Burgh turned against him, and that he soon agreed to give even a larger slice of his territory to the Crown.

As to John de Courcy, we have the independent account of Roger de Hoveden that he was treacherously entrapped in this year (1201) by Hugh de Lacy, his late compan-
[190] ion-in-arms, into his castle[21] 'for the purpose of delivering him up to the King of England, who had long wished to take him', but that John de Courcy's men ravaged the lands of the de Lacys until their lord was delivered up to them.[22]

On November 2, 1201, the king gave a secret commission to Meiler Fitz Henry, William de Burgh, and Geoffrey de Costentin, and commanded the barons of Meath to have faith in what these commissioners should tell them on the king's behalf.[23] This may have been the way the new policy of supporting Cathal Crovderg was communicated. At any rate, Cathal himself, on being released, went to William de Burgh, who, in accordance with the new policy, early in 1202, accompanied by Murtough Finn, Conor Roe, and Fineen Mc Carthy, marched with Cathal Crovderg into Connaught and proceeded to fortify himself at the monastery of Boyle. While the fortification was going on, Cathal Carragh was killed in a skirmish in the neighbourhood. Thus the war came to an end. The O'Briens and Fineen Mc Carthy returned to their homes, William de Burgh's troops were billeted throughout Connaught, while William himself and Cathal Crovderg went in all friendship to spend Easter at Cong.

[191] But to secure peace it is not always enough for rulers to agree, if their peoples are not friendly at heart. Besides, in this case it was Cathal's people who had to pay in the coin of cows for past services. On a false rumour that William was dead the Connaught men acted 'as if they had taken counsel together', and each tribe killed the foreign soldiers billeted upon them, to the number altogether of 900 or more. We may acquit Cathal of all treachery in this matter, and yet not wonder that this massacre led to a rupture between him and William de Burgh.[24]

21 This was no doubt the castle of Nobber, to which, as stated in the Annals of Clonmacnois, Cathal Carragh (*recte* Cathal Crovderg) was also at first taken. The Annals of Inisfallen mention that John de Courcy 'was taken prisoner by the sons of Hugh de Lacy, by the advice of the King of England'. 22 Roger de Hoveden, 1201. 23 Rot. Pat., 3 John, p. 2 b. 24 Ann. Loch Cé, 1202. In describing this massacre as the consequence of a plot by de Burgh against Cathal's life, Miss Norgate does not display her usual care; nor in calling William a double-dyed traitor does she show her usual restraint of language (John Lackland, p. 139). The account in the Annals of Loch Cé, 1202, hints indeed at an uneffected plot, but as the direct consequence, not the cause, of the massacre. Even the entries in the Annals of Clonmacnois followed by the Four Masters (a much inferior authority, especially for Connaught) do not warrant this harsh judgement on William de Burgh. It is true that he twice changed his alliances; once apparently in consequence

So far William de Burgh had clearly acted in accordance with the new arrangement with Cathal Crovderg, but now, early in 1203, accompanied by the sons of Conor Maenmoy, he entered Connaught, probably to take possession, in spite of Cathal [192] Crovderg, of some lands which he had been granted there, perhaps by King John in 1195, perhaps by one or other of the Cathals. He erected a castle at Meelick, near the Shannon, in the County Galway, 'and the spot where the castle was erected was round the great church of the place, which was filled round about with earth and stones up to the gables.'[25] In other words, it seems that the church of Meelick was used as the core of a mote for the new castle. From this castle William de Burgh and his Connaught allies devastated the country, going as far as Knockmoy, Mayo, and Cong. Cathal was unable to resist him, until Meiler Fitz Henry, the justiciar, and Walter de Lacy summoned William to Limerick in the name of the king.

Evidently the Crown still held by the arrangement with Cathal Crovderg. William then submitted, recalled the garrison of Meelick, and surrendered Limerick and his Munster castles to Meiler as the king's representative.[26] In the July of this year the king gave William a safe conduct to and from the king's court, provided he answered the complaints made against him by Meiler.[27] At the same time the custody of Lim- [193] erick was given to William de Braose.[28] By October William de Burgh had been to the king and was so far restored to favour that the lands he had pledged and the castles of Kilfeakle and Askeaton were to be restored to him, but the justiciar was to keep in safe custody William's sons and other hostages.[29]

Evidently John was not very angry with William de Burgh. Meiler, however, formulated complaints against him, and he against Meiler. In March 1204 the king took the unusual course of appointing a special commission to try and determine the cross plaints between Meiler and William.[30] A month later John virtually overrode the jurisdiction of this commission by respiting all plaints against William de Burgh (whom he intended at the time to take to Normandy with him) and commanding the justiciar to give full seisin to William or his agents of all his lands except the land of Connaught, which was to remain in the king's hand.[31] It would appear, however, that this mandate [194] was not immediately carried out, as it was virtually repeated in the September following. William had undertaken to stand his trial in the king's court in Ireland to answer all appeals, and Connaught was to be retained in the king's hand (theoretically, we must suppose) pending the result of the trial.[32] How the trial ended, or whether it ever took place, does not appear. William returned to Ireland, but only to die in the winter

of the changed policy of his lord, and again in consequence of the treacherous massacre of his troops. If for such changes he deserved to be called 'a double-dyed traitor', what words are left for, say, Donnell O'Brien? **25** Ann. Loch Cé, 1203. I have given the words their literal meaning, and this rendering brings out the nature of the work more clearly than the editor's rendering. **26** This is evident from the statement in the Annals of Loch Cé (1203) of what occurred, when read in connexion with the records. Up to this period William de Burgh had the confidence of the king. **27** Rot. Pat., 5 John, p. 31 b. **28** Rot. Chart., 5 John, p. 107. **29** Liberate, 5 John, p. 67. Askeaton, as we have seen, must have been granted to William de Burgh after Hamo de Valognes' death or forfeiture. **30** Rot. Pat., 5 John, p. 39 b. The commissioners were Walter de Lacy, Henri de Londres, then archdeacon of Stafford, Godfrey Lutterel, one of the king's trusted officers, and William Petit. **31** Rot. Pat., 5 John, p. 41 b. **32** Rot. Pat., 6 John, p. 46.

of 1205–6.[33] In April 1206 Meiler Fitz Henry was ordered to take into the king's hand all William's lands.[34] His son Richard was a minor, and did not get seisin until 1214.[35]

The annalist of Clonmacnois, a place which William de Burgh had plundered from his castle of Meelick, shows his animus against him and exhibits the prevailing superstition of the time by ascribing his death to a loathsome disease inflicted on him by God and the patrons of the churches he had plundered. But the translator adds: 'These and many other reproachful words my author layeth down in the old book, which I was loath to translate because they were uttered by him for the disgrace of so
[195] worthy and noble a man as William Burke was, and left out other his reproachful words which he (as I conceive) rather declared of an evil will he did bear towards the said William than any other just cause.' O'Donovan, assuming, as has been usually done, that William de Burgh was the same person as William Fitz Audelin, endeavours to defend the annalist as against the translator by adducing the unfavourable description of Fitz Audelin given by Giraldus.[36] It is strange that O'Donovan did not perceive that this description could not possibly apply in its entirety to William de Burgh. Giraldus again and again sneers at the slothfulness and cowardice of William Fitz Audelin,[37] but these qualities were surely alien to the 'William Burke' of the annalists. William de Burgh was probably neither better nor worse than other vigorous spirits of the age, but no man could master two provinces of Ireland in the course of a decade, as he did, without being both energetic and brave.

As to the plundering of churches and monasteries so often laid to the charge of eminent Anglo-Norman leaders—and indeed to Irish chieftains too—by the monkish annalists, a further word of explanation may be advisable. If we may judge from the number and magnificence of their religious foundations in Ireland, these leaders were certainly not wanting in piety as understood at the time, while the plunder and destruction of churches, as such, was obviously not a military measure. But it was the custom of the Irish to store their corn and other property within the sanctuary of a church, presumably as being safer there than elsewhere. In proof of this we have not only the direct statement of Giraldus that this was the custom, and that in view of it Cardinal Vivian, the papal legate, in 1177 gave permission to the English, on any expedition when they could not get supplies elsewhere, to take what they found in the churches on payment of a just price.[38] At this particular time, however, the men of Connaught, by way of creating desolation before the advance of Miles de Cogan, with their own hands burned what provisions they could not conceal, together with the churches in which they were stored.[39] But the Irish annals themselves afford other
[197] instances. Thus in the very passage describing the harrying of Connaught by Cathal

33 Ann. Loch Cé, 1205. 34 Rot. Pat., 7 John, p. 60 b. 35 Ibid., 16 John, p. 118 b. Another son, Hubert, became Prior of Athassel and afterwards (1223) Bishop of Limerick. 36 Four Masters, 1204, note *o*. 37 Giraldus speaks of Fitz Audelin as 'Imbellium debellator, rebellium blanditor; hosti suavissimus, subdito gravissimus' (v. 338); he also exclaims at his unfitness for a lord-marcher, 'strenuitate carens' (p. 352), one whose maxim was 'Hostibus illaesis semper spoliare subactos' (p. 391), and much more to the same effect. 38 Gir. Camb. v. 346; cf. the statement on p. 137 that the Irish, not having any castles, used to seek protection for themselves and for their goods in churches. 39 The Annals of Loch Cé, 1177, here virtually corroborates Giraldus, see above, p. 27 [p. 162].

Carragh and William Burke and the two O'Briens, it is said that they carried off 'all the property, stock, or food that was in the churches, without regard to saint or sanctuary or any earthly terror.'[40] In 1214 Thomas Mac Uchtry and Rory Mac Rannall 'carried off the precious things (goods) of the community of Derry, and of the north of Ireland besides, from the middle of the great church of the monastery.'[41] In 1236 Richard de Burgh, endeavouring to quell disturbances in Connaught, went to Tuam and Mayo and other ecclesiastical centres, 'and not a stack of seed or corn of all that was in the great *relig* (churchyard) of Mayo, or in the *relig* of the church of Michael the Archangel, was left without being taken away; and threescore or fourscore baskets were brought out of these churches.'[42] Now to reduce to submission an enemy that will not meet you in the field, and that possesses no castles or fortified towns which might be taken and held against him, almost the sole, and certainly the most merciful, military measure is to cut off his provisions and destroy his property. At the present [198] day we are perhaps more soft-hearted, but certainly not more pious than the Normans, and if circumstances should render the taking of a church a measure of prime military importance there is no general who would hesitate to sound the assault. It was not the methods of William de Burgh, but his policy, that the Irish annalists viewed with disfavour. Had he been an Irishman with the same record he would have been described as 'Flood of the glory and prowess of the Western World.' By some Irish writers he is called 'William the Conqueror', and though he did not fully earn that title he was at least the 'King-maker' of Connaught. No one there could stand against him, and the subsequent kings of Connaught remained subject, and in general obedient, to the English Crown.

40 Ann. Loch Cé, 1200, p. 212, where the words of the text for what was carried off are *cach crodh ocus cach eallach nó bhídh is na templuib.* 41 Ann. Loch Cé, 1213; Ann. Ulster, 1214. The word here, *sét*, translated 'precious things', was used to designate goods and chattels of any kind: O'Donovan's supplement to O'Reilly's Dictionary. 42 Ann. Loch Cé, 1236, p. 339.

[199] # CHAPTER XX

WILLIAM THE MARSHAL IN IRELAND, 1207–13

At the commencement of the year 1206 William de Burgh and Theobald Walter were both dead. They were succeeded by minors, and their lands were taken into the king's hand. John de Courcy, too, had been banished from Ulster. The leading figures among the Anglo-Normans were Hugh de Lacy, now Earl of Ulster; his brother Walter, Lord of Meath; Meiler Fitz Henry, the justiciar in Dublin; and in Munster, Walter de Lacy as seneschal for William de Braose, and Geoffrey de Marisco, Thomas Fitz Maurice, and other large landholders there. But early in 1207 there appeared in Leinster a William greater than any of these in the person of William Marshal, as he is usually called, Earl of Pembroke and Striguil and Lord of Leinster. Writers of Irish history have said little about this great man, and that little in important points wrong, partly because until recently not much was known of his doings in Ireland. Now, however, we have a most valuable biography of William Marshal in the form of an Old French
[200] poem or rhymed chronicle.[1] From its concluding verses the editor infers that it was composed by a professional *trouvère* at the request of William Marshal the younger, from materials, which probably took the form of written memoirs, supplied by John d'Erleé, one of the Marshal's most faithful followers.[2] The work appears to have been completed about the year 1226. For us it supplies several new facts concerning William Marshal in Ireland, throws fresh light on an obscure page of the history of the country, and helps us to form a true estimate of King John's character as displayed in his dealings with his Irish barons.

William Marshal was born about the year 1144. His father, John, son of Gilbert, succeeded to the office of Marshal of England granted to Gilbert by Henry I. The
[201] office was hereditary, and supplied a surname for the family. In 1152, when about eight years old, William was given as a hostage to King Stephen, then besieging Newbury. His life, according to the rules of war, became forfeit, and it was proposed to place him in the sling of a *pierrière* and hurl him into the castle. But Stephen, won over by the trustful ways of the child, who asked to be given a swing in the machine, would

1 L'Histoire de Guillaume le Marechal, Comte de Striguil et de Pembroke, ed. Paul Meyer, 1891–1901.
2 John d'Erlée received his name from a village now called Early in Berkshire, not far from Reading. In Latin documents it appears as Erleia, Erleya, Erleg', Erlegh'. He is first mentioned in the Histoire in 1188, when he was William's esquire, and he appears frequently afterwards. He accompanied his lord to Ireland in 1207 (Rot. Pat., 8 John, p. 69), and was given the custody of Southern Leinster when William was summoned back by John. He witnessed the Marshal's charters to Tintern, Dunbrody, Duiske, and Kilkenny, and was granted lands in the County Kilkenny, where the parish name Erleystown (now corruptly Earlstown) long preserved his name.

not allow him to be injured, and then we have the pretty picture of the king in his tent playing at jack-straws with the little boy.[3] William is said to have grown to be a well-formed man, perfect in limb as a beautiful statue, with brown locks and a presence that would grace a Roman emperor. 'He who made him,' says the poet, 'was a great Master.'[4] During the years 1170–83 he was a member of the household of Henry 'the young king', a victor in many a tournament, and ever faithful to his lord—even in his revolt against his father—up to the day of his death. He then went to the Holy Land in vicarious fulfilment of the young king's vow, and after his return was one of King Henry's most faithful followers to the last.

It was about May 1189 that Henry, lying ill at Le Mans, promised William the hand of Isabel de Clare, the heiress of Leinster, in recompense for his good service,[5] and ordered Hubert Walter, then Ranulf de Glanville's clerk, to give him possession of the [202]
lady and her land on his return to England. When in the following month Henry was flying from Le Mans with the Marshal guarding the rear, Richard of Poitou overtook them. The Marshal turned and spurred towards Richard. 'God's limbs! Marshal,' cried Richard, 'slay me not. That would be foul. I have no hauberk.' 'Nay,' replied the Marshal, 'may the Devil slay thee, for I will not'; and with that he plunged his lance into the horse, threw the rider, and stopped the pursuit.[6] When less than a month later Richard met William beside Henry's bier at Fontevrault, he not only bore him no ill will, but confirmed his father's gift to him of the *damisele d'Estregoil*, and sent him on an important mission to London.[7] On the way he visited the Pays de Caux to take possession of his bride and of some lands there to which she was entitled by inheritance.[8] Then, after accomplishing his mission in England, he married Isabel in London, at the house of the sheriff.

Soon afterwards we have an instructive scene. John refused to give the Marshal seisin of his Irish lands, and the latter had to seek the king's intervention. Richard [203]
insisted, and John reluctantly consented, 'provided,' he said, 'the grants of lands I have made to my men hold good and be confirmed.' 'That cannot be,' said the king. 'For what would then remain to him, seeing that you have given all to your people?' Finally, John asked that the land he had given to Theobald Butler (*au boteillier Tiebaut*) should be left to him. To this the king consented, provided Theobald held of the Marshal in chief.[9] This was not the only case in which John endeavoured to create tenancies to be held of himself in chief in lands which he only possessed in wardship. As we have seen,[10] he seems to have done the same thing in Cork with the lands of Miles de Cogan, and there were probably other cases both in Meath and Leinster.

3 Histoire G. le Mar., ll. 467–650. 4 Ibid., ll. 715–36. 5 Ibid., ll. 8303, &c. 6 Histoire G. le Mar., ll. 8837–49. Gerald de Barry (viii. 236) alludes to this incident, though without mentioning the Marshal's name. 7 Ibid., ll. 9321–71. 8 Ibid., ll. 9455–62. Longueville was the *caput* of the fief, which came to Isabel through her father. 9 Ibid., ll. 9581–618. John in Henry's reign had granted Arklow to Theobald Walter, and William Marshal, probably in pursuance of the above arrangement, made a similar grant with additions including Tullow. See Carte's Ormond, Introd., p. xlvi, where Carte was puzzled by the two grants of the same place by different persons. The above scene explains the difficulty. 10 *Supra*, pp. 45–6 [pp 168–9].

William Marshal did not go to Ireland to take possession of his fief, but sent Reinalt de Kedeville as his bailiff or seneschal for that purpose. The writer of the Histoire calls
[204] Reinalt a rogue, and intimates that he played false to his lord.[11] William himself was now appointed by Richard one of the subordinate justiciars of England, first under Hugh, Bishop of Durham, and then under William de Longchamp, and he held some office of this kind during the whole time Richard was absent from England.[12] Modern writers, following Walter Harris's Table of Chief Governors of Ireland, place William Marshal in that capacity from 1191 to 1194.[13] But, as we have seen, Harris's list, in the early portion at any rate, is full of errors. As for William Marshal, no authority has been pro-
[205] duced for inserting him in the list, no charters executed by him as governor are forthcoming, not a single act is anywhere ascribed to him in Ireland at this time, and his position and doings in England during these years seem to negative the possibility of his holding office in Ireland. Moreover, it was very much against his will, and only at the king's command, that John put William Marshal in possession of his lands; and we shall find John, when king, refusing William permission to go to Ireland to visit his fief, intriguing against his interests there, and endeavouring to thwart him in every way. The appointment, if made, must have come from John, and John is unlikely to have made it.

After Nottingham was surrendered to Richard in person in 1194, the chancellor (meaning, apparently, William de Longchamp) called upon Walter de Lacy to do homage to the king for his land in Ireland. This Walter did. Then the chancellor called upon William Marshal to do the same. But William refused, saying that it would be felony to John, to whom he had done homage for all that he held of him, and that he would deceive nobody by flattery. The king thereupon said he was right and the barons approved. William added: 'If any man in the world seeks to obtain Ireland, I shall range myself with all my force on the side of him whose man I am. I have faith-
[206] fully served our lord the king here for the land I hold of him, so that I have nothing to fear.'[14] One does not know which to admire most, the fearlessness of the Marshal or the good-humoured toleration of the king.

William appears to have been almost continually in Normandy with Richard up to the time of the king's death. He was one of the principal supporters of John's succession, and received from John the formal investiture of the earldom of Pembroke and a confirmation of the office of marshal of the household.[15] He may have paid a brief

11 Hist. G. le Mar., ll. 9619–30. In the lines 'Reinalt de Kedevile, un fals / Veirement fu de Kedevile / Quer toz diz le servi de gile' there is an evident play on the name, which puzzled the editor. Might not the place-name have suggested the word *chétif* to the *trouvère*? The place intended may have been, as M. Meyer suggests, Quetiéville (formerly Chetivilla, Ketelvilla, Keteuvilla) or Quetteville, both in Calvadoz. Probably the 'caitiff' played into the hands of John in his intrigue with Meiler against the Marshal's lands. 12 Walter of Coventry, vol. i, pp. 378, 388, 432. William was given the custody of Nottingham Castle on July 28, 1191 (ibid., p. 462), and was acting against William Longchamp in the following October (ibid., vol. ii, p. 5). In March 1193 he was besieging Windsor with his Welsh followers: Roger de Hoveden, iii. 206; Gerv. Cant., vol. i, p. 515; Hist. G. le Mar., l. 9898, &c. 13 Harris did not invent the statement; for though Ware and Hanmer are silent, Cox makes William Marshal governor from 1191 to 1197. 14 Hist. G. le Mar., ll. 10289–340. 15 Roger de Hoveden, iv. 90; Rot. Chart, 1 John, p. 46. On November 12, 1207, John granted to William Marshal's nephew, John Marshal, the marshalcy of Ireland and the cantred of Kilmeane near Roscommon: ibid., 9 John, 173 b.

visit to Ireland in the winter of 1200–1.[16] Certain Latin annals place the founding of the monastery de Voto or Tintern (County Wexford) in this year, stating that William, when in peril by sea, vowed that if he reached land in safety he would erect a monastery to Christ and His mother Mary.[17] This he did at the head of Bannow Bay, and we may conjecture that the Marshal's ship found refuge in the bay not far from [207]
where Robert Fitz Stephen first landed in Ireland. William brought monks from the Cistercian house of Tintern in Monmouthshire to supply the Monasterium de Voto, and hence the latter came to be known as 'Tinterna Minor'. As to the date, however, the charter by which William endowed his new foundation has been preserved to us in an inspeximus and confirmation of the time of Richard II,[18] and from the names of the witnesses it would seem to belong to the period 1207–13, during which William was almost continuously in Ireland. The vow, of course, may have been made some years earlier.

We need not here follow William Marshal's career in Normandy and England during the early years of John's reign. Suffice it to say that he became more and more estranged from the king. When through John's supineness Richard's 'Saucy Castle' [208]
had fallen and Normandy was hopelessly lost, William was one of those who thwarted John's belated efforts to lead an expedition against Philip, and this no doubt contributed to John's ill will. But John was jealous of William's reputation, power, and independence, and would have humbled him if he could. William's unswerving loyalty and tact, however, gave him no opportunity.

About the close of the year 1206 the Marshal sought John's leave to go to Ireland to visit his lands there. The king gave an unwilling consent. He had been often asked to grant this leave, but hitherto had always refused.[19] William had not got beyond his castle of Striguil, however, when he was overtaken by a messenger from the king demanding his second son as a hostage. William's eldest son was already a hostage in the king's hands, and a less prudent man than William would have refused this new demand. Disregarding the advice of his countess and his barons, he told the messenger that he would gladly send all his sons to the king if he desired it; 'but,' he added, 'tell me, for the love of God, why he acts thus towards me?' The messenger replied [209]
that the king desired above all to prevent the Marshal going to Ireland. 'By God,' said the Marshal, 'for good or for ill I shall go, since he has given me permission.' On the morrow he sent his son Richard to the king and set sail for Ireland.[20]

16 He can be traced with John's court every month up to the 3rd September 1200, but from this date to March 1201 we seem to lose sight of him in the records. 17 Annals, Laud MS., Chart. St. Mary's, Dublin, ii. 307, and cf. ibid., p. 278. 18 Chartae Priv. et Immun., p. 80. The names of the witnesses mentioned are those of William's feudatories: Jordan de Saukvill, John d'Erlée, John Marshal, William and Maurice de Londres, Walter Purcell, Baldwin and Robert Keting, William Chevre, Nicholas Brun, and Philip the Cleric. Of these John Marshal was sent by his uncle to Ireland in 1204 to take over the seneschalship of his lands and castles: Rot. Pat., 5 John, p. 42. John d'Erlée came to Ireland with his lord in 1207; Rot. Pat., 8 John, p. 69. Jordan de Sauqueville and Walter Purcell were in Ireland with the earl in 1207–8; Hist. G. le Mar. (*infra*, p. 211 [p. 235]). Compare, too, the witnesses to the earl's charters to Kilkenny, Dunbrody, and Duiske, all of which seem to date from about the same time. 19 Hist. G. le Mar., ll. 13311–20. The writer says that William had never seen his lands; but if the date (1200) assigned for the founding of the Monasterium de Voto (or even for the vow) be correct, this statement cannot be accurate. 20 Hist. G. le Mar., ll. 13335–422.

And now opens a story of intrigue against the Earl Marshal which we should never be able to piece together without the Histoire, but which, confirmed as it is on many points by the records (which it explains), we may confidently accept as in all essentials true.

When the Earl Marshal landed in Ireland, most of his men, we are told, welcomed him with honour, but some there were who in their hearts were much chagrined at his coming. Foremost among these was Meiler Fitz Henry, the justiciar. It appears indeed from the records that Meiler, while in general only carrying out John's orders, had by his high-handed action in one way or another aggrieved many of the magnates of Ireland and despoiled them of their rights. His action towards William de Burgh was hardly justified by the king. He had, as we have seen, taken Limerick by force from
[210] Walter de Lacy, who held it for William de Braose, and the king had not scrupled to profit by the violence.[21] He had also by John's orders taken into the king's hand the whole of the kingdom of Cork and made a number of new grants there, which were subsequently confirmed by the king, and which apparently ignored the seignory of the heirs of the original grantees, and perhaps disallowed the rights of some of the former tenants.[22] In Leinster, on no apparent legal grounds, he had taken Offaly into the king's hand, and, as we shall see, he seems also to have taken possession of Fircal in Meath; and when the barons of Meath and Leinster attempted to get redress they were indignantly reprimanded by the king.[23] William Marshal's name is not mentioned, but he was aggrieved by the seizure of Offaly, and presumably supported his barons. At any rate, Meiler is said to have told the king that if he permitted the Marshal to remain long in Ireland it would be to his detriment. John summoned both the Marshal and Meiler to his presence. This was probably in October 1207. Meiler reached the king early in November, apparently before the earl.

[211] Anticipating disturbance, the earl made his arrangements. He gave the custody of his lands to Jordan de Sauqueville and John d'Erlee, and left with them his cousin, Stephen d'Evreux, and some of the knights he had brought with him, and bade them act by the advice of Geoffrey Fitz Robert, Walter Purcell, Thomas Fitz Anthony, and Maillard, his standard-bearer.[24] Then the earl summoned his barons to Kilkenny. Leading his countess by the hand before them, he said: 'My lords, you see here your rightful lady, daughter of the earl who liberally granted you your fiefs when he had

The king's protection for the lands of William Earl Marshal while in Ireland is dated Feb. 19, 1207: Rot. Pat., 7 John, p. 69. He was accompanied by Henry Hose and John d'Erlée. **21** *v. supra*, p 177 [pp 221–2]. **22** *v. supra*, p. 45 [p. 168], and see Meiler's grants in Desmond referred to in Rot. Pat., 8 John, p. 71 b. **23** This was on May 23, 1207: Rot. Pat., 8 John, p. 72. The barons were charged with establishing a 'new assize'. Perhaps Meiler had been summoned to answer for his conduct before the chief courts of the Liberties; cf. Rot. Pat., 9 John, p. 76 b, translated, Early Statutes (Berry), p. 3. **24** Hist. G. le Mar., 13424–512. Stephen d'Evreux (or de Ebroica, Chart. St. Mary's, Dublin, ii. 183) was perhaps founder of the family of Devereux in co. Wexford. Geoffrey Fitz Robert [see *Add.*] had been, and perhaps still was, the earl's seneschal: Reg. St. Thomas's, p. 125. He has been confounded with, but must be distinguished from, his namesake, the second husband of Basilia de Clare. He speaks of his wife, Eva de Bermingham, as living, in a charter witnessed by Hugh le Rous, Bishop of Ossory, i.e. after 1202. Basilia's husband was living 1199–1201: Reg. St. Thomas's, no. cxxix; and she seems to have survived him: ibid., cxxvii, cxxxvi.

conquered the land. She abides here in your midst *enceinte*. Until God brings me back again I pray you all to guard her well and loyally, for she is your lady. I have naught here except through her.' They all promised to do right, but some of them failed to keep their words.[25]

No sooner had the earl landed in Wales on his way to the king than Meiler's men [212]
and kinsfolk raided his territory. They burned his granges at his newly formed port, now known as New Ross, slew twenty of his men, and carried off a prey from the town. And thus the disturbances commenced.[26]

Meanwhile Meiler was with the king at Woodstock on the 8th of November, when the new grants in Cork were confirmed. According to the biographer of the Earl Marshal, Meiler offered to raise a host at his own cost and take both William de Braose and William Marshal prisoners and bring them to the king. As a preliminary he got the king to send letters summoning to England John d'Erlée, Stephen d'Evreux, Jordan de Saukeville, and other leading followers of the Marshal,[27] under penalty of losing the lands which they held of the king in England. The king, too, gave permission to [213]
Meiler to return to Ireland,[28] but when the Earl Marshal afterwards asked for leave to return it was refused.

Meiler, on arriving in Ireland, found that matters had not gone well with his friends, several of whom were in prison for their misdeeds. He summoned the earl's men to a parley at Castledermot,[29] and there the king's messenger gave them the royal letters recalling them to England. They took counsel together and were convinced that the king meant to disseise their lord. Accordingly they decided to remain in Ireland and defend the land which the earl had entrusted to them. They then sought aid from [214]
Hugh de Lacy, Earl of Ulster, who speedily came with 65 knights and 1,200 men, and they devastated Meiler's lands.[30] Here we have a confirmation with fresh details in the Irish annals. 'The sons of Hugo de Lacy,' we are told, 'and the English of Meath marched to the castle of Ardnurcher, and continued to besiege it for five weeks, when it was surrendered to them, as was also the territory of Fircal, and Meiler was ban-

25 Hist. G. le Mar., ll. 13527–50. **26** Hist. G. le Mar., ll. 13551–74. M. Meyer is unfortunate in his suggestion that the *novele vile* of l. 13569 is Newtownbarry, a town which only got its name from an ancestor of Lord Farnham in the latter part of the sixteenth century. It is undoubtedly the *villa novi pontis*, or New Ross, where John stopped on June 21, 1210—a town which clearly owed all its early importance to William Marshal. **27** Ibid., ll. 13575–670. The editor could find no trace of these letters, but that they were actually sent appears from the Close Rolls. On February 20, 1208, John wrote to the Earl Marshal as follows: 'We have ordered that the land which John de Erleg' held of your fee and which was taken into our hand be restored to you. We caused him to be disseised because for more than two months he failed to come to us after being ordered to do so We desire you to send back him and the others whom we lent you, and that they come to us since we have need of their service, and until they return we shall hold their lands in our hand': Rot. Claus., 9 John, m. 8, p. 103. On March 19, 1208, John ordered the sheriff of Buckinghamshire to deliver Jordan de Saukeville's land to William Marshal (ibid., p. 106 b); and on the 20th there is a similar order as to John d'Erlée's English lands (ibid.). **28** Meiler probably returned to Ireland soon after Nov. 14, 1207, when he was with the king at Gloucester. The events next related must have taken place before the end of March 1208, when the king became reconciled with the Earl Marshal. **29** The text of the Histoire is here corrupt, and the placename disguised. Meiler held his *parlement hors ceiste* [or *teiste*] *de mot* (1. 13697); but we can confidently restore *tristerdermot*, the usual Anglo-Norman form of the Irish 'Disert Diarmada', now Castledermot. **30** Hist. G. Ie Mar., ll. 13680–786.

ished from the country.'[31] Ardnurcher had been granted to Meiler by the elder Hugh de Lacy, but from this entry it would seem that Meiler claimed Fircal (an adjoining district in King's County, but belonging to Meath), adversely to Walter de Lacy—just as he claimed Offaly adversely to William Marshal, and Limerick adversely to William de Braose. Probably Meiler had acted according to John's directions throughout. If so, we must regard this widespread disaffection among the Irish barons at this time as the Irish counterpart of the disaffection which grew to a head among the barons of England a little later, and as due to the same cause: the capricious, oppressive, and, as we
[215] would now say, unconstitutional action of the Crown.

Meanwhile, Earl William, who was following John in his movements in England, knew nothing of what was going on in Ireland. Indeed, as seems to have often happened, all communication with Ireland was cut off during the winter.[32] One day at Guilford[33] the king asked the earl if he had heard any good news from Ireland. On the earl replying in the negative, John told an imaginary tale of how the countess had been besieged at Kilkenny by Meiler, how Meiler had at last been beaten, but John d'Erlée, Stephen d'Evreux, and Ralph Fitz Pain had been killed. The earl was much grieved at this, but wondered to himself how the king could have got the news. When Lent came both king and earl learnt the facts: that Meiler had been beaten and taken Meiler prisoner, and had been obliged to make peace with the countess and give his son Henry as a hostage, and that Philip de Prendergast and the rest who had taken Meiler's part had also given hostages.[34]

Having failed to humble the Earl Marshal by means of Meiler, John executed one
[216] of his rapid changes of front. He took both William Marshal and Walter de Lacy into favour, restored to them their lands, discredited Meiler, and before long superseded him in the office of justiciar. The steps by which this change was effected are all attested by the records. On the 7th of March, 1208, probably soon after the authentic news came from Ireland, John informed Meiler that William Earl Marshal had shown himself sufficiently submissive to the king's will, and ordered the justiciar to observe the existing peace in Ireland, adding that if any raids had been made by the justiciar's people on the earl's land the justiciar should make the best amends he could, the earl having given a reciprocal undertaking.[35] This mandate and the authenticity of the letters recalling the marshal's chief men go far to confirm the story told in the marshal's biography. On the 19th John gave a similar order with regard to Walter de Lacy.[36] On the 20th he sent Philip of Worcester and others to see that his orders were carried out.[37] On the 21st he ordered Meiler to give seisin to the earl of the land of Offaly with
[217] its castles, for which, however, the earl was to give 300 marks;[38] and on the 28th he gave

31 Four Masters, 1207; cf. Ann. Loch Cé, 1207. Perhaps the beginning of 1208 was the true date. In this latter year the annals also mention Geoffrey Mareis or de Marisco as defeating some of Meiler's men at Thurles: Ann. Laud MS., Chart St. Mary's, Dublin, ii, p. 311. 32 It is said in the Histoire, ll. 13672–5, that Meiler's was the only ship that crossed over from Michaelmas (1207) to *la Chandelor* (February 2, 1208). 33 John was at Guilford, January 25–27, 1208. 34 Hist. G. le Mar., ll. 13787–888. 35 Rot. Claus., 9 John, p. 105. Probably the earl at this time assented to the restrictions on behalf of the Crown afterwards inserted in the new charter of Leinster. 36 Ibid., p. 106 b. 37 Ibid. They were to be summoned to the councils of the justiciar: ibid., p. 107. 38 Rot. Pat., 9 John, p. 80 b.

to the earl a new charter of his land of Leinster.[39] This was followed a few weeks later by a similar charter to Walter de Lacy of his land of Meath.[40] The exact date of Meiler's supersession is unknown, but according to the Annals of Inisfallen Hugh de Lacy was appointed justiciar in this year.[41]

The earl returned to Ireland, landing at Glascarrig probably in April. He dealt generously with those of his men who had acted against him,[42] and restored to them their hostages. Afterwards Meiler, no longer justiciar, came to terms with him. He agreed to give up to him at once his castle of Dunamase, the remains of which (or rather of some later reconstruction) may still be seen crowning a rock in Queen's County, and after his death all the rest of his land[43]—a pretty clear admission that it had been wrongfully [218]
taken.

In the next chapter we shall see that Earl William, through his sheltering William de Braose from John's wrath, once more fell under that capricious king's ill will, but with the exception of a campaign in Wales in 1211, when William fought for his unworthy master, he seems to have remained in Ireland until early in 1213. He was then once more summoned to England by John, who, when in difficulty, knew his real worth and (almost excessive) loyalty to the throne. After this it is doubtful if he ever resided in Ireland again. At most he can only have visited his lands for brief periods. From this time up to the death of the king the earl appears to have been one of John's principal coun- [219]
sellors, and certainly when regent for Henry III he did not leave England.

I have dealt with the life of the great Earl Marshal, so far as it was concerned with Ireland, in some detail, because trustworthy details concerning him, though not generally known,[44] happen to be forthcoming, and we are thus able to form a completer picture of him than of any other Anglo-Norman leader of his time. He must not, however, be taken as an average example of an Anglo-Norman feudal lord, but rather as one of the finest human products of the feudal system: brave, generous, upright, and ever true to his lights, the highest realized type of chivalry. So far as appears, with the exception of the skirmish carried on by his men to baffle the intrigues of King John and Meiler, he engaged in no wars or fighting in Ireland. His work was entirely one of construction—to build up and perfect, so far as he could, the feudal organization which was to give to his Liberty of Leinster, for about a century, a peace and pros-

39 Rot. Chart., 9 John, p. 176. For the restrictions inserted in this charter see Appendix to this chapter. 40 Ibid., p. 178. 41 There seems to be no reason to doubt this appointment. Harris places it in October 1208, which may be right. Hugh de Lacy can only have held the appointment for a few months, as by favouring William de Braose he soon fell from the king's good graces. John de Gray appears to have been justiciar from about the close of 1208. 42 Philip de Prendergast and David de la Roche, both of Flemish descent from South Wales, were the principal of these. They had just received large grants in Desmond, probably through Meiler's influence: Rot. Chart., 9 John, pp. 171 b, 172 b. 43 'A lui en tel guise fina / Que son boen chastel otreia, / Donmas al conte en heritage. / Apres le jor de son aage / Li otreia tote sa terre.' Hist. G. le Mar., ll. 14127–31. The editor, ignorant of Irish topography, supposes Donmas to be the *caislen na Dumach* (*recte Dumhcha*), or Dough Castle, in the Co. Clare, referring to O'Donovan's note to Four Masters, 1422. It is undoubtedly the castle of Dunamase (Irish, *Dun Masc*), as to which see vol. i, p. 375 [p. 142]. John took the castle into his own hand in 1210 (Hist., ll. 14330 et seq.), but it was ordered to be restored to the earl in 1215–16 (Cal. Docs. Ireland, vol. i, nos. 644, 664, 684), and afterwards became the chief castle of his successors in Leix.

perity and a reign of law hitherto unknown in Ireland. So far indeed as this peace was infringed within his fief during this period, the infringement, as we shall see, was almost entirely due to dissensions among the feudal lords themselves. His connexion
[220] with Ireland, indeed, was only a comparatively uneventful episode in an eventful life. With the government of the country he had little or nothing to do, but only with that of his liberty. He was too upright and too independent a man for John, while his will was unfettered, to choose as his minister. Almost to the last John viewed him with unmerited jealousy and suspicion. But when the deserted king found himself in dire straits he made use of the marshal's extraordinary loyalty and known integrity to help him out of his difficulties. It would have been well for the success of the new regime in Ireland had William Marshal been invested with the chief official power, but he was called away, even from the humbler work of organizing and developing his fief, to greater issues elsewhere.

As throwing a further light on the mind of this great man, the final scene, gleaned from his biography, may be referred to here, though much was to happen before it took place. In May 1219, as he lay on his death-bed, his faithful follower Henry Fitz Gerald, probably inspired by some cleric, said to him: 'Sire, it is right to think of your salvation. Death is no respecter of persons, and the clergy teach us that nobody shall be saved who does not restore what he has taken.' The Marshal replied: 'Henry, listen
[221] to me a moment. The clergy are too hard on us. They seek to shave us too close. I have taken in my time 500 knights, and have retained their arms, horses, and accoutrements. If the kingdom of heaven is closed to me for this, there is nothing to be done; for I cannot give them back. I can do no more for God than give myself up to him, while repenting of all the wrongs I have done … Either the clergy are wrong in their reasoning or no man can be saved.' 'Sire,' said John d'Erlée, 'that is the very truth; but I warrant there is hardly one of us who in his last days would dare to say as much.'[45] The marshal's sentiments have indeed a surprisingly modern ring about them. A little later, when it was a question what should be done with the rich robes and furs he had for ceremonial purposes, a cleric named Philip suggested that they would fetch a great sum for purchasing his salvation. 'Hold thy peace, bad man,' said the earl. 'I have had too much of your counsel, and want no more of it. A plague on bad counsellors! It will soon be Whitsuntide, when my knights will want their robes. It will be the last time that I shall give them to them, and you seek to cajole me out of them!' And then he ordered the robes to be distributed among his men, and more to be procured if there were not enough for all.[46] Yet it would be a great mistake to suppose that William
[222] the Marshal had freed himself generally from mediaeval ideas about the Church. He was its firm friend and munificent patron. He had founded and endowed monasteries at Tintern, Duiske or Graig-na-Managh, and Kilkenny, in Ireland, and he remembered them handsomely in his will. It was to the Pope's legate that he handed over the guardianship of the young king. One of his last acts, touchingly described by his biographer, was to take an affectionate farewell of his wife, and symbolically give himself

44 Miss Norgate has made good use of the Marshal's biography in the 'Angevin Kings' and 'John Lackland'. 45 Histoire, ll. 18461–501. 46 Ibid., ll. 18675–716.

up to God and become a Templar. But with all his extraordinary loyalty to throne and Church, he never feared to withstand either king or priest when his reason and conscience forbade him to perform their will.

We shall now describe the earl's principal dealings with his fief, so far as we can ascertain them:—

From the spring of 1207, then, to the spring of 1213, William the Marshal abode almost continuously in Ireland, and it is to this period that most of his doings there are to be referred. He chose Kilkenny as his principal place of abode, and made it the chief centre of his whole lordship, and to him and his son William the early greatness of that town is mainly due. Indeed, the rapid development of Ossory, which in the course of a generation completely outstripped the other divisions of Leinster, progressive as they too were, may be traced to his influence.

As we have seen, Strongbow made grants of lands at the two extremities of Ossory, [223]
at Aghaboe and Iverk.[47] It is probable, too, that in his time were erected the motes of Castlecomer and Odagh, which afterwards became centres of important seignorial manors.[48] He even erected a similar mote at Kilkenny, which was, however, abandoned by its garrison and destroyed by Donnell O'Brien, the bitter foe of Ossory, in 1173.[49] During the minority of Isabel de Clare, John, as *Dominus Hiberniae*, appears to have made further grants of lands on the borders of Ossory. To him should, perhaps, be ascribed the grant of Gowran to Theobald Walter, as well as grants of lands to Manasser Arsic, Richard Fitz Fulk, and others in the north of the present County Kilkenny.[50]

As early as 1185 John erected the mote-fortress of Tibberaghny on the south-western frontier, and this afterwards became the centre of a de Burgh manor. In Central Ossory, however, Donnell Mac Gillapatrick seems to have ruled undisturbed, under [224]
English protection, up to his death in 1185.[51]

How or exactly when the MacGillapatricks were ousted from Central Ossory we do not know. Certainly we hear of no fighting or violent expulsion, and it may have been a gradual process. Of Melaghlin, Donnell's successor, nothing is recorded except his death in 1193.[52] When next we hear of the family they were located near Slieve Bloom, where they were probably assigned lands, and where they lived as Irish chieftains for centuries, at first apparently in amity with their English neighbours.[53]

47 *Supra*, vol. i, pp. 388–9 [p. 147]. 48 For the grounds of this suggestion and for the Anglo-Norman settlement in Ossory generally, see my paper on 'Motes and Norman Castles in Ossory', Journ. R.S.A.I. 1909, pp. 318–42. 49 *Supra*, vol. i, p. 332 [p. 125]. 50 See John's charter to Jerpoint confirmatory of grants to that monastery prior to c.1189, and for the identification of the places mentioned see Journ. R.S.A.I., as above, p. 315. 51 He made a grant of Kilferagh, near Kilkenny, to John Cumin, Archbishop of Dublin, between 1181 and 1185 (Crede Mihi, no. xxxiii); and about the same time he granted numerous lands to Jerpoint (see John's confirmatory charter, c. 1189, in Dugdale's Monasticon Angl.). He has indeed been usually regarded as the founder of Jerpoint, but there appears to have been a Cistercian monastery here, from which sprang the monastery of Killenny prior to 1165: Facsimiles Nat. MSS. Ireland, pt. ii, pl. lxii, and Carrigan's History of Ossory, vol. iv, pp. 279–84. It is probable, however, that the splendid abbey church of Jerpoint was commenced soon after the monastery was endowed by King Donnell and the Norman benefactors mentioned in John's charter. Some features of the existing ruins seem to indicate this period for their original construction. 52 Ann. Loch Cé, 1193. 53 In 1213 Donnell Clannagh Mac

[225] In 1192, soon after Earl William Marshal obtained seisin of his lands, a castle is said to have been built at Kilkenny.[54] Perhaps this castle was little more than a strengthening or reconstruction of Strongbow's mote. Whatever may have been its precise form, the original mote appears to have been preserved, and even as late as the year 1307 formed part of the precincts of the castle.[55] From about the time of the erection of this castle we may probably date the commencement of the sub-infeudation of Central Ossory. It must have been about this time that the earl gave Geoffrey Fitz Robert a grant of lands on the King's river, which formed the 'Barony' of KELLS. Here Geoffrey erected a mote, which still remains with the later stone walls of the castle-bawn running up towards it. A small town grew up in connexion with the castle. Close by he founded the great priory of Kells, to rule which he brought four canons from the
[226] priory of Bodmin, in Cornwall.[56] Geoffrey was the earl's seneschal of Leinster at the beginning of the thirteenth century,[57] and perhaps earlier. Higher up the King's river was formed the seignorial manor of CALLAN. Two of the Marshal's followers, John d'Erlée, his biographer, and Maillard, his standard-bearer, were given lands at Erleystown, now corruptly Earlstown, and at Mallardstown, between Callan and Kells. Other probable feoffees of the earl were Thomas Fitz Anthony, afterwards his seneschal, and William de St. Leger. The former founded the priory of Inistioge, and held the manor of Grenan, or Thomastown, as the vill came to be called after its founder. The latter, besides the manor of Rosconnell in the north, held lands at Tullaghanbrogue, near Kilkenny.

Kilkenny itself, though not mentioned in the early centuries for which we have annalistic records, and, so far as is known, not at any time the seat of the kings of
[227] Ossory, must have been an ecclesiastical site of some importance in pre-Norman times, as is shown by its ancient ecclesiastical round tower, and by some slight remains which have been discovered of a Romanesque church.[58] From 1192, when the first castle of the Marshals was built, we may trace the beginnings of the civil importance of the town. At this time the church at Aghaboe was the cathedral church of the diocese of Ossory, and it is stated to have so remained up to the death of Bishop Felix O'Dulany

Gillapatrick and other Irish chieftains 'gave an overthrow to Cormac Mac Art O'Melaghlin', a determined foe of the English and one who had recently defeated the justiciar, John de Gray, in Fircal: Ann. Clonmacnois, 1212 (*recte* 1213). 54 Ann. Inisfallen, Dublin MS., and Ware's Annals, 1192. A castle at Kilkenny is alluded to in a grant by Felix O'Dulany (ob. 1202): Hist. of St. Canice, Graves and Prim, p. 29. 55 In an Extent of the lands and tenements in the burgh of Kilkenny which belonged to Joan, Countess of Gloucester, who died April 19, 1307, it was found that she held in the vill of Kilkenny a castle in which were 'una aula, quatuor turres, una capella, una mota, et alie domus diverse ad idem castrum necessarie': Inquis. P. M., 35 Ed. I, no. 47, rm. 34. 56 The Registrum Chartarum Monasterii B. M. de Kenlis in Osseria is only known to us by an abstract made by Sir James Ware, of which there are copies, T.C.D., F. 4. 23, and Brit. Mus., Lansdowne, 418. No foundation charter is forthcoming, but the register contains a sort of confirmatory memorandum by Geoffrey referring to his grant and its confirmation by Earl William Marshal. This memorandum must be dated after 1202. The date usually assigned for the foundation of the monastery is 1193. For the charter to the town of Kells, see Chartae, &c., p. 16. 57 He was seneschal when Meiler Fitz Henry was justiciar: Reg. St. Thomas's, Dublin, p. 125. 58 The burning of Cill Cainnigh, meaning probably the church and ecclesiastical buildings of Kilkenny, is recorded by the Four Masters under dates 1085 and 1114. In 1169 Maurice de Prendergast and his band of about 200 men lodged for the night at Kilkenny: Song of Dermot, l. 1311.

in 1202.[59] The new bishop, Hugh le Rous, one of the canons brought from Bodmin to rule the new priory at Kells, was no doubt readily persuaded by Earl William to move the seat of the bishopric from the march-lands of Aghaboe to the new seignorial centre at Kilkenny. He gave the see-lands of Aghaboe to the earl in exchange for other lands in more settled districts near Kilkenny,[60] and also granted to him, 'to enable him to enlarge his vill of Kilkenny,' some of the land on which the present town is built.[61] [228]
Between 1207 and 1211 the earl granted a full charter of liberties to the burgesses of Kilkenny, which must have already become an important town.[62] He is said to have built a castle there after 1207,[63] and, though no early authority is quoted for this statement, it is probable that when he came to dwell in Kilkenny he built a regular stone castle for his habitation.

The beautiful cathedral of Kilkenny was probably completed about the middle of the thirteenth century, but the precise date of its commencement is uncertain. The architecture of the nave is certainly later than Earl William's time, but in spite of the statement in a sixteenth-century compilation,[64] that Hugh de Mapilton (bishop from [229]
1251 to 1260) was the first founder of the church, it is on architectural and general grounds probable that the choir, at least, was built in the time of Earl William or of his eldest son. To the elder William Marshal is attributed the foundation of the priory of St. John the Evangelist on the left bank of the river at Kilkenny, and this is perhaps in substance correct, but the charter granting a new site and rich endowments to the priory, quoted as evidence thereof, was actually given not by him, but by his son, William Marshal junior, probably about 1223.[65] Besides founding the Monastery de Voto, or Tintern Minor, already mentioned, and confirming the charter of Dunbrody, the elder William Marshal founded another Cistercian house known as Duiske, or as it was [230]
afterwards called Graig-na-managh.[66] Other foundations attributed to the earl are the

59 Nomina Episcoporum Ossoriensium, &c., Brit. Mus., Sloane MS. 4796. Transcribed in Carrigan's History of Ossory, Appendix, vol. i. 60 For the deeds effecting this exchange see Journ. R.S.A.I. 1858–9, pp. 327–9. The bishop's name is usually written 'de Rous', but seemingly on no contemporary authority. As it was translated Rufus, I have ventured to restore 'le Rous', O. Fr. for le Roux. 61 Liber Albus Ossoriensis; Cal. Docs. Ireland, vol. ii, no. 861. The portion of land granted is described as 'extending from Keuerocke's well to the river called Bregath running under Coterel bridge'. Keuerocke's well probably represents *Tobar Chiarog* or St. Ciaran's well. It has been identified with a well near the centre of the town, south of the old market, in the garden of what is supposed to have been the house of the famous Kyteler family. Coterel bridge is represented by the Watergate bridge over the Bregagh river, which henceforth separated the Irish town from the High or English town. 62 Chartae Priv. et Immun., p. 33. 63 Hanmer, p. 173; Cox, p. 54. 64 Nomina Episcoporum Ossoriensium, &c., Sloane MS. 4796, Brit. Mus. 65 From this charter (Dugdale, vi. 1143) it appears that the friary buildings had previously been commenced close to St. John's Bridge. The friars were here prior to 1202 as is evidenced by a charter of Felix O'Dulany contained in the cartulary of the priory. This site may have been given them by the elder William Marshal. His son moved them 'ad caput parvi pontis de Kilkennia', i.e. to the site of the present St. John's church, near the bridge over the millstream in St. John's Street. The charters of these two earls are frequently confused, but a comparison of the witnesses to the undoubted charters of the younger William Marshal, Reg. St. Thomas's, no. 137, and the second charter to Kilkenny, dated April 5, 1223 (Chartae Priv. et Immun., p. 34, and cf. p. 80), with the charters to St. John's Priory (Dugdale, vi. 1143) and to the burgesses of Carlow (Chartae, &c., pp. 37–8), will show that these four charters were executed by the same person and about the same time. 66 Facsimiles Nat. MS8. Ireland, vol. ii, no. lxix.

priory of St. John at Wexford for knights of the Hospital, and an Augustinian priory at Kilrush in the County Kildare.

But more important for the temporal prosperity of Leinster than the numerous religious houses founded by the earl and the greater landholders about this time, were the efforts made to foster trade and commerce and civic life, which, together with the advance in agriculture, changed the whole conditions of living in the province. Now that Leinster was really under one lord increased use was made of the great river-ways for transport, and the rivers themselves were bridged in places, not with a view to plunder, but to facilitate peaceful intercourse and trade. One of the earl's first cares was to establish a port on the Barrow in his manor of Ross, and to give it an independent existence, at the same time bridging the river at this point, so as to connect the new town with the road to Kilkenny. The place was variously called 'William Marshal's town', 'the town of the new bridge of Ross', or 'Rosponte', and afterwards New Ross, to distinguish it from Old Ross, as the seat of the manor came to be called.
[231] Situated within the tidal way, New Ross was within reach of the largest merchant vessels of the time. From it, too, in boats of light draught, goods could be brought up the Nore to Inistioge and Thomastown, if not to Kilkenny, and up the Barrow to St. Mullins, Graig-na-managh, Carlow, and even as far as Athy.[67] Thus New Ross became the port of South Leinster. In the course of the thirteenth century its trade far outstripped that of Wexford, and appears even to have surpassed that of Waterford, in spite of the royal favour shown to the latter town.[68]

Indeed, the formation of towns was perhaps the most significant feature of the new régime. Apart from the Scandinavian seaports, which themselves were the first to expand under Norman rule, small towns grew up in the time of the Marshals under the protection of the castles at the seignorial manors of Ferns, Old Ross, the Island, Carrick on Slaney, and Bannow, in the County Wexford; at Carlow, Forth
[232] O'Nolan, and St. Mullins, in County Carlow; at Kilkenny, Callan, Castlecomer, Odagh, and Aghaboe, in Ossory; at Kildare; and at Dunamase; and the same thing in a less degree followed on the erection of many of the castles of subordinate grantees. Thus may be said to have commenced civic life in Ireland, and this civic life rendered possible the growth of trade, and *pari passu* with that growth the towns themselves grew and prospered.

67 Cal. Justiciary Rolls (1298), p. 202. The jurors presented that the passage of boats that used to come from Ross to Athy was obstructed by a weir. 68 Thus for the five years following May 4, 1275, the receipts from the 'new custom' granted to the Crown amounted in New Ross to £2632, in Waterford to £1865, and in Wexford to only £22: Cal. Docs. Ireland, vol. ii, no. 1902, and Irish Pipe Rolls, 36th Rep. Dep. Keeper, which makes some corrections and additions.

[233]

NOTE

King John's charters of Leinster and Meath

King John's confirmatory grant of the land of Leinster to William Marshal, Earl of Pembroke, is dated the 28th of March, 1208 (Rot. Chart., 9 John, p. 176). It is nearly similar in form to the confirmatory grant of the land of Meath to Walter de Lacy four weeks later (ibid., p. 178). Both grants contain reservations to the Crown of rights which seem not to have been reserved in the original charters of Henry II, or in the charter by which John, when Earl of Mortain, restored the land of Meath to Walter de Lacy. Henry had granted the land of Meath to Hugh de Lacy to hold from the king and his heirs 'as Murchardus Hu Melachlin or any other before or after him better held the same', and Hugh was to have 'all liberties which Henry had or was able to give there'. But now John took care, both in the case of Leinster and of Meath, expressly to reserve to himself and his heirs the pleas of the Crown, namely of treasure-trove, rape, forestalling, and arson, and the plea where one appeals another for felonious breach of the peace, and he provided for appeals to the king's court in case of default of justice in the lord's court, and in the case of complaints of injury done by the lord himself or his court. Cross-lands and dignities appurtenant to them (i.e. church-lands and the higher ecclesiastical preferments) were also reserved to the Crown. One disputed case of feudal incidents seems to have been provided [234]
for favourably to the lord of the liberty. Where a tenant-in-chief died, leaving heirs who were minors, the Crown latterly seems to have claimed the custody of all his lands, even of those which he held of some mesne lord, and this was one of the grievances of the barons of England. John now granted to Walter de Lacy and William Marshal that in such a case they should have the custody of fees held of themselves, but that the 'marriages' of the heir should belong to the Crown.

[235] CHAPTER XXI

KING JOHN IN IRELAND, 1210

At the commencement of the year 1210, King John, in his home dominions at least, was to all appearance at the height of his personal power. It is true that he had lost nearly all his ancestral possessions in France, that England lay under the papal interdict, and that he himself was excommunicate, but the loss of his heritage over sea caused him to concentrate his attention upon his island dominions, and the fulminations of the Pope, for the moment at all events, served as a pretext for enriching himself at the expense of the fugitive clergy. In Ireland indeed, to which the interdict did not apply, these fulminations hardly resounded at all.[1] In the summer of 1209 William the Lion was forced to come to terms with John, and in October—'what had never
[236] been heard of in times past'—all the Welsh nobles came to him at Woodstock and did him homage. In the same year, too, the king received homage from all his free tenants, and even from boys of twelve years of age, throughout the whole kingdom, and after they had done fealty he dismissed them with the kiss of peace.[2] 'There was not a man in the land,' complains one chronicler, 'who could resist his will in anything.'[3] Another, with reference to the clergy, bitterly says: 'When they saw the wolf coming they quitted the sheep and fled.'[4]

There was one baron, however, who failed to give the hostages required in 1208, and who fled to Ireland to escape the king's wrath. When the king's messengers came to William de Braose and demanded hostages, William's wife, Matilda de St. Valery, with feminine boldness taking the word out of her husband's mouth, replied: 'I will not deliver up my son to your lord, King John, for he basely murdered his nephew Arthur, when he should have kept him in honourable custody.' Her husband reproved her foolish tongue and offered, if he had offended, to give satisfaction according to the judgement of his peers. But this was of no avail. When the king heard of it he secretly
[237] sent soldiers and bailiffs to seize William and his whole family. The latter, however, forewarned, fled with his wife and sons to Ireland.[5]

In a document[6] which John put forward to the world in 1210, and which was evidently intended by him as a justification of his actions towards William de Braose, a different complexion is sought to be given to the matter. William de Braose owed a

1 [See *Add.*] So little did the Irish clergy enter into the spirit of the contest of their class in England against the king that Eugenius the Primate (who, like Stephen Langton, had been designated by the Pope in opposition to the royal nominee) accepted in July 1207 a commission from the king to execute the episcopal office in the see of Exeter, left derelict owing to the Interdict: Rot. Claus., 9 John, m. 17 (p. 88). 2 Roger of Wendover, vol. ii, pp. 50–1. Rymer's Foedera, vol. i, pt. 1. p. 103. 3 Gerv. Cant., vol. ii, p. 100. 4 Roger of Wendovor, vol. ii, p 48. 5 Rog. Wend., vol. ii, pp. 48–9, *sub anno* 1208.

large sum to the king in respect of the lordship of Limerick, which, owing to the opposition of the barons already in occupation under grants from the Crown, had doubtless brought him no profit. John represents his action as arising out of William's defaults in payment and resistance to the processes of the law. According to the above document, John ordered his bailiff, Gerard de Athiis,[7] to distrain on William's Welsh property for the amount of the debt, which John characteristically exaggerates.[8] An arrangement is then said to have been made by which William surrendered his castles [238] in Wales to be held by the king, mortgaged all his lands in England, and gave hostages, until his debts should be paid. Nevertheless, William attempted with a large force to enter his castles, and, failing in this, burned half the town of Leominster. Whereupon John sent Gerard de Athiis to capture him, but William fled with his family to Ireland, and was there harboured by William Marshal and Walter and Hugh de Lacy. The latter undertook that William would make satisfaction, and that if he failed to do so they would no longer harbour him. This promise not being kept, the king raised an army with the intention of going himself to Ireland.

It is not difficult to accept John's version of the facts as in the main correct, though exaggerated and misleading, and yet believe that the true motive for his vindictiveness against William de Braose was personal animosity connected with the tragic fate of Arthur of Brittany. William de Braose had been given the custody of Arthur before he was handed over to Hubert de Burgh, and perhaps William knew more about the real end of Arthur than we do.

It was in the hope of finding a refuge with his son-in-law, Walter de Lacy, that [239] William de Braose fled with his family to Ireland. This was probably in the winter of 1208–9.[9] He was driven by stress of weather to Wicklow, where Earl William Marshal was then sojourning, and the earl gave him and his family kindly shelter and entertained them for twenty days. When the justiciar, John de Gray, heard of it he at once informed the earl that he was harbouring the king's traitor, and on the part of the king ordered the earl to deliver him up to him without delay. The Marshal replied that he had only sheltered his lord,[10] as he was bound to do, and that he did not know that the

6 Rymer's Foedera, vol. i, pt. 1, p. 107. 7 It is worth noting that one of the provisions wrung from John by Magna Carta was: 'Nos amovebimus penitus de balliis parentes Gerardi de Athyes quod de cetero nullam habeant balliam in Anglia.' 8 In 1205–6 William owed £2865 6*s*. 8*d*. (Pipe, 7 John, Rot. 8), and the account stood at the same figure in 1209–10: ibid., 11 John, Rot. 1. John says that William owed 5,000 marks, which was the sum originally agreed to be paid at the rate of 500 marks a year. William had already paid £468, which John omits to notice. John also claimed five years of the farm of the city of Limerick (at 100 marks a year, from 1208), but he omits to notice that during part of this time Meiler held the city for the king. 9 The flight of William de Braose to Ireland is placed in 1208 by Roger de Wendover (vol. ii, p. 49) and by the Laud MS. Annals, Chart. St. Mary's, Dublin, vol. ii, p. 310; cf. Brut y Tywys. 1207. Miss Norgate, however, places it in 1209, but without giving her authority: John Lackland, p. 150. From the passage in L'Histoire de G. le Marechal immediately referred to it appears that the flight took place when John de Gray was justiciar. Unfortunately, in the absence of the Patent and Close Rolls for 1209, the date of John de Gray's appointment is uncertain. The Four Masters place it in 1208 (*recte* 1209). He was certainly in Ireland at the close of 1209 (Rot. Misae, p. 144), and Hugh de Lacy, if appointed justiciar in the autumn of 1208, would probably have been soon superseded owing to his connexion with William de Braose. 10 How William de Braose was the Marshal's *seignor* is obscure. Possibly it was in respect of some of the de Clare property in Wales.

[240] king was otherwise than well disposed towards him. To deliver him up now to the bishop would be a treachery which he refused to commit. Accordingly he conducted him safely to Walter de Lacy.[11] The Marshal was prepared to resist John's will and risk the loss of his fief rather than do a dishonourable act.

According to his own account, then, it was simply to chastise William de Braose and his aiders and abettors, and to enforce payment of a crown debt, that John made his expedition to Ireland in the summer of 1210. This may seem a mean and paltry motive for the royal expedition, but John's motives were often mean and paltry. Moreover, he certainly did not come to quell dissension among the barons, for he had received the dissentient barons into favour two years previously, and since Meiler was discredited and superseded there were no further dissensions. Nor was there any turbulence among the barons, except what had been excited by John's relentless persecution of William de Braose, his family, and those who sheltered them. Even more certainly he did not come either to protect the Irish from aggression or to put down their revolt, though all these causes have been alleged. There had been no inter-racial conflicts for some years, while, as we shall see, the policy of his new minister, John de
[241] Gray, was first to obtain control in Connaught, and next to subdue the chieftains of the north. It will be seen, too, that all John's military efforts, when he was in Ireland, were expended in taking possession of the lands and castles of the de Lacys, and in endeavouring to capture their persons, as well as to hunt down Maud de Braose and her family.

As to William de Braose himself, John in his elaborate statement goes on to say that William came to the neighbourhood of Pembroke, where the king was with his army, and offered by his intermediaries 40,000 marks for the king's peace. But the king replied that he well knew that William was not his own master at all, but was ruled by his wife, who was in Ireland,[12] and proposed that William should accompany him to Ireland and that the matter should be settled there. William, however, remained in Wales. Evidently he feared to put himself into John's power.

One incident of disturbance is indeed usually here mentioned as having taken place in 1209, namely, a massacre of 300 of the citizens of Dublin, who were making holiday near the town on a certain Easter Monday. This day, remembered as Black Monday, is
[242] said to have been celebrated in Elizabeth's time by the mayor, sheriffs, and citizens feasting on the spot, and daring the enemy to come and attack them. But the sole authority for this story is Hanmer,[13] who, it should be needless to say, is no authority for the thirteenth century. His account of the period is often a mere travesty of the facts, and sometimes dull invention. Black Monday may have been celebrated in Hanmer's time, as he says, and the tradition of a massacre on the spot may have been well founded, but there is good reason for thinking that in ascribing it to the year 1209 tradition (or Hanmer) antedated it by half a century at least, as we have no evidence of any raids of the O'Birnes or the O'Tooles until near the close of the reign of Henry III.

11 Histoire, ll. 14137–232. 12 So I understand the passage: 'Quod bene novimus quod non erat omnino in potestate sua, sed magis in potestate uxoris suae quae fuit in Hibernia': Rymer's Foedera, vol. i, pt. i, p. 107. 13 Hanmer's Chronicle (1633) p. 86. Hanmer died in 1604.

We shall now endeavour to follow John in his progress in Ireland. Unfortunately there is at this period a great gap in the series of enrolments which from the beginning of John's reign have thrown authentic light on affairs in Ireland. The Patent, Close, Charter, and Fine Rolls for the eleventh to the thirteenth years of John's reign are missing. Also the Close Rolls for the tenth John. Had these been preserved we should probably have a much clearer idea of what had happened in Ireland immediately prior to John's visit, and of his transactions during his visit. Covering the period of his stay in Ireland we have indeed the Prestita Roll of the twelfth regnal year. This contains [243]
accounts of payments made to the Earl of Salisbury and other officials, for their fees and for the pay of soldiers and sailors and others connected with the expedition. It gives long lists of the knights and others who accompanied the expedition, and, above all, from it we can glean an authentic itinerary of the king's visit.[14] We are thus enabled to follow John's course almost from day to day, to note some of his transactions, and, by requisitioning information from other scattered sources, form a correct, though no doubt incomplete, idea of the purpose, scope, and results of his expedition.

From the 3rd to the 16th of June John was at Cross on the sea, below Pembroke, the usual place of embarkation.[15] Here he was busy making final arrangements for the expedition, and made payments to knights, mariners, amounting to £1,433 13*s*. 6*d*. His half-brother, William Longsword, Earl of Salisbury, supposed to be son of Henry II by Rosamond Clifford, was in chief command of the army. John landed at Crook, near Waterford, on June 20, thus following precisely the route which his father had adopted [244]
thirty-nine years before, and which he himself seems to have taken in 1185. At Crook he was joined by the justiciar, the Bishop of Norwich, with a body of Irish troops. John, no doubt, visited Waterford, where, we are told, Donough Cairbrech O'Brien repaired to make his submission, and received a charter for Carrigogunnell and the lordship thereunto belonging at a yearly rent of sixty marks.[16]

On June 21 John was at New Ross,[17] having perhaps come from Crook or Waterford by river. This town owed its origin to William Marshal, or perhaps, following tradition, we should say, to the Countess Isabel. It is generally supposed, indeed, to have been the site of a great monastery founded by St. Abban in the sixth century, but the identification is very doubtful, and in any case this monastery seems to have disappeared before the arrival of the Normans. Situated on the banks of a great navigable river, New Ross soon became the principal port of the lordship of Leinster, in the race for trade outpacing the old Scandinavian port of Wexford, and rivalling the king's vill of Waterford. So keenly did the latter port feel the rivalry that for nearly two centuries it endeavoured to deprive New Ross of the privileges of a trading port. Already at the [245]
date of John's visit William Marshal had spanned the river with a wooden bridge at the spot, thus facilitating the connexion with Kilkenny. Hence, the town was called

14 The Rotulus de Prestito does not account for all of the 53 dozen skins of parchment which John brought with him to Ireland: Rot. Misae, 11 John, p. 167. 15 'Apud Crucem subtus Penbroc' or 'super mare'. Cf. Song of Dermot, l. 2590, note; where, however, delete the suggestion that Carew Cross marks the place. More probably it was near Pembroke Dock. 16 Ann. Inisfallen (Dublin MS.), 1209. As to this grant see *ante*, p. 168, note 2 [p. 218, note 63].

villa novi pontis, or *villa de Rosponte*. The *caput* of the manor, however, throughout the century was at Old Ross, some five miles to the east, where a mote still marks the original castle-site.

Next day John was at a wood near the land of Thomas Fitz Anthony.[18] He was one of William Marshal's principal tenants, and at a later period his seneschal. Thomastown, situated at a bend of the river Nore about ten miles above its junction with the Barrow, preserves the name of Thomas Fitz Anthony. He founded a monastery for canons regular at Inistiogue.[19] There is a mote here, and it may have been the *caput* of the manor at the time of John's visit, and the wood where he halted and made a payment for 'six galleys going with Geoffrey de Lucy in search of pirates' may be now represented by Woodstock demesne. He probably went on to Earl William Marshal's
[246] castle of Kilkenny for the night. Here he and his host were entertained by the earl, who had accompanied him from Pembroke.[20] We have already noted the early history of this castle, so far as it is ascertainable, and have shown that what became known as the 'High town' or 'English town' of Kilkenny owed its origin and incorporation to the earl. It was the earl's chief seat in Leinster, and the river was already spanned by a bridge connecting the town with the new foundation of the priory of St. John's on the north-eastern side.

On June 24 John was still at Kilkenny, and on the 26th he was at Naas.[21] At this time the baron of Naas was William Fitz William.[22] In a pedigree in the Gormanston Register he appears as second son of the William to whom John confirmed Naas in 1185, but he must have been older than his brother David, whom he preceded in the barony.

On June 28 John was at Dublin. Here he probably stayed at the rich abbey of St.
[247] Thomas,[23] founded thirty-three years before. At Dublin he gave audience to some of the barons of Meath, who came to intercede on behalf of their lord, Walter de Lacy. In his name they offered his complete submission, endeavoured to dissociate him from the action of his brother Hugh, and prayed the king to relax his ire.[24] The intercession was of no avail. John now proceeded to take possession of Walter's principal castles in Meath (as well as Hugh's), and it was not until 1215 that he came to an agreement with Walter for the restoration of his lands.

On June 30 John advanced as far as Greenoge, in the barony of Ratoath and county of Meath, June 30 and on July 2 he was at Trim. He must therefore have passed by Ratoath, where Hugh de Lacy had an important mote-castle, which was now seized

17 'Apud pontem novum,' also referred to as 'villa Willielmi Marescalli'. 18 'Apud Boscum juxta terram Thome filii Antonii'. He is called seneschal of Leinster in 1215 (C.D.I., vol. i, no. 673). He probably succeeded in that office Geoffrey Fitz Robert, baron of Kells, who died circa 1211. 19 Circa 1206, Dugdale, Mon. Angl., vol. ii, p. 1041; but according to Archdall, circa 1210. 20 Hist. G. le Mar., ll. 14259–66. John probably arrived at Kilkenny on the evening of the 22nd June and left on the morning of the 24th: Rot. de Prest., pp. 247 and 179. 21 From Kilkenny to Naas must have been two days' journey. One night was perhaps spent in tents: 'quando dominus Rex jacuit in papilionibus': Rot. de Prest., p. 181. 22 Cal. Docs. Ireland, vol. i, no. 448, and cf. no. 89. He married the widow of Philip de Braose; ibid., no. 962. [See *Add.*] 23 A battlemented building here was known in 1634 as 'King John's chamber' (Journ. R.S.A.I. 1907, p. 395). 24 These barons of Meath were William le Petit, Richard de Tuit, Richard de Feipo, Richard de

by the king. Indeed, Hugh, as we have seen, held the whole barony of Ratoath (as well as that of Morgallion) of his brother Walter.[25] By a deed which may be confidently assigned to this period John granted the whole of Ratoath to Philip of Worcester for [248]
the service of one knight. Among the witnesses, who we may infer had not risen to arms with the de Lacys, were Richard Tyrell, Richard de Tuit, William le Petit, Peter de Meset, Richard de Feipo, Martin de Mandeville, and Adam Dullard.[26]

John was now accompanied by a considerable force, including, besides Flemish mercenaries, an Irish contingent from Munster and Desmond, and troops which came with Geoffrey de Marisco, Thomas Fitz Maurice, and others. At Trim, where John remained until July 4, he, no doubt, took Walter de Lacy's castle into his hands. It was one of those restored in 1215. What sort of castle it was is obscure. Probably the original mote-fortress had been vastly strengthened by stone walls, but it would seem that, like other Irish castles, it was too small for John to hold his court in it. Accordingly here, as in several other cases, his writs are dated at a mead (*pratum*) near the place. He evidently held his court under a tent in the open field. The keep, the oldest part of the existing castle-ruins at Trim, is of a peculiar plan. It may be described as a square with [249]
a square tower projecting from the middle of each of the four sides, thus forming a twenty-sided figure. It resembles in plan the keep of Warkworth castle in Northumberland, which is a square with a semi-octagonal projection in the middle of each side. The latter keep is said to have been built in 1200, but the keep at Trim is probably somewhat later. It may be ascribed with much probability to about the year 1220.[27]

From Trim John moved by way of Ardbraccan to Kells. At Ardbraccan, Cathal Crovderg O'Conor, King of Connaught, made submission to King John, and accom- [250]
panied him as far as Carrickfergus.[28] John's prests on the 4th and 5th July are dated 'at a mead near Kells'. It is doubtful whether there was any castle here at this time. It was

Capella, and Hugh Hose: Cal. Docs. Ireland, vol. i, no. 402. According to William of Newburgh (vol. ii, p. 511), 'Walterus de Lacy se et sua omnia ei reddidit, quod illum postea poenituit, quia illum praedictus rex abjurare omnia tenementa et terras et redditus quos habebat in Hibernia fecit, ipsumque postea et omnes suos de Anglia depulit.' **25** *Supra*, p. 76 [pp 247–8]. **26** Gormanston Register, f. 6. The castle of Ratoath was restored to Walter de Lacy in 1216: Rot. Pat., 18 John, p. 194. The large grant made about the same time to Philip of Worcester in Munster may perhaps be regarded as compensatory. **27** To this year is assigned the building of the castle of Ath Truim in the Annals of Inisfallen (Dublin MS.). So in Hanmer's Chronicle (which is followed by Ware), with the confused addition that it was after the wars between William Marshal and Hugh de Lacy, when Trim was besieged and brought to a lamentable plight, 'to prevent after-claps and subsequent calamities, the castle of Trim was builded' (p. 189). But the siege of Trim took place in 1224, and as the castle then withstood successfully for seven weeks all the efforts of so skilful a commander as William Marshal the younger, we must infer that it was an exceptionally strong castle (see Royal Letters, ed. Shirley, vol. i, p. 500). Moreover, in the previous March, when the castle was in the king's hand, the justiciar was commanded to allow 'Walter de Lacy to have the hall, houses, and chambers in the castle of Trim, in which he and his retinue may dwell while he is fighting the enemies of the king and himself': Rot. Claus., 8 Hen. III, p. 591). From this mandate we may not only infer that a strong and well-provided castle then existed, but that the *turris* or keep was to be retained by the king's constable. All this bears out the date given in the Annals of Inisfallen. **28** Ann. Clonmacnois, where Cathal is said to have 'come to the king's house' at 'Tibreydultan called Ardbracken in Meath'. St. Ultan's well (*Tioprait Ultáin*) is still pointed out at Ardbraccan close to the church. Land here as well as at Navan had been given to Jocelin de Angulo. A lofty mote on an esker-knoll at Navan, and a small mote on high ground near the church and village of Ardbraccan, mark the Norman centres.

not one of those restored, and at any rate its site is unknown. Here John dispatched a small expeditionary force under John Marshal, probably to take possession of some other de Lacy strongholds. John himself now turned northwards to Uriel—probably taking possession of the castle of Nobber, which belonged to Hugh de Lacy, on the way—and stopping on the 7th at his own vill of Louth. There is a small mote at Louth, formerly connected with the town trench which marks the site of the castle.[29]

[251] On the 8th John was seemingly at Dundalk,[30] the chief manor of Nicholas de Verdun. Here he made a prest for 400 soldiers lately come [to their allegiance], who had been with Hugh de Lacy. Evidently in the face of the king's advance Hugh could no longer command the allegiance of all his followers. We are told that Hugh, 'when he found that the king was going north, burned his own castles in Machaire Conaille and Cuailgne (the baronies of Upper and Lower Dundalk) before the king's eyes, and also the castles which had been erected by the Earl of Ulster [John de Courcy ?] and the men of Uriel, and he himself fled to Carrickfergus, leaving the chiefs of his people burning and destroying the castles of the country.'[31] It is probable, then, that the mote-castle of Dundalk was one of those burned by Hugh de Lacy at this time. In spite of the agreement with Thomas de Verdun to which reference has already been made, Hugh seems to have claimed the castelry of Dundalk,[32] but King John gave it to Nicholas de Verdun with the whole barony of Lower Dundalk, and Nicholas was now in John's army.

From Dundalk John went to Carlingford, where he seized the castle, which
[252] belonged to Hugh de Lacy. The existing ruins, in the main Edwardian, stand on a rock overlooking Carlingford Bay. It was retained as a royal castle until 1226, when it was restored to Hugh de Lacy.[33] Here John stayed for three days (July 9–11), and made payments for carpenters, quarriers, ditchers, and miners, probably for the repair of injuries made by Hugh de Lacy on abandoning the castle.

So far John had advanced without meeting any opposition, and, seemingly, had not unsheathed a sword. Hugh de Lacy, however, evidently hoped to defend his lordship of Ulster against him. The only practicable approach by land into Lecale was by a long and difficult detour between the Mourne Mountains on the south and those which culminate in Slieve Croob on the north. This was called the gate of Lecale, and it was already guarded by the castle of Dundrum, then known as the castle of Rath.[34] As its
[253] ruins still bear witness, this castle was a formidable structure, built on a rock, and consisting of a massive circular donjon-keep surrounded by stout walls and rock-hewn trenches. Here, if anywhere, Hugh de Lacy must have prepared to make a stand. But John had collected a large fleet of transports. He threw a bridge of boats across Car-

29 For this and other motes in the neighbourhood see my paper on 'Motes and Norman Castles in County Louth', Journ. R.S.A.I. 1908, pp. 241–69. John paid his huntsmen on July 7 'apud pratum juxta Luvet' (Louth): Rot. de Prest., p. 248; but after leaving Kells he made prests for his army 'apud pratum subtus aquam quandam que vocatur Struthe': ibid., p. 192. 'Struthe' represents the Irish *sruth*, 'a river,' perhaps the Dee near Nobber. **30** 'Apud pratum juxta Cadelac' (Cather Delgan ?). **31** Ann. Inisfallen, Dublin MS. 1211. This passage is quoted by O'Donovan, Four Masters, vol. iii, p. 164, note. **32** *Supra*, p. 121 [p. 198], and see Reg. St. Thomas's, Dublin, p. 9.

lingford Lough, probably at Narrow-water, and sent the main body of his troops across the bridge to advance round the mountains towards the castle of Rath, while he himself with the rest went by sea. He landed first at Ardglas, where he was on the 12th at Jordan de Saukeville's castle, and then he immediately turned back to the castle of Rath, which appears to have been for the moment the objective.[35] Probably its defenders, seeing themselves out-manoeuvred, retreated before retreat was cut off. At any rate, on the 14th the castle was occupied by John, apparently without resistance, and [253]
Hugh de Lacy's supporters concentrated at Carrickfergus.

On the 12th, while at Ardglas, John made a prest to 'Mariadac, King of Limerick'. This was Murtough Finn, son of Donnell O'Brien, who had apparently come with a contingent from Thomond. Jordan de Saukeville appears to have been disseised of his lands at Ardglas, Holywood, and other places in Ulster at this time, as in 1217 his lands there were restored to him.[36] A mote on the 'Ward of Ardglas', a promontory forming the southern boundary of the harbour, probably represents the original castle-site, but even at this early period the town, as the principal seaport of Lecale, must have risen to some importance, and a stone castle may have been already built there.[37]

At Rath, or Dundrum, John also set his carpenters, quarriers, and ditchers to work, probably, as at Carlingford, to repair the damage done by Hugh de Lacy. The castle was left in the custody of Roger Pipard, and was retained as a royal castle for seventeen years.[38]

On the 16th John was at Downpatrick, the seat of the bishopric, and formerly the [254]
caput of John de Courcy's lordship. But now the objective was Carrickfergus. This was Hugh de Lacy's strongest castle, and the remnant of his followers were gathered together in it, apparently prepared for a siege. John, however, made a great concentration of his forces here, both by sea and by land, and the castle soon surrendered. A large number of knights and gentlemen, feudatories of the de Lacys, and their retainers, were taken prisoners in the castle and deprived for the time of their lands.[39] Hugh de Lacy himself, however, at the king's approach, escaped in a boat to Scotland, and at [255]
the same time Maud de Braose and her sons William and Reginald also fled. Maud,

33 Rot. Pat., 17 John, m. 19 (p. 148), and Cal. Docs. Ireland, vol. i, nos. 742, 1015, 1386. We have already seen (*supra*, p. 121 [p. 199]) that Hugh de Lacy obtained the barony of Lower Dundalk from Thomas de Verdun. Probably Hugh built the first castle of Carlingford. He afterwards granted the castle to his daughter Matilda, together with all the lands which he had received with her mother in 'Cole et Ergalea' (Cooley and Uriel) on the occasion of Matilda's marriage with David, baron of Naas: Gormanston Register, f. 191 dors. 34 For the identification of the castrum de Rath with the castle of Dundrum see my paper, Journ. R.S.A.I. 1909, pp. 23–9. 35 That there was some such manoeuvre appears to follow (1) from the statements in the Annals of Inisfallen (see Four Masters, *sub anno* 1209), which after mentioning Hugh's retreat says that the king at Carlingford 'made a bridge of his ships across the harbour by which he landed some of his troops on the other side and proceeded thence to Carrickfergus partly by sea and partly by land'; (2) from the recorded itinerary of the king; and (3) from general topographical considerations. John brought a vast number of *pontes*—I suppose materials for making pontoon bridges —with him to Ireland, as many as 155 from York and still more from Dorset and Somerset: Pipe Roll, 12 and 13 John. 36 Rot. Claus., l Hen. III (p. 304 b). 37 A well-preserved castle at Ardglas, known as 'Jordan's castle', is, however, of later date. In 1220–1 Jordan de Saukeville obtained respites 'in fortifying his land': Rot. Claus., 4 Hen. III (p. 413 b), and 5 Hen. III (p. 455). These, however, may have referred to other lands of his. 38 See my paper, as above, note 34.

her son Williarn, and others of the family were immediately captured by Duncan of Carrick, uncle of Alan of Galloway, but Hugh de Lacy and Reginald de Braose succeeded in escaping. The king, informed of this while still at Carrickfergus, sent John de Courcy (seemingly the former lord of Ulster) and Godfrey de Craucumbe to convey the prisoners to him, which they did.[40]

At first sight it may seem strange that the king should have become reconciled with John de Courcy, and should bring him on this expedition to his former lordship, without intending to reinstate him; but John's ways were not as other men's ways, and he probably derived a malign pleasure, first in using against Hugh de Lacy the man
[257] whom he had supplanted, and then in withholding from John de Courcy the lordship of which he had been deprived.[41]

As to Maud de Braose, according to John's own statement, when she was brought before him she offered 40,000 marks for life and limb of her husband, her family, and herself, her husband to quit-claim to John all his lands and castles. It is obvious that these preposterous conditions must have been imposed by John, not with any expectation that they could be fulfilled, but in order that their non-fulfilment might form a pretext for confiscation and outlawry. Ultimately the terms were agreed to and ratified, but default was made in the first payment, Maud declaring that she had not the money. Thereupon William de Braose was declared an outlaw. So far, with many additional details to emphasize his forbearance, John gives his account of the matter, and as the document is attested by the Earl of Ferrers [see *Add.*], nephew of William de Braose, and by Adam de Port, his brother-in-law, as well as by several eminent men, we may accept the facts stated as formally correct though misleading. John does not tell the sequel, however. William de Braose died next year, an exile in
[258] France, while his wife and eldest son were starved to death in prison by order of the king.[42]

39 Upwards of thirty are mentioned by name in the Rolls as having been taken prisoners in the castle, and subsequently, at different times extending over six years, as being released on payment of a fine. Among those connected with Ulster may be mentioned William and Luke de Audley, a name which survives in Audley Castle on Strangford Lough; Walter de Logan, witness of John de Courcy's charter to the church of Down, and one of the magnates of Ireland in 1221; Robert de Weldebuef, whose land called Edereskel lay between Holywood and Ballyoran (Reeves, Eccl. Tax., pp. 359, 361); Robert and Thomas Talbot, who had lands at Irewe and Brakenberg (Reeves, Eccl. Tax., p. 57); and Ralph de Rossal (Russell). Among those connected with Meath were Hubert Hose of Galtrim, Lucian de Arquilla, and Gilbert de Weston, who had lands in the honour of Nobber; John de Feipo, son of Adam de Feipo of Skreen; Michael, son of Adam le Gros, and Walter Sancmesle, both of whom were again in rebellion in 1224. On the other hand, several names of those who either at this time or soon afterwards were landholders in Ulster, Uriel, or Meath appear among the knights who supported John, e.g. Robert and Thomas le Savage, Robert de Mandeville, Ralph Gernun, Eborard de Vernun, Hugh de Bernevall; besides Nicholas de Verdun and Roger Pipard, tenants *in capite* in Uriel. 40 Rymer's Foedera, vol. i, pt. i, p. 108. There is just an element of doubt as to the identity of this John de Courcy, as there was another John de Courcy, son of Roger of Chester, who had been one of the hostages of the conqueror of Ulster (*supra*, p. 139, n. [p. 206, note 62], and who early in the next reign claimed his father's lands in Ulster: Cal. Docs. Ireland, vol. i, no. 833. But for reasons already given (*supra*, p. 143 [p. 207]) there can be little real doubt that it was the former lord of Ulster who accoompanied King John. 41 Before John left Ireland a prest of 20 marks was made to John de Courcy, presumably for his services: Rot. de Prest., p. 227. 42 So much seems certain. The story of

As for the de Lacys, a story is told in some late Latin annals to the effect that on being expelled from Ireland they fled for refuge to the monastery of St. Taurin in Normandy, and worked there, unknown, in menial employment until at length the abbot discovered who they were; that at the abbot's intercession the king restored them to their former rank and lordships; and that Walter de Lacy, out of gratitude, gave to the abbot's nephew, John Fitz Alured, the lordship of Dengyn, and brought monks from St. Taurin and gave them farms and the cell called Foure.[43] Though most of the details of this story can be shown to be apocryphal, it is not improbable that the de Lacys did actually seek shelter and hospitality from the monks of St. Taurin at Evreux. It appears, however, that it was Hugh de Lacy the elder who granted to those monks the churches and tithes of Fore, and the mill of St. Fechin there, and a wood near the town for their habitation;[44] while Thomas and Walter, sons of Alured, made [259]
grants of the church of Laracor (the parish in which Dengyn, now Dangan, is situated) at dates preceding the expulsion of the de Lacys.[45] This already established connexion may have induced the de Lacys to seek shelter with the monks of St. Taurin.

John was at Carrickfergus from the 19th to the 28th of July, and we have long lists of the knights to whom he made payments, dating from the 20th, when we must suppose the castle was in his hands. As at Carlingford and Rath, he made payments to carpenters and stoneworkers, apparently for repairs to the castle. Indeed these three castles were the principal —perhaps the only—regular stone castles in the lordship. Carrickfergus is a well-preserved example of the keep and bailey plan, situated on a rocky headland. It is doubtful whether the keep should be ascribed to Hugh de Lacy or to John de Courcy, but it is probable that the latter had a castle here.[46] The gateway and mural towers are later. While at Carrickfergus John sent a force to seize the castle [260]
of Antrim, and directed John de Gray to have two galleys built there for service on Lough Neagh. He gave Carrickfergus Castle to the custody of Geoffrey de Serland, and it was retained in the king's hand up to 1226.[47] Having made provision for the custody of his prisoners, and having dismissed his Irish auxiliaries, he now returned southwards.

On the 29th John was at Holywood, on the southern shore of Belfast Lough. This place, as well as Ardglas, appears to have belonged to Jordan de Saukeville,[48] and until

John's vengeance is told with many variants by the chroniclers. See Miss Norgate's John Lackland, p. 288, where the statements are collected and examined. 43 Laud MS. Annals, printed in Chart. St. Mary's, Dublin, vol. ii, p. 311. The story has been reproduced in the Book of Howth, p. 121, Grace's Annals, &c. 44 Cal. Docs. France (Round), vol i, p. 105. The charter is by Hugh de Lacy the elder, with the witnesses compare those of the elder Hugh's grant to William le Petit (one of whom was Thomas Fitz Alured): Song of Dermot, p. 310. Walter de Lacy further endowed the monks of Fore, but, in part at least, before his expulsion. 45 Reg. St. Thomas's, Dublin, p. 42. The name Fitz Alured became Fitz Averay, and a Thomas Fitz Averay was lord of the manor of Dengyn (now Dangan) in 1300: ibid., p. 421. 46 From a letter of Reginald, Bishop of Connor, c.1224, it appears that John de Courcy endowed the House of St. Mary of Carrickfergus to the use of canons of the Premonstratensian Order, and conferred on them the church of St. Nicholas at Carrickfergus, which he had probably built: Royal Letters, Cal. Docs. Ireland, i, no. 1225. From this it seems probable that John de Courcy defended the place with a castle. 47 Rot. Pat., 10 Hen. III. Geoffrey de Serland was succeeded as constable by William de Serland, who in 1223 was appointed Seneschal of Ulster: Rot. Pat., 7 Hen. III. 48 Rot. Claus., 1 Hen. III (p. 304 b).

recently there was a mote in the town. He visited 'Balimoran', probably now Ballymorran, a townland in the parish of Killinchy, barony of Dufferin, where 'White's Castle' stands on an earlier earthwork. Probably about the same time he seized the castles of Ballymaghan and Dundonald in the neighbourhood, as these castles were in the
[261] king's hand in 1221.[49] On the 2nd and 3rd of August John was again at Downpatrick, and on the 4th at the river Bann. The exact spot on the river was probably at the place now called Hilltown, in the parish of Clonduff, where there is a mote. It lies on the direct route from Downpatrick to Narrow Water, where John probably crossed the inlet on his way back to Carlingford, which he reached on the 5th. Here he sent an officer to the Isle of Man 'to guard the king's supplies there', but, according to unofficial accounts, the island was plundered by John's men at this time.[50]

On the 8th John was at Drogheda, where the castle on 'the Millmount' guarding the bridge was taken into his hand and retained permanently. On the 9th he went on to Duleek, on the 10th to Kells, and on the 11th to Fore, where he took Walter de
[262] Lacy's castle into his hand.[51] On the 12th he reached Granard, the mote-castle of Richard de Tuit,[52] on the north-western frontier of the lordship of Meath. He now turned south, and was at Rathwire on the 14th. It belonged to Robert de Lacy. The remains show that it was a mote and bailey castle, and that a stone castle was afterwards built in the bailey.

At Rathwire Cathal Crovderg came to meet John, according to arrangement, but failed to satisfy him. The relations between Cathal and John at this time are somewhat obscure. Cathal, as we have seen, owed his crown to the support given to him by William de Burgh and the English king—a support which was not given for nothing. When William de Burgh turned against Cathal after the massacre of his men in 1203, John, through Meiler Fitz Henry, forced William to give way, and continued to support Cathal, retaining in his hand, however, the rights acquired by William in Connaught. In March 1204 the king sent Meiler and the Archdeacon of Stafford (Henri de Londres, the future Archbishop of Dublin), along with Walter de Lacy to arrange matters with Cathal.[53] We have records of two proposals made to regulate Cathal's
[263] position. The first was communicated by Meiler in August 1204. By it Cathal was to quit-claim two-thirds of Connaught to the king and retain the remaining third as an estate of inheritance at a rent of 100 marks.[54] John's rapacity probably caused the negotiations to fail. In December 1205 a new proposal was presented by an Irishman[55]

49 Called 'Dundunnelan and Balimichgan': Rot, Pat., 6 Hen. III. 50 In the Annals of Loch Cé it is stated that, after taking Carrickfergus, John sent a fleet of his people to the Isle of Man and 'they plundered it and killed its people'. So William of Newburgh, vol. ii, p. 511, 'insulam Man destruxit.' In May 1212 John granted to Reginald, King of Man, a knight's fee near Carlingford and 100 seams of wheat to be received yearly at Drogheda, and the two kings reciprocally bound themselves to punish acts of violence of their subjects on each other's territory: Rot. Chart., 14 John, p. 186 b; Rot. Pat., 14 John, p. 92 b. 51 Fore (Irish, *Fabhar*, latinized *Favoria*) was restored to Walter de Lacy in 1215: Rot. Pat., 17 John, p. 148 b. 52 Apud Grenard, called 'castrum Ricardi de Thuit': Rot. de Prest., 12 John, p. 248. It was restored to Walter de Lacy along with other castles in 1215, but Richard de Tuit was killed in 1211, and the castle may in consequence have been in the king's hand. 53 Liberate, 5 John, p. 83. 54 Rot. Claus., 6 John, p. 6 b, Cal. no. 222; Rymer's Foedera, vol. i, pt. i, p. 91. 55 The Irishman's name is printed Deremunt. It is proba-

on Cathal's behalf, namely that he should hold in fee of the king a third of Connaught as a barony at 100 marks a year, and for the remaining two-thirds he should render a tribute of 300 marks. He was to grant to the king two cantreds with their villeins to farm or do his pleasure therein.[56] A charter appears to have been granted on some such terms, and is referred to in a later document.[57] In 1207 the king made grants of lands in Connaught to John Marshal and Gilbert de Angulo.[58] These lands appear to have been (partly at any rate) comprised in the baronies of Athlone and Longford, in the counties of Roscommon and Galway respectively. When John came to Ireland, Cathal [264] Crovderg accompanied him with a force to Carrickfergus. On their return from the north it was arranged that Cathal was to meet John in a fortnight and bring his son Aedh with him as a hostage, and that John would grant him a charter, framed apparently so as to include Aedh, for the third part of Connaught. O'Conor, on reaching home, however, adopted the advice of his wife not to take his son to the king, 'although,' says the annalist, 'this was the worst counsel.' Accordingly, when Cathal came to Rathwire without his son, John was evidently enraged, and seized four important members of O'Conor's retinue, and took them with him as hostages.[59] Later in the year, as we shall see, O'Conor was forced to come to terms with John de Gray, the justiciar, and to give his son Turlough as a hostage.

On the 18th of August John was back at Dublin. Here he stayed for six days before his departure, and we have a long list of his knights to whom he made payments. On [265] the 24th he was at a mead near Dublin, perhaps at Ringsend (if this was the place of his embarkation), and on the 26th he was at Fishguard.

When John was in Dublin after the surrender of Carrickfergus, he charged the Earl Marshal with having sheltered William de Braose, his mortal enemy, and having aided his escape. The earl made much the same answer as he had previously made to the justiciar, adding that if any one except the king accused him he was ready to defend himself according to the judgement of the court. As had happened once before, no one accepted the challenge. The king then demanded hostages, and named Geoffrey Fitz Robert, Jordan de Sauqueville, Thomas de Sanford, John d'Erlée, and Walter Purcell, and required that the castle of Dunamase should be delivered up to him. Only the two last named were present. These readily consented to give themselves up as hostages, and the earl delivered them and his castle to the king. John was still unsatisfied, and insisted on getting security from all the earl's barons who were present for the complete fulfilment of his demand. All agreed except David de la Roche, who was

ble that the individual was Dermot Mac Dermot, King of Moylurg, who accompanied Cathal to Rathwire and was seized as a hostage. **56** Rot. Claus., 7 John, p. 62, Cal. no. 279. **57** Ibid., 8 John, p. 78 b, Cal. no. 311, confirming Cathal's grant of Maenmagh to Gilbert de Angulo. **58** Ibid., 9 John, pp. 173, 173 b. **59** Ann. Loch Cé, 1210. The men seized as hostages were Dermot Mac Dermot, King of Magh Luirg, Conor O'Hara, King of Luighne, Find O'Carmacan and Toirberd, officers of O'Conor's household. They were released next year when Cathal's son was sent. John stopped at Castellum Bret on the 17th. Its position is uncertain. Milo le Bret had lands near Dublin for which an exchange was ordered to be given him in 1207: C.D.I., vol. i, nos. 360, 361. His principal seat seems to have been at Mainclare, said to be Moyclare in Meath: Chart. St. Mary's, Dublin, vol. i, 128–9.

regarded with contempt by the rest.[60] When John returned to England he bailed out
[266] his hostages in various places there. Next year the Marshal fought for the king against Llewelyn in Wales, and then the king restored to him his hostages, but to Geoffrey Fitz Robert death came before liberty.[61] The earl returned to Ireland and remained there until the beginning of the year 1213, when he was again summoned to England in view of the threatened invasion of England by Philip Augustus. Then at last the king handed over the earl's two sons, one to John d'Erlée and one to Thomas de Sanford.[62]

John was about nine weeks in Ireland. During this time he had crushed William de Braose, expelled the de Lacys, and confiscated their lands. Even from Earl William Marshal he had exacted a number of hostages and taken the castle of Dunamase. In the course of his progress he had seized the principal castles of the lordships of Meath and Ulster, including the following: in Meath, Trim, Drogheda, Ratoath, Nobber, Fore, Granard, Loughsewdy, and Clonard; and in Ulster, Carrickfergus, Antrim, Car-
[267] lingford, Dundrum, and others.[63] Those in Meath, except Ratoath and Nobber (which had belonged to Hugh de Lacy) were restored to Walter de Lacy for a fine of 4,000 marks in 1215, while the castles of Ulster were not restored to Hugh de Lacy until after 1226. Of the de Lacy feoffees John had taken a large number prisoners at the surrender of Carrickfergus, and these he committed to the custody of various persons in England. It would seem that by far the major part of the lands of the barons of Meath and of Ulster were confiscated or held to ransom, and in several cases new grants were made to those of John's adherents whom he wished to reward. Thus John immediately granted to Duncan, son of Gilbert, lord of Carrick, who had captured Maud de Braose and her son, 'the town of Wulfrichford' (the Ulfreksfiordr of the Northmen, now Larne), and all the lands which Roger de Preston and Henry Clemens held near Wulfrichford' and as far as Glenarm.[64] Other grantees had afterwards to give up for an exchange the lands granted to them when the former owners were restored.[65]

[268] John was not ignored on this visit by the Irish princes, as he had been on his visit twenty-five years before. Indeed, the difference in their attitude is the measure of the growth of Anglo-Norman influence during the interval. At his summons the kings of Limerick or Thomond, Connaught, and Tirowen all appear to have led contingents to Carrickfergus. Aedh O'Neill was ready enough to assist in expelling his enemy Hugh de Lacy, but he managed to return home without giving hostages to John.[66] Cathal Crovderg's position was less independent, and, as we have seen, he was forced to give hostages. Murtough O'Brien [67] and his brother Donough were entirely depen-

60 Histoire, ll. 14283–446. 61 Histoire, ll. 14447–86. This was the Welsh war of 1211: Rog. de Wend., vol. ii, p. 58. 62 Ibid., ll. 14487–578, and cf. Rot. Claus., 14 John, p. 132 b. 63 This, the main result of John's progress in Ireland, has not, I think, been duly noticed. Even so perspicacious a writer as Dr. G.T. Stokes describes John as merely 'personally inspecting the fortresses from Carrickfergus in the north . . . to Waterford in the South': Anglo Norman Church, p. 242. 64 Cal. Canc. Hib., vol. ii, p. 354, and see Rot. Claus., 3 Hen. III, p. 402 b, where the charter is stated to have been inspected. 65 Thus Sir William le Pugneor, 'the king's knight,' had to give up the land of William de Cusac in Ulster when the latter was reinstated: Rot. Pat., 18 John, p. 191 b; and so of Godfrey de Serland, constable of Carrickfergus: Rot. Claus., 18 John, p. 271. 66 Four Masters, *sub anno* 1209. 67 A prest of 10 marks was given to Mariadac,

dent on English support. According to Roger de Wendover, more than twenty kinglets came to meet John in Dublin, and these, stricken with fear, did him homage and fealty. A few, however, who dwelt in inaccessible places scorned to come to the king,[68] and the king, it may be added, in the spirit in which he had lost Normandy, seems to have scorned to subdue them.

After this expedition, John was in a very literal sense *dominus Hiberniae*, meaning [269]
by Hibernia the parts occupied by the English. The lordships of both Ulster and Meath, with their castles, were in his hand. Even the fiefs of most of the subordinate barons had been confiscated, only to be redeemed on payment of fines, and many of the owners were his prisoners. The settled parts of the kingdoms of Limerick and of Cork had been dealt with at one time or another almost at his will, and the principal tenants there held directly of him. The counties of Dublin (including most of Wicklow) and Waterford were from the first crown-lands. No great fief remained in the hands of his barons except the lordship of Leinster. This indeed he had endeavoured to curtail, and had it been in the hands of any one less strong, less patient, less upright, and less unswervingly loyal to the throne than William Marshal, he would assuredly have found some excuse for confiscating it also. Even of the Irish kinglets there were none except the chieftains of Irish Ulster and Irish Uriel that were not more or less dependent on his favour. From the greater part of these vast territories he enforced not only the feudal dues recognized as of right belonging to the immediate lord, but also in many cases those increases and arbitrary exactions which in a short time banded the barons of England together to wring from him the Great Charter.

Had John really established the domination of the Crown over 'the five-fifths of [270]
Ireland', Celtic and Norman, and left behind him an organization and a government capable of maintaining peace, much might be said for this curbing and crushing of the Irish barons. But he personally made no attempt to do anything of the kind. The net result of his personal interference in Ireland would seem to have been to disturb and weaken the settlement which had already been effected, and to divert a considerable portion of the issues and profits of the land into his own coffers.

But John is credited with introducing English laws into Ireland, organizing the administration of justice, parcelling out the parts of Ireland subject to his jurisdiction into counties, and appointing sheriffs to execute the judgements of the courts. Let us examine how far this was so. The principal authority on the subject is an English chronicler whose cursory notice of John's visit to Ireland certainly contains one misstatement of fact. He says that John 'established there the laws and customs of England, appointing sheriffs and other officers to administer justice to the people of that kingdom according to English laws.'[69] This statement, as it stands, is probably not incorrect. It is, however, vague and perhaps misleading. On the one hand, it must not be inferred that English laws and customs were introduced into Ireland for the first [271]
time in 1210; and on the other, the statement as to sheriffs and other officers is no

King of Limerick, at Ardglas: Rot. de Prest., p. 196. Indeed the Irish contingents must have been considerable: there was a prest of £100 to the Bishop of Norwich for Irish soldiers he had retained, ibid., p. 178; and again £40, ibid., p. 188. 68 Rog. of Wendover, vol ii, p. 56. 69 Rog of Wendover, vol. ii, p. 56.

authority for the definite assertion, made first apparently by Hanmer at the close of the sixteenth century,[70] then by Sir John Davies in 1608,[71] and since blindly repeated by a host of writers, that John 'made twelve shires in Leinster and Munster, namely Dublin, Kildare, Meath, Uriel, Carlow, Kilkenny, Wexford, Waterford, Cork, Limerick, Kerry, and Tipperary'.

Whether by a formal ordinance to that effect or by mere implication, Henry had undoubtedly introduced English laws and customs into Ireland, so far at least as the new settlers, who were alone prepared to accept them, were concerned. His grants of the lordships of Leinster and Meath to be held on feudal conditions would alone show that English law and custom were to rule, and it seems unnecessary to labour the point;[72] but, except in the court of the justiciar and as regards the lands retained by the Crown, the administration of law would seem to have been left to the lords of the liberties themselves.

[272] The dominating note of John's policy in Ireland was the increase of the power of the Crown and the weakening of that of the lords of the great liberties. In 1204 he granted authority to the justiciar that 'his writs should run throughout the king's entire land and dominion of Ireland', namely the writs of Right, of Mort d'Ancestor, of Novel Disseisin, of Fugitives and Villeins, and for Making Bounds;[73] and in 1207, at the time of the dissensions between Meiler and the barons, he forbade his subjects to answer in any court respecting their free tenements or on any plea of the Crown, save only before the king or his justiciar, or before the justices whom they should send for the upholding of the law.[74] These ordinances appear to have been directed against the courts of the liberties, which had apparently assumed a co-ordinate jurisdiction with the justiciar's court. When in 1208 John granted confirmation charters to William the Marshal and Hugh de Lacy, he introduced, as we have seen, some express exceptions and reservations not contained in the previous charters, and provided for appeals in certain cases to the king's court.

[273] It seems that when John came to Ireland in 1210 he took some formal steps to enjoin and secure the observance of English laws and customs. There are several allusions to this in the rolls of Henry III. Thus in 1228 the king commanded the justiciar Richard de Burgh to read before a specially convened assemblage 'the charter of the lord King John, our father, to which his seal was appended, which he caused to be made and to be sworn to by the magnates of Ireland concerning the observance of the laws and customs of England in Ireland', and to enjoin again obedience to those laws and customs;[75] and in the year 1233, in another ordinance, concerning pleas of lay fee and advowsons of churches, the king refers to 'the laws and customs of the realm of England which the lord King John our father of happy memory, with the common consent of all men of Ireland, ordained to be kept in that land.'[76] Here again it would

70 Hanmer's Chronicle, first ed., p. 188. Hanmer (ob. 1604) was clearly only amplifying in his usual way Roger de Wendover's statement. 71 Sir John Davies's Discovery (ed. 1787), p. 93; first published 1612. 72 See Lynch's Institutions, c. i. 73 Rot. Pat., 6 John, p. 47 b. 74 Rot. Pat., 9 John, p. 76 b; cf. the king's reprimand of the barons of Leinster and Meath for attempting to create a new assize. Rot. Pat., 8 John, p. 72. 75 Rot. Claus, 12 Hen. III, m. 8; Early Statutes (Berry), p. 23. 76 Rot. Pat., 18 Hen. III. m. 17; Early

seem that, though no doubt the whole common law of England was included by the terms of this ordinance, the main object was to settle the jurisdiction and procedure of the various courts.

The appointment of justices in eyre probably dates from about this time. Itinerant [274] justices are alluded to in John's charter to the city of Waterford in 1215,[77] and in an ordinance of Henry III certain assizes are directed to be taken 'in the same form and plan and before the same judges as assizes were taken from the time when King John established English laws and customs in Ireland'.[78] But the jurisdiction of these justices, except as regards pleas of the Crown, was limited to the settled districts outside the great liberties, and was probably only gradually extended over even this restricted area, and proceeded with the formation of counties in the strict sense of sheriffdoms. As long as a liberty existed ordinary legal processes therein were executed by the officers of the lord of the liberty, and not by a sheriff appointed by the Crown. Indeed, the touchstone of a true liberty was that in it the king's writs were addressed to the lord of the liberty or to his seneschal, and not to the king's sheriff.

The assertion that John divided Leinster and Munster into twelve counties in the [275] sense of administrative units subject to sheriffs, is demonstrably incorrect. Sheriffs may have been appointed by the Crown or by the justiciar for the districts retained in the king's hand from the first, but there is no clear evidence of this until after John's visit. Soon after this we find Geoffrey Luterel, who was one of John's officers on his Irish expedition, described as *vicecomes Dubliniensis*,[79] and we read of the counties (*comitatus*) of Waterford and of Cork or Desmond, which, however, were given to the custody of Thomas Fitz Anthony, who no doubt appointed his own legal officers. Uriel and the forfeited liberty of Ulster are called bailiwicks in 1215, when they were in the custody of Roger Pipard as seneschal.[80] Meath, until restored to Walter de Lacy in 1215, may have been similarly treated. The honour of Limerick does not appear to have been revived, though the castle and city of Limerick were granted to the custody of Reginald de Braose, son of William de Braose, by Henry III in his first year at 'the old farm', and the lands of his father were restored to him. When Limerick was first treated as a county under the jurisdiction of a sheriff does not appear, but in the Pipe Roll of the 19th year of Henry III (1235)[81] we have the accounts of sheriffs for the [276] counties of Dublin, Munster (or Cork), Limerick, Uriel, Waterford, and Kerry. In 1261 there were in addition sheriffs for the counties of Tipperary and Connaught,[82] from which last named was afterwards distinguished the county of Roscommon. So the list remained until the year 1297, when the first council of the magnates of Ireland which deserves the name of a parliament assembled. The writs summoning this par-

Statutes, p. 24. By 'all men of Ireland' is of course meant the Norman or English magnates. To have imposed English laws on the Celtic chieftains and their tribesmen would have been an utterly impossible task. 77 Chartae Priv. et Immun., p. 13, where the charter is wrongly dated the 7th instead of the 17th John; cf. Cal. Docs. Ireland, vol. i, no. 580, and the witnesses to John's Dublin charter of 1215 and to his grant to Thomas Fitz Anthony, July 3. There appear to have been justices in eyre in Ulster in 1218: Cal. Docs. Ireland, vol. i, no. 833. 78 Rot. Claus., 10 Hen. III, m. 2. Up to 1221 only a single justice went on circuit: Rot. Claus., 5 Hen. III, p. 451. 79 Chart. St. Mary's, Dublin, vol. i, p. 249; Reg. St. Thomas's, p. 17. 80 Rot. Pat., 17 John, p. 148. 81 35th Rep. Dep. Keeper Ireland, pp. 34–7. 82 Ibid., pp. 40, 44.

liament, called Wogan's first parliament, were addressed to the sheriffs of Dublin, Louth, Kildare, Waterford, Tipperary, Cork, Limerick, Kerry, Connaught, and Roscommon, and to the seneschals of the liberties of Meath, Wexford, Carlow, Kilkenny, and Ulster.[83]

It would be out of place here to pursue this inquiry further. Enough has been said to show that the formation of counties (in the sense of administrative units where pleas were heard before itinerant justices and legal processes were executed by a sher-
[277] iff appointed by the central government) was a very gradual process, and did not extend to the liberties included in the 'twelve counties' mentioned for many generations. A beginning, however, was probably made about the time of King John's visit, but for this and other administrative improvements, as well as for an improved coinage, credit should probably be given not directly to John, but to his minister, John de Gray, whom he left behind him as justiciar. The appointment to the chief office in Ireland of a cultivated English ecclesiastic, trained in affairs, and with a practical knowledge of legal and administrative machinery, was the best thing John did for Ireland at this time.

83 Early Statutes of Ireland (Berry), p. 195. The text is given in Irish Arch. Soc. Misc., p. 15. Kildare here appears for the first time as a sheriffdom. It had been recently surrendered to the king, so that the liberty had merged in the Crown: Cal. Docs. Ireland, vol. iv, no. 365. By this parliament Kildare was constituted a separate county.

CHAPTER XXII [279]

EPISCOPAL VICEROYS, 1210–16

When King John departed from Ireland he left behind him his faithful minister, John de Gray, Bishop of Norwich, as justiciar.[1] By the Irish annalists he is usually designated 'the Foreign Bishop'. The epithet, whether so intended or not, may serve to recall the facts that he was the first episcopal viceroy and, with one or two unimportant exceptions, the first chief governor who had not already thrown in his fortunes with Ireland and was not a great Irish landholder. Meiler Fitz Henry was a brave soldier and an able commander, and one well adapted to the rough-and-tumble work of the 'first conquest', but he had not developed the qualities of a statesman, and possessed neither the prudence, the tact, nor the authority requisite to guide and control the barons of Ireland. In the course of his ten years' tenure of office he had fallen foul [280]
of, and even come into armed collision with, William de Burgh, William de Braose, Walter and Hugh de Lacy, Geoffrey de Marisco, and William Marshal. He had not even the territorial status to enable him, apart from his office, to take his place among the greater barons. He held lands about Dunamase in the lordship of Leinster and about Ardnurcher in the lordship of Meath, but he was tenant *in capite* only of some distant and unprofitable lands in the west of Kerry. Nor, so far as we can judge, was he always justified in his opposition to the great barons. It may indeed be said that he was always loyal to the Crown, and was at worst only the tool of a capricious and tyrannical master; but there is reason to think that in some cases, at any rate, he was not merely a willing tool, but that in the counsel he gave to his sovereign he aimed rather at advancing his own interests than at promoting the general weal.

The new justiciar, whatever his imperfections as an ecclesiastic may have been, was a trained statesman and man of affairs, and something of a military strategist besides. He regarded the colony as a whole, set about strengthening the weak parts in its defence, and by diplomacy backed by military measures endeavoured to win the submission of those Irish chieftains who still retained more or less of their independence. [281]
He at once saw the strategic importance of Athlone. Whoever held the passage over the Shannon here held the gate between Connaught and Meath. This indeed had long been perceived by the O'Conors. As long ago as 1129 they had erected a fort of some sort here, and had again and again, in 1120 and subsequent years, thrown wicker-bridges across the river in order that, as one Irish annalist explains, 'they might at their

1 The Four Masters in recording the bishop's appointment under the year 1208 (which may be right) add: 'and the English were excommunicated by the successor of St. Peter for sending the bishop to carry on war in Ireland'—a novel reading of papal motives in proclaiming the interdict!

pleasure have access to take the spoils of Westmeath'. As often as built, however, the bridges at the first opportunity had been destroyed by the O'Melaghlins of Meath, whose land was threatened thereby.[2]

[282] Athlone had been occupied by the English before 1199, when, we are told, the bawn there was burned by Cathal Crovderg;[3] and it seems probable that the mound of earth, to this day contained by the curtain walls of the castle, represents the mote thrown up in connexion with this bawn. Possibly the original wooden tower and wooden defences were no longer in existence in 1210. At any rate, immediately after the king's departure John de Gray commenced to build a bridge—no doubt a wooden bridge—and a strong castle at Athlone.[4] We are expressly told by one Irish annalist[5] that the castle was of stone, from which we may infer that such a castle was even then a novelty, at least in this neighbourhood. It included 'a stone tower' or keep, built, no doubt, on the summit of the mote where its successor stands to-day. This tower, perhaps owing to the looseness of the artificial foundation, fell next year, and in its fall killed Richard de Tuit and eight Englishmen besides. He was the Richard de Tuit at
[283] whose castle of Granard King John had stopped on August 12, 1210, and was probably the same Richard de Tuit to whom the elder Hugh de Lacy had granted 'a rich feoffment'. According to some of the Irish annals he was left in Ireland as Lord Chief Justice in 1211, when John de Gray and the magnates of Ireland were summoned by the king to attend the expedition undertaken in that year against Llewelyn of Wales. This statement is probably correct, and Richard de Tuit was probably concerned with the castle of Athlone in his capacity as deputy at the time of his tragic death.[6]

2 Here are the notices in the annals of the Four Masters of the bridge of Athlone, which has been strangely described as 'a work of much merit and utility in those days':— 1120: Bridge built by Turlough O'Conor, after making 'a false peace' with Murrough O'Melaghlin. 1125: Bridge destroyed by the men of Meath. 1129: Bridge and castle built by Turlough. 1133: Bridge and castle destroyed by O'Melaghlin and O'Rourke. 1140: A wicker-bridge made by Turlough, and 'he devastated the west of Meath'. 1153: The wicker-bridge destroyed by Melaghlin O'Melaghlin and its fortress (*daingen*) demolished. 1155: A wicker-bridge was made by Turlough 'for the purpose of making incursions into Meath'. It was destroyed in the same year, and its fortress (*longport*) burned by Donough O'Melaghlin. 1159: A wicker-bridge made by Rory O'Conor 'for the purpose of making incursions into Meath'. The forces of Meath went to prevent the erection of the bridge, and a battle was fought at Athlone. 3 Ann. Loch Cé, 1199, where the *bodhun Atha*, 'the bawn of the ford,' seems clearly to refer to Athlone. It was probably by way of reply to this attack that the cantred in Connaught known as Tir Fhiachrach bhfeadha, or the Faes of Athlone, was granted in the next year to Geoffrey de Costentin: Rot. Chart., 2 John, p. 79 b. 4 Ann. Loch Cé, 1210. 5 Ann. Clonmacnois: *caislen cloiche—tor cloiche*. 6 See Ann. Clonmacnois and Four Masters, 1210 (the true date was 1211: Ann. Loch Cé; Laud MS. Ann., Chart. St. Mary's Abbey, Dublin). O'Donovan, on quite insufficient grounds, questions the statement that Richard de Tuit was justiciar at the time, but though the date is wrong and the entry in the Four Masters confused, it is pretty clear that John de Gray and the magnates were summoned for the campaign of 1211 (described by Rog. de Wendover, vol. ii, p. 58), as they certainly were for the abortive one of 1212 (Rot. Claus., 16 John, p. 131 b). In the Histoire de Guillaume le Marechal it is expressly stated (ll. 14447–86) that William Marshal fought for the king against Llewelyn in the year after John's Irish expedition. From the Pipe Roll, 13 John, it appears that the Bishop of Norwich brought the king's money from Ireland in that year, and Roger de Wendover includes him among the king's *consiliarii iniquissimi* at the time (Aug. 30, 1211) when Pandulf the papal legate absolved John's subjects from their allegiance. During the absence from Ireland of the Bishop of Norwich somebody must have been appointed justiciar or deputy in his room, and there is no reason to doubt that this was Richard de Tuit.

The castle of Athlone was soon rebuilt, and perhaps the mote was this time revetted [284] with masonry, similarly as we see it to-day, so that the disaster should not recur. The castle has been altered from time to time to suit later military requirements. It was tremendously shattered by Ginckell in 1691, and since restored. Yet it remains to-day in essentials much as we may suppose it to have been left by John de Gray: a great platform of earth, raised some twenty five feet above the river-bank, held in position by strong retaining walls, and bearing on top a massive decagonal donjon-tower. The reconstructed castle was given to the custody of Geoffrey de Costentin, to whom John had previously given lands in the neighbouring district on the Roscommon side, and except for a comparatively brief period in the fifteenth century, when the Crown lost possession of it, it has always remained a royal castle.[7]

While John de Gray was building this castle and bridge at Athlone in 1210, an expedition, probably authorized by the king, was led into Connaught by Geoffrey de Marisco, Thomas Fitz Maurice, and the English of Munster, supported as usual by Donough Cairbrech O'Brien and his men. Aedh, one of the sons of Rory O'Conor, was brought with them, in case it should be necessary to play off a rival claimant to the [285] throne. Cathal, however, showed no fight, and on his agreeing to meet the justiciar all depredations were stayed. At Athlone peace was concluded between the justiciar and Cathal. The latter was now prepared to satisfy King John's demands. The obligation to pay rent or tribute was again acknowledged, and Cathal gave his son Turlough and the son of another noble as hostages.[8]

The terms of the Peace of Athlone were apparently more favourable to Cathal than the arrangement of 1205. They were finally embodied in the charter of 1215, by which John granted and confirmed to Cathal all the land of Connaught to hold of the king in fee during good service, and so that the King of Connaught should not be disseised of his land without judgement of the king's court, rendering for ever to the king 300 marks, and saving to the king the castle of Athlone.[9] The grant, however, was per- [286] sonal to Cathal, and he was liable to be disseised by judgement of the king's court in default of good service. In pursuance of this treaty two cantreds in the neighbourhood of Roscommon, which had been granted under the former arrangement to John Marshal and Philip de Angulo respectively, appear to have been restored to Cathal and the feoffees compensated.[10]

7 See my paper, 'Athlone: its early history,' Journ. R.S.A.I. 1907, pp. 257–76. 8 Ann. Clonmacnois, 1208 or 1209 (*recte* 1210); Ann. Loch Cé, 1210. Next year (1211) the four hostages forcibly taken by John at Rathwire were restored (ibid. 1211). Cathal kept Christmas probably in 1212 with the deputy in Dublin (Ann. Clonmacnois, 1211). Cathal's son, Turlough, died in restraint with the Englishmen (ibid. 1213). 9 Rot. Chart., 17 John, p. 219. Cathal was to pay 5,000 marks for this charter; Rot. Claus., 17 John, p. 228 b. At the same time an alternative charter was prepared granting to Richard de Burgh all the land of Connaught which William his father held of the king: Rot. Chart., 17 John, m. 3 (p. 218 b). This charter, we must suppose, was to be delivered only if Cathal failed to take up the other, and in the events which happened became for the time a dead letter. It is, however an example of John's double-dealing. 10 Rot. Claus., 17 John, p. 223, Cal. no. 630, where 'the cantred of Roscoman' appears to be equivalent to Moy Ai, and Rot. Pat.,17 John, p. 152, Cal. no. 537 where 'Kilman' is probably now represented by the parish of Kilmeane, where we may perhaps see a trace of Anglo-Norman tenure in the demesne of Mote Park; cf. the grant to John Marshal in 1207 (Rot. Chart., 9 John, p. 173 b) 'of the cantred in which the vill of

The Peace of Athlone seems to have been on the whole loyally observed on both sides until after Cathal's death in 1224. Cathal remained a faithful vassal of the king, sending petitions to him directly or through the English justiciar, and in common with other tenants *in capite* receiving the king's mandates.[11] Though he was attacked more
[287] than once by the sons of Rory, these aspirants to the throne of Connaught received no assistance from the English. Once indeed in 1221 Walter de Lacy made an attempt to build a castle at Athleague, a ford over the Shannon to the north of Lough Ree, but he was at once compelled by Cathal to desist;[12] and once in 1219 Richard de Burgh, who had hereditary claims to parts of Connaught, privately sought to obtain a charter curtailing Cathal's rights,[13] but this proposal was for the time rejected, and to the end Cathal remained King of Connaught, owing tribute to, and receiving protection from, the English Crown.

The ultimate aim of John de Gray's policy, like that of Henry VIII more than three centuries later, seems to have been to convert the Irish kings who were still independent into feudal barons holding their several tribe-lands directly from the English Crown. No attempt was made to impose feudal law on the tribesmen, and though the charter to Cathal was in form similar to the grant of a liberty to an English baron, reserving the pleas of the Crown, it is probable that no attempt was made to hold these pleas or interfere in any way as long as Cathal 'served the king well'. A rent of 300 marks was exacted and an occasional aid demanded, as from the English barons. In
[288] return letters of protection were granted, and, as we have said, during Cathal's lifetime the treaty seems to have worked well. It was certainly an improvement on the Treaty of Windsor, which left the other Irish kings subordinate to the King of Connaught, and tributary, through him, to the English Crown. This, as we have seen, was from the first unworkable. But even if John de Gray had succeeded in making similar arrangements with the northern chieftains, we may well doubt whether the aim of the policy could have been effected. On the one hand there was the constant pressure of English barons seeking more land and offering better security to the Crown for rents and services, and on the other there was a constant temptation, if not to the actual chiefs, at least to some aspirant to the throne, to gain popularity and power by refusing to pay tribute, throwing off the slight restraints imposed by the treaty, and carrying out some successful raid against the foreigners. Above all, the effect of granting the tribal territory as an hereditary fief to the existing chieftain was to introduce the feudal rule of descent and to disappoint the roydamnas, other than the chieftain's eldest son, of all hope of succession.

Having thus secured the allegiance of the King of Connaught, while that of the O'Briens of Thomond was already assured, John de Gray next turned his attention to the chieftains of the north of Ireland. Aedh O'Neill, the most powerful of these, had,
[289] as we have seen, joined the expedition to Carrickfergus to expel his dangerous neighbour Hugh de Lacy, but he avoided giving the hostages to King John—perhaps he

Kylmien is situated'. 11 Royal, &c., Letters, Hen. III (Shirley), vol. i, pp. 165, 183, 223; Rot. Claus., 3 Hen. III, p. 390 b, and 5 Hen. III, p. 476 b. 12 Ann. Loch Cé, 1221. 13 Rot. Claus., 3 Hen. III, p. 401, Cal. no. 900.

refused to give them. We may conclude that John had directed his justiciar, after securing Cathal's allegiance, to take measures to enforce the submission of the north. It was a difficult enterprise, as the whole history of Ireland shows, and, with the scanty means at the bishop's disposal, an impossible one. Nevertheless the bishop seems to have laid his plans well. The recalcitrant chieftains were attacked from three different quarters. First of all a hosting of Connaught men, presumably by agreement with Cathal, was sent under the leadership of Gilbert Mc Costello (who had long been in Cathal's service, and held land in Connaught) to Assaroe, at the debatable borderland between Connaught and Tirconnell. Here, somewhere in the district known as Caol-uisce (Narrow Water), where the waters of Castle of Lough Erne begin to narrow into the river, they erected a castle.[14] This was the gate of Connaught from the north, and the scene of many a battle with the Cinel Connell. Cathal may have consented to the erection of a castle here to protect Connaught from his hereditary foes, while John de [290]
Gray's object may rather have been to obtain a basis for action in this direction against the northern chieftains. About the same time the bishop led an English force to Clones and erected a castle there, with the object, according to an Irish annalist, 'of taking possession of the North of Erinn'. Clones was an ancient ecclesiastical centre in Irish Uriel, and lay outside the area of English domination, the limits of which in this region seem to have been marked by Roger Pipard's castle of Donaghmoyne. There is a steep mote at Clones which may be regarded as a memorial of this expedition. The attempt, however, failed. Mac Mahon, chieftain of Uriel, checked the advance into Tirowen, and Aedh O'Neill completed the defeat.[15]

Lastly, the bishop probably countenanced, if he did not actually plan, an incursion made in this year by the Scots of Galloway to Derry and Inishowen against the Cinel Owen. John, as we have seen, had rewarded Duncan of Carrick's capture of Maud de Braose by a grant of territory between Wulfrichford (near Larne) and Glenarm in Antrim. He also, it seems, promised a huge grant of lands in the northern part of the lordship of Ulster to Alan Fitz Roland, Earl of Galloway, Duncan's nephew.[16] Some time in the spring of 1212 the bishop met at Carrickfergus emissaries from Alan, [291]
including Alan's uncle, and there assigned to Alan on the king's behalf 140 fees, extending apparently over the whole north-east of Ulster from the river Foyle to the Glynns of Antrim. From this grant were excepted ten fees on each side of the Bann near the castle of Kilsantan, which were to be retained in the king's hand; also all church-lands, and the lands already granted to Duncan of Carrick.[17] It can hardly be a mere coincidence that in this same year Alan's brother, Thomas, Earl of Athol, and some of the Mac Donnells came with a fleet of seventy-six ships to Derry, and in com-

14 Ann. Ulster, Ann. Loch Cé, 1212; Four Masters, 1211. In 1214 the territory of Carbury (Co. Sligo) [see *Add.*], not many miles south of Assaroe, is called by the Four Masters the possession of Philip Mac Costello. 15 Ann. Loch Cé, Ann. Ulster, 1212; Four Masters, 1211. 16 'Alanus filius Roulandi' accompanied John's army in Ireland: Rot. de Prest., 12 John, p. 186. 17 Rot. Pat., 14 John, p. 98; C.D.I., vol. i, no. 427. See this document transcribed with annotations by Bishop Reeves: Eccl. Ant. Down, Connor, and Dromore, pp. 323-5. The grant to Alan was confirmed by John in 1215 (Rot. Chart., 17 John, p. 210), and by Henry III in 1220; Rot. Claus., 4 Hen. III, p. 420 b.

pany with O'Donnell spoiled Inishowen.[18] Indeed the expeditions of the men of Gal-
[292] loway mentioned in the annals are regularly followed by grants from the Crown to the leaders engaged. Thus the expedition of 1212 was rewarded in July 1213 by a grant to the Earl of Athol of that part of Derry which belonged to O'Neill.[19] Again, in 1214 Thomas Mac Uchtry (as the Irish annalists call the Earl of Athol after his grandfather, Uchtred or Gothred) built the castle of Coleraine, 'and they threw down all the cemeteries and clochans (probably dry-stone beehive-shaped cells) and buildings of the town, excepting the church alone, in order to build this castle.'[20] It was evidently of stone. On the same day as King John confirmed the charter to Alan of Galloway (June 27, 1215) he granted another to his brother Thomas, including Kilsantan and the cas-
[293] tle of Coleraine, with ten knights' fees on both sides of the Bann.[21] Thus early were the Scots planted in the north-east of Ireland, where they lived for centuries and formed a clan distinct from, but hardly less turbulent than, the Irish clans of Tirowen.

Notwithstanding these comprehensive plans, the attempt to enforce the submission of Aedh O'Neill was a failure. Not only did he repulse the advance into Tirowen from the newly erected castle of Clones, but in the following year, 1213, he burned the castle itself.[22] About the same time, at his instigation, the subordinate chieftain of Fermanagh, named O'Hegney, whose daughter Benmee was married to Aedh, burned the castle of Caol-uisce and killed its garrison, including Gilbert Mc Costello;[23] and in
[294] 1214 Aedh 'dealt a red slaughter' on the foreigners of Ulidia.[24] In fact, during a long reign of upwards of thirty years, though his territory was frequently raided by the for-

18 Ann. Ulster, 1212; Ann. Loch Cé, 1211; Four Masters, 1211. There can be little doubt that the true date of all three expeditions, to Caol-uisce, Clones, and Derry, was 1212. The entries in the Four Masters at this period are regularly antedated by a year. Inishowen, the peninsula between Lough Swilly and Lough Foyle, was for centuries debatable land between the Cinel Owen and the Cinel Connell. It had been plundered by John de Courcy in 1197, and seems to have been taken by O'Neill from O'Donnell after a bloody battle in 1209 (Ann. Ulster, &c.). **19** Rot. Chart., 15 John, m. 3 (p. 194), where 'Talachot' is perhaps Tullyhoe in the parish of Tallaght-Finlagan, Keenaught, and not, as has been supposed, Tullaghoge near Dungannon. There are indications that this grant was not wholly inoperative. There were Mac Donnells in Derry in the middle of the thirteenth century. Thus in 1259 Aedh O'Conor went to Derry to espouse the daughter of Dugald, son of Sorley Mac Donnell, and he brought home eight-score men with her, together with Alan Mac Sorley; Ann. Loch Cé. **20** Ann. Ulster, 1214; Ann. Loch Cé, 1213. In the previous year O'Kane, the petty King of Ciannacta and Fir na Craibhe, districts west of the Bann which had been granted to Alan, was killed by the Foreigners; and in 1214 Thomas of Galloway and Rory Mac Raghnall (Mac Donnell) again plundered Derry and carried off the loot to Coleraine. **21** Rot. Chart., 17 John, pt. i, m. 10 (p. 210). The castle of Coleraine was demolished by Hugh de Lacy and Aedh O'Neill in 1222 (Ann. Ulster, 1222; Ann. Loch Cé, 1221). When Hugh de Lacy's lands were restored in 1226–7 it would seem that the restoration was made 'saving the seisins of Alan and Thomas de Galloway' (C.D.I., vol. i, nos. 1372, 1498). In the town of Coleraine on the west side of the Bann is an artificial mound known as Gallows Hill, near the church of Killowen. This was probably the site of Thomas of Galloway's castle, and also of a later castle, called Drum Tairsigh, erected in 1248. **22** Ann. Ulster and Ann. Loch Cé, 1213. **23** Ibid. O'Hegney's name is given, Ann. Clonmacnois and Four Masters, 1212. Benmee died 1215. **24** Ann. Ulster and Ann. Loch Cé, 1214. O'Neill is said at the same time to have burned 'the Carlongphort'. This has been taken to refer to Carlingford, but it can hardly mean the castle, which seems to have been at this time safe in the custody of Roger Pipard (Rot. Pat., 17 John, p. 148), and it may be doubted whether it refers to that place at all, which is elsewhere always called Cairlinn in the Annals. Perhaps some minor fortress or fortified camp (*longport*) in the neighbourhood of Coleraine was intended.

eigners, and though he had many conflicts with the Cinel Connell, with Connaught, and even with his own tribesmen, Aedh O'Neill remained to the last 'a king who gave neither pledge nor hostage to Foreigner nor Gael'.[25]

After his repulse by Mac Mahon and O'Neill in 1212, John de Gray's attention was diverted by disturbances in the south-western portion of Meath, which it will be recollected was at this time in the king's hand. The ancient kingdom of Meath extended into the western part of the modern King's County, where the barony of Garrycastle represents the Irish district of Delvin Mac Coghlan, and the baronies of Ballycowan, Ballyboy, and Eglish represent the district of Fircal. The remaining western baronies, Ballybritt and Clonlisk, were included in Ely O'Carroll, which was reckoned part of Munster, and in the diocese of Killaloe. Since 1184, when Art O'Melaghlin, King of West Meath, was killed, Melaghlin Beg, or 'the Little', was king of the Irish of that region. In recent years, like the Kings of Thomond and Connaught, he seems to have [295] acquiesced in the Norman policy of 'pacific penetration', in the building of castles and planting of English settlements in various parts of his reduced kingdom, and we find Norman baron and subordinate Irish chieftain living in amity as neighbours. But there were among the 'roydamnas' some who resented the submission of their rulers, and perhaps thought by a 'spirited foreign policy' to earn for themselves the succession to the chieftainship. Such were Murtough, son of Brian O'Brien of Slieve Bloom, and Cormac, son of Art O'Melaghlin. Brian of Slieve Bloom had been for a brief period, in 1168–9, King of Ormond, when he was blinded by his brother, Donnell Mor O'Brien,[26] and thus Murtough had through his father special claims on Ormond, including presumably Ely O'Carroll, or the territory to the west of Slieve Bloom. This district was included in the grant to Theobald Walter; but he died in 1206, and as his son was a minor[27] the fief was taken into the king's hand. In 1207, however, John gave Matilda le Vavasour, widow of Theobald Walter, in marriage to Fitz Warin, with seisin of one-third of Theobald's land in dower.[28] How far Theobald had exploited his Irish [296] lands cannot be stated with certainty,[29] but he gave a large grant in Ely in frank-marriage to his daughter Beatrice (by a former marriage) and Thomas de Hereford,[30] and we may perhaps infer that the castles in Ely to be mentioned presently were erected by Theobald's feoffees. Fircal, as we have seen, seems to have been claimed by Meiler Fitz Henry adversely to Walter de Lacy, but in the winter of 1207–8, in the course of his dispute with William Marshal and the de Lacys, Meiler was driven out of Fircal and out of his castle of Ardnurcher. Soon afterwards, taking advantage, no doubt, of the falling out of the invaders to endeavour to regain the territory near Slieve Bloom, Murtough O'Brien destroyed the castles of Kinnity, Birr, and Lothra—perhaps Lorrha, in County Tipperary, or perhaps the place now known as the Mote of Laragh (Ir.

25 Ann. Loch Cé, 1230. 26 Ann. Tigernach Continuation, 1168; Four Masters, 1169. See Pedigree of the O'Briens, *supra*, p. 151 [p. 211]. 27 This son, Theobald II, came of age and obtained seisin in 1221: Rot. Claus., 5 Hen. III, p. 463 b. 28 Rot. Claus., 9 John, p. 92 b. 29 We can trace Theobald exercising acts of ownership at Caherconlish and Abbeyowney in County Limerick, at Nenagh, Thurles, and perhaps Lorrha, in County Tipperary, as well as in Ely. He also held lands at Arklow, Tullow, and Gowran, in Leinster, and at Ardmulchan in Meath. 30 These lands included Corcatenny (now the parish of Tem-

[297] *Lathrach*), in Upper Ossory.[31] This was in 1208. In the preceding year the sons of Art O'Melaghlin, who was the predecessor of Melaghlin Beg in the titular kingship of Meath, preyed the town of Ballyloughloe and burnt part thereof. Melaghlin Beg and certain English forces overtook the marauders, but were discomfited, and a son of the king was slain.[32] In 1212 Cormac, one of the sons of Art O'Melaghlin, again became very active. He was opposed not only by the English settlers, but sometimes by Irishmen as well, but he was generally successful, especially over the English. He wrested Delvin Mac Coghlan from them, probably early in 1212. Thereupon 'the foreign bishop' hastened to Leinster, and, joined by the forces of Munster under Donough Cairbrech O'Brien, delivered battle at a place called Kilnagrann in Fircal, but was defeated with loss of 'cows, horses, gold, silver, and other things'.[33] Next, in 1213, a
[298] purely Irish combination, consisting of an O'Brien of Thomond, an O'Melaghlin of Meath, an O'Dempsy of Clan Malier, and a Mac Gillapatrick of Upper Ossory, succeeded in giving Cormac 'an overthrow'.[34] Evidently Cormac was a discontented roydamna, who tried to win a principality, or at least plunder, for himself, and cared not at whose expense. Then the Englishmen of Meath combined against him, but once more were overthrown at the same battlefield of Kilnagrann in Fircal. Among the names of those slain we can recognize Piers Messet, Baron of Lune in Meath. This time Cormac was assisted by Aedh, son of Conor Mainmoy, and Melaghlin, son of Cathal Carragh, disappointed 'roydamnas' like himself.[35] They formed a sort of 'cave of Adullam'. On the side of the English was Geoffrey de Marisco, who was perhaps
[299] temporarily appointed *custos* or deputy in the place of the Bishop of Norwich, prior to the arrival of the new justiciar, Archbishop Henri de Londres.[36]

Henri de Londres had been recently appointed Archbishop of Dublin in succession to John Cumin, who died about the close of 1212. He had been a trusted minister of King John from the beginning of his reign. He was an experienced lawyer, and

plemore) and Ikerrin in County Tipperary: Reg. St. Thomas's, Dublin, pp. 196–7. Beatrice afterwards married Hugh Purcell, baron of Lochmoe (ibid., p. 193). Roger Poer was another of Theobald's feoffees in Ely (ibid., p. 198). 31 Ann. Clonmacnois, 1207. At this time Murtough O'Brien, with the sons of O'Conor of Connaught, also spoiled the castle of Athronny in Leix, identified by O'Donovan with Ballyroan in Queen's County. There are, or were, motes at these four places: Journ. R.S.A.I. 1909, p. 336. 32 Ann. Clonmacnois, 1206. Ballyloughloe (Ir. *Baile locha Luatha*, 'the town of the lake of ashes,' i.e. dried-up lake?) is six miles east of Athlone. There is 'a typical Norman mote here fashioned out of an esker ridge, and apparently untouched since it bore its wooden tower and wooden palisades': Journ. R.S.A.I. 1907, p. 273. 33 Ann. Clonmacnois, 1211; Ann. Loch Cé, 1212. 34 Ann. Clonmacnois, 1212. These chieftains had all probably made terms with the English. They were Murtough O'Brien of Thomond, Donnell, son of Donnell Bregach O'Melaghlin, the recognized tanist of Melaghlin Beg of West Meath, Cuilen O'Dempsy of Clan Malier, and Donnell Clannagh Mac Gillapatrick of Upper Ossory. All of them were left in possession of parts of their territories. 35 Ann. Loch Cé, 1213; Ann. Clonmacnois, Four Masters, 1212. The editor of the Annals of Loch Cé, following O'Donovan, suggests that the two entries as to Kilnagrann refer to the same battle, but the details as well as the dates are different. The second battle probably took place after John de Gray's return to England in July 1213. Obit Petrus Messet, 1213, Chart. St. Mary's, Dublin, i, p. 31. 36 The Bishop of Norwich, with 500 knights and many horsemen from Ireland, attended the great muster at Barham Down near Canterbury, May 4–6, 1213, and appears not to have returned to Ireland: Rog. of Wend., vol. ii, p. 67. Archbishop Henri did not reach Ireland before the end ef July, when he came as justiciar.

had acted as an itinerant justice in Berkshire and as a judge of the king's bench at Westminster. He was a skilful diplomatist, and had been employed on various embassies to foreign countries. He had served as a treasury official, and it is probable that his experience as such was not the least of his recommendations for his new post in his master's eyes, now that Ireland was becoming a considerable source of revenue to the Crown. He was not unknown in Ireland. As Archdeacon of Stafford he had formed one of a special commission sent to Ireland in 1204 to adjudicate on the cross plaints of Meiler Fitz Henry and William de Burgh, and at the same time he was commissioned along with Meiler Fitz Henry to negotiate with Cathal Crovderg concerning the future tenure of Connaught.[37] He was again sent to Ireland in June 1212,[38] but [300]
for what purpose does not appear. And now, on July 23, 1213, three days after the ceremony of the king's absolution from the papal excommunication, John thanked the prelates and magnates of Ireland for their good and faithful service, which had been commended by the Bishop of Norwich, and notified to them the appointment of Archbishop Henri as justiciar.[39] At this time the archbishop retained the office of justiciar for barely two years, when he was summoned to the king's presence and stood by the king at Runnymede on June 15, 1215.[40] On July 6, Geoffrey de Marisco was formally appointed justiciar in his stead,[41] and it was not until July 1221 that the archbishop was again in complete control, under the king, of the government of Ireland.[42] As justiciar, and still more indelibly as archbishop, he has left his mark on the country. At present, however, we are only concerned with his doings during his first tenure of office, when he was more of a statesman and less of an ecclesiastic than he afterwards [301]
became.

The new justiciar arrived in Ireland about the beginning of August 1213, and had at once to deal with the disturbances in Ely O'Carroll, Fircal, and Delvin. Carrying out the plans of castle-building initiated by his predecessor, he first of all built or completed a castle at Roscrea.[43] The situation, near the southern end of the Roscrea Slieve Bloom Mountains, was well chosen to command and keep open at this critical point the main route from Dublin and Kildare to the newly settled districts in Ormond and Limerick. It was on the line of the ancient Irish road known as *Slighe Dala*. The old but now probably disused monastery of St. Cronan, still marked by the ruins of a round tower and Romanesque church, formerly existed at Roscrea, and the church-lands on which the castle was built belonged to the see of Killaloe, in which the ancient bishopric of Roscrea had been recently merged. An inquisition taken in 1245[44] informs us of the circumstances in which the castle was built, and is substantiated on all essential points by the annals. It is interesting, too, as showing incontrovertibly that even at this period the Normans, sometimes at any rate, built castles of [302]
the mote and bretesche type. The inquisition was evidently taken at the request of

37 Rot. Pat., 5 John, p. 39 b; Rot. de Lib., 5 John, p. 83. 38 Rot. Claus., 14 John, m. 8. 39 Rot. Pat., 15 John, p. 102. 40 Rog. of Wend., vol. ii, p. 118. 41 Rot. Pat., 17 John, p. 148. 42 Cal. Docs. Ireland, no. 997. Prior to this, in 1217, Geoffrey de Marisco was ordered to abide by the archbishop's counsel, especially as to disbursements from the Exchequer, and do nothing without his assent: ibid., no. 780. 43 Four Masters, 1212 (*recte* 1213). 44 Inquis. P. M., 29 Hen. III, no. 43; Cal. Docs. Ireland, vol. i, no. 2760.

Donatus or Donough O'Kennedy, then Bishop of Killaloe, with a view to obtaining compensation for the church-lands occupied by the castle. The jurors found that in time past Murtough MacBrien ravaged the land of Ormond and Ely O'Carroll, and levelled five castles there, whereupon the king's force and council assembled at Roscrea to expel Murtough. The king's council commenced fortifying a castle in the vill of Roscrea, by erecting a mote and bretesche (*mota et britagium*). The lands at the time belonged as of right to the bishopric of Killaloe, and the bishop, Cornelius or Conor O'Heney, hearing that Archbishop Henri had by King John's direction repaired to the vill, came thither and forbade, under penalty of excommunication, the continuing of the work. The justiciar thereupon besought Bishop Cornelius on behalf of the king that he might be allowed for the common good to fortify the mote and bretesche until the termination of the war, undertaking in the king's name that the bishop should then have the vill and its appurtenances, or the just value thereof. The bishop thereupon granted permission accordingly. The jurors further found that the lands were worth thirty-five marks a year, and that the custodian of the castle received the marches as
[303] his fee. Whether the bishop obtained compensation immediately as a result of this finding does not appear, but ultimately, in 1280, when an Edwardian castle, the ruins of which remain, was being built at Roscrea, the matter was settled by the bishop, Matthew O'Hogan, granting to the king the manor of Roscrea, and the king 'releasing' to the bishop three carucates and 84 acres of land in the manor of Newcastle de Leuan in the vale of Dublin.[45]

After building the castle the English forces fought a battle with Murtough, son of Brian of Slieve Bloom, at Killeigh, a little to the south of Tullamore, in which Melaghlin, son of Cathal Carragh, was killed.[46] We hear no more of Murtough.

Next year (1214) Cormac, son of Art O'Melaghlin, continued his raids and succeeded in taking spoils from the castles of Ardnurcher and Kinclare. Then a great muster was made of all the forces of the English 'together with all the Irish forces that owed service to the King of England', and at last Cormac suffered a defeat at their hands, probably at Clara, in the barony of Kilcoursy, and Cormac was banished from Delvin.[47] Then the English built a castle at Castle Clonmacnois, where a mote and bai-
[304] ley surrounded by a deep ditch still support the ruins of a later stone castle. They also repaired or re-erected the castles of Durrow, Birr, and Kinnitty,[48] so that the whole district was ringed round with castles, all probably of the mote and bretesche type. The wooden defences of these castles, once they were carried, were easily destroyed, but the earthworks remained and were almost as easily re-fortified.

Like the castles of Athlone and Roscrea, the castle of Clonmacnois was built on churchland, and for all three compensation was duly paid to the ecclesiastical owner. In the case of Athlone the tithe of the expenses of the castle was ordered to be paid to the prior, and four cantreds in the fee of Loughsewdy, confiscated from Walter de

45 Rot. Chart., 8 Ed. I; Cal. Docs. Ireland, ii, 1663, 1664. 46 Ann. Clonmacnois, Four Masters, 1212 (*recte* 1213). 47 Ibid. 1213 (*recte* 1214). 48 Ibid. In the Annals of Loch Cé, 1214, is mentioned the building of the castles of Clonmacnois and Durrow, and further depredations of Cormac, son of Art, including the burning of the bawns of the castles of Ballyboy in Fircal and of Birr.

Lacy, were assigned to him, and when these lands were restored to Walter an exchange was ordered to be made. For many years an annuity of ten marks for 'the vill, castle, mill, and fishery towards Connaught' was paid to the prior of Athlone.[49] In the case of Roscrea, as we have seen, the compensation appears to have been delayed, but when given at last it was given with a generous hand. In the case of Clonmacnois the justi- [305]
ciar was ordered to compensate the bishop for his land occupied in fortifying the castle, for his fruit-trees cut down, his cows, horses, oxen, and household utensils taken away or 'commandeered' during the carrying on of the works.[50]

This favourable treatment of church property, and indeed of the rights of the Church generally, by the Normans in Ireland contrasts strongly with their comparative disregard of the rights and property of laymen, whether princes or peasants, and whether native or foreign, and indeed is a complete inversion of more modern notions on the subject. Laymen of Norman blood were disseised by the Crown, in John's reign at all events, on the slightest pretext. Irish tribe-lands were disposed of even before the tribes were subdued, but in the grants made, whether by the Crown or by the barons, church property was habitually respected. In Ireland, as elsewhere, the clergy enjoyed under the Normans many rights and exemptions denied to laymen, and occupied in the eye of the law an exceptionally favourable position. These and other considerations make it impossible to believe that the plundering of churches so frequently recorded by the monkish annalists, especially in the earlier years of the invasion, was due to [306]
want of piety or due respect for the Church. We have already given positive proof, both from English and from Irish sources, that it was usual, at any rate in times of disturbance, to store provisions and goods of all sorts in churches, or within the sanctuaries of churches, for their better protection.[51] To seize these was an ordinary military measure, and does not evince a sacrilegious spirit. Nor was it a measure adopted only by the Normans. Cormac, son of Art O'Melaghlin, we are told, 'went to the castle of Birr, burned its bawn, and burned the entire church and took all its food (*biadh*) out of it, in order that the Foreigners of the castle should not get food in it.'[52]

It is probable that about this time the first stone castle in Dublin was completed. There was indeed a castle here of some sort from the early days of the Norman occupation. According to the Song of Dermot, when Henry was leaving Ireland he gave the custody of the city of Dublin and of the castle and the keep (*e le chastel e le dongon*) to Hugh de Lacy.[53] These are the very words with which the same writer describes the mote-fortress erected soon afterwards for Hugh de Lacy at Trim, and the inference is that the fortress at Dublin was of the same type. The *porta castelli* is mentioned in one [307]
of Strongbow's grants.[54] To judge by the analogy of other walled towns, Wexford, for instance, the mote would have been erected adjoining the walls at some one point so as to form part of the general enceinte for defensive purposes against outside attack, and yet be separated by its ditch from the town, so as to be capable of defence in this direction also. That the castle of Dublin was surrounded by a ditch and approached

49 Rot. Claus., 16 John, p. 170 b; 18 John, p. 273; Cal. Docs. Ireland, vol. i, no. 2289. 50 Rot. Claus., 18 John, p. 273. 51 *Supra*, pp. 195–8 [pp 229–30]. 52 Ann. Loch Cé, 1214. 53 Song of Dermot, l. 2715. 54 Reg. St. Thomas's, Dublin, no. 419. *Supra*, vol. i, p. 370. [p. 140]

by a bridge prior to John's reign we know from a curious record of the year 1200. This was a criminal pleading which came before the king concerning the murder of William le Brun, who was struck on the bridge of Dublin Castle by a man with a hatchet, and fell into the castle-ditch.[55] This description, so far as it goes, harmonizes with the supposition that the castle was of the mote type. Further, that it was not a strong stone castle appears from a mandate of King John to Meiler Fitz Henry in 1204, directing him to build one.

This mandate was to the following effect: 'You have informed us that you have no fit place for the custody of our treasure, and inasmuch as for this and for other purposes we need fortalices at Dublin, we command you to construct a strong castle there with
[308] good ditches and strong walls in a suitable place for the governance and, if need be, the defence of the town; but first you are to construct a tower or keep (*turris*), where afterwards a castle and bailey (*castellum et baluum*)[56] and other necessary works may conveniently be constructed. For this at present you are to take 300 marks which Geoffrey Fitz Robert owes us.'[57] This keep may have been built by Meiler, but we have no proof. The works, however, appear to have extended over several years, and it is probable that John de Gray, who, as we have seen, was an energetic castle-builder, had much to do with pushing on its construction. At all events, the king's castle of Dublin was in existence at the close of John de Gray's term of office, when its custody was ordered to be delivered to Archbishop Henry, the new justiciar.[58] To the archbishop, indeed, the building of the castle is ascribed in the annals of St. Mary's abbey, but probably he only completed the works. To make room for the fortifications of the castle certain churches
[309] were cleared away, for which the archbishop received a grant of two cantreds without Dublin as compensation.[59] This castle, of the keep and bailey plan, occupied part of the site of the present castle, and it seems probable that the Record Tower still preserves in its lower stages some of the masonry of the original keep.

During the years that followed John's visit to Ireland the barons there, unlike the English barons, seem to have been thoroughly loyal to the Crown. This may have been in part due to the severe lesson which John had given to the de Lacys and William de Braose, but their loyal conduct, for which the king thanked his Irish barons more than once, should also be attributed to the skilful handling of the justiciar, John de Gray, and above all to the example and leading of the greatest of them, William Marshal. Two remarkable letters from the king, and a still more remarkable manifesto of the barons, are evidence of this loyalty. It is difficult to date these documents precisely, or even to determine their relative sequence, but on the whole it is probable that the manifesto preceded the letters, which seem rightly ascribed to about October 1212.[60] This

55 Cal. Docs. Ireland, vol. i, no. 116. 56 This is a good example of the distinction at this time between the *turris* or keep and the *castellum* or enclosing walls. So in the Song of Dermot we have the expression *donjon e chastel*, and in Irish *tech ocus caislén*. 57 Rot. Claus., 6 John, p. 6 b. The debt of 300 marks had not been recovered from Geoffrey Fitz Robert by March 6, 1206, when Meiler was ordered to distrain Geoffrey's lands for it: C.D.I., vol. i, no. 287. 58 Rot Pat., 15 John, p. 105 b. 59 Rot. Pat., 1 Hen. III, m. 2; Cal. Docs. Ireland, no. 805. 60 From its opening words the manifesto apparently followed the Pope's action in absolving or threatening to absolve the king's subjects from their fealty to the king. This appears to have been done either by Pandulf on the failure of his negotiations with John on the 30th August, 1211

manifesto purports to proceed from William Marshal, Earl of Pembroke, and [310] twenty-six of the principal magnates of Ireland on behalf of the rest. 'Moved with grief and astonishment,' they say, 'they had lately heard that the Pope proposed to absolve the subjects of the king from their fealty, because the king resisted the injury done to him regarding the matter of the church of Canterbury.' They go on to defend the king's action as directed to preserve the liberty and dignity which the Crown had hitherto enjoyed, and conclude by stating that 'with the king they are prepared to live or die, and to the last they will faithfully and inseparably adhere to the king.[61]

John's letter to the Bishop of Norwich commends the discretion of the bishop, thanks him and the barons of Ireland for the oath of fealty which the barons lately tendered, and repeats the substance of his letter to the Earl Marshal. In this latter John returns special thanks to the earl as the prime mover in the matter (which we can well [311] believe), begs him to remain in Ireland to assist the bishop in expediting the king's affairs, sends a transcript of letters (about which nothing further is known) made to the king by the magnates of England, and prays the earl with the other barons of Ireland to put their seals to similar letters. Finally, he alludes to the Marshal's counsel about establishing peace with the Church, and desires him to notify under what form it seems meet to the common council of the king's faithful subjects of Ireland that peace should be made without injury to the king's rights.[62]

Early in 1213 King John issued a general summons to all who owed him fealty to muster at Dover at the close of Easter. This was in view of the meditated invasion of the French king. The muster took place, and the troops, said to be 60,000 strong, were reviewed at Barham Down near Canterbury, early in May. Among those assembled were Bishop John of Norwich and Earl William Marshal, with 500 knights and many other horsemen from Ireland.[63] That Ireland could be denuded of such a force without any disturbance arising, beyond a continuance of the petty raids of the disap- [312] pointed roydamnas, is a noteworthy proof of the strength of the English colonists when not divided against themselves, and a striking indication of the general contentment of the Irish among them with the new order of things.

On May 15 John met Pandulf the papal legate at the house of the Templars near Dover, where 'of his own free-will and by the common counsel of his barons', as he says, he surrendered to the Pope the realms of England and Ireland to receive them back and hold them as a feudatory of the Roman Church. He also swore fealty to the Pope and undertook to pay to the Roman Church 1,000 marks annually, 700 for England and 300 for Ireland. Among the witnesses to this humiliating charter were Henry, Archbishop of Dublin, John, Bishop of Norwich, and William, Earl of Pembroke.[64] This took place a few days before Ascension Day. Verily the hermit Peter, who proph-

(Ann. of Burton), or, more probably, by the Pope himself on the return of his envoys (Rog. de Wendover, ii. 59). Doubt has been thrown on this story by Sir James Ramsay (Angevin Empire, p. 430), but it would seem to have been believed at the time in Wales: Brut y Tywys. (1212), p. 273. 61 Cal. Docs. Ireland, i, no. 448, from the Red Book Exchequer, Q. R. 62 Rot. Claus., 14 John, p. 132 b. 63 Roger of Wendover, vol. ii, p. 67. William Marshal, when summoned to John, is said to have advised this muster: Hist. G. le Marechal, vol ii, p. 161; where 'le mont de Brandone' no doubt represents Barham Down. 64 Roger of Wendover, vol. ii, pp. 74–6.

esied that on that day John would no longer be king, might claim that his prophecy had come true. The immediate effect, however, was to disperse the storm that was gathering both at home and abroad, and fix John's crown more securely on his head. In Ireland, indeed, John's reconciliation with the papacy had no more effect than his
[313] previous quarrel. The interdict did not apply to Ireland, and there were now no disloyal barons. They had expressed their indignation at the Pope's sentence of deposition and their determination to adhere to the king, but at the same time they had apparently counselled him to make peace with the Church, and their leader and spokesman, William Marshal, stood by John's side when the submission was made. In Ireland there was certainly no indignation at the surrender, if indeed that sentiment was widely felt anywhere at the time.

In the wringing of the Great Charter from John the Irish barons, though they had suffered much from his exactions, extortions, and oppressions, played no part. It may be, however, that, while the chief credit for that achievement must be assigned to the firmness and far-sighted statesmanship of Stephen Langton, John was actually induced to sign the document by the upright, wise, and loyal counsel given him by William the Marshal, who stood by his side and acted as intermediary, rather than by the bluster and threats of the revolted barons. John in his adversity had at last learned to value and trust in the earl as one who would give him disinterested, if not always palatable, advice, and for the last three years of his reign kept him pretty constantly at his side.

In the weeks that followed the signing of the Great Charter, John made a large
[314] number of grants to towns and individuals in Ireland of a beneficial nature. The object in view may have been to keep the Irish barons steadfast in their loyalty, or even largely to obtain money, but in the wise attention bestowed on Irish affairs at this time we may perhaps detect the influence of William Marshal and of the Dublin archbishop, both of whom were among the king's diminished counsellors.

Some of these grants we may here mention. To the citizens of Dublin John granted the city with the provostship to be held in fee-farm at an annual rent of 200 marks, adding some new privileges and confirming all liberties and free customs previously conferred.[65] To the citizens of Waterford he gave a charter defining the extent of the port of Waterford and granting a number of liberties and free customs similar to those given to Dublin by the charter of 1192, and in addition a declaration that all ships or boats entering the port between Rodybanke (Red Head, near Dunmore) and Ryndowane (the Hook) should load and unload at the Quay of Waterford and nowhere
[315] else within the port.[66] William Marshal, who witnessed this charter, cannot at the moment have foreseen how unfairly this exclusive privilege would work against his own port of New Ross, for there was no way of reaching it except between Red Head and the Hook. A few weeks later he obtained a mandate from John authorizing shipping to come to New Ross, 'provided no injury should thereby accrue to the king's vill

65 Rot. Chart., 17 John, p. 210 b. 66 Chartae Priv. et Immun., p. 13, where the charter is wrongly dated 3rd July [see *Add.*], a. r. vii, instead of 3rd July, a. r. xvii. It is witnessed by H[enri] Archbishop of Dublin and others who were all present at court on the 3rd July, 1215.

of Waterford';[67] but the proviso virtually nullified the concession, and century-long disputes resulted. To the burgesses of Dungarvan John granted all the liberties and free customs of Breteuil,[68] a town in Normandy. This expression has been misunderstood. Following the precedent of Henry's charter to Dublin, it became customary in Ireland, when granting charters to towns for the first time, to grant to them 'the law of Bristol' [see *Add.*]. Thus John in Henry's lifetime seems to have granted to the citizens of Cork the same free laws and free customs as the citizens of Bristol enjoyed.[69] After 1188, when John granted an extended charter to Bristol, the law of Bristol would include the liberties and free customs mentioned in that charter. These were substantially the liberties and free customs expressly included in John's Dublin charter of [316]
1192. In 1213, however, John granted to the burgesses of Drogheda the law, not of Bristol, but of Breteuil, with all the liberties and customs appertaining to that law.[70] And now in granting a charter to Dungarvan a similar phrase is used. What these customs of Breteuil exactly were we do not know, but they were probably not dissimilar from those granted to Bristol in 1188. In the first year of his reign John granted a charter to his burgesses of Breteuil (*de Bretolio*), on account of the great loss they had incurred in his service, that they might buy and sell throughout his land by the same liberties as were enjoyed by the burgesses of Verneuil (near Breteuil).[71] The feudal lords in Ireland, however, in granting charters for the first time, granted liberties' according to the law of Bristol'. Thus Walter de Lacy granted the law of Bristol to his burgesses of Trim and Kells, and we find the burgesses of the archiepiscopal towns of Rathcoole, Ballymore, and Holywood holding according to the same laws and liberties.[72]

Whatever the motive may have been, John's grants of charters to the seaport towns [317]
of Ireland gave a great impetus to the growth of Irish trade.

His grants and restorations of lands to individuals at this time were no less remarkable, and did something to restore the sense of security which must have been shattered by his wholesale confiscations in 1210. The lordship of Ulster was not restored to Hugh de Lacy,[73] but many of the freeholders there and in Meath who had been taken prisoners in the castle of Carrickfergus were restored on payment of fines to their liberty and their lands. About the same time large grants of lands in the north of Ulster were, as we have seen, made to Thomas and Alan of Galloway and their uncle, Duncan of Carrick. With Walter de Lacy, however, the king now came to terms, and, in consideration of a fine of 4,000 marks, restored to him his lands and castles, except

67 Rot. Pat., 17 John, p. 153 b. 68 Rot. Chart., 17 John, p. 211: 'omnes libertates et liberas consuetudines de Bretoill[io],' absurdly taken by Sweetman, Cal., vol. i, no. 578, as meaning 'bridge-toll'. 69 See Council Book of Cork (Caulfield), p. x, referring to Harleian MS. no. 441. 70 Rot. Chart., 17 John, p. 194: 'legem de Breteill[io] cum omnibus libertatibus et consuetudinibus ad eandem legem pertinentibus.' 71 Rot. Chart., 1 John, p. 5: 'ut emant et vendant per totam terram nostram per easdem libertates quas burgenses nostri de V[er]nolio habent.' 72 For Trim and Kells see Chartae Priv. et Immun., p. 10; for Rathcoole, ibid., p. 33; for Ballymore and Holywood, Cal. Lib. Niger, Proc. R.I.A., xxvii (c), pp. 60, 62. 73 There appear to have been negotiations for the restoration of Ulster to Hugh, but the stipulated fine (the amount is not stated) was not paid, so the king announced that he could only convert the land of Ulster to his own profit: Rot. Pat., 16 John, p. 134.

the castle of Drogheda, which was retained as a royal castle.[74] In Leinster John made, or purported to make, a tardy restitution to William the Marshal by repeatedly order-
[318] ing that the castle of Dunamase, and all his fees in the lands held by Meiler Fitz Henry, should be restored to him.[75] It seems, however, that these orders were not entirely carried out in John's lifetime.[76] In Munster John granted to Thomas Fitz Anthony and his heirs the custody of the counties of Waterford and Desmond and of the city of Cork, and of all the demesnes and escheats of the king in those counties, for the yearly rent of 250 marks.[77] John appears to have treated the southern portion of the present county of Tipperary as his demesne or escheat, probably as having been demesne of William de Braose, and for a fine of £100 he now granted to Philip of Worcester 'to maintain him on the king's service' five cantreds in this district, and the castles of Knockgraffon, Kiltinan, and Ardmayle.[78] The honour of Limerick was not
[319] revived, but Richard, son of William de Burgh, Maurice, son of Gerald Fitz Gerald, and Hamo, son of Hamo de Valognes, were given seisin of their respective fathers' lands;[79] while the cantred of Okonach (Coonagh),which seems to have been also demesne of William de Braose, and the vill and cantred of Tibrary (Tipperary) were granted to Archbishop Henry.[80] As regards Connaught, John made the grant to Cathal Crovderg to which we have already referred.[81]

John made several other grants and concessions to his Irish subjects during the last year of his reign, but we have mentioned the most important. Altogether the fines payable for them amounted to a considerable sum, which was badly needed for 'the Barons' War'. One of his very last acts indicates remorse for one of his many crimes. On the 10th of October, 1216, he granted to Margaret de Lacy a site whereon to build a monastery for the good of the souls of her father, William de Braose, his wife and son.[82] John died on the 18th of October, 1216.

It has been the fashion, especially with writers who have seldom a good word for English policy in Ireland, to bestow a considerable measure of praise upon the action of King John in that country. But if we have correctly read the record of his rule, this
[320] praise was wholly undeserved. We need not recall his disastrous boyish visit in 1185, nor dwell on the obscure period that elapsed before his accession to the throne. But from the commencement of his reign until near its close, when by his conduct in England he had alienated almost all support and could no longer make his will prevail, his action in Ireland seems to have been swayed by capricious favouritism or by vindictive personal animosity, without any regard for the general weal of his Irish dominion. For the native Irish themselves, in common with too many of his contemporaries, he had

74 Rot. Pat., 17 John, p. 181. 75 Cal. Docs. Ireland, vol. i, nos. 644, 647, 664, 684, 689, 691. 76 On December 2, 1216, a few weeks after John's death, Meiler's service for his land in Leinster was ordered to be restored to the earl in a remarkable mandate: Rot. Pat., 1 Hen. III, m. 16. It would appear from Rot. Pat., 17 John, pp. 161 b and 180, touching the restoration of Dunamase, that John employed certain secret signs (*intersigna*) without which his justiciar was not to carry out his ostensible orders. 77 Rot. Chart., 17 John, p. 210 b. 78 Rot. Pat., 17 John, p. 147 b. The castle of Ardmayle, however, had belonged to Walter de Lacy and was afterwards restored to him. For Knockgraffon see *supra*, p. 147 [p. 210]. 79 Rot. Pat., 16 John, p. 118 b; 17 John, p. 147. 80 Rot. Chart., 17 John, p. 213. 81 *Supra*, p. 285 [p. 264]. 82 Rot. Pat., 18 John, p. 199.

no sort of regard. But while always ready to grant away their territories (for a consideration) to his favourites, he gave the latter no assistance in making his grants effective, and no support in establishing their rule. On the contrary, with or without pretext, he again and again overrode his own grants in the most capricious manner. To recall only the principal examples: He first parcelled out the kingdom of Limerick among a number of tenants-in-chief of the Crown, and then, without any regard to the rights so conferred, sold the whole honour of Limerick to his favourite for the moment, William de Braose. A few years later he remorselessly hunted down William de Braose and his family, because he was unable to pay the stipulated consideration. He encouraged Hugh de Lacy to make war upon John de Courcy, and when Hugh had suc- [321]
ceeded, loaded him with honours and granted him the lands which his victim had won and organized. Then five years later he led a great army into Ireland, expelled both Hugh and his brother Walter, and confiscated their lands, on no better pretext than that they had endeavoured to shelter the objects of his tyranny. He similarly encouraged his justiciar Meiler Fitz Henry to make private war on William Marshal, and it was only when Meiler failed that he grudgingly acknowledged the earl's rights. Had John dared, however, we can hardly doubt that the fief of Leinster would have gone the same way as those of Limerick, Ulster, and Meath. John, in a word, was the same man in Ireland as in England: capricious, vindictive, tyrannical, only that in his tyranny he was even less under control. But when he found himself almost alone and in need of the support of his Irish barons, then he did something to undo the evil he had done, to reinstate those he had dispossessed, and to grant a number of charters favourable to the trade of the seaport towns. Among the first acts of the new boy-king, or rather of his great regent Earl William Marshal, was to extend to Ireland the liberties which had been wrested from John for England, and to further the work of undoing, so far as might be, the wrong that John had done.

[323] CHAPTER XXIII

AFTER FIFTY YEARS

Not quite half a century had now elapsed since the Norman invader first set foot on Bannow Island, and in the course of that brief period a great change had taken place over at least two-thirds of Ireland. In the eastern parts of Ulster and Uriel, throughout the whole of the ancient kingdoms of Meath, Leinster, Ossory, Desmond, and Limerick, the Normans dominated almost everywhere. In each lordship, after the first few years of resistence, a period of comparative peace and order commenced such as Ireland had never known before. It was a veritable 'pax Normannica', and was co-extensive with Norman sway. It was not produced by strong legionary forces encamped at strategic points, nor by armed garrisons within impregnable castles of stone. Wooden fortresses protected by earthworks were indeed erected on almost every manor, but except as a safe retreat in the event of a sudden rising or for a last stand in the face of overwhelming odds, they were of little military avail, and in most cases after
[324] a generation or so were either converted into stone castles or fell into disuse. The conquest, rendered inevitable by the previous anarchy, was effected primarily by superior weapons and better discipline in the field, but the position won was maintained and peace secured by that instinct for organized rule which is the mark of progressive races all the world over, and which, for the time at any rate, in the districts named, led to a general acquiescence in the change of rulers.

Some disturbances, no doubt, took place within this region, especially along the marches or borders between 'the land of peace' and 'the land of war', as the English and Irish districts were sometimes respectively called;[1] but they were of small moment in comparison with the desolating raids that went on with little rest before the strong hand of the Normans stayed them. Above all, there were no more interprovincial wars in this region. Neither an O'Brien, nor an O'Conor, nor an O'Rourke, came swooping down with their hosts over Leinster or Meath, carrying off whatever booty they could lay hands on. Nor was the lordship of Ulster subject any longer to periodical devastation at the hands of the Cinel Owen. Only in those districts where the Normans were
[325] not supreme did the turmoil of the past continue—a turmoil now caused partly, but not exclusively, by the efforts of the new-comers to extend their domination. Some of the leading barons, indeed, opposed armed resistance to the forces of King John's first justiciar, and writers have dwelt on these conflicts as evincing the innate turbulence of the Normans. We have traced these disturbances, such as they were, to him who

1 The use of the term 'English Pale' to denote the districts dominated by the English prior to the fifteenth century is a misnomer and an anachronism.

appears to have been their real author; but in any case they were as nothing to the 'Barons' War' which broke out in England a few years later from the same cause. On the whole, with one or two exceptions, the barons of Ireland stood faithfully by each other and by the common cause of the colony.

As to the treatment of the Irish by the invaders I do not propose to consider the question from the moral point of view. This is emphatically one of those questions which cannot be fairly or usefully discussed with a tacit reference to modern standards. In any case we must first of all find out, if we can, how the Normans did in fact treat the Irish. Then those whose knowledge of history is sufficient for the comparison may, if they wish, compare the action of the Normans with that of other conquering races in similar conditions elsewhere. To the preliminary investigation, which is encompassed by much difficulty, we may make the following tentative contribution.

From what is known of the sub-infeudation of Leinster, Meath, and Uriel—and [326]
the same is probably true of other districts also—each of the larger sub-grants appears to have generally comprised the territory of a distinct sept, or smaller tribe, and to be now roughly represented by the baronial divisions. The few surviving charters or transcripts of charters show that the lands were conveyed under their old denominations without any express mention of boundaries, and often as some particular sept or chieftain of a sept held the same. The former chieftain, whether of a sept or of a group of septs or larger division, was of course deprived in whole or in part of his ancient privileges. Where he resisted the invaders he either fell in the conflict or was expelled, or perhaps retired into a monastery.[2] In most cases, however, even in Meath and Leinster, and apparently still more often in Ulster and Munster, the more important chieftains submitted to terms, accepted portions of their former territories, and continued to rule there according to Irish law. Thus the O'Melaghlins in part of Westmeath, the O'Byrnes and O'Tooles on the skirts of the Wicklow Mountains, the Mac Murroughs about the northern borders of their former principality, the O'Conors Faly and the [327]
O'Mores in the western parts of their territories, the Mac Gillapatricks in Upper Ossory, and other smaller chieftains, continued their tribal rule and organization, though in much more confined areas. In Munster, and perhaps in Ulster, English and Irish districts seem to have been still more closely intermixed. As an example of the gradual expropriation of an Irish chieftain we may mention the case of Donnell O'Faelain, lord of the Decies of Munster, who in 1204 quit-claimed to the king the province of Dungarvan, one of the three cantreds held by him, on condition that the other two should remain with him, one for his life, and the other as an inheritance.[3] Somewhat similar arrangements were made, as we have seen, with the Mac Carthys, the O'Briens, and the O'Conors. There is also at least one example—that of Donnell Mac Gillamocholmog—of an Irish chieftain who became a feudal lord, and whose grandson, by intermarrying with the Geraldines and dropping the Irish surname, became almost indistinguishable from his Norman neighbours.[4] Of the smaller chief-

2 Faelan MacFaelain, lord of Offelan, died in the monastery of Old Connell founded by Meiler Fitz Henry: Four Masters, 1203. 3 Rot. Claus., 6 John, p. 6 b: 'ita quod alii duo sibi remaneret, scilicet alter eorum in vita sua et alter hereditarie.' 4 *Supra*, vol. i, p. 368 [p. 139], and see Gilbert's History of Dublin,

[328] tains some may have been treated similarly. Others perhaps were driven into the Irish districts at once. Sooner or later, throughout large parts of the east and south of Ireland, the lands held in severalty were expropriated, and probably became the demesnes of early Norman manors.

Thus in many parts of the region nominally dominated by the Normans, as well as in the parts where they had effected no settlement, there remained Irish districts where the former Irish tribal organization was continued, where the ancient Brehon law was observed, where the former ruling families still continued to draw the allegiance of the tribesmen, and where the king's writ did not run. Even when these Irish districts were quiet and at peace with the Normans there was at first no amalgamation of the two peoples; and, except so far as the Irish may have adopted from their neighbours some improved methods of building and perhaps of agriculture, or have taken advantage of the greater facilities now offered for trade, they seem to have participated but little in the increased prosperity of the rest of the country. On the other hand, these Celtic tribes interspersed among the feudalized districts had always the feeling rankling in their minds that the invaders had robbed them of the best lands, and they remained always ready, when opportunity should occur, to raid and plunder as of old, and if possible recover the land they had lost.

[329] But though sooner or later most of the free tribesmen were thus in one way or another cleared off the feudalized districts, it was not so with the actual tillers of the soil. Every inducement was offered to them to remain on the newly settled land, and a variety of evidence goes to show that the inducements offered were effective. We have not only the express statement of Giraldus that it was a prime object with Hugh de Lacy to invite back to peace the rural inhabitants who had been driven out in the course of the reprisals that followed the rising of 1174, and to restore to them their farms and pasture lands, but we can see from the Treaty of Windsor with Rory O'Conor in 1175,[5] and from the mandate to the justiciary in 1204, 'to cause the villeins and fugitives from the province of Dungarvan to return with their chattels and retinue,'[6] that measures were taken to enforce the return to their homes of those who had fled when their tribe-land was first overrun. Moreover, from the surviving extents and accounts of manors dating from about the middle of the thirteenth century and from other sources, it appears that a class of Irish farmers called *betagii* or betaghs was generally to be found on each manor. Thus in the earliest Irish Pipe Roll that has been preserved we find in the crown-lands near Dublin considerable sums paid as rent by
[330] the betaghs of Othee, Obrun, and Okelli, tribe-lands on the skirts of the Dublin and Wicklow mountains.[7] In some manors the rents of the betaghs were the principal source of income,[8] and we can hardly doubt that they were very numerous, especially in the settled districts more remote from Dublin.

vol. i, pp. 230–5, and Mr. Mills's paper, Journ. R.S.A.I. 1894, p. 162. 5 *Supra*, vol. i, p. 350 [p. 132]. 6 Rot. Claus., 6 John, p. 6 b. 7 Irish Pipe Roll, 13 Hen. III, 35th Rep. D. K., p. 29. 8 See the account of the manor of Lucan, Pipe Roll, Ed. I, summarized by Mr. Mills, Journ. R. S. A. I. 1894, p. 174; and for further evidence as to the position of betaghs, the same writer's notice of the manor of St. Sepulchre, ibid. 1889, pp. 31-41, and 1890, pp. 54-63; and the extents of certain Munster manors, Cal. Docs. Ireland, vol. i, nos. 2607 (Kilsheelan) and 3203, vol. iii, no. 459.

Betaghs are identified as regards their legal status with the *nativi* or villeins of feudal law.[9] In the Rolls of Court they are often termed *hibernici* in a technical sense—in full phrase, *hibernici servilis conditionis*.[10] Probably they represented the 'daer-stock tenants' or 'base vassals' of the Brehon law, who, as we have seen, were bound to pay food-rents and provide refection for their lord, to whom they had parted with their honour-price, and against whom they could not bear witness.[11] Similarly in the Anglo-
Irish courts it was a valid plea in bar that the plaintiff was a betagh or *hibernicus* who [331]
had not obtained the right to use English laws;[12] and again similarly the Anglo-Irish lord could recover damages for the killing, assaulting, or robbing of his *hibernici*.[13] It would seem, then, that the Normans, in not admitting betaghs to the full rights of freemen, were not lowering their status. The *hibernicus* might, however, be enfranchised by the king, or by his immediate lord,[14] and in most of the cases that came before the courts such enfranchisement was in fact proved, and the plea in bar failed. Betaghs were perhaps at first *adscripti glebae*, like the sept of Macfeilecan, transferred with the land of Baldoyle by Dermot's charter to the canons of All Saints, Dublin,[15] but some of them seem to have risen into the class of *firmatii*, whose position was regulated by contract.

Besides betaghs there was a large class of Irish agricultural labourers, including the
lord's churls, who worked on his farms, and who perhaps represented the *fuidhirs* or [332]
bondsmen of the Celtic chief. Above these classes were Irish artisans of various sorts, who, though *hibernici*, were not of servile condition, and could sue and recover damages even against their employers.[16] Mr. Mills, the present deputy-keeper of the records in Ireland, who has studied the condition of the inferior agricultural classes in the thirteenth century, considers that their condition 'was steadily improving where the power of the Norman colony was least disturbed, and while it retained anything of its pristine vigour'.[17]

To modern minds, however, the withholding the benefit of the laws of England from the Irish is the greatest blot on the record of the Normans in Ireland. Sir John Davies puts it in the forefront of 'the defects in the civil policy and government which impeded a full conquest'. To take the most glaring case, 'it was often,' he says, 'adjudged no felony to kill a mere Irishman in time of peace.'[18] This is a difficult subject, which has never
been adequately treated, and cannot here be fully discussed. It may, however, be [333]
observed, in the first place, that it would have been quite futile to attempt to extend

9 Stat., 14 Ed. II and 5 Ed. III, § 3; Early Statutes (Berry), pp. 292, 325; and cf. Harris's Ware, Antiquities (1764), p. 157. 10 Justiciary Rolls, Pref., p. viii. This double meaning of the term *hibernicus* has misled many writers. 11 *Supra*, vol. i, p. 116 [p. 40]. It would seem that the name must be connected with *biathad*, the word used in the Book of Rights for refection. *Orba biatach* is applied in the Brehon Laws, vol. iv, p. 44, l. 10, to lands set apart for providing food for the chief. The *biatach coitchenn*, or 'public hospitaller', must, however, be distinguished from these ordinary betaghs: Four Masters, 1225, note *s*; and cf. the *lánbiatach* of the Ann. Ulster, 1178. 12 Justiciary Rolls, pp. 82, 454, &c. 13 Ibid., pp. 156, 162, 221, &c. 14 Ibid., p. 271, where Walter Otothel (O'Toole) produced a charter of enfranchisement given to his great-grandfather by William Marshal, Earl of Pembroke, in the tenth year of King John. 15 Reg. All Hallows, I.A.S., p. 50. 16 See Just. Rolls, p. 342. A case where the jury found that the plaintiff and his father were *hibernici* (Irishmen) and millers of the defendant and his father, but not *hibernici* (villeins) of the defendant. The plaintiff was therefore capable of suing, and in fact recovered damages. This is a good example of the double meaning of *hibernicus*. 17 Journ. R.S.A.I. 1890–1, p. 62. 18 Discovery (1787), pp 75-7.

English laws over all Ireland without having first established adequate machinery to enforce them. The laws would have been contemptuously disregarded by the Irish themselves. Sir John Davies in fact inverts cause and effect. Until the conquest was perfected it was obviously impossible to maintain sheriffs and enforce judgements in Irish districts. It was difficult enough to do so after the Elizabethan wars. If an Irishman living in an Irish district killed an Englishman in time of peace we may be quite sure that, unless caught by the English, he would either be not punished at all or at most be liable under the Brehon law to pay a fine for the homicide. With the Irish it was certainly no felony to kill an Englishman. This being so, we can hardly wonder that in the converse case an Englishman could not be hung. Again, in the case of Irishmen of servile condition living under a lord in a feudalized district, it would be unreasonable to expect the Normans, at the period we have reached, at any rate, to grant them, as a body, liberties which they had not enjoyed under their former chieftains, and that, too, at a time when similar classes in England were in a state of serfdom. The lord of the betagh, as we have
[334] seen, had his remedy in damages for any violence done to his men. There remains then only the case of those Irishmen who had enjoyed freedom under the Brehon laws and who remained in the feudalized districts. Probably these free-born Irishmen so remaining were not very numerous, and probably, too, the right to use English laws was granted to most of them individually, though here again, perhaps following the unfortunate precedent of the Brehon law, the English law 'as to life and limb' seems not at first to have been included in the grant—so slow were the Normans to admit any class of Irishmen to equality with themselves.[19]

A wider experience has gradually taught the western world that to make a united and contented nation equal rights before the law must be secured to all. Such a conception was, however, entirely beyond the ken of the statesmen of the twelfth and thirteenth centuries, and indeed could not have been realized in Ireland without a complete conquest and a rooting up of old customs, which would have inevitably entailed, for the time at any rate, immense hardship. But had the Normans been wiser in their generation, they would have spared no pains to induce as many as possible of the free-born
[335] Irishmen to remain amongst them, and by good faith and liberal treatment have won them over to the support of the new regime. This, indeed, appears to have been the idea of Giraldus.[20] They might, we should imagine, have converted them into feudal owners, living in their midst, and thus have enormously strengthened their own position, and, while preserving their own more advanced ideas of order and government, have made a commencement in the amalgamation of the two races. But it is plain that the Normans regarded the Irish as an uncouth and barbarous people and the fit spoil of their conquerors, and those who guided the destinies of the colony were not far-seeing enough to perceive the ultimate effect of a half-conquest carried out in such a spirit.

The Ostmen of the seaport towns were perhaps more ready than the Irish to accept the new regime, and were treated more liberally; but in their case it is obvious the same

19 It was extended to them by Stat., 14 Ed. II; Early Statutes, p. 292; cf. Rot. Claus., 12 Hen. III, m. 8; ibid., 23–4. **20** See his condemnation of the taking away 'the lands of our Irishmen who had faithfully stood by us from the first', vol. v, p. 390, and his opinion (p. 398) as to how Ireland should be governed.

difficulties did not arise. In Dublin they were given a district to inhabit on the north side of the river, outside the walls. This was long known as the *villa Ostmannorum*, Ostmantown, or (corruptly) Oxmantown. In Waterford they were given a charter by Henry II entitling them to the law of the English,[21] and, perhaps after the revolt of [336]
1174, they were settled in a quarter of their own outside the town.[22] Henry III took them under his protection, and Edward I confirmed his great-grandfather's charter.[23] The Ostmen of Limerick, however, as we have seen, remained in the city and supplied the first mayor to the newly chartered town. In all cases the Ostmen seem to have had full rights of holding and inheriting property and of suing in the courts, though sometimes they had to prove that they were not Irishmen, and to petition for a recognition of their rights as Ostmen.[24]

The cantred of the Ostmen both at Cork and at Limerick was retained in the king's hand along with the cities. At Limerick forty carucates of this land were afterwards granted to the citizens in burgage tenure.[25] Most of the Ostmen mentioned in the [337]
records belonged, as might be expected, to the towns, but some of them were to be found in rural parts as agriculturists. Thus about the year 1283 a Wexford jury found that there were in the time of the Marshals 100 well-to-do Ostmen, possessed of cattle, who had to pay certain dues to the provosts of Wexford for the lord of the liberty, and that provided they paid these dues they were free to hold of any lord in the county they chose. Some forty of these, reduced in wealth, survived in the time of William de Valence, when they were freed from the aforesaid burdens, and given licence to hold land of any lord in the county at rents and services proportionate to their reduced numbers and means.[26]

It is quite certain then that there was no general clearance of the native population. There is no sign of any considerable influx of foreigners into the rural parts of Ireland. Land without inhabitants was obviously of no value to the Anglo-Norman lords, and it was their aim to retain as many of the former cultivators of the soil as possible. To the mass of these the Anglo-Norman settlement meant little more than a change [338]
of territorial rulers. Instead of the exactions of their former chiefs, some small rents and certain services were required by their new lords. Some liberties might be lost, but in return they obtained greater security for their cattle and a better market for their produce. Though East Meath was more fully occupied by the foreigners than perhaps any other rural part of Ireland (with the possible exception of the parts near Dublin and the south-east corner of the County Wexford), and though that occupation remained unchecked through the centuries, Irish continued to be the language spoken

21 A transcript of this charter is among the Carew Papers: Cal. Misc., p. 466. 22 The vill of the Ostmen near Waterford is referred to in Cal. Docs. Ireland, vol. ii, p. 426. The finding of a jury in 1310 as to the cause of the expulsion of the Ostmen of Waterford cannot, I think, be taken as correct. See Facsimiles Nat. MSS. of Ireland, vol. iii, Introd. vi, pl. vii, and App. iii, and *supra*, vol. i, p. 336 [p. 126]. 23 Cal. Docs. Ireland, vol. ii, no. 2134, where Henry II's charter is stated to have been inspected. For *Custmanni* read *Oustmanni*. 24 See the petition of Philip Mac Gothmond, 'an Ostman and Englishman' of Waterford, for himself and 400 of his race: Cal. Docs. Ireland, vol. iii, p. 305; also of Maurice Macotere, ibid., p. 306. 25 Rot. Chart., 17 John, p. 211. 26 See this document transcribed in an interesting paper on the English and Ostmen in Ireland by E. Curtis, Eng. Hist. Rev. 1908, p. 217.

by the mass of the people, and in process of time even by some of the descendants of the foreign settlers, up to at least the middle of the seventeenth century, and it only finally died out amongst the old people within living memory.

We have mentioned that the mote-castles of the first settlers served only a temporary military purpose, but as manorial centres they or their successors soon became the foci of new activities, agricultural, industrial, and commercial. Demesne lands were marked out, commons were set apart, in some few cases forests were reserved for game. Grants of lands were made to a number of free tenants of foreign birth, to be held for military service, and subordinate manors were created. Lands were also let to
[339] farmers at a rent, and these were in some cases of Irish extraction. Improved methods of agriculture were introduced on the home farms. The manorial courts in their several degrees administered justice and settled disputes. Vills sprang up under the protection of the castles and grew to be towns where new industries were carried on, and where no doubt the foreign element predominated. Many of these are still among the chief towns of Ireland, while the memory of others which have entirely disappeared survives in persistent local tradition. Lands in the vicinity of the towns were divided among the burgesses at low fixed rents as burgage-land, and charters were granted to the more thriving towns to encourage trade and secure improvements. Even where the Norman mote now rises lonely amid the fields we often find records or traces or traditions of a town close at hand, and, except in cases where the manorial centre seems to have shifted at an early date, it is rare not to find the remains of a later castle, the ruins of a church with some Early English features, and the evidence of an ancient mill-site, in close proximity to the grass-grown mound. Navigable rivers were now used for commerce, and not for raids, and were bridged in places for the same purpose, The Church was at the same time better organized and more adequately endowed, and her temples were re-erected on a grander scale and in the new transitional or, later,
[340] in the Early English style. New monastic establishments were founded and endowed with indeed reckless profusion. Large sums were paid into the English exchequer, which, if of no benefit to Ireland, were at least a proof of growing wealth; and again and again a feudal host was dispatched to the aid of the king in his wars in France, in Wales, and against his own revolted subjects.

Thus in the course of two generations the whole face of two-thirds of Ireland became changed. The seaport towns in particular, most of which owed their origin and small beginnings to the Norsemen, rapidly expanded and became centres of a growing foreign trade. In a future work we hope to trace the development of this new life and to analyse the causes which ultimately checked and defeated its earlier promise. Here it must suffice to note two weak points in that feudal organization which for the first time rendered these peaceful activities possible. It did not extend all over Ireland within the four seas. It embraced in a firm grasp only the eastern parts of the island. It had a weaker hold on the south, while most of the north and west lay practically beyond its control. Moreover, the keystone of the structure was lacking, and its place filled by a weak substitute. The strong restraining hand of the *Dominus Hiberniae* was far away, and he was too fully engaged with other concerns, [continued on p. 288]

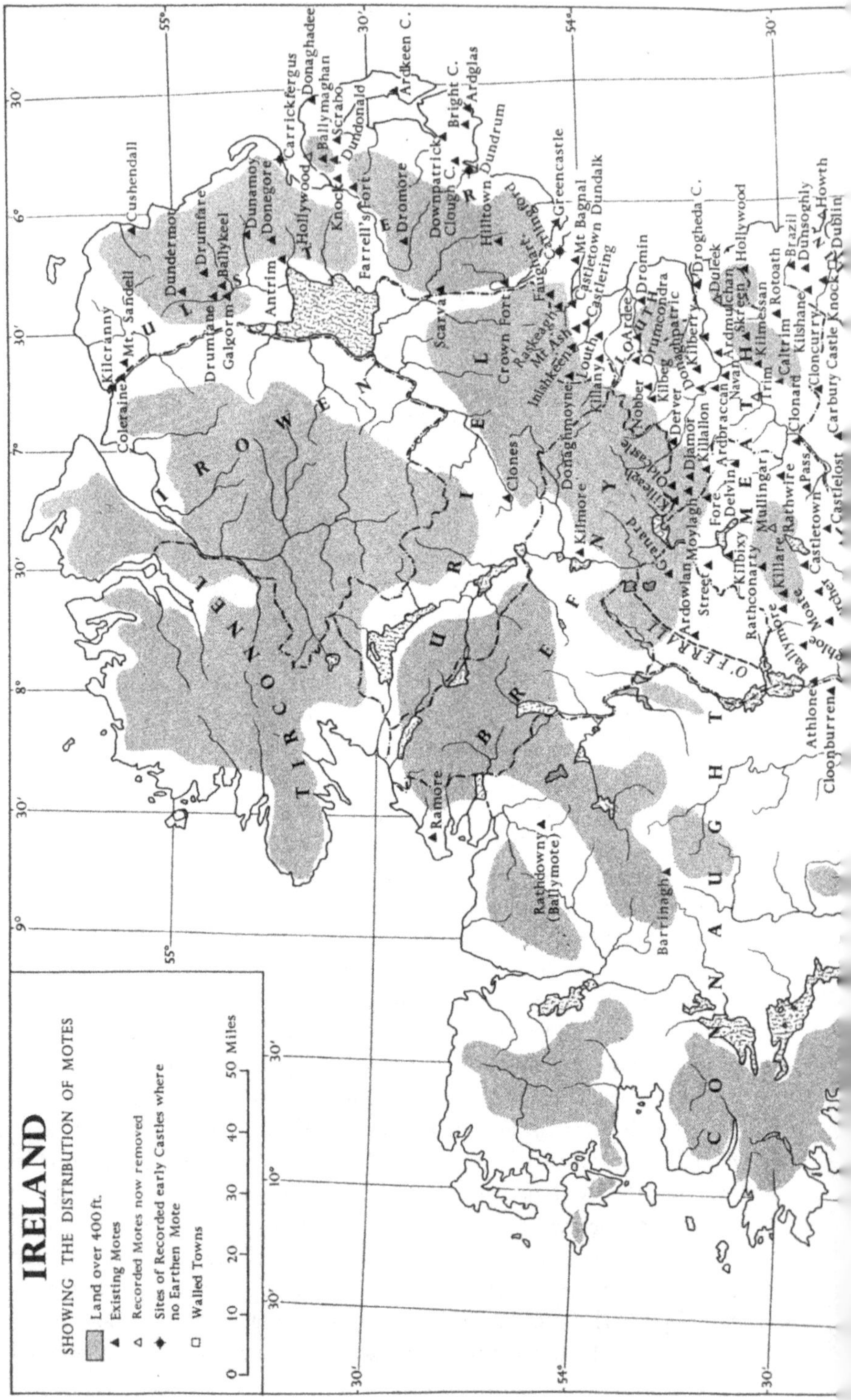
IRELAND
SHOWING THE DISTRIBUTION OF MOTES
Land over 400 ft.
Existing Motes
Recorded Motes now removed
Sites of Recorded early Castles where no Earthen Mote
Walled Towns
0 10 20 30 40 50 Miles
TIRCONNELL
TIROWEN
ULSTER
URIEL
BREFFNY
MEATH
CONNAUGHT
O'FERRALL
LOUTH
Coleraine
Kilcranny
Mt. Sandell
Cushendall
Dundermot
Drumfare
Ballykeel
Drumtane
Galgorm
Dunamoy
Donegore
Antrim
Carrickfergus
Donaghadee
Ballymaghan
Scrabo
Hollywood
Knock
Dundonald
Farrell's Fort
Dromore
Ardkeen C.
Bright C.
Ardglas
Downpatrick
Clough C.
Dundrum
Hilltown
Greencastle
Scarva
Crown Fort
Mt Bagnal
Castletown Dundalk
Castlering
Louth
Mt Ash
Inishkeen
Killany
Clones
Donaghmoyne
Kilmore
Dromin
Drumcondra
Drogheda C.
Duleek
Hollywood
Skreen
Ardmulchan
Navan
Kilberry
Donaghpatric
Kilbeg
Nobber
Derver
Killallon
Ardbraccan
Trim
Kilmessan
Rotoath
Brazil
Dunsoghly
Howth
Dublin
Caltrim
Clonard
Kilshane
Cloncurry
Carbury Castle
Knock
Castlelost
Pass
Rathwire
Mullingar
Delvin
Fore
Moylagh
Kilbixy
Rathconarty
Killare
Castletown
Ardowlan
Street
Ballymore
Moate
Athlone
Cloonburren
Ramore
Rathdowny (Ballymote)
Barrinagh

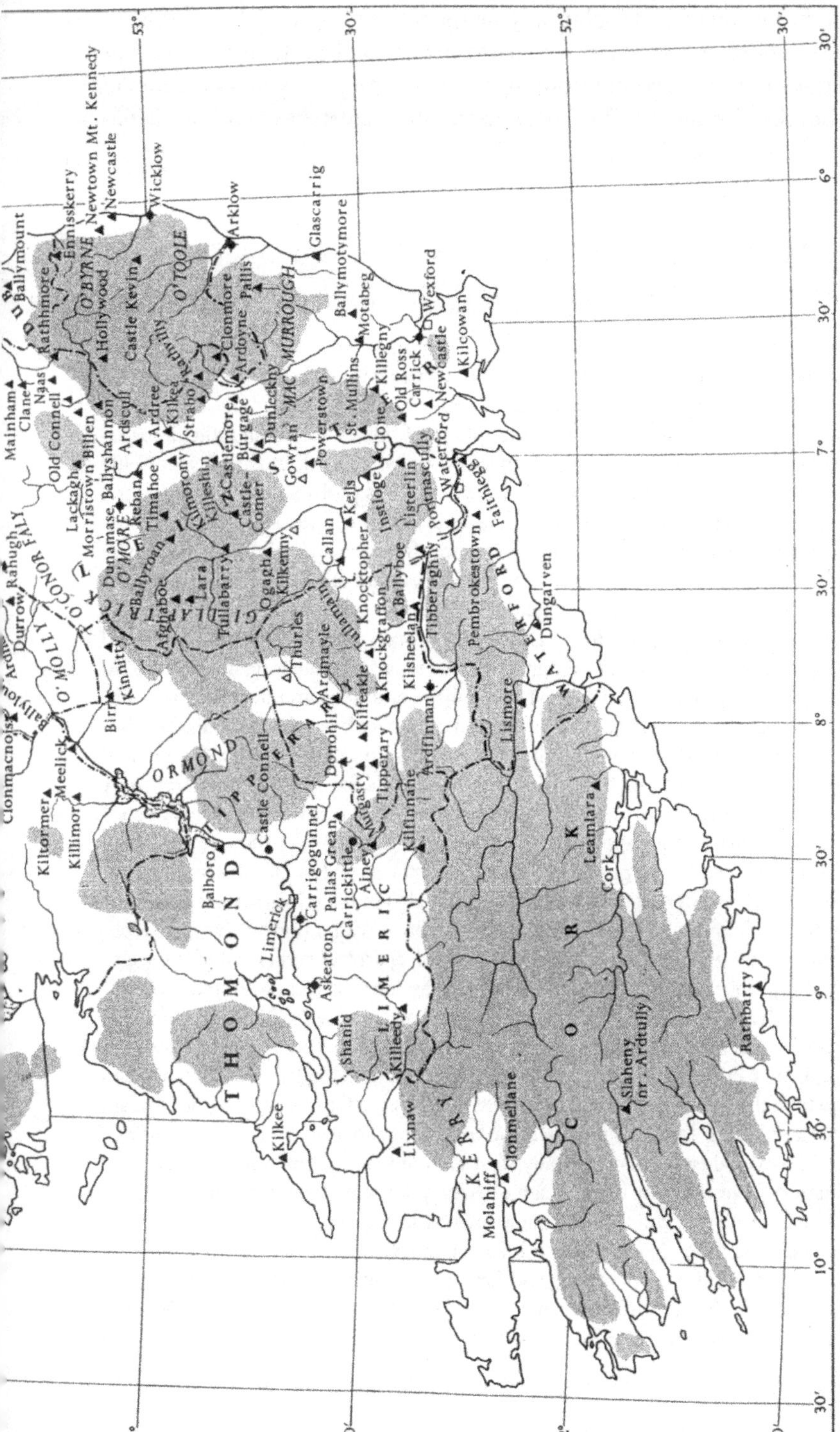

THOMOND
ORMOND
TIPPERARY
LIMERICK
KERRY
CORK
WATERFORD
O'MOLLOY
O'CONOR FALY
O'MORE
O'BYRNE
O'TOOLE
MAC MURROUGH
Wicklow
Newcastle
Newtown Mt. Kennedy
Enniskerry
Ballymount
Rathmore
Hollywood
Castle Kevin
Arklow
Glascarrig
Ballymotymore
Motabeg
Wexford
Kilcowan
Newcastle
Carrick
Old Ross
Killegny
St. Mullins
Clone
Powerstown
Dunleckny
Clonmore
Ardoyne
Pallis
Naas
Clane
Mainham
Old Connell
Billen
Ballyshannon
Ardscull
Ardree
Kilkea
Strabo
Castlemore
Burgage
Gowran
Lackagh
Morristown
Dunamase
Reban
Timahoe
Kilmorony
Killeshin
Castle-Comer
Ballyroan
Lara
Kilkenny
Callan
Kells
Instioge
Listerlin
Waterford
Faithlegg
Pembrokestown
Dungarven
Lismore
Tibberaghny
Ballyboe
Knockgraffon
Knocktopher
Ogagh
Tullabarty
Aghaboe
Kinnitty
Birr
Durrow
Rahugh
Clonmacnoise
Meelick
Killimor
Kiltormer
Thurles
Ardmayle
Kilfeakle
Donohill
Tipperary
Muligasty
Ainey
Carrigogunnel
Castle Connell
Balboro
Pallas Grean
Carrickittle
Kilfinnane
Ardfinnan
Kilsheelan
Limerick
Askeaton
Shanid
Killeedy
Lixnaw
Kilkee
Clonmellane
Molahiff
Slaheny (nr. Ardtully)
Cork
Leamlara
Rathbarry

and indeed, in the person of King John, was not morally equipped, either to rule his [341]
barons with justice or to restrain them from harsh treatment of his Irish subjects. The first shock to the structure came not from the Gael, not even, if we go to the root of the matter, from the Norman barons, but from the alternate neglect and capricious interference of the *Dominus Hiberniae* himself.

NOTE TO MAP SHOWING THE DISTRIBUTION OF MOTES [343]

This map must be regarded as only a tentative survey. For want of space, and because they are of minor importance, I have not inserted all the true motes known to me in Leinster and Meath. Moreover, I have not personally inspected the greater number of those marked throughout Ireland, and in many cases have had to rely on the descriptions of others. It is often difficult to distinguish between a mote, the fortifications of which have been obliterated, and an ancient Celtic mound erected for sepulchral, ceremonial, or other purposes. It is probable, too, that in several cases the Norman mote occupies the site of an earlier Celtic fort which was adapted for the purpose, and this adaptation may account for some divergences from the normal type, especially in the plan and defences of the bailey or enclosure at foot. These and other circumstances sometimes render it doubtful whether we should regard a given earthwork as a mote or not.

Outside the area of Eastern Ulster, Meath, Leinster, Tipperary, and Waterford, I have aimed at marking all earthworks which should be regarded as belonging to the type in question. In some of these districts, especially in parts of Mayo, Galway, and Roscommon, there are a few earthworks which appear from early Anglo-Norman times to have been called motes, but they are distinguishable in type as not containing a high enclosed mound. They generally consist of a rectangular platform, sometimes artificially or naturally raised a few feet, and surrounded by ditches and ramparts rectangular in plan. Though from their features and sites, taken in con- [344]
nexion with the data of history, they appear to be Norman or English works, they are distinct in type from the high motes, and were probably formed at a later period, under different conditions, and with a somewhat different object. I have accordingly not included them.

With the above qualifications and explanations the map shows with, I think, substantial accuracy the distribution of motes in Ireland, and this distribution, apart from other evidences, seems to offer a conclusive proof of their Norman origin. They are found thickly scattered throughout the lordships of Meath, Leinster, and Ulster, at the chief manorial seats. There are some fine examples, also at early manorial centres, in Southern Tipperary, and a few in other parts of the south of Ireland. In all Connaught there are only a very few rather degraded examples, while in the districts to which the Normans did not penetrate there are, so far as is known, none at all. Even in Leinster and Meath the areas to which the Irish tribes appear to have been confined show no motes. The map, therefore, incidentally serves not only to indicate the general area of Norman domination about the close of the reign of King John, but also to mark nearly all the more important centres of manors and sub-manors formed at that period.

For some of the evidence of Norman mote-building in Ireland, and for a description of a mote, see *supra*, vol. i, pp. 338–43 [pp. 127–9]; and for further evidence on the subject, and references to the writings of others, consult the papers mentioned in the note [40] to p. 342 [p. 129]. In chapters xi and xv, and elsewhere, allusion has been made to many of the motes marked on the map.

[15] CHAPTER XXIV

THE MINORITY OF HENRY III, 1216–26

'John, King of the Saxons, was deposed by the Saxons in this year, and died of a fit. The son of the King of France assumed the sovereignty of the Saxons and obtained their pledges.'[1] Such is the literal rendering of an entry in one of the older Irish annals under the year 1216. Couched in the phrases usually employed by native writers to record dynastic changes in Ireland, it expresses the view of contemporary events in England taken by an Irish onlooker. As it turned out indeed there was no dynastic change, but at the moment the statement seemed to be warranted by the facts.

At the time of King John's death, England was in a state of anarchy recalling the worst days of of King Stephen. The greater number of the earls and barons of England were in arms against the Crown, and had called to their aid the Dauphin of France. Louis had landed in England with a formidable army, the citizens of London had opened their gates to him, and most of the barons had done him homage. Alexander of Scotland and Llewelyn of Wales had taken the opportunity of throwing off their allegiance, and both of these princes, from motives of their own, favoured the
[16] barons' cause. Of the earls of England, Randolph of Chester, the earls of Derby and of Albemarle, and William Marshal alone supported the royal cause. The lords of the Welsh March were on the same side, and many of the royal castles were garrisoned for the king, but the northern, eastern, and south-eastern counties were all in the hands of Louis and the revolted barons. Throughout one half of England the king's writ no longer ran.

The royal cause had indeed benefited by the moral support of the Pope, who had annulled the Great Charter, excommunicated Louis and all his adherents, and sent Cardinal Gualo as legate to support the Crown with all the authority of the Church. The papal prohibition, however, had been ineffectual to prevent the French invasion, and though all clerical opposition had been silenced, the immediate effect was to remove from the conflict a moderating influence and to exasperate the barons still more.

It was indeed a time of great peril for England and for the boy-king, who was only nine years old. King John, on his death-bed at Newark, was well aware of the danger impending over his house. With unerring instinct he pointed out the only man who could save the situation. 'For God's sake,' cried the dying king to those around him, 'pray the Marshal to pardon the wrongs I have done him. He has always served me loyally and has never requited me ill for the ills I have done to him. And because I am

1 Ann. Loch Cé, 1216.

more sure of his loyalty than of that of any living man, I pray that he may always take charge of my son, for the lad will never be able to hold his own without the Marshal's aid.'[2] The great Earl Marshal was full of years, but by his character and antecedents [17]
he was clearly marked out as the fittest person to undertake the regency. Urged by the unanimous voice of the king's Council, he took up the perilous task and carried it through to a successful issue. As *Rector regis et regni*, by his conciliatory policy, he gradually won over many of the revolted barons to the young king's side. Then by his energy, courage, and military skill he succeeded, in spite of scanty resources, in inflicting damaging defeats upon his foreign opponents. Finally, by the moderation of his conditions,[3] he induced the French prince to give up his great undertaking and depart with his army whence he came.

During all this period of disturbance and danger in England peace and comparative quiet seem to have reigned in Ireland. In after times, as has often been said, 'England's difficulty was Ireland's opportunity.' Now if ever was the moment for Ireland to throw off the yoke if she found it galling. But it is a clear indication of the strength of the Anglo-Norman position in Ireland at this early period, and of the general acquiescence in Anglo-Norman rule, that, at a moment when the Regent was summoning every man he could obtain from the castles and garrisons far and near to aid the child-king, there was no rising of native tribes to expel the foreigner from Ireland, no attempt by the native chieftains to recover the independence they had lost.

The Irish policy of the new government is outlined in a letter to Geoffrey de [18]
Marisco, the justiciar, written (probably, as the phraseology indicates, by the legate Gualo) in the name of the young king soon after the Council of Bristol (November 11). After announcing the death of his father and his own coronation, the king proceeds to state that it was his wish to remove for ever and forget the angry feelings which formerly arose—whether with or without cause he knew not—between his father and some of the nobles, and if any such feelings existed against himself he was ready and anxious to purge them away, and by giving to every one by the advice of his subjects what reason should dictate, by uprooting evil customs, and by the introduction of liberties to restore the gracious days of his noble ancestors. Then, after alluding to the reissue of the Great Charter, the king promised that his subjects in Ireland should enjoy the same liberties as had been granted to his subjects in England.[4] This promise was soon fulfilled by the extension of the Great Charter to Ireland.[5] It must be remembered that the Charter had been repudiated by John and denounced by the pope. Its re-enactment in England and its extension to Ireland at this moment—in each country in a somewhat curtailed form, it is true—must have been mainly due to [19]
the political sagacity of William Marshal, who, with the earls of Chester, Derby, and

2 L'Histoire de Guillaume le Maréchal, ll. 16170–90. 3 Among these conditions was an indemnity to Louis of 10,000 marks. Towards finding this sum the king's advisers borrowed 6,000 marks from two merchants of St. Omer, and the Earl Marshal pledged all the lands he held of the king of France for the repayment of the debt due to them. For fuller particulars see Minority of Henry III (Norgate), pp. 83–4. 4 Foedera, vol. i, pt. 1, p. 145. It further appears from this letter that the Irish Council had prayed that either the Queen-Mother or the king's brother might be sent to Ireland, thus early intimating a desire, often since vainly repeated, for the establishment of a royal residence there. 5 Early Statutes (Berry), pp. 5–19. The

Albemarle, alone represented the nobility. The presence of the papal legate and eleven bishops, however, proves that the Church had come round to the liberal policy. Among the other magnates present were Walter de Lacy, lord of Meath, John Marshal, Earl William's nephew, and several of the lords of the Welsh border.

Notwithstanding preoccupations in England the Regency during this period devoted much attention to Ireland. The work of undoing John's confiscations, already commenced under the influence of William Marshal in John's lifetime, went on under the same influence with quickened pace in the early years of the new reign. The injury done to William himself was now redressed. The service which Meiler Fitz Henry owed for the earl's lands in Leinster, and which King John had taken into his hand as security for the earl's service, was once more ordered to be restored to the earl, 'who', say the king's advisers in a memorable phrase, 'had proved himself in time of need like gold in the furnace.'[6] These were apparently the lands in Leix and Offaly, which, as we have seen, Meiler, with King John's concurrence, had held adversely to the earl and
[20] about which disturbances had arisen.[7] The fief of Leinster was now once more restored to its original extent. To Walter de Lacy, whose personal loyalty was unquestioned, the king provisionally restored the castle of Drogheda and the land of Ardmayle (Co. Tipperary) to hold to the king's fourteenth year. Meanwhile a jury was to determine whether the castle of Drogheda belonged to the king or to Walter.[8] Geogrey de Marisco delayed to perform the mandate for livery. It was repeated more than once, and livery of the castle of Blathach near Limerick was also ordered.[9] Ultimately, in August 1220 an arrangement was made by which the castle and vill of Drogheda (which presumably had been found to belong by right to Walter)[10] were to be retained by the king, while Walter was to receive £20 a year as compensation.[11] Similarly, twenty marks a year were to be paid to Walter for the castle of Blathach, which it appears, when in the king's hand, had been granted to Archbishop Henry, and by him conferred on his niece Matilda before her marriage with William de Marisco.[12] In Uriel or Louth the castle of Dundalk was restored to Nicholas de Verdun, and seisin
[21] was also given to him of half the cantred of Ferrard.[13] Reginald de Braose, son and (since the death of his brother Giles, bishop of Hereford) heir of the ill-fated William de Braose, became reconciled to the new king, and in June 1217 the justiciar was

charter was apparently sent to Ireland on February 6, 1217, with a covering letter to the archbishops, barons, &c., commending the loyalty which they had shown to the king's father and would show to the king: Patent Roll, 1 Hen. III, p. 31. 6 Pat. Roll, 1 Hen. III, m. 16, pp. 9–10: *tanquam aurum in fornace, sic se in necessitate probavit.* It is noteworthy that these two mandates are addressed by the young king himself to Geoffrey de Marisco and Meiler Fitz Henry and are sealed not, as usual, with the seal of William Marshal (who was an interested party), but with the seals of the Legate and the Bishop of Winchester, who take the opportunity of expressing their high estimation of the Marshal. 7 *Ante*, vol. ii, pp. 210, 317–18 [pp. 235, 277]. 8 Pat. Roll, 1 Hen. III, m. 13 (p. 26). 9 Ibid., 2 Hen. III, pt. 1, m. 3 (p. 157): *Castrum de Blathac iuxta Limeric.* 10 An inspeximus of Walter de Lacy's grant in 1194 of the law of Breteuil to his burgesses of Drogheda next the castle, i.e. *ex parte Midie*, will be found in Pat. Roll, 14 Edw. III, p. 2, m. 26. 11 Close Roll, 4 Hen. III, p. 427b. 12 These compensatory payments were continued to Walter and his heirs for upwards of a century, before which time the true site of the castle of Blathach was forgotten and it was confused with the castle of Drogheda: see my notes in Journal R.S.A.I., vol. xxxix (1909), p. 40, and vol. xliv (1914), pp. 167–70. 13 Patent Roll, 1 Hen. III, p. 74.

ordered to give him the custody of the castle and city of Limerick and seisin of all the lands which belonged to his father in Munster.[14] It is very doubtful, however, if anything was done in pursuance of this order. It was repeated six months later. The original grant to William de Braose had been bitterly opposed by the Munster feoffees of whom Geoffrey was one, and now they would be equally opposed to its revival in favour of William's son. Certainly no restoration of the honour of Limerick was effected.[15] Lastly, within a month of the death of King John, an attempt was made to induce Hugh de Lacy, whom King John had hunted out of Ulster, to return to his allegiance.[16] But this had no effect, and though some of the subordinate tenants were [22]
restored to their lands in Ulster, the lordship was for many years administered by royal seneschals, who held in the king's name the castles of Carrickfergus and Dundrum. Hugh de Lacy appears at this time to have been taking part in the crusade against the Albigenses,[17] and perhaps had more attractive booty in view than any to be found in Ireland; but the failure to undo King John's work here was the cause of the first disturbance to the peace of the colony in the new reign.

Geoffrey de Marisco or de Mareis (Marsh), whose appointment as justiciar dated from 1215, was left undisturbed in his office under the new king. He was now one of the principal figures in Irish history. He held lands in County Limerick under the Crown,[18] and by his marriage with Eva de Bermingham, heiress of Offaly and widow of Gerald Fitz Maurice, he held that barony for his life under the lords of Leinster.[19]
He was a strong supporter of the de Burghs and of all who had least scruple in their [23]
methods of extending English rule over Ireland, but he was jealous of the power in Ireland of the great lords of the Welsh March. He seems to have been a crafty but plausible man, who generally succeeded in getting his way with the king and council even after their doubts as to his policy and suspicions as to his integrity had been aroused. It is clear that the Regency was not altogether satisfied with Geoffrey's administration, and it endeavoured to provide a check on his action and to secure a

14 Ibid., pp. 72–3. 15 I have found no subsequent trace of the De Braoses in Munster. Limerick Castle was one of those surrendered to the king by Geoffrey in 1221, and was committed to the custody of Richard de Burgh as seneschal of Munster in 1223: Pat. Rolls, 6 Hen. III, pp. 316, 375. The principal lands in question were in southern Tipperary, and had been regranted to Philip of Worcester (*ante*, vol. ii, pp. 175, 318 [pp. 221, 277]). In 1218 they were taken into the king's hand, and eventually, in 1225, four of the five cantreds were granted to Philip's nephew, William of Worcester: Close Roll, 9 Hen. III, p. 35 b. Irish officials viewed with apprehension the recognition of the heirs of William de Braose: Royal Letters (Shirley), vol. i, p. 60, c. 1219. 16 Pat. Roll, 1 Hen. III, m. 16, p. 4, dated November 18, 1216, where the following remarkable admission of John's wrongdoing occurs: ' licet vero bone memorie I. pater noster in aliquo erga vos deliquerit, ipsius delicti debemus esse immunes nec delictum suum aliquatenus nobis debet imputari'. 17 He can be traced in this crusade at intervals from 1211 to 1219; Recueil des Historiens de la France, vol. xix, pp. 145, 170, 181, and cf. Ann. Mon., vol. iii, p. 75. William de Lacy, Hugh's half-brother, appears to have taken possession, presumably on Hugh's behalf, of the castles of Rath and Carlingford, but early in 1217 he was ordered to deliver them to Geoffrey de Marisco, the justiciar (Pat. Roll, 1 Hen. III, m. 13, p. 26), and this appears to have been done. 18 See *ante*, vol. ii, p. 169 [p. 219]. 19 For the evidence as to the marriages of Eva de Bermingham and the devolution of the barony of Offaly see the writer's paper on 'The Fitz Geralds, Barons of Offaly', in Journal R.S.A.I., vol. xliv (1914), pp. 39–105. Geoffrey also held Holywood in Wicklow and Killorglin in Kerry; Cal. Docs. Ireland, vol. i, no. 2228. There was a dispute with the Crown as to Holywood ('Seinbois' or 'de Sancto Bosco'); ibid., nos. 139, 276.

better control over the revenue of Ireland, all of which passed through his hands. There is, indeed, evidence that he gave some of the escheats of the Crown to his own friends, and that he delayed to execute and even ignored some of the direct mandates of the distant English Government. In April 1217 it was ordered that the rents and fines of Ireland should be received only at the Exchequer, and should be safely kept by the treasurer until the king otherwise directed,[20] and about the same time Henry de Londres, Archbishop of London, was sent to Ireland 'to expedite the king's business there', and Geoffrey was ordered 'to abide by the archbishop's counsel, without whose assent nothing was to be done'.[21] As may be easily understood, relations between the justiciar and the archbishop soon became strained. A year later Geoffrey was reprimanded for not coming to England as required 'to render homage and certify concerning the state of Ireland', and he was again bidden to come and bring as much money as possible towards liquidating the debt owed to the dauphin and the arrears of
[24] tribute due to the Pope.[22] Geoffrey, however, on one excuse or another, seems to have postponed going to England until August 1220, when a stringent agreement was entered into between the king and Geoffrey for the future regulation of his office.[23]

By this convention, which was made in the presence of Pandulf, the new papal legate, Henry de Londres, Peter des Roches, and others of the King's Council, account was to be made in future at the Exchequer for the escheats, wards, fines, gifts, tallages, reliefs, and aids accruing in Ireland, and the proceeds thereof were to be rendered to the king at his mandate. Out of the assessed revenue and other profits of Ireland Geoffrey was to maintain the custody of the king's land and castles there, under the surveyance and by the counsel of the Archbishop of Dublin, Thomas Fitz Adam, and Richard de Burgh, and account at the Exchequer for any surplus revenue and profits; and the clerks of the king appointed for the purpose were to keep a counter roll of all these things. The constables, appointed by the justiciar to the king's castles, were to swear fealty to the king, and to give hostages into the hands of the archbishop and the Earl Marshal; while the justiciar gave his two sons as hostages, and pledged all his lands as security for his observance of the stipulations.

Geoffrey, however, failed to perform his part of these stipulations, and within a year
[25] he was superseded by Archbishop Henry. On July 17, 1221, the king, or rather the regency, still dominated by Pandulf, the papal legate, announced to the Irish kings and tenants in chief Geoffrey's dismissal and the appointment of the archbishop in a remarkable letter containing the following statements: that since the death of King John the king had received nothing from the demesne-lands or assessed rents or escheats of Ireland; that Geoffrey had failed in his undertakings to restrict the expenditure of the keepers of the king's castles and to give security for their fidelity; and that instead of the revenue of Ireland being paid into the exchequer to be dealt with as the

20 Rot. Claus., 1 Hen. III, p. 306. **21** Patent Rolls, 1 Hen. III, m. 8, p. 57. **22** Rot. Claus., 2 Hen. III, p. 376 b. In July 1218 a sum of nearly £500 was sent to the English exchequer by Thomas Fitz Adam and Richard de Felde, Crown officials in Ireland, Cal. Docs. Ireland, vol. i, no. 843. This probably represented the proceeds of the special aid imposed in the previous November on the kings of Ireland and the tenants in chief; ibid., no. 810. **23** Rot. Claus, 4 Hen. III, m. 3 d, pp. 463–5.

king should order, Geoffrey had caused it to be received in his chamber and had disposed of it more at his own will than according to the king's commands.[24]

That it should have been thought necessary to give such justificatory reasons for Geoffrey's supersession suggests that some opposition was apprehended in Ireland. In England at this time the regency experienced considerable difficulty in recovering the king's castles from the custody of those to whom they had been entrusted by King John, and a similar opposition may have been anticipated in Ireland. None however occurred. Before the end of October, Geoffrey, by his agents, formally surrendered to the king the following castles: Dublin, Limerick, Roscrea, Clonmacnois, Athlone, Drogheda, Dundrum, Carlingford, Dundonald, Balimichgan (Ballymaghan?),[25] Car- [26]
rickfergus, and Antrim, and the king, on the other hand, 'for the faithful service which Geoffrey rendered to King John and himself', quit-claimed to Geoffrey the sum of 1,080 marks and all quest touching his office.[26] Geoffrey was, in fact, absolved from any supposed reflection on his loyalty, but his supersession marks an attempt to obtain a better control over the revenue of the Crown, and in particular, through a reformed exchequer, a more adequate account of receipts and expenditure.

To this task the new justiciar set himself with inconvenient energy. He was immediately ordered to take into the king's hand all the king's demesnes and escheats, both new and old, unless the holders had special letters of the king or charters of his predecessors.[27] It was perhaps owing to his efforts to perform this mandate that the archbishop received the nickname 'Scorchevileyn' or 'Flay the Serf', by which he was known to contemporaries in Ireland. According to the story, as we first have it in a fifteenth-century compilation, the archbishop summoned his tenants to answer by what tenure they held of him. They accordingly produced their letters and charters, which he straightway threw into the fire. Hence the freeholders used always to call him Scorchevileyn.[28]

To Archbishop Henry is ascribed the building of Dublin Castle. He was certainly [27]
compensated for the loss of some churches, the sites of which were included in the castle-area, but, as we have seen, Meiler Fitz Henry was ordered to build the keep of a strong castle in Dublin in 1204, and the custody of the castle of Dublin was given to the archbishop on his first taking office in 1213. Probably the building of the *enceinte*

24 Rot. Claus., 5 Hen. III, p. 476 b. 25 This castle was presumably near the ecclesia de Balimichgan in the deanery of Blaethwyc (Newtownards): see Reeves, Eccl. Antiquities, p. 12, where the editor says that the church, of which there are no remains, is known to have 'occupied the ground at present under the orchard which belongs to the Moat House'. This is two miles south of Holywood. The castle was probably a 'mote-castle'. 26 Pat. Roll, 6 Hen. III, m. 6, p. 316. 27 Rot. Claus., 6 Hen. III, p. 478 b. 28 Laud MS. Annals, Chart. St. Mary's Abbey, vol. ii, p. 312. The sobriquet has been written by later writers 'Scorchvillaine' and 'Burnebill' from a supposed literal reference to the burning of the deeds, but the first element in the name is clearly the Old French *escorcher* (*excorticare*, 'to flay'), and it was the tenants who were metaphorically flayed or despoiled. Curiously enough the archbishop's niece Matilda, wife of William de Mariscis, is called in a Plea Roll of the time of Edward II 'Matilda Scorchevyleyn', thus showing that the nickname was not confined to the archbishop personally. See Chart. St. Mary's Abbey, vol. ii, Prefaee, p. cxxii, rote 4. Dr. Berry would connect the sobriquet with the Old French *vent escorchevel*, 'a wind which would skin a calf' (Journ. R.S.A.I., vol. xxii, p. 178); but the second element would seem to be 'vilein' (*villanus*).

occupied several years.[29] Archbishop Henry's charter (to which we have already referred), founding and endowing the offices of dean, precentor, chancellor, and treasurer, at the collegiate church of St. Patrick, thus giving it the status of a cathedral, must be ascribed to the year 1219.[30] The archbishop was a zealous upholder of clerical privileges and, in particular, of those appertaining to his own See. He endeavoured to extend the jurisdiction of his Ecclesiastical Court and his liberty of St. Sepulchre, and in doing so, both before and after he was made justiciar, infringed the liberties of
[28] the citizens of Dublin.[31] For this, in 1223, he was severely reprimanded by the king,[32] and the matters in dispute were settled next year by agreement between the archbishop and the citizens, mainly in accordance with the contentions of the latter.[33] He was also very tenacious of the property of the See, which he left much richer than he found it. He came into conflict with Thomas Fitz Adam, the king's forester, concerning the forest of Coillacht, a mountainous region on the southern border of County Dublin, which the archbishop claimed against the king and eventually succeeded in retaining for his See.[34] Indeed, nearly the whole mountainous district from the border of County Dublin to the lands attached to the fiefs of Wicklow, Arklow, Imaile, Naas, and Rathmore, was afterwards, in 1229, freed from the forest laws and acknowledged to belong to the archbishopric.[35] The possessions of the united Sees of Dublin and Glendalough were very extensive, and during the thirteenth century of increasing value. At the death of Archbishop Henry in 1228 the income of the See-lands seems to have been about £600,[36] while at the commencement of the reign of Edward I it
[29] averaged about £1,250.[37] The principal manors at the earlier period were Swords, Finglas, St. Kevins (afterwards called St. Sepulchre, near the city), Shankill, 'Salvum Keyvini' (afterwards Castlekevin, near Glendalough), Tallaght, Clondalkin, Newtown, Ballymore, 'Bretaschia' (now Brittas), and Rathcoole.

Meanwhile up to the death of William Marshal no serious trouble anywhere arose. The earl himself, indeed, had a dispute with Albin O'Mulloy, bishop of Ferns, concerning some lands alleged by the bishop to have been wrongfully appropriated by the earl. The bishop prosecuted his claim at Rome, whither he went to attend the Fourth Lateran Council, and he obtained from Innocent III, shortly before his death, a letter directing the archbishops of Tuam and Dublin to warn the earl and his accomplices to restore the possessions and property of the church of Ferns under threat of excommunication.[38] We are nowhere directly told where these lands lay, but it appears prob-

29 *Ante*, vol. ii, p. 306 [p. 272]. From the sheriff's account for 1228–9 it appears that works of construction at the towers of Dublin Castle were still going on; 35th Rep. D. K., p. 30. 30 *Ante*, vol. ii, p. 63 [p. 175]. The cathedral establishment was confirmed by Honorius III in 1221; Theiner's Vetera Monumenta, no. xlv, p. 18. 31 Royal Letters (Shirley), vol. i, p. 108. 32 Close Roll, 7 Hen. III, p. 570. 33 Chartae Priv. et Immun., p. 20. 34 Cal. Docs. Irel., vol. i, nos. 892, 926, 932–3 and 1317. The land of Coillacht had been expressly granted to the archbishop by King John in 1213 *in baroniam*, on condition 'that the king, when he goes to Ireland, may exchange it for land of the same value'; ibid., no. 475, and see *ante*, vol. ii, pp. 71–3 [pp. 178–9]. 35 Ibid., vol. i, nos. 1757, 1769. The king, however, retained the park or forest of Glencree, which was part of the territory of Obrun (in *Briuin*) 36 Irish Pipe Roll, 13 Hen. III, 35th Rep. D. K., p. 32 37 Ibid., 36th Rep. D. K., pp. 36, 41. 38 See the archbishops' letter reciting that from the Pope, preserved amongst the evidences of the monastery of Reading and transcribed in Journ. R.S.A.I., 1864, p. 138. Honorius III, in 1218, bade the parties come to an agreement: Theiner, Vetera Monumenta,

able that they included the lands which, in 1227, Philip de Prendergast, 'in pursuance of a decree of the ecclesiastical court and compelled by the authority of the Apostolic See, resigned for peace's sake' into the hands of John de St. John, successor of Albin O'Mulloy in the bishopric of Ferns. These lands were in the neighbourhood of Templeshanbo and Ferns, where two of the (subsequent) episcopal manors lay.[39] For the moment the suit against Earl William was respited on the ground that the king, who [30]
would be called to warrant the earl's title, was under age.[40] Many years later, however, after the death of the earl, and the death without issue of all his five sons, Matthew Paris tells a story which attributes the extinction of the family in the male line to the maledictions of the defrauded bishop. While, therefore, we must regard some of the details of the story as an *ex post facto* invention, the story is so characteristic of a mediaeval Irish ecclesiastic, and fits so well into authentic facts, that it seems worth repeating.

Under the year 1245, when all the sons of William Marshal were dead without issue, Matthew Paris writes that after the death of the earl [1219], the Bishop of Ferns came to the king and complained of the injury done to him by the earl in unjustly depriving him of two manors. For this he had excommunicated the earl, and he now begged the king to restore the manors to him, so that the deceased might obtain absolution. The king then asked the bishop to go to the earl's tomb and absolve him, promising that he would himself see that satisfaction was given to the bishop. The bishop then went to the tomb, and, as though addressing a living person, said: 'O William, who doth lie buried here bound in the bonds of excommunication, if what thou hast wrongfully taken from my church be restored to me by the king or by thy heir I absolve thee. If not, I confirm thy sentence, so that, wrapt up in thy sins, thou mayst for ever remain damned in hell.' The king was angry at the bishop's severity, but [31]
nevertheless endeavoured to induce the earl's eldest son and heir to restore the manors. He and his brothers, however, proved obdurate. Whereupon the bishop, enraged all the more, confirmed the sentence, and prophesied the extinction in a single generation of the earl's name, and the scattering of his inheritance within the king's lifetime.[41]

The death of the five sons of the earl, one after the other, without issue, was indeed such an unexpected event, and one so fraught with bad consequences to the English in Leinster, that we cannot wonder if it was regarded as having been brought about by supernatural means.

In August 1220, Walter de Lacy, who had now been re-seised of substantially all his lands and castles, came once more to Ireland. The castle of Trim, the principal seat of his liberty, is stated to have been built in this year, and it seems possible that the great stone keep still standing there, though afterwards extensively remodelled, dates from

p. 6; and probably the papal excommunication was never pronounced. 39 A deed by Gerald de Prendergast confirming his father Philip's agreement was enrolled by Sir H. Wallop in 1595 (Pat. Roll (Ireland) 37 Eliz.). For a full translation see Journ. R.S.A.I., 1864–6, pp. 147–8 note, and for the present writer's comments thereon see Hore's Hist. of Wexford, vol. vi, pp. 342–5. 40 Pat. Roll, 2 Hen. III, pp. 148–9. 41 Matt. Paris, Chron. Mai., vol. iv, pp. 493–4. 42 See ante, vol. ii, p. 249 [p. 250]. The keep of Warkworth

this time.[42] The gateway, towers, and enclosing walls, however, are clearly of later construction. But the lord of Meath did not confine his activities to strengthening his position in Meath. He also made an attempt to dominate Breffny, where it appears his vassals had already effected some settlements. This district, comprising the present counties of Leitrim and Cavan, at the time of the invasion was the principality of
[32] Tiernan O'Rourke, Dermot Mac Murrough's arch-enemy, but afterwards it was divided between the ruling septs of O'Rourke and O'Reilly. The territory of the former comprised County Leitrim and the two adjoining baronies of County Cavan, while the remainder of County Cavan was O'Reilly's country. In the past the chieftains of Breffny sometimes gave hostages to O'Conor and sometimes to O'Donnell, but more often were practically independent.

Now it seems that from an early period some Nangles of the Normans of Meath had a footing in Breffny. Before 1196, Gilbert de Angulo, or de Nangle, to whom the elder Hugh de Lacy had granted Nobber in Meath, held some land 'beyond the lakes of Therebrun' (*Tirbriúin*), meaning probably Lough Oughter in Cavan, and on his outlawry in that year John, Count of Mortain, gave the same to Walter de Lacy.[43] In the same year the English of Meath made a hosting into Breffny, but were defeated by Ualgharg O'Rourke.[44] In 1214, after the death of Gilbert de Nangle, we find his nephew Phillip, now lord of Navan, established in the south of Breffny, where his lands were plundered by O'Rourke.[45] Also the castle of Kilmore in Cavan was one of those restored to Walter de Lacy after the confiscation of 1210.[46] At that period it must have been a seignorial castle of some importance, but its origin is obscure.[47] It was near
[33] Lough Oughter, and its site is probably marked by the mote—exceptional in this territory—in what was afterwards the episcopal demesne at Kilmore.[48] In 1219 O'Donnell led an army into Breffny and took hostages from both O'Rourke and O'Reilly,[49] and it was probably in consequence of the submission of these chieftains to O'Donnell and to support the settlers in Breffny that the lord of Meath now interfered there.

According to the Irish annals, Walter de Lacy in 1220 'performed a great hosting to the crannog of O'Reilly. He went upon it and obtained hostages and great power'.[50] A crannog was, properly speaking, an artificial island, and it was usually formed by driving one or more circles of piles into the bed of a shallow lake and filling up the interior with layers of stone, marl, and rods, until a solid platform arose over the surface of the water. O'Reilly's crannog appears to have been in Lough Oughter in County Cavan, where the ruins of an early castle known as Cloch Oughter still stand.

Castle, however, the plan of which is there compared to that of Trim, is referred by good authorities to about the year 1400 or even later: 'Border Strongholds' by Cadwalader Bates; and see Early Norman Castles (Armitage), p. 377. 43 Gormanston Register, f. 5 dors. 44 Ann. Loch Cé, 1196. 45 Ibid., 1214. The Four Masters in the parallel entry call this territory Crich Cairpri, which O'Donovan takes to be Carbury in Co. Sligo, but it was clearly Crich Cairpri in Tethba, the region about Sliabh Cairpri on the border of Counties Leitrim and Longford. 46 Rot. Pat. 17 John, p. 148 b. 47 O'Reilly of Tirbrun, having been dispossessed by Tiernan O'Rourke, consistently supported Strongbow (Song of Dermot, ll. 1750 and note, 1788, 1909). He was probably reinstated, and it may have been through his influence that the Normans first got a footing in Breffny. 48 See English Historical Review, vol. xxii (1907), p. 342. 49 Four Masters, 1219. 50 Ann. Loch Cé, 1220.

This castle is described as 'circular in plan, the internal diameter being 35 feet and the thickness of the outer wall 7 feet'. The principal entrance 'was at a height of 15 feet from the ground', and appears to have been defended by 'the usual corbelled projection' above. The island on which the castle stands is an artificial island or ancient crannog, 190 by 140 feet – that is to say, 'stakes or small piles are visible all round its margin, and even some of the horizontal beams are exposed to view when the water is [34]
at summer level'.[51] Of course there may be, and probably is, a rock or other solid foundation beneath the castle. The ground at the base of the walls is about 10 feet above the water. As we shall see this castle comes prominently into notice (together with the castle of Kilmore) in 1224, and is mentioned on several subsequent occasions.[52] It seems probable that it was erected by the de Lacy's at about this time, in connexion with the movement to dominate Breffny.

That nothing less was intended is evident from a deed made by Walter de Lacy next year (1221), by which he purported to grant to Philip de Nangle all the land which Ualgharg O'Rourke held in Breffny from Lough Oughter to the Shannon, and (apparently) from some place on Lough Erne (presumably the southern end of the Upper Lake) to Slieve Carbury in the northern extremity of County Longford.[53] This included at least the southern half of County Leitrim with the barony of Tullyhunco in County Cavan. This was no doubt a 'speculative grant' to induce the lord of Navan, [35]
who had hereditary claims in part of this region, to endeavour to substitute Norman for Celtic domination over the whole of it. It was provided by the same deed that William de Lacy should build three stone castles for Philip, and that when the lands should be let to farm, Philip should render the service of three knights. As we afterwards hear of 'Mac Costello's castle in Breffny'[54] we may infer that this undertaking was in part at least accomplished.

To complete, so far as our scanty materials allow, the story of this attempted settlement in Breffny by 'the sons of Jocelin', we may here mention that Philip de Nangle was followed in this district by his son Miles, who married a daughter of Hugh de Lacy, Earl of Ulster.[55] In 1245 Miles built a castle at Ath-an-chip, a ford on the Shan-

51 'For plan and description see Journ. R.S.A.I., vol. xxi (1890–1), p. 294. 52 It is usually called *Cloch locha uachtair*, or 'the Stone keep of Lough Oughter'. It is mentioned in 1327 (Four Masters), in 1369 and 1390 (Ann. Loch Cé), and in 1487 (Ann. Ulst.). It was the castle in which Bishop Bedell was confined in 1641. It was no doubt more than once restored. 53 This deed was enrolled in 32 Elizabeth: Cal. Pat. and Close Rolls, Ireland (Morrin), p. 197. It was witnessed by James, Legate and Penitentiary of the Apostolic See, then in Ireland, Geoffrey de Marisco, justiciar, &c., which fixes the date (1221). See Ann. Ulst. 1221 and note. The names of the extreme boundaries and of the included territories are given. As printed, they are corrupt, but the territories included Muinter Eolais (barony of Mohill), Magh Nissi (in barony of Leitrim), Muinter Cinaith (in Drumahaire), Cenel Luachain (in Carrigallen), and Tellach Dunchadha (Tullyhunco in Co. Cavan). 54 Ann. Loch Cé, 1242. Members of this family were called by the Irish *Mac Goisdealbh*, anglicized Mac Costello, i.e. son of Jocelin. The eponymous Jocelin came from Nangle or Angle in Pembrokeshire and was enfeoffed in lands at Navan (*ante*, vol. ii, p. 84 [p. 183]), where the name Nangle (in Latin documents *de Angulo*) survived. 55 Ann. Loch Cé, 1253. The relationship of the various early members of this family is rather obscure, but from Plea Roll, 16 Edw. II (see Betham's Excerpta, vol. ii, p. 224, in Ulster's Office), it would seem that this Miles de Nangle and his father Philip, son of William, son of Jocelin, were on the senior line of the lords of Navan, and that the line of Castlemore, Co. Mayo, separated from that of Navan in the sons of Miles.

non somewhere near Carrick. In 1247 he expelled Cathal Mac Rannell from the woods of Conmaicne in the south of Leitrim, but with the whole clan Costello was himself expelled in the same year by the sons of Aedh O'Conor. We hear no more of the Mac
[36] Costellos in County Leitrim,[56] but they had already been enfeoffed in County Mayo, where they held their own for three centuries and gave their Irish name to the barony of Costello in that county.

In the same year (1221), Walter de Lacy attempted to build a castle at Athleague, where there was a ford across the Shannon just above the entrance of the river into Lough Ree. The name is partly preserved in Ballyleague, as the western suburb of Lanesborough is called. A castle here would have been a protection to the southern part of Annaly (County Longford), where some Norman settlements had been made. The Connaught men, however, with whom there were at this time peaceful relations, naturally resented the presence of another castle on the Shannon. They marched into Annaly and obtained the abandonment of the castle as the price of peace.[57]

[37] Meanwhile no restitution had been made to Walter de Lacy's brother Hugh, the dispossessed Earl of Ulster. Negotiations went from time to time, but without result. In September, 1221, a safe-conduct was given to Hugh and his retinue in coming to England to the king.[58] Fifteen months later the terms offered to him by 'the majority of the king's council' were that he should have the lands which Walter his brother gave to him (Nobber and Ratoath), and the lands which formed the marriage portion of his wife, Lesceline de Verdun (in the north of Co. Louth).[59] Hugh, however, was not satisfied with these terms, and demanded the restoration of Ulster as well. The king in council offered to commit the land of Ulster and its castles to the Earl of Chester, Walter de Lacy, and others for five years, provided they would pledge their lands to restore them to the king at the end of the term, if the king so pleased. The proposed guarantors, however, were unwilling to take the risk, and nothing was done. By this time, June 1223, Hugh had lost patience and was plotting to invade Ireland. The king sent to the Archbishop of Dublin the Pope's letter of excommunication against Hugh and his accomplices if he should invade the land, and, what was more useful, gave orders to victual and man the castles of Ulster.[60]

56 Nevertheless three centuries later Sir Thomas Nangle, baron of Navan, in a plaint before the king's council stated that Mc Rannell refused to pay him '100 kyne yearly, with a knight's fees', which the baron's ancestors claimed out of Muinter Eolais, and ultimately a decree was made by consent that Mc Rannell should pay to the baron a yearly rent of £6 out of the lands: Pat. Roll (Ireland), 5 Edw. VI (Morrin), p. 259. 57 Ann. Loch Cé, 1221. A castle was, however, erected at Athleague by William de Lacy and the English of Meath in 1227: Ann Clon. It was broken in 1271: Ann. Loch Cé. Lands, now represented by Keel and Clooncallow in the barony of Shrule, were granted by the elder Hugh de Lacy to William le Petit: see the charter transcribed Song of Dermot, p. 310. Here was built the *Caislén nua*, now Newcastle, mentioned in this very year 1221, Ann. Loch Cé. We also hear of the castle of *Ard abla*, now Lisardowlan, a few miles east of Longford: see Journ. R.S.A.I. (1910), p. 223, for the mote site here. Annaly (*Anghaile*) was undoubtedly part of the ancient kingdom of Meath. The castle of Moybrachry or Street, built by Herbert de la Mare, was also in existence. For the site and remarkable key found there: see ibid., pp. 214–22. 58 Pat. Roll, 5 Hen. III, p. 301. 59 Rot. Claus., 7 Hen. III, p. 527 b, and see *ante*, vol. ii, pp. 121–3 [p. 199]. 60 Ibid., p. 549 b. William de Serland was given the custody of Carrickfergus and appointed seneschal of Ulster: Cal. Docs. Ireland, vol. i, 1124. John de Tiwe was given the custody of Dundrum (Rath) (ibid.

It was soon after this, in the latter half of the year 1223, that Hugh de Lacy crossed over to Ireland to assert his claims by the strong hand.[61] He seems to have gone to Meath, where, aided by William de Lacy, and other local lords, he ravaged the country and even threatened Dublin, so that, it is said, Archbishop Henry was obliged to purchase a truce to the following summer.[62] [38]

About this time, when Hugh de Lacy was active in Meath, Cathal Crovderg O'Conor, King of Connaught, wrote a remarkable letter to King Henry, which has been calendared as follows:— 'Hugh de Lacy, enemy of the king, of the king's father, and of Cathal, whom King John by Cathal's advice expelled from Ireland, has without consulting the king come to that country to disturb it. Against Hugh's coming Cathal remains, as the Archbishop of Dublin knows, firm in his fidelity to the king. [39] But the closer Cathal adheres to the king's service, the more he is harassed by those who pretend fealty to the king, and, as the justiciar knows, shamefully fail against the enemy; so that between Hugh de Lacy on the one hand and those who pretend to be faithful on the other, Cathal is placed in great difficulty. Wherefore, unless it is better that the peace of Ireland should be subverted by this disturber and by default of some of the king's subjects, Cathal prays the king to send a force thither to restrain Hugh's insolence.'[63]

By 'those who pretend fealty to the king', but who nevertheless harassed Cathal, the King of Connaught may perhaps have had in view Richard de Burgh and his supporters. Cathal had indeed good reason to regard Richard de Burgh as his enemy. At this time Richard was again urging his claim to Connaught under his charter of 1215, or at least seeking compensation from the king in lieu thereof, and the king, to satisfy Richard, had ordered the justiciar to press Cathal for an increased rent.[64] But, as another letter to be presently mentioned shows, Cathal also viewed with apprehension the attempt on behalf of Walter de Lacy to annex Breffny, the overlordship of which the kings of Connaught had disputed with the O'Donnells. The immediate answer to

1128), but was afterwards taken prisoner: ibid. 1162. In October 1223, John Marshal, cousin of Earl William Marshal, was given the custody of Ulster with the king's castles therein: ibid. 1140. In March 1224 Roger Waspail was made seneschal of Ulster: ibid. 1158. 61 Ann. Mon., vol. iii, p. 85. There is confusion in the Irish annals as to the date of Hugh's arrival and some consequent uncertainty as to the order of his proceedings. The entry in Ann. Ulst. 1222 (which is copied in Ann. Loch Cé and Four Masters, 1221) is clearly misplaced and relates to the events of 1223–4. It is the only entry in Ann. Ulst. and Four Masters touching the war. The entry is virtually repeated in Ann. Loch Cé at the true date, 1224, and refers to the close of William Marshal's campaign, the date of which is fixed to the summer of that year. Hugh can hardly have landed until after June 1223, when orders were given to resist his coming: Rot. Claus., 7 Hen. III, p. 549 b. There is no earlier mention in the records of Hugh's activity in Ireland. 62 The statement in the Annals of Dunstable (Ann. Mon., vol. iii, p. 85), that the archbishop purchased a truce in 1223, is perhaps supported by entries in the Close Rolls to the effect that the archbishop borrowed £366 from the citizens of Dublin 'to maintain the war against Hugh': Cal. Docs. Ireland, vol. i, nos. 1265, 1463. 63 Cal. Docs. Ireland, vol. i, no. 1174, where the letter is ascribed to 'about March 1224', also Royal Letters, vol. i, p. 183 (Shirley), where the editor, probably relying on the Annals of Ulster, dates the letter May 1222. It must, however, be dated after June 1223, when the first intimation appears on the Rolls that Hugh was plotting to invade Ireland. 64 Rot. Claus., 8 Hen. III, p. 584. For the two inconsistent grants of Connaught of 1215 see *ante*, vol. ii, p. 285 and note [p. 264 and note 9].

[40] Cathal's letter was a renewed grant of protection 'to endure so long as the King of Connaught should faithfully serve the king'.[65]

Early in 1224 Cathal, evidently feeling his end approaching, sent another letter to the king, accompanied by a recommendatory letter from Archbishop Henry. In this letter, after reaffirming his fidelity, Cathal prays for a renewal of the charter of Connaught to his son Aedh in fee. The dying king was evidently desirous of securing the land to his own line on feudal terms, foreseeing, no doubt, that Aedh's succession would meet with opposition, from different motives, at the hands of both English and Irish. He further prays 'that the king will deliver to his son the land of Ui Briuin, Conmaicne, and the Caladh (Breffny and part of County Longford), detained by William de Lacy, Cathal's enemy and kinsman of the king's enemy'.[66] On June 14, presumably on the advice of William Marshal, now justiciar, the king ordered seisin of these lands to be given to Aedh 'for his maintenance on the king's service',[67] but this order was certainly not carried out, and in all probability was not communicated to Aedh.

[41] Meantime, on May 28, 1224, Cathal died,[68] and his son Aedh assumed the government of Connaught. One of Aedh's first acts was to lead a hosting into Annaly, take and burn the castle of Ard-abhla, and 'kill every one whom he found in it, both Foreigners and Gael'. The site of this castle is marked by a mote and bailey earthwork called Lisardowling, about five miles east of the town of Longford.[69] It was in O'Farrell's country, or Annaly, and may have been recently erected by the English. By this action, characteristic of a newly-made Celtic chieftain not quite certain of his popularity, Aedh put himself in the wrong with the English crown and gave his enemies a handle against him.

To deal with the transgressions of Walter de Lacy's men of Meath 'in harbouring Hugh de Lacy, pillaging and burning the king's land, killing and holding his men to ransom', the king's council at first adopted the strange expedient of employing Walter de Lacy against his kith and kin. In March 1224 it was agreed that Walter should deliver to the king Ludlow Castle in England and Trim Castle in Ireland to hold for two years, that Walter should go to Ireland and with the king's force fight the transgressors in Meath, that the king should hold their lands when recovered for a year and a day, and that afterwards it should be done to Walter as the king's court should decide. For the purpose of fighting the king's enemies Walter was to have free access to the castle of Trim.[70]

[42] Before any important steps were taken to carry out this agreement the conduct of operations was placed in abler and more independent hands. On May 2 William Mar-

65 Cal. Docs. Ireland, vol. i, no. 1164 (March 5, 1224). 66 Ibid., no. 1184; Royal Letters (Shirley), vol. i, p. 223. Ui Briuin was the generic name for O'Rourke's and O'Reilly's territory; Conmaicne (Maighe Rein) seems to have been another name for Muinter Eolais, or Mc Rannell's country and the Caladh was co-extensive with the barony of Rathcline, Longford. 67 Rot. Claus., 8 Hen. III, p. 604 b. 68 Ann. Loch Cé, 1224, where there is an extraordinary eulogy on Cathal. But even this is surpassed in a tract ascribed to Torna O'Mulconry, where, among many other things, it is said that 'he was a man who burned the greatest number of homesteads and took the greatest number of preys from both the English and the Irish who opposed him ... It was he who blinded, killed, and chastised the greatest number of rebels and enemies. He was the most gentle and peaceable of all the kings that ever reigned in Ireland'. 69 Journ. R.S.A.I., vol. xl (1910), p. 223. 70 Pat Rolls, 8 Hen. III, p. 483.

shal the younger, Earl of Pembroke, one of the foremost commanders of the time, was appointed justiciar in the place of the aged Archbishop of Dublin, and on June 19 he landed at Waterford. Among the followers whom he brought with him from England was John d'Erlee, his father's faithful vassal and virtual biographer. On August 5 the earl sent a military dispatch[71] to the king, which has happily been preserved, and from it, supplemented by some other records, we can form an authentic and fairly adequate idea of the campaign.

From Waterford the earl proceeded to Dublin, collecting no doubt on the way his Leinster vassals. At Dublin he was invested with the office of justiciar by the archbishop. His first difficulty was to provide for his army. Twelve citizens of Dublin had already lent the archbishop £366 to aid the king in defending Ireland against Hugh de Lacy,[72] and the archbishop had also taken 300 marks which had been deposited in the cathedral of Dublin.[73] These sums, however, appear to have been already spent. The earl got 600 head of cattle and 40 marks from the Cistercians of Mellifont and £200 from the same Order in Dublin,[74] but as he says that he spent during the siege of Trim upwards of £16 a day these items did not go very far.

The earl lost no time in Dublin, but rode to Trim, where he found the castle held [43] by certain knights and others against the king. Aided by Walter de Lacy, who accompanied him, he straightway besieged the castle.[75] On hearing of the earl's arrival, the barons who were holding a parley with the King of Connaught in the west of Meath, came to the earl and rendered their service; and the earl, quite in the manner of a modern general, requested the king to commend Geoffrey de Marisco and the other Irish barons as well as the citizens for their prompt service. While at Trim the earl dispatched his cousin, William le Gras, the elder,[76] with a small force to relieve Carrickfergus, which was being besieged by Hugh de Lacy. The party safely reached the castle by water, though Hugh sent eight boats to harass them on the way. Hugh then raised the siege and retired, probably to seek assistance from O'Neill. Meanwhile the earl sent a party of horse against William de Lacy, who with difficulty escaped to the moors and had to throw himself on the mercy of the Irish. At this time O'Reilly, chieftain of Cavan, who had recently come to the king's peace, was besieging the castle called Crannog O'Reilly[77] in Lough Oughter (already mentioned), where William de [44] Lacy had placed for security his wife (daughter of Llewelyn), his mother (daughter of Rory O'Conor),[78] and the wife of his half-brother, Thomas Blund. O'Reilly applied to

71 Royal Letters (Shirley), vol. i, pp. 500–3. 72 Orders were given in 1225 and 1226 to repay this sum (Cal. Docs. Irel., vol. i, nos. 1265 and 1463). In 1229 the citizens quit-claimed to the king £312, part of this loan in return for licence to elect a mayor annually: ibid., no. 1689. 73 Royal Letters (Shirley), vol. i, p. 325. 74 Cal. Docs. Ireland, vol. i, nos. 1245, 1266. 75 'Et dictum castrum una cum domino W. de Lascy, qui nobiscum venit, dedimus obsidioni.' Sweetman's rendering would lead one to suppose that William de Lacy was besieged in the castle, whereas the meaning clearly is that Walter de Lacy assisted the earl in the siege: Cal. Docs. Irel., vol. i, no. 1203. 76 'Misimus dominum W. Grassum primogenitum, consanguineum nostrum'—not 'W. le Gros, his eldest cousin', as rendered by Sweetman. He was called *primogenitus* to distinguish him from his brother of the same name. He was the earl's seneschal in Leinster at this time: *infra*, p. 50 [pp. 305–6]. 77 See *ante*, p. 33 [pp. 277–8]. 78 She was the elder Hugh de Lacy's second wife whom he married in 1181; see *ante*, vol. ii, p. 54 [pp. 172–8]. She must have afterwards married a Blund.

the earl for succour, and in reply the earl sent some soldiers with Walter de Ridelsford and Richard de Tuit, who took the castle. The ladies were taken into custody, and Rory O'Conor's daughter appears to have been employed to induce her nephew, Aedh O'Conor, now King of Connaught, to return to the king's peace. As we have seen he had taken advantage of the disturbance to enter Annaly and burn the castle of Ardowlan. His aunt's intercession, however, seems to have had effect, as we find him soon afterwards joining the army against Hugh de Lacy in the march to Dundalk. The earl's knights then besieged and took the castle of Kilmore, which was held by Henry Blund, another half-brother of William de Lacy. Three or four castles in Meath, including the de Lacy castles of Ratoath and Rathfeigh, had been taken before the earl's arrival, and at the date of his dispatch Trim Castle was to be surrendered after a six weeks' siege on the following August 11.

The disaffection in Meath was thus quickly suppressed with little bloodshed and, incidentally, a check was put upon the aggressive movement into Breffny, but Hugh de Lacy was still at large in Ulster, and had obtained the powerful support of Aedh O'Neill. Together they demolished the castle of Coleraine,[79] which belonged to the
[45] Earl of Athol, and deprived Duncan of Carrick of his land.[80] Here were the elements of a bargain between Hugh and O'Neill, for these Scottish nobles had also been given land in O'Neill's territory.[81] Hugh would aid O'Neill in ousting the Scots from Ireland, and O'Neill would assist Hugh in recovering his earldom from the Saxon king. Unfortunately we have no further dispatch from the Earl Marshal to elucidate what followed, but from the Irish annals it appears that, supported by the Kings of Connaught, Thomond and Desmond, he led an army to the borders of Ulster at Dundalk.[82] Here Hugh de Lacy had ravaged the lands of his brother-in-law Nicholas de Verdun,[83] and now with O'Neill he held the passes, always difficult to force, into Ulster. Neither side, however, wished to push matters to extremities and there was no fighting. It was obviously important to detach Hugh from his Irish ally, and probably the Marshal was able to assure Hugh that no very severe terms would be imposed. At any rate Hugh surrendered to the Marshal, and was sent to the king to abide by his award.[84] This was probably in October. Early in November, William Marshal was summoned to the king, and the management of affairs in Ireland was temporarily entrusted to Geoffrey de Marisco.

Though we have described the disturbance caused by Hugh de Lacy at some length
[46] its importance should not be exaggerated. It did not affect adversely the mutual relations of English and Irish. Indeed the circumstances show the strength of the Anglo-Norman position at this period. Not only was Hugh unable to get any support from the Irish except from O'Neill, but the other provincial kings all actively supported the Crown against him. There was no serious split among the barons of Ire-

79 See the misplaced entry Ann. Ulst. 1222 and note *supra*, p. 38 [p. 300]. The castle of Coleraine was rebuilt in 1228: Ann. Ulst. 80 Close Rolls, 8 Hen. III, pp. 615, 640. 81 See *ante*, vol. ii, pp. 290–3 [pp. 266–7]. The grants to Alan of Galloway and Duncan of Carrick had been confirmed by Henry III: Rot. Claus., 4 Hen. III, p. 420 b and 8 Hen. III, I p. 587. 82 Ann. Loch Cé, 1224. 83 Rot. Claus., 8 Henry. III, p. 618. 84 Ann. Loch Cé, 1224; Ann. Dunstable, pp. 91–2, and cf. Cal. Docs. Ireland, vol. i, no. 1219.

land. Even in Meath, with the exception of the junior branches of the de Lacys and some others, the principal tenants were loyal. It was essentially a personal quarrel between Hugh and the Crown, and should be regarded as an example, rare up to this time on Irish soil, of the struggle which had been going on in England for several years between the Crown and a section of the barons that championed an extreme form of feudal independence.

Some time elapsed before terms were settled with the de Lacys. As regards Walter, it was arranged in May 1225 that he should make 'a fine with the king of 3,000 marks, to have seisin of the lands of his knights and free tenants in Ireland taken into the king's hand, because they went against the king in Hugh de Lacy's war'. The castles of Trim and Kilmore in Ireland, and Ludlow in England, were to be restored to him, but the king was to retain the castles of Ratoath, Nobber, and Drogheda.[85] He was held responsible for the transgressions of his tenants, but, with three exceptions, he was to keep the fines which these tenants should make with him to have their lands again, so that Walter's fine may be in part regarded as a convenient way of collecting these fines [47]
for the king. Nevertheless, coming on the top of the fine of £4,000, imposed by King John in 1215, it was a heavy burden, and in 1234–5 Walter owed £2,747 1*s*. 10*d*. for the two fines,[86] and at his death he was still in debt to the Crown. About the same time, at the instance of the Earl Marshal, the king gave Hugh de Lacy 200 marks until he should further provide for him.[87] But it was not until a year later that an arrangement was made for Hugh's benefit, by which Walter received the custody of the castles of Carrickfergus, Antrim, and Dundrum, with all the land which Hugh formerly held in Ulster, also all the lands which Hugh held of Walter's fee, with the castles of Ratoath and Nobber, and also the lands which he held of the fee of Nicholas de Verdun and had in marriage with Lesceline his wife, with the castle of Carlingford—all these lands and castles to be restored to the king at the end of three years, unless meanwhile Hugh should obtain of the king's grace their restoration to himself.[88] These terms do not appear to differ in substance from those to which the king's council was ready to assent in 1223, but now the requisite sureties were forthcoming. Indeed, elaborate precautions were taken to insure fulfilment of the terms. Hostages were given, including Walter and Roger, sons of Hugh de Lacy, and many of the highest nobles of England became sureties that Walter and his son Gilbert would surrender the castles and lands, if the conditions were not fulfilled.[89] William Marshal himself was a surety both for this arrangement, and for the former one concerning Walter's lands. Though Hugh [48]
de Lacy had joined Llewelyn against him in Wales, and though they had been opposed in Ireland, it is evident that William Marshal bore his opponent no ill will, but acted generously towards him, and even risked something to enable him to obtain restoration to favour. This generous conduct was ill repaid by Hugh de Lacy, in the part he took a few years later in bringing about the tragic death of Richard Marshal, the earl's brother and successor.

85 Rot. Claus., 9 Hen. III, p. 39 b. 86 Pipe Roll (Ireland), 19 Hen. III, 35 Rep. D. K., p. 34. 87 Close Roll, 9 Hen. III, p. 37 b. 88 Pat. Roll, 10 Hen. III, p. 31. 89 Ibid., pp. 75 8.

[49] CHAPTER XXV

THE SONS OF WILLIAM MARSHAL, 1219–45

William Marshal, the younger, Earl of Pembroke, is prominent in Irish history as the commander who successfully curbed the turbulence of the supporters of Hugh de Lacy in Meath and Breffny, and as the statesman who removed the cause of disaffection by bringing about the peaceable restoration of Hugh to his earldom. These public actions have been sufficiently described in the preceding chapter. The latter action was forgotten by the de Lacys, while the former was remembered against the earl and his successors, as was also his unsuccessful protest against the policy of confiscation adopted with regard to Aedh, son of Cathal, King of Connaught, to be mentioned in chapter xxvii. Before telling the story of the fatality which befell the male members of his father's house and brought about the breaking up of Strongbow's great fief, we shall here notice some traces of his work as lord of Leinster.

The earl's seneschal in Leinster in 1223, when he granted charters to Carlow and Moone, and made an addition to his father's charter to Kilkenny, was Thomas Fitz
[50] Anthony,[1] who had been his father's seneschal; but in 1224 his seneschal was William le Gras, called *primogenitus*, or senior,[2] to distinguish him from his brother William le Gras, junior. This family, from which descended the Graces of Tullaroan, has been strangely mishandled by our genealogists. On no better ground apparently than the supposed identity of the sobriquet, it has been alleged to have sprung from Raymond Fitz William, nicknamed 'le Gros', in spite of the clear evidence that Raymond left no children.[3] On a similar ground, and through an apparently mistaken interpretation of his nephew's charter to Sodbury in Gloucestershire, William le Gras, 'primogenitus,' has been identified with William 'le Gros', the Earl of Albemarle, who died in 1179.[4] From his charter to Bradenstoke, however, granted shortly before the death of the elder William Marshal (who with his son William witnessed it), it appears that William Grassus or le Gras, 'primogenitus,' was the eldest son of another William le Gras

1 Chartae Privilegia et Immunitates, pp. 34, 38; also charter to Moen, Justiciary Roll, vol. i, p. 371. 2 Gormanston Register, f. 209. This change of seneschal is important for the dating of many charters. 3 Memoirs of the Grace Family, by Sheffield Grace. 4 Journal R.S.A.I., vol. xxxii (1902), pp. 64–7. This Sodbury charter (undated) is apparently only known by an extract given in Rudder's Gloucestershire: 'Willelmus Crassus primogenitus [?] filius Willelmi Crassi iunioris salutem. [Sciant, etc.] nos concessisse . . . burgensibus nostris de Sobbur' [Sodbury] totum quod Willelmus Crassus primogenitus, avunculus noster, eisdem fecit [viz. the laws of Breteuil].' Possibly the first 'primogenitus' has crept into the text by error. At any rate it is pretty clear that the grantor was the son of the William, junior, and nephew of the William, 'primogenitus', of the Bradenstoke charter and of the Irish documents. William le Gras, primogenitus or senior, obtained a market at Sodbury in 1217: Close Roll, 2 Hen. III, p. 368.

(Grassus), and that his brothers were William le Gras, junior, Hamo le Gras, Anselm [51] le Gras, then treasurer of Exeter, and Robert le Gras, then dead.[5] This Anselm le Gras was consecrated Bishop of St. David's in 1231, and is described as nephew of the elder William Marshal,[6] while the younger William Marshal, as we have seen,[7] calls William le Gras, primogenitus, 'his cousin'. From these facts we may conjecture with probability that William le Gras, father of the above-named brothers, married a sister of the elder William Marshal, which would account precisely for the stated relationships, and that in all probability he was the William le Gras who was appointed by King John seneschal of Normandy on August 19, 1203.[8] William le Gras, primogenitus, was still seneschal of Leinster in December 1224.[9] As he was succeeded in Sodbury by his [52] nephew William, son of his brother William, junior, we may perhaps infer that he died without issue;[10] and that it was his nephew who appears in 1247 as holding lands of Richard, Earl of Gloucester, son of Isabel Marshal, in Offerlane, Queen's County, and at Tullaroan, County Kilkenny,[11] and who was, no doubt, ancestor of the Graces, barons of Courtstown near Tullaroan.

The younger William Marshal was in Ireland in the winter of 1222–3, but left early in April 1223, on account of the aggressive action of Llewelyn on the English border.[12] He came again to Ireland as justiciar in June 1224, and was there nearly continuously[13] for two years, when he was superseded by Geoffrey de Marisco. He returned to Ireland in a private capacity about the end of August 1226, and seems to have remained [53] there until about May 1227.[14] In his time (1219–31), and indeed ever since the settling of the dispute between his father and Meiler Fitz Henry in 1208, the peace in Leinster appears to have been quite unbroken. The younger earl followed in the footsteps

5 This charter is given in Dugdale's Monasticon, vol. ii, p. 208 'Sciant, etc., quod ego Willielmus Grassus primogenitus Willielmi Grassi Deo et canonicis de Bradenstoke concessu Willielmi le gras iunioris et Hamonis Gras et Anselmi Gras Thesaurarii Exoniensis fratrum meorum et aliorum parentum meorum pro salute Roberti le Gras fratris mei ibidem requiescentis totam terram illam in villa de Wales quam dedi praefato Roberto le Gras fratri meo, etc. Testibus domino Willielmo Marescallo, comite Penbrochie, Willielmo Marescallo filio suo, Willielmo le Gras iuniore, Hamone le Gras, Anselmo le Gras Thesaurario Exoniae, fratribus meis, etc.' 6 Annales Monastici, vol. iv, p. 422, and cf. Register St. Thomas's Abbey, Dublin, p. 137, where Anselmus nepos comitis [Penbrochie] is one of the witnesses to a grant by William Marshal I. 7 *Supra*, p. 43 [p. 302]. 8 According to L'Histoire de Guillaume le Marechal, the elder William Marshal had two sisters who were 'richement mariées', 1. 398. From ll. 7265 *et seq.* it would seem that one of the sisters was married to Robert del Pont de l'Arche and had five daughters then living (c. 1184), whom she was concerned to marry. William le Gras is mentioned (ibid., l. 4713) at a tournament at Lagny-sur-Marne. 9 Gormanston Register, f. 209. 10 From Fine Roll, 4 Hen. III, p. 40, it appears that in December 1219 William Crassus, primogenitus, made a fine for having to wife Hawise, daughter and heir of Thomas de London, and that William Marshal II and others of his family and friends were pledges for the fine; but from an entry dated June 11, 1223 (Cal. Patent Rolls, vol. i, p. 376), it would seem that the marriage did not take place, and that Walter de Braose married Hawise with the king's consent. 11 See Chart. St. Mary's, vol. ii, p. 405. The family of Welond had some claims to lands at Tullaroan, which in 1283 were released to William le Gras (who had previously held the lands of the gift of William Welond) in consideration of receiving from him Sodbury in exchange: Cal. Docs. Ireland, vol. ii, no. 2158. 12 A charter of his is dated at Kilkenny, April 5 a. r. 7 Hen. III (1223); Chartae Privil. et Immun., p. 31, and cf. inspeximus, p. 80. The earl appears to have landed in Wales on April 10; see Minority of Henry III (Norgate), p. 192 note. 13 He went to the king for a short time in November 1224; Cal. Docs. Irel., vol. i, no. 1224. 14 Cal. Docs. Irel., vol. i, nos. 1440, 1506.

of his father, building castles, encouraging the formation and growth of towns, endowing religious establishments, and developing generally his great fief. To assist him in the work of incastellation, the king granted to him the service which he owed for the year 1222–3, and again, when the earl was justiciar, the service which he owed for the year 1225–6.[15] Orders of this kind were not uncommon in Henry's reign, and they sometimes afford indications as to the dates of the first stone castles. It would seem, however, that the earl never got this latter service, as the order was afterwards postponed until after Richard de Burgh should have acquired the land of the King of Connaught.[16] The last of these orders was for his service of forty days, due to the king for one year to fortify the castle of Cumbre (Castlecomer), but this was shortly before William's death, and the first stone castle here was probably not erected until later.[17] Perhaps, however, to the younger earl should be ascribed the erection or completion
[54] of the first stone castles at Ferns and Carlow. They are first mentioned in, or immediately after, his time, and the existing ruins seem to point to about this period.

The castle somewhat hurriedly constructed at Ferns by the sons of Maurice Fitz Gerald in 1177 was, as we have seen, destroyed in the interest of the Mac Murroughs.[18] A seignorial manor was, however, subsequently formed here, probably by the elder William Marshal, and this seems to have been the subject of his dispute, to which we have already alluded, with Albin O'Mulloy the last Irish Bishop of Ferns.[19] The elder earl may have built or commenced to build the castle, and this supposition would harmonize with his dispute with the bishop, but the first time we hear of it is in 1232, when 'the manor and castle of Ferns' were offered by Richard Marshal as part of the dower of his brother's widow.[20] It may therefore have been built or completed by the younger Earl William. Albin O'Mulloy died in 1222, and John de St. John, who had been a trusted minister of the Crown in Ireland since 1212, and held the offices of Treasurer and Escheator, was appointed in his place. The dispute as to the church-lands was in part, at all events, settled or compromised between him and Philip de Prendergast in 1227,[21] but though the bishop had a manor at Ferns and was granted
[55] a fair there in 1226,[22] the manor attached to the castle of Ferns remained a seignorial manor, and until near the close of the century was the most lucrative manor of the lordship of Wexford.[23] There is indeed ample evidence that throughout the thirteenth

15 Ibid., nos. 1030, 1269. 16 Ibid., nos. 1439, 1515. 17 Ibid, nos. 1809, 1866. Cumbre was an important manor at the time of the partition of Leinster and went with Kildare. There was a stone castle here in the time of Edward I, but nothing now remains except the mote, which is partially revetted; see Journ. R.S.A.I., 1909, pp. 318-19. 18 *Ante*, vol. ii, p. 8 [p. 154]. 19 *Supra*, vol. iii, p. 29 [pp. 295–6]. 20 Close Roll, 16 Hen. III, pp. 144–5. Eleanor's dower was, however, fixed at £400 a year, leviable in case of non-payment out of the earl's English lands: Cal. Docs. Irel., vol. i, no. 2041. From this it would seem that at this time the fief of Leinster was valued at £1200 a year. 21 *Supra*, vol. iii, p. 29 [p. 296]. 22 Rot. Claus., 10 Hen. III, p. 127. £11 10*s*. 9¼*d*. was received from the episcopal manor of Ferns (including Clone) when in the king's hand for five months in 1282; Hore's History of County Wexford, vol. vi, p. 191; and see Irish Pipe Roll, 10 Ed. I, 36th Rep. D. K., p. 61. 23 At the partition of Leinster, Ferns was valued at £81 15*s*. In 1307 when an inquisition on the lands of Joan de Valence was taken there were 160 burgages in the town paying £8 0*s*. 4*d*., free tenants paying formerly £18 0*s*. 3*d*., and fifty-four carucates of land (no doubt largely let to Irish holders) formerly worth £59 9*s*. 2*d*. The total, however, had then depreciated to £38 16*s*. 6*d*. The inquisition taken after the death of Aymer de Valence in 1324 shows that the manor was then of

century the greater part of the ancient kingdom of Okinselagh, and the subordinate territories in the present County Carlow, were extensively settled and the whole district normally peaceful and prosperous, though early in the succeeding century the Mac Murroughs, Kavanaghs, Kinsellas, and others of the Irish who had not been expelled, once more began to dominate much of the northern part of their ancient territories.

In plan the castle of Ferns was a rectangle of 90 by 65 feet, with three-quarter projecting round towers, 32 feet in diameter, at the corners. The walls of the towers are 8 feet thick, and the remaining south wall is 7 feet thick. The castles of Kilkenny, Carlow, Wexford, and Enniscorthy, though varying considerably in dimensions, seem all to have followed a similar ground-plan, and were probably all erected at about the same period.

The ruined chancel of the Anglo-Norman Cathedral at Ferns bears testimony to the skill and taste of the age. It belongs to the early part of the thirteenth century, and [56]
was perhaps the work of John de St. John, who is said to have been 'one of the principal benefactors of his Church, as well for his structures as for the privileges obtained for his See'.[24] The church when complete must have been a stately structure of about 180 feet long. The present building was roughly formed in the time of Queen Elizabeth by walling up the central portion of the nave, without the side aisles, some of the original pillars of which are embedded in these walls. To this in 1816 a piece was added joining the building with the tower, which had previously stood separate.[25]

The younger Earl William granted an extended charter to the town of Carlow in 1223.[26] It mentions the castle, and follows closely the form of his father's charter to Kilkenny. He also granted a similar charter to the burgesses of Moone in County Kildare,[27] but both these boroughs were established earlier, as the rent of one shilling for each burgage was fixed by Geoffrey Fitz Robert, his father's seneschal.

As regards religious foundations, the earl in 1227 confirmed his father's grant to the Cistercian monastery de valle Sancti Salvatoris, situated on the Barrow at Duiske, or Graig-na-managh as it is now called. A large number of documents relating to this convent are preserved at Kilkenny Castle, and have been edited by Dr. Bernard, now [57]
Provost of Trinity College, Dublin.[28] From these it appears that in 1227 the Abbot of Froidmont, acting on behalf of the general chapter of Citeaux, decreed that the neighbouring convent de valle Dei, or Killenny, on account of its poverty should be incorporated with that at Duiske. Killenny was a daughter house of Jerpoint, and owed its first endowments to a grant from Dermot O'Ryan, lord of Idrone, which was confirmed by Dermot Mac Murrough before the Normans came. Its absorption by Duiske, though confirmed by all the highest authorities spiritual and temporal among the latter being William Marshal), was for a long period contested by Jerpoint, and the contest was not finally settled until the year 1289, when the sum of 1,300 marks was

little or no value 'owing to the war of the Irish'. **24** Ware, Bishops. **25** Hore's History of Co. Wexford, vol. vi, pp. 165–9. These facts became manifest during the recent (1901–3) restoration, and some of the embedded pillars are now partially exposed to view. **26** Chartae Privil. et Immun., p. 37. **27** Justiciary Roll, 30 Ed. I, pp. 369-71 (Mills). **28** Proc. R.I.A., vol. xxxv (c), pp. 1–188.

paid to Jerpoint by way of compensation. During the thirteenth century Duiske was a prosperous monastery, essentially Anglo-Norman in *personnel* and tone, but early in the next century it suffered from the disturbed state of the country. It became more and more Irish in character, and its last abbot was a son of Donnell Reagh Kavanagh, self-styled King of Leinster. To judge by such of the remains as have not been mutilated it must have been a fine example of Anglo-Norman architecture, the abbey-church resembling in plan that of Strata Florida. The earl also granted a new site to the Prior and monks of St. John the Evangelist at Kilkenny, and richly endowed the house.[29] Part of the ruined chancel of this church still stands on the site so
[58] granted, and contains some beautiful early thirteenth-century work. It should be compared with that of the church of St. Mary at New Ross, which was appropriated by the younger Earl William to the Prior of St. John's, and must date from about the same time.[30] The choir and transepts of the stately cathedral of St. Canice already, perhaps, adorned the 'Fair citie by the Nore,'[31] and now a new foundation, the convent for Dominicans, usually called the Black Abbey, was added by the earl to the religious foundations of the city.[32] The church which is still used, has suffered much from violence and tasteless rebuilding, and little of architectural interest remains. Indeed, in all these churches in Leinster, Ferns, Graig-na-managh, St. Mary's, St. John's, the Black Abbey, and Gowran, as in many others throughout Ireland, it is humiliating to contrast the simple grace and beauty of the original thirteenth-century architecture with the clumsiness and want of taste displayed in the structures that have partially replaced them. In the cathedral of St. Canice alone has the pristine beauty of the edifice been worthily preserved or restored.

In May 1230 Earl William accompanied the king on his fruitless march to Bordeaux, and in October he was left behind at Nantes with Randolph, Earl of Chester, and a small force when the king returned to England. Early in April 1231 the earl was
[59] back in London and was present at the nuptial festivities of his sister Isabel, Countess of Gloucester,[33] with Richard, Earl of Cornwall, the king's brother. A few days afterwards he died unexpectedly, in the flower of his age, and was buried in the New Temple beside his father.[34] Though twice married, first in 1214 to Alice, daughter of Baldwin de Betune, titular count of Aumale,[35] and again in 1224 to Eleanor the king's sister,[36] then only nine years old, he left no issue.

29 *Ante*, vol. ii, p. 229 [p. 242] note [65], where the charter is shown to belong to the younger Earl William and to have been executed in 1223. 30 See my pamphlet on New Ross in the thirteenth century (1911), p. 11. The Lady Chapel of St. John's, called by reason of its many lofty lights 'the Lantern of Ireland', was not completed until 1290: Liber Primus Kilkenniensis. It was finally demolished when the present church was built. 31 *Ante*, vol. ii, p. 229 [p. 242]. 32 Ware. 33 Her first husband, Gilbert de Clare, Earl of Gloucester and Hertford, died in October 1230. 34 Roger of Wendover (Coxe), vol. iv, p. 220; Ann. Waverley, 309. The tradition that he was buried at Kilkenny must be rejected. 35 Alice de Betune's mother was Haweis, daughter and heir of William le Gros, Count of Aumale, who died in 1180. Baldwin de Betune was her third husband and an old companion of the elder William Marshal: L'Histoire de G. de Marechal, l. 14968. Alice was betrothed to the younger William Marshal in 1203, when she was only about six years of age: Rot. Chart., vol. i, pp. 112 b, 113 a. The marriage appears to have taken place in 1214, and Alice died about a year afterwards. 36 Rot. Pat., 8 Hen. III, vol. i, p. 426; Gerv. Cant., vol. ii, p. 113. Eleanor afterwards (1238) married Simon de Montfort, the victor at Lewes.

The king immediately, on April 11, announced the death of the earl to the constables of his castles of Kilkenny, Odagh, Wexford, Old Ross, Dunamase, Carlow, Kildare, Carrick on Slaney, and the Island (in the parish of Kilmokea, County Wexford),[37] and ordered them to give up the custody of the castles to Walerand le Teys, or Teutonicus, the king's bailiff.[38] There was some opposition to the execution of this mandate [60] which, seeing that the heir was not a minor, was somewhat unusual. On May 31 the king wrote to explain that his action was not directed to injure Richard Marshal, the earl's brother and heir, but as Richard was liege to the King of France, the king's chief enemy, the king intended to hold in his hand the earl's land until Richard should come before him and do his duty in regard to the inheritance.[39] When, however, Richard came to proffer his homage, the king, by the advice of Hubert de Burgh, refused to accept it on the plea that his brother's widow might have a posthumous child, and on the more serious ground of his association with the king's enemies in France, ordered him to leave the kingdom within fifteen days. Thereupon Richard is said to have gone to Ireland, prepared to enter upon his inheritance without the king's consent.[40] Ultimately on August 8 the king took Richard's homage and ordered seisin to be given to him.[41]

Notwithstanding the ill turn done to him by Hubert de Burgh, Earl Richard Marshal was one of those who, after Hubert's fall in July 1232, saved him from the worst [61] consequences which the malice of his enemies had prepared for him. He then became the leader of the opposition to Peter des Roches and the Poitevin counsellors of the king, who had taken all offices of trust and emolument into their own hands. In bold language he remonstrated with the king for having summoned these foreigners to his councils, to the oppression of the kingdom and of his native-born subjects, and to the subversion alike of laws and liberties. The Poitevins accordingly turned their animosity upon the earl and his supporters, and poisoned the king's mind against them. The story of their vengeance on the earl is told at great length and with righteous indignation by Roger of Wendover, and repeated with some literary embellishments by Matthew Paris.[42] As we shall see, this story, though true in the main, must be taken with considerable reserve. We shall first give a brief summary of the leading events as narrated by these writers, and while noting certain details which seem incorrect or incredible, reserve more general comments for the close.

37 Patent Roll, 15 Hen. III, p. 429. For the first seven castles see *ante*, vol. i, pp. 373–7 [pp. 141–3]. Carrick castle was on the site of Robert Fitz Stephen's earthen fort: ibid., pp. 232–3. The Island had been the *caput baroniae* of Hervey de Montmorency: ibid., p. 393; but had escheated to the lord of Leinster. 38 Pat Roll, 16 Hen. III, p. 429. 39 Pat. Roll, 15 Hen. III, p. 435. Richard had been assigned his father's estates in Normandy: Magni Rot. Scacc. Norm., vol. ii, cxxxviii (Stapleton); Cartulaire Normand, no. 285 (Delisle). Apparently Henry expected Richard Marshal to renounce his allegiance to Louis of France 'a cuius ligancia si ipse Ricardus recedere velit, adhuc ignoramus'. 40 Roger of Wendover (Coxe), vol. iv, p. 225. 41 Close Roll, 15 Hen. III, p. 541. Earl Richard was in Ireland in 1233 when, on April 1 (his fatal day), at his castle of Old Ross, he restored to the Cistercians of Dunbrody the wood of Duncannon: Chart. St. Mary's, Dub., vol. ii, p. 160. About the same time he delimited his forests of Ross and Taghmon: ibid., p. 154. This deed is of great topographical interest and shows that the southern half of County Wexford up to the limits of these forests was well settled at the time. 42 See Roger of Wendover (Coxe), vol. iv, pp. 270–308; Matthew Paris, Chronica Maiora, vol. iii, pp. 246–79.

A conference was summoned at London for August 1, 1233, when Earl Richard, who had come to take part in it, was warned by his sister, wife of Richard, Earl of Cornwall, that his enemies were plotting to take him prisoner and serve him as they had served Hubert de Burgh. Accordingly at nightfall the Earl Marshal withdrew to Wales, where he was joined by others. The king, without trial, declared the fugitive
[62] barons to be exiled and proscribed men, gave their lands to the Poitevins, and ordered their persons to be seized. Henry himself led a host into Wales, but the Marshal, now in open rebellion, with the aid of his Welsh allies not only eluded all attempts to overpower him, but, while avoiding direct conflict with the king, succeeded in inflicting great losses on the Poitevins. At last, about January 1234, the Bishop of Winchester, Peter of Rivaux, and others of the king's counsellors, finding that they could not gain their end by open fighting, had recourse to treachery. They induced the king to affix his seal to letters, of the purport of which (as he afterwards swore) he was ignorant, addressed to Maurice Fitz Gerald, the justiciar, Walter and Hugh de Lacy, Richard de Burgh, Geoffrey de Marisco, and others, the Marshal's sworn but faithless men,[43] bidding them seize Richard Marshal if he should come to Ireland and bring him dead or alive before the king, and promising that if they should effect this, all the Marshal's possessions in Ireland, now at the king's disposal, would be granted to them to be divided amongst them. Accordingly these Irish mag-
[63] nates, having first received from the king's advisers a grant sealed with the royal seal (surreptitiously obtained from the chancellor), setting forth the possessions of the Marshal assigned to each, invaded the Marshal's territory, took some of his castles, and divided the booty amongst them.

When the earl heard that some of his castles in Ireland had been taken and his lands plundered, he at once sailed for Ireland with only fifteen knights. This was about February 2, 1234. He was met by Geoffrey de Marisco his liege-man, but now said to be faithless to him and in league with his enemies. He pretended, however, to adhere to the earl, and urged him to make war upon his enemies and to subdue Ireland, intimating, according to Matthew Paris, that Ireland belonged to him by hereditary right as the descendant of Strongbow.[44] This treacherous advice was adopted with such success, that not only were some of his own castles recovered, but Limerick[45] was taken

43 *Homines eiusdem Marescalli iuratos sed infideles.* But this sweeping statement is far from correct. Neither Walter de Lacy, Lord of Meath, nor Hugh de Lacy, Earl of Ulster, nor Richard de Burgh, whose lands lay in Munster and Connaught, held any lands of the Marshal. Maurice Fitz Gerald's principal lands lay about Croom in Limerick and in Imokilly, while his lands of Maynooth and Rathmore in Leinster were held directly of the barons of Naas (*ante*, vol. i, p. 380 [p. 144]). Geoffrey de Marisco, indeed, at this time seems to have held the lands of Lea and Geashil in Offaly of the Marshal as tenant by the curtesy in light of his (late) wife Eva de Bermingham, but his principal lands lay in Munster, where he held the manors of Ainy and Adare in Limerick of the Crown (*ante*, vol. ii, p. 169 [p. 219]), and Killorglin in Kerry (*infra*, c. xxvii).
44 This sophistical argument was not one that would appeal to Richard Marshal, who, like his father, felt strongly the mutual obligations of the feudal relation. The passage does not appear in Roger de Wendover's account. 45 It is quite certain that the Marshal never went to Limerick or outside his own fief. There is, however, some evidence that Limerick was attacked about this time, or more probably a little later, by Donough Cairbrech O'Brien, but he was acting in concert with Felim O'Conor against Richard de Burgh, and quite independently of Richard Marshal: *vide infra*, c. xxviii [p. ___].

after a four days' siege, some castles belonging to his enemies were captured, and the Irish nobles, not daring to meet the earl, retired to collect additional forces.

When they had collected a strong force, the Irish magnates sent some Templars to the earl to tell him that they could not without infamy suffer him to continue acting as [64] a traitor towards the king, and to ask for a truce while they inquired whether the king meant to defend Ireland; for if the king determined to abandon it they would give up the whole country to the earl without opposition.[46] To this the earl replied that he was no traitor, 'for', said he, 'the king unjustly and without trial has deprived me of my office of Marshal, banished me from England, and burned and destroyed my property. Twice he has bidden me defiance, though I was always ready to appear in his court and abide by the judgement of my peers. Therefore I am no longer his man,[47] but have been absolved from allegiance to him, not by my own act, but by his'. As regards a truce the earl invited the magnates to meet him in colloquy on the morrow on a certain mead. (This was the Curragh of Kildare.) The Irish nobles agreed to this, knowing that they had superior forces and determined not to return without a battle. The Marshal was for granting a truce, but he was overborne by the treacherous counsel of Geoffrey de Marisco and of his own vassals, about eighty in number, who had all been bribed to deceive him.[48]

On the morrow, the 1st of April, the parties met on the Curragh. The earl's opponents were attended by 140 picked knights chosen for the purpose of slaying him, [65] while, with the exception of the fifteen knights of his household who had accompanied him from Wales, the earl's men only pretended to be his adherents. The Templars, as before, acted as intermediaries. The earl demanded the restoration of his castles before granting a truce. This was refused, and the Irish nobles prepared for battle, secure of victory. Then Geoffrey advised the Marshal to concede the truce, 'for', said he, 'my wife is sister of Hugh de Lacy and therefore I cannot fight against him with whom I am allied'.[49] The Marshal then knew that he was betrayed, but disdained to concede through fear what, by Geoffrey's advice, he had refused to grant for favour. 'I know', he said, 'that I am betrayed unto death this day, but it is better to die with honour in the cause of justice than to fly the field and incur perpetual infamy.' He then gave orders for his young brother Walter to be brought for safety to the castle (of Kil-

46 It is incredible that such terms could have been proposed. The earl's reply, however, probably states correctly enough the defence of his attitude against the king. 47 It would have been considered disgraceful for either lord or man to attack the other while there was affiance between them. Hence the king 'defied' the Marshal before waging war against him, and the Marshal argues that the feudal nexus has been broken. 'Rebellions and wars are conducted on quasi-legal principles': Pollock and Maitland, Hist. of Eng. Law, vol. i, p. 303. 48 Again a reckless statement which can be proved untrue by the punishment afterwards meted out to his vassals. 49 This excuse, futile even if true, was perhaps a mere invention of Roger de Wendover. Geoffrey's wife in 1218 was Eva de Bermingham (Rot. Claus., 2 Hen. III, p. 363), and she was still alive in 1223 (ibid., 7 Hen. III, p. 649 b), and died presumably shortly before December 1226. See Journ. R.S.A.I., vol. xliv (1914), p. 103. Seeing that even in 1226 the elder Hugh de Lacy had been dead for forty years, it is very improbable that Geoffrey afterwards married his daughter. Moreover, Geoffrey was specially commended by Earl William Marshal in 1224 for his services against Hugh de Lacy, 'whom he in no way favours': Royal Letters (Shirley). All this must have been known to Earl Richard, and the excuse can hardly have been made.

dare ?) hard by, so that all of his family might not perish, and exhorting his men to follow him, dashed bravely against the ranks of his foes. But his sworn men in whom he
[66] trusted, as had been arranged by the conspirators, voluntarily, without a blow, surrendered themselves as it were to friends, or fled unwounded to churches and convents, and only the fifteen knights of his household remained to support the Marshal. An unequal combat followed in which the Marshal fought with desperate courage and consummate skill, so that for a long while no one dared to come near him. At length after fighting all day and performing prodigies of valour he was overwhelmed by a host of common people armed with lances, pitchforks, hatchets, and pole-axes, who succeeded in houghing his steed and thus bringing horse and rider to the ground. Then rushing on him they raised his hauberk and gave him a mortal stab in the back.

His nearly lifeless body was borne to the castle (of Kilkenny?) which Maurice the justiciar had recently taken, and there he was kept in custody. After a few days he so far recovered that he was able to eat and drink, play at dice, and walk about his room. His wounds, however, grew worse. A physician sent to him by the justiciar, 'rather', it is said, 'to kill than to cure him', probed them with a heated instrument and acute fever set in. On the 16th of Aplil the ill-fated earl died.

Such in brief is the story of the tragic end of Richard Marshal, as told by Roger of Wendover. It is evidently coloured by a strong animus against the Marshal's enemies. It has been uncritically adopted by modern writers, and by some the ugly shadows have been even further deepened.[50] In substance we must accept the story as in the
[67] main true, but not only, as we have pointed out, is it apparently incorrect in many important details which prove the writer's ignorant imagination, but as regards the worst features of the episode material modifications of the view presented seem to be warranted by attested facts.

In the first place, we cannot acquit the king of responsibility for what occurred on the plea that he was ignorant of the contents of documents to which he put his seal. On March 7 he gave orders that Maurice Fitz Gerald should have out of the king's treasure in Dublin whatever might be necessary and expedient to keep the peace of Ireland and maintain war against the king's enemies.[51] This can only refer to the earl's war. A word to the Marshal at this time that the king was meditating a change of counsellors would have stayed the war. On March 27 the king wrote to the Mayor and citizens of Dublin thanking them for what they told him concerning the arrival of the earl in Ireland, which, he says, was not unknown to him, and stating that he had convened a council for April 9 to treat concerning that and other matters touching the state of the realm, and would communicate to the mayor what might be done on that day.[52] Next day, March 28, he notified to his officers in Wales that he had granted a truce to Llewelyn and the Earl Marshal until the Sunday after Easter,[53] but no such notification appears to have been sent to Ireland. When on April 9 the king finally yielded to the counsel of the archbishop and sent him to Wales to make peace with Llewelyn and the earl, he well knew that the latter was in Ireland, and no doubt he had

50 See Gilbert, Viceroys of Ireland, pp. 95 9, and Stokes, Ireland and the Anglo-Norman Church (1889), pp 297-306. 51 Cal. Pat. Rolls, 18 Hen. III, p. 40. 52 Close Roll, 18 Hen. III, p. 395. 53 Ibid., p. 555.

been kept informed of the struggle going on there. Moreover, we cannot believe in the sincerity of the king's lamentations at the news of the Marshal's death—perhaps Matthew Paris does not intend us to believe it—seeing that not only had he proscribed him and sought in person to compass his destruction in Wales, but after the horrid deed was done in Ireland he thanked and rewarded those who had had a hand in it, and punished by heavy fines those who had taken the earl's side. Nor does the king's grief and supposed contrition tally with the expressions put into his mouth five years later, when he called Earl Richard 'a bloody traitor', ' whom', he said, ' I took fighting against me in deadly war in Ireland, and who, deservedly disinherited, was kept wounded in prison until by the vengeance of God he ended his life'.[54] [68]

Secondly, though we have formed no high opinion of his character it is impossible to believe that Geoffrey de Marisco played the false and despicable part assigned to hirn. Subsequent events show that he did not confederate with the earl's enemies. He himself, two of his sons, and three of his nephews were taken prisoners on the field, were ordered by the king to be securely guarded, and were heavily fined.[55] Moreover, next year William de Marisco, Geoffrey's son, was outlawed for avenging the earl by killing in London one Henry Clement, clerk to Maurice Fitz Gerald, who had boasted [69] that he had caused the earl's death.[56] This was not the act of a traitor to the earl.

Thirdly, we cannot on the mere statement of the chroniclers of St. Albans attribute the action of the earl's Irish opponents to the mean motives of cupidity and greed, or stigmatize it as stained with treachery. No portion of the Marshal's great fief was as a matter of fact obtained by any of the them, and none of the leaders owed him feudal allegiance, except (indirectly) Maurice Fitz Gerald, and he was the king's justiciar, specially bound to execute the king's mandates. Richard Marshal was an outlaw in open war against the king, the feudal army was summoned against him, and the Irish barons must be credited with supposing that they were carrying out the king's order to take him alive or dead. Nor is there any good reason to suppose that he was killed otherwise than in fair fight. This was the view taken by the Irish annalist. 'Richard son of William Marshal raised a war against the King of the Saxons in Saxon-land and came across from the east and went into Leinster; and the foreigners of Erin assembled against him on behalf of the King of the Saxons. . . . They all proceeded to the Curragh and fought a fierce obstinate battle against the Marshal; and Richard son of William Marshal was slain there, and Geoffrey Marshal (*recte*, de Marisco, Mareis, or Marsh) was taken prisoner. And there was no one fighting this battle towards the end [70] but himself alone, after he had been abandoned by his own people. And this deed was

54 Mat. Paris, Chron. Mai., vol. iii, pp. 523–4. This was said by Henry in one of his outbursts against Gilbert Marshal. 55 Cal. Docs. Irel., vol. i, nos. 2119, 2222, 2300. Geoflrey was ultimately outlawed (ibid., no. 2683) and his lands confiscated. His manor of Adare appears to have been granted to Maurice Fitz Gerald, and was certainly held by his representatives for many generations. He died in 1245, 'exul miser et profugus, expulsus a Scotia, foris bannitus ab Anglia, exheredatus in Hibernia': Mat. Paris. 56 Royal Letters (Shirley), vol. i, pp. 469–71; Mat. Paris, Chron. Mai., vol. iii, p. 327; Close Roll, 19 Hen. III, p. 180. William de Marisco and his followers fled to Lundy Island, where they maintained themselves as pirates for some years, but eventually in 1242 he was captured and hung: Mat. Paris Chron. Mai., vol. iv, pp. 193, 195.

one of the greatest deeds committed in that time.' We do not indeed suppose that no personal consideration weighed with the Marshal's opponents. Their names show that nearly all of them were barons who held lands outside of Leinster. There was the old jealousy, never quite extinct, on the part of the Geraldines and other descendants of the early conquerors against new-comers from France or England; and—probably the deciding factor—most of them were engaged in the conquest and partition of Connaught and had a grudge against the Marshal family touching their plans there, for the late earl had, as we have seen, opposed their movement. The de Lacys too had their special grudge against the brother of the man who had recently curbed and controlled them and thwarted their advance into Breffny. The desire to pay off old scores was more likely to have influenced them than the futile hope of uprooting the strongest settlement in Ireland.

Lastly the odious charge of treachery to their lord, levelled against the earl's men, seems to have but slender foundation. There is no evidence that, apart from the case of the justiciar and of Walter de Ridelisford,[57] both of whom were also tenants of the
[71] Crown, any of his Irish vassals turned against the earl. They did not by all accounts fight desperately to the death, as their lord did. They were not of his heroic mould, and they did not make his quarrel wholly their own; but the long list of those who were punished for taking his part refutes the charge that they were traitors in the pay of his enemies. Contemporary records show that the following leading feudatories of the Marshal sided with their lord and had to pay large fines before they were given back their lands: Roger de la Hyde (his seneschal), Hugh Purcell, David Basset, Matthew Fitz Griffin, Miles de Rochfort, Stephen de Hereford, Geoffrey de Norrach, Robert de Grendon, Robert Whittey, Maurice de Londres, John le Chenu (Canutus or le Hore), and Henry Walsh.[58] Moreover the Irish Pipe Roll for 19 Hen. III, in an account of the County and City of Limerick by Hugh de Barry then sheriff, contains a list of thirty-three names of landholders who were fined in large sums for 'being against the king in the war with the Richard Marshal'. These names include Geoffrey de Marisco and William his son 3,000 marks, three of Geoffrey's nephews, viz. William, son of Jordan de Marisco £200, Richard de Marisco £100, and John Travers £200, also David baron of Naas (he held lands in County Limerick) 300 marks, and others at fines varying from £10 to 400 marks. Also a list of two hundred names of persons fined half a mark or more 'because they did not come at the summons of the king to the army against Richard Marshal'. These facts show how coloured and exaggerated is the story of the affair given by the chroniclers of St. Albans. Yet when all is said to put this 'great deed' in its true light, the death of this fearless knight, fighting
[72] for justice and the liberties of England against the autocracy of the Crown and its alien advisers, at the hands of men who, had they been true to the interests of their class,

57 Walter de Ridelisford seems to have been on the side of the king: Cal. Docs. Irel., vol. i, nos. 2139, 2253–5. He was tenant of the Crown of lands at Bray and in the vale of Dublin, and he was one of those interested in the expected division of Connaught, but he also held the manors of Tristeldermot and Kilkea in Leinster. One of his daughters was married to Hugh de Lacy. 58 Cal. Docs. Irel., vol. i, nos. 2129, 2139, 2201, 2224, 2226, 2345–6, 2362, and 2418. The list is not complete.

would have ranged themselves under his banner, cannot but be regarded as a cruel tragedy and a blot on the fame of the chivalry of Ireland.

Earl Richard is described as 'an excellent knight, well versed in letters, and graced becomingly by his manners and virtues . . . and one who so shone among the sons of men in the beauty of his person that Nature would seem to have vied with the Virtues in his composition.'[59] He was buried at Kilkenny, probably in the precincts of the Dominican Convent founded by his brother, where tradition long pointed out the tomb of 'the Knight of the Curragh',[60] and where to this day is preserved as a precious relic a skull ascribed by tradition to one of the Marshals.[61]

By an added touch of tragedy, while Earl Richard lay on his death-bed the cause for which he had fought was, without his knowing it, won. On the 2nd of February, about the time when the Marshal set sail for Ireland, Edmund Rich, Archbishop elect of Canterbury, and his suffragan bishops formulated a heavy indictment against the king's foreign advisers, and in plain terms told the king that he was estranging the [73]
affections of his people, 'as was evident from the conduct of the Marshal, who', they said, 'was the best subject in his dominions'. Then they warned the king under threat of ecclesiastical censure to dismiss his foreign advisers and govern by the assistance of his own faithful subjects. The king postponed a decision for the moment, but at the next council, on April 9, when the archbishop, now duly consecrated, repeated his former warning, the king at once yielded to him in everything. In a few days the Poitevins were ignominiously dismissed, and the archbishop himself was sent to Wales to make peace with Llewelyn and the Marshal.[62]

It was not until May 12, when at Woodstock on his way to meet the archbishop, that the king heard the news of the Marshal's death and shed too late the tears of repentance. Influenced by the archbishop, he lost no time now in pardoning the proscribed nobles and in giving them the kiss of peace.[63] He at once invited Gilbert, Walter, and Anselm Marshal, the deceased earl's remaining brothers, to his presence to seek his favour, and on May 28 he restored to Gilbert his hereditary possessions, received his homage, and shortly afterwards girded him with the knight's belt, and delivered to him the wand of the marshalship. The reconciliation was, for the time, apparently complete.

About the same time, however, the king, whose double dealing and insincerity is [74]
manifest, thanked Richard de Burgh for his strenuous resistance to Richard Marshal, and declared himself ready to bestow an adequate reward after he had conferred with Maurice Fitz Gerald, Hugh de Lacy, and the Bishops of Ferns and Meath, whom he

59 Roger of Wendover (Coxe), vol. iv, p. 308; cf. Ann. Waverley, p. 818. 60 Hanmer (ed. 1533), p. 174. Journ. R.S.A.I., vol. i, p. 457. Roger of Wendover says that Richard Marshal was buried 'in oratorio fratrum Minorum apud Kilkenni ubi ipse adhuc vivens sepulturam elegerat'; but on this point the authority of the Laud MS. Annals, supported by tradition, is preferable. 61 On visiting the church I was told by the custodian that the relic was the skull of the second William Marshal, but he was buried in the Temple in London. 62 Mat. Paris, Chron. Mai., vol. iii, pp. 269-72. 63 Cal. Pat. Roll, 18 Hen. III, p. 48. On June 8, 1234, the king declared the sentence of outlawry against Hubert de Burgh, Gilbert Basset, Richard Seward, Philip Basset, and others who favoured the Earl Marshal, should be annulled, 'eo quod iniuste et contra legem terrae in eos fuit promulgata': Close Roll, 18 Hen. II p. 667.

at the same time summoned to his presence.[64] This reward, as we shall see, took the form of the restoration to Richard de Burgh of his land of Connaught. Maurice Fitz Gerald was evidently apprehensive for his safety, for though summoned more than once he did not come until after he had obtained a safe-conduct from the Archbishop of Canterbury.[65] In September Maurice was with the king and fully retained his favour for many years. Peace was made between Gilbert Marshal and the Irish magnates, and the terms on which those who had sided with Richard Marshal should be restored to their lands were finally settled. The dismissal of the Poitevins and the closing of this episode were due to the wisdom and courage of Edmund Rich, Archbishop of Canterbury, who, in the historical temple of those who have striven for British liberty, merits a small niche between the lofty pedestals of Stephen Langton and Simon de Montfort.

But neither Archbishop Edmund nor Earl Gilbert had quite the qualities for leading successfully the baronial opposition or keeping the king to good resolutions, which were merely the outcome of the policy of the moment and not of any settled conviction. Upon the king's marriage with Eleanor of Provence new foreigners— Savoyards
[75] and Provençals—gained the king's ear, to be followed later on by a new invasion of Poitevins. More than once the king quarrelled with Earl Gilbert, and on the earl's death, which occurred through an accident at a prohibited tournament in 1241, the king refused for a time to grant seisin to the fourth brother, Walter. Earl Walter died on November 24, 1245, and eleven days later Anselm, the fifth and sole remaining brother, breathed his last at Strigul. The strange fatality that cut off all the male descendants of the great Earl Marshal was now complete.

The great fief of Leinster was now divisible among the five daughters of the elder Earl William Marshal or their representatives. These five daughters had all married great English lords, and by May 1247, when the partition was effected, only the eldest, Matilda, widow first of Roger Bigod, Earl of Norfolk, and then of William, Earl Warenne, was alive. Of the shares of the deceased daughters, one became divisible among seven co-heiresses, and another among three co-heiresses, so that the primary division into fifths became in two cases subject to a further subdivision. Herein was exemplified one of the weaknesses of the feudal system. That a great fief, viewed simply as property, should be parted among several proprietors, may seem to us no bad thing; but the feudal baron was much more than a mere landed proprietor. He was the head of a great organization, the representative and protector of a large social unit. Under the king, and within defined limits of law and custom, he was the virtual ruler of his domain. His courts were open to all his tenants for the settlement of their disputes, and in the great liberties, except so far as the pleas of the Crown were reserved
[76] and appeals to the king's court were allowed, criminal jurisdiction was in the lord's hand. In short the lord of the liberty and his officials occupied in large measure the place of our modern civil service. Nay more in Ireland in the thirteenth century the social units depended on the barons' swords and the military power at their command for protection against the border clans ever on the look out for a weak place to attack and plunder. This great power was no doubt often abused, but in practice it was

64 Close Rolls, 18 Hen. III, p. 561. 65 Cal. Docs. Irel., vol. i, nos. 2146-8.

almost the only barrier against anarchy. When, therefore, a great fief became divided among female heirs whose husbands were absentees with greater interests elsewhere, or when, during minorities, it was in the hands of the Crown and was administered by bailiffs or seneschals with no permanent interest in its welfare, the disruptive forces, whether internal or external, were apt to gather head and become difficult of restraint.

Another source of weakness was the extravagant provision made for the widow of the preceding feudal lord. One third of his lands of inheritance was normally assigned to her as dower. This greatly crippled the power of his successor. In the case of the partition of Leinster there were no fewer than three widows to be provided for. Firstly, Eleanor, the king's sister, widow of William Marshal, and now the wife of Simon de Montfort, Earl of Leicester. In 1233 Richard Marshal agreed to pay her £400 a year in name of dower.[66] In 1244 the king became surety for Walter Marshal, and undertook in case of default to pay this sum and raise the amount out of the earl's lands in Ireland.[67] The Countess of Leicester survived her second husband and died *c.*1275. [77]
Secondly, Margaret, Countess of Lincoln and Pembroke, widow of Walter Marshal. To her was assigned in dower the whole county of Kildare, the manor of Forth in the county of Carlow, and lands of the value of £62 17*s.* 9*d.* in the manor of Oboy in Leix. To these were afterwards added the castles of Kildare and Carbury.[68] The seven daughters of Sibyl Marshal, to whom the county of Kildare was assigned on the partition, had now to be given compensation out of the shares of other heirs, so that the burden of the Countess of Lincoln's dower might fall equally on all the five shares.[69] This involved much litigation and expense. Thirdly, Matilda de Bohun, widow of Anselm Marshal and afterwards wife of Roger de Quency, Earl of Winchester. As her husband had not obtained seisin when he died she does not appear to have been entitled to dower, but, by some arrangement, to her belonged the new and the old vill in the County Kilkenny[70] (Jerpoint?). She died in 1252 when these lands became divisible among the co-heirs. Margaret of Scotland, widow of Earl Gilbert Marshal, died in 1244, and Earl Richard was unmarried.

Whatever disadvantages were inherent in the devolution of a Celtic chieftainship— and from the point of view of social order and progress they were many and grave— the system was at least free from these evils of feudal succession. Hence it was that [78]
while the larger Norman fiefs sooner or later became divided to the point of weakness and, burdened with widows' dowers, devolved upon absentee lords, or became merged in the Crown, to be regranted in smaller parcels, the headship of a Celtic tribe or tribe-group passed unimpaired (it might be after a period of internal conflict) to the chosen or victorious agnatic successor,[71] and the allegiance of the undivided tribe or tribe-group would be given to an adult, resident, male protector.

66 Close Roll, 17 Hen. III, p. 310. 67 Cal. Pat. Roll, 28 Hen. III, pp. 415–16. In 1259-60 most of the heirs were in arrear from the time ot the partition: Cal. Docs. Ireland, vol. ii, p. 104. 68 Cal. Pat. Rolls, 33 Hen. III, p. 40. 69 Cal. Docs. Ireland, vol. i, nos. 2949, 2988. Margaret countess of Lincoln died between Michaelmas 1268 and March 1271: Cal. Docs. Ireland, vol. ii, nos. 850, 896. 70 Cal. Docs. Ireland, vol. ii, no. 110. 71 It was not until the next century that, with a view to avoiding the evils of a disputed succession, the custom of electing a tanist as successor in the lifetime of the ruling chief was gradually introduced.

[79] CHAPTER XXVI

THE PARTITION OF LEINSTER, 1247

In this chapter (which may be omitted without interruption of the narrative) I propose to give a detailed account of the partition of the great fief of Leinster among the five daughters of the elder William Marshal (or their representatives), and to trace the devolution of the several shares up to the opening years of the fourteenth century. I shall note the pedigree of the family[1] only so far as is necessary to indicate successive owners, and shall direct attention mainly to the division of the inherited lands, the situation and value of the various seignorial manors, and the names of the principal sub-feoffees.

The partition was finally made in the king's court at Woodstock on May 3, 1247;[2] each share was so arranged as to be of the estimated annual value of £343 5*s*. 6½*d*. The total annual value of Leinster must therefore have been estimated at £1,716 7*s*.
[80] 8½*d*. Each share included a chief borough, the future *caput baroniae*, to which (except in the case of Dunamase) was appurtenant the *corpus comitatus* or 'body of the county'. The *comitatus* may be regarded as a tract of land, or as the community of landholders on it. The word was also commonly used as here for the county court at which those landowners owing suit of court were bound to attend. In these liberties the county or rather seignorial court was presided over, not by the king's sheriff, but by the seneschal or other officer of the lord of the liberty. The monetary value seems to have consisted of the estimated annual profits derived from court-fees paid, amercements imposed, fines made, feudal dues exacted, and other issues of the county. Then there were certain manors in demesne with the rents and services appurtenant thereto allotted to each share, and in several cases these were detached or outlying manors situated in what was topographically a different county. Finally, to make the shares exactly equal, the excess-value of those that exceeded the average was assigned out of some specified vill to make up the deficiency of those that fell below it. A further complication was introduced by the temporary readjustments which, as already mentioned, had to be made, owing to the assignment of dower to Walter Marshal's widow, mainly out of the county of Kildare. In fact, simply to say, as is generally done, that the five purparties consisted of the four counties of Carlow, Wexford, Kilkenny, and Kildare, and the territory about Dunamase, would be to give a very inaccurate conception of the actual complications of the partition.

1 The Marshal pedigree for this period has been elaborately examined by Mr. Hamilton Hall, F.S.A., in Journal R.S.A.I., vol. xliii, pp. 1–29, and to his paper, which I have found useful, I may refer my readers for further genealogical details. 2 For a note on the MS. authorities see App. I to this chapter.

Matilda or Maud, the eldest and at the time of the partition the only surviving daughter, had been twice married, firstly in 1207 to Hugh Bigod, Earl of Norfolk, who died in 1225, and secondly to William, Earl Warenne, who died in 1240. [81]

Her share was as follows:

	£	s.	d.
Katherlak burgus	24	12	4
Corpus comitatus cum assisis et perquisitis	24	1	11
Ballidunegan (Ballidongan *Babc*)	11	17	2
Futhered (Fothyrd *Bbc*)	53	5	2
Tamulyn (Thamolyn *Ba*)	38	18	1
Castrum de Ros	72	3	4½
Elurgus de Ros	52	13	4
Insula	43	6	0
Balisex (Balisax *Ba*)	28	5	7
Total (correct)	£349	2	11½

To which is added a note to the following effect: This total exceeds the fifth part (viz. £343 5*s*. 6½*d*.) by £5 17*s*. 5*d*. [correct], which amount is assigned out of the vill of Balisax to the purparty of Dunamase.

The places mentioned are as follows:

The town of Carlow. Here the castle was probably built or completed by the younger William Marshal who granted a charter, which mentions it, to the town.[3] Opposite the castle in 1307 was a hall in which the pleas of the county and assizes were held.[4] The perquisites of assizes were then worth in common years, after deducting the fees of the seneschal and other ministers, £40,[5] and these formed the principal issues of the *comitatus*. There were 160 burgages in the town.

'Ballidunegan.' The name seems now to be represented by Dunganstown or Bestfield, a townland close to the town of Carlow on the north and adjoining Oak Park demesne, which was no doubt the park of the manor. The manor appears to have [82] passed to Richard de Burgh, who held it in 1305,[6] and his successors in title held it of the Crown up to at least 1391.[7]

'Futhered', *Fotharta ui Nualláin*, included the barony of Forth and part of that of Rathvilly, Co. Carlow. The precise *caput* of the manor is marked by the mote of Castlemore, about two miles west of Tullow. It had been the principal manor of Raymond le Gros, but on his death without issue it had reverted to the lordship of Leinster.[8] In 1307 the town of Castle Fothered contained 79 burgages and 29 cottages. There is now no town or village there.

3 *Ante*, [vol. iii] p. 66 [p. 313]. 4 Justiciary Rolls, vol. ii, p. 345. 5 Ibid., p. 347. The serjeants of the county used to render 20 marks for their serjeancies. 6 Justiciary Rolls, vol. ii, p. 136. The manor was probably granted by the king to Richard de Burgh, c. 1302, when the Earl of Norfolk's lands were in the king's hand and before they were restored as estates tail (bound to terminate with his life): Cal. Docs. Ireland, vol. v, no. 87. The king owed Richard de Burgh £4,000: ibid. no. 371. 7 Cal. Pat. Roll (Ireland), 15 Richard II, p. 147 b (12). There are several previous references to Balydongan, Co. Carlow, in the same volume. 8 *Ante*, vol.

'Tamulyn', *Tech Moling*, now St. Mullins. The vill of Techmulin belonged to William de Carew, lord of Idrone, *c.*1200, seemingly under a grant from his uncle Raymond le Gros to Odo de Carew, William's father.[9] It must have reverted to the lordship before 1247. In 1307 it was held of the Earl of Norfolk by Richard Talun. There is an important mote and long rectangular bailey at St. Mullins overlooking the Barrow near the head of the tideway.

'Castrum de Ros.' This was at old Ross, four miles east of New Ross. There is a
[83] mote in the 'castle field' near an ancient mill-race, but no remains of the stone buildings mentioned in the extent of 1307. It had probably been a seignorial centre from Strongbow's time.[10] It was surrounded by the forest of Ros, which, as delimited by Richard Marshal, embraced rather more than the present parishes of Old Ross, Kilscanlan, and Carnagh.[11]

'Burgus de Ros.' This was the *villa novi pontis* or de Rosponte, now New Ross, to which reference has already been made. In 1265 owing, it is said, to disturbances consequent on a feud between Walter de Burgh and Maurice Fitz Maurice, the town was hastily enclosed with a fosse and vallum,[12] and by 1279 it had walls and gates.[13] The rent paid by the burgesses was £25 6*s.* 8*d.*, and as the usual burgage rent was only twelve pence, this implies upwards of 500 burgages. A charter was granted to New Ross by Roger le Bigod, Earl of Norfolk, *c.*1279, but it appears from it that the burgesses claimed to have received a charter from William Marshal, Earl of Pembroke (probably the first earl), granting them as full liberties as the burgesses of Bannow, or Kilkenny, or Wexford, or any burgesses of Leinster enjoyed. These liberties were set forth and confirmed to the burgesses of New Ross by Richard II on December 12, 1389.[14]

'Insula.' This is the place now known as the Great Island in the parish of Kilmokea,
[84] Co. Wexford. It, however, is no longer an island, the Barrow now flowing only on its western side. It was the *caput baroniae* of Hervey de Montmorency's fief, and much of the lands of the baronies of Shelburne and Bargy were held of it.[15]

'Balisex.' Ballysax, a parish in Kildare to the south of the Curragh. This was a detached manor.

Matilda Marshal died in 1248. She was succeeded by her son Roger, fourth Earl of Norfolk and Marshal of England. He died without issue in 1270, when his nephew Roger, the fifth earl, son of his brother Hugh, succeeded. Nearly 100 rolls of accounts of the bailiffs of his Irish manors have been preserved, and from them we can glean a great deal of rare information about the management and working of his lordship of Carlow.[16] In 1302 he surrendered his Irish lands to the king, receiving them hack as an

i, p. 387 [pp. 146–7]. 9 Chart. St. Mary's Abbey, Dublin, vol. i, pp. 112–13, and cf. ibid., vol. ii, p. 98. 10 *Ante*, vol. i, p. 374 [p. 141]. 11 Chart. St. Mary's, vol. ii, p. 154. 12 See the old French poem, the text of which was printed in Archaeologia, vol. xxii, and again with L.E.L.'s (Mrs. George Maclean's) spirited rendering in Crofton Croker's 'Popular Songs of Ireland', pp. 277–304. 13 See Hore's Hist. of Wexford, vol. i, pp. 142, 148. 14 Chartae Privilegia et Immunitates, pp. 84–6. 15 *Ante*, vol. i, p. 393 [p. 149]. In 1307 there were about 110 burgages in the town of the Island: Just. Roll, vol. ii, p. 349. Much of the original grant to Hervey de Montmorency had been alienated in 'free alms' to the monasteries of Dunbrody and Tintern; also to the Templars. 16 See Hore's History of Old and New Ross, pp. 142–61, also my pamphlet on New Ross in the thirteenth century, and Mr. James Mill's paper, Journ. R.S.A.I., vol. xxii (1892).

estate in tail, and he died without issue on December 11, 1306. According to the inquisitions taken in 1305 and 1307[17] his lands were worth beyond reprises and costs of custody £343 0*s.* 1½*d.*, so that up to this date there was no falling off in value.

In addition he held advowsons to the value of £38, and 35½0 knights' fees were held of him. His principal tenants by knights' service were (in Co. Carlow) Edmund [85] le Boteller, who held 4 knights' fees at Tullow, Nicholas de Carew, who held 5 knights' fees in Idrone, William de St. Leger, who held 6 knights' fees in Obargy,[18] and Reginald de Dene, who held 2 knights' fees in Kellistown. In County Wexford there were a number of smaller tenants holding of the Earl of Norfolk by knights' service, of which the following were among the most noted: Maurice de Caunteton at Glascarrig, Nicholas Brown at Mulrankin, Nicholas Keating at Kilcowan, the heir of Reginald de Dene in the barony of Keir or Keyrey (*Cloch na g-caerach*, where the old manorial centre is, now called Wilton),[19] and John de Sutton at Ballybrazil.[20]

On the death of Earl Roger without issue his vast estates reverted to the Crown and, including the honour of Carlow or the greater part of it, were afterwards regranted to Thomas of Brotherton, son of Edward I, who was created Earl of Norfolk and Marshal of England. In his hands and those of his successors the lordship soon became much depreciated in value.

Joan Marshal, the second daughter, married (after 1219) Warin de Munchensi (Monte Caniso), but she was dead at the time of the partition and was represented by her son John de Munchensi. John died shortly afterwards, and his heir was his sister Joan, already married to William de Valence, the king's half-brother, and on August 13, [86] 1247, seisin was ordered to be given to them.[21] This share appears to have been as follows:

	£	*s.*	*d.*
Weseford burgus	42	1	5
Corpus comitatus, ut supra	50	12	6
Odoch (Odogh in com. Kilken. *Bb*)	42	10	4
Rosclar	68	19	11
Karrec (Carryk; *Ba*)	23	15	0
Fernes	81	15	0
Banno[22]	31	0	10
In the vill of Taminie (Taghmone *Ba*) from the surplus of Kildare	1	15	2½
Total of above items[23]	£342	10	2½

17 Cal Docs. Irel., vol. v, nos. 367, 617; and Justiciary Rolls, vol. ii, pp. 41, 344–50. Cal. Inquis. P. M., Ed. I, vol. iv, pp. 304–9. 18 Obargy, *ui Bairchi*. The manor here, with centre at Killeshin, would seem to have been formed by John de Clahull, Strongbow's marshal: *ante*, vol. i, p. 385 [p. 146]. William de St. Leger married Joan, daughter and heir of Hugh Purcell. 19 Inquis. Lagenie, Wexford, no. 16 Jac. I. 20 For the inquisitions taken in 1307 see Cal. Justiciary Rolls, vol. ii, pp. 344–50. 21 Cal. Docs. Irel., vol. i, no. 2900. 22 This item omitted in *A* is supplied fiom *Babc*. 23 The total given in A is £341 10*s.* 4½*d.*; that

Of these places Wexford was a walled town of the Ostmen at the time of the Invasion. The mound on which the later castle stood just touched the southern extremity of the walls, and was probably the first addition to the defences thrown up by the Normans. We first hear of a (stone) castle at Wexford on the death of the younger William Marshal in 1231,[24] but it may have been erected by his father or earlier. A charter to the borough (known through an inspeximus) was granted by Aymer de Valence on July 25, 1317, but from it we learn that Geoffrey Fitz Robert, who was seneschal of the
[87] elder William Marshal, *c.*1200, founded the borough and fixed the burgage rent at twelve pence.[25] In this respect it was like New Ross, Kells, and other boroughs.

'Odoch' (*ui Duach*), now Odagh on the Nore, about five miles above Kilkenny. The mote here close to the parish church probably dates from Strongbow's time.[26] The castle is mentioned in 1231. There were 110 burgages in 1307. This was the only detached manor of this purparty.

'Rosclar' (probably *Ros a(n) chláir*, 'the peninsula of the plank-bridge'), now Rosslare, Co. Wexford. From the high value of this manor and from the inquisition on the lands of Aymer de Valence it would seem that a large part of the barony of Forth, let to tenants at rents, was appurtenant to the manor.

'Karrec', now Carrick on Slaney or Ferry Carrick, two miles above the town of Wexford. The castle, which was built on the site of Robert Fitz Stephen's 'chastel sur Slani',[27] is one of those mentioned in 1231. It was still in existence in 1307, but was *vacuum et fractum*, with ruined hall and chapel, in 1324. There were about 112 burgages here in 1307, of which three were waste in 1324.

'Fernes': for the castle and seignorial manor of Ferns see *ante*, p. 54 [p. 307]. The castle, which was still intact though needing repair at the death of Aymer de Valence,
[88] when the surrounding country was in the hands of the hostile Irish, seems finally to have fallen into the hands of the Kavanaghs in 1359.[28]

Banno': the Irish name for Bannow Bay was *cuan an bhainbh*, 'the harbour of the sucking-pig', a name probably to be connected with 'Banba', a bardic name for Ireland. This was the landingplace of Robert Fitz Stephen in 1169. The borough was seemingly formed here and granted privileges by Geoffrey Fitz Robert, seneschal of the elder William Marshal. In 1307 there were nearly 160 burgages here. In 1324 the manor was valued at about £26. In the middle of the seventeenth century there were a number of thatched houses here arranged along named streets and possessed and owned by people of English or Flemish name,[29] but now there are no visible remains

in Babc is £343 5*s.* 11½*d.*, which is almost precisely the aliquot part of the whole, but neither total is made up by the items given. **24** *Ante*, p. 59 [p. 309]. In 1324 there was 'a stone castle at Wexford with four towers roofed with shingles', also a hall similarly roofed and two houses roofed with straw, all in bad state of repair: Inquis. P. M. (Aymer de Valence), July 26, 18 Ed. II. I quote from a transcript in my possession. **25** Chartae Privilegia et Immunitates, p. 47. At the death of Joan de Valence (1307) there were 365½ burgages formerly worth £18 6*s.* 6*d.*, but then only £11 18*s.* 6*d.*, because 127 burgages were waste: Inquis. P. M., 1 Ed. II. At the death of Aymer de Valence there were only 110 burgages. **26** *Ante*, vol. i, p. 232 [p. 85]. 'A mote upon which are two houses roofed with straw' is mentioned at Odagh in 1324: Inquis. P. M., Aymer de Valence. **27** *Ante*, vol. i, p. 376 [p. 142], and Hore's History of Wexford Town, pp. 22–35. **28** Cal. Close Roll (Ireland), 33 Ed. III, p. 77 b (31). For the interim history of the castle see Hore's Wexford (Ferns), p. 10. **29** See Hore's History of Wexford (Duncannon, &c.), pp. 459–61.

of the town except the ruined church of St. Mary and a thirteenth-century stone coffin-lid.

'Villa de Taminie' (read Tamune): Taghmon (*Tech Munna*). This vill was assigned to the purparty of Kildare, but the sum of £1 15*s*. 2½d. out of it was assigned to the purparty of Wexford.

William de Valence was created Earl of Pembroke in 1264 and died in 1296.[30] Joan, Countess of Pembroke, died in 1307,[31] when her heir was Aymer de Valence, who died *s. p.* June 23, 1324.[32]

In the inquisition taken in 1307 after the death of Joan de Valence her lands were [89]
valued at £324 10*s*. 9½*d*. The manor of Ferns, in the north of the county, had become reduced in value by more than one half, but on the other hand the manor of Roslare, which included the barony of Forth, had increased in value to £114 18*s*. 7*d*. There were tenants holding by military service 294 knights' fees, but their names are not given. At the death of Aymer de Valence in 1324 a marked depreciation had occurred, and his lands were valued at £214 15*s*. 10½*d*. In particular the seignorial manor of Ferns, which included 19,200 acres formerly yielding £80, was now waste on account of the war of the Irish. There were several tenants holding by military service in the southern half of the county belonging to families which for centuries were prominent there, e.g. D'Evreux or Deveroys at Adamstown, Whittey at Ballyteigue, Keating at Kilcowan, Stafford at Ballymacarne, Synnot at Ballybrenan, Lamport at Ballyhire, De la Roche in Shelmalier West, Codd at Carnsore, French at Tacumshin. The manor of Roscarlan (now Rosegarland), formerly belonging to Maurice de Londres, was held by George le Poer in right of his wife Matilda de Londres, from whom it passed to Matilda's son and heir (by a former husband), Thomas Lynet, and from him to his daughter Isabel, wife of Simon Nevill.[33] But most of the fiefs held on military tenure in the northern part of the county no longer rendered royal service 'because they were waste and destroyed by the war of the Irish'. Among these we may recognize the large fiefs held by Maurice de Rochfort in the Duffry in connexion with Enniscorthy Cas- [90]
tle,[34] and by George de Roche in Shelmalier and about Courtown near Gorey.[2] Other fiefs were held by Gilbert, son of William fitz Ely, at Cherlegonay (Killegny ?),[36] by Reginald de Nyvel at Gorey and Balyconewy (Ballycanew),[37] and by Hoel, son of

30 Pipe Roll (Ireland), 25 Ed. I, 38th Rep. D. K., pp. 41–2; Inquis. P. M., 24 Ed. I, Cal. Docs. Irel., vol. iv, no. 306. 31 Inquis. P. M., 1 Ed. II, no. 56; Cal. Inquis., vol. v, p. 22 32 Inquis. P. M., 18 Ed. II, no. 518; Cal. Inquis., vol. vi, pp 324–7. 33 Close Roll (Ireland), 32 Ed. III, p. 68 (28), and 9 Rich. II, p. 128 b (19). 34 Enniscorthy Castle, after the death of John de Rochfort (before 1377), was in the king's hand and was held by Matthew Fitz Henry up to the close of the fourteenth century, when it seems to have fallen into the hands of the Mac Murroughs: Hore's Hist. of Wexford, vol. vi, p. 352. 35 He held 4 knights' fees 'in Schyrmal and Kynalo'. The former is perhaps Shelmalier, but the latter name is puzzling. 'Curtun in Kinelahun, or Kinelaon, in the County of Wexford' was held before 1281 by Christiana de Mariscis, and by her then granted to the king: Cal. Docs. Irel, vol. ii, nos. 1801, 2339, and p. 462. Adam John de Roche then applied for a grant of it: ibid., p. 561. This was probably the place, now Courtown near Gorey. For subsequent records see Hore's Hist. of Wexford (Ferns, &c.), p. 342. 36 'Kylaugy' (or better, Kylangy), Co. Wexford, was held for life by Maurice Fitz Maurice (died 1286) of the inheritance of Maurice de Rochfort: Cal. Docs. Irel., vol. iii, no. 463. There is a mote at Killegny. 37 'Ballyconnoe, alias Baronscourt, alias Nevelscort': Inquis. Lagenie (Wexford), no. 53 Car. I (anno 6), showing that after a lapse of

Stephen, at Carrickbyrne,[38] and there were several others at places more difficult to identify.

Isabel Marshal, the third daughter, married *c.*1217 her cousin Gilbert de Clare, Earl of Gloucester and Hertford, and in 1231 Richard, Earl of Cornwall, the king's brother. Both she and her first husband were dead at the time of the partition and were repre-
[91] sented by their son, Richard, Earl of Gloucester and Hertford. His share is given as follows:

	£	*s.*	*d.*
Kilkennly burgus	73	3	10
Corpus comitatus, ut supra	130	16	3
Dunfert	37	16	3
Locmadran (Loghmethran *Ba*, Loghmera *Bbc*)	19	8	6½
Grenan (Brenan *Bab*, Brenan *Bc*)	10	8	11
Callan[39]	10	8	10
The total is given in all versions as	£346	7	4½

To which is added a note to the effect that this total exceeds the fifth part (£343 5*s.* 6½*d.*) by £3 1*s.* 10*d.* [which is correct], and this amount is assigned out of the vill of Callan to the purparty of Dunamase. But as the items given, even including the valuation of Callan, only amount to £282 2*s.* 7½*d.*, it is clear that there are important omissions. In the extent of the lands of Joan, widow of Gilbert, Earl of Gloucester and Hertford, taken in 1307, in addition to the above, the following seignorial property is included: the old and the new vill of Jerpoint, the manor of Palmerston (near Kilkenny), the boroughs of Coillauch (Coolaghmore ? in the barony of Kells), and Kilmanagh (in the barony of Crannagh); the lands of Ballycallan, &c. (in Crannagh), and the vill of Rosbercon.[40] We may conjecture that some or all of these places have been omitted.

Of the places mentioned, the chief points of what is known of the origin of the
[92] town and castle of Kilkenny have already been noted.[41] In 1307 the castle consisted of 'una aula quatuor turres una capella una mota et alie domus diverse ad idem castrum necessarie'. There were then about 330 burgesses in the town, and the total value, including perquisites of assizes, was £130 4*s.* 0½*d.*

'Dunfert' (*Dún Ferta*, 'the dun of the cemetery),[42] now corruptly Danesfort in the barony of Shillelogher. A natural esker-mound surrounded by a shallow ditch and low

three centuries the fermer ownership of the Nyvel or Neville family still left its trace. 38 On the western slope of Carrickbyrne Hill is 'Courthoyle', where there are remains of a castle and also earlier earth works. The *capella* and *domus* of 'Hoel of Karrothobren' are mentioned in the deforestation Charter of Richard Marshal: Chart. St. Mary's Abbey, Dublin, vol. ii, p. 155. 39 'Callan' omitted in A is supplied from *Babc*. 40 Cal. Docs. Irel., vol. v, no 653, &c. Besides the above, 'Hillyd', i.e. Ullid in Iverk, had reverted to the countess, and the manor of Fermaille, i.e. Fermoyle in the parishes of Durrow and Rosconnel, had been purchased by the earl from William de St. Leger: ibid. 668, 670. 41 *Ante*, vol. ii, pp. 223–8 [pp. 240–2]. 42 For *ferta* see the Book of Armagh, f. 12vo., where Tirechan tells the strange story of the conversion and death of the daughters of King Laeghaire and proceeds: 'Et sepelierunt eas . . . et feerunt iossam rotun-

outer rampart seems to be the original Dunfert. In appearance as well as in name it suggests a pre-Christian burial site. But the extent of 1307 states that 'there are in the manor within the enclosure one hall, one chamber, one dairy, one grange, one bretage beyond the gate, and other wooden houses'. Further on a dovecot is valued. This description suits the remains at Danesfort Cross Roads better than the ancient Dunfert. If this was the site, as I think it was, the 'bretage' was built within a small circular fort fifty paces in diameter and artificially raised about ten feet, and the other buildings mentioned were in a very large circular enclosure close by, surrounded by a deep ditch and inner bank and containing traces of buildings. Between the small raised fort and this enclosure are the ruins of a columbarium fifteen feet in diameter and with seventeen tiers of pigeon-holes.[43]

'Locmadran': now Loughmerans in the parish of St. John near Kilkenny. Here in [93]
1307 there were a bretage, grange, stable, sheepfold on posts, in bad condition and ruinous. The earthworks of the bretage, easily discernible, look from the neighbouring railway like a mote, but may be more properly classed as a promontory fort, fully forty feet high, jutting out into the dried-up lake. It has a roughly triangular space. twenty-three paces by thirteen, on top, cut off by a wide ditch from a rectangular bailey.[44]

'Grenan': this is now the name of the townland on which the ruins of the castle of Grenan stand.[45] The neighbouring town on the Nore appears to have been at first called Grenan, but was for centuries known as Thomastown and called by the Irish *Baile mic Antáin* both names referring to its founder, Thomas Fitz Anthony, who appears to have granted it a charter under the name of Grenan.[46] In 1307 the burgesses of a fifth part of the vill of Thomastown held their burgages of Joan, Countess of Gloucester and Hertford,[47] and it would seem that there were then about 215 burgesses in the town.[48]

'Kallan': Callan on the King's River above Kells. The elder William Marshal
granted a charter to this town. There was a castle here in 1247 and in 1307. A large [94]
mote in the demesne of Westcourt adjoining the town on the north side of the river probably marks the original site.[49]

Among the tenants by military service of Richard, Earl of Gloucester, in 1247, the most notable were the following:[50] Stephen of Hereford, presumably the son of that name of Adam of Hereford, at Rathdowny in the barony of Clandonagh in Upper Ossory; William le Gras, son of 'William Crassus, junior', and ancestor of the Grace family, at Offerlane and Tullaroan; William de St. Leger at Rosconnell and Tulla-

dam in similitudinem *fertae*. Sic faciebant Scotici homines et Gentiles; nobiscum autem *rel*[ic] vocatur'. *Relic* (Latin *reliquiae*) = a cemetery. 43 See Journal R.S.A.I., vol. xxxix (1909), p. 321. I have since visited and now distinguish the ancient *Dún Ferta*. 44 Ibid. Since writing this paper I have visited the site and identified the bretage. 45 Ibid. 46 Ibid., vol. iv (1856–7), p. 85. 47 Cal. Docs. Irel., vol. v, p. 191. Perhaps Thomastown was included in the New and Old Vill of Jerpoint, assigned as dower to Maltilda, widow of Anselm Marshal, and on her death in 1252 was divided into fifths among the co-parceners; cf. Cal. Docs. Irel., vol. ii, no. 110, and the grant by Humphrey de Bohun, Carew Cal. Misc., p. 369, 447. 48 Chartae Privilegia et Immunitates, p. 68. 49 Journal R.S.A.I., vol. xxxix (1909), p. 319. 50 For the complete list see Chart. St. Mary's, Dublin, vol. ii, pp. 404–6.

ghanbrogue; William Fitz Maurice, 'baron of Kiltrany' or Burnchurch; John de Valle, a name which became Wale or Wall, at Tulachany; the heir of John Fitz Geoffrey, younger son of Geoffrey Fitz Robert and heir to his brother, William Fitz Geoffrey, at Kells; Raymond Fitz Griffin, brother and heir of Matthew Fitz Griffin, at Knocktopher; William de Dene, afterwards (1260–1) justiciar of Ireland, at 'Ogenty' in the parish of Columkille near Thomastown;[51] Theobald Butler III at Gowran; and Miles Fitz David, great grandson of David Fitz Gerald, Bishop of St. David's, in Iverk.

Richard, Earl of Gloucester and Hertford, son of Isabel Marshal, died in 1262 and was succeeded by his son Gilbert, who in 1290 married (secondly) Joan of Acre, daughter of Edward I. As part of the marriage-treaty Gilbert surrendered all his lands
[95] to the king, who regranted them to Gilbert and Joan and the heirs of their bodies.[52] Joan outlived her husband, married Ralph de Monthermer in 129d, and died on April 19, 1307, and from the inquisitions taken soon after her death it would seem that her lands in the liberty of Kilkenny had not decreased in value.[53] The heir of Joan and Gilbert was their son Gilbert de Clare, last Earl of Gloucester and Hertford. He was slain at Bannockburn in 1314,[54] when his heirs were his three sisters, namely, Eleanor, wife of the younger Hugh Despenser and afterwards of William la Zouche; Margaret, widow of Piers Gaveston and afterwards wife of Hugh d'Audley; and Elizabeth, widow of John de Burgh, eldest son of Richard de Burgh, Earl of Ulster.[55] It was this Hugh Despenser's namesake and successor in title who in 1391 sold Kilkenny Castle to James Butler, third Earl of Ormonde.

Soon after the death of Earl Gilbert, about 1317, a partition was effected between his three sisters. To Hugh Despenser and Eleanor were assigned the castle of Kilkenny, the borough of Rosbercon (which since the separation of New Ross from the lordship of Kilkenny had become a port of importance and had received a charter[56] from the late earl), the manors of Dunfert and 'Kyldermoygh',[57] some rents and lands at Callan, and the serjeancy of Iverk. To Hugh d'Audley and Margaret were
[96] assigned the boroughs of Kilkenny, 'Coyllagh',[58] Thomastown, and Newtown Jerpoint, the manors of Ballydowel[59] and Clontubbrid,[60] the pleas and perquisites of the manor of Callan, and the serjeancy of Odagh. To Elizabeth de Burgo[61] fell the castle of 'Offarelan' (i.e. Castletown, Offerlane, *ui Fairchellain*, in Upper Ossory), which was not extended or valued because it was in the march, the manors of Fermoyle (in the parishes of Durrow and Rosconnell), Ballycallan, Palmerstown, Loughmerans (all three not far from Kilkenny), and 'Shillercher',[62] the boroughs of Callan and Kil-

51 Inquis. Lagenie (Kilkenny), no. 20 Jac. I. 52 Cal. Docs. Irel., vol. iii, nos. 620, 629. 53 Ibid, vol. v, nos. 653–70. 54 The issues of two-thirds of his Irish lands in the king's hand for about a year ending February 1316 amounted to £341: 42nd Rep. D. K., p. 60. 55 See 43rd Rep. D.K., p. 44. 56 Chartae Priv. et Immun., p. 39. 57 Now the parish of Killermogh in Upper Ossory, adjoining the parish of Durrow. 58 Probably Coolaghmore in the barony of Kells. 59 Probably Ballydowel in the parish of Ballinamara. 60 Formerly a parish, but now a townland in the parish of Sheffin and barony of Crannagh. 61 As no husband is mentioned we may infer that at the date of this partition Elizabeth de Clare was a widow. John de Burgh, her first husband, died in June 1313. She married Theobald de Verdun II in February 1316, but he died in the following July. Afterwards she married Roger d'Amory. See Journ. R.S.A.I., vol. xliii (1913), p. 16. 62 Shillercher represents *Sil Faelchair* (Onom. Goed.), where the *f* would be silent and the *l* eas-

managh, 'with the capital messuage and park of Callan and the demesne lands of the manor there', and the serjeancy of Offerlane and Shillercher.

The services of the military tenants were distributed amongst the three parceners, and here we may note some new names afterwards famous in the history of the county. James Butler, soon to become first Earl of Ormonde, had superseded two Geraldine [97] families which had become extinct in the male line, namely, the descendants of Miles Fitz David, who were barons of Iverk, and those of Griffin Fitz William, who were barons of Knocktopher. We also meet for the first time as holders of knights' fees the names of Forestall, l'Ercedekne (Archdeacon or Mc Odo), Cantwell, Shorthall, and Utlagh.[63] Some of these names indeed occur at a much earlier period, but not, I think, as military tenants in Ossory.[64]

Sibyl Marshal, the fourth daughter, who had married William de Ferrers, afterwards Earl of Derby, was dead at the date of the partition, leaving as her heirs seven daughters, viz. Agnes, wife of William de Vescy, Isabel, wife of Reginald de Mohun. Maud de Kyme, a widow, afterwards wife of William de Fortibus, Sibyl, wife of Francis de Bohun of Midhurst, Eleanor, wife of William de Vaux, Joan, wife of John de Mohun (son of Reginald de Mohun by a former wife), and Agatha, afterwards wife of Hugh Mortimer.

The undivided share of these co-parceners was as follows: [98]

	£	s.	d.
Kildar burgus	23	2	4
Corpus comitatus, ut supra	73	11	0
Karberie	60	19	8
Ballimadan	53	19	10
Mon	83	13	9[65]
Kumbre	32	1	6
Tamminie (Thaghmon, *Ba*)	7	16	2
Clumena (Clonmen, *Ba*)	9	18	8
Total (as given in all versions)	£345	3	11

ily commuted with *r*. It is now, in the form Shillelogher, the name of a barony in Kilkenny. In 1358 it appears as the 'cantred of Sileyrthir', and perhaps included the barony of Crannagh as well as that of Shillelogher: Cal. Pat. and C1. Rolls (Ireland), p. 74 (64 and 66). Where precisely the seat of the manor was is obscure to me. 63 The above notes on the partition of c. 1317 are taken from Add. MS. Brit. Mus. 4791, ff. 64–72, collated with Carew MS. 635, ff. 40–41. 64 Odo Archiedekne witnessed the elder William Marshal's charter to Kilkenny c. 1208: Chartae Priv. et Immun., p. 34. He was probably the eponym of the Mc Odos (later Cody), as the Archdeacons were called by the Irish. Stephen Ercedekne witnessed Walter Marshal's charter to Dunbrody (1241–5). He married Desiré, one of the daughters of Thomas Fitz Anthony. G. de Kentewell (Cantwell) witnessed the charter of Theobald Walteri I to Wodeny: Chartae Priv. et Immun., p. 11. Geoffrey and William 'Scortall' witnessed John Fitz Geoffrey's charter to Kells: ibid., p. 17; and the family appears at Ballylarkin before 1218: see History of the Cathedral of St. Canice (Graves and Prim), p. 167. 65 So in *Ba*. With these figures the items amount to 1*s*. less than the total given. A has £84 13*s*. 9*d*.

Then follows a note (*Babc*) to the effect that this total (viz. £345 3*s.* 11*d.*) exceeds the fifth part by £1 18*s.* 4½*d.* (correct), of which £1 15*s.* 2½*d.* is assigned out of the vill of Taghmon to the purparty of Wexford, and 3*s.* 1*d.* out of the vill of Mon to the purparty of Dunmas.

The partition of this fifth into sevenths was perhaps not made immediately. At any rate, as we have mentioned, the whole county of Kildare was assigned as (part) dower to Margaret Countess of Lincoln, widow of Walter Marshal, and in consequence a new (temporary) division of Leinster was ordered so that each of the earl's heirs should have his due portion.[66] We are nowhere given a connected account of this compensatory readjustment, but we can gather from various entries that Isabel and Reginald de Mohun, Joan and John de Mohun and Sibyl and Frank de Bohun were assigned manors out of the purparty of Wexford. Their interest in these manors was
[99] however bought out by William de Valence for an annual payment during the life of the countess.[67] Similarly Maud (de Kyme) and William de Fortibus received compensation out of the purparty of Kilkenny.[68] Of the other coheiresses Agatha de Ferrers (afterwards Mortimer) was assigned the manors of Taghmon and Clonmines in Co. Wexford,[69] and Eleanor de Vaux the manor of Castlecomer,[70] as part of their permanent shares, and presumably had no claim to compensation. Similarly Agnes de Vescy seems to have been given ten librates of land in Kildare before the manor of Kildare was assigned as dower to Walter Marshal's widow.[71]

With reference to the places to be divided among the seven daughters of Sibyl Marshal:

It is stated in a late inquisition that the castle of Kildare was built by the elder William Marshal on land belonging to the episcopal see, and that afterwards the earl (apparently the younger William), to make peace, gave to Bishop Ralph of Bristol and his successors ten marks a year by way of compensation.[72] The site consists of a raised platform, partly artificial, on the border of the town. One late tower remains.

After the death of the Countess of Lincoln (*c.*1270) Agnes de Vescy became entitled to the castle and manor of Kildare and the principal share of the *corpus comitatus*,
[100] including profits of pleas and other issues of the county, but her sisters Matilda, Eleanor, and Agatha, also shared in the corpus and there was litigation concerning their rights. This was settled in 1275, when the co-parcenary of the three surviving sisters (Eleanor had died without issue) was recognized.[73] Agnes was dead by June 1290, and was succeeded by her son William de Vescy, who was appointed justiciar in the following September. In 1297 William surrendered his lands, including the castle manor and county of Kildare, with all its liberties to the king.[74] By a parliament held in this year it was enacted that 'the county of Kildare, which was formerly a liberty

66 Cal. Docs. Irel., vol. i, nos. 2949, 2988. 67 Ibid., vol. ii, nos. 29, 103, 628. It was not a purchase of their original shares under the partition, as Mr. Hall seems to have thought (Journ. R.S.A.I., vol. xliii, pp. 19, 21, 23, 24), but only of their compensatory shares during the life of the Countess of Lincoln (Cal. Docs. Irel., ii. 139). 68 Ibid., vol. ii, no. 30. 69 Ibid., vol. ii, nos. 1109, 1330; vol. v, no. 538. 70 36th Rep. D. K., p. 31. 71 Cal. Docs. Ireland, vol. i, no. 2951. 72 Ibid., vol. v, no. 132. 73 Cal. Docs. Ireland, vol. ii, nos. 935, 1096. 74 Ibid., vol. iv, nos. 365, 373–5, and (extent) 481.

intentive to the county of Dublin, be henceforth a county by itself' with a separate sheriff.[75] In 1316 Edward II granted the town and castle to John Fitz Thomas of Offaly on his creation as Earl of Kildare.

'Karberie': Carbury, a barony in the northwest corner of Co. Kildare. The cantred had been granted by Strongbow to Meiler Fitz Henry, but on his death had escheated to the Marshals.[76] The manor of Carbury was assigned to Matilda de Kyme,[77] but the Mohuns also had interests in lands in Carbury. Matilda died in 1299, when her share was again subdivided into four parts among her coheirs, each of whom accordingly obtained one 140th part of the lordship of Leinster.

'Ballimadan': the name survives as Maddenstown in the parish of Ballysax. The manor included the marchlands between the marches of Kildare and Reban.[78] It was assigned to Sibyl Ferrers and Frank de Bohun.[79] Their son John sold it and his inter- [101]
est in Castlecomer to John de Saunford, Escheator of Ireland and afterwards Archbishop of Dublin. The archbishop died 1297, a bastard and without heirs, when the king seized the lands, but restored them in 1302 to James, son of John de Bohun.[80] At his death in 1306 the lands were worth £55 16*s.*[81] In 1323 John, son of James de Bohun, obtained seisin.[82]

'Mon' (*Moin Coluimb*): Moone, now the name of a barony united with that of Kilkea. The lands included Ardscull (where in 1282 there were 160 burgages), Mullaghmast, Belan, and Glassely. The younger William Marshal granted a charter to the town-of Moone.[83] Near the town, in the demesne of Moone-Abbey House, are the remains of an ancient castle. William son of Isabel Ferrers and Reginald de Mohun held at his death in 1282 lands in the manor of ' Grange Mohun', or the grange of Moone, and also in Carbury and 'Aliwine' or 'Alewyn' (*Almu* g. *almhuine*, a name surviving in the Hill of Allen) in Co. Kildare, and at 'le Cumbre' (Castlecomer, Co. Kilkenny).[84] In 1297 his lands were partitioned between his daughters Mary and Eleanor, wives respectively of John de Merriet and John de Carew.[85] In 1299 John de Mohun, grandson of the John de Mohun who married Joan Ferrers, surrendered all [102]
his lands in Ireland to the king.[86] These lands seem to have been in the same manors as those of William de Mohun.[87] They were valued in 1305 at £58 9*s.* 8½*d.*

'Kumbre' (*an Comar*, 'the confluence'): Castlecomer, Co. Kilkenny. The mote which marks the castle-site remains.[88] The manor, as we have said, seems to have been originally assigned to Eleanor de Vaux, but after her death it was divided among the other heiresses.

'Tamminie' (we should probably read here and elsewhere in *A* Tam[m]une): *Tech Munna* now Taghmon, Co. Wexford. A square tower of uncertain date remains. The

75 Early Statutes (Berry), p. 199. 76 *Ante*, vol. i, p. 378 [p. 143]. 77 Pipe Roll (Ireland), 31 Ed. I, 38th Rep. D. K., p. 81. 78 Cal. Docs. Ireland, vol. iii, p. 267. 79 36th Rep. D. K., p. 32. 80 Justiciary Rolls, vol. i, pp. 272, 456; Cal. Docs. Ireland, ii, 183, iii, 480, v. 361. 81 Justiciary Rolls, vol. ii, p. 291; Cal. Docs. Ireland, v, 530; 39th Rep. D. K., p. 23. 82 Pipe Roll (Ireland), 18 Ed. II, 42 Rep. D. K., p. 58. 83 Justiciary Rolls, vol. i, pp. 369–71. 84 Cal. Docs. Ireland, vol. ii, nos. 1963, 2324; Pipe Roll (Ireland), 26 Ed. I, 38th Rep. D. K., p. 38. 85 Cal. Docs. Ireland, vol. iv, nos. 437, 499. Cf. the pedigree of the Carews of Idrone; *infra*, p. 155 [pp. 156–7]. 86 Cal. Docs. Ireland, vol. iv, nos. 566, 677. 87 Ibid., vol. v, 335; Justiciary Roll, vol. ii, pp. 28–30. 88 *Ante*, vol. i, p. 376 [p. 142].

manor, along with that of Clonmines, was assigned to Agatha Ferrers and Hugh Mortimer.[89]

'Clumena' (*Cluain mín* ?): Clonmines, Co. Wexford. The form Clonmines only appears in quite late documents, and is probably due to a false etymology, as some lead and silver mines were worked here in the middle of the sixteenth century.[90] The site is now remarkable for a group of castles and churches, none of which, however, appears to date from the thirteenth century. A franchise or liberty appears to have been granted to the town by William Marshal, and was claimed by Agatha Mortimer as against the liberty of Wexford.[91] Besides Taghmon and Clonmines, Agatha held at her death in 1306 parcels of land in Carbury, Co. Kildare, and at Newtown-Jerpoint, Co. Kilkenny.[92]

[103] The services due in respect of the twelve knights' fees held by the barons of Naas were divided into four parts. Three of these parts were rendered to William de Vescy, John de Mohun, and William de Mohun respectively, and the fourth presumably to one of the other coheirs. The most notable of the other tenants by knight's service of William de Vescy at the time of his death in 1297, were Ralph Pipard at Leixlip and other places, Waleran de Wellesley at 'Kynheygh' (Kineagh in the parish of Kilcullen ?), Robert Percival, William's seneschal, and Geoffrey le Bret, who married one of the heiresses of the barons of Naas.

Eva Marshal, the fifth and youngest daughter, married William de Braose, grandson of the William de Braose who was persecuted by King John. They were both dead at the partition, leaving three daughters as coheiresses, viz. Maud, wife of Roger Mortimer of Wigmore, Eva, wife of William de Cantilupe, and Eleanor, wife of Humphrey de Bohun, eldest son of the Earl of Hereford.

The share of Roger Mortimer and his parceners was as follows:

	£	*s.*	*d.*
Dummas burgus	104	19	1
Obboy (Oboy *Bab*)	82	6	5½
Achkbo	72	6	5
Karnebo (Carneboth comitatus Weysford *Babc*)	74	8	3
In the vill of Balisex of the surplus of Katherlak	5	17	5
In the vill of Kallan of the surplus of Kilkenny	3	1	10
In the vill of Mon of the surplus of Kildar		3	1
Total (correct)	£343	4	6½

[104] Of these places 'Dummas' (*Dun Masc*) is now written Dunamase. The ruins of a strong castle crowning a precipitous rock, with three walled baileys descending the hill-slope, are still to be seen, but the existing remains are apparently of later date than

89 Cal. Docs. Ireland, vol. ii, nos. 1299, 1445. **90** See Hore's Hist. of Co. Wexford (Tintern, &c.), pp. 233–62. **91** Cal. Docs. Ireland, vol. ii, no. 1330. **92** Ibid., vol. v, no. 538. **93** See *ante*, vol. i, p. 375 [p. 142]; vol. ii, p. 217 [p. 238].

the thirteenth century.[93] The honour was assigned to Maud and Roger Mortimer, and the latter at his death in 1282 held lands in right of his wife valued at £171 7*s*. 6½*d*., a sum which indicates an advance in value. At this period there were 127 free burgages in the New Town of Leix.[94] The very site of this borough has been forgotten, but it may, not improbably, have been on an adjoining hill, a little to the west of the Rock of Dunamase, where 'site of ancient village' is marked on the Ordnance Survey (Index) Map. The services due in respect of the twelve knights' fees held by the barons of Offaly were equally divided between the three daughters of Eva Marshal. Besides his share in these, to Roger Mortimer were assigned the services of Walter de Ridelisford at Castledermot and Kilkea, of Walter de l'Enfant in Allewyn (Allen), and of Robert de St. Michael in Reban.[95] Edmund Mortimer, son and heir of the above-named Maud and Roger, died in 1304. His son and heir was the Roger Mortimer who married Joan of Geynville, heiress of the liberty of Trim. He was created Earl of March in 1328, and met a traitor's doom in 1330, when the honour of Dunamase escheated [105]
to the king.

'Obboy' (*ui Buidhe*): the name of a deanery in the diocese of Leighlin, approximately the barony of Ballyadams, Queen's County. In the townland of Castletown near the church is a mote. This was the 'Balliscaslan O'Moy' or 'Castletown O'Moy' of later times,[96] and probably marks the manorial centre. William de Cantilupe (d. 1254) was succeeded by his son George, who died in 1273, soon after coming of age.[97] His heirs were John de Hastings, son of his sister Joan, and his sister Milicent, wife of Eudo la Zouche. A partition was ordered,[98] and in 1277 the custody of the manor of Oboy (where the lands of John de Hastings lay) was given to Miles of Down.[99] In 1283 John de Hastings obtained seisin.[1] He married a sister of Aymer de Valence, and in 1339 his grandson Lawrence Hastings was created Earl of Pembroke.

'Achkbo' (*Achadh-bó*): Aghaboe in Queen's County.[2] In 1278, Milicent (as heir of George de Cantilupe) and Eudo la Zouche successfully claimed the presentation to the church of Aghaboe against the Bishop of Ossory,[3] and from this we may infer that the advowson of Aghaboe was part of their share of the Cantilupe inheritance. Milicent's heir was her son William la Zouche, who did homage for his mother's lands in March [106]
1299.[4] In February 1300, however, Gilbert de Bohun, late seneschal of Kilkenny, held the manor of Aghaboe,[5] under grant from his brother Humphrey de Bohun, Earl of Hereford. So we may conclude that the Cantilupe lands were mostly confined to Oboy.

'Karnebo': this place more often written 'Carneboth', appears to have been within the liberty of Wexford and on the confines of the liberty of Carlow.[6] The Irish form

94 For the extent of Roger Mortimer's lands see Cal. Docs. Ireland, vol. ii, no. 2028. 'Maimolieth', where there were betaghs, probably represents *Magh Muilchiath*, in Leix, where a battle was fought in 1042 (Four Masters). Many other place-names, hard to identify, are mentioned in the extent. 95 For the early records of the manors of Castledermot and Kilkea see *ante*, vol. i, p. 386 [p. 146], and for the manor of Reban, ibid., p. 383 [p. 145]. 96 Fiants, Elizabeth, nos. 5147, 5424; Inquis. Lagenie (Queen's Co.), no. 22 Jac. I. 97 Cal. Docs. Ireland, vol. ii, no. 985, and cf. 956. 98 Ibid., no. 1008. 99 Ibid., no. 1401; cf. 38th Rep. D. K., p. 71. 1 Ibid., no. 2107. 2 For the site and early history of the manor of Aghaboe, see *ante*, vol. i, pp. 388–9 [p. 147]. 3 Cal. Docs. Ireland, vol. ii, no. 1450. 4 Cal. Docs. Ireland, vol. iv, no. 599. 5 Justiciary Roll, vol. i, p. 397. 6 See Justiciary Rolls, vol. i, p. 142.

of the name appears as *Carnbuada*, 'the Carn of Victory', in the grant by Donnell Reagh Kavanagh Mac Murrough, Lord of Leinster, to the Abbey of Duiske in 1473.[7] We need have little hesitation in identifying it with Carnew, a parish partly in Co. Wexford and partly in Co. Wicklow. It was assigned to Eleanor and Humphrey de Bohun.'[8] Eleanor's son and heir Humphrey in 1274 succeeded his grandfather as Earl of Hereford and Essex, and granted his lands in Carneboth, Aghaboe, and Moone, to his brother Gilbert.[9]

The 100 services originally reserved in the grant of Leinster were, in the reign of Edward I and previously, distributed as follows: 33⅓ services (⅓ of the whole, or in money value £66 13*s*. 4*d*.) were due from the liberty of Kildare, and the remaining 66⅓ services were divided evenly between the liberties of Carlow, Wexford, and
[107] Kilkenny, so that each owed £44 8*s*. 10 2½*d*.[10] This seemingly unequal arrangement appears to have originated as follows. When the partition was made, Margaret Countess of Lincoln, widow of Walter Marshal, held her dower lands (which as already mentioned consisted of 'the whole county of Kildare, the manor of Fothered, and lands of the value of £62 17*s*. 4*d*. in the manor of Oboy') subject to ⅓ of the 100 services,[11] and the lords of the other three liberties were each subject to ⅓ of the remaining ⅔. After the widow's death this arrangement was continued, and the county of Kildare bore ⅓ of the whole. Why the honour of Dunamase did not bear its share of the services is perhaps not quite clear, but for some reason it was not constituted a separate county, but was regarded as in the county of Kildare. In the inquisition taken in 1283, after the death of Roger de Mortimer,[12] 'Dumasek' (Dunamase) is described as 'in the tenement of Leys (Leix) in the county of Kildare'. For the same reason in the partition of 1247 there is no item 'corpus comitatus' in the purparty of Roger de Mortimer and his parceners. Nevertheless from the same inquisition it appears that Roger de Mortimer rendered to the king the service of 6⅔ knights, i.e. ⅓ of ⅕ of 100 services, or his full proportionate share, and presumably his two parceners were each subject to a similar burden. Whether the services of the honour of Dunamase were all included in the 33⅓ services of Kildare, or whether by some arrangement between the lords of the liberties they were so distributed that each of the five honours really bore only 20 services, I have not been able to discover.

7 Proc. R.I.A., vol. xxxv (c), p. 149. 8 Cal. Docs. Ireland, vol. i, no. 2973. 9 Cal. Carew MSS. (Miscellaneous), p. 447. 10 See Exchequer Memoranda, English Historical Review, vol. xviii (1903), p. 505; and Irish Pipe Rolls, *passim*. 11 Pipe Roll (Ireland), 46 Hen. III, 35th Rep. D. K., p. 42. 12 Cal. Docs. Ireland, vol. ii, no. 2028.

APPENDIX I [108]

Note on the Authorities for the Partition of Leinster

There are several versions of this partition, all of which may, I think, be referred to one or other of two originals. I group them as follows:

A. Chancery Miscellaneous Roll, no. 320, m. 3 dors., calendared by Sweetman, Cal. Docs. Irel., vol. ii, no. 933. This is undated, but referred to the time of Henry III.

An inspeximus of the same by Ed. III (1347–8), transcribed by Gilbert, Chart. St. Mary's Abbey, Dublin, vol. ii, App. 1, and 'Viceroys', pp. 616–18. In this version the honours are arranged in the order Kilkenny, Wexford, Kildare, Carlow, Dunamase, and are ascribed respectively to the daughters Isabella, Johanna, Sibilla, Matilda, Eva (or their representatives), but nothing is stated as to the seniority of the daughters.

B. (*a*) Brit. Mus. Add. MS.4791, ff. 64–72 (a Clarendon MS.), headed 'In quodam antiquo rotulo'. The account of the partition is here preceded by some annalistic entries mainly concerning the Marshal family and substantially identical with those contained in the Register of Dunbrody (Chart. St. Mary's Abbey, Dublin, vol. ii, pp. 140–4), and is followed (1) by an entry giving the division of Killkenny among the three daughters of Gilbert de Clare, Earl of Gloucester, and Joan his wife (c. 1317), stated in the margin (by another hand) to be taken from the book of the Convent of the Friars Minors of Kilkenny; (2) by a transcript of the royal patents for Gilbert de Clare and Joan (1247), similar to that published in Chart. St. Mary's Abbey, Dublin, vol. ii, pp. 403–6; (3) by some biographical notes concerning the families of the daughters of William Marshal similar to those in the Register of Dunbrody, pp. 144–6, but including the family of the fifth daughter Eve.

(*b*) Carew MS. 635, ff. 140, 141 b. Here the account of the partition of 1247 is also followed by an account of the partition of 1317 between the daughters of Earl Gilbert and Joan, and this is followed by genealogical notes, similar to those above-mentioned, touching the families of the [109] daughters of William Marshal.

(c) Carew MS. 608, ff. 38 b, 39, calendared in the Miscellaneous volume, pp. 373–4.

All three B. versions (probably of monastic provenance) purport to give the partition made in the court of King Henry III at Woodstock, May 3, a.r. 31 (1247), and both the several shares and the genealogical notes are expressly arranged in the order of the seniority of the daughters, viz. Matilda (Carlow), Johanna (Wexford), Isabella (Kilkenny), Sibilla (Kildare), and Eva (Dunamase). Matilda is called primogenita filia, and the others, in the above order, secunda, tertia, quarta, and quinta. That Matilda was the eldest is also shown by Close Roll, 30 Hen. III, m. 7 (July 22, 1246), from which it appears that the Marshalcy was assigned to her *que habet esneciam hereditatis*, and there is no valid reason to doubt tbe correctness of the order assigned in the B. versions to the other daughters. It is true that in the account of the daughters given in L'Histoire de Guillaume le Marechal (ll. 14916–06) the order observed is Maud, Isabel, Sibyl, Eve, Joan, but the order appears to be that of their marriages, and Joan (though the second daughter) was married last—after her father's death. Maud was married to Hugh Bigod a little before Lent 1207, when her father went to Ireland; ibid., 13349; cf. Cal. Docs. Irel., vol. i, no. 313.

I have dwelt on the evidence touching the order of the daughters' birth because Mr. Hamilton Hall in the paper to which I have referred (Journal R.S.A.I., vol. xliii (1913), pp. 1–29) expresses considerable doubt on the subject. But Mr. Hall seems to have been unaware of the above B. versions, and to have assumed without sufficient grounds that 'Carlow was the least

considerable of the Irish Honours'. On this last point it may be remarked (1) that the Irish honours were all made of equal monetary value, and (2) that the honour of Carlow comprised a large slice of the present County Wexford including the port of New Ross, while the great waterway of the Barrow connecting the town of Carlow with the sea may have given it an actual or prospective value over Kilkenny, notwithstanding the greater importance of the latter town.
[110] The order followed in the A. version may have been arbitrarily adopted by the commissioners when making their valuations and adjustments before the several shares were allotted to the coparceners, and may have been afterwards followed by the court in the document which recorded the allotment irrespective of the order of birth which is not here given. Or again it may be that as Matilda got the *esnecia* of the whole inheritance in the castle of Strigul, she was not given first choice amongst the Irish honours.

I have not noticed all the MS. variations in the monetary values assigned to the items, but, except where otherwise stated, have followed the A. version as being the most authoritative and seemingly the most correct.

CHAPTER XXVII [111]

THE GERALDINES IN MUNSTER IN THE THIRTEENTH CENTURY

From the time when Maurice Fitz Gerald and his kith and kin first set foot on the Wexford coast no family has so continuously played an important part in the drama of Irish history as the Geraldines. Sprung from the stock of Gerald of Windsor and Nest of Wales, they spread out in many branches and covered large tracts of the island in nearly all directions. The heads of the two principal branches became earls of Kildare and earls of Desmond respectively, but there were many important offshoots, such as the Fitz Williams, barons of Naas; the Fitz Maurices, barons of Kerry; the Carews, barons of Idrone; the Fitz Mileses, barons of Iverk; the Fitz Griffins, barons of Knocktopher; the Fitz Gibbons or white knights; the knights of Glinn; the knights of Kerry, and many others only less notable. The earlier members of the family, along with their kinsmen of the half-blood, took a pioneer's part in the first conquest, and to the literary productions of one of them, Gerald de Barry, we owe much of our knowledge of the early struggle. In the course of the centuries many members of the family have held the highest offices of state.

In their respective districts the heads of some branches have ruled at times with almost regal authority. They exercised the right of private warfare, and some of them [112]
with disastrous results to themselves even bore arms against the Crown. Like other families, they have had their ups and downs of fortune, and some lines have become extinct or indistinguishable, but it is hardly too much to say that there has not been a moment in the history of Ireland for seven centuries past when some descendant of Gerald of Windsor has not been conspicuous among Irishmen for his position, his power, or his abilities. To track out this great family through all its numerous ramifications is of course beyond the scope of this or of any purely historical work, if indeed it be within the power of man; but it is essential for the student of Irish history to keep these several lines distinct, and it is therefore more than a matter of mere genealogical interest to ascertain the precise starting-points of the main branches from the ancestral trunk.[1]

It will be remembered that Strongbow's grant to Maurice Fitz Gerald included the middle cantred of Offelan, a name which soon dropped out of use, but must be care-

1 For some corrections in the heretofore received pedigrees of the Geraldines in the twelfth and thirteenth cenluries, see my papers on 'The Fitz-Geralds, Barons of Offaly', in Journal R.S.A.I., vol. xliv (1914), pp. 99–112; and on 'The Origin of the Fitz Maurices, Barons of Kerry and Lixnaw', in Eng. Hist. Review, vol. xxix (1914), pp. 302–15; and also a correction touching the Barons of Naas, in a review of the Gormanston Register, ibid., vol. xxxi (1916), pp. 488–9.

[113] fully distinguished from Offaly.[2] This cantred, lying in the northern part of the pre-
sent County Kildare, descended to Maurice's eldest son, William, who retained in his
own hands the honour of Naas, of which he is reckoned first baron, while he gave half
the cantred with centres at Maynooth and Rathmore to his brother Gerald.[3] This Ger-
ald Fitz Maurice, who was ancestor of the earls of Kildare, was also entitled at his
death in 1203 to the castles and lands of Lea and Geashill,[4] the principal Anglo-Nor-
man centres in Offaly, and as such has rightly been regarded as first Geraldine, Baron
of Offaly. The barony of Offaly, however, had been granted by Strongbow to Robert
de Bermingham, and Gerald appears to have acquired it by his marriage with Eva de
Bermingham, who was presumably daughter and heiress of Strongbow's grantee.[5]
Gerald also held lands in Imokilly, County Cork, which he presumably derived,
[114] directly or indirectly, from his uncle, Robert Fitz Stephen,[6] and here later on we find
his descendants lords of thc manor of Inchiquin and with seignorial rights in the town
of Youghal.

When dealing with the primary infeudation of the present county of Limerick,[7] we saw that three of the sons of the first Maurice Fitz Gerald obtained lands there. These in the order of birth were William, Baron of Naas, who obtained Carrickittle in the barony of Small County, Gerald, Baron of Offaly, who obtained Croom in the valley of the Maigue, and Thomas, who obtained Shanid, 'the most ancient house' of his successors, the earls of Desmond, in Connello. It is indeed a noteworthy fact that the extension of the Anglo-Norman settlement into the territory of the O'Briens, as indeed afterwards into the territories of the Mac Carthys and the O'Connors, was not brought about by new-comers, but was principally the work of those who had already obtained a foothold elsewhere in Ireland. In fact, the little band of kinsmen and neighbours that came from South Wales—Cambro-Normans and Flemings rather than Anglo-Normans—settled, increased, and multiplied principally in the province of Munster. From the very first it was their complaint, voiced with some exaggeration by Gerald de Barry, that they, who were the pioneers of the conquest, were given the remoter lands on the Irish marches, while the more profitable lands near the coasts of Leinster were reserved for new-comers. The grant of the kingdom of Cork in 1177 to

2 Offelan, *Ui Faelain*, divided into three cantreds, included roughly the northern half of the County Kildare; while at this time Offaly, *Ui Failghe*, included the present King's County east of Tullamore, and the two northern baronies of Queen's County, but I think very little, if any, of the present baronies of Offaly in Co. Kildare. 3 *Ante*, vol. i, pp. 379–80 [p. 144]. The cantred of Wicklow was also included in Strongbow's grant, but the castle of Wicklow was resumed by the Crown after Maurice's death. The barons of Naas, however, retained lands there (Cal. Docs. Irel., vol. i, no. 1757), some or all of which David Fitz William, third baron of Naas, granted to his brother Maurice to be held by the service of one knight: Gormanston Register, f. 190 d. This grant was confirmed in 1234: Cal. Docs Irel., vol. i, no. 2169. 4 Rot. Pat. 5 John p. 38, Cal. no. 195. 5 For this marriage and presumed origin of the Fitz Gerald property in Offaly see my paper on 'The Fitz Geralds, Barons of Offaly', as above. Eva de Bermingham, Gerald's widow, afterwards married (1) Geoffrey Fitz Robert, lord of Kells in Ossory, and (2) Geoffrey de Marisco, who held Offaly in her right and, after her death, by 'the curtesy of England'. So I understand Patent Rolls, 11 Hen. III, p. 96, Cal. no. 1458; cf. Close Rolls, 25 Hen. III, p. 215, Cal. no. 2493, where Robert de Mariscis, Geoffrey's son, is called brother (of the half-blood) of Maurice, the justiciar, son of Gerald. 6 *Ante*, vol. ii, p. 44, note 3 [p. 168, note 32]. 7 *Ante*, vol. ii, pp. 164–5 [p. 217].

Robert Fitz Stephen and Miles de Cogan determined many of them—Barrys, Carews, Cauntetons, Barrets, Fitz Geralds—to settle there, and they were soon afterwards fol- [115] lowed by Prendergasts and Roches, who had been their Flemish neighbours about Haverford. It was the adventurers from South Wales that seemingly first penetrated under Meiler Fitz Henry into Kerry, and it was men of the same stock who in the kingdom of Limerick south of the Shannon ultimately secured the lion's share of the spoil. Even in Connaught the first permanent settlers in the beginning of the thirteenth century were Gilbert, son of Jocelin of Angle in Pembrokeshire, or Mac Goisdelbh (Costello), as he came to be called, and the 'Welshmen of Tirawley'; and though Richard de Burgh was the chief figure in the final conquest of that province, among his principal supporters, who obtained large grants of lands there, were Fitz Geralds, Prendergasts, Roches, Barrys, and others of half-Welsh extraction or provenance.

Wherever these semi-Cambrians went they retained racial characteristics distinct from both Anglo-Normans and native Irish. The long training which they and their ancestors had undergone in somewhat similar conditions among hostile Welsh tribes had taught them the best methods of coping with the Irish in war, while when peace was made their half-Welsh origin inclined them the more readily to intermarry with the families of Irish nobles and to conform to Irish modes of life. Though it is an exaggeration to say that they ever became as a body 'Hibernis ipsis hiberniores', yet even in the thirteenth century these Cambro-Normans were less removed from the Irish in habits and sentiments than were the new-comers of more purely Anglo-Norman origin, and to diverse racial characteristics may in part at least be ascribed the antagonisms which from time to time broke out between them and the Marshals, lords of Leinster, the de [116] Burghs, lords of Connaught, and the Butlers, lords of Kilkenny and Ormond.

Hereafter we shall have occasion to mention other branches of the Geraldines, but we are now principally concerned with the descendants of Thomas, one of the younger sons of the first Maurice Fitz Gerald. This Thomas 'of Shanid', as we may call him, was one of the principal tenants of the Crown in County Limerick.[8] He is said to have married a sister of Geoffrey de Marisco, but for this marriage no good authority is forthcoming.[9] He was, however, closely connected with Geoffrey, who shared in the exploitation of Limerick, and soon after 1211 married Eva de Bermingham, widow of his brother Gerald. Along with Geoffrey he led a contingent from Munster to join King John's army in Ireland in 1210,[10] and in the same year he took part in the expedition led by Geoffrey into Connaught which resulted in the King of Connaught submitting to King John's will.[11] He was one of the magnates of Ireland who protested their loyalty to the king in 1211,[12] and he died about the close of 1213.[13]

8 He appears as juror on two important inquisitions held in Limerick in 1201: 'Black Book of Limerick' (Mac Caffrey) pp. 27, 29. 9 Burke, 'Extinct Peerages'. Lodge (Archdall) makes Thomas, father of John of Callann, marry Ellinor, daughter of Sir William Morrie, but the widow of Thomas Fitz Maurice is called Sabina (usually a latinized form of the Irish *Sadhbh*) in Fine Roll, 16 John (Hardy), p. 527, when she and Nicholas Fitz Leon fined for the custody of his land and heir. The custody was, however, given to Thomas Fitz Anthony in l 215. 10 Rot. de Prest. (Hardy), pp. 188, 202; *ante*, vol. ii, p. 248 [p. 250]. 11 Annals of Clonmacnois, p. 223; *ante*, vol. ii, p. 284 [p. 264]. 12 Cal. Docs. Irel., vol. i, no. 448; *ante*, vol. ii, p. 310 [p. 274]. 13 Rot. Claus., 16 John, p. 186; AnD. Inisfallen (Dublin MS.) where he is called *Tomás*

[117] The heir of this Thomas, as is well known, was John Fitz Thomas, often called by late writers 'John of Callann' from the scene of his death in 1261, to distinguish him from his namesake, but hardly contemporary, John Fitz Thomas of Offaly, afterwards first Earl of Kildare. It would be better, however, to speak of the former as 'John Fitz Thomas of Desmond', as he was ancestor of the earls of Desmond and was himself the first of the family to hold lands there. But Thomas of Shanid had another son Maurice, who was in all probability the real founder and eponymous progenitor of the house of Fitz Maurice of Kerry, as to the origin of which our professed genealogists have been strangely astray.[14] To these sons of Thomas Fitz Maurice we shall return by and by, but so much having been premised about the Geraldines up to this point, it will be necessary briefly to review the rival forces in South Munster, before piecing together, so far as our scanty authorities permit, the story of the Anglo-Norman attempt—for it was only partially successful—to gain control in Desmond.

Early in the thirteenth century the eastern part of the present county of Cork, as well as the present county of Limerick, seems to have been in the hands of English landholders and to have been thickly settled by them. The original seignories granted
[118] to Robert Fitz Stephen and Miles de Cogan, so far at least as there had been an effective occupation in pursuance of the grant, seem to have devolved upon a Carew and a de Courcy respectively, though the precise connexion of the new tenants in chief with the original grantees is matter of conjecture.[15] In 1207, however, Philip de Prendergast and Richard de Cogan received extensive grants from the Crown, the former in the district between Cork and Inishannon, where the important manor of 'Beuver' (Beauvoir) or Carrigaline was afterwards formed, and the latter in Muskerry, where his descendants long held the manors of Dundrinan and Carrigrohane More.[16] By these grants and some others of 1207 the lands were to be held of the king in chief, and the seignories of the heirs of the original grantees were ignored—perhaps because no effective settlement had been made in these districts.

From the inquisition taken on the death of Gerald, son of Philip de Prendergast, in 1251, we can gauge the importance of the manor of Beuver. There were eleven tenants who held by knight's service, besides many free tenants at rents, and there were two mar-
[119] ket-towns, Carrigaline and Douglas, each with a large district of burgage lands.[17] In 1207 the Abbey de Albo Tractu was founded for Cistercians at a place about two miles south

Mac Muiris mic Gerailt, and this description confirms the position assigned to him in the more recent pedigrees of the line of Desmond. 14 See my paper on 'The Fitz Maurices, Barons of Kerry and Lixnaw, afterwards Earls of Kerry', as above, where the alleged descent from Raymond le Gros is clearly disproved, and the true descent from this Maurice Fitz Thomas of the Geraldines indicated with reasonable confidence. 15 *Ante*, vol. ii, pp. 47–50 [pp. 169–70]. As regards Robert Fitz Stephen's moiety, further research has established other links in the chain, and the probable devolution in the line of Carews is given in an appendix to this chapter. 16 Rot. Chart., 9 John, pp. 171 b and 173. Dundrinan is to be identified with Castlemore in the parish of Moviddy on the river Bride in East Muskerry: Cox's Description of Cork, c. 1685, in Journal R.S.A.I., vol. xxxii (1902), p. 363. It must be distinguished from the 'Castle of Mora', where John de Cogan, senior, had a grant of a fair in 1252: Cal. Chart. Rolls, Hen. III, vol. i. p. 412. The latter was near Mourne Abbey (Mainister na Mona), and lay on the direct line between Buttevant and Cork; cf. Cal. Docs. Irel., vol. iii, pp. 267, 275. 'Mora' is Latin for the Irish *móin móna*, 'a moor'. 17 Cal. Docs. Irel., vol. i, no. 3202.

of Carrigaline. The monks came from Ty Gwyn or Alba Landa, now Whitland near Tenby,[18] and the foundation may confidently be connected with the settlers from South Wales. Gerald de Prendergast also held of David de Barry a large manor at Ballacha in Orrery in the extreme north of the county. This place, after passing to the de Cogans, was long known as Rathcogan. In 1662, however, the first Earl of Orrery changed what he called 'the heathenish name of Rathgoggan' to Charleville, which he thought more euphonious and more appropriate to the times.[19] The lands of Gerald de Prendergast passed through his daughters to John de Cogan, junior (son of John de Cogan, senior, and grandson of Richard de Cogan), and to Maurice de Rochford, the former obtaining the Cork manors,[20] and the latter those in counties Wexford and Limerick.

Among the numerous landholders in County Cork who were not at first regarded as tenants in chief, the Barrys stand out prominently. The senior line, descended from Philip de Barry, nephew and feoffee of Robert Fitz Stephen,[21] held the manors of [120]
Castlelyons and Carrigtohill in the barony of Barrymore, and Buttevant in that of Orrery, while an offshoot, perhaps a little later, was seated at Rathbarry and Timoleague in the barony of Barryroe. Then there were the Roches in Fermoy, the Barretts and Cauntetons (Condons) in the baronies bearing their names, and the Fitz Geralds, the Carews, and others in Imokilly. In fact Eastern Cork became dotted over with small manorial towns, and in 1299 there were at least thirty-eight, the names of which are known, where markets were held.[22] There were, no doubt, many Irish *betaghs* distributed about the various manors, and in some districts, as for instance in East Muskerry (which, however, belongs rather to West Cork) whole septs seem to have remained, subject to rent; but so far as appears no Irish chief exercised sway in Eastern Cork.

The position was very different in West Munster. Here the Normans had hardly anywhere penetrated, but great movements had recently taken place amongst the Irish clans. We have already seen how the hereditary feud between the Dalcassians and the Eoghanachts manifested itself on the morrow of the battle of Clontarf, and how the conflict was for the moment averted owing to the quarrel which arose between the Eoghanacht leaders, Cian, son of Molloy, and Donnell, son of Duvdavorenn.[23] Now Cian's son Mahon was eponym of the O'Mahonys, and Donnell's son Donough was eponym of the O'Donoghues. Both families belonged to a powerful tribe-group whose original territory is now represented approximately by the baronies of Kinalmeaky and Kinalea near Cork.[24] In the course of the eleventh century the O'Donoghues were dri- [121]
ven out by the O'Mahonys and migrated to the region about Killarney, whence they drove the O'Carrolls and other earlier occupants westwards to Iveragh. Here, in the barony of Magunihy, the O'Donoghues eventually formed two branches, whose chief-

18 Brut y Tywys, 1224, and annals in Chart. St. Mary's Abbey, Dublin, vol. ii, p. 235. 19 Smith's 'Cork', vol. i, p. 303. Thus do places run the risk of losing their historical associations. The Irish name 'Ballacha' seems to survive in the neighbouring parish of Ballyhay. 20 Cf. Pipe Roll (Ireland), 10 Ed. I, 36th Rep. D. K., p. 62, 'Beuver'. In 1439, the representative of the de Cogans granted all his possessions in Cork, including the original Prendergast property, to James Fitz Gerald, Earl of Desmond: Cal. Carew Papers, Misc. 362. 21 *Ante*, vol. ii, pp. 41, 43–4 [pp. 167–8]. 22 Justiciary Rolls, vol. i, p. 265 [000]. 23 *Ante*, vol. i, pp. 32–4 [pp. 6–7]. 24 For these clans consult 'The O'Mahonys of Kinelmeky and Ivagha', by Canon O'Mahony, in the Cork Historical and Archaeological Journal (1907).

tains respectively were O'Donoghue Mor, with centre at Ross Castle on the lower lake of Killarney, and O'Donoghue of the Glens, about the upper reaches of the river Flesk. The O'Mahonys would now appear to have been supreme in Kinalea and Kinalmeaky until extruded by the Prendergasts and Cogans, but even before the coming of the Normans the clan is said to have extended westward up the Bandon River to West Carbery, where they wrested some lands from the O'Driscolls, O'Cowhigs, and others. As we shall see, the O'Mahonys were eventually subjected to a branch of the Mac Carthys, and confined by them to the district between Bantry Bay and that known by the unhappy name of Roaring Water.[25]

In 1178 and subsequently the O'Briens expelled the O'Donovans from Croom and Bruree in the valley of the Maigue, and other Eoghanacht septs from different parts of County Limerick, and their expulsion paved the way for the Geraldine settlement
[122] there.[26] The O'Donovans fled southward across Mangerton and settled in the northern parts of Carbery, where Castledonovan preserves their name and marks their principal centre. The O'Driscolls and their kinsmen, thus pressed by the O'Donovans and the O'Mahonys on the northwest, and afterwards by the Normans on the east, were eventually confined to the district between Ivahagh and Castlehaven, only a comparatively small portion of their ancient tribe-land, which is said to have been at one time conterminous with the diocese of Ross.[27]

To the forward movement of the Anglo-Normans through southern Tipperary in 1192[28] may presumably be ascribed the expulsion of the O'Sullivans from the valley of the Suir about Clonmel and Caher. They subdued the earlier occupants[29] of two of the great peninsulas in Kerry and Cork, and became divided into two main branches. O'Sullivan Mor held sway over a large district between Dingle Bay and Kenmare River, and O'Sullivan Bere eventually occupied most of the peninsula between Kenmare River and Bantry Bay. Similarly the O'Keefes of Fermoy, who settled in Duhallow, were presumably driven out of their former seat by the Roches, who seem to have been settled in Fermoy before the close of the twelfth century.[30]

[123] The above is necessarily an imperfect outline of the principal movements of the Irish clans into Desmond, and their positions there prior to the second decade of the thirteenth century. Contemporary authorities are few, and inferences from subsequent events more or less doubtful. It seems clear, however, that at the opening of the century the population-groups of Desmond were still in a state of flux. Septs that from of old had possessed the land were disappearing or becoming obscure. New and more vigorous ones had reduced them to subjection or driven them further afield. Over all, the Mac Carthys of the royal line of South Munster, which had been associated with Cashel, were recognized as overlords, and as such possessed demesne lands in differ-

25 This district became known as Ivahagh, an anglicized form of *Uibh Echach*, the tribal name of the O'Mahonys; also as *Fonn Iartharach*, 'the western land'. According to Canon Mahony their tribe-lands were at one time co-extensive with the Diocese of Cork, and extended from Mizen Head to Lough Mahon, but were cut in two by the O'Donovans and the Mac Carthys. **26** *Ante*, vol. ii, pp. 160–1 [pp. 215–16]. **27** Consult 'Genealogy of the Corca Laidhe' in Miscellany of the Celtic Society, App. E, and O'Donovan's remarks, pp. 141–2. **28** *Ante*, vol. ii, p. 145 [p. 209], &c. **29** These were O'Sheas, O'Moriartys, O'Connells, and others: Topog. Poems, p. 109. **30** *Ante*, vol. ii, p. 45 [pp. 168–9].

ent parts of Desmond and received dues of varying amount from the different clans.[31] Only in Kerry north of the river Maine, which properly speaking does not belong to Desmond, had some slight settlement been effected by Meiler Fitz Henry in pursuance of a grant made to him by King John in the year 1200.[32] The de Cogans had penetrated into East Muskerry, the de Prendergasts were forming manors in Kinalea, [124]
and the de Courcys seem to have been established about Kinsale; but notwithstanding some earlier dealings by the Normans with land along the southern coast, it seems doubtful if they had made any effective settlements elsewhere in West Munster.

Of affairs in Desmond during the first half of the thirteenth century little is to be learned from the printed Irish Annals, but the manuscript Annals of Inisfallen preserved in Dublin, though a late compilation in Irish and not to be implicitly trusted, embodies some early sources of Munster history not to be found elsewhere.[33] Checked and supplemented by occasional entries in the records and such other contemporary sources as are available, these annals enable a slight outline, trustworthy as far as it goes, to be drawn.

After the death in 1206 of Donnell, son of Dermot Mac Carthy, there were from time to time rival claimants among the Mac Carthys for the position of head of the ruling family. The chieftain, though still sometimes called King of Desmond, may more properly be described by his Irish title of Mac Carthy Mor. Donnell left three sons who figure in succeeding years, namely, Dermot called 'of Dundrinan',[34] Cormac Finn or 'the Fair', ancestor of the line of Mac Carthy Mor, and Donnell Got or 'the [125]
Stammerer', ancestor of the line of Mac Carthy Reagh. There was also an uncle, Fineen, who at first succeeded to the chieftainship, but he was deposed immediately by Dermot of Dundrinan, and slain by the O'Sullivans in 1209. Dermot of Dundrinan now became king, but in 1212 he was taken prisoner by the English of Cork, and his brother, Cormac Finn, stepped for the moment into his shoes. Dermot, however, seems to have come to terms with the men of Cork. He married an English lady of that county, Petronilla or Peronelle Bloet,[35] and the Cork people henceforth appear to have supported him against his brother, Cormac Finn.

31 For a detailed account of 'The Lordship of Mac Carthy Mor', as disclosed by the Survey of Desmond with accompanying maps (1597) in vol. 625 of the Carew MSS., Lambeth Library, see the careful papers of Prof. W. F. Butler in Journal R.S.A.I., 1906–7. 32 Rot. Chart., 2 John, p. 77 b, where the parcels are two cantreds in 'Kery', namely 'Akunkerry' (or better Akmikerry, i.e. *aicme Charraighe*, a name partly preserved in the thirteenth-century deanery of Hackmys and in the present barony of Trughanacmy), and 'Hyerba' (*Ui Ferba*, also anglicized Offerba and Offeriba about the coast of Tralee Bay), and a third cantred in Cork, namely 'Yoghenacht Lokhelen' (*Eoghanacht Locha Lein*, a district in the barony of Magunihy about the lakes of Killarney). This third cantred is stated in the same record to belong to 'Humeriedae', i.e. O'Moriarty. So we must conclude that the O'Donoghues had not yet effected a complete conquest. 33 Writing on December 23, 1845, O'Donovan says with reference to the compilers of these annals: 'They had, however, some Munster annals which we have not, and from these they have extracted various passages relating to Desmond not to be found in any other compilation that I know of. There are several copies of these annals. The best Irish text is T.C.D. MS. H. 1. 7. They are of course to be distinguished from the ancient Annals of Inisfallen preserved in the Bodleian Library (Rawlinson 503). 34 So called apparently, as was the habit with this Munster annalist, from the place of his death. In these annals indeed his name is always written *Diarmaid duna Dronáin*, but *dún draighnin* seems the proper form. It was anglicized Dundrinan, Eccl. Tax., Cal. Docs. Irel., vol. v, p. 321. 35 In March 1217 a mandate was issued to Geof-

An attempt was now made by the English to gain control over the whole of Desmond. The movement seems to have proceeded from the settlers in County Limerick aided by the Government, rather than from the settlers about Cork. First we
[126] are told, under date 1214, that 'Donough Cairbrech O'Brien and the sheriff, with the English of Munster and Leinster, marched to destroy Desmond on Dermot of Dundrinan'.[36] As usual the invaders supported one Irish claimant against the other, and Cormac Finn was in their host. 'Dermot, joined by the English of Cork, came at the head of an army to Durrus, where he encamped for twenty days against Cormac Finn, who was at the other side of Mangerton all that time.'[37] We do not hear of any collision between the two forces, but Dermot put to death the sons of Donnell Mor O'Sullivan, who, we may infer, supported his opponent. Then under date 1215 is a remarkable entry, including a record of castle-building in Desmond, which certainly was not all accomplished in one year, but was probably spread over a longer period of time. This entry may be rendered as follows: 'A great war broke out between Dermot of Dundrinan and his own brother Cormac Finn, the English assisting on both sides. In the course of this war the foreigners overran all Desmond and gained much territory and power, and built castles and strongholds for themselves against the Gael.'

[127] Following this is the list of castles.[38] Giving the places mentioned their modern names, we may group them as follows: (1) A string of castles was built along the valley of the river Maine in Kerry at Currans, Molahiffe, Clonmellane, Castlemaine, and Calanafersy, and the line was completed to the sea by a castle at Killorglin near the mouth of the river Laune. This was the line which for centuries separated Kerry proper from Desmond, and the castles were evidently intended to protect the settlement in Kerry to which we have referred from attacks of the Irish of Desmond. These castles seem to have been erected by John and Maurice, sons of Thomas of Shanid, and grandsons of the first Maurice Fitz Gerald, whom we soon find as the principal landowners in Kerry.[39]

(2) A castle was also built by the same Geraldines at Dunlo to the west of the lower lake of Killarney, and another by a Roche somewhere in the level district to the east of the lakes. These were also in territory formerly granted to Meiler Fitz Henry, which

frey de Marisco, the justiciar, to cause Petronilla Bloet, wife of Dermot Mac Carthy, King of Cork, to have her *maritagium* which Thomas her brother gave to her; Rot. Claus., Hen. III, p. 302. The doubt probably arose because Dermot in this year took the newly-built castle of Timoleague: Ann. Inisfallen, 1217. Many writers have absurdly identified Petronilla's husband with the old King Dermot slain in 1185: see *ante*, vol. ii, p. 100 [p. 190]. Thomas Bloet was an official of King John, and in 1211 he fined to have the lands of Milo de Cogan with his niece (or granddaughter) in marriage: Cal. Docs. Irel., vol. i, nos. 422, 1504. He was one of the magnates who joined in the declaration of loyalty in 1212: ibid., no. 448. His heirs held a knight's fee under the Prendergasts: ibid., no. 3203. 36 Ann. Inisfallen, as above. Who was 'the sheriff'? If the date be correct he *may* have been Geoffrey de Marisco; but if, as is more probable, 1215 was the true date, 'the sheriff' was probably Thomas Fitz Anthony, the newly appointed seneschal of Decies and Desmond. 37 Ibid. Durrus is the name of a parish in West Carbery, Co. Cork. It is twenty-two miles south of Mangerton. In July 1216 'Connac Lechaune', a corruption, I suspect, of Cormac le Chanu (*canutus*), i. e. Cormac Finn, made a fine of 100 marks to have land in Cork: Fine Rolls, 17 and 18 John, p. 556. This entry seems to point to 1215 as the true date, and at any rate throws light on the events recorded in the annals of Inisfallen. 38 Compare O'Donovan's note (y) to Four Masters, 1215. 39 'The castle of the Maine' (Castlemaine) and that at Killorglin are expressly ascribed to *Muiris mac Tomáis mic Gerailt*, and

presumably was now given as an escheat to John Fitz Thomas, who held it at his death.[40]

(3) Another group, consisting of the castles of Dunkerron Capanacush and Ardtully, was erected by a Carew about the head of the estuary of Kenmare, and he also erected another castle at Dunnamark near Bantry. The name of this Carew is not given, but he was presumably head of the branch of Carews that settled in Imokilly. As is shown in the appendix to this chapter, there was a Richard de Carew, possibly a younger son of Odo de Carew, eldest brother of Raymond le Gros, but more probably an illegitimate son of Raymond himself, who held lands in Imokilly about the close of the twelfth century. He married Raghenild, 'daughter of Mac Carthy,'and was father of Robert de Carew, who was one of the chief magnates of the county in 1221, and ancestor of the Carews who held the Fitz Stephen moiety of Cork in the last quarter of the thirteenth century. The Mac Carthy marriage would have facilitated the acquisition of lands in Desmond. This Richard de Carew, however, seems to have died in 1205, and his son Robert seems to have come of age shortly before 1216, so that probably the latter was the castle-builder about the heads of the estuaries of Kenmare and Bantry. [128]

(4) Lastly, a number of castles were placed along the south coast of County Cork at important natural harbours or inlets, namely, one at Muntervary,[41] the tongue of land between Bantry Bay and Dunmanus Bay, one at Baltimore, the ancient *Dún na séad,* [129] and another on Ringarogy Island near by;[42] two in the neighbourhood of Glandore,[43] ascribed to a Barrett; and two more at Timoleague and Dundeady (or Galley Head) by Nicholas Boy (*buidhe*) de Barry. Hitherto the most westerly castles on the south coast would seem to have been the de Courcy strongholds at Ringrone opposite Kinsale, and at Oldernass or the Old Head of Kinsale.

From this account of the castle-builders in Kerry and Desmond, and of the places where the castles were erected, it appears that the settlers were mainly Geraldines; that the district in Kerry proper, the escheated lands of Meiler Fitz Henry, were now

the othors more vaguely to *mac Muiris mic Gerailt*, which must mean grandson of Maurice Fitz Gerald, as no son of his was alive in 1215. 40 I identify the 'Yoghenacht Lokhelen' (*Eoghanacht Locha Léin*) of the grant to Meiler (Rot. Chart., 2 John, p. 77b) with 'Ogenathy Donechud' (*Eoghanacht ui Donnchada*) of the inquisition touching the lands of John Fitz Thomas (Cal. Inquis. P. M., 11 Ed. I, no. 437). The district is now roughly represented by the barony of Magunihy, or part of it. Dunlo is written *dún lóich*, as in Four Masters, 1570. Roche's castle is said to have been in 'Airloch', a name hitherto unidentified. I think it represents the large district known as *Airluachair* or *Irlochir*, 'O'Keefe's Country' (Book of Rights, p. 75, note; Onom. Goed.), or more particularly the plain of Luachair belonging to O'Dunadhaigh (a name which, according to O'Donovan, was anglicized Denny): Topog. Poems, p. 114 and notes, and see *infra*, p. 138, n. 3 [p. 349, note 70]. The particular Roche was probably Gerald de Roche, to whom was given in marriage another of the daughters of Thomas Fitz Anthony. 41 This castle is ascribed to Mac Cuidighthe, evidently a name given by the Irish to some Anglo-Norman, as in cases of Mac Feorais, Mac Muiris, &c. Probably it represents Mac Odo, and refers to Stephen, son of Odo, l'Ercedekne (or Archdeacon). Like John Fitz Thomas and Gerald de Roche, he married one of the daughters of Thomas Fitz Anthony, and his descendants were often called 'McOdo', or later, ' Cody ', by the Irish. 42 These are ascribed to *Sleibhneach*, meaning perhaps the heir of Robert Fitz Stephen: cf. *infra*, p. 134, note 3 [p. 347, note 56]. 43 William Barrett held at his death 'Clardor' of Maurice de Carew: Justiciary Rolls, vol. i, p. 228. This was probably the district about Glandore.

guarded by the castles on the line of the river Maine; and that the castles on the harbours of Desmond were seemingly placed with a view to the domination of that part of the kingdom of Cork originally granted to Robert Fitz Stephen and Miles de Cogan, but hitherto not brought under control.

Considerable further light is thrown on this movement and on the persons who guided it by the public records of the period. In the summer of 1215, immediately
[130] after the Great Charter was wrung from him, King John, as we have already noticed,[44] paid unwonted attention to the pacification of Ireland, and in particular made a number of grants to individuals, restoring to them the lands of which he had deprived them, and removing many possible causes of disaffection and disturbance. We have mentioned the most important of these grants and have attributed them to the influence of the great Earl Marshal, whose wisdom and fidelity the king in the time of stress and danger had at last learned to appreciate. We may perhaps further see the finger of William Marshal in the policy now pursued with regard to Desmond, where the peace was disturbed by the conflict between the rival Mac Carthys. Hitherto little or nothing had been done to bring Desmond, as distinguished from the rest of the ancient kingdom of Cork, under the effective control of the Crown. But now, on July 8, 1215, the king granted to Thomas Fitz Anthony and his heirs the custody of the counties of Waterford and Desmond and all the king's demesnes in those counties and all escheats therein for a rent of 250 marks; and it was provided that Thomas should guard at his own cost the said counties, castles, and the king's lands in the march and elsewhere, and should be reimbursed the expense of fortifying castles in any of the king's escheats of which he had the custody.[45] Now Thomas Fitz Anthony held the manor of Grenan or Thomastown (as it came to be called) in Kilkenny of the Earl
[131] Marshal, and he was one of his most trusted men. He was at this time seneschal of the earl's lands in Leinster.[46] The earl was one of the witnesses of the king's grant, and we may be sure that the selection of Thomas Fitz Anthony was due to the earl's counsel.

At the same time the king, for a fine of 600 marks, gave to Thomas Fitz Anthony the custody of the lands and heirs of Thomas Fitz Maurice,[47] and committed to Geoffrey de Marisco (who had just been appointed justiciar in place of Archbishop Henry) Maurice, younger son of Thomas Fitz Maurice, to be taken with him to Ireland. He had been a hostage for his father, but was now liberated.[48]

There can be little doubt that the forward movement resulting in the incastellation of the coasts of Desmond was directly connected with this comprehensive grant to Thomas Fitz Anthony, and that Geoffrey de Marisco was instructed to assist him in obtaining as full seisin as possible. To pacify the Mac Carthys and further the object, arrangements seem to have been made with Cormac Finn, who for a fine of 100 marks

44 *Ante*, vol. ii, pp. 313–19 [pp. 275–7]. 45 Rot. Chart., 17 John, p. 210 b. In the king's *entourage* at this time were many Irish magnates, including William Marshal, Henry de Londres, Geoffrey de Marisco, Richard de Burgh, Roger Pipard, Ralph Petit, Walter de Ridelisford (the younger), and others. 46 Rot. de Finibus, 17 and 18 John, p. 551. 47 Rot. Pat., 17 John, p. 147 (July 4). 48 Ibid., p. 148 b (July 7), where he is called *Mauricius filius Thome filii Mauricii*. There can really be no doubt about his identity. There is no other Thomas, son of Maurice, of the Geraldines known to history at this time.

was to obtain a grant of lands in Cork from the king,[49] while his brother Dermot was recognized as king of the Irish of Desmond.

By the above grant Thomas Fitz Anthony and his heirs obtained only the custody of the counties of Waterford and Desmond (or Cork), and though great powers were given to him to reimburse himself out of the king's escheats for the expense of forti- [132]
fying castles, yet it would seem to have been contemplated that, subject to such reimbursement, the escheats would inure for the benefit of the Crown. But Thomas Fitz Anthony, the custodian of Desmond, and Geoffrey de Marisco, the justiciar, seem to have made King Henry's grant of the kingdom of Cork to Robert Fitz Stephen and Miles de Cogan the basis of the new tenures now created. The obvious reason for so doing was to avoid subjecting the lands to the liability of increased rents and services to the Crown which would result if the lands were treated as escheats of the Crown. Accordingly, Robert de Carew and Patrick de Courcy were regarded as entitled to the benefit of Henry's grant, while the interest of the Crown was confined to the sixty services originally reserved. How their titles were made out has long been a moot point, and several untenable hypotheses have been from time to time put forward. For reasons given in the appendix to this chapter it seems probable that Patrick de Courcy married Margery de Cogan, granddaughter and heiress of Miles de Cogan (and seemingly widow of Thomas Bloet), and that Patrick in her right and his issue by her became entitled to the de Cogan moiety; while Richard, father of Robert de Carew, was either nephew or more probably illegitimate son of Raymond le Gros (who we are told succeeded to the inheritance of Robert Fitz Stephen), and was regarded by the barons from the motives above-mentioned as entitled to the Fitz Stephen moiety. In any case there was a flaw in his title, for if, as seems to have been the fact, Robert Fitz Stephen was a bastard and died without leaving legitimate issue, his moiety cannot have passed by inheritance. In fact, as we shall see, more than a century later the [133]
Crown took advantage of this flaw in the Carew title to confiscate the castle and manor of Dunnamark and a moiety of the lordship of Desmond, then in the hands of the first earl.

To this period, too, should be ascribed the acquisition by the sons of Thomas Fitz Maurice of their lands in Kerry. Meiler Fitz Henry, to whom these lands had been granted by King John (in apparent derogation of his father's grant of the kingdom of Cork from Brandon Head to Lismore), was now an old man without legitimate children, and about this time he entered the monastery of Old Connell in Kildare, founded by himself, and his lands in Kerry, as elsewhere, became escheats.[50] He had given the cantred of Offerba in Corcaguiny to John de Clahull, who was now confirmed therein by the Crown.[51] Here the family of de Clahull can be traced for some generations, and in their lands about Tralee Bay they enjoyed the right (often abused) of wreck of the sea.[52] Judging from later documents the distribution of other cantreds

49 Rot. de Finibus, 17 and 18 John, p. 556. 50 Rot. Claus., 18 John, p. 272; Cal. Docs. Ireland, vol. i, no. 691; and cf. no. 3082. 51 Rot. de Finibus, 18 John, p. 598, and see English Historical Review, vol. xxix (1914), p. 307. 52 In 1284 Geoffrey de Clahull was granted the sergeancy of Kerry and wreck of the sea in his land of Offerba: Cal. Docs. Ireland, nos. 2194, 2198.

in Kerry seems to have been as follows: the cantred of Ossurys, the western extremity of Corcaguiny, was given to Robert, son of Geoffrey de Marisco,[53] the cantred of
[134] Acmikery, now Trughanacmy, to John Fitz Thomas,[54] and the cantred of Altry, afterwards known as Clanmaurice, to Maurice Fitz Thomas, while Geoffrey de Marisco himself retained the Castle of Killorglin.[55] Even here, in spite of King John's grant to Meiler Fitz Henry ignoring the de Cogan seignory, there is evidence that some at any rate of Meiler's lands were not treated as escheats of the Crown, but that the former seignory was now revived. In the inquisition taken in 1282 as to the lands of which John Fitz Thomas was seised at his death in 1261, it was found that he held the cantred of Acmikery of Miles de Courcy (son and heir of Patrick de Courcy) by the service of two knights.[56] It was apparently for their dealings with these escheats in Kerry and Desmond to the prejudice of the Crown that Geoffrey de Marisco in 1221 was superseded as justiciar, and that Thomas Fitz Anthony in 1223 and later was reprimanded by the Regency, and eventually deprived of the custody of Decies and Desmond. It is at any rate clear that the sons of Thomas Fitz Maurice owed their first footing in Kerry to the influence and favour of Geoffrey de Marisco and Thomas Fitz Anthony. The former was married to their uncle's widow, Eva de Bermingham, and
[135] the latter was their guardian, and he gave one of his daughters in marriage to John Fitz Thomas. Indeed, as already inferred, he seems to have made provision in Desmond for two of his other sons-in-law, namely, Gerald de Roche and Stephen l'Ercedekne (Archdeacon or Mc Odo).

Thus by putting together these various, but quite independent, sources, namely, the entries in the Annals of Inisfallen, the records as to the grants to Thomas Fitz Anthony, the evidence as to the recognition of the seignory of Desmond in the persons of Robert de Carew and Patrick de Courcy, and as to the dealings with the escheat of Meiler Fitz Henry's lands and the subsequent tenure of the same by John Fitz Thomas and his brother Maurice, we can obtain a trustworthy outline of when and how the Geraldines and others obtained lands in Kerry and Desmond. There was apparently no prolonged fighting, and certainly no considerable displacement of Irish septs, but the sites of these castles outside of Kerry, and no doubt considerable portions of land in their vicinity, were, as usual elsewhere, the rewards which the foreigners secured for their services to the chieftains they had assisted.

There were intermarriages, too, between the leading families of the two races, and these intermarriages are further indications that the settlement was effected with the consent and by the aid of some of the principal chieftains of Desmond. King Dermot, as has been mentioned, married a sister of Thomas Bloet, who was the first husband

53 Rot. Claus., 33 Hen. III, m. 16; Cal. Docs. Ireland, vol. i, no. 2976, where Ossuris is absurdly equated with Ossory. It represents the Irish *Aes Irruis*, 'people of the promontory': Onomasticon Goedelicum.

54 See Inquis. P. M. as to the lands of John Fitz Thomas: Cal. Docs. lreland, vol. ii, p. 429, and Cal. Inquis. P. M., Ed. I, vol. ii, no. 437; also English Historical Review) 'Origin of the Fitz Maurices, Barons of Kerry and Lixnaw,' vol. xxix (1914), p. 312, where my map, p. 305, shows the situation of these territories.

55 Cal. Docs. Ireland, vol. i, no. 2228.

56 The same inquisition states that John held half a carucate at Corleleye (*Corca Laidhe*) of [the heir of] Robert Fitz Stephen for the service of one knight: about Baltimore ?

of Margery Cogan, and Richard de Carew married Raghenild, daughter probably of the same King Dermot by a former wife, and he is said to have given a daughter in marriage to Dermot O'Mahony, one of whose sons appears to have been named [136]
Richard.[57] Dermot Mac Carthy's position as chieftain of the Irish and quasi-tenant of the Crown was recognized, and for about thirty years amicable relations with the Mac Carthys seem to have been generally maintained. In 1221, when Archbishop Henry superseded Geoffrey de Marisco as justiciar, letters of credence were addressed to Dermot Mac Carthy and to other Irish chieftains in the king's peace, as well as to the principal feudal tenants,[58] and in 1224 Dermot accompanied the feudal host against Hugh de Lacy, then in rebellion.[59] In 1229 he founded a Franciscan convent in Cork, and in the same or the next year he died.[60]

At about this time Thomas Fitz Anthony died, leaving heavy debts, and five daughters as co-heiresses.[61] The king, indeed, had been dissatisfied both with him and with Geoffrey de Marisco for their dealings with escheats. In 1223 he ordered the custody of Decies and Desmond to be taken into the king's hand, as Thomas had not come to him with his charter when summoned and 'had detained some of the king's escheats'; and in 1226–7 he committed the said custody to Richard de Burgh.[62] [137]

Dermot of Dundrinan was succeeded by his brother Cormac Finn, ancestor of the line of Mac Carthy Mor. In 1230 he took part in Richard de Burgh's campaign in Connaught when Felim, son of Cathal Crovderg O'Conor, was made king.[63] Taking advantage of the disturbances caused by the quarrel with Earl Richard Marshal in 1234, the Irish attacked Tralee, where they were defeated, seemingly by John Fitz Thomas, and Dermot, son of Cormac Finn, and others were slain.[64] About this time Cormac Finn imprisoned his brother Donnell Got, but soon afterwards liberated him, whereupon the latter 'committed an unneighbourly act' on O'Mahony by killing his sons and dispossessing him of his territory in Carbery.[65] This was the origin of the separate territory of Mac Carthy Reagh, or 'the Swarthy', a line descended from Donnell Got and in general independent of Mac Carthy Mor. In 1244 Cormac Finn was summoned by the king to join the intended expedition against the Scots,[66] and shortly before 1248 he died in the habit of a grey monk at his own 'longport' at Mashanaglass[67] near Macroom.

After the death of Cormac Finn there were renewed disputes between Donnell Got [138]
and his nephews about the chieftainship, and English settlers took part on different

57 See Cork Archaeological Society Journal, 2nd ser., vol. xiv, p. 79 58 Rot. Claus., 5 Hen. III, p. 476 b. 59 Ann. Loch Cé, 1224, where he is called Dermot 'Cluasach' Mac Carthy, from some peculiarity of his ears. 60 Ibid., 1230, and Four Masters, 1229. In the Annals of Inisfallen he is said to have been killed by lightning at Dundrinan. Hence the distinguishing name given to him in that compilation. 61 Before July 20, 1229: Cal. Docs. Irel., vol. i, no. 1714. His daughters were all married, and their husbands were Gerald de Roche, William de Cantilupe, Geoffrey de Norragh, John Fitz Thomas, and Stephen Archdeacon: Ir. Pipe Roll, 16 Hen. III, transcribed in Report of Record Commissioners, vol. i, pp. 333–6. 62 Cal. Docs. Irel., vol. i, nos. 1001, 1108, 1462, 1502. 63 Ann. Inisfallen, as above. 64 Ibid. The presence of John Fitz Thomas may be inferred from Cal. Docs. Irel., vol. ii, no. 89. 65 Bodleian Annals of Inisfallen, as quoted by O'Donovan, Celtic Miscellany, p. 142. 66 Close Rolls, 28 Hen. III, p. 255; Cal. Docs. Irel., vol. i, no. 2716, where he is called Cormac lethan (*Liathánach*) Mac Carthy, as in the Bodleian Annals of Inisfallen; see Celtic Soc. Miscellany, p. 13, note. 67 Ann. Inisfallen, R.I.A.

sides. Fineen, son of Dermot of Dundrinan, slew Geoffrey de Cogan, brother of John de Cogan, and some other settlers, and did great damage to the English until he was himself slain by his uncle Donnell Got and the Cogans in 1250.[68] Donnell Got, though under the protection of the king of England,[69] was slain next year by John Fitz Thomas,[70] who appears to have supported his rival Donnell Roe, son of Cormac Finn. This deed had serious consequences. Another Fineen, son of Donnell Got, described as usual from the place of his death as 'Fineen of Ringrone', now broke out in violence and rebellion. He burned to death O'Donoghue, his wife, brother, and three sons, in their house near Killarney. Then, assisted by O'Donovan, he slew Dermot O'Mahony near Enniskeen, thus consolidating and extending his possessions in Carbery. In 1259 he raided Kerry and there made 'great slaughters, burnings, and plunderings of the English'. Next year he burned the English castles at Dunnamark, Ringarogy Island,
[139] Dundeady, Rathbarry, and others.[71] Clearly he had his own ambitions to serve as well as his father's death to avenge.

Up to the recent disturbances the attempt to control Desmond by building castles in favourable positions on the coasts and harbours had seemingly met with considerable success. The castles built in 1215 had become centres of English influence, and others had been built since. An unwonted peace had prevailed. In 1244 John Fitz Thomas had obtained a grant of free chase and warren in Kerry, Muskerry, Magunihy, and Iveragh, as well as in his lands about Shanid;[72] and in 1252 John de Cogan had got a grant of a market and fair at his castle of Mora in Desmond.[73] But the dispute about the succession to Cormac Finn, and especially the outbreak of Fineen, son of Donnell Got, threatened to ruin the whole settlement.

In 1261, however, a great effort was made to crush Fineen. William de Dene, late sheriff of Cork and now justiciar, led the feudal host into Desmond. It consisted mainly of the Munster barons who undertook to finance the expedition,[74] and conspicuous
[140] amongst them was 'Clann Gerailt' or the Geraldines. John Fitz Thomas was clearly the prime mover in the expedition. In November 1259 he had obtained a grant in fee from Prince Edward of the lands of Decies and Desmond, the custody of which had formerly been held by his father-in-law, Thomas Fitz Anthony;[75] and just as the forward

68 Ann. Inisfallen, and Four Masters, 1250; and see Cal. Docs. Irel., vol. i, no. 3145, and vol. ii, no. 129. 69 Ibid., vol. i, no. 3160 (June 22, 1251). 70 Ann. Inisfallen, according to which Donnell Got is said to have been treacherously killed in Roche's house at Bally O'Denny, *a m-baile hui Dionuighe a tig an Roistigh*. O'Dionuighe seems to be another form of O'Dunadhaigh (Denny), chieftain of the plain of Luachair, the level part of the barony of Magunihy; see Topographical Poems, p. 114, and notes. If so, this confirms the identification given above, p. 127, n.2, of Airloch, where a castle was built in 1215 by Gerald de Roche. It would seem that while John de Cogan favoured the claims of Donnell Got, John Fitz Thomas supported his rival Donnell Roe, son of Cormac Finn, ancestor of the line of Mac Carthy Mor. 71 Ann. Inisfallen, as above, where the place-names are '*Dún-na-mbarc, Dún na n-Gall, Dún deide, Rath an bháraigh, Inis Eoghnain* [Inishannon?], and Caislean uabhair ('the fort of pride', perhaps Dunour in the parish of Kilcrohane?)'. In the Pipe Roll accounts for 1259–61, among the names of those owing fines is 'Fynyn, son of Dermot (?) Got Mac Karthy': 35 Rep. D. K., p. 37. 72 Cal. Docs. Irel., vol. i, no. 2680, where these places appear as 'Okonyl, Muskry, Kery, Yonach, and Orathat', i.e. *ui Conaill*, *Muscraighe*, *Ciarraighe*, *Eoghanacht*, and *ui Raihach*. It is not clear what *Mucscraighe* is intended, probably *Muscraighe tri maighe* in the barony of Orrery. 73 Ibid., vol. ii no. 121. 74 See Cal. Close Rolls, 3 Ed. I, p. 240. 75 Cal. Pat. Rolls (Ireland), 44 Hen. III,

movement of 1215 to gain control over Desmond followed close on the grant to Thomas Fitz Anthony, so the renewal of the grant to John Fitz Thomas was followed by an attempt to quell the growing turbulence of the Irish, who were not unnaturally chafing at their restricted bounds. Arnong the ranks of the English was Donnell Roe, son of Cormac Finn Mac Carthy, of the rival house of Mac Carthy Mor, with all the Irish he could muster—not very many perhaps, as 'the chiefs of the tribe of Eoghan' were with his cousin of Carbery. The opposing forces met on July 24, 1261, at a place called Callann of Glen Ruachtain (Glanarought) in the *tuath* of Kenmare. The site of the battle is still pointed out, where a mountain torrent called the Slaheny river rushes down through a narrow glen to join the Roughty, a little above Ardtully, where a castle was built about the year 1215 by a Carew.[76] We have no details of the battle, but it is probable that Fineen waited to be attacked in a position which he had chosen, where the enemy's cavalry could not operate. In the result 'a great battle and unspeakable slaugh- [141]
ter ensued between them, and the English were entirely defeated, and John, son of Thomas Fitz Gerald, seneschal of Munster, and Maurice his son, were slain, together with eight barons and twenty-five knights and many of the English besides'.[77]

Fineen made the most of his victory. The Annals of Inisfallen give a list of a dozen castles, including Macroom, Dunnamark, Killorglin, and Dunlo, and several on the southern coast which he levelled and broke, killing most of the foreigners that were in them. This was the time when, in the expressive language of Dr. Meredith Hanmer, 'the Carties plaied the Divells in Desmond, where they burned, spoiled, preyed, and slue many an innocent; they became so strong and prevailed so mightily that for the space (so it is reported) of twelve yeeres the Desmonds durst not put plow in ground in his owne Country'.

Fineen, however, did not live long to enjoy the fruits of his victory. Emboldened by his success he now attacked Ringrone (*Rinn Róin*), the castle of the de Courcys, at the western side of Kinsale Harbour. The lord of Kinsale at this time was Miles, son of Patrick de Courcy. Miles de Cogan is said to have come to his assistance, and 'a great defeat and overthrow was given to Fineen's people, in which Fineen himself and a great number of the chiefs of Desmond were slain'.[78]

William de Dene, the justiciar, died soon after the battle of Callann, whether from [142]
wounds received in the fight or from natural causes does not appear. He was succeeded about October 1261 by Richard de la Rochelle, who had been Lord Edward's seneschal

'Antiquissime', no. 32, and cf. no. 17; also Cal. Docs. Ireland, vol. ii, no. 629, and vol. iii, no. 10–51. It appears that the justiciar, Stephen de Longespée, refused to give John seisin on the ground that he had deceived the Lord Edward, whereupon John took seisin on his own account: Cal. Docs. Ireland, vol. ii, pp. 279, 426. 76 There is an earthwork of the promontory-fort type near the reputed site of the battle which may perhaps mark the position of Carew's castle. 77 Ann. Inisfallen, as above. The entry in Annals of Loch Cé, 1261, is to the same effect. Among those slain was the 'Barrach Mór', i.e. David de Barry, grandson of Philip de Barry, and lord of Castlelyons, Carrigtohill, and Buttevant. For the precise date of the death of John Fitz Thomas, July 24, 1261, see Cal. Docs. Irel., vol. ii, p. 426. His account for Cork County covered a period up to July 22: Ir. Pipe Roll, 45 Hen. III, 35th Rep. D. K., p. 37. 78 Ann. Inisfallen. A Miles de Cogan witnesses grants by Gerald de Prendergast, c. 1230–50: Reg. St. Thomas's Abbey, pp. 186, 189. He was probably brother of Geoffrey de Cogan, slain by another Fineen as already mentioned.

and lieutenant in Ireland under John Fitz Geoffrey. In 1262, joined by Walter de Burgh with a feudal army and 'a great number of the Irish', he advanced into Desmond to give battle to Cormac, Fineen's brother, and avenge the slaughter of Callann. The opposing forces met on the slopes of Mangerton, at a place henceforth known as Tuairin Cormaic. Here Gerald Roche, 'the third best baron in Erin', was slain, but this, we are told, was 'joy with sorrow to Desmond', for Cormac, son of Donnell Got, was slain on the same day, and great losses were suffered on both sides.[79]

In spite of such two-edged victories the battle of Callann, for good or for evil, effectually prevented the establishment of Anglo-Norman rule in Desmond. It is true that owing to dissensions among the Irish tribes the earls of Desmond eventually 'overtopped them all', but in the region from which they drew their title they had more of
[143] the character of a Celtic chief than of a feudal lord, and it was left for more resolute Tudor statesmen and more ruthless Tudor generals to break down the clan-system there. The settlement in Kerry, however, was not permanently affected. Maurice, son of John Fitz Thomas, left by his wife, Matilda de Barry,[80] a baby son named Thomas. Late writers have called him *Tomás an Ápa*, or 'Thomas of the Ape', a soubriquet which they say he obtained from an incident which occurred when news of the fatal battle of Callann reached the castle of Tralee. A panic seized the garrison, which was only allayed by the strange sight of a pet ape on one of the turrets of the castle carefully carrying the infant heir in its arms. This was hailed as a good omen—a sign from heaven that they should rally round their new lord. As a somewhat similar, but even more picturesque, ape-story is told of the infant John Fitz Thomas, afterwards first Earl of Kildare—a story which accounts for the ape-supporters on the family crest—it may be doubted to which branch of the family the legend really belongs.

Thomas Fitz Maurice came of age early in 1282, and from the inquisition then taken[81] we learn many details about his grandfather's lands. His most lucrative property was in County Waterford, but he also held valuable manors at Shanid, Killeedy, and Glenogra, in County Limerick. His property in Desmond at the time of the inquisition was of little value, but, as we have mentioned, he held in Kerry the cantred
[144] of Acmikerry (Trughanacmy), worth in his time £100, where a little later[82] were the valuable manors of Killorglin, Castle-Island, and the New Manor near Tralee. John Fitz Thomas is said to have founded the Dominican convent at Tralee in 1243,[83] and here, after the disaster of Callann, he and his son Maurice are said to have been buried.

After a time relations with the Mac Carthys appear to have improved. About the year 1284 Donnell Roo Mac Carthy, 'lord of the Irish of Desmond,' who had fought

79 Ann. Loch Cé, 1262, and Ann. Inisfallen. Presumably the Gerald Roche who married one of the daughters of Thomas Fitz Anthony. Unfortunately we are not told who the first and second 'best barons' were. Perhaps John Fitz Thomas and the Barrach Mór. Irish writers had a great fancy for 'triads'. For a similar example see Ann. Loch Cé, vol. i, p. 391. Walter de Burgh was allowed 250 marks in his Connaught account for his expenses in this campaign; 35th Rep. D. K., p. 47. 80 Inq. P. M., 28 Ed. I, p. 264. Her dower-lands were at Tralee and the New Manor in Kerry. One of the ignorant additions to the Annals of Inisfallen (Dublin) states that this Maurice's widow was a daughter of Geoffrey Mareis. 81 Cal. Docs. Irel., vol. ii, no. 1912; Cal. Inquis. P. M., Ed. I, vol. ii, no. 437. 82 Cal. Docs. Irel., vol. iv, nos. 551, 727; Cal. Inquis. P. M., Ed. I, vol. iii, no. 596. 83 Ware, Dowling's Annals, 1261.

on the side of John Fitz Thomas at Callann, wrote to Edward I, 'vehemently desiring to be subjected to the king's domination and wishing beyond measure to acquire the king's friendship by his service';[84] and in 1285 he obtained a safe-conduct to go to the king in England.[85] He seems, however, to have failed to carry out to the letter his vehement desire and measureless wish. In 1288 he and other Irishmen of Desmond were in a hostile state, when the Keeper of Ireland, Archbishop John de Sanford, held a parley with them and admitted them to the king's peace.[86] About this time his son Donnell Og Mac Carthy was outlawed for several robberies on the prosecution of William de Barry and Gilbert le Waleis, and was subsequently pardoned. Whereupon the prosecutors complained to the king that they had been prejudiced by the pardon and prayed a remedy; 'for if such things may be,' they said, 'law cannot avail us'[87]—a [145]
complaint which has often found an echo since.

In 1292 the king granted to Thomas Fitz Maurice and Margaret his wife (described as the king's cousin) and their heirs the custody of the a castle of Dungarvan and the homages, rents, and services of all tenants, as well English as Irish, belonging to the lands of Decies and Desmond.[88]

Perhaps this was the king's answer to the complaint of William de Barry and Gilbert Walsh. It was a repetition with some modifications of the previous grants to Thomas Fitz Anthony and John Fitz Thomas, but its effect in establishing English law in Desmond was not conspicuous. In 1297 the sheriff of Cork returned that Donnell Og, who was appealed for the death of John de Courcy, tenant in chief, 'would not submit to justice and had nothing in the land of peace whereby he might be distrained,' whereupon the sheriff was ordered to attach him.[89] A few months later the sheriff returned that Donnell 'was not found, but was among the Irish in waste land where no serjeant or bailiff of the king dared go to attach him'.[90] In fact, neither Thomas Fitz Maurice nor his titled successors made English law of much avail in Desmond.

Of Maurice, younger brother of John Fitz Thomas, and ancestor of the long line of the Fitz Maurices, lords of Kerry, we know little beyond what has been mentioned. [146]
He appears to have held the manor of Altry in the barony afterwards known as Clan-Maurice. The manorial centre was at Lixnaw. His son, Thomas Fitz Maurice, founded the Franciscan friary of Ardfert in 1253.[91] Judging from architectural evidence the cathedral of Ardfert must have been rebuilt about the same time, when the builders had the good taste to preserve the earlier Romanesque doorway.[92] Thomas was succeeded, *c.*1280, by his son Maurice,[93] who appears to have been tenant in chief of the Crown, but long afterwards the earls of Desmond of the senior line claimed to

84 Cal. Docs. Irel., vol. ii, no. 2362. 85 Ibid., vol. iii, no. 61. 86 Ibid., p. 266. Donnell Roe had to pay a fine: ibid. p. 277. 87 Ibid., no. 817. Gilbert le Waleis was one of the pledges for Donnell Og: 37th Rep. D.K., p. 54 (account 1290–5). 88 Ibid., no. 1051. Margaret, 'the king's cousin', was daughter of Sir Thomas de Berkeley by Joan, daughter of William de Ferrers, Earl of Derby. She was descended from King John's illegitimate son Richard: see 'Complete Peerage'. 89 Justiciary Rolls, vol. i, p. 101. 90 Ibid., p. 143. 91 Four Masters, 1253. 92 See a paper by Arthur Hill, B.E., Journal R.S.A.I., 1883–4, p. 294, and compare illustrations, ibid., p. 312. 93 This Maurice, called second baron of Kerry, died at

be lords of the Fitz Maurices—a claim which led to many bitter disputes. Throughout the thirteenth century—from 1232 at any rate[94]—Kerry was a separate shrieval county and was regularly visited by justices in eyre. At the close of the century its
[147] export trade from the port of Dingle was appreciable, and seems to have exceeded even that of Limerick.[95] From the manors of the Bishop of Ardfert, when in the escheator's hands for thirteen months in 1288–9, the sum of £80 6*s*. 4*d*. was received,[96] and the diocese was valued in the ecclesiastical taxation of 1306 at £178 16*s*. 6*d*. The lords of Kerry are said to have often intermarried with the families of the O'Conors of Kerry, the O'Briens of Thomond, and the Mac Carthys of Desmond, but throughout the dark period of Irish history the English settlement in Kerry, though but slightly controlled by the central government, never lost its identity.

APPENDIX I

The seignory of Cork

When treating of the occupation of Cork in the twelfth century, we briefly considered the difficult question of the devolution of the moieties of the 'kingdom of Cork' granted by Henry II to Robert Fitz Stephen and Miles de Cogan respectively (*ante*, vol. ii, pp. 46–50 [pp. 169–170; see *Add*. ref. vol. ii, pp. 48–50]). Further research has enabled me to add some links in the chain of descent of the Carews who are found in possession of the Fitz Stephen moiety in the latter part of the thirteenth century, and also to put forward more confidently the suggestion that Patrick de Courcy married a de Cogan heiress and thus acquired the de Cogan moiety.

The Carews, tenants in chief in Cork, were of a different line from the Carews of Idrone in County Carlow, though both had no doubt a common ancestor in William de Carew, eldest son of Gerald and Nesta, who died in 1173. The Carews of Idrone were identical with the senior line, the lords of Carew Castle in Pembrokeshire, while the Carews of Cork, as will be shown,
[148] were descended from a Richard de Carew who held lands in Cork about the close of the twelfth century, but whose parentage is obscure. In both cases the land was held at an earlier period by Raymond le Gros, a younger son of the first William de Carew. He was enfeoffed in the Carlow lands by Strongbow, and we are told (Giraldus Cambrensis, v. 350) that he succeeded to the inheritance of his uncle Robert Fitz Stephen in Cork. As we have said (*ante*, vol. i, p. 387 [pp. 146–7]), Raymond appears to have enfeoffed his nephew William, eldest son of Odo de Carew (son of William, son of Gerald of Windsor), in Idrone. On Raymond's death without legiti-

Moyflayth (Molahiff) in April 1305. He was then owner of Lixnaw: Justiciary Rolls, vol. ii, p. 422. For these early Fitz Maurices see my paper (above referred to), English Historical Review, vol. xxix (1914), pp. 302–15. I may here correct another error in the Fitz Maurice pedigree as given by Lodge (Archdall, vol. ii, p. 18b). It appears from Plea Roll, no. 68 m., 29 P. R. O., Dublin, that the first wife of this Maurice, and mother of his son and heir Nicholas, was Elena, daughter and heir of William Fitz Elie, and that his second wife's name was Sibilla. So that the statement in the MS. pedigree referred to by Lodge, viz. that the mother of Nicholas, third lord of Kerry, was a daughter and heir 'to Sir John M'Cleod of Galway, chief of his name (whose kindred are since commonly called M'Eligott)', must be rejected. **94** See Pipe Roll, 19 Hen. III 35th Rep. D.K., p. 37. **95** See accounts of the 'New Custom', 37th Rep. D.K., p. 24, &c. **96** Ibid., p. 34.

mate issue his Carlow lands reverted to Strongbow's heiress Isabel de Clare, and henceforth Raymond's feoffees, inciuding William de Carew and his successors, held immediately of the lords of Leinster, but as regards the Cork lands there was no superior lord except the Crown.

The clue to the descent of Maurice de Carew, who during the last quarter of the thirteenth century was recognized as holding the seignory of Fitz Stephen's moiety of Cork is to be found in a suit recorded in the Justiciary Rolls (vol. ii, pp. 372–3). From this it appears that Maurice recovered by writ of right some tenements in Imokilly 'of the seisin of his *abavus* Richard de Carew'; that this Richard married Raghenild, daughter of Mc Carthy, and that his eldest son was named Robert. Richard de Carew who married Raghenild may with probability be identified with the Richard de Carew whose widow Regina (a latinized form of Raghenild) had dower out of her late husband's tenement in Leinster in 1205 (Rot. de Finibus, 7 John, p. 321); and also with the Richard de Carew who granted a burgage in the suburbs of Cork to the Abbey of St. Thomas before 1206, and is the first witness to the confirmations by M., Bishop of Cork, of several early grants of benefices in Cork to the same Abbey (Reg. St. Thomas's Abbey, Dublin, pp. 213, 220–1). This M., Bishop of Cork, was not (as supposed by the editor) Marianus O'Brien who was translated to Cashel, in 1224, but probably Murrough O'Hea who died in 1206: Ann. Loch Cé. Four of the principal witnesses were contemporaries of Miles de Cogan, who died in 1182. Richard's son and heir was Robert, who fined £100 for his relief in 1216 (Rot. de Finibus, 18 [149]
John, p. 598) and was therefore a tenant in chief, and with Patrick de Courcy was one of the chief magnates of Cork in 1221–35 (Cal. Docs Ireland, nos. 1001, 2285). Robert was then presumably born *c.* 1195, and Maurice de Carew, the recognized tenant in chief, who was a minor in the king's custody in 1273 and given seisin of Castlecor in 1276 (36th Rep. D.K., p. 31, and 38th Rep. D. K., p. 30), was born *c.* 1255. In view of these dates it seems probable that *abavus* in the Justiciary Roll means great-grandfather, and not, as in classical usage, great-great-grandfather. There is therefore only one link in the pedigree to be supplied, and this appears to be the Richard de Carew who, presumably as superior lord, confirmed to the Abbey of St. Thomas a number of churches in Co. Cork, including that of Castlecor (now Middleton), the principal manor of the Carews: Reg. St. Thomas, p. 200. This deed must be dated between 1240, about which time the first John de Cogan and Maurice Fitz Maurice came of age, and 1261, when the first David de Barry was killed at the battle of Callann, these persons being among the witnesses.

We also meet this Cork line of Carews in Connaught, and the references to them there confirm the above pedigree. It is probable that Robert de Carew, and perhaps his son Richard, joined in the conquest of Connaught under Richard de Burgh in 1235, as both names appear as witnesses to the deed by which Gerald de Roche granted to Maurice Fitz Gerald part of Conmaicne Culi in Connaught, not very long after the conquest (Red Book of the Earl of Kildare, f. vi d). In 1234 Robert de Carew sided with Richard de Burgh against Earl Richard Marshal (Cal. Docs. Ireland, vol. i, nos. 2266, 2285), and he seems to have been enfeoffed by Richard de Burgh in lands in Southern Tirawley, as we find his son Richard, before November 1255, giving warranty to William Barrett of his lands in Bredagh in that district (Cal. Docs. Ireland, vol. ii, no. 474). And again in 1300 'Maurice, son of Richard de Carew' summoned another William Barrett to do suit and service in Bac and Glen and Bredagh. The claim was admitted by Barrett, but was disputed by the Earl of Ulster (Plea Roll, 28 Ed. I, 47, m. 13 d, and see *infra*, vol. iii, c. xxix). This William Barrett also held the land of Clardor (i.e. probably Glandore in [150]
Co. Cork, *supra*, p. 129 [p. 344]) of Maurice de Carew (Justiciary Roll, vol. i, p. 228), further indicating the dentity of these two lines.

The remainder of the pedigree is well authenticated and the whole may be tabulated side by side with the Carews of Idrone as below, at the end of this note.

It remains to inquire who was this Richard de Carew who died *c.* 1205, and was ancestor of the Carews who in the thirteenth century and later held the *dominium* of a moiety of Cork. The

field of inquiry is not large. He must have been either son or grandson of the first William de Carew who died in 1173, and (as his son and heir Robert was born about 1195) presumably grandson. William de Carew's attested sons were Odo, his heir, Raymond le Gros, once at any rate called Raymond 'de Karreu' (Cal. Christ Church Deeds, no. 3), and Griffin. Of these Raymond had no legitimate children; Griffin had four sons: Gilbert, Matthew, Raymond, and Griffin. They generally appear with the patronymic 'Fitz Griffin', and the first three at any rate seem to have left no male issue (Cal. Docs. Ireland, vol. iii, p. 294, and consult Journ. R.S.A.I., vol. xxiii (1893), p. 186). Odo's son and heir was William, who succeeded to Idrone, and Odo had other sons: Stephen *filius Odonis de Carew* (Reg. St. Thomas, p. 205), Tancard, named from his mother's father, and perhaps Adam and Baldwin, mentioned in charters in tlle Register of St. Thomas's Abbey. As far as dates go Richard de Carew may have been another younger son of Odo, but there is no proof or indication that this was so, and even if Odo had a younger son named Richard he could not normally have succeeded to Raymond's 'inheritance'. But though Raymond left no legitimate issue, it appears from some charters in the Chartulary of St. Mary's Abbey (though the fact has not hitherto been noticed) that he left two sons, whom we must suppose to have been illegitimate, named Walter and Richard. These charters concern Tilechstelan, a parish near Glencullen, County Dublin, and by them William de Carew (Raymond's nephew) and 'Walterus filius Reimundi' confirm (with possibly additions) a former grant to St.
[151] Mary's Abbey made before 1185 by Raymond le Gros (Chartulary, vol. i, pp. 106–11, and and cf. p. 86). Among these are three grants by *Walterus filius Reimundi*: the first (no. 89) is witnessed by Gerald Fitz Maurice, who was dead by January 1204 (Cal. Docs., vol. i, no. 195), and by Meiler Fitz Henry, who is not called justiciar, therefore before 1199, and another witness is 'Richard de Carew'. By the second (no. 90) Walter grants and confirms the church of Tilechstelan with the land which his father Raymond had granted to it, and this is witnessed (*inter alios*) by 'Richard his brother'. The third (no. 91) commences: *Sciant, &c., quod ego Walterus filius Reimundi commendavi cartas meas quas habeo de Comite* [Strongbow] *et de patre meo Reimundo in manu monachorum monasterii Marie iuxta Dublin.*, &c. It seems a necessary infercnce that this Reimundus was Reimundus filius Willelmi, commonly called le Gros, and that therefore Walter and Richard were his (illegitimate) sons. *Ricardus filius Reimundi* also witnesses a grant by Basilia, Raymond's widow, in 1199–1200 (Reg. St. Thomas, p. 111).

It is, moreover, a fair conjecture that this Richard, natural son of Raymond, was the Richard de Carew whose parentage we are seeking. On his father's death shortly after 1188 there was no one but the Crown who could legally take advantage of the escheat of Raymond's claim to the Cork seignory. At this time it was probably not of much value, and it was no one's interest to dispute the succession of Raymond's natural son. About then, or soon afterwards, he married Raghenilda, daughter of Mc Carthy, and with her he, no doubt, obtained a foothold among the Irish of Desmond. It was not, however, until after the bridling of Desmond with castles in 1215 and the following years that his son Robert de Carew and Patrick de Courcy were recognized as successors to the original grantees, and this was probably effected by Thomas Fitz Anthony and the other barons interested, with the design that the original service to the Crown of sixty knights' fees for the whole of Cork should not be increased to their disadvantage. It is to be noted, however, that Philip de Prendergast and his heirs always appear as tenants in chief of the Crown under the grant of 1207, and owed the services of one and a half knights' fees.

As regards the de Cogan moiety, Margarita, only daughter and heiress of Miles de Cogan,
[152] and widow of Ralph Fitz Stephen who was slain in 1182 (*ante*, vol. ii, p. 40 [pp. 166–7]), appears to have had a daughter (Margery) for whose marriage, together with 'all the land of Miles de Cogan', Thomas Bloet before 1211 made a fine of 500 marks (Cal. Docs. Ireland, vol. i, nos. 422, 452). This fine was still unpaid in 1227 (ibid., no. 1504). Thomas Bloet was an official of King John, and was employed by him in 1207 to summon John d'Erlee

CAREWS OF IDRONE AND CAREWS TENANTS-IN-CHIEF IN CORK

[154]

WILLIAM DE CAREW, s. and h. of Gerald f. Walter and Nest of Wales; d. 1173 at Carew Castle.

Odo, = Margaret, dau. of Richard f. Tancred, Castellan of Haverford.
living with monks at St. Mary's Abbey, Dublin, in 1202.

William,
succeed to Idrone by 1202;
confirmed in Mulesford and Carew, May 25, 1213;
d. before Sept. 17, 1213.

Richard,
lord of Carew.

Raymond 'le Gros',
c. 1174 enfeoffed by Strongbow in Idrone, Co. Carlow;
c. 1182 succeeded to the inheritance of Robert f. Stephen in Co. Cork;
d. s. p. c. 1188.

Richard I = Raghenild, dau. of McCarthy, also called Regina.
(Probably an illegimate son of Raymond le Gros),
held lands in Imokilly; granted a burgage near Cork, to the Abbey of St. Thomas before 1206;
d. c. 1205.

Robert,
1216 fined for his relief;
built Dunnamark and other castles in Desmond;
1221 magnate in Cork;
1234 sided with Richard de Burgh against Earl Richard Marshal; c. 1235 enfeoffed in lands in Tirawley.

William,
lord of Carew,
1247 held five knights' fees in Pembroke.

Nicholas,
lord of Carew,
1278 went to Ireland;
1306 held five knights' fees in Idrone;
d. 1311.

John,
Before 1312 enfeoffed by his father Nicholas in his Carlow lands: Close (Ireland) 5 Edw. II (41).
= Eleanor, dau. of William de Mohun.

Richard II,
c. 1250 confirmed grants of churches in Cork, including church of Castlecor, to St. Thomas's Abbey;
c. 1255 called to warranty by William Barrett in Tirawley.

Thomas,
d. seised of Castlecor before 1274.

Maurice,
16 May 1276 given seisin of Castlecor; pays 30 services as tenant-in-chief in Cork;
1305 pardoned £400 arrears of services for Desmond;
1307 recovers lands in Imokilly of the seisin of his *abavus*, Richard de Carew, who married Raghenild.

Thomas,
16 July 1320 obtained seisin of the lands which his father Maurice held in chief: Close (Ireland) 14 Edw. II (51);
1336 quit-claimed *dominium* of Olethan to David f. David f. David de Barry: Ibid., 32 Edw. III (26, 27, 82);
Before 1329 enfeoffed Maurice f. Thomas, afterwards Earl of Desmond, in a moiety of the lordship of Desmond, but this was held invalid on the ground that Robert f. Stephen was a bastard, and died without heirs: Cal. Fine Rolls, vol. iv p. 286.

and other followers of William the Marshal in pursuance of the intrigue against the earl, of which we have given an account: *ante*, vol. ii, pp. 212–16 [pp. 236–7]. He appears as a great Munster lord in 1210, when he joined King John with a large force from Munster (Prest. Rolls, p. 188), and he was one of the magnates who joined in the declaration of loyalty to the king in 1211 (Cal. Docs. Ireland, vol. i, no. 448). He must have been dead by February 1217, when a fine of 100 marks was accepted from Margery de Cogan 'to have the land of her inheritance in Desmond' (ibid., no. 758). This Margery was, I think, the granddaughter of Miles de Cogan, now a feme-sole and widow of Thomas Bloet, and there was presumably no issue of the marriage. It is a reasonable conecture that soon after this date she was married to Patrick de Courcy. There is indeed no direct evidence for this marriage, but in 1221 Patrick de Courcy and Robert de Carew were the principal tenants in chief in Cork, and they[97] and their respective descendants for several generations appear to have been held liable in equal moieties for the sixty services reserved in the original grant to Miles de Cogan and Robert Fitz Stephen.

In my former note (*ante*, vol. ii, p. 50 [p. 170]) I confused this Margery de Cogan with the *Margarita filia Milonis* who made a grant in Rosselethry (*Ros Ailither*, now Rosscarbery) to St. Mary's Abbey (Chart., vol. ii, p. 4), but I now think that the former was daughter and heiress of the latter. Margarita's grant was perhaps a death-bed gift which did not take effect. The [153]
whole cantred, saving the bishop's demesnes, had been given by King John to David de Roche in 1207. Margarita's grant or confirmation is witnessed by Geoffrey de Marisco, justiciar, i.e. between 1215 and 1221, and should, I think, be placed before February 14, 1217, when her daughter Margery fined for inheritance in Desmond. At this date her mother, whose heir she was, must have been dead.

97 That Patrick de Courcy and Robert de Carew were so held liable is evidenced by the fact that, in the Pipe Rolls and Exchequer accounts, payments for these services were entered under their names (as was not unusual) long after they were both dead. See e.g. Cal. Docs. Ireland, vol. iv.

APPENDIX II

[156] ANCESTORS OF THE FITZGERALDS, EARLS OF DESMOND, AND OF THE FITZMAURICES, BARONS OF KERRY AND LIXNAW

Thomas f. Maurice,
younger son of Maurice f. Gerald I *qui obiit* 1176.
He obtained Shanid, c. 1197: *ante*, vol. ii, p. 164 [p. 217];
died 1218.

John f. Thomas, = Margt., dau. of Thomas f. Anthony.
succeeded to Shanid;
held cantred of
Acmikery: supra, p. 133 [p. 347];
given Decies and Desmond
in 1259: supra, p. 140 [p. 349]; killed
at Callann in 1261.

Maurice f. John, = Matilda, dau. of David de Barry I.
killed at Callann in
1261.

Thomas f. Maurice, = Margt. dau. of Thomas de Berkeley.
came of age in 1282;
given Decies and
Desmond in 1292:
supra, p. 145 [p. 352];
died 1298.

Maurice f. Thomas, = Katherine, dau. of Richard de Burgh, Earl of Ulster.
obtained seisin in
1314; created Earl
of Desmond in 1329;
died in 1356.

Maurice f. Thomas, sent
to Ireland in 1215 with
Geoffrey de Marisco:
supra, p. 131 [p. 345]; held
manor of Altry.

Thomas f. Maurice,
founded Franciscan
Convent at Ardfert,
in 1253: F.M.;
died *c.* 1280.

Maurice f. Thomas, = Elena, dau. of Wm. f. Elie.
held manor of
Altry: supra, p. 146 [p. 352];
died in 1304.

Nicholas f. Maurice,
knighted in 1313 by
John f. Thomas,
of Offaly: Laud MS.,
p. 342.

Maurice f. Nicholas,
positus ad dietam in 1339, by
the Earl of Desmond:
Laud MS. and Clyn.

John f. Nicholas,
still alive in 1375:
Pat. (Ireland) 49 Edw. III,
no. 168.

APPENDIX III

The Mac Carthys of Desmond

(based on the pedigree in MS. 4. 1. 17, f. 137 d, T.C.D.

Dermot, s. of Cormac, s. of Muiredach, s. of Carthach *qui obiit* 1045: A.U.
K.D. 1145–85. Submitted to Henry II in 1171: *ante*, vol. i, p. 259 [p. 95]; obtained aid from Raymond le Gros against his son Cormac in 1176: *ante*, vol. i, p. 355 [p. 134]; slain by the English of Cork in 1185: *ante*, vol. ii, p. 100 [p. 190].

- Cormac, *Liathánach*. Took his father prisoner in 1176, and was afterwards slain by his own people: F.M.
- Donnell Mór, *na Curradh*, K.D. 1185–1206. Expelled (temporarily) the English from Limerick in 1195: *ante*, vol. ii, p. 157 [p. 214]; died 1206: AL.C.
    - Dermot 'of Dundrinan', K.D. 1209–30. Opposed by Cormac Finn in 1214: *supra*, p. 125; joined Wm. Marshal against Hugh de Lacy in 1224: A.L.C., died 1230: *ib.* = Peronelle, sister of Thomas Bloet: Close, 1 Hen. III, p. 302.
        - Fineen, slew Geoffrey de Cogan, *c.*1248, and was himself slain in 1250 by Donnell Got and the Cogans: *supra*, p. 138 [p. 349].
    - Cormac Finn, K.D. 1230–48, died *c.*1248: *supra*, p. 137 [p. 348]. Ancestor of MacCarthy Mór.
        - Donnell Roe, K.D. 1262–1302. Fought for the English at Callann in 1261: his letter to K. Edward, 1284; *supra*, p. 144 [p. 352]; died 1302: A.L.C.
            - Donnell Óg, K.D. 1302–3: A.L.C.
                - Cormac, K.D.; died *c.*1320.
                - Dermot, K.D.; killed at Tralee in 1325 by William f. Nicholas f. Maurice of Kerry: Clyn, p. 17.
    - Dermot, Got, 'the stammerer' of Carbery, K.D. 1248–51. Deposed O'Mahony and took possession of Carbery in 1233: *supra*, p. 137 [p. 348]; slain in 1251 by John f. Thomas: *supra*, p. 138 [p. 349]. Ancestor of MacCarthy Reagh.
        - Fineen, *Rinna Roin*, K.D. 1251–61. Defeated John f. Thomas at Callann in 1261: *supra*, p. 141 [p. 350]; slain at Ringrone in same year.
        - Donnell Maol, K.D. 1261–2: F.M.
        - Cormac, slain at Mangerton in 1262: A.L.C.
- Fineen, *Lice Laichtin* (of Lislaughtin), K.D. 1206–9. Aided William de Burgh against Cathal Carrach in 1202: *ante*, vol. ii, p. 190 [p. 227]; slain by his own people in 1209: A.L.C.

[158] CHAPTER XXVIII

THE CONQUEST OF CONNAUGHT, 1224–37

Ever since the beginning of the thirteenth century Cathal Crovderg O'Conor had remained in undisturbed possession of Connaught, holding it, since 1215 at any rate, by charter in fee during good service as a vassal of the Crown, subject to an annual rent of 300 marks.[1] Viewed as a feudal fief, Connaught on Cathal's death would pass under John's charter in ordinary course to his eldest son Aedh, and, as we have seen,[2] Cathal just before his death in 1224 was anxious to obtain from Henry III a confirmatory charter to Aedh in fee. No such confirmation appears to have been actually obtained, but on Cathal's death Aedh, we are told, 'assumed the government of Connaught ... for he had been a king in dignity beside his father previously, and the hostages of Connaught were at his command'.[3] From this and other indications it may be inferred that Aedh was not inaugurated 'O'Conor' by the twelve chieftains of the Sil Murray according to ancient custom. In ordinary course it was more usual for the chieftainship to pass to a brother, brother's son, or cousin of the deceased chieftain—
[159] to some near male agnate otherwise qualified. In recent times, however, it had become increasingly common for a son to secure his father's vacant throne, and, if he proved himself 'the best man', to obtain or enforce recognition from the 'urrighs' or subordinate chieftains. Aedh would no doubt have preferred to owe his position to the free choice or the strong arms of his followers, rather than rely on English charters or English support, and it was perhaps to gain popularity with the clansmen that he burned the castle of Ardowlin and killed its occupants. But as he had to call upon the justiciar to support his claim to the throne, his succession may perhaps be regarded as the first important example of a Celtic chieftainship descending as a quasi-feudal fief from father to son.

King Aedh, son of Cathal, though apparently supported by the English, had rivals and enemies among his own kith and kin at home, ready to dispute his succession. Even before Cathal's death, Dermot, son of Rory O'Conor, the last ard-rí, made an abortive attempt to gain the sovereignty of Connaught,[4] and now, early in 1225, Turlough and Aedh, also sons of Rory, obtained the assistance of Aedh O'Neill to contest the throne. The Sil Murray clans, with the exception of the Mac Dermots, together with the O'Flahertys and others, joined in the rebellion against Aedh, son of Cathal. After pillaging Eastern Connaught as far as the woods of Athlone, O'Neill marched

1 *Ante*, vol. ii, pp. 189, 263, 285–7 [pp. 227, 255–6, 266–7]. 2 *Supra*, p. 40 [p. 301]. 3 Ann. Loch Cé, 1224. 4 Ann. Loch Cé, 1221.

to Carnfree, where he made Turlough O'Conor king.[5] This was the beginning of a [160] series of desolating wars which ended in the Anglo-Norman domination of Connaught under Richard de Burgh and his followers.

Meanwhile Aedh, unable to resist his enemies by himself, went for assistance to Athlone, where the English were at the time holding a court, 'and every one of them', we are told, 'was a friend of his, for his father's sake and his own, for he and his father before him were very liberal in wages to them. And he brought with him the justiciar[6] and as many of the foreigners of Erin as he thought sufficient'. Donough Cairbrech O'Brien and O'Melaghlin of Meath also assisted him with their forces. There is an unusually elaborate account of this campaign, apparently derived from contemporary reports, in the Annals of Loch Cé, but we need not follow it in detail. The first forces which were operating in the north of the province came to no regular engagement, but there was a good deal of harrying and plundering the land. In fact the Irish malcontents were unable to face the Normans in the field of battle, while Aedh, son of Cathal, was unable to cope with his enemies without Norman aid. O'Neill, we are told, 'went on a quick march to his house on hearing that a large army of foreigners and Munstermen were coming against him'.[7] The forces of the sons of Rory dispersed, and were mainly concerned 'to protect their cows and people and to make peace for [161] their sake until his foreigners should depart from Aedh son of Cathal.'[8] At the same time a second army of foreigners, led by Murtough O'Brien and 'the sheriff of Cork', entered Connaught from the south and harried the land. Aedh, son of Cathal, we are told, 'disliked their coming into the district, for it was not he who had invited them; but when they heard of all the spoils the justiciar with his foreigners had obtained, envy and jealousy seized them.'[9] By 'the sheriff of Cork' is, no doubt, intended Richard de Burgh. He had recently been appointed seneschal of Munster,[10] and this office would seem to have included that of sheriff. The King of Connaught would naturally have preferred to do without the aid of William de Burgh's son, but, on the other hand, it would have been very strange if Richard de Burgh, with his hereditary pretensions, did not have a finger in the open pie. The sons of Murtough O'Conor, another brother of Rory the late *ard-rí*, submitted to Aedh, son of Cathal, 'for the sake of their cows and people'. They formed a distinct sept known as Clan Murtough, and were at this time seated in Carra, County Mayo. O'Flaherty also submitted for the same reason, and was obliged to yield up the island fortresses[11] in Lough Corrib and [162]

5 Ann Ulst. 1225. In Ann. Loch Cé there is a double entry: first under 1224 (following the Annals of Ulster even in a blunder as to an important verb), and again at greater length from another source, under 1225, probably the true date. The Four Masters, 1225, combine the two sources and correct the faulty verb. 6 William Marshal the younger was justiciar up to June 25, 1226, when he was superseded by Geoffrey de Marisco: Pat. Roll, 10 Hen. III, p. 47. Geoffrey, however, conducted this campaign (Ann. Ulst., 1226) as deputy of the Earl Marshal. who had been summoned to England in November 1224: Rot. Claus., 9 Hen. III, vol. ii, p. 96 b. 7 Ann. Ulst., 1225. 8 Ann. Loch Cé, 1225, pp. 279, 281. 9 Ibid., 1225, p. 281. 10 Cal. Docs. Irel., vol. i, nos. 1114, 1216, 1288. We usually read of the seneschal of a liberty, such as Leinster or Meath, and the sheriff of a county, such as Dublin or Waterford; but at this time Munster does not seem to have been divided into separate shire-grounds. In the Irish Pipe Roll for 19 Hen. III we find the sheriff of Munster's account, but no separate sheriff of Cork is mentioned. 11 *Inis-cremha*, or 'Wild Gar-

the boats on the lake. On the other hand, Donough O'Brien was forced to submit to Aedh, son of Rory, and to make peace and 'drowning of candles' with him to effect the release of some of his chief men who had been captured. But in every case the submission was insincere.

No sooner were the foreigners, except a small band, departed from Aedh than O'Flaherty and the sons of Murtough and other 'royal heirs' raised the standard of revolt and once more joined the sons of Rory. Aedh accordingly dispatched messengers to the English requesting additional forces. His request was readily granted, 'for', adds the annalist, 'these expeditions were profitable to the foreigners, who used to obtain spoils and used not to encounter danger or conflict'. The English on this expedition were led by 'William Cras and the sons of Griffin'. By the former was meant William le Gras senior, cousin and seneschal of the Earl Marshal, and the latter were the sons of Griffln Fitz William, brother of Raymond le Gros. The elder of these, Matthew Fitz Griffin, held the manor of Knocktopher of the Earl Marshal. Evidently the earl, who had by this time returned to Ireland, entrusted the leadership of the campaign to his own men. This change of commanders is perhaps a premonitory symptom of that estrangement between Richard de Burgh and the lord of Leinster, which grew in strength next year and broke out with fatal consequences to the earl's brother a few years later. As before, there was no regular fighting, but much harrying of the land. The sons of Rory, once more deserted by the Connaught tribes (who went to protect their cows and people), sought refuge with O'Neill 'and there resulted noth-
[163] ing to them from this hosting, but that the best territory in Erin was injured and destroyed through them'.[12] Famine and plague followed the plundering: 'Quidquid delirant reges plectuntur Achivi.' It is ever thus, especially when the weaker side will neither submit nor face the 'trial by battle'.

Hitherto Aedh O'Conor had been supported by the forces of the Crown, but now (in 1226) a change of policy on the part of the English Government took place. A plan which had been from time to time proposed by Richard de Burgh, but which had hitherto been rejected, or at least laid aside, was now put into operation. This was nothing less than the confiscation of the land of Connaught, and the granting of the greater part of it by royal charter to Richard de Burgh. The English Government may have been persuaded that Aedh, son of Cathal, was incapable of retaining the mastery of Connaught, that in view of the dissensions among the O'Conors and the Connaught clans, as to the succession to the throne, it was hopeless to expect peace in the province[13] under any native ruler, and that the present was a favourable opportunity for extending English domination over it. But when all is said that can fairly be said in favour of the new policy, the fact remains that it involved harsh treatment of King

lic Island', and *Oilen na circe*, or 'Hen Island'. See O'Flaherty's West Connacht, p. 25. 12 Ann. Loch Cé, 1225 (p. 289). It will be observed that throughout the long-disputed succession to the throne of Connaught between the sons of Rory and the sons of Cathal Crovderg, the former, when driven out, sought protection and aid from O'Neill, while the latter had recourse to O'Donnell. Lassairfhina, daughter of Cathal Crovderg, was wife of this O'Donnell: Ann. Loch Cé, 1239. 13 In this very year (1226) fighting went on between the clan-groups of Connaught, and several chieftains were killed.

Cathal's son, and was not unnaturally regarded by him and his followers as an act of [164]
treachery and deception. Nor was this view confined to his Irish followers. Many of the Norman barons resented this treatment of an Irish king whose cause they had supported, and by whose side they had fought. At their head was Earl William Marshal, till now the justiciar, and the facts established by a study of the authorities show beyond a doubt that the earl's refusal to endorse the new policy was the true cause of his supersession at this time by Geoffrey de Marisco, as well as of the opposition to that policy which speedily manifested itself among the earl's vassals.[14]

As has been mentioned,[15] when King John, in 1215, gave to Cathal Crovderg O'Conor a confirmatory charter of all the land of Connaught except the castle of Athlone, he made an alternative grant to Richard de Burgh of 'all the land of Connaught which William his father held of the king'. These two grants were mutually inconsistent, but the latter grant was held in abeyance, presumably to come into operation in the event of Cathal's default and forfeiture, and seisin was not given in pursuance of it. In 1219 Richard, then with the king in England, made a new offer for a charter materially curtailing for his own benefit Cathal's rights;[16] but this offer was [165]
rejected, and renewed protection was granted to Cathal for four years.[17] In 1220 Richard returned to Ireland [18] and received a general mandate for seisin of all the lands of which his father had been disseised, and this mandate was repeated in 1223.[19] In terms these mandates would seem to include Connaught, but no immediate steps to give seisin were taken. Apart from Connaught, Richard de Burgh inherited several valuable manors in the present counties of Limerick and Tipperary, and at his death these manors were valued at £332 14*s*. 4*d*.[20] Prior to 1225 he had allied himself to the [166]
de Lacys by his marriage with Egidia, daughter of Walter de Lacy and he had received

14 Miss Norgate (Minority of Hen. III, p. 2630) rightly sees in Geoffrey's appointment the hand of Hubert de Burgh, Richard's uncle (not 'brother' as she says), but she can only attribute 'the jealousy of the de Burghs' to Earl William's 'successes in Wales and Ireland and his marriage with the king's sister'. These things may have partly influenced Hubert, but as regards Ireland, Richard de Burgh had a much stronger motive. He well knew that as long as William Marshal was justiciar he could not carry out his long-cherished scheme for the confiscation of Connaught. 15 *Ante*, vol. ii, p. 285, note [p. 264, note 9]. 16 Rot. Claus. 3 Hen. III, p. 401. 17 Cal. Docs. Irel., vol. i, no. 928. 18 Four Masters, 1219. 19 Rot. Claus. 4 Hen. III, p. 427, and 7 Hen. III, p. 551. 20 Cal Inq. P. M., 27 Hen. III, no. 19. These manors, besides Esclon, Castleconnell, Kilfeakle, and Kilsheelan, mentioned *ante*, vol. ii, pp. 166–9 [pp. 217–18], were 'Wethemtire', more correctly Wetheni-tire, *Uaithne tire*, now represented by the barony of Owney, County Tipperary, and to be equated with the manor of Castle Amory (Irish Pipe Roll, 1 Ed. I, 36th Rep. D.K., p. 22, where the names mentioned can be found in this barony; cf Eccl. Taxation, Cal. Docs. Irel., vol. v, p. 281); 'Tristelaweran and Balihodan', now Inch St. Lawrence and Ballyhobin in the barony of Clanwilliam, County Limerick; 'Castrum Wilekin', *Caislen Uilcin* (Four Masters, 1200), according to O'Donovan, Castle Erkin in the same barony; Tiperacht, Tibberaghny near Carrick-on-Suir (Rot. Chart. 2 John, p. 71 *b*), 'Cloncridan', Clonkerdin in the parish of Whitechurch, County Kilkenny. 'Lisrothorach', now Lisronagh (Cal. Docs. Irel., vol. v, p. 307, where the older form of the name is given); 'Oleithach', *Ui Luighdhech*, the ancient barony of Ileagh, where Borrisoleigh retains the name and marks the Norman site (see Four Masters, vol. v, p. 1749, note); 'Lother', *Lothra*, Lorrha (the manor along with 'Tyrdeglas' or Terryglass belonged to the Earl of Ulster prior to l 333, Inquis. P. M., 'William de Burgo', 7 Ed. III); 'Grellach', perhaps Grallagh in the parish of Dolla, Upper Ormond. Castle Amory and these last five manors have not, I think, hitherto been identified.

with her the cantred of Ardmayle in County Tipperary.[21] Through the influence of his uncle Hubert de Burgh, justiciar of England, he was now high in favour with the king. In 1225 he was appointed seneschal of Munster and custodian of the castle of Limerick, and the Crown rent of 250 marks out of Decies and Desmond was assigned to him for his maintenance in the king's service.[22]

Next year the new policy was declared. On June 25, 1226, Earl William Marshal was superseded in the office of justiciar of Ireland by Geoffrey de Marisco.[23] No reason is assigned for this supersession, but five days later the new justiciar obtained the required orders to summon Aedh, son of Cathal, late King of Connaught, before the king's court in Dublin 'to surrender the land of Connaught, which he ought no longer to hold on account of his father's and his own forfeiture'. If Aedh refused to surrender, the justiciar was to ascertain by the court the truth of the forfeiture, and if it was found that Aedh had forfeited the land, the justiciar was to take it into the king's
[167] hand.[24] He was then to grant seisin thereof to Richard de Burgh, to hold of the king at the rent of 300 marks for the first five years and 500 marks subsequently. Five of the best cantreds nearest to the castle of Athlone were to be retained for the king's use.[25]

By the contemplated procedure the King of Connaught was to be treated as if he were simply a feudal tenant in chief of the Crown. No doubt this was his strict legal position. Under the charter granted to his father, Aedh held Connaught in fee during good service, and was not to be disseised of his land without judgement of the king's court. No feudal tenant on a charge of forfeiture could do more than demand to be tried by his peers. The precise act of forfeiture charged against Aedh is not stated. His sacking of Ardowlin and massacre of the garrison in 1224 was presumably an act of forfeiture, but seeing that the justiciar William Marshal afterwards aided him to recover his throne, it would seem to have been condoned. There may indeed have been other breaches of feudal obligation, and Aedh probably well knew or was informed that he had no adequate defence, and that he must rely on his own right arm if he was to retain his position. Irish kings who were ready to accept the protection afforded by a charter from the Crown, and the military assistance given to them, were seldom equally ready to observe the corresponding obligations, or to accept the consequences of default. When confronted with these consequences they would fall back upon their status as tribal chieftains, which they did not regard as impaired by their submission to the Eng-
[168] lish king. And indeed, seeing that feudal law, even if applicable between Aedh and the Crown, did not affect Aedh's relations with his Irish subjects, the analogy between Aedh's position and that of an ordinary feudal baron was far from complete.

As already intimated, Aedh was not alone in resenting this striet application of feudal law to his case. William Marshal, who was ever zealous in defending the rights of

21 Rot. Claus. 9 Hen. III, p. 35 *b* (Cal. no. 1208), where Ioganach Cassel, *Eoghanacht Caisil*, is to be equated with the cantred of Ardmayle restored to Walter de Lacy in 1217; Cal. no. 743. As Egidia de Lacy survived Richard, and as his sons were minors at his death in 1243, the statement that he married a daughter of Aedh, son of Cathal, who was the mother of his younger sons, made by an Irish genealogist (see 'West Connaught', Hardiman's note, p. 38) and followed in 'The O'Conors of Connaught' (p. 97), must be dismissed as apocryphal. 22 Cal. Docs. Irel., vol. i, nos. 1288, 1292. 23 Ibid., vol. i, nos. 1380, 1383. 24 Patent Roll, 10 Hen III, p. 48. 25 Ibid., p. 49.

the aristocracy of England against the Crown, took immediate action in his defence. With a chivalry and a daring worthy of his sire, but without, perhaps, his sire's incomparable temper and tact, he seems to have warned Aedh of what was in store for him, directed his bailiffs to withhold delivery of the royal castles, and started on his way to Ireland, apparently with the intention of thwarting the new justiciar and Richard de Burgh. The king, however, intimated his displeasure at William's going to Ireland, and ordered him before doing so to surrender his castles of Caermarthen and Cardigan.[26] Consequently William did not continue his journey. He was not prepared to carry his opposition to the new policy to the point of a direct conflict with the king, his brother-in-law. He surrendered the castles, met the king in August, in the Welsh Marches, and submitted to his will. Then he went to Ireland with letters of protection on the king's service,[27] presumably to deliver the royal castles held by his bailiffs to Geoffrey de Marisco.

Meanwhile, probably in July, Geoffrey de Marisco landed at Waterford. From his letter to the king, written shortly after his arrival in Dublin, we learn both his proceedings and the attitude of the Irish barons with regard thereto. He was about to pro- [169]
ceed to Dublin to communicate the mandates to the king's subjects when he heard that Earl William, by the agency of Theobald Walter, was about to oppose his passage with all the force of Leinster. Having at length arrived at Dublin, he held a council, when all assembled rendered their oaths of fealty, except William Baron of Nass, Walter de Ridelisford, Matthew Fitz Griffin, and John de Clahull—all leading vassals of the earl. Theobald Walter too excused himself from taking the oath, asserting that he could not part with the custody of the castles confided to him by the earl without his mandate. 'All the [king's] castles of Ireland', says the justiciar, 'are fortified against the king, save the castle of Limerick in the custody of Richard de Burgh, who always assists the justiciar in the king's affairs.' This loyal assistance on the part of Richard de Burgh is not surprising, seeing that the king's affairs in Ireland at this time were virtually directed by Hubert de Burgh in his nephew's interest. 'All the Irish', adds Geoffrey, 'are so banded together and so wheedled by William Crassus (i.e. William le Gras, the Earl Marshal's seneschal) that they cannot be recalled from their conspiracy.' He goes on to state that the King of Connaught, 'at the instigation of William Crassus', had become heedless of the king's mandates; that he, Geoffrey, had summoned him to Dublin, but that as the king did not come he had appointed a day for him at Athlone. Thus far Geoffrey's letter.[28] In the Annals of Loch Cé, however, it is stated that when Aedh was summoned before the court in Dublin, 'he was betrayed in that court, until [170]
William Marshal, his own friend, came with his forces into the midst of the court; and they carried him out of it by force and conveyed him safely to his own country'.[29] Geoffrey's letter and other facts seem inconsistent with this dramatic action. Aedh did not appear when summoned, and it would seem that William Marshal was not in Ireland at the date of Geoffrey's letter. Nevertheless the entry is valuable as giving the

26 Patent Roll, 10 Hen. III, p. 30 (July 10). 27 Ibid., p. 59 (August 27). 28 Royal Letters (Shirley), vol. i, p. 290. 29 Ann. Loch Cé, vol. i, p. 293. There is some confusion as to the date. The text gives 1226, which seems to be the true year, but the indicia supplied point to 1227.

Irish view of the diverse sympathies of Anglo-Irish political parties. Probably the substratum of fact was that William Marshal, through his seneschal William le Gras, warned Aedh of what was intended against him, and advised him not to appear. The submission of William Marshal to the king's will was speedily followed by the withdrawal of opposition on the part of his vassals. William Marshal took no further part in Irish politics, but by his opposition to the scheme for the confiscation of Connaught he had sown the seeds of enmity towards his house which eight years later bore bitter fruit in the tragic death of the 'Knight of the Curragh'.

For what happened at Athlone we may rely on the Annals of Loch Cé. The meeting took place near a marsh outside Athlone.[30] William de Marisco, Geoffrey's son, appeared on behalf of the justiciar with eight horsemen. Aedh came across the marsh
[171] with a few of his chief men, and 'remembering the treachery and deception practised against him at Dublin', immediately seized William. Aedh's people actively supported him; the constable of Athlone was slain, and three of the deputation from the Glovernment were taken prisoners and carried across the marsh. Then Aedh and the Connaught men plundered and burned the town of Athlone. 'This', says the short-sighted annalist, 'was a felicitous act for all the Connaught men, for they obtained their sons and daughters and the hostages of Connaught [in exchange for the prisoners], and peace for the Con naught men afterwards.'[31] The peace, however, was only for the moment, and this outbreak gave Aedh's enemies the pretext for which they were looking. He had now committed a clear act of forfeiture. In May 1227 the grant of Connaught in fee to Richard de Burgh on the terms already settled was formally executed,[32] and the tenants in chief of Ireland were summoned for an expedition into Connaught with a view to punishing Aedh and giving Richard seisin.[33] The whole of Connaught was soon overrun by the English. They brought with them the sons of Rory, whom they had previously opposed. Richard de Burgh himself, with Aedh, son of Rory, plundered the country about Inishmaine on Lough Mask and took hostages. The justiciar, Geoffrey de Marisco, with Turlough, son of Rory, took the hostages of the Sil Murray in the northern part of the present County Roscommon,
[172] and erected the castle of Rinnduin[34] on the shores of Lough Ree. Other detachments went against the O'Flahertys in the west of County Galway, into Carra in the middle of County Mayo, and to the country about Sligo, taking hostages and cattle.[35] Aedh, son of Cathal, fled to O'Donnell, and Connaught was for the moment reduced to submission without any serious opposition.

As for Aedh, he returned from Tirconnell in the same year with his wife and his brother Felim. His wife was captured by the sons of Rory and handed over to the English, while Aedh himself a little later was killed in the house of Geoffrey de Marisco. There was a natural suspicion of 'an ugly treachery', but it is clear that he was de-

30 The Irish name of the place, *Lathach-caech-tuaithbhil*, 'the northern blind slough', is still partly preserved in that of the village of Bellaugh (*bel láthaigh* = 'entrance to the marsh'), lying west of Athlone. 31 Ann. Loch Cé, 1227 (*recte* 1226). 32 Cal. Chart. Roll, 11 Hen. III, p. 42. 33 Scutage was exacted from those who failed to attend, see Cal. no. 1581. 34 For description and early history of the Castle of Rinnduin, see my paper on Athlone Castle, Journ. R.S.A.I., 1907, pp. 274–6. 35 Ann. Loch Cé, 1227.

throned by the Connaught men themselves, and it is said that he was killed in a fit of jealousy by an Englishman with whose wife Aedh had taken liberties, and that the Englishman was hanged next day by Geoffrey for the deed.[36]

Though possibly unconnected with this affair, there was now another change in the office of justiciar. On Febrnary 13, 1228, Geoffrey de Marisco was superseded by Richard de Burgh. The king, when announcing the new appointment, stated that Geoffrey had expressed a wish to retire.[37] There are indications, however, that Geoffrey [173] had quarrelled with Richard at this time. Geoffrey took no further part in the conquest of Connaught and was not one of those rewarded by a grant of lands there, and, as we have seen, he was opposed to Richard de Burgh and the other enemies of Earl Richard Marshal in 1234. Now in 1226–7 Richard de Burgh had been given the custody of the Crown lands in Decies and Desmond previously held by Thomas Fitz Anthony.[38] Richard complained to the king that the lands had been so alienated by Thomas Fitz Anthony that the residue did not suffice to yield the service due. Accordingly, in August 1227, the king ordered Geoffrey as justiciar to take in the king's hand and deliver to Richard all the lands which had been so alienated, and to certify their value and the amount of the residue, so that the king might enjoin what was just.[39] As Geoffrey in his former justiciarship had got into trouble about the dealings with these lands, and as he and some of his friends appear to have benefited by the alienations, we have here a probable source of his quarrel with Richard de Burgh.

But Richard de Burgh had many friends and was now the leading figure among the Anglo-Normans. His grant of Connaught soon became effective, and constituted a partition of the province between him and the King of England. The five cantreds reserved to the latter bordered along the Shannon from the river Suck northwards to Lough Allen, and thence to Lough Gill in County Sligo. They were known as Omany, Tirmany, Moy Ai, the Three Tuaths, and Moylurg and Tirerril considered as one cantred. Together they comprised nearly the whole of the present County Roscommon [174] with parts of the adjoining baronies in County Galway, and the barony of Tirerril in County Sligo.[40] The remainder of the kingdom of Connaught, reckoned as twenty-five cantreds, was assigned to Richard de Burgh. As yet, however, he was far from having obtained 'quiet enjoyment' of his great fief, and unfortunately we have few indications of how he proposed to obtain it. There was certainly no immediate attempt at colonization on a large scale. There never was any question of a wholesale clearance of population from any part of the land; and it was not proposed to do without the intervention of an Irish king. The difficulty seems to have been to find a king who would accept a subordinate position, with a restricted territory, while permitting

36 Ann. Ulst. 1223. In the Annals of Clonmacnois it is stated that Aedh 'came to an atonement' with Geoffrey, and was by him restored to the kingdom of Connaught, and being afterwards in Geoffrey's house was killed, &c., as above. There is no other authority for Aedh's restoration to the throne. It is not improbable, however, that he came to Geoffrey with overtures for assistance, and even that these overtures were favourably received by Geoffrey. 37 Pat. Roll, 12 Hen. III. 38 Cal. Docs. Ireland, vol. i, nos. 1462, 1602. 39 Rot. Claus. 11 Hen. III, p. 195 *b*. 40 For an attempt at a more precise demarkation see a paper by Mr. H. T. Knox, Journ. R.S.A.I., 1901, p. 365.

the Normans to make settlements in the country, and who, at the same time, would be able to command the obedience of the leading Irish tribes.

Now that Aedh, son of Cathal, was out of the way, it might be supposed that the Connaught clans would have united under the house of Rory; but 'a great war broke out in Connaught between the two sons of Rory, for (Aedh) the younger son did not yield submission to (Turlough) the elder, and they destroyed Connaught between them'.[41] Indeed what might be superficially regarded as the 'War of the Connaught Succession' between members of the O'Conor family, but what was in fact the 'War of the Conquest of Connaught' by Richard de Burgh, lasted, with brief intermissions, [175] from its commencement, in 1225, for altogether twelve years, and did not terminate until a king was found who was willing to hold the Saxon king's five cantreds as his territory and leave the rest of Connaught to the domination of Richard de Burgh. It would be unprofitable to follow minutely all the fortunes of this war, though for most years the annalistic materials for doing so are unusually abundant; but in order to understand how the Normans became dominant in Connaught—or rather perhaps how it was that the change of rulers was so long in coming about—it is essential to note the chief phases of the conflict and the influence of English political changes in postponing the inevitable result.

On returning to Ireland as justiciar, Richard de Burgh, like his father before him, became the King-maker of Connaught. At first he favoured Aedh, son of Rory, and he 'was made king by the election of the justiciar and the chiefs of Connaught in preference to Turlough his elder brother'.[42] But it seems that the war between the sons of Rory went on. 'The churches and territories of Connaught were pillaged by them, and its clergy and folk of learning were expelled into foreign countries.'[43] The year 1229 is a blank in the annals as regards affairs in Connaught,[44] but the Close Roll shows that in July the king ordered Richard de Burgh to retain as demesne of the king the best [176] lands in the five cantreds and to take counsel as to settling the residue to the king's advantage, and that a grant was made by the king to Adam de Staunton, lord of Moone in County Kildare, of five knights' fees about Dunamon on the river Suck.[45] It is probable that Richard also made some grants, and that it was in this year he erected the castle of Meelick on the Shannon, where his father in 1203 seems to have utilized the church as the core of a mote.[46]

Probably, however, the actual settlement had not proceeded far when next year (1230) King Aedh, son of Rory, turned against Richard de Burgh. This he did at the instigation of Donn Óg and Cormac Mac Dermot, 'for', says the annalist, 'they pledged their word that they would not belong to any king who would bring them into the house of the foreigners'.[47] Presumably Richard de Burgh, in pursuance of the king's mandate, had been trying to induce them to become tenants of the English

41 Four Masters, Annals of Boyle, 1228. 42 Four Masters, 1228. The entry in the Annals of Loch Cé is that 'Aedh son of Rory assumed the sovereignty of Connaught, and his brothers along with him'. 43 Ann. Ulst., 1228. 44 The entries in the Annals of Loch Cé, 1229, touching the plundering of Rinnduin, &c, are misplaced. They are repeated under 1236, the true date. 45 Close Roll, 13 Hen. III, m. 7, p. 194. 46 *Ante*, vol. ii, p. 192 [p. 228], Felim was imprisoned here in 1231. 47 Ann. Loch Cé, 1230.

Crown. Aedh and his followers set about plundering the new settlements made by the English in Tirmany and the lands of the Mac Costellos. Richard de Burgh now took up the cause of Felim, son of Cathal Crovderg, representative of the rival branch of the O'Conors. He entered Connaught from the south, accompanied by Felim, and supported, not only by the English barons, but also by the kings of Thomond and Desmond with their Gaelic forces.[48] After skirmishing somewhat ineffectually with the O'Flahertys near Galway, and obtaining pledges from Manus O'Conor of Clan Murtough in the region about Clew Bay, they marched through the southern part of [177]
the present County Sligo and over the Curlieu hills, with the object of forcing an engagement with Aedh, son of Rory, and the Sil Murray, who were in a wood near Lough Key. At length, contrary to the advice of King Aedh, whose plan was to clear the cattle from the country and avoid a battle, Donn Óg Mageraghty resisted the march of Richard de Burgh and was slain and his force routed. Thereupon Aedh fled to O'Neill; the cattle of the Sil Murray, which had been driven off for safety across the Shannon to the glens of Slieve-anierin in County Leitrim, were rounded up; and Felim was made king by the justiciar.[49]

Felim apparently proved no more tractable than Aedh, son of Rory, and was imprisoned next year (1231) by Richard at his castle of Meelick. We are left to conjecture the cause, but probably like Aedh he resented his subordinate and circumscribed position. Aedh now made peace with Richard, whose terms, whatever they were, he must have accepted and was once more made king (1232). In this year Richard erected a castle at Galway, and Adam de Staunton commenced another at Dunamon.

But now a change took place as the immediate result of political changes in England. On July 29, 1232, Hubert de Burgh, who with all his shortcomings was the most faithful minister of the Crown since the death of the great William Marshal, and after Stephen Langton its most patriotic adviser, was dismissed and disgraced, and the king [178]
fell under the influence of his old guardian, Peter des Roches, Bishop of Winchester, and his Poitevin nephew (?) Peter of Rivaux. A clean sweep was made of the old officials, lucrative posts were showered on the creatures of Peter des Roches, and bands of Poitevin mercenaries were brought into England. At the same time the baronial party, naturally incensed at their exclusion from the councils of the king, were weakened by the deaths of the younger William Marshal and Randolf, Earl of Chester. The former, who had proved himself a not unworthy successor of his father, died prematurely in May 1231, and the latter, who had long headed the old feudal aristocracy, died in October 1232.

Two important consequences to Ireland followed from this change in the king's advisers. We have already dealt with the revolt and tragic death of Earl Richard Marshal, which was directly traceable to Poitevin intrigues. The more immediate conse-

48 Annals of Inisfallen, 1230 (Dublin MS.). 49 Annals of Loch Cé, Ulster, Boyle, and Clonmacnois, 1230. The account given in Roger of Wendover (Coxe, vol. iv, pp. 213–14), apparently of this battle, receives no support from the detailed statements of the Irish annalists, and is certainly wrong in stating that Geoffrey de Marisco was then justiciar and leader of the English forces.

quence was the fall of Richard de Burgh and the temporary undoing of his work in Connaught.

At first an attempt was made to save Hubert de Burgh from his enemies by appointing him Justiciar of Ireland, with his nephew, Richard, as deputy,[50] and thus leaving open a retreat for him there. But the appointment was a dead letter. Before the end of July 1232 almost all the offices at the king's disposal in Ireland were lavished upon Peter of Rivaux, and Hubert was ignominiously dismissed. In Ireland Peter was given for life the offices of treasurer and chamberlain of the Exchequer, the king's
[179] prisage of wines, the custody of all the king's ports and coasts, the custody of the king's Jews, also the custodies of the king's escheats and wards, of the king's castles of Athlone, Drogheda, and Randown, with the king's five cantreds in Connaught, the custody of all vacant archbishoprics and bishoprics, of the city of Limerick with its castle, of Decies and Desmond with the city of Cork and the king's vill of Dungarvan.[51] Never before had such power in Ireland been concentrated in the hands of one man—and he an untried foreigner resident in England. The Chancery of Ireland was conferred on Ralph Neville, Bishop of Chichester and Chancellor of England, to be administered by deputy.[52] The office of justiciar was indeed committed during pleasure to Maurice Fitz Gerald, grandson of the first Maurice, but the office was shorn of most of its powers, and Maurice was to call in the aid and counsel of Peter's bailiffs and the Deputy Chancellor in the king's affairs, and without their presence nothing was to be done.[53]

With the fall of his uncle, the Earl of Kent, Richard de Burgh speedily lost the king's favour. In August he was peremptorily ordered to release Felim on his finding sureties to abide any charge that might be made against him,[54] and to deliver up the royal castles to Peter of Rivaux. On September 2 he was superseded in the office of justiciar by Maurice Fitz Gerald. Richard released Felim, with consequences which
[180] did not make for the peace of Connaught, and after some delay surrendered the castles; but a special commission was appointed to audit his accounts and to prosecute the king's plaint against him,[55] and the justiciar was afterwards ordered to take into the king's hand the land of Connaught and keep it for the king's use.[56] Richard refused to surrender his castle of Meelick, and the king gave orders first to the justiciar and then to Felim O'Conor to take it by force.[57] This, however, was not done, and in the spring of 1234 Richard de Burgh regained the king's favour, if he did not add to his own reputation, by the action he took against Richard Marshal.

Meanwhile Felim O'Conor made use of his liberty to destroy his rivals. Acting with the Mac Dermots and others, he organized a hosting into Connaught, in the course of which Aedh, son of Rory, King of Connaught, one of his brothers, and two of his nephews, were slain, and witll them fell for ever the sovereignty of this branch of the

50 Pat. Roll, 16 Hen. III, p. 487 (July 1). 51 Cal. Chart. Roll, 16 Hen. III, m. 3, p. 166. 52 Close Roll, 16 Hen. III, p. 112. Geoffrey de Turville, the chancellor's deputy, had been chamberlain of the Exchequer from 1226. He was appointed treasurer in 1234, an office which he honourably filled up to his death in 1250. He was elected Bishop of Ossory in 1244. 53 Ibid., pp. 102–3. 54 Ibid., p. 101. 55 Cal. Patent Roll, 17 Hen. III, p. 10 (Feb. 4, 1233). 56 Close Roll, 17 Hen; III, p. 306 (May 3, 1233). 57 Ibid., and Cal. Patent Roll, 17 Hen. III, p. 17.

O'Conors. Felim then proceeded to destroy the castles that had been erected by Richard de Burgh and the sons of Rory, namely, the castles of Galway and Dunamon, the Hen's castle and the Hag's Castle, the two last island castles probably those in Lough Corrib and Lough Mask respectively.[58] He now 'assumed the sovereignty and government over the Connaught men', and, owing to the king's quarrel with Richard de Burgh, he was not interfered with. Indeed it was in May of this year that the king fatuously invited Felim to take the castle of Meelick from Richard, while at the same [181]
moment he was urging the justiciar to subjugate to the king's power the whole of Connaught. Such futile and virtually inconsistent mandates show how little the king understood of the real position of affairs in Connaught and give us the measure of his intellect, which never knew how to adapt rneans to ends. By this time indeed (July 1233) Henry began to make preparations for an immediate expedition in person to Ireland.[59] This was certainly a wise projeet, but on August 28, having on his hands the more pressing task of countering the revolt of Richard Marshal in Wales, Henry changed his purpose and countermanded the preparations.[60]

The capricious change in Henry's attitude towards Richard de Burgh had effects outside the borders of Connaught. In 1234 the Mac Carthys, as we have seen., attacked Tralee, Felim advanced into Westmeath and burned Ballyloughloe and Ardnurcher, where the Normans had mote-castles from early times,[61] and — more ominous still— Donough Cairbrech O'Brien, King of Thomond, who had for so many years worked loyally with the de Burghs and fought by their side, now allied himself with Felim, attacked the eity of Limerick, and plundered O'Heyne, a chieftain in the [182]
south of Galway who had remained faithful to Richard in his adversity.[62]

But Felim's day of independence lasted only as long as the royal ire against Richard de Burgh, or rather, perhaps we should say, while the Poitevins controlled Henry's emotions. In April 1234 the Bishop of Winchester and Peter of Rivaux were dismissed from their offices. In May Richard regained the king's favour as a reward for his action against the Earl Marshal, and in September his land of Connaught was restored to him as before. The justiciar, Maurice Fitz Gerald, was ordered to give him seisin, and Richard himself was to exert himself strenuously to take possession of the land.[63] In fact the conquest of Connaught had to be begun over again.

Next year (1236) there was a general muster of the feudal host under Maurice Fitz Gerald to obtain once more the submission of Connaught. Among the leaders expressly named were Richard de Burgh, Hugh de Lacy, Walter de Ridelisford, and John de Cogan. To these we may probably add Gerald de Prendergast, Gerald de

58 Ann. Loch Cé, 1233. 59 Close Roll, 17 Hen. III, pp. 316–17. At the same time the king ordered that (Cormac Finn) Mac Carthy should be restored to the state from which he was removed by Richard de Burgh. 60 Ibid., p. 322. 61 Ann. Clonmacnois, 1234. For the mote at Ballyloughloe (*Baile locha ıuatha*) see Journal R.S.A.I., vol. xxxvii (1907), p. 273. It is probably to be identified with the castle of 'Lagholachon' restored to Walter de Lacy in 1215: Rot. Pat., 17 John, p. 148 *b*. For the castle of Ardnurcher see *ante*, vol. ii, p. 89 [p. 185]. 62 Ann. Loch Cé, 1235. In the Pipe Roll for 19 Hen. III may be found a reference to O'Brien's defection. Hugh de Barry, sheriff of Limerick, took credit for expenses 'in repairing the injuries caused by D. Carebrach at Limerick': 35th Rep. D. K, p. 85. 63 Close Roll, 18 Hen. III, pp. 625, 561. The king bade him 'quod de terra predicta perquirenda viriliter et potenter e intromittat'.

Roche, Peter de Bermingham, Matthew Fitz Griffin, and John le Botiller. All of these shared in the exploitation of Connaught, and nearly all were now or later connected by marriage. Thus Hugh de Lacy married as his second wife Emeline, daughter of
[183] Walter de Ridelisford; John de Cogan married a daughter of Gerald de Prendergast; Gerald married as his second wife a daughter of Richard de Burgh; while Richard was married to Egidia, daughter of Walter de Lacy. At first the feudal host went northwards from Athlone by Roscommon and Elphin to Boyle Abbey. They failed, however, to come to close quarters with Felim, who well knew their strength, and only succeeded in carrying off the cattle of the Sil Murray, which had as usual been driven for safety to the glens of Leitrim. Then they turned south into Thomond to punish O'Brien for his defection. Felim followed them to succour his ally,[64] but their joint forces were defeated, and O'Brien at once made peace and returned to his allegiance, while Felim fled to O'Donnell. O'Flaherty also made peace, and he and O'Heyne assisted the foreigners with their boats in ravaging the islands in Clew Bay.[65] Here Manus O'Conor, head of Clan Murtough, who alone in the lands of Richard de Burgh seems to have resisted, had retreated with his cattle.

After punishing O'Donnell for granting asylum to Felim, the army assaulted the island-rock of Lough Cé, which belonged to Mac Dermot. This assault is peculiarly interesting, not only as being an almost, if not quite, unique case of the Irish at this period defending a fortress, but also as showing that the Normans employed siege-engines, when required, in Ireland. They appear to have mounted on ships some small *pierriers*, or engines for discharging large stones, and to have constructed galleries
[184] or covered ways to protect the men working the engines.[66] With these they threw many stones into the island-fortress, but without avail. They then made some rude boats out of the timber of some neighbouring houses, filled them with combustible materials, bound them together into a large raft, and tied empty barrels around it to keep it afloat. When all was ready a large vessel protected by a plank-house towed the whole construction towards the fortress to set it on fire. The garrison, however, smitten with fear at these stratagems, surrendered on terms. The justiciar put a ward in the fortress, but twenty days later one of them treacherously locked out the rest, and they fled to Trinity Island, to the protection of Clarus Mac Mailin, Archdeacon of Elphin, whom they had previously befriended—an ignominious ending to a successful siege.

As the result of this campaign Felim 'made peace with the justiciar and obtained the king's five cantreds out of which he was to receive rent and customs',[67] and Mac

64 It was probably at this time that Felim broke down the castle of Meelick: Ann. Loch Cé, vol. i, p. 333.
65 See O'Flaherty's West Connaught, p. 51. As there stated the boats must have been drawn overland from Lough Corrib to Leenane in Killary Harbour. 66 Ann. Loch Cé, 1235, p. 328. Compare the curious phonetic passage in the Annals of Boyle as given in O'Grady's Catalogue of Irish MSS. The editor of the Annals of Loch Cé misunderstands the technical terms *go ngailleribh ocus co pirrélaibh*, which are probably loan-words from the French. A *pirrél* was, presumably, a small *pierrier* (Lat. *petraria*), a general term here denoting a *trébuchet*, or a mangonel, as it was more often called in England, and *gailler* is probably *galerie*. The word *créfal*, which the editor takes as 'an earthen wall', appears in the Annals of Connacht and in the Annals of Boyle as *crebannach*. It probably denoted some sort of wooden mounting for the *pierrier*, and was carried on board ship. The dauphin brought a *trébuchet* to England in 1217: see Minority of Henry III (Norgate), p. 27. 67 Ann. Loch Cé, 1235.

Dermot submitted at the same time. This amounted to a recognition by Felim of the [185]
partition of Connaught between himself and Richard de Burgh, the latter indeed getting the lion's share, but each holding as a tenant of the Crown at a definite rent. The Four Masters however state that Felim was given 'the king's five cantreds free of tribute or rent', but it is quite certain that this was not the fact. In this year Felim paid £90 13*s.* 4*d.* towards his fine for the farm of the five cantreds, and his rent at this time seems to have been £400 a year.[68] At a later period he paid a rent of £300 for a reduced territory. This rent eventually fell into large arrears, but it seems to have been paid with tolerable regularity as long as Felim lived.[69] Felim and his successors no doubt enjoyed the empty title of King of Connaught, but apart from all question of rent, their rights and jurisdiction were confined to the cantreds which they held of the King of England, and owing to their outbreaks as time went on these cantreds were reduced in number. These facts, absolutely vital to the understanding of the subsequent history of Connaught, have been too often ignored or obscured by writers on the sub- [186]
ject.[70] The rent of Richard de Burgh for his share of Connaught consisting of twenty-five cantreds was 500 marks a year. He had also made a fine of 3,000 marks for the recovery of his land and for acquittance of his account when justiciar. In June 1236, however, Richard went to England to confer with tlle king, and he obtained a remission of £1,000 out of his fine, and easier terms for the payment of the balance.[71]

While Richard de Burgh was in England, the justiciar, Maurice Fitz Gerald, for some unexplained reason[72] once more banished Felim and gave the possession of the five cantreds to Brian, son of Turlough, son of Rory. Felim, however, soon returned, and a bitter contest followed between the descendants of Cathal Crovderg and those of Rory. Felim succeeded in crossing the bawn of the castle of Rinn-duin,[73] where his rival Brian was installed, and driving off the cattle which had been collected in 'the [187]
island' beyond— i.e. on the point of the peninsula cut off by a large ditch (which may still be seen) connected with the lake—and in the lighting that ensued 'a multitude of the host of cursed candle-extinguished [excommunicated] people were slain in the

68 Pipe Roll (Ireland), 19 Hen. III, 36th Rep. D. K., p. 37. For the two and a half years ending with Easter term 1236 Master Stephen de Turri 'accounts for £1,000 rent of Connaught, viz. at £400 per year'. Most of the money was expended on works at the bridge of Athlone and the castles of Randown, Athlone, and Ardnurcher. 69 The next extant account is in the Pipe Roll for the 46th year of Henry III, P. R. O. Dublin, from which tho following is taken: 'Fethelmus Okonechor (Felim O'Conor) [owes] £600 for the farm of the said three cantreds (viz. Mackny, Tyrthotha, and Maylurg, i.e. *Magh n-Ai*, *Trituatha*, and *Magh Luirg*) for this and the preceding year, as is contained in the bond of the said Felim which is in the treasury, and £1,050 arrears of the same for several preceding years, as is contained in roll 44.' That is to say, at Michaelmas 1262, Felim owed five and a half years' rent at £300 a year. 70 Mr. Knox is perhaps the only writer who has recognized the true position of Felim and his suceessors. 71 Cal. Docs. Ireland, vol. i, no. 2342. 72 A consequence if not the cause of this quarrel was the erection 'against Connaught' of a castle called 'Muille Uanach' (probably in Onagh, a townland in the parish of Taghmaconnell on the east side of the river Suck, due west of Athlonc), pcrhaps to kcep the way open from Athlone to Galway: Ann. Loch Cé,1238. It is called 'Mayllonaeh' in 1245: Cal. Docs. Irel., vol. i, no. 2792. 73 The castle of Rinn-duin was not entered, nor probably the inner ward. The ditch of the innet ward is connected with a ditch running south-west and cutting off the point of the peninsula. For a description of the existing remains aud a slight sketch of the early history of the castle see Journ. R.S.A.I., 1907, pp. 274–5. New works had been going on there in the previous year: Pipe Roll (Ireland), 19 Hen. III, *loc. cit.*, p. 37.

island and outside'.[74] From this expression we may infer that Felim had the spiritual support of the local church.

When Richard de Burgh returned from England he still supported Felim. He appears, however, to have left the justiciar to deal with the king's five cantreds and went to quell or disperse those in his own part of Connaught who had turned against Felim.[75] This was done without much trouble, but the contest between Felim and the sons of Rory, though confined to the five cantreds, went on during this year and part
[188] of the next, when it ended in the final dispersal of the surviving descendants of Rory, 'so that they had no residence in Sil Murray'.[76]

The annalist sums up the whole of this disturbed period as follows: 'During the period of twelve years down from the war of O'Neill [1225] were the Foreigners and Gael plundering in turn, without sovereignty or supremacy being possessed by one beyond the other, but the Foreigners able to destroy it [Connaught] every time they came into it; and the King and royal heirs of Connaught pillaging and profaning territories and churches after them.' From the point of view of the invaders the main trouble was with the O'Conors. The Normans had no difficulty in overrunning the country, and the lesser chieftains seem to have been ready enough to submit and become vassals of Richard de Burgh, but as soon as an O'Conor was set up as king, he either rebelled or was attacked by rival O'Conors of the same or, more usually, of a different branch of the family. The agony of the province incident to the change of masters was further prolonged for several years owing to the capricious change in English politics which brought about the temporary fall of Richard de Burgh in 1232. At last, in 1237, peace was once more made by Maurice Fitz Gerald with Felim O'Conor, and the five cantreds were once more given to him. From this time up to Felim's death in 1265, though in his later years, in consequence of the outbreaks of his son Aedh, some of his
[189] territory was taken from him, Felim personally remained a loyal vassal of the Crown, and Connaught, especially in the territory of the de Burghs, enjoyed comparative peace.

In the course of these twelve years Richard de Burgh made at least three great campaigns in Connaught: one in 1227 against Aedh, son of Cathal, another in 1230 against Aedh, son of Rory, and a third in 1235 against Felim, son of Cathal. Each time he banished the king who tried to thwart him, and each time he had the whole country at his mercy, until at last he forced Felim to accept his terms. But he did much

74 Ann. Loch Cé, 123. 75 The passage in the Annals of Loch Cé, vol. i, p. 837, is rather confused, but probably it should be rendered thus: When Mac William heard of the defeat inflicted on those of his people who had turned against him [i.e. Felim], he joined O'Connor [i.e. Felim] and went to expel or subdue them.' The annalist then tells how Dermot, son of Maghnus [son of Turlough] O'Conor went for protection to Maghnus of Clan Murtough, and how Richard pursued him and forced him to submit. This Dermot had apparently fought against Feliin. The annalist would not call Brian, son of Turlough, son of Rory, 'O'Conor' simply, as supposed by Mr. Knox (Hist. of Mayo, p. 87), whereas he frequently in this same year calls Felim by that title. The above interpretation is virtually that of the Four Masters. The editor of the Annals of Loch Cé supposes that Richard went to attack or pacify Felim, but that is just what he did not do. In these events we may probably see the first sign of that jealousy between the de Burghs and the Geraldines in Connaught which in after years manifested itself more openly. 76 Ann. Loch Cé, 1237. Brian, son of Turlough, son of Rory, the justiciar's protégé, seems to have retired to the monastery of Knockmoy, where he ended his days in 1267.

more than this, as we shall see in the next chapter. He introduced into the districts he had subdued a new class of proprietors, or as they might more aptly be termed local rulers, who, whatever their faults, were much more modern in their ideas of political subordination, social order, and rural economy, than those who had preceded them, and the settlement thus established, more firmly in some places than in others, but influencing directly or indirectly at least three fourths of the province, made on the whole for order and progress for at least a century. To Richard de Burgh, rather than to his father,[77] critical history will give the title of 'Conqueror of Connaught'.

77 See *ante*, vol. ii, p. 198 [p. 230].

[190] CHAPTER XXIX

THE SUB-INFEUDATION OF CONNAUGHT, 1237, AND AFTERWARDS

Richard de Burgh had now a free hand in Connaught, and though sundry attempts at occupation had been made at various times since the beginning of the century, the effective settlement of Anglo-Normans in the province may be said to have commenced in 1237. In that year, says the Irish annalist, 'the barons of Erin came into Connaught and commenced to build castles in it'. In the following year 'castles were erected in Muinter Murchada (the northern half of the barony of Clare, County Galway), Conmaicne Cuile (the barony of Kilmaine, south of the river Robe, County Mayo), and in Cera (the barony of Carra, County Mayo) by the aforesaid barons'.[1] Save for personal quarrels among the O'Conors themselves the peace was unbroken.

Unfortunately there is no contemporary summary of Richard de Burgh's enfeoffments, such as the Song of Dermot gives of those of Strongbow and the elder Hugh de Lacy, and though there are transcripts in the 'Red Book of the Earl of Kildare' and in the 'Gormanston Register' of several charters of this period, we are largely depen-
[191] dent on indications in the annals, and on inferences from later documents and records for our knowledge of the Anglo-Norman settlement in Connaught. Indeed the first comprehensive account is to be gleaned from the Inquisitions taken in 1333[2] after the murder of William de Burgh, Earl of Ulster, fifteen years after the great disruption caused by the Scottish invasion under Edward Bruce, and at a time when the royal power in Ireland had begun to wax faint.

Richard de Burgh's principal manor was at Loughrea, where the castle which he built in 1236[3] became the chief seignorial seat of the lordship. In Earl Walter's time there were four carucates of demesne land at Toolooban near Dunsandle, and prior to 1333 even more, all arable land under the lord's plough. Richard had also a castle and

1 Ann, Loch Cé, 1237–8. 2 Chancery Inquisitions p. m., 7 Ed. III, no. 39 These inquisitions are very voluminous and deal with the lands of the earl in Carlow, Uriel, Meath, Munster, and Ulster, as well as those in Connaught. For full abstracts and a careful study of those relating to Connaught see the papers by Mr. H. T. Knox in Journal R.S.A.I., vols. xxxii, xxxiii (1902–3). 3 Ann. Clonmacnois, 1236. Loughrea was in the cantred of Maenmagh, which had been given by Cathal Crovderg to Gilbert de Nangle in 1195: *ante*, vol ii, p. 155 [p. 213]. In February 1207, King John confirmed this grant, but in the following November he made a grant to Gilbert of lands further to the east, no doubt in substitution for Maenmagh. This new grant included *Muinter Maelfinnain*. This, too, eventually passed to the de Burgh lord, but in conformity with the above it is stated in the inquisition of 1333 that it was not held in chief of the Crown like the rest of the lordship. Presumably the title was traced through Gilbert de Nangle.

manor at Meelick on the Shannon. This was in O'Madden's country, where the Irish chiefs seem always to have been friendly with the de Burghs. We also hear of the earl's [192] castle at Portumna, where the ferry was valuable. The castle at Galway, erected in 1232, though destroyed by Felim next year, was no doubt rebuilt immediately on Richard's return to power. Not far off he formed a small manor in the parish of Ballinacourty, where the land juts out into the bay to the south-east of the town.[4] Apart from the demesne-lands, the cantreds comprised in the present baronies of Loughrea, Leitrim, and Longford, and the district about the town of Galway, appear to have been granted to free tenants for rent service,[5] or on minor tenures in comparatively small lots, and to have been strongly colonized. This was the territory which from about the middle of the fourteenth century became known as 'Clanrickard's country'. But the remainder of County Galway and the whole of the counties Sligo and Mayo were granted in large fiefs to be held by military service and a money rent. In general the reservations were at the rate of twenty marks, and the service of two knights per cantred. In the reservation of a money rent the subinfeudation of Connaught differed [193] from that of Leinster and Meath.

Owing presumably to the loss of most of the Irish Pipe Rolls for the reign of Henry III, we have no wardship accounts[6] relating to the manor of Loughrea until the beginning of the reign of Edward I, when for eight years it was in the king's hand during the minority of Richard the Red Earl of Ulster. This was a disturbed time and the accounts are not complete, but the sum of £2,210 9*s*. 2*d*. was received for the king from the manor of Loughrea, and the sum of £129 14*s*. from the town fisheries, &c., of Galway.[7]

It was probably immediately after his decisive campaign of 1235 that Richard de Burgh set about rewarding those who had supported him, by granting them large fiefs in different parts of Connaught, to be held by knight's service and low rents. First of all to Hugh de Lacy he granted five cantreds, namely, Corran, Carbury-Drumcliff,

4 This manor appears as 'the land of Metherye' when restored to the second Richard de Burgh in 1247: Close Roll, 31 Hen. III, p. 534. The name represents the Irish *Medhraighe*, famous as the western extremity of the *Eiscir Riada*, and has survived as 'Maäree': Four Masters, vol. vi, p. 2198, note. At Ballynacourty near the church are the remains of the basement of an early castle. 5 For example: Rathgorgin, where there are remains of an early castle, was held by John Dolfin, in 1271, and by Thomas Dolfin in 1333, at a rent of £3 6*s*. 8*d*. In the adjoining townland of Oldcastle is a good example, rare in Connaught, of the mote-type of earthwork, perhaps dating from the time when Gilbert de Nangle held Maenmagh: see Journal, Galway Arch. and Hist. Soc., vol. ix, pp. 33–44. In 1585 twenty-seven quarters of land about here were known as 'Eraght Dolphine': West Connaught, p. 325. 6 Yet there was a minority before each succession. Richard le Burgh died in 1243. His eldest son Richard came of age in February 1247, when seisin was granted to him (Cal. Docs. Irel., vol. i, no. 2865). The Connaught lands then held by the custodians are described as 'the land of Miloc' (Meelick, barony of Longford), 'land of Metherye' (now Ballinacourty), 'land of Iochorye' (probably a blundering form of Loch Riach, Loughrea), the 'castles of Caylly and Kyrky' (*caislén na Caillighe* in Lough Mask and *caislén na Circe* in Lough Corrib), and the islands in the two lakes (ibid., 2908). The second Richard de Burgh died before November 5, 1248, and was succeeded by his brother Walter in May 1250 (ibid., no. 3050). Walter died in 1271, and was succeeded by his son Richard the Red Earl in January 1280 (ibid., vol. ii, no. 1629). The Red Earl died in 1326, and in 1328 his grandson, William, the Brown Earl, when only sixteen years of age, was put into possession of his estates. 7 Pipe Roll (Ireland), 9 Ed. I, 36th Rep. D.K., p. 63.

[194] Tireragh on the Moy, Luighne, and Slieve Lugha, for the service of ten knights and the annual rent of 100 marks.[8] This grant was in substitution for a previous inoperative grant of ten cantreds given by William de Burgh to the same grantee about the beginning of the century.[9] It included rather more than the present county of Sligo less the barony of Tirerril. Hugh de Lacy, however, died in 1243. His last years were much occupied by affairs in Ulster, and he seems to have at once parted with most of his Connaught lands. He formed, indeed, a manor at Meelick in the south-eastern portion of the barony of Gallen, included at this time in Luigne.[10] This manor was assigned to his widow Emeline as her dower out of her lord's five cantreds, and was by her given to the second Richard de Burgh in exchange for his Munster manor of Tristelaurent, now Inch St. Lawrence in County Limerick.[11]

[195] Of these cantreds Hugh de Lacy soon granted Carbury[12] and the northern half of Luighne[13] (as well as his claims as Earl of Ulster on Tirconnell)[14] to Maurice Fitz Gerald. This was the nucleus of the Geraldine manor of Sligo, but it was afterwards, as we shall see, increased in two directions. Maurice obtained from Jordan of Exeter a moiety of the southern half-cantred of Luighne, which with the northern half-cantred made up the present barony of Leyney, and his son and successor in Connaught, Maurice Fitz Maurice, acquired the cantred of Corran, which was originally granted to Gerald de Prendergast. Thus the Geraldine manor of Sligo included approximately the present baronies of Carbury, Leyney, and Corran. In 1238 Maurice Fitz Gerald, then justiciar, and Hugh de Lacy dethroned Donnell Mac Loughlin, king of the Cinel Owen, and set up Brian O'Neill in his place, and in the next year Maurice plundered Carbury, which at this period was subject to O'Donnell. At Sligo Maurice built a castle in 1245, and here, in 1253, he founded a Dominican Friary.[15] In 1244 he obtained a
[196] grant of free chase and warren in 'Luyne' (Leyney),[16] and probably about this time built the castles of Banada and Arderee.[17] Before his death in 1257 Maurice enfeoffed

8 Gormanston Register, f. 189., where the cantreds appear as 'Korn, Karbridrumclef, Tirfichre Omoly, Lune, and Clefluuethe', and the witnesses are Maurice Fitz Gerald, then justiciar, Walter de Ridelisford, Gerald de Prendergast, Peter de Bermingham, and Matthew Fitz [Griffin], all of whom probably accompanied Richard and Huh on this campaign and were directly or indirectly rewarded. 9 *Ante,* vol. ii, p. 156 note [p. 214, note 24], and cf. p. 187 note [p. 226, note 18]. 10 The northern part of Gallen, called Coolcarney (*Cuil Cernadha*), was included in Tir Fhiachrach, but Meelick (*Milic*) and even Athlethan were in Luighne in the larger sense of that denomination. Luighne, indeed, was an alias for the diocese of Achonry, which included the parishes of Leyney, Corran, Gallen, and part of Costello: Ann. Loch Cé, vol. i, pp. 279, 355. In the inquisition of 1333 I take 'the half cantred of Lowyn' in which was 'Adlayn' (*Ath lethan*) as standing for Luighne, not Sliabh Lugha as supposed by Mr. Knox: Journ. R.S.A.I., 1902, p. 398. The barony of Gallen was ultimately formed out of the Mac Jordan de Exeter lands. 11 Cal. Docs. Irel., vol. i, no. 3006. 12 Red Book of the Earl of Kildare, f.v*d*: 'cantredum Carebri Drumclef . . . faciendo servicium duorum militum et reddendo viginti marcas . . . et unum accipitrem sorum.' 13 Ibid. f. vi: 'dimidium cantredum de Luyne, illam [*sic*] videlicet que iacet versus aquilonem proxima de Esdaro (Ballysadare) ... faciendo servicium unius militis et reddendo decem marcas argenti.' The kingdom of Luighne appears to have been co-extensive with the diocese of Achonry, and included, besides the barony of Leyney, the greater part of Gallen and the northern part (Sliabh Lugha) of Costello. 14 Ibid. f. v *d*: 'Tyrconyll per rectas metas divisas inter Keneleon et Tyrconyll . . . faciendo servicium quatuor militum pro omni servicio.' 15 For the above events see Ann. Loch Cé, *sub annis.* 16 Cal. Docs. Ireland, vol. i, no. 2680. 17 Under the year 1265 the Annals of Loch Cé record the destruction by Aedh O'Conor of the castles of *Benn-fhada* (Banada) and *Rath-aird-craibhe* (Ardcree in Kilvarnet parish), as well as of the castle of Sligo.

his second son Maurice in all his land of Carbury, with the castle of Sligo as well as with his lands of Tirconnell and Fermanagh.[18] Maurice Fitz Maurice gave Banada to his younger brother Thomas,[19] father of John Fitz Thomas of Offaly. After the death of Maurice, son of Mauriee Fitz Gerald, in 1286, Maurice's lands were partitioned between his daughters Juliana, wife of Thomas de Clare, and Amabil. The latter gave her share to her cousin John Fitz Thomas, afterwards first earl of Kildare.[20] In settlement of the dispute which arose between John FitzThomas and the Red Earl, all the [197]
lands of the former in Connaught seem to have been surrendered to the latter,[21] and in the inquisition taken on the death of Earl William in 1333, the manor of Sligo appears as belonging to the de Burghs. Its value before the recent disturbances was assessed as high as £333 6*s*. 8*d*.[22] About this time, however, the O'Haras recovered possession of Leyney.

The southern half of the cantred of Luighne (including the greater part of the barony of Gallen (*Gailenga*)) was apparently given by Hugh de Lacy to Jordan of Exeter.[23] In 1240, however, Jordan, as we have mentioned, granted a moiety of his half-cantred to Maurice Fitz Gerald.[24] In the other moiety, in what is now the barony of Gallen in County Mayo, Jordan formed the manor of Athlethan, now Ballylahan, where the ruins of a thirteenth-century castle still stand on a spur projecting from the [198]
high ground above a ford on the Moy. In 1253 he was granted a fair at the town,[25] which is said to have been incorporated, and at about the same time he founded a Dominican Friary at Strade,[26] not far off. In 1249, apparently when sheriff of Con-

They were all, no doubt, rebuilt—that of Sligo in 1269, and again by Earl Richard in 1310. **18** Red Book, f. viii. See the essential parts of this deed (which has been misinterpreted) transcribed in my paper on the Fitz Geralds, barons of Offaly ', in Journal R.S.A.I., vol. xliv (1914), p. 107 (where 'pro quiet' clam' quam [*sic*],' &c., should have been expanded into 'pro quieta clamacione quam,' &c.). **19** Ibid. f. xxii: 'Ego Mauricius filius Mauricii dedi, &c. Thome filio Mauricii fratri meo totam terram meam de Bennede in cantredo de Lune cum castro et omnibus pertinentiis excepto castro de Rathardkreth cum tribus villatis terre ad dictum castrum pertinentibus viz. Rathardkrath Rouelan et Clarath et excepto dominio Roberti de Prendirgast habend' &c. adeo plenius prout dominus Mauritius filius Geraldi pater meus illam terram cum castro . . . tenuit . . . et mihi dedit Reddendo umum ostorium sorum . . . et faciendo sectam ad curiam meam de Rathardkreth,' &c. **20** See the several deeds mentioned in the Red Book from Amabil to John, son of Thomas, H. M. C., 9th Rep., pt. 2, pp. 266–7. In the partition most of the Connaught lands seem to have been assigned to Amabil. **21** See the agreement set out in Cal. Justiciary Rolls (1299), pp. 285–6. **22** Journal R.S.A.I., vol. xxxiii (1903), p. 61. **23** In 1333 a rent of 10 marks was received from Adlayn (Athlethan or Ballylahan) for half the cantred of Lowyn (Luighne) from John of Exeter. **24** In the Red Book, f. 62 *d*, is an agreement dated at Ardrathan, September 10, 1240, by which Jordan agreed to give to Maurice 'medietatem dimidii cantredi de Luyna quod [*sic*] dictus Iordanus tellet de comite Ultonie . . . tenend' de eodem Iordano in feodo per servicium unius militis per redditum centum solidorum. Et proper hoc debet predictus Mauricius firmare quoddam castrum ad opus Iordani in Winterclerekyn (perhaps = *Druim ui Cleirchein*; Four Masters, vol. ii, p. 934, now Dromin between Athlacca and Uregare, Geraldine manors in Co. Limerick) de magnitudine et simultudine castri eiusdem Iordani quod habet in tenemento de Ardrath,' &c. Jordan de Exeter held the two vills of 'Donncolyn and Rothbethach' (Dunkellin and Roevehagh in the parish of Killeely) of the Geraldine manor of Ardrathan: ibid., f. xvi *d*. **25** Cal. Docs. Ireland, vol. ii, no. 250. **26** Ann. Loch Cé, 1253. It is believed that the Annales de Monte Fernandi were writton in this House. According to the Register of the Dominican Friary of Athenry, the Convent of Strade was originally founded for Franciscans, but was transferred to Dominicans at the instance of Basilia, daughter of Meiler de Bermingham, and wife of Stephen, son of Jordan of Exeter.

naught, he routed a force under the sons of Aedh O'Conor which came to attack Athenry. He was again sheriff in 1258, when he was killed while endeavouring to arrest a piratical fleet from the Western Isles under 'Mac Sorley'.[27] The family became very numerous in Connaught, where one branch became known as Mac Jordan and another as Mac Stephen. Like the Costellos, they maintained their position for upwards of three centuries, and in the composition of 1585 the Mac Jordan Dexeter of the day was assigned the castle of Ballylahan and eight quarters of land.

The cantred of Corran appears to have been granted by Hugh de Lacy to Gerald
[199] de Prendergast. Gerald granted it to 'David, son of Maurice',[28] in frank-marriage with Gerald's daughter Matilda. This David was an unnoticed son of Maurice Fitz Gerald, the justiciar. He died before St. Patrick's Day, 1249, when Matilda was still under seven years of age.[29] After Gerald's death in 1251 Matilda was given in marriage to Maurice, son of Guy de Rochford, 'the king's groom.'[30] He died before May 1258,[31] and shortly afterwards his widow Matilda was married to Maurice Fitz Maurice. This marriage, unnoticed in the pedigree of the Fitz Geralds, is proved by a letter of the year 1259 from Pope Alexander IV to the Bishop of Cloyne, directing the bishop not to harass Maurice Fitz Maurice on account of the former contractual relations of his wife Matilda, daughter of Gerald de Prendergast, with his deceased brother David.[32] The marriage accounts for the possession by Maurice Fitz Maurice of the cantred of Corran, one-third of which descended to his daughter Amabil (presumably Matilda's heir), and was by her given along with other lands in Connaught to John Fitz Thomas
[200] of Offaly in 1289.[33] From John Fitz Thomas, Corran, with the other Geraldine lands in Connaught, passed to Richard de Burgh, Earl of Ulster, and here at Ballymote in 1300 the earl built a great castle. The small town which grew up about the castle was burned, and the castle itself broken during the disturbances caused by the invasion of Edward Bruce. Probably there was no considerable settlement of the English in the district, and in 1338, after the murder of Earl Richard's son Edmond, the Irish regained control over Corran.

Though no sub-grant of the cantred of Tireragh is forthcoming, there can be little doubt that Hugh de Lacy gave it to Piers de Bermingham. The whole district 'from the river Moy eastwards ha to Ballysadare Bay' was called 'Mac Feorais's country' as

27 Ibid., 1258, where Jordan of Exeter is called Siúrtán dEissétar. In Ann. Ulst., 1258, he is called *Siurtan Gaileang* from his fief. Another Jordan of Exeter was sheriff of Connaught in 1269–72: 36th Rep. D. K., p. 28. By Mac Somhairle (Sorley) we must understand a *descendant* of Somerled. The person meant was probably Dugald, son of Ruaidhri, son of Ragnall, son of Somerled, whose daughter Aedh O'Conor married next year: Ann. Loch Cé, 1259, where the above Dugald is called Dubhgall Mac Somhairle. 28 Red Book of the Earl of Kildare, f. vii *d*: 'cantredum de Coron . . . duas partes scilicet dicti cantredi in dominico et tertiam partem in homagio et servicio . . . reddendo xx marcas argenti . . . et faciendo servicia duorum militum (in quibus xx marcis cum serviciis predictis ego et heredes mei Ricardo de Burgo tenemur ad redditus et servicia de predicto cantredo versus dominum Regem acquietando),' &c. 29 For Matilda's age see Cal. Inquis. P. M., 36 Hen. III, no. 254. 30 Cal. Docs. Ireland, vol. ii, nos. 80, 84, 165. 31 Ibid., no. 580. No. 852 is misdated, cf. no. 116. 32 Theiner, Vetera Monumenta, no. ccxi. 33 Red Book of the Earl of Kildare, f. xxiv *d*. The marriage also accounts for the fact that Maurice Fitz Maurice held for his life Gerald de Prendergast's lands at Tobernea, Co. Limerick, Corbyn, Co. Cork, and Killegny, Co. Wexford: Cal. Docs. Ireland, vol. iii, no. 463.

early as 1249, when Aedh, son of King Felim, broke out in rebellion and plundered it.[34] Here, as elsewhere, Mac Feorais was the Irish name for the sons or descendants of Piers de Bermingham, and from certain Plea Rolls of the time of Edward I it appears that both the Tethmoy and the Athenry branches of the family held lands here.[35] The principal castles were at Ardnarea and Castleconor, both on the Moy, but there was another at Buninna,[36] near Ballysadare Bay. In 1333 Tireragh appears to have consisted of two cantreds, 'Tyromoy' (*Tir Fhiachrach Maidh*) and 'Con[or]dunmor' (Castle-
conor). Each paid twenty marks to the earl, but the tenants names are not given.[37] The [201]
English seem to have maintained themselves here until 1371, when the castles of Ardnarea and Castleconor were taken by O'Dowd, and the English that were in them were driven out.[38] Ardnarea, however, appears to have been held by the Burkes long after this.[39]

Slieve Lugha, the last of the de Lacy cantreds, comprised the northern part of the barony of Costello. The O'Garas were the native chieftains, but there is no mention of any fighting with them. The cantred was held at his death by Miles de Nangle or Mac Costello. He was son of Philip, son of William, son of Jocelin de Nangle, first Baron of Navan.[40] He married a daughter of Hugh de Lacy, Earl of Ulster, and it is a probable conjecture that Hugh gave him Slieve Lugha in frank-marriage with her. She died in 1253 and was buried in the abbey of Boyle.[41]

Miles is surnamed *Bregach* by MacFirbis, indicating that he came directly from Meath (Breg). He died in 1259. His descendants in the barony of Costello, the whole of which they ultimately obtained, were very numerous. His younger son, Philip, who appears to have been the sheriff of that name of Connaught in 1277,[42] was ancestor of the clans Mac Jordan Duff and Mac Philip. The principal castle in the barony was
known as Castlemore Costello and was very famous. There was another at Kilcol- [202]
man.[43] From their position on the borders of the Irish districts the MacCostellos were frequently fighting with the O'Conors, the Mac Dermots, the O'Haras, and others. Yet for upwards of 300 years they maintained their position, and in 1586 John McCostello, 'captain of his nation,' having obtained a regrant from the Crown of numerous manors and lands in the barony, sold the same to his kinsman Tibault Dillon,[44] and what was once a feudal holding and then a quasi-Celtic chieftainry, became a modern landed estate.

The southern part of the barony of Costello included most of the country of the Ciarraighe (Kerry), an ancient tibe to whom was assigned as eponymous ancestor Ciar, son of Queen Meave, and the Ultonian hero Fergus Mac Roig. John Fitz Thomas of

34 Ann. Loch Cé, 1249. 35 In 1297 Peter, son of James de Bermingham of Tethmoy, released his whole right and claim in the vill of Castleconor and three carucates there to Eustace le Poer, who claimed through a Bermingham-Poer marriage: Plea Roll, 24 Ed. I. In 1302 Eustace got a grant of free warren in Kenmoy and Castleconor: Cal. Chart. Rolls, 30 Ed. I, p. 24. 36 *Bun finne.* See Ann. Loch Cé, 1308, 1310 37 Journal R.S.A.I., vol. xxxiii (1303), p. 59. 38 Four Masters, 1371. 39 Ann. Loch Cé, 1532–3. 40 See the Plea Roll, 16 Ed. II, cited *supra*, p. 35, note 2 [p. 298, note 55]. The senior line in Meath was continued from Miles in successive generations, by Hugh, Jordan, and John. We have already mentioned the attempt of Philip de Nangle and his son Miles to get a foothold in County Leitrim: *supra*, pp. 32–6 [pp. 297–9]. 41 Ann. Loch Cé, 1253. 42 Cal. Docs. Irel., vol. ii, p. 266. 43 Ann. Loch Cé, 1270. 44 Fiants, Eliza-

Desmond held the lands of Kerry Loch-narney under Maurice de Londres, who may have been the first grantee. Thomas Fitz Maurice, grandson of John Fitz Thomas, gave the lands, subject to a rent of £33 3*s*. 8*d*., to Henry de Roche in exchange for the manor of Mallow.[45] These lands were about Lough Mannin, where, on a small peninsula, there
[203] are some remarkable earthworks and a small round keep resembling, on a smaller scale, the keep of Shanid, and seeming to date from the thirteenth century.[46] There is a tradition that the monastery at Ballyhaunis was founded on the site of a de Barry manor-house,[47] and archaeological evidence indicates that the site had been fortified by the Normans. There is a roughly rectangular mote at Annagh, not far from Ballyhaunis, recalling some examples in the east of Ireland, and indeed what appear to be minor Norman earthworks abound in this part of Connaught.[48] At a later period we find the Mac Jordans (Duff), a branch of the McCostellos, in this district as well as in Kerry Oughter or Upper Kerry (parishes of Aghamore and Knock), and members of this family founded a house for Austin Hermits at Ballyhaunis and one for Dominicans at Urlare.

South of these Kerry districts, in the parishes of Kiltullagh and part of Kilkeevin, was the cantred of Sil Maelruain, of which the O Flynns were chiefs. The death of 'Piers Ristubhard, lord of Sil Maelruain, a noble baron', is recorded in 1264,[49] but his identity is uncertain. He may have been a Rochford, as in 1272–80 the fourth part of
[204] a cantred in 'Silmorne' (Sil Maelruain ?) was held by Henry de Rochford.[50] There is a mote called Sheeaunbeg in the townland of Barrinagh (parish of Kiltullagh) which seems to belong to the early Norman period,[51] but the O'Flynns were always energetic fighters, and probably no strong settlement was formed here. A strong castle was, however, built in the neighbouring parish of Toberbride, now Ballintober, County Roscommon. Curiously enough nothing is known about its origin, but in the inquisition of 1333 it is grouped with the cantred of Sil Maelruain and is described as 'an old castle surrounded by a stone wall, which would be very useful for keeping the peace' if repaired and garrisoned. Here there were three hundred acres of arable land under the lord's plough, a hundred-court, water-mills, burgages at Toberbride and Rathfernan and many free holdings, all formerly valued at £84 per annum, but then, owing to the recent disturbances, at £10 only.[52] It had evidently been an inportant seignorial

beth, nos. 4898, 4902. For the sale to Dillon see Ann. Loch Cé, vol. ii, p. 477 (anno 1586), and O'Flaherty's West Connaught (Hardiman), p. 339. 45 Inquisition on the lands of John Fitz Thomas (1282): Cal. Docs. Irel., vol. ii, p. 429. See, too, Inquisition after the death of Thomas Fitz Maurice (1298): ibid., vol. iv, pp. 258, 340. Maurice de Londres held the manor of Roscarlan (Rosegarland) in County Wexford from the Marshals: see Chart. St. Mary's Dub., vol. ii, p. 155. He probably sprang fron the family that owned Kidwelly Castle in Carmarthenshire, and he may have been related to Henry de Londres, archbishop of Dublin. 46 For plan and description see Journ. Galway Arch. Soc. (1902), vol. vii, p. 115. Lough Glinn Castle, in the adjoining parish of County Roscommon, is also said to have been built by the Geraldines: Hib. Dominicana, p. 311. 47 Hy Fiachrach, p. 161, note. 48 Some Connacht Raths and Motes (H. T. Knox), Journ. R.S.A.I., vol. xli (1911), p. 301 et seq. 49 Ann. Loch Cé, 1254. The name Ristubhard is taken by the editor to refer to de Ridelisford, as in 1235 'Ualdar Ritabhard, high baron of Leinster', clearly refers to Walter de Ridelisford, but there is nothing to connect his family with the district. Perhaps the entry is a blundered double of the preceding obit of 'Piers Pramister' (Bermingham). 50 Irish Pipe Roll 36th Rep. D. K., p. 63. Henry de Rochford was sheriff of Connaught in 1280: ibid.. p. 66. 51 For plan and description see Journal R.S.A.I. vol xli (1911), pp. 307–9. 52 Journal R.S.A.I., vol. xxxiii (1903), pp.

manor. In 1305 Earl Richard sought and obtained the king's licence to found and endow a chantry there and at Loughrea notwithstanding the statute of Mortmain. The jurors in recommending the proposal said that 'it would be of great advantage, if for no other reason, for the teaching of children in those parts where learning was too scarce'.[53] The remains of the castle of Ballintober are Edwardian in plan—a quadrangle with polygonal towers at the corners and gateway towers, all surrounded by a wet ditch—and indicate great strength.[54] The original building may with probability be [205] referred to about the last quarter of the thirteenth century. It was well situated to overawe the O'Conor kings. The town was burned in 1315, but seemingly not the castle. In 1362 we first hear of an O'Conor taking possession of it.[55] It remained generally in their hands, and after many vicissitudes the castle was restored and occupied by the O'Conor Don in the sixteenth century.

It is a probable conjecture that the castle was held by William 'Liath' de Burgh, the powerful cousin of Earl Richard; that after his death in 1324 it was held by his son Walter; and that on Walter's forfeiture and death in prison in 1332 it came into the hands of Earl William. The ownership by William 'Liath' of this strong castle so near the Sil Murray fits in remarkably well with his action in 1309–10 in reference to the kings of Connaught, and also with his son Walter's doings in 1328–31.[56]

Sligo was not the only manor of Maurice Fitz Gerald in Connaught. He also obtained extensive grants in the counties of Galway and Mayo. For his assistance in the campaign of 1235 Richard de Burgh rewarded him out of the territory of O'Heyne in parts of the baronies of Dulkellin and Kiltartan, County Galway.[57] Here the manorial centres were at Ardrahan and Kilcolgan, and here in 1241 Maurice obtained a grant of [206] free warren in his demesne lands and of a market and fair at Kilcolgan.[58] From an interesting agreement transcribed in the Red Book it appears that at first 'half the cantred of Ogehethie' was granted to Eoghan O'Heyne, but that on May 26, 1252, at Clare, in the presence of Florence Mac Floinn, archbishop of Tuam, and others, O'Heyne surrendered the half-cantred to Maurice saving the tenures of his feoffees, viz.: Conor O'Heyne, Master Maurice, Thomas Malet,and Nesta, daughter of Thomas, son of Robert. In consideration of this surrender Maurice granted to O'Heyne 'the villata of Tillog and Punchedath in the tenement of Ardrahan' with eight cows and forty marks of 'old Flemish money'.[59] The O'Heynes and O'Shaughnessys assisted Richard de

59–60. 53 Cal. Docs. Ireland, vol. v, nos. 436, 510. 54 See Journal R.S.A.I. (1889), pp. 24–30, for plan and description. 55 Ann. Loch Cé, 1362. 56 See *infra*, vol. iv, c. xxxviii. 57 Red Book, f. vi, where the grant is transcribed. The parcels are 'duo cantreda terre de Ofecherath [*ui Fiachrach* (*Aidhne*)] sicut Rothy Ohethyn [Ruaidhri O'h-Eidhin] ea . . . tenuit salvo et in manu mea retento cantredo de Kenoloth' [*Cenel Aodha*, 'O'Shaughnessy's country] to be held by the service of four knights and the rent of 40 marks. Among the witnesses are Hugh de Lacy, Walter de Ridelisford, Gerald de Prendergast, Mathew Fitz Griffin, Richard de Tuit, Peter de Bermingham, Nicholas Power, John de Cogan and others—pointing to the year 1235. This was the only land held by Maurice Fitz Gerald directly of the de Burghs. The two cantreds were, seemingly, *Coill ua bh-Fiachrach* aud *Oga Bethra*. 58 Cal. Docs. Ireland, vol. i, no. 2550, and Red Book, f. ii. 59 Red Book, f. xix. Eoghan O'hEidhin died next year; Ann. Loch Cé, 1253. 'Ogehethie': *Oga Bethra*, a territory in the northern part of Aidhne; Hy Fiachrach, pp. 53, 63. 'Tillog': *Tul oighre* ? 'hill of the heir' (Joyce, vol. iii), Tulleyre (Fiants Eliz., 5808), now Tullira in paish of Ardahan.

Burgh more than once, accepted their subordinate position, and were left in possession of parts of their territories. Small thriving towns grew up about the castles of Ardrahan and Kilcolgan. In 1289, after the death of Maurice, son of Maurice Fitz Gerald, the lands were partitioned between his daughters Juliana, wife of Thoms de Clare, and
[207] Amabil, the former getting Ardrahan and the latter Kilcolgan. The demesne lands of the undivided manors were valued at £49 6*s*. 8*d*., and the rents of freeholders at £33 12*s*. 0½*d*. The burgesses of Ardrahan paid a rent of £4 1*s*. 0*d*. for their burgage land, and those of Kilcolgan £7 6*s*. 8*d*.[60] Another inquisition taken in 1321, after the death of Thomas, son of Richard de Clare (younger brother of the first Thomas), shows that the lands of Ardrahan were then worth a little over £40.[61]

The lands of Maurice Fitz Gerald in Mayo were mainly in the barony of Kilmaine, south of the river Robe.[62] He obtained them not directly from Richard de Burgh, but partly from Gerald de la Roche[63] and partly from Raymond, brother and heir of
[208] Mathew Fitz Griffin.[64] Here he formed the manor of Lough Mask, built a castle,[65] and in 1244 received a grant of free chase and warren.[66] The principal towns were at Ballinrobe and Shrule. The manors of Lough Mask and Dunmougherne were ceded along with his other Connaught lands by John Fitz Thomas to Earl Richard in 1299,[67] and the manors of Lough Mask and Shrule were among those granted by the earl in 1308 to his son John and Elizabeth de Clare.[68]

60 Red Book, ff. xvi-xviii, where full details are given, including tenants' names. denominations of lands, and tenures. The lands held of the manors extended beyond the present parishes of Ardrahan and Kilcolgan. 61 For an abstract of this inquisition and plan of the earthworks about the castle see Galway Arch. Journal, vol. vii, pp. 73–83. In the Red Book, ff. vii and xiii, there are two grants from Conor [Mac Murray], bishop of Kilmacduagh (d. 1247), to Maurice Fitz Gerald of lands near the vill of Kilcolgan in exchange for other lands. Since this chapter was written, full abstracts of my transcripts (from the Red Book of the Earl of Kildare) of all the above-mentioned documents relating to Kilcolgan and Ardrahan have been edited and annotated by Mr. H. T. Knox: ibid., vol. ix, pp. 129–77. 62 The Robe was the boundary between the territory of Conmaicne-Cúile and that of Cera. 63 The parcels in Gerald's grant are 'dimidium cantredi de Conmacnekuly unacum redditu quinque marcarum quas Ricardus Cosin michi reddere consuevit annuatim de terra quam de me tenuit in Tirnathyn'. (To be dated before 1246); Red Book, f. vi *d*. *Tir nechtain* was in the Prendergast district of Clanmorris (Inquis. 1333). 64 The parcels in Raymond's grant are castrum de Struther (*Sruthair*, Shrule) cum dimidio cantredi terre ibidem; Red Book, f. xviii *d*. 65 Lough Mask Castle was probably one of those built in 1138, Ann. Loch Cé. It was certainly in existence in 1264, when it, along with the castle of Ardrahan, was seized by Walter de Burgh in consequence of his dispute with Maurice Fitz Maurice (ibid., 1264); see infra, p. 241 [p. 402]. 66 Cal. Docs. Ireland, vol. i, no. 2680. 67 Cal. Justiciary Rolls, vol. i, pp. 235–6. The name Dunmougherne appears to be obsolete. It is the *Dún-mughorn* of Ann. Loch Cé and Four Masters, 1133, where it is mentioned as having been demolished with Dunmore, from which it was evidently not far distant. O'Donovan there confuses it with *Dúnmudhord* or *Dúnmighdhord*, now Doon near Westport mentioned in the same annals in 1235. But in the anglicized form 'Dunmochern' it was one of the lands granted by Amabil to John Fitz Thomas (Red Book, f. 26 *d*, not 'Dannocharne' as in Index, 9th Rep. H. M., p. 267 *a*), and as 'Dunmougherne' it is the name of the Geraldine manor surrendered by John Fitz Thomas to Earl Richard. In Historia et Genealogia Familiae de Burgo it appears as 'the bally of Dunmuirne', where it is mentioned with places in the parishes of Kilmainemore and Kilmainebeg (Knox, History of Mayo, p. 353). The remains of the *dún* should be sought in this neighbourhood. Perhaps it is the place now called Roundfort: see Journal R.S.A.I., vol. xxxi (1901), p. 32, where, however, Mr. Knox treats the name incorrectly, having only the faulty form, 'Dannocharne', before him. 68 Cal. Close Rolls, Ed. III, vol. ix, p. 442, and Ir. Pipe Roll, 43rd Rep. D. K., pp. 22, 24. Hence these manors do not appear in the inquisitions of 1333, being still

The barony of Clanmorris in County Mayo takes its name from a Maurice whose [209]
descendants were called by the Irish *Clann Muiris na m-Brigh*, i.e. Clan Maurice of Brees Castle in this barony. The doubt whether the Mac Maurices of Brees were Fitz Geralds or Prendergasts is of old standing,[69] but it seems certain that they were Prendergasts, though the exact line of descent of this branch of the family is obscure. In 1335 the family is called in the Annals of Loch Cé 'Clan Maurice Sugach (or 'the Merry') son of Gerald',[70] and as Gerald de Prendergast, who died in 1251, is called in the same annals Gerald 'Sugach',[71] we might infer from this alone that the Clan Maurice of Brees were Prendergasts. This inference is confirrned by the inquisition of 1333, which found that the cantred of Crigfertur (*Crích fer tíre*, now the barony of Clanmorris) was then held immediately of the earl by William de Prendergast and the heir of John de Prendergast.[72]

How, precisely, these Prendergasts of Clanmorris were related—as they presumably were—to Gerald de Prendergast is a more difficult question to answer. Gerald, [210]
as we have seen, left no male issue. His heirs were his two daughters or their representatives, and at his death he seems to have held no land in Connaught. He had parted with the cantred of Corran, given to him presumably by Hugh de Lacy, but it would be very strange if he had not also been rewarded for his assistance in the conquest by Richard de Burgh, whose daughter he married as his second wife in or before 1240. It seems highly probable that he was given the cantred of *Crích fer tíre* (or Clanmorris, as it came to be called) by Richard de Burgh. Gerald, however, was a large landholder in the counties of Cork, Limerick, and Wexford, where several of his kinsmen held knights' fees under him, and as in the case of the cantred of Corran he probably parted with *Crích fer tíre* in his lifetime to one or more of his kinsmen. A Maurice de Prendergast was one of the witnesses to Gerald's grant of Corran, and he held half a knight's fee from him in Ballacha (near Charleville, Co. Cork).[73] He may have been a brother[74] of Gerald and eponym of the County Mayo family, but it is also possible that Maurice de Prendergast, 'the first conqueror', was eponym of the whole clan.

The castle of Brees was strongly situated on a hill (*bri*, an old word meaning *tulach* or hill). Some tumbled ruins of it remain. It continued for many centuries to be the chief centre of the Mac Morrises of Mayo, and here in 1585, 'Richard Mac Moryse [211]
of the Bryse, chiefe of his name,' still had his seat when he entered into the composition with Sir John Perrot.[75]

in the hands of Elizabeth de Clare. 69 See the Composition of 1685: 'Mac Morys, otherwise surnamed Fitz Gerald or Prendergaste': West Connaught (Hardiman), p. 336. 70 Ann. Loch Cé, 133; cf. Ann. Ulst. and Four Masters. All the editors assume that Fitz Geralds were intended. The editor of the Annals of Ulster departs from his text, following the ignorant translator of the Annals of Clonmacnois, where the only true word is 'falsam', probably an intelligent comment which has crept into the text. 71 Ann. Loch Cé, 121, where the editor supposes that some unknown Fitz Gerald is intended. 72 Journal R.S.A.I., vol. xxxii (1902), p. 397. If further proof of identity is needed see Ann. Loch Cé and Ann. Ulst. 1300, where 'Seonin Oc Mac Muiris' and 'Ioan Prondarcass ' evidently denote the same John Prendergast, there being a double entry of his death. 73 Red Book, f. vi, and Cal. Docs. Ireland, vol. i, p. 477. 74 If we can trust implicitly Annals of Loch Cé, 1335, where the family is called *Clann Muiris t-sucaigh mic Gerailt*, the eponymous Maurice was a son (presumably illegitimate) of Gerald de Prendergast. Mac Gerailt has been rendered Fitz Gerald as a surname; hence the confusion. 75 West-Connaught (Hardiman), pp. 331, 336,

Piers de Bermingham, head of the family of Tethmoy in Offaly, was presumably the first grantee of the barony of Dunmore in County Galway. He witnessed several Connaught charters, both of Richard de Burgh and of Hugh de Lacy,[76] and no doubt took part in the expedition of 1235. He was given the custody of part of Richard de Burgh's Connaught lands, and of all the lands of his son Richard, at their respective deaths.[77] He died in 1254, when he is called by the Irish annalist, 'Piers Pramister, lord of the Conmaicne of Dunmore'.[78] The senior line of his descendants, however, though retaining the lordship of Dunmore, was connected with Offaly rather than with Connaught. His grandson, Peter, son of James, whom we shall have occasion to mention again, was a famous warrior and joined in some of the expeditions of Edward I from 1294 to 1301. He fought also against the O'Conors in Offaly, and at his death in 1308 is described as 'nobilis debellator Hibernicorum'. His son and heir, John de Bermingham, Earl of Louth, was even more famous as the conqueror of Edward Bruce. At his death in 1329 he held the manor of Dunmore in Connaught as well as Tethmoy in Offaly.[79] He left
[212] three daughters as coheiresses, the eldest of whom was married to Eustace le Poer.[80]

The castle of Dunmore is situated on an artificially shaped mound, presumably the site of the Irish *dún*. A small town soon grew up beside it and was enclosed with walls in 1280.[81]

Meiler de Bermingham is the first that can be definitely connected with Athenry, where he is said to have founded the Dominican Friary in 1241.[82] He was granted a fair at Athenry in 1244,[83] and the town with its castle soon became of importance. In 1249 Turlough, son of Aedh O'Conor, who had been made king by the justiciar in place of Felim, led a hosting to Athenry to plunder it, but his forces were routed by Jordan of Exeter, sheriff of Connaught, and his 'terrible mail-clad cavalry'.[84] Meiler de Bermingham married Basilia, daughter of William of Worcester, who brought him some lands in County Tipperary, and there was a long litigation, originating between him and William de Prendergast, about some of them.[85] He is stated in the Register of the Convent of Athenry to have died in 1252, but the pleadings in the above litigation
[213] show that he was living in 1264. He was succeeded in Athenry by his son Peter. His son William was Archbishop of Tuam from 1289 to 1311. In 1316 Athenry was the scene of the crushing defeat of the Irish of Connaught, who had seized the opportunity of Bruce's invasion to rise against the English. Richard de Bermingham, grandson of Meiler, led the victorious army. Richard died in 1322. In 1333 the half-cantred of Clantayg (including Athenry) was held in fee by the heir of Richard de Bermingham.[86] This was his son Thomas, who seems to have been still a minor.

and cf. Fiants, Eliz., no. 4669. 76 Red Book and Gormanston Register. 77 Cal. Docs. Ireland, vol. i, nos. 2908, 2975. 78 Ann. Loch Cé, 1254. 79 Pipe Roll (Ireland), 8 Ed. III, 44th Rep. D.K., pp. 32, 37, 38. 80 Clyn's Annals, 1331. 81 Pipe Roll (Ireland), 8 Ed. I, 36th Rep. D. K., p. 47. For a description of the castle-mound and remains of the castle, see Journal R.S.A.I., vol. xli (1911), p. 305. 82 A late compilation known as Registrum Monasterii Fratrum Predicatorum de Athenry gives many particulars about the benefactors of this Friary, but it cannot be implicitly trusted. The existing ruins of the church are of various dates. Some early lancet windows in the chancel probably belong to the original building. For a full description see Prof. Macalister's paper in Journal R.S.A.I., vol. xliii (1913), pp. 197–222. 83 Cal. Docs. Ireland, vol. i, no. 2674. 84 Ann. Loch Cé, 1249. 85 Cal. Docs. Ireland, vol. ii, no. 1163. 86 Journal

Walter de Ridelisford, successor and presumably son of Strongbow's vassal of the same name in South Kildare, obtained the northern part of the barony of Clare, County Galway. This was the territory known as Muinter Murchadha, the tribe-name of the O'Flahertys, where a castle, presumably at Headfort, was built as early as 1238. Some arrangement must have been made with the O'Flahertys, who were not expelled until 1273. Here were formed the manors of Athmekin, or Headford,[87] and Corrofin. Walter died about 1240, leaving as his heirs his daughter Emeline, widow of Hugh de Lacy and wife of Stephen Longespée, and his infant granddaughter, Christiana de Mariscis.[88] To Emeline was assigned Corrofin,[89] and to Christiana, Athmekin. Chris- [214]
tiana afterwards granted all her lands to the king, and from the Extent taken in 1281 it appears that the lands about Athmekin were then well colonized, and that the issues of the manor amounted to £73 11*s.* 4*d.*[90] The manor of Corrofin descended to Emeline's daughter Emeline and her husband Maurice, son of Maurice Fitz Gerald.[91]

John de Cogan, head of the family in County Cork, took part in the Connaught campaign of 1235 and obtained the southern part of the barony of Clare. In 1252 he was granted a market and fair at his manor of Clare in Galway as well as at Castle Mora in Desmond.[92] He married one of the daughters and heiresses of Gerald de Prendergast, and his son John inherited one half of Gerald's lands. In 1290 his grandson, John de Cogan, founded a Franciscan Friary at Clare-Galway, the beautiful ruins of which in the early pointed style of the thirteenth century still exist.[93] De Cogans [215]
also held from an early period some lands in the baronies of Leitrim and Longford, County Galway, where the patronage of the churches of Portumna, Lickmolassy, and Muinter Maelfinnain were given before 1254 by William de Cogan to the Abbey of Dunbrody.[94]

Adam de Staunton, lord of Moone in County Kildare,[95] obtained the cantred of Cera, i.e. the southern part of the present barony of Carra, County Mayo, and that

R.S.A.I., vol. xxxii (1902), p. 896. For further details touching the early Bermingham Pedigree see my 'Notes' in Journal, Galway Areh. and Hist. Soe., vol. ix, pp. 195–205. **87** The name appears as *Ath-mac-Cing* in the Circuit of Muircheartach Mac Neill, 1. 143, and as *Ath-cind* and *Ath-mic-Cind* in an ancient treatise on 'O'Flaherty's Country' (transcribed in West Connaught, p. 371). Headford is an attempted translation of the Irish name. **88** Cal. Docs. Irel., vol. i, no. 2730. Christiana's father was Robert de Mariscis. **89** Cal. Docs. Ireland, vol. ii, no. 112. This Corrofin descended to Emeline's daughter of the same name, wife of Maurice Fitz Maurice, and from her to her daughter Juliana, wife of Thomas de Clare. It has been confounded with Corrofin in Co. Clare. **90** Ibid., vol. ii, nos. 1801, 2340, where with the help of the above-mentioned treatise on 'O'Flaherty's Country' most of the names can be identified. In 1295 the manor was committed to a Walter de Ridelisford to farm, and the issues were upwards of £60 a year: 88th Rep. D K pp. 69, 95. **91** Ibid., vol. ii, no. 1249; vol. iii, no. 463. **92** Cal. Charter Rolls, vol. i, p. 412; cf. Cal. Docs. Ireland, vol. ii, no. 121 (no. 853, ibid., is misdated, and should be assigned to the same date as no. 121). For the castle of Mora in Desmond see *ante*, p. 118, note 2 [p. 339, note 16]. **93** For description and drawings see Journal R.S.A.I., vol. xxxi (1901), pp. 324–32. There were three successive Johns de Cogan. The first was son of Richard de Cogan (Milo's brother?): Cal. Docs. Ireland, vol. iv, p. 44; the second was born in 1243, ibid., vol. i, p. 477, and married Juliana, daughter of Gerald, son of Maurice Fitz Gerald, and died before 1276: ibid., vol. ii, no. 1279; the third came of age shortly after Feb. 20, 1281: ibid., no. 1789. **94** Chart. St. Mary's Abbey, Dublin, vol. ii, pp. 119 and 196–8; and cf. Pipe Roll (Ireland), 10 Ed. I, 36th Rep. D. K., p. 63. The lands were known as Muinter Maelfinnain, O'Lomain, and Cinel Feichin. 'Maysketh in Kinalegham,' where John de Cogan I was also granted a fair in 1252, was probably a place in Cinel [Fh]eicin. **95** Adam de Staunton of Moone was son of Miles de Staunton who

part of the barony of Kilmaine which lies north of the river Robe. In 1247 we read of 'Clan Adam (Staunton) and the English of Cera'. The names Castlecarra and Burriscarra indicate the thirteenth century manorial centre. Adam, son of Philip, son of Adam de Staunton, died in 1300 without male heirs, and his lands in Connaught,
[216] Leinster, and Wales were partitioned among his five daughters.[96] In 1312 the Connaught lands were assigned to his daughter Nesta and her then husband Fromund le Brun.[97] At his death in 1329, John de Bermingham, Earl of Louth, held 'the manor of Kerre' (Carra), when the rents and issues were at first received by Bernard de Staunton, but on July 9, 1333, the custody of both Dunmore and Carra was given to Edmund, son of Earl Richard de Burgh.[98] Some of the Stauntons appear to have been implicated in the murder of this Edmund in 1338.[99] A junior branch of the family, said by MacFirbis to have been descended from Sir Bernard Staunton, became known in Carra as MacEvilly (*mac in Mhilidh*, 'son of the knight'), and at the close of the sixteenth century, though the Burkes held much of the barony, 'Myly Mc Evily chief of his name' was one of those who entered into the composition of 1585.[1]

The northern part of the barony of Carra, known as *Clann Cuain*, is believed to have been first granted to a de Barry, who has left his name in Castlebar, i.e. *caislén an Bharraih* or 'the Barry's Castle'.[2] Before 1333, however, the freeholder was a de Cogan.

The primary enfeoffment of the baronies of Erris and Tirawley is complicated and
[217] obscure. The traditional account given by Duald MacFirbis[3] is confused and mixes up distinct events (which, however, can, I think, be disentangled), and trustworthy records are scanty. There were rival claims among the settlers founded apparently on inconsistent grants, and these led to disputes. From such facts and indications as can be gathered from early records and from the annals it appears that some time about the beginning of the thirteenth century, when William de Burgh was treating Connaught as a conquered province, he made a grant to Nicholas le Petit of the cantred of Tirawley, or the northern part of the present barony, including the tuath of Bredagh,[4] and that Nicholas afterwards enfeoffed Adam Cusack 'senior' of some or all of these lands.[5] It is, however, improbable that there was any effective occupation of the lands

succeeded to the lands of Thomas the Fleming, one of Strongbow's feoffees and was probably his son: Song of Dermot, l. 3112; *ante*, vol. i, p. 386 [pp. 145–6], and Register of St. Thomas's Abbey, Dublin, pp. 161–3 and 167. The family seem to have taken their name from Stainton in the hundred of Roose, near Haverford, whence the Prendergasts, Roches, and other Flemings came. 96 Ann. Loch Cé, 1300. For his five daughters see Justiciary Rolls, 1300, pp. 305–6. The marriage of Margaret, the youngest daughter, was sold by the king to John Wogan the justiciar for £60: Cal Docs. Ireland, vol. iv, no. 828. 97 Cal. Close Rolls (Ireland), 6 Ed. II, no. 37 98 Pipe Roll (Ireland), 8 Ed. III, 44th Rep. D. K., p. 37. 99 O'Flaherty's West Connaught, p. 47. 1 Ibid., p. 331. Bernard de Staunton, knight, was foreman of the jurors at Athenry on two of the de Burgo inquisitions of 1333. 2 Castle-Barry is described by Downing, c. 1680, as 'the most western corporation, and a very fair large bawn and two round towers or castles therein'. See Hy Fiachrach, p. 160, note. 3 Hy Fiachrach, pp. 325–39. 4 Bredagh comprised the parish of Moygawnagh and a part of that of Kilfian: ibid., p. 229 n. 5 This is stated expressly by Earl Richard in a pleading of the year 1300: Plea Roll, 30 Ed. I, no. 62, m. 14 d, cited in Knox's 'Mayo', p. 291. Nicholas le Petit was probably the brother, so named, of William le Petit, the elder Hugh de Lacy's feoffee in the cantred about Mullingar (Chart. St. Mary's, Dublin, vol. i, p. 69), and Adam Cusack, senior, was presumably the contemporary lord of Killeen in Meath (ibid., pp. 201–2). A grant by William de Burgo to William le Petit of a cantred in Connaught is entered on Pat. Roll, 28 Eliz. (Morrin, p. 113), but it seems to have concerned

until after the conquest by Richard de Burgh. At this time, *c.*1237, Richard de Burgh appears to have granted lands in the barony, including at any rate the cantred of Bac and Glen, or the southern part of the barony, and the tuath of Bredagh, to Robert, father of Richard de Carew of Cork, who enfeoffed William Barrett. Bredagh was thus [218]
the subject of inconsistent grants. Afterwards, apparently in the time of the second Richard de Burgh, *c.*1247–8, William Barrett ejected Adam Cusack, senior, from Bredagh, and when Cusack's immediate lord, Adam le Petit, recovered judgement, William Barrett violently resisted the execution of the decree. In 1255 there was a renewed order to give Adam le Petit seisin, but there is no sign that it was carried out.[6]

In 1281 a new dispute arose between another William Barrett and another Adam Cusack, presumably sons or other kinsmen of the former disputants. A parley between them at Moyne (*Maighin*) near Killala ended in a fight, with the result that Barrett was captured and died in Cusack's prison.[7]

The king then took into his hand the lands of William Barrett, both in Cork and [219]
Tirawley, and of Adam le Fleming in Erris,[8] and heavy fines were exacted from members of the Barrett faction,[9] showing that they were considered in the wrong, and that at this time the arm of the law could reach the wrong-doer even in the uttermost parts of Connaught. In 1299 seisin in wardship of the lands of William Barrett was given to Richard de Burgh, Earl of Ulster, and the heir, a third William Barrett, who was born in 1280, was soon afterwards let into possession. At this time the intermediate tenancy

Ciarraighe Maighe n-Ái, *Clann Connmaigh*(?), and *Sil Máilruain*, in the present County of Roscommon. It was, no doubt, inoperative, but it is one of many proofs that William de Burgh attempted to sub-infeudate Connaught. 6 Cal. Docs. Irel., vol. ii, nos. 292, 474, and Plea Roll, 30 Ed. I, as above. William Barrett called to warranty Richard de Carew, thus showing the intermediate tenancy. The Petits and Cusacks were Meathmen, while the Carews and Barretts, though coming immediately from Co. Cork, were by extraction from Pembrokeshire. One William Barrett was called *Breathnach*, i.e. *Cambrensis*. See, too, Owen's 'Old Pembroke Families'. A racial difference perhaps accentuated the land-feud between the families. 7 Justiciary Rolls, vol. i, pp. 227–8, and Ann. Ulst., Ann. Loch Cé, 1281. In the Latin annals (Laud MS., Grace, Dowling) Adam Cusack is expressly called 'minor' or 'junior'. None of these annals mention the place where the battle was fought, but it is given in the Historia familiae de Burgo as 'apud Mayn de Kilro'. Mac Firbis (Hy Fiachrach, p. 329) speaks of the 'great battle of Maighin' as having been won by William Fionn (Barrett) of Kilcommon (in Erris), whom he here identifies with William Mor (Barrett) na Maighne, and states that 'the Cusack' fell with many of his people. He goes on to tell how this William then took the great court of Meelick near Moyne, drove out the Cusacks, and divided the country between his own kinsmen. He mentions, however, that he has more than one account before him. I think he tries to combine accounts relating to events separated by more than thirty years. In his pedigree of the Barretts (given in Knox's Mayo, p. 416) he starts with three successive Williams, viz. William Fionn of Kilcommon, William Mor na Maighne, and William Og—so far perhaps correctly. It was probably the first William who drove out the Cusacks, c.1247–8, possibly killed Adam Cusack, senior, and divided the country among his own kinsmen; and it was his son William who was defeated and killed by Adam Cusack, junior, at Maighin in 1281, and was therefore, according to a common usage, called by subsequent writers William Mor na Maighne. The death of Adam Cusack is entered in the Annals of Ulster under the year 1287. There was an Adam Cusack, lord of Killeen in Meath, in 1280: Cal. Gormanston Register, p. 28. 8 Justiciary Roll, vol. i, pp. 228, 312. 9 There are numerous entries among the Exchequer Receipts, 1285–97, of payments by Batin Barrett of his fine for having peace, and in 1292 his account stood at the sum of £163 18*s.* 6*d.*: Pipe Roll (Ireland), 20 Ed. I, 37 Rep. D. K., p. 45.

of Maurice, son of Richard de Carew, was recognized,[10] but by 1333 it had disappeared, and 'the heirs of William Barrett' held Bac and Glen directly from the earl at a rent of twenty marks, the usual chief rent for a cantred.

[220] The Barretts spread far and wide in Tirawley and overflowed into Erris. They became divided into several families or clans, as Mac Wattin (Mac Bhaitin), descended from Batin Barrett, who obtained the great court of Meelick, Clan Andrew of Bac, Clan Toimin and Clan Philpin of Erris, and others. There were also Merricks, Lawlesses, Lynotts, and others. Mac Firbis gives some account of these and of the districts in which they settled, and as he came of a family who were hereditary historians of the O'Dowds, head chieftains of Tirawley, his account is likely to be substantially correct, though, as we have seen, he seems to err as to the precise period of the first settlement, and actually reverses the immediate result of the fracas at Moyne.

MacFirbis also tells the gruesome tale, immortalized by Sir Samuel Ferguson, of the blinding of the Lynotts by the Barretts, and of the cunning revenge of the victims.[11] The story, however, receives no support from the annals, and on the face of it was devised to account for the fact that in later ages the Burkes had scattered estates over the Barrett country. For the credit of the Welshmen of Tirawley we may hope that the story is not true.

At the composition of 1595 Sir Richard Burke was to have 5*s.* out of every quarter of 160 quarters of freeholders' lands in Tirawley, viz. the freehold lands of the Barretts, Burkes, Lynotts, Clanpaidyne, Cusacks, Carews, and Clandonnells.[12] Of these, Clanpaidyne was a sept of the Barretts, and the Clandonnells were Scottish gallo-
[221] glasses. Indeed nearly all the freeholders of County Mayo mentioned in the composition with Sir John Perrot were of other than Irish extraction.

As to Erris still less is positively known. It was in 1273 that Donnell, son of Manus O'Conor of Clan Murtough, was expelled by the English from Erris, and after this, at any rate, the English would seem to have dominated the cantred. Adam le Fleming, who sided with William Barrett and was killed in the battle of Moyne in 1281, seems to have held the greater part of the cantred. His lands were taken into the king's hand,[13] and appear to have been set to farm to Jordan of Exeter—the same Jordan as held Affane in County Waterford of the Crown and Ballylahan in Mayo of the earl.[14] One of the tenants was John Butler, who held the manor of Ballycroy from Jordan by knight's service.[15] In 1333 the cantred was held of the earl by John, son of Jordan of Exeter, at the usual rent for a cantred, viz. twenty marks. But, as we have noticed, the Barretts spread from Tirawley over Erris, and in 1593 the Queen's commissioners found 'by ancient testimony and witnesses of great credit that the whole barony of Erris was and is the lawful inheritance of Edmund Barrett', some of the Burkes, however, had 'usurped upon part of it, and being traitors were slain in open rebellion'.[16]

10 Plea Roll, 28 Ed. I, no. 47, m. 13 d. For all these transactions consult Knox's History of Mayo. pp. 291–2. 11 Hy Fiachrach, pp. 335–9. 12 West Connaught, p. 335. For the rights and possession of Mac William Eighter in Tirawley, c. 1684, see the extracts from Historia Familiae de Burgo printed in Hy Fiachrach, pp. 455–61. 13 Justiciary Roll, vol. i, pp. 312. 330. 14 Cal. Docs. Ireland, vol. iv, pp. 314, 374, and vol. v, p. 25. 15 Knox's History of Co. Mayo, p. 298, referring to the Plea Rolls. In the composition of 1585, Ballycroy is said to belong to the Earl of Ormonde: West Connaught, p. 333. 16 Cal. Pat.

Umhall, or 'the Owles', now the baronies of Burrishoole and Murisk, seems to have been granted to Henry le Boteler. Burrishoole, as the name indicates, must have been [222] a Norman borough, and it was in all probability the *Burgheis cinn trachta*,[17] 'the burgage at the head of the strand', which was burned in 1247 by some of the Clan Murtough of Munster (O'Conors) who had recently settled in Umhall. Next year there was a formidable outbreak of the clan, and 'the castle of Mac Henry [Butler] was burned by them and its constable taken'.[18] Jordan of Exeter (the sheriff of Connaught), John Butler,[19] Robin Lawless,[20] and others made a counterattack, and Mac Henry, who was lord of Umhall—'for it belonged to him and he was residing in it'—came with a large army, made peace with Donnell, son of Manus O'Conor (head of Clan Murtough), and with his aid suppressed those who had turned against him. Twenty-four years later (1272) 'Henry Butler, lord of Umhall', presumably the same person or his son, was slain by another member of Clan Murtough. This led to the expulsion of the clan from Umhall and Erris in the succeeding year. In 1333 John le Botiller held the cantred of 'Owyl Botiller' of the earl at a rent of £10, and certain [223] townlands there were held by de Burghs, Robert Lawless, and O'Malley, apparently the Irish chieftain of Murrisk. The value to the earl of the whole cantred of Owyl was £52 13*s*. 4*d*. The claims of the Butlers were never forgotten, though they must have been in abeyance for a long time, and in the composition of 1585 Thomas, Earl of Ormond and Ossory, was said to be seised of forty quarters of land belonging to the manor of Burrishoole, and the same were assigned to him free.[21]

From this survey of the primary enfeoffment of Connaught it will be seen that the first feoffees were all, or nearly all, great feudal lords who already held fiefs in other parts of Ireland. For the campaigns of 1227 and 1235, at any rate, it appears that the feudal host who owed royal service had been summoned, and Richard de Burgh naturally rewarded those who were most active in their assistance. In some cases, however, the barons did not personally exploit their acquisitions, but created new tenures of their lands, making the new tenants liable for the rents and services due to Richard de Burgh and reserving perhaps a profit rent to themselves.[22] In process of time such intermediate tenures tended to disappear. But in most cases the Connaught lords, like their overlord Richard de Burgh and his successors, continued for some generations at least to hold their new acquisitions along with their former fiefs. Such were the Fitz Geralds of Offaly, the Berminghams of Tethmoy, the Ridelisfords of Castledermot, the Exeters of Affane, the Stauntons of Moone, the Cogans, Barrys, and Barrets of [224]

Roll (Morrin), 40 Eliz., pp. 503–4. **17** Not Burriscarra, as suggested by O'Donovan. That place belonged to the Stauntons. **18** Ann. Loch Cé, 1248. The Four Masters, in copying this passage, explain Mac Henry by Piers Poer (perhaps because this name occurs in 1249), but this is an error, as the entry of 1272 indicates. Henry le Buttiler is mentioned in 1235 in a list (probably) of those who fought against Earl Richard Marshal. Most of them, however, are known to have been engaged in the Connaught campaign of 1235 or in the settlement that followed. The Henry of 1285 may have been the Henry Pincerna mentioned in 1215: Cal. Docs. Irel., vol. i, no. 610 **19** John Pincerna (Butler) witnessed grants made in Connaught, c. 1235–7, by Hugh de Lacy, Richard de Burgh, and Gerald de Roche: Red Book. **20** Robert Lawless held seven townlands in Owyl in 1333. **21** West Connaught, p. 335. **22** e.g. Hugh de Lacy, Gerald de Prendergast, Maurice de Londres, the Fitz Griffins, and the Carews of Cork.

County Cork, the Nangles and Cusacks of County Meath, &c. In this respect the settlement in Connaught, though paralleled to some extent by that in Munster, differed from the settlement in Ulster, where John de Courcy's followers were previously for the most part landless men.

THE O'CONORS AND 'THE KING'S CANTREDS' IN CONNAUGHT, 1235–74

After the confiscation of Connaught, in 1227, none of the kings of Connaught held of the Crown any portion of the province outside the five cantreds reserved to the English king. There were indeed O'Conors in other districts. Some of the sons or other descendants of Turlough Mor, who was slain in 1156 and who is credited with a numerous progeny, had been allotted territories or had imposed themselves on weak clans in various parts of the province previous to the partition. Henceforward the most noteworthy of these were the descendants of Murtough 'of Munster' and of Brian 'of Luighne', both sons of Turlough Mor. The former came to be known as 'Clan Murtough', and in course of time formed a disturbing element, often at variance with their kinsmen of the lines of Cathal Crovderg and of Rory, the last *ard-rí*, as well as with the Anglo-Norman settlers. They seem to have established themselves in the west of County Mayo, about Clew Bay and in Erris, whence they were expelled in 1273. Soon after this, however, four of the clan succeeded in becoming kings of Connaught (i.e. of the Sil Murray districts) for brief periods. The descendants of Brian of Luighne [226]
were more peaceably settled under the Fitz Geralds and afterwards under the de Burghs in the cantred of Carbury, County Sligo, and from this line descended the O'Conors Sligo. The king's five cantreds, however, or a progressively diminishing portion of them, were granted to the O'Conor who for the time being was called 'King of Connaught', though he had no jurisdiction outside the lands held of the Crown. These he held at an agreed rent during good serviee or at the king's pleasure.

Such was the legal position; but at times the royal power was so faint that the English king could not exercise the pleasure which we may suspect he would have felt in determining the grant which he had made. The king's dealings with the cantreds reserved to him can only be understood in connexion with the history of the O'Conor kings and their varying attitudes of tranquillity and turbulence.

In 1235, as we have mentioned, Felim paid £90 13*s*. 4*d*. towards his fine for the farm of the five cantreds, and a rent at the rate, seemingly, of £400 a year.[1] At this time the king appears to have retained only the castle of Athlone, with some land in its neighbourhood, and the castle of Randown on the western shore of Lough Ree. Next year, however, the justiciar erected a castle at Onagh on the river Suck, and, as already noted,[2] this and possibly the retention of some adjoining land was the consequence, if not the cause, of the justiciar's temporary quarrel with Felim. In 1240 Felim went to

1 *Supra*, p. 185 [p. 374]. 2 *Supra*, p. 186, note 3 [p. 374, note 72].

the king in England, 'to complain to him of the Foreigners and Gael in Ireland, and
[227] he received great honour from the king on this occasion and came home safely, joyfully and contentedly.'[3] Unfortunately we have no authentic account of what passed at this interview, for the account given by Matthew Paris[4] does not harmonize with established facts and is quite untrustworthy. In 1245 another castle, called the castle of Suicin, was erected at or near Ballinasloe.[5] This was probably done with Felim's consent, for it was in this year that Felim joined the expedition under Maurice Fitz Gerald to assist the king in Wales. The object of this castle, as of that at Onagh, was presumably to keep control of the route between Athlone and the English settlements about Loughrea.

In January 1245 the king announced to Maurice FitzGerald that David, son of Llewelyn, late Prince of North Wales, had revolted against him, and besought the jus-
[228] ticiar and the king's subjects in Ireland to aid him with men, money, and supplies, as he 'wished Ireland to share in his conquest'.[6] The expedition was delayed, but by August the king was at the mouth of the river Conway, fortifying the castle of Gannock, as it is called in the English records. It was on the site of the ancient fortress of Dyganwy, once a royal residence, on the north-eastern shore of the harbour or estuary, within view of the Cistercian House of Aberconway, which forty years later was replaced by the Edwardian castle. On August 29 the king wrote to the men of Dublin, Waterford, Drogheda, Limerick, Cork, and Carrickfergus, urging them to send immediately victuals of all kinds, of which his army stood in great need.[7] How great the need was appears from a private (uncensored) letter written from the camp about the close of September and transcribed by Matthew Paris.[8] 'We are dwelling', the writer says, adapting the language of St. Paul, 'round the castle in tents, employed in watchings, fastings, and prayers, and in cold and nakedness. In watchings, through fear of the Welsh suddenly attacking us by night; in fastings, on account of a deficiency of provisions, for a farthing loaf now costs five-pence; in prayers, that we may return home safe and sound; in cold and nakedness, because our houses are of canvas and we
[229 are without winter clothing.[9] The writer goes on to give a graphic description of

3 Ann. Loch Cé, 1240. 4 Chron. Maj., vol. iv, p. 57. According to Matthew Paris, Felim complained of the devastation of his territory by John [*sic*] de Burgh, stated that he had paid an annual rent of 5,000 marks [*sic*] ever since King John, who subdued him [*sic*], had confirmed him in his kingdom, and besought the king not to suffer him to be disinherited by an ignoble adventurer. Thereupon Henry ordered Maurice Fitz Gerald, who was then present, to uproot the evil plantation made in those parts by Hubert de Burgh and restore Felim to his kingdom. Perhaps Matthew Paris confused the events of 1232 with Felim's visit of 1240. Certainly no such order was executed at the latter date. 5 Ann. Loch Cé, 1246. The parish of 'Sukyn' in the diocese of Clonfert (Eccl. Tax., Cal. Docs. Ireland, vol. v, p. 221) seems equivalent to the present parish of Creagh, in which Ballinasloe, east of the Suck, is situated. The manors of Aughrim and Suicin were evidently near each other: ibid., vol. iv, nos. 766, 814. O'Dollovan's location of this castle near the head of the Suck in Co. Mayo (Four Masters, vol. iii, p. 316, note) must be rejected. 6 Close Roll, 29 Hen. III, m. 16 dors. (p. 348). The king also ordered eight wooden towers (*bretachiae*) to be prepared (pp. 285, 289). David was Henry's nephew, his mother being Joan, illegitimate daughter of King John. 7 Close Roll, 29 Hen. III, m. 4 dors. (p. 362). Henry also ordered the justiciar to expend 500 marks in buying corn and flour to be shipped as quickly as possible, and to cause as many merchants as he could to come to the army with wine and provisions, also masons and other workmen: ibid. 8 Chron. Maj., vol. iv, p. 481. 9 Ann. Loch Cé, 1245. Clearly the bulk of the force was composed of the Irish of Connaught, but

how a ship under the command of Walter Byset, bringing provisions from Ireland, grounded in the mud opposite the castle, but unfortunately on the Welsh side of the estuary; and how after much fighting the Welsh got possession of the greater part of the cargo, consisting of 'sixty hogsheads of wine besides other much-desired and seasonable provisions'.

Meanwhile Maurice Fitz Gerald had succeeded in raising a force of upwards of 3,000 men in Ireland, including in particular Felim O'Conor, 'accompanied by a great army of the Gael',[9] but they seemingly did not arrive at Gannock until October 20, when the season for fighting was over, and the king was already preparing to return. They landed on the Isle of Anglesea and ravaged the whole island.[10] On their return journey they put to the sword and burned all that remained there. Indeed the main force can have reached Gannock only a few days before the camp broke up. On October 1, Geoffrey de Turville, bishop of Ossory and treasurer of Ireland, paid to the king at Gannock the sum of £397 10*s*. 6*d*. of Irish treasure,[11] and on October 21 he was ordered to cause the 3,000 foot-soldiers who came from Ireland to the king's service at Gannock to have their pay of 2*d*. a day for ten days from the 20th to the 29th of October.[12] This was a poor recompense for the pains and perils of their journey, but probably they eked out their scanty pay by the plunder of Anglesea. Maurice Fitz Gerald, [230]
too, was harshly treated. The king was angry, ostensibly because he arrived too late to save the expedition from being a failure, and on November 4, 1245, superseded him as justiciar by John Fitz Geoffrey. Felim, however, was treated with honour by the king and received letters of protection until Henry's 'arrival in Ireland'.[13]

John Fitz Geoffrey, the new justiciar, was a son of Geoffrey Fitz Peter, Earl of Essex,[14] who had been for many years King John's justiciar in England. He was already connected with Ireland by his marriage with Isabel, widow of Gilbert, son of Walter de Lacy. Her first husband died in 1230, and we first hear of John Fitz Geoffrey in Ireland in 1234, when the justiciar was ordered to give him and his wife seisin of the 'manor of Conhal',[15] Isabel's *maritagium*, of which she and her husband had been disseised in the war of Richard Marshal.[16] Isabel, it seems, was a daughter of Matilda Marshal and Hugh Bigod, Earl of Norfolk.[17] Jolm Fitz Geoffrey was one of those added at the instance of the English barons to the Privy Council in 1237, on the occa- [231]
sion of a grant to the king of a thirtieth of their movables, in the vain effort to counteract the influence of the king's foreign advisers,[18] and he seems always to have

Peter de Bermingham and Adam de Staunton accompanied Maurice. 10 Chron. Maj., vol. iv, p. 486. 11 Cal. Pat. Rolls, 29 Hen. III, m. 2 (p. 461). 12 Ibid., m. 1. 13 Cal. Patent Rolls, 29 Hen. III, m. 1 (October 21). 14 Fine Rolls, 11 Hen. III, m. 5, vol. i, p. 158 (Roberts). 15 This was probably Conall, now Old Connell in Co. Kildare. Meiler Fitz Henry's lands there, other than those with which he endowed the Priory of Conall (i.e. Great Connell), must have escheated at his death to Earl William Marshal, Isabel's grandfather. 16 Close Roll, 18 Hen. III, m. 22 (p. 430). On April 12, 1234, the castle and honour of Ewias Lacy were restorod to John Fitz Geoffrey and Isabel his wife as being the dower of the latter in the lands of her late husband: Cal. Pat. Roll, 18 Hen. III, m. 15 (p. 42). 17 Dugdale's Monasticon, vol. v, p. 371, from the Tintern Chronicle; but the account given of the Bigod family from this chronicle is manifestly incorrect. Another corrupt account is printed in Chart. St. Mary's Abbey, Dublin, vol. ii, p. 313. 18 Matt. Paris, Chron. Maj., vol. iii, p. 383.

favoured the baronial cause. In this very year he was chosen with his brother-in-law Roger Bigod, Earl of Norfolk, and others, and sent to the Council of Lyons to protest against the papal tribute, and also against the oppressive proceedings of Master Martin,[19] a rapacious envoy of the Pope.

No trouble occurred with Felim after his return from Wales until 1249, when his son Aedh broke out in rebellion. At this time Peter de Bermingham had the custody of the lands and castles of the second Richard de Burgh[20] during the minority of his brother and heir, Walter. By means of an ambuscade Aedh cut off a small party of mounted men who were going in front of Peter de Bermingham to the lately erected castle of Sligo, and then plundered all the Bermingham lands in Tireragh. He also treacherously killed 'Geroitin Mac Feorais', who was probably a son of Peter de Bermingham. To punish Aedh, Maurice Fitz Gerald mustered his forces and retrieved some of the spoil. Felim, fearing the consequences of his son's outbreak, fled to O'Neill. The justiciar, John Fitz Geoffrey, also led an army by way of Athlone into Connaught and joined Maurice at Elphin. Together they ravaged the Sil Murray districts and made Turlough, son of Aedh, son of Cathal Crovderg, Felim's nephew, king. Turlough, however, was not able to restrain his kinsmen, the other 'sons of the
[232] kings of Connaught', or 'roydamnas', who against his will attacked Athenry, but were badly defeated by Jordan of Exeter, the sheriff. Next year Felim returned with a force of the Cinel Owen and expelled Turlough, who fled to the English. The government, however, in accordance with their usual policy, accepted the claimant who proved the strongest and best able to control the rest, and Felim was restored.[21]

His son's escapades cost Felim the cantred of Omany, in which the king now began to make permanent grants. Before 1253 Richard de la Rochelle, who was a nephew of John Fitz Geoffrey[22] and afterwards seneschal of Prince Edward and justiciar of Ireland, held the manor of Aughrim in Omany, which with subsequent additions was developed into a large estate held by the service of seven knights and a rent of £125.[23] Another grantee in the same cantred was Jordan of Exeter, Lord of Ballylahan, who had recently defeated the 'roydamnas' at Athenry.[24]

[233] About this time indeed a suggestion seems to have been made for the confiscation of some or all of the lands of both Felim O'Conor and of Conor O'Brien, for on May 23, 1253, when Henry was preparing for his expedition to Gascony, he wrote to say that it was not his intention to commit to any person the lands of the king of Con-

19 Ibid., vol. iv, pp. 420, 441. 20 Cal. Docs. Ireland, vol. i, no. 2975. 21 Ann. Loch Cé, 1249, 1250. 22 In a quit-claim to the advowson of the church of Kenles in Fothered, Richard de la Rochelle calls John Fitz Geoffrey his *avunculus*: MS. Kilkenny Castle, dated 1264. 23 For the grant of lands about Aughrim and subsequent additions see Cal. Docs. Ireland, vol. ii, nos. 35, 223, 226, 823. (The last entry is bungled in the Calendar. 'Thoyth' = *tuath*, i. e. the tuath of Clan Uadach.) Richard's son Philip found the conditions of the holding oppressive and petitioned for relief in 1282: ibid., no. 1986. Philip appears to have sold twenty-five villates, including the manors of Aughrim and Suicin, to his 'cousin' Theobald Butler IV (who had married a daughter of John Fitz Geoffrey): ibid vol. iv, nos. 765–7, 814. In 1305 Edmund, son of Theobald Butler IV, petitioned for a reduction of rent: ibid., vol. v, no. 198. In 1585 the Earl of Ormonde held 24 quarters of land in the barony of Kilconnell about Aughrim: West Connaught (Hardiman), p. 319. 24 Ibid., vol. ii, no. 228.

naught or of the king of Thomond.[25] But Henry's intentions were seldom consistently held for long. Seven weeks later he promised that 'if he should not wish to retain the four cantreds which Felim held at the king's pleasure', Stephen de Longespée should have, as we would say, the refusal of them;[26] and on February 11, 1254, three days before his grant of all Ireland to his son Edward, Henry, when in Gascony, ignoring both Felim's possession and his own promise to Stephen, granted in fee to his Poitevin half-brother, Godfrey de Lusignan, 500 librates of land (i.e. lands worth £500 a year) in 4½ cantreds in Connaught.[27] Lands in Connaught at the king's disposal could only come, if at all, out of the king's five cantreds, and in June 1255 the king, 'to avoid ambiguity', ordered that two of these cantreds (i.e. that selected as the best by the Lord Edward and that in which were the castles) should remain to Edward, and that of the remaining three cantreds Godfrey should select two. There was, however, to be 'no question regarding the land which Felim held on lease'.[28] But seeing that Felim appears to have held on lease, or at least at the king's pleasure, four of these cantreds, the ambiguity was sufficiently glaring. The king, in fact, seems to have been ordering [232]
a quart to be drawn out of a pint pot. Felim naturally protested,[29] and the king replied that no injury had been done to him by giving Godfrey two cantreds in Connaught, seeing that 'some of Felim's relatives, who would not derogate from his right, if any, to those lands, had offered to the king large sums of money for the grant of them'.[30] This *argumentum ad consanguinitatem* was not likely to convince Felim. Afterwards Prince Edward waived his own claims and made a grant to Godfrey of the cantreds of Tirmany and Moylurg-Tirerril, with the homage and services of the existing tenants in chief in Omany.[31] Even this arrangement, which would have displaced Felim in two cantreds, was abandoned, and Godfrey was eventually compensated with manors in the Crown-lands of Louth and in England,[32] while Felim retained the four cantreds up to his death.

But Felim, though himself peaceably inclined, was unwilling or unable to restrain the impetuous spirit of his son Aedh. The latter was a warrior of the old reckless heroic mould. In 1253 and subsequent years he fought with and conquered the O'Reillys, and afterwards the O'Rourkes, of Breffny. As his house had lost its ancient domination over the greater part of Connaught, he thought, no doubt, to obtain compensation in the line of least resistance towards the east, and to revive the ancient claims of the kings of Connaught to the overlordship of Breffny. Moreover the Eng- [235]
lish of Meath had made settlements in Breffny and had built some castles there, one of which was at a ford on the Shannon leading into the O'Conor territory.[33] The O'Reillys, too, were inclined to be friendly with the English, and as recently as 1250 had joined Maurice Fitz Maurice in an expedition against O'Neill. In 1256 there was

25 Ibid., vol. ii, no. 189. **26** Ibid., no. 237. **27** Ibid., no. 321. **28** Ibid., nos. 447–8. **29** Ann. Loch Cé, 1255. **30** Cal. Docs. Irel., vol. ii, no. 457, July 29, 1255. **31** Ibid., no. 478 (Nov. 9, 1255). **32** Ibid., no. 524 (Nov. 8, 1256). For the motes at these manors in Louth, see Journal R.S.A.I., vol. xxxviii (1908), pp. 250–6, and for the finding of a remarkable thirteenth century prickspur, perhaps connected with Godfrey's tenancy, in one of them, see ibid., vol. xl (1910), pp 217–18. **33** At Ath-an-chip near Carrick-on-Shannon. See *ante*, p. 35 [pp. 298–9].

fighting between the O'Reillys and the O'Rourkes in Breffny, in which the O'Reillys suffered most. But this was only 'a drop before the shower' of tribulation in store for them. The O'Rourkes obtained the assistance of Aedh O'Conor, while the O'Reillys sought aid from Walter de Burgh and Miles de Nangle. But before the latter could effect a junction of forces with them, O'Conor and O'Rourke, on the Festival of the Cross (September 14), fell upon the O'Reillys in the plain of Moy Slecht, near Ballinamore in County Leitrim, and utterly routed them. In recounting 'the brave destructive heroic battle' that was fought between them, one annalist, speaking of Aedh O'Conor, falls into the bombastic inflated style of the later shanachies, telling how he 'had the glowing fury of a prince, the firmness of a champion, and the valour of a lion on that day', and how 'no one could gaze on the face of the arch-prince, for there were two broad-eyed enormous royal torches flaming and rolling in his head'.[34]

Notwithstanding, or perhaps in consequence of, this evidence of Aedh O'Conor's
[236] power and aggressive designs, the new justiciar, Alan la Zuche, made peace with him at Randown, and promised that the O'Conor territory (i.e. seemingly the four cantreds) should not be diminished while he was justiciar.[35] Next year indeed it is stated in the annals that a charter of the king's five cantreds was granted to Felim, but it may be doubted if this entry is quite correct, as large grants had already been made in Omany and were not resumed. Presumably the entry refers to the abandonment, already mentioned, of the impossible plan of providing for Godfrey de Lusignan out of the five cantreds without infringing on Felim's interests.

From about this time forward Aedh was virtually king, and he became more aggressive and more truculent than ever. In 1257 he blinded two possible rivals, descendants of his uncle the late King Aedh, son of Cathal Crovderg.[36] In 1258 he gave hostages to Brian O'Neill, and joined in the confederacy which conferred on O'Neill the sovereignty of the Gael of Erin, and was evidently aimed at the expulsion of the English.[57] In return for his submission, Aedh was given the hostages of Breffny 'from Kells to Drumcliff'. He had now a free hand in Breffny, where he proceeded to dethrone and set up kings, without, however, preserving the semblance of order in that country.

In 1259 Aedh went to Derry to marry a daughter of Dugald Mac Sorley, and he brought home with her a band of eight-score warriors (*ógláigh*) under Alan Mac Sorley.[38] Dugald and Alan were seemingly sons of Rory, son of Ranald, son of Somerled,
[237] and represented one branch of the family of the Lords of the Isles.[39] Donald and Rory, sons of Ranald, in company with Thomas of Galloway, plundered Derry in 1212 and 1214,[40] and there may have been some settlement of Clan Ranald there. Probably Dugald was the 'Mac Sorley' who led a pirate fleet in 1258 from Innsi-Gall, and passed round Erin westwards to Connemara, where they plundered some islands and a merchant vessel, and treacherously killed the sheriff, Jordan of Exeter, and 'other

34 Ann. Loch Cé, vol. ii, p. 413. What seems to be another account of the same fighting follows on p. 417. 35 Ann. Loch Cé, p. 421. 36 Ibid., 1257. 37 Ibid., 1258, and see *infra*, pp. 274–5 [pp. 418–19]. 38 Ibid., 1259. 39 See Skene's Celtic Scotland, vol. iii, pp. 293–4, and *Genealach Mhic Ruaidri* (from the Books of Ballymote and Lecan), ibid., p. 471, and the Appendix to this chapter. 40 Ann. Ulst. *sub annis*; and see *ante*, vol. ii, pp. 290–3 [pp. 266–7].

good men'.[41] The foreign soldiery who accompanied Dugald's daughter formed perhaps the first band of *Gallógláigh*, or Galloglasses (as the name came to be written in English), to appear in Ireland. They were professional heavy-armed foot-soldiers, and their employment did much to increase the military power of the semi-independent Irish chiefs and stiffen their resistance to absorption in the feudal organization. There were other intermarriages between the families of Irishmen and the Clandonald of Scotland,[42] and in course of time bands of Galloglasses formed body-guards for many Irish chiefs, especially in the north, and the Mac Donalds and other Scottish clans [238]
began to send offshoots to various parts of Ireland. The Government was not blind to the dangers likely to accrue from the influx of Scottish bands into Ireland. In February 1256 the king ordered his bailiffs and subjects in Ireland not to allow Angus Mac Donald (i.e. Angus Mor, Dugald's cousin), or other Scottish malefactors whose names the King of Scotland would communicate, to be received in Ireland.[43] This was the boy-king Alexander III, who was already married to Henry's daughter Margaret, and who afterwards succeeded in uniting the Western Isles to the Scottish Crown. Again, on April 29, 1260, shortly before the battle of Down, at which probably Aedh's 'foreign youths' fought, the justiciar was ordered not to permit persons from Scotland to be received in Ireland, and if he should find any such seeking confederacies with the Irish, to arrest and keep them in custody.[44]

In 1260 Aedh O'Conor joined Brian O'Neill in the combined attack on the English of Ulidia, which ended in the fatal battle of Down on May 14, 1260. When we come to treat of affairs in Ulster we shall describe in greater detail this formidable attempt against the growing English supremacy. O'Neill and many of the chief men of Tirowen and Connaught fell, and the hopes of the confederacy fell with them. Felim O'Conor could hardly have expected to escape implication in his son's action, but he seems to have thought that in diplomacy, at any rate, the offensive was the best defensive. Accordingly, soon afterwards he complained to the king of some losses which Walter de Burgh had caused to him and to the church of Elphin in this year, and in a [239]
subsequent letter, to be dated about August 1261, he prayed the king to cause Walter to render him full justice, protesting that 'for no inducement offered to him by the Irish had he receded, or would he recede, from faithfully serving the king and his son'.[45] But Felim may here be suspected of 'protesting too much'. The reply of the

41 Ann. Loch Cé, 1258. The death of Dubhgall Mac Ruaidhri, king of Innsi-Gall and Airergaidhel, is recorded in 1268: ibid. 42 About this time Donnell Og O'Donnell, who had been fostered in Scotland, appears to have married a lady of Clandonald, and to have introduced *gallógláigh* into his household; and they, in 1290, secured the succession of her son Turlough: Ann. Loch Cé, 1290. Angus Og, Lord of the Isles, grandson of Donald, married a daughter of Cumhaighe O'Cathain. His grandson Eoin Mor, 'the Tanist,' married Mairi Byset, and through her his descendants succeeded to the Glynns of Antrim. 43 Cal. Pat. Roll, 40 Hen. III, m. 16 (p. 462). 44 Ibid., 44 Hen. III, m. 3. 45 Royal Letters (Shirley), vol. ii, p. 199; Cal. Docs. Ireland, vol. ii, no. 713. Felim's first complaint was made when William de Dene was justiciar, i.e. between *c*.October 1260 (ibid., no. 683) and the battle of Callann, July 27, 1261 when, or soon afterwards, William de Dene died. His subsequent letter was written soon after the latter date, when Richard de la Rochelle was justiciar. The Annals of Loch Cé, 1260, mention the hosting of Walter de Burgh against Felim to Roscommon, when he plundered some districts in Tirmany and also the people of the bishop (of Elphin). There was a bitter dispute going on at this time about the succession to the bish-

Government came early in 1262 in the form of a 'prodigious hosting of the Foreigners of Erin' against Felim and Aedh. The latter drove the greater number of their cattle into Tirconnel, and remained to defend them and their people at Inisaimer, an island on the Erne near Ballyshannon, while Richard de la Rochelle, the justiciar, accompanied by John de Verdun and joined by Walter de Burgh, plundered what was left in the O'Conor territory, and marked out the site of a castle in Roscommon. Aedh retaliated by plundering and burning the English homesteads between Balla and Slieve Lugha, and also in the district between Tuam and Athlone, and 'they killed all the men
[240] they found between those places'. Notwithstanding all this violence, the armed forces did not come into confiict. The English are said to have opened negotiations, and peace was concluded between the parties at Derryquirk near Tulsk, and Aedh and Walter de Burgh, we are told, 'slept in the same bed', in token of amity.[46]

From the account, however, of Meiler de Roche, sheriff of Connaught for the period ending at Michaelmas 1262, it appears that Felim was amerced in 600 marks for himself and Aedh for having the peace of Lord Edward, and that he bound himself in a fine of 5,000 marks and 200 cattle for getting the fee farm of three cantreds, namely, Moy Ai, the Three Tuaths, and Moylurg, at a rent of 300 marks. He was also charged with rent for Tirmany.[47] This fine for peace and the large fine for the restoration of his land were no doubt imposed on Felim because of Aedh's complicity in the revolt of Brian O'Neill, and were presumably the terms of the peace of Derryquirk. From this time until after the death of Aedh very little, if any, rent was paid by the king of Connaught, and the amount of arrears and fines mounted up and were duly carried forward.

[241] But fines entered on Pipe Rolls, though not collected, only served to exasperate Aedh O'Conor still further, and the peace was soon broken again. In 1264, there was another meeting between the English leaders, including Richard de la Rochelle, justiciar, Walter de Burgh, now Earl of Ulster, and Maurice, son of Maurice Fitz Gerald, on the one side, and Felim and Aedh on the other. The latter came in great force, and, according to the annals, 'fear and consternation seized the English', who forthwith concluded peace.

Near the close of 1264 a quarrel broke out between Walter de Burgh, now Earl of Ulster, and Maurice FitzMaurice, who represented the Geraldines in Connaught. The quarrel is said to have caused great disturbances in Ireland, but authenticated facts are few. On December 6 at Castledermot in County Kildare, Maurice Fitz Maurice and his nephew Maurice Fitz Gerald, third lord of Offaly, made prisoners of Richard de la Rochelle, then justiciar, Theobald Butler and John de Cogan, and confined them in

opric of Elphin (see Cal. Docs. Irel., vol. ii, nos. 646, 650, 690, 721, and Ware's 'Bishops'), and it is probable that Walter's action was concerned therewith. 46 Ann. Loch Cé, 1262. As confirmation of Aedh's raid to Athlone we may note that in his account of the issues of Athlone for the years 1262–6, Richard de la Rochelle 'answers nothing for issues of five acres outside the rampart of the castle because it was devastated by' Felim and Aedh his son: 35th Rep. D. K., p. 48. 47 Irish Pipe Roll, 46 Hen. III, 35th Rep. D. K., p. 44. have examined the original roll, from which it further appears that Felim owed £1,050 arrears of rent of three cantreds, besides two years' rent of Tirmany, the amount of which is not stated.

the castles of Lea and Dunamase.[48] Earl Walter seized the castles of Lough Mask, Ardrahan, and others belonging to Maurice Fitz Maurice in Connaught, and each party seems to have plundered the other's lands. How widespread the disturbances were is illustrated by the contemporary poem in Old French on the entrenchment of the town of Ross in County Wexford. It recounts how in February 1265, all the inhabitants, instituting an extensive system of 'dilution of labour', aided the hired workmen [242] in hurriedly enclosing the town, in dread of the consequences of the feud between 'Sir Maurice and Sir Walter'.[49] The cause of this feud between the de Burghs and the Geraldines, which broke out again in the next generation, is nowhere stated, but there are indications which make it pretty plain how it originated.

The root-fact was that the Fitz Geralds in Connaught were too ambitious and too powerful to remain loyal vassals of the de Burghs, and the latter for their part were jealous of the power of their Geraldine rivals. Though Maurice Fitz Gerald, father of Maurice Fitz Maurice, held directly from Richard de Burgh only the lands about Ardrahan and Kilcolgan in the south of County Galway, he had acquired from other grantees a large holding about Lough Mask in County Mayo, as well as from Hugh de Lacy extensive lands in County Sligo connecting up with Tirconnell and Fermanagh, to which he also had claims under Hugh de Lacy's grant. He was in fact by far the largest subordinate landholder in Connaught. His position, too, as justiciar during the remainder of Richard's lifetime gave him additional power, and there are not wanting signs that jealousy and variance of political policy arose between the two from the outset of the occupation.[50] After the death of Hugh de Lacy in 1243 the land of Ulster [243] was taken into the king's hand, and as regards his claims to Tirconnell and Fermanagh, at any rate, Maurice had no superior lord between him and the Crown. When in 1247 seisin was granted to the second Richard de Burgh, Walter's elder brother, the *dominium* of the Sligo lands does not seem to have been included.[51] In 1253, after Walter had succeeded to his brother, he arraigned Maurice Fitz Gerald on an assize of mort d'ancestor,[52] probably in respect of the Sligo seigniory, but with what result is not known. Soon after 1258 Maurice Fitz Maurice, who now held his father's Connaught lands, acquired in right of his then wife, Matilda, daughter of Gerald de Prendergast, the cantred of Corran in County Sligo.[53] In 1263 Walter de Burgh built a castle at Ath Anghaile somewhere in Corran,[54] and this intrusion in his domain, though possibly justified, is likely to have been unwelcome to Maurice. When about this time or in the

48 Clyn's Annals and Ann. Loch Cé, 1264. The Annales de Monte Fernandi (Strade) give the day of the justiciar's caption, 'in die Sancti Nicholai', and its accuracy is shown by the pleading in Cal. Docs. Irel., vol. ii, p. 205, though in that pleading the regnal year is given as forty-eight, apparently by error for forty-nine. 49 For the text of this poem see Archaeologia, vol. xxii and for a spirited rendering by Mrs. George Mac Lean (L.E.L.), see Crofton Croker's Popular Songs of Ireland, pp. 291–304. The disturbance, originating at Castledermot, where the justiciar was presumably holding a court, extended to the County Wexford, because Maurice Fitz Maurice held some lands there in right of his Prendergast wife: Cal. Docs. Ireland, vol. iii, no. 463. 50 See *supra*, p. 187, note 2 [p. 375, note 75]. 51 *Supra*, p. 193, note 1 [p. 378, note 6]. 52 Cal. Docs. Ireland, vol. ii, no. 282. 53 *Supra*, p. 199 [p. 381]. 54 Ann. Loch Cé, 1263. It probably stood at a ford over the Owenmore river, near where it leaves the Templehouse lake, which appears to have been formerly known as Lough Awnally (*Ath anghaile*). It was near to, but distinct from the castle of Tech Templa mentioned in 1271: see Proc. R.I.A., vol. xvi (c), p. 368.

next year Walter de Burgh was made Earl of Ulster by Prince Edward and given the lands of Hugh de Lacy there, Maurice must have greatly resented the interposition of his rival as superior lord between him and the Crown. Probably a decision in the justiciar's court at Castledermot adverse to Maurice, touching the rights of the parties in
[244] Ulster and perhaps in Sligo, was regarded as unjust by Maurice, and in the abeyance of the royal power consequent on the battle of Lewes, he and his kindred did not scruple to use force against the king's representative.[55]

It appears that Geoffrey de Geynville led force on behalf of the government against the Geraldines in 1265,[56] and this indicates the side Prince Edward thought was in the wrong. By June 10 the king had heard that the discord between the parties had been appeased,[57] and it was ordained in regard to the restoration of lands that all persons should have the same estate as they had when the disturbance began.[58]

It was not to be supposed that Aedh O'Conor would sit quiet while this feud was being waged between the magnates. Accordingly we read that in 1266 in company with O'Donnell he demolished the castles of Sligo, Banada, and Ardcree.[59] These were Geraldine castles. In the same year, his father, King Felim, died—'a man full of distinction and honour in Erin and Saxon-land'—and he was buried in the Dominican Friary in Roscommon, where his sepulchral effigy, battered by time and neglect,
[245] is still pointed out. For thirty years Felim had been, on the whole, in difficult circumstances, personally loyal to the king of England. He had accepted the settlement of 1235, by which he held the five cantreds from the English Crown. He had visited King Henry in England and had aided him in his war in Wales. But in his later years he had found himself unable to curb the aggressive spirit of his warrior son, and he had seen in consequence one of his cantreds taken from him.

Aedh now suceeeded Felim as actual king, and just as Cuchullin on first receiving arms must needs sally forth from Emain 'to redden his weapons' on friend or foe, so Aedh on assuming the sovereignty 'executed his royal depredation' in Offaly, where he committed many burnings and killings, and on his return to Athlone he blinded Cathal, son of Teig O'Conor, who died after having been blinded.[60] Such is the view taken by the annalists of Aedh's expedition to Offaly, and it is endorsed by O'Donovan. But it may be asked, why did Aedh select distant Offaly for his 'royal depredation'? Why not Loughrea, for instance? It is impossible not to note that Offaly (or part of it), like Sligo, where he had just destroyed the eastles, was a Geraldine district, and that in both cases Aedh was apparently despoiling the opponents of Walter de Burgh. lf this was done with Walter's connivanee, it was a short-sighted as well as a dishonourable policy—

55 It is perhaps not irrelevant to note that Richard de la Rochelle and Theobald Butler IV were connected by marriage with Walter de Burgh. Both Walter and Theobald were married to daughters of John Fitz Geoffrey, formerly justiciar (Cal. Docs. Ireland, vol. iv, no. 638): and Richard de la Rochelle was his nephew. As for John de Cogan, who was also imprisoned, he married the elder daughter of Gerald de Prendergast, half-sister of Matilda, then wife of Maurice Fitz Maurice. But there had already been disputes between these half-sisters about their shares in Gerald's lands: Cal. Docs. Ireland, vol. ii, no. 166. 56 36th Rep. D. K., p. 37. 57 Docs. Ireland, vol. ii, p. 126. 58 Ibid., p. 205. 59 Four Masters, Ann. Loch Cé, 1265. The latter annals do not mention O'Donnell. 60 Ann. Loch Cé, Four Masters, Ann. Clonmacnois, 1265. Cathal was grandson of Felim's elder brother Aedh and had the senior claim to the kingship.

'Non tali auxilio nec defensoribus istis tempus eget'.
[Nor such aid nor such defenders does the time require.]

As might have been expected, Aedh did not long confine his attentions to Walter's quondam foes. Next year (1266) several attacks were made on the English settlers. The castle of Tiaquin[61] was breached and the district about Dunmore laid waste. Ardnarea and the borough of Ballintogher were burned. A raid was made by Aedh's people against the Britons and Leinstermen of the west of Connaught—meaning presumably the Welsh men of Tirawley and their neighbours from Meath and Dublin—and thirty-nine of their heads were presented to O'Conor. One consequence of these exploits was that the king resumed the cantred of Tirmany and made grants therein.[62] [246]

We must suppose that Aedh O'Conor would have been checked in his turbulent career before this, had not Henry and his ministers been preoccupied with greater issues in England. The great struggle of the English barons to secure a reform in the administration of the realm—a struggle which commenced in 1258, and came to a crisis in the capture of Henry and his son Edward at Lewes in 1264—did not end with the death of Simon de Montfort at Evesham in the next year, but lingered on until the summer of 1267 was over. [247]

In 1268, Aedh was once more summoned to a conference at Athlone, but as before he came in force, and this time employed the argument of weapons with some effect on those who had summoned him. In September, Robert d'Ufford came to Ireland on affairs of Prince Edward, and next year as justiciar he began to build a castle at Roscommon. This was a sign for all to read that the king had definitively resumed the cantred of Tirmany. Aedh was ill at the time, but it is clear that he had no intention of tamely submitting to this further encroachment on his already circumscribed domain. About the same time Maurice Fitz Maurice rebuilt the castle of Sligo.

In 1270, O'Donnell burned Sligo and war broke out with Aedh O'Conor. Earl Walter, accompanied by Richard of Exeter, deputy-justiciar,[63] led a large force, including

61 Ann. Loch Cé, 1266. Tiaquin (*Tech Dhachoinne*) was in O'Kelly's country, and but for this entry we should not know that there was a castle here. It was probably held in connexion with Dunmore. 62 Cal. Pat. Roll, 51 Hen. III, p. 85, where 'Thoyth' probably represents the Irish *tuath*, viz. Clann Uadach. Sweetman mistook it for the name of a person: Cal. Docs. Ireland, vol. ii, no. 823. This explains the statement in Ann. Loch Cé, 1267, that Walter de Burgh plundered Tir Maine and Clann Uadach. Ho was taking possession for the king. Clann Uadach was O'Fallon's territory and lay in the parishes of Camma and Dysart in the barony of Athlone: Four Masters, vol. iii, p. 236. Both this land and 'Crohon in Tirmany' (*Creamhthainn*, sometimes anglicized Cruffon, in the barony of Killian, County Galway) afterwards belonged to Richard de la Rochelle: 36th Rep. D. I., p. 56, and Cal. Docs. Ireland, vol. ii, no. 878; and see the grant by Richard de la Rochelle to the little known Cistercian abbey De Diserto iuxta Briolam, i.e. Briole in the parish of Dysart: Chart. St. Mary's Abbey, Dublin, vol. i, p. 254. Other grantees in Tirmany (later) were John de Saunford, Escheator (ibid., no. 2115) in Clann Conmaigh in the barony of Ballymoe; and Richard de Exeter, deputy of Robert de Ufford. ibid., no. 1704; cf. vol. iv, no. 806, and vol. v, nos. 209, 316. His castle was at Athleague on the Suck. For further details and other grantees see Knox, Journal R.S.A.I., vol. xxxiii (1903), pp. 284–94. 63 The annalists mention the justiciar, but do not give his name. Robert d'Ufford seems to have returned to England and left Richard of Exeter as his deputy before the battle, which took place in die sancti Pantaleonis (July 28, 1270): Annales de Monte Fernandi, Tracts, I. A. S., vol. ii, p. 15.

[248] an Irish division, by way of Roscommon to Elphin, and so to the Shannon, somewhere near Carrick or Jamestown. Aedh was encamped in Moy Nissi, in the south of County Leitrim, and the earl, leaving the justiciar behind him, crossed the Shannon and marched to near Aedh's camp. He then opened negotiations with Aedh, and sent his own brother, William Og, as a hostage to Aedh's people, 'while Aedh should be in the earl's house arranging the peace'. Aedh's people, however, at once took the earl's brother prisoner, and killed John Dolphin and his son, who were in attendance. This treachery was enough to show that it was vain to negotiate with Aedh, and the earl, either not being in sufficient force to fight or fearing for the life of his brother, retreated towards the Shannon.

O'Conor, we are told, harried the retreat, 'as a furious raging, tearing lion goes about his enemies when killing them, so that he permitted them neither to eat, sleep, nor be at rest'. When the English reached the ford across the Shannon at Ath-an-chip,[64] Turlough O'Brien,[65] who was fighting on O'Conor's side, overtook them. Earl Walter slew him in single combat. But now the Connaughtmen came up, forced the earl's rearguard, and turned the retreat into a rout. Nine knights were slain and a hundred caparisoned horses were left on the field. Clearly the earl was badly mauled.
[249] Aedh then killed William de Burgh, the earl's brother, in his captivity 'as an eric', or rather in revenge, for the death of Turlough O'Brien, though the latter appears to have fallen in fair fight. True to the feline analogy, Aedh paid no attention to the conventions of warfare. Subsequently he followed up his success by demolishing the castles of Ath-Anghaile, Slieve Lugha, and Kilcolman, and burning Roscommon, Randown, and Owenagh. Clearly Aedh was a formidable opponent to the English domination of Connaught, and yet Prince Edward, the *dominus Hiberniae*, set so little store on the peace of his lordship, that in this year he set out on a crusade to the Holy Land, and did not return to England until four years had passed.

In 1271, after a week's illness, Earl Walter died in his castle of Galway, on the first anniversary of his defeat at Ath-an-chip. His lands were now taken into the hand of Prince Edward, soon to be king, for nine years during the minority of his eldest son Richard, afterwards known as the Red Earl of Ulster. As for Aedh O'Conor, he broke in this year the castle of the Templars (now Templehouse in Leyney), the castle of Sligo, and the castle of Richard of Exeter at Athleague; and in the next year he broke the castle of Roscommon, and made a raid into Meath as far as Granard, burned the town of Athlone, and broke down the bridge across the Shannon. But the end of this great warrior was approaching,and he died on May 3, 1274. Though he hardly ever ventured into the more fully colonized parts of Galway and Mayo, which during all this time enjoyed comparative peace, his frequent forays into Sligo and the lands bordering on his cantreds, wasted these districts from time to time, and greatly interfered with their progress and prosperity. Even the Irish annalists, usually indiscriminate in their
[250] eulogies of deceased kings, give him a double-edged obituary [continued on p. 408]

64 Ath-an-chip, 'vadum trabis', was near Carrick on Shannon, but the precise site is uncertain. Miles de Nangle built a castle here in 1245, but it had long since been abandoned. 65 He was perhaps a son of Brian Roe O'Brien, king of Thomond, who also turned against the English at this time.

MAIC SOMHAIRLE

Based on pedigree in the Books of Ballymote and Lecan, as given by Skene, with identifications, dates, and references to Irish Annals, &c.

Somerled, chieftain of Airer-Gaedhel = dau. of Olaf, king of the Isles.
c. 1156, obtained the southern Isles from Godfred, s. of Olaf;
1164, killed at Renfrew, where he was supported by Galls from Dublin: A.U.

Dubhgall (Dougall),
lord of Lorn, Morvern, and Mull;
a quo Clan Dougall.

Raghnall (Ranald, Reginald),
lord of Kintire, Cowall, Isla,
and the islands of the Clyde.

Angus,
slain in 1210 by the sons
of Raghnall: Skene.

Donchadh (Duncan).

Domhnall (Donald),
a quo Clan Donald,
lord of Kintire and Isla;
ravaged Derry and Inishowen
in 1212: A.U.; slain fighting for
O'Donnell in 1247 (?): A.L.C.

Ruaidrí (Rory, Roderick)
a quo Clan Rory,
lord of Bute, Arran, and Garmoran;
ravaged Derry and Inishowen
in 1212: A.U.: and again in 1214.

Eogan (Ewen)

Angus Mór,
not to be received in Ireland, 1256: supra,
p. 238; present at Scottish parliament of
1284; swore to keep the peace, July 1292:
Cal. Docs. Scot., ii. 622; safe-conduct for
him, his son Alexander, and his merchants,
in Ireland: Cal. Docs. Irel., iii. 1137;
died 1294: Skene.

Alan,
1259, went with 160 *óglàigh*
to Connaught: A.L.C.;
present at Scottish
parliament, 1284.

Dubhgall,
with a pirate fleet
off Connemara,
1258: A.U.;
died 1268: A.L.C.

Alexander, safe-conduct to trade in Ireland, 1292: Cal. Docs. Irel., iii. 1136; killed Alexander, son of Angus Mor, 1299: A.L.C.; received into peace, 1301: Cal. Docs. Scot., ii. 430.

Angus Óg, married a dau. of Covey O'Cahan: Book of Clanranald; supported Robert Bruce; slain at Faughart in 1318 (?): A.L.C., A.U.

Lochlan, married a dau. of Alexander of Lorn, received into peace, 1301: Cal. Docs. Scot., ii. 430; slain at Faughart in 1318 (?), A.L.C., A.U.

Ruairdrí

a dau., married to Aedh O'Conor in 1259: A.L.C.

Eoin (John) commanded the fleet at Dublin acting against the Scots in 1315: Cal. Docs. Scot., iii, nos. 447, 450.

Eoin d. 1387: A.U. = (2ndly) Margt., dau of Robert, the High Steward of Scotland.

Anna or Amie = John of the Isles. (1st wife)

Domhnall 'of Ile', lord of the Isles.

Eoin Mór, the tanist, ancestor of the Earl of Antrim: Keating, vol. iv, p. 105 = Mairi Byset, who brought the Glynns of Antrim to the Mac Donalds.

notice: 'A king who emptied and wasted Connaught against the English and Gael who opposed him; a king who inflicted frequent great defeats on English and Gael, and a king who demolished their courts and castles; a king who took the hostages of the Ui Briuin and Cinel Connell; the most formidable triumphant king of the kings of Erin; the destroyer and improver of all Erin during the period of his own renown, dignity, and time.'

Aedh O'Conor was at any rate a strong king, though a ruthless one. In his time no rival O'Conor dared to contest the throne with him, but immediately he was gone the old factions ran riot. He attained this immunity from revolt by reviving the odious practice, then happily becoming rare, of blinding possible opponents, and at least three members of the house of his uncle, the former King Aedh, son of Cathal Crovderg, suffered thus at his hands. The English government made no sustained effort to control him. Again and again he broke out into acts of violence beyond his borders, but each time, after at most a show of force, an ineffectual peace was made with him. But King Henry himself was partly to blame for Aedh's irreconcilable attitude. His fatuous attempt to provide an income for his half-brother out of the five cantreds, at a time when Felim was loyal and contented, was the way to breed distrust, discontent, and disloyalty. Indeed, Henry's dealings with these reserved cantreds were marked throughout by political ineptitude. While excluding the de Burghs from the district, he made no attempt to rule it himself. He neither controlled the O'Conors, nor (apparently) allowed Walter de Burgh to punish them for raids into his lands. On the other hand, he did not leave them in undisturbed possession of their enclave. From time to [251]
time, in view of an outbreak, a cantred or a piece of one would be withdrawn from them, or a large fine would be imposed before admitting them to peace. The imposition of fines was, however, the less of a deterrent as they were seemingly never paid, but by granting the withheld lands to officials and favourites who were absentees, and made little or no attempt to castellate, colonize, and govern their lands, the king of England lost the good will of the king of Connaught without appreciably strengthening English influence in the province.

It may indeed be said that the record of the O'Conors throughout the thirteenth century shows that none of them could ever keep the rest in order, but this was an argument for depriving them of their dominion altogether, and not for continually irritating them by piecemeal dismemberment and by what seemed to them unwarranted exactions.

[254] CHAPTER XXXI

THE EARLDOM OF ULSTER, 1227–71

The complete restoration of Hugh de Lacy to the lands of which he had been deprived by King John took place in April 1227.[1] Besides the extensive lordship which John de Courcy had established in Ulster, these lands included the manors of Ratoath and Nobber in Meath, which Hugh had held of the gift of Walter de Lacy, and the castle of Carlingford with the land in the north of the present county of Louth, which Hugh had acquired with his wife Leceline de Verdun.[2] The monetary value of the lordship of Ulster at this period, in normal years, must have been considerable, and the implied prosperity of the feudalized districts very great, for, in spite of the recent disturbances, the sum of £936 was received by Robert de Vaux, the king's bailiff, in the space apparently of little more than a year prior to June 1226.[3]

[255] Moreover this sum apparently did not include the issues of Coleraine and the Twescard (*Tuaiscert*), or the northern part of the present county of Antrim, afterwards the most lucrative part of the earldom. At this time the northern district was held directly of the Crown. As we have seen,[4] large tracts here, extending along the northern coast as far as Derry, had been granted by King John to Alan, Earl of Galloway, and his brother Thomas, Earl of Athol, and the latter had built a castle at Coleraine. Hugh de Lacy, however, in company with Aedh O'Neill, had recently destroyed the castle of Coleraine[5] and had harried the lands of the Scottish nobles who were opposing his attempt to recover his lands by force. They were, therefore, naturally apprehensive of the consequences to them of Hugh's reinstatement and appealed to the king.[6] In the arrangements made in 1226 with a view to the restoration of Hugh's lands, it was expressly provided that the seisins of these Scottish nobles should be saved.[7] What became of their tenures is, however, obscure. In 1228 the castle of Coleraine was rebuilt,[8] but by whom we are not told. Matthew Paris mentions that Alan of Galloway was married to a daughter of Hugh de Lacy, so we must suppose that the two became

1 Patent Roll, 11 Hen. III, p. 118. 2 For Ratoath see *ante*, vol. ii, p. 76 [p. 180]; for Nobber ibid., p. 84; and for Carlingford, p. 251. For the remarkable agreement by which Hugh acquired lands in Uriel with his wife Leceline, ibid., p. 121. The lands in Uriel included the ancient district of Cooley (*Cuailnge*), in which, on a high river bank close to the graveyard of Newtown-Cooley, are the earthworks of a mote and bailey fortress, now known, after a much later tenant, as ' Mount Bagnall'. They presumably mark the first Anglo-Norman site in the district. 3 Rot. Claus., 11 Hen. III, p. 205. 4 *Ante*, vol. ii, pp. 290–2 [pp. 266–7]. Among the magnates of Ireland to whom, in July 1221, Henry III announced the supersession of Geoffrey de Marisco as justiciar by Henry de Londres, Archbishop of Dublin, was 'Thomas de Galweie earl of Athoyl': Rot. Claus., 5 Hen. III, p. 476 *b*. 5 Ann. Ulst. 1222. 6 Cal. Docs. Irel., vol. i, nos. 1218, 1219, 1473. 7 Rot. Pat., 10 Hen. III, pp. 76–8. 8 Ann. Ulst. 1228.

reconciled; but the same writer tells us that after Alan's death in 1234, Hugh assembled [256]
a force from Galloway, the Isle of Man, and parts of Ireland, and that after entering into a blood-covenant according to the old barbaric rites, the confederates attempted to deprive Alan's three daughters of their inheritance in Galloway in favour of a male successor.[9] They were utterly defeated by the Scottish king in 1236, but it may have been in consequence of this quarrel that Hugh put an end to the Scottish tenures in the Twescard. In 1242, Patrick, son of Thomas of Galloway, was murdered in Scotland, and Walter Byset and his nephew John, accused of the crime, were outlawed and fled to Ireland.[10] Here they obtained, presumably from Hugh de Lacy, lands about Glenarm, in the parishes of Carocastle and Ardclinis, in the district of Carey and in Rathlin Island.[11] These lands certainly included the better part of those formerly granted to Duncan of Carrick and Alan of Galloway. The feud between these families seems to have lasted for some years longer, as in January 1252, Alan, son of Thomas, Earl of Athol, was pardoned for killing some of John Byset's men in Ireland.[12]

John Byset, 'destroyer of churches and of the Gael', perished of a sudden death in 1257.[13] He was succeeded by his son John, who, however, seems to have died in 1260, leaving three daughters as coheiresses.[14]

Hugh de Lacy had spent a large part of his life campaigning, not only in Ireland east and west, but in Languedoc against the Albigenses, and in Wales on the side of Llewellyn, and he did not now remain peaceably within the borders of his recovered [257]
earldom. He took part, as we have seen,[15] with Richard de Burgh in his great campaigns in Connaught in 1230 and 1236, and was rewarded by a grant of five cantreds in the northern part of that province. He immediately enfeoffed Maurice Fitz Gerald and others in most of his lands there, retaining, so far as appears, only the manor of Meelick in the present barony of Gallen.[16] In 1234, forgetting what he himself had suffered at the hands of a capricious monarch, and unmindful of the generous treatment meted out to him when he was in the power of the late Earl William Marshal, he played the treacherous game of the king and his Poitevin counsellors against Earl William's brother, the fearless champion of constitutional government, and must share the disgrace of the foul deed by which that chivalrous, if imprudent, knight was done to death. In this ugly episode, as in that of the downfall of John de Courcy thirty years before, we cannot acquit Hugh de Lacy on the plea that he was merely repressing disorder at the command of his lord the king—he could be disorderly and rebellious enough himself when it suited him— nor can we fail to suspect that he was in each case actuated by personal motives.

As long as Aedh O'Neill, the ally of his rebellious days, was alive, Hugh made no attack upon Tirowen. But Aedh died in 1230— 'a king who gave neither pledge or hostage to foreigner or Gael'—and soon the old struggle for the kingship between the O'Loughlins and O'Neills broke out again, accompanied by much fighting between the Cinel Owen and the Cinel Connell. In 1238 Maurice Fitz Gerald, then justiciar, and [258]

9 Matthew Paris, vol. iii, p. 64. 10 Ibid., vol. iv, pp. 188–9, and Fordun's Chronicle. 11 Cal. Docs. Ireland, vol. ii, no. 1500. 12 Ibid., no. 2. 13 Ann. Ulst., 1257. 14 Cal. Docs. Ireland, vol. ii, no. 1500. 15 *Supra*, p. 182 [pp. 372–3]. 16 *Supra*, pp. 193–201 [pp. 378–82].

Hugh de Lacy dethroned Donnell O'Loughlin, and gave the sovereignty to a son[17] of Aedh O'Neill and obtained the hostages of the two northern kingdoms. It was probably as a reward for Maurice's services on this occasion that Hugh enfeoffed him in Tirconnell, and perhaps in the district about the lower end of Lough Erne, and in part of Fermanagh as well.[18] If Maurice could make good his claim to these latter districts, as well as to what Hugh had given him in Connaught, he would have a continuous stretch of territory from Banada in Leyney to Fanad on Lough Swilly. He seems to have made the attempt. From this time forward he frequently appears fighting in Tirconnell, which became, as we should say, a Geraldine sphere of influence. Thus in 1242, supported by Felim O'Conor, he entered Tirconnell, and the chieftains of the Cinel Connell came into his house and gave him hostages.[19] These submissions for the time seem to have been real and not merely nominal. In July 1244 Henry III invited the kings of Tirconnell and Tirowen, and the principal chiefs of Eastern Ulster and Uriel (as well as those of Connaught and Munster), to join him in an expedition against the Scots.[20]
[259] As peace was made with Alexander II, the expedition was countermanded, but the king, while thanking the Irish chiefs for the good service they were prepared to render, asked them to be ready for service by the ensuing summer. Next summer (1245) Maurice Fitz Gerald led a force to assist the king in Wales, and this force included Felim O'Conor, 'accompanied by a great army of the Gael',[21] but whether any of the northern Irish were persuaded to join does not appear. The expedition was a failure. Henry advanced to the river Conway, and during a stay of over two months there fortified the castle of Dyganwy, but his army effected nothing and suffered great privations. The Irish contingent under Maurice Fitz Gerald arrived late,[22] and this is the reason assigned by Matthew Paris for the supersession of Maurice as justiciar by John Fitz Geoffrey, which now took place. Matthew Paris adds that 'Maurice patiently endured all this, because since the death of his son he despised all the glories and dignities of this world'. This was his eldest son, Gerald, who until recently has been strangely mis-
[260] placed in the received pedigree of the Leinster Geraldines. He had accompanied King Henry in the disastrous expedition to Poitou in 1242 and never returned.[23]

17 Apparently Brian *catha an Dúin*: Ann. Loeh Cé, 1238. 18 The grant of 'Tyrconylı . . . per reetas metas et divisas inter Keneleon et Tyrconyll . . . faciendo . . . servicium quatuor militum', &c., is in the Red Book of the Earl of Kildare, f. v. *d*. In 1293 Amabil, one of the two daughters and coheirs of Maurice Fitz Maurice, quitted claim to John Fitz Thomas 'in medietate cantredi de Crycarbry ubi Slygath iacet et in duobus cantredis et duobus teodhis de Tirconyll et medietate de Locherny et in septem teodhis de Fermanath que terre mihi ex iure hereditario acciderunt': ibid., f. viii. 19 Ann. Loch Cé, 1242. 20 Close Roll, 28 Hen. III, p. 265. The northern chieftains sumtnoned were Dovenald king of Tirchunill; Felim, son of late king [of Connaught]; Oraly (*O'Raghallaigh*); O'Hanlon (*O'hAnluain*); Brian O'Nel, king of Kinelun (O'Neill of *Cinel Eoghain*); O'Chatan (*O'Cathain*, O'Kane); O'Hynery (*O'hInneirghe*); Donald Mackadmel (*MacCathmail*, Mac Cawel); Mac Anegus (*Mac Aenghusa*, Mc Guiness); Mac Kartan (*Mac Artain*); Mac Gilemuri (*Mac Gilla Muire*, Gilmurry); O'Flen (*O'Floinn*); Mac Mathaven (*Mac Mathghamain*, Mac Mahon); and Mac O'Calmery (the son of *O'Glailmredhaigh*, O'Gormley). 21 Ann. Loch Cé, 1245; cf. Foedera, vol. i, p. 257. 22 Payment at the rate of *2d*. a day was ordered to be made to 3,000 foot-soldiers who came with the justiciar to the king's service at Gannock for the ten days prior to October 29 (Cal. Pat. Rolls, 29 Hen. III, p. 461), when the camp was broken up. 23 Cal. Docs. Irel., vol. i, no. 2573; Clyn's Annals, 1243, and see my paper on the 'Fitz Geralds Barons of Offaly', Journal R.S.A.I., vol. xliv (1914), pp. 105–8.

By this date indeed most of the leading figures that occupied the stage of Ireland during the first half of Henry's reign had disappeared. Before the close of 1245 not only all the male representatives of the elder William Marshal, but Richard de Burgh, and both Walter and Hugh de Lacy were dead, and in every case there was no adult male heir to fill the vacant place. Walter de Lacy died early in 1241, infirm and blind and burdened with debts to the Crown.[24] Three years earlier he had acknowledged his grandson, Walter, son of Gilbert de Lacy, as his heir,[25] but at his death his heirs were his two granddaughters, Margaret and Matilda, daughters of his son Gilbert. By 1244 Margaret was given in marriage to John de Verdun, son of Rohesia de Verdun and the second Theobald Butler, and Matilda to Peter de Genevre,[26] a Provençal of humble origin thus promoted by the king. Peter, however, died in 1249,[27] and by August 1252 Matilda was the wife of [261]
Geoffrey de Geynville, or Joinville, brother of the historian of Louis IX. By this time Meath had been partitioned between the two coheiresses, and eventually Trim became the caput of the de Geynville moiety, in which the liberties and free customs enjoyed by Walter de Lacy prior to 1224 were restored,[28] while Ballymore of Lough Sewdy (*Baile mór locha semhdidhe*) was the principal manor of the de Verdun moiety, where the franchises of the liberty seem to have been more frequentily withheld by the king.[29]

Like the eldest son of Maurice Fitz Gerald, Richard de Burgh died in the king's service on the ill-fated expedition to Poitou in the winter of 1242–3.[30] He left by his wife Egidia, daughter of Walter de Lacy, three sons, Richard, Walter, and William, all minors. Richard was given seisin of his father's lands in February 1247, but was dead without issue by November 5, 1248. His brother Walter was still a minor, and Peter de Bermingham was given the custody of his lands and castles.[31] [262]

The year 1242 saw also the last of Donough Cairbrech O'Brien, king of Thomond,[32] who had joined Richard de Burgh on many an expedition. His brother Murtough died three years earlier.[33] The latter seems to have married a daughter of Richard de Burgh, for in February 1243 the king at Bordeaux, evidently at the request of Richard, who lay

24 Matthew Paris, Chron. Mai., vol. iv, p. 93. On March 5 Walter de Godarville was given the custody of Walter's lands in Ireland: Cal. Pat. Rolls, 25 Hen. III, p. 246. 25 Ibid., 22 Hen. III, p. 220. 26 The issues of Walter's lands in Meath were restored to these couples on May 14, 1244, to hold without partition till further orders: Close Rolls, 28 Hen. III, m. 10. John de Verdun, if as usually supposed son of Theobald Butler II, was not of full age in 1244, as Rohesia did not marry Theobald until after Sept. 4, 1225: Rot. Claus., 9 Hen. III, p. 60. He had presumably attained twenty-one by May 3, 1247, when he was given seisin of his mother's lands: Rot. de Finibus, 31 Hen. III, m. 7, p. 11. 27 Matthew Paris, Chron. Mai., vol. v, p. 90; where Peter is said to have had a son and a daughter by Matilda. 28 Cal. Docs. Ireland, vol. ii, no. 60, and Cal. Chart. Rolls (1262), p. 401. 29 See Cal. Docs. Irel., vol. ii, nos. 810, 1646, 1670. No record of the partition of Meath seems to have been preserved. Speaking generally, the eastern portion fell to Geoffrey de Geynville and the western to John de Verdun. Duleek, however, in East Meath, was a de Verdun manor, as were also Ballymore of Lough Sewdy (Sunderlin) in West Meath, Incheleffer (?), Moydow in Co. Longford, and 'Adleck' (*Athliag*, now Ballyleague or Lanesborough on the Shannon), where fairs and markets were granted to Theobald de Verdun in 1284: ibid., 2303–4; while the services of Mullingar and some other manors in the eastern baronies of Westmeath were assigned to the de Geynville moiety: Gormanston Register, pp. 10–13. 30 Before March 7, 1243, when Egidia was given dower in his Munster lands, as to which see *supra*, p. 165 [p. 364]. His death was the result of hardships endured at sea: Matt. Paris, Chron. Mai, vol. iv, pp. 198–9. 31 Cal. Docs. Irel., vol. i, nos. 2865, 2975, 2978. 32 See *infra*, vol. iv, c. xxxiv. 33 Ann. Loch Cé, 1239.

dying there, ordered that Alice, Richard's daughter, should have her dower according to the law and custom of Ireland out of the lands of Murtough O'Brien.[34]

The same year that witnessed the deaths of the last two sons of Earl William Marshal the elder saw also the miserable end of Geoffrey de Marisco. He had been a prominent figure in the reign of King John and in the earlier part of the reign of his successor, and had twice held the office of justiciar, but he had sadly fallen from his high estate. The part he played in the occurrences which led to the death of Earl Richard Marshal in the spring of 1234, though perhaps not quite so discreditable as the chroniclers of St. Albans represented it, seems to have left him with no friends in Ireland. In August 1235 the king indeed 'remitted his ire' against him for siding with Richard Marshal, restored him to his lands or some of them, and gave him easier terms for the payment of the fine of 3,000 marks which had been imposed upon him.[35] But
[263] about the same time Geoffrey got into trouble with Hubert de Burgh, brother of Richard de Burgh and Bishop of Limerick, who excommunicated him for certain alleged injuries to the church of Limerick. The quarrel did not come before the civil courts, and its details can only be inferred from some documents preserved in the Black Book of Limerick. It concerned the town of Kilmallock and some neighbouring lands which belonged to the see and were held by Geoffrey. The Bishop of Lismore, commissioned by the Pope in 1235 to investigate the matter, found that though Geoffrey had received a hundred marks for the quit-claim of the town, the issues of which were valued at £32 3*s*. 4*d*., he nevertheless detained it for twenty years and more. Acts of violence were also alleged, but this seems to have been the ground-cause of the dispute. The damages to the see were estimated at 1,500 marks, and the sentence of excommunication was confirmed until satisfaction should be made.[36] In the same register there is an undated deed by which Geoffrey acknowledged that he had done homage to Bishop Hubert for Kilmallock and the other lands, and would pay an annual rent for the same of £11 3*s*. 4*d*.[37] This seems to have been the original agreement. In 1236 the king issued a mandate to the justiciar to give seisin to Geoffrey of his land of Kilmallock, which had been wrongfully claimed by the bishop as an escheat owing to the outlawry of Geoffrey's son William, who was tenant under Geoffrey of the land.[38] But in any case the bishop had not to wait very long for a legal ground of escheat. William de
[264] Marisco, as already mentioned,[39] was charged with the death of Henry Clement in 1235 and was outlawed. In 1238 he was accused of instigating an attempt on the king's life. These charges, however, were vehemently denied and were never proved. But William, driven to desperation, maintained himself for some time as a pirate on Lundy Island, and in 1242 was captured and ignominiously executed.[40] His father, Geoffrey, seems to have been outlawed about the same time,[41] but in what circumstances does not appear.

34 Cal. Docs. Irel., vol. i, no. 2603. 35 Cal. Fine Rolls, 19 Hen. III, p. 286. 36 Black Book of Limerick (Mac Caffrey), nos. clvii, clxi (anno 1235), and clviii (anno 1237); and cf. Cal. Docs. Ireland, vol. i, nos. 2267, 2268 37 Black Book of Limerick, no. xxv, p. 29. 38 Cal. Docs. Ireland, vol. i, nos. 2837, 2386. 39 Supra, p. 68 [p. 314]. 40 Matt. Paris, Chron. Mai., vol. iv, pp. 193, 195. 41 His outlawry is referred to in a mandate of June 11, 1244: Cal. Docs. Ireland, vol. i, no. 2683. It would seem to have taken place at least a year and a day previously.

According to Matthew he died in 1245, 'a wretched exile and wanderer, expelled from Scotland, banished from England, and disinherited in Ireland'.

Lastly, before February 1243 Hugh de Lacy, Earl of Ulster, died, and his land of Ulster reverted to the Crown. The legal basis of this reversion is obscure. There is no doubt that Hugh left at least one daughter, Matilda, by his first wife, Leceline de Verdun. Soon after Hugh's restoration she was married to David Fitz William, baron of Naas, and Hugh gave her the castle of Carlingford and all the land which he had with her mother in Cooley and Uriel and in the county of Limerick, also all his land of Morgallion (the manor of Nobber) in Meath.[42] She died shortly before Easter 1281.[43] [265]
Hugh's second wife, whom he seems to have married late in life, was Emeline, daughter and eventual coheiress, with her sister, of Walter de Ridelisford, but he had no issue by her. She was granted her dower out of Hugh's lands in Ireland, 'except the county of Ulster which was to be retained in the king's hand'.[44] She was given in remarriage to Stephen Longespée,[45] son of the Earl of Salisbury who commanded the army when King John expelled Hugh de Lacy from Ireland. She survived until 1278, when her heir to the lands which came to her from her father was her daughter by Stephen, then the wife of Maurice, second son of Maurice Fitz Gerald.[46] King John's grant to Hugh de Lacy was 'to him and his heirs', but we do not know the precise terms on which Hugh's lands were restored to him.[47] His renewed estate may have been limited to his life, or to him and his heirs male. It seems clear that Hugh left no legitimate male issue, and that in any case the resumption of his Ulster lands by the Crown was not contested.

It is, however, stated in some late fourteenth-century annals, and has been long supposed, and is asserted even by writers of our own day, that Walter de Burgh succeeded [266]
to the earldom of Ulster in right of his wife, who was daughter and heir of Hugh de Lacy.[48] But contemporary evidence is inconsistent with this title. Walter de Burgh obtained the county of Ulster under a grant from Prince Edward in exchange for the manor of Kilsheelan and other Munster lands.[49] This grant appears to have been made

42 Gormanston Register, f. 191 *d*. It is not clear on the face of it that this grant was made on the occasion of Matilda's marriage, though perhaps it was. Shortly before his death Hugh granted all his land of Morgallion and his manor of Nobber to Albert, Archbishop of Armagh, and his successors: Chartae, &c., p. 24. It is not easy to reconcile these grants. There was litigation in 1302 between Matilda's granddaughter and Nicholas, Archbishop of Armagh, about Nobber: Justiciary Rolls, vol. i, pp. 432–9; and cf. Chartae, &c., p. 40. The issue of the litigation is not clear, but the manor passed to Matilda's descendants: Gormanston Register, f. 1. 43 Cal. Docs. Irel., vol. ii, no. 1741. 44 Ibid., vol. i, no. 2663. 45 Ibid., no. 2600. 46 Ibid., vol. ii, no. 1249. 47 The king on April 25, 1243, ordered the manor of Nobber to be kept in his hand 'until he should be certified regarding the agreements made between the king and the earl touching that manor and the earl's other lands': Close Roll, 27 Hen. III, p. 23. 48 The statement, which does not appear in the notice of Hugh de Lacy's death in Clyn's Annals (1349), appears first in a modified form in the Laud MS. Annals (Chart. St. Mary's, Dublin, vol. ii, p. 315), where it is simply stated that Hugh left a daughter as his heir, whom Walter de Burgh, who was Earl of Ulster, married. But the full statement appears in Grace's Annals (c.1537), and was followed by Hanmer (ed. 1571), Dowling (ob. 1613), Cox (1690), Ware (ed. 1706), Leland (1773), Gilbert, who added new errors of his own (1865), Joyce (1893), D'Alton (1910), &c. 49 Prince Edward's feoffment is mentioned in a letter from the king in 1269: Cal. Docs. Irel., vol. ii, no. 860. It was in exchange for the manor of Kilsheelan (ibid., nos. 1520, 1548), and probably for the vills of Kilfeakle and Clonmel and the de Burgo lands in Estermoy (Clanwilliam), which thus came into Edward's hand and were granted along with Kilsheelan to Otho de Grandison when

in 1264,[50] twenty-one years after Hugh de Lacy's death, when Walter is first called Earl of Ulster.[51] Walter had obtained seisin of his Connaught and Munster lands in May 1250, after having given security that he would not marry without the king's licence.[52]
[267] At his death in 1271 his widow was Avelina, daughter of John Fitz Geoffrey,[53] who was justiciar from 1245 to 1256 and died in 1258. Richard de Burgh, Walter's son and heir by Avelina, was nearly, if not quite, of age in January 1280, when he obtained seisin.[54] He was born therefore about 1259, and Walter must have married Avelina not later than 1258–9, and perhaps some years earlier. A previous marriage, if such can be supposed to have taken place, with a daughter of Hugh de Lacy cannot therefore have been the occasion of Walter's obtaining Ulster.

From the time of Hugh de Lacy's death in the winter of 1242–3 Ulster was in the king's hand and was administered by the king's seneschals up to 1254, when with the rest of Ireland it was given by the king to his son Edward as part of his appanage on his marriage with Eleanor of Castile.[55] Ulster was then administered by Prince Edward's seneschals for a further period of about ten years, until it was granted to Walter de Burgh, as already mentioned. During the period when Ulster was in the king's hand some attempts were made to defend the English borders both on the east and on the west against the northern chieftains, and to make the king's suzerainty over them a real-
[268] ity. In 1245 Maurice Fitz Gerald, with the aid of Felim O'Conor, erected the castle of Sligo[56] as the manorial centre for his lands in the north of Connaught. In the following years, when no longer justiciar, Maurice repeatedly invaded Tirconnell, which had also been (nominally) granted to him by Hugh de Lacy, took hostages and set up kings, but the kings he set up proved no more amenable than those he had deposed. In 1248 John Fitz Geoffrey, the justiciar, built a bridge across the Bann at Coleraine and erected a castle at Drumtarsy (now Killowen) on the western side of the river,[57] and, 'since the power of the foreigners was over the Gael of Ireland', the Cinel Owen gave hostages to the justiciar.[58] In 1252 Maurice Fitz Gerald rebuilt the castle of Caol-uisce on the Erne in Fermanagh, while John Fitz Geoffrey rebuilt the castle of Moy Cova in Iveagh, Co. Down.[59] At the same time Brian O'Neill once more submitted to the justiciar and deliv-

Richard de la Rochelle was justiciar (1261–5). This last-mentioned grant was confirmed and extended in 1281 (ibid., no. 1847). 50 'Walterus de Bourgh factus fuit comes Ultoniae': Chronicle of Henry of Marleburghe under the year 1264; Collectanea Hiberniae, MS. T.C.D., E. 3. 10. 51 Ann. Loch Cé, 1264. The document in Cal. Docs. Irel., vol. i, no. 2561, is altogether misplaced. It should be dated 1269. The Royal Letter, calendared, ibid., vol. ii, no. 860, is the king's reply. See *infra*, p. 283 [pp. 422–3]. 52 Excerpta Fine Rolls (Roberts), vol. ii, p. 78. 53 Inquis. p. m. on lands and heir of Richard Fitz John, 27 Ed. I (Cal. Inquis. Ed. I, vol. iii, no. 507), from which it appears that Amelina or Avelina, widow of Walter de Burgh, and 'of whom was born Richard de Burgh', was sister and one of the heirs of Richard, son of John Fitz Geoffrey, to whom the cantred of the Isles (in Thomond) had been granted. Cf. Cal. Docs. Ireland, vol. iv, no. 289. 54 Cal. Docs. Irel., vol. ii, no. 1629. 55 Cal. Docs. Ireland, vol. ii, nos. 326, 371. On July 23, 1263, all Ulster and its issues were assigned by the king to Eleanor the Queen Consort in dower (ibid., no. 255), but this assignment was superseded by the grant of 1254. 56 Ann. Loch Cé, 1245. 57 Ann. Ulst., 1248. For the identification of Drumtarsy see Reeves, Colton's Visitation, p. 131. 58 Ann. Loch Cé, 1248. 59 The castle of Caol-uisce (i.e. Narrow Water), originally built by Glilbert de Nangle in 1212 (*ante*, vol. ii, p. 289 [pp. 265–6]), was in Fermanagh (Red Book, f. viii) on the Erne, near its exit from the lower lake. Both O'Donovan and Hennessy confuse it with Narrow Water, Co. Down. The castle of Magh Cobha, originally erected by John de Courcy before 1188, is almost certainly marked by the great mote of Dro-

ered his own brother as a hostage. But this submission was no more sincere than former ones. Next year Brian destroyed the castle of Moy Cova and other castles, and made a destructive raid into the plain of Down where some undefended towns were burned.[60]

For the period during which Prince Edward was *Dominus Hiberniae* there is a [269] marked decrease in the number of records relating to Ireland, and it is therefore difficult to ascertain whether the 1254 change in the administration was responsible for bringing about the unrest which undoubtedly ensued in the districts occupied by the Mc Carthys, the O'Briens, the O'Conors, and the northern chieftains. When making over Ireland to his son, the king retained to himself the jurisdiction concerning the cross-lands, the custodies of vacant ecclesiastical benefices, and the rights of the Crown in the matter of preferments, and there are many mandates from the king touching these. He also sent numerous mandates as to the provision for Godfrey de Lusignan, his half-brother, of four and a half cantreds in Connaught,[61] which, though eventually not carried out, probably contributed to the unrest in that quarter. But though there are many mandates from the prince in 1255 for the sending to Gascony of moneys from the issues of Ireland and various supplies for his army in Gascony,[62] few directions from him touching the administration of his new dominion appear on the rolls. In July 1255, while still in Gascony, Prince Edward sent his seal to Ireland, 'in order', as he says, 'that he who is deputed to the offlce of chancery in that country might use it in his place,[63] and in May 1256 the king recalled his own seal, and ordered his subjects in Ireland to [270] be intentive to Edward's seal as they were wont to be to the king's seal.[64] Nevertheless some of the king's writs appear to trespass on his son's province, and there is no doubt that for some years the king kept the government of Ireland under his control, while it is probable that many of Edward's writs and grants were never enrolled in England and, if enrolled in the chancery of Ireland, have been lost.[65]

In November 1264 a mandate was sent from Bayonne, where the prince was, to Richard de la Rochelle, his seneschal in Ireland, to direct his attention to the pacification of Ulster, where, as we have seen, Brian O'Neill had made a destructive raid in the preceding year. The seneschal was authorized to take £100 from the prince's treasure for that purpose, and ordered to collect retainers and an aid from the country and to certify to the prince 'on his arrival in Ireland' the names of those persons who refused to come to his peace.[66] It seems that some further attempt was made to pacify O'Neill and that he again nominally submitted, for we find, duly entered in a subsequent pipe roll[67] that he owed £100 aid to the king for his war in Gascony, and a fine of 3,092 cows,

more, Co. Down: *ante*, vol. ii, p. 117 [p. 197] and note [19], and see Journal R.S.A.I., vol. xliv (1914), p. 53. It was clearly the work of the justiciar: Cal. Docs. Irel., vol. ii, nos. 32 and 124. 60 Ann. Loch Cé, 1253: *ocus sráid bhailedha do loscad*. The Four Masters turn this into *loisctear an Sradbaile*, meaning Dundalk. The 'street-towns', i.e. undefended towns, included some in Dufferin: see Cal. Docs. Ireland, vol. ii, no. 411. 61 See *supra*, p. 233 [p. 398]. 62 Cal. Docs. Ireland, vol. ii, nos. 419, 442, 446. 63 Ibid. 453. Ralph of Norwich was chancellor at this time. 64 Cal. Docs. Ireland, vol. ii, no. 500. 65 In January 1267 the king superseded a writ of Edward's on the ground of informality: ibid., no. 529, and cf. no. 696. 66 Cal. Docs. Ireland, vol. ii, nos. 411, 412. Peter de Repenteny was at this time seneschal of Ulster, but Henry de Mandeville seems to have held the office in the Twescard. 67 Facsimiles of National MSS. of Ireland,

and these entries were probably carried forward from 1254–5. There are several other allusions to Edward's intention to visit Ireland and spend some time there, but unfor-
[271] tunately, like the good intentions of his father, the programme was never carried out. At this moment Edward was of course too young and inexperienced to institute a wise policy. He had yet to gain his political schooling at the hands of his opponents in the Barons' War. But had a ruler, such as Edward afterwards proved himself to be, given his whole attention, even for a short period, to the actual business of governing Ireland on the spot, he could not have failed to perceive that there were several parts of Ireland which required 'pacification' to enable an orderly government to be carried on there, and that such pacification was not to be produced by the magic of mandates from Gascony or even from Westminster, or to be enforced by the entry of fines on the pipe roll, but that the problem was one calling for the highest efforts of statesmanship, backed by adequate military power, and guided by principles of justice and fair dealing.

In 1256 Alan la Zuche was justiciar. He had been justiciar in the parts of Wales adjoining Chester prior to the grant to Edward, and he was sent to Ireland on Edward's service about the end of March. It was seemingly due to him that the attempt to provide for Godfrey de Lusignan at the expense of the king of Connaught was abandoned, for the Irish annals of that year state that the justiciar made peace with Aedh, son of Felim, on condition that the territory of O'Conor should not be diminished while he was justiciar.[68] This arrangement, however, did not prevent Aedh from immediately endeavouring to extend the territory of O'Conor, both in Connaught and in Breffny, at
[272] the expense of his neighbours whether Irish or Eng lish. It seems that Edward was now prepared to adopt a more spirited policy of his own and contemplated the appointment of a justiciar—perhaps Walter de Burgh—who would endeavour to curb the aggressive tendencies of Felim's son. In June 1268, having learnt that Edward intended to make a justiciar in Ireland and to commit his castles to constables without consulting the king, Henry took the extreme step of commanding his subjects in Ireland not to be intentive to any justiciar, constable, or keeper not appointed by the king's letters patent.[69] The dispute, however, appears to have been amicably settled, and by October Stephen Longespée, the king's cousin, was justiciar,[70] and the writs of both Henry and Edward were directed to him. It was in Stephen's time that the disturbances in Munster between the Mc Carthys of Carbury and the English settlers broke out. In 1259 Fineen, son of Donnell Got Mc Carthy, raided Kerry, and probably it was in consequence of this that the Lord Edward on November 7 of that year made the grant Decies and Desmond to John FitzThomas in the hope that he would be able to control the Irish there. But, as we have seen,[71] the effort ended disastrously in the battle of Callann.

Meanwhile a greater danger threatened the English in the north of Ireland. Following upon O'Neill's incursion over the eastern border of the Irish territories, Goffraigh O'Donnell in 1257 penetrated into the Geraldine district in the west, razed the castle
[273] of Caol-uisce, burned the town of Sligo, and in a fight at Credran in the Rosses, in

Part II, plate 73. See *infra*, pp. 277–8 [p. 420]. 68 Ann. Loch Cé, 1256. Alan la Zuche was killed in Westminster Hall by Earl Warenne in 1259: Mat. Paris. 69 Foedera, vol. i, p. 373. 70 Cal. Docs. Ireland, vol. ii, no. 600. 71 *Supra*, p. 140 [pp. 349–50].

which he was sorely wounded, routed a pursuing body of the English.[72] The northern chieftains in fact were determined to resist the extension of English rule and to maintain their independence, but, unfortunately for their objects, the kindred clan-groups were fired with greater animosity against each other than against the foreigners, and this feeling precluded all possibility of joint action. When in 1258 O'Donnell was lying on his death-bed from the wounds he had received at the battle of Credran, O'Neill took advantage of his hapless plight to demand the submission of the Cinel Connell. But though O'Donnell's body was stricken unto death, his spirit was unbroken. Borne on a bier at the head of his men he defeated the Cinel Owen on the banks of the Swilly, and soon afterwards died 'the death of a hero who had at all times triumphed over his enemies'.[73] Once more O'Neill demanded the hostages of the Cinel Connell, and while [274]
the petty chiefs were deliberating what they should do, for they had no lord since Goffraigh O'Donnell's death, Donnell Og O'Donnell, youngest son of Donnell Mor, a youth of only eighteen years, appeared amongst them on his return from Scotland, where he had been fostered by the Lord of the Isles. His coming at this crisis is likened by the annalist to the coming of Tuathal Techtmar over the sea from Alban, in the penumbral period of Irish story, after the extirpation of the royal race of Erin by the servile tribes. The chieftainship was immediately conferred on Donnell Og, and he proudly rejected O'Neill's demands, replying to his emissaries, in the words of a Scottish proverb, that 'every man should have his own world'.[74] In this retort the very spirit of the clans found utterance, a spirit incompatible with political unity.

And yet it was political unity that O'Neill sought to bring about. At this very time he was trying to form a confederacy of the Gael against the English, and to revive in his own person the long lapsed office of *Ard-rí*. He had before his eyes the successful example of Llewelyn, who had recently united the Welsh people in both the north and the south of the ancient principality and had assumed the title of Prince of Wales. With a like object in view, Brian held a conference at Caol-uisce, but the attempt was doomed to failure. Aedh O'Conor, the warrior son of Felim, king of Connaught, and virtual leader of the Sil Murray clans, submitted to him and gave him hostages on condition of getting a free hand in Breffny,[75] but it is clear that neither Conor O'Brien, king of [275]
Thomond, as represented at the conference by his warlike son Teig, nor Donnell Og, the youthful chieftain of Tirconnell, would consent to subordinate himself to O'Neill. Teig indeed is said to have insisted on obtaining the position of *Ard-rí* for himself, while

72 Ann. Loch Cé, 1257. The statement in Four Masters that O'Donnell and Maurice Fitz Gerald, who is spoken of as being the justiciar, met in single combat and severely wounded each other, is certainly inaccurate and probably without foundation. Maurice, who had not been justiciar since 1245, died in 1257 in the habit of a monk at the Franciscan Friary of Youghal, which he had founded (Clyn and Dowling). His *obit* is entered before O'Donnell's raid in the older Irish annals, and they make no mention of the single combat or of his presence. According to Matthew Paris he died before Ascension, 1257, i.e. before May 27. Maurice obtained seisin in 1216, and must have been at least sixty-two years of age in 1257. He had given his lands in Sligo, Fermanagh, and Tirconnell to his son Maurice some time before his death: Red Book, f. viii; and see Journal R.S.A.I., vol. xliv (1914), p. 107, where the deed of enfooffment is transcribed and explained. 73 Ann. Ulst., vol. ii, p. 324, MS. D, note; and Four Masters, 1258. 74 Ann. Ulst., vol. ii, p. 325, MS. D, note; and Four Masters, 1258. 75 Ann. Loch Cé, 1268.

O'Donnell, as we have seen, had rejected O'Neill's demands and held aloof from the confederacy.

The outcome of this conference appeared in 1260, when Brian O'Neill, described as 'King of the Gael of Erin', supported by Aedh O'Conor, advanced as far as Drumderg near Downpatrick, and there on Sunday, May 14, met with 'a terrible defeat' at the hands of the English of Down.[76] Brian himself was killed, and with him fell 'many of the best' of Tirowen and Connaught. Brian indeed had little title to be regarded as king of the Gael. Not only was he not joined by the southern Irish, but it would seem that even in his own province he had a rival[77] and was not supported by the chieftains of Tirconnell, Fermanagh, or Irish Uriel (with the exception of O'Hanlon), while the Irish of Eastern Ulster held aloof or opposed him. The confederacy was defeated, not by the feudal host, which was not summoned, but by 'local levies of the commonalty of the city and county of Down' under the leadership of Sir Roger des Auters and the mayor of that city.[78]

[276] These leaders were accordingly rewarded by grants of land.[79] But though O'Neill's attempt thus signally failed, the combination of the kings of Tirowen and Connaught was the most formidable native effort that the English in Ulster had to meet in the thirteenth century. Brian's death is lamented in a remarkable dirge[80] by Gilbride Mac Namee, hereditary bard of the O'Neills, commencing with the following quatrain (translated):

> Death of my heart! The head of Brian
> In a strange country under cold clay!
> O head of Brian of Slieve Snaght,[81]
> Eire after thee is an orphan!

It is not without other pathetic verses, but, as the editor remarks, the victories of O'Neill and his ancestors, of which the bard proudly boasts, were mostly gained in their own province over their immediate neighbours and kindred. The principal exception was the winter raid of Murtough 'of the Leather Coats', who in the year 942 carried off the king of Leinster and made chessmen of his bones, exacted tribute from the Danes, fettered the king of Cashel, burned the palace of Kincora, and carried captive the king of Con-
[277] naught.[82] If this was the model that Brian had in view in his effort to make himself *Ard-*

76 Ann. Loch Cé, Ann. Ulst., 1260. For the precise date see Clyn's Annals. 77 In 1259 Aedh Buidhe O'Neill, Brian's rival and successor, had accompanied O'Donnell in a devastating raid through Tirowen and Irish Uriel: Four Masters, 1259, Ann. Ulst., vol. ii, p. 327, note. 78 See the king's letter to his son: Cal. Docs. Ireland, vol. ii, no. 661. The statement, frequently made, that O'Neill was defeated by the justiciar Stephen Longespée, is not found in any early authority and is inconsistent with the above letter. It appears to have originated in the blunder of a copyist. In the Laud MS. Annals under the year 1259 are two entries: 'Stephanus de Longa Spata venit iusticiarius Hibernie. Item, interfectus est Oneyl apud Doune'. Of these entries Dowling makes one: 'Stephanus de longe espee iusticiarius Hibernie anno 42 Henrici 3 interfecit O'Nel cum 352 eius familiaribus in vico de Down'. Subsequent writers seem to have blindly followed him. 79 Cal. Docs. Ireland, vol. ii, nos. 677–8. 80 Miscellany, Celtic Society, pp. 146–183. 81 *Sliabh Sneachta* (Mons nivium), a mountain in Inishowen. 82 See the 'Circuit of Ireland, by Muircheartach Mac Neill', in Tracts, vol. i, Irish Archaeological Society.

rí, Ireland was happy in the battle of Down. The poem indeed affords an instructive insight into the limits of the patriotism which animated the Irish clans—limits which effectually barred the way to Irish unity. The contemporary dirge by Fearghal Og Mac an Bháird on the deaths of the O'Cahans[83] slain in the same battle, though a slighter effort, is more full of tender human touches. The bard sorrows most for his foster-brothers, Maghnus and Eachmarcach O'Cahan, and dwells with fond memory on the days when in their sports they used to place Maghnus on a mound and inaugurate him as their chieftain, while Eachmarcach (i.e. 'horse-rider') would be a horse to carry the hereditary bard as his rider thrice round the mound. It is curious, too, to note that as the body of O'Cahan was not recognized among the slain, the bard supposes that the fairies may have carried him off: 'In fairy mound west or east,/Who knows but he may still be living!'—and he quotes traditional examples of fairy abduction.

The Irish Pipe Roll for the year 1260–1[84]—one of the few for the reign of Henry III which has been preserved—throws some light on the profits of the lordship of Ulster, then in Prince Edward's hands, and on the relations with Brian O'Neill and other Irish chieftains. The farm of Ulster, except the Twescard or northern part of County [278]
Antrim, then in separate custody, was let to the seneschal, Nicholas de Dunheved, at 300 marks a year. Accordingly there are no entries of rents paid, but the account consists mainly of fines for defaults, trespasses, &c., both English and Irish. Brian O'Neill appears to have held the territory of Tirowen subject to a rent of 400 cows, which may be regarded as equivalent to £66 13*s*. 4*d*.[85] But this rent was very irregularly paid, as eight years arrears are debited to him. He is also charged with £100 aid to the king for his war in Gascony (1253–4), and '3,092 cows of a fine made with the justiciar'—probably with John Fitz Geoffrey, in consequence of Brian's raid into Ulidia in 1253, when the castle of Moy Cova was destroyed. These were clearly bad debts. Some of the Irish chieftains of Ulidia—Mac Guiness, Mac Artain, Mac Duilechain, &c.—were debited with smaller fines in cows.

For the Twescard there is the more detailed account of Henry de Mandeville, the *custos*, for the four terms ending November 1, 1262.[86] From this district in the north of County Antrim, corresponding probably to the Deanery of Twescard in the ecclesiastical organization, the custodian accounts for the considerable sum of £464 9*s*. 4*d*. It had evidently been well settled by the Normans and was in a prosperous condition; and this conclusion is borne out by the ecclesiastical taxation of 1302–6, when the churches [279]
of the deanery were valued at £217, while the deanery of Lecale, the next highest in Ulidia, yielded only £108. The principal town was Coleraine, where the burgage rent was £23. There were manors at or including the places now known as Portstewart, Portrush, Bushmills, Dunluce, Dunseverick, Armoy, Mount Sandal, and Loughguile. The last-named was an important manor, seemingly belonging to the Savage family, but now, during a minority, set to farm at £64 a year. The inland portion of the Twescard

83 Miscellany, Celtic Society, pp. 404–14. 84 See Facsimiles of National MSS. (Ireland), part ii, plate 73. 85 From another entry it appears that 3*s*. 4*d*. was the equivalent of a cow. 86 Exact information regarding the Norman settlement in Ulster in the thirteenth century is so scanty that I have given an abstract of this account, with some elucidatory notes, as an appendix to this chapter.

was largely held by the free-tenants of this manor. The issues of the lord's mills and of the fisheries of the Bann were very lucrative.

About this time, seemingly just before O'Neill's attempt, repairs were effected at some of the principal castles of Ulster. Timber was brought to make *hurdicia* (wooden galleries) for defending the walls of Greencastle at Narrow Water. The hall of the keep (*aula turris*) was roofed with shingles, but lead brought from Drogheda was also employed. At Carlingford quarried stone and lime-mortar was used for the works at the castle. Freestone was brought from Down and iron from Drogheda to repair the gates and doorways of the castle of Rath (Dundrum).[87]

In October 1261 Richard de la Rochelle, Prince Edward's former seneschal, was appointed justiciar in succession to William de Dene, who died soon after the defeat at Callann, and in the course of the suceeeding year, supported by Walter de Burgh, he
[280] led two expeditions, one to punish Aedh, son of Felim O'Conor, for his share in the battle of Down, and the other to check the Mac Carthys, who since the battle of Callann were carrying all before them in Desmond. By the former expedition the site of a castle at Roscommon was marked out, indicating the meditated confiscation of some land there, but peace for the moment was made with Aedh. By the latter expedition Cormac Mac Carthy, brother of Fineen, was slain.[88]

But from about this time and for some years the lord of Ireland was too much engrossed with the serious state of affairs in England to pay due attention to his Irish dominion, and this may have induced him to revive the earldom of Ulster and put that part of Ireland in the hands of Walter de Burgh, who had showed himself an able and energetic supporter of the justiciar. Early in 1264 hostilities broke out between the barons who followed Simon de Montfort and the royalists, and on May 14 was fought the battle of Lewes, which left the king a prisoner in Earl Simon's hands, while soon afterwards Prince Edward surrendered himself as a hostage for the good behaviour of the marcher lords. From this date up to the battle of Evesham (August 4, 1265) the royal authority was in commission, and the few more important writs concerning Ireland, though issued in Henry's name, must be regarded as carrying out the will of Earl Simon.[89] It would have been strange if there were no echo in Ireland of the Barons'
[281] War. The Irish annals for 1264 with customary exaggeration of phraseology, speak of 'a great war between Mac William Burk (i.e. the new Earl of Ulster) and Mac Gerailt (i.e Maurice Fitz Maurice), so that the greater part of Erin was destroyed by them'. When dealing with affairs in Connaught at this period we gave an account of this quarrel, and of the disturbances that followed the imprisonment of the justiciar, Richard de la Rochelle, and others, and we indicated the probable cause of this unprecedented act of violence on the part of the Geraldines.[90] Here it may be noted that the disturbance

87 Pipe Roll (Ireland), 46 Hen. III, account of Robert Gelous of money received at the Exchequer, Hilary 1260; see Rep. Record Commissioners of Ireland, vol. i, plate 2 (between pp. 56 and 67) 88 Ann. Loch Cé, 1262, and see *ante*, pp. 239 and 142 [400–1 and 351]. 89 Thus on September 24, 1264, the king, with the consent of his son, commands Walter de Burgh and others to give seisin to the Earl of Gloucester, who had just come of age, and who at this time was one of Earl Simon's principal supporters: Cal. Docs. Ireland, vol. ii, no. 750. 90 *Supra*, pp. 241–4 [pp. 401–3].

in Ireland should probably not be altogether dissociated from the revolutionary movement which had just taken place in England. In their action against Lord Edward's justiciar and his newly created earl, the Geraldines were following at a distance the example of Simon de Montfort, if they were not actually instigated by him. Maurice Fitz Maurice indeed, as was shown, probably had some personal dispute about his Connaught and Ulster lands with Walter de Burgh. His father had held both Sligo and Tirconnell under grants from Hugh de Lacy, and Maurice may have claimed to hold them independently of Earl Walter. The justiciar would probably decide against this claim on legal grounds, and in the general anarchy of the moment Maurice and his kindred may have seen an opportunity of asserting his supposed rights by force. It seems, however, clear that Earl Simon was anxious to replace Edward's justiciar. On February 16, the king, presumably at the earl's instance, wrote to Fulk de Saunford, Archbishop of Dublin, referring to the disturbances likely to occur owing to the discord prevailing among the magnates of Ireland and praying him to undertake the office of justiciar.[91] [282]
On March 19 Roger Waspail was sent over on a confidential message, and the archbishop was to certify the state of Ireland and 'how the magnates bear themselves in regard to their fealty';[92] and on May 6 Richard de la Rochelle was summoned to the king, and the custody of Ireland was entrusted to Roger Waspail, assisted by the counsel of the Archbishop and the Bishop of Meath.[93]

On May 28 Prince Edward escaped from custody and went over to the marcher lords, with whom Earl Gilbert of Gloucester was now acting, and on June 10 more peremptory letters were sent by the king and the Earl of Leicester (who was evidently their real author) to the prelates of Ireland, and to Walter de Burgh, Maurice Fitz Glerald, Maurice Fitz Maurice, Richard de la Rochelle, and Geoffrey de Geynville, stating that Edward, the king's son, 'at the instigation of him who strives to sow the seeds of discord' (meaning apparently the Earl of Gloucester), had against the ordinance and his own oath gone over to certain marchers and rebels, and had therefore, according to the rigour of the law, forfeited his right to the kingdom and to all his demesnes, and commanding that the recipients be intentive to Hugh, Bishop of Meath, as justiciar, and do not aid or obey Edward or his bailiffs.[94] On August 4, however, the battle of Eve- [283]
sham restored the royal power, Richard de la Rochelle appears still as justiciar,[95] and the government of Ireland was carried on (or neglected) much as before the recent changes.

In 1269 Thomas de Liddell, Bishop of Down, complained to the king that he was harassed by Walter de Burgh, Earl of Ulster, with unprecedented exactions, and that because the bishop would not answer in the earl's court, the earl had given judgement despoiling him of his manors. The bishop, after stating that 'from the first coming of the English into Ulster the king's name had been commemorated in each mass

91 Cal. Pat. Rolls, 49 Hen. III, p. 406. 92 Cal. Docs. Ireland, vol. ii, no. 766. 93 Cal. Pat. Rolls, 49 Hen. III, p. 422. The entry in Cal. Docs. Ireland, vol. ii, no. 727, summoning Richard de la Rochelle and also Geoffrey de Geynville, Walter de Burgh, and Maurice Fitz Maurice to the king, seems to be misplaced, and should apparently be dated May 5, 1265. 94 Cal. Pat. Roll, 49 Hen. III, p. 432. 95 Richard de la Rochelle was still justiciar in April 1266 (ibid., no. 793). He was superseded by David de Barry by Michaelmas 1266: 35th Rep. D. K., p. 48.

throughout the Down diocese, where there are more priests and religious than in any other part of equal dimensions in Ireland', threatened that if the king did not speedily find a remedy he would leave his diocese under an interdict and seek a remedy at the court of Rome.[96] In response to this appeal the king peremptorily commanded the earl to desist from his oppressions and restore to the bishop the amerciaments he had taken.

During Earl Walter's time there was peace throughout his Ulster lands. In Connaught, as we have seen,[97] nothing could restrain the bellicose spirit of Aedh, son of Felim, now, in 1265, king of Connaught in succession to his father; and with him Wal-
[284] ter de Burgh came into frequent conflict. But the relations of the earl with Aedh Buidhe O'Neill, the new king of the Cinel Owen, were friendly. Aedh Buidhe, or Hugh Boy, i.e. 'Hugh the Yellow', was eponymous ancestor of the Clannaboy (*Clan Aedha Buidhe*) O'Neills, who about the middle of the next century occupied part of Eastern Ulster.[98] He had recently married a cousin of Earl Walter. and in 1265 accompanied him in an expedition into Tirconnell.[99] A document dated October 2, 1269, which by a rare chance has survived,[1] shows the subordinate position of the king of the Cinel Owen relative to the Earl of Ulster at this time. It indicates that the debts of cows due from Brian O'Neill in the account already quoted were not exceptional, and prepares us for the position held by subsequent Ulster chieftains as stated in the inquisition of 1333. This document is in Latin, and the material parts are thus rendered: '53 Hen. III, Oct. 2, Antrim. Odo Onel Rex Kenlean (Aedh O'Neill, King of *Cenél Eoghain*) is bound to the nobleman, his lord W. de Burgh, Earl of Ulster and lord of Connaught, 3,500 cows to be paid as follows ... And he is bound to deliver to the said earl four hostages ... If he cannot do this, then he is bound to return and revert to the said earl and subject him-
[285] self in all things to his person and will. And he has promised to bind himself under pain of excommunication to keep Aleanor his wife, cousin of the said earl,[2] honourably and faithfully, furnishing her with necessaries; and all her rights, as well in lands as goods, which are considered to belong to her according to the use and custom of his country, he will cause to be rendered to her. To keep this agreement he has sworn on holy relics to the earl. If he break the agreement the earl may drive him from his regality, which he is bound to hold of him, and give or sell it to any one else.'

Earl Walter died in Galway Castle in the year of 1271, when he was only about forty-two years of age. Though he had failed to restrain the turbulence of Aedh, son of Felim, in Connaught, by supporting Aedh Buidhe O'Neill against his rivals of the house of Brian O'Neill and against his powerful neighbour O'Donnell, he had gained

96 Cal. Docs. Ireland, vol. i, no. 2551, where the entry is entirely misplaced. The bishop's election was finally confirmed on November 5, 1266 (ibid., vol. ii, no. 804), and the king's answer to his complaint is dated December 22, 1269: ibid., no. 860. 97 See *supra*, p. 243 et seq [pp 402ff]. 98 See Journal R.S.A.I., vol. XIV (1915), pp. 132–7. Aedh Buidhe was descended from Aedh O'Neill, nicknamed *Macamh* Tóinlesc, who was king of Cinel Owen for a time in 1177: Ann. Ulst., vol. ii, p. 186, and Four Masters, 1281. 99 Ann. Ulst., vol. ii, p. 339, Four Masters, 1265. 1 It is among the MSS. of Lord de L'Isle and Dudley, H.M.C., 3rd Rep., p. 231. In the same collection is a document which, though corrupt, appears to be a bond of about the same date from M. O'Flynn, king of Tuirtri, to assist Hugh Bissett to recover a cattle-spoil from Eachmarcach O'Kane, king of Keenaght. 2 The relationship appears to have been as fol-

an unwonted control in Tirowen, and apparently over the whole province,[3] and had laid the foundation for the great power afterwards wielded over the northern chieftains by his more famous son.

APPENDIX II [*repositioned for this edition*] [288]

The Account of Henry de Mandeville, *custos* of Twescard, for the four terms ending November 1, 1262, abstracted from Pipe Roll (Ireland), 19 Henry III, with annotations.

The rents from the places named and other issues were as follows:

	£	s.	d.	
'Dundrif' (probably for Dunlif,[4] now Dunluce)	26	13	4	
'Dunsumery' (probably Dunseverick, the Irish *Dún sobhairche*), including 87½ crannocks of oatmeal sold for £5 16*s*. 8*d*.	17	0	0	
and one mark of the old increase		13	4	
'Portkarman' (now included in the parish of Dunluce to the west of the river Bush)[5]	20	0	0	
'Portros' (Portrush, i. e. the parish of Ballywillin)	40	0	0	
Land in 'Villa Ohatheran'[6] (now Agherton or Ballyaghran parish) for three terms when it was assigned to Robert de Beumes	3	0	0	
'Villa que vocatur La Pere' (i.e. La Pierre, perhaps Ballyclogh, 'the town of the stone' or 'stones', in the parish of Dunluce	4	0	0	[289]
'Villa Ossandali' (perhaps Mount Sandall,[7] a promontory fort near the Salmon Leap on the Bann)	10	13	4	
'Erthermoy '(*Airther-maighe,* the parish of Armoy)	20	0	0	
'Ardbegan' (part ot the possessions of the Dominican Friary of Coleraine at the dissolution)	2	13	4	
Burgages of 'Coulrath' (*Cuil rathain,* Coleraine)	23	0	8	

lows: Aedh married a 'daughter of [Miles] Mc Costello' (Ann. Ulst., 1263, vol. ii, p. 337), and Miles Mc Costello's wife was 'daughter of the earl of Ulster', i.e. Hugh de Lacy (Ann. Loch Cé, 1263). Walter de Burgh's mother was Egidia, daughter of Walter de Lacy, Hugh's brother. Therefore Walter de Burgh and Eleanor Mc Costello were second cousins. 3 Earl Walter's widow Avelina was endowed (*inter alia*) with five castles in the marches and almost all the homages of the Irish of Ulster: see Cal. Patent Rolls, 1 Ed. II, p. 7. 4 The name appears in the inquisition of 1333 as 'Dundelyff'. The castle is called *caislén dúin-libsi* in Ann. Ulst., vol. iii, p. 510, and *dún Lipsi* in Ann. Loch Cé, vol. ii, p. 464. It was latinized by Colgan 'Dunlifsia'. The Four Masters, vol. v, p. 1324, have *caislén dhúinlis*. 5 Reeves, Eccl. Ant., p. 77. 6 'O'Haugharn's land' was confiscated after the battle of Down, 1260 (Cal. Docs. Ireland, vol. ii, no. 677), and was granted by Prince Edward, under the form 'Hochageran', to Robert de Beumes (de Bello Manso): ibid., nos. 1782, 1976. It appears as 'Hathrantone' in the Ecclesiastical Taxation, and 'Harggdon' in the inquisition of 1333. 7 Mount Sandall was probably the site of the castle of Kilsantan or *Cill Santail* erected by John de Courcy on the Bann near Coleraine in 1197: *ante*, vol. ii, p. 135 [p. 204], and see English Historical Review, vol. xxii (1907), p. 443.

'Villa monasterii' (probably the church lands[8] formerly belonging to the monastery of Coleraine) . .	4	0	0
'Drumtarsy' (now Killowen, a parish to the west of the Bann adjoining Coleraine)	16	0	0
'Loch Kel' (Loughguile)[9] with the demesnes thereof set to farm	64	11	4
Increase thereof		16	6
From Henry de Mandeville for two carucates in Drumtarsy	2	0	0
For 410 crannocks of the greater hundred measure of oatmeal of the issues of the mills of Twescard and of the mill of Ohatheran	147	0	0
Issues of the fishery of the Bann	40	6	8
[290] Issues of the fishery of the Lynne (i. e. the Salmon Leap, now called the Cutts of Coleraine): see Cal. Pat. Roll (Ireland), 5 Rich. II, no. 151	1	6	8
Land which Alan de Logan holds in 'Drumgenath' and 'Drumcarbri' which before the last year was waste	15	0	
Pleas and perquisites	19	19	2
Total [correct]	£464	9	4

8 For these church-lands, which had been occupied by the Anglo-Normans, Hugh de Lacy in 1241 granted to Albert of Cologne, archbishop of Armagh, as compensation, the manor of Nobber in Meath: Chartae Privilegia et Immunitates, pp. 24, 40. 9 This important manor was, I think, in the prince's hand during the minority of Henry le Savage, who died in 1277 (Cal. Docs. Ireland, vol. ii, no. 1328, where the extent £63 10*s*. 4*d*. is given). Lisanoure Castle marks the manorial centre.

APPENDIX I

De Lacy Pedigree, showing the devolution of Meath

(1) Roheis de Monemue = Hugh de Lacy = (2) a dau. of Rory O'Conor.
enfeoffed in Meath by Henry II, killed 1186.

Robert de Lacy enfeoffed in Rathwire by Hugh (probably) his brother. Probable ancestor of the Lacys of Rathwire: *temp.* Bruce's invasion.

Children of Hugh de Lacy:

- (by his first wife) Walter, lord of Meath, ob. 1241. = Margery, dau. of William of Braose.
- (1) Lesceline, dau. of Bertram de Verdun. = Hugh, created earl of Ulster 1205; ob. 1243. = (2) Emeline, dau. of Walter de Ridelisford, by whom Hugh had no issue.
- (by his second wife) William, C.D.I. i. 1203.

Children of Walter and Margery:

- Gilbert ob. c.1230. = Isabel, dau of Hugh. Bigod and Matilda Marshal; she married 2ndly, John Fitz Geoffrey.
- Egidia = Richard de Burgh, lord of Connaught.

Children of Hugh, earl of Ulster:

- Walter, Roger: living 1226; ob. v.p.s.p.
- Matilda = David f. William, baron of Naas. (Matilda succeeded to her father's Louth lands.)
- dau. = Alan of Galloway.
- dau. = Miles de Angulo.

Children of Gilbert and Isabel:

- Walter, living 1238: ob. s.p., viv. avo.
- Margaret = John de Verdun, ob. 1274 (C.D.I. ii. 1061). (Margaret coheir of her grandfather, Walter (C.D.I. i, 2662).)
- Matilda = (1) Peter de Genevre, d. 1250 (Mat. Paris). = (2) Geoffrey de Geynville, held a moiety of Meath after the death of Matilda, until 1308, when he surrendered it to Roger de Mortimer and Joan (Close Roll (Ireland), 2 Ed. II, no. 413). (Matilda coheir of her grandfather, Walter, ob. 1302.)

Nicholas = Basilia, dau. of John de Cogan I (C.D.I. ii. 1635)
sl. 1271, s.p. (Ann. Loch Cé).

John
sl. 1271, s.p. (C.D.I. ii. 2274).

Theobald de Verdun I;
he was deprived of his liberty in Meath in 1280, and again in 1291, ob. 1309.

Peter de Geynville,
ob. 1292 (Chart. St. Mary's, ii, p. 321).

Theobald de Verdun II, = (1) Maud, sister of Roger Mortimer (2) Elizabeth de Clare, widow of John de Burgh.
justiciar 1314, ob. 1316.

Joan = Roger Mortimer,
heir of Matilda, her grand-mother
justiciar, 1317 and 1319; hanged 1330.

John = Thomas, Lord Furnival

Elizabeth = Bartholomew de Burghersh.

Margery = Sir William le Blunt.

Isabel = Henry, Lord Ferrers.

Edmund Mortimer,
ob. 1331.

Roger Mortimer,
restored to his Irish lands in 1355, ob. 1360.

Edmund Mortimer, Earl of March and Ulster and Lord of Meath; ob. 1381.
= Philippa, dau. of Lionel, Duke of Clarence, and Elizabeth, dau. and heir of William de Burgh, Earl of Ulster.

Edmund Mortimer,
ob. s.p. 1424.

Anne = Richard, Earl of Cambridge,
beheaded 1415.

Richard, Duke of York;
sl. 1460.

King Edward IV.

HENRY III, 1216–72

Henry III died on November 16, 1272. During his long reign of fifty-six years the area of Anglo-Norman rule in Ireland had been greatly extended. The earldom of Ulster had been strengthened, and the earl's influence began to assert itself over the northern kings. The conquest of Connaught had been finally effected, and the sway of her native kings was restricted to a broad belt about the upper reaches of the Shannon. A beginning was made of the occupation of a portion of Thomond. The barons of County Limerick had established a strong colony in Kerry, and with those of County Cork had erected castles on advantageous sites beside the natural harbours of the south and south-west coasts, and in some inland places. The barons of Ireland were seldom interfered with by the government. They were in general loyal to the Crown—too loyal it may be thought in the affair of Richard Marshal—and the king had no conflict with them comparable to that which arose with the barons of England during his reign. With the exception of the long-drawn-out contest in Connaught, there was no serious conflict between the Crown and the native kings up to the year 1260, and in spite of local disturbances the wealth and trade and general prosperity of Ireland had greatly increased.

In the latter part of Henry's reign, however, while England was distracted by the [292] struggle between the Crown and the baronage, disaffection among the native princes came to a head in the north, south, and west of Ireland. In the north there was the futile attempt of Brian O'Neill to revive the high-kingship of Erin. In the south there was the more effective movement of Fineen Mc Carthy to resist the encroachments of the Munster barons into Desmond. In Thomond the O'Briens were beginning to be restive, while in Connaught nothing could restrain the turbulence of Aedh O'Conor, which threatened to revive the former anarchy.

In estimating Henry's personal influence on periods of affairs in Ireland it is necessary to distinguish three periods of his reign in which that influence had very different weights. First the period of about ten years from his accession (October 28, 1216), when he was only nine years old, to the beginning of 1227, when, having declared himself to be of legal age, he announced before a council at Oxford that from henceforth, freed from wardship, he would take a leading part in directing the affairs of the Crown.[1] During this period the civil government was controlled at first by William Marshal, and after his death by Hubert de Burgh, and the king's influence

1 Roger of Wendover (Coxe), vol. iv, p. 139.

was practically negligible. Secondly, the period of twenty-seven years from his coming of age to February 1254, when he granted Ireland, together with the other outlying possessions of the Crown, to his son Edward on the occasion of his marriage. During this period the king was legally his own master, but for the first few years he
[293] was clearly much influenced by Hubert de Burgh, and afterwards at times by his foreign advisers. Nevertheless, it was mainly during these years that his personal influence on Irish policy made itself felt. Lastly, the period of eighteen years, from February 1254 to his death. During this time Prince Edward as *Dominus Hiberniae* was primarily responsible. Henry, however, not only kept throughout ecclesiastical affairs in his own hands, but, especially at first, naturally advised most of the measures taken in his son's name, and even occasionally superseded his son's orders. Moreover, it must be remembered that from the time of the battle of Lewes (May 14, 1264) to that of the battle of Evesham (August 4, 1265), the royal power was practically in abeyance, or was exercised by direction of Simon de Montfort.

Henry's defects as a ruler in Ireland were negative rather than positive. From the time when the Regency, which managed things better, came to an end, neglect of kingly duty, instability of purpose, and lack of any consistent policy marked his government. In July and August 1233, he made elaborate preparations for an armed expedition to Ireland, but at the last moment he announced that he had 'changed his purpose'.[2] The change at this time was, no doubt, occasioned by the quarrel with Richard Marshal now coming to a head. In ensuing years, however, Henry repeatedly referred to his intention to visit Ireland, and in September 1240 he announced 'his firm purpose' to go after the following Easter, and ordered his manors and castles to
[294] be provisioned, and his houses to be repaired and improved.[3] In April 1243, with a view to his long postponed visit, he ordered a hall to be constructed in the castle of Dublin, 120 feet in length and 80 feet in breadth, with glazed windows after the manner of the hall of Canterbury. There was to be a round window, 30 feet in diameter, in the gable beyond the dais, a painting of the king and queen sitting with their baronage, and a great portal at the entrance of the hall.[4] All this was characteristic of Henry's artistic proclivities, of which we can see proofs in parts of Westminster Abbey and elsewhere. In January 1244 he ordered the work to be stopped, 'because he was much in want of money'.[5] In November 1245 he ordered the hall to be completed with a supply of water in a pipe from the city conduit, 'so that at the approaching summer he might find the hall complete'[6]—but the king never set foot in Ireland.

In not even visiting his Irish dominion, Henry's example was too often followed by his successors on the throne, most of whom had still less excuse for this neglect of kingly duty; but in his attitude towards the great outstanding event of his time in Ireland, the confiscation, conquest, and partition of Connaught, the defect of instability

2 Cal. Docs. Ireland, vol. i, pp. 305–6. 3 Close Roll, 24 Hen. III, p. 225 4 Close Roll, 27 Hen. III, p. 23. One of the charges made, c. 1285, against Stephen de Fulburne, bishop of Waterford and justiciar of Ireland, concerned 'the pillars of marble taken from the king's hall in the castle of Dublin and carried to Dunbro', the bishop's manor in Co. Dublin: Cal. Docs. Ireland, vol. iii, p. 13. 5 Ibid., 28 Hen. III, p. 152. 6 Cal. Patent Rolls, 30 Hen. III, p. 467.

of purpose is more strikingly illustrated, and its consequences were fraught with more serious evils. In 1226, while still under the influence of Hubert de Burgh, he replaced the younger William Marshal, who, both as soldier and as statesman, had just success- [295]
fully dealt with the dangerous situation arising out of Hugh de Lacy's return, by the appointment as justiciar of the already discredited Geoffrey de Marisco, and he authorized Geoffrey and Hubert's nephew, Richard de Burgh, to carry out the latter's design for the overthrow of the king of Connaught. Six years later, when the conquest of Connaught had been all but accomplished, he abandoned his old minister Hubert to his enemies, and with him Richard de Burgh, and, while giving Felim O'Conor a free hand in Connaught, prepared to hand over the government of the whole kingdom to the Poitevins. When compelled by the English barons, headed by Edmund, Archbishop of Canterbury, to dismiss the Poitevins, he once more took Richard de Burgh into favour for no better reason than because he had been instrumental in bringing about the tragic death of Richard Marshal, and once more threw over the king of Connaught, thus by his shifty policy prolonging the turmoil in that province. With similar caprice Henry, in 1245, dismissed Maurice Fitz Gerald after thirteen years loyal service as justiciar, apparently because he was mortified at his own want of success against David of Wales, in the region of Conway, and must needs find a scapegoat to carry his sins. Finally, in 1254, he handed over Ireland to his inexperienced son without making effective provision for his residing there or paying due attention to its affairs, but having first characteristically attempted to make an impossible provision for his Lusignan half-brother at the expense of the much-tried king of Connaught. In making the youthful Edward *Dominus Hiberniae*, Henry was following the unfortunate example of his grandfather, and in both cases the motive seems to have been to make [296]
a family provision out of what was regarded as the private property of the Crown, rather than to select a suitable governor to forward the public interests of the country to be governed. Edward was, however, a very different man from John, and had he been given Ireland alone, and taken up his residence there, the consequences would probably have been very different; but he was given Gascony and Wales (not to speak of other places) as well, and these countries preoccupied his energies.

But in spite of these capricious changes the barons of Ireland had no reason to complain of Henry's justiciars. They were men who spent most if not all of their lives in Ireland, who held lands there and had the interests of the colony at heart, and who, if they took little thought of the interests of the native Irish population, at least understood them and their ways as no official from England could do. Though Geoffrey de Marisco undoubtedly was more careful to feather his own nest than to safeguard the rights of the Crown, there is no reason to suppose that he neglected the interests of his peers. Archbishop Henry de Londres, while very zealous in furthering the wealth and power of his see, was a more watchful guardian of the revenue of the king, and indeed caused some irritation by his activities on behalf of the Church and the Crown. He was superseded by Earl William Marshal, because a military commander was needed to quell the disturbance caused by Hugh de Lacy. Once order was effectively restored, the Earl Marshal showed a wise statesmanship in enabling Hugh de Lacy, on

giving adequate security for his loyalty, to recover his confiscated lands; but he was
[297] opposed to the new policy of the confiscation of Connaught and had to give way to less scrupulous men. Richard de Burgh and Maurice Fitz Gerald tarnished their reputation in the eyes of posterity, but not in their sovereign's eyes, by their unchivalrous action against Earl Richard Marshal, but they succeeded in subduing Connaught and greatly extending the area of Anglo-Norman domination in Ireland, and in this they had the support of most of the Irish barons. Maurice Fitz Gerald, and, after him, John Fitz Geoffrey, ruled the eountry with a fair measure of success for altogether twenty-four years. The long periods during which they continued in office contrast favourably with the rapid changes in the next sixteen years when Edward as *Dominus Hiberniae* was responsible for the choice of justiciars. During this period there were at least eight occupiers of the office, and they were nearly all strangers to Ireland. It was a period in which there were risings of the Irish in many districts, and one serious disturbance, coincident witll the war of Simon de Montfort, among the barons themselves.

There are indeed indications that on more than one occasion Henry was dissatisfied with his son's choice of justiciars and claimed to overrule his son's measures. We have mentioned his mandate of 1258 bidding his subjects in Ireland not to be intentive to any justiciar unless appointed by his own letters patent, and his efforts in 1225— perhaps inspired by Simon de Montfort—to supersede Richard de la Rochelle.[7] But a little later a more drastic interference with Edward's administration
[298] was attempted. On July 12, 1268, after referring to the grant to his son of the whole of Ireland 'so that the land should not be separated from the Crown of England', and stating that Edward without the king's licence had made alienations of Crown-lands in that country, the king empowered his nephew, Henry of Almaine, son of his brother Richard, to revoke all alienations of lands made by Edward in Ireland and take the same into the king's hand.[8] The principal alienations of Crown-lands made by Prince Edward were the feoffment of Decies and Desmond to John Fitz Thomas of Shanid in 1259,[9] and the feoffment of Ulster to Walter de Burgh in 1264.[10] The lands included in the former grant would seem to have been in the king's hand from tlle death of John Fitz Thomas in 1261 until the grant was virtually renewed in 1292 to his grandson, Thomas Fitz Maurice, and Margaret his wife, the king's cousin;[11] while the feoffment to Walter de Burgh was not revoked. In fact it does not appear that anything was done in pursuance of this mandate. Robert d'Ufford was appointed justiciar about the following Michaelmas, and Henry of Almaine started with the prince for the Holy Land in 1270, and on his return journey was slain by the sons of Simon de Montfort.

What little legislation there was for Ireland in Henry's reign, as in the reigns of his predecessors, took in general the form of writs and ordinances addressed by virtue of the royal prerogative to the justiciar or other executlve officers or to his subjects in Ireland generally. In a few cases enactments made by the king and council in England

7 See *ante*, pp. 272 and 281–2 [pp. 417 and 421–2]. 8 Cal. Docs. Ireland, vol. ii, no. 844. 9 See *ante*, p. 140 [pp. 349–50]. 10 See *ante*, p. 266 [pp. 414–15]. 11 Cal. Docs. Ireland, vol. iii, no. 1051.

were by the king's authority trancribed and transmitted for observance in Ireland. [299]
Thus the Great Charter, as reissued in England under date November 12, 1216, was extended to Ireland with some slight variations to suit the case of that country.[12] What at first sight appears to be another reissue of the Great Charter, resembling generally, but differing in some respects from what is known as the second Charter of Henry III (1217), is transcribed in the Black Book of Christ Church, Dublin.[13] But this transcript, though dated November 6, 1217, contains some significant variations from Henry's second charter which point clearly to its manufacture at a date subsequent to the third charter of 1220. Thus to mention only the most important variations, the phrase in the preamble *spontaea et bona voluntate mea* is singularly inappropriate as applied in 1217 to the boy-king of ten years of age, and seems to have been taken from the charter of 1225, where its appearance is intelligible. The omission indeed of the reference to the demolition of the unlicensed castles built during the war between King John and the English barons might be explained as being inapplicable to Ireland, where there was no war with the barons.[14] But the statement as to the grant of a fifteenth of goods, which is not contained in the printed charter of 1217, also appears, in the same terms, in the charter of 1225, and while true of the latter year, it was not apparently true of either England or Ireland in 1217. In England other plans for rais- [300]
ing money were adopted, while in Ireland a toll was imposed on the cities, boroughs, and demesnes of the king, and an aid sought from the Irish kings and the barons and knights who held in chief.[15] Finally the formula of the dating clause ('datum per manum . . . R[icardi de Marisco] Dunholmensis episcopi cancellarii nostri'), as Mr. Powicke has shown, almost certainly implies that the original bore the great seal, but this was not in existence in 1217. At that period all important documents including Henry's second charter and the Forest Charter issued at the time and place mentioned in the dating clause of the transcript, were sealed with the seals of the Legate Gualo and of Earl William Marshal. We must conclude then that the transcript does not represent an unknown original, but that the text has been compiled and edited from more than one revision of the Great Charter with a few additional words taken from the Charter of Forests.

The command in general terms that English laws and customs were to be observed in Ireland was more than once repeated in Henry's reign, and in 1236 the constitutions of Merton were transmitted and ordered to be observed in Ireland. Other ordinances were concerned either with procedure, or with declarations of the substantive law on special points on which doubts had arisen in the Irish courts. In this way the law was declared as to tenancy by the curtesy, coparceners, the jurisdiction of Courts Christ- [301]

12 See *ante*, p. 18 [p. 290]. 13 See 'An unnoticed charter of Henry III (1217)' by Dr. Lawlor: English Hist. Rev., vol. xxii (1907), p. 514. Dr. Lawlor was inclined to consider the charter genuine, but the question was again examined with a different result by Mr. F. M. Powicke: ibid., vol. xxiii (1908), p. 232. 14 In the previous February the Irish barons had been commended for the fealty which they had manifested to the late and to the present king: Pat. Roll, 1 Hen. III, p. 31. 15 Rot. Claus. 2 Hen. III, p. 370 (November 10, 1217). On July 8, 1218, the receipt was acknowledged at the exchequer of London of £493 2*s*. 10*d*., sent from Ireland : Cal. Docs. Ireland, vol. i, no. 843. This was probably the proceeds of the toll and aid.

ian, persons born before wedlock, and a bastard dying without heirs. In one case only, so far as appears from Dr. Berry's edition of Early Statutes, an enactment having the character of statute-law was made in Ireland, during Henry's reign. This was a provision made in 1269 for establishing uniform weights and measures 'as they are appointed and approved in the city of London'. It is expressed to have been enacted by the justiciar and council 'with the consent of all the magnates and the entire commonalty of Ireland',[16] but how this consent was signified does not appear.

Owing to the fragmentary state of the accounts it is not possible to give even an approximate estimate of the amount of the revenue of Ireland which found its way into the English Exchequer in Henry's reign. Probably in many years the ordinary revenue was almost entirely absorbed in Ireland. We have seen that in 1221 the king complained that since the death of King John 'nothing had been received from the demesne lands, rents of assise, or escheats of Ireland',[17] but the interests of the Crown were more faithfully looked after by subsequent justiciars. Certainly there were many orders for payments unconnected with the administration to be made out of Irish treasure, and the justiciars were frequently urged to bring or send to the king all the money they could. In November 1249, the king ordered that all the profit issues of
[302] Ireland for two years should be given to Simon de Montfort, seneschal of Gascony, to make fortifications there,[18] and considerable sums of money seem to have been paid for this purpose. In August, following the grant of Ireland to Prince Edward, sums amounting to £1,900 of the issues of Ireland were transmitted to Gascony,[19] and in July 1255 a further sum of 600 marks was acknowledged by the prince,[20] while in May 1257 the king ordered the escheator of Ireland to pay 2,200 marks out of the issues of vacant sees to the citizens of Bordeaux,[21] but we cannot be sure that this and similar orders were carried out.

Henry's unpractical schemes and injudicious meddling in foreign affairs, as well as his love of display and his desire to finance his own and his wife's relatives, led him into great expense and extravagance, which could not be met out of the ordinary revenues of the kingdom, and there was always the annual incubus of the Papal tribute. Consequently he had recourse again and again to subsidies and aids, both lay and clerical, which in England caused great irritation and aroused the opposition of both barons and clergy, and the king's necessities were made the occasion of demands of constitutional reform. In Ireland these subsidies were less frequently sought and were perhaps not so harshly pressed. Certainly they led to no open conflict with the Crown. We may note the following. Besides the toll and aid imposed in the young king's name
[303] in 1217, to which reference has already been made, and which seems to have produced nearly £500,[22] an aid was requested in September 1220 from the tenants in chief to

16 Early Statutes, p. 36. A provision with a similar object was contained in the Great Charter of Ireland. In it the measure of corn was to be 'the quarter of Dublin': Ibid., p. 14. 17 *Supra*, p. 25 [p. 293–4]. 18 Cal. Docs. Ireland, vol. i, p. 451. In July following, 700 marks were sent to the New Temple: ibid., nos. 3069, 3078; and there were orders to pay 550 marks to Simon de Montfort for fortifying castles in Gascony: ibid., no. 3099; and 1,000 marks to the mayor of Bordeaux for the king's debts: ibid., no. 3128. 19 Ibid., vol. ii, nos. 381–2. 20 Ibid., no. 455. 21 Ibid., no. 547. 22 *Supra*, p. 300 [p. 432].

pay the king's debts to the Pope, Queen Berengaria, Louis of France, and others. This aid produced the sum of £1,693 2*s*. 8*d*.[23] In January 1226, Pope Honorius III issued a bull exhorting the clergy of Ireland to yield a subsidy to the king, urging that 'Ecclesiastical liberty is not injured, but defended, when aid is freely given to its protector in time of need',[24] and in the following November the king, referring to the Pope's order, prayed the archbishops to induce the inferior clergy to grant a sixteenth of the annual value of their benefices to enable him 'to seize the opportunity of the death of the King of France (Louis VIII) to recover his rights'.[25] Owing to the opposition of Hubert de Burgh, justiciar of England, the expedition was postponed, and up to June 1229, at any rate, this aid was not paid.[26] In November of that year the king besought the Cistercian abbots for an aid in place of the sixteenth demanded from them and the clergy, and at the same time he sent a mandate to assess a toll on the tenants in chief.[27] If any money was collected it was expended on Henry's futile march in 1230 from Nantes to Bordeaux and back.

In November 1236, the king asked for an aid both lay and clerical to pay his debt to the Emperor Frederick II for the marriage of the king's sister Isabella, and also his debt to the Pope; but the justiciar was not to communicate the king's request to the [304]
Irish magnates unless he believed that they would comply without repining and without complaining of the losses which they had suffered for the king in the war [of Connaught].[28] In July 1238, 2,000 marks were sent by the justiciar, Maurice Fitz Gerald, to England, presumably as proceeds of this aid.[29] In June 1243, the king, when again at Bordeaux on another futile expedition to Gascony, in the course of which Richard de Burgh, Gerald Fitz Maurice, and other Irish leaders lost their lives, thanked the Irish clergy for complying with his request that they would grant him a subsidy to enable him to continue his war.[30] In May 1253, the king, while ordering the justiciar to induce the barons and others of Ireland to meet the king at Bordeaux for his expedition into Gascony, also ordered him to require a competent aid from those unable to come.[31] In July nearly £4,000 of Irish treasure, new and old money, was received by the king.[32] It is impossible to say how much (if any) of this sum was the proceeds of the aid, or whether it was merely the surplus revenue of Ireland. The king, however, wanted more, and on August 11 asked for an additional 1,000 marks of Irish treasure wherever it could be obtained, and failing that, loans of 400 marks 'out of the money of the crusaders', and of 600 marks out of the issues of the mint.[33] About this sum of Irish treasure was paid into the Exchequer at Westminster on December 10.[34] [305]

It is clear that Henry had already cast covetous eyes on the Crusade-money. To tell the whole story of the nefarious dealings with this fund would be out of place here. Suffice it to say generally that the popes wanted money for their secular struggle with

23 Patent Roll, 5 Hen. III, p. 296. 24 Ibid., 10 Hen. III, p. 80. 25 Ibid., 11 Hen. III, pp. 100, 103. 26 Ibid., 13 Hen. III, p. 254. 27 Close Roll, 14 Hen. III, p. 383. 28 Close Roll, 21 Hen. III, p. 512. In October 1237 the king wrote direct to the magnates requesting this aid: ibid., p. 574. 29 Ibid., 22 Hen. III, p. 75. 30 Cal. Docs. Ireland, vol. i, no. 2622. 31 Patent Roll, 37 Hen. III, p. 229. 32 Ibid., p. 216. 33 Cal. Docs. Ireland, vol. ii, no. 293. 34 Patent Roll, 38 Hen. III, p. 361.

the emperor, the king aided the pope in despoiling the Church of England, and the pope rewarded the king by giving him a share in the spoil, while for both pope and king the Holy Land was used as a mere bait for collecting money. To confine ourselves to Ireland:—In 1250 the king, having 'assumed the cross', prayed the archbishops to have the cause of the crusade preached throughout Ireland and the letters of Pope Innocent IV, granting 'boons' to the promoters, published.[35] In March 1251 the king besought the Archbishop of Dublin to co-operate with Master John de Frusinon, who was sent by Pope Innocent IV to collect a tithe from the clergy 'for three years before the passage of the king for the Holy Land'.[36] In March 1253 the pope's order was repeated. It is impossible to say how much Ireland contributed in pursuance of these repeated orders, but the Dean of Hereford's account alone (1258) shows that 3,065
[306] marks were collected in Ireland for the pious purpose.[37] But the pope was more anxious to gain control over the kingdom of Sicily than to free the Holy Land from the infidel. Henry eagerly accepted for his nine-year-old son Edmund the proffered crown, to be held as a fief of the Holy See, and undertook to pay the pope the huge sum of 135,000 marks for his expenses in the war; and in return the pope released Henry from his crusading vow and authorized the diversion of the tithes and obventions collected for the crusade to the prosecution of the Sicilian adventure.

Henry owed much in the early years of his reign to the influence exercised on his behalf by Popes Honorius III and Gregory IX, and his natural piety inclined him to avoid conflict with either the Church or the papal curia. During the regency, however, a conflict arose with Donat O'Lonergan, Archbishop of Cashel. In December 1218 the archbishop complained that Geoffrey de Marisco, the justiciar, had disseised him of the new vill of Cashel, and a year later the archbishop ordered that the province be placed under an interdict, and that the justiciar be excommunicated unless restitution should be made.[38] Archbishop Henry, the papal legate, advised that, to avoid disturbance, restitution be made until the king's coming of age. It appeared, however, 'by the finding of a jury of the highest station and most worthy of faith' that the vill had rightly come into the king's hand,[39] and for some years Cashel is specifically mentioned in the king's writs along with other royal boroughs. In 1222 Pope Honorius ordered the archbishop to
[307] relax the interdict,[40] and next year the archbishop resigned. In 1228, however, when Henry was his own rmaster, he remitted his claim to the new archbishop, Marianus O'Brien, and granted him the new vill for 3300 marks.[41] Marianus thereupon granted a charter to the existing provost and burgesses of the town and their successors, reserving only the bakehouse and shambles and a chief rent of nine marks.[42] The town, though held of the archbishop, was organized after the model of an English borough, and extensive franchises were granted to it by subsequent kings.[43]

35 Cal. Docs. Ireland, vol. i, no. 3067. 36 Cal. Docs. Ireland, vol. i, no. 3115; cf. Mat. Paris, Chron. Mai., vol. v, pp. 324–32. 37 Ibid., vol. ii, no. 605. 'For an account of the whole episode see 'Edmund earl of Lancaster' by W. E. Rhodes, Eng. Hist. Rev., vol. x (1895), pp. 20–7. Innocent IV died before the bargain was completed, but his policy was pursued by his successor, Alexander IV. 38 Royal Letters (Shirley), vol. i, p. 72. 39 Rot. Claus., 4 Hen. III, vol. i, p. 435 (Jan. 24, 1220). 40 Ibid., 6 Hen. III, vol. i, p. 517. 41 Close Roll, 13 Hen. III, pp. 127–8. 42 Chartae Privilegia et Immunitates, p. 21. 43 Irish Pat. Roll, 26 Eliz., m. 26 (Morrin, p. 82, and cf. pp. 236–9).

In 1230 Henry ordered all who held pools and fisheries within the archbishopric of Dublin to pay tithes for the same, as 'he did not wish to imperil his soul by withholding such tithes',[44] an expression, used more than once, which indicates the power wielded by the Church. He was more courageous, however, when it was the soul of another that was imperilled, and could express his astonishment that, in a dispute between the bishops of Emly and Cloyne touching a tenement, Maurice Fitz Gerald should defer giving judgement through fear of being excommunicated by one of the parties.[45] In 1245 he was induced by the magnates of England to make a protest against the exactions and oppressions which Master Martin, a papal envoy, made on the clergy to enable the pope to carry on his war against the emperor, and at the same time he ordered Maurice Fitz Gerald, the justiciar, not to allow Master Martin, or his emissary, [308] John the Red, to make similar exactions and oppressions in Ireland.[46] Nevertheless, according to Matthew Paris, John the Red extorted 6,000 marks from Ireland, and, as we have seen, a few years later Henry did not scruple to collude with the same pope in despoiling the Church for the sake of furthering the mad Sicilian project.

It has already been mentioned that the jurisdiction claimed by Archbishop Henry in respect of his manor of St. Sepulchre clashed with the liberties claimed by the citizens of Dublin, and that in 1223 the archbishop was severely reprimanded for some of his proceedings against the citizens.[47] In 1233 King Henry had occasion to issue a mandate to his subjects, both lay and clerical, in Ireland that, in conformity with the law in England, no pleas should be held in an ecclesiastical court concerning advowsons, or lay fees, or chattels, not connected with testamentary matrimonial matters.[48] A conflict of jurisdictions, lay and clerical, again broke out when Fulk de Saunford was Archbishop of Dublin. In 1260 Fulk went to Rome, and in November 1261 Pope Urban IV wrote to the king submitting complaints made by the archbishop regarding the king's justiciars and bailiffs in Ireland and threatening ecclesiastical censure. These complaints were, briefly, to the following effect:—that the justiciar and bailiffs prevent the archbishop, his suffragans, and officials from hearing and deciding causes between laymen, who are subject to them, concerning money, or possessions, or defamation, though by ancient custom they had cognizance of such causes; that they even prevent [309] clerks from summoning clerks before an ecclesiastical judge in pecuniary causes, and rectors from summoning other rectors in causes concerning chapels belonging to their churches or concerning tithes; that they do not allow those properly fined for contumacy or offence to be compelled to pay their fines, nor suffer the archbishop, &c., to punish usurers, or in cases of divorce to compel restitution of dower; that they hinder the fulfilment of testamentary gifts to the Church by citizens and burgesses of their burgages, and by betaghs of their goods; that they punish by fines, and sometimes even by imprisonment, ecclesiastical judges whom the king has inhibited from proceeding further with a cause, even if they obey the inhibition, also judges who are found by inquisition to have taken cognizance of any causes which are not either mat-

44 Cal. Docs Ireland, vol. i, no. 1798. 45 Ibid., no. 2741. 46 Cal. Docs. Ireland, vol. i, no. 2746. 47 *Supra*, p. 27 [pp. 294–5]. 48 Early Statutes (Berry), p. 24, from Patent Roll, 18 Hen. III, m. 17.

rimonial or testamentary; and that they inhibit any ecclesiastical judge, who in the course of any question before him has pronounced sentence of excommunication on a layman, from proceeding with the cause, and they prevent the layman from being shunned as excommunicate.[49]

We do not know what answer at the time was given to these complaints, or what precise form the controversy took. Probably the archbishop relied, in part at least, on the liberties granted to his predecessors or enjoyed by them in respect of the archiepiscopal manors. However this may have been, inquiry was made into the secular jurisdiction and liberties actually exercised by his predecessors in the manors of the see.
[310] On an inquisition made in June 1264, at 'a parliament' held at Castledermot before Richard de la Rochelle, chief justiciar, and other officers of the king, into the alleged usurpation of pleas of the Crown and liberties by Fulk Archbishop of Dublin to the prejudice of the Lord Edward and his liberties, the jury found that Luke, the preceding archbishop, held all pleas of the Crown in his court except forestalling, rape, treasure-trove, and arson, and that Archbishop Fulk made no purpresture, but used the same pleas and liberties.[50] This finding was itself based on the findings of inquisitions held at the archbishop's manors of St. Sepulchre, Shankill, Castlekevin, Ballymore, Clondalkin, Rathcoole, and Swords.[51]

At this time, a month after the battle of Lewes, neither king nor prince was free to deal with the questions at issue, but on June 27, 1268, Edward, as Lord of Ireland, sent letters patent to the archbishops, bishops, and judges ordinary or delegated by the Apostolic see in Ireland, prohibiting the holding of pleas in Courts Christian, either against the citizens of Dublin or generally, concerning chattels or debts, except such as might arise out of testamentary or matrimonial matters,[52] thus virtually following the king's mandate of 1233. Two days later he authorized the mayor and bailiffs of Dublin to prevent the execution, 'hateful to the Lord', of the ecclesiastical sentence of
[311] public fustigation through the streets of the city.[53] In the following April the archbishop appealed in person to the king, but succeeded only in getting a mandate in general terms that he might enjoy the same liberties and quittances as his predecessors had used, and should have all ordinary jurisdiction in his archbishopric.[54] The mayor and citizens of Dublin, however, evidently carried out with zeal Prince Edward's mandate, for on February 29, 1268, Ottohon, Cardinal dean of St. Adrian and papal legate, commanded the bishops of Lismore and Waterford to excommunicate the mayor and citizens because, among other 'enormities', they claimed to restrict or mitigate public penances, and 'with damnable presumption' declared that matrimonial and testamentary causes alone should be tried in ecclesiastical courts.[55] In the following November the dispute as to public fustigation was arranged before Robert d'Ufford, justiciar, and

49 Crede Mihi, f. 84, transcribed in Gilbert's Historic and Municipal Documents of Ireland, pp. 172–8. 50 'Alani Registrum, f. 63v°, transcribed by Gilbert (as above), pp. 141–3. 51 Ibid., transcribed (as above), pp. 143–66. 52 Dublin Recorder's Book, f. 167: transcribed by Gilbert (as above), p. 179. 53 Transcribed by Gilbert (as ahove), pp. 179–82, from the original in the archives of the Municipal Corporation of Dublin. 54 Cal. Patent Roll, 51 Hen. III, m. 20 (p. 54). 55 Crede Mihi, f. 101, transcribed by Gilbert (as above), p. 180.

resulted in a compromise on the whole favourable to the citizens. Only for a fourth offence of a grave and public nature was the offender to be denounced to the mayor and bailiffs, 'so that he might be banished from the city or whipped through it'.[56] It would seem, however, that some of the citizens were too zealous in resisting clerical pretensions, and in July 1270 Edward bade the mayor assist in repressing their excesses, so that the archbishop might peaceably exercise his office, so far as regards ecclesiastical discipline'.[57] Moreover, except in some particulars where there was a con- [312]
flict of jurisdiction between the archbishop and the citizens of Dublin, the liberties, franchises, and secular jurisdiction of the archbishops in respect of their manors do not appear to have been curtailed.

The rule as to the free canonical election of bishops and abbots, subject to the king's licence to elect having been first obtained, and his assent to the election being subsequently given, was generally observed in Ireland in the reign of Henry III and his successor, and what was perhaps more important, the temporalities were taken into the king's hand during vacancies. This was the rule established by King John in 1213, when he conceded the right of free election, and it was afterwards confirmed by Magna Carta. The conditions mentioned were immediately enforced by the regency in 1217, in the case of a vacancy in the see of Armagh,[58] and in 1226 the king sent letters to the four archbishops commanding them not to admit to cathedral churches until they had been apprised that the king's licence and assent had been given.[59] Even in the more remote dioceses of the provinces of Cashel and Tuam, the king's licence and assent seem to have been normally sought and obtained, but in certain purely Irish dioceses in the province of Armagh, the king's right to the temporalities during vacancies was not exacted by Henry III, and the rule as to elections was not regularly enforced,[60] but was allowed to lapse. Probably the king's right could not easily be [313]
enforced in these dioceses, and in any case the monetary value of the temporalities was small, as these districts had only to a small extent participated in the economic advance which elsewhere followed the coming of the Normans. Edward I, however, endeavoured to establish a uniform practice, and in spite of the protest of the archbishop, on a writ of *duo warranto* in 1289, the temporalities of the five sees in question, namely, Derry, Raphoe, Clogher, Dromore, and Kilmore, when vacant, were adjudged to the king.[61] Probably even after this the king's right was not regularly enforced, but as regards the see of Derry, at any rate during the remainder of Edward's reign, the king's licence and assent were regularly sought and obtained.[62] That some supervision was advisable is suggested in this case by the fact that for the preceding century the see had been monopolized by a single family, named O'Carolan.

56 Dublin Chain Book, f. 32; transcribed by Gilbert (as above), p. 182. 57 Alani Registrum, f. 24; transcribed by Gilbert (as above) p. 183. 58 Cal. Docs. Ireland, vol. i, nos. 750, 797, 839. 59 Ibid., no. 1455. 60 Nevertheless the king's assent was obtained to the election of the Bishop of Dromore in 1227 (Cal. Docs. Irel., vol. i, no. 1500), and again in 1245 (ibid., 2774), and the king's licence to elect to the See of Kilmore was granted in 1250 (ibid., 3046). In 1241 Henry endeavoured to unite the See of Clogher with that of Armagh 'on account of the poverty of each see' (ibid., 2505). In other cases the justiciar may have given the king's assent (ibid., 1519). 61 Cal. Docs. Irel., vol. iii, p. 251. 62 Ibid., vol. iv, nos. 94, 175, 195, 371, 401, 417.

Unlike his father, Henry was neither malicious nor tyrannical. His private life was blameless, and his disposition was naturally amiable. He had, however, an exaggerated idea of his capacity both as soldier and as statesman, and of his importance as a continental potentate. This was probably due to the fact that he succeeded to the throne at so early an age. He remained something of a spoilt child throughout. He would fly into
[314] an impotent rage when he could not get what he wanted, and he often wanted what was unattainable. Easily led—and led astray—by self-seeking foreign relatives who flattered his foibles, he would turn a deaf ear to the warnings and advice of his natural counsellors, who were really in advance of their times in discerning and advocating the best interests of the kingdom. He was, perhaps, never consciously unjust, but while a great stickler for his own rights, in an apparent clash of interests he was incapable of understanding the position of others. He would fain be an autocrat, but he was without the capacity which sometimes serves to make autocracy successful and popular. He was guilty of many arbitrary acts, and was led to resist the constitutional movement of the barons of England. As regards Ireland, however, Henry's influence was too slight for these defects to bear their full fruit. Except the passing quarrel with Richard de Burgh, and the more fateful contest originating in England with Earl Richard Marshal, the king after he came of age had no serious conflict with his barons in Ireland. In general they were allowed to go pretty much their own way. He neither gave them efficient support, nor kept them in sufficient control, while the want of a considered and consistent policy in the difficult matter of the relations of the Crown with the semi-independent Irish chieftains led to disorders in many parts of Ireland. Dante recognizes the mediocrity of Henry's character by placing him in purgatory, 'the king of simple life, sitting alone, who left issue better than himself'.[63]

63 Purgatorio, vii. 131.

CHAPTER XXXIII [8]

EDWARD I AND HIS JUSTICIARS, 1272–1307

During the last eighteen years of the reign of Henry III, insufficient attention was paid to the growing unrest of the semi-independent Irish chieftains.[1] This neglect was no doubt due in part to the division of responsibility between the king and his son, but mainly to the preoccupation of both in the conflict with the barons of England. At the close of this period Aedh O'Conor, unchecked since the death of Walter de Burgh, was destroying the castles and plundering the districts held by the English near his territory in Connaught; Brian O'Brien was in revolt in Thomond; the dispute between the Mandevilles and the new seneschal, William FitzWarin, led to some disturbance in the north of Ulster; while nearer the capital the O'Byrnes and the O'Tooles of Wicklow were for the first time beginning to give trouble. Before leaving for the Holy Land in 1270, Edward appointed as his lieutenants in England Walter Gifford, Archbishop of York, Philip Basset, Roger Mortimer, and Robert Burnell, afterwards Bishop of Bath and Wells, and from 1273 to 1292, chancellor of England. It was probably these lieutenants who, in September 1270, after the defeat of Walter de Burgh at Ath-in-chip, appointed James d'Audley justiciar. His accounts show that he was [9]
engaged during his term of office in succouring and victualling the castles of Roscommon, Athlone, and Randown, against Aedh O'Conor, in bringing O'Neill and O'Cahan to the king's peace, and in endeavouring to repress the revolt of Brian O'Brien in Thomond.[2] In this last expedition he met with his death through a fall from his horse on June 23, 1272,[3] and Maurice Fitz Maurice, eldest surviving son of Maurice Fitz Gerald, was deputed by Prince Edward's lieutenants as justiciar in his place. Edward on his accession was still absent from England, and merely confirmed the appointments of Maurice Fitz Maurice as justiciar of Ireland, and of William Fitz Warin as seneschal of Ulster. In 1273 Maurice led a force into Thomond, when 'he took hostages and obtained sway over O'Brien',[4] but in August he was superseded by Geoffrey de Geynville, lord of the liberty of Trim, who had been with Edward in the Holy Land. From about this time the king infused justiciar, a new vigour into the government of Ireland. He provided funds for the administration by directing that the issues

1 For Edward's actions with regard to Ireland before he came to the throne see in particular *ante*, vol. iii, pp. 269–83 [pp. 416–23]. 2 See the account rendered by his son and heir William de Audley: Cal. Docs. Irel., vol. ii, no. 890. He obtained hostages (who seem to have been soon afterwards restored) from Brian Roe O'Brien. 3 Annales de Monte Fernandi (Strade, Co. Mayo): Laud MS. Annals, Chart. St. Mary's Abbey, vol. ii, p. 317; and cf. Ann. Loch Cé, 1272. 4 Ann. Loch Cé, 1273. He borrowed £861 9*s*. from the citizens of Dublin 'to maintain war against the king's enemies': Cal. Docs. Ireland, vol. ii, no. 1139; also 100 marks from a citizen of Cork for the army against O'Brien: ibid., p. 180.

[10] of the escheatry, as well of wards as of vacant sees and abbeys, should be at the justiciar's disposal,[5] and he strengthened the justiciar's hands by giving him power to appoint and remove sheriffs, and to call for the delivery to him of castles in the hands of the escheator, or of the seneschal of Ulster.[6] Indeed throughout Edward's reign there seems to have been a lack of money for carrying on the government, and large sums were expended in building and strengthening castles. The accounts of Geoffrey de Geynville show that he was engaged in repairing and strengthening the castles of Athlone, Randown, Roscommon, Roscre, and Newcastle Mc Kynegan, and in other defensive works, as well as in expeditions into Connaught and against the Irish in the Wicklow mountains.[7]

In another chapter we shall give an account of the numerous dynastic contests that followed the death of Aedh, son of Felim, king of Connaught, and ultimately provoked the interference of the English. Here we shall endeavour to describe the position in Wicklow, where the Irish, during the next three centuries, were a chronic source of peril, becoming intermittently acute, to the English of the surrounding districts.

From the time of their expulsion by Dermot MacMurrough and his Norman auxiliaries from the plains of Kildare, we hear little or nothing of the O'Byrnes and O'Tooles. They seem to have lived peaceably on the lower slopes and wooded valleys of the Wicklow mountains, where they carried on their clan life and organization.
[11] Ancestors of their ruling families had been chieftains of Offelan and Omurethy respeetively, and in a more remote past had supplied several of the kings of North Leinster, but since the invasion their lands in Kildare were held by Fitz Geralds and de Ridelisfords, and those of the former inhabitants, who did not remain as tenants under the Norman lords, migrated to the defiles of the Wicklow mountains.

Here they were hemmed in on all sides by the English settlers. In the north-east at Bray there was the castle and extensive manor of the de Ridelisfords. South of this, in the half-barony of Rathdown, the descendants of Donnell Mac Gillamocholmog were left in undisturbed possession. He was the chieftain of South Dublin, who sat on the Thingmount during the Norse attack in 1171, and joined in with the winning side.[8] His son Dermot *c.*1207 gave Kilruddery, south of Bray (now the beautiful demesne of the Earl of Meath), to Richard de Felda, from whose son, after a lawsuit, it passed to the abbot of St. Thomas.[9] John, son of Dermot, married Clarice, daughter of Gilbert Fitz Griffin, a nephew of Raymond le Gros, and the family, now thoroughly anglicized, continued to hold the manor of Rathdown at a rent of two otter-skins for some generations.[10] More to the west and nearer to the mountains, was the territory known
[12] as Obrun (*ui Briúin Cualann*), extending from Ballycorus to Delgany. It was inhabited by Irish betaghs, and was usually let to farm at a rent of £51 11*s*. 6*d*.

5 Cal. Pat. Roll, 1 Ed. I, p. 29. 6 Ibid., 2 Ed. I, p. 57. 7 See his accounts from August 15, 1273, to Michaelmas 1270: 30th Rep. D.K., pp 40, 41; also the escheator's accounts of payments: ibid., p. 33. 8 *Ante*, vol. i, p. 241 [p. 89]. 9 Reg. St. Thomas, p. 150; the rent reserved was two bezants or 4s. In 1256 the abbot let the manor to Ralph de Nottingham for his life at a rent of 12 marks, and in 1259 to Hugh de Taghmun, Bishop of Meath, for twelve years at a rent of 15 marks (ibid., pp. 175–9), showing the increasing value of the land. 10 Consult Journ. R.S.A.I., vol. xxiv (1894), p. 1.

Further south was another extensive Irish territory called Othee (*ui Teigh*)[11] farmed in the reign of Henry III at £56 11*s*. 6*d*. a year. Near by was formed at an early date the royal castle and manor of Newcastle, to protect the king's demesnes in the north-eastern portion of County Wicklow, then included in County Dublin. It was called Newcastle Mc Kynegan,[12] to distinguish it from other 'Newcastles', and especially from Newcastle de Leuan (now Newcastle Lyons) in County Dublin, which also belonged to the king. The site of the castle was a low natural ridge overlooking the 'King's Way' from Bray to Wicklow. The extremity of the ridge was cut off from the remainder by a deep fosse and vallum, and the portion so isolated was scarped round and raised, so as to form a mote with an unusually roomy platform for the castle buildings. These buildings were, no doubt, at first of wood. The manor was usually let to farm at £31 2*s*. 6*d*. The castle had a long and troublous history, a slight sketch of which is given elsewhere.[13]

The whole cantred of Wicklow, except the comote (*tuath*) of Arklow, was among the lands granted by Strongbow to Maurice Fitz Gerald.[14] From him it passed by [13]
descent to the barons of Naas,[15] and from them by marriage about the close of the thirteenth century to the family of de Londres. The castle of Wicklow, which was probably originally built by the Northmen, was situated at the extremity of a small rocky promontory jutting out into the sea, where its ruins buffeted by the waves may still be seen. It does not figure, however, in the wars of the thirteenth century, though it afterwards had some importance. Arklow was given by Prince John, *dominus Hiberniae*, to the first Theobald Butler,[16] and the ruins of a Butler castle still stand on a bluff overlooking the river-mouth.

Much of the more mountainous land had belonged to the Abbey of Glendalough, and 1229 an extensive tract was freed by the Crown from forest laws, and acknowledged as part of the possessions of the see of Dublin.[17] It consisted of three denominations: (1) 'Saufkevin or *Salvum Kevini*',[18] presumably the region about the ecclesiastical centre at Glendalough; (2) ' Fertir' (*Fir tíre*), a name surviving in the Vartry, and comprising the wide upper basin of that river, and seemingly that of the river of Annamoe, from Luggalaw to Castle Kevin;[19] (3) 'Coillach', a forest district on the western side of the main water-parting about the upper reaches of the Liffey and [14]
the Dodder. To keep order in this vast region, which so far as it was inhabitable was occupied mainly by Irishmen, the archbishop had a castle and manor at Castle Kevin, about one mile south-east of Annamoe, near the entrance to Glendalough, and here he held a court and, as in his other manors, exercised an almost unrestricted civil and

11 Both Obrun and Othee lay to the east of the mountainous district: Cal. Docs. Ireland, vol. i, nos. 1757, 1769. 'O Ceallaigh is over East Ui Teigh': O Huidrin, Topogr. Poems, p. 89. This chieftain's name seems to be preserved in Farrankelly, a townland south of Delgany. 12 It is called in the Annals of Connacht *Caislén nua ui Findacáin* (Ann. Loch Cé, vol. ii, p. 112), so that Mc Kynegan probably represents 'Mac Fhinnagain', where the initial 'f' would be silent. 13 See the paper by the present writer in Journ. R.S.A.I., vol. xxxviii (1908), pp. 126–40. 14 'Gormanston Register, f. 190; and see Giraldus Cambrensis, vol. v, p. 314. 15 David Fitzwilliam, Baron of Naas, gave some of the lands there to his brother Maurice c. 1234: Gormanston Register, f. 190 *d*. 16 See *ante*, vol. i, p. 371 [p. 140], vol. ii, p. 203, note [p. 232, note 9]. 17 Cal. Docs. Ireland, vol. i, nos. 1757, 1769. 18 So called in the Pipe Roll, 19 Hen. III, where *salvum* seems to be used as equivalent to *sanctuarium*. 19 See 'Lagenia' (Wicklow), no. 17 Car. I.

criminal jurisdiction.[20] The remains of the castle, consisting of the ruins of small mural towers, stand on a square mote with steep sides—once apparently revetted with masonry—and surrounded by a deep ditch. There was a bailey to the east, and a small lake, now a morass, to the north.[21] Both this castle and Newcastle figure in the military operations at the commencement of Edward's reign.

Parallel to and south of the valley of Glendalough is Glenmalure (*Glenn Maoilughra*) or Glyndelory, as it is usually called in Anglo-Irish documents. It appears, from a deed transcribed in the Register of Archbishop Alan, that Fulk de Saunford, who was Archbishop of Dublin from 1256 to 1271, gave 'Glandelure' to Murtough O'Toole.[22] It proved to be an unfortunate grant for the peace of the district. The upper part of the valley runs straight between precipitous rocky walls into the heart of the mountains, while the lower part, where it is more open, was rendered difficult of
[15] access by dense woods, some of which remain. It became the principal fastness of the rebels in Wicklow, of whom at this time the O'Tooles were the chief. It was destined to be the scene of many a reverse to English arms, and three centuries later it was the stronghold of the O'Byrnes under their redoubtable leader Feagh Mac Hugh.

The cause of the outbreak at the commencement of Edward's reign does not appear. The rule of the archbishops over this wild region, to judge by the inquisitions into their secular powers, was not calculated to promote order. They seem to have habitually admitted to peace, for money-payments, outlaws (both English and Irish) guilty of homicide and robbery. On the other hand, from 1271 to 1279, during the period of the disturbances, the temporalities of the see were in the king's hand, in the custody of Master Thomas de Chaddesworth, who seems to have taken hostages of the O'Tooles and O'Byrnes from the first,[23] and as in other cases it is not improbable that the harsher rule of the king's seneschals was the immediate cause of the rising.

There were several expeditions to Glenmalure about this time. They are not mentioned in the regular Irish annals, and it is not always easy to assign the scattered references in the records to the particular expedition to which each belongs. The first advance was in 1274, when Geoffrey de Geynville was justiciar, and it ended in disaster. William Fitz Roger, Prior of the Hospital of St. John of Jerusalem at Kilmainham, who seems to have been in command, Oliver le Gras, sheriff of County Limerick, and
[16] others, were taken prisoners, and many were slain.[24] The prisoners were soon released, probably in exchange for the hostages of the Wicklow clans who were brought from Dublin to Glenmalure at this time.[25] Next year 'Morydagh' was captured at Norragh

20 See Historic and Municipal Docs. (Gilbert), p. 150: Inquisition made at Castle Kevin on the secular powers of the archbishop. 21 For a fuller description with illustrations of Castle Kevin and a historical account of the place see the author's paper in Journal R.S.A.I., vol. xxxviii (1908), pp. 17–27. 22 See Journal R.S.A.I., vol. xxvii (1897), p. 420, from the Liber Niger Alani. 23 See his account, Cal. Docs. Ireland, vol. ii, p. 313. 24 Laud MS. Annals, Chart. St. Mary's, vol. ii, p. 318, and Clyn's Annals; and cf. Pipe Roll (Ireland), 4 Ed. I, 36th Rep. D.K., p. 33, where the expedition of a. r. 2 is distinguished from that led by Thomas de Clare in a. r. 4. 36th Rep. D.K., p. 37, where Thomas de Chaddesworth takes credit for 'expenses for the Prior of Kilmainham and Oliver le Gras when they came out of the prison of Glyndelur'; and ibid., p. 40, where Geoffrey de Geyoville in his account ending Michaelmas a. r. 2, takes credit for 'the cost of bringing the hostages from Dublin to Glyndelure'. In June 1175 William Fitz Roger was in England, and apparently reluctant to venture again into Ireland: Cal. Docs. Ireland, vol. ii, no. 1146.

in County Kildare by Walter l'Enfant.[26] The name stands for Muircheartach or Murtough, and it seems that he was Murtough Mac Murrough,[27] styled King of Leinster at this time. The circumstances of his capture are not given, but it appears from the Escheater's accounts that there was an expedition to Glenmalure in this year,[28] and presumably the Mac Murroughs rose in sympathy with the Wicklow clans. This Murtough Mac Murrough and his brother Art, who are believed to have been grandsons of Donnell Kavanagh,[29] held lands within the liberty of Carlow under the second Roger Bigod, Earl of Norfolk, with whom they were clearly on good terms. Art is spo- [17]
ken of as a kinsman of the earl.[30] They had in fact a common ancestor in King Dermot. Even after these disturbances, in 1279–81, Art was given a fee by the earl, presumably for policing the Irish districts within the liberty, and received gifts of wine and robes.[31]

There was another expedition to Glenmalure early in 1276. This time the principal opponents seem to have been the MacMurroughs.[32] They were probably led by Art MacMurrough, who had his brother's capture to avenge and, if possible, his liberation to effect. Geoffrey de Geynville himself led 2,000 vassals from his lordship of Meath, while Maurice Fitz Maurice brought a contingent of 'Connaught hinds'.[33] The chief command in the field, however, was committed to Thomas de Clare, Maurice's son-in-law. He had a personal interest in the success of the expedition, for he was promised a general summons of knights' fees or other services due to the king's army, to pacify his newly-granted land of Thomond, conditionally on the men of Glenmalure coming to the king's peace.[34] Supplies were sent to Newcastle Mc Kynegan, which seems to have been the base of operations. The expedition appears to have fared as badly as that of 1274. If we can trust the Annals of Clonmacnois, Mac Murrough 'gave a great overthrow to the Deputy and killed many of his army and [18]
wounded himself [the Deputy] grievously. He also took hostages of the Englishmen and caused them to eat their horses in Glen [malure] for famine'. Certain it is that there was now a change of justiciars and a new expedition was deemed necessary. In June 1276 Robert d'Ufford was appointed justiciar for the second time with a salary of £500 a year and very ample powers. All the issues of Ireland were placed at his disposal for the custody and amelioration of the land, and all the king's castles were to be committed to his nominees.[35] Before Michaelmas 1277, with Thomas de Clare and other magnates, he led another army to fight the rebels and king's enemies of Glenmalure, this time using Castlekevin, nearer to the scene of operations, as base.[36] Before

26 Laud MS. Annals, Chart. St. Mary's, vol. ii, p. 318. 27 In 1289 Walter l'Enfant in a petition to the king states that he was aggrieved with expenses for (among other things) the taking of 'Macmonvyth' (i. e. Mac Murrough): Cal. Docs. Ireland, vol. iii, p. 249. 28 36th Rep. D.K., p. 33. 29 According to Duald Mac Firbis and Keating, Murtough and his brother Art were sons of Donnell, son of Donnell Kavanagh. This is possibly correct, but their father could not have been the son of Donnell Kavanagh who was killed as a hostage by Rory O'Conor in 1170, as carelessly assumed by O'Donovan: Journal R.S.A.I., vol. iv, (1856–7), p. 121. 30 Cal. Docs. Ireland, vol. ii, no. 1873. 31 See the accounts of the earl's ministers: Hore's History of County Wexford (Old and New Ross), pp. 14–18, and 143–6. 32 36th Rep. D.K., p. 37, where the expedition of a. r. 4 is called 'the war of the Macmurchys', and cf. Ann. Clonmacnois, 1276. The regular Irish annals do not mention these Wicklow risings. 33 Cal. Docs. Ireland, vol. ii, no. 1389. 34 Ibid., no. 1191 (January 26, 1276). 35 Cal. Patent Rolls, 4 Ed. I, pp. 149–50. 36 36th Rep. D.K., p. 36;

the year was out, the justiciar was able to report to the king that 'his affairs in Ireland were much improved', and that 'the thieves who were in Glendelory had departed, many of them having gone to another strong place'.[37]

The new castle of Mc Kynegan was now rebuilt, and it seems that the original wooden buildings and palisading were replaced by a stone tower and other edifices.[38] [19] Castlekevin was also fortified and constructed anew.[39] Parts of the lands of Obrun and Othee were given to Englishmen on permanent tenures,[40] and among these it seems probable that now or a little later the lands in Obrun, famed for their beauty, and known to-day and for many centuries past as Powerscourt, were granted to a Le Poer. The original grant does not appear to be forthcoming, but in 1296 Eustace le Poer, who was ancestor of the Le Poers of Curraghmore in County Waterford, and had taken part in the victorious carnpaign in Scotland in this year, received a grant from the Crown of free-warren in his demesne-lands of (amongst other places) Obrun, in the then County of Dublin,[41] and probably from him the name of Powerscourt became attached to the place. At the same time the king gave him some deer from the neighbouring royal park of Glencree to stock his demesne.[42]

We hear no more of disturbances in Wicklow till 1295, but the MacMurroughs seem to have broken out again. In 1281 Murtough Mac Murrough was a prisoner in Dublin,[43] and next year compensation was paid to the Irish betaghs and others in the vale of Dublin for depredations made by Art MacMurrough.[44] A price was put on Art's head, and the two brothers were put to death by the English at Arklow on July [20] 21, 1282.[45] Such are the bare facts to be gleaned from the records and annals, but the circumstances are obscure. The Earl of Norfolk, who visited his lands in Ireland in 1279–80, obtained a safe-conduct for Murtough and Art to go with him to England in July 1280, and for Art and others in November 1281, to go to him in England and return,[46] with a view no doubt to their coming to the king's peace. It seems that Murtough took advantage of the earl's friendly offices,[47] but in April 1283 the earl complained to the king of the justiciar's action with regard to Art's 'head-money', stating that Art's head had not been proclaimed with his consent (as lord of the liberty of Carlow), and that Art was at peace with the king before his death.[48]

Edward did not confine his efforts merely to repressing disorders and strengthening the military defences of Ireland; he also exhibited a sagacious concern in promoting its economic interests. Thus among the instructions that he gave to Geoffrey de

Cal. Docs. Ireland, vol. ii, p. 267. 37 Cal. Docs. Ireland, vol. ii, no. 1400. 38 Ibid., pp. 309, 422–3, 440, 535–6; and 36th Rep. D.K., pp. 53, 59. For further details and a sketch of the history of 'Novum Castrum Mc Kynegan' see the author's paper, Journal R.S.A.I., vol. xxxviii (1908), pp. 126–40. 39 Ibid., p. 267, and 36th Rep. D.K., p. 36, and the author's paper with illustrations 'Castrum Keyvini', Journal R.S.A.I. (as above), pp. 17–27. 40 In 1283 Ralph le Mareschal was granted lands at Balimacorus in Obrun: Cal. Docs. Ireland, vol. ii, no. 2069; and William le Deveneys other lands there: ibid., 2070; while in 1284 William Burnell was granted lands in Glencappy (Glen of the Downs ?) in Othee: ibid., no. 2199, and cf. no. 2329, where 'Othe' is identified with 'Howth'! 41 Charter Roll, 25 Ed. I, m. 3; Cal. Docs. Ireland, vol. iv, no. 347, where the editor ignorantly identifies Obrun with Brownstown, wherever that may be. 42 Ibid., no. 362. 43 Cal. Docs. Ireland, vol. ii, p. 401. 44 Ibid., p. 440. 45 Laud MS. Annals and Ann. Loch Cé. 46 Cal. Docs. Ireland, vol. ii, nos. 1716 and 1873. 47 Ibid., vol. iii, p. 70. 48 Ibid., vol. ii, no. 1919; and cf. ibid., nos. 2383 and 2338.

Geynville, the first justiciar of his personal choice, was a mandate to proclaim throughout Ireland that all merchants might securely come to that country with their merchandise, and freely carry on their trade subject to lawful and ancient customs without further exaction.[49] The substitution of a fixed impost for arbitrary exactions was a great encouragement to foreign merchants, and there was a large increase in for- [21]
eign trade during Edward's reign. In the first general parliament held at Westminster in April 1275, including knights of the shire and representatives of the market-towns, the magnates and commonalty, 'at the instance of the merchants' themselves, granted the king a custom on the export of wool, woolfells, and leather.[50] In the same year a similar grant was made in Ireland,[51] and the result was a considerable increase to the revenue, while the principle was introduced of making foreign commerce bear a share of the burden hitherto borne almost exclusively by the land.

While Geoffrey de Geynville was still justiciar, the king thought to put an end to the anarchy in Thomond by granting the whole territory to Thomas de Clare. In another chapter we shall follow in some detail the fortunes of this experiment. During the lifetime of Thomas de Clare it met with some success, but the O'Brien factions were as bitterly opposed to each other as the O'Conor factions, and one of them proved an uncompromising opponent of the English settlers. After forty years of precarious existence the English colony, which never extended much beyond the confines of the barony of Bunratty Lower, was practically wiped out.

In his report to the king referring to the departure of 'the thieves' from Glendelory, Robert d'Ufford, the justiciar, goes on to state that the Irish offered 7,000 marks for a grant from the king of the common laws of the English, and to request the king's plea- [22]
sure thereupon.[52] To this the king replied that it seemed meet to him and his council that a grant of English laws should be made, 'because the laws which the Irish use are detestable to God, and so contrary to all law that they ought not to be deemed laws'. The king therefore commanded the justiciar to ascertain the opinion of the prelates and magnates of Ireland and having bargained for a higher fine and a supply of foot-soldiers, to arrange what might seem most for the king's honour and advantage.[53] The sincerity of Edward's desire that all the Irish should be governed by English law is beyond question. At this very time he was attempting to override the laws and customs of Wales in the four cantreds ceded to him by Llewelyn, and to introduce English law there—an attempt which, it is significant to note, was the immediate cause of the revolt of 1282.[54] It was, however, easier to lead armies into Wales than into Ireland, and Edward's energy soon served to effect the conquest of the Principality, and to girdle his newly-won lands with stronger castles than had ever been seen in the country before. But he was not prepared to take equally effective steps in Ireland. In June 1280, however, he returned to the subject which he had at heart, and with greater emphasis

49 Cal. Pat. Rolls, 1 Ed. I, m. 5. This, indeed, had been provided by the Great Charter of Ireland 1216: Early Statutes (Berry), p. 16; and a mandate in 1220 directed the justiciar not to take prises from foreign merchants without giving satisfaction at once: Rot. Claus., 4 Hen. III, p. 341. 50 Parliamentary writs 1, 2. Stubbs's Select Charters (ed. 1913), pp. 440–4. 51 Cal Docs. Ireland, vol. ii, no. 1117. 52 Cal. Docs. Irel., vol. ii, no. 1400. 53 Ibid., no. 1408; Foedera, vol. i, p. 540. 54 See The Political History of England, 1216–1377 (T.F. Tout), pp. 160–1, and England in the Later Middle Ages (K.H. Vickers), pp. 23–4.

commanded the magnates to debate the question whether he could make the concession without prejudice to them, and to lay before him all the circumstances touching [23] the concession with their advice.[55] We do not know their answer, but presumably they pointed out the unreality of the proposal and the utter impracticability of its enforcement over large tracts in Ireland, if, indeed, the actual proposal was correctly interpreted or rightly understood by the king, which is more than doubtful. Inasmuch, however, as this supposed wilful refusal to extend the laws of England to all Irishmen has been made the subject of a grave charge against the Irish government, or against the magnates of Ireland, it seems necessary to examine the grounds of the charge a little further.

Sir John Davies, attorney-general in Ireland, writing in 1612, contends that one of the chief defects of the civil policy in Ireland which impeded the perfection of the conquest was 'that the Crown did not from the beginning give laws to the Irish'. We have already considered this criticism and showed that Sir John inverts cause and effect, that it was clearly impossible to subject the Irish to English law until the conquest had been perfected,[56] as it may be said to have been shortly before Sir John's time. By way, indeed, of meeting the obvious objection, that the Irish would have resisted to the uttermost the imposition of English law, Sir John refers to a petition mentioned by Edward III in 1328, and said to have been made by 'divers men of Ireland' to the effect that all Irishmen who should wish it might use English laws, without the necessity of obtaining from the Crown charters for that purpose.[57] Sir John [24] argues from a part—and a very small part—to the whole, and ignores the plain teaching of Irish history. Some modern writers further misrepresent the facts, and press still further the faulty argument. Thus, one writer states that ' on two well-known occasions—meaning that referred to by Sir Robert d'Ufford and the petition of 1328—the general body of the Irish petitioned the king that an act might be passed to make all the Irish subject to the English law'.[58] But it is quite certain that on neither occasion was there any request made by 'the general body of the Irish', and that in particular no intimation was reeeived from the independent or semi-independent Irish of their willingness to abandon the Brehon Law for the Common Law of England. There was, indeed, no person or body corporate who could speak for the Irish in general, while we know that there was nothing the Irish clung to with more tenacity than their traditional laws and customs. It is probable that Sir Robert was speaking only of the Irish of Wicklow with whom he was in fact dealing. He may have been approached by some of the more peaceably inclined leaders of the O'Tooles and O'Byrnes who remained in Wicklow, when 'the thieves' (i.e. their more turbulent rivals) had for the moment departed, and who were anxious to secure their lands in that district, and obtain the protection of English laws, and the assistance of English arms against their rivals. But

55 Cal. Docs. Ireland, vol. ii, no. 1681; Foedera, vol. i, p. 582. 56 *Ante*, vol. ii, pp. 332–5 [pp. 282–4]. 57 'Discovery' (edition 1787), pp. 87, 88, and see Cal. Close Rolls, 2 Ed. III, p. 312. Sir John does not refer to the report of Sir Robert d'Ufford in 1277 and the king's mandates thereon, though these would seem at first sight to be more to his purpose. 58 Joyce, Short History of Ireland, vol. i, p. 298.

in the light of the subsequent history of the Wicklow clans it is difficult to believe that, however friendly the chiefs may have been, they could have persuaded their clansmen [25]
to give up their communal rights for the land-system of England, or to authorize English judges to hang their evildoers. If such were the object, the negotiations were doomed to failure. It seems clear, at any rate, that the question mooted in 1328 was a much smaller as well as a more practical one, and was virtually whether all Irishmen in the feudalized districts might plead in the king's courts on equal terms with Englishmen, or whether, as theretofore, the privilege should be confined to those Irishmen to whom it had been specially granted by the Crown. The whole tendency of judicial decisions had been towards restricting the efficacy of the plea that the plaintiff was *Hibernicus servilis conditionis*. In every reported case the plea failed. Such was the result in all the cases, save one, cited by Sir John Davies.[59] In the excepted case the defendant charged with the killing of an Irish-man, though not convicted of 'felony', was committed to gaol until he should find pledges for a fine of five marks to be paid to the king. This, the usual punishment in such cases, may be compared with the 'eric' of Irish law. The plea was regarded by the judges as an *exceptio odiosa*, to be construed strictly against the person relying upon it, and where it was unsuccessful the plaintiff in general won his suit without further trial, and the defendant who failed in the plea was often committed to gaol.[60]

Before 1328 some further steps towards widening the enfranchisement of *hibernici* [26]
in the feudalized districts had been taken. Power had been given to Roger Mortimer, Lord of Meath, Thomas, Earl of Kildare, and John de Bermingham, Earl of Louth, to receive into English law all their men and tenants;[61] and in 1321, all who were admitted to use English law were to use the English law of life and limb, and were to be treated according to the custom of the English, saving the lord's rights in the goods and chattels of betaghs so admitted.[62] Finally, the question raised in 1328 was expressly decided three years later, when it was enacted 'that one and the same law be made as well for the Irish (meaning necessarily the Irish in districts where the king's writ ran) as for the English, except the service of betaghs in the power of their lords in the same manner as is used in England concerning villeins'.[63] If this law, which seems a wise and just one, was not always observed, it was only one of the many examples of the decay of English power in Ireland which set in rapidly from about this time. The problem which then confronted the Irish government was not how to induce the Irish generally to submit to English law—that without the application of force was always hopeless—but how to prevent the English in Ireland from adopting Irish law and its 'lewd [27]
customs' and disregarding the law of England.

59 Discovery, &c. (edition 1787), pp. 78–84. 60 See Justiciary Rolls, vol. i, p. 168, and consult Index of Subjects. 61 Cal. Patent Rolls, 12 Ed. II, pp. 339, 342. It would seem that the lords of liberties had this power from early times. Thus, in 1299 Walter O'Toole produced in court a charter from Earl William Marshal granting to his great-grandfather and his heirs that they might use English laws: Justiciary Rolls, vol. i, p. 271. 62 Early Statutes (Berry), p. 292. 63 Ibid., 5 Ed. III, p. 325. In England the distinction in the law of *murdrum* pointed out in the Dialogus de Scaccario, between the case of freemen and that of men *servilis conditionis*, was not finally repealed until 1339.

But in spite of dynastic disputes among both the O'Brien and the O'Conor factions, and of disturbances caused by the Wicklow clans, the trade, wealth and general prosperity of the districts where English rule was effective—that is to say in about two-thirds of Ireland—advanced at this period by leaps and bounds. In the final chapter of this volume we shall adduce evidence of the growing trade and increasing wealth of Ireland under Anglo-Norman rule. Here we shall say something about the revenue.

From the beginning of the reign of Edward I the accounts of the treasurer, the justiciar, the escheator, and the various sheriffs have been better preserved, and were seemingly more strictly audited than at any previous time, and they suffice to show that large and increasing sums were received, and for the most part expended, in Ireland. In the year 1276 the escheator accounted for £3,155, issues of vacant bishoprics and of wardships in the king's hand,[64] and this was exclusive of the issues of the Archbishopric of Dublin, which was vacant owing to a double election for seven years and a half from 1271, and was in separate custody. Its issues during this period amounted to about £1,300 a year.[65] The escheators accounts appear at irregular intervals, and some are missing. The next account, in continuation of the above, was in 1282, when the receipts amounted to £7,280.[66] The receipts of the justiciar, Geoffrey de Geynville,
[28] from August 1273 to Michaelmas 1276 amounted to £7,916,[67] while those of his successor, Robert d'Ufford, from July 1276 to Mareh 1280 were £11,290.[68] The receipts, acknowledged by the treasurer in the four years ending with Michaelmas 1278, amounted to £14,662,[69] or on the average £3,665 a year, and in the six years ending June 1284 amounted to a little over £35,000,[70] or about £5,840 a year.

Unfortunately the treasurer's receipts afford no true index of the revenue for two reasons: In the first place the whole revenue did not pass through the treasurer's hands. Both the escheator and the various sheriffs paid considerable sums to the justiciar, or expended them by his direction on military expeditions, works of fortification, &c. And, secondly, because the accounts of this treasurer were seriously challenged. He was Stephen de Fulburne, brother of the Hospital of St. John of Jerusalem in England. He was sent by the Crown to Ireland in 1270 to collect the ecclesiastical tenth. In 1274, 'at the king's request', he was elected bishop of Waterford, and in September of that year the office of the treasury of the exchequer was committed to him.[71] He was *locum tenens* of Robert d'Ufford during the latter's visits to England, and in November 1281, when Robert d'Ufford had become incapacitated
[29] by infirmity, was appointed to succeed him as justiciar. Clearly Brother Stephen was a highly-trusted servant of the Crown. Nevertheless, many complaints amounting to charges of peculation were made against him, and when his accounts were audited in 1285, great omissions and irregularities were noted, and in the result he was found to owe to the king £13,235.[72] He was superseded in the office of treasurer by Nicholas de

64 Pipe Roll, 36th Rep. D.K., pp. 30–3. 65 Ibid., pp. 36–7 and 40–1. 66 Ibid., pp. 60–4. 67 Pipe Roll, 36th Rep. D.K., pp. 40–1. 68 Ibid., pp. 35–6 and 48–9. 69 Cal. Docs. Ireland, vol. ii, nos. 1038, 1294, 1389, 1496. 70 Ibid., no. 2327. Of course in computing the revenue we cannot simply add together the receipts of these various officials, as some of the escheator's receipts were paid into the treasury, and most of the justiciar's receipts issued from the treasury. 71 Cal. Docs. Ireland, vol. ii, noi. 1009, 1034. 72 For

Clere, who had been one of a commission to inquire into the state of the exchequer, and to make a view of the treasurer's accounts, but he did not altogether lose the king's confidence, as (subject to a bond to the king for £4,000) he was pardoned all arrears, and was retained in the office of justiciar at a salary of £500.[73] In July 1286 he was promoted to the archbishopric of Tuam, and he died in July 1288.

It does not seem possible at present to ascertain with precision the total amount of the annual revenue of Ireland in the reign of Edward I. It varied from year to year, and the proceeds of some sources of revenue cannot be fixed. The Pipe Rolls and certain exchequer memoranda, indeed, contain much more plentiful materials for this purpose than are available for any former time, but these await full publication, exarnination, and analysis, before they can be made to yield all the information they may contain. Without attempting to examine and analyse incomplete documents, some fur- [30]
ther figures may be given which will help to form a rough estimate.

Some memoranda of the exchequer, compiled about the year 1287, probably in connexion with the audit of the accounts of Stephen de Fulburne, contain a detailed statement of the amounts usually received from certain particular sources.[74] From these memoranda it appears that what are called the 'profits of the counties', i.e. of the various county courts, amounted at the highest to £365 7*s*. 6*d*. Some of the figures given can be verified from the Calendar of Pipe Rolls, but it is manifest from the sheriffs' accounts that these profits bore only a small proportion to the amount received by them from other sources, and paid into the treasury or otherwise expended on the administration. Then the rents of assize given in Assize detail, i.e. the fixed rents at which the various royal cities, boroughs, manors, and other Crown-lands were usually let to farm, amounted to £2,476 0*s*. 11¼*d*. The money value of the military services due to the king when summoned (the service in respect of each knight's fee being valued at forty shillings) amounted to £837. Then there were the prisage of wines, and the profits of the mint, the values of which were too uncertain or too obscure to be set down. Over and above these sources there were the issues of the escheatry, averaging [31]
about £2,000 a year, the proceeds of the custom on wool and hides, which were upwards of £1,500 a year, and occasional aids and subsidies, and the king's share of the Papal Tenths, to be mentioned hereafter. Altogether we shall probably not be far wrong if we make a rough estimate of the revenue of Ireland during the last quarter of the thirteenth century as exceeding £10,000.

The king was absent in France from May 1286 to August 1289, and during his absence his cousin, Edmund Earl of Cornwall, was regent. Affairs in Ireland, as in

the charge against Stephen de Fulburne, see Indexes to Cal. Docs. Ireland, vols. ii and iii. For the 'view of his account' see ibid., vol. ii, nos. 2284, 2327, and vol. iii, nos. 42 and 59. In judging the validity of these charges it must be borne in mind that Stephen's principal accuser was Nicholas de Clere, who superseded him, and against whom still graver charges were made in 1290–2. 73 Cal. Docs. Ireland, vol. iii, nos. 117, 121, 122, 129. 74 See in particular Cal. Docs. Ireland, vol. ii, no. 2329. A nearly similar statement of 'rents of assize', with a detailed account of the 'royal services', is transcribed (with many errors) in the Book of Howth, pp. 228–34, and also in a MS, preserved in Corpus Christi College, Cambridge. This last, which contains some additional matter, has been edited by Miss Mary Bateson in English Historical Review, vol. xviii (1903), pp. 497–513.

England, got somewhat out of hand. Officials took advantage of the greater laxity of control to misuse their positions for the purpose of private gain, and there were numerous charges and complaints of peculation, extortion, and oppression against the justiciar, the treasurer certain sheriffs, and others. On his return Edward at once took steps to investigate these charges and complaints, and to see that justice was done.[75] In particular Nicholas de Clere, the treasurer, was imprisoned, and a fine of 500 marks imposed on him for his transgressions.[76]

Meantime, on the death of Stephen de Fulburne, John de Saunford, Archbishop of Dublin, was Saunford, appointed by the king's council Keeper of Ireland until the king should otherwise provide. He was brother of Fulk de Saunford, a former Archbishop of Dublin, and had been escheator of Ireland from 1271 to 1285. During the
[32] two years of his tenure of offlce he visited many parts of Ireland with a view to keeping or restoring order, but he was principally engaged in defending the English of Leinster against the depredations of the Irish of Offaly and Leix, who had recently begun to give trouble.[77]

In the partition of Leinster, the honour of Dunamase, which included the greater part of the territory of Leix in the present Queen's County, fell to the lot of Roger de Mortimer of Wigmore, in right of his wife, one of the three daughters of Eva Marshal.[78] There were several free tenants, but much of the land seems to have been let to the Irish, who up to about the time of the death of Roger de Mortimer in 1282, seem to have been generally peaceable.[79] Offaly, which lay to the north of Leix had been granted by Strongbow to Robert de Bermingham, and, as we have seen,[80] had come to the Geraldines through the marriage of Gerald, son of the first Maurice Fitz Gerald, with Eva de Bermingham, heiress of Strongbow's grantee. Settlements were soon effected by the barons of Offaly in the southern strip of the district, where their principal castles were at Lea on the Barrow, above Monasterevin, and at Geashill. John Fitz Thomas of Desmond held from them the *tuath* of Iregan, still further to the west, near Slieve Bloom, and, as early at least as 1234, we find Peter de Bermingham holding Tethmoy, apparently under Maurice Fitz Gerald, the justiciar.[81] Tethmoy was the
[33] name by which the north-eastern corner of Offaly was known, and the parish of Castro-petre or Monasteroris preserves the name of Peter (de Bermingham) in the Latin and the Irish form respectively.[82] After the death of the third Maurice Fitz Gerald, who was drowned when crossing the Channel in 1268, there was a long minority, and it would seem that Gerald his son and heir had to fight for his inheritance. In 1284, when Gerald was at most just of age, the castle of Lea was burned by the Irish of Offaly, and next year Gerald himself was taken prisoner by them.[83] In 1286, Calvagh

75 See the king's answers to the numerous petitions apparently invited by him at this time: Cal. Docs. Ireland vol. iii, nos. 558, 622. 76 Ibid., vol. iv, no. 472. For the many charges against Nicholas de Clere see ibid., vols. iii and iv, index. 77 See the archbishop's detailed account of his journey and expeditions, ibid., vol. iii, no. 559. 78 *Ante*, vol. iii, p. 104 [p. 332]. 79 See the Inquisition taken at his death: Cal. Docs. Ireland, vol. ii, no. 2028; Cal. Inquis. P.M., vol. ii, pp. 267–8. 80 *Ante*, vol. iii, p. 113 [p. 337]. 81 Close Roll, 18 Hen. III, p. 157. Tethmoy represents the Irish *Tuath dá Muighe*. 82 The Berminghams were called by the Irish 'Mac Feohrais', 'Son of Piers', and the monastery which was founded by John de Bermingham, Earl of Louth, was called *Mainistir (Fh)eorais*. 83 Clyn's Annals, Laud MS. Annals, *sub annis*.

O'Conor, one of the chiefs of Offaly, was captured and imprisoned in Dublin Castle, but he seems soon to have escaped. In 1287, when he was not more than twenty-three years of age, Gerald Fitz Maurice died,[84] possibly from wounds received in fight with the Irish of Offaly. While he lay on his death-bed at Rathangan on June 26 he made over the castle of Lea,[85] and (it is said) all his inheritance, to the son of his 'Welsh uncle', John Fitz Thomas, who now, since the death in 1286 of Maurice FitzMaurice, [34]
was his nearest representative in the male line. In 1288, John Fitz Thomas, now lord of Offaly, and his liege-man Peter, son of James de Bermingham of Tethmoy and grandson of the above-mentioned Peter,[86] were commissioned by the justiciar, John de Saunford, to guard the marches from Tethmoy to Rathangan. They were, however, worsted in an encounter with Calvagh O'Conor, and in the autumn of 1289, after many vain parleys with the rebels, the justiciar led the feudal host of Leinster against the Irish of Offaly, with the result that they came to the king's peace.[87] Nevertheless, from about this time we may begin to trace the growing independence of the O'Conors of Offaly and the O'Mores of Leix.

On September 12,1290, Sir William de Vesey was appointed justiciar. As son and heir of the eldest of Sibyl Marshal's seven daughters he held the castle manor and liberty of Kildare. Except for recurrent risings of the Leinster clans, the Irish were com- [35]
paratively quiet during his term of office and indeed during the remainder of Edward's reign, but the justiciar had much litigation with the Abbot of St. Thomas's, the Bishop of Kildare and others,[88] as well as a violent dispute with John FitzThomas, to which we shall refer when we come to describe affairs in Connaught at this period. In 1294, probably taking advantage of this dispute, the men of Offaly took the castle of Kildare and Calvagh O'Conor burned all the rolls and tallies of the county.[89] The O'Conors of Offaly and some adjoining clans continued to harass their English neighbours on all sides. In the summer of 1299 the magnates of Meath and Kildare agreed to aid Peter de Bermingham 'to maintain his war which the Irish felons of the parts of Offaly raised against him and to repress the malice of the Irish the themselves and to clear their passes'. The aid consisted in the payment of £100 as wages for 400 footmen in addition

84 Clyn's Annals, 1287. It is indeed stated in the Dublin copy of the Annals of Inisfallen, that Gerald Fitz Maurice was killed along with Thomas de Clare in battle with Turlough O'Brien, but this statement appears to have been due to the blunder of the compiler and must be rejected: see *infra*, pp. 99–104 [pp. 483–5]. 85 A letter of attorney from Gerald, son of Maurice, lord of Offaly, appointing John, the clerk, formerly provost of Lea, to deliver full seisin of the manor of Lea, to John, son of Thomas, and dated at Rathymegan June 26, 1287, is transcribed in the Red Book of the Earl of Kildare, f. x *d*. Clyn says: 'hereditatem suam dedit domino Iohanni filio Thome filio adwunculi sui.' John was son of Gerald's paternal great-uncle. 86 See my 'Notes on the Bermingham Pedigree': Galway Archaeological Journal, vol. ix, p. 198. There is an interesting deed of fealty in the Red Book of the Earl of Kildare (f. iii *d*), dated April 26, 1289, by which Peter, son of James de Bermingham, acknowledges that he has sworn 'quod fidelis ero Iohanni filio Thome, auxilium meum consilium et servicium contra omnes gentes, salva fide regea [*sic*], in omnibus suis negotiis et agendis integre et fideliter eidem prestando . . . eidem etiam Iohanni familiaris ero quoad vixero, robas suas capiendo et portando pro me et duobus sociis pro voluntate mea eligendis.' 87 See Cal. Docs. Ireland, vol. iii, no. 559, where the archbishop gives a detailed account of the expenses of his numerous journeys to divers parts of Ireland in the years 1288–90. For the encounter with Calvagh see Ann. Loch Cé, 1289, where John Fitz Thomas is apparently meant by 'Mac Muiris'. 88 Cal. Docs. Ireland, vol. iv, pp. 52–7. 89 Laud MS. Annals, p. 323.

to Peter's own men to be levied off the free-tenants of Meath and Kildare.[90] We hear of no immediate fighting, but in 1305 Peter de Bermingham earned his £100 and a bad name in history by the action he took against the common enemy. According to the Irish Annals, Murtough O'Conor Faly, Maelmora his kinsman, and Calvagh [his brother] with twenty-nine others were killed by him in his castle 'through treachery and
[36] deceit'.[91] The monastic annals ascribe the deed to Jordan Comyn at Peter's castle of Carrick in Carbury.[92] The merit or demerit of the deed, however, rests with Peter, for on July 2, 1305, John Wogan, the justiciar, authorized the payment to Peter of £100 granted to him 'to subdue Irish felons of Offaly of the race of O'Conors and to decapitate the chiefs of the same race'. Peter, it is added, had already sent the heads of Murtough and Maelmora O'Conor and of sixteen others to Dublin.[93] It is clear that a price had been put on their heads. Nor was this the only example in Edward's reign of this pernicious policy, sure to induce unscrupulous men to resort to discreditable means of winning the reward. A price was put upon the heads of Murtough and Art MacMurrough in 1282, and some time before on the head of Donnell Og O'Donnell. The latter, however, fell in fair fight at the battle of Disertcreaght in 1281.

But it was not only English settlers who suffered from the raids of the O'Conors Faly and other neighbouring clans. In January 1306, O'Dempsey, chieftain of Clanmalier, a territory lying on both sides of the Barrow in the present baronies of Portnahinch and Upper Philipstown, in a petition to the justiciar and council showed that the O'Conors of Offaly, O'Dunn of Iregan (now the barony of Tinnahinch), Mac Gillapatrick of Upper Ossory, Mageoghegan of Kenaliagh (the barony of Moycashel, Westmeath), and O'Molloy of Fircall (the baronies of Eglish Ballyboy and Ballycowan in King's County) and their confederates 'do not cease to fight and injure him and others who adhere to the king's peace', and he prayed aid against them. This was granted,
[37] and provision was made on a small scale for a joint expedition by him and John Fitz Thomas.[94] In the following June, John Fitz Thomas, Peter de Bermingham, and O'Dempsey received payment for beheading divers felons, including O'Dunn.[95]

In October 1294, William de Vescy was superseded as Justiciar by William de Oddingeseles, who is said to have come from Maxstoke in Warwickshire.[96] He had, however, been already employed on the king's service in Ireland. For some time prior to August 1290 he held the custody of the king's castles of Roscommon and Randown, and in Easter week 1289, with Walter l'Enfant, he had acted as lieutenant of John de Saunford, the justiciar, in some operations taken in conjunction with Manus O'Conor, king of Connaught, against O'Melaghlin of Meath.[97] The king now granted to him the land and castle of Dunamon near Roscommon,[98] but he died in April 1295, after only six months' tenure of office.

90 Justiciary Rolls, vol. i, p. 286. 91 Ann. Ulster, Ann. Loch Cé. This act was cited as an example of the perfidy of the English by Donnell O'Neill and his associates in their letter to Pope John XXII, when giving reasons for seeking aid from Edward Bruce and constituting him king and lord in Ireland. 92 Laud MS. Annals, p. 332. 93 Cal. Docs. Ireland, vol. iv, no. 434; Justiciary Rolls, vol. ii, p. 82. 94 Justiciary Rolls, vol. ii, p. 215. 95 Ibid., p. 270. 96 See Gilbert's 'Viceroys', p. 112. 97 Cal. Docs. Ireland, vol. iii, no. 683; and p. 270, where *a. r.* 18 seems to be a mistake for *a. r.* 17; cf. p. 269 and Ann. Loch Cé, 1289. 98 Cal. Docs. Ireland, vol. iv, nos. 177, 184.

Thomas Fitz Maurice of Desmond, son of the Maurice who, with his father John, was slain at Callann in 1261, was now appointed by the King's Council in Dublin as keeper of Ireland. The imprisonment of the Earl of Ulster by his turbulent tenant and rival, John Fitz Thomas of Offaly, in the previous winter (to which we shall return in a later chapter) had created a great commotion,[99] and in the spring of 1295 the Mac Murroughs and the Wicklow clans, taking advantage of the general disturbance, again [38]
broke out and laid waste Newcastle Mc Kynegan, and some other towns in Leinster.[1] Thomas Fitz Maurice now organized an expedition on a considerable scale against the insurgents. The feudal services were proclaimed, and amongst others the Earl of Ulster and John Fitz Thormas attended with their contingents.[2] Though the feud between them was unappeasod, both were willing to co-operate with the justiciar against the Irish enemy. The muster-ground was at Castledermot. Newcastle Mc Kynegan, Castlekevin, Ballymore, and other places on the skirts of the mountains were strongly guarded. We have no record of the fighting, but in the result, on July 19, the justiciar received to the king's peace Maurice (Murrough), son of Murtough Mac Murrough 'with all his nation and following' on condition of his giving certain hostages for the Mac Murroughs, O'Tooles, and O'Byrnes respectively, paying a penalty of 600 cows, and making satisfaction for damages done to the betaghs and other tenants of the king or of the archbishop, the betaghs and others making like satisfaction to Mac Murrough.[3] Finally Mac Murrough swore under forfeiture of his hostage that he would with all his power make war upon the O'Byrnes and O'Tooles if either should attempt anything against the king or infringe this covenant.[4] The covenant, however, was infringed and the oath violated in the winter of 1301–2.[5]

Though Thomas Fitz Maurice had been favoured by the king, who had given him [39]
'his cousin' in marriage and had granted him the lands of Decies and Desmond,[6] he was not long retained in office. Perhaps it was thought unsuitable to have a Geraldine in office while the quarrel between John Fitz Thomas and the Earl of Ulster was not settled. On October 18, 1295, the king appointed John Wogan and on the same day commanded both John Fitz Thomas and the earl not to inflict any evil on each other whereby the peace might be infringed.[7]

Unlike his immediate predecessors, Sir John Wogan retained his post almost continuously for the long period of eighteen years. He belonged to the Pembrokeshire family of that name and was lord of Picton Castle near Haverford.[8] He may have owed his favour with King Edward to his lord and patron, William de Valence, Earl of Pembroke and uncle of the king. It was perhaps his Cambro-Norman extraction and connexions that enabled him to understand the temperament of both native Irish chieftains and Anglo-Norman settlers, so that during his long term of office there was

99 See infra, pp. 116–19 [pp. 492–3]. 1 Laud MS. Annals. 2 Cal. Docs. Ireland, vol. iv, pp. 123–4. 3 Here we have an example of betaghs fighting against an independent Irish clan and being protected by their lords. 4 Justiciary Rolls, vol. i, p. 61. 5 Cal. Docs. Ireland, vol. v, p. 5. 6 See *ante*, vol. iii, p. 145 [p. 352]. 7 Cal. Docs. Ireland, vol. iv, nos. 267–8. 8 In 1302 he founded the Wogan chantry in the chapel of St Nicholas in St. David's Cathedral, then describing himself as 'dominus de Pykton et capitalis iusticiarius de Hibernia'. See Arch. Cambrensis, Fifth Series, vol. xv, p. 228, and Owen's Old Pembroke Families, pp. 40–1. His precise position in the Wogan family is obscure.

but little disturbance on the Irish marches and no conflict between the Irish magnates and the Government, or between the Irish magnates themselves. In his time, too, the king's influence in Ireland was perhaps greater than at any other period prior to the
[40] reign of Henry VIII. Immediately on his arrival he tactfully effected a truce between the Earl of Ulster and John Fitz Thomas and enlisted the services of both, along with those of other Irish lords, in the campaign of 1296 against Balliol, King of Scots.[9] Indeed the frequency with which in the next few years forces and provisions in considerable quantities were dispatched from Ireland to assist the king in his wars in Scotland, Flanders and France, is strong testimony to Wogan's success in preserving the peace of Ireland and in maintaining the loyalty and goodwill both of the magnates and of the Irish population in general towards the Crown.

Sir John Wogan is best remembered as the justiciar who in 1297[10] summoned the first assembly in Ireland that really deserved the name of a parliament, though of course the credit of the constitutional advance which marked this parliament should be attributed to his lord and master, King Edward, who had himself learned the great principle of government by elected representatives in the school of Simon de Montfort. To this council of Ireland not only were summoned the archbishops, bishops,
[41] abbots, and priors, whose presence seemed to be thereunto necessary, as well as the earls, barons, and other chief persons (optimates) of the land, but it was ordered that the sheriffs of Dublin, Louth, Kildare, Waterford, Tipperary, Cork, Limerick, Kerry, Connaught, and Roscommon, each in his full county court, and the seneschals of the liberties of Meath, Wexford, Carlow, Kilkenny, and Ulster, each in his full court of the liberty, by the assent of his county or liberty, should cause to be elected two of the most honest and discreet knights of the several counties and liberties, that they might be present with full powers.[11] Here then we have an assembly which exercised legislative functions and consisted virtually of lords spiritual, lords temporal, and knights of the shires, this last element involving the representative principle which in its development has rendered possible the establishment of orderly democracies. The cities and boroughs were indeed unrepresented in 1297, but this defect was remedied in the parliaments of 1300 and 1310.

As has already been noticed,[12] legislation for Ireland in previous reigns consisted mainly of royal ordinances issued by virtue of the king's prerogative. The laws of England were in general terms ordered to be observed in Ireland, and in a few cases particular statutes passed in England were, by the king's authority, transmitted to Ireland

9 Laud MS. Annals (Chart. St. Mary's Abbey, Dublin, p. 326). For those summoned see Cal. Docs. Ireland, vol. iv, no. 276. On May 13, the king entertained the Irish leaders at a great feast in the castle of Roxburgh: Laud MS. Annals (as above), p. 326. **10** There should be no doubt about the year. The act provided that 'the county of Kildare, formerly a liberty intentive to the county of Dublin, be henceforth a county by itself'. This must have been done between February 1297, when William de Vesci surrendered the liberty of Kildare to the king (C.D.I., iv, nos. 365, 373), and the following July when Kildare had 'newly been made a county by itself': Just. Roll, vol. i, p. 145. 11 Particulars concerning this parliament and its enactments are known only from an entry in the Black Book of Christ Church, Dublin. See Irish Archaeological Society's Miscellany, pp. 15–33; also Early Statutes (Berry), p. 195. **12** *Ante*, vol. iii, pp. 298–301 [pp. 431–3].

for observance there. Similarly in 1279 the Statute of Mortmain of that year was obdained to be observed in Ireland,[13] and in 1285 all the great legislation of Edward I [42] directed to restrain the corruption, extortion, and oppression of sheriffs, king's officers, and others in authority; or designed for the improvement of legal procedure, for the protection of widows and wards, and for the better recovery of debts and the redress of other grievances, was extended to Ireland.[14] The statute of 'Quia Emptores', which was professedly intended to secure the feudal rights of the Crown and baronage by stopping the sub-infeudation of lands held in fee simple, but which has had far-reaching effects in facilitating the division of estates and in multiplying tenures in chief of the Crown, does not seem to have been transmitted to Ireland in its entirety. In 1293, however, the king sent among other ordinances one forbidding tenants in chief from making feoffments, save to be held of the king in chief and by leave of the king or of his justiciar. Nothing is said about the feoffments of mesne tenants, and even as regards tenants in chief an exception was made of those whose lands 'lay in the land of war or in the marches'. They were to have power to enfeoff others to hold of the feoffors for the defence of the land until the king advised otherwise.[15] This then is an example of an English statute having been materially modified to suit the special requirements of Ireland.

So far as appears then, the first legislation originating in Ireland was that enacted in Wogan's Parliament of 1297. By it Kildare (no longer a liberty since its surrender by William de Vesey to the king) was made a county by itself under a sheriff; but the [43] most characteristic clauses were those directed towards inducing the English (under penalties for default) to guard the Marches and act together in defending themselves and their neighbours against risings and plundering raids of the Irish. Other clauses forbade any one from leading out an army through the land of peace without licence from the justiciar, from keeping more kerns and idle men than he could support out of his own resources, and from attacking any Irishman who was at peace. There was also an order for the clearing of ancient highways which passed through woods, and for the repair of bridges and causeways. Finally, it was already deemed necessary to forbid Englishmen from attiring themselves in Irish garments, and particularly from wearing their hair after the manner of the Irish *culan*.[16] In subsequent reigns there was to be much further legislation with the same double object of resisting Irish outbreaks and restraining men of English descent from falling into the turbulent ways of the Irish. Two centuries later indeed we find Edmund Spenser inveighing against the Scythian (i.e. Gaelic) custom 'of the wearing of mantles and long glibbes, which is a thicke curled bush of haire, hanging downe over their eyes, and monstrously disguising them', both of which he describes as 'fit rnasks for a thief'.

But though this parliament of 1297 was the first in Ireland that deserves the name, it is clear, in spite of much that has been written to the contrary, that much of the legis-

13 Early Statutes, p. 37. 14 Early Statutes, pp. 47–177. 15 Ibid., p. 192. We have mentioned (*ante*, vol. ii, p. 48 [pp. 169–70]) that through neglect of this ordinance Maurice de Carew in 1302 was held to have forfeited the seignory of Fermoy. 16 The *culan* seems to have been a wisp of hair allowed to grow long, and brought from the back forwards over the forehead and down to the eyes.

[44] lation for Ireland, both before and for many years after this date, consisted of ordinances issued by the king in virtue of his prerogative, or by the king and council in England, or of acts of the English parliament transmitted to Ireland and ordered by the king to be proclaimed and observed there. As Dr. Berry says in the Preface to his edition of Early Statutes, 'at what period or in what reign the king's ordinances completely yielded to the more constitutional authority of parliamentary enactments has never yet been precisely ascertained'. So far indeed as appears, it was not until 1460 that an Irish parliament claimed that Ireland was not bound by acts of the parliament of England, saving only such as were accepted by the great council or the parliament of Ireland.

But this declaration, though no doubt popular at the time in Ireland, was made when Richard, Duke of York, had assumed the governorship, and should be regarded as part of the parliamentary armour put on by the duke for his protection against the Lancastrian parliament, by which he had been attainted.

In June 1299, Edward sent a writ patent to the justiciar forbidding the introduction into Ireland of divers bad moneys known as pollards or crokards, and by other names, and ordering that wardens be appointed to carry out the ordinance.[17] The sheriff of Cork returned a list of thirty-eight market-towns and ports in his bailiwick in which

[45] wardens were appointed.[18] These must all have been centres of trade, and the list indicates the highly developed state of County Cork at that time. Unfortunately we have no similar lists from other parts. By the same writ the export of good silver coin and of silver in plates, without special licence, was forbidden, and in 1300 this ordinance was made more absolute, and no money other than sterlings of the king's coinage was to be henceforth current in the kingdom.[19] The operation of the economical law that bad money has a tendency to drive out good was already perceived.

In 1299, too, there was an anticipation, in a less drastic form, it is true, of the famous Statute of Labourers which was passed after the Black Death in 1349. Complaints having been made that servants, ploughmen, carters, threshers and others, 'on account of the fertility of the year',[20] refused to serve as accustomed, it was provided by the justiciar and council in Dublin that such servants should serve as they were accustomed to do, and stay with their lords and receive the same liveries and wages as in other years, and that no lord should give greater liveries or larger wages heretofore, or draw away the servants of another without his will.[21] The Statute of Labourers was occasioned by the scarcity of labour owing to the Black Death; while the great fertil-

[46] ity of 1299 induced a demand for extra labour to secure the increased harvest, at a time when the cheapness of food enabled many labourers to avoid work. But though the conditions were different, the actual result (for the moment) was the same. The sup-

17 Early Statutes, 27 Ed. I, p. 221. In the previous Easter term the justiciar in council had made some provisions for the seizure of such foreign moneys if not up to a certain standard (ibid., p. 213), but these provisions were superseded by the king's ordinance. **18** Justiciary Rolls, vol. i, p. 265. **19** Early Statutes, p. 239. In February 130l, the king having learnt that money and silver were clandestinely exported in sacks of wool, &c., sent letters to John Wogan again forbidding the export: Cal. Docs. Ireland, vol. iv, no. 776. **20** In a memorandum of this ordinance preserved at Cambridge, its occasion is said to be ' quod famuli . . . non curaverunt servire propter vile forum bladi': see Eng. Hist. Rev., vol. xviii (1905), p. 508. **21** Early Statutes (Berry), p. 215.

ply of labour did not meet the demand, and the competition of employers tended to raise wages abnormally. But there was this difference: the result of the Black Death was felt for many years, while the fertility of 1299 was no doubt exceptional, and was certainly more than counter-balanced by the famine of 1315–17. Hence in spite of the Statute of Labourers wages increased in the years following 1350, but there is no sign of any general increase of wages, in Ireland at any rate, for many years after 1299.[22]

By exercising a greater control over officials and a more strict audit of their accounts, by the imposition of the fixed custom on the export of wool, and by his encouragement of trade and commerce, Edward greatly increased the revenue of Ireland; and notwithstanding a liberal expenditure on defensive works there and on salaries, he succeeded in obtaining large sums for building and provisioning castles in Wales and supplying his armies there and in Scotland. This was effected, in Ireland at least, without having recourse so frequently as his father had done to irritating subsidies. In 1292, however, the Irish magnates granted to the king a fifteenth out of their goods and chattels,[23] and in the course of the next seven years the sum of £11,369 14*s*. [47]
81*d*. was collected in respect of this assessment.[24]

On January 18, 1300, the king asked for a subsidy from his faithful people of Ireland to aid him for 'repressing the rebellion of the Scottish enemies and rebels'. Scotland in fact was not subdued by the defeat of Wallace at Falkirk, and a new expedition was necessary to carry out the king's designs. A parliament was summoned at Dublin, consisting not only of the prelates and magnates, but also of the elected representatives of the communities of the counties, and likewise of the communities of the cities and boroughs. But the power of representatives to bind their constituents was not yet established, and even prior to the assembling of the parliament, the justiciar, Sir John Wogan, went to a number of the principal cities and boroughs and obtained directly from each community sums varying presumably according to their wealth. When the parliament assembled, divers of the magnates and representatives, excusing themselves (for the moment) from giving a subsidy, prayed the justiciar to go with them through the various communities, and promised that they would assist in inducing the communities to contribute, and that they (except the prelates) would then contribute. This was done, and a long and interesting list of counties, liberties, tenants on ecclesiastical or abbatial lands, and boroughs contributed a total of £2,361 6*s*. 8*d*.[25] John [48]
Wogan, John Fitz Thomas, Peter de Bermingham and many others headed contingents on the expedition to Scotland of 130l, but as an Irish annalist cautiously observes, 'they obtained not complete sway in it'.[26]

22 The wages paid on the Earl of Norfolk's Irish manors, *c.*1279–86, were very similar to those paid on the farms of the Priory of the Holy Trinity, *c.*1344. See Journal R.S.A.I., vol. xxii (1892), p. 57, and Account Roll of the Priory, 1337–1346, ed. James Mills. **23** Cal. Docs. Ireland, vol. iii, no. 1090. **24** An examination of the rolls of receipt published in the Calendar, vol. iv, shows that £3,278 16*s*. 8*d*. was collected in Trinity term 1293 (no. 48), £3,294 7*s*. 9¼*d*. in the three terms ending Easter 1294 (no. 130), and £4,796 10*s*. 3¼*d*. between that date and Easter 1299 (no. 612). **25** Early Statutes, pp. 229–37; Justiciary Rolls, vol. i, p :303, and cf. Irish Pipe Roll, 32 Ed. I. An analysis of of the above total shows that the counties and liberties contributed £1,361 6*s*. 8*d*.; the tenants on ecclesiastical and abbatial lands £197 13*s*. 4d.; and boroughs £817 13*s*. 4*d*. Ulster and Connaught were not represented. **26** Ann. Loch Cé and Laud MS.

The ecclesiastical taxation of Ireland, *c.*1302, made with a view to the levy of the 'Papal tenths', affords some index of the relative prosperity of the districts under Anglo-Norman and Irish rule respectively. For instance the dioceses of Down and Connor, covering only the county of Antrim and the eastern half of the county of Down, but comprising nearly all the feudalized parts of the lordship of Ulster, were taxed at £1,051 14s. 7½*d.*, while the rest of the whole province of Ulster, though covering an area at least six times greater, was taxed at about £300. Similarly in Connaught the diocese of Elphin, including rather more than the district in which the O'Conors held sway, was taxed at £69 7*s.* 10*d.*, while the adjoining dioceses of Clonfert and Kilmacduagh, comprising approxi-mately the district afterwards known as Clanrickard, though of smaller area, were valued at £268 5*s.* 11*d.* A comparison of the valuation of the Irish districts in Wicklow, Offaly, and Desmond, with that of neighbouring districts under Anglo-Norman rule, gives similar results. Everywhere the valuation of the benefices in the Irish districts was relatively much lower; and this result
[49] cannot be attributed solely to inferiority in the quality of the land, but was primarily due to the disturbed state of the districts under Irish rule. In some cases the churches are described as waste owing to war, and of no value.

In all the feudalized districts the common law of England, as modified or supplemented by statutory enactments and royal ordinances, was administered throughout the great liberties in the courts of the lords of the liberties, and elsewhere in the courts held by the chief justiciar or by itinerant justices. Only a few of the plea rolls of Edward's reign have survived, and of these only those pleas held by the chief justiciar in the period from 1295 to 1307 have been published. During this period the justiciar held courts not only in Dublin and at several places in the adjoining counties of Louth, East Meath, Kildare, and Wicklow, and at the cities of Waterford, Cork, Limerick, Cashel, and Kilkenny, but also at the following smaller and more remote towns, viz. Tralee, Ardfert, and Duagh, in County Kerry; Mallow, Buttevant, Ballyhay, and Ardskeagh, in County Cork; Kilmallock, Rathkeale, and Ardagh, in County Limerick; Clonmel, Carrick, Nenagh, and Aherlow, in County Tipperary; Dungarvan, Tallow, and Stradbally, in County Waterford; Castlecomer, Callan, Thomastown, Gowran, Graig-na-managh, and Rosbercon, in County Kilkenny; Carlow, Tullow, Wells, and New Ross, in the former liberty of Carlow;[27] Mullingar, Loughseudy, and Rathwire, in Westmeath; the New Town of Leix, and Roscommon. The pleas heard before the justiciar ranged over all kinds of offences, civil and criminal, from cases of
[50] homicide to disputes about rights of way, and a case where a man was found to have stolen two goats, value 11*d.*, but was acquitted 'for the soul of the king', as he was not accustomed to do evil, but was impelled solely by hunger. The court reviewed proceedings of all inferior courts, while its proceedings were in turn liable to review in the king's court in England. Sometimes what was called a 'parliament' was held before the justiciar and council. Its proceedings included the making of enactments and the hearing of petitions.

Annals, 1301, cf. Cal. Docs Ireland, vol. iv, 785. The Earl of Ulster did not go: Ann Ulst. 1301. **27** The only liberties recognized in Leinster and Meath at this time were Wexford and East Meath.

Edward generally kept escheats and wardships in his own hands, instead of selling them to the highest bidder or giving them to favourites. When, as in the case of Ulster, Thomond, and Desmond, he did make large grants to individuals, it was with the political object of securing more effective control and better order in Gaelic districts, and not from the mere personal motive of rewarding his followers. He also obtained possession of several manors by surrender from the owners. Sometimes this was effected by giving the owner an equivalent in English lands, as in the case of Christiana de Mariscis, one of the coheirs of the Riddelisford lands, who surrendered manors in Connaught, about Bray, and at Castledermot and Kilkea,[28] and of Ralph Pippard, who surrendered the manors of Donaghmoyne and Ardee in Uriel, Leixlip in Co. Kildare, and Dysart in Westmeath.[29] In other cases the surrender was obtained in other ways. Thus in 1290 Edward gave his daughter, 'Joan of Acre,' in marriage to Gilbert, Earl of Gloucester, on condition that the earl should surrender his lands both in England and Ireland and receive them back entailed on the issue of tlle marriage, or [51]
in default on the heirs of Joan.[30] In 1297 William de Vesey surrendered the castle, manor, and county of Kildare to the king in consideration of a pardon for his Crown debts. A few months later the lands were given back to him for his life, and on his death very shortly afterwards the whole inheritance vested in the Crown.[31] In 1202 the king induced Roger Bigod, Earl of Norfolk, who though twice married was childless, to surrender all his castles and lands in Ireland (as in England) and receive them back with reversion to the king in the event of the earl's death without heirs of his body.[32] The result was that on the earl's death in 1308 his vast estates, to the disherison of his brother, reverted to the Crown. Thus did the king gain control over three of the great Leinster liberties. This policy may have enabled the king to counteract the baronial opposition in England, but in Ireland, where there was no marked conflict between the barons and the Crown, the ultimate consequence of weakening the baronial power was to encourage the border Irish clans to make raids into Leinster and Meath.

Whatever may have been Edward's shortcomings from the modern ideal of a ruler governing in the interests of the governed, Ireland under his rule reached a degree of order, wealth, and prosperity never attained before, and never even distantly approached in pre-Norman times. His reign in Ireland was in fact the culminating period of the whole Anglo-Norman epoch, when the wave of mediaeval progress which followed the partial organization and comparative order introduced by his great- [52]
grandfather reached its high-water mark. Guided by England, Ireland was taking her place, a subordinate but no mean one, among the progressive countries of Western Europe, and with England was participating in the new ideas of state-government and social organization, the new activities in agriculture, industry, trade, and commerce, the new developments in art and architecture and tlle amenities of life generally, which marked the thirteenth century as a period of great achievement and still greater promise.

28 Cal. Docs. Ireland, vol. iii, nos, 1798–1801. **29** Ibid., vol. v, 149, 167. **30** Ibid., vol. iii, nos. 620, 659. **31** Ibid., vol. iv, nos. 374, 414, 426. **32** Ibid., vol. v, nos. 54, 87.

[53] CHAPTER XXXIV

THE NORMANS IN THOMOND

From the close of the twelfth century, when the Normans first permanently occupied the city of Limerick and began to settle extensively in the present county to the south of the Shannon, grants were also made by the Crown of some lands to the north of the estuary, in the present county of Clare—the district to which the name of Thomond came henceforth to be more specifically confined. Thus, seemingly before the accession of King John, Arnold Keting had received a grant of the cantred of Tradry (Bunratty Lower), while the king retained for his own use the three cantreds of Corcovaskin (Moyarta, Clonderalaw, and part of Ibrickan). In 1199 Arnold Keting exchanged Tradry for the middle cantred of Corcovaskin,[1] and about the same time Thomas Fitz Maurice, ancestor of the Desmond Fitz Geralds, was granted five knights' fees on the northern bank of the Shannon near Limerick.[2]

It would seem that, as in the case of the lands in County Limerick, these cantreds along the northern shores of the estuary of the Shannon were left at the disposal of
[54] the English Crown by agreement with the sons of Donnell O'Brien. As we have seen, Donough Cairbrech O'Brien in 1197 brought the English into Thomond, where they slew Covey Macnamara, Conor O'Quin, and many others.[3] It was probably in return for Norman assistance in quelling the opposition of these powerful chieftains[4] that Donough relinquished his overlordship of Tradry, the richest land in Thomond, to his allies. The principle adopted by the Government, here and elsewhere, was to confirm the Irish chieftain in part of his former territory as a quasi-tenant in chief, while reserving another part for the disposal of the Crown as immediate overlord.

About the time of King John's expedition to Ireland (1210), or soon afterwards, a further Donough arrangement seems to have been made. After a dispute with his brother Murtough, Donough O'Brien seems to have been finally recognized as king of about a moiety of Thomond subject to a rent, and to have obtained a lease of Carrigogunnel or Esclon then in the king's hand,[5] while four cantreds in Thomond, viz. Ogashin (Bunratty Upper) and the three cantreds of Corcovaskin, were placed at the disposal of the justiciar, John de Gray, Bishop of Norwich. The bishop made grants

1 Cal. Docs. Irel., vol. i, no. 106. 2 Rot. Chart., 1 John, p. 19b: in *thwedo de Huamerith quod est in Thomunt super aquam de Sinan*; the *ui Aimrit* of Topogr. Poems, p. 128; seemingly north of Cratloe on the way to Ballymulcashel; *Caithréim*. p. 122. 3 *Ante*, vol. ii, p. 159 [p. 215]. 4 The Mac Namaras, whose hereditary privilege it was,' to name O'Brien' at Magh Adhair, were chiefs of Ui gCaisin or Ogashin (approximately Bunratty Upper), and the O'Quins were chiefs of Muintir hIfernain, about Corrofin. 5 *Ante*, vol. ii, p. 150 [p. 212], and p. 168 [p. 218] note [63].

of some of these lands,[6] but it is improbable that any effective colonization was made [55] at the time. The grantees, no doubt, met with opposition from the local chieftains, for in 1215, by the advice of some of the grantees, a proposal was made to give the four cantreds to Murtough O'Brien, saving the interest of the feoffees in two of them.[7] This particular arrangement fell through, but seemingly an alternative offer from Donough was accepted.[8]

The death in 1216 of Conor O'Heney, Bishop of Killaloe, seemed to give an opportunity for appointing an Englishman to the vacant see, and accordingly, on January 14, 1217, the king's approval was given (by the regency) to the 'canonical election' of Robert Travers, nephew of Geoffrey de Marisco, and he was consecrated by the bishops of Waterford, Emly, and Limerick.[9] About the same time Geoffrey de Marisco erected a castle at Killaloe for the bishop.[10] The election of an English bishop, though sanctioned by King Donough, was, however, disputed,[11] and in 1221 the pope's legate deposed the bishop and sent him to Rome.[12] 'Perpetual silence' was imposed upon him, and another consecrated in his place.[13] At the time of the election of Robert Travers an endeavour was made to establish the rule that no Irishman should be promoted [56] to a cathedral church, on the ground that disturbances were likely to ensue from such appointments,[14] but this exclusive principle was, as a matter of fact, never strictly carried out. On the other hand, when Henry III in 1250 complained to Pope Innocent IV that archbishops and bishops in Ireland and their chapters had ordained that no Englishman should be received as a canon in their churches, the pope issued a bull commanding the ordinance to be revoked.[15]

In 1217 Geoffrey de Marisco, the justiciar, was ordered to assist Thomas Fitz Adam to build a castle in his land of Corcovaskin.[16] At Kilkee there is an earthwork of the mote type[17]—a very unusual thing in County Clare—and it is possible that it represents this castle. Tradry was retained for the king's use, and lands there were to be assigned to Miles de Cogan and Walter Bluet, knights,[18] while Cratloe was sold to Geoffrey Lutterel, from whom it passed to his son-in-law, Philip Marc.[19]

We have no further information as to these early attempts to enfeoff parts of Thomond, and it is probable that, outside of Tradry at any rate, they did not meet [57] with any success. In 1222, however, a clearer light is thrown on the subordinate position of the Irish king. In that year Donough, king of Thomond, received a new grant of the land which he had previously held (called afterwards a moiety of Thomond) at

6 The bishop granted the moiety of Ogashin, 'which O'Grady had formerly held', to Reginald Finegal (who also held lands of the Talbots of Malahide), and among tho bishop's feoffees in Corcovaskin were Thomas Fitz Adam (an official of the Crown) and Robrrt Petit, brother of Nicholas Petit of Meath: Cal. Docs. Irel., vol. i, nos. 607, 629. 7 Ibid., nos. 629, 669, and cf. no. 2191. 8 Ibid, no. 673. About the same time King John, as overlord, confirmed to the Archbishop of Cashel a grant which Donough had made to him of five vills in Thomond: ibid., no. 649. 9 Ibid., no. 738. Papal Letters, vol. i, p. 50. 10 Ann. Clonmacnois. 11 Theiner, Vetera Monumenta (1864), pp. 5, 11, 25. 12 Cal. Docs. Ireland, vol. i, nos. 1026, 1037. The bishop of Ardfert, an English Benedictine, was at the same time similarly deposed. 13 Theiner, Vet. Mon., p. 26. 14 Cal. Docs. Ireland, vol. i, nos. 736, 739. 15 Ibid., no. 3084. 16 Rot. Claus., 1 Hen. III, p. 310. The mandate was repeated in 1220; ibid., p. 427b. 17 See Journal R.S.A.I., vol. xxxix, p. 116. It has a souterrain, however, a feature unusual in Norman motes. 18 Cal. Docs. Irel., vol. i, no. 690. The Cogans and Bluets were landowners in Co. Cork. 19 Ibid., nos. 560, 633, 821, 881. Geof-

an annual farm of 130 marks. He was now to hold it of the king during good service, until the king's full age, at the increased rent of £100 a year and a fine of 200 marks.[20] On the expiration of this lease in 1228 Murtough O'Brien offered 80 marks increased rent and £1,000 to have the moiety of Thomond, hitherto leased to Donough at £100 a year, and he moreover offered to build a castle in the land for the king's use, and maintain at his own cost the force placed in it by the justiciar (Richard de Burgh).[21] Though the king accepted this offer, it does not appear to have been acted on. The brothers were ready to bid against each other to get a lease from the Crown, but as before Donough was successful. In 1225, and again in 1230, Donough assisted Richard de Burgh in his campaigns in Connaught; but in 1234–5, taking advantage of the cleavage among the barons caused by Earl Richard Marshal's revolt, Donough allied himself with Felim O'Conor against Richard de Burgh, and ravaged the Crown-lands of Thomond up to Limerick.[22] Defeated by Richard de Burgh, he made a timely peace, and for a fine of 400 marks recovered his position.[23] At this time, in addition to
[58] his moiety of Thomond, he held Corcovaskin, and probably Ogashin, on lease from the king, and the feoffees of the Bishop of Norwich or their representatives were compensated.[24]

Donough O'Brien died in 1242, when he is called by an Irish annalist 'the maintainer of the faith and renown of Leth Modha, and the pillar of the dignity and nobility of the South of Erin'.[25] The foundation of the Cistercian house of Sancta Maria de Petra Fertili, or Corcumroe, the remains of which stand on a green spot in the desolate Burren of Clare, has been variously attributed to Donough and to his father, Donnell Mor.[26] Perhaps each had a hand in the buildings, as the architecture of the abbey-church, which has been well preserved, points to slightly different periods.[27] Donough was at any rate a benefactor of the Cistercians. A grant from him of two marks yearly to the mother-church at Citeaux, in aid of procuration for the Irish abbots attending the general chapter there, is still extant at Dijon.[28] To Donough has also been attributed the foundation in 1227 of the Dominican Convent at Limerick, but this again is doubtful, as not only had Donough no jurisdiction in Limerick at this date, but Edward I in 1285 made a special grant of ten marks a year to the Dominican
[59] friars of Limerick, 'whose house', he says, 'was founded by the king's ancestors and the king himself'.[29]

Whatever may be thought of Donough's conduct towards his hereditary foes of the seed of Eoghan, towards his neighbours the kings of Connaught, and above all with

frey Lutterel was sheriff of Dublin in 1213: Hist. et Mun. Docs. Irel. (Gilbert), p. 473. Both he and Philip Marc were faithful servants of King John. For the latter see 'Minority of Henry III' (Norgate), p. 75. **20** Rot. Claus., 6 Hen III, p. 505b; Rot. Pat., 6 Hen. III, p. 336. **21** Rot Claus., 13 Hen. III, p. 126. **22** See *ante*. vol. iii, pp 181–2, [p. 372]. **23** Cal. Patent Roll, 18 Hen. III, p. 71. **24** Cal. Docs. Irel., vol. i, nos. 2191, 2193. **25** Ann. Loch Cé. **26** Ware, Chart. St. Mary's Abbey, Dublin, vol. ii, p. 237. **27** For descriptions and illustrations see Journ. R.S.A.I. (1895), p. 280, and (1900), p. 299. **28** See my note on 'Some Irish Cistercian Documents', Eng. Hist. Rev. (1913), p. 307. The deed must be dated 1223–4. It is witnessed by the bishops of Limerick, Emly, Kilfenora, and Ross, by the heads of the Cistercian houses at Monasteranenagh, Holycross, Inishlounaught, and Corcumroe, and by several chieftains in Thomond. **29** Cal. Docs. Irel., vol. iii, no. 97; and cf. Ancient Dominican Foundations in Ireland (Coleman, 1902), p. 52.

regard to the preservation of his patrimony (which is said to have formerly extended from Cuchullin's Leap (Loop Head) to the ford of Boruma (near Killaloe), from Birr to Knockainy, and from Cashel to Burren), it must be admitted that in difficult circumstances he was on the whole a faithful vassal of the English Crown, and that in his time there was comparative peace in Thomond.

The peace continued for several years under Donough's son, Conor. He was one of those summoned by the king in 1244 to a projected expedition against the Scots which, however, did not take place.[30] In 1250 the king directed that for a fine of 2,200 marks Conor was 'to hold during good service the land which his father held by charter from King John', i.e. a moiety of Thomond. The justiciar, John Fitz Geoffrey, was also authorized to commit to Conor the land which he held to farm.[31] For this last-mentioned land, presumably Corcovaskin and Ogashin, Conor afterwards offered a fine of £500 to get the fee.[32] The precise terms were not settled when, in July 1253, Conor complained that he was much troubled by the king's bailiffs in Thomond and harassed by his suit at the court of Limerick. He made at the same time a threefold [60]
offer for the land which he held on lease in Thomond, and the king, while ordering the bailiffs to desist from troubling Conor, sought the advice of the justiciar as to Conor's proposals.[33] One marvels at the ineptitude of this haggling over monetary terms when the vital point was to secure a ruler who would be a faithful vassal of the king and at the same time be accepted by the clansmen as their chieftain. Some terms were eventually settled, as there is an entry in the Pipe Rolls for the year 1260–1 that Conor owed £514 17*s.* 5*d.* 'for having a moiety of Thomond',[34] and from the Exchequer memoranda of the time of Edward I it appears that Conor O'Brien was wont to render 140 marks a year for the same.[35]

While these negotiations with Conor O'Brien were proceeding, some grants leading to permanent settlements in the cantreds reserved to the Crown were made. In 1248 Tradry was granted in fee farm to Robert de Muscegros at a yearly rent of £30, which was remitted for two years to enable Robert to build castles—presumably the first castles at Bunratty and Clare.[36] In 1252 an extended grant was entered on the charter-roll. It conferred unusual immunities on the grantee. The cantred was to be quit of all pleas and plaints of sheriffs, bailiffs, and other ministers of the king, who were not to enter except for the four pleas of the Crown.[37] Robert was afterwards granted a fair and market at his vills of Bunratty and Clare and free warren in his demesne-lands of Tradry [61]
and 'Ocormok' (the district about Clare, which went with Bunratty), and 260 oaks from the king's forests for building.[38] He died before February 1254, when he was succeeded by his son, John de Muscegros, who was sheriff of Limerick, perhaps continuously, from 1261 to his death in 1275.[39] The castle and manor of Bunratty were then in the king's hand up to April 26, 1276, when, by arrangement with another Robert de Muscegros, they were delivered to Thomas de Clare.[40]

30 Cal. Docs. Irel. vol. i, no. 2716. 31 Ibid., no. 3054. 32 Ibid., no. 3114. 33 Cal. Docs. Irel., vol. ii, nos. 272–3. 34 Pipe Roll (Ireland), 45 Hen. III, 35th Rep. D.K., p. 40. 35 Cal. Docs. Irel., vol. iii, p. 550. 36 Ibid., vol. i, no. 3126. 37 Ibid., vol. ii, no. 4. 38 Ibid., no. 51, 155–6. 39 Ibid., vol. ii, no. 325, and Pipe Rolls (Ireland) for 45, 46, and 51 Hen. III and 1 Ed. I, 'accounts for Limerick County'. His rent seems to have been reduced to half a mark a year: ibid., p. 549. 40 Ibid., nos. 1202–4, and Pipe Roll (Ireland), 4

In 1253 the cantred of the Isles in Thomond, now included in the barony of Islands, was granted to the justiciar, John Fitz Geoffrey, at a rent of 43 marks, with immunities similar to those contained in the grant of Tradry, and John and his heirs were to have power to build castles and create markets, fairs, and warrens.[41] John Fitz Geoffrey died in 1258, and the cantred passed in 1260 to his son John, and then in 1276 to another son, Richard Fitz John, on whose death, c. 1297, it became divisible among female heirs.[42] Probably the cantred was never actually colonized, but in time of peace a rent of two marks from each of forty villatas was received from the Irish tenants.

In the year 1257 we hear for the first time in this century of fighting between the
[62] Irish of Thomond and the English, and then it seems to have been Teig, the warlike son of King Conor, that instigated his father to revolt. It is noteworthy that from about this period relations between English and Irish were embittered in Connaught and in Desmond as well as in Thomond, and in every case it was the next claimant to the throne that was dissatisfied with the 'peaceful penetration' of the foreign settlers. In Connaught it was Aedh, son of King Felim, that rebelled, and in Desmond it was Fineen, son of Donnell Got Mac Carthy. There were rival claimants in each case, and the 'heir presumptive' presumably thought that the best way to secure popularity and the succession was to lead the clansmen on a successful plundering expedition against the foreigners. But the root of the irritation was the attempt to treat the remaining semi-independent kings of Ireland as if they were ordinary feudal tenants in chief. They were subjected to substantial rents and heavy fines (not always paid, however) for the portions of their former territories left during good behaviour under their control, and then every outbreak of the restless tribes, impatient of any control, was made the occasion of fresh fines and further deprivation of territory.

In the year 1257, we are told, a great slaughter was inflicted by Conor O'Brien on the foreigners of Munster and a great depredation was committed on them by his son Teig.[43] Next year Teig attended the meeting at Caoluisce on the Erne, where Brian O'Neill attempted to form a confederation of the Gael under himself as *ard-rí*. Aedh O'Conor gave hostages to O'Neill and a partial confederacy was formed, but though
[63] we might expect that Teig would be ready to fall in with the project, a local writer, seeking to glorify Teig, tells how he disdained to accept a gift of two hundred caparisoned steeds from O'Neill, the usual symbol of submission, thus breaking up the meeting.[44] In the same year Conor O'Brien attacked the English in the south of County Galway and burned the towns of Ardrahan and Kilcolgan, then belonging to Maurice Fitz Maurice.

The reply to Conor's revolt was a further diminution of his territory. It seems to have been in this year (1258) that John Fitz Thomas of Shanid entered Thomond, no doubt to punish Conor, and was granted the cantred of Ogashin, half the cantred of

Ed. I, 36th Rep. D.K., pp. 32, 33. 41 Cal. Docs. Irel., vol. ii, no. 289, and cf. nos. 392–3, 410. 42 Ibid., vol. iv, nos. 638, 673–4. 43 Ann. Loch Cé, 1257. 44 Ann. Loch Cé, Ann. Clonmacnois (where for 'O'Bryans' read Ui Briúin), 1258, and see the passage from the Caithréim *Thoirdhealbhaigh* in Miscellany Celtic Soc., pp. 177–9. This account has been doubted (Four Masters, vol. iii, p. 368 n.), and the authority

Omulloid near Killaloe, and thirteen vills in Corcumroe. John Fitz Thomas nominally held these lands at his death in 1261, but they were then waste[45] (i.e. no profit was obtainable from them), and his grandson surrendered them to the king.[46] The date of acquisition seems to be given by an inquisition taken at Limerick in 1275, where the jurors state that 'from the time when Sir John Fitz Thomas first entered Thomond, to wit seventeen years ago', the citizens had received no profit from certain of their lands on the Thomond side of the bridge.[47] Evidently this was a disturbed period in [64]
Thomond.

Teig died in 1259. His father Conor lived for another nine years, but 'he was filled', we are told, 'with despondency and no longer cared to play the king'. The consequence was that some of the subject clans, 'puffed up with increase of gear and goods, consequent on their not having been harried or preyed for a long time, omitted to send him his royal rent and lawful dues' and broke out in rebellion against him.[48] While endeavouring to subdue O'Loughlin's country in the Burren of Clare, Conor was slain with several members of his family by his cousin Dermot, son of Murtough O'Brien.[49] He was buried in the abbey-church of Corcumroe founded by his ancestors, and his sepulchral effigy is still pointed out in the beautiful transitional chancel there.[50] He resided at Clonroad (near Ennis), where he had built 'a permanent stronghold with earthworks,'[51] and near by on the banks of the Fergus, where the town of Ennis now stands, he is said to have founded the Franciscan Friary.[52]

Conor's son, Brian Roe, succeeded. He was given two cantreds of Corcumroe for a fine duly entered on the Pipe Roll, but probably never paid. In 1270 he turned against [65]
the English and took the castle of Clare near Ennis,[53] which belonged to John de Muscegros. Hostages were exacted from him in 1272 by James d'Audley, the justiciar,[54] and again in 1273 by Maurice Fitz Maurice, his successor, who led an army into Thomond and 'obtained sway over O'Brien'.[55]

And now with the advent of Thomas de Clare begins a new chapter in the history of Thomond. Descended from the senior line of the great house of Clare, Thomas was brother of Gilbert, Earl of Gloucester and Hertford, and grandson of the Earl Gilbert who married Isabel Marshal. He was thus, through his grandmother, fourth

is certainly not a good one; but it is to be noted (1) that the Irish annals do not mention Teig as one of those giving hostages, (2) that a subsequent meeting took place next year between O'Conor and O'Neill, and (3) that (though Teig himself was dead) the O'Briens did not join in the battle of Down (1260), the outcome of the confederacy. 45 Cal Docs. Irel., vol. ii, p. 429. Inq. P.M., 10 Ed. I, p. 437. 46 Cal. Docs. Ireland, vol. ii, no. 1622. 47 Cal. Docs. Ireland, vol. ii, p. 214. These lands were part of the cantred of the Ostmen, which had been given by King John as burgage land to the citizens of Limerick. 48 Caithréim, p. 5. 3 49 Ann. Loch Cé, 1268. 50 Journal R.S.A.I., vol. xxx (1900), p. 302. 51 *longport comnaide criad*: Caithréim (text), p. 4. Clonroad (*cluain ramfada*) is close to Ennis on the east, but no earthworks seem to have been noticed here. 52 Four Masters, 1247. The Caithréim (p. 32) in an extravagant passage ascribes its foundation to Turlough, son of Teig. For description see Journ. R.S.A.I., vol. xxv (1895), pp. 135–54. 53 Four Masters, 1270; *Clár atha dha charadh*: 'the plankbridge of the two weirs'. Hence the name of the County Clare. 54 Cal Docs. Irel., vol. ii, p. 148. 55 Ann. Loch Cé, 1273, and cf. Cal. Docs. Irel., vol. ii, p. 180 (payments to Maurice Fitz Maurice and John de Muscegros), and Pipe Roll, 1 Ed. I, 36th Rep. D.K., pp. 24, 25.

in descent from Strongbow. With his brother, the earl, he had rallied to the royal cause before the victory at Evesham, which was won largely by their aid, and Prince Edward, as *dominius Hiberniae*, had rewarded Thomas with a grant of the custody of the lands of Maurice Fitz Gerald, third baron of Offaly, who was drowned in the Irish Channel in 1268.[56] Thomas, being about to depart for the Holy Land with the prince, sold this custody for 3,500 marks to William de Valence, the king's half-brother.[57] He came to
[66] Ireland near the close of 1274, and was employed by the new king in a judicial capacity and as a commissioner in important positions of trust.[58] About this time he married Juliana, daughter and prospective heiress of Maurice Fitz Maurice, and thus allied himself to the Geraldines.[59]

On January 26, 1276, the king granted to Thomas de Clare the whole of the land of Thomond to hold in tail, with advowsons, wards, reliefs, and liberties, by the service of ten knights (reduced during Thomas's life to five), saving to the king his royalty and *crociae* (or episcopal and abbatial investitures), the four pleas of the Crown, and the fees of English knights.[60] The justiciar, Geoffrey de Geynville, was ordered to give Thomas the hostages of Thomond,[61] and as soon as the O'Tooles and O'Byrnes of Glenmalure were brought to the king's peace, Thomas was to have the general summons of the military services due to the king in Ireland, 'to pacify his land of Thomond'.[62] As far as lay with the king, Thomond was to be the liberty of Thomas de Clare, to hold as fully as the Earls Marshal had held their liberties, and by an arrangement with Robert de Muscegros, who was given lands in England in exchange, the castle of Bunratty, with the cantred of Tradry, and the *tuath* of Ocormok (about
[67] Clare Castle) were also granted to him, to hold of the king in chief.[63]

To give a connected account of the fortunes of the de Clares in Thomond we must in part rely on a tract called *Caithréim Toirdelbaig* or 'The Triumph of Turlough'. The original composition of this piece must at any rate be placed after 1364, as it refers to the death of Dermot, king of Thomond, who died in that year, while the earliest existing manuscript—a fragment—is dated 1509.[64] It is professedly the work of John, son

56 This Maurice Fitz Gerald was grandson, in the senior line, of Maurice Fitz Gerald, the justiciar, who died in 1257. His widow was Agnes de Valence, the king's cousin. See my paper on 'The Fitz Glerelds, Barons of Offaly': Journal R.S.A.I., vol. xlix (1914), pp. 105–9. 57 Cal. Docs. Irel., vol. ii, nos. 867, 957, 970, 1039. 58 Cal. Docs. Irel., nos. 1059, 1091, 1185, 1163. 59 He was married before February 18, 1275, when he was given by his father-in-law the manor of Inchiquin and the vill of Youghal in special tail; ibid., vol. iii, p. 498. 60 Ibid., vol. ii, no. 1194. In the following July Thomas was given power to enfeoff knights and others in Thomond; ibid., no. 1261. 61 Ibid., vol. ii, no. 1197. Among the hostages was Donough, the king's son and future king: ibid., p. 239. 62 Ibid., nos. 1191, 1476. He does not seem to have got the service until 1281. 63 Cal. Docs. Irel., nos. 1167, 1202–4, 1223–4. Bunratty was delivered to Thomas de Clare on April 26, 1276; 36th Rep. D.K., p. 32. It was at the moment seemingly of small value. The receipts in the hands of the Escheator for the preceding nine months were only £7 3*s*. 4*d*. 64 The earliest MS. is that in the Royal Irish Academy marked $\overline{Q}\,\frac{23}{16}$. It was written in 1509, but is unfortunately very imperfect. It contains thirty-three leaves. The best late text (modernized) is by Andrew Mac Cruitin, made in 1721 for a deseendant of the MacNamaras (H.1, 18, T.C.D). He supposed that the original was written in 1459, as appeared 'at the 19th folio of the same very old book' from which he worked, but it seems probable that he was misled by the exemplar before him, and that the original was composed nearly a century earlier. There are several other copies. Through the courtesy of Sir Norman Moore I have been

of Rory Magrath. The Magraths were hereditary poets or historians in Thomond, but this particular Magrath has not been identified with certainty.[65] But besides not being [68]
a strictly contemporary composition, the work is stamped throughout as a partizan eulogy of one of the O'Brien factions, and a 'hymn of hate' against the foreigners, and in particular against the de Clares, who were guilty of supporting the rival faction. The dates supplied in the existing manuscripts, generally by a later hand, are often quite wrong, and the distortion of some episodes and the omission of others can be proved. Nevertheless, the work is full of verifiable topographical details, showing the writer's intimate acquaintance with Thomond. He refers to the annals of Clan Cuilean's accomplished bard, and quotes poems of local shanachies contemporary with events from 1259 to as late as 1318. Moreover, the broad outline of the story as regards the de Clares can in general be corroborated from authentic sources, while there is no reason to doubt the turmoil it discloses among the Irish chieftains themselves. Occasional side-lights on the manners and sentiments and methods of warfare of the Irish are particularly valuable, as they, at any rate, were not set down in malice. Used with caution, the tract often throws light on what would otherwise be obscure or unknown. It is written in a turgid style overladen with numerous compound epithets. In Mr. O'Grady's spirited rendering this defect is to a large extent concealed—generally by the simple device of omission.

It appears from the Caithréim that about the time of the grant to Thomas de Clare Thomond was in a state of anarchy. After Brian Roe had reigned successfully for nine years, the Mac Namaras and O'Deas revolted against him, drove him into exile, and set up as king his nephew Turlough, son of Teig of Caoluisce. From this time for very many years the O'Briens were divided into two factions, which came to be known as [69]
Clan Brian (Roe) and Clan Turlough (Mor) respectively. With the advice of those who remained faithful to him, Brian sought aid from Brian Thomas de Clare, 'then residing in Cork and claiming authority over the English of Munster',[66] and promised him all the land between Athsollus[67] and Limerick (i.e. the present barony of Bunratty Lower) in consideration of his assistance. Thus was confirmed, in part at least, by the Irish chieftain the grant of the English king, but, as often happened elsewhere, though the legitimate Gaelic chieftain might be willing to make a peaceful accommodation with the Norman baron, some of the *urrighs* and subordinate clans would always be ready to support a rival to the chieftainship who showed fight.

In pursuance of the agreement, Thomas de Clare aided Brian to recover Clonroad and Quin, while Turlough fled to Connaught for assistance. According to the Caithréim, Thomas then 'built at Bunratty a castle of dressed stone, girt with thick outer wall, containing a roofed impregnable donjon, and having capacious white-lined

enabled to use the text as edited and rendered by Standish Hayes O'Grady, which, it is hoped, will soon see the light. 65 A Rory Magrath, the poet (*in file*), is mentioned in the text (p. 120), as directing the burial of those who fell in the battle of Corcumroe in 1317. He was probably the Rory Mag Craith, *ollamh* of Leth Mogha, who died in 1343, and may have been the author's father (Four Masters). But as many members of this family are mentioned as poets or historians in Thomond, the inference is uncertain. 66 Caithréim, p. 6. Thomas de Clare was sheriff of Limerick, seemingly at this time; 36th Rep. D.K., p. 39. 67 *Athsolais*, now Ardsollus, is on the extreme north of the barony of Bunratty Lower, about a mile S.W. of Quin.

appurtenances'. Afterwards he strengthened the castle and precincts with a broad-based, high-crested rampart, with ditch running from the stream (the Raite river, now Owenogarney, near its mouth) to the sea (the Shannon estuary).

Turlough soon obtained assistance from the Turlough O'Maddens and O'Kellys of
[70] Connaught, and from some of the de Burghs,[68] who were jealous of the Fitz Geralds and their new powerful ally. He then, in 1277, re-entered Thomond, and joined by the Mac Namaras and O'Deas, defeated King Brian in a battle in which amongst others 'Patrick Mac Maurice', described as 'son and heir of Mac Maurice of Kerry and own brother of De Clare's wife', was slain.[69] Unfortunately the description is inconsistent with itself, and this error shakes our faith in the accuracy of this, the only detailed, account of the episode. If Patrick Fitz Maurice was brother of Juliana, wife of Thomas de Clare, he was son of Maurice Fitz Maurice of the Offaly line, and only distantly related to the Fitz Maurices of Kerry. However that may have been, Brian fled to Bunratty. Here, we are told, when Thomas de Clare had positive news of his people's great losses,[70] frenzy and rage possessed him ... The whole fortress rang with the women's cries of woe, Thomas's wife exclaiming 'that through O'Brien she had lost her good brother, and that never would God's blessing rest on any place where he should be'. All this so maddened Thomas, that 'to satisfy his wife and Fitz Maurice'
[71] [her father], who was in the house, he rashly and of evil motion caused O'Brien to be hanged on the spot.[71]

This deed—seemingly motiveless,[72] the result of blind fury—was given a prominent place in the indictment drawn up on behalf of Donnell O'Neill and other Irish chiefs against the English, and sent to Pope John XXII in 1318, but it cannot have been regarded at the time in Thomond as an unpardonable offence, as within a year Donough O'Brien, son of the murdered Brian Roe and successor to his claims, renewed the alliance with Thomas de Clare. According to the Caithréim, Thomas sent a message to Donough expressing regret at the death of Brian, and offering 'as an eric' to assist Donough in his efforts to recover his father's throne. Donough accepted the offer, and Turlough once more fled before the allied forces.[73] He returned, however, as soon as he had collected his supporters, and the fighting went on between the rival kinsmen.

68 Earl Walter and Maurice Fitz Maurice had a quarrel in 1264, and possibly bitterness between the families survived in 1277, when Earl Richard was a minor and William 'the Grey' was the chief power in Connaught. 69 Caithréim, p. 9: 'Patraic Mag Muiris i. mac agus oigre Meg Muiris chiarraide, agus ba derbráthair do mnái in Chláraig in degdamna sín.' Patrick Fitz Maurice is not mentioned in the Red Book of the Earl of Kildare, nor anywhere else so far as I am aware. He may, possibly, have been an unnoticed son of Maurice Fitz Maurice, in which case the only error would be in describing the latter as of Kerry. 70 It would seem from this that Thomas de Clare was not present at the fight. He was with the justiciar, Robert d'Ufford, at Glenmalure in 1277, before Michaelmas: Cal. Docs. Irel., vol. ii, p. 267. 71 Caithréim, p. 10. In the Annals of Loch Cé, 1277, it is stated that Brian 'was apprehended in treachery by the son of the earl of Clare, after they had poured their blood into the same vessel, and after they had formed gossipred, and after they had exchanged mutual vows by the relics, bells, and croziers of Munster, and he [Brian] was afterwards drawn between steeds by the earl's son'. 72 Maurice Fitz Maurice may have had a grudge against Brian Roe for the burning of the towns of Ardrahan and Kilcolgan in 1258. 73 Caithréim, pp. 10–11. This was probably early in 1278. On July 29 of that year the king repeated the order

The savage character of the warfare may be illustrated from an incident described [72] at length in the Caithréim. Turlough and his brother Donnell surprised Mahon O'Brien and the O'Gradys, faithful supporters of Clan Brian, at Clare Abbey, and put them to flight. Turlough followed in pursuit, while his brother Donnell, being unopposed, rounded up the cattle of the O'Gradys, 'and having taken so many as they got of their men, their fair-haired women, their little boys and other members of their families, their servants, kerne, horseboys, and herdsmen, they made of them one universal litter of slaughter, a deed which shall long live as "the Carnage of Clare".' When Thomas de Clare came up to stay the marauders, Donnell, before retiring, 'bade bring the prisoners and cattle out upon *Móin na sead* (the heifers' moor) and indiscriminately massacre them, thus providing that when he abandoned them, the enemy, on finding them in his hands, should not have any great cause of self-gratulation'.[74]

Desultory fighting between the rival kings seems to have ensued at frequent intervals until 1280 or 1281, when, we are told, Donnell Roe Mac Carthy, king of Desmond, induced Turlough to consent to a partition of Thomond with Donough, and this compromise was afterwards confirmed by the young Earl of Ulster, 'a very Conn for wisdom', who intervened and ordered that four hostages be given to Thomas de Clare—thus recognizing his supremacy in Thomond and his position as guardian of the peace—and that one half of the country be restored to Turlough.[75] As about this time, early in 1281, a feudal force was led by Robert d'Ufford, the justiciar, and Theobald Butler against 'the disturbers of the king's peace in Thomond',[76] we may infer that the [73] settlement was really the result of the intervention of the government. A brief interval of peace followed, and Thomas de Clare set about building the great castle of Quin[77] to defend his northern border. According to the Caithréim, while this work was going on, Donnell O'Brien, Turlough's brother, the hero of the 'Carnage of Clare', was treacherously slain by one of the workmen engaged in the building. In November 1282, the king specially commended Thomas de Clare for his diligence in preserving the peace of Ireland, and promised that when Thomas should come to the king in England he would favour the matters which Thomas desired to promote. He also approved of his retaining Thomas Fitz Maurice (of Desmond) to resist those who infringed the peace.[78]

But neither king of England, chieftain of Desmond, earl of Ulster, nor lord of Bunratty, could keep the O'Brien factions from flying at each other's throats. The struggle between the 'half-kings' soon broke out again. At first, according to the Caithréim, Thomas de Clare 'patched up a hollow peace' between the combatants, and

for Thomas de Clare to have a general summons of the military tenants to bring peace to his land of Thomond, but it appears that he did not get it until 1281; Cal. Docs. Irel., vol. ii, no. 1476, and p. 410. Thomas de Clare was in England for some time prior to November 16, 1278, when he was about to return to Ireland; ihid., no. 1508. 74 Caithréim, pp. 13, 14. 75 Ibid., pp 18, 19. 76 Cal. Does. Ireland, vol. ii, pp. 393, 400, 410. This was the first time that Thomas de Clare obtained the assistance of the military services due to the king. The expedition took place in a. r. 9 before St. John the Baptist's Day. Theobald Butler was allowed £128 16*s*. 2*d*. for his expenses. The cost was partly recouped by the sale of 340 cows, the prey of Thomond: 36th Rep. D.K., p. 53. 77 For this castle see Appendix. 78 Cal. Docs. Ireland, vol. ii, no. 2005. In February 1284, seisin was ordered to be given to Thomas Fitz Maurice of the cantred of Ogashin and the half-cantred of Omulloid, which had belonged to his grandfather: ibid., no. 2175.

[74] fixed a boundary line between their shares.[79] This was probably in 1283, shortly before November, when Thomas went to England with the expectation of remaining there for three years.[80] But Turlough was not satisfied with his 'half-kingship', and at last in 1284, while Thomas Donough was apparently still in England, he treacherously killed Donough at a conference on the banks of the Fergus.[81]

It may have been this event, or the ravaging of Tradry that followed, which brought Thomas de Clare back to Ireland in October, but there is no indication, either in the Caithréim or elsewhere, that he opposed Turlough or supported a rival in Donough's place. On the contrary, to this time should probably be assigned the arrangement in existence at Thomas de Clare's death, when Turlough O'Brien held seven cantreds and sixteen vills in Thomond, subject to a rent of £121 11*s*., and was the only Irish king recognized there.[82] As long as Thomas lived there seems to have been little further disturbance in Thomond. He is not mentioned in the Caithréim elsewhere as taking any part in affairs there after 1283, when he 'patched up the hollow peace' and went to England. On August 16, 1285, he was named with the justiciar, the Arch-
[75] bishop of Dublin, and Geoffrey de Geynvill, on an important commission to deal with the king s waste land in Connaught.[83] He was again named on a commission in Cork in April 1286,[84] and we do not hear of him again until his death—apparently from natural causes on August 29, 1287.

I have stated the few facts known about Thomas de Clare and his movements in these last few years with particularity, because they have been misstated, and baseless inferences as to his actions and motives have been founded on the misstatements. He has, indeed, been represented as the prime instigator of all the civil strife in Thomond since 1276—a strife said to have culminated in his defeat and death in battle at the hands of Turlough.[85] But a sober judgement, based on a critical review of the authorities to which I have referred, and the conditions of the case, will, I think, show that the efforts of Thomas de Clare were repeatedly directed towards any settlement between the rival factions which promised peace in Thomond, and a peace which was, indeed, essential to his interest—while the sole authority for his defeat and death in battle is an entry in the slovenly compilation known as the Dublin continuation of the Annals of Inisfallen, compiled in the latter half of the eighteenth century—an entry,
[76] as shown in the appendix to this chapter, certainly incorrect on some points and not borne out—nay, virtually inconsistent with—the source from which it was evidently derived.

At the death of Thomas de Clare, Bunratty was a considerable town with 226 bur-

79 Caithréim, p. 20. 80 Thomas de Clare went to England before November 8, 1283, when he appointed attorneys to act for him in Ireland for three years, and his letters of protection were for the same period: Cal. Patent Rolls, 11 Ed. I, p. 86. He seems to have remained in England until after October 2,1284, when he was about by the king's licence to depart for Ireland: ibid., 12 Ed. I, p. 134. 81 Caithréim, p. 24. Ann. Loch Cé, Ann. Clonmacnois, 1284. 82 Cal. Docs. Ireland, vol. iii, p. 208. 83 Cal. Patent Rolls, 13 Ed. I, p. 188. In Cal. Docs. Ireland, vol. iii, no. 135, 'Thomas de Clare' seems to be an error for 'Nicholas de Clere': see Cal. Patent Rolls, as above. 84 Cal. Docs. Irel., vol. iii, no. 206. 85 See Mr. Westropp's account of the events from 1283 onwards, Journal R.S.A.I., vol. xxi (1890–l),pp 291–2, and Transactions R.I.A., vol. xxxii, pp. 175–7. Reference to the documents on which he relies will show how he misconceives them.

gages.[86] The lands of the manor, which seem to have comprised nearly all the present barony of Bunratty Lower, were mostly let to free tenants or held by military service. Turlough O'Brien held seven cantreds and six vills in Thomond at a rent of £121 11*s*. Six vills at Quin and a few others were waste.

The total income was £171 4*s*. 6*d*., not counting the value of advowsons and knights' services. Besides Bunratty, Thomas de Clare held (amongst others) the important manor of Inchiquin, including the vill of Youghal, in County Cork, and the manors of Knockainy and Mahoonagh, in County Limerick.[87] His heir was his son Gilbert, then in his seventh year.[88] His widow Juliana, daughter and one of the heirs of Maurice Fitz Maurice, soon afterwards married Adam de Creting, to whom the lands of Bunratty were committed in wardship. After Adam's death, from December 1295 to April 1299, the manor (including Juliana's dower) yielded £613, of which Turlough's rent amounted to £3374 13*s*. 6*d*.[89] This account does not show much falling off in value, notwithstanding that it embraced the period of the siege of Bunratty to be [77]
mentioned by and by.

Meantime, apparently in the autumn of 1287, and probably after the death of Thomas de Clare, who is not mentioned,[90] Turlough passed in a desolating raid through the Butler territory of Owney and Ormond and the eastern extremity of County Limerick. The writer of the Caithréim in language of bitter irony exults over the destructive work. At Caherconlish, for example, where from the commencement of the century there was a castle of the Butlers,[91] the foreigners, we are told, advanced to meet the invading host. But their efforts were vain, 'for first they were soundly gashed in the fray, then for their hurts presently after had the actual cautery, a severe remedy which nevertheless yielded scant relief, seeing that it was furnished by a raging fire which greeted them at their return, and from bawn to bridge very soon wrapped the entire fortress ... And a grand exploit it was for them [the Irish] that out of the gloomy pile in which for scores of years before the tongue-tied strangers[92] had unmolested dwelt, they now had fashioned (as it were) ladies' lightsome bowers, radiant with brave ornament of red'.[93] And so of many a prosperous settlement in Ely and Ormond.[94] [78]

This raid was mainly directed against the lands of Theobald Butler, then in the king's custody, and it may be regarded as in revenge for the expedition made by

86 The burgages in Bunratty seem to have been rather more numerous than those in Youghal, and nearly equal to those oceupied in Wexford in 1307 (Inquisition P.M., Joan de Valence). Mr. Westropp's summary of the De Clare inquisition, by an unfortunate slip, states that 'the burgesses of Bunratty held no burgages': Trans. R.I.A., vol. xxxii (c), p. 193. 87 Cal. Inq. P.M., 16 Ed. I, no. 696; Cal. Docs. Irel., vol. iii, no. 459. 88 Ibid., vol. iv, no. 819. Gilbert was born on February 3, 1281. 89 Cal. Pipe Roll, 26 Ed. I, 38th Rep. D.K., p. 39. 90 The precise date of this raid is hard to fix. The outside limits are the death of Theobald Butler IV, in September 1285, and the death of the justiciar, Stephen de Fulburne, on July 3, 1288. The references to it in the records seem to point to the autumn of 1287 or the winter of 1287–8; see below. The Caithréim gives the date 1304, which is manifestly wrong. 91 For the lands of Theobald Butler IV, see Pipe Boll (Ireland), 16 Ed. I, 37th Rep. D.K., p. 35, and cf. Rot. Pat., 16 John, p. 120 b. 92 *Balbh-gaill*: dumb or stammering foreigners, so called because they 'had little Irish'. 93 Caithréim, p. 25. In his account from Easter 1287 to Easter 1289 the Escheator takes credit (inter alia) for expeniditure on the wooden tower at Carkenlys (Caherconlish): 37th Rep. D.K., p. 36. 94 The places specifically mentioned in the Caithréim are *Inis Amblaoibh* (?), *Fiadh Mogháin* (?) or *Tiadh Mogain* (Timoney (?) in Iker-

Theobald into Thomond in 1281, and as an attempt to recover the old extended kingdom of Donnell Mor O'Brien. To check or punish the raiders, Stephen de Fulburne, the justiciar, led a force, which seems to have mustered at Cashel, against Turlough.[95] We do not hear of any fighting, but there was a parley at Limerick, and Turlough was subjected to a fine of 600 marks for having peace for himself and his retainers, for which he delivered four hostages.[96] According to the Caithréim, indeed, Turlough was
[79] only persuaded to desist from his enterprise by the Earl of Ulster (who very probably was present at the parley in Limerick), and were it not for this, Tullough 'for a surety had been all Ireland's king'. So at least a fairy maiden, 'the Sovereignty of Erin', proclaimed to Turlough, while prophesying, 'woe to him who has robbed me of my gentle lover, of Turlough, man of dreadful prowess'.[97]

Turlough, now undisputed king of Thomond and enjoying the favour of the great Earl of Ulster, was more powerful than ever, but he seems in general not to have interfered with the English. Only on two occasions during the rest of Turlough's reign do we hear of the collisions between the Irish and English of Thomond. About 1290, in consequence of a fracas at 'the round-towered stone-substantial town of Quin', in which two of the O'Liddys were killed, Cumea Mac Conmara attacked the castle: 'its ditch was crossed, earthworks carried, great gate battered in; its strong walls were breached, its English stammerers captured . . . and in the actual great castle a huge pile of stuff was given to the flames that ran riot till the whole became a black-vaulted
[80] hideous cavern'.[98] Again early in 1298, for some unexplained reason, Turlough besieged the castle of Bunratty, then in the king's hand. The siege lasted for five weeks, when the castle was relieved by expeditions from Limerick by land and water under John Wogan, justiciar.[99]

rin), *Magh n-Ailbh* (Moyaliff in Kilnamanagh), *Bealach Acaille* (Ballykelly (?) near Timoney), *Leitrach Odhran* (Latteragh, in Upper Ormond), and *Ceallmore Araidh* (Kilmore (?) south of Nenagh). 95 See Cal. Docs. Irel., vol. iii, p. 251, Petition of Robert de Callan (1289). The muster seems to have been at Cashel: 37th Rep. D.I., pp. 24, 27. In November 1290, the abbot of Wetheny (founded by the first Theobald Walter, *tempore* Richard I) was fined 60 marks for harbouring the Irish of Thomond: Cal. Docs. Irel., vol. iii, no. 802. 96 Pipe Roll (Ireland), 16 Ed. I, 37th Rep. D.K., pp. 33, 37. One of the hostages appears to have been Turlough's eldest son Donough, afterwards his successor. On August 6, 1290, the king commanded that the custody of the eldest son and heir of Turlough should be delivered to the Earl of Ulster; Cal. Docs. Irel., vol. iii, no. 756; and for a further fine Donough was soon afterwards delivered to Turlough: Pipe Roll, 20 Ed. I (as above), p. 51. 97 Caithréim, p. 28. The symbolism of a wedding with the sovereignty of Ireland is very old. See Rhys, Celtic Heathendom, pp. 414–16, where the term *Lug-nassad* is explained as Lug's wedding. So in Ann. Loch Cé, vol. i, p. 474, Aedh Mac Cathail is said to have been 'a husband to Cruachan'. 98 Caithréim, p. 30. The burning of Quin Castle took place before September 1292 (Cal. Docs. Irel., vol. iii, p. 498), and probably in the year ending Easter 1291, when the Escheator's account mentions journeys to treat with Turlough and the Irish of Thomond: 37th Rep. D.K., p. 42. Whatever damage was done to the castle at this time seems to have been repaired, as in the inquisition taken in 1321 after the death of Thomas, son and heir of Richard de Clare, it is stated that the 'Castle of Quin was thrown down during the lifetime of the said heir', who was a minor at his death. Moreover the Escheator's account for the three years ending Easter 1299, includes payments for the custody of the castles of Bunratty and Quin: 38th Rep. D.K., p. 42. 99 The siege of Bunratty lasted from January 27, 1298, to March 3 following: 38th Rep. D.K., p. 42. The sum of £117 17*s.* 7½*d.* was expended on this expedition: ibid., p. 45, and Cal. Docs. Irel., vol. iv, no. 521. The Caithréim represents the siege of Bunratty as separated only by a brief interval from the burning of Quin, and states that Turlough forebore to take the

Turlough died in 1307, and was succeeded by his son Donough.[1] In an extravagant passage, overladen with epithets, Magrath states that Turlough raised three goodly structures: the regal edifice of his hospitality, i.e. the palace of Clonroad, the Franciscan Monastery at Ennis, and 'Heaven's own refulgent holy mansion that he won'.[2]

In 1307, according to the dates supplied in the Caithréim, but possibly a year or two later, war broke out between the clan-groups in Thomond. It originated in the lawless conduct of the Mac Conmaras, who not only killed one of the Earl of Ulster's constables—an act which might have been overlooked in Thomond—but pillaged the termon-lands of Moynoe, and thus brought upon themselves the hostility of their old enemies, the Ui Bloid, by whom the church was venerated.[3] To follow all the details of [81] the conflict, known to us only through the Caithréim, would be unprofitable. At first Clancullen got the best of it, but a formidable confederation of 'all who nourished a spite against Donough Mac Conmara', chief of the clan, including a disappointed aspirant to that position, rose up against them. In the result Clancullen, divided against itself, was beaten, and its chief treacherously slain by some of his own men.[4] Early in 1311 King Donough assisted by the de Burghs, entered the scene and defeated the confederates, who now included the shattered remnants of Clancullen and were led by Dermot, son of Donough, son of Brian Roe, representative of Clan Brian. Thereupon Richard de Clare, who had succeeded his brother Gilbert in 1308, came to the aid of Clan Brian, and with them and 'the two divisions of Clancullen' harried the territory of the supporters of King Donough.[5] Thus what was at first a conflict between local clans became virtually a war between the two O'Brien factions, in which each side was supported by a great Anglo-Norman house.

About May 7, 1311,the King of England ordered Edmund Butler and others to [82] prohibit Richard de Clare and Donough O'Brien, 'who calls himself king of the Irish of Thomond', from continuing to wage war against each other.[6] But before this order could be carried out the de Burghs in company with King Donough invaded Tradry, and on May 20 William de Burgh and Richard de Clare came into actual conflict near Bunratty. Richard was driven back on his castle, but William de Burgh was taken prisoner, and then King Donough fled.[7] In the same year King Donough was slain near

castle only in consequence of the counsel of the Earl of Ulster. 1 Ann. Loch Cé, 1306. 2 Caithréim, p. 32. 3 Ibid., p. 35. The name *Ui m-Bloid* (pronounced with the eclipsing *m*) is preserved in the deanery of 'Omúlloid' in the East of Co. Clare. Belonging to the tribe were the O'Kennedys, the O'Shanahans, the O'Aherns, and others. They seem to have consistently supported Clan Brian, and were in general friendly to the de Clares. 4 Caithréim. 5 Ibid., pp. 43, 44. Cf. the Irish annals, 1311. The Caithréim slurs over, while admitting, the defection of Clancullen from King Donough, but the Irish annals, which lump together events separately described in the Caithréim, state it quite plainly. Maccon and Sheeda MacConmara, brothers of the late chief Donough, were, however, not happy in the new alliance and retired to the rugged region of Slieve Aughty; but Loughlin (another brother) and Donnell 'Mac mic Chon', who seem to have been chiefs respectively of the two divisions of Clancullen, with the mass of the clansmen continued to support Clan Brian. 6 Cal. Pat. Roll (Ireland), 3 and 4 Ed. II, p. 17 (84). Though the mandate is undated, the position on the roll shows that it belongs to May 1311, not 1309, as stated by Mr. Westropp in Journal R.S.A.I., 1890–1, p. 383, nor 1310 as stated by the same writer in Trans. R.I.A., vol. xxxii (c), p. 179. 7 Irish annals; Caithréim, p. 44. There should be no doubt about this precise date, May 20, 1311. All the Irish annals and the Laud MS. annals place the battle in 1311, the latter giving the day,

Corcumroe by the treachery of some of his own men,[8] and the war for the moment was ended.

Richard de Clare now succeeded in getting all the clans 'to unite together for concord', and Dermot Dermot of Clan Brian was chosen sole chief by acclamation, and duly proclaimed 'O'Brien' by Loughlin Mac Conmara at the inauguration mound of
[83] Moy-Ar.[9] But in the following autumn Sir William de Burgh, with the assent of the earl, again interfered and destroyed the fair prospect. Entering Thomond in great strength the de Burghs defeated Dermot, who had to take refuge at Bunratty, and set up Murtough of Clan Turlough, brother of the late King Donough, as chief.[10] Murtough, however, found little support in Thomond, except from the Mac Conmaras under Loughlin, who now rejoined Clan Turlough, and he was soon driven out by Richard de Clare.

We may pause here for the moment to inquire into the motives which induced the pursue the apparently suicidal policy of weakening a neighbouring baron in face of 'the Irish enemy'. But in the first place it must be observed that the O'Briens had nearly always been friendly to the de Burghs. The first William de Burgh had married a daughter of Donnell Mor O'Brien,[11] and Donough Cairbrech, son of Donnell Mor, had consistently aided Richard de Burgh in the conquest of Connaught. William *Liath* de Burgh is said to have married Finola, daughter of Brian Roe O'Brien, and Edmund, one of Earl Richard's sons, married Sláine, daughter of Turlough O'Brien and sister of Murtough, the chief opponent of Richard de Clare.[12] Then it seems probable that
[84] Thomas de Clare, through his Geraldine wife, incurred some of the enmity which existed between the de Burghs and the Fitz Geralds, and which from time to time broke out into open violence. But apart from these personal grounds of antagonism, there were other motives which led the de Burghs to interfere. Thomond lay like a wedge between their lands in County Limerick and those in County Galway, and from their point of view it was desirable that the kings of Thomond should be under their influence. This object was most readily maintained by favouring Clan Turlough as against de Clare's proteges of Clan Brian. Nevertheless it was a narrow and short-sighted point of view, and the attitude of the de Burghs is an example of that want of solidarity among the English settlers which was a contributory cause of the subsequent failure of England for nearly three centuries to maintain the position that had been won in Ireland.

A guerrilla warfare ensued between the rival factions. The de Burghs gave shelter to Murtough and his men in Maenmagh, and from this base the Mac Conmaras made raids into Thomond, while they confined their chief prisoners in the earl's castle at

'tertio decimo Kal. Iunii', i.e. May 20. Clyn gives the wrong year, 1310, but adds 'in die Ascensionis', which in 1311 (but not in 1310) fell on May 20. About June or before July 8, 1311, the king issued a further mandate relating to the discord between William de Burgh and Richard de Clare, but the actual order is illegible: Cal. Pat. Roll (Ireland), 3 and 4 Ed. II, p. 17b (92). 8 Ann. Loch Cé, &c., 1311, Caithréim, p. 46. He was slain by Murrough, son of Mahon O'Brien. 9 Caithréim, p. 47. 10 Ibid., p. 48. This Dermot is called *Diarmaid cleirech*, or 'the cleric', in Ann. Loch Cé, 1311. He seems to have been son of Donough, son of Brian Roe. He died in 1313. 11 *Ante*, vol. ii, p. 148 [p. 210]. 12 For the marriage of Sir William

Loughrea.[13] At last a conference was held between the earl and Richard de Clare, and a partition of Thomond between the O'Briens was arranged.[14] But nothing could keep the Mac Conmaras and Ui Bloid carrying on the feud by any means, fair or foul, when either party had the other in his power, and by All Hallows the chiefs were at war [85]
again. Early in 1313 King Dermot died.[15] But the struggle was carried on between his cousin, Donough of Clan Brian,[16] and Murtough of Clan Turlough.

In 1314 a partition of Thomond was made between Murtough and Donough on terms favourable to Murtough, and Richard de Clare (like his father in 1283), 'seeing the country as it were patched up', sailed for England. But no sooner had he gone than Clan Turlough broke the pact and made the rent in the country worse than ever.[17] Murtough got assistance from William de Burgh, Thomas le Botiller, and the Comyns, as well as from the O'Kellys and O'Maddens, and endeavoured to obtain the forcible submission of the clans that owed allegiance to his rival. His methods were no less barbarous than those of Turlough in his struggle with Donough, son of Brian Roe. The following example recalls 'the Carnage of Clare'. Clancullen (the Mac Conmaras), having routed Cinel Donnaly (the O'Gradys), came upon a stockaded enclosure in a forest where the latter had placed the cattle for safety. 'Clancullen', we are told, 'in the late rout had failed to have all their appetite of the runaways to slaughter them; now therefore they stormed the strong boolies of the Cinel Donnaly, and on that clan did grievous killing that played havoc with them: women and boys and whole families included; whereby that murderous far-secluded area became a mere heap of carnage thickly-stacked. There in abundance they had young men lying on their faces, women [86]
in lamentation, kine that bellowed deafeningly; and by this red raid Clancullen effectually relieved Cinel Donnaly of all care in respect of their cattle and young people.'[18]

On the return of Richard de Clare later in the year, Clan Brian with his assistance once more expelled Murtough, who 'remained with the earl in the fringe of Connaught'. Early in 1315 William de Burgh granted Murtough a hosting to win the country for him, but the levies before reaching Thomond were recalled,[19] evidently because they were wanted for greater issues elsewhere. Meanwhile throughout 'the dark-visaged winter' (1314–15) Clancullen was in danger of being overwhelmed by Clan Brian. Accordingly in the early spring they made a pretended submission to King Donough and gave him hostages.

But now, as a result of the general upheaval in Ireland caused by the invasion of Edward Bruce, there was brought about a regrouping of the clans in Thomond and a shifting of alliances. In particular Richard de Clare turned against Clan Brian and gave

Liath see Register of the Abbey of Athenry, Add. MS. 4784, Brit. Mus. It ia rather remarkable that both these ladies seem to have married Turlough O'Conor, king of Connaught, after the deaths of their respective de Burgh husbands: Ann Loch Cé, 1335,1339. In order to marry Sláine (who was his aunt, Ann. Ulst., 1343) Turlough put away his existing wife, daughter of Aedh O'Donnell. 13 Caithréim, p. 50. Loughrea was in the middle of the cantred of Maenmagh, which had been thoroughly colonized by the de Burghs, and it was with them, and not with the O'Kellys, as supposed by O'Grady, that Murtough took refuge. 14 Ibid., p. 5. 15 Ibid., p. 55, Ann. Loch Cé, 1313. 16 He was son of Donnell, son of Brian Roe. Caithréim, p. 70, and cf. Ann. Inisfallen (Bodleian), quoted by Mr. Westropp: Transactions R.I.A., vol., xxxii (c), p. 184. 17 Caithréim, p. 70. 18 Caithréim, p. 71. Note the characteristic irony. 19 Ibid., p. 75.

his support to his former enemy Murtough. The author of the Caithréim does not explain the cause of this change of policy, but the facts he states, coupled with what we otherwise know, make it plain enough. In the spring of 1315, Richard, we are told, 'ordered a hosting for distant service in the land of Leinster to destroy it'.[20] Thus does the author of the Caithréim refer to the response of Richard de Clare to the summons of the feudal host of Leinster and Munster by the justiciar, Edmund Butler, to resist
[87] the invasion of the Scots. Clan Brian, however, 'unanimously voted rather to make war on the English (settlers) and their domains'. These confederates, we are told, 'turned to generalize the war, to make their doings illustrious and furnish people with somewhat to say about them', that is to say, they were preparing to take advantage of the Scottish invasion to join in a general rising for the extermination of the English in Ireland.

As will be seen when we come to tell in detail the story of Edward Bruce's invasion, the forces under the justiciar were not employed immediately against the Scots in Ulster. That task was left to the Earl of Ulster, whose forces were routed at Connor in County Antrim on September 10, while the army under Edmund Butler, with whom was Richard de Clare, appears to have been engaged in suppressing risings in the marches of Leinster.[21]

When Richard de Clare returned to Thomond he found Clan Brian apparently supreme in that territory, but the clans were seething with plots and counter-plots. Murtough, perhaps at this moment, was in Connaught, where he met the defeated earl,[22] but could get no help in that quarter. For in Connaught, too, at the instigation of Edward Bruce, the war for the expulsion of the English was in full swing. Felim
[88] O'Conor, who was still friendly with the earl, had been dispossessed, and his successful rival of the house of Rory, under the instigation of Edward Bruce, had burned the English towns and many of their castles from Sligo to Athlone. De Clare now finally threw over Clan Brian as being in league with the Scots and supported Murtough, who either from opposition to Donough or through the persuasion of the earl was ready to oppose them. First de Clare secured the adhesion of the Mac Conmaras by granting to their chief a charter of Ogashin.[23] Afterwards in company with Murtough and the Mac Conmaras he subdued the O'Shanahans, obtained the submission of the O'Deas, and eventually drove Donough into Connaught, where he found refuge with Teig O'Kelly.[24]

When we come to describe events in Ireland connected with the invasion of Edward Bruce, we shall tell how Felim O'Conor, early in 1316, with the help of the barons of Connaught, overcame his rival in battle, and how he then turned against his

20 Ibid., p. 76. **21** There are allusions to this army in Pipe Roll (Ireland), 9 Ed. II, 39th Rep. D.K., p. 70, &c. According to a Memorandum Roll of the Exchequer, cited by Mr. Westropp (Trans. R.I.A., vol. xxxii (c), p. 185), Richard de Clare was given 100 marks for his services against the rebels in the marches of Leinster in 1315. He was again thanked and rewarded on May 16, 1316: Cal. Pat. Roll, 9 Ed. II, p. 459. **22** Ann. Loch Cé, vol. i, p. 571 (1315). **23** Caithréim, p. 77. **24** Ibid., pp. 79–82. These events took place (presumably) after February 1316, when Edward Bruce returned to Ulster from his winter raid in Meath and Leinster, and (certainly) before August 10, 1316, when Donough O'Brien and Teig O'Kelly shared the defeat of Felim O'Conor at Athenry and when Teig was among the slain.

allies and formed a confederacy, including Donough O'Brien and Teig O'Kelly, to expel the English from Connaught, but was defeated and killed in the following August at the bloody battle of Athenry. More fortunate than most, Donough escaped from this battle, and, according to the Caithréim, went to Ulster to solicit aid from the Scottish invaders. And now in March 1317 'the overwhelming wave ... of close-packed Scots' were entering Munster, and 'clan Brian Roe closely accompanying the King of [89] Scotland and Edward Bruce his brother on that hosting'... 'for yonder in Ulster Donough, son of Donnell, son of Brian Roe had been with the Scots intreating them that they would come on this progress.'[25] By the end of the month the Scots had reached Castleconnel, and the feudal host, under Edmund Butler, Richard de Clare, the Earl of Kildare, and others, which had been hanging on their rear, was at Ludden[26] near Caherconlish, about eight miles to the south. There was some skirmishing, but no important fighting. Richard de Clare and Murtough O'Brien had Thomond well in hand, and consequently there was no rising of the Irish. On receiving news that Roger Mortimer had landed at Youghal and was advancing towards them with a fresh force, the Scots suddenly retired,[27] having accomplished nothing in this direction by their raid.

Clan Brian, though 'left stranded' by the retreat of the Scots, was strong enough to force Clan Turlough from Quin to Bunratty, when Richard de Clare effected 'a cessation of arms' between the rival chiefs, and for a while all parties observed it.[28] Richard then went to Dublin to attend a parliament—probably that which met on June 27, when the Earl of Ulster was finally liberated.[29] According to the Caithréim he went 'to purchase peace for Clan Brian'; whereat Murtough was sent to the same session 'to [90] confute his sly devices'.[30] While they were absent Dermot, brother of Murtough, who was left with the chiefry, took the question at issue into his own hands, and on August 15, 1317, summoned the tribes to take measures for the destruction of Brian.[31] Into the mouth of Donough, when he heard of the intended attack, are put words which, if not prophetic of Thomond, were applicable to many other parts of Ireland: 'To universal Gaeldom', he said, 'this story will be a tale of woeful import, and this encounter is big with sorrow for the Erinachs; seeing that for the free-born clans of Brian's seed . . . and the other children of Conall, son of Cas, to come to one place for unsparing mutual destruction is merely to give the pale English charters and conveyance of all countries of the Gael.'[32]

Signs and omens multiply as the hapless king approaches his doom, and the poet-historian tells how Donough sees a loathly crone [33] washing skulls in a mountain-tarn, and how he learns that it is his own skull and those of his companions that she is washing. The battle, which was then fought near the abbey of Corcumroe, is described at great length and was disastrous for Clan Brian. Donough himself was

25 Caithréim. 26 Clyn's Annals, 1317: In *Paschate*. Easter in 1317 fell on April 3. 27 Annals printed in Chart. St. Mary's, Dublin, vol. ii, p. 301. 28 Caithréim, p. 89. 29 Laud MS. Annals, Chart. St. Mary's, Dublin, vol. ii, p. 355. 30 Caithréim, p. 86. 31 Ibid., p. 87. The tribes met at Ralahine in Tradry. 32 Ibid., p. 90. 33 The writer here surpasses himself, and uses about ninety epithets to picture the hag.

killed and most of the leaders, 'so that of Clan Turlough's foemen none save a bruised and battered few escaped with Brian Bane Mac Donnell O'Brien over Burren northwards'.[34]

[91] After Murtough's return all Thomond, 'save a small fraction which, to serve de Clare's own purposes, Mahon O'Brien had of him', rallied to Murtough. He kept quiet during the winter, 'but', we are told, 'it wrung his heart to have Mahon in his (Murtough's) father's hold (the island-castle in Inchiquin lake); and he found it a hard thing to have Irrus and the Dunes (Corcovaskin) and Ibrican, a slice of West Corcumroe, and half of the Upper Cantred (part of Inchiquin), Ui Flannchada (part of the barony of Islands), and Western Kinelea (the district about Kilmacduagh, now in County Galway)—all of them bulked together without a break from Cuchullin's Leap eastwards to Kilmacduagh— subject to Mahon as de Clare's vice-gerent.'[35] From this it would seem that an arrangement had been made, perhaps in Dublin, by which Murtough, as in 1314, was to hold Eastern Thomond with Clonroad and the cantred about Ennis, while Western Thomond was to be held by Mahon O'Brien, who had been a consistent supporter of Clan Brian, under Richard de Clare. Murtough soon began to make petty raids on Murtough Mahon, and in the beginning of the spring of 1318 Richard summoned them both to appear before his court. Murtough refused to appear without a safe-conduct, which Richard, it is said, refused.[36] Murtough thereupon took the law into his own hands, swept the country from Loop Head to Kilmacduagh, and banished Mahon.[37]

The barons at Limerick appointed a meeting to settle the dispute. All parties
[92] appeared, Murtough and Mac Conmara under the protection of Edmund Butler, Maurice Fitz Thomas (afterwards first Earl of Desmond), and 'William Óg' de Burgh. The meeting, however, came to nothing. Murtough was probably not prepared to admit the seignory of Richard de Clare in Thomond, nor to make suitable restitution and reparation to Mahon O'Brien. 'They propounded their terms', we are told, 'with guarantee of the barons that they should have effect; but de Clare refused the security, and insisted rather that they should submit themselves to his honour, i.e. their tender of reparation to be duly carried out at maturity, or [failing that] themselves to lie in his hands as pledges of fulfilment.'[38] Richard knew, from repeated experience, that Murtough's promises without hostages for their performance were valueless, and he was naturally unwilling to give the barons a right to interfere in his barony.

The arbitrement of the sword alone remained, and for this Richard de Clare was at the moment ill-prepared. Murtough left him no time for preparations, but immediately began to raid Richard's cattle, while the baron looked on helpless to interfere. Richard now sent messengers to William Og de Burgh to ask him to escort Mahon O'Brien and the O'Gradys to Kilnasoolagh. He seems to have prepared to comply and got as far as Ardrahan. On the same day Richard marched to Quin. His small force

34 Ibid., pp. 92–114. 35 Ibid., p. 118. 36 Ibid., p. 119. 37 Ibid., p. 120. 38 Caithréim, p. 121. The text (p. 137) has 'Sir Muiris fái Thomas agus Sir Uilliam og a Bure', where *fái* must, I think, represent the French *fiz*.

appears to have been mainly English, his tenants in Tradry, but he had with him Mahon O'Brien's two sons and Brian, son of Donnell, son of Brian Roe, and brother of the late King Donough, the last representative of that family. His object, presum- [93] ably, was to recover possession of Inchiquin for Mahon O'Brien, and he may have expected to form a junction with Mahon's forces. He had, however, first to obtain the submission of the O'Deas who lay in his line of march.

Conor O'Dea, having notice of Richard de Clare's approach, sent urgent messengers to Felim O'Conor of Corcumroe, and to Loughlin O'Hehir in the northern part of the barony of Islands, for help. Like Donough before his doom at the battle of Corcumroe, Richard de Clare, according to the Caithréim, passed on his march the banshee, Badhbh, dipping the blood-stained trappings of himself and his knights into a stream. Undeterred by such omens he advanced next day, May 10, 1318, towards Disert O'Dea. On the way he had to cross a stream, beyond which Conor O'Dea had set an ambush of his men. When the English came up they saw a detachment of horse and foot driving a prey across the stream into O'Dea's country. A fight ensued, and Richard, impetuously urging on his troops, put himself at their head. His opponents gave way, and Richard with a portion of his men crossed the stream after them. Then the men in ambush arose. Some held the ford and checked the main body of English troops, while the rest fell upon those who had already crossed and overwhelmed them. Richard was killed, and those with him were cut down to a man. The disaster did not end here. While the fight with the main body of the English forces was still going on, and O'Dea's men were being surrounded and hard pressed, first Felim O Conor, then Loughlin O'Hehir, and finally Murtough himself—all with fresh forces—came to the rescue and completed the rout of the English.[39] Only a few escaped from the battlefield to Bunratty, whither Murtough [94] followed them—to find the town 'deserted, empty, wrapped in fire'. For when his wife and household received tidings that Richard was killed, 'with one consent they betook them to their fast galleys', carrying off with them 'the choicest of the town's wealth and valuable effects, and having at all points set it on fire. From which time to this', adds the exultant chronicler, 'never a one of their breed has come back to look after it'.

There is no reason to suppose that either Thomas or Richard de Clare were other than brave and chivalrous Norman knights, just and honourable according to the ethics of their times. They belonged to a class impregnated with the best traditions of feudalism. They were not like the turbulent barons of the Welsh Border, ready on occasion to make common cause with the natives against the Crown. Though not subservient courtiers, they were loyal vassals of the king, respecting his prerogatives, but also scrupulously demanding respect for their own rights, both from superior lord and inferior vassal. But this class of proud and loyal feudalists was just the class that was

39 Caithréim, pp. 126–9. For the date see Laud MS. Annals, Chart. St. Mary's, Dublin, vol. ii, p. 358, where it is further stated that four knights, viz. Henry de Capella, Thomas de Naas (or rather, as in Clyn, Thomas de Lesse), and James and John de Caunton, were also slain, and that the body of Richard de Clare was said to have been cut into small pieces through hatred. In the Escheator's account (Pipe Roll, 12 Ed. II, 42nd Rep. D.K., p. 20) it is stated that James and Henry de la Chapelle and Thomas de Lees, tenants of Richard de Clare, died on May 9; while according to Clyn the battle was fought on Thursday morning, May 11, 1318.

least happy in its relations, both with the old Anglo-Irish lords and with the native
[95] Irish princes. The former regarded them with the jealousy and dislike not uncommonly felt towards 'superior people' of the same class, while the latter, proud and sensitive in their own way, resented their masterful manner and their foreign exclusiveness. The Geraldines with their half-Welsh extraction and long familiarity with Celtic usages, and the Burkes and others long settled in Connaught, had become much more akin to the Gael in sentiment and manners. They intermarried with the families of Irish chieftains and knew how to humour the Irish, so that a contemporary Irish writer could speak of them as 'those princely English lords who were our chief rulers, and who had given up their foreignness for a pure mind, their surliness for good manners, their stubbornness for sweet mildness, and their perverseness for hospitality'.[40] The de Clares had given up none of these things, and had nothing in common with the turbulent clans of Thomond whom they tried in vain to reduce to order. It was, however, no part of their policy to abolish the native chieftainship or to interfere with native rules and customs. What they aimed at was to secure as their quasi-feudal tenant-in-chief a Gaelic chieftain who would be loyal to the Crown and able and willing to restrain the turbulence of the native clans, so that they themselves might be left undisturbed to develop the resources of the manor of Bunratty. Unfortunately in this aim they were continually thwarted by the jealous barons of Connaught.

[96] Thomas, son and heir of Richard de Clare and the last male representative of his house, was a minor at his father's death and died three years later,[41] when his lands were divided between his aunts.[42] Quin Castle was overthrown during his minority. Bunratty was held for some years by constables appointed by the justiciar,[43] but in 1332 the castle was taken by Murtough O'Brien and the Macnamaras,[44] and was levelled to the ground. The existing castle would seem to have been built on the same site, but on a different plan, after this date.[45]

Thus was finally extinguished all hope of establishing Anglo-Norman rule in Thomond, and for upwards of two centuries the influence there of the English Crown was negligible, until in 1543 the 'treshault et puissant Seigneur', Murrough O'Brien, submitted to Henry VIII and was created first Earl of Thomond.[46] Indeed, a generation later a writer on the state of Connaught and Thomond could point to Ennis, Quin, Clare, Bunratty, and other towns in the newly-formed county of Clare and say, 'In old times these were good market towns and had English jurisdiction in them, and
[97] were governed by portriffes and other officers by the authority of the King of England; but now they are all wasted and destroyed in a manner, saving the castles, and no part of the towns left but old houses of stone-work, broken gates, and ruinous walls.[47]

40 Hy Many, Irish Arch. Soc., p. 186. 41 He died Feb. 28, 1321: 42nd Rep. D.K., p. 37. The lands were committed to the custody of Maurice Fitz Thomas and Maurice de Rochford. 42 These were Matilda, wife of Robert de Wells, and Margaret, wife of Bartholomew de Baddlesmere. 43 e. g. Herbert de Sutton and James de Beaufoy in 1326: Cal. Close Roll (Ireland), 20 Ed. II (141). 44 Clyn, Laud MS. In this year an expedition was led by Anthony de Lucy, the justiciar, into Thomond, September 9 to October 10 (43rd Rep. D.K., p. 56), but we do not know the result. 45 See Note B, at the end of this chapter. 46 Carew Cal. (1516–74), p. 203. 47 Ibid. (1601–3), p. 475, a document ascribed to the year 1574.

[98]

APPENDIX I

CLAN TURLOUGH AND CLAN BRIAN ROE

- Donough Cairbrech O'Brien, K.T., d. 1242
  - Conor Roe, K.T.: slain by Dermot, s. of Murtough, 1268.
    - Teig, called 'of Caoluisce'; d. 1259.
      - Turlough, K.T. (with intermissions) 1276–1306; supported by the Earl of Ulster.
        - Donough, K.T. 1306–11; supported by Wm. de Burgh.
        - Murtough, K.T. (with intermissions) 1311–43; supported by Wm. de Burgh.
        - Dermot, defeated and killed Donough, s. of Donnell, 1317.
      - Donnell; killed at Quin Castle, 1281.
    - Brian Roe, K.T. 1268; expelled by his nephew, Turlough, 1276; reinstated and afterwards 'executed' by Thomas de Clare, 1277.
      - Donough, Half K.T. 1278–84; supported by Thomas de Clare; killed by Turlough, s. of Teig.
        - Dermot 'the cleric' K.T. 1311–13; supported by Richard de Clare.
      - Donnell.
        - Donough, Half-king 1313–17; supported by Richard de Clare.
        - Brian Bán, escaped to Ara after death of Richard de Clare, 1318.
      - Turlough; d. 1305.

[99] APPENDIX II [NOTE A]

The death of Thomas de Clare

The evidences touching the death of Thomas de Clare are as follows: From the proof of the age of Gilbert, his son and heir, taken on September 22, 1302, it appears that Thomas died on August 29, 1287.[48] Three of the witnesses use this date in their calculations of Gilbert's age. One of them, Sir Maurice de Lees, was a member of Thomas's household at the time, another was in his custody, and the third was his servant. None of them speaks of Thomas's death in battle, as they surely would have done had it been the case.

Of the annalists, Friar Clyn, who died in 1349, writes: '1287. Mortuus est Geraldus filius Mauricii, capitaneus Geraldinorum: hereditatem suam dedit domino Iohanni filio Thome, filio adwunculi sui; hic Iohannes primus de hac natione factus est comes Kildarie. Obiit dominus Thomas de Clare.' Henry of Marlborough, vicar of Balscaddan, County Dublin, wrote annals in Latin which he commenced in 1406.[49] His entry (translated) is: 'Anno 1287, deceased Richard Deciter, Gerald Fitz Maurice, Thomas de Clare, Richard (*sic*) Taff, and Nicholas Telinge Knights.' This entry is reproduced in Ware's Annals. Some annals copied in the Book of Howth (p. 171) have: 'Sir Thomas de Claro, Sir Nicholas Tathe, and Sir Nicholas Telinge died 1287.' In the Annals of Clonmacnois the entry is: '1287 . . . Thomas de Clare died.' In the Laud MS. Annals under the date 1286 is: 'Obiit dominus Thomus de Clare.' So in Grace's Annals, 1286: ' Obiit Thomas Clarus'; and Camden translates 'The Lord Thomas de Clare departed this life'. Cox (Hibernia Anglicana, p. 77) states: 'This year 1286 was fatal to many
[100] Noblemen, viz. Maurice Fitz Maurice who died at Rosse, as Girald Fitz Maurice Og did at Rathmore; and the Lord Thomas de Clare could not escape the Common Fate, to which the Lord Justice himself [Stephen de Fulbourne] was forced to submit.' In all these entries there is no suggestion that Thomas de Clare died otherwise than in the course of nature, or that the obits mentioned were in any way connected with each other beyond occurring in the same year.

In short the sole authority, so far as I am aware, for Mr. Westropp's statement is the compilation made in the latter half of the eighteenth century known as the Dublin copy of the Annals of Inisfallen. There are several copies of this compilation written in Irish. In MS. 23 F. 9, R.I.A., the passage in question is rendered as follows: '1287. The Earl Thomas de Clare, who was the protector of the English in Munster, and the knights Gerald Mc Muiris, Riocard Taafe, Riocard Decetir, and Niocalas Teling were slain in Thomond in battle which they fought against Turlough son of Teige, Caoluisge O'Brien, and the forces of Thomond.'

Concerning these annals, O'Donovan, writing December 23, 1845, says: 'It appears from a letter (prefixed to the copy in the Academy) in the handwriting of Theophilus O'Flannagan that the Dublin copy of the Annals of Inisfallen was manufactured by the Rt. Rev. John O'Brien, some time R.C. Bishop of Cloyne, the author of the Irish Dictionary, who employed an Irish scholar of the name of Conry or Mulconry to arrange the language for him and make the copy ... O'Flannagan in his letter says that Dr. O'Brien made the Bodleian copy of the Annals of Inisfallen the ground-work of this compilation, but many entries have been added from sources good, bad, and indifferent.'

From the identity of the names it is pretty certain that the source of this last entry was the entry in Marlborough's chronicle, and that the addition, were slain in battle, &c.', is not authorized thereby, or indeed by any known authority, any more than the title of 'earl' given to Thomas de Clare.

48 Cal. Docs. Ireland, vol. iv, no. 819. 49 Harris's Writers of Ireland, pp. 322–3.

But let us examine this isolated entry to see if by any possibility it correctly represents a fact unnoticed elsewhere. Gerald Fitz Maurice, who was baron of Offaly, met with a signal defeat [101]
in 1285 at the hands of the Irish of Offaly, when he and 'about three score knights and free-holders' were taken prisoners 'with a great slaughter of the inferior sort'.[50] On June 26, 1287, at Rathangan he made a Letter of Attorney appointing John the clerk, formerly provost of Lea, to deliver seisin of the manor of Lea (i. e. his lands in Offaly) to John Fitz Thomas or his attorney.[51] This was part of that transference of his inheritance mentioned in the obituary entry in Clyn's Annals quoted above, and it formed, as we know, the basis of the claim of John Fitz Thomas to the succession. Gerald was only about twenty-three years of age, and it is very unlikely that he would have parted with his inheritance had he not been dying. Probably he never recovered from wounds received in the battle of 1285 or from the effects of his subsequent imprisonment, and the gift to his cousin John Fitz Thomas was in the nature of a *donatio mortis causa*. If this be so, it is clear that he did not fall fighting in Thomond on August 29 following. Indeed it would seem that he was dead before July 22 next, as on that day John Fitz Thomas made a Letter of Attorney authorizing Friar Roger, Abbot of Rosglas (Monasterevin), to take over seisin of the manor of Lea.[52] The case of Sir Richard of Exeter is still clearer. He is a well-known man. He was a justice of the King's Bench before the death of Henry III and afterwards.[53] He was deputy justiciar of Ireland at intervals from 1270[54] to 1277. He held the manor of Derver in Co. Louth and also lands within the king's cantreds in Connaught, and he died on or before September 25, 1286, when by reason of his death his lands were in the king's hand to October 14 same year, when the manor of Derver was delivered to his son and heir.[55] [102]
We have therefore contemporary record evi dence that he was not slain fighting in Thomond in 1287. Sir Richard Taafe is unknown, and the name is probably correctly preserved in the Book of Howth, which has Sir Nicholas Tathe (i.e. Taafe). He was justice of the Common Pleas at Dublin along with Richard of Exeter. I cannot fix the precise date of his death, but it was after March 14,1286, and before Christmas 1289.[56] It is highly improbable that he died in battle in Thomond. I cannot identify Sir Nicholas Teeling.

It is certain then that the entry in the so-called Annals of Inisfallen is faulty in several particulars and cannot be trusted as an authority. If any one should nevertheless maintain that probably Bishop O'Brien did not draw wholly on his imagination, but may have had some authority no longer existing, for the statement as far at least as the death in battle of Thomas de Clare is concerned, I can deduce only negative evidence to the contrary, but its force in the circumstances seems irresistible. Had Thomas de Clare been defeated and killed in battle by Turlough O'Brien we should expect to find some allusion to the catastrophe in the numerous records which concern his death; the Irish annalists too could hardly have failed to notice Turlough's victory; and above all the author of the Caithréim would surely have surpassed himself in exultation over this crowning triumph of his hero. Turlough, we may add, would surely have followed up his victory by ravaging all Tradry and burning Bunratty, but we know from the inquisition post-mortem that this was not done.

Mr Westropp indeed seems to have been so perplexed by this last omission that he was led to suppose a break in the Caithréim and to suggest that the lost pages told of the defeat and death of Thomas de Clare in 1287. This brings me to another important correction. So far as

50 Ann. Clonmacnois, Clyn, Laud MS. 1285. 51 Red Book of the Earl of Kildare, f. x. 52 Ibid. 53 Cal. Docs. Irel., vol. ii, p. 148, nos. 947, 1285. 54 3th Rep. D.K., p. 54; Ann. de Monte Fernandi (Stradel, 1270). There are several entries about him in these annals. His first wife died in 1202: ibid. He would have been at least fifty years of age in 1287, had he been then alive. 55 Pipe Roll (Ireland), 16 Ed. I, 37th Rep. D.K., p. 35. He was succeeded by his son of the same name, but this Richard was still alive in 1302: Cal. Docs. Irel., vol. v, no. 106. 56 Cal. Docs. Irel., vol. iii, no. 203 and p. 252.

I can discern there is no sign of any break in the language of the Caithréim (MacCruitin's MS., [103] T.C.D., H.1. 18), and there is no unusual gap in the events recorded. The suggestion of such a gap seems to have arisen from the faulty dates ascribed by a later hand in the margin of Mac Cruitin's MS. Donough's death, the real climax of the struggle with Turlough, is ascribed to 1283 instead of 1284, as in the annals. ' Next spring'—which may have been 1285, as Mr Westropp supposes—'Turlough raided all Tradry.' Then at the new paragraph (p. 25 of O'Grady's text, before the words *Tangatur tra*) there is a marginal note in a later hand: 'Hic evidenter patet defectus satis extensus.' But there is no evident defect. An account of the raid through Theobald Butler's territory comes next, and this, as already shown,[57] took place about 1287 and not, as in the marginal date, in 1304. Later on, in 1305, according to the marginal date, there is an account of the burning of Quin Castle, but this took place before the summer of 1292, when Juliana, daughter of Thomas de Clare, stated on an inquisition that a certain charter was lost at the burning of the said castle.[58] Then Turlough burned the town of Bunratty and besieged the castle there. This was clearly the siege which lasted from January 27, 1298, to March 3 following.[59] Afterwards Turlough defeated an attempt by his namesake and cousin Turlough, son of Brian Roe, probably in or shortly before 1305;[60] and then in 1306 (the correct date here appears in the margin) Turlough died. Thus when the true dates are supplied there [104] is no marked gap in the series of events, nor any reason (except the alleged killing of Thomas de Clare) to suppose that any pages have been lost.

There is therefore no historical ground for this particular 'triumph' of Turlough, and we cannot wonder that Mr James Frost and Mr George Stackpoole Mahon 'failed to identify the battlefield', and found 'no tradition of de Clare existing among the peasantry of Tradry'.[61] Unfortunately Mr Westropp's authority has misled subsequent writers on this point.

APPENDIX II [NOTE B]

The castles of Bunratty and Quin

The first stone castle of Bunratty was probably built by Robert de Muscegros before 1254, when he died. It was certainly in existence, though out of repair, in 1276, when it was delivered to the king on condition that when peace should be restored and Robert de Muscegros [II] should have repaid the cost of repairing, defending, provisioning, and holding the castle in the king's hand, the king would restore it to him.[62] Early next year, however, a new arrangement was made, and the king gave the whole of Thomond, with the castle of Bunratty and the cantred of Tradry, to Thomas de Clare. Thomas is stated in the Caithréim to have 'built a castle at Bunratty, containing an impregnable donjon', but the building was probably a restoration and

57 *Supra* p. 77 [p. 472]. Mr. Westropp places this raid (which he mistakenly supposes concerned 'other possessions of de Clare') in 1285 (Trans. R.I.A., vol. xxxii, p. 176), but his only authority for this date (Cal., vol. iii, p.79) concerns the expedition of 1281: cf. ibid., vol. ii, pp. 393 and 410. 58 Cal. Docs. Irel., vol. iii, p. 498. The burning probably took place within the two years ending Easter 1291, as the Escheator's account for that period includes payments for journeys to treat with Turlough O'Brien and the Irish of Thomond: 37th Rep. D.K., p. 42. 59 38th Rep. D.K., p. 42. 60 This Turlough, son of Brian Roe, died in that year: Ann. Loch Cé, 1305; where the editor wrongly supposes that King Turlough is intended. 61 Journal R.S.A.I., vol. xxi, p. 292, note 3. 62 Cal. Docs. Ireland, vol. ii, no. 1167.

strengthening of the castle of de Muscegros. However this may be, no part of the castle of the de Clares now remains. The entry in the Laud MS. Annals under date 1332 is as follows: 'Castrum de Bunrat capitur et ad terram prosternitur per Hibernicos Totemonie mense Iulii'; and though such expressions do not preclude the possibility of restoration on the same lines, the plan of the existing castle and some of its essential features point to a later date than the latter [105] half of the thirteenth century. It is of a uniform plan, a rectangle about 63 x 42 feet with boldly projecting square towers at the corners, the towers being connected on the north and south faces by lofty arches flush with the projections. The outside measurement of the whole building is about 70 x 90 feet. Quin Castle, on the other hand, which was certainly built by Thomas de Clare, *c.* 1280, was a quadrangle of 122 feet with three-quarter projecting round towers at the corners, such as may be seen on a larger scale at the castle of Roscommon, built a little earlier.[63] The bases of three of these towers remain, and part of the curtain walls, 9 feet thick, are embodied in the beautiful church of the Franciscan Friary, founded on the site of the castle by Sheeda Cam Macnamara in 1402.[64] Between Easter 1287 and Easter 1289, after the death of Thomas de Clare, the Escheator effected some repairs at Bunratty. He was allowed £11 10*s*. 8*d*. for making 25 perches of a fosse round the castle and erecting a palisade, also £5 3*s*. 9*d*. for covering the great tower and the chamber near the water, buying new locks for the gate, and constructing and raising a wooden tower beyond the gate.[65] Apart from these slight repairs and additions we may infer that the buildings were intact. Now the expression great tower, *magna turris*, could hardly be used to describe a castle of the existing type. The same expression recurs in the inquisition of 1321, taken after the death of Richard de Clare.[66] Both it and the 'impreg- [106] nable donjon' of the Caithréim point to a round donjon tower, such as is to be seen (disfigured by an absurd open-work arcade recently erected on the top) at Nenagh. In fact, according to MS. authority quoted by Mr G.U. Macnamara, in 1353 Sir Thomas de Rokeby, justiciar of Ireland, 'caused both Thomond and Munster with their rulers, to wit Mac Conmara and Mac Dirmuid [Mac Carthy], to submit to him, and he rebuilt the castle of Bunratty'.[67] The present castle, though greatly modernized in the seventeenth century, may perhaps date in essentials from this time, and a stone found in the castle, bearing a date which has been variously read 1357 and 1397, affords some support to this view.

About 100 yards west of the castle is a rectangular platform of earth, 20 x 14 paces, and about 12 feet high, with traces of a surrounding ditch. It appears to have been a slight work intended as the platform for a 'bretesche' (*britagium*) or wooden tower, and was presumably used as the basis of the wooden tower mentioned by the Escheator. It may, however, have been originally thrown up by one of the early feoffees at the beginning of the century.

All that remains of Clare Castle is a mural tower round on the outer side, and part of the bawn wall.

63 Roscommon Castle was built by Robert d'Ufford, justiciar in 1269, Ann. Loch Cé. It was broken (*do brissed*) by Aedh O'Oonor in 1272 (ibid.) and rebuilt early in the reign of Edward I: 36th Rep. D.K., p. 33. It was thrown down (*do legad*) in 1277 (Ann. Loch Cé), and repaired and strengthened in 1278–9: 36th Rep. D.K., p. 48. For ground-plan, 224 x 177 feet, see Journal R.S.A.I., vol. xxi, p. 546. 64 Quin Friary is described and illustrated and the remains of the castle indicated by Mr. T. J. Westropp: Journal R.S.A.I., vol. xxx, pp. 427–39. 65 Pipe Roll (Ireland), 16 Ed. I. Escheator's account from Easter 1287 to Easter 1289. 66 Inquis. P.M. Thomas, son of Richard de Clare, May 26, 1321. 67 See Journal North Munster Archaeological Society, vol. iii, pp. 220–327, and Antiquarian Handbook Series, no. vii, R.S.A.I., pp. 105–20, where Mr. Macnamara refers to Cotton MSS., Vesp. B. ii, fol. 126, and Domit. xviii, fol. 856. For the later history of Bunratty consult these papers.

[107] CHAPTER XXXV

O'CONORS, DE BURGHS, AND FITZ GERALDS IN CONNAUGHT, 1274–1315

In the half-century that followed the death of Aedh, son of Felim O'Conor, in 1274, there were no fewer than fourteen successive so-called 'Kings of Connaught'. With the exception of one who ended his reign by a natural death, and another who, having turned against the English at the critical period of Bruce's invasion, was slain at the battle of Athenry, all of these kings were either killed or deposed by their own kinsmen or followers. The several branches of the O'Conor family, who were descended from Turlough Mor, king of Ireland,[1] were in fact inveterately jealous of one another and incapable of uniting under any one chief. This was so even of members of the same branch. There are few years during this period in which the Irish annals do not record some outrage or act of violence by an O'Conor against an O'Conor.

The numerous descendants of Rory O'Conor, the last *ard-rí* of Ireland, had either been exterminated by their rivals or had sunk into obscurity, and, as we have seen, the
[108] kingship had passed to the descendants of Cathal Crovderg. In the previous fifty years, two of Cathal's sons, Aedh (d. 1228) and Felim (d. 1265), and one grandson, Aedh, son of Felim (d. 1274), had been kings. In 1274 it seems that there was no eligible descendant of King Felim, except an illegitimate son known as Aedh 'of Munster',[2] who was passed over for the moment; but there were some members of the senior line, grandsons of Aedh, son of Cathal Crovderg, who had hitherto escaped death or blinding at the hands of their rivals. Of these grandsons, Owen, son of Rory, was made king, but within three months he was killed by his cousin, Rory, son of Turlough, in the church of the Friary at Roscommon. Aedh, son of the blinded Cathal[3] (son of Aedh, son of Cathal Crovderg), next held the sovereignty—or, as the bard expresses it, was 'husband to Cruachan'—for a fortnight, when he was slain. He was followed by Teig,[4] brother of the Rory who had slain Owen. Thus there were three new kings

1 Appended to this chapter is a Table showing the descent and relationship of the kings of Connaught descended from Turlough Mor up to the middle of the fourteenth century. 2 *Aedh Muimhnech*, so called because he was nourished and brought up in Munster: see Four Masters, vol. iii, p. 424, note. He was fathered on Felim after that king's death; Ann. Clonmacnois, 1276. 3 Cathal *Dall*: he was one of those blinded by Aedh, son of Felim, in 1257: Ann. Loch Cé, Four Masters, where he is called *Cathal Cuircech* or *Cairceach*; see O'Donovan's note. 4 Of this Teig there is a record in 1275 when the king authorized Geoffrey de Geynville, then justiciar, to treat with him regarding his petitions for a lease of Connaught: Cal. Docs. Ireland, vol. ii, no. 1135. The Irish Pipe Roll of Ed. I (36th Rep. D.K., p. 40), contains entries of some payments in 1274 from Eugenius and Tatheg O'Konechor, i. e. Owen and Teig, grandsons of Aedh; and before Michaelmas 1277, £193 6*s*. 6*d*. was received as a fine from O'Konechor: ibid., p. 54.

of Connaught in this year. Teig thought it necessary to imprison his brother Rory, but he had a more formidable opponent in Aedh of Munster, the base son of Felim, who, [109] in 1278, entered Connaught to claim the chieftainship against King Teig, and was supported by the Mac Dermots. There were burnings and depredations on all sides. Next year Aedh, with the help of O'Donnell, threw down the newly-built castle of Roscommon, and in 1278 both Teig and his brother Rory were slain, and Aedh of Munster assumed the sovereignty. Robert d'Ufford, the justiciar, now spent the sum of £3,200 in strengthening the castle of Roscommon, and the ditch round the town there, and in works at Randown and Athlone. He also sent a force to punish O'Donnell,[5] but does not seem to have interfered with the new king of Connaught.

As may be imagined, the O'Conor territory during these years was the scene of almost incessant internecine warfare, which, however, did not extend to the de Burgh portion of Connaught. Hanmer relates that the king, in 1278, hearing of these 'civill warres', sent for the justiciar, Robert d'Ufford, 'to yeeld reason why he would permit such shameful enormities under his government'. The justiciar 'satisfied the king that all was not true that he was charged withall, and for further contentment yeelded this reason that in policie he thought it expedient to winke at one knave cutting off another, [110] and that would save the king's coffers and purchase peace to the land; whereat the king smiled, and bid him return to Ireland'. It is indeed clear from the Irish annals that at this period the English in no wise interfered in these contests for the kingship.[6]

Another branch of the O'Conors, known as Clan Murtough, now came to the front. They were not descended from Rory, the *ard-rí*, nor from Cathal Crovderg, but from Murtough 'of Munster', another son of Turlough Mor. They had been left undisturbed in Erris and the district about Clew Bay (Co. Mayo) until 1273, when, in consequence of an outbreak in the previous year against the Butlers of Burrishoole, they were expelled.[7] In 1280 King Aedh was killed by them, and Cathal, son of Conor Roe, son of Murtough, son of Turlough Mor, was made king—the fifth aspirant who had won the perilous position in six years.

By this time Robert d'Ufford had completed the restoration of the great castle of Roscommon. As may be seen from the extensive ruins which have survived to this day, it formed a large quadrangle, with projecting round towers at the corners, and two gateway towers. In 1303–4 it had three drawbridges and portcullises for two gates, also two outward bridges and gates. There was a great hall inside, and a carefully con- [111] structed well. It is on low ground, and there was formerly a lake close to the castle,

5 See his account, 36th Rep. D.K., pp 48–9. This O'Donnell was Donnell Og, as to whom see *ante*, vol. iii, p. 274 [p. 418]. His father married Lassairfhina, daughter of Cathal Crovderg, and both father and son befriended Cathal's descendants against their rivals. His action against Roscommon Castle perhaps brought upon him the enmity of the Government. A price was put on his head (Cal. Docs. Ireland, vol. ii, no. 2049), and he was slain in battle in 1281 by Aedh Buidhe O'Neill and Thomas de Mandeville: Ann. Ulst., 1281. 6 Hanmer's Chronicle, p. 204 (ed. 1633). It was in May 1279 that Robert d'Ufford went to England to confer with the king: Cal. Docs. Irel., vol. ii, no. 1567. Gilbert (Viceroys, p. 109) characteristically quotes this story as indicating that the justiciar had adopted 'the policy of sowing dissension among the Irish septs', a charge which it does not support and for which there is not a tittle of evidence. 7 Ann. Loch Cé, 1273; and see *ante*, vol. iii, p. 222 [392].

which was partly supplied with water brought in a conduit from St. Bridget's well.[8] With this lake the castle-ditch was presumably connected. This castle, and those of Athlone and Randown, protected the cantreds of Omany and Tirmany, which were no longer leased to the O'Conors. These two cantreds, comprising the southern part of the present county of Roscommon, together with a considerable strip lying to the west of the River Suck in the county of Galway, were held in large lots by Philip, son of Richard de la Rochelle, Richard of Exeter, John de Saunford, and others, at rents which, however, they found difficult to pay.[9] Two cantreds and a half, comprising the north-eastern part of County Roscommon and the barony of Tirerrill in County Sligo, were leased to Cathal O'Conor from Michaelmas 1281.[10] These cantreds were held by him and succeeding kings of Connaught at a reduced rent of one hundred marks, but 'the Irish rarely paid the whole farm and often nothing'.[11]

In 1284 the O'Conors were once more interfering beyond the bounds of their cantreds, and King Cathal threw down the castle of Kilcolman belonging to the Mc Costellos.[12] Next year, Manus O'Conor, the king's brother, defeated the Cusacks at Ballysadare, and Philip, son of Miles Mc Costello, retaliated for the destruction of his
[112] castle by defeating Manus in the mountains,between Leyney and Tireragh. The disturbance did not continue, and before the year was out Cathal entered into a bond with the king for one thousand marks to have his portion of the king's cantreds, and once more promised for himself and his men henceforth to keep firm peace.[13]

In 1286 Richard de Burgh, the young Earl of Ulster and Lord of Connaught, led a force into the latter province, where 'he obtained sway in every place through which he passed, and received the hostages of all Connaught, and he afterwards took with him the army of Connaught, and obtained the hostages of the Cinel Owen and the Cinel Connell'.[14] This is the first time that we hear of Earl Richard in Connaught. Perhaps he came to receive for the Government the pledges which King Cathal promised with his bond, but he may also have had occasion to enforce his rights against his own vassals, English and Irish. It must be remembered, too, that his principal tenant, Maurice Fitz Maurice, died this year, leaving female heirs, and the earl would naturally come to regulate the succession.

The Clan Murtough proved to be no more united than the other branches of the O'Conors, and in 1288 Manus O'Conor forcibly deposed his elder brother, King Cathal, and assumed the sovereignty himself. Some fighting ensued among the O'Conor factions, and then the earl came with a force as far as Roscommon to deal with Manus. Here, near the border of Moy Ai, he found John Fitz Thomas[15] of Offaly
[113] supporting Manus and his people, and 'they challenged the earl to pass beyond that place' into the O'Conor cantreds. The earl, who was always reluctant to settle disputes by the arbitrement of the sword, did not take up the challenge, but left the country and dispersed his army. This is the first indication we have of the dispute between John

8 Cal. Docs. Ireland, vol. v, p. 106. 9 See *ante*, vol. iii, pp 232, 246 [pp. 397, 404]. 10 Irish Pipe Roll, 15 Ed. I, 37th Rep. D.K., p. 24. 11 Justiciary Rolls, vol. ii, p. 134. 12 Four Masters, 1284. 13 Cal. Docs. Ireland, vol. iii, no. 172. 14 Ann. Loch Cé, 1286. 15 He is here (as generally) called by the annalists 'Mac Gerailt', but there can be no doubt as to the person intended.

Fitz Thomas and Earl Richard, which came to a head in 1294, and was not finally appeased until several years later.

Since the deaths of Maurice Fitz Maurice (1286) and the third Gerald Fitz Maurice (1287), John Fitz Thomas was making a claim as head of the Geraldines to the vast Geraldine estates in Connaught and elsewhere—a claim which, as regards Connaught, it seems that the earl was unwilling to admit. John Fitz Thomas was certainly not the heir of either Maurice Fitz Maurice or Maurice Fitz Gerald, but he seems to have been the nearest male agnate to both;[16] and it was not until about 1293 that he obtained the grants, entered in the Red Book of the Earl of Kildare, of the greater part of the Geraldine inheritance from the female heirs. The Earl of Ulster was the most powerful man in Ireland, and John Fitz Thomas the most ambitious, and the feud which arose between them, whatever precisely was its origin, first manifested itself in the desire which each entertained to control the king of Connaught. Obviously neither had any legal right to interfere in the ' king's cantreds', unless specially commissioned by the king; but we cannot wonder if they both thought that the policy of
'winking at one knave cutting off another' had already been pursued too long—more [114]
especially as the disturbances to the peace had recently begun to extend beyond the O'Conor borders. Unfortunately divergent interests or arnbitions prevented them from uniting in support of the same Irish chieftain.

Manus O'Conor, however, was not disturbed, but was recognized as king by the Government. In 1289 John de Saunford, Archbishop of Dublin and justiciar, obtained the aid of Manus and a force from Connaught in some operations against Carbry O'Melaghlin, chief of the Irish in the western parts of Meath. The expedition was under the command of Richard Tuit, a Meath baron, while the archbishop's headquarters were at the castle of Randown. The result was a victory for O'Melaghlin, who behaved himself with such lion-like valour as to be compared to Hector. Richard Tuit, 'the noblest baron at that time in Erin', was slain, and his brothers along with him.[17]

In 1291 there was more fighting among the O'Conors. An attempt was made to depose Manus, but, assisted by the English of Roscommon, he maintained his position. Next year the earl again intervened, and Manus personally submitted to him, though this submission was against the wishes of his people and, it would seem, of John Fitz Thomas.

In 1293 Manus died after an illness—the only king in the half-century under
review whose reign was terminated by a natural death. The justiciar, William de Vescy, [115]
then intervened and made Aedh, son of Owen, of the line of Cathal Crovderg, king, but on the tenth day after his election, John Fitz Thomas, with an excess of Geraldine audacity, took him prisoner and slew fifty of his men. Cathal Roe now reassumed the sovereignty, but he was slain before the end of a quarter by a kinsman of the same branch, and Aedh, son of Owen, was restored by the justiciar.[18] This was presumably

16 The position of John Fitz Thomas in the Offaly family will be seen in the pedigree of the Barons of Offaly in Appendix II this chapter. 17 Cal. Docs. Ireland, vol. iii, pp 268–70; Annals of Clonmacnois and of Loch Cé. The battle was fought near Lismoyny in Mageoghegan's country. Carbry O'Melaghlin was slain next year by his neighbours the Mac Coghlans of Garrycastle. 18 Ann. Loch Cé,

the origin of, or at least an incident in, John Fitz Thomas's quarrel with William de Vesey, which broke out about the same time as his quarrel with Richard de Burgh, and was probably connected therewith.

John Fitz Thomas, having restored the castle of Sligo, the seat of the great Geraldine manor in the north of Connaught now in his possession, went to England,[19] where he charged William de Vescy with treasonable practices. William, who had been superseded by Walter de la Haye as keeper of Ireland, appealed John of defamation before the King's Council in Dublin on April l, 1294, and there was a wager of battle between the two. The king summoned the parties to Westminster, and on the day named, July 24, 1294, William appeared as an armed knight ready to do battle. John, however, made default of appearance, whereupon William demanded judgement. So
[116] much appears from the Coram Rege roll.[20] Some Anglo-Irish annals, however, give a different version of the affair. They state that William, refusing the battle, fled to France, and that the king gave to John all William's Irish possessions.[21] It must not be supposed that John Fitz Thomas, who was a born warrior ready to appeal to arms at any moment, was personally a coward. His default appears to have been explained, and the whole proceedings annulled for informality. But it is certain that Kildare was not given to John Fitz Thomas until twenty-two years later, when he was made an earl by Edward II, in reward for his services against Edward Bruee. It is also clear that the charge of treason cannot have been credited, as William de Vescy was immediately employed by the king in a mission concerning the affairs of Gascony. Except that several writers have adopted and embellished the false version of this episode it would not be worthy of notice here.

The quarrel with Richard de Burgh, Earl of Ulster, led to more serious consequences. During the same year (1294) the fighting among the O'Conor factions went on, and King Aedh, son of Owen, threw down the newly-restored castle of Sligo.[22] This outrage seems to have maddened John Fitz Thomas, who probably suspected that it was instigated by the earl. However this may be, on December 11, 1294, John took the earl prisoner and detained him in the castle of Lea in Offaly up to March 12, 1295, when his liberation was effected by the Parliament held at Kilkenny on that
[117] date.[23] This whole episode, even in some of its details, closely resembles the quarrel between Maurice Fitz Maurice and Earl Walter de Burgh thirty years previously, when the former imprisoned the justiciar, Richard de la Rochelle, and when another King Aedh burned the castle of Sligo.[24] In fact it seems certain that the later dispute was a recrudescence of the former one and had the same origin. It may be remembered that the grant of Sligo was not derived immediately from Richard de Burgh, the earl's grandfather, but from Hugh de Lacy, and it seems that both Maurice Fitz Maurice

1293. The kinsman who slew Cathal Roe was Rory, son of Donough Reagh O'Conor, who was son of Magnus, son of Murtough 'of Munster', see ibid., 1288. The Four Masters, following the Annals of Ulster, have a confused entry here, evidently compounded from two sources. **19** Ann. Ulst., 1293. **20** Cal. Docs. Irel., vol. iv, no. 147, and cf. nos. 135, 137. **21** Laud MS. Annals in Chart. St. Mary's Abbey, Dublin, vol. ii, p. 323. **22** Ann. Loch Cé, 1294. **23** Clyn, p. 10; and Laud MS. Annals p. 323. **24** See *ante*, vol. iii, pp 241–4 [pp. 401–3].

and John Fitz Thomas resisted the claims of subsequent earls of Ulster to the immediate overlordship of the district.[25] In fact when John Fitz Thomas liberated Earl Richard from imprisonment he made him release all his claim, both in demesne and in other respects in the land which John had in Connaught,[26] and this enforced release, though afterwards annulled and the position of the parties actually reversed, shows clearly what John's claims were.

In consequence of the earl's caption, 'all Erin', we are told, 'was thrown into a state of disturbance'.[27] With his liegeman, Peter de Bermingham, John attempted unsuc- [118]
cessfully to depose Aedh. The castle of Kildare was taken, apparently by Calvagh O'Conor Faly, who burned all the records of the county, and the surrounding district was wasted by both English and Irish. The Wicklow tribes seized the opportunity of the discord to rise and burn some of the towns that had grown up round the castles,[28] and Thomas Fitz Maurice of Desmond, keeper of Ireland, the Earl of Ulster, Theobald Butler, John Fitz Thomas, and others were engaged in suppressing the Leinster rebels in the summer of 1205.[29] By August John Fitz Thomas, who had been impleaded in the king's court at Westminster touching the caption of the Earl of Ulster and other transgressions, had submitted to the king's will and bound himself and twenty-four mainpernors (whom he should find) to fulfil faithfully whatever the king should order.[30] In October the king sent over John Wogan as justiciar, and he not only succeeded in making a truce between the disputants, but managed to induce them both to join the expedition against Balliol, King of Scots, in the spring of the following year.[31] For their good services in this campaign both were pardoned for all transgressions in Ireland excepting those against each other.[32] At length after further [119]
postponements, on October 22, 1298, the seals of the parties were put to an agreement by which Sir John acknowledged his trespass, put himself at the earl's will, and agreed to render to the earl all his lands in Connaught, Uriel, and Ulster. These lands were to be valued, and 120 librates thereof (i.e. lands of the yearly value of £120) were to remain to the earl and his heirs as amend for Sir John's trespass, and for the lands beyond that amount the earl was to make an exchange to Sir John of lands of equal value in Leinster and Munster.[33] John, however, made default in appointing valuers,

25 It was of course as lords of Connaught and not as earls of Ulster that Walter and Richard de Burgh claimed to be overlords of the Fitz Geralds in Sligo. But the latter may possibly have relied on a grant from the Crown to Hugh de Lacy. See *ante*, vol. ii, p. 187, note [p. 226, note 18]. 26 This release is transcribed in the Red Book of the Earl of Kildare, f. iii d. By it the Earl released to Sir John, 'totum ius et clamium nostrum quod habuimus tam de dominico quam aliis occasionibus in omnibus terris et tenementis que idem Iohannis habet in Connacia . . . Datum apud Kilkennium die dominica proxima post festum Sancti Gregorij Pape a. r. Regis Edwardi vicessimo tertio. Hiis testibus domino Theobaldo le Botiller Thome filio Mauricii'. The date (March 13, 1294) agrees with that indicated in the Laud MS. for the earl's release. 27 Ann. Loch Cé. On account of the war and the caption of the earl nothing was received in Hilary term, 1295, in respect of the fifteenth granted to the king: Cal. Docs. Ireland, vol. iv, no. 191. 28 Laud MS. Annals, Chart. St. Mary's, vol. ii, pp 323–4. 29 Cal. Docs. Ireland, vol. iv, pp 123–4. For the conditions on which the Leinster tribes were admitted to peace, see Justiciary Rolls, vol. i, p. 61. 30 Cal. Close Rolls, 23 Ed. I, p. 457. 31 Cal. Docs. lreland, vol. iv, nos. 267, 270; Ann. Ulst., 1296; Laud MS. Annals, pp 325–6. 32 Ibid., nos. 315, 344. 33 Justiciary Rolls, vol. i, p. 235.

and on March 16, 1299, before Sir John Wogan, the justiciar, he gave the earl in amend for his trespass the following manors, viz.: Loughmask, Dunmougherne (Co. Mayo), Kilcolgan, Sligo, Banada, Carbury, and Fermanagh.[34] These were seemingly all the lands he had in Connaught and Ulster, except Tirconnell, to which his claim was probably nominal, and it does not appear that any other lands passed between the disputants. This surrender gave the earl undisputed control in Connaught and greatly increased his already great power.

In 1296 Aedh, son of Owen, was deposed by his own sept, aud Conor, son of Cathal Roe of Clan Murtough, was made king. The deposed king obtained assistance from the de Burghs, who endeavoured to make peace between him and his revolted *urrighs*. But 'though they promised peace, they did not observe it', but sided again with Clan Murtough. After some fighting, however, Conor Roe was slain and King Aedh restored,
[120] mainly through the potent influence of Mac Dermot, who reverted to his side.

In 1300 the earl commenced to build a castle at Ballymote in Corran. It was a strong castle with towers at the corners, and was designed to afford further protection for the great Sligo manor, the possession of which the earl had recently acquired from John Fitz Thomas in the circumstances already mentioned. This district was always the first to suffer from the outbreaks of the O'Conors and the Sil Murray clans.

ln 1305 Earl Richard, in a petition to the king, after stating that 'O'Conor an Irishman, who had perpetrated many homicides and robberies in the earl's land', held in farm of the king the land of Sil Murray in Comlaught, prayed the king that the said land might be granted to him or another Englishman at the yearly rent the said Irishman was accustomed to pay. Thereupon the king ordered John de Wogan, the justiciar, to inquire if the king without injury to himself or other might enfeoff the earl or other Englishman, and how much the land was worth yearly. The inquisition was taken at Castledermot on October 13, and the jurors, consisting of twenty-eight knights and free-tenants of the counties of Connaught, Tipperary, Louth, and Meath,[35] said that Felim O'Conor held five cantreds of King Henry III, rendering 500 marks, and that all his life he kept the peace and faithfully paid his rent. But 'after his death his son arose and became a felon of the king, and slew the lawful Englishmen of
[121] those parts, and moved common war against the present king, and threw down his castles of Roscommon and Randown . . . on account of which he was outlawed and died a felon'. And that Robert d'Ufford 'again fortified the castle of Roscommon and demised to O'Conor (meaning Cathal Roe O'Conor) two and a half cantreds of the said land, viz. the cantred of Moylurg and Tirerril, the cantred of the Three Tuaths, and the half cantred of Moy Ai, rendering to the king yearly 100 marks, and so divers justiciars to divers Irish of that name by the like farm demised the two and a half cantreds; but the Irish rarely paid the whole farm and often nothing'. And they said that the two and a half cantreds were worth 100 marks in times of peace, and 'that if the Irish were driven from those parts, and the land assessed to faithful men', they would be worth 250 marks yearly; but this, they said, 'cannot be done without a great

34 Ibid., p. 236. For Dunmougherne see *ante*, vol. iii, p. 208, note [p. 385, note 67]. 35 It is perhaps noteworthy that many of the jurors summoned did not come.

force of the king and inestimable expense exceeding the value of the land; especially as O'Conor is one of the five Irish captains of Ireland'. And they said that 'the king without injury to himself or other might enfeoff the earl, or other whom he will', of the said cantreds, and that 'it would be to the advantage of the king and his faithful people of those parts if the king gave the land to the earl in exchange for 100 marcates of land or rent in land of peace; especially as the earl has his lands in Connaught and Ulster and a great force of English and Irish adjoining that land, by which he would be better able than another to chastise the Irish of that land'.[36]

It does not appear that any action was taken on this finding. Certainly no immediate attempt was made to oust the O'Conors. Nevertheless, as we shall see, there are [122]
passages in the Irish annals which suggest that in 1310 William de Burgh, called 'Liath' or 'the Grey', the earl's cousin, and in 1330–1 William's son, Walter de Burgh, both aimed, as the annalist in the latter case puts it, 'at seizing the sovereignty of Connaught for himself'. The later attempt was discountenanced by the then earl, and Walter de Burgh was imprisoned; but possibly the earlier action of William de Burgh was countenanced by both the earl and the Government. Indeed, seeing the long-continued disunion of the O'Conor families, their turbulence, and their inability to keep order among their own men, it would not be surprising if many thought that the only way to secure peace and order in the province was to put an end to the rule of the O'Conors and place them and the Sil Murray chieftains under the de Burghs.

Next year (1306) civil war again broke out in Connaught between King Aedh, son of Owen, of the line of Cathal Crovderg, and Aedh, son of the former king, Cathal Roe, of the line of Murtough of Munster. The latter is generally distinguished as Aedh of Breffny, probably because he was nurtured there. He was at any rate supported by the men of Breffny as well as by many of the sons of chieftains of Connaught. He occupied the Three Tuaths—the cantred along the Shannon including the present barony of Ballintober North—and made raids therefrom and burned the king's palace of Cloonfree near Strokestown. King Aedh held his own for a time, but promiscuous fighting went on among the O'Conors—Aedh of Breffny fighting even against his own brother Rory—until at length in 1309 King Aedh, son of Owen, and many of his principal men were slain by his rival. Up to this time the de Burghs do not [123]
seem to have interfered.

But now a confused situation arose. The Three Tuaths at once submitted to Aedh of Breffny, but he met with opposition elsewhere. Mulrony Mac Dermot, king of Moylurg, the most powerful of the *urrighs*, entered Sil Murray with his household troops to defend the claim of his foster-son Felim, son of the late king, then only sixteen years of age. Both parties sought to obtain the support of the de Burghs. William de Burgh and his brothers came to Rathcroghan, invited by Mac Dermot, who was endeavouring to win the support of the local chieftains on behalf of Felim.[37] But the Sil Murray chieftains appear to have eventually given the lordship to Rory, brother of Aedh of Breffny.[38] Rory came with O'Flynn to the Plain of Connaught, and one of the

36 Justiciary Rolls, vol. ii, pp 133–4; Cal. Docs. Ireland, vol. v, no. 437. 37 Ann. Loch Cé, Ann. Clonmacnois, 1309. 38 This appears in Ann. Ulst. and Four Masters.

Berminghams was killed by him. Whereupon, after an abortive conference, William de Burgh expelled Rory, and made forays into Leitrim and Sligo against Clan Murtough. Meanwhile Aedh of Breffny had gone to Meath to solicit the support of the earl, but without effecting his object. On his return he fought for his own hand. In 1310 he attacked Mac Dermot and burned and spoiled his country. William de Burgh now came to the assistance of Mac Dermot to Killummod near Boyle. Aedh secretly sent his brother Rory with a band to Bunina on Ballysadare Bay to destroy the castle there which William had left, and while this was being done Seonac Mac Uighilin[39]
[124] (Johnnock Mac Quillin), captain of a mercenary band that acted as Aedh's bodyguard, assassinated him. This deed is said to have been done at the instigation of William de Burgh, and on the *cui bono* principle this seems not improbable. William William now billeted Mac Quillin and his two hundred de Burgh mercenaries on the Sil Murray. 'And,' says the annalist, 'there was not a town in all Sil Murray without habitual *bonaght*, nor a district without exaction, nor a prince without oppression, during William Burk's rule over them'.[40] Aedh of Breffny is described at his death as the worthy 'makings' of an archking of Connaught and 'the best son of a king that came from Murrough, son of Brian Boru, downwards', but he does not appear to have been formally inaugurated king. In fact during the period (1309–10), from the death of Aedh, son of Owen, to the inauguration of Felim, there was anarchy in Connaught.

Meantime William de Burgh took no steps to inaugurate Felim. It is indeed suggested that he was endeavouring to take into his own hands the government of the O'Conor territory. But when Mulrony MacDermot 'perceived that his fosterson Felim was ignored' and that he himself was given little power—'for the English were convinced that if he were weak the whole province would be under their sway'—he brought Felim on his own authority to Carnfree and had him in augurated there according to ancient custom. If William de Burgh, who seems throughout all this period to have exercised the earl's power in Connaught, had any designs against the
[125] O'Conor territory—as is not unlikely—he abandoned them after Mac Dermot's action. Felim was recognized as king and, except for some attacks from Clan Murtough, was undisturbed up to the year 1315, when, as we shall see, he joined the earl's expedition against Edward Bruce.

When we come to tell of the upheaval caused by Bruce's invasion we shall mention in greater detail how Felim was dethroned in his absence by Rory, son of Cathal Roe O'Conor of Clan Murtough, how Connaught was thrown into sheer anarchy, and how Felim, though he owed the recovery of his crown to the English, turned against them and was defeated and killed in the critical battle of Athenry (1316). Felim's cousin, Rory 'of the Faes', was now made king, and he and all the Sil Murray, except Mac Dermot, made peace with William de Burgh, who soon came to assert his supremacy. The exception was all-important, however. Mac Dermot was strong and stubborn and

39 Mac Quillin: this is the first mention of a family afterwards famous in Twescard. They were clearly not of Irish descent, and the fact that they then held former Mandeville lands suggests that they were Mandervilles. Possibly the descendants of Hugh de Mandeville, mentioned in 1274 (Cal. Docs. Ireland, vol. ii, no. 1088), were called 'Mac Uighilin'. 40 Ann. Loch Cé, 1310.

rightly suspicious of William de Burgh, and his allegiance was given to Turlough, brother of the late King Felim. In vain did William de Burgh ravage his country. Mac Dermot would not come to terms, and when the English army departed he deposed Rory, and Turlough was made king (1317).

Turlough appears to have been recognized as king by the English Government,[41] but he was dethroned in 1318 by a claimant belonging to a new line, namely, Cathal, son of Donnell of Clan Andrias, a sept descended from Brian 'of Luighne', a son of Turlough Mor. Cathal, who was ancestor of the O'Conors Sligo, reigned for six years, when he was slain by the deposed Turlough, who now resumed the kingship. Turlough, though once more temporarily deposed, reigned altogether twenty-one years, and after a chequered career was slain in 1345. He saw the virtual breaking of the link which connected Connaught with the English Crown, but this fact did not make much difference to the extent of territory subject to his sway, except that the English tenants in Roscommon gradually disappeared. The Burkes of Mayo and Galway were too strongly established to be dispossessed, and the English tenants grouped themselves under them, while most of the Irish chieftains outside the five cantreds, who did not do the same, became practically independent.

41 It would seem that he was the O'Conor to whom on March 8, 1318, the king granted that he should have the lands of Silmurray, the Faes or woods near Athlone, and the king's lands of Tirmany at the accustomed rents during good behaviour, except the lands of the English and the burgage lands of the towns: Irish Pat., 11 Ed. II, p. 23 (103).

[127]

APPENDIX I

Turlough Mór O'Conor, King of Conaught and Ardrí, sl. 1156

He is said to have had 23 sons. The following were kings or ancestors of kings of Connaught.

- Rory, K.C. 1156–86; Ard-rí, 1166–71; d. 1198.
  - Conor Maenmagh, K.C. 1186–9; sl. by his own people.
    - Cathal Carrach, K.C. 1189–1202; sl. by Cathal Crovderg.
  - Turlough, K.C. 1225; d. 1239.
  - Aedh, K.C. 1228–33; sl. by Felim.
- Cathal Crovderg or Red-Hand, KC. 1202–24.
  - Aedh, K.C. 1224–28; sl. 1228.
    - Rory
      - Owen. K.C. 1274; sl. by his cousin Roy.
        - Donough; d. 1292.
          - Rory 'of the Faes', K.C. 1316; sl. by his cousin Cathal
        - Aedh, K.C. 1293–1309, sl. by Aedh 'of Breffny'.
          - Felim, K.C. 1310–15; sl. at battle of Athenry, 1316.
          - Turlough, K.C. 1317–18, and again 1324–25, sl. by Clan Murtough.
          - Cathal; d. 1361.
    - Turlough; d. in monastery of Knockmoy, 1266.
      - Teig, K.C. 1274–8; sl. by Mac Dermott
      - Rory, sl. by McClancy, 1278.
    - Cathal Dall, blinded by Aedh, s. of Felim, 1257.
      - Aedh, K.C. 1274; sl. by Mageraghty.
  - Felim, KC. 1233–65; d. 1265.
    - Aedh, K.C. 1265–74; d. 1274.
    - Aedh 'of Munster', K.C. 1278–80, sl. by Clan Murtough.
- Murtough 'of Munster' a *quo* Clan Murtough; d. 1210.
  - Conor Roe; sl. by his steward, 1245.
    - Cathal Roe, K.C. 1280–8; deposed by his brother Manus.
      - Conor Roe, K.C. 1296; sl. by Mac Dermott.
      - Aedh 'of Breffny', K.C. 1309–10; sl. by Mac Uighilin.
      - Rory, K.C. 1315–16; sl. by Felim.
    - Manus, K.C. 1288–93; d. 1293.
- Brian of Luighne, sl. 1181; ancestor of O'Conor Sligo.
  - Andrias.
    - Brian
      - Donough, sl. by Aedh of Breffny, 1307.
        - Cathal, K.C. 1318–24; sl. by Turlough, s. of Aedh, s. of Owen.

APPENDIX II

THE BARONS OF OFFALY

Maurice f. Gerald I,
enfeoffed in the middle cantred of Offelan and the cantred of Wicklow by Strongbow; d. 1176

William f. Maurice, s. and h., 2nd baron of Naas.

Gerald f. Maurice I, enfeoffed in moiety of Offelan, including Maynooth, by his brother William; obtained Croom, Co. Limerick, and lands in Imokilly; 1st baron of Offaly; d. 1203–4. = Eva, dau. and heiress of Robert de Bermingham; she brought Offaly to her first husband and his heirs; she married (2) Geoffrey Fitz Robert, baron of Kells, and (3) Geoffrey de Marisco; she d. *c.* 1226.

Thomas f. Maurice, obtained Shanid, Co. Limerick.

Maurice f. Gerald II, = Juliana .... (?): Reg. All Hallows, p. 16.
2nd baron of Offaly;
1215 obtained seisin of his father's lands;
1235 given extensive lands in Connaught by Hugh de Lacy and Richard de Burgh;
1232–45 justiciar of Ireland;
d. 1257.

Gerald f. Maurice II; d. *vivente patre* 1243.

(1) Matilda, dau. of Gerald de Prendergast, and widow of Maurice de Rochford: Theiner, Vet. Mon. ccxi. = Maurice f. Maurice, obtained the Connaught lands by his father's feoffment; Red Bk., f. viii; justiciar 127; 1276, did fealty for the lands of his 2nd wife's inheritance; d. 1286. = (2) Emeline, dau. of Stephen Longespée, heiress of a moiety of the lands of her grandfather, Walter de Ridelisford.

Thomas f. Maurice, enfeoffed in Banada, Co. Sligo, by Maurice f. Maurice: Red Bk., f. xxii; d. 1271.

Maurice f. Gerald III, grandson and heir of Maurice f. Gerald II; 3rd baron; drowned at sea 1268. By his first wife (whose name is unknown) he left one son: Red Bk. = (2) Agnes de Valence; d. s.p. 1310.

Juliana = John de Cogan II, gave her inheritance in Cos. Kildare and Limerick to John f. Thomas: Red Bk.

Amabil, gave her inheritance in Connaught to John f. Thomas: Red Bk.

Juliana = Thomas de Clare.

John f. Thomas = Blanche de Roche. He got in all hereditary claims of Juliana de Cogan and Amabil. 5th baron of Offaly. 1316 created Earl of Kildare; d. Sept. 8, 1316.

Gerald f. Maurice III, 4th baron of Offaly; granted Lea to John f. Thomas: Red Bk. d. s.p. 1287. = Joan, dau. of Geoffrey de Geynville.

John de Cogan III.

Thomas f. John, 2nd Earl of Kildare = Joan, dau. of Richard de Burgh, Earl of Ulster; d. 1328.

CHAPTER XXXVI [130]

THE EARLDOM OF ULSTER, 1271–1315

One of the difficulties of writing in any detail the the history of Ireland in the thirteenth century is that there was little or no history common to the whole country. Each province and sometimes even smaller districts must be treated more or less separately. For though there was a central government nominally supreme over all, its influence and activities, while fully maintained in some parts, were almost unfelt in others. Not only did the relative strength of the English and the Irish inhabitants vary enormously in different regions, but even in parts dominated by the English the actual organization of society varied greatly. A similar difficulty no doubt faces the historian of Ireland in earlier times, but the secular struggle for the head kingship and the inter-provincial wars and alliances incident thereto serve to maintain a certain epic unity in the story. But all this was now a thing of the past, and though the general progress of English domination affords some substitute for the struggles of the provincial kings, the affairs of each province were in general little affected by events outside its borders.

This aloofness of certain districts is particularly true of the province of Ulster.
Indeed it is noteworthy that throughout the whole historical period, and, so far as we [131]
can see, even in the penumbral age before the dawn of authenticated history, the peoples of Ulster, broadly speaking, kept very much to themselves, and except on rare occasions interfered but seldom with the rest of Ireland. Yet both in the legendary and in the historical period their pre-eminence as warriors is acknowledged. Even when the nominal *ard-rí* was no longer as a matter of course one of the race of Niall Mor, they never, except perhaps momentarily, submitted to any other aspirant to the head kingship. When Henry II came to Ireland the Ultonian princes alone scorned to offer their submission, and though that fearless fighter, John de Courcy, forced the Ulidian chiefs of North-East Ulster (believed to belong to an older race) to submit to him, the great clan-groups of the rest of the province continued to preserve their independence in a marked degree.

The isolation and independence of control of the English of Ulster in the thirteenth century is even more marked. First we see John de Courcy, 'Princeps Ulidiae', as Jocelyn calls him, reigning in Ulster like an independent king. At length he is displaced by Hugh de Lacy, at the bidding of King John, whom he had flouted. But that king soon finds that Hugh de Lacy is no more amenable to control than his predecessor, and he has to lead a great expedition in person to expel the earl he had created. This was the first important interference of the Crown in Ulster and it was the last.

In the next reign Hugh de Lacy comes to his own again, and the earldom is as independent as ever of the Crown. So again it is when the earldom is renewed in the persons of the de Burghs. English Ulster stands aloof from Ireland, and Ireland from her.
[132] In other parts the great families of Leinster and Meath obtain lands, first in Cork, then in Tipperary and Limerick, then in Kerry and Desmond, and finally in Connaught. The same families can be traced as leading feoffees in all these districts, but the followers of John de Courcy are not found elsewhere, and there is little or no further infiltration into this north-eastern corner of Ireland, though it was a 'land of peace'. Even the Geraldines who permeate everywhere else obtain no foothold in Ulster. What new blood is found there comes for the most part by sea from Galloway and the Isles. Except in the brief periods when Ulster is 'in the king's hand' under royal seneschals—themselves usually Ulstermen—the justiciar never goes there, nor do itinerant justices, nor sheriffs, nor other officers of the Crown. Aids and subsidies do not appear to be levied in Ulster, and the Ulster barons do not figure in the feudal array. The Red Earl indeed, as we shall see, brings large forces to aid King Edward in his wars, but only after making, as man to man, a hard bargain for his reward. Even in face of the deadly peril of the Scottish invasion of Ulster, the earl, to his own discomfiture, is too jealous to accept the aid of the justiciar's army, and chooses to fight alone.

Now what was the cause of this persistent independence and aloofness of Ulster whether partly dominated by Gael or by Norman? It may have been partly due in each case to a racial difference, but it was made possible by certain physical conditions which rendered Ulster not easily accessible by land. North-eastern Ulster in particular can be approached from the south only through mountainous defiles north of the
[133] plain of Louth, where a handful could withstand a host. Against the west it is bounded by the Newry River, Lough Neagh, and the Lower Bann, and what might seem the weakest point, south of Lough Neagh, was a difficult country of woods and bogs[1] and was further artificially defended in prehistoric times by the so-called 'Dane's Cast', and in Anglo-Norman times by the mote-castles of Moy Cova at Dromore, and the Crown Rath near Newry. Similarly, what seems to have been the southern boundary of the ancient kingdom of Ulaid was marked by great lakes and rivers and mountains and bogs, linked together by a great prehistoric ditch and rampart known generally as 'The Black Pig's Dyke'.[2]

When Earl Walter de Burgh died in 1271 his son and heir Richard, afterwards known as the 'Red Earl', was a minor about twelve years old. in the custody of the king, and once more we have an example of the evils attendant on a minority. It needed the strong hand of a resident lord to keep order in a great feudal fief, and a seneschal appointed by the king, even if an upright man, lacked the necessary prestige and power. On the earl's death William Fitz Warin was appointed by Prince Edward's deputies as

1 These were 'Kilulto' (*Coill Ultach*), Kilwarlin (*Coill uairlinne*), and Clonebrassel (*Clann Bresaill Mic Duilecháin*). See Edmund Hogan's Description of Ireland in 1598, pp 7–9. 2 See Proc. R.I.A., vol. xxvii (c), no. 14, and xxxiii (c), no. 19, where Mr. W. F. De Vismes Kane has traced the dyke across Ireland in three partly divergent lines which seem to represent three successive defences of a gradually shrinking Ulster.

seneschal of Ulster, but his authority was challenged by Henry de Mandeville, who had been bailiff of the Twescard, or northern portion of the present county of Antrim, [134]
before Ulster was granted to Walter de Burgh.[3] Henry now seized the bailiwick of Twescard, but was deprived of it by the new seneschal. This was the beginning of a quarrel between William Fitz Warin and the Mandevilles, which was not finally appeased until after Earl Richard was given possession of his lands. According to the finding of a jury on an inquisition held before William Fitz Warin on December 27, 1272, Henry de Mandeville, when previously bailiff of Twescard, had been guilty of many extortionate, unjust, and violent proceedings therein set forth, and three days later 'the commonalty of Ulster, as well of English as of Irish', sent letters to the deputies asserting that Henry de Mandeville had been justly dispossessed of his bailiwick and strongly upholding William Fitz Warin's action.[4] The king confirmed the appointment of William Fitz Warin, and on receiving the finding on the above inquisition ordered him to take such amends for the trespasses of Henry de Mandeville as justice might require.[5] The Mandeville party, however, did not submit. In a letter to the king in 1273, the mayor and commonalty of Carrickfergus report that Aedh O'Neill, king of Cinel Owen, and Cooey (Cumhaighe) O'Cahan, king of Keenaght, at the instance of the Mandevilles and their friends, had 'hostilely entered the king's land and brought into it homicide, burning, and robbery', but 'were driven to confusion by the valour of the seneschal, Hugh Byset, and their friends'.[6] About the same time several [135]
Irish chieftains,[7] including in particular those whose lands lay among the English, also wrote to the king and took credit to themselves for having assisted the seneschal by pursuing and routing the king's Irish enemies. For this they said some of the king's council were endeavouring to oppress them, but they besought the king to confide in the testimony of the seneschal whom they were ready to obey as the king himself.

In the course of this quarrel it appears that Henry de Mandeville was slain. For his death and the disinherison of his sons, William Fitz Warin was prosecuted before the king's court, but was acquitted. This was before 1276. But when Richard de Burgh was given seisin of his lands in 1280, he appointed Thomas de Mandeville as his seneschal, and, at the instance of the sons of Henry de Mandeville, took into his hands all William's lands in Ulster, though said to be held of the king in chief, and seized and destroyed his chattels. In October 1281, peace was made between Earl Richard and William, and Thomas de Mandeville was ordered to restore the chattels. This, however, was not done, and further acts of pillage were committed on William's property by the Mandeville party, and William himself barely escaped with his life. In July
1282, an inquisition was taken by John de Saunford, escheator of Ireland, and in the [136]

3 See *ante*, vol. iii, p. 278 [p. 420]. 4 Cal. Doc. Ireland, vol. ii, no. 929. 5 Ibid., nos. 941, 954–5. 6 Ibid., vol. ii, no. 952; Foedera, vol. i, p. 520. 7 Cal. Docs. Ireland, vol. ii, no. 953. These chieftains were N[iall Culánach] O'Neill, 'king of Incheun' (Inishowen), Mac Dunlevy, king of the Irish of Ulster (Uladh), O'Flynn, king of Tuirtre, O'Hanlon, king of Uriel [he is usually styled lord of Orior, but he had slain in this year Mac Mahon, king of Uriel: Four Masters], D[ermot] MacGilla Muire, 'chief of Anderken' (*ui Derca Céin*), and Mac Artain, 'king of Onelich' (?), perhaps 'Ouelich', representing *Abhalaigh*, 'a place full of apple-trees', now Ouley, a townland in Iveagh, where Mac Artain was at this time chieftain.

finding of the jury the above facts and the various acts of pillage and violence are set forth. The escheator then formed a court before which William Fitz Warin presented his complaint. The defendants answered that they could not plead without the earl, 'whose tenants both they and the plaintiff were'. There was thus a question of tenure involved,[8] in which the earl seems to have gained his point. For ultimately it was arranged that the matter should be tried in the earl's court, and that only if right were denied him there should William seek right before the king.[9] We hear no more of the dispute and may suppose that justice was done by the earl. The whole episode shows what slight control the Crown had in English Ulster, even when in the king's hand during a minority.

In the absence of any more stirring events the quarrel between the Mandevilles and William Fitz Warin looms large in the records, but the dispute was mainly confined to the Twescard, and the damage to the property of the disputants.[10] That the earldom generally did not suffer much, and was even then a lucrative property, would appear
[137] from the account of William Fitz Warin for a little less than two years ending January 1276, when he accounts for £1,379 10*s*. 3½*d*, summarized as follows:—[11]

	£	*s.*	*d.*
Rent of the demesnes, burgages, mills, &c., of Carrickfergus manor, with pleas and perquisites, works of betaghs, &c.	176	7	4
From demesnes, pastures, fisheries, &c., of the manors of Lochkel (Lough guile) and Culrath (Coleraine) in Twescard	259	17	10
Rent of demesnes, burgages, &c., of the manors of Portros (Portrush), Portcoman (Bushmills), and Antrim	178	9	10
From the manor of Artken (Ardkeen Upper Ards), with the fishery of 'Balimithegan'	60	19	8
From the manor of Dun (Downpatrick)	76	9	7
From different Ulster counties, viz. Maulyn (Magh Linne), Carrickfergus, &c.	18	10	0
From farm of Ulster	608	16	0

8 In the king's writs William's lands are stated to have been held of the king in chief. In 1305 in a plea between Alan, son of William Fitz Warin, and William de Mandeville, the former produced a charter from King John to William de Serland, 'his great-grandfather whose heir he was', of some lands including Drumroan in the Grange of Kiltullagh: Justiciary Roll, vol. ii, pp. 11 and 64. William de Serland was constable of Carrickfergus in 1213–15 and seneschal of Ulster in 1223. 9 Cal. Docs. Ireland, vol. ii, no. 1918. 10 Henry de Mandeville's lands lay waste in 1277: 36th Rep. D.K., p. 32; and William Fitz Warin was allowed £105 13*s*. 4*d*., for decrease of rents owing to the war: Cal. Docs. Ireland, vol. ii, no. 2130. 11 Pipe Roll (Ireland), 9 Ed. I, 36th Rep. D.K., p. 54. The items amount to £4 more than the total given.

Owing to the differences in the grouping of the various denominations and to the changes which took place in the manors held at the time by the lord of Ulster, it is impossible to make an exact comparison between the values here set down, and those which, according to the inquisitions of 1333, appeared in the extent taken after the death of Earl Richard in 1326; but after making allowances it would seem that there was no very marked disparity between them. The total value in 1326 was about £442 a year, omitting the value of the military tenures, while in 1276, omitting the last item, 'farm of Ulster', it amounted to about £385 a year. This large item, farm of Ulster, [138]
amounting to £304 a year, probably represents the rents then payable by the chieftains of the various Irish territories in the province—rents which it would seem from the account of Nicholas de Dunheved in 1260–61[12] were paid (if at all) in cows; but in Earl Richard's time it appears that the condition of their tenures was changed to that of the quasi-military service which, as hereinafter mentioned, was in force at his death, and the monetary value of which was estimated at £55 a year.

The above account of William Fitz Warin does not include wardships and escheats, which are separately accounted for by the escheator, John de Saunford, and amount to upwards of £70.[13] Moreover at this time considerable portions of Ulster were held in dower, and the issues thereof do not appear in this account. The countess Emeline, widow of Hugh de Lacy and afterwards wife of Stephen de Longespée, died in 1276, and by her death the important manor of Dundonald came into the king's hand, as well as the castles of Antrim and Rath (Dundrum) and the sheriffdoms of Down and Nova Villa (Newtownards).[14] Also Avelina, widow of Earl Walter, was at first 'improperly endowed' with five of his castles in the marches of Ulster, 'which belonged to its defence', and of almost all the homages of the Irish of Ulster, 'which likewise belonged to its defence'.[15] A new arrangement was made, and Avelina was endowed [139]
with other lands, including the castle of Galway. This is one of many examples tending to show that feudal law of dower was not only a great tax on the successor, but was a fertile source of military weakness.

In January 1280, Richard, son and heir of Earl Walter de Burgh, was given seisin of his father's lands and castles, when he was nearly if not quite of age.[16] He had evidently been brought up in the king's household, and in the same year is called 'the king's groom'.[17] At Christmas 1283, he was knighted by the king at Rhuddlan in Wales.[18] In the same year he married his distant cousin, Margaret de Burgh, great granddaughter of Hubert de Burgh, earl of Kent. The king now gave him the dower-lands in Ulster of Emelina, late countess, formerly wife of Hugh de Lacy, and

12 *Ante*, vol. iii, p. 278 [p. 420]. 13 Pipe Roll (Ireland), 4 Ed. I, 36th Rep. D.K., p. 32. 14 Ibid., and Cal. Docs. Irel., vol. ii, no. 2073. This last entry shows that William Fitz Warin's salary as seneschal was 100 marks per annum, and that he received £54 for his robes and those of his two associates during his term of office. 15 Cal. Pat. Rolls, 1 Ed. I, p. 7. Sweetman's rendering (Cal. Docs. Irel., vol. ii, no. 950) is faulty. The point was that castles in the marches and services appertaining to the defence of the land should not have been assigned to a woman. As we shall see 'the homages of the Irish of Ulster' in Earl Richard's time included an arrangement by which a certain number of the earl's troops were billeted among them. 16 Cal. Docs. Irel., vol. ii, nos. 1629, 1632. 17 Ibid., no. 1769. 18 According to Justiciary Rolls, vol. i, p. 452; but evidence given in proof of age cannot always be trusted.

the queen gave to him and his wife in special tail Hugh de Lacy's former manor of Ratoath in Meath, while he was also replaced in seisin of the former de Burgh property in Owney, County Limerick.[19] The young earl and his bride were evidently high in favour in the king's court.

[140] In 1286 the Earl of Ulster led an army into Connaught. At this time Cathal Roe O'Conor of Clan Murtough was king. The annalists state that the earl 'obtained sway in every place through which he passed, and received the hostages of all Connaught; and he afterwards took with him the army of Connaught and obtained the hostages of Cinel Connell and Cinel Owen, and he deposed Donell, son of Brian O'Neill and gave the sovereignty to Niall Culánach O'Neill'.[20] Hugh Boy O'Neill, who had lived on terms of amity with Earl Walter, and with the support of Thomas de Mandeville and the English of Ulster had curbed the power of the O'Donnells in 1281, in a decisive battle at Desertcreaght, near Dungannon,[21] was himself slain in 1283 by Brian Mac Mahon, chieftain of Irish Uriel. He was succeeded by Donnell O'Neill, son of Brian 'of the battle of Down', but the earl presumably thought that Niall Culánach, who is said to have been a brother of Hugh, would be more amenable. In 1290 Donnell expelled Niall and assumed the sovereignty. Next year the earl again deposed Donnell and reinstated Niall, but no sooner had the earl left the country than Donnell, determined this time 'to mak sicker', killed Niall. He did not, however, gain his ulterior object immediately, for Brian, son of Hugh Boy, was now made king 'with assent of
[141] the earl by Mac Martin (a Mandeville) and Mac Eoin (a Byset)',[22] and Donnell was once more expelled.

We have already given an account of the quarrel which arose in Connaught between the Earl of Ulster and John Fitz Thomas, head of the Geraldines of Offaly and the earl's principal tenant in Connaught. It came to a crisis in December 1294, when Sir John captured and imprisoned the earl. But, as Sir John in amend for his trespass had to surrender all his Connaught manors to the earl, the ultimate result was greatly to consolidate and increase the earl's power over the whole north of Ireland from Galway Bay to Carlingford Lough. In Tirowen, however, Donnell O'Neill, taking advantage of the momentary weakness of the earl owing to the dispute, slew Brian, son of Hugh Boy, and 'great havoc was wrought of English and Gael along with him.[23] So far as appears, Donnell was left in undisturbed possession of the chieftainry until the period of the invasion of Edward Bruce, whom he supported. We have no direct information of the attitude of Donnell O'Neill during these twenty years, but no hostile act is recorded, and as he was one of those summoned by the king to the Scottish war in 1314, his attitude, even then, cannot have been openly hostile.

19 Cal. Docs. Irel., vol. ii, nos. 2099, 2102, 2103. **20** Ann. Ulst., Ann. Loch Cé, 1286. **21** Ann. Ulst., 1281. The 'Mac Martain' here mentioned and again in 1291 was, I think, Thomas de Mandeville, seneschal of Ulster, who, by a mandate dated February 14, 1283, was 'to be paid what was due to him for the head of O'Donnell proclaimed to be cut off:' Cal. Docs. Irel., vol. ii, no. 2049. Martin de Mandeville, who held lands in the time of King John in Mandevilleston (now Mansfieldstown), Co. Louth, was probably the eponym: Cal. Docs. Ireland, vol. i, nos. 1284, 1621. **22** Ann. Ulst., vol. ii, p. 375. **23** Ann. Loch Cé, 1295.

In May 1296, John Wogan, the justiciar, the Earl of Ulster, Theobald Butler, John Fitz Thomas and others, with their forces, joined the king in his campaign against Balliol king of Scots, and on Pentecost Day the king feasted the leaders at Roxburgh Castle.[24] About the same time James the Steward of Scotland gave in his submission,[25] and [142] a marriage was arranged between him and the earl's sister Egidia. On October 10 the king confirmed a charter by which the earl granted to James and Egidia in frank-marriage his Castle of Roo, the borough and demesne belonging to the said castle, the lordship services and rents of the lands of the English enfeoffed by the earl in Keenaght, and all the earl's land of Rennard (*Rinn Arda Magilligain*).[26] This is the first we hear of the manor of Roo, which was clearly already well established. It was in O'Cahan's territory of Keenaght, and the castle is probably to be identified with that long afterwards known as O'Cahan's Castle of Limavady. It was situated on a high projecting cliff on the right bank of the river Roe, near the Dog's Leap, which, in its Irish form, gave its name to the castle and old town of Limavady (*Leim an mhadaigh*). The manor must have reverted to the earldom, for from the inquisition of 1333 it appears that though then waste, it used to bring in to the late earl the considerable sum of £72 per annum.[27]

We have already mentioned that Cooey O'Cahan, king of Keenaght, made a raid into the Twescard in 1273, when he was driven out by the seneschal William Fitz Warin. Probably Cooey was dispossessed by the seneschal at about this time, as five years later, by a deed which is extant, Dermot O'Cahan, king of *Fir na Craibhe* (at this time the name of the district about Limavady),[28] surrendered 'all the land of Oconc- [143] ahil, which he held of the earl immediately, to hold to the earl in fee'.[29] The place-name has not been identified, but it was clearly in O'Cahan's territory, and the surrender may have been the origin of the earl's manor of Roo.

In this connexion it may be noted that Angus Og (MacDonald), lord of Bute and Islay and Cantire, is said to have married a daughter of Cumhaighe (Cooey) O'Cahan, and, according to the Scottish tradition, being anxious to plant with settlers some portion of his lands, he accepted as dowry with his wife seven score men out of every surname under O'Cahan. Among these, it is said, were the Munroes, 'so-called because they came from the innermost Roe Water in the County Derry, their names being formerly O'Millans'[30] [O'Meallain ?]. Whatever may be thought of this origin of the name Munro,[31] the tradition may have been based on an actual exodus of some [144]

24 Laud MS. Annals, p. 326. 25 His is the first name on the 'Ragman's Roll': Cal. Docs. Scotland, vol. ii, no. 823. 26 Cal. Pat. Rolls, 24 Ed. I, p. 208. 27 For these and further particulars concerning the castle and manor of Roo see the writer's paper on 'The Normans in Tirowen and Tirconnell', Journal R.S.A.I., vol. xlv (1915), pp. 283–6. 28 When the territory of Tyrone (including the present County of Londonderry) was reduced to shire-ground in 1591, 'Faranycryve' was one of the subdivisions of the barony of Limavady, now Keenaght; the others were Ardmagilligan, now Magilligan, and Kenaght, about Dungiven: see Colton's Visitation (Reeves), p. 129. 29 From the MSS. of Lord de L'Isle and Dudley, H. M. C. 3rd Rep., p. 231. The deed is dated apud Novam villam de Blawic (Newtownards), 6 Ed. (I), December 1. 30 Book of Clanranald, translated in Skene's Celtic Scotland, vol. iii, p. 401. 31 It is countenanced by Alexander Macbain, 'Gaelic Personal Names and Surnames', p. 18, where he says: 'In the fourteenth century the name is "of Monro", which shows it is a territorial name, explained as *Bun-roe*, the mouth of the Roe, a river in County Derry, Ireland, whence the fam-

O'Cahan septs from the valley of the Roe. This exodus would harmonize in date,[32] and may well have been connected with the Red Earl's settlement in the same district.

The earl, with many others, was summoned to join the king's ill-timed and fruitless expedition to Flanders in the summer of 1297. He seems to have made preparations to go with John Fitz Thomas and others, but on October 23 the king found the conditions of the agreements made with the justiciar very hard, and preferred that the earl and John should remain in Ireland, and bade the justiciar 'recede from them in the most courteous manner he could, so that no one might have reason to be displeased'.[33] But the earl seemingly was displeased, and when he was summoned to the Scottish expedition of 1301, though the king besought his assistance in a remarkable message, he made unacceptable conditions and did not go.[34] He took an important part, how-
[145] ever, in the Scottish campaign of 1303, when he seems to have been given his own terms, and before setting out he is said to have made thirty-three knights in Dublin.[35] This campaign seemed at the time to have effected the conquest of Scotland, and the earl was one of the principal negotiators of the terms of peace.[36] In consideration of his services the king wiped out all the earl's debts at the exchequer, and these are said to have exceeded £11,600.[37]

In 1305 the earl erected the castle of Northburgh in Inishowen.[38] This peninsula between Lough Swilly and Lough Foyle had long been debatable land between the Cinel Owen and the Cinel Connell, and had often been raided both by Normans and by Scottish Gaels. The castle stood on a rock which rises at the entrance of Lough Foyle just opposite Magilligan Point, where the land also belonged to the earl in connexion with the manor of Roe. The keep, of which the basement and part of the upper walls remain, is a massive rectangular structure, 51 feet by 45 feet, with walls 12 feet thick at the ground level. It projects from the land side of an oblong courtyard, about 280 feet by 100 feet. At the entrance of the courtyard are two polygonal towers. The
[146] earl obtained lands in the parishes of Moville (in which the castle was situated), Inch, and Fahan in Inishowen,[38] as well as the temporal control of the city of Derry, from Godfrey Mac Loughlin, who was Bishop of Derry from 1297 to 1315,[39] and he

ily are represented as having come in the eleventh [*sic*] century'. 32 Angus Og must have been born about the middle of the thirteenth eentury. See Pedigree of Maic Somhairle: *ante*, vol. iii, chapter xxx, Appendix [p. 406–7]. In a canopied niche in the ruined church of Dungiven, the centre of the O'Cahan's territory of Keenaght, there is a tomb with a recumbent effigy of a warrior on the top, and below on the upright front the figures of six *gallóglaigh*, or galloglasses. It is traditionally ascribed to *Cumhaighe na n-Gáll*, or 'Cooey of the foreigners', and it probably represents this Cooey, whose connexion with the Gall-Gaidheal of the Isles would account for the epithet. 33 Cal. Docs. Irel., vol. iv, nos. 396, 404, 452. Nevertheless John Fitz Thomas seems to have gone, *ibid*., 436, and there were many Irish foot-soldiers in the king's army: Rishanger, p. 414. 34 In the Annals of Loch Cé, 1301, it is expressly stated that the earl did not go. See too the account of John de Hothum: 38th Rep. D.K., p. 54. For the king's message to the earl, see Cal. Docs. Irel., vol. iv, no. 849. This message should be dated *c.*April 1301; cf. nos. 785, 788, 799. It seems to be again abstracted with additions (out of place) in vol. v, p. 60 (first memorandum). 35 Laud MS. Ann., Chart. St. Mary's, Dublin, vol. ii, p. 331. For a list of those about to go to Scotland with the earl, see Cal. Pat. Roll (Ireland), 31 Ed. I, p. 5 (21). 36 Cal. Close Rolls. 29 Ed. I, p. 169; cf. Cal. Docs., Scotland, vol. ii, nos. 1419, 1451. The earl dined repeatedly with the Prince of Wales: ibid., no. 1516. 37 Cal. Docs. Irel., vol. v, no. 340, and cf. p. 61. 38 Ann. Loch Cé, 1305, where it is called the New Castle of Inishowen. 39 See Pat. Roll (Ireland), 3 and 4 Ed. II, p. 18 (128). In 1327 Bishop

obtained some neighbouring lands from the Bishop of Raphoe.[40] The castle was a garrison castle, and the earl used to receive £60 a year from Irish tenants of the manor, but no settlement of English tenants seems to have been made here.[41]

In the same year (1305) the earl obtained a grant of free chase in all his demesne lands in Tuirtri, Keenaght, Cinel-Owen, Inishowen, Moy Cova (about Dromore), and Mourne in the earldom of Ulster, as well as in his recently acquired lands in Owney and Estermoy (Clanwilliam) in County Limerick.[42] The population of the above districts in Ulster was almost exclusively Irish, and the grant is some indication of the widespread domination of the earl. But we have a surer guide to the extent of the Red Earl's possessions in Ulster, in Connaught, and elsewhere in the inquisitions[43] of 1333. [147]
These inquisitions, indeed, were taken before Ulster had time fully to recover from the havoc and devastation caused by the invasion of Edward Bruce, and at a moment when the murder of the last de Burgh, Earl of Ulster, and the consequent reprisals and punishments had once more let loose the dogs of war throughout the province, so that the picture presented by the Ulster inquisitions is in several districts one of the waste and ruin of what had been a promising civilization. A measure of this waste and ruin may perhaps be found in the fact that, according to the jurors, the monetary value of the earl's interest in Ulster had decreased to about one-third of what it was when the last extent had been taken, i.e. presumably soon after the death of Earl Richard,[44] and from such indications as are forthcoming it would seem that even at the time of the earlier extent the value was very much less than it had been before 1315. The inquisitions in general state where the farmers and free-tenants of the seignorial manors and the tenants by knight service held lands, though it is not always easy to identify the place-names or to determine the extent of the lands so held. It is, however, pretty clear that all the baronies lying along the coast from the Bann at Coleraine round to Carlingford Lough, as well as a broad central patch about Antrim and the Six Mile water, [148]
were strongly held by English tenants. The earl's principal castles seem to have been at Northburgh, Coleraine, Antrim, Belfast, Dundonald, Greencastle, Dundrum, and Carlingford. Carrickfergus was a royal castle. In Connaught the earl's principal castles were at Loughrea and Meelick in the south, at Ballintober near the O'Conor territory in the middle, and at Sligo and Ballymote in the north.

Michael MacLoughlin complained to the Pope that the earl, 'supported by the favour of the temporal power', had constrained his predecessor to consent *verbaliter sed non cordialiter* to an agreement under which the earl had held for twenty years a certain part of the city of Derry and the temporal jurisdiction there, and certain advowsons and tenements, which belonged to the church of Derry, and the bishop prayed restitution: Theiner's Vetera Monumenta, p. 237; and Papal Letters (Bliss), vol. ii, p. 256. 40 See Cal. Pat. Rolls, Ed. II, pp. 292, 293. 41 For the above and further particulars concerning the Castle of Northburgh, see the writer's paper already mentioned, in Journal R.S.A.I., vol. xlv (1915), pp. 286–8. Also, same vol., pp. 124–7. 42 Cal. Charter Rolls, 1305, p. 53. 43 For full abstracts with annotations of the inquisitions of 1333, relating to Connaught, see five papers by Mr. H. T. Knox in Journal R.S.A.I., vols. xxxii and xxxiii (1902–3), and for similar abstracts of those relating to Ulster, see four papers by the present writer, ibid., vols. xliii-v (1913–15). 44 On August 14, 1326, John Darcy, the justiciar, went to Ulster to take into the king's hand the castles and lands of Richard de Burgh, deceased, and make extents of the same: Close Roll (Ireland), 20 Ed. II, p. 35 (47).

But not the least instructive part of these inquisitions is the section which discloses the former relations between the earl and the Irish chieftains of the province of Ulster. All the northern chieftains with the exception of O'Donnell[45] (who is not mentioned) are stated to have held their lands of the earl by the service of maintaining a fixed number (varying from 20 to 80) of 'satellites' (followers) appointed by the earl for the time being, and 'whenever the earl should wish to have them in his army they should be at his will, ready and equipped for whatever wars he might choose to assign them'. The chieftains mentioned are the representatives at the time of O'Cahan, O'Neill, Maguire, Mac Mahon, O'Hanlon, Mac Artain, Mac Gilmurry, and O'Flynn. The total number of 'satellites' was 345, and the monetary value of the services was estimated at £355. In ordinary times they would presumably form permanent bodyguards for the chieftains favoured by the earl to protect them against rivals and hostile neighbours, while as long as the system worked smoothly the earl would have the nucleus of a standing force ready at his call to supplement that supplied by his English tenants.
[149] This right exercised by the earl seems to have been an adaptation of the Irish custom of coigney (*coin-mheadh*) or billeting which appertained to the tribal chief, but like the military service of feudal law it was grafted on tenure.

The earl's children were married into the highest families of the three kingdoms. In 1302 his daughter Elizabeth was given in marriage to Robert Bruce, Earl of Carrick, and soon afterwards king of Scots.[46] In 1308 John de Burgh, the earl's eldest surviving son and heir apparent, married Elizabeth de Clare, daughter of Gilbert, late Earl of Gloucester, and through her mother, Joan of Acre, granddaughter of King Edward.[47] Upon their marriage the earl enfeoffed his son and daughter-in-law in a large number of manors, both in Ulster and in Connaught.[48] In the same year another tie was formed with the house of Clare, by the marriage of the Earl of Ulster's daughter Matilda with Gilbert de Clare, the young Earl of Gloucester, who afterwards fell fighting with reckless bravery at the battle of Bannockburn.[49] In 1312 the two great houses of the
[150] Geraldines were linked with that of de Burgh, by the marriages of the earl's daughters, Catherine and Joan: the former to Maurice Fitz Thomas, afterwards created Earl of Desmond; and the latter to Thomas, son of John Fitz Thomas of Offaly, and afterwards second Earl of Kildare,[50] thus sealing the reconciliation between these great Irish houses. The earl's daughter Avelina was married to John, son of Peter de Bermingham

45 O'Donnell may have held at a rent included in the aid to the earl at Northburgh Castle by Irishmen there. 46 Laud MS. Annals, Chart. St. Mary's, Dublin, vol. ii, p. 331. After Bruce's revolt in 1306 his wife and daughter Marjory (by a former marriage) were taken prisoners, and brought to England, and it was not until after Bannockburn that they were restored to Bruce in exchange for the Earl of Hereford: 'The Bruce' (Barbour), iv, 39, &c., and xii, &. 47 The earl's eldest son Walter died in 1304, and the earl's wife died in the same year: Ann. Loch Cé, 1304. His son John died on June 18, 1313, leaving one son, William, afterwards earl, born September 17, 1312: Laud MS. Annals as above) pp. 342–3. 48 For a list of these manors, see Cal. Close Rolls, 26 Ed. III, p. 442, and Pipe Roll (Ireland), 2 Ed. III, 43rd Rep. D.K., pp. 22, 24. 49 There was no issue of the marriage, and Earl Gilbert's heirs were his three sisters, viz. Eleanor, wife of Hugh Despenser, Margaret, widow of Piers Gaveston and wife of Hugh d'Audley, and Elizabeth, widow of John de Burgh (d. 1313) and afterwards wife of Theobald de Verdun (d. 1316), and then of Roger d'Amory. For the partition of the lands in Co. Kilkenny between these sisters, see *ante*, vol. iii, p. 95 [p. 327]. 50 On July 3, 1329, John Darcy, justiciar, married Joan de Burgh, Countess of Kildare: Laud MS. Annals, p. 371.

of Tethmoy, afterwards Earl of Louth;[51] and finally, another daughter (Alicia?) was married to Sir John de Multon of Egremont, who possessed extensive estates in Cumberland, Lincolnshire, and other English counties, and acquired with his wife some manors in Munster.[52]

In January 1306 Robert Bruce killed his rival, 'the Red Comyn', and stirred up the Scottish revolt against English domination. On March 25 he was crowned king of Scotland. Defeated on June 26 at Methven by Aymer de Valence, Earl of Pembroke, [151]
he went into hiding. We hear of him seeking refuge with Angus Og, 'the heir of mighty Somerled', who sheltered him in the castle of Dunaverty in Cantire; but according to Barbour, 'ever fearful of treachery', he stayed Robert there only three days, and then crossed the stormy sound to 'Rauchryne'[53] (now Rathlin Island), off the north coast of Antrim. Here he is said to have commandeered victuals for three hundred men every day while he lay there 'till the wyntir neir wes gane'. Then he sent James of Douglas to Arran, and followed himself in ten days.[54] At this time Rathlin Island (as well as Glenarm) appears to have belonged to Hugh Byset. Now, before January 29, 1307, the king directed Hugh Byset to procure shipping, men, and all necessaries, and to join John de Menteith without delay, and proceed to repress the malice of Robert Bruce, hiding in the islands on the coast of Scotland. Arrangements were made to collect, equip, and pay a force of 600 men, but it was May 2 before they departed from Carrickfergus.[55] There is a curious irony in the appointment of Hugh Byset to hunt for Bruce in the Scottish islands at a moment when, if Barbour can be trusted, he was still hiding in Hugh Byset's land. It is hard to refrain from suspecting that there was a secret understanding between hounds and hare, and this suspicion is [152]
strengthened by the facts that eight years later John Byset accompanied Edward Bruce in his invasion of Ireland,[56] and that Hugh Byset's lands of Glenarm and Rathlin were confiscated on account of his adherence to the Scots.[57] But suspicion is not proof. During the struggle for Scottish independence many leading men changed sides, and chronology is not Archdeacon Barbour's strong point.

Once more before the Scottish invasion of 1315 we hear of Bruce in Ireland. At the end of May 1313, he sent some galleys to the coast of Ulster on a plundering expedition, but the Ulstermen resisted valiantly and put them to flight. It was, however, said that Bruce himself landed by leave of the Earl of Ulster to make a truce.[58]

51 See Papal Letters (Bliss), vol. ii, p. 209, from which it appears that John de Bermingham (whose marriage had been granted by the king to Richard de Burgh: Cal. Pat. Rolls, 1 Ed. II (1308), p. 76) was at first betrothed to the earl's daughter Matilda, but as she was afterwards chosen by the envoys of the Earl of Gloucester, as being the fairest, Avelina was assigned to him in her place. This necessitated a papal dispensation. 52 The marriages of the six daughters of the Earl of Ulster are given in Clyn's Annals, p. 18; also in the Gormanston Register (Cal., p. 2), where too a table is given of the descendants of John de Multon of Egremont (p. 15), and the partition of the Munster manors between his daughters is set out at length, p. 111. 53 Irish *Rechru Rechra* (genitive, *Rechrann* or *Rechrainne*, from which Rathlin is a corruption). The island is still called by the natives 'Baghery', representing the old nominative. 54 Barbour's 'Bruce', book iii, ll. 659–762; book iv, ll. 338, 460. 55 Justiciary Rolls, vol. ii, pp. 332–4; Cal. Docs. Ireland, vol. v, no. 710; and 39th Rep. D.K., p. 25, account of Richard de Wodehouse; Cal. Docs. Scotland, vol. ii, nos. 1888–9. 56 Laud MS. Annals, p. 344. He died in the following year. 57 Cal. Patent Rolls, 12 Ed. II, p. 313. 58 Laud MS. Annals, p. 342; Ann. Loch Cé, 1313.

Up to the period of Edward Bruce's invasion the Earl of Ulster was not only the most powerful man in Ireland, but in some respects he exercised a greater influence on affairs than the justiciar. It was to him that the king appealed in particular when he sought in Ireland for forces and subsidies for his foreign wars. His influence, moreover, was not confined to those of English birth or extraction. According to an Irish writer his mere word was enough to stay the king of Thomond in a career of conquest which would otherwise have carried him to the throne of Ireland.[59] But, perhaps, just because he was so powerful, it was thought wiser not to add to his power by making him justi-
[153] ciar. Once, indeed, during the temporary absence of Sir John Wogan in the autumn of 1299, the earl acted as his *locum tenens*,[60] and again on June 15, 1308, he was actually appointed by Edward II to be the king's lieutenant in Ireland, but on the very next day Peter de Gaveston received a similar appointment and a writ of aid was directed to Richard de Burgh.[61] The explanation of this change seems to be that at the last moment the king devised this method of saving his favourite from the full effect of his banishment from England, which had been inexorably fixed by the barons and bishops of England for June 25. Some late writers state that there was bickering between the earl and Gaveston, but there seems to be no foundation for the statement.[62]

Peter de Gaveston, Earl of Cornwall, came to Ireland accompanied by his wife, Margaret de Clare, eldest sister of the Earl of Goucester, and a splendid retinue. We are told that in 1309 he subdued the O'Byrnes, rebuilt Newcastle Mc Kynegan, and Castle-Kevin, and cleared the pass through the woods from the latter castle to Glendalough.[63] The subjugation of the O'Byrnes, however, was only for the moment, as in
[154] 1311 they broke out again along with the O'Tooles, and a large force had to be sent to attack the robbers lurking in Glenmalure and other woody places; while the statement about the rebuilding of Newcastle may be doubted, as the Pipe Roll accounts, while showing that it was strongly garrisoned from May 20 to July 16 (1309), do not indicate that any works were in progress there. At Castle-Kevin, however, which had been burned by the Irish in the preceding year, rebuilding was effected, towards which the archbishop elect of Dublin, to whom the castle belonged, contributed £100.[64] Gaveston returned to England on June 23, 1309. His position in Ireland as king's lieutenant was anomalous, as throughout his term of office William de Burgh is repeatedly mentioned as *locum tenens* of John Wogan, justiciar, and he was paid his fee as such up to April 1309, at the rate of £500 a year, with £100 in addition as the king's gift.[65]

59 Caithréim, *supra*, p. 79 [pp. 470–1]. 60 Justiciary Rolls, vol. i, pp 287–98. 61 Cal. Pat. Rolls, 1 Ed. II, p. 83. 62 See Campion, Cox, Leland, and Gilbert. The supposition seems to be founded on the entry in the Laud MS. Annals that the earl *venit contra Petrum Gaveston apud Drogheda* on August 14. Probably the earl went to meet Gaveston to give him counsel and aid according to the king's mandate. The two were closely allied through the marriages with the house of Gloucester, and it was at Gaveston's instance that on September 12 following, payment to the earl of £2,150 15*s*. was ordered for arrears of pay: Irish Close Roll, 2 Ed. II, p. 7 b (16). The earl seems to have been absent from Ireland from this time up to Christmas 1309. 63 Laud MS. Annals, p. 338. 64 Pipe Roll (Ireland), 3 Ed. II, 39th Rep. D.K., p. 34. For a detailed account of Castle-Kevin and Newcastle Mc Kynegan, see the writer's papers in Journal R.S.A.I., vol. xxxiii (1908), pp. 17–27, and 126–40. 65 Close Roll (Ireland), 2 Ed. II, nos. 40, 68, and 109.

Edward II, from the time of his accession, practically abandoned his father's energetic policy regarding Scotland, and Bruce, taking advantage of the discord aroused in England by the opposition of the barons to Gaveston, was gradually mastering the kingdom. In August 1309, the Earl of Ulster was appointed to treat with Bruce for terms of peace,[66] but nothing came of the negotiations. About this time the earl, for his good services to the late king, was pardoned the yearly rent of 500 marks for his Connaught lands, and was given the custody of the king's castles of Roscommon, [155]
Randown, and Athlone.[67] He appears, however, to have left the direction of affairs in Connaught to his kinsman William de Burgh (the Grey), who at this time seems to have been aiming at the control of the O'Conor cantreds, and who in 1311, as we have seen, when dealing with affairs in Thomond, came into conflict with Richard de Clare.

In February 1310 a full parliament assembled at Kilkenny. The writs were addressed to the Earl of Ulster and eighty-seven magnates, whose names have been preserved, and the sheriffs were commanded to summon of every county two knights, and of every city and burgh two citizens or burgesses. At the suggestion of the king's council, the assembly, as being too cumbrous, delegated their powers to sixteen of their members, who passed many ordinances which, in the words of an annalist, 'would have been very useful had they been observed'. The disturbed state of the country occupied their attention. In Leinster, in particular, the growing power and turbulence of the Wicklow clans on the one side, and of those of Leix and Offaly on the other, had set an example of lawlessness which was now being followed by some of English name. The counties of Kildare and Carlow were no longer franchises, and there were now no longer lords of the liberties to organize resistance to the encroachments of the Irish or to keep order among the English. It was accordingly ordained that 'every chieftain of great lineage' (i.e. the magnates of high birth) should chastise those of his own family and of his own surname who trespass against the peace, and should take and render amenable to justice at the King's Court all malefactors and their adherents [156]
who should be found in his lordship in land of peace.[68] It is not to be wondered at if this sweeping ordinance, which sought to shift on to private shoulders the first duty of the State (as we conceive it), was not effectively observed. It was repeated in slightly variant forms in subsequent statutes, and penalties were added,[69] and in the reign of Henry VI it was reduced to the more reasonable ordinance that 'every man should answer for his sons and hired men'.[70] It seems probable that the principle of this enactment was taken from the Brehon Laws, which provided that, if a malefactor absconded, the liability for his crime (*cin*) should fall upon his father and certain relatives, and, if they could not be caught, upon the chief.[71] This was in fact 'the auncient Irish custome of Kincogish', to which Edmund Spenser alludes as having been made Statute-law.[72]

66 Cal. Pat. Rolls, 3 Ed. II, p. 189. 67 Cal. Pat. Rolls. 3 Ed. II, p. 182. 68 The Patent Roll on which this ordinance is preserved (Early Statutes, p. 267) has been obliterated in many places, but from 19 Ed. II (ibid., p. 313), which purports to repeat the enactment, the above would seem to have been its substance. 69 Ibid., pp. 307, 313, 379, and 449. 70 Statute, 23 Hen. VI, c. 22. 71 Brehon Laws, vol. iv, p. 241. 72 'State of Ireland', p. 54 (reprint 1810). 'Kin-cogish' is the exact phonetic equivalent of *Cin cómhguis*, or *comhfhoguis*, 'the crime of relatives', meaning the liability of relatives of a

There was also a clause directed against the prises of great lords who 'take what they will without making reasonable payments', and 'lodge with the good people of the country to their impoverishment'—herein, too, following the custom of Irish chiefs,[73]
[157] though in this case the practice was forbidden, and the Crown was to prosecute, if others dared not. There were also ordinances, similar to those of the parliament of 1297, against keeping 'Kernes and Idle-men' at the cost of tenants in time of peace;[74] against supplying victuals or aid to rebels, or receiving them to a separate peace; and with reference to guarding the marches—thus showing the ineffectiveness of former provisions with these objects.

Even now the principal sanction provided for the new ordinances was the excommunication pronounced by the bishops present against those who should break the king's peace or violate the ordinances.

In the time of Earl Richard, up to 1315, was comparative peace both in Ulster (in the large sense of the term) and in Connaught. The districts occupied by the English were no longer liable to the raids of Irish tribes, and the only disturbance of importance was a domestic one, arising out of the imprisonment of the earl in 1294. The families of the O'Donnell's, the O'Neills and especially the O'Conors, were at times torn by rival claimants to their respective thrones; but these disturbances were generally kept within the boundaries of their respective territories. There were no inter-provincial, not even any inter-tribal, wars. The earl during this period exercised a power never held by any one man in Ireland before, and he seems in general to have
[158] exercised it wisely and with moderation. The kings of Tirowen were his nominees. All the chieftains of Ulster, with the exception of O'Donnell, appear to have acknowledged that they held their territories of the earl, and to have submitted to the billeting of a small force upon them, ready at all times for his service. It seemed as if the Pax Normannica was at last beginning to extend over the entire north of Ireland, but the insecure fabric was shaken to its foundations by the Scottish invasion, and finally fell with the fall of the house of de Burgh.

wrong-doer for his crimes. 73 See *ante*, vol. i, p. 117 [p. 40]. 74 In these practices of billeting Kern (*ceithearn*, 'a band of foot-soldiers') and taking prises we seem to have the germ of the customs of "Coigney and Livery' which were forbidden by Statute (Early Statutes, p. 521) and bitterly denounced by Davies (pp 131, 142). 'Coigney' represents the Irish *coinmheadh*, 'billeting': see the quatrain in Four Masters, vol. ii, p. 969, and as a verb, p. 1109, also Ann. Loch Cé, vol. i, p. 552. "Livery' is presumably the French *livrée*.

PEDIGREE OF THE HOSUE OF DE BURGH

William de Burgh = dau. of Donnell O'Brien, K.T.,
brother of Hubert de Burgh, justiciar of England;
d. 1207

Richard I, obtained seisin 1214; d. 1242. = Egidia, dau. of Walter de Lacy

Hubert, Bishop of Limerick, 1223–51.

William; d. 1247.

Children of Richard I:

Richard II, obtained seisin 1247; d. s.p. 1248.

Walter, obtained seisin 1250; Earl of Ulster 1264; d. 1271. = Avelina, dau. of John Fitz Geoffrey.

William Og, killed in captivity by Aedh O'Conor, K.C., 1270.

Margery = Theo. Butler II.

A daughter = Gerald de Prendergast.

Children of Walter:

Richard III The 'Red Earl' of Ulster, obtained seisin 1280; d. 1326. = Margaret de Burgh, g.-granddau. of Hubert de Burgh, Earl of Kent.

Theobald; d. 1303.

Egidia = James Steward of Scotland

Descendant of William Og (dotted line):

William *Liath* (the Grey); d. 1324. = Finola, dau. of Brian Roe O'Brian, K.T.

Children of Richard III:

Walter; d. 1304, s.p.

John d. 1313. = Elizabeth, dau. of Gilbert Earl of Gloucesceter.

Thomas' d. 1316

Edmund; killed 1338, ancestor of Clanwilliam in Munster.

6 daughters, for whose marriages see *supra*, pp. **149–50**.

Son of John:

William the Brown Earl; killed 1338. = Matilda, dau. of Earl Henry of Lancaster.

Daughter of William the Brown Earl:

Elizabeth = Lionel Duke of Clarence, from whom King Edward IV was descended.

Children of William Liath:

Walter; d. 1332

Edmund Albanach; d. 1375; Mac William Eighter.

Ulick; d. 1353

3 other sons

Gyle = Richard de Manderville.

Son of Ulick:

Richard Og; d. 1387 Mac William Oughter.

[160] CHAPTER XXXVII

THE INVASION OF EDWARD BRUCE, 1315–18

The invasion of Ireland by Edward Bruce in the year 1315 has been rightly recognized as the turning-point of English influence in mediaeval Ireland. Up to this time in spite of some back-sets, notably during the troubled period in England caused by the Barons' War, the Anglo-Norman occupation had steadily progressed and Anglo Norman domination was beginning to control more or less completely the whole of Ireland. The century preceding was, indeed, the period of Ireland's awakening, when she found herself more closely linked by ties political, ecclesiastical, economical, with the family of European nations, when her intestinal feuds became rarer and less disastrous, when her wealth increased and her foreign trade expanded, when her cities grew in strength and beauty and self-sufficiency, and small thriving towns arose round mediaeval castles over three-fourths of her area. There was every prospect that Ireland would continue to share in the movement of progressive countries, but the sequel showed that this prospect was largely delusive. In those days of difficult communication the king of England was too remote and too much absorbed in multifarious pro-
[161] jects to fulfil his function as nerve-centre of the feudal system of a separate island. The Anglo-Irish feudal lords were themselves jealous of English control, while, above all, their lack of sympathy with the Irish, whom they regarded as an inferior race, prevented them from establishing their power on the firm basis of a contented people.

Into the causes of the decay of this early Anglo-Irish civilization it is not proposed to enter further here; but as Bruce's invasion marks its commencement, and was at least its occasion, it is important to piece together as full an account of his campaigns as can be gleaned from authentic sources.

The brothers Robert and Edward Bruce were grandsons of Robert Bruce, one of the competitors in 1291 for the Scottish throne, and were of Anglo-Norman descent; but through their mother, daughter and heiress of Neil, son of Duncan, Earl of Carrick, they had the blood of the Scots of Galloway in their veins and could even claim a shadowy descent from the legendary ancestors of Irish kings. Through his great-grandfather, Duncan of Carrick, Robert Bruce may have had some hereditary claims to lands about Larne and the Glens of Antrim.

After the crowning victory of Bannockburn King Robert of Scotland was able to take a vigorous offensive against England, and he naturally turned to strike his foe in the most vulnerable spots. He raided Northumbria, but he could not safely go very far in that direction. Ireland seemed an easier prey. Ireland had sent contingents of men and large supplies to aid the king of England against the Scots. To invade her shores

would at once be a pleasing act of vengeance and would tend to cripple England for the future. It was seemingly not a difficult task, as Bruce might count on the assistance of the native Irish, with some of whom he was in correspondence,[1] and who were no [162]
doubt represented as everywhere ready to join him. Moreover, if we are to believe the Scottish account, King Robert was glad to have a new field for the ambition of his brave brother, Edward, who, according to Archdeacon Barbour,

> Thocht that Scotland too litill was
> Till his brothir and him alsua,

and who would otherwise perhaps demand an inconvenient share of the newly won kingdom.[2] Accordingly he supplied his brother with a select army for the invasion of Ireland, and promised to join him with further troops by and by.

On May 26, 1315, the Scots, to the number of 6,000 men under Edward Bruce, landed at the haven of Larne.[3] Among the leaders were Thomas Randolph,[4] Earl of Moray, and the following knights: Philip de Mowbray, John de Soulis, John Steward, [163]
Ramsay of Ouchtirhouse, Fergus of Ardrossan, John de Menteith, John Campbell, and John Bisset. Having overcome the resistance of Thomas de Mandeville and other local lords, and having been joined by Donnell O'Neill,[5] king of Tirowen, and some of the lesser northern chieftains,[6] Bruce advanced along the Six Mile Water, on either side of which there were many prosperous manors and demesne lands to be plundered and laid waste.[7] He then proceeded southwards,, forced the Moiry Pass[8] between Newry and Dundalk in spite of the opposition of the local Irish chiefs, and on June 29 took and burned the town of Dundalk.[9] From this he ravaged the surrounding coun- [164]

1 The Bruce, xiv. 8-15. This probably refers to Donnell O'Neill, king of Cinel Owen. See his Letter to Pope John XXII; Fordun's Scotichronicon. 2 The Bruce, xiv. 4-5; cf. Fordun, Gesta Annalia, cxxxiii: 'Iste Edwardus . . . nec voluit cohabitare fratri suo in pace nisi dimidium regni solus haberet, et hac de causa mota fuit guerra in Hibernia.' 3 According to Barbour (xiv. 33) they landed at 'Vaveryng Fyrth' or 'Wokingis Fyrth', corruptions apparently of one of the many names of Larne Haven which owe their origin to the Norse occupation: see Reeves, Eccl. Ant., p. 265. The Laud MS. says they landed at 'Clondonne'. This take to be Clondu[n]males, 'Lying between Oldersfleet and the town of Larne'; Inquis. Ultonie Antrim, 7 Jac. I. It was the seignorial manor of Dunmalys of the Inquisition of 1333, now Drumalys, a townland in the Curran of Larne: see Journal R.S.A.I., vol. xliii, p. 139. The two accounts therefore virtually agree. The supposed identity of 'Clondonne' with the Glendun river in the NE. of Antrim has led to confusion. 4 Thomas Randolph and John, son of Neil or Nigel Campbell, were King Robert's nephews. Philip de Mowbray held Stirling Castle against Bruce, but after Bannockburn joined the Scottish side. John de Menteith and Nigel Campbell were sent as envoys by Bruce to Richard de Burgh, Earl of Ulster, to treat of peace in 1309: Cal. Pat. Rolls, 3 Ed. II, p. 189. 5 Donnell was son of Brian O'Neill who was killed at the battle of Down in 1260. 6 See *Cath Fhochairte Brighite*, Louth Archaeological Journal, vol. i, p. 81. 7 This was the ancient *Magh Line* (Moylinny). The castle of Dunedergale (Dunadry, in the Grange of Nilteen) was broken at this time by the Scots (Inquisition 1333, see Journal R.S.A.I., vol. xiiii, p. 141). Also the neighbouring Rathmore of Moylinny: Ann. Loch Cé, 1315. 8 Called by Barbour the pass of Endwillane (The Bruce, xiv. 113) or Inderwillane (ibid. xvi. 62). It led, we are told, to Kilsaggart (ibid. xiv. 133), now Kilnasaggart, famous for its inscribed pillar stone, and this identifies the route with Moyry Pass. Cf. Journal R.S.A.I., vol. xliii, p. 40. It was probably the route of the ancient *slighe Midluachra*. The Irish chiefs who opposed Bruce were Mac Artain of Iveagh and Mac Duilechain of Clanbrassil (Co. Down). 9 Laud MS., Ann. Loch Cé. Barbour tells of a stubborn fight taking place in the

try, killing all who resisted, and even burning the church of Ardee when full of refugees, men, women, and children—an early fourteenth-century example of the 'policy of frightfulness'.

Meantime Edmund Butler, the justiciar, with the feudal host of Munster and Leinster, and Richard, Earl of Ulster, accompanied by Felim O'Conor and the forces both English and Irish of Connaught, were converging against Bruce. About July 22 the earl met the justiciar in the hilly district to the south of Ardee,[10] but while they were arranging plans for annihilating or capturing the Scottish forces, who were clearly inferior in numbers, the latter gave them the slip and retreated northwards. Thereupon the earl, over-confident of his power to rid Ireland of the invader, and perhaps jealous of vice-regal interference in his earldom, unwisely dispensed with the assistance of the viceroy and undertook to bring Bruce, dead or alive, to Dublin. This was the first great mistake of the campaign. That night the earl reached Ardee in pursuit of Bruce, who was then some ten miles further north at Inishkeen. Next day the earl advanced to the town of Louth, but though there was some skirmishing between the earl's advance guards and the Scots, who lay in a wood near Inishkeen, Bruce, persuaded by O'Neill, declined a pitched battle and they retreated 'by regular marches northwards to Col-
[165] eraine, and to the border of Inishowen, and they broke down the bridge' over the Bann 'before (or against) the earl'.[11] The earl followed him and encamped at Coleraine, and for some time the two armies were unable to encounter each other, separated as they were by the deep river, and each employed itself in ravaging its own neighbourhood.

So much is clear from the Annals of Loch Cé. But those who would fain track out the precise movements of Bruce and understand the strategy by which for upwards of three years he succeeded in baffling his opponents, will inquire further into this movement, its meaning, and its direction. Did Bruce simply run away from the earl,[12] and did the earl, who certainly had a superiority in horse, pursue Bruce all the way from the plains of Louth to Coleraine without overtaking him? What was the line of Bruce's retreat? Was it east or west of Lough Neagh and the Bann? And did the earl follow in Bruce's footsteps? Let us see if the Scottish account throws any light on these obscure points.

Now 'The Bruce' was written sixty years after the event, and the story of the Irish campaigns as told therein by Archdeacon Barbour is vague, incomplete, and in some respects demonstrably in correct. His chronology is at fault. He omits the winter cam-
[166] paign of 1315-16. He exaggerates Bruce's victories. He misnames the English leaders, and his estimates of their forces are simply ridiculous. The historical value of his nar-

streets of Dundalk between the Scots and the feudal host. A fight there probably was, but from better sources it would appear that the feudal host had not yet assembled. 10 Sliabh Bregh: Ann. Loch Cé, vol. i, p. 564. The name was applied to the chain of hills extending from Clogher Head, Co. Lough, to Rathkenny, Co. Meath: Four Masters, vol. vi, p. 1922, note. 11 *Re haghaid in Iarla:* Ann. Loch Cé, vol. i, p. 566. The expression does not imply the presence of the earl at the moment. 12 This seems to be the view taken in Vita Ed. II auctore Malmesberiensi, Chronicles Ed. I and Ed. II (Stubbs), vol. ii, p. 211 'In primo congressu fugati sunt Scoti ad montana quasi greges ovium dispersi per pascua.' Then follows a description of the pastoral state of the Hibernienses sylvestres', leading up to the opinion, 'si comes de Hulvestre fuerit fidelis non est enim timendum ab eorum insidiis'.

rative is therefore slight. But he relates a number of incidents, which he certainly did not invent, and which may quite probably have occurred; he tells of some of the stratagems employed by Bruce, helps us to picture the character of the fighting, and occasionally throws some light on what our better sources have left obscure.

Several of the above points are illustrated in Barbour's account of this movement to Coleraine.[13] According to it, a few days after the taking of Dundalk, Bruce and his men were in a great forest called Kilros, which may be identified with part of the district west and north of Inishkeen.[14] Here they are attacked by 'Richard of Clare, that wes the Kyngis luf-tenand', with 50,000 men. In this passage and elsewhere 'Richard of Clare' is simply a blunder, often repeated, for Richard de Burgh, who, however, was not at this time the king's lieutenant.[15] We are given a picture of the fight:

> The Scottis all on fut war then,
> And thai on stedis trappit weill,
> Sum helyt[16] all in irne and steill.
> Bot Scottis men, at thair metyng,
> With speris perssit thar armyng,
> And stekit hors and men doune bar
> Ane felloune fechting wes than thair.

This was the skirmishing between William de Burgh and the Scots near Inishkeen to [167]
which we have referred. It was a cavalry reconnaissance, in some force perhaps, but Barbour speaks of it as a battle between the two hosts in which the English were rudely routed. Bruce, however, does not allow his men to pursue the foe, but retires into the forest, and we hear no more about 'Richard of Clare' at this time, except that he was preparing for another attack. Obviously there had been no decisive battle. Then Bruce goes to meet Odymsy,

> Ane Erische kyng that ayth had mayd
> Till Schir Edwarde of fewte.

But Odymsy turns out to be a 'fals tratour'. He leads the Scots across a great river, makes them encamp in a low-lying place, and then, under pretext of going to get them food, opens a dam which he had previously made and lets out the waters so as to flood the camp, and the men are nearly drowned. Now Odymsy is a name unknown in Ulster, but it was the name of the well-known chief of Clanmalier in the Irish Offaly, and this incident, which is told with much humour, is clearly misplaced. It belongs in all probability to the winter campaign of 1315–16, when, as we shall see, Edward Bruce

13 The Bruce, xiv. 239–382. 14 Kilros, coili rois, 'the forest of Ros', was presumably in the territory of Ros, somewhere in the barony of Farney, Co. Monaghan. Its precise limits are unknown, but the name seems to survive in Magheross (*machaire rois*), the parish in which Carrickmacross (*Carraig machaire rois)* is situated, and perhaps in Ballyrush, a little north of Inishkeen. 15 Edmund Butler was justiciar from January 4, 1315, to November 23, 1316. 16 'covered'.

passed through O'Dempsy's country. This is the simple explanation of a topographical difficulty which has misled commentators.

Barbour next tells us that the Scots were between two impassable rivers. One of these he names:

> The Bane, that is ane arme of se,
> That with hors may nocht passit be,
> Wes betuix thame and Ullister

[168] Ulster at this time was the district east of the Bann, Lough Neagh, and the Newry River so it is evident that Bruce was to the west of the Bann near its mouth. Moreover, Barbour next tells us how Thomas of Dun, 'a scummar of the se' (i.e. a pirate, whom we shall meet with again), sailed up the Bann with four ships and carried them over to the earl's dominions. This must have been below Es Craibhe, or the Cutts of Coleraine. The other river mentioned, but not named, by Barbour was, I think, the Foyle, including its great estuary. Thus Bruce's destination in his northern march, as indicated by Barbour, agrees precisely with that recorded in the Annals of Loch Cé, viz. 'Coleraine and the borders of Inishowen', i.e. Lough Foyle. In this region there were many English settlements west of the Bann near Coleraine, and the earl, as we have seen, had an important manor at Roo close to Limavady. These were the places Bruce now ravaged. It was probably at this time, too, that siege was laid to the earl's castle of Northburgh in Inishowen. It held out, however, until the next year.

Now this strategic retreat northwards (for such it clearly was) was of O'Neill's devising, and he would certainly have brought Bruce through friendly Irish territories, viz. O'Hanlon's country in County Armagh, and O'Neill's own territory in County Tyrone, i.e. as nearly as possible due north from Inishkeen. He may have hoped to entice the earl to follow them through these Irish districts. But in any case the earl was too prudent to fall into this trap. He no doubt went by Newry through his own dominions east of Lough Neagh, to Coleraine, where he was checked by the broken bridge
[169] over the Bann. This, I think, is the explanation of the fact that in no account, Irish, Scottish, or English, is there any sign of contact between the two armies until they were face to face on opposite sides of the Bann about Coleraine. Here for some time the opposing forces continued in sight of one another, but without effective conflict.

Bruce now utilized the opportunity to exercise his diplomacy. He sent secret messages to King Felim offering him undivided power over Connaught if he would steal away from the earl to defend his own province.[17] With this seductive arrangement Felim appears to have been only too ready to fall in, but unfortunately for him the earl, his partner, as it were, in the lordship of Connaught, was not his sole, nor indeed at the moment his most formidable, rival. Rory, son of Cathal Roe O'Conor, representative of the line of 'Murtough of Munster', brother of Cathal Crovderg, saw in the absence of Felim an opportunity of asserting his own claims to the province. He went through

17 Ann. Loch Cé, vol. i, p. 567.

Tirconnell to Coleraine to enlist the support of Edward Bruce, and Bruce is said to have given him a free hand to expel the English from Connaught provided he did 'not commit spoliation on Felim or go into his land'. This, however, was not what Rory did. He had no intention of fighting the English merely for Felim's benefit. He went right into Felim's territory, claimed sovereignty over Molrony Mac Dermot (who, however, gave neither pledge nor hostage), took the hostages of the Sil Murray, and had himself inaugurated king at Carnfree in Felim's room.[18] When Felim heard that Rory was [170]
returning to Connaught to contest the sovereignty for himself, he besought the earl to return with him to defend Connaught, but the earl had pledged his word to deal with Bruce and was not to be turned from his purpose. Felim thereupon left the earl and endeavoured to lead his host back to Connaught. He had to fight his way through Eastern Ulster and Uriel, where no doubt he was regarded as a deserter, and it was with reduced forces and exhausted strength that he reached the abode of his uncle, O'Farrell, in Annaly (County Longford). Here, feeling himself no match for Rory, he released his *urrighs* from their allegiance and permitted them to submit to Rory rather than be wanderers with him. 'But if I am again powerful', he said, 'you shall be with me.'[19]

When Earl Richard found himself deserted by Felim and the Irish of Connaught he retired towards Connor, which was the base of his supplies. About the same time Bruce crossed the Bann unperceived,[20] presumably with the assistance of the 'scummar of the se', as before mentioned. Here Barbour tells how the Earl of Moray captured a provision-train on its way from Connor to the English camp, some ten miles off. Moray then bethought him of 'a juperdy' or daring adventure. Having arrayed his men in the prisoners' garb, and keeping the English pennons flying, he advanced in [171]
the dusk towards the English camp. A number of the English, suspecting nothing, came out to meet the supposed victuallers, when

> The Erll and all that with him war,
> Ruschit on thame with wapnys bar,

and the fields were strewn with the slain.[21]

Earl Richard now hastily retreats to Connor and sends throughout the country to summon those of his men who were absent. Moray learns all the enemy's plans from a scouting party which he has captured, and that same night comes within half a mile of Connor, before his foes are fully assembled.[22] Next morning, September 10, the armies meet for the first time in a regular battle. Some English scouts are chased back

18 Ibid., p. 569. The burning of the English towns and castles in Connaught, mentioned in this passage, seems to have taken place a little later, after the news arrived of the earl's defeat at Connor: Laud MS., p. 346. 19 Ann. Loch Cé, vol. i, 569. Shane O'Farrell, Felim's mother's brother, lived at *Coill na n-amus*, 'the wood of the mercenaries', now Kilnaneawse near Edgeworthstown: Four Masters, vol. iii, p. 529, note. 20 'Nane of the land wist quhar thai lay': The Bruce, xiv. 386. 'Quod percipiens (the earl's retirement) Brus *caute* dictam aquam (de Banne) transivit sequens eum': Laud MS., p. 346. 21 The Bruce, xiv. 388-446. 22 Ibid., 447-98.

into the town, and the English host issues forth in battle array. Once more the ever-resourceful Scottish leaders employ a ruse. Leaving their camp and baggage-gear just as usual with banners flying over it, the Scots take up positions on either side out of sight, and when the English horse charge into the deserted camp, the Scots fall upon their flanks and take them at a disadvantage, encumbered as they were in the midst of the baggage.[23]

After a stubborn fight, graphically described by Barbour, the English were completely routed, and the Scots entered the town of Connor. The earl's cousin, Sir William de Burgh, and two of the Mayo Stauntons were taken prisoners. On the other side Sir John Stewart was wounded through the body with a spear-thrust. Some of the
[193] English fled to Carrickfergus, but the earl returned to Connaught, where, as we have seen, Rory, son of Cathal Roe, was carrying all before him.[24]

Thus ended the first attempt to defeat Edward Bruce. Its failure resulted in the first instance from the earl's over-confidence in his own resources and unmerited trust in the fidelity of his Irish troops, but credit must also be given to the prudent strategy of O'Neill, the resourceful tactics of the Scottish commanders, and the stubborn valour of the Scottish troops. The earl's defeat was the signal for the rising of the Irish of Connaught and Meath. Rory, son of Cathal Roe, burned the castles of Kilcolman, Ballintober, and Dunamon, and plundered the towns of Sligo, Ballymote, Roscommon, Randown, and Athlone. Moreover, the earl's retreat left the whole of Ulster at the mercy of Edward Bruce, and it is clear that not only did the Irish in Ulster generally now throw in their lot with Bruce, but some of the English had no alternative but to make terms for their lives with the successful invader. Carrickfergus Castle, however, held out, and Bruce, having sent the Earl of Moray with the prisoners and four ship-loads of spoil to Scotland to seek reinforcements, laid siege to the castle 'full stalwardly'. It proved, however, a tough nut to crack and held out for more than a year.

On November 13, Bruce, with the main body of his troops, left Carrickfergus, and
[173] having been joined by the Earl of Moray and a fresh band of 600 men, marched to the region about Dundalk, and thence to Nobber in Meath. Here (November 30) he left a garrison to secure his retreat, if necessary, and advanced on Kells,[25] where Roger de Mortimer of Wigmore, lord of East Meath in right of his wife, had assembled a large, but untrustworthy, force to oppose him. The engagement was soon over. The de Lacys in particular are said to have early fled from the field. Mortimer, who was not wanting in courage, was left alone with a few and had to fly to Dublin, while Walter Cusack[26] retired to Trim to hold the castle there.

23 Ibid., xv. 1-40. 24 The Bruce, xv. 41-97. Ann. Loch Cé, vol. i, p. 671. Laud MS., p. 346, where Roger de Sancto Bosco (Holywood, Co. Down) is also mentioned as having been killed at Connor. Barbour says that besides 'Richard of Clar' (i.e. Richard de Burgh), 'the Butler with the Erllis twa of Desmund and Kildar war tha'; but (apart from the fact that there were then no such earls) he is certainly wrong. 25 The Laud MS. Annals embodies two conflicting accounts as to the order of the battles of Kells and Ardscull, but there can be no doubt that Mortimer's defeat at Kells took place before Bruce advanced into Kildare. Not only is this order alone consistent with topographical considerations, but a letter from Sir John de Hotham to the king, written immediately after the battle of Ardscull (Jan. 26), states that the preparations for that battle were made after Mortimer had left Ireland: Cal. Docs. Scotland, vol. iii, no. 469. 26 Wal-

Bruce now burned Kells, and, while making no attempt to take the strong castle of Trim, advanced through Westmeath as far as Granard in County Longford. This place, where the Tuits had a manor, Bruce burned, and he plundered the neighbouring monastery of Larha, and burned the English town of Finnea[27] on the boundary between Westmeath and Cavan, and going south-west through the English settlements in Annaly or County Longford he burned Newcastle[28] in Shrule, and reached Bally- [174]
more Loughsewdy, the *caput* of the de Verdun moiety of Meath, where he kept Christmas. He made no long stay, however. He had to feed his army, and soon after Christmas, having burned the place,[29] he set out to seek new farms to plunder in Leinster.

Now it was that the de Lacys parleyed with Bruce, and, according to their own account,[30] confirmed by the jury before whom they were arraigned, craftily led him through Irish territories (presumably Mageoghegan's country and the Irish Offaly), where he spent fourteen days and lost a great number of men and horses in approaching Leinster, when he might have marched through the English districts of Meath in a couple of days. Thus they accounted for the fact that Rathwire and other de Lacy manors were not injured by the Scots. By this route Bruce reached the Bermingham district of Tethmoy[31] and the Fitz Gerald lands of Rathangan and Kildare, where, however, the castle successfully withstood a three days' assault.[32] Thence he went as [175]
far south as Castledermot, and returned by Athy and Reban, burning and destroying everything in his course, but not without some loss of men.[33]

On January 26, 1316, Bruce was at Skerries near the mote of Ardscull,[34] about three miles east of Athy. Here a formidable force opposed him under Edmund Butler the justiciar, John Fitz Thomas, baron of Offaly, and Arnold Power, seneschal of the liberty of Kilkenny. Any one of these lords, says the annalist, would have sufficed to conquer Edward Bruce, but unfortunately discord arose among them and, breaking up in confusion, they left the field to their foes.[35] There were some losses on both sides, but it is clear that there was no stubborn fighting. Of the English, Hamon le Gras and William de Prendergast were slain, and of the Scots, Fergus of Ardrossan, Walter of

ter Cusack was father of John Cusack, who was rewarded for his services at the final battle of Dundalk: ibid., nos. 640-1. **27** 'Fynnagh': Laud MS. (as above), p. 347. The Irish name is given in Four Masters, vol. iii, p. 544 (1330), as *Fiodh-an-atha*, 'the wood of the Ford'. **28** Geoffrey O'Farrell had levelled this castle, called *caislen in Baile-nua*, in 1295: Ann. Ulst. **29** The manors of La Roche (Co. Louth) and Loughsewdy 'were so burned and destroyed by the Scotch and Irish that (in 1316-17) no profit could be received from them': Pipe Roll (Ireland), 12 Ed. II, 42nd Rep. D.K., p. 24. **30** See Plea Roll, 10 Ed. II (Jan. 31, 1317), printed in Chart. St. Mary's Abbey, vol. ii, pp. 407-9. The de Lacys and their following were then pardoned suit of peace for a fine of £200. The finding of the jury, it may be noted, confirms the order here given of Bruce's battles. **31** To reach Tethmoy by this route Bruce must have passed through O'Dempsy's country or Clanmalier, and to this time should probably be ascribed the treacherous action of that chieftain mentioned by Barbour as occurring during the retreat to Coleraine in the previous summer: see *supra*, p. 167 [p. 518]. O'Dempsy was habitually loyal to the English: see *supra*, p. 36 [p. 453]. **32** Rot. Parl. Angl., 14 Ed. II, quoted in Viceroys (Gilbert), p. 529, and see Cal. Pat. Rolls, 9 Ed. II, p. 457. **33** Laud MS. Annals (as above), p. 347. **34** 'Skethyr iuxta Arscoll' (ibid.). Adam Bretoun, seneschal of Carlow, was allowed 20 for the loss of a horse in a deed of arms against the Scots in the district of 'Sketheres': Pipe Roll (Ireland), 10 Ed. II, 39th Rep. D.K., p. 73. **35** Laud MS. Annals (as above), p. 347. Clyn says that only five of the English were slain, but of the Scots about seventy.

Moray, and others. John of Hotham, who had been commissioned by the king in the previous September to make arrangements for the expulsion of the Scots,[36] sent a report of this affair to the king, in which, after describing the strong force collected, he says: 'but by bad luck the enemy kept the field, losing, however, some of their good
[176] people, while the king's forces lost only one, thanks to God'[37]—thus discreetly distributing praise and blame so as to offend nobody, while, after the manner of bulletins, concealing the facts and minimizing the defeat.

This was the third army defeated or dispersed by Edward Bruce within nine months of his arrival in Ireland. Bruce's men were veterans whose lives had been spent in fighting against England, and who had just come through a victorious war, and they were led by skilful and experienced commanders. Edward Bruce himself and the Earl of Moray had each headed a division at Bannockburn. The English of the eastern half of Ireland, on the other hand, had little or no experience of serious warfare. For three generations they had lived at peace, interrupted only by an occasional summons to punish or repress some petty raid or rising of the Irish on the border. The mass of the English host were mere country-folk—'a gadering of the cuntre' as Bruce disparagingly called them—not trained soldiers. By the Scottish veterans they were quite outclassed. Had the great lords acted together and been loyally supported by their vassals they might, no doubt, by sheer force of numbers, have surrounded and overcome Bruce's Scottish bands, but for several generations they had not felt the need of co-operation. There was no outside pressure, no eommon danger to make them forego their rivalries and jealousies, or if there really was such they were blind to it. The old feud between the de Burghs and the Fitz Geralds had indeed been quieted by inter-
[177] marriages and rearrangement of spheres of interest, but it is clear that the Red Earl was still regarded with jealousy by some of the Irish magnates, and that his Ulstermen were viewed with distrust and dislike by the inhabitants of Dublin and the neighbourhood. John Fitz Thomas had given one of his daughters in marriage to Edmund Butler, but there are signs that the jealousy between the Butlers and the Le Poers and the southern Geraldines, which afterwards broke out in violence, had already begun to work, while there was a chronic antagonism between the resident Anglo-Irish lords and the Dublin officials, who for the most part were new-comers appointed in the interests of the Crown. At this moment, however, after the fiasco at Ardscull the great lords of Leinster and Munster felt the necessity of standing together, and on February 4 they put their seals to a solemn declaration undertaking to defend the king's right against all men, and to do their best to destroy his enemies the Scots.[38]

But though Bruce was able to ravage the country and disperse his opponents, he was clearly much weakened by this winter campaign. Apart from the ravages of war,

36 Cal. Pat. Rolls, 9 Ed. II, p. 347. 37 Cal. Docs. Scotland (Bain), vol. iii, no. 469. Hotham gives the date, 'Monday before Chandelour', i.e. Jan. 26, 1316, thus confirming the accuracy of the Laud MS., p. 145. 38 Rymer's Foedera, vol. ii, pt. 1, p. 283 (ed. 1818). This document, written in French on February 4, 1316, and sent to the king, was sealed by John Fitz Thomas, lord of Offaly, Richard de Clare, Maurice Fitz Thomas (afterwards Earl of Desmond), Thomas, son of John Fitz Thomas, John le Poer, Baron of Dunoyl, Arnold le Poer, Maurice de Rochford, and David and Miles de la Roche. All the above, with the exception of Richard de Clare, were present at the affair of Ardscull.

there was a severe famine in the years 1315-16, which was not confined to Ireland.[39] Owing to excessive rains the corn in many parts never ripened, and dearth, famine, [178] and pestilence followed. Having burned the castle of Lea, the Scots on February 14 were preparing to attack the castle of Geashill, while the English were assembling not far off in the neighbourhood of Kildare. But the Scots were perishing of hunger, and did not await the approach of the enemy. They suddenly retreated northwards to Fore in Westmeath, where more of them died of hunger and exhaustion, and it was a weakened remnant that Bruce led back to Ulster near the end of February.[40]

The Earl of Moray was now once more sent to Scotland for reinforcements, while Edward Bruce is said to have held pleas in Ulster. This has been regarded as an indication of orderly government, but his decrees seem to have merely taken the form of hanging those who had opposed him. About mid-Lent (March 21) he seems to have paid a short visit to Scotland, bringing Alan Fitz Warin with him as a prisoner. Carrickfergus Castle still held out, and on Thursday in Holy Week (April 8) Thomas de Mandeville relieved the castle by sea from Drogheda and gained some successes against the besiegers, but was slain shortly afterwards.[41] About May 1 Edward Bruce is said to have caused himself to be crowned king Edward of Ireland at (or near) Dun- [179] dalk, perhaps on the hill of Faughart where he afterwards met his doom,[42] but we have no trustworthy details. As the Chronicle of Lanercost sarcastically says, 'he reigned (in Ireland) as many kinglets reign there'. About the same time he took Greencastle opposite Carlingford, but this was soon recovered by the men of Dublin and garrisoned for the king. At some time in this year he also took the earl's castle of Northburgh in Inishowen.[43]

But though Bruce did not venture out of Ulster again this year, the success of his winter raid encouraged the Irish of Leinster to rise sporadically. The O'Byrnes and the O'Tooles plundered the coast towns in Wicklow, the Irish of Imaile attacked Tullow, the O'Mores devastated part of Leix, and the O'Hanlons ravaged the country near Dundalk. But there was no concert among the different insurgent clans. Each people simply took the opportunity of the general disorganization to plunder their nearest English neighbours, and each was separately punished.[44]

One trivial though daring attempt on Dublin itself is worth noting, as perhaps it was the origin of the curious celebration of Black Monday described by Hanmer as

39 See Walsingham's Historia Anglicana, vol. i, pp. 144-5, and Roger's Six Centuries of Work and Wages, pp. 215-17. In Ireland in Mid-Lent 1316 wheat was sold for 18*s.* the crannock, and at Easter for 11*s.*: Laud MS. Annals, p. 350. In ordinary years the price varied from 5*s.* to 6*s.* 8*d.* Nevertheless, in May 1316 Earl Thomas of Lancaster bought wheat and oats at Drogheda and Dalkey for victualling Lancaster Castle: Historical and Municipal Docs. Ireland (Gilbert), pp. 388-91. 40 Laud MS. Annals (as above), p. 349. 41 Ibid., p. 350. This incident is also told with further details in 'The Bruce', xv. 101 et seq., where it is said to have taken place during a truce, and is mentioned immediatelv after the battle of Connor. Barbour in fact omits all mention of Bruce's campaign in the winter of 1315–16. 42 This was the Irish tradition preserved in a late tract, *Cath Fhochairte Brighite*, published in Louth Arehaeological Journal, vol. i, p. 86. For the date see Laud MS. p. 345. 43 Laud MS. Annals (as above), p. 349. In October 1316 the king's victuallers were ordered to supply forty crannocks of wheat for Northburgh Castle and thirty crannocks for Carrickfergus: Hist. and Mun. Docs. Ireland (Gilbert), p. 335; but the supplies were diverted to Whitehaven and Skinburness,: ibid., p. 341. 44 Laud MS. Annals.

[180] taking place in his time, though, as already remarked, he seems to have altogether antedated its origin in ascribing it to the year 1209.[45] An entry in the Laud MS. Annals mentions that on Monday before the feast of the Nativity of the Virgin (September 6, 1316), David O'Toole and twenty-four men hid themselves all night in Cullenswood (in the southern suburbs of Dublin), and in the morning advanced on Dublin, when Sir William Comyn with the citizens issued forth and put them to flight, killing seventeen of them and mortally wounding others.[46] The identity of the day of the week (though not of the month), the attacking party, and the precise place from which the attack was made, seem to indicate an identical occurrence. Sir William Comyn had been recently appointed 'captain of a guard for defending Dublin from the malice of the Irish of the mountains of Leinster'.[47]

While these events were happening in the east of Ireland, Connaught was thrown into a state of sheer anarchy. To the earl on his return flocked harried English settlers and dispossessed Irish chieftains in the hope that he would relieve them from oppression, but he was apparently powerless to restore order. The great earl is described as being 'without sway or power throughout Erin this year'. The chief combatants among the O'Conors were Rory, son of Cathal Roe O'Conor, the newly-proclaimed king, representative of Clan Murtough, Felim, the dispossessed king, representative
[181] of the line of Cathal Crovderg, and the sons of Donnell O'Conor of Clan Andrias now coming into prominence. Then there were rival Mac Dermots in Moylurg and O'Kellys in Omany. O'Donnell too, after the manner of neutrals, joined in to secure a share of the spoil and levelled the castle of Sligo, recently rebuilt by the earl, and plundered Drumcliff and its churches. The whole province was convulsed, and to add to the misery there were 'numerous wonderful diseases throughout Erin this year and a destruction of people in *great* numbers in it, and famine and various distempers and slayings of people and a curious anti-climax—intolerable, destructive, bad weather also in it'.[48]

At last, in February 1316, Felim O'Conor assembled a great army of English and Irish, including 'Mac Feorais' (Sir Richard de Bermingham of Athenry) and Mulroney Mac Dermot and the sons of Donnell O'Conor. A pitched battle was fought near Ballymoe, and 'the superior numbers of the hands and weapons together with the mail armour of the English', vanquished King Rory, son of Cathal Roe, who was slain, and Felim regained his kingdom.[49] But though he owed the recovery of his crown to English aid, Felim, intoxicated with the vision of undivided sovereignty held out to him by Edward Bruce, soon afterwards turned against his allies and proceeded to expel
[182] the English of the west of Connaught. He first forced the Irish on the borders of the Sil Murray (who were friendly to the English) to give hostages, then burned Ballyla-

45 Hanmer's Chronicle, p. 186 (1633 ed.), and see *ante*, vol. ii, p. 242 [p. 247], where, if I am now right, I should have said that 'tradition (as Hanmer) had antedated the occurrence by more than a century'. People do not celebrate their defeats in the way described by Hanmer. 46 Chart. St. Mary's Abbey, vol. ii, p. 351; cf. ibid., p. 297. 47 Historical and Municipal Documents, Ireland (Gilbert), p. 381. 48 Ann. Loch Cé, vol. i, p. 579. 49 Ibid., p. 5-31. The battle was fought at *Tóchar móna Coinnedha*, 'the causeway of Coinnidh's bog', from which the parish of Templetogher, between Dunmore and Ballymoe, takes its name; and the date, according to the Annals of Ulster, was February 23, 1316.

han and killed its lord, Stephen of Exeter, with other English knights, and plundered all the country from Ballymote to Ballinrobe, and demolished the castle of Meelick on the Shannon.[50]

By this time, about the end of July, Sir William de Burgh, released from Scotland,[51] had arrived in Connaught and had joined Richard de Bermingham at Athenry. Felim now made a great muster of Connaught men to expel William de Burgh, and obtained assistance from the Irish chiefs of Thomond, Meath, Breffny, and Conmaicne. A pitched battle was fought at Athenry on August 10, 1316,[52] when the Irish were totally defeated and Felim and a host of his supporters killed. To judge by the long list of eminent Irishmen slain, this must have been the bloodiest battle fought in Ireland for many a long day. It had a permanent effect in weakening the O'Conors of Connaught, and it was their last effort to expel the English from the province.

A contemporary Irish writer, referring to Owen O'Madden, chieftain of Sil Anm- [183]
chadha, who sided with the English, utters a noteworthy opinion (which must have been held by many far-seeing Irishmen) with regard to Bruce's invasion and the attitude of other Connaught chieftains:— 'In his time foreigners less noble than our own foreigners arrived; for the old chieftains of Erin prospered under those princely English lords, who were our chief rulers, and who had given up their foreignness for a pure mind, their surliness for good manners, their stubbornness for sweet mildness, and their perverseness for hospitality. Wherefore it was unjust in our nobility to side with foreigners who were less noble than these, in imitation of the Eoghanachs [i.e. the O'Neills of Ulster] who first dealt treacherously by their own lords on this occasion, so that at this juncture Erin became one trembling surface of commotion, with the single exception of the territory of Eoghan O'Madden, who took care not to violate his truth by acting treacherously towards his lord without strong reason.'[53]

Meanwhile the heroic defenders of Carrickfergus held out. So reduced were they for want of food that they are said to have chewed skins and even eaten the bodies of some of their prisoners, At last, after a year's siege, in September 1316, they surrendered on terms of safety to life and limb.[54]

Since the failure of the great lords in the early months of the year no combined [184]
action had been taken against Bruce. The local magnates had all they could do to

50 Ann. Loch Cé, 1316. Stephen of Exeter was also lord of Athmethan (Affane), Co. Waterford: 42nd Rep. D.K., pp. 23, 24. Mac Firbis places him as son of Jordan Óg, and grandson of the Jordan who formed the manor of Ballylahan (*ante*, vol. iii, pp. 197–8 [pp. 380–1]), but the descent is not clear: consult Knox, History of Mayo, pp. 306–10. Miles de Cogan (son and heir of John de Cogan III), William de Prendergast, John de Staunton, and William Lawless were also slain. News of Felim's action reached Dublin on July 20: Laud MS. Annals (as above), p. 296. 51 Laud MS. Annals, u. s., p. 352. He left his son (Edmond Albanach ?) in his stead. 52 'On the day of St. Laurence the Martyr': Ann. Loch Cé. The Laud MS. Annals say, 'in the week following the Feast of St. Laurence', calculated probably from the time when the news reached Dublin. Wherever we can test them the precise dates so often given about this time in the Laud MS. seem remarkably accurate. 53 Hy Many, p. 136. O'Donovan's rendering. On June 14, 1320, Owen O'Madden, two of his brothers, and a nephew, and their heirs, at the instance of the Earl of Ulster, were granted the use of English laws: Irish Pat. Roll, 13 Ed. II (93). 54 Laud MS. Annals, p. 297. By a 'slim trick' on June 24 they had seized and imprisoned thirty Scots sent according to agreement to receive their submission, p. 350.

defend their own lands from the attacks of the Irish. No help was obtained from the Crown, which did nothing beyond sending an embassy to Rome to seek spiritual aid against the Scottish enemy.[55] The weak and humiliated king and his cousin, the incompetent self-seeking Earl Thomas of Lancaster, were more concerned in thwarting each other than in upholding the honour of England in Northumbria, in S. Wales, or in Ireland. Some efforts were indeed made by the local lords whom Bruce had dispossessed in Ulster. About the end of October, John Logan and Hugh Byset[56] obtained an advantage over the Scots in Ulster and slew three hundred men-at-arms; and on December 5 Alan Stewart, who was taken prisoner by John Logan and John Sandale, was brought to Dublin Castle. But by the close of the year[57] Robert Bruce with many 'galloglasses' had joined his brother at Carrickfergus, and a new and more formidable campaign was in prospect.

[185] About February 13, 1317,[58] the two brothers, at the head of an army refreshed and strengthened, and supported by a large body of the Northern Irish, arrived without warning at Slane in Meath[59] and threatened Dublin. An event now occurred which has never been satistactorily explained, and, indeed, is rather puzzling. On the 21st Robert of Nottingham, Mayor of Dublin, forcibly seized the Earl of Ulster and some of his relatives who were then in St. Mary's Abbey and imprisoned them in Dublin Castle. It is clear that the citizens suspected the earl of complicity with Bruce, but the grounds of their suspicion are obscure, and it may be doubted whether they were well founded. The entry in the annals, in which the Dublin view is given, seems to say that the Scots reached Slane without being perceived, though the army of Ulster was in their presence, and that they ravaged the whole country before their eyes,[60] the implication apparently being that the army of the Earl of Ulster had not done its duty in opposing the Scots. A different light is thrown on this event by the narrative in 'The Bruce'. Barbour there states at great length (what is not mentioned elsewhere) that Richard de Clare [i.e. Richard de Burgh, Earl of Ulster] had assembled 40,000 men [no doubt a reckless exaggeration] to oppose the Scots on this occasion. Not daring to
[186] meet them in the open, however, he laid an ambuscade for them on the line of march. He allowed Edward Bruce and the vanguard to pass, but attacked the rearguard under King Robert, with the result that a hard battle—according to Barbour, the hardest fighting of all the war—ensued. At last the earl had to give way and fled to Dublin.[61] It is clear that the earl's forces, consisting mainly of his Gaelic levies, were dispersed,

55 Papal Letters, vol. ii, pp. 127–32. 56 It was seemingly after this that Hugh Byset adhered to the Scots. 57 Circa Natale Domini: Clyn. This approximate date for the arrival of Robert Bruce may be accepted. The Irish annals place it among the first entries of 1317. An undated entry in the Laud MS. (p. 352) would seem to place it before the surrender of Carrickfergus, but the entry records a mere rumour. According to Barbour (xvi. 38–48), who is utterly vague, Carrickfergus was in the hands of Edward Bruce when his brother arrived (cf. ibid., xv. 259). 58 *Circa festum Carniprivii* (i.e. February 13, 1317), Laud MS. Annals. There can be no doubt about the date yet Barbour (xvi. 63) says that the two brothers advanced 'in the month of May, Quhen byrdis singis on the spray' &c. 59 It is noteworthy that the Bruces made no attempt on the walled town of Drogheda: 'Thai raid evin forrouth Drouchyndra,/And forrouth Devilling syne alsua.' The Bruce, xvi. 261–2. 60 Laud MS. Annals (as above), p. 298. The words are: 'Circa festum Carniprivii venerunt Scoti oeculte usque Slane cum viginti millibus armatis, et exercitus Ultonie coram illis, et cepredaverunt ante ipsos totam patriam.' 61 The Bruce, xvi. 74–213.

and it is possible that some of them deserted to Bruce and gave him their allegiance.[62]

There are many other allusions in the Laud MS. to the 'Ultonienses', and all show the distrust and dislike with which the men of Dublin regarded them. Their natural lord was now in prison, and those who did not join Bruce were outcasts, dispossessed of their homes and deprived of their leader. In March 2,000 of them at their own request were enrolled under the banner of the king, but, we are told, 'they did more harm than the Scots, and ate meat throughout Lent, and ravaged the country, for which they deserved the malediction of God and man'.[63] They were afterwards, as we shall see, placed under the leadership of the young Earl of Kildare, but the famine of 1317 was even worse than that of the previous year, and we read of 'the marvellous vengeance' that befell the Ulstermen early in 1318 for the damage they had done in Ireland and for eating meat in Lent; for 'they were reduced to eating one another, so that out of 10,000 there remained only about 300 who escaped the vengeance of God'. [187]
They even exhumed the dead and cooked the flesh in the skulls and ate it, and their women devoured their own children from hunger.[64] It may be that with some of them, as in the case of Dante's Count Ugolino, 'fasting got the mastery of grief', but the malign exaggeration of this gruesome tale, if indeed it had any foundation, is manifest. Bad as the famine was, it did not cause a dearth of pots!

Of possible grounds of suspicion against the earl himself, we may note that his daughter Elizabeth was the wife of Robert Bruce. Taken prisoner by the English in 1306, she had been restored to her husband in an exchange of prisoners after Bannockburn and was now the Scottish Queen. Moreover, in the previous July the earl had interfered with the sailing of some ships from Drogheda to re-victual Carrickfergus, but this action appears to have been part of a bargain for the release of his cousin Sir William de Burgh from captivity in Scotland.[65] No other facts are known which might be thought to throw doubt upon his loyalty. He had undoubtedly failed to overcome Edward Bruce in the first campaign, probably owing to the defection of Felim, and now he had failed to stay the course of the victorious brothers, probably owing to a similar defection; but other Anglo-Irish lords had equally failed against the Scots, and even the chivalry of England had been broken to pieces in the vain attempt to break the Scottish 'schiltroms' at Bannockburn. On the other hand, he had for years been fighting against the Scots, in their own country as well as in Ulster, and no one person in Ireland had lost more through the Scottish invasion than the lord of Ulster [188]
and Connaught or had stronger motives for repelling the invaders.

The king had trusted him fully and had often thanked and rewarded him for his services,[66] and now sent mandates ordering an inquiry into the causes of his imprisonment, and even directing that he should be sent under safe-conduct to England.[67]

62 John, son of Nicholas of Slane, forfeited his lands for adherence to the Scots: Cal. Pat. Roll (Ireland), 13 Ed. II (86). 63 Laud MS. Annals (as above), p. 300. 64 Laud. MS. Annals (as above), p. 357. 65 Ibid., p. 296. 66 On August 21, 1309, Richard de Burgh had been appointed commissioner to treat for terms of peace with Robert Bruce, whose envoys were John de Menteith and Neil Campbell: Cal. Pat. Rolls, 3 Ed. II, p. 189. About the same time, for his good services, the yearly rent of 500 marks for his Connaught lands was remitted, and he was given the custody of the king's castles at Roscommon, Randown, and Athlone: ibid., p. 182. 67 Cal. Close Roll, 10 Ed. II (1317), pp. 404–5, transcribed Hist. and Mun.

Yet it was not until May 8 that, after much debating, he was at length liberated.[68] On the whole it seems reasonable to conclude that the action of the citizens in imprisoning the earl was inspired by panic and was persevered in from fear of his vengeance. They had good grounds for distrusting his ability to protect them. They owed him no allegiance, they were jealous of feudal claims, and viewed with alarm the presence of the magnates in their city. But they had no real grounds for doubting his fidelity, and their precipitate action was not calculated to confirm the loyalty of his followers.

It is, indeed, certain that the citizens were thoroughly alarmed at the near approach
[189] of the Scots and took hurried measures for the protection of their city. The old north wall of the town, which still in part exists, and has recently been exposed to view by the removal of some old houses, ran on either side of the still existing St. Audoen's Gate and past a gate which then stood in Wine Tavern Street, parallel to but some distance south of, the present river embankment. A strip of land had been reclaimed between this wall and the river,[69] and houses had been built thereon, including the Dominican Convent, thus weakening the defence in this direction and perhaps exposing the bridge-end. The citizens now pulled down the church of the Dominicans and with the stones built a wall along the quay,[70] and connected it at the west end with the old west wall near Gormon's Gate, thus enlarging the town towards the north and protecting the bridge-end. They also threw down the belltower of the church of St. Mary del Dam near the walls, and used the stones for the repair of the castle.[71]

On February 23 Bruce advanced towards Dublin, but stopped at Castleknock,[72]
[190] where he took Hugh Tyrrell and his wife prisoners, but released them on ransom. The same night the citizens of Dublin fired the western suburbs about St. Thomas's Street, to prevent the Scots obtaining shelter therein from which to assault the city. The fire extended further than was intended, and altogether four-fifths of the suburbs were destroyed.[73] When Bruce saw the desperate measures taken by the citizens and learned that the city was well fortified to resist assault, he turned aside to Leixlip, where he remained four days, burning and plundering.

At this period of the relative evolution of attack and defence, castles and walled towns, if adequately garrisoned and provided, were not easily taken by assault—unless

Docs. Irel. (Gilbert), pp. 397-401, also Foedera, ii. 326, 327. It appears from these mandates that Gilbert and Hubert de Burgh were also imprisoned. A Hubert, son of Gilbert de Burgh, was a juror on one of the inquisitions taken in 1333 after the murder of Earl William de Burgh. **68** Laud MS. Annals, p. 354. **69** I was informed by the foreman of the works that when removing a portion of this wall, east of School-House Lane, a layer of shells was found close up to the foundations on the side facing the river, thus indicating that at one period the river flowed by the wall. **70** Laud MS. Annals, p. 363. Richard Stanihurst in his Description of Ireland (c. 1585) mistakenly supposes that it was the wall by St. Audoen's Gate and Wine Tavern Gate, which was built at this time; but, apart from the positive statement in our annals, there are clear references to these gates at an earlier period. **71** Historical and Municipal Docs. Irel., pp. 405-6. The church was pre-Norman: see vol. i, *ante*, p. 242 [p. 89]. **72** Bruce is said to have arrested his march here on learning of the taking of the Earl of Ulster. This may have been the supposition of those who imprisoned the earl, but, if he could have taken Dublin, Bruce would not have left so important a place intact in his rear, and his ultimate change of objective is better explained, as is done later, by the measures taken for the defence of the city. **73** For this burning of their suburbs the mayor and citizens were pardoned, July 20, 1318 (Cal. Pat. Rolis, 12 Ed. II. p. 192), and relieved of 100 marks a year for five years out of the farm due to the exchequer: ibid., p. 204.

indeed a surprise could be effected—and a long siege, such as had been found necessary at Carrickfergus, did not suit Bruce's plan of campaign. Rapid movement was essential to its success. His army had to be fed off the country, and he preferred to swoop down upon the rich demesnes and manorial centres of the great Anglo-Norman lords. Accordingly he marched southwards to Naas, the de Lacys, it is said, contrary to their recent oaths conducting him,[74] and on to Castledermot, where he [191] plundered the Franciscan monastery, and thence by Gowran to Callan, which he reached on March 12. Wherever the Scots went they plundered the rich monastic houses, and even burned or broke the churches, 'But to gif battale nane thai fand'.

At this time, however, Edmund Butler, the justiciar, Thomas Fitz John, the second Earl of Kildare, Richard de Clare, Arnold le Poer, John le Poer, Baron of Dunoyl, and Maurice Fitz Thomas of Desmond were at Kilkenny assembling their forces, but they did not dare to meet the Bruces in the open field, while the latter, on the other hand, as in the case of Dublin and Drogheda, made no attempt against the well-walled city on the Nore.

From Kells near Callan Bruce proceeded to Cashel and thence to Nenagh, where he stayed to burn and destroy the lands of the justiciar. The English magnates, adopting Fabian tactics, hung about his rear, but failed to stay his destroying hand. Then in the first week in April the Bruces were induced by Donough O'Brien, who had recently been expelled from Thomond, to march towards Limerick, no doubt with the object of destroying the lands of Richard de Clare and the other English settlers in Thomond, and in the expectation, perhaps, of a general rising of the Irish in the west, if not with the hope of taking Limerick itself. They got as far as Castleconnell on the Shannon, while the magnates, with whom was Murtough O'Brien, Donough's rival, advanced to Ludden near Cahirconlish about eight miles to the south.[75] The latter [192] were now joined by 'the meat-eating cattle-raiding' band of Ulstermen who were placed under the Earl of Kildare, but though there was some skirmishing,[76] there seems to have been no fighting of any moment.

But now an abler and more ruthless commander than Edmund Butler was at hand. On April 7 Roger Mortimer of Wigmore, who had been appointed king's lieutenant with extensive powers, landed at Youghal with a fresh force and hastened towards the scene.[77] He sent a dispatch to Edmund Butler to do nothing before his arrival. The

74 Sir Hugh Canon, who had been sheriff of Kildare and was a justice of the king's bench, is said to have directed his brother-in-law, 'Wadin le Whyte', i.e. Walter le Blund (probably descended from the first Hugh de Lacy's widow: see *ante*, vol. ii, p. 111, note [p. 195, note 2]), to guide the Scots through the country. Hugh Canon was killed next year by Andrew Bermingham, and Walter le Blund was outlawed along with the de Lacys. See Chart. St. Mary's Abbey, Dublin, vol. ii, pp. 299, 357, 411; and Cal. Pat. Roll (Ireland). 11 Ed. II, p. 23 b (119). 75 Clyn's Annals, p. 13. This was *in Paschate*. Easter Sunday in 1317 fell on April 3 and Palm Sunday on March 27. Some of the marginal dates added by Gilbert to his transcript of the Laud MS. are wrong. Edmund Butler was allowed 200 marks (beyond his fee of £500) for wages and expenses in connexion with his expedition to 'Lodene' to encounter the Scottish and Irish felons: Pipe Roll (Ireland), 12 Ed. II, 42nd Rep. D.K., p. 12. He was at 'Lodyn' on April 10, 1317: Cal. Pat. Roll (Ireland), 11 Ed. II, p. 21b (28-9). 76 Adam Bretoun, seneschal of Carlow, was allowed £20 for good service ... in fighting against the Scots in the district of Lodyn in the company of Thomas, son of John, Earl of Kildare: Pipe Roll (Ireland), 10 Ed. II, 39th Rep. D.K., p. 73. 77 On Jan. 4, 1317, John de Hastings and

toils were now gathering around the Scots. They were far from their base in Ulster.
[193] Two years of fighting and famine had beggared the country, and it was becoming more and more difficult to feed the army. There was, moreover, no sign of any general rising of the Irish. The blow at Athenry had crushed Connaught, and the mangled remnants of the Gaelic clans were at variance among themselves. Even in Thomond Murtough O'Brien had for the moment thrown in his lot with Richard de Clare and the English, and his exiled rival Donough was powerless to provoke a rising.[78] When about the middle of April Bruce received intelligence of the advent of Mortimer, he slipped away in the night and retreated towards Kildare. Here Barbour tells the well-known story of how King Robert halted his army rather than leave behind a poor laundress who was overtaken by the pains of childbirth:

> This was a full gret curtasy
> That sic a king and swa mychty
> Gert his men duell on this maner
> Bot for a full pouir laynder.

With that want of solidarity which marks all the operations of the English, the Munster forces now dispersed, and the Scots were followed as far as Naas by the Earl of Kildare and his Ulster band alone, while Mortimer and the magnates at Kilkenny failed to take any steps to intercept the retreat. Bruce rested in a wood near Trim for a week to refresh his men, who were perishing with hunger and fatigue, and on May 1 finally retired into Ulster.[79]

Like the raid of Edward Bruce into Meath and Kildare in the winter of 1315–16, this raid of the two brothers also took place in the winter. The choice of season was
[194] deliberate. The strength of the feudal army rested mainly in their horse, and summer-time suited it best, when the ground was hard and grass was plentiful. But the strength of the Scottish forces lay in their trained bands of pike-men, who were comparatively little affected by weather conditions. In winter they would have more opportunities of protecting their flanks by marshy ground, where the enemy's cavalry could not operate, while the scarcity of fodder would be a constant difficulty for their foes.

But this winter raid of the two Bruces, like the previous raid of Edward Bruce, however disastrous to the feudal lords and their humbler dependents, and however fatal to the prestige of the Crown, was also disastrous to Edward Bruce and fatal to his projected kingdom. For him it had simply resulted in the wasting of a second army. Beyond weakening his enemy he had gained no military advantage. His victories were Pyrrhic victories.

fourteen others were ordered to go to Ireland in person or send men-at-arms according to the extent of their lands in that country . . . to be at Haverford at the Purification next (Feb. 2). . . the king having ordered Roger de Mortimer of Wigmore to proceed thence to Ireland to repel the invasion of Edward Bruce: Cal. Close Rolls, 10 Ed. II (1317), p. 451; Foedera, vol. ii, p. 309. Roger de Mortimer was appointed Keeper of Ireland on Nov. 23, 1316: Cal. Pat. Rolls, 10 Ed. II, p. 563; Foedera, vol. ii, pp. 301-2. **78** *Supra*, pp. 88–9 [pp. 477–8]. **79** Laud MS., pp. 301-2.

He had not taken, or at least had not held, a single important town or strategic point outside of Ulster. The Irish in general did not welcome him as a deliverer, and there was no concerted rising in his favour. A few took advantage of the disturbance to plunder their English neighbours, but were speedily repressed. The native kings in the west and south who had rebelled at his instigation, or trusting to his assistance, had been crushed. Robert Bruce, no doubt, saw that nothing was to be gained by his remaining in Ireland, and accordingly about Pentecost (May 22) with the Earl of Moray[80] he returned to Scotland to carry on the border warfare there. Edward Bruce indeed remained for the time safe in Ulster, but he was henceforth powerless outside its borders.

Mortimer now came to Dublin, and on May 8 the Earl of Ulster was released by [195]
the council on his undertaking not to do any injury to the citizens on account of his imprisonment except by process of law. He took no legal proceedings, however, and on June 27 he gave his oath and found sureties that he would obey the mandates of the law and repel the Irish and Scottish enemies of the king.

Mortimer now summoned the de Lacys to surrender to the king's peace, but they slew his emissary and defied him. He accordingly assembled a force and drove them into exile, and on July 18, 1317, at Mortimer's instance they were proclaimed felons by the council at Dublin and their lands confiscated.[81] Mortimer next set about the restoration of order in Meath and Leinster. He went to Drogheda, where some of the starving Ulstermen were punished for cattle-stealing, but he made no attempt to recover Ulster. He forced O'Farrell of Annaly to sue for peace and give hostages, and then proceeded to punish the Irish of Imaile and Okinselagh (?).[82] The chieftain of the O'Byrnes surrendered himself, and the Archebolds were mainprised by the Earl of Kildare. On June 28 John of Athy was appointed admiral of the fleet destined for service against the Scots,[83] and on July 2 he succeeded in capturing Thomas of Down, [196]
the 'scummar of the se' mentioned by Barbour, and forty of his men.[84]

On February 2, 1318, the Papal Bull ordering a peace for two years between the King of England and Robert Bruce under pain of excommunication was read in Dublin in the church of the Holy Trinity.[85] Bruce refused to open the papal letters because they were not addressed to him as King of Scotland, and, so far from consenting to a cessation of hostilities, proceeded to press the siege of Berwick. Interdicts and threats of excommunication followed, but in the result papal interference on behalf of the English king had little or no effect.

80 Chron. Lanercost (Maxwell), p. 218, gives the date. 81 After the disgrace and death of Mortimer the legality of this outlawry was questioned at the instance of Edmund, son and heir of Almaric de Lacy; see the Plea Roll of 1384 transcribed in Chart. St. Mary's Abbey, Dublin, vol. ii, pp. 409–16, where all Mortimer's proceedings are recited, but the result of the appeal is not given. Cf. Laud MS., p. 356, and Cal. Pat. Roll (Ireland), 11 Ed. II (119). In 1331 Hugh de Lacy was pardoned and returned to Ireland: Laud MS., p. 374. 82 The Laud MS. has 'Glynsely'. Grace reads ' Olinseli'. 83 Cal. Pat. Rolls, 11 Ed. II, p. 165. 84 Laud MS., p. 355, here described as *fortissimus latro*. About Easter 1316 the king ordered the men of Drogheda to provide ships for an expedition against 'Thomas Dun': Hist. and Municipal Docs. Ireland (Gilbert), p. 377. 85 Laud MS., p. 357. For this Bull see Rymer's Foedera, vol. ii, pt. 1, p. 327; cf. p. 364, and Papal Letters, vol. ii, p. 427 &c.

Meanwhile, since the battle of Athenry Connaught was torn by the rival factions of the O'Conors contending for the vacant throne. At first for a brief period a cousin of the late King Felim was made king, but early in 1317 he was deposed and afterwards killed, and Turlough O Conor, Felim's brother, succeeded,[86] only, however, to be supplanted next year after a fierce battle by the representative of the Sligo O'Conors now
[197] coming more prominently into notice. The fighting was almost confined to the Irish districts. The English settlers headed by Sir William de Burgh and Richard de Bermingham, Baron of Athenry, seem in general to have held their own. In Thomond it was otherwise. The death of Richard de Clare on May 10, 1318, in a skirmish near Dysert O'Dea, put an end to the hope of English control in that region.

In May 1318, soon after the capture of Berwick by the Scots, Mortimer was recalled to England, and the custody of Ireland together with the chancellorship was entrusted to William Fitz John, Archbishop of Cashel. During his period of office there was no further attempt made by the Scots in Ireland. The harvest was exceptionally good, a welcome relief after the famine of the last two years. Bread from new flour appeared as early as July 25, a thing rarely or never known before, and the price of corn fell from sixteen to seven shillings. On October 9 Alexander de Bykenore, who had been consecrated Archbishop of Dublin by the Pope at Avignon in the previous year, entered Dublin as justiciar.

And now on October 14, 1318, came the end of this fateful episode. Edward Bruce, of whom we have heard nothing since May in the previous year, and who seems to have been for part of the time in Scotland, was once more advancing southwards out of Ulster. He was accompanied by his faithful knights Philip de Mowbray, Walter de
[198] Soulis,[87] and John Steward,[78] but the resourceful Earl of Moray was no longer with him. He was, however, now openly supported by Walter, Hugh, Robert, and Almaric de Lacy, Walter le Blund,[89] and John de Caermarthen.[90] The Scots numbered between 2,000 and 3,000 men,

> Outane the kyngis off Erischry
> That in gret rowtis raid hym by.[91]

Bruce entered the county Louth, as before, by Moiry Pass. An English force had been hastily collected to oppose him under the command of John de Bermingham.[92]

86 William de Burgh and the English supported Turlough O'Conor, and on March 8, 1318, the king granted to Turlough the lands of Sil Murray, the Feths, near Athlone, and the king's lands of Tirmany (excepting the lands of the English and the burgage lands of the towns) to hold during good behaviour at the accustomed rent: Cal. Pat. Roll (Ireland), 11 Ed. II, p. 23 (103). 87 So in Laud MS., p. 359. Barbour, however, speaks of John de Soulis as killed in the battle (xviii. 110), but John appears to have been already dead, c. 1316: Cal. Docs. Scot., vol. iii, no. 530. 88 So in The Bruce, xviii. 31. He had been wounded at the battle of Connor, but was healed at Montpelier: ibid., xv. 83. 89 For Walter le Blund or White, see *ante*, p. 190, note [p. 530, note 78]. 90 John de Kermerdyn was also outlawed along with the de Lacys in July 1317, and his lands of Aghaviller, Co. Kilkenny, confiscated: Pipe Roll (Ireland), 12 Ed. II, 42nd Rep. D.K., p. 19. 91 The Bruce, xviii. 8–9. Barbour reckons the Irish as 'weill forty thousand neir!': ibid., 89. 92 John de Bermingham was son and heir of Peter de Bermingham of Tethmoy (not of Peter of Athenry, as stated in Dict. Nat. Biog. and elsewhere); see Papal Letters, vol. ii, p. 245, where it appears that he was

With him were some of his relatives and some local lords and officials and their levies. Richard de Tuit,[93] Milo de Verdun, Hugh de Turpilton, Herbert de Sutton and John [199]
de Cusack are mentioned. To these were added a chosen band of the townsfolk of Drogheda under Walter de la Pulle, sheriff of Louth. Roland Joce, Archbishop of Armagh, was also present and gave the army absolution.[94] None of the chief lords of Ireland were engaged. With the exception of the Leinster Berminghams the army seems to have been composed of the common people of the neighbouring districts mustered under their lesser lords and local officials. We cannot tell their numbers,[95] but while it would seem that they were more numerous than the Scots without their Irish allies, their numerical superiority, seeing how the army was got together, cannot have been very great.

North of Dundalk, beyond the low-lying land near the harbour and river, the [200]
ground rises first gradually and then more rapidly, up to the hill of Faughart. This was the site of the battle, but we have few trustworthy details of the fight. The English appear to have broken the Scottish ranks with a rush, and all who stood their ground were slain. Edward Bruce himself was found dead under the dead body of John Maupas, one of the Drogheda contingent. Walter de Soulis and John Steward were also slain, and Philip de Mowbray was mortally wounded. Among the leaders who were slain we may also add, from the Irish annals, MacRory, king of the Innsi-Gall, and Mac Donnell, king of Argyle.[96] Hugh and Walter de Lacy were among the few who escaped. John de Bermingham brought Bruce's head to the king and was created Earl of Louth with the barony of Ardee in recognition of his services.[97]

the founder of Monasteroris in Tethmoy. On the death of Peter, Richard de Burgh, Earl of Ulster, was granted the marriage of John: Cal. Pat. Rolls, 1 Ed. II, p. 76; and the earl afterwards gave his daughter Avelina in marriage to John: Papal Letters, vol. ii, p. 209. According to Clyn he had assisted Roger de Mortimer in expelling the de Lacys from Meath, and had been knighted by him. The Book of Howth states at length that he owed his appointment to Alexander de Bicknor, the new archbishop-justiciar, who only reached Dublin five days before the battle. 93 Richard de Tuit and Walter de la Pulle held at this time the custody of some of the lands of Theobald de Verdun, deceased, and Nicholas de Verdun and his brother Milo held the residue: Pipe Roll (Ireland), 11 Ed. II, 42nd Rep. D.K., pp. 16, 24. Walter de la Pulle was sheriff of Louth from May 10, 1318: ibid., p. 64. He had been implicated in the Verdun riot of 1312, but had seemingly obtained pardon: Plea Rolls printed in Chart. St. Mary's Abbey, vol. ii, App. III. He was escheator in 1324 (Cal. Close Roll (Ireland), 18 Ed. II, no. 27), and was succeeded by Herbert de Sutton: ibid., 20 Ed. II, no. 139. Hugh de Turpilton had already been given the manor of Martry (Co. Meath), forfeited by Walter de Say (Cal. Pat. Roll (Ireland), 11 Ed. II, no. 51), and was afterwards further rewarded: ibid., no. 154 and Cal. Pat. Rolls, 2 Ed. III, p. 345. John de Cusack was sheriff of Louth in 1315-16: Pipe Roll (Ireland), 9 Ed. II, 39th Rep. D.K., p. 67. He had 'sixty men at arms, the best of his own surname and lineage, at Dundalk when Edward Bruce was killed', and was rewarded with a grant of land: Cal. Docs. Scotland, vol. iii, no. 640-1. 94 Laud MS., p. 360. 95 In Marlborough's Chronicle it is said with curious precision that the English numbered 1,324 men, but as the entry goes on to state that they slew 8,274 of Bruce's men, we cannot rely upon it. Barbour's statement that 'Richard of Clare' had with him at Dundalk 'of trappit hors tuenty thousand' besides footmen (xviii. 17), in all 40,000 and more (ibid. 93), is obviously, like nearly all his numerical statements, worthless. 96 *Mac Ruaidhri rí Innsi-Gall agus Mac Domnaill rí Aerther-Ghaidhel*: Ann. Ulst. The persons intended would seem to be Lochlan, son of Alan of Clan Rory and Angus Og of Clan Donald (see Pedigree of Maic Somhairle, *ante*, vol. iii, appendix to chapter xxx [pp. 406–7), but I am not aware of any other authority for their deaths in this battle. 97 Laud MS. Annals, pp. 359-60.

So much we learn from contemporary sources, but can we not gain some trustworthy idea of the tactics of this memorable battle from the later accounts which have come down to us?

According to Barbour, Bruce's knights urged him not to fight immediately, but to
[201] await some reinforcements reported to be near at hand.[98] But Edward Bruce never willingly shirked a fight, and this time, at all events, would not suffer his inclination to be overborne by prudent counsels:

> Now help quha will, for sekirly
> This day, but mair baid, fecht will I.
> Sa na man say, quhill I may dre,
> That strynth of men sall ger me fle!

It was bravely though foolishly spoken. 'So be it', quoth the knights in effect, 'we shall abide what God has in store.' But the Irish kings, when they found that Bruce's resolution was not to be shaken, warned him plainly not to count on them, saying:

> For our maner is of this land
> To follow and ficht, and ficht fleand,
> And nocht till stand in plane melle
> Quhill the ta part discumfit be.

Accordingly they took their stand on the heights above the battlefield where they could watch the issue. They did not indeed join in with the victors in the field. They gave succour to some of Bruce's party who fled. On the other hand, the victors are said not to have attacked the Irish. The few Scots who escaped from the field met the reinforcements who came too late, and made their way to the ships at Carrickfergus, but, according to Barbour,

> that wes nocht forouten pane,
> For thai war mony tymes that day
> Assailit with Erischry.

How are we to account for this alleged withdrawal of the Irish forces from this cru-
[202] cial engagement? It cannot have been due to cowardice. The Irish were born fighters. It is true that they often adopted Fabian tactics against the English, but it is not the fact that they never stood in plain *mélee* until one side was discomfited. Only two years

98 The Bruce, xviii. 51-3. The Scalacronica of Sir Thomas Gray similarly says that Bruee 'would not wait for reinforeements, which had lately arrived and were not more than six leagues distant'. But the Lanercost Chronicle speaks of Bruce arriving at Dundalk 'with his Irish adherents and a great army of Scots which had newly arrived in Ireland to enable him to invade and lay waste that land'; and the *Cath Fhochairle* speaks of Bruce having been 'joined by another army from the north', apparently in the middle of the fight.

had elapsed since the carnage of Athenry. They may well, however, have agreed with the Scottish knights in thinking that the occasion was not a favourable one for a regular pitched battle, but we cannot rely implicitly on Barbour's account of their conduct.

The Irish are not mentioned in the accounts of the battle given in the Irish and Anglo-Irish annals, but it is otherwise in the *Cath Fhochairte* Tract.[99] Here, as in the Lanercost Chronicle,[1] Bruce's forces are represented as in three battalions. The host of the Gaels were northwards (i.e. near the brow of the Hill of Faughart), the Galls and Gaels of Meath in the centre (i.e. lower down the slopes), and the Scottish host in a position southwards (i.e. nearest to Dundalk). The English archers poured their arrows on the Gaels, so that 'they were forced from their position', and many of them were killed or wounded. The heavy cavalry charged the Galls of Meath and drove them back on to the brow of the hill, while Bermingham himself made a vigorous [203]
onset against the Scottish battalion, 'so that it suffered much more than the other divisions of the army'. Nevertheless the southern and central divisions rallied under Bruce and forced the enemy to the foot of the hill. When the Gaels perceived this brave charge, they rushed upon the archers, whose arrows were spent, and routed them. The broken columns now united and, having been 'joined by another body of forces from the north'—clearly the Scottish reinforcements which Barbour says were near at hand, but had not arrived, and the Lanercost Chronicle says had already joined Bruce—forced back their foes and restored the fortune of the day to the Scottish side.

But now, according to this account, all was lost through the death of Bruce. His forces, secure of victory, had sat down to refresh themselves and take food, while the king himself walked about alone on the field inspecting the dead. At this moment a Gall, disguised as an idiot juggler, came up to Bruce, and pretending to perform a trick for his amusement, killed him with an iron ball attached to a chain, and then took to his heels and escaped. Taking advantage of the confusion and disorganization that followed the death of the king, the English completely routed their opponents.

We must, however, reject this story[2] of the death of Edward Bruce. It is improbable in itself. It is inconsistent with the entry in the earlier Irish annals that Bruce was slain by the English 'through the power of battle and bravery', and it is contradicted [204]
by the specific statement in the Laud MS. that John Maupas slew him in the battle 'viriliter cum magno honore', and was afterwards found dead over the dead body of the king. It would certainly have found ready credence with the Scots and would have been enshrined in Barbour's verse had there been any foundation for it. Its genesis, moreover, is easily understood. A simple people cannot bring itself to believe that its

99 Printed in The Louth Archaeological Journal, vol. i, pp. 87–9. 1 This tract is published from a transcript written by Bryan Geraghty in 1845, but evidently from a much older original. It is composed in full sympathy with Edward Bruce's attempt to become king of Ireland, and gives an independent but fairly correct account, so far as it goes, of his movements. It preserves some Irish traditions not otherwise known. The Lanercost Chronicle does not state the composition of the three columns or battalions, but says they were so far apart that each was disposed of before the next could come to its assistanoe. 2 The story is, however, at least as old as Thady Dowling, Chancellor of Leighlin, who died in 1628. See his Annals under date 1314, where, breaking into English, he writes: 'Mappas, a jugler, knocked him with ij bullets in a bagg and killed him.'

hero has been overcome in fair fight. Barbour himself tells a story, hardly consistent indeed with this Irish tradition, but owing its origin, no doubt, to similar feelings. He says that Bruce did not wear his coat-of-arms that day, but gave it to his faithful follower, Gib (or Gilbert) Harper, who bore it in his stead. In the result the latter was mistaken for Schyr Edward, and it was really Gib Harper's head that was brought 'by Johne Mawpas' to King Edward in England.[3] But Bruce's appearance was well known both in England and in Ireland, and a mistake as to the identity of the head could not have occurred. The story is merely an attempt to spare the Scottish people the painful thought that their hero's body was mutilated and failed to obtain honourable burial.

Apart, however, from this Irish tradition of the precise way in which Edward Bruce met his fate, there seems no reason to doubt the substantial correctness of this account of the tactics of the battle and of the part played in it by the Irish. I gather from it that Bruce chose the ground, and drew up his three divisions, as stated, at intervals on the
[205] descending slopes of the hill. The English did not advance through Dundalk—where the bridge and narrow causeway leading northwards from the bridge could have been easily defended—but crossed the Castletown stream somewhere higher up. Thus approaching from the southwest, their three divisions engaged the three divisions of the enemy nearly at the same time. It is noteworthy that their heavy cavalry was not employed against the Scots, but against the de Lacys and the Meathmen. John de Bermingham had evidently learned the lesson of Bannockburn, repeated, no doubt, many times in Ireland, that heavy-armed horse would only shatter itself in vain against the Scottish 'schiltroms', and he probably relied on the rush of a superior force of footmen. His archers served to disperse the Irish contingent, who were presumably protected only by their 'bright saffron shirts'. They did not shirk the fight, as stated by Barbour, but suffered with the rest.

At the same time there are good grounds for thinking that even the Irish of the north, never quite whole-hearted in their support of Bruce, had come to see that his presence in Ireland brought them nothing but evil—sword, famine, and pestilence—and that the sooner the last Scot quitted the shores of Ireland the better for all concerned. The Papal Bulls, too, excommunicating Bruce and his adherents, though despised by Bruce himself, may have influenced many and caused them to leave him to his fate. The actual assistance given by those of the Irish who were present at the final scene was perhaps negligible, and the Scots had good reason for thinking that the Irish failed to support Bruce at the last.

A contemporary Dublin record expresses the feeling of relief which came over the
[206] English community at the result of the battle of Dundalk: 'sic per manus communis populi et dextram Dei deliberatur populus Dei a precognita et machinata servitute'.[4] But the relief was not confined to the English. The Irish annalist is even more emphatic: 'Edward Bruce, the destroyer of all Erinn in general, both English and Gael, was slain by the English of Erinn through the power of battle and bravery at Dun Delgan . . . and no better deed for the men of all Erinn was performed since the beginning

3 The Bruce, xviii. 94-8, 162-74, 221-8. 4 From the Red Book of the Exchequer, Dublin, quoted by Sir John Davies, 'Discovery' (ed. 1787), p. 65.

of the world, since the Fomorian race was expelled from Erinn, than this deed; for theft, and famine, and destruction of men occurred throughout Erinn during his time for the space of three years and a half, and people used actually to eat one another throughout Erinn.'[5]

Thus ended Edward Bruce's dream of founding a kingdom of his own in Ireland. It never had any chance of realization. The Irish themselves gave him little effective support and showed no enthusiasm for a mere change of masters. Had he driven every person of Norman or English descent out of Ireland he would still have been faced by the far more difficult task of welding the warring Celtic clans into one nation under his rule, and, with the might of England against him, it is not likely that he could have gained even the measure of success attained by Strongbow and his followers.

5 Ann. Loch Cé, 1318.

[207] CHAPTER XXXVIII

THE EBBING TIDE, 1318–33

Though the Scottish invasion marks the commencement of the ebb of English influence in mediaeval Ireland, its immediate effect, even in Scottish Ulster, was moral and economical rather than political. Sword, famine, and pestilence had brought in their train a general impoverishment which affected both races and all classes alike. The bonds of society were relaxed, and a new spirit of turbulence gradually appeared among the English settlers. But there was no considerable recovery of their lands by the Irish. In Ulster, as long as the earl and his grandson lived, there was no marked political change, but there was many a ruined homestead, and much of the prosperity of the English districts was gone. Much of Leinster and Meath had suffered in the same way, but the border-clans were kept in better control than they had been for many years. In Connaught, the battle of Athenry had effectually weakened the O'Conors, with the result that the de Burghs and Berminghams were relatively stronger, and the lesser Irish clans more independent. In Desmond, Maurice Fitz Thomas gradually became the chief power, though his lands lay mostly outside of Desmond proper. In Thomond, however, though Bunratty and Tradry were not immediately lost, the
[208] defeat and death of Richard de Clare left Murtough O'Brien, who enjoyed the friendship of the de Burghs, more powerful than before; while in part of Ormond, Brian Bán O'Brien, grandson of Brian Roe, was becoming a power which threatened both the Butlers and the de Burghs.

For some years, however, matters went smoothly in Ireland. Rewards were given to those who had been conspicuous in resisting and defeating the Scots, and compensation was given to some of those who had suffered injury from the movements of armies. In particular John de Bermingham, who commanded at Faughart, was created Earl of Louth, and was given all the issues of the entire county and the office of sheriff for life, with knights' fees, &c., as fully as Thomas Fitz John (son of John Fitz Thomas) held the county of Kildare. To this was afterwards added cognizance of all felonies.[1] John of Athy, admiral of the fleet serving against the Scots, was given the manor of Glenarm in Ulster, forfeited by Hugh By set for adherence to the Scots.[2] Amongst others who were rewarded with lands for special services against the Scots were Hugh de Turpilton, John de Cusack, Edmund de Bermingham, Miles de Verdun, and Adam le Bretoun, seneschal of Carlow.[3] As we have seen, the de Lacys of Meath, believed to have been descended from Robert de Lacy, brother of the first

1 Cal. Pat. Rolls, 12 Ed. II, p. 334; Foedera, vol. ii, pp. 393, 397. 2 Ibid., p. 313. He had already been given the manor of Dissard in Meath: ibid., 11 Ed. II, p. 126. 3 Cal. Pat. Rolls, 12 Ed. II, p. 343; Cal. Pat. Roll

Hugh and lord of Rathwire, were declared felons and their lands confiscated. There were some other confiscations, but they do not appear to have been numerous, and several Ulster men who, probably under compulsion, had joined the Scots were pardoned.[4] Part of the rent of the city of Dublin was remitted in consideration of the costs to which the citizens had been put in erecting defences against the Scots and of their losses through the burning of the suburbs, and allowances were made to several officials and others for good services rendered or for losses sustained in the course of the war. [209]

Even in the impoverished times that followed the Scottish invasion there were some achievements in the cause of progress. Few of the larger rivers of Ireland were as yet spanned by anything more permanent than wooden bridges resting on piles, and some of these were probably wrecked in the late war; but now, in 1319, a bridge of stone was built across the Liffey at Kilcullen, and in the following year another across the Barrow at Leighlin.[5] These were on the high road from Dublin to Carlow and Kilkenny. In a different sphere of human activity there was a yet more ambitious enterprise, which must have seemed to the best minds of the day full of promise, but which now, [210] in the light of history, is seen to have been doomed to failure. This was an attempt made in 1320, to keep Ireland abreast of the educational movement in England by the establishment of a university in Dublin after the example of that at Oxford. It appears that in 1311, John de Leche, Archbishop of Dublin, had obtained a bull from Pope Clement V empowering him to establish in Dublin a university of scholars and a general school (*studium generale*) in every science and lawful faculty, in which masters might freely teach, and scholars attend and study, and such as should be admitted to the honour of the doctorate might obtain a licence in any of the said faculties.[6] Owing, however, to the death of John de Leche in 1313, to disputed elections to the archbishopric, and to the disturbances caused by the Scottish invasion, nothing came of the project until the year 1320, when Alexander de Bykenore, the new archbishop, obtained from Pope John XXII a confirmation of the former bull, and drew up rules for the governance of the university, and the granting of licences in each faculty.[7] We need not look for the university buildings. If the university had any local habitation it was in connexion with St. Patrick's Cathedral, where the doctors in divinity were to deliver their lectures. The first doctors of divinity belonged either to the Franciscan or to the Dominican order, and Master William Rodyard, Dean of St. Patrick's, promoted to the degree of doctor in canon-law, was the first chancellor.[8] For lack of funds to [211]

(Ireland), 11 Ed. 11, p. 21 (5). 4 Among these were Henry de Logan, Walter de Kilkevan, John and Robert le Savage, Robert de Kendale, Alan Fitz Warin, Michael de Kilkevan and John his son: Cal. Pat. Rolls, 12 Ed. II, pp. 313, 580. 5 Laud MS. Annals, p. 361, where the bridges are said to have been constructed by Master Maurice Jak, canon of the cathedral of Kildare. In 1233 eighty marks were required to complete the bridge at Athlone, and the masonry work at the castle of Randown was suspended to enable the work at the bridge to proceed: Cal. Docs Ireland, vol. i, no. 2043. For the bridge across the Nore at Treadingstown (now Bennett's Bridge) there was a grant of customs for three years: ibid. vol. iii, no. 73. 6 For a transcript of the original from the *Registrum Alani* see Mason's History of St. Patrick's, App. VII, §1. 7 Ibid., § 2. In 1318 Pope John XXII granted a bull to the University of Cambridge. 8 Laud MS. Annals, Chart. St. Mary's Abbey, Dublin, vol. ii, p. 361.

maintain the students the university never flourished, though it appears to have lingered on until the temporary suppression of the cathedral in the reign of Henry VIII,[9] and it was not until the year 1592, that by the energy of Archbishop Loftus and some Dublin citizens,[10] who obtained a charter from 'the most serene Queen Elizabeth', by the liberality of the Dublin Council, who granted the splendid site of the dissolved monastery of All Hallows, and by the munificence of the gentry of Ireland, who first subscribed funds, the present college of the Holy and Undivided Trinity was founded 'near Dublin'. But though this movement for the establishment of a university in Dublin did not meet with much success, the fact that the attempt was made is proof that there were men in high places in Ireland who were really in advance of their times, and is further evidence of that precocity of thought and action which manifested itself in many departments in the thirteenth century.

In 1320 a parliament was held in Dublin under Roger Mortimer who had returned to Ireland as justiciar. It took cognizance of the fact that there were bands of evildoers roving throughout the country, lodging with honest folk against their will, and taking their goods; also others who were or pretended to be men of birth, who collected companies of idle men and went from town to town demanding under threats presents of
[212] money, corn, and other victuals; and it was ordained that when any such appeared hue and cry should be raised against them and they should be apprehended and committed to prison. Also it was further ordained that no one should exact rents from persons for being under his 'avouery and protection', that henceforth none should grant protection except the king and lords of liberties; and that no one should take victuals from their tenants or others against their will. By the same statute it was provided that in each county should be assigned a justice—'a man of court, wise, lawful and powerful'—who with two knights of the county should hold assizes and gaol delivery, and also inquire how sheriffs and others had performed their offices upon the articles aforesaid.'[11]

This legislation is one of many indications that a considerable number of people had been ruined by the Scottish depredations and had been rendered lawless and desperate men. Unfortunately economical conditions, to which the impoverishment was partly due, did not improve. The famine of 1316–17 was followed by a murrain followed among the cattle, recorded in the years 1321, 1324, and 1325, and there were epidemics among the people of small-pox in 1327 and of something like influenza[12] in 1328, and great dearth of corn in 1328, 1330, and 1331. These calamities following on the havoc of the recent war tended further to weaken the moral fibre of the English settlers. Many of the leading figures who had occupied the stage of affairs in Ireland
[213] immediately before and during the Scottish invasion passed away about this time. The second Theobald de Verdun, who was lieutenant in Ireland in 1314, died in July 1316,

9 See Mason's History of St. Patrick's, c. xiv; Ware's Antiquities (ed. Harris), p. 242 et seq. 10 Especially Henry Ussher, Archdeacon of Dublin and afterwards Archbishop of Armagh, and Luke Challoner. Both had been educated at Cambridge. See The Book of Trinity College, Dublin, p. 4. 11 Early Statutes (Berry), p. 281. 12 Called *slaedán*, a term now used for 'a cold', 'it lasted for the space of three or four days with every person whom it attacked, so that it was next to death with him': Ann. Loch Ce, 1328.

and his numerous lands in England as well as in Meath and Louth were ultimately divided among his four daughters. John Fitz Thomas, who had pushed his way to the headship of the Geraldines of Offaly, and had recently been created Earl of Kildare, died in the following September, when he was succeeded by his son Thomas. Richard de Clare, as we have seen, was slain in May 1318, leaving an infant son who died three years later, the last male representative of the family. Edmund Butler, who had been justiciar during the darkest days of the invasion, died in 1321, leaving as his heir his son James, a minor, afterwards created Earl of Ormonde; and in the same year died John Wogan, who with a few intermissions had been a successful justiciar from 1295 to 1312. Richard de Bermingham, the victor of Athenry, died in 1322, and William de Burgh, who had shared in that victory, closed an active career of combat in 1324. Finally Richard de Burgh, the 'Red Earl' of Ulster, now feeble health, attended his last parliament at Kilkenny in 1326, and having given a great feast to both magnates and common people, retired to the monastery of Athassel, where on July 29 he breathed his last.[13] He is described by Friar Clyn as 'a knight prudent and witty, wealthy and wise and full of years', and by the Irish annalists as 'the choicest of all the English of Ireland'. His heir was his grandson William, son of John de Burgh and Elizabeth de Clare, then a minor [214]
of about fourteen years of age. Whatever his faults may have been, the great Earl of Ulster had kept order among his feudatories throughout his vast domains for forty-six years. There had indeed been quarrels between the de Burghs and the Geraldines, but the earl had been satisfied to arrange them before the courts without bloodshed and to seal the reconciliation by intermarriages. But now his strong hand was removed from the provinces of Ulster and Connaught, while Thomond and Meath and Louth, and indeed large parts of Munster and Leinster, were without a resident lord with power and authority to keep order.

The disappearance of the great feudal lords might not have been an unmixed evil if the central Government had been strong and well organized and ready to take their places in the maintenance of order and the administration of the law. But from the moment of the accession of Edward II the hand that held the reins of government was weak, irresolute, and capricious. The signs were many and manifest. We may here note in particular three cases in which the mishandling of affairs in England had evil consequences in Ireland. These were Edward's irresolute action with regard to Scotland, his weak yielding to the nefarious condemnation of the Templars, and his capricious selection of chief ministers and advisers, to the estrangement of the barons of England.

In the first place, early in his reign Edward practically abandoned his father's energetic policy in Scotland, without adopting the logical alternative of acknowledging the Scottish king and living in amity with him. Instead of frankly recognizing the inevitable, [215]
he virtually forced what friends he had in Scotland to make terms with his rival, and then, when it was too late, made futile and costly attempts to recover the lost ground. The immediate consequence to Ireland of this vacillation, ending with the *débâcle* of Bannockburn, was the scourge of the Scottish invasion with which we have already dealt.

13 The precise date is given by Clyn, who describes him as 'miles prudens, facetus, dives et sapiens, plenus dierum'.

Secondly, against his own better judgement and without any national pressure, Edward weakly acquiesced in the base conspiracy of Philip le Bel and Pope Clement V against the Templars, and ordered their suppression and the confiscation of their goods. The Templars in Ireland shared the betrayal of the Order elsewhere. They had indeed made little mark in the history of the country. Unlike the Prior of the Hospitallers, the 'Master of the Knighthood of the Temple in Ireland' does not appear in the lists of justiciars and other high officials, though he was occasionally employed to audit ministers' accounts, to take charge of crown-moneys, and on other special duties. But the position of the Order, under the continued favour of king and pope, was one of extraordinary privilege. They were freed from all kinds of tolls, taxes, and onerous customs, from tithes, and even from the terrors of excommunication and interdict locally pronounced, while they exercised complete civil and criminal jurisdiction over their own vassals and tenants. Their privileges indeed attracted to their lands the tenants of others to the detriment of their neighbours. Though a military order they held their lands in frankalmoign and not by military service. They were free from assessment for
[216] the defence of the land,[14] and they are not mentioned as fighting in any of the Anglo-Irish wars. They were a class apart, and as such were employed by the royalist barons in 1234 as intermediaries between them and Earl Richard Marshal. They were careful managers of their property, acute business men, and honourable bankers, but their privileges, their pride, and above all their wealth created enemies both lay and clerical. The young king of England, too weak to resist the mandates of the pope, before the close of 1307 ordered their arrest and the sequestration of their property;[15] and now that pope and king had turned against them, the clergy, especially the mendicant orders, pursued them with redoubled hatred and malice. The charges of heresy, idolatry, and evil practices, made against the Templars were not supported, in Ireland at any rate, by any evidence worthy of the name, but the dissolution of the whole Order was decreed in 1312 by an apparently reluctant pope under pressure of the French king.

The wealth of the Templars was not so great as has been supposed. In Ireland their principal manors at the time of the dissolution were as follows: Clontarf in County Dublin and Crook and Kilbarry in County Waterford, granted to them with some other property in 1172 by Henry II, whose charter was confirmed by John, Henry III, and Edward I, the last-named king adding many immunities;[16] Cooley and Kilsaran in County Louth, the former (and perhaps the latter) granted to them by Matilda de
[217] Lacy, widow of David, Baron of Naas;[17] Kilcork and Rathbride in County Kildare; Kilclogan in County Wexford; Clonaul, now Clonoulty, in County Tipperary; and Teach Templa, now Templehouse, in County Sligo. In addition to the manors they

14 Justiciary Rolls, vol. i, p. 409. 15 Cal. Close Rolls, 1 Ed. II, p. 48 (December 20). 16 For the date of Henry II's charter see *ante*, vol. i, p. 274, note [p. 101, note 47]. It was produced along with Edward's confirmation in a plea between the Abbot of Dunbrody and the Master of the Templars in 1287: Cal. Docs. Ireland, vol. iii, p 329, 17 Matilda de Lacy's grant of her tenement of Coly with the advowson of the church of Carlingford is transcribed from Plea Roll no. 64 (30 Ed. I, m. 19) by Mr. Herbert Wood: 'The Templars in Ireland', Proc. R.I.A., vol. xxvi (c), p. 37. To this paper the reader is referred for further details on the subject.

held a considerable number of churches to their own use, and at various times other lands as well. The total annual value of the lands and advowsons held by the Templars at the time of dissolution seems to have been little more than £450,[18] and the total value of their goods and chattels was about £750.[19] At first most of their lands were farmed out by the Crown, but the issues of Crook, Kilclogan, and Kilbarry were assigned for the sustenance of the imprisoned Templars, while the manors of Clontarf and Kilsaran were actually granted to the Earl of Ulster (though eventually surrendered to the Hospitallers), and other lands were claimed by the feudal lords as escheats. In the year 1324, however, in accordance with papal bulls, an Act was passed in England [218]
assigning all the lands of the Templars to the knights of St. John,[20] thus further enriching that already rich Order. The goods of the Templars passed through many hands, and some of the custodians, in particular Alexander de Bykenore, Archbishop of Dublin and treasurer, were not above levying toll by the way, so that altogether not much of the property of the Templars went to enrich the king of England, while apparently not all of their lands were acquired by the knights of the Hospital.

A curious outbreak of religious persecution which took place at Kilkenny at this date (1324) may perhaps be regarded as having been suggested and inspired by the success of the proceedings against the Templars. In that year Alice le Kyteler[21] and several others were accused of heresy, idolatry, and sorcery, before Richard Ledred, Bishop of Ossory. Dame Alice, though known hy her maiden name, had been four times married. Her first husband, William Utlagh or Outlaw, was a wealthy banker and money-lender in Kilkenny, and their son, William Outlaw junior,[22] followed his father's [219]
business with eminent success, and it seems probable that, as in the case of the Templars, the great wealth of the family was their real sin.

The bishop's proceedings are detailed at great length, from his point of view, in a contemporary narrative,[23] which in essentials is supported by the annals of Friar Clyn and other monastic annals. As one reads this narrative one marvels at the pertinacity

18 This is the amount (in round numbers) of the items given by Mr. Wood, in the paper above cited, from the certificate sent from the Irish to the English Exchequer in 1327, and from one or two minor sources; but the value of some of the lands mentioned in Mr. Woods' list (Appendix A) is not given. Professor Clarence Perkins estimates the total annual value as not exceeding £411 11*s*. 2d.: Eng. Hist. Rev., vol. xxv (1910), p. 223. **19** According to the above-mentioned certificate the goods were valued at £716 16*s*. 6½*d*. (Woods, as above, p. 348), but the items given by Mr. Woods in his Appendix amount to £750 9*s*. 2½*d*. He gives a transcript of the inventory regarding Clonaul. An abstract of that concerning Kilclogan is given by Mr. Hore in his History of County Wexford. **20** Statutes, 17 Ed. II (2). For an account of 'The Hospital of St. John of Jerusalem in Ireland' see the paper under that title by Caesar Litton Falkiner in Proc. R.I.A., vol. xxvi (c), pp. 276-317. See, too, *ante*, vol. i, p. 366 [pp. 137–8], where a flaw is pointed out in Mr. Falkiner's argument as to the date of Strongbow's grant of Kilmainham. **21** The Kyteler family seem to have come from Ypres. In 1277 William le Kyteler of Ypres and his men had a safe-conduct in carrying his goods and merchandise into Ireland and trading there: Cal. Pat. Roll, 5 Ed. I, p. 223. A William de Kyteler, perhaps the same, was sheriff of the liberty of Kilkenny in 1302, when he had a dispute with Dame Alice, then the wife of Adam le Blund of Callan, touching £3,000: Cal. Pat. Roll (Ireland), 31 Ed. I, nos. 3 and 4; and cf. Justiciary Rolls, vol. ii, p. 335. There was a 'villa Flamingo-rum' at this time in Kilkenny: Journ. R.S.A.I., vol. i, p. 39. **22** William Outlaw was one of a few in Ireland from whom in April 1322 the king sought a gift or loan of money in aid of the Scottish campaign: Cal. Close Rolls, 15 Ed. II, p. 530. **23** A contemporary Narrative of the Proceedings against Dame Alice Kyteler in 1324 (edited by Thomas

of the prelate 'in the cause of faith'. Neither Arnold le Poer, seneschal of Kilkenny, nor the chancellor of Ireland, nor the treasurer, nor even the vicar-general of his own metropolitan could temper the bishop's ruthlessness. Not satisfied with having secured the condemnation of Dame Alice (who, however, aided by friends managed to escape), and with having scourged into confession and burned at the stake in the market-place at Kilkenny one of her alleged 'pestiferous companions'—the first case of the kind in Ireland[24]—he summoned her son William Outlaw on a charge of 'heresy and consorting with heretics', caused him to be imprisoned, and at length consented to his release only
[220] on his finding sureties in £1,000[25] that he would roof the chancel of the cathedral at Kilkenny and St. Mary's chapel therein with lead, perform various acts of penance, and provide a perpetual priest to celebrate mass at the said chapel. Even this triumph, as we shall see, did not end the bishop's activities 'in the cause of faith'.

Thirdly, from the beginning of his reign Edward had alienated the barons of England by dismissing his father's counsellors and elevating to the highest posts self-seeking favourites, first Piers de Gaveston, who was murdered in 1312, and afterwards the two Despensers, father and son. This ill-advised conduct led to disorders and civil war in England. The baronial opposition was crushed for the moment at Boroughbridge in 1322, when the blood of Gaveston was avenged by the defeat and execution of Earl Thomas of Lancaster and many of his principal followers. For a few years the Despensers triumphed, but their enemies were numerous, and troubles multiplied about them and the king; and when in September 1326 the unscrupulous queen and her paramour Roger Mortimer landed in England with an invading force, the end of the Despensers and of the unfortunate king was at hand. As in other cases, these disorders, and even it would seem these rival factions, had their counterparts in Ireland, where though comparatively unimportant at the time, they were ultimately more disastrous because attended by more permanent results. For in Ireland not only were disorder and private warfare more difficult to repress, but Irish clans were ever ready to
[221] take advantage of disunion among the magnates to regain their own freedom from control and to reduce the area in which the king's writ ran.

The feud among the Irish barons arose before June 18, 1325, when writs were issued to Arnold le Poer and Maurice Fitz Thomas commanding them to desist from assembling men-at-arms and foot-soldiers for the purpose of attacking each other.[26] At a parliament held at Kilkenny on July 11 following, the ordinance to which we have already referred, bidding the magnates to chastise those of their families and names who should break the peace, was confirmed, and the penalty of a fine at the king's will was imposed on non-compliance.[27] In spite of writs and ordinances some disorders must have ensued, as on July 14, 1326, Maurice Fitz Thomas, and John, son of Peter le Poer,

Wright), Camden Society, 1843. **24** It was soon imitated. In 1328 an unfortunate Irishman, Adam Duff O'Toole, was burned at Le Hogges near Dublin for alleged heresy and blasphemy: Laud MS. Annals, p. 366. **25** On Jan. 25, 1325, Roger Outlaw, prior of St. John of Jerusalem, and ten of the principal landllolders in County Kilkenny acknowledged that they were bound to the Bishop of Ossory in £1,000: Cal. Close Roll (Ireland), 18 Ed. II (50). These were the sureties for William Outlaw: see ibid., 20 Ed. II, no. 16. **26** Cal. Close Roll (Ireland), 18 Ed. II (99–100). **27** Early Statutes (Berry), 19 Ed. II, p. 313.

Baron of Dunoyl, Co. Waterford, had licence to treat with felons of their respective families, surnames, and following, up to the end of November, and meantime the sheriffs of Cork, Waterford, Limerick, and Tipperary were ordered not to arrest the said felons.[28] But this period of grace seems to have been utilized by the opposing magnates in strengthening their respective factions by confederacies, for on December 11, the same sheriffs were ordered to issue proclamations forbidding all such confederacies, and special writs were issued to Maurice Fitz Thomas, John de Bermingham, Earl of Louth, Arnold de Poer and others, not to join such confedera- [222] cies or aid them in any way.[29] But denunciatory proclamations and writs, in the absence of the power to enforce them, were waste paper. In 1327 the dispute came to a head. Maurice Fitz Thomas was supported by the Butlers and the Berminghams, and Arnold le Poer by the de Burghs. Maurice first attacked the de Burghs, killed some of them, and drove the rest into Connaught, and then towards the close of the year he or his allies turned and laid waste Arnold's lands in counties Tipperary and Waterford, and at Kells in Ossory, so that Arnold with the Baron of Dunoyl had to take refuge in the city of Waterford.[30]

The Earl of Kildare, who had been appointed justiciar in the beginning of the year, named a day for the parties to come before the council, but Arnold Power, instead of appearing, crossed to England about February 2, 1328, while his opponents continued to harry and burn his lands. The towns now began to be alarmed lest they should be attacked, but Maurice and his allies sent messengers to the king's council to say that they would come to Kilkenny, and there clear themselves and show that they had no intention of harming the king's lands, but only of avenging themselves on their enemies. The right of private warfare was seldom more openly claimed. When, however, Maurice and his followers appeared before the justiciar and council at Kilkenny and sought the king's charter of peace, the council cautiously took time until a month after Easter to consider their answer.[31] Meantime in Easter week the justiciar died and was [223] succeeded in his office by Roger Outlaw, Prior of Kilmainham.

The monastic annals, the only ones which notice this quarrel, give no indication of its real cause. They say indeed that Arnold le Poer, using monstrous language (*enormia verba*), called Maurice Fitz Thomas 'a Rymour', and that this led Maurice, James Butler and William de Bermingham to ravage Arnold's lands. The sting of the gibe lay in the fact that Irish rimers or bards used their art to incite the native clans to attack the English at every opportunity and recover their ancient inheritance.[32] But this gibe, like the nicknames Gaveston bestowed on his opponents, was obviously a symptom of the quarrel, not its cause, for which we must search elsewhere. Now Arnold le Poer was

28 Cal. Pat. Rolls (Ireland), 20 Ed. II (20 and 21). This was subsequent to the parliament which met at Kilkenny on May 11, 1326, when the community of Co. Tipperary granted an aid (assigned by the king to the Earl of Louth) to repress the felons and rebels in that district: ibid.. no. 22. 29 Cal. Close Rolls (Ireland), 20 Ed. II (60, 61). 30 Laud MS. Annals (as above), pp 364–5; Clyn, p. 19. 31 Laud MS. Annals (as above), p. 365. 32 They also came among the English as spies: Statute of Kilkenny, c. 15. Those who are familiar with their savage incitements at a later age—e.g. to wipe out the inhabitants of the Pale, 'so that a woman from Meath may munch out a morsel of her first child's heart'—will understand the secular detestation with which the loyal English regarded Irish rimers.

seneschal of Kilkenny, where the castle and liberty were held up to this time by the younger Hugh Despenser in right of his wife Eleanor, eldest daughter and one of the coheirs of the late Earl of Gloucester. Hugh coveted the earldom of Gloucester and had intrigued against his parceners, Hugh d'Audley and Roger d'Amory, husbands of the other Gloucester heiresses, who were therefore his bitter enemies. It is not improbable that some of the odium which attached to Hugh Despenser adhered to his seneschal, and this possibly accounts for the hostility of the Butlers who were the prin-
[224] cipal freeholders in the county. When in October 1326, Mortimer let loose the dogs of war against the Despensers, the hunted king with his favourite set sail from Chepstow with, it is said, the intention of seeking refuge in Ireland—presumably in Hugh Despenser's castle—but they were driven back by contrary winds. We should not, however, be warranted in thinking that the causes which produced the cleavage among the English barons were precisely those which operated to bring about a similar cleavage in Ireland. It is more probable that disorder spread by infection, as it were, from the one country to the other, and that in Ireland diverse local interests and jealousies determined the sides men took. The Poers held lands in the Decies and may have come into conflict with Maurice Fitz Thomas who was overlord there. In the politics of Thomond and County Limerick, Maurice now occupied the place of the de Clares, having been given during pleasure in 1321 all the castles and lands of Richard de Clare 'for the better preservation of peace in the marches'.[33] This grant inevitably brought him into antagonism with Murtough O'Brion, king of Thomond, and with the de Burghs (who always supported Murtough), and, as a necessary consequence, into alliance with Murtough's rival of the house of Brian Roe, Maurice's ally, William de Bermingham, had married Joan, widow of Richard de Clare. Nevertheless, it must be noted that the fortunes of the two parties in Ireland, at least as affected by governmental action, rose and fell with the rise and fall of the corresponding parties in England. Thus, as long as the Despensers ruled the kingdom, custodies and other
[225 emoluments were bestowed on Arnold le Poer,[34] while in 1328–9, when Roger Mortimer had triumphed over the Despensers and was the virtual ruler, Arnold le Poer was left to die in prison, while James Butler was created Earl of Ormonde,[35] and Maurice Fitz Thomas, Earl of Desmond.[36] When Mortimer in his turn was overthrown, William de Burgh, Earl of Ulster, was taken into high favour, and the Earl of Desmond and William de Bermingham were thrown into prison.

Arnold le Poer, indeed, was imprisoned at the instance of the implacable Bishop of Ossory, who stated that he (Arnold) had been convicted before him of heresy. The bishop, however, failed to appear on the day fixed for the civil inquiry, alleging that his

33 Cal. Close Rolls (Ireland), 14 Ed. II (98). 34 See Cal. Patent and Close Rolls (Ireland), Close, 18 Ed. II (57 and 164); Pat., 20 Ed. II (5), and Close, 20 Ed. II (168). These grants were all between January 1325 and August 18, 1326. 35 This was at the parliament of Salisbury in October 1328, when Mortimer had himself created Earl of March. About the same time James Butler was given in marriage the king's niece, Eleanor, daughter of Humphrey de Bohun, Earl of Hereford. 36 This was on August 27, 1329. The creation of John de Bermingham as Earl of Louth in 1319 was also probably due to the favour of Roger Mortimer, who was then in power and justiciar of Ireland.

enemies were lying in wait for him on his route. At the same time Roger Outlaw, the justiciar, was defamed by the bishop for favouring heresy and abetting Sir Arnold in his heretical pravity. The justiciar was allowed to clear himself, which he did effectually, but Arnold died in the castle of Dublin on March 14, 1329, and lay for a long time unburied.[37] It is vain to attempt to unravel all this tangled skein of intrigue, of which [226]
we can see clearly only a few threads, and yet it seems probable that ecclesiastical persecution of this unfortunate man was not unconnected with the baronial feud. The bishop was, indeed, charged with fomenting feuds amongst the magnates, and on June 18, 1329, when an inquiry was about to be made into his conduct, he fled from Ireland and, when summoned before the king in England, set out for Rome. The king accordingly wrote to the pope to warn him not to believe the bishop's representations.[38] It is some satisfaction to know that ten years later, by an appropriate revenge, the bishop was himself accused of heresy by his metropolitan.[39] He was not finally restored to favour until near the end of the year 1354. The merit, however, is ascribed to him of having much adorned his cathedral in erecting anew and glazing all the windows, 'among which the east window was beautified with such excellent workmanship that the like was not in Ireland'.[40]

We cannot wonder that while these feuds divided the magnates, attempts were made by the Irish in Leinster to recover the province.

Early in 1328, for the first time since the days of Strongbow, we hear of the various clans of Leinster assembling together to make a king (namely, Donnell, son of Art McMurrough)[41] who proposed to inaugurate an era of conquest. The movement was [227]
checked for the moment by his capture and that of the leader of the O'Tooles, but friendly relations with the Leinster clans were further off than ever.

In the spring of 1329, at a parliament held in Dublin, peace was made between the young Earl of Ulster (who now appears on the scene for the first time) and Maurice Fitz Thomas, and the magnates and the king's council once more ordained that the king's peace should be maintained by each magnate punishing the wrongdoers among his own kindred and men.[42] Thus did the government once more confess its inability to perform its primary function, and once more put the responsibility on the magnates individually—and this in spite of the fact that the magnates had hitherto evinced an inveterate predilection for punishing each other's wrongdoers rather than their own. The usual feastings followed, but the king's peace was not long preserved.

A further example of the demoralization that had set in among the Anglo-Irish was

37 Laud MS. Annals, pp. 368–9. The indignity to the body of this unfortunate man was in accordance with the fifteenth article of the Constitutions of Bishop Ledred, which declares that any one who (*inter alia*) 'impedes the jurisdiction of the bishop' shall not receive ecclesiastical burial, and if buried in ignorance shall be exhumed and cast on a dunghill: Liber Ruber Ossoriensis, Proc. R.I.A., vol. xxvii (c), p. 168. 38 Rymer's Foedera, vol. ii, p. 767. 39 Ibid., pp. 810, 1082. 40 Ware's 'Bishops'. 41 Laud MS. Annals (as before), pp. 365–6. This Donnell was probably son of the Art Mc Murrough who was slain in 1282: *supra*, p. 19 [p. 445]. According to Keating, from this Art sprang the race of Dermot Lavderg Kavanagh, i. e. the septs of St. Mullins, and Polmounty, and, later, of Borris; but see notes to Four Masters, vol. iii, p. 647, and vol. iv, p. 830. King Donnell escaped from the castle in January 1330: Laud MS. Ann., p. 372. 42 Ibid., pp. 369.

afforded in the the following June by the massacre of the Berminghams. At Braganstown in Co. Louth John de Bermingham, the recently created Earl of Louth, two of his brothers, and about nine of his kindred and name, together with 160 others, were slain by Gernons, Cusacks, Hadsors, Clintons, and others of the oldest families in the
[228] county. According to the defence put forward, Robert de Bermingham, brother of the earl, and other evil doers gathered a multitude of armed men, by assent of the earl, and committed homicides, arsons, &c., and upon hue and cry, the sheriff with the posse followed the evildoers to Braganstown and commanded the earl not to receive them, but the earl with armed force assaulted the sheriff and slew several of their following, in which proceedings the earl and the rest were slain.[43] The perpetrators of the deed were pardoned, but whatever their pretext may have been, contemporary opinion was probably correct in assigning as their real motive their unwillingness that the earl 'should rule over them'.[44]

Sir John Darcy was now again appointed justiciar, and on July 3 he married Joan de Burgh, widow of Thomas Fitz John, late Earl of Kildare. The principal matters which engaged the attention of this active justiciar and his movements during the next six months are known to us through the accounts of the paymaster of his forces,[45] and they serve to show the disordered state of the country at the time and the scanty forces at the disposal of the justiciar for restoring order. By the conditions on which he held office he was bound to maintain twenty men-at-arms in his suite, and the men whose
[229] wages were paid by the paymaster were in addition. These last and the times and purposes for which they were employed were as follows: 25 men-at-arms in the justiciar's company going from Dublin to Kilkenny to establish peace between the Earl of Ulster and the Poers and Barrys of the one part, and the Earls of Ormonde and Desmond and William de Bermingham of the other part (July 6–14).[46] From another roll it appears that a tribunal of three judges and arbitrators was appointed by the justiciar between the parties[47]—78 men-at-arms, 291 hobelers, and 285 footmen setting out with the justiciar to subdue the O'Byrnes (August 16–24);[48] 18 men-at-arms, 12 hobelers, and 18 footmen in the justiciar's company going again to Kilkenny to establish peace between the said magnates and settle divers discords between them (September 22–October 22);[49] 53 men-at-arms, 98 hobelers, and 63 footmen setting out with the justiciar to subdue the O'Dempsys and O'Mores who were against the king's peace (October 28–31); 89 men-at-arms, 217 hobelers, and 72 footmen setting out with the
[230] justiciar to subdue William Mageoghegan and persons of the name of the de Lacys

43 Cal. Pat. Rolls, 4 Ed. III, p. 531. 44 Clyn's Annals, p. 20. Both Clyn and the Irish Annals state that Mulroney Mac Carroll. a blind or squint-eyed minstrel—'the most choice tympanist in the world', 'a phoenix in his art'—was killed along with the Berminghams. The precise date was June 10, 1329, though the Irish annals place the deed in 1328. 45 Pipe Roll (Ireland), 2 Ed. III, 43rd Rep. D.K., p. 28. 46 Cf. Four Masters (1329): ' Mac William Burke (i.e. Walter, son of William Liath de Burgh) and the Earl of Ulster made peace with Mac Thomas (i.e. Maurice Fitz Thomas, Earl of Desmond).' 47 See 43rd Rep. D.K., p. 65. 48 Compare Laud MS. Annals (as above), p. 371, where Sir John Darcy is stated to have set out on the precise day, Aug. 16, for Newcastle McKynegan and Wicklow against the O'Byrnes. It is noteworthy that Murtough O'Toole was one of the leaders against the O'Byrnes. 49 On Oct. 14 a general pardon was issued to Maurice Fitz Thomas, Earl of Desmond, and on Nov. 1 power was given to the justiciar to admit the earl's men to the king's peace for a reasonable fine: Cal. Pat. Rolls, 3 Ed. III, p. 457.

who in the parts of war had revolted against the king (November 10–22);[50] 77 men-at-arms, 240 hobelers, and 65 footmen setting out with the justiciar to subdue the O'Byrnes who were once more against the king's peace (December 10–18). The wages for each man-at-arms was 12*d.* per day,[51] for each hobeler, 4*d.*, and for each footman 1½*d.*, and the total for all expeditions amounted to £314 19*s.* 8*d.* The leaders seem to have been mostly County Dublin men with some from Meath and Kildare. The old feudal array was a thing of the past, and the money commutation for military service was difficult to collect and quite inadequate to present needs.

Notwithstanding the justiciar's energy, all his objects were not attained. In January of next year (1330) he called upon Maurice Fitz Thomas, the newly-created Earl of Desmond, to come with an army to subdue the king's enemies at the king's costs. Maurice came with his army and Brian O'Brien (who can hardly have been welcome to all the magnates) was with him. The force is said to have numbered 10,000 men, mostly, no doubt, consisting of Irish kerne. We cannot trust the figures, but we may be sure that the army was very much more numerous than any force the justiciar could muster. Maurice first attacked the O'Nolans, defeated them, took a great spoil, burned their lands, and obtained hostages from them. Then he went against the O'Mores and [231]
obtained their hostages. He also recovered the castle of Lea which had been captured by O'Dempsy.[52]

This Brian O'Brien who accompanied the Earl of Desmond into Leinster is usually called in the Irish annals Brian Bán O'Brien. He was grandson of Brian Roe O'Brien, and, as has been mentioned, he had shared the defeat of Richard de Clare at Dysert O'Dea in 1318. He then held Thomond, where Murtough O'Brien of the rival clan was now supreme, and had since been carving out for himself a principality in the northern part of County Tipperary mainly at the expense of the de Burghs and the Butlers. As the representative of Clan Brian Roe he had claims to the chieftainship of Thomond, and he seems to have been supported by the Earl of Desmond against Murtough O'Brien of the opposite faction. In July 1329, he defeated at Thurles a formidable army mustered by the young Earl of Ulster, with whom were the kings of Connaught and of Thomond, and he followed up his success by burning the towns of Athassel and Tipperary, and devastating a large tract of the surrounding country.[53]
Though fighting indiscriminately for his own hand, he was a formidable opponent to [232]
the English, and to bring such a man with his wild Irish forces into Leinster to quell

50 On the preceding August 9, Thomas Butler, Lord of Dunboyne, and a number of Meathmen were killed in a fight with William Mageoghegan: ibid., p. 370. 51 In the above statement the knights and other leaders who are mentioned by name, are included in the number of men-at-arms. Their pay seems to have been the same, 1*s.* per day, but many of them were allowed various sums in consideration of good service. 52 Laud MS. Annals (as above), p. 372. 53 Clyn, p. 21 (14 Kal. Augusti, 1329): Ann. Loch Cé, Ann. Ulst., 1328(?). At first sight the Irish annals seem to preserve the true date, as up to July 14,1329, Darcy, the justiciar (as already mentioned), was establishing peace between the magnates at Kilkenny, when the Earl of Ulster was presumably present. But perhaps the earl was not present when his army was defeated, and the burning of Athassel 'in the first week of August, 1329 (Clyn)' may have caused the discords which necessitated the second intervention of the justiciar in the September of that year. At this time Clyn's dates are very accurate. He died apparently in 1349.

the border clans there, was a novel departure, which must have excited more resentment than gratitude from the English magnates. Indeed the recrudescence of the feud between the de Burghs and the Earl of Desmond, which now seemed imminent, was apparently due to their diverse relations with Brian O'Brien.

In the May following his performance in Leinster Brian O'Brien was engaged in what was probably the more congenial task of resisting James Beaufo (Bellofago), sheriff of Limerick, and killing him together with 120 liege subjects of the Crown. To punish this new outrage and expel Brian O'Brien from Thurles, which he seems to have occupied, a large army[54] was led against him in July by Roger Outlaw, the deputy-justiciar, the Earls of Ulster and Ormonde, William de Bermingham, and Walter de Burgh. No decisive result was obtained, and the forces dispersed to their several homes. Then Walter de Burgh with his Connaught men proceeded to ravage some lands of the Earl of Desmond, presumably because he suspected him of abetting Brian O'Brien. Thereupon
[233] the justiciar committed both the Earl of Ulster and the Earl of Desmond to the custody of the Marshal at Limerick. The latter earl escaped, and the former appears to have been soon released. Early next year (1331) he went to England. Probably neither earl was directly responsible for this new breach of the peace, but pursuant to the recent ordinance it was sought to make each accountable for the acts of his kindred.

Meanwhile great changes in political forces had occurred in England. On November 29, 1330, Roger Mortimer after four years of inglorious rule suffered a traitor's death at Tyburn, and the young king took into his own hands the reins of government. On March 3, 1331, a number of ordinances were made in the parliament at Westminster for the reformation of the Irish government. Some of these were virtual repetitions of clauses in the Act of 1297. Others had for their aim a better control over sheriffs and other officers. We have already noted and commented on the most important new ordinance, that 'one and the same law be made as well for the Irish as the English, except the service of betaghs in the power of their lords', who were to be treated in the same manner as was used in England concerning villeins.[55] But there were also some clauses which seem to have been suggested by recent events: e.g. one forbidding the justiciar to grant pardon for homicides or for any robberies and burnings (except for robberies and burnings committed before Easter 1331), without first ascertaining the king's will thereon; and another forbidding any person of whatever state or condi-
[234] tion to maintain favour or defend Irishmen or any other person whatever rising against the king's peace, under penalty of being himself held a felon.[56]

Two days later the king issued a mandate to the justiciar ordering the resumption of all castles, lands, liberties, &c., granted by him since his accession, the reason assigned being that matters concerning the state of the kingdom 'by certain of our then coun-

54 Laud MS. Annals, pp. 373–4; Clyn, p. 21. See too the account of the paymaster for this expedition: Cal. Pipe Rolls (Ireland), 4 Ed. III, 43rd Rep. D.K., p. 43. There are several references in the Pipe Rolls to the royal services exacted for this 'army at Athissel', as it is called. It is not quite certain that Thurles was the place occupied by O'Brien. The Laud MS. has 'Urlyfe iuxta Cashell', and Clyn says that O'Brien defeated the Earl of Ulster, &c., in 1329 'at Yrlef'. O'Donovan takes this as a mistake in the transcription of Thurles (Ir. *Durlas*) which he supposes was written with the thorn-letter. 55 *Supra*, p. 26 [p. 448]. 56 Early Statutes (Berry), pp. 323–9.

cillors had been carried out to our injury and dishonour and the impoverishing of the people of the said kingdom'.[57] The reference of course was to the rule of Roger Mortimer, and one of the principal persons affected in Ireland was the Earl of Desmond.

Shortly before this time the king had appointed Anthony de Lucy,[58] a Cumberland baron already noted for his rigour, justiciar of Ireland, with William de Burgh, Earl of Ulster, as his deputy.[59] The latter was to take, with the advice of the justiciar and council, all measures necessary for the preservation of peace. Evidently the young earl, who seems to have been in England at the time, was fully trusted by the king. He was the king's kinsman and contemporary. He had been brought up in England, was knighted by the king, and had been given in marriage the king's cousin Matilda, daughter of Earl Henry of Lancaster. And now his father-in-law had been the moving spirit in helping [235] the young king to free himself and the kingdom from the incubus of his mother's paramour.

Sir Anthony de Lucy came to Ireland on June 3. He summoned a parliament at Dublin for July 1, but as several of the magnates failed to attend, he adjourned it to meet at Kilkenny on August 1. The Earl of Desmond, William de Bermingham, and others who had ignored the first summons now came and submitted themselves to the king's grace. We are then told that 'the king (i.e. the justiciar), so far as it lay with him (*quantum sibi incumbebat*), graciously pardoned them, under a certain form, for the evils they had done in the land'.[60] Evidently the pardon was not absolute. There was some reservation. Presumably the pardon was given by the justiciar subject to the king's confirmation, which was not obtained. According to the ordinance of the preceding March, the justiciar was forbidden to grant such pardons without first ascertaining the king's will thereon. It would have been better for his reputation if the justiciar had adhered more strictly to this rule. Fifteen days later the justiciar took the Earl of Desmond prisoner at of Limerick and afterwards confined him in the castle of Dublin.

There were, no doubt, good legal grounds for imprisoning the Earl of Desmond with a view to bringing him to trial for his warfare against the Poers and de Burghs. But there seems to have been no trial. Probably the Government knew that they could not get a conviction from the earl's peers even though the facts were against him. They proceeded to undermine the earl's power in a more discreditable way. On November 6, [236] 1331, the king sent a mandate to the justiciar 'to take into the king's hand the castle and manor of Dunnamark[61] with the demesne lands there, with a moiety of the lordship of the land of Desmond, pursuant to an inquisition taken by him showing that Henry II enfeoffed Miles de Cogan and Robert Fitz Stephen by charter of his whole demesne of Desmond; that Miles and Robert divided the lordship between them; that Robert died

57 Ibid., p. 331. 58 He was hitherto known to history as the man employed in 1323 to capture Andrew de Harcla (or of Hartley), the victor of Boroughbridge, lately created Earl of Carlisle and warden of the Scottish marches. Virtually abandoned by Edward II, Andrew of Hartley had been obliged to make terms with Robert Bruce, and in consequence, though not a traitor at heart, he suffered a traitor's death: see England in the Later Middle Ages (Vickers), p. 125, and the article by J.E. Morris there referred to. 59 Foedera, vol. ii, p. 811. 60 Laud MS. Annals (as before), p. 375. The words in Grace's Annals are 'qui transacta eis *fere* condonavit' 61 Printed 'Dunumcark', but evidently Dunnamark (*dún na mbarc*) near Bantry, where a Carew founded a castle, c. 1215, was intended. See *ante*, vol. iii, p. 128 [p. 344].

seised, a bastard and without heirs of his body; and that Thomas de Carew, asserting that he and his ancestors were heirs of the said Robert (though they were not, because Robert died without heirs, &c.), enfeoffed by charter Maurice Fitz Thomas before Maurice was Earl of Desmond, without licence'.[62] Now it is quite certain that Thomas de Carew and his ancestors held a moiety of the seignory of Desmond for upwards of a century. Their position is attested by their own grants, by inquisitions and legal decisions,[63] and above all by the fact that the Crown again and again claimed and obtained from them the thirty services reserved in the original grant to Robert FitzStephen.[64] But
[237] it was now objected that FitzStephen had no legal heirs. This was probably the fact. But it was also a fact that in 1182, at a moment when all the lands comprised in the grant were on the point of being lost to the grantees and to the Crown, Raymond le Gros, in the eyes of the world Fitz Stephen's nephew, saved the situation, and afterwards (whether there was a fresh grant from the Crown or not) was allowed to succeed to his uncle's interest. Similarly from Raymond the half-seignory was allowed to descend to Richard de Carew (whose parentage, however, is uncertain), and from him the regular descent to Thomas de Carew can still be traced, and, as we have said, was often recognized and never questioned.[65] To rely on the technical informalities in the earlier descent was a political blunder as well as a monstrous injustice, and was certainly not the way to make the Earl of Desmond a loyal subject of the Crown.

In the beginning of the following year Anthony de Lucy led a force into Munster 'to repress the malice of certain malefactors there'.[66] We have no further details of this expedition, but it was apparently on this occasion that he took William de Bermingham and his son Walter prisoners at Clonmel and brought them also to Dublin Castle. William de Bermingham was brother of the late Earl of Louth. He and his son Walter had done good service at the battle of Faughart, but he had supported Maurice Fitz
[238] Thomas in his warfare against the Poers and the de Burghs; and more recently he had been concerned in various acts of violence.[67] On July 11, 1332, to the consternation and grief of the community, who were not accustomed to see laws enforced, William de Bermingham was hanged by order of the justiciar. The Anglo-Irish annalist calls him the noblest and best of knights among thousands, and with a cry of grief exclaims, 'Who in telling of his death can refrain from tears?'[68] It seems, indeed, to have been one of those spasmodic acts of severity which, coming after a long period of utter laxity, inflame rather than allay passions. The king appears to have awakened to the danger of

62 Cal. Fine Rolls, vol. iv, p. 286, 5 Ed. III, November 6, 1331. **63** See Justiciary Rolls, vol. i, pp. 154–5 and 383–5; also Cal. Close Rolls (Ireland), 32 Ed. III, nos. 25, 26, 27, and 37. **64** As recently as 1305 Maurice de Carew (father of Thomas) for his good service in Scotland was pardoned £400 'arrears of services due for lands which he held *in capite* in Desmond': Docs. Ireland, vol. v, no. 41.3. **65** See *ante*, vol. iii, chapter xxvii, appendix: 'The seignory of Cork' [pp. 356–7]. **66** The sum of £226 5*s*. 6*d*. was expended for men in the justiciar's army in Munster between January 20 and May 2, 43rd Rep. D.K., pp. 53–4. **67** For these, see Clyn, pp. 22–3, where it also appears that in the summer of 1331, William de Bermingham presided over the nuptials of his niece Matilda, eldest daughter and heiress of the Earl of Louth, with Eustace, son of his late enemy Arnold le Poer. Matilda was the king's ward, but if the marriage was without licence, as is probable, the irregularity was afterwards condoned, and a third of the manor of Ardee was delivered to Eustace le Poer in right of his wife on September 22, 1332: 44th Rep. D.K., p. 38. **68** Laud MS. Annals (as before), p. 377.

the situation and at once put a check on the ruthlessness of the viceroy. On August 4 he ordered that execution against any magnates who might be imprisoned for felonies should be stayed until his arrival in Ireland, as he had granted to Roger Outlaw, Prior of Kilmainham, power to treat with both English and Irish about 'coming into the king's peace and favour',[69] and on September 30 Anthony de Lucy was superseded as justiciar by John Darcy. Meanwhile, some three months after the arrest of the Earl of Desmond, another arrest was effected which led to even more serious consequences.
In November 1331 Walter de Burgh and two of his brothers were taken prisoners in [239]
Connaught by, or by the authority of, the Earl of Ulster, and in the following February were brought to the castle of Northburgh in Inishowen,[70] where in the course of the year Walter died in prison.[71] According to the Irish annals he died of hunger, meaning apparently that in accordance with the inhumane custom still sometimes practised, he was as the phrase goes, 'put upon diet' and starved to death,[72] but there is no suggestion of this in the Anglo-Irish annals, and it may be doubted.

As the event which marks the final shattering of English influence over the greater part of Ireland—namely, the murder of the young Earl of Ulster—was connected with the fate of Walter de Burgh, it is important to ascertain as clearly as may be Walter's position and proceedings in Connaught, and his relations with the earl. He was eldest son of William de Burgh, called '*Liath*' or the Grey, who died in 1324,[73] and is described by the annalists as 'son of William Mór'. He was probably son of Earl Walter's brother William, who was killed at Athanchip in 1270.[74] If so, he was first cousin
to the Red Earl. On October 29, 1326, after the death of Earl Richard, his eldest sur- [240]
viving son, Edmund, and Walter, son of his cousin William, were appointed guardians of the peace in the counties of Connaught, Tipperary, and Limerick, and also custodians of the lands of the late earl in those counties.[75] In May 1327, however, the manors of the earldom, except those assigned in dower to the widow of John de Burgh, were delivered to the young earl,[76] but Walter de Burgh, like his father in his later years, seems to have exercised a very free hand in the affairs of Connaught, and to have forwarded a policy of his own without regard to the earl's wishes. Thus we are told that in (seemingly) the very year when Turlough O'Conor, king of Connaught, accompanied the earl in his expedition against Brian O'Brien, Walter de Burgh plundered a number of Turlough's principal retainers.[77] In the same year there was a parley between Walter de Burgh and Gilbert Mc Costello on the one part, and Mulroney Mc Dermot and his son Tomaltagh and Tomaltagh Mc Donough, lord of Tirerril, on the

69 Cal. Close Rolls, 6 Ed. III, p. 484. 70 Laud MS. Annals (as before), p. 376. 71 Clyn, p. 24 where the statement is *obiit in carcere* (1332), and so, on p. 25, when giving the report that the murder of the earl was instigated by Gyle de Burgh, he states as her motive *eo quod fratrem eius Walterum de Burgh et alios incarceravit*. 72 John, son of Walter de Lacy, was so punished by Mortimer in 1318: Laud MS., p. 368; where it is said of him, *adiudicatus fuit ad dietam et in carcere moriebatur.* 73 Clyn, p. 16. The Irish annals seem to have two entries of his death, one in 1322 and the other in 1324. 74 Both Duald Mac Firbis and the Historia et Genealogia de Burgo make William *Liath*, son of Richard *Óg*, an unnoticed son of the first William de Burgh who died in 1206. But see Galway Arch. Journ., vol. vii, pp. 1–28. 75 Cal. Pat. Rolls (Ireland), 20 Ed. II (13). 76 Pipe Roll, 2 Ed. III, 43rd Rep. D.K., pp. 22–3. 77 Ann. Loch Cé, *sub anno* 1328; but as the expedition against O'Brien and the murder of the Earl of Louth, recorded in the same year, really took place in 1329, the latter is, perhaps, the true date.

other part.[78] The meeting came to blows, in consequence seemingly of a blood feud between two members of the Mc Donough clan, but Walter's aim was to enlist the Mc Dermots against King Turlough. Past experience had shown how important it was to secure Mc Dermot's aid in all attempts at dynastic change. Nor apparently was Walter
[241] de Burgh altogether unsuccessful, for in 1329 there was war between King Turlough and clan Mulroney. In the same year Turlough's brother, Cathal, was forcibly expelled from the Faes of Athlone and from Tirmany 'by the order of Walter de Burgh', imposed upon the O'Kellys.[79] This was in apparent derogation of the grant made in 1318.[80] Of these districts (which were included in 'the king's cantreds') to the king of Connaught. In 1330 Turlough made an attack on Walter de Burgh, who was encamped in Mc Dermot's territory. Gilbert Mc Costello, Tomaltagh Donough, and apparently Tomaltagh Mc Dermot came to Walter's assistance, and O'Conor was forced to withdraw. Walter now mustered 'the armies of all Connaught, both English and Irish, with the object', says the annalist, 'of seizing the sovereignty of Connaught for himself'. This, however, was not what Mc Dermot wanted, and 'he turned against' Walter and made 'a prudent amicable peace' with O'Conor.[81] O'Conor then went to the earl to complain of Walter's proceedings, and to seek the earl's assistance against him. This is stated by the Four Masters. The Annals of Loch Cé state that 'Turlough O'Conor was slain by the people of Walter Mac William Burk (i.e. Walter de Burgh) when coming from the earl's house', and following this source the Annals of Clonmacnois expressly call Turlough 'King of Connaught', thus identifying beyond doubt the individual said
[242] to have been slain. But King Turlough lived for many years and was killed in 1345. There is therefore here some copyist's error. Perhaps Walter did attack Turlough when returning from his mission to the earl, and even slay some of his retinue, and, if so, we can the more readily understand the earl's subsequent treatment of Walter.

However this may have been, it will be remembered that after the campaign against Brian Bán O'Brien in the July of this year Walter de Burgh ravaged the lands of the Earl of Desmond, and that this was followed by the committal of the two earls to the marshal, the Earl of Ulster's going to England (probably to clear himself), and his appointment on March 3, 1331, as deputy to the new justiciar, Sir Anthony de Lucy. Next the Irish annalists state that in 1331 Walter de Burgh led a host against Tomaltagh Mac Dermot, now king of Moylurg, and burned his entire country, while the Four Masters add that Tomaltagh and Walter afterwards made peace with one another. The addition is probably correct, as in the next year (1332, though the date can hardly be right) the Irish annals record a victory by 'the earl's son' (i.e. Edmund de Burgh, son of Earl Richard) over Tomaltagh Mac Dermot and Mac William Burk (i.e. Walter de Burgh). This was probably the occasion of the arrest of Walter, which was effected by Edmund de Burgh by order of his nephew Earl William in November 1331.

From this survey of the proceedings of Walter de Burgh in Connaught it is clear

78 Ibid., and Ann. Clonmacnois. 79 Ann. Loch Cé, 1329. The translator of the Annals of Clonmacnois and the editors of the Annals of Ulster and of Four Masters so understand this entry. The cantred of Tirmany was perhaps at this time subject to the O'Kellys. 80 See *ante*, p. 125, note [p. 496, note 40]. 81 Ann. Loch Ce, 1330, and so Four Masters.

that he had been playing his own game in the province, and that the authority of the young earl was ignored. The Red Earl in his later years had left the conduct of affairs in Connaught to Walter's father, who, as we have seen, often played the kingmaker [243]
there, and once at any rate was suspected of trying to do away altogether with an Irish king. His son thought to follow in his father's footsteps, and he had the support of the large majority of the English settlers in Connaught. Beyond keeping constables in the castles of Roscommon and Randown, the Irish Government had long ceased to exercise control even in 'the king's cantreds', which, as we have seen, had been given up to Turlough O'Conor in 1318. But the young Earl of Ulster, imbued with English notions of order and owing much to the favour of Edward III, while ready to check Irish aggression on his lands, was determined to quell the turbulence of his own barons. The conflict between him and his men was inevitable.

Edward III proposed to visit Ireland in person in the summer of 1332. In the previous November he summoned the Earls of Ulster and Ormonde, William de Bermingham, and Walter de Burgh to England to advise with him concerning his intended visit.[82] Possibly the real object of summoning the two last-named, who no doubt did not attend, was to gain control of their persons. He also bade the Earl of Norfolk and twenty other absentee lords to send men for the defence or recovery of their possessions, intimating that, if when he came to Ireland he found their lands in the hands of the enemy, he might retain them as his conquest.[83] The king's departure was afterwards postponed to Michaelmas. Elaborate preparations were ordered for shipping at Holyhead on that date, and for the storing in Dublin of wine and provi- [244]
sions,[84] and for the assembling of 1,000 foot soldiers in Wales. But the visit never took place.

In December 1332 the English Parliament decided that it would be dangerous for the king to leave the country in view of the possibility of the Scots invading England. Who can say how the history of Ireland might have been changed had Edward devoted his restless energy, not to barren victories on the moors of Scotland and in the plains of France, but to giving good government to Ireland and fulfilling the promise of the thirteenth century!

Besides the Munster expedition when William de Bermingham was arrested, Anthony de Lucy led expeditions into Leinster to recover and repair the castles of Clonmore and Arklow, which had been captured by the Irish in the previous year, and into Thomond where the castle of Bunratty had been levelled to the ground by Murtough O'Brien and the McNamaras.[85] The castle of Ferns had also been taken by the Irish through some treachery, and was recovered in this year. The manor of Ferns, however, was of little value, and even at the death of Aymer de Valence, in 1324, was nearly all in the hands of the Irish.

82 Foedera, vol. ii, p. 828; Cal. Close Rolls, 5 Ed. III, p. 400. 83 Ibid., 826. 84 Cf. 43rd Rep. D.K., pp. 59–60; Cal. Close Rolls, Ed. III, pp. 483, 487–8. 85 Clyn, p. 24; Laud MS. Annals (as above), p. 376; and see the paymaster's accounts for these expeditions: 43rd Rep. D.K., pp. 53–6. It is interesting to note that the person who supplied the largest number of troops for the expedition to Clonmore was Lysagh O'More of Leix.

John Darcy, the new justiciar, did not come to Ireland until February 13, 1333. One of his first acts was to release the Earl of Desmond from prison, where he had been
[245] detained for a year and a half. He was liberated on the mainprise of twenty-six earls, barons, knights, and others headed by the Earls of Ulster and Ormonde, who rendered themselves liable to forfeiture of life and lands if he should make any attempt against the king and they should fail to produce his body.[86] Walter de Bermingham was released at about the same time.[87] The paroxysm of severity was over.

And now the tragedy occurred which may be regarded as closing this epoch of Irish history. On June 6, 1333, William de Burgh, Earl of Ulster and lord of Connaught, was murdered by his own men. It appears that the earl, who was only in his twenty-first year, was going from Newtown-Ards to Carrickfergus when he was treacherously slain at Le Ford—a name which in its Irish dress survives as Belfast.[88] John de Logan, Robert, son of Richard de Mandeville, and Robert, son of Martin de Mandeville, are mentioned as the actual perpetrators of the crime, but the deed created a great commotion, and there must have been many sympathizers. The Countess Matilda of Lancaster had to fly by sea to England with her infant daughter, destined to be the ancestress of kings. Darcy, the justiciar, had been collecting shipping and an army to join the king's campaign on behalf of Edward Balliol, the new puppet-king of Scotland—whither too the earl had intended to go—but now, on July 1, by counsel of the
[246] magnates in Dublin, he brought his army by sea to Carrickfergus to avenge the earl's death. The perpetrators of the murder had called to their assistance some of the Irish, who were only too ready to befriend the enemies of the loyal English. A petty war ensued, but Darcy's force, with the aid of John de Mandeville[89] and other loyal settlers, made short work of the insurgents, though not before much property was destroyed.[90] The justiciar then departed with his army for Scotland, leaving the treasurer, Thomas de Burgh, as his deputy.

The motive which actuated the perpetrators of this crime, like all motives, can only be inferred. Frian Clyn, indeed, says that the crime was ascribed as usual to the influence of a woman, Gyle de Burgh, sister of Walter de Burgh and wife of Richard de Mandeville, and that she had instigated the murder because the earl had imprisoned her brother Walter and others. This vindictive motive may of course have actuated Walter's sister and may have caused her to incite her husband's family to the deed, but the suggestion does not account for the earl's leading vassals in Ulster taking up a blood-feud that was not theirs, nor for their joining in or assenting to a deed which, so long as feudal ideas prevailed, was regarded as peculiarly disgraceful, nor does it harmonize with the hurried flight of the countess and her infant daughter. If the earl's
[247] vassals generally had been faithful, she was in no danger. The earl was clearly justified

86 Laud MS. Annals (as before), p. 378. The names of the mainpernors are given on p. 387 under the year 1346, when by another act of spasmodic rigour most of them were (for the moment) deprived of their possessions. 87 Ibid., p. 379. 88 *Bel-feirste*, 'the month of the *fearsad*', *vadum* vel *traiectus* (Joyce). There was a castle and manor here: Inquis. 1333. 89 John de Mandeville was appointed sheriff of Co. Down in 1326, after the death of Earl Richard. At the same time Richard de Mandeville was *custos pacis* in the bishoprics of Commr and Derry: Pat. Roll (Ireland), 20 Ed. II (7, 12). 90 Especially about the manor of Le Ford, which was laid waste by 'John Logan's war': Inquisition of 1333, Journal R.S.A.I, vol. xliii (1913), p. 139.

in punishing his turbulent vassal in the interests of good faith and order, and there is no suggestion that he acted illegally. Mere vengeance for Walter's death, then, cannot have been the motive of the conspiracy. The circumstances show that the feudal sentiment of fealty to the lord was by this time dead, that the feudal organization was everywhere breaking down, and that, as in the case of the massacre of the Berminghams in Louth, the real motive which actuated the conspirators was the desire to free themselves from the control of a feudal superior. That this motive was at work will be plain to those who have studied the history of the next few years and have seen how the opportunity of the earl's death was seized by the brothers of Walter de Burgh[91] in Connaught to become virtually independent, and how Edmund de Burgh, the Red Earl's son, to whom the custody of the lands of the infant heir was entrusted, was also foully murdered, and in Ulster how the Countess Matilda was unable to obtain the issues of her dower-lands.[92]

But though the motive which actuated the conspirators was probably the same in each case the murder of the Earl of Ulster was a much more glaring breach of the feudal code than that of the Earl of Louth. Even if we discount the defence put forward in the latter case, it must be remembered that the newly-created Earl of Louth was imposed as superior lord over men who for many years had known no superior except the Crown itself. This was always viewed as a grievance. When King John created the [248]
honour of Limerick for William de Braose, the crown-tenants there, though only quite recently enfeoffed, bitterly resented it, and some of them opposed their new lord in arms.[93] John de Bermingham too, though a successful commander who had done welcome work in the defeating of Edward Bruce, came of a subordinate line of barons remarkable mainly for their fighting qualities combined with a turbulence which often brought them into conflict with their English neighbours, and in one recent case the family escutcheon is said to have been stained by an act of bad faith towards the Irish.[94] But William de Burgh came of a line famous in the annals of the conquest of Connaught, and for nearly seventy years he and his ancestors had held the one ancient earldom of Ireland and had brought a measure of order and prosperity to the wilder and more backward parts of the island unknown before. He was the sole link which connected the Crown with two of 'the five Fifths' of Ireland, the sole head of a great organization, incomplete and unwieldy indeed, but better than the anarchy of the past and susceptible of improvement, and when he was removed in this violent fashion the Crown was unable to take his place.

Personally Earl William seems to have been a man of great promise. Young as he was, he had been employed in more than one mission of state. He enjoyed the complete confidence of his sovereign, and was clearly prepared to aid the energetic young king in putting a stop to the factions and disorders which had sprung up owing to the [249]
weak and capricious rule of the preceding reign. When grounds of dispute arose between his kinsmen and the Earl of Desmond, he succeeded in allaying the recrude-

91 These brothers were Edmund Albanach, from whom were descended the Mac Williams Eighter (Lower) of Mayo, and Ulick, whose son, Richard Óg, was the first Mac William Oughter (Upper) of Galway. 92 See Close Rolls, 8 Ed. III, p. 248. 93 See *ante*, vol. i pp. 172–8 [pp. 62–4]. 94 *Supra*, pp. 35–6 [pp. 452–3].

scence of an ancient feud by submitting the points at issue to the arbitration of judges, and he did not hesitate to take the part of Turlough O'Conor against his own kinsmen when he thought that they were in the wrong. Friar Clyn says of him that he was a man *subtilissimi ingenii, reipublicae et pacis amator*. This high praise, not at all in common form, has a ring of truth about it and is borne out by all we know of him.

Though what are called 'epochs of history' are never in reality sharp]y marked off, but merge more or less gradually into one another, and though the gradual decay of the best elements of feudalism and the disruption of society caused by the Scottish invasion, with consequent growing insubordination and disorder, were already for some years past undermining the vigour of Anglo-Norman rule in Ireland, yet, in view of its circumstances and far-reaching effects, the murder of the young Earl of Ulster may fairly be regarded as marking the close of the feudal period introduced by Strongbow and Henry II, and signalizing the opening of a new epoch, distinguished by the recrudescence of Celtic tribalism and its spurious imitation by many of Anglo-Norman descent. The door was now finally closed on a century and a half of remarkable progress, vigour, and comparative order, and two centuries of retrogression, stagnation, and comparative anarchy were about to be ushered in.

CHAPTER XXXIX [250]

ONE HUNDRED AND SIXTY YEARS OF NORMAN RULE, 1173–1333

In a a former chapter[1] a slight survey was made of the character of the great change effected in Ireland by the Anglo-Normans in the half-century that followed the invasion. Now that their doings have been traced for upwards of a century and a half it will be possible to estimate more adequately the results of that change, the good it brought with it, and the evil, if any, it carried in its train, and to discern some of the causes which brought about the decay of the feudal organization and put a stop to continuous progress on the lines laid down.

There has been a strong tendency amongst Irish writers to assume that nothing but evil resulted to Ireland from Anglo-Norman rule. They have in mind the troubled history of Ireland in much later times, learnt perhaps in pages which lay all the faults at the door of England, which ignore historical perspective, and take no account of the political, social, and moral environment of the statesmen and soldiers whom they condemn. Their righteous indignation has been stirred by the recital of the ruthless Tudor wars, the stern Cromwellian repression, the wholesale confiscations, the iniq- [251]
uitous trade restrictions, the Williamite wars of religion, the long-continued Catholic disabilities. In spite of the fact that in all these troubles leading descendants of the Anglo-Norman settlers suffered as much as any one else, these writers are ready to find the origin of these evils in the Anglo-Norman occupation, and are not in a frame of mind to inquire dispassionately into the actual results of Anglo-Norman rule while it was effective. In their eyes, too, the one bright spot in the later history of Ireland is Grattan's Parliament, but they ignore the fact that the class represented in that parliament were the spiritual successors of the old Anglo-Norman settlers. An independent study of the primary sources has, however, led the present writer to think that the direct and more immediate results of Anglo-Norman domination were on the whole distinctly beneficial to Ireland. To consider possible indirect and more remote consequences, while ignoring the proximate causes of these, would serve no useful purpose, while an adequate consideration of all contributory causes would practically involve the re-writing of the whole history of Ireland.

When estimating the effects of Norman rule in Ireland it is necessary to have in our minds an adequate picture of the state of Ireland before the Normans came. Without such a picture comparison is impossible and judgement worthless. Here, however, it would be out of place to do more than recall the leading impressions produced by a study of the pre-Norman period and supplement in some respects the sketch already made.[2]

1 *Ante*, vol. ii, c. xxiii. 2 *Ante*, vol. i, chapters i, ii, and iv.

Historical criticism and archaelogical research have reduced to comparatively hum-
[252] ble proportions the exaggerated notions of native writers as to the antiquity and the degree of civilization in early Ireland. Nevertheless, in the centuries following the introduction of Christianity to her shores there was what may fairly be called a 'Golden Age of art and learning' in Ireland. Amid the welter of the break-up of the Western Empire under the pressure of Germanic tribes, Ireland, undisturbed as yet by barbarian inroads, had opportunities of developing cultural ideas which she had received mainly through the channel of the Church. Christian missionaries had brought to her the Latin alphabet, and the monasteries founded by them became in course of time centres of theological learning, to which students flocked from England and the Continent for study and a contemplative life. In her turn Ireland sent forth her missionary sons to foreign lands and helped to keep alive for the world what survived of the faith and learning of the later Imperial Rome. But the monastic scribes and writers did not confine themselves to reproducing copies of the Gospels and composing lives of the saints in the Latin language. The customary laws of Ireland, modified to some extent under Christian influence, were noted down and became the text-books to be explained and expanded by the Brehon lawyers. The heroic tales of pagan Ireland—probably for the most part, as has been said, 'myths tinged and distorted by history'—which had been orally handed down from a remote past, were now written in the vernacular, given a quasi-historical setting, and thus preserved to become the spiritual heritage of the Irish race. New or improved arts and handicrafts,
[253] too, were practised in these monastic centres, and are attested by the marvellous ornamentation of some of their manuscripts, by the intricate metal-work on many a shrine and reliquary, by the panelled crosses in their graveyards, and by the delicate ornamentation of the portals, pediments, and arcades of many a small stone-roofed temple. But when all is said that can fairly be said, it may reasonably be doubted whether this outburst of art and learning penetrated appreciably beyond the cloister and the immediate patronage of the Church so as to make any permanent impress on the people as a whole.

At any rate, this early promise did not lead to full fruition. In the ninth and tenth centuries Ireland, for the first time in the historic period, became the prey of barbarian invaders, and her monasteries, in particular, were again and again plundered and burned. Possibly the picture drawn by the monastic annalists of the destruction caused by the Scandinavian raids is exaggerated, while historians have scarcely given due credit to the Norse settlers for the great advance they made in forming seaport towns and in opening up a foreign trade; yet it seems clear, as already remarked, that the march of civilization in Ireland was arrested, nay turned backwards, by the fierce depredations of the Viking hordes. The century and a half which elapsed between the battle of Clontarf and the coming of the Normans was a period of increasing moral and political anarchy in Ireland. The Church, which had suffered most, had lost her early zeal, and though she numbered some saintly men among her prelates, she had become unfitted in the altered times for the due fulfilment of her mission. The political nexus was broken. The shadowy authority of the *ard-rí*, instead of becoming more substantial, was no longer acknowledged throughout the island, and even the theory [254] of a pentarchy, evolved by historians, seldom, if ever, represented the facts. It was during this period that England under the Normans was consolidated into a strong centralized monarchy, while towards its close a great king, by his wise statesmanship and far-seeing administrative reforms, had established order and security; and had devised a machinery for carrying on the business of government which subsequent ages have done little more than extend and develop.

The relatively backward state of Ireland during this period is manifest. The whole country was broken up into numerous shifting groups of tribes, often at war with each other, but with no group powerful enough to obtain and hold the mastery over the rest. Their legal conceptions had never been recast in the Roman mould, but were primitive and unsuited to a progressive society. The idea of the State was unknown and with it the conception of crime as an offence against the community. There was no machinery for making new laws, and the ancient customary laws expounded by the Brehons, though containing much 'natural equity', had no effective sanction. There was nothing but public opinion—the popular 'boycott'—to compel the offender to submit to the arbitration of a Brehon or to abide by his award. Other peoples had passed through a similar stage of evolution, but in the twelfth century the Irish lagged far behind the more progressive nations of Europe.

A somewhat similar absence of governmental interference found indeed advocates among a few political reformers of the last century in England, and the framework of society in twelfth-century Ireland curiously resembles the aggregation of 'amorphous [255] communes', to attain which the Russian anarchist Bakunin was ready to sink modern civilization in blood. But saner minds have seen that to attain the greatest freedom, freedom must be surrendered. Without state-control there can be no security to the individual. In the general insecurity which followed from the absence of state-control in Ireland, agriculture could not thrive, even if the communal land system had offered better inducement for steady work. Cattle-rearing, then even more than now the main industry of the country, was carried on under the ever-present peril that the stock of the business might be 'lifted' by some hostile tribe. There was no Celtic coinage, and inter-tribal commerce must have been greatly restricted. What foreign trade there was seems to have been confined almost entirely to the Scandinavian seaports.

Into this disordered and divided land, where there was little sense of patriotism, as we understand the term, where each man's 'country' was the territory of the tribe or at most the tribe group to which he belonged, there burst, in the latter part of the twelfth century, a band of Norman adventurers with their retainers, bent on seeking sword-land for themselves.

I have called these adventurers Normans or Anglo-Normans for convenience and as best indicating their most distinctive qualities, but it should be borne in mind that the term is loosely applied. Most of the first invaders came directly from South Wales, and some of them had Welsh blood in their veins, while others were Flemish by extraction, and to these racial elements in their composition, and especially to their Welsh environment, may be ascribed certain divergences of character and conduct [256] which have been already noted. Nevertheless, broadly speaking, all the settlers, in the country parts at least, had retained or taken on the Norman culture and traditions.

Who then were these Normans and what were their traditions? In the past four centuries they had made their mark on Western Europe and in more than one country had changed the course of history. From about the year 800, issuing from their northern homes, bands of Scandinavian sea rovers had swooped not only upon Ireland, but upon the islands, coasts, and rivers of Scotland, Britain, and Gaul. Wherever the Northmen appeared they plundered and ravaged, especially the monasteries, and carried off with them whatever they could lay hands on, so that the terror-stricken Irish would welcome an angry sky and say,

> Bitter is the wind to-night,
> It tosses the ocean's white hair:
> To-night I fear not the fierce warriors of Norway
> Coursing the Irish Sea—

and a new petition was added to the litany of nations: *a furore Normannorum libera nos Domine*!

But the period of mere piracy had long ago ended. As we have said, 'from pagans and pirates they became Christians and traders'. They settled and formed orderly governments in Iceland, in the Orkneys and the Western Isles of Scotland, in the seaport towns of Ireland, in the north and east of England, and above all in the country henceforth known from them as Normandy. This last in their hands became a powerful well-organized state in nominal subjection to the king of the Franks. Here in the
[257] course of the tenth century they forgot their native language and shed nearly all of their Scandinavian habits and customs, while they took on the French tongue and absorbed what survived of Latin civilization. In the eleventh century they kept their swords sharpened in the Crusades, and some of their bolder spirits formed the brilliant but short-lived Sicilian kingdom, of which Professor Haskins has said that 'it stood well in advance of its contemporaries in all that goes to make a modern type of government'; and most far-reaching feat of all, they conquered Saxon England, and welded the country into a strong monarchical state, which a century later, in the words of the same accomplished writer, 'was the most highly organized and effective government of its time in Western Europe'.

Such, in brief, was the history and such the tradition behind the invaders of Ireland. They had among their forbears two marked types, occasionally united in varying proportions in the same person, but in general quite distinct: the soldier-type, brave and chivalrous, but lustful of conquest and often unscrupulous, and the statesman type with a great capacity for organization and the ruling of men, but prone to seek his ends by diplomacy, craft, and intrigue, rather than by even-handed justice. In the early conquerors the former qualities predominated, but they were followed by others in whom the characteristics of the latter class were more marked, while all were imbued with the pride of race and the consciousness of superiority. To these men the conquest and domination of Ireland must have seemed a natural development of the past.

In preceding pages, so far as our materials allowed, we have traced the steps by which the invaders gradually accomplished their objects. As usual in their aggressions [258] they covered their self-seeking aims with a veneer of legality. It was the tribute which, ever since moral principles began to prevail, vice has been wont to pay to virtue. They came to reinstate a dispossessed chieftain who had approached them as a suppliant, and they had the licence of their own king. The utter lack of cohesion among the Irish tribes rendered any sustained general resistance impossible. Like the Gauls of Caesar's time, *dum singuli pugnant universi vincuntur*, and as in the case of the Gauls, there were always powerful native chieftains who, on various occasions, gave the invaders their assistance against their own particular foes. The conquest of Leinster and Meath was soon effected. The feudal relation between the conquerors and King Henry was recognized and established. Nearly all the native kings acknowledged the overlordship of the English monarch, while the native Church welcomed the new regime. The possession of the eastern sea-board facilitated the arrival of newcomers and the transmission of supplies, and the expansion of the Norman settlers as far as Downpatrick, Cork, and Limerick soon followed. By the fourth decade of the thirteenth century Connaught was finally brought within the feudal organization, and the sway of its king, as a quasi-tenant of the Crown, confined to a comparatively small portion of his former territory. In the last quarter of the same century the flow of Norman influence had reached its high-water mark. All Ireland, nominally at least, acknowledged the supremacy of the English Crown.

But to get a true conception of the relative strength of the forces of feudalism and tribalism we must look more closely at the distribution of the land. If we consider the [259] map of Ireland in the reign of Edward I, we find that about three-fourths of the country were actually dominated by Anglo-Norman lords. In these districts nearly all the best land—that is to say, roughly speaking, land other than woods and bogs with an elevation of not more than 500 feet—was parcelled out among their vassals, and here the feudal organization and feudal land-system prevailed. It must not, however, be supposed that the Irish were entirely expelled from these regions. In many parts, especially in the feudal lordships of Connaught and Ulster, entire Irish septs continued to hold their lands or part of them in more or less real subjection to the Anglo-Norman lord, and, as already shown,[3] most manors throughout the country included among the tenants numerous Irish *betaghs* (the *nativi* or villeins of feudal law) and other unfree classes. As in England the Norman landholders formed a ruling aristocracy, but unfortunately for the amalgamation of the races, Celtic freeholders in feudalized Ireland were more rare than Saxon freeholders in England. In the remaining fourth the Irish clans continued to be virtually autonomous. In their territories the families of their chieftains, and those of their *urrighs*, or subordinate chieftains, formed the aristocracy, the Brehon law prevailed, and English judges, sheriffs, and other officers of the Crown never made their appearance.

3 *Ante*, vol. ii, pp. 329–32 [pp. 281–2].

The territories of three main groups of virtually autonomous clans may be distinguished: (1) The greater part of the present province of Ulster, viz. all except the present counties of Down and Antrim, the northern part of County Derry, and the
[260] peninsula of Inishowen. Even here, however, the Irish chieftains at the time of which we speak acknowledged the overlordship of the Earl of Ulster, and were in general peaceful. (2) A broad strip about the upper reaches of the Shannon where the O'Conors, nominally vassals of the Crown, were left to wrangle among themselves over the shadow of their ancient power. (3) Desmond or southern Kerry, and western Cork, mostly mountainous country, where, since the battle of Callann in 1261, the MacCarthys and others were practically supreme until the Earl of Desmond 'overtopped them all', but rather as a quasi-Celtic chief than as a feudal lord. With the possible exception of Desmond, where some few of the earlier settlers seem to have retained or recovered their possessions, these territories were almost exclusively inhabited by native Irishmen.

Besides the above, there were some other Irish territories nominally subject to Anglo-Norman lords where some settlements had been made, but these were too few and too scattered to influence the essentially Irish character of their surroundings. These were (1)Thomond, now County Clare, where the O'Brien kings, at first loyal, had lately cast off their allegiance, and though the whole country had been granted to Thomas de Clare to govern as a sort of liberty, the only part actually held by his Norman tenants and organized on a feudal basis was little more than the barony of Bunratty Lower. (2) A large tract having for centre the mountainous region of Slieve Bloom. Here the principal Irish territories to the north-east, east, and south—Offaly, Leix, and Upper Ossory—were nominally subject to the lords of Leinster. There were
[261] castles at Geashill, Lea, Dunamase, Offerlane, and other places, and the king had recently caused a strong castle to be built at Roscrea, but only the eastern parts of Offaly and Leix, and the southern half of Upper Ossory were held by Anglo-Norman tenants. In the remaining parts the Irish clans, under the O'Conors Faly, the O'Mores, and the Mac Gillapatricks, were becoming more and more independent, and at times made raids across the border. The territories to the immediate north-west of Slieve Bloom were reckoned in Meath, but here again the native clans were kept in very imperfect control. (3) The Wicklow mountains and adjoining valleys and uplands. In this region the O'Byrnes and O'Tooles, once powerful clans who had supplied kings to North Leinster, had been confined by Strongbow. Early in the reign of Edward I they had become increasingly restless, expeditions were led against them in their mountain fastnesses, and the castles of Newcastle Mc Kynegan and Castlekevin were 'constructed anew' as a defence against their raids.

The distribution of the districts which remained practically independent of Anglo-Norman rule was largely determined by topographical conditions. Each of them included a difficult mountain region into which the Irish could retire with their cattle when a punitive expedition was sent against them. But after all deductions and explanations have been made, the fact remains that Anglo-Norman rule in Ireland throughout the thirteenth century, and especially towards its close, was a very real thing. It wrought a great change in every department of life. It was an all-pervading dynamic force introducing new ideas—political, social, economical, and moral—which were all in the direction of what humanity generally regards as civilization and [262] progress. It remains to point out in detail the principal changes thus brought about, and to indicate, so far as is possible at this stage, the causes which deprived Anglo-Norman rule of its full effectiveness, and ultimately defeated much, but not all, of its earlier promise.

In the first place, the most important result of the Norman occupation was what I have ventured to call a 'Pax Normannica'. Comparative peace was, indeed, a necessary condition of all progress. It may be said not to have been seriously broken until 1315-18, when the Scottish invasion, though ultimately unsuccessful, disclosed the weakness of England's hold on Ireland. It was not, of course, absolute over all the country. It extended only in a modified form to the districts which remained under Irish rule. Here the old contests between rival factions over the succession to the local chieftainships broke out from time to time, and the settlers by favouring one or other of the claimants, with a view to increasing their own influence, not infrequently added to the turmoil. The subjugation of Connaught involved a decade of intermittent warfare in that province, and there were attempts at domination not permanently successful in other territories. But during the whole period up to 1315, the lordships of Leinster, Meath, Ulster, and Connaught, and the greater part of the province of Munster were free from the desolating raids to which, mainly owing to contests for the provincial kingships, or to struggles to obtain the high-kingship of Ireland, these districts were frequently subject in the pre-Norman period.[4] Feudalism, indeed, as introduced into Ireland had a distinctly integrating effect. Wherever it prevailed it made [263] the country one in a sense unknown before. Some quarrels and consequent disturbances arose among the Anglo-Irish lords, but they were few and trivial as compared with the devastating conflicts of former Irish chiefs, or even with the discords and risings against the Crown of their English compeers. On the whole the barons of Ireland stood by each other and were conspicuous for their loyalty to the king of England.

Secondly, this freedom from the peril of external raids brought with it for the first time the possibility of social advance, and in particular gave security to the cattle-rearer and the tiller of the soil. As already mentioned, there is no indication of any general clearance from the feudalized districts of the mass of the Irish labouring population. To the Norman settlers land without men to work it was valueless, and we have many proofs of their desire—nay, of their exercising pressure—to keep Irishmen from migrating from the occupied lands.[5] There is, indeed, ample evidence that the Norman occupation led to a great increase in the area of agriculture, and to greatly improved methods of husbandry. This was largely due to the fashion of 'landlord cultivation' then in vogue in England. Each manor had extensive demesne lands which were worked as a home-farm, partly by means of the customary services of the

4 In the Book of Rights, among the prerogatives of the kings of Munster are included the right to raid 'the cattle of Cruachan at the singing of the cuckoo', and the right 'to burn North Laighin', p. 5. 5 *Ante*, vol. ii, pp. 329–32 [pp. 281–2].

betaghs, but to an increasing extent by hired labour. There were thus only two economic classes concerned in the culture of these demesnes, and the produce in many
[264] cases formed the principal part of the lord's income. There are still extant certain early thirteenth century farming manuals written originally in Anglo-Norman French, such as 'Le Dite de Hosebondrie' by Walter of Henley, and Les Reules Seynt Robert' by Robert Grosseteste, Bishop of Lincoln, the most independent thinker and scholar of the age. These are practical treatises embodying the wisdom of the time concerning rural economy, the keeping of estate accounts, the duties of the various estate officers, and the management of the household. Walter of Henley's work retained its pre-eminence for upwards of two hundred years, and even now may be read with interest. The Rules of Bishop Grosseteste were written for Margaret, Countess of Lincoln, who, in 1242, married Walter Marshal, Earl of Pembroke, and they must have been familiar to those concerned in the management of the great fief of Leinster. From the accounts of the ministers of Roger Bigod, Earl of Norfolk, and lord of the liberty of Carlow,[6] we have full information as to the way in which a great estate in Ireland was managed in the latter part of the thirteenth century. A seneschal of knightly rank with a salary of £100 a year presided over the court of the liberty at Carlow. He was head of the executive, and had under him for police and military purposes the constables of the castles of Carlow, Fothered (Castlemore near Tullow), Fennagh, Old Ross, and the
[265] Island (Kilmokea). There were two lawyers (*narratores comitis*) to assist the seneschal, and a chief sergeant to execute the processes of the baronial court. There were also hundred-courts at the principal manors. The chief fiscal officer was the treasurer, to whom at the castle of Carlow the provosts of the burghs and various bailifs and receivers of the lordship rendered their accounts. Husbandry, with which we are here principally concerned, was carried on for the earl on his demesne lands and particularly at Old Ross. At this manor there were remaining in 1281, at the close of the season, 921 wethers, ewes, hoggets, and lambs.[7] 261 had been sold in the course of the year. Sheep sold at 8*d*. to 1*s*., and lambs at 4*d*. These are low prices, but wool sold at 2*d*. and 3*d*. a lb., a price which (if we multiply by fifteen to get the approximate equivalent in modern currency) will compare favourably with recent pre-war prices. In 1283 the earl had at Old Ross besides sheep 4 common horses ('afers'), 39 oxen, 1 bull, 29 cows, 14 calves, 5 pigs, 9 swans, and 11 pea-fowl. He sold 231 stone of cheese at 8*d*. a stone, and his garden produced leeks, herbs, and apples. Cows and common horses cost about 10*s*., but for agriculture oxen were principally employed. A team of draft oxen cost from 25*s*. to 31*s*. In 1282–8,[8] 15½ acres were sown in wheat, 28½ acres in rye,
[266] and 82 acres in oats at Old Ross, besides 32 acres of oats at 'Baliconwr' somewhere in the neighbourhood. At the present day in Ireland this would be considered a large

6 Mr. Philip H. Hore in his History of Co. Wexford, vol. i, pp. 9-39 and 140-61, has given copious extracts from these accounts so far as they relate to that county. He has also kindly lent me his MS. transcripts. See too a paper by Mr. James Mills, Deputy Keeper of the Records of Ireland, in Journal R.S.A.I., vol. xxii (1892), pp. 50–62. 7 In subsequent years the stock of sheep increased. In 1283-4 the total stood at 1,397, and in 1285-6 at 1,442. In 1288 2,160 sheep were sheared. 8 An account of supplies for the army in Wales, sent in 1282 to the Earl of Norfolk, as marshal, from his Irish manors, includes large quantities of grain, meat, fish, wine, beer, cheese, salt, onions, &c.: Cal. Docs. Ireland, vol. ii, no. 2009.

amount of tillage for one farm. Wheat sold at 5s. to 6*s*. 8*d*. a crannock. Taking the crannock at eight bushels, or one quarter, this would give the price of wheat as estimated in our money at from 75*s*. to 100*s*. a quarter. Oats sold at 4*s*. to 6*s*. a crannock, and rye at 6*s*. The wages of the regular farm servants—usually eight plough men, four shepherds, a cowherd, a reaper, a waggoner, and a watchman or overseer—were four shillings a year each and four pence a week allowed for food. Occasional unskilled labourers received a penny a day. But much was done, particularly at harvest-time, by specially hired labour and piece-work. The average yield of grain was low, apparently not quite three times the amount sown.

The accounts written in Latin are a model for any modern farmer or land-steward. To take for example the account of David Trillec, provost of the manor of Old Ross, for the year commencing Michaelmas 1283—he begins by debiting himself with the arrears of the previous account. Then follows the amount produced by sales of cattle, sheep, wool, cheese, corn, &c. (every item being separately entered), the sums received for pleas and perquisites of the court of the manor, feudal incidents and miscellaneous receipts. The total with the arrears is shown. Next come the expenses, e.g. iron for the repair of ploughs, agricultural implements, wages of smith, hiring of harrowers, &c. Then the keep of the regular farm hands and their wages. Then the cost of work at the farm buildings and enclosures, every item, whether for labour or materials, being separately entered. Then small miscellaneous expenses, including twelve pence the [267]
usual present to the servants at Christmas. In a separate heading are the harvest charges for winnowing last year's grain, and for harvesting the current crop. The various operations appear to have been done mainly by piece-work, the particulars of which are supplied. Ninepence was paid for the 'hocmet', or harvest-feast, of the servants. The total of expenses is then shown, credit is taken for payments to the treasurer at Carlow, &c., and the balance is debited to the provost. On the back of the roll is a full account of the produce of the grange and of the stock. The exact amount of grain—wheat, rye, oats—produced or bought is stated, and every bushel, whether sold or used for seed or fodder, is accounted for. And so of the stock, the number of each kind remaining as stated in the last account, and the increase are accounted for—so many died, so many sold, and so many remaining.

There is no reason to suppose that the farming at Old Ross was in any way exceptional, or even that it was a particularly favourable example of prosperous husbandry. To the accident that Roger Bigod's lands passed to the king in 1306 we owe the exceptional preservation of these accounts, and we are thereby enabled to obtain authentic details which would otherwise have been difficult or impossible to collect. But the earl was an absentee, and only once visited his Irish lands. It is certain that many resident landowners had larger and even more prosperous farms. From a brief memorandum of the chattels left by Maurice Fitz Maurice at his death, in 1286, it appears that he had at Inchiquin in Imokilly ten teams of ploughing oxen, and all the corn of as many carucates in granges and haggards (neither amount nor value stated), a stud of horses [268]
of the value of £100, 300 two-year-old cattle, besides war-horses;[9] while he left at five

9 From £5 to £20 was usually paid as compensation to those who lost a war-horse in the service of the king:

other manors altogether nineteen ploughing-teams and the corn of as many carucates of demesne land, all valued at £170.[10] Many inquisitions show that in the thirteenth century large areas of arable land were held in demesne, and cultivated by the tenants in chief. Thus the inquisitions taken in 1333 concerning the lands of the ill-fated William de Burgh, Earl of Ulster, state that at Toolooban[11] in the Loughrea district, previous to the recent disturbances, no fewer than 570 acres were under the lord's plough, besides thirty-two acres of meadow, each acre being equivalent to at least two modern statute acres, and this was only one, though the principal, of the earl's manors. We may be sure that the lesser occupying tenants in their degree followed the example of their lords, and the large quantities of grain exported from Ireland (instances of
[269] which will be presently cited) are the best proof that in the new order and comparative security of the thirteenth century agriculture became vastly increased and was very profitable to all concerned.

Some legal proceedings taken in 1295 afford an indication of the accumulated wealth in goods and chattels of various kinds to be found in one of the less important manors of County Tipperary. It appears that the castle of Donohill,[12] which belonged to Silvester l'Ercedekne (Archdeacon), was forcibly entered by the sheriff, Hugh Purcell, acting on information that certain felons were being harboured there, and the jurors found that he and his followers took in the castle twelve marks in money of Lady Johanna l'Ercedekne, and they took robes, clothes, &c., to the value of £40.... They say also that they took 300 cows, 120 afers, 28 mares, 4 horses, 500 sheep, 200 lambs, 100 pigs, 100 goats, 40 kids, which cattle were found within the castle [i.e. in the bawn]. They took also 28 oxen in a field outside the castle. In his plaint Silvester l'Ercedekne alleges in greater detail that the sheriff broke chests and coffers and took goods to the value of £500, viz. £50 in money, robes, table-clothes, napkins, coverlets (*coopertoria tapeta,* tapestries?), sheets, fallings [Irish cloaks], hacquetons, gambisons, habergeons,[13] helmets, spears, bows, and other armour, 68 charters of feoffment, 48
[270] bonds of debtors to the value of £100, cups and silver spoons, gold rings, precious stones, brooches, girdles woven with silk, and other jewels, brass pots, cauldrons, and dishes, basins, and other vessels'. He also alleged that even more cattle, &c., were taken than the jurors allowed.

Thirdly, another remarkable step in advance directly due to Norman rule and organization was the growth of towns throughout the feudalized districts. In the first place

Cal. Docs. Ireland, vol. iv, no. 320. 10 Great roll of the Irish exchequer, P.R.O., London, Bundle 58/250. Sweetman in each case translates 'good carucates', reading no doubt *carucatas bonas* (Cal. Docs. Ireland, vol. iii, no. 463), but Mr. Philip H. Hore kindly informs me that the true reading is *caruc'bou* (i.e. *carucatas boum*), meaning ploughing teams of oxen. This is, no doubt, correct, as it was chattel property, not land, that was concerned. Where land is meant the phrase is usually *carucatas terre.* 11 Journal R.S.A.I., vol. xxxii (1902), p. 133. For a description of the bawn at Toolooban—a rectangular enclosure, 237 by 219 ft., surrounded by a stone wall and having a stone building at the entrance—see Journal Galway Archaeological and Historical Society, vol. xi (1906), p. 127. 12 Justiciary Rolls, vol. i, p. 6. Some remains of this castle are still to be seen, built (like Shanid) on the summit of a high mote in the townland of Moat Quarter and parish of Donohill. In the bawn or bailey foundations of buildings have been traced. The fosses and earthworks are much defaced. 13 'Falling', Irish *falaing*, a mantle; 'hacqueton', a variety of gambison or quilted tunic; 'habergeon', a short hauberk or coat of mail.

the seaport cities of Scandinavian origin, Dublin, Waterford, Cork, and Limerick, were enlarged, strengthened, and given a new impetus under royal charters to an expanding trade. To these was soon added the town of Drogheda, taken over by the king from Walter de Lacy.[14] These communities held well together in defence of their common interests. In 1252 a compact was entered into between the burghers of Drogheda and the citizens of Dublin, providing for the joint furtherance of matters of advantage to either community, and for the settlement of disputes which might arise between individual burghers and citizens;[15] and in 1286 a more extended compact was made between the citizens of Waterford, Dublin, Cork, and Limerick, and the burghers of Drogheda, for the maintenance of their liberties, and for a triennial meeting at Kilkenny with a view to common action in matters affecting them.[16] But it was not only these royal cities and boroughs, including also the boroughs of Athlone, Dungarvan, and Louth, that grew and prospered under Norman rule, but wherever [271]
the principal settlers built their castles and established their manorial seats a small town generally grew up and throve under their protection. The nucleus would be formed by the castle, the church—either an ancient one restored or one built anew—the mill, and the houses of the officials, artisans and traders, whose services would be required. If the surrounding settlement attained sufficient importance, a weekly market, and an annual fair, would be established by patent, and the town would receive a charter from its lord, giving it many valuable rights and immunities, and thus further attracting merchants and traders. Burgage land would be set apart for the townsfolk, who usually paid the small fixed rent of one shilling for their burgages. In the course of time several of these towns were walled or otherwise enclosed. In the thirteenth century, however, a mere town-ditch seems to have been considered a sufficient protection. With few exceptions the murage-grants, of which there were many, belong to the fourteenth century or later. The towns were inhabited largely by men of English rather than of Norman blood, and the names of the burgesses very often denoted a trade.[17] Irishmen too were occasionally made burgesses, and then, as in England in the case of serfs, they became by custom free.[18] Where the towns received a charter, the [272]
burgesses usually elected their own mayors or provosts and other officers, held their own courts, established trade-guilds, and while paying their burgage-rents and certain small dues to the lord, were practically exempt from feudal burdens and feudal control. Others might more properly be described as thriving manorial villages possessing franchises of varying degrees of importance. These towns and manorial villages were very numerous. We have already mentioned a list of no fewer than thirty-eight market-towns and ports in County Cork alone where, in 1299, wardens chosen by the several communities were appointed to carry out the ordinance as to bad moneys;[19]

14 These towns paid annually for their privileges as follows: Dublin 200 marks, Waterford 100 marks, Limerick £73 6*s*. 8*d*., Cork 80 marks, and Drogheda on the side of Uriel £40, and on the side of Meath 40 marks. 15 Historical and Municipal Documents (Gilbert), p. 130. 16 Ibid., p. 196 17 See the lists of names derived from trade, mostly of townsfolk, collected by Mr. Mills in his two volumes of Justiciary Rolls (Index of Subjects). Among the provosts of New Ross were L'Aurifaber (Goldsmith), Le Faber (Smith), Le Napper (till lately extant there), Le Gaunter (Glover); also in the same town, L'Espicer, Le Hoser, Le Teynturer, Le Verrur, Le Taillour, &c. 18 See Justiciary Rolls, vol. ii, p. 352. 19 Justiciary Rolls, vol. i,

also a list of thirty of the more important towns of the counties of Cork, Limerick, Tipperary and Waterford, which in 1300 contributed to the subsidy for the war in Scotland.[20] A long list might be compiled of towns known to have received charters
[273] either from the king or from their lords, or at which fairs or markets were established by patent. Indeed it is probably not too much to say that the vast majority of the existing towns in the greater part of Ireland—as well as some others that have since disappeared—owed their origin and early prosperity to the Anglo-Norman settlement. Most of these towns were indeed diminutive in size, but in their small way they formed centres of industry and trade, and of free orderly municipal life, even, in many cases, when the surrounding country had become subject to a disorderly form of feudalism, or lay at the mercy of predatory Irish tribes.

Fourthly, *pari passu* with the growth of towns proceeded the growth of trade, inland and foreign. To the Normans, indeed, was due the introduction into general use of coined money, without which trade cannot advance very far. The Norsemen, it is true, had minted silver coin, but their coinage does not seem to have been widely current in Ireland, and the Irish kings do not appear to have had mints of their own. As late as the year 1157 we read in the Annals of large offerings being made to the newly consecrated church of Mellifont in cows and ounces of gold. Indications of the expansion of trade under the Anglo-Normans are numerous. We shall here mention only a few. The various grants of customs for the purpose of building or repairing the walls of the larger towns, and, at a somewhat later period, of many of the smaller ones, indicate the principal articles of trade. These murage grants, though, as might be expected, containing many items in common, usually vary with the circumstances of each town, and in cases of successive grants to the same town the list of customable
[274] articles becomes progressively much more extensive.[21] It is, clear, in fact, that the lists were, at first at any rate, drawn up locally with a view to the special trade of each town, though later there seems to have been a tendency to adopt a common form.

As an example we may take the Dublin murage-charter of August 26, 1295. It included custom duties on the following articles sold in the city: corn; horses and cat-

p. 265. This list (the names being put into modern form) is as follows:—Cork, Youghal, Timoleague, Carrigtohill, Buttevant, Charleville, Middleton, Castlemartyr, Cloyne, Mogeely, Tallow, Corkbeg, Castlelyons, Glanworth, Shandon, Mallow, Fermoy, Mourne, Carrig, Kilworth, Brigown or Mitchelstown, 'Newtown of Olechan'?, Carrigrohane, Castletown?, Doneraile, Dunbulloge, Inishannon, Grenagh, Ballyhooly, Kinsale, Athnowen, Dundanion, Ringrone, Rincorran, Ballinaboy, Beaver or Carrigaline, Douglas, and Fayth (near Cork). With the exception of Cork and Cloyne, all these towns grew up in connexion (seemingly) with Anglo-Norman manors. **20** The towns mentioned in Co. Limerick are Limerick, Emly, Adare, Rathkeale, Askeaton, Ardagh, Croom, Kilmallock, Darragh, Aherlow, Knockainy, Pallas Grean, and Caherconlish. Those in Co. Tipperary are Cashel, Clonmel, Athassel, Carrick, Ardfinnan, Nenagh, Modreeny, Thurles, Fethard, and Modeshil. Early Statutes (Berry), pp. 231–7. **21** The former variation may be seen, for instance, by comparing the murage-grant to Waterford on June 7, 1234, with that to Drogheda a week later (Cal. Docs. Ireland, vol. i, nos. 2133, 2135), or either of them with that of Dublin in the previous October (ibid., no. 2068); or, again, that of Kilkenny in 1282 with that of Cork in 1284 (ibid., vol. ii, nos. 1913, 2248). For the latter variation compare the grant to Dublin by Henry III in 1233 with that by Edward I in 1295 (Historic and Municipal Documents, ed. Gilbert, pp. 99, 191), or the grant to Drogheda in 1234 with that in 1296 (Cal. Docs. Ireland, vol. iv, no. 311).

tle; hides, fresh, salted, or tanned; salt-meat; bacon; fresh salmon; lampreys; goats and hogs; fleeces; woolfels and skins of many animals; salt, cloth of many kinds, linen cloth, canvas, Irish cloth, cloth of Galloway in Scotland (*Galeweythe*) and of Worstead in Norfolk (*Worthstede*), cloth of silk and gold, of samite,[22] diaper,[23] and baudekyn,[24] cloth of silk without gold, and pieces of embroidered sendal;[25] sea-fish; wine; *cineres* [charcoal?]; honey; wool; iron; lead and tin; tan; avoirdupois [anything sold by]; suet [275]
and fat; wood; alum and copperas; onions; garlic; herrings; boards; mill-stones; flour; cheese and butter; coal; fire-wood; brewing cauldrons; cordwain; roofing nails; horse-shoe iron and cart-clouts; other nails; and any kind of merchandise exceeding the value of 2*s*.[26]

Some of the above articles were imported. For instance, salt[27] (except what was produced by solar evaporation), coal, the finer kinds of cloth, and probably all the metals and chemicals, though in the reign of Edward I attempts were made to work some metalliferous mines in County Tipperary. The principal import trade was in wine,[28] and the amount shipped to Ireland from the royal dependencies of Anjou, Aquitaine, and Gascony was very great. Not only was there enough to supply the king's castles in Ireland, the justiciar's expeditionary forces, and the private cellars of ecclesiastics, Norman barons, and Gaelic chieftains, but large quantities were from time to time re-shipped to supply the Welsh castles and the armies led into Wales and Scotland. Thus in December 1298 the king ordered 1,000 hogsheads of wine for the coming Scottish expedition, and 'if these were not found in Ireland the justiciar and the treasurer were to treat with some merchants in order to have them sent from Glascony'.[29]
In January 1300, 3,000 hogsheads of wine were ordered from Ireland to be sent to [276]
Skinburness.[30] Waterford seems to have had the largest share in this trade, but all the other principal ports participated in it in greater or less degree.

As regards exports, Ireland shared in the wool trade between England and the weavers of Flanders and other places. Even before the coming of the English, Ireland clothed her sons in woollen garments of her own weaving,[31] and the Flemish colony about Haverford in South Wales, from which many of the early settlers came, is described as 'a people well versed in commerce and woollen-manufacture, a people anxious to seek gain by sea or land in defiance of fatigue and danger';[32] but though there is some evidence that in the thirteenth century Ireland exported cloth and cloaks of her own making to England and other places,[33] the trade seems to have been incon-

22 Samite: a rich silk stuff, woven with six kinds of threads. The word is derived, through the French, from the Greek εξάμιτον. 23 Diaper: Old French, *diaspre, diapre*; from the Greek δίασπρος meaning 'pure white'. 24 Baudekyn: silk interwoven with threads of gold, originally made at Bagdad (O.F. *Baudas*). 25 Sendal or Cendal: a rich thin silken stuff from the Sanscrit *Sindhu*=the river Indus, through Low Latin and French. 26 Historic and Municipal Documents (Gilbert), pp. 191-4. The Dublin murrage-charter of 1312 contains even a longer list: ibid., pp. 308-12. 27 Salt was imported from the pits of Bordeaux and Poitou. Its abundance is noted in 1318 in contrast to the scarcity of the preceding disturbed period: Laud MS. Annals, p. 359. 28 Ireland imported wine from the time of St. Ciaran of Clonmacnois in the sixth century, probably in exchange for skins, wolf-dogs, and possibly hawks. 29 Cal. Docs. Ireland, vol. iv, no. 570. 30 Cal. Docs. Ireland, vol. iv, no. 716. 31 Ante, vol. i, p. 136, note 1 [p. 47, note 78]. 32 Giraldus, Itin. Kamb. 33 Small quantities of Irish cloth, white, green, yellow, and red, were sent to England from the time of King John: Cal. Docs. Ireland, vol. i, nos. 420, 462, 500; vol. ii, no. 2009. In 1305, Irish cloth and

siderable. It was mainly the raw material that was sent abroad for others to manufacture, and wool, leather, and skins of various kinds were her principal exports. A good index of the export trade of Ireland and of the relative importance of the principal ports is given by the receipts of 'the great new custom' granted by the magnates to the
[277] king in 1257. It consisted of half a mark on each sack of wool (forty-two stone), half a mark for each sack of 300 wool-fels, and one mark for each last of hides (twelve dozen).[34] Henceforth throughout Edward's reign this was an important source of revenue. In the first five years the foreign merchants, who were collectors of the custom, appear to have received from it upwards of £7,522.[35] The receipts for two years from Michaelmas 1280 were as follows:[36]

	£	*s.*	*d.*
From the port of New Ross	880	17	3¾
Waterford	690	18	0½
Cork	525	9	3
Dublin[37]	325	8	2
Drogheda	294	2	2
Youghal	152	4	11¾
Galway	75	8	5¾
Limerick	21	5	2
Total	£2,965	13	7

That New Ross should head the list, as she did up to the year 1292, will not be sur-
[278] prising if we consider its suitable position, near the junction of the water-ways of the Barrow and the Nore, for drawing from the greater part of Leinster, where the Anglo-Irish, to whose energy the trade was mainly due, were most thickly settled. In the absence of good roads and numerous bridges, the water-ways of Ireland had an importance not easy to realize.[38] Other accounts show that there were receipts in respect of this custom, though of comparatively small amount, at the ports of Wexford, Kerry (Dingle), and of North-East Ulster (Dundalk, Carlingford, Strangford, Carrickfergus, and Coleraine).

fallyngs (cloaks) were exported to Bayonne: Justiciary Rolls, vol. ii, pp. 157-8. See, too, Mrs. Greens note, 'The Making of Ireland' (2nd edition), Appendix, p. 508, which, however, mostly refers to a later period. 34 Cal. Docs. Ireland, vol. ii, no. 1117. Grants seem to have been made separately by the great Irish landholders. For William de Valence see Parliamentary Writs 1, 2, cited in Select Charters (Stubbs), p. 443. The price of Irish wool at this time varied from 2*s.* to 3*s.* a stone. 35 Cal. Docs. Ireland, vol. ii, pp. 414-17, from which it appears that Bonesius of Florence received upwards of £800 before April 1277, when he was killed by malefactors in Ireland (ibid., no. 1336), Hugh of Lucca received £1,551 during the same period, and Percival of Lucca received £6,171 between April 1277 and Michaelmas 1280. Cf. no. 2325, and 36th Rep. D.K., pp. 28, 29, and 48. 36 36th Rep. D.K., pp. 54-6 and 73. 37 Great ships could not come to land at the port of Dublin (owing to the river-bar) until in part discharged. They used to anchor at Dalkey and there in part unload before proceeding to the precincts of the city (Ringsend ?): Justiciary Rolls, vol. ii, p. 316; Cal. Records, Dublin, vol. i, p. 19. 38 In 1298 a jury at Kildare presented that the passage of boats, which were accustomed to come from Ross to Athy, was obstructed by a weir, to the injury of the whole country. The obstruction was ordered to be removed: Cal. Justiciary Rolls, vol. i, p. 202.,

But Ireland's exports were not confined to wool and leather. Sawn timber was sent to England for building purposes,[39] and to make ships and oars,[40] and *bretachiae* or wooden towers were sent to Wales and Gascony for military objects.[41] But above all, contrary to what might be supposed, judging from the evidence of both earlier and more recent times, Ireland in the latter half of the thirteenth century and the beginning of the fourteenth exported large quantities of grain. As early as 1225 the Mayor of London bought 1,000 crannocks of wheat from the second Earl William Marshal in Ireland,[42] and there are other examples of the private export of grain to England, Scotland, and France. But the principal cases of the export of grain and other victuals that come under notice were to supply the king's armies in Gascony, Wales, and Scot- [279]
land. Thus, to take a few out of many examples, in 1255 2,000 crannocks of wheat were ordered to be sent from Ireland to Gascony.[43] In 1277 600 quarters of wheat and 1,000 quarters of oats were to be bought in Ireland and sent to Chester,[44] and in about the year 1280 the treasurer expended £1,980 18*s*. 4*d*. on victuals for Wales. Entries of supplies from Ireland for Edward's castles in Wales are numerous. As for Scotland, in December 1298 8,000 quarters of wheat, 10,000 quarters of oats, 2,000 quarters of ground malt, 1,000 hogsheads of wine, 600 carcases of salt beef, 1,000 fat pigs, and 20,000 dried fish were ordered from Ireland to be at Skinburness by the following Pentecost.[45] This was for the expedition that was to avenge the defeat inflicted by Wallace at Stirling Bridge. In the first half of the next year sums amounting to £4,383 were paid in Ireland towards these victuals.[46] For all the subsequent expeditions to Scotland to the end of Edward's reign (1300–1307) large supplies of similar victuals were obtained from Ireland.[47]

All this trade in wool, leather, cloth, timber, and grain must have benefited the native Irish producers as well as the Anglo-Norman settlers, though its existence and volume is clearly traceable to the industry, energy, and connexion with England of the latter.

Fifthly, under the new régime the Church was brought into closer conformity with [280]
that of Western Europe and into more intimate relations with the papal see; its wealth was greatly increased, its status raised, and important immunities secured to the clergy.

To estimate the effect of Norman rule on the Church it will be necessary to review briefly the previous state of the Irish Church and the tendencies of recent movements therein—a subject we have hitherto hardly touched.

The essentially monastic character impressed on the Irish Church from the first, together with her geographical position, had a profound influence upon her subsequent history. The peace and seclusion of her cloisters rendered possible that high position for learning to which she attained in the seventh to the ninth centuries, while the comparative isolation of the country induced that independence of external con-

39 Cal. Docs. Ireland, vol. i, nos. 1196, 3090. 40 Ibid., no. 1232. 41 Ibid., vol. i, nos. 2735–6, and vol. ii, no. 446. 42 Ibid., vol. i, no. 1285. 43 Ibid., vol. ii, no. 446. 44 Ibid., vol. ii, no. 1318. 45 Ibid., vol. iv, no. 570. 46 Ibid., vol. iv, pp. 284 and 304. In the same year 401 quarters of wheat were supplied to the castles in Wales: ibid., no. 597. 47 Ibid., vol. iv, nos. 716, 836; vol. v, no. 251, pp. 108–9, no. 506, &c.

trol and those peculiarities of custom and observance which distinguished her from the Churches of England and Western Europe. As we have said, the Church took the mould of the tribe.[48] The 'comarb' (heir or successor) of the founder of any particular monastic house succeeded to the government of the institution and held the church property by virtue of his abbatial office and not of his episcopal rank. In fact he was not necessarily a bishop; and hence the line of bishops in some places is difficult to trace. Bishops, though holding a subordinate place in the monastic regime, were, however, essential for the ceremony of ordination. They were appointed in great numbers, apparently as a recognition of merit, whether there was a vacant see or not,
[281] and often seemingly without connexion with any see. Their sees were in consequence often small, temporary, and fluctuating. There was, in fact, no regular diocesan distribution of the country[49] and no generally acknowledged hierarchical organization. Even the primatial authority of the see of Armagh, though an attempt was made in a document called the *Liber Angeli*[50] to represent it as divinely ordained, and on the faith of this document it was confirmed in respect of Munster by King Brian Borumha,[51] appears to have been seldom exercised prior to the twelfth century beyond the northern province, and even then was rejected by the Ostman communities of Dublin, Waterford, and Limerick.

It was indeed these Ostman communities that made the first inroad on the ecclesiastical independence of Ireland. In 1074 on the death of Dunan or Donatus, first Bishop of Dublin, Patrick, chosen by the clergy and people of Dublin as his succes-
[282] sor, was sent to Lanfranc, Archbishop of Canterbury, for consecration, and to Lanfranc his profession of canonical obedience was made.[52] Indeed there are some grounds for thinking that Dunan, his predecessor, elected c.1040, was likewise consecrated at Canterbury. Not only might we expect that the Norsemen of Dublin, who called their city 'the metropolis of Ireland', would prefer to apply to the metropolitan of their kinsfolk in England—the country from which it seems they received their Christianity[53]—rather than admit the supremacy of the Celtic Bishop of Armagh, but also it is expressly stated in the annals of St. Mary's Abbey that Patrick made his profession of obedience at Canterbury 'after the manner of his predecessors'.[54] Certainly Patrick's three successors were all consecrated by Archbishops of Canterbury and all made professions of obedience to that see. Similarly Maelisa O'hAinmire or Malchus, first Bishop of Waterford, was consecrated by Anselm in 1096. It is not known who

48 *Ante*, vol. i, p. 26 [p. 4]. 49 A synod held probably in 1118, under Gillebert, Bishop of Limerick, limited in number and defined in area the dioceses of Ireland, but the arrangement then made was not acquiesced in everywhere: Keating (Irish Texts Soc.), vol. iii, pp. 299-307, referring to the Annals of Clonenagh. The see of Dublin was omitted because, says Keating, 'it was not customary for its bishop to receive consecration except from the Archbishop of Canterbury in England'. 50 See Book of Armagh (ed. Dr. Gwynn, 1913), pp. 40-42, and Introduction, pp. lxxv, lxxviii, where the learned editor says 'the *Liber Angeli* is evidently a document deliberately framed with intent to establish the prerogatives and possessions of Armagh, and its primatial jurisdiction and supremacy, on the basis of an alleged divine ordinance ... In its present form it can hardly be placed before the last quarter of the eighth century.' 51 According to an interesting insertion in the Book of Armagh: ibid., p. 32. Brian's visit to Armagh in 1004 is mentioned in the Annals of Ulster and Four Masters. 52 Ussher's Sylloge (ed. 1696), no. 29 and p. 120. 53 Consult Halliday's Scandinavian Dublin, pp. 122–6. 54 Chart. St. Mary's Abbey, vol. ii, p'349.

consecrated Gille, or Gillebert, first Bishop of Limerick, but his successor, Patrick, about the year 1140, was consecrated by Archbishop Theobald.[55]

Prior to this, early in the twelfth century, an energetic party arose in Ireland, including some of these bishops of the Ostman cities, whose aim was to bring the Irish Church into closer conformity with Rome. Eminent among them was Gillebert, [283]
Bishop of Limerick and papal legate, apparently the first so appointed in Ireland. He had become acquainted with Anselm at Rouen and corresponded with him, and he wrote a treatise de *Statu Ecclesiae* expounding the hierarchical system as developed at Rome and Canterbury.[56] Then there was Malchus, who had been a monk at Winchester before he was consecrated by Anselm as Bishop of Waterford, with which see, at this time, Lismore seems to have been united. Most famous of all was Maelmaedhog O'Morgair, or Malachy. He belonged to the Northern province, but became thoroughly imbued with the teaching of the Romanizing party at the famous school of Lismore, then presided over by Bishop Malchus. Of Malachy we know much, principally from the writings of his intimate friend and biographer, St. Bernard, Abbot of Clairvaux.

It would have been strange if, in the period following the Scandinavian raids, the Irish Church had not reflected the political anarchy of the time. In the view of the most eminent contemporary writers it was in a condition of administrative chaos, and religion in a state of decay. We have already alluded to the letters of Lanfranc and Anselm, addressed to Irish kings, censuring the laxity of sexual relations in the districts subject to their rule.[57] Other charges made by these prelates were that bishops were consecrated by a single bishop and were appointed without any fixed sees, that infants were baptized without consecrated chrism, and that holy orders were given by bishops for money. In his Life of St. Malachy the Abbot of Clairvaux makes more [284]
sweeping statements. Thus in describing the condition of the diocese of Connor, to which Malachy was appointed in 1124, he says,[58] 'It was not men but beasts that this man of God had to deal with. Nowhere yet had he met with the like in the most savage place; nowhere had he found people so profligate in their morals, so ungodly in their faith, barbarous as to their laws, stiff-necked against discipline, filthy in their lives, Christians in name—in reality pagans.' When he comes to particular charges we hear that 'they did not pay tithes, nor first-fruits, nor keep to lawful wedlock, nor go to confession ... There were very few ministers of the altar ... No voice of preacher or chanter was heard in the churches'. Possibly the writer darkens the shadows to throw into stronger relief Malachy's successful efforts at the reform of his diocese: 'The barbarian laws are abolished, those of Rome are introduced . . . the temples are rebuilt and the clergy ordained in them. The solemn rites of the sacraments are duly celebrated, confessions are attended to, the people crowd to church, the marriage ceremony gives its sanction to the intercourse of the sexes; in fine, everything is so much changed for

55 See Ussher's Sylloge, as above, nos. 33, 40, and pp. 12–21. It is possible that Gille was an Ostman. Haliday (Scandinavian Dublin, pp. 129–34) gives reasons for thinking that the Gaelic *giolla* was borrowed from the Scandinavian settlers. 56 Ussher's Sylloge, as above, no. 30. 57 *Ante*, vol. i, p. 129 [pp. 44–5]. 58 *Vita Malachie*, cap, viii, as rendered by Robert King, Church History of Ireland, vol. ii, pp. 462–4.

the better that', in the words of the prophet, 'they who before were not my people, are my people now.'

One of the great stumbling-blocks to reform was the practice as to the succession of the 'comarbs' of St. Patrick at Armagh. St. Bernard speaks of this in his usual indignant terms: 'A scandalous custom',[59] he says, 'had been introduced by the dia-
[285] bolical ambition of certain nobles, that the holy see [of Armagh] should be obtained by hereditary succession. For they allowed no one to be promoted to the bishopric unless such as were of their own tribe and family; nor was it for any short period this execrable succession had continued, as nearly fifteen generations [or rather successions of bishops] had already passed away in this villainy ... In fine there had been already before the time of Celsus eight individuals who were married and without orders, yet still men of education. Hence arose all that neglect of church discipline throughout the entire of Ireland which we have already mentioned; hence that relaxation of censures and wasting away of religion; hence, too, that wild savage spirit that stole into the place of Christian meekness, nay a sort of Paganism introduced under the Christian name.'[60]

An end was at last put to this 'execrable succession' by the promotion (not without opposition from the noble family aforesaid) of Malachy in 1134 to the see of Armagh. After three years, however, when peace and order were restored, he resigned his position and was succeeded by Gilla Mac Liag or Gelasius, a worthy man who was still primate when the Normans came. But Malachy, though now in the subordinate position of Bishop of Down, remained the real leader of the Irish Church, which he laboured unceasingly to reform and to bring more and more under the influence and authority of Rome.

Such a man would inevitably be drawn to visit Rome, and to Rome in 1139 Malachy went. On his way, both going and returning, he stayed for a time with St. Bernard at
[286] Clairvaux, and, leaving some of his companions there to be trained in the ways of that monastery, he made arrangements for the introduction of the Cistercian order into Ireland. His aim was accomplished in 1142 by the foundation of the great Cistercian Monastery of Mellifont,[61] destined soon to be the mother of a numerous progeny of the same order. At Rome, Malachy was appointed papal legate in place of the aged Gillebert, but the principal object of his journey was to obtain from Pope Innocent II the honour of a *pallium* for the primatial see of Armagh, and also his confirmation of the erection by Celsus of 'another metropolitan see' to be subordinate to Armagh, and the bestowal on it too of a *pallium*. This subordinate metropolis is not named in the Vita Malachie. Eminent writers[62] on the early history of the Church in Ireland have assumed that Cashel was intended, but it seems much more probable that it was Dublin. There

59 A similar 'bad custom' prevailed in many of the churches in Wales: Giraldus, Itin. Kamb., book ii, c. 4. 60 *Vita Malachie*, c. x, in Migne's Patrology (Robert King's rendering, as above, p. 465). 61 The first abbot was Christian O'Conarchy, who had been trained at Clairvaux and was sent over by St. Bernard: Sylloge, no. 40. He was afterwards made bishop of Lismore and papal legate; he presided at the Synod of Kells in 1162, and at the Synod of Cashel twenty years later. 62 Professor G.T. Stokes states without comment that Cashel and Armagh were the sees in question: Ireland and the Celtic Church, p. 345; and so does the Rev. Thomas Olden: Church of Ireland, p. 231.

is no authority for the supposition that Celsus erected (or attempted to erect) Cashel into a metropolitan see, and, indeed, it seems to have been generally considered such long before his time. On the other hand, the Annals of St. Mary's Abbey Dublin, when paraphrasing the passage in the *Vita*, explain the unnamed see as Dublin.[63] Moreover, the Irish annals state that on the death of Samuel, Bishop of Dublin, in 1121, 'Cellach [287]
(Celsus), comarb of Patrick, assumed the bishopric of Dublin by the choice of Gall and Gael'.[1] The Annals of St. Mary's Abbey interpret this entry to mean that Celsus constituted Dublin a new metropolis, subject nevertheless to the see of Armagh and to its archbishop as primate.[65] It is clear, however, that the majority of the burgesses and clergy of Dublin refused to submit to Celsus, and, as on previous vacancies, sent one of their own choice, named Gregory, to Canterbury for ordination, with an intimation that the bishop 'who resides at Armagh' was very jealous of them 'because they were unwilling to submit to his ordination',[66] evidently alluding to the attempt to subject Dublin to Armagh. This view that Dublin was the other metropolitan see in question explains at once the zeal displayed by Malachy, the cautious action of the Pope, and the long delay in settling the matter. Malachy wished to correct the anomalous position of Dublin, and he hoped to overcome the opposition to the policy of Celsus by the Pope's authority and the dignity of the *pallium*. The Pope, while confirming the constitution of the metropolis, is said to have withheld the bestowal of the *pallia* until a general council of bishops, clergy, and nobles of the land should have manifested the consent and common desire of all. Evidently the Pope feared that Malachy's proposal might lead to dissension in Ireland. On his return Malachy found that there was still opposition to the arrangement—this time, perhaps, proceeding from the sees of Tuam and Cashel—and it was not until the year 1148 that a synod was held at Holmpatrick to consider the [288]
questions at issue. We are not told precisely what was decided there, but Malachy, by the advice of the synod, once more set out to confer with the new Pope, Eugene III. He died on the journey at Clairvaux, and did not live to see his long-cherished wish gratified. In 1152, however, Cardinal Paparo, the papal legate, brought, not two, but four *pallia*, and constituted, not two, but four metropolitan sees, Armagh, Dublin, Cashel, and Tuam. This arrangement probably carried out the advice of the synod of Holmpatrick and the final proposals of Malachy. By distributing the honours it was sought to mitigate jealousy and overcome opposition. By this synod the diocesan organization of Ireland was established as it has substantially remained ever since, and all Ireland by implication acknowledged the spiritual supremacy of Rome.

There are some to whose eyes the surrender of the independence of the Irish Church, which they attribute vaguely to the Anglo-Normans, was a misfortune only equalled in the eyes of others by the surrender of Ireland's political independence; but the former surrender (as indeed the latter) was bound to come sooner or later, and, as we have shown, was in a fair way to accomplishment before Henry II came. Henry was instrumental only in completing, rendering more effective, and setting the seal of permanence to what had already been done.

63 Chart. St. Mary's Abbey, vol ii, p. 259. 64 Ann. Loch Cé, Ann. Ulst., Four Masters, 1121. 65 P. 254. 66 Ussher's Sylloge, no. 40.

The papal documents which we have previously examined[67] show that an improvement in the position of the Church and the reformation of morals were among Henry
[289] II's professed objects in the proposed subjugation of Ireland. Even if we regard Henry's professions as merely intended to conceal purely political designs, he knew that the influence of the Church was in general on the side of order and moderation and respect for the plighted word, and as a statesman he must have wished to stand well by it and to gain its support. The Irish clergy, indeed, were not slow to recognize the advantages held out to them, and at once accepted Henry as their lord, and indeed, throughout the period under review at any rate, generally threw the weight of their influence on the side of the Crown. One of Henry's first acts was to summon a synod of the Irish clergy at Cashel under the presidency of Christian O'Conarchy, Bishop of Lismore and papal legate. We have already given an account of this synod and the substance of the decrees there promulgated. Besides those directed to the reform of irregularities in the matter of marriage, &c., these decrees ordained the payment of tithes to the parish churches; the freedom of church-property from secular exactions, including certain oppressive refections and food-rents that used to be enforced by the Irish chieftains; exemption of clerics from sharing the liability to *eric*-fines imposed upon their kindred for homicide; regulations concerning wills of movables, so that one third or one half of the movables of deceased persons (according as they did or did not leave both a wife and children) should be reserved to the Church, ostensibly for their
[290] obsequies.[68] Some of these regulations, in particular the payment of tithes,[69] appear to have been recognized before by the Brehon lawyers, but they had clearly not been generally observed, and there can be little doubt that their solemn enactment by the heads of the Irish Church with the king's sanction, thus making them legally enforceable, was an important gain to the Church and tended to increase its wealth and raise its status. Finally it was laid down generally that all the offices of the Church should henceforth be conducted according to the observances of the Anglican Church. Wherever Anglo-Norman influences prevailed we may be sure that this ordinance was substantially observed.

Church lands were as a rule scrupulously respected in the grants made by the Crown, and compensation was paid whenever any of it was taken, even for the sites of the king's castles.[70] This was in marked contrast to the more arbitrary dealings with the rights of Irish chieftains in the lands over which they held sway, and indeed with the lands of Anglo-Norman tenants, which were often confiscated under the feudal regime on the pretext of some offence, or even of some supposed irregularity in title.

But the Norman settlers did much more for the Church and religion. At the close
[291] of the twelfth and in the thirteenth century many splendid monastic establishments

67 *Ante*, vol. i, c. ix. 68 The Church endeavoured to retain control over this third or half— 'the dead man's part'—by refusal of ecclesiastical burial to those who 'defrauded the Church, their creditors, and their own souls', and by suspension of entrance to the church of legatees who benefited thereby: see the constitutions of Ledred, Bishop of Ossory (1317), Cal. Liber Ruber of Ossory, Proc. R.I.A., vol. xxvii (c), p. 168. 69 *Corus Bescna*, Brehon Law Tracts, vol. iii, pp. 33-9, and Introd., p. liii. 70 For Dublin Castle see Cal. Docs. Ireland, vol. i, nos. 805, 1790; for Athlone, ibid., no. 693; for Clonmacnois, ibid., no. 694; for Roscrea, ibid., vol. ii, nos. 1663-4; for Kildare, ibid., vol. v, no. 132.

were founded and handsomely endowed by them. Parish churches were restored or rebuilt. Judging by such ecclesiastical and monastic registers and charters as have survived, it would seem that there were few settlers who did not devote some portion of their lands towards the endowment of some religious house. The movement of the mendicant orders which commenced in the third decade of the thirteenth century was also encouraged by the king and the Irish lords. In fact nearly all the great houses of these orders in the period under review were founded by the Anglo-Normans. To some modern minds, however, this revival and extension of monasticism may seem anything but a gain to humanity. The monks, it may be thought, were mere parasites living on the sweat of others. But though monasticism may be justly regarded as a false ideal for human activity, and though monasteries did not always live up to even their imperfect ideals, yet in the conditions of mediaeval society they performed functions which, had it not been for them, might have been left undone. The Dominicans were learned preachers, and to some extent supplied the place of our modern professors and lecturers. The Franciscans, also learned, were pioneers in social work and the practice of medicine among the poor of the towns. The Benedictines were foremost in the art of illuminating manuscripts. The Cistercians vied with the Norman barons in setting an example of improved agriculture. The Templars were trusted bankers and accountants. The Priors of the Hospital of Kilmainham often led the feudal array to repress disorder, and sometimes themselves held the office of justiciar. The principal abbots and priors were generally summoned, along with the prelates of the [292]
Church, to the great councils or parliaments as spiritual peers. The nunneries were places where the daughters of the well-to-do classes could receive such education as was then deemed suitable. The monasteries as a whole helped to fill the void of inns where travellers could obtain lodging and refreshment, and by inculcating charity supplied —not altogether satisfactorily—the want of a system of poor-relief. They offered a place of retreat from the turmoil of the world to many a Norman baron and Irish chieftain in his old age, and above all they were centres of such learning as there was in the country, and by their intercourse with foreign houses, and their use of the common Latin tongue, they formed a link with the learning and art of Western Europe. To them we owe various annalistic records, written in Latin, which throw much light on the history of Ireland during the thirteenth and fourteenth centuries.

Sixthly, a great advance was made by the Anglo-Normans in architecture, and especially in ecclesiastical architecture. The mote-castles with their wooden towers and palisading and earthen defences, which the invaders at first constructed wherever they settled, and which in themselves were a great advance in security over the native *dúns* and ring-forts, were replaced in the reigns of Henry III and Edward I by stone keeps and walled baileys enclosing the great halls, kitchens, and other necessary or convenient offices. These, as we have said, became centres of small towns and added greatly to the security of the country. In the larger towns the walls were enlarged and strengthened with mural towers and towers at the gates and bridgeheads, and we now hear of public buildings therein, such as guild-halls and tholsels, as well as of the [293]
domus lapideae of the principal citizens. But it was in ecclesiastical architecture that

here, as elsewhere and at all times, the greatest effort was made. Precious from their rarity in other lands as are the tiny oratories of early Ireland, and even beautiful in their humble way as are many of her pre-Norman churches with their delicate romanesque ornamentation, it must yet be admitted that, from their diminutive size alone, they were quite unsuited for congregational worship. This was felt by the Cistercians who began to form settlements in Ireland before the Normans came, and to build on a much more bounteous scale. But the great impetus to the movement was given by the Normans themselves. New and more spacious and more splendid fanes were now erected in the transitional or, a little later, in the early English style: such as the cathedrals of Dublin, Downpatrick, Kildare, Kilkenny, Ferns, Waterford, and Limerick, and a vast number of monastic churches for the Benedictine, Cistercian, Franciscan, Dominican, and other orders; many fine parish churches too, such as still in part remain at Youghal, New Ross, Gowran, St. John's (Kilkenny) and other places, the simple grace of which contrasts favourably with structures of a later age.

It was not only in the great art of architecture that Ireland owed a debt to the Anglo-Normans. It must be remembered that in the thirteenth century Anglo-Norman and Angevin art of many kinds reached a high-water mark of development. Whatever his faults as a ruler may have been, Henry III was a sincere lover and intel-
[294] ligent patron of all kinds of art. Mural painting, stained glass, sculpture in the form of sepulchral monuments, metal-work, manuscript-illumination, weaving and embroidery, all reached a degree of perfection not attained by any other country at the time, and in some branches, in the opinion of good judges, never since surpassed. Ireland cannot have failed to share to some extent in this aesthetic movement, though the ravages of time and the more destructive ravages of man have left us little but a few fragments of architecture by which to judge. The numerous guilds of arts and crafts that arose, not only in Dublin, but in some of the lesser towns as well, afford some indication that this was so. Nothing was produced in Ireland comparable to Henry III's palace at Westminster with its famous 'painted chamber', but we have seen that Henry had a 'great hall' built at Dublin Castle after the manner of the hall at Canterbury, with large rose-window, mural painting, and a marble portal, the last-named feature valuable enough to excite the cupidity of an episcopal viceroy.[71] The east window of the cathedral of Kilkenny is described by a writer in the early part of the seventeenth century (believed to be David Both, Roman Catholic bishop of Ossory) as being 'divided by two piers furnished with columns of solid stone, the light streaming through glass of many colours, on which is most skilfully depicted the history of the entire life, pas-
[295] sion, resurrection, and ascension of the Lord'.[72] The window so described is believed to have been erected in 1346 by Bishop Richard de Ledred, and it no doubt was the window for which Cardinal Rinuccini three centuries later offered the large sum of £700. The offer was not accepted by Bishop Roth— unfortunately, as it turned out, for a few years afterwards the 'fanatick Limbs of the Beast' (so Bishop Williams terms

71 *Ante*, vol. iii, p. 294 [p. 429]. About the same time the king ordered glass windows to be made for the chapel of St. Edward the Confessor in Dublin Castle: Cal. Docs. Ireland, vol. i, no. 2581. 72 History and Antiquities of the Cathedral of St. Canice (Graves and Prim), p. 69.

the Cromwellians), among other enormities, broke down all the windows and carried away every bit of the glass, that, they say, was worth a great deal'.[73] Some fragments of thirteenth and fourteenth-century glass were discovered in 1846 in the course of excavations outside the northern windows of the choir at Kilkenny, and some similar fragments have been found outside the magnificent east window of the Collegiate Church of St. Mary at Youghal, which was destroyed by the Earl of Desmond in 1579.[74] With regard to sepulchral monuments, Ireland indeed has nothing to show equal to the best examples of this period in England, but for simple piety and refined taste our Anglo-Norman memorials of the dead compare favourably with many much more modern constructions. These monuments take in general one of two forms:

(1) A coffin-shaped slab with chamfered edge, bearing generally a graceful floreated cross and simple inscription, either in Latin or more often in old French, as for instance at the Dominican Friary of Kilkenny: MESTER : ROBERD : DE : SARDELOVE : CIT : ICI : DEV : DE SA ALME : AIT : MARCI : PAG. NR.

(2) A recumbent effigy of the deceased, whether prelate of the Church in episcopal robes, or knight in chain armour with emblazoned shield and sword, as at Timo- [296] lin, Kilfane, Graiguenamanagh, and the so-called Strongbow effigy at Christ Church in Dublin. This effigial style of monument was also adopted at about the same time by some of the Irish chieftains.

Seventhly, among the results making for progress that followed the Anglo-Norman occupation may be reckoned the undermining, so far as it went, of Celtic tribalism. Like the occupation it was only partial, and even in districts dominated generally by the Normans there were large patches where the Irish were allowed to remain under their old chieftains, with their antiquated organization and their archaic legal customs. The complete uprootal of the tribal system and substitution of English law everywhere and in all things could not have been effected without arousing fierce opposition, and was perhaps beyond the power of England to effect. Yet the tribal system had to be outgrown before any general and permanent progress could be assured. History everywhere had shown or was showing that national unity was impossible in a loose political organization which involved rivalries leading to violence in the succession to each chieftainship, jealousies leading to war between tribe and tribe, and insubordination leading to governmental weakness between every link in the chain from the petty chief up to the nominal *ard-rí*. Further, that economic progress was impossible where the hereditary principle of succession—not necessarily primogeniture—was not established, but the land of the sept was subject to chronic redistribution. And finally, that safety to life and limb could not be secured or blood-feuds extinguished under a juridical system which merely aimed at imposing a fine on the family the evil-doer. This [297] loose tribal organization and these primitive legal customs were not the peculiar product of Ireland. They were a stage in the early history of many other countries. The comparative isolation, however, of the westernmost island had favoured their survival into a period when progressive humanity had dimly discerned that for their prosperity, and even for their continued existence, it was necessary for small independent and

73 Ibid., pp. 42-3. 74 Journal R.S.A.I., vol. xxvi, p. 240.

semi-independent groups to shed these hampering customs, surrender some of their freedom, and coalesce into strong centralized states. It is a process which has been going on up to our own times. What progress Ireland would have made under her tribal system if the Normans had never settled there may perhaps not unfairly be estimated by the nearly stationary condition of the more purely Gaelic districts in the north of the country. These were the most powerful and the least disorderly of all the ancient divisions of Ireland, and they were also the least affected by the coming of the Normans, and yet between the upper reaches of the Shannon and the Bann, up to the age of Elizabeth, there was hardly a place deserving the name of a town.

Finally, the connexion with England brought Ireland into closer contact with the art and thought and life of Western Europe, and opened a channel by which she might share more readily in the intellectual heritage of all the ages. Such a channel, as we have seen, had indeed been formed by Christian missionaries and monastic schools at a much earlier period, but in the stormy times of the Scandinavian inroads the channel so formed had been silted up, and the art and learning previously introduced and devel-
[298] oped, cut off from rejuvenating influences, had languished, and when the Normans came was hardly alive. We have noted Ireland's gain by this new channel in trade and agriculture, in architecture and ecclesiastical organization, but it was still more manifest in the whole scheme of civil government, legislative, executive, and judicial. Norman rule in Ireland, in short, marks the introduction into a country which had never been through the school of Roman domination, of ideas of state-governance and organization which, as developed in the British Isles, have become the model for all the free governments of the world, and which in final analysis humanity owes to Imperial Rome.

We have now touched on some of the more important results of early Norman rule in Ireland. They constitute a great and rapid advance on the lines of mediaeval progress. Viewed broadly and as a whole, the thirteenth century was a great period in the history of Ireland, great in its performance and even greater in its promise. A new and greater Ireland was being developed, an Ireland fitted to co-operate in all that was making England great and to share in her greatness.

But why, it will be asked, was this progress not maintained and this promise not fulfilled? or rather, why was there a marked retrogression from some of the points attained? For a full answer to this question a study in detail of the next two centuries would be a necessary preliminary. But already we can see in operation some of the causes of failure. In the first place, however, it may be remarked that the cause is not to be found in any special iniquity in the conquest as such. Even up to our own times in Europe there has been no general agreement as to the ethics of conquest, and in the twelfth century the blessed words 'democracy' and 'self-determination' were
[299] unknown. Large districts in Europe frequently fell to new rulers, sometimes by naked conquest, sometimes as a marriage bargain or otherwise, without any reference to the wishes of the inhabitants. Henry had a better title to Ireland than his great-grandfather had to England. His vassal was already in possession of one whole province by agreement with its late king. He had the Pope's licence to enter the land and subject the people to his dominion. It is true that by Irish law Dermot exceeded his rights in

bartering away the succession to his throne, and that to our thinking the Pope had still less right to interfere in the temporal affairs of Ireland; but to the feudalists of the twelfth century neither action was without its precedent, and at any rate, apart from any such disputable title, when Henry came he was at once accepted by the prelates of the Church, and nearly all the kings of the land swore fealty to him. He had no occasion to unsheath a sword. To the mass of the Irish people it seemed to make little difference who was *Ard-rí*. We must seek for the seeds of failure elsewhere.

The Norman settlers, especially at first, and the new-comers from England for many centuries, regarded the Irish as an inferior race, instead of (as they were) a race in a very different, and what was no doubt in some respects a less advanced, stage of culture. This view, it is true, did not prevent some intermarriages with the families of Irish chieftains. Thus following perhaps Strongbow's example, the elder Hugh de Lacy married as his second wife a daughter of Rory O'Conor, king of Connaught, and the first William de Burgh is said to have married a daughter of Donnell O'Brien, king of Thomond. Donnell's son Murtough married a daughter of Richard de Burgh. Richard de Carew mar- [300]
ried Raghenilda, daughter of Dermot Mac Carthy, king of Desmond, and Dermot himself married Peronelle, sister of Thomas Bluet. There were no doubt other intermarriages, but there is no indication that they were common in the thirteenth century. There were legal difficulties. An English lady, in case of her survival, would gain no right of dower in her Irish husband's lands; while an Irish lady, except perhaps as the result of a pre-nuptial arrangement, would not bring any rights in land to her husband. There were indeed, in many other matters, immense difficulties in treating the Irish on an equality with the English before the law. It was impossible to reconcile the differences of law and custom. To enforce the abandonment of the tribal system, even if possible, would have led to increased bitterness of feeling. It was easier and involved less hardship to treat the chieftain as a quasi-feudal tenant of a circumscribed area, holding either of the Crown or of some great lord, leaving his relations with the tribesmen untouched, and giving him protection so long as he was loyal, and able and willing to prevent raids outside his borders. This was in fact done in many cases with at first a certain amount of success, but the plan in no way facilitated the amalgamation of the races, and these Irish enclaves sooner or later became centres of local disaffection and disturbance. Often this was not the fault of the ruling chieftain, but of some 'roydamna' or rival, who sought to gain popularity and secure his succession by a 'spirited foreign policy', which generally took the form of a successful plundering raid against the foreigner. The government had no adequate machinery for rapidly repressing disorder, and was often disinclined to incur the inevitable expense, while the lords of the neighbouring districts, [301]
which were alone immediately affected, even if sufficiently powerful, were not impartial agents in the settling of disputes.

For this failure to amalgamate the Irish themselves were not free from blame. Not only did they continue to fight among themselves (on a smaller scale than of yore it is true), but they could not keep faith nor give up their predatory habits. They would submit again and again, solemnly pledge themselves to keep the peace, and as often break out afresh and raid the homesteads across their borders. They had indeed one great excuse. Whatever may have heen the merits of any particular dispute, they saw the foreigner in possession of much of the best land of the country, and this was a continual source of irritation.

Nevertheless in the course of the thirteenth century a certain amount of amalgamation of a wholesome kind went on. We hear of more intermarriages in high quarters. The families of the White Knight, the Knight of Glyn, and the Knight of Kerry, sprang from the union of John Fitz Thomas of Desmond with a daughter of O'Conor of Kerry. In the north, Aedh Buidhe O'Neill, king of Cinel Owen, eponymous ancestor of the Clannaboy O'Neills, married a cousin of Walter de Burgh, Earl of Ulster. In Connaught, Sir William (Liath) de Burgh married Finola, daughter of Brian Roe O'Brien, king of Thomond, and Edmund de Burgh, son of the Red Earl, married a daughter of Turlough O'Brien, a later king of Thomond. It seems probable that in the feudalized districts any Irishman of proved loyalty could obtain licence to use English
[302] laws, if he wished it. Moreover, many of the lesser chieftains, while retaining their own laws and customs, preserved in general friendly relations with their new overlords in all parts of Ireland. Thus in Connaught O'Heyne, O'Shaughnessy, O'Flaherty, O'Madden, and O'Kelly were usually loyal to the de Burghs. There was no general combination against the English of Connaught until the time of the invasion of Edward Bruce, when the confederates suffered a severe defeat at the battle of Athenry. It was with reference to their defection at this crisis that a contemporary Irish writer, in a passage already quoted, upbraided the Irish chieftains who sided with the Scots against 'their princely English lords' under whose rule they had prospered. It is indeed certain that at least up to this period the lrish gained under the new regime greater security from attack, obtained a better market for their produce, and had examples before them of improved husbandry, new industries, better housing, and many things that add to the conveniences and amenities of life.

It must, however, be admitted that even in the thirteenth century Gaelic Ireland went on very much in its old way, little influenced by contact with new habits of thought and new modes of life It seems indeed to be one of the most marked characteristics of the Celtic temperament in its native land to be ever looking backward to a supposed golden age in the past, while paying little heed to the actual conditions of the life of the day and making the best of them. But in the lapse of time this purely Celtic temperament has to become modified through the mingling of the races—for in spite of futile and mischievous legislation they have intermingled. The ground for this leg-
[303] islation was that the descendants of the Normans who intermarried with the Irish or whose children were nurtured among them became turbulent and 'degenerate', or, as the phrase went, *Hibernis ipsius hiberniores*. But the real remedy for this, as for the turbulence of the Irish, was a more effective machinery for preserving order, a more consistent and less selfish policy with regard to the Irish, and a firmer and more impartial rule all round. In spite, however, of the default of the central government and of their own real or supposed degeneracy, the Anglo-Irish, while gaining something from the quick, sympathetic imagination of the Celt, never lost that energy of character, that power of initiative, and that capacity for leading and controlling men which they either

inherited from their Norman ancestors or imbibed from the Norman tradition. Hence perhaps it is that so many great generals, distinguished statesmen, and eminent pro-consuls of the British Commonwealth have sprung from an Anglo-Irish stock, and that with very few exceptions even the great leaders of Irish national movements from the time of James II to quite recent days have been of Anglo-Irish descent.

History shows that feudalism was a necessary stage in the evolution of a well-ordered progressive state, but it had in its laws relating to inheritance, wardship, and dower certain inherent defects as compared with tribalism. These laws begat frequent minorities, encumbered successors, and sooner or later partition among female heirs, who (in the case of Ireland) were often wedded to absentee lords. The result was to place the greater feudal fiefs at a distinct disadvantage in face of the homogeneous tribe or tribe-group with its resident adult, male, successor to the chieftainship, and its unimpaired territory. To avoid this disadvantage various attempts were made, by settlement [304]
or otherwise, to exclude females from succession.[75] Thus John Fitz Thomas of Offaly pushed his way to the Geraldine succession, though there were female heirs entitled by the law of England to succeed,[76] and the same reluctance to admit the right of a female heir probably influenced the de Burghs of Connaught in their action after the death of Earl William in the critical year 1333. But they and other English settlers, especially in parts outside Leinster,[77] found that they could not hold their own against Irish clans unless they adopted an agnatic succession framed somewhat on the Irish model; and soon we find persons of Norman or of English descent styled 'captains of their nations (or names)'. By the middle of the fourteenth century this system was recognized even in Leinster by the justiciar, before whom persons of the names of Harold, Archbold, Laghles, Howel, and Walsh, presumably of Saxon or Welsh descent, were sworn as chiefs of their respective names.[78]

From a military point of view feudalism in Ireland gradually lost much of the advantage it originally possessed in better equipment and greater cohesion in the face of the foe. From the first, indeed, the invaders were always greatly out-numbered; but [305]
this disadvantage was more than counterbalanced by their superior weapons, offensive and defensive—especially the hauberk and the bow—their use of cavalry, and their better discipline and tactics. But the Irish soon learned to avoid regular engagements in open country, and in the course of time the conditions became more equalized, while towards the close of the thirteenth century the bodies of heavy-armed 'galloglasses' from Scotland that were engaged by the chieftains of the north and west of Ireland formed a nucleus of professional soldiers that added much to the strength and discipline of the Irish forces. Finally, the success which attended the early campaigns of the Bruces showed that the English were not invincible, and, while the impoverishment that followed the ravages of the Scots and the accompanying years of famine

75 A similar motive in Scotland led to the attempted disinherison of the daughters of Alan of Galloway in 1234: *ante*, vol. iii, p. 256 [p. 410]. 76 See *ante*, c. xxxv, p. 113 [pp. 489–90], and Appendix II. 77 Even in Leinster in 1299 two of the Rochfords, by an agreement, sought to arrange that on failure of heirs male 'the most noble, worthy, strong, and laudable, of the pure blood and name of the Rochfordeyns' should be chosen to succeed to the 'indivisible' barony of Okethy: Cal. Justiciary Rolls, vol. i, p. 326. 78 See English Historical Review, vol. xxv, p. 16.

affected both races alike, the Irish who had the least to lose were the first to regain something approaching their former state. The weak rule of Edward II and the neglect, interrupted by spasms of misplaced severity, of Edward III utterly disheartened the loyal settlers, who saw that they could no longer rely upon the Government for the preservation of order. Not only was the tide of immigration stayed, but many settlers gave up their ruined homesteads and returned to England or Wales, while those who remained lapsed more and more into the disorderly ways of their Irish neighbours.

Thus, even in the period under review, among the many benefits that Norman rule implanted in Ireland we can clearly trace the germination of some of the evil seeds whose growth choked and defeated the promise of the thirteenth century. In particular the treatment of the Irish generally as an inferior race, and a short-sighted disre-
[306] gard of their welfare; the inability of the Irish themselves to face the facts, shake off old hampering customs, and accommodate themselves to the larger life opening before them; and the weak, selfish, and inconsiderate policy of the central authority. But above and beyond all such seeds of failure, the two systems of Norman feudalism, held in imperfect restraint, and Celtic tribalism, in a condition of arrested development, could not long exist side by side. One or other must have given way. The weakness and neglect of a distant and preoccupied Government decided which it was to be, and for upwards of two centuries tribalism, which now extended to some of Norman descent, regained much of its former sway. Then at a time when feudalism, in the proper sense of the term, was a thing of the past, the inevitable work of the supersession of tribalism had to be undertaken by England in very self-defence at the cost to Ireland of much pain and hardship.

[307]

ADDENDA ET CORRIGENDA TO VOLUMES I AND II

Vol. i, p. 16; vol. ii, p. 114 [p. xvi]. 'Joint justiciarship of Peter Pipard and William le Petit':—There is doubt about the date, *c.* 1198–9, assigned to this joint justiciarship. The charter on which I relied (Chart. St. Mary's Abbey, Dublin, vol. i, p. 143; vol. ii, p. 28) is a confirmation by Thomas O'Conor, Archbishop of Armagh, of a previous grant of land at Balibachel (Ballyboghill, Co. Dublin) to St. Mary's Abbey, and is witnessed by several bishops and archdeacons, and by 'Peter Pipard and William Parvus, at that time justiciars'. One of the witnesses is John, Bishop of Leighlin, and a bishop of Leighlin of that name was elected in 1198, but his predecessor's name is not known with certainty. Professor H.J. Lawlor, however, who has paid a close attention to episcopal successions in Ireland, informs me that there are some grounds for thinking that this predecessor's name was also John. Now the date indicated for the charter in question by the other clerical witnesses would fall within the years 1192–4. In particular Simon [de Rochford] is described as 'Elect of Meath', while according to Ware he was consecrated *c.* 1194. Moreover, there is independent evidence that Peter Pipard was justiciar in 1194 (*ante*, vol. ii, p. 112 [**195**]), and that, probably about the time of the archbishop's confirmation, the boundaries of 'Balibackil' were perambulated and marked out 'in the presence of William Parvus, justiciar' (Chart. St. Mary's, Dublin, vol. i, p. 175). It is, therefore, not improbable that it was in, or shortly before, 1194 that, following the precedent of May 1181, these two were appointed joint justiciars.

Vol. i, p. 18 [26]; vol. ii, pp. 165, 246 [217, 249]. 'William, son of William [**sic**], Baron of
[308] Naas':—It was William, third Baron of Naas, son of William, the second baron, who married Matilda of Pont de l'Arche. She was widow of Philip de Braose: Close Roll, 11 Hen. III, p. 199. This William Fitz William has been hitherto omitted in the received pedigrees, but in a review of the Gormanston Register (English Hist. Review, vol. xxxi (1916), pp. 488–9) I have established his position. His father, William, son of Maurice, who married Alina, daughter of Strongbow, was dead before *c.* September 1199 (Rot. de Obtalis, 1 John, m. 15, p. 26). The third baron is often called simply 'William, Baron of Naas', hence the confusion; but his patronymic appears in several documents, e.g. Cal. Gormanston Register, pp. 154, 200, 204; and Cal. Docs. Ireland, vol. i, p. 448. David Fitz William, fourth Baron of Naas, was his son and heir by 'Mahaut de Pontearch (Matilda de Pont de l'Arche): Cal. Gormanston Register, p. 163.

Vol. i, p. 33 [6]. 'Stuffed their wounds with moss':—It would seem that the absorptive and curative properties of 'sphagnum', of which we have had much recent evidence, was known and utilized at this time by the Irish.

Vol. i, pp. 104, 121: [35, 41]—For 'Aryan family of races' read 'Aryan-speaking peoples'.

Vol. i, p. 140, note 1 [49, note 88]:—For a description of Rathgall, see my paper in Journal R.S.A.I., vol. xli (1911), pp. 138–50; and for an attempted identification with the *Dún Galion* of the Book of Leinster and the 'Dunum' of Ptolemy, see Proc. Roy. Irish Academy, vol. xxxii (c), pp. 41–57.

Vol. i, p. 268 (last line) [99]:—For 'the law of Bristol' read 'law of Breteuil', and see *infra*, corrigendum to vol. ii, pp. 315–16.

Vol. i, p. 281, l. 14 [104, l. 13]:—For 'in the preceding July' read 'on June 14, 1170'.

Vol. i, p. 287, l. 7 [107, l. 4]:—For some information about Stephen White, see Text-book of Irish Literature (Eleaonor Hull), vol. ii, pp. xix and 183.

Vol. i, pp. 323–4, and note to the latter page [121–2, and note 13]. 'The foundation-charters of Dunbrody':—Another and more probable solution of the difficulty concerning the dates of these charters to Dunbrody is that the confirmation of Hervey's charter ascribed to 'Earl Richard, son of Earl Gilbert', is, like some other monastic charters, a forgery. It is not [309] mentioned in the agreement of November 1, 1182, when the Convent of Buildwas made over all their rights under Hervey's grant to St. Mary's Abbey, Dublin (Chart. St. Mary's Abbey, vol. i, pp. 354–6), nor by Prince John in his confirmation in 1185 (ibid., vol. ii, p. 166), nor in the confirmation by Albin O'Molloy, Bishop of Ferns, after 1186 (ibid., p. 168), nor in the Bull of Pope Celestine in 1195 (ibid., p. 98), though all of these mention or recite Hervey's charter, and the three last mention the grants of subsequent donors as well. Strongbow's charter is first mentioned *c.*1207 in the confirmation by Earl William Marshal the elder (ibid., p. 158), in view of obtaining which it may have been manufactured. On this supposition there is no difficulty in assigning Hervey's charter to a date between 1178, when Felix [O'Dullany], Bishop of Ossory, one of the witnesses, was consecrated, or at any rate when the preceding bishop, Donnell O'Fogarty, died (Four Masters, 1178), and November 1, 1182, when the Convent of Buildwas made over their claims to the site which Hervey had lately (*nuper*) given them. Dr. H.J. Lawlor in a criticism of this passage, which led me to reconsider the solution of the difficulty I had noted, suggests that both Hervey's and Strongbow's charters are forgeries, but I see no reason to doubt the authenticity of the former, or its ascription to a date within the limits above mentioned. Indeed, the very description given to Hervey in his charter as 'Mariscallus Domini Regis de Hibernia et Senescallus de tota terra Richardi comitis', points to a period soon after the earl's death (May 1176), when the same influences which led William Fitz Audelin, the justiciar, to seek 'to humble the pride of the Geraldines and scatter their shields' (Gir. Camb., vol. v, p. 335), led not improbably to the promotion of Hervey. It may further be noted that the impossibility of placing Strongbow's alleged charter before Hervey's, which it confirms, may have led the compiler of some inaccurate chronicles concerning the lords of Leinster, inserted in the Register of Dunbrody (Chart. St. Mary's Abbey, vol. ii, p. 141), to post-date the death of Richard Fitz Gilbert by two years. His obiit is there placed in 1178, and it is added that he and Hervey founded the House of Dunbrody. Thus Strongbow's lifetime is incorrectly extended [310] so as to cover the earliest date to which Hervey's charter can be assigned—probably its actual date.

Vol. ii, pp. 48–50 [169–70]. 'Descent of the seignory of Cork':—For a further examiantion of this subject, with some corrections and additions, see vol. iii, pp. 147–55 **[000]**.

Vol. ii, p. 59 (last line) [174, l. 19]:—There seems to be no early authority for calling John Comyn 'a monk'.

Vol. ii, p. 67, 1. 20: [177, l. 15]—For 'Hugh de Lucy' read 'Hugh de Lacy' [corrected in text].

Vol. ii, p. 78 [181]. Kells (Meath) charter:—Though the printed transcript to which reference is made has 'legem Bristolli', it is not improbable that the original charter conferred the 'Law of Breteuil'.

Vol. ii, p. 79. 'Drogheda castle' [181]:—From the inspeximus of 1340 (Pat. Roll, 14 Ed. III, pt. 2, m. 26; Cal., p. 525) it appears that by a charter dated in June 1194 Walter de Lacy granted 'to his burgesses of Drogheda dwelling on the side of the bridge next his castle, namely the southern side', their burgages as assigned by a jury, with a frontage for each burgage of fifty feet, and three acres of land; and that the river Boyne should be free from all obstacles from the sea to the bridge of Trim, so that the burgesses might come and go with their boats and mer-

chandise. He also granted them 'the free Law of Breteuil' (*liberam legem Britolli*). This charter strongly supports the position originally taken up by me in a paper read before the Royal Society of Antiquaries of Ireland at Dundalk (see Journal, vol. xxxviii (1908), pp. 246–50), and at the time received with noisy incredulity, that Walter de Lacy's castle of Drogheda was situated on the artificial mound there known as the Mill-mount on the southern side of the Boyne overlooking the bridge; and seeing that Walter appears to have got seisin of his lands for the first time in 1194 (*ante*, vol. ii, p. 112 **[195]**), the charter also bears out my inference that the castle was built by his father Hugh. While therefore I am grateful to Professor Tait for calling my attention to this charter, of which I was ignorant, and also for noticing some other slips and omissions in my former two volumes, which he reviewed with great care and sympathy, I cannot accept his position that the grant of 1203, by which the custody of the Bridge of Drogheda
[311] was committed to Nicholas de Verdun, 'had nothing to do with the castle on the Meath bank of the Boyne—but only with the northern *tête de pont* in Louth, which was known as Bridge of Drogheda' (see his review of 'Ireland under the Normans', in English Historical Review, vol. xxvii, January 1912). If by *tête de pont* is meant any kind of fortification on the northern side, I can only say that no trace of such has been anywhere noticed, and that if any such fortification existed it would surely be anomalous to have it and the castle on the other side of the bridge in different hands. It would have been more exact if I had stated that what John gave in custody to Nicholas was 'Pons de Drocheda cum pertinenciis', and explained at length that by this was meant the town of Drogheda, including in particular the castle on the Mill-mount, which, no doubt, was the primary object of the custody. Professor Tait seems to think that the name 'De Ponte' was confined to the part of the town lying to the north of the river. But this was not so. (See e..g. Register of All Hallows, Dublin, p. 66, 'consensu proborum de Ponte ex parte Midie'.) This Latin name for the town seems to have arisen in this way. *Droichead átha*, the Irish name, means 'the bridge of the ford', but the town was locally called simply *an droichead*, 'the bridge' (see O'Donovan's note *h* to Four Masters, vol. iii, p. 349). This was at first latinized 'Pons', or 'villa de Ponte', or (to distinguish it from other bridge-towns) 'de ponte de Drocheda', though that expression was tautological. Later on, the Latin element was usually dropped, and when a distinction had to be made between the two parts of the town (which had received separate charters), the northern part was described as 'Drogheda versus Uriel', and the southern as 'Drogheda versus Midiam'.

With regard to the castle, with which I was more particularly concerned, it is often called simply the Castle of Drogheda, but it appears as 'Castrum de Ponte de Drocheda' when, along with the other royal castles, it was surrendered by Geoffrey de Marisco, the justiciar, on his quitting office in 1221 (Pat. Roll, 6 Hen. III, pt. 1, m. 6, p. 316), and by the same description Walter de Lacy's former castle was in 1225 permanently retained by the king (Close Roll, 9
[312] Hen. III, p. 39b). It was clearly the same castle throughout. Why it was in the king's hand in 1203 does not appear—though we may conjecture that it was on account of the proceedings of John de Courcy and 'W. de Lacy' referred to in Oblate Roll, 1 John, p. 74—but, indeed, it is evident from many documents that not only King John, but the advisers of Henry III, were resolved that a castle at this strategic point in the defence of the vale of Dublin should not be left in private hands.

In conformity with the untenable view that 'Bridge of Drogheda' meant exclusively the northern town, Professor Tait also assumes that when John in 1213 gave his burgesses 'de Ponte de Drocheda' the Law of Breteuil he was enfranchising the northern town alone. I see no reason to think that the grant was so confined, even if there was any considerable town at that time north of the river. It appears, no doubt, that Walter de Lacy had made a similar grant to his burgesses (on the Meath side) many years before, but the king had confiscated Walter's lands, and the burgesses would naturally seek a new grant from their new lord.

Vol. ii, p. 104, l. 14 [192, l. 10]:—For 'Earls of Leinster' read 'Earls of Kildare and Dukes of Leinster'.

Vol. ii, p. 119, l. 2 [198, l. 4]. 'Barony of Ardee':—Perhaps Peter Pipard, the justiciar (1194), believed to be brother of Gilbert and Roger, was the first grantee. Christinus, Bishop of Louth, quit-claimed the advowsons of Clonkeen and Drumcar to Peter Pipard by a deed to be dated 1187–8. (See Professor Lawlor's paper, Proc. R.I.A., vol. xxxii (c), p. 37. From this it may be perhaps be inferred that at this date Peter Pipard was the baronial lord.

Vol. ii, pp. 121–2 [199]. 'Agreement between Hugh de Lacy and Thomas de Verdun':—In 1235 Hugh de Lacy, in consideration of £200, quit-claimed for his life to Roesia de Verdun all his right under this agreement: Cal. Gormanston Register, p. 161.

Vol. ii, p. 165 [217]:—Insert 'his grandson' before 'Thomas' in l.3 [15], and 'in 1295' after 'the justiciar' in l.4[16].

Vol. ii, p. 165, 1.7 [217. l. 18]:—I have found no early authority for the statement usually appearing in the pedigrees that Gerald, son of the first Maurice Fitz Gerald, married a daughter of Hamo de Valognes. The mother of his son and heir, Maurice, was Eva de Bermingham; [313] see *ante*, vol. iii, p. 113 [337], and references there given.

Vol. ii, p. 166 [218]. 'Ardpatrick and the cantred of Fontimel':—Mr. T.W. Westropp, whom I hesitatingly followed, identified the castle built at Ardpatrick in 1199 with Knockpatrick in the parish of Robertstown (Proc. R.I.A., vol. xxvi (c), p. 240), but he has since abandoned the identification (ibid., vol. xxxiii (c), pp. 36–8). It is clearly the Ardpatrick in the barony of Coshlea (south of Kilmallock), and about it the cantred of Fontimel or 'Fontymchyll', as the name subsequently appears, must be placed.

Vol. ii, p. 187 [226]:—For 'Earl of Mortain' read 'Count of Mortain'.

Vol. ii, p. 211, note 1 [235, note 24]:—Geoffrey Fitz Robert, Baron of Kells and seneschal of Leinster, may be identical with Geoffrey Fitz Robert, second husband of Basilia de Clare. The statement of the editor of the Register of St. Thomas's Abbey, to the effect of that Geoffrey pre-deceased Basilia (Preface, p. xiv), is not borne out by the charters to which he refers. Geoffrey appears to have been husband of Basilia in the time of John, Bishop of Leighlin, 1199–1201 (ibid., p. 112). He cannot have married Eva de Bermingham until after the death of Gerald Fitz Maurice, her first husband, *c.*1203 (Pat. Roll, 5 John, p. 38), and Basilia may have died in the interim.

Vol. ii, p. 235 [245, note 1]:—Delete note 1. Exeter was one of the vacant sees in 1207–8, but the commission to Eugene, Archbishop of Armagh, to execute the episcopal office there, preceded the proclamation of the interdict by eight months.

Vol. ii, p. 257, l. 21 [253]:—for 'Earl of Ferrers' read 'William of Ferrars, Earl of Derby'.

Vol. ii, p. 289, note [266, note 14]:—'Co. Sligo' is O'Donovan's addition, but the Carbury intended was probably the district about Sliabh Cairbri in counties Leitrim and Cavan. See ante, vol. iii, p. 32 [297].

Vol. ii, p. 314, note 2 [275, note 66]. 'John's Waterford Charter':—Adolphus Ballard (British Borough Charters, 1042–1216, p. 255) notices, as I have done, that John's charter to Waterford is wrongly dated, but he adds that the charter is suspect on other grounds, as containing a number of clauses not found in any genuine charter of the same date. His argument seems convincing, and, if so, the clause directing that all shipping entering the port between Rodybank and Ryndouan should load and unload at the Quay of Waterford and nowhere else—a clause which gave rise to the age-long dispute between New Ross and Waterford—would seem to be a forgery. The clause does not appear in the charter granted to Waterford by Henry III in 1232 (Chartae, Privilegia, et Immunitates, p. 22), nor is John's charter mentioned in the confirmation of Henry's charter by Edward II in 1308 (ibid., p. 42), nor does John's charter appear to be quoted subsequently. Many mandates and counter-mandates on the subject were, however, issued from the time of Henry III, and a similar clause appears as a new concession in a charter from Edward III in 1356 (ibid., p. 60). Not until the reign of Richard II, if then, was the dispute finally settled on the basis of allowing ships to proceed to either port at the option of the merchants (ibid., p. 74).

Vol. ii, pp. 315–16 [276]. 'The Law of Breteuil':—Professor James Tait, in his review already mentioned of the first two volumes of this work, notes with not unnatural surprise my complete unconsciousness of Miss Bateson's investigations into the Laws of Breteuil, published in the English Historical Review. To this charge of ignorance I must plead guilty; but then I may be allowed some small credit for having independently discerned that it was the Law of Breteuil (not of Bristol or 'Bridge-Toll') that was granted by King John to Dungarvan and Drogheda. (The names im the charters, 'Bretoill' and 'Breteill', are, as Professor Tait points out, Anglo-French forms, and I should not have expanded them as if they were Latin.) In describing the de Lacy charters to Trim and Kells, and those of the archbishop to Rathcoole, Ballymore, and Holywood, I followed the reading of the only sources available. But in these and in some other cases Miss Bateson was probably justified in suspecting that the original charters referred to the 'Law of Breteuil'. An example not noticed by Miss Bateson was perhaps Mungret, to the burgesses of which a bishop of Limerick is said to have granted *la ley de Brutolle*: Statute Rolls, Ireland, 3 Ed. IV, c. 12.

[315] Miss Bateson's inferential reconstruction of the customs of Breteuil has, however, since met with criticism from Dr. Hemmeon in his 'Burgage Tenure in Mediaeval England', and more recently the late Adolphus Ballard, author of British Borough Charters (1913), has reviewed the question and thrown doubt on many of the supposed Bretollian clauses: English Historical Review, vol. xxx (1915), p. 646 et seq. He points out the patchwork character of English charters, states that the differences between them and the French charters are much more numerous than the resemblances, and that in some respects the English charters show an advance, and he concludes with the remark that the great attraction to settlers in towns of the Law of Breteuil was that the amercement for all offences, with few exceptions, was limited to 12*d*.

IRELAND
CIRCA 1300 A.D.
Anglo-Norman Liberties & Counties, & subordinate districts predominantly Anglo-Norman are shown in roman capitals.
Semi-independent Irish Territories and smaller districts predominantly Irish are shown in italic capitals
Principal towns, castles and manorial centres thus:-Trim
Principal Irish ruling families thus:- O'Neill
English Miles
0 10 20 30 40 50
Land over 500 ft. Land over 1000 ft.
TIRCON
O'Donnel
O'Conor Sligo
Caoluisce
CARBURY
Sligo
BRE
TIRERAGH
Castleconor
Ardcree
TIRAWLEY
Ardnaree
LUIGHNE
Ballymote
CORRAN
Banada
SLIEVE LUGHA
Castlemore
ERRIS
Borrishoole
Castlebarry
UMHALL
TREDS
MOYLURG
Loch Cé
O'Conor
Moy
CONNAUGHT
CARRA
Brees
CLAN-MORRIS
COUNTY
SILMAILRUAIN
Toberbride
Athleague
Roscommon
TIRMANY
O'Kelly
Randown
Dunmore
Lough Mask
Shrule
Tuam
Athmekin
Corrofin
CONNAICNE MARA
O'Flaherty
THE
Clare
Athenry
OMANY
Galway
Kilcolgan
Loughrea
Meelick
Ardrahan
O'Madden
Corcomroe Abbey
O'Heyne
Portumna
Lorrha

Ragery
Portcaman
Dunseverick
Dunluce
Portrush
TWESCARD
INISHOWEN
Northburgh Castle
Ballylough
Coleraine
Kilsantail
Armoy
EARLDOM OF ULSTER
Roo
Lough Guile
Derry
Dunaghy
Glenarm
KEENAGHT
O'Cahan
ONNELL
Donnell
Raphoe
TUIRTRY
Larne
Connor
Antrim
MOYLINNY
Carrickfergus
TIROWEN
O'Neill
Holywood
Dundonald
Lelord
Newtown-Blathwic
Grey Abbey
Moy Cova
Ardkeen
Inch Abbey
Audley's Castle
Armagh
Down
FERMANAGH
Maguire
IVEAGH
Mc Artan
Rath
Ardglas
ORIOR
O'Hanlon
URIEL
Mac Mahon
Newry
O'Rourke
Greencastle
Lough Oughter
O'Reilly
Dundalk
Carlingford
Kilmore Castle
Louth
Ardee
Nobber
Granard
Kells
Slane
Drogheda
Navan
Moydow
Fore
Athboy
Duleek
MEATH
Delvin
Kilbixy
Trim
LIBERTY
Ratoath
Mullingar
Lough Sewdy
Rathwire
Dysart
Galtrim
Dunboyne
Swords
Malahide
Athlone
O'Melaghlin
Ardnurcher
CARBURY
Castleknock
Howth
Mageoghegan
O'Conor Faly
Maynooth
Leixlip
Dublin
TETHMOY
DELVIN
Mc Coghlan
Geashill
Kill
Rathangan
Naas
Rathmore
Bray
FIRCAL
O'Molloy
O'Dunn
OFFALY
O'Dempsy
KILDARE COUNTY
Kildare
Lea
DUBLIN COUNTY
Newcastle
Lorrha
Dunamase

CARRA
Brees
CLAN-MORRIS
COUNTY
SILMAILRUAIN
Toberbride
Athleague
Roscommon
Dunmore
TIRMANY
Lough Mask
O'Kelly
Randown
Shrule
Tuam
CONMAICNE MARA
Athmekin
THE
Corrofin
O'Flaherty
Clare
Athenry
OMANY
Galway
Kilcolgan
Loughrea
O'Madden
Meelick
Ardrahan
Corcomroe Abbey
O'Heyne
O'Shaughnessy
Portumna
Lorrha
Terryglass
INCHIQUIN
SILMAEL
FINNAN
O'Brien
OGASHIN
Dysert
THOMOND
Nenagh
Clonroad
Clare
Quin
Killaloe
TRADRY
Bunratty
Castleconnell
CORCOVASKIN
Limerick
Esclon
Askeaton
Caherconlish
Glin
Shanid
Adare
Grean
LIMERICK
Croom
Ainy
O'Conor Kerry
Ardagh
COUNTY
Tipperary
Mahoonagh
Kilmallock
KERRY
Duagh
Lixnaw
Killeady
Ardpatrick
Ardfert
ALTRY
ACMIKERRY
Rathcogan
Ardfinnan
Tralee
COUNTY
Brigown
Currans
Buttevant
Molahiff
O'Keefe
Castlemaine
Mallow
Dingle
Fermoy
Killorglin
Castle Mora
Loch Lein
O'Donoghue
CORK
O'Sullivan Mor
MacCarthy Mor
Macroom
Cork
Carrigtohill
Callann
Ardtully
Cloyne
Dundrinan
Douglas
Beuver
COUNTY
Inishannon
Kinsale
O'Sullivan Bere
O'Donovan
Dunnamark
Timoleague
Ringrone
O'Mahony
O'Driscoll
Baltimore

Kells
Slane
Drogheda
Navan
Duleek
Moydow
Fore
Athboy
Delvin
M E A T H
Trim
Kilbixy
L I B E R T Y
Ratoath
Lough Sewdy
Mullingar
Rathwire
Galtrim
Dunboyne
Swords
Malahide
Dysart
Athlone
O'Melaghlin
Ardnurcher
CARBURY
Maynooth
Castleknock
Howth
Mageoghegan
O'Conor Faly
TETHMOY
Leixlip
Dublin
Kill
DELVIN
Mc Coghlan
Geashill
Rathangan
Naas
Rathmore
Bray
FIRCAL
O'Mulloy
O'Dunn
OFFALY
KILDARE
DUBLIN
O'Dempsy
Lea
Kildare
COUNTY
COUNTY
Newcastle
UPPER
OSSORY
Dunamase
Norragh
Glendalough
Reban
Castle Kevin
Wicklow
ELY
O'Carroll
LEIX
Athy
IMAILE
Glenmalure
Roscrea
O'More
O'Toole
Aghabo
Castledermot
OBOY
Carlow
ERARY
Comar
Tullow
Arklow
KILKENNY
BARGY
Mac Murrough
Borrisoleigh
CARLOW
Odagh
FORTH
Gorey
Thurles
Tullaroan
Kilkenny
LIBERTY
Courtown
UNTY
Gowran
LIBERTY
Ferns
Ardmayle
Glascarrig
Kells
WEXFORD
Callan
Duiske
Cashel
Jerpoint
DUFFRY
Enniscorthy
Kilfeakle
Knocktopher
Grenan
St. Mullins
LIBERTY
New Ross
Caher
Carrick
Clonmel
IVERK
Wexford
Taghmor
Dunbrody
Rosclare
WATERFORD
Waterford
BARGY
Bannow
FORTH
COUNTY
Dunhill
Baginbun
Stradbally
Rindooan
Lismore
Dungarvan

INDEX

This index is an integration of the indexes provided in the original edition – that appeared in volume 2 (for vols. 1 and 2) and volume 4 (for vols. 3 and 4). Entries in the original indexes that obviously refer to the same matter have been consolidated. The original index for vols. 3 and 4 notes that: 'Members of the same family are placed, as nearly as may be, in the order of descent, or (in the case of Irish kings) in the order of their succession'. **All the page numbers given here are those of the parent edition, which appear within brackets in the margins of the present edition.**